World Atlas

CENSUS EDITION

RAND McNALLY & COMPANY

Chicago / New York / San Francisco

Contents

Human Patterns and Imprints
4A-42A

Maps, photographs, and text are combined to give meaning to the world's population distribution, human settlement, use of resources, and the challenges posed by the earth's environment.

Photo Credits: 4A, United States Geological Survey; 9A, Bob and Ira Spring; 12A, left, 13A, National Aeronautics and Space Administration; 12A, right, FPG/Wendler; 18A, George Hunter; 19A, 34A, Brazilian Embassy; 22A, Apollo Photo Group/Perceval; 23A, 24A, upper, Photo Researchers, Inc./G.R. Roberts; 24A, lower, PFI/Charles E. Rotkin; 25A, Howard S. Sochurek; 26A, 38A, Marvin W. Mikesell; 28A, Grant Heilman; 33A, left, Woodfin Camp/ Marc and Evelyne Bernheim; 33A, right, John LaDue; 35A, Illinois Department of Transportation; 36A, Weyerhaeuser Company; 39A, Harold M. Mayer; 40A, Embassy of Japan.
Map Credits: 12A, After Lester E. Klimm; 32A, 33A, After Brian J.L. Berry.

Human Patterns and Imprints

Marvin W. Mikesell

Professor of Geography, University of Chicago

No part of the earth is beyond the reach of human activity. We have climbed Mount Everest, penetrated the densest jungle, camped at the North and South poles, and explored the depths of the oceans. Now, when we are reaching out to the most distant planets of the solar system, we may believe that the earth has been effectively tamed and settled.

People have been almost everywhere, but human settlements are not distributed evenly or randomly over the earth, nor are the patterns and imprints of our occupancy the same from place to place. In fact, our cities and farms, villages and industries occupy only limited areas of the world, and even these regions are unevenly settled. For example, the great sprawling cities along the eastern seaboard of the United States lie near miles of uninhabited land, some of it virtual wilderness.

The Human Mosaic. The high altitude infra-red image of the Goodland, Kansas, area illustrates a variety of humanity's patterns and imprints. Vegetation shows red, lack of vegetation blue and green.

The dense rural population of Egypt is concentrated in a narrow valley surrounded by the vast desert of northwestern Africa. For every "boom town," with its vigorous and rapid growth, there is a "ghost town," abandoned when resources ran out. And our impressive ability to improve and alter the environment is countered by air and water pollution, soil erosion, and other processes that destroy some areas or make them unfit for human habitation. Our environment, part natural and part artificial, still presents a major challenge to human understanding.

The World and Human Geography

We will attempt to build a foundation for understanding our world by looking at the historical distribution of human population, the patterns of settlement and land use, and the ways we have modified nature to suit our needs. The detailed maps in this atlas illustrate many of the varied patterns of human activity. While the maps give us a broad perspective of our world, they show us only part of the story. Much of what follows is an attempt to deal more fully with the features that appear as

lines or colored areas on the maps and illustrations. Perhaps the starting point for an understanding of our world is the general belief among many scholars that there is a fundamental order and logic in the distribution of people and their activities and creations, a "human geography" controlled by nature and culture. If we can increase our understanding of this order and logic, perhaps we can deal more intelligently with some of the problems facing us now.

Photographs taken from satellites and other spacecraft reveal the varied patterns and imprints of the human race, how we have marked and changed the earth's surface. Our first task is to try to understand why human population

---

...Our environment, part natural and part artificial, still presents a major challenge to human understanding...

---

is so unevenly distributed. Although different growing seasons and levels of rainfall help explain the worldwide contrast between crowded and empty areas, various cultural factors also must be considered.

In our exploration of how humanity has used the earth, the year A.D. 1500, just before European expansion overseas, serves as a particularly important landmark. The progressive settlement of the Americas was a continuation of the process started by early European explorers. The recent pioneer settlements in Brazil, Siberia, and Australia continue that process today.

Modern patterns of land use, contrasting forms of rural and urban settlements, the location of industries, and the availability of energy sources all influence where people will settle. The last of our human patterns, vast transportation and communication networks, is another important factor indicating economic development and determining patterns of land use.

Satellite photographs have also made us more aware that our environment, the earth and its atmosphere, is a closed system, intricately balanced and often highly vulnerable to human activity. That we have destroyed as well as built is evident in the many scarred areas people have left behind them. The decline of air and water quality has been a consequence of the Industrial Revolution that began in the 18th and 19th centuries. But deforestation and erosion are equally serious and are much older problems, dating back some 10,000 years to the beginning of farming in the Near East. In the 20th century, we tend to think of artificial environments—heated and air conditioned—as the answer to our search for more comfortable

---

...Our environment is a closed system, intricately balanced and often highly vulnerable to human activity...

---

habitats. While opportunities in this area may seem limitless, management of the real world outside our structures remains a serious challenge to human ingenuity. Realizing that the world is a closed system may help us find solutions to our energy and population problems that will work with and not against the earth's environment.

The task of describing and interpreting our world is a continuous one, for the patterns and imprints we try to explain are always changing. Our study of the past can help us understand the present and perhaps allow us to see a few years into the future. But beyond that point, we cannot tell where our human ingenuity will take us.

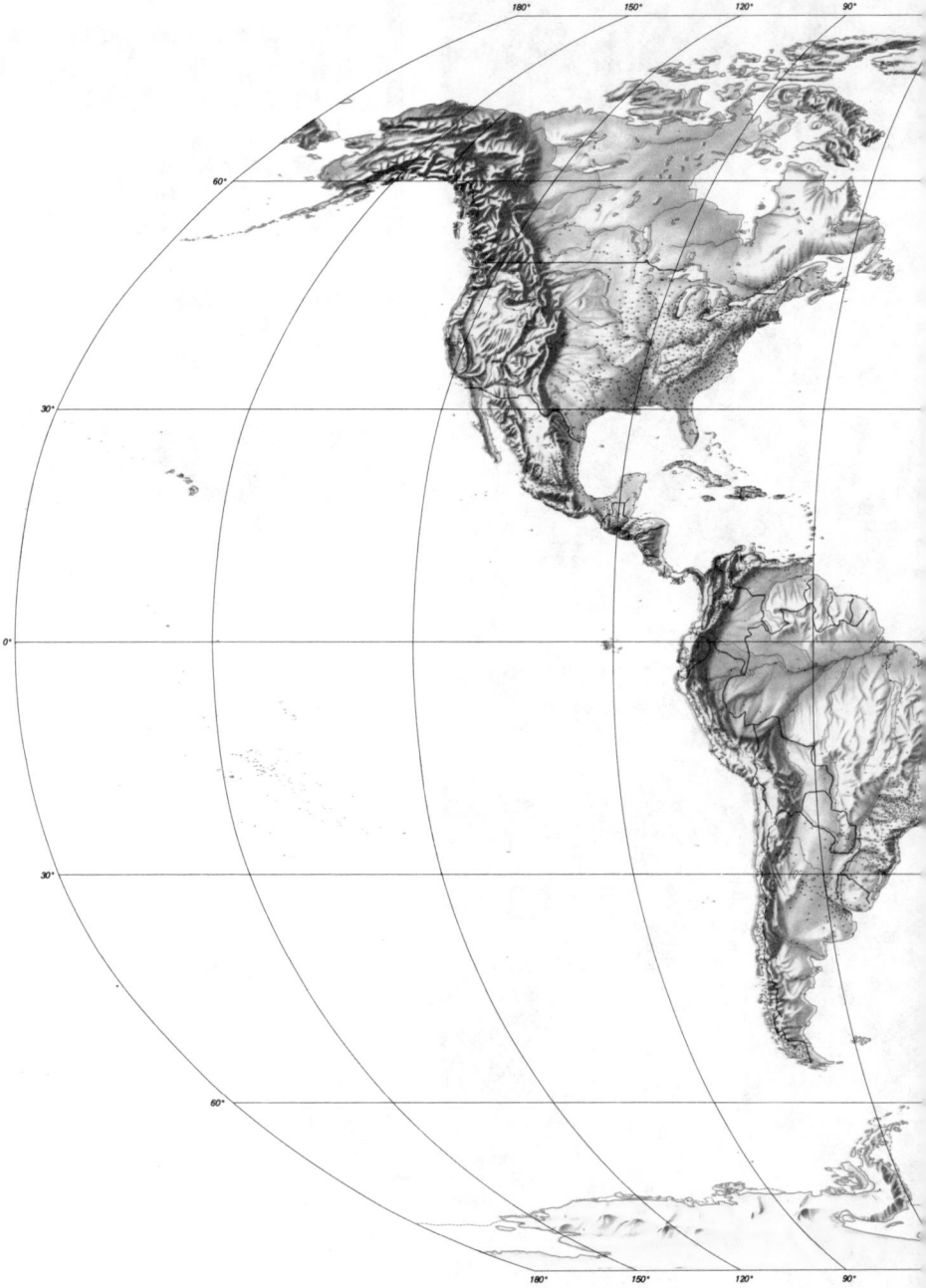

Crowded and Empty Areas of the Earth

Everyone knows that the world is experiencing a human "population explosion." Faced with this challenge, we may forget that substantial regions of the earth are *under*populated or virtually empty.

The most densely settled parts of the earth appear in two dissimilar regions: the industrial areas of Europe, the United States, and Japan; and the predominantly rural areas of India, China, and Southeast Asia. The industrial regions date from the mid-18th and 19th centuries, when emerging technology increased people's productive capacity and encouraged

WORLD POPULATION
One dot represents 100,000 people

0   1000   2000 Mi.

0   1000   2000   3000 Km.

Copyright © by Rand McNally & Co.

the development of large urban districts. The heavily populated rural areas of India, China, and other Asian countries reflect nearly 4,000 years of an agricultural civilization.

Other regions of the world offer striking contrasts between crowded and open places. In the Soviet Union, a narrow band of population stretches along the Trans-Siberian railway. The crowded area of Canada's southern Ontario is a dramatic counterpart to the open stretches far-

... regions of the world offer striking contrasts between crowded and open places...

ther north. In Japan, the well-populated island of Honshū lies just south of the more sparsely settled island of Hokkaidō. The eastern shores of the Mediterranean Sea, with the crowded coastal fringe of Israel, Lebanon, and Syria, stand out sharply against the barren land beyond. But perhaps the clearest illustration is the dramatic difference between Java and Iceland, two countries approximately equal in size but vastly different in population.

The United States, with slightly over 226,000,000 inhabitants and an area of about 3,600,000 square miles (9,500,000 square kilometers), is only moderately crowded. Settlement is fairly dense from the major urban areas along the Atlantic seaboard and the Great

Contrasts in the Distribution of Humanity. Densely settled areas in Southwest Asia, Southeast Asia, and China are rural-agricultural populations. In western Europe, northeastern United States, and parts of Japan, high density regions are urban-industrial in character. Sparsely inhabited or virtually empty areas often lie close to dense settlements.

Lakes to as far west as Texas, Oklahoma, Kansas, Nebraska, and the Dakotas. Beyond that point, until reaching the urban areas of the Pacific Coast, lack of adequate rainfall restricts settlements to river valleys, along transportation lines, and near sites of valuable resources.

Natural Limits on Growth. To explain the uneven distribution of humanity, we must look at several natural and cultural factors. Perhaps the most important are the limits that nature imposes on agricultural development. Many areas are too dry or too mountainous or have growing seasons too short to support a large,

stable population. While people have settled in harsh climates such as the Sahara, northern Siberia, and Antarctica, such settlements are small and likely to remain so. Thus, for the most part, we can mark off the earth's rich and fertile regions as the effective limits of the habitable world.

Growing Season. The most severe limitation on human settlement is the length of the growing season. Areas with less than 90 days free of frost are not suitable for most forms of agriculture. Without an adequate local supply of food, settlements cannot grow beyond a certain population size. Inadequate growing seasons

. . . To explain the uneven distribution of humanity, we must look at several natural and cultural factors. . .

partly explain why large areas of Canada and Siberia remain empty, but other factors also limit settlement in the world's northlands. Portions of these regions are extremely dry, which limits plant growth. The vegetation of the Arctic zone consists of mosses, sedges, lichens, and other species, which are referred to as tundra. The lack of trees is explained by the short growing season and the permanently frozen subsoil. Move southward and you will find tundra replaced by taiga, a forest of fir, spruce, larch, and other conifers. These vast forested regions constitute an important resource in Canada, Scandinavia, and the Soviet Union. Unfortunately, the thin, acidic soil that develops under such forests is too infertile to sustain permanent agricultural settlements.

Aridity. Human settlement is also seriously limited by the lack of adequate precipitation. In general, farming is not practical where annual rainfall averages less than 10 inches (25.4 centimeters). In areas where rainfall occurs mainly in the hottest part of the year and averages less than 20 inches (51 centimeters) annually, farming may be marginal.

The great arid and semiarid regions of the world were once populated by bands of nomadic farmers and herders and by oasis dwellers. Today, nomadism is declining as a way of life and in some areas has disappeared altogether, making the great desert regions of North Africa and Southwest Asia more desolate than ever before. In contrast, population in the desert areas of the United States has increased sharply. Air conditioning and water piped in from underground reservoirs have made cities such as Tucson, Phoenix, and Las Vegas more attractive. Converting salt water to fresh, a practical but still expensive process, will eventually enable more acres of arid and semiarid land to be cultivated.

Mountainous Regions. A substantial part of the world is too mountainous or simply too high for people to settle. The "timberline" on mountains is similar to the forest-tundra boundary of the Arctic region. This line varies with latitude, from about 8,000 feet (2,438 meters) in the European Alps to about 14,000 feet (4,267 meters) in the tropics. Above the line, growing seasons are too short for cultivation, although alpine pastures may be grassy enough to raise domestic herds. Also, many areas of the earth are too rough or rocky to support farming. Settlements in these regions are too scattered to appear on the map. Although Tibet has about 1,300,000 inhabitants, it is sparsely populated for its size. The upper slopes of the Alps and many other mountain ranges are also virtually without human habitation. Only when mountains are exposed to rain-bearing winds, as in Southwest Asia, can they support large, populous settlements.

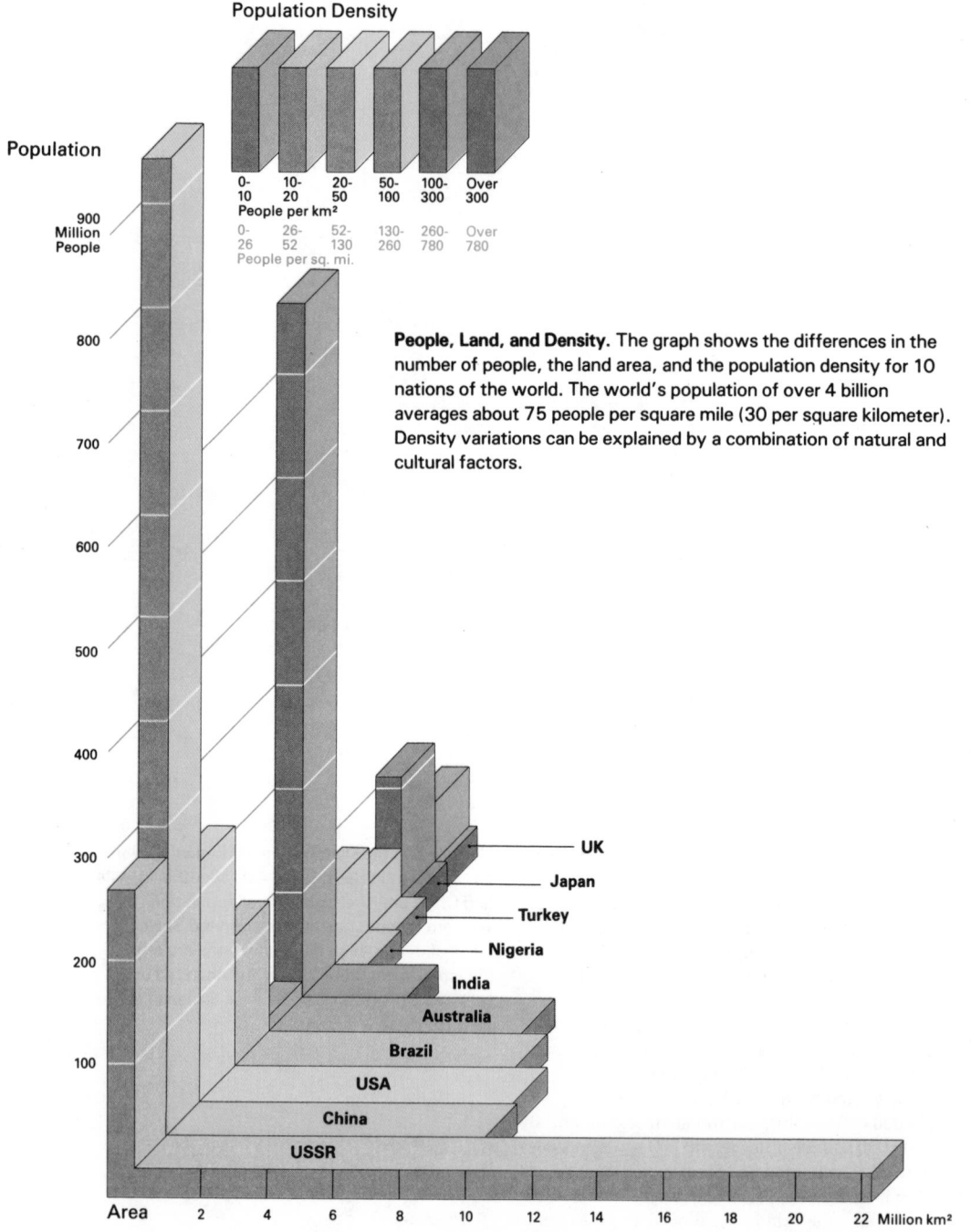

Population Density

0-10	10-20	20-50	50-100	100-300	Over 300

People per km²

0-26	26-52	52-130	130-260	260-780	Over 780

People per sq. mi.

People, Land, and Density. The graph shows the differences in the number of people, the land area, and the population density for 10 nations of the world. The world's population of over 4 billion averages about 75 people per square mile (30 per square kilometer). Density variations can be explained by a combination of natural and cultural factors.

Population

900 Million People

800

700

600

500

400

300 — UK

— Japan

— Turkey

200 — Nigeria

— India

Australia

100 Brazil

USA

China

USSR

Area   2   4   6   8   10   12   14   16   18   20   22 Million km²

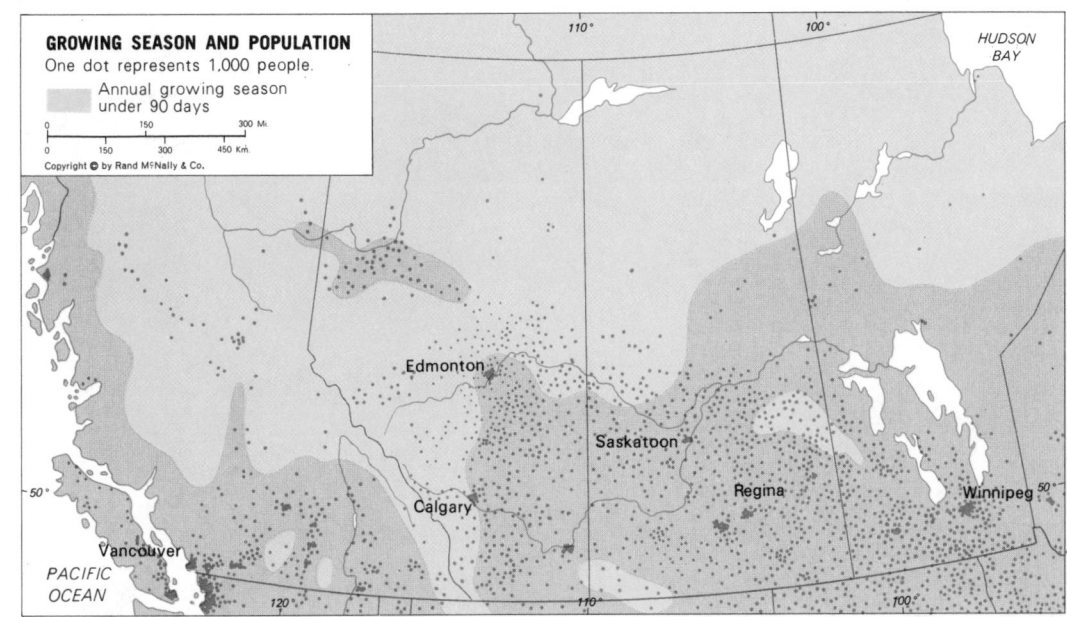

GROWING SEASON AND POPULATION
One dot represents 1,000 people.
Annual growing season under 90 days

0 150 300 Mi.
0 150 300 450 Km.
Copyright © by Rand McNally & Co.

Short Growing Season. A short growing season restricts agriculture in western Canada. Occupations such as hunting, trapping, lumbering, mining, and fur-trading account for some of the scattered population outside the limits of farming. These settlements—though nonagricultural—are like the oases of the arid zone.

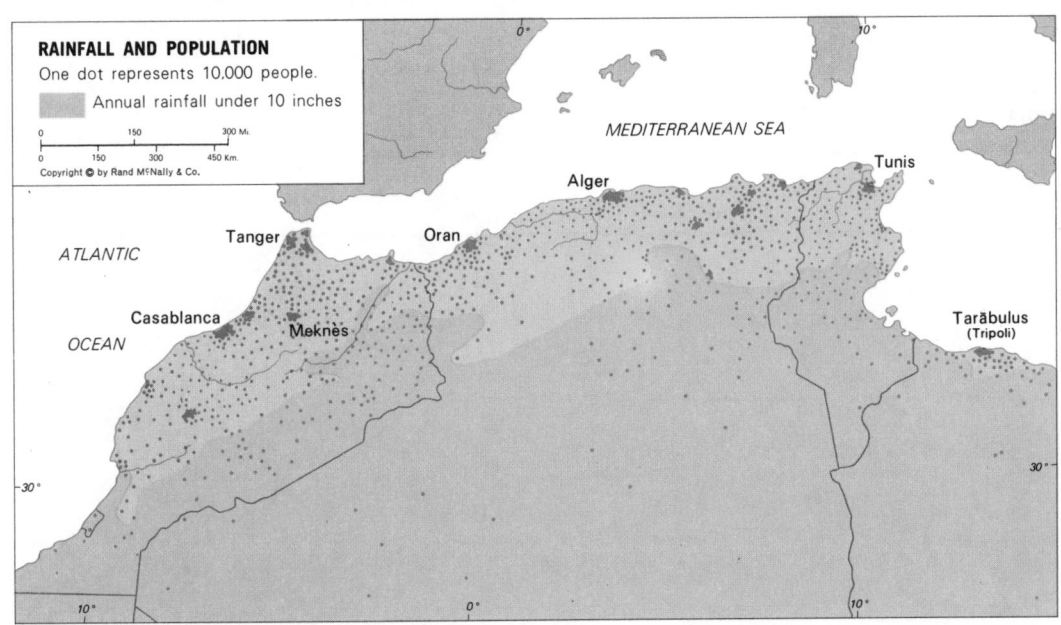

RAINFALL AND POPULATION
One dot represents 10,000 people.
Annual rainfall under 10 inches

0 150 300 Mi.
0 150 300 450 Km.
Copyright © by Rand McNally & Co.

Too Dry. Cereal farming in northwestern Africa requires at least 10 inches (25.4 centimeters) of rainfall each year. As a result, the dense rural population has settled mainly in the coastal hills. But rural settlement does not terminate abruptly, for wells and dams supply water for irrigation. Nevertheless, population is sparse where average rainfall drops below 10 inches a year.

Humanity's Boldness. In sight of the Myrdals Glacier, a farmer in Iceland has succeeded in extending the limits of the habitable world. Cultural developments, such as hybrid crops that mature faster, make farming—and permanent settlement—possible in these harsh northern latitudes.

Living on the Edge. Maps on page 9A emphasize the importance of natural limits on population distribution. Length of growing season in Canada and precipitation in northwestern Africa restrict the number and range of settlements in both areas. Since non-agricultural opportunities are limited in these regions, population centers reflect where farmers have successfully cultivated the lands.

In western Canada a short growing season has restricted settlement. There can be little agriculture except that based on grazing where the growing seasing is less than three months long. But settlement does not end abruptly, for some appears in the colder zone. Hunting, trapping, fishing, fur-trading, lumbering, mining, and transportation and government jobs account for the scattered population outside the limits of farming.

In northwestern Africa, cereal farming requires abundant rainfall. As a result, the dense rural population has settled mainly in the coastal hills. However, as in western Canada, settlement does not end abruptly, for wells tap underground water and dams divert streams flowing from the Atlas Mountains. Nevertheless, irrigation farming is more restricted than rain agriculture. The pattern of population distribution shows a break where average precipitation drops below 10 inches (25.4 centimeters) a year.

Perhaps nowhere else in the world is the contrast between inhabited and uninhabited land so dramatic as in the Nile Delta and surrounding desert lands. The photograph taken from an orbiting spacecraft highlights the stark contrast between the fertile valley and the bleak, arid land to the west and south. Average annual rainfall at Cairo, at the southern edge of the delta, is only slightly over 1 inch (2.54 centimeters). At Alexandria, on the northern edge, moist winds from the Mediterranean Sea raise the total to 7 inches (17.78 centimeters), still insufficient for farming without irrigation. As a result, the population of Egypt is confined to the floodplain and delta of the Nile River—the crowded homeland of 40,000,000 Egyptians.

Culture and Human Settlement. Cultural factors also influence where people are likely to settle. The contrast between major urban areas and uninhabited land in the northeastern United States is a good example. A vast and almost continuous zone of urban development,

---

. . .A vast and almost continuous zone of urban development stretches from Washington, D. C. to Boston. . .

---

a megalopolis, stretches from Washington, D. C., to Boston. This region offers innumerable employment opportunities, has an intricate network of communication, and can boast of all the facilities and resources associated with one of the world's greatest concentrations of popu-

lation. This complex of homes, schools, industry, stores and supermarkets, highways, parking lots, train and air terminals, and hospitals is a zone best described as a cultural landscape.

This urbanized area, as so many other built-up areas, has its counterpart in uninhabited or sparsely settled lands close by. Urban zones are limited mainly by their network of communication and transportation. People will commute an hour, even two, to their jobs, but not three or four hours. Outlying regions, beyond the range of commuting, especially in hilly or poorly drained areas, serve as sites for resorts, retirement communities, and small market towns. In general, the persistence of these communities runs counter to the trend for people to move

from rural to urban areas. And, in the past decade, cities in the North and Northeast have been losing their populations to the less urbanized South and Southwest. For some, milder climate has become more attractive than commercial opportunities. Also, rising labor and energy costs have forced many businesses to relocate in the so-called Sun Belt—in some instances, taking their workers with them.

The association of crowded and empty land is also evident in Europe. As in the United States, the first areas to be abandoned were those where agriculture was poor. The pattern included shifts from mountain land to lowland, dry land to irrigated land, and poorer land to richer land. Many people gave up rural liveli-

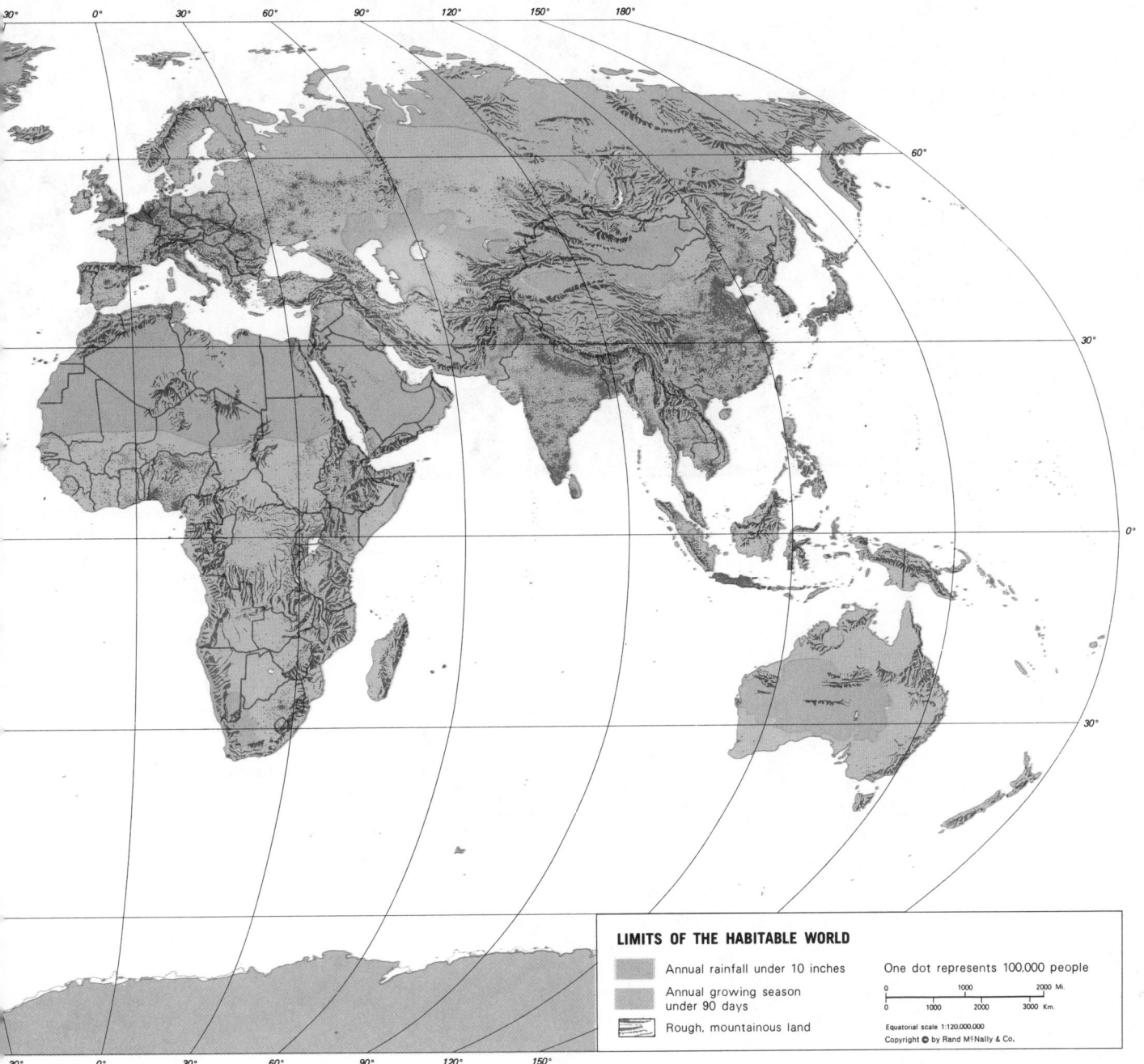

LIMITS OF THE HABITABLE WORLD

Annual rainfall under 10 inches

Annual growing season under 90 days

Rough, mountainous land

One dot represents 100,000 people

0 — 1000 — 2000 Mi.
0 — 1000 — 2000 — 3000 Km.

Equatorial scale 1:120,000,000

Copyright © by Rand McNally & Co.

hoods for the greater promise of commerce and industry. For example, the trend to settle the alpine slopes was reversed when industries keyed to water power sprang up in the valleys. Since the industrial process that encourages this shift in population is not yet evident in many areas of the world, we cannot speak of a global trend toward rural depopulation.

Our "Permanent" Patterns. We are so used to thinking of ourselves as "conquerors of the world," it is well to remember that many of our imprints and settlements have not lasted. Each generation has left a new pattern of ghost towns and abandoned land. To understand the complex forces behind our patterns of settle-

. . . It is well to remember that many of our imprints and settlements have not lasted. . .

ment and abandonment, advance and retreat, we must bear in mind that the earth's resources are exhaustible and that each generation is governed by its own goals and values. The current energy crisis has made us keenly aware of how dependent our great urban and industrial centers are on adequate energy supplies. Should those supplies be disrupted or destroyed, the megalopolis could rapidly become a "ghost town."

Most Desirable Regions. As the map illustrates, humanity has chosen to settle in the richest and most fertile regions of the earth. These areas combine adequate rainfall and growing season with terrain that is neither too rough or mountainous. Abundant mineral deposits as well as people's ability to develop natural resources also explain settlement preferences. In contrast, regions with less hospitable climates, such as deserts, equatorial zones, and the poles, have discouraged dense settlement.

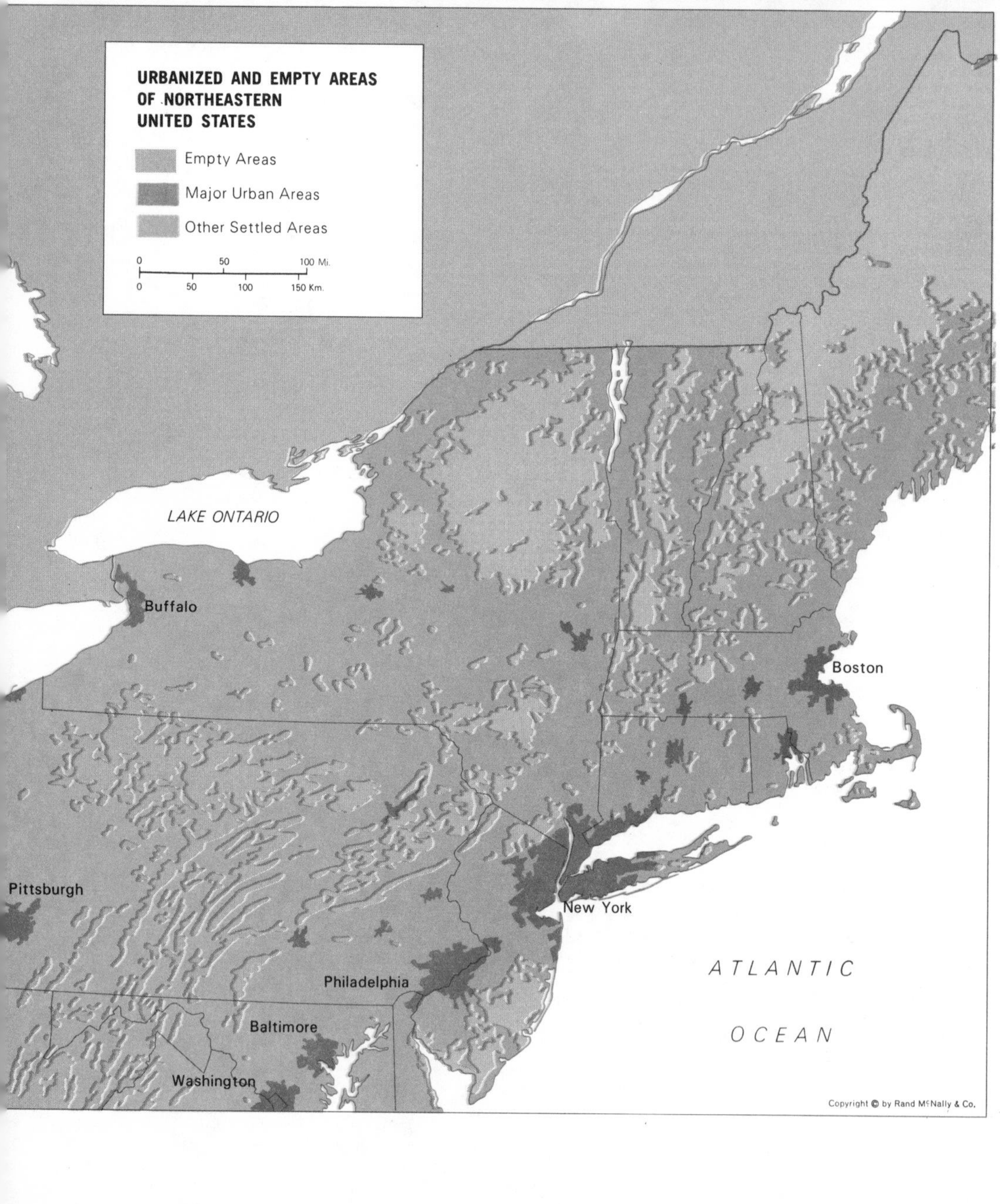

Urban Crowding. New York City (above left) is an example of the densely settled human urban landscape that develops when multiple factors are present to offer employment opportunity. It is a typical setting for the life and work of many Americans and others in the world living in industrial-commercial societies.

Humanized Rural. The part of Vermont shown above typifies the "empty" regions adjacent to the heavily populated northeastern metropolitan areas of the United States. The soil, terrain, and climate limit economic opportunity and thus permanent settlement, even though scenery and recreational potential make it an attractive place in which to live. It is sobering to realize that despite our great urban centers, sparsely inhabited land accounts for the major portion of the earth's surface.

URBANIZED AND EMPTY AREAS OF NORTHEASTERN UNITED STATES

- Empty Areas
- Major Urban Areas
- Other Settled Areas

0   50   100 Mi.
0   50   100   150 Km.

LAKE ONTARIO

Buffalo

Boston

Pittsburgh

New York

ATLANTIC

OCEAN

Philadelphia

Baltimore

Washington

Cultural and Natural Factors Combine. Cultural incentives such as employment opportunities found in the cities of the northeastern United States help explain the dense urban settlement along the seaboard. Gray areas near these urban sprawls outside the commuting range depict hilly or poorly drained land with little economic potential. This natural restriction, together with the cultural factor of better employment opportunities in cities, has accelerated the movement of people from rural to urban areas.

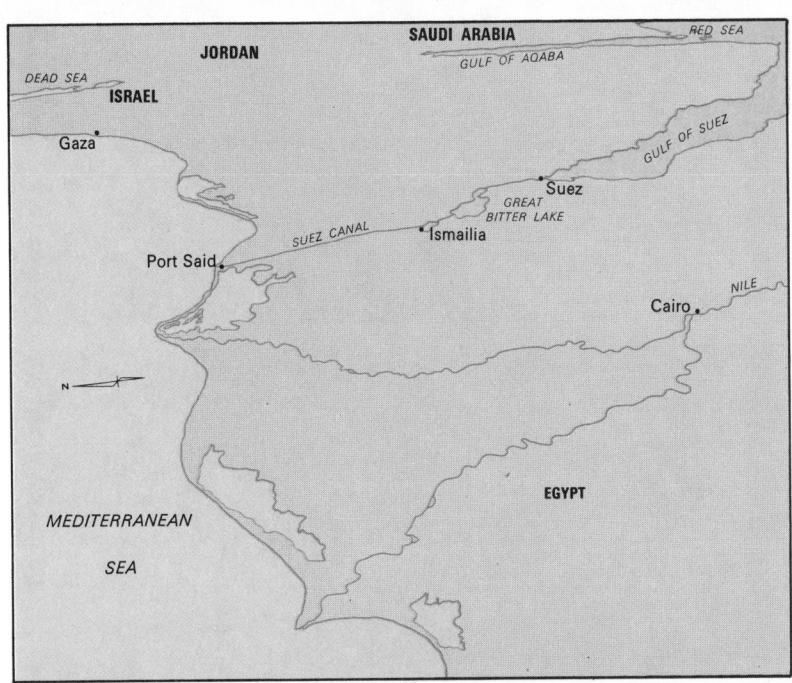

Map of the Nile Delta shown in the photograph below.

An Astronaut's View. The photograph of the Nile Delta, taken from the spacecraft Gemini IV, points out the sharp contrast between crowded, fertile land in the foreground and the desert beyond. An average annual rainfall of only 1 to 7 inches (2.54 to 17.78 centimeters) in this region cannot support agriculture without irrigation. As a result, the population of Egypt lives on the floodplain and delta of the Nile River.

Historical Forces

Before giving further consideration to the factors that influence the distribution of human settlement and economic activities, we must go back several centuries. The human geography of our world cannot be adequately explained without taking into account the forces that have shaped it over many hundreds of years.

Patterns of Land Use—A.D. 1500. Perhaps the most significant event in the evolution of the world's cultural landscapes is the extraordinary expansion of European culture. We can best show the impact of this expansion by looking at the pattern of land use at about A.D. 1500, on the eve of the European movement into Africa, Asia, and the Americas. The nearby world map depicts only the most significant features of that pattern: the distribution of agricultural and nonagricultural livelihoods, including the ranges of important natural resources.

Eight Major Centers. By 1500, agriculture had spread over most of the Old World and a substantial part of the New World. The diffusion of crops and domesticated animals came primarily from eight major regions or centers in the world. Scholars have not yet been able to

---

. . . The diffusion of crops and domesticated animals came primarily from eight major centers in the world. . .

---

determine the exact ages of these centers and their possible connections with one another. Yet archaeological evidence suggests that cereal farming, especially wheat, barley, and maize, may have been practiced before other types of cultivation. In any case, each of the centers contributed several plant foods, and many contributed various domestic animals, to world agriculture.

From the standpoint of Western culture, the most important center was located in Southwest Asia and the Mediterranean region. Here the cultivation of cereals, vegetables, and tree crops, and the herding of sheep and goats, provided the foundation for what may have been the world's oldest system of agriculture. In contrast, Europe was not an important center of innovation. Only one significant crop, oats, is thought to have been domesticated north of the Alps. Most of Europe's crops were introduced from Southwest Asia. The crop complexes of East, South, and Southeast Asia spread throughout these regions and also into Africa.

Livelihood Patterns in the Old World. Agricultural civilizations took several forms. In Europe, Northwest Africa, Southwest Asia, and Central Asia, cereal farming, horticulture, and livestock used for plowing were common features. In the tropical regions of Africa and Asia, root crops were combined with cereal farming and, in some cases, replaced it. Plows were supplanted by hoes and other hand tools. Population density was heaviest in East and South

The Birth of Agriculture. The wide-ranging agricultural landscapes of the earth in A.D. 1500 owed their origins to eight major centers of origin from which domesticated crops and animals had been disseminated for many hundreds of years.

Plural endings, e.g., onions, indicate several varieties.
Question marks indicate uncertainty as to area or areas of origin.

Southwest Asia and Mediterranean

almonds	onions	dromedary
barley	peas	camel
date palm	rye	goat
fig	wheat	pig
grapevine	cattle?	pigeon
olive	dogs	sheep

Northeast Africa

coffee	melons	sorghums
cotton	millets	cats
cucumbers	peas	donkey
lentils	sesame	dogs

Central Asia

apple	onions	bactrian camel
cherries	pears	dogs
hemp	peas	horse
lentils	turnips	reindeer
melons	walnut	yak

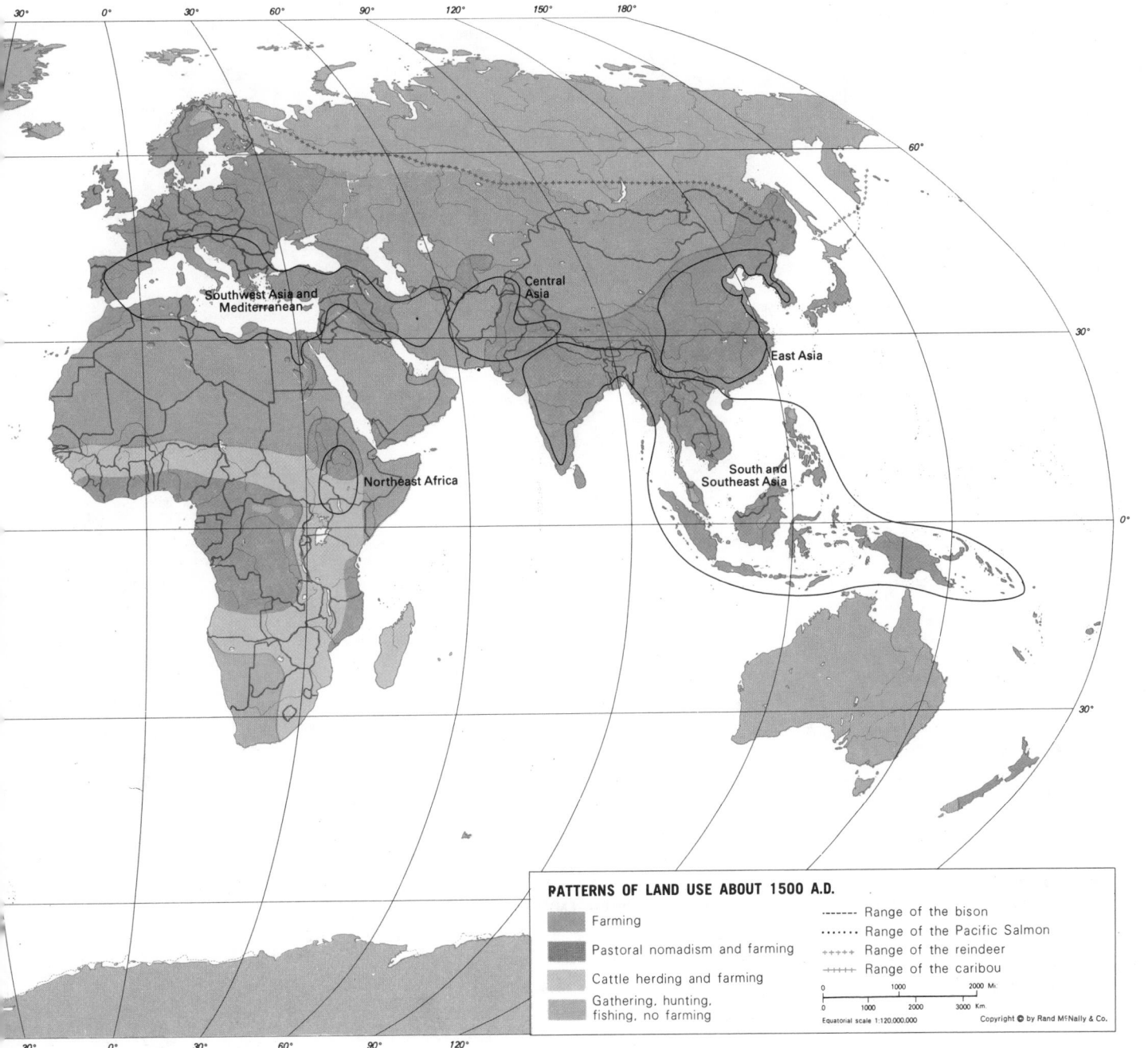

South and Southeast Asia

banana	taro	ducks
black pepper	yam	goose
citrus fruits	cats	pig?
eggplant	cattle?	water buffalo
mango	chicken	
sugar cane	dogs	

East Asia

apricot	persimmon	dogs
cabbages	plums	chicken?
millets	radishes	pig?
mulberry	rice	
peaches	sorghums	

Eastern South America

cocao	peanut	tobacco?
cashew	pineapple	dogs
beans	squashes	ducks
manioc	sweet potato	

Andean Highlands

oca	squashes	guinea pig
potato	ulluco	llama
strawberry	alpaca	

Mexico and Central America

avocado	red pepper	dogs
beans	squashes	turkey
maize	tomatoes	

The World Stage Set for Development. Just prior to the expansion of European culture into almost every area of the world, people's livelihoods were related to various forms of farming, hunting, fishing, and plant gathering. The map shows the likely distribution of these activities and the eight major centers of innovation. Most of these areas had also developed sophisticated urban centers.

PATTERNS OF LAND USE ABOUT 1500 A.D.

Farming

Pastoral nomadism and farming

Cattle herding and farming

Gathering, hunting, fishing, no farming

------ Range of the bison
······ Range of the Pacific Salmon
+++++ Range of the reindeer
+++++ Range of the caribou

Equatorial scale 1:120,000,000   Copyright © by Rand McNally & Co.

Asia and in Europe. Although somewhat less populated, the area of North Africa and Southwest Asia included densely settled river valleys where cultivation depended on irrigation. By 1500, most of these regions had developed cities or urban districts. The agricultural areas of the Old World had also witnessed the development of several major religions, different systems of writing, and the rise and fall of kingdoms and vast empires. On the eve of its expansion overseas, Europe was evolving from a rather backward peninsula of Asia into a formidable military, political, and economic power.

The nonagricultural areas of the Old World were restricted to the northern part of Europe and Asia, where growing seasons are too short for farming. Certain isolated patches of nonagricultural areas were also found in the tropical forests of Central Africa and Southeast Asia. Pygmy and Negrito tribes in these latter areas lived by hunting and by gathering wild plants. A more specialized livelihood based on herding reindeer was practiced by some of the people in Scandinavia and the Arctic fringe of Siberia. Nonagricultural livelihoods were also found in the arid and semiarid regions of Southwest Africa. While the cereal-farming, pastoral, and oasis economy of North Africa would have suited the southwest area as well, the economy could not spread through the humid tropical environment of Central Africa. Agriculture also failed to move beyond the East Indian islands into Australia.

Diffusion of Crops in the New World. At the time of the first voyages across the Atlantic, agriculture had already spread over substantial areas of the New World. For the most part, it involved the diffusion of two crop complexes. One from Central America included maize, beans, and squashes, and the other from South America consisted of manioc and sweet potatoes. The crop complex of the Andean highlands—potatoes and potatolike plants (oca, ulluco)—provided the food base for the vast Inca empire.

To the north, agriculture was restricted to Central America and Mexico (the Mayan and Aztec civilizations), the forest lands of the eastern half of the United States and along the rivers in the southwestern United States. The crop complex of Mexico and Central America could not survive in the short growing season

---

...The most impressive example of the diffusion of agriculture was the extraordinary distribution of maize, from Chile to the St. Lawrence...

---

north of the Great Lakes, nor did it spread into the semiarid lands of the Great Plains. The most impressive example of the diffusion of agriculture was the extraordinary distribution of maize, from southern Chile to the St. Lawrence Valley and the Great Lakes region of North America, a chain spanning two continents.

The nonagricultural areas of the New World

included the semiarid environment of central Argentina, which could not support tropical crops, as well as the colder regions of southern Argentina and Chile. In restricted areas of the tropical forests, throughout South America, scattered groups practiced hunting, fishing, and plant gathering to support themselves. In North America, salmon and bison provided the basis for some groups' livelihoods, but for the most part people obtained their sustenance from plants as well as from fish or game. The richest source of plant food was probably acorns from the oak forests of California.

Livelihood patterns of people in the New World can help us distinguish between civilized and primitive areas. Mexico, Central America,

---

...Except for weaknesses in military technology...New World civilization might have been able to resist the Europeans...

---

the northern fringe of South America, and the Andean highlands—areas where agriculture was well established—all had advanced civilizations, with urban areas, elaborate political organizations, distinct social levels, and sophisticated art and architecture. In many ways, these areas compared favorably to civilized regions of the Old World. Except for weaknesses in military technology—absence of rid-

PATTERNS OF EUROPEAN EXPANSION

European culture hearth

Extension of European Settlement

European plantation development

Mixed European and native settlement

Areas of European influence or control

Limited or no European settlement

Equatorial scale 1:120.000.000

Copyright © by Rand McNally & Co.

ing animals, iron, and gunpowder—these New World civilizations might have been able to resist the Europeans.

European Expansion and Colonization. From the time of Columbus until the middle of the 17th century, Europeans did not try to establish many settlements overseas. They were more interested in acquiring the spices, silks, tea, and other goods of the Orient, and the gold and silver of Central and South America. As in the Spanish conquest of the Aztec and Inca empires, the motto "God, gold, and glory" seemed to inspire most early European ventures abroad.

In time, European occupation of new lands assumed two forms: "farm colonization" in the temperate regions of North America, Australia, New Zealand, and South Africa, and "plantation colonization" in the tropical regions of Central and South America, Central Africa, and Asia.

Farm Colonization. Farm colonization began when fur trading, fishing, and other commercial enterprises gave way to subsistence farming. As more and more settlers immigrated to the New World, they reproduced the European settlement patterns of hamlets, villages, and

---

. . . European occupation of new lands assumed two forms: "farm colonization" and "plantation colonization". . .

European Influence Causes Change. After A.D. 1500, European settlement and the associated culture had its most dramatic extension in North America and South America. Europe's influence and control, however, touched most areas of the world, including many regions that have achieved independent statehood in recent decades. Only China and Japan remained outside the main sphere of European influence until the late 19th and early 20th centuries.

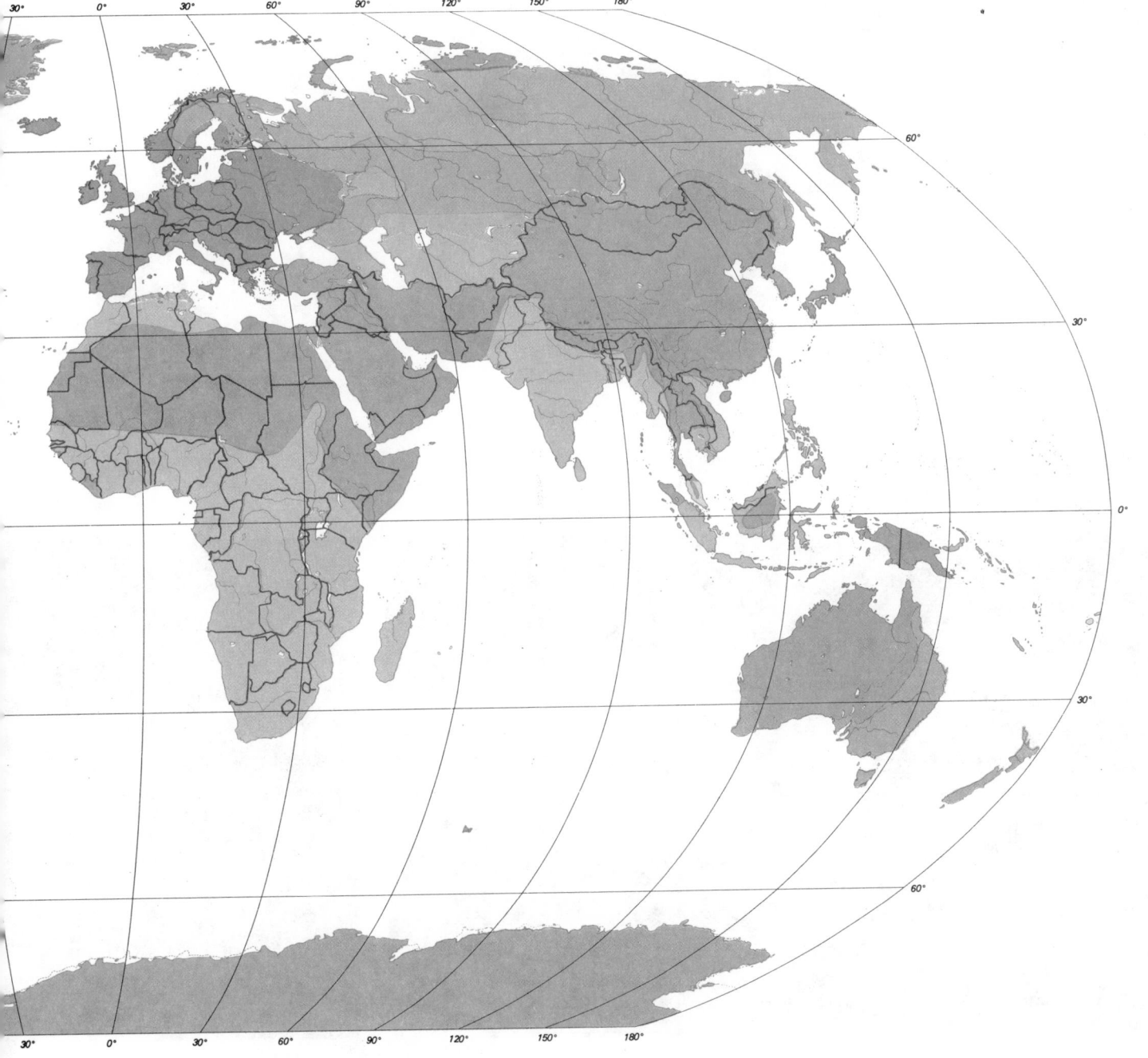

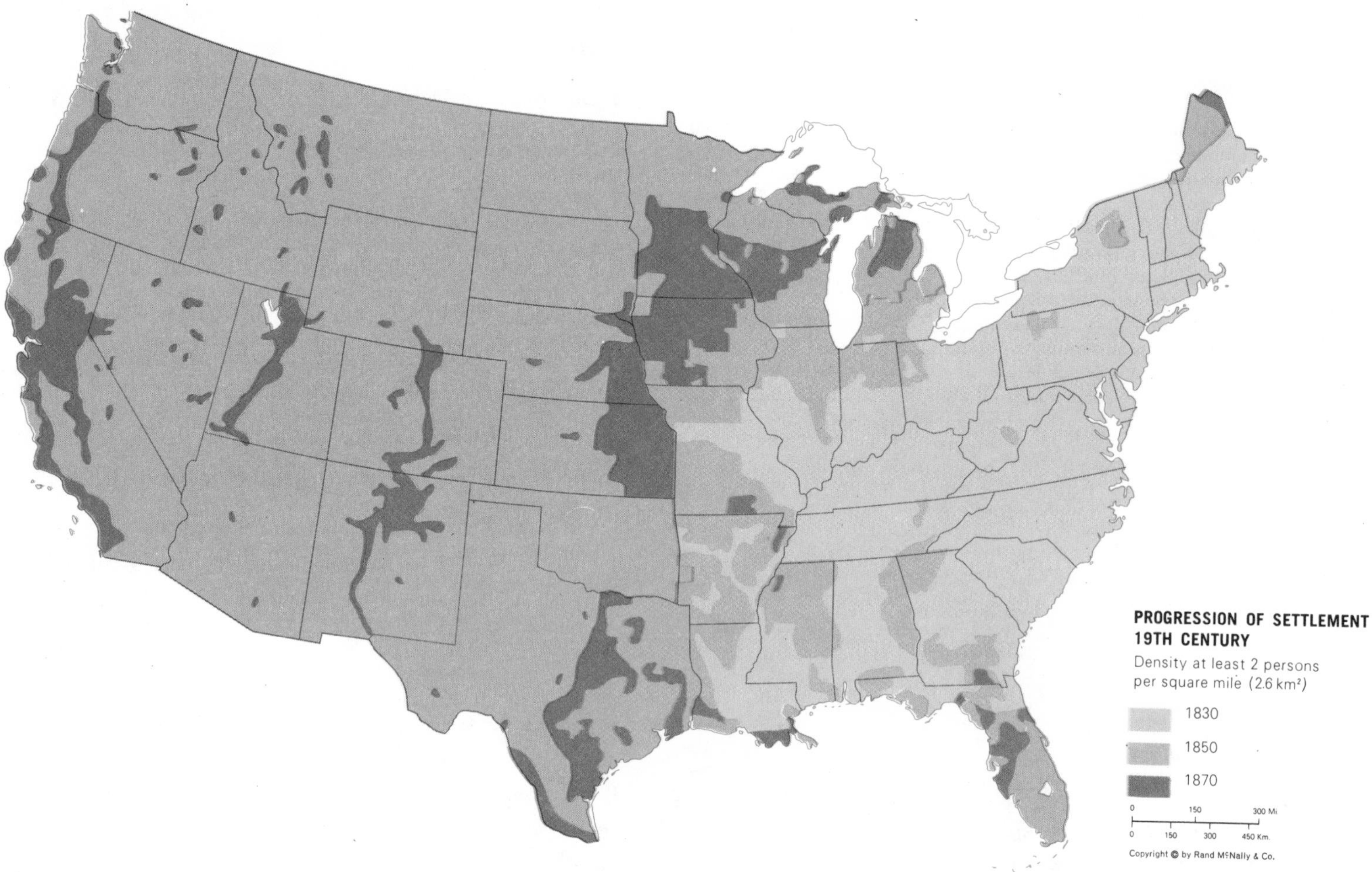
PROGRESSION OF SETTLEMENT
19TH CENTURY
Density at least 2 persons
per square mile (2.6 km²)
1830
1850
1870
0 150 300 Mi
0 150 300 450 Km.
Copyright © by Rand McNally & Co.

Pioneering the Arctic Fringe. Houses and service connections of Inuvik, Northwest Territories, Canada, are lifted above the pemanently frozen land. Strong governent support is needed to establish settlements on the world's arctic lands in Alaska and the Soviet Union as well as this area of Canada.

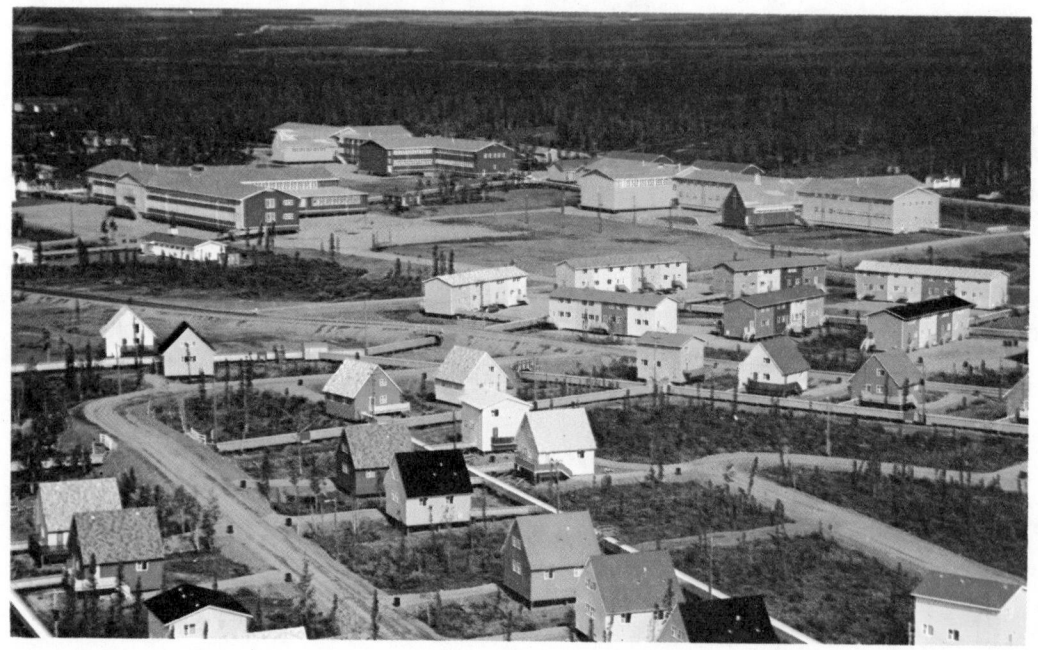

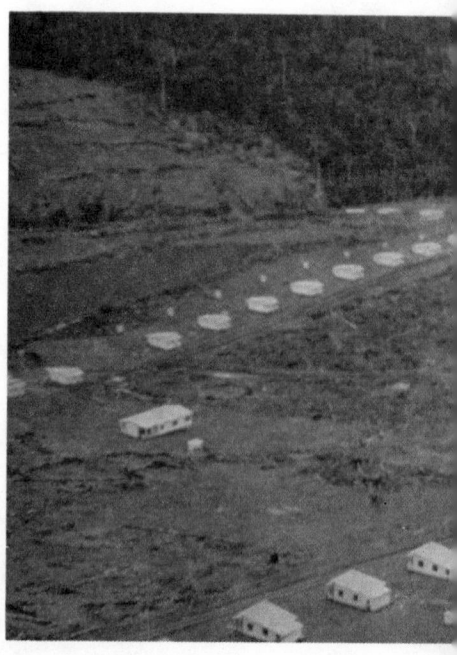

The Moving Frontier. The gradual settlement of the United States in the 19th century illustrates a process that occurred in most areas of farm colonization. From the eastern seaboard, settlers moved westward into the rich agricultural lands between the Appalachian Mountains and the Great Plains. Expansion after the late 1800s was confined to scattered pockets of irrigated land and newly discovered mineral deposits.

Edge of a Tropical Frontier. This agricultural village in the state of Pará, Brazil, is one of many government-sponsored attempts to permanently settle people in one of the last land frontiers on earth.

towns. This population pushed steadily westward and eventually occupied territories larger and richer than the European homeland.

Plantations. Plantation colonization developed in areas that possessed valuable natural resources for European markets but were less attractive as permanent settlements. The plantation economy was generally based on certain crops or raw materials, such as sugar cane and rubber, which were grown or collected for export. Europeans acted as overseers of native laborers, usually local people but later slaves from West Africa. Plantations worked best in the tropics, where cheap labor, year-long growing seasons, and a host of valuable crops or raw materials insured a handsome return for colonists involved in the enterprise. The European plantation economy persisted into the 19th century in the Americas and even later in Africa and Asia. Eventually, the abolition of slavery; competition from beet sugar, artificial dyes, new fibers, and textiles; and the rise of nationalism brought the age of European colonization to a close.

New "Frontiers". The vast lands opened to pioneer settlement in the 19th century have all been occupied. Frontiers today are marginal or remote areas that earlier settlers passed by: the interior of Brazil, the eastern flanks of the Andes, the drier edges of the cultivated areas of the Soviet Union, the tropical environment of northern Australia, and the mining frontiers of Canada and Siberia. Although these frontiers are not likely to attract many people, some government attempts to settle people in the tropical areas of Brazil are in the experimental stage. For the most part, however, it is not an exaggeration to suggest that the age of European exploration and settlement in the 19th century marks the last chapter in the history of our occupation of the earth. Since then, population movement has meant concentration rather than expansion, as more and more nations experience the effects of rapid industrialization and urban development.

Modern Patterns of Land Use

European expansion encouraged patterns of land use substantially different from those in existence before Columbus's time. Vast areas are still relatively empty, but within most of the habitable world, rural landscapes have been significantly modified.

Vanishing Ways of Life. Livelihoods based on hunting and gathering, once practiced over large parts of the New World in A.D. 1500, are now limited to the northern fringe of Canada and a few isolated areas in the tropical forests of South America. Elsewhere in the world, this most primitive form of livelihood is practiced by only a few thousand people in Europe and Asia, many living on reservations. By the end of this century, hunting and gathering as a way of life may disappear altogether.

Nomadic life, which once prevailed over the deserts and steppes of the Old World, has also

declined. In the Soviet Union, it has all but disappeared. It is discouraged, officially or unofficially, in most of the countries in North Africa and Southwest Asia. Nomads are no longer able to serve as sovereigns of oases or guardians of trade routes; these responsibilities have been assumed by governments. In many parts of the world, old trade routes have been abandoned and transportation mechanized: Impoverished by the loss of their privileged social and economic positions, nomadic peoples have become more willing to seek employment in towns and cities. At present, nomads are predominant in only two countries: Mauritania and Somalia. Elsewhere, even in Saudi Arabia, suppression combined with increased opportunities for settled life is discouraging this ancient livelihood.

Commercial Farming. The decline of pastoral nomadism has not affected the world's production of meat, milk, hides, and other animal products. Commercial stock raising is an important feature of the economy in the semiarid regions of Argentina, Australia, Mexico, and the United States. Beef or pork production is an essential part of agriculture in the American Midwest and most of Europe. And dairy farming is not only a major economic factor in such countries as Denmark, Switzerland, the Netherlands, Ireland, and New Zealand, it is often a conspicuous feature of land use near most cities in the Western world.

In some regions, particularly the United States, industrialization has transformed crop raising. Many small, family-owned farms have given way to huge commercial agri-business firms. Using advanced methods of fertilization and mechanized harvesting, these agricultural businesses can raise enough food to feed the population of the United States and still export tons of surplus to other countries.

Subsistence Farming. It would be a mistake, however, to believe that rural life has undergone profound changes everywhere in the world. The semiindustrial agriculture of Europe and the United States is not characteristic of much of Africa, Latin America, or Asia. In these regions, subsistence farming is still the main way of life. It may shift from one area to another, as in the tropical forest of Africa and Southeast Asia, or serve as the basis for peasant village economies found in many areas of the non-Western world. Subsistence

---

. . . Rich land does not necessarily mean rich people, for such regions are often seriously overcrowded . . .

---

farming usually means that food is produced for local consumption only. But farmers may also practice a certain amount of specialization in raising livestock or crops and trade their surplus for a variety of other products—including imports from the outside world. For example, at tribal markets in remote areas of North

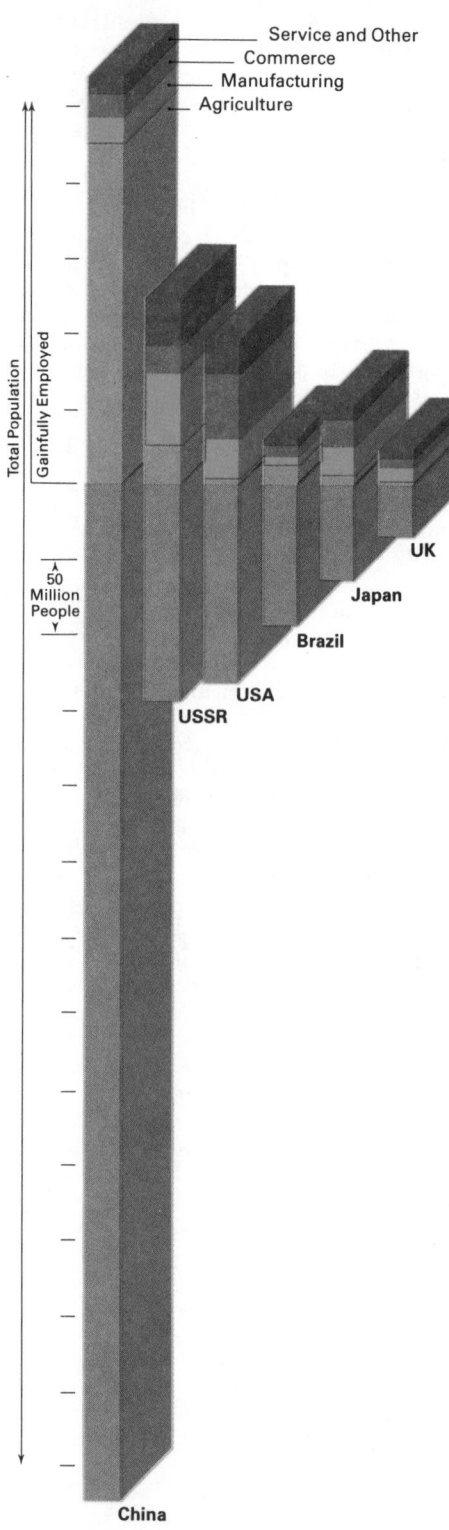

Service and Other
Commerce
Manufacturing
Agriculture

Total Population

Gainfully Employed

50
Million
People

UK

Japan

Brazil

USA

USSR

China

Contrasting Livelihoods. Differences in how people in various countries earn a living is illustrated by this graph. The extreme dependence upon agriculture for a livelihood in China contrasts sharply with the United Kingdom and the United States. Comparing the total employed population to the total number of people in each country gives an idea of the relative importance of the work force to the country.

Africa you will find tea, kerosene, ballpoint pens, sunglasses, and a host of other items from around the globe.

Nevertheless, the large areas devoted to subsistence farming represent small, essentially closed economic systems. It is in these areas that the challenge of economic development is greatest, for this type of farming is often the struggle of an impoverished people to wrest a living from tiny plots of land. Even rich land does not necessarily mean rich people, for such regions are often seriously overcrowded. Few areas in the world are more fertile than the Nile and Ganges valleys, and few areas have experienced more poverty and suffering.

Release from such grinding poverty and toil is possible only where industries can provide an alternative to rural life and where systems of transportation and storage permit farming on a large scale. For example, the source of food for cities in the United States is incredibly complex—potatoes from Maine, citrus fruits from Florida or California, coffee from Brazil, bananas from Central America, and so on. However, underlying and supporting this pattern of consumption is the mechanized agriculture of the United States, a system that yields maximum results from a relatively small investment of labor. While not as mechanized, Western Europe farming follows the same pattern.

Hunger versus Plenty—a Worldwide Problem.
The various categories on the land use map provide a basis for distinguishing between regions

... The social and political implications of hunger and poverty constitute a grave threat to the stability of the world ...

of hunger and plenty, tradition and innovation, and above all between areas of declining rural livelihood and places where no other way of life is possible. Such contrasts may seem remote to people in the United Kingdom or the United States, where only 5 to 10 percent of the population is employed in food production. But the social and political implications of hunger and poverty constitute a grave threat to the stability of the world, a threat that wealthier nations cannot afford to ignore.

Manufacturing and Commerce. Only a small portion of the earth's surface is devoted to manufacturing and commerce—the foundation of wealth and national power. These areas coincide with major urban districts. In the United States, cities account for slightly over 1 percent of the territory, yet provide employment and residence for nearly 70 percent of the population. Australia, a large and sparsely populated country, is even more highly urbanized. Only in the United Kingdom, the Netherlands, and West Germany do urban areas cover a substantial part of the land. This situation, perhaps more than any other, demonstrates the truth of our earlier generalization that the people of the earth are distributed unevenly over the face of the globe.

Today. Only small portions of the earth, corresponding to dense urban populations, are devoted to manufacturing and commerce. Yet these areas control much of the world's wealth and political power. Agricultural surplus is possible where mechanization and relatively low population allow high productivity yields per person. In some fertile Asian lands, overpopulation means that many people exist at starvation levels, even though crop yields are high. Vast arid, equatorial, polar, and mountainous regions still sustain human settlement but only at subsistence level. Development of these zones offers one of the greatest challenges to our ingenuity for extending the area of human settlement.

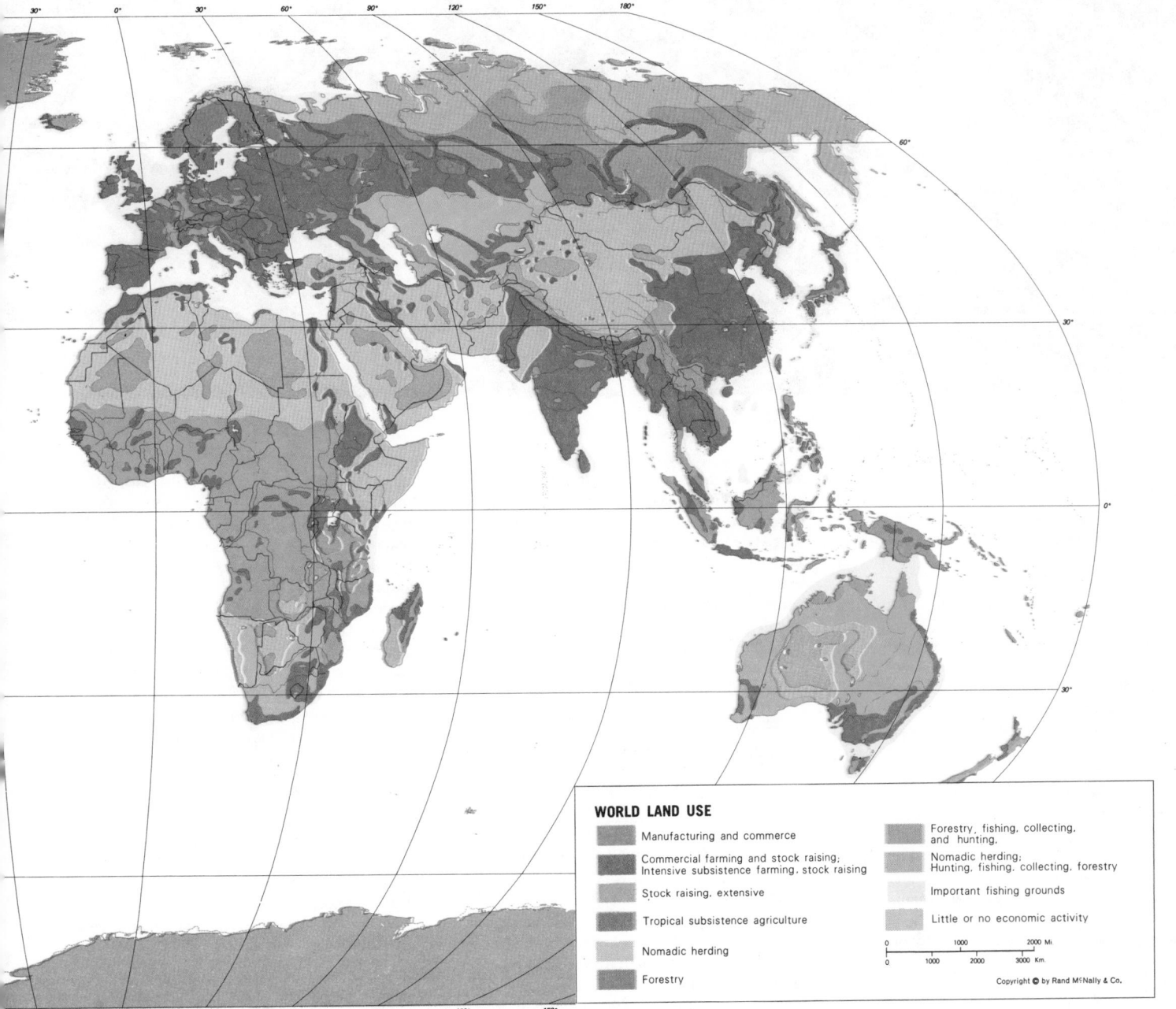

WORLD LAND USE

- Manufacturing and commerce
- Commercial farming and stock raising; Intensive subsistence farming, stock raising
- Stock raising, extensive
- Tropical subsistence agriculture
- Nomadic herding
- Forestry
- Forestry, fishing, collecting, and hunting.
- Nomadic herding; Hunting, fishing, collecting, forestry
- Important fishing grounds
- Little or no economic activity

0   1000   2000 Mi
0   1000   2000   3000 Km

Copyright © by Rand McNally & Co.

Settlements

Human settlement is either concentrated into hamlets, villages and cities or dispersed into scattered farmsteads.

Patterns of Rural Settlement. Every culture has created its own distinctive pattern. Throughout history, wherever rural people live together and travel to their fields, the settlements are in tight clusters, usually near lines of communication and reliable sources of water. Dispersed settlements may be strung out along roads, on dikes in poorly drained areas, or along rivers and coastlines.

Scattered settlements are found in many parts of the world: Australia and New Zealand, the British Isles, Argentina, and most of Canada and the United States. Often such settlements reflect widely dispersed sources of water or hilly terrain. They may also be the result of a particular system of land subdivision, an explanation that accounts for the way farm communities are scattered in the United States.

However, environment or methods of land subdivision alone do not explain patterns of rural settlement. When all factors are considered, the most basic issue is culture, the particular style and preferences of a people. Some prefer to live in compact villages and commute to their fields; others prefer to settle on the banks of rivers; and still others are content to live in widely scattered houses in the midst of their fields. Also, settlement patterns tend to reflect cultural tradition more than personal choice. In most parts of the world, and espe-

---

. . . Settlement patterns reflect cultural tradition for people tend to live in the manner of their ancestors . . .

---

cially in rural areas, people tend to live in the manner of their ancestors.

Urban Development Patterns. The pattern of urban development also varies from culture to culture. In most of North America, most cities are laid out in a grid pattern, with streets intersecting one another at right angles. Other fea-

tures include a distinctive profile, with tall buildings in the heart of the city giving way to lower structures and then to single-family and apartment dwellings. American cities usually have well-defined zones: residential, industrial, commercial, and so on. The quality of residences tends to improve as you travel to the outskirts of the city. In these outlying regions, urban and rural areas may blend into an "urban sprawl." In a culture strongly influenced by the automobile, such as the United States, it is not surprising that newer shopping districts are usually built in suburban areas or as narrow strips along highways.

In Europe, the pattern of city development is more complex. The basic structure of most European cities was established long before the automobile arrived on the scene, and streets tend to be more irregular and narrow. Zoning is usually less distinct, with more specialty shops and fewer well-defined central business districts or "downtown" areas. The focal point of such cities tends to be religious or political rather than commercial. As a result, urban sprawl is less evident, and there is usually a sharper distinction between urban and rural

Clustered Settlement. In many areas of Europe, rural settlement consists of a tight cluster of houses and other buildings located in the midst of surrounding fields. Varennes, France, shown in this photograph and map, is such a settlement. Numerous factors have contributed to the development of these rural clusters: local water supplies, the convergence of communication lines, the mutual need for protection, and social or economic circumstances that encourage close residential communities.

The lighter, wedge-shaped area on each map represents the region pictured in the accompanying photograph.

Scattered Settlement. When farm buildings and houses are situated on the individual farmstead they serve, as shown by the map and photo near Taunton, England, a dispersed pattern of settlement develops. A common feature of the agricultural landscape of the United States and Canada, this scattered form of settlement can also be seen in Europe and many other parts of the world.

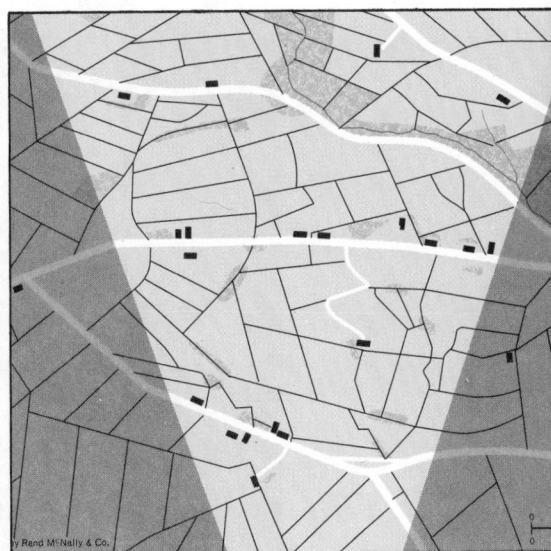

Linear Settlement. A special linear settlement pattern near Beauharnois, Canada, developed under the seignorial, or landlord, system in the French-speaking areas of Canada during the latter half of the 17th century. Narrow strips of land, some only 100 yards (60 meters) wide, fronted the St. Lawrence River and extended back from the banks for a half mile or so. This type of rural settlement contrasts with those in northern France, the homeland of most pioneer settlers of the St. Lawrence Valley.

Rectangular Grid Pattern. Although widespread in the world, the rectangular, or grid, street pattern is most characteristic of cities in the United States and Canada. San Francisco, even though built on hilly terrain, is an example of the north-south and east-west orientation of streets intersecting at right angles; this layout was chosen in response to a uniform national survey system.

Radial Pattern. This photograph and map of Paris, France, illustrates the world's most notable example of a radial plan. It was used in the 19th-century redevelopment of the French capital with the Arc de Triomphe at its center. Based on the principle of a wheel hub and spokes, the plan was conceived in the 18th century by the architect L'Enfant for the capital of the United States.

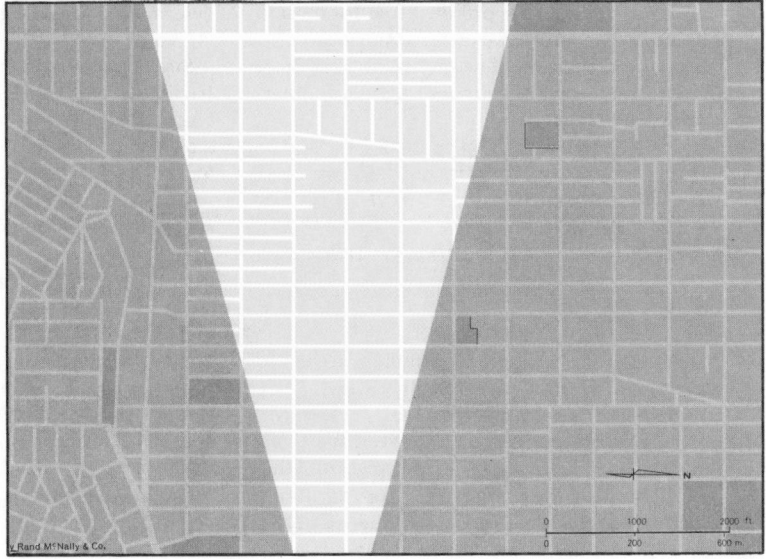

Irregular City Pattern. Many traditional urban developments in North Africa and Southwest Asia resemble this medieval walled city of Fès, Morocco. Compact and seemingly haphazard arrangements of narrow streets, twisted alleys, low houses, and tiny courtyards characterize these cities. The lack of more substantial thoroughfares indicates that such towns were designed long before motor traffic came on the scene.

landscapes. Since the skyscraper does not yet dominate European cities, the urban profile is less clearly outlined than in the United States. If a geometric pattern is evident, more often than not it has been imposed on an older, more haphazard design.

Once we move beyond the realm of Western civilization, we encounter widely different city patterns, as the photograph of Fès, in Morocco, clearly illustrates. Since Fès is walled, it begins and ends abruptly. Its profile is low, for most buildings have only two or three stories. Streets are narrow alleys, often with dead ends, since they were built without regard for motor vehicles.

. . . One of the most important principles of human geography is that each culture has a distinctive urban style. . .

Fès has several quarters, but these are culturally rather than economically defined. The Andalusian quarter was founded by refugees from the Christian reconquest of Spain, while the Kairouani quarter takes its name from the original inhabitants, who came from the Tunisian city of el-Kairouan. Unlike American or European cities, Fès has no clear distinction

between residential and commercial or industrial districts. Crafts and trade activities are spread along particular lanes; craft workers and merchants usually live above or behind their shops. The focal point of the entire city, as with many cities of the Middle East, is a large mosque containing the tomb of the patron saint of the city. Several smaller mosques serve as focal points for particular quarters. But as a visitor to Fès, you would have a hard time determining where the "downtown" of the city is located.

Similar urban patterns can be found in the traditional cities of the Middle East and elsewhere in Asia. Modern quarters, of course, have a different character. The new quarter of the ancient city of Damascus is laid out in wide, regular streets not unlike those found in an American city. Where European influence has been strong, especially in former colonial areas, two distinctly different cities often exist side by side. Old and New Delhi and the ancient and modern quarters of Jerusalem are particularly striking examples of this dual pattern. In the course of time, contrasting styles may eventually blend. Nevertheless, it is still possible to speak of "Western" and "Eastern" patterns of urban development. This fact illustrates one of the most important principles of human geography—that each culture has a distinctive urban style.

Distribution of World Industry

The process of industrialization, which began in Europe in the 18th century, so thoroughly transformed society that it has often been described as a revolution. Perhaps "evolution" would be an equally appropriate term, for the inventions, economic changes, and social transformations of the process of industrialization have helped shape history during the past three centuries.

Key Inventions of the Industrial Revolution. The Industrial Revolution was founded on a series of key inventions. Perhaps the most influential were improved spinning and weaving machines, the steam engine, the railway locomotive, and the factory system of production characterized by specialized tasks.

The significance of these technological advances cannot be overestimated. They constitute the foundation of the modern economy in Europe, the United States, Japan, and the Soviet Union. It is striking to note that a large number of major inventions occurred over a fairly brief time, and most of them can be cred-

---

. . . The industrial revolution was founded on a series of key inventions. . .

ited to Europeans and Americans. The Industrial Revolution is indeed an achievement of Western civilization, and it may be the only such achievement destined to spread over the entire world.

Taken together, several technological changes had far-reaching effects on the nature of production and employment in the Western world. These include (1) the use of new basic materials, especially steel; (2) the use of new sources of energy (steam engines, petroleum, electricity, and internal combustion engines); (3) a great increase in production with a smaller investment of labor; (4) a radical reorganization of work, from small, family enterprises to large factories with elaborate subdivisions of labor; (5) important developments in transportation partly needed to carry raw materials to factories and ship finished products to markets; and (6) an increased application of science to industry.

These innovations not only permitted the mass production of goods but meant an increased use of certain natural resources such as oil, natural gas, coal, aluminum, and other minerals. Population tended to concentrate in those areas where abundant raw materials were discovered.

Resources and Manufacturing. Europe and the United States, with their large deposits of coal and iron ore, have the raw materials necessary for steel production. The United States is also well endowed with petroleum and natural gas. The extraordinary abundance of resources in the United States was underscored in World War II. The interruption of international commerce resulted in only minor shortages of critical raw materials such as rubber and tin. In contrast, Germany's economy was seriously hampered when the country could no longer get adequate petroleum supplies. The Japanese Empire, whose industry depended on imports of raw materials, lost the war when it lost command of the sea. Control of or access to the resources required for heavy industry, and especially steel production, is necessary for any country that hopes to be a major world power. The United States and the Soviet Union—great rivals since World War II—are particularly rich in this regard.

But natural resources alone do not account for the distribution of manufacturing in the world. For example, tiny Switzerland is a major producer of watches and other precision instruments, whereas the Middle East, with its huge reserves of petroleum, has few other important industries. Besides raw materials, power, and fuel, industrial development requires a skilled labor force; sufficient capital for construction, maintenance, and research; transportation facilities; and access to effective markets. Also, government planning, tariffs, monetary incen-

. . . Control of or access to resources required for heavy industry is necessary for any country that hopes to be a major world power . . .

tives, and economic or political alliances influence industrial development. Thus, the existence of one of the world's major deposits of natural gas in the Sahara does not mean that Algeria will automatically develop a vast petrochemical industry. Nor is the impressive waterpower potential in central Africa likely to promote large-scale industries in the near future. On the other hand, government policies may encourage industrial developments that other countries would not consider efficient. For example, the steel mill at Karabük in Turkey is not economical by European or American standards. Yet the foundry is regarded as a national asset by the Turkish government.

Location of Industrial Areas. Thus, an entire range of factors influences the location of industries and industrial development. Neither the general pattern nor specific cases of industrialization can be adequately explained without keeping these factors in mind. Yet we can make some general observations about the location of industrial regions.

Indelible Imprint. Near Hibbing, Minnesota, the mining of iron ore—the most useful of the world's metals and a foundation of the industrial strength of the United States—has been carried on for over 100 years. Open-pit mining of iron ore and strip mining of coal have radically altered the earth's surface in many areas—vivid evidence of human modification of the environment.

Keys to Industrial Development. Of all the world's natural resources, fossil fuels have been the most essential for industrial development. (The map shows their distribution favors countries in the northern hemisphere.) Even with rising costs, fossil fuels continue to serve as major energy sources because of abundant reserves and the recent discovery of vast new deposits. Though scattered and less accessible than previously uncovered reserves, these deposits are still cheaper to develop and transport than newer sources of energy, including electricity.

The Americas. In North America, industrial sites coincide with concentrations of resources or with urban districts large enough to provide adequate markets for finished goods. This is especially true of the diversified industrial districts of the Pacific Coast. The main centers of steel production—the Lower Great Lakes region, southeastern Canada, and the northeastern United States—profit from large deposits of iron ore and the transportation network of the Great Lakes. This region, heavily populated, is also blessed with abundant labor and a large market. On the Atlantic Coast, the Piedmont has replaced New England as America's leading textile center and is now a diversified district similar to those on the West Coast. The Gulf region benefits from its port facilities and rich deposits of petroleum and natural gas.

In South America, industrial districts are confined primarily to the main urban centers of the continent: Rio de Janeiro-São Paulo, Buenos Aires, and Santiago. (One exception is the development of the Brazilian rain forest currently under way.) Only Rio de Janeiro and São Paulo have profited from readily accessible deposits of iron ore and coal. Venezuela has important reserves of petroleum and iron ore but lacks an adequate labor force or national market to sus-

tain major industrial development. The same can be said for Chile's abundant copper deposits.

Europe, the Soviet Union, and Japan. Four of the major industrial districts of Europe—Midlands-Lancashire, Belgium and northern France, the Ruhr basin, and Silesia (Ślask)—coincide with significant deposits of iron ore or coal. The Po Valley in Italy profits from abundant and accessible hydroelectric power. Yet the presence in this area of the Fiat automobile works is not a reflection of natural resources but of individual initiative and collective skills. Also, the southern industrial district of Sweden, while developing the rich deposits of iron ore in the north, is not tied to this one resource.

On the other hand, the pattern of industrial development in the Soviet Union is directly tied to resources. One exception is the Moscow-Gorki district, which—like Buenos Aires or the Po Valley—is more a reflection of local labor supplies and large urban markets than of abundant raw materials. Both the Donbas and the Kuzbas basins have large reserves of coal, with the Donbas also rich in iron ore and hydroelectric power. The Urals region is blessed with a variety of industrial resources, including iron

ore, coal, and petroleum. In southern Manchuria, local supplies of coal and iron ore—originally developed by the Japanese—now serve as the base for China's major manufacturing region.

Japan itself is nearly equal to the United States and the Soviet Union in overall industrial production, followed closely by West Germany. Indeed, the impressive growth in Japan in shipbuilding, electrical and optical industries, textiles, automobiles, and many other enterprises is the result of human rather than natural resources. Japan lacks important sources of coking coal, iron and other metallic ores, petroleum, and many other resources essential to modern industry. Yet skillful management and abundant, relatively cheap labor have enabled the Japanese to meet the high costs of importing raw materials and still compete with resource-rich West Germany, the United Kingdom, and the United States.

Other Regions. Industrial development in other areas of the world reflects a mixture of natural resources and cultural influences. India has only one major industrial district, the product of government encouragement and local supplies of iron ore and coal. Australia's development is virtually coincident with its

Key Inventions (1764-1964) These and many other technological innovations revolutionized the nature of production and employment and greatly increased the use of natural resources. Since 1964 people have been aided in their use of the world's resources by widespread use of computer technology, earth-monitoring satellites, and breakthroughs in genetic research.

1764	Spinning Jenny	ENGLAND
1765	Steam Engine	ENGLAND
1769	Self-propelled Steam Vehicle	FRANCE
1783	Puddling Iron Furnace	ENGLAND
1785	Power Loom	ENGLAND
1786	Threshing Machine	SCOTLAND
1793	Cotton Gin	UNITED STATES
1802	Steamboat	UNITED STATES
1811	Cylinder Printing Press	GERMANY
1824	Portland Cement	ENGLAND
1825	Steam Locomotive	ENGLAND
1831	Electric Generator	ENGLAND
1834	Reaper	UNITED STATES
1839	Vulcanization of Rubber	UNITED STATES
1839	Photography *(Daguerreotype)*	FRANCE
1844	Telegraphy	UNITED STATES

1846	Rotary Printing Press	UNITED STATES
1850	Corn Picker	UNITED STATES
1851	Refrigerating Machine	UNITED STATES
1855	Bessemer Process Steel	ENGLAND
1859	Gas Engine	FRANCE
1859	Oil Well Drilling	UNITED STATES
1861	Passenger Elevator	UNITED STATES
1866	Open-hearth Steel Furnace	UNITED STATES
1867	Reinforced Concrete	FRANCE
1869	Railway Air Brake	UNITED STATES
1876	Telephone	UNITED STATES
1876	Four-cycle Gas Engine	GERMANY
1879	Incandescent Light	UNITED STATES
1882	Steam Turbine	FRANCE
1884	Photographic Roll Film	UNITED STATES
1884	Linotype	UNITED STATES
1884	Artificial Silk *(rayon)*	FRANCE
1888	Pneumatic Tire	IRELAND
1892	Diesel Engine	GERMANY
1892	Electric Motor *(A.C.)*	UNITED STATES
1892	Gasoline Automobile	UNITED STATES
1893	Motion Pictures	UNITED STATES
1895	Wireless Telegraphy	ITALY
1900	Caterpillar Tractor	UNITED STATES

1903	Airplane	UNITED STATES
1906	Radio Vacuum Tube	UNITED STATES
1907	Plastic *(Bakelite)*	UNITED STATES
1911	Air Conditioning	UNITED STATES
1913	Radio Receiver	UNITED STATES
1913	Talking Motion Pictures	UNITED STATES
1925	Television	SCOTLAND - UNITED STATES
1926	Liquid-propelled Rocket	UNITED STATES
1928	Autogiro	UNITED STATES
1931	Cyclotron	UNITED STATES
1935	Radiolocator *(radar)*	SCOTLAND
1937	Nylon	UNITED STATES
1937	Jet Aircraft Engine	ENGLAND
1937	Xerography	UNITED STATES
1939	Helicopter	GERMANY - UNITED STATES
1942	Nuclear Reactor	UNITED STATES
1946	Computer	UNITED STATES
1947	Transistor	UNITED STATES
1956	Nuclear Power Station	ENGLAND
1957	Earth-Orbiting Satellite	SOVIET UNION
1959	Fuel Cell	UNITED STATES
1960	Laser	UNITED STATES
1962	Communications Satellite	UNITED STATES
1964	Microcircuitry	UNITED STATES

MAJOR INDUSTRIAL RESOURCES

- Major coal and lignite deposits
- Major petroleum producing areas
- Major gas fields
- Major hydroelectric plants
- △ Major iron ore deposits
- ○ Major bauxite deposits

Equatorial Scale 1:180,000,000

Copyright © by Rand McNally & Co.

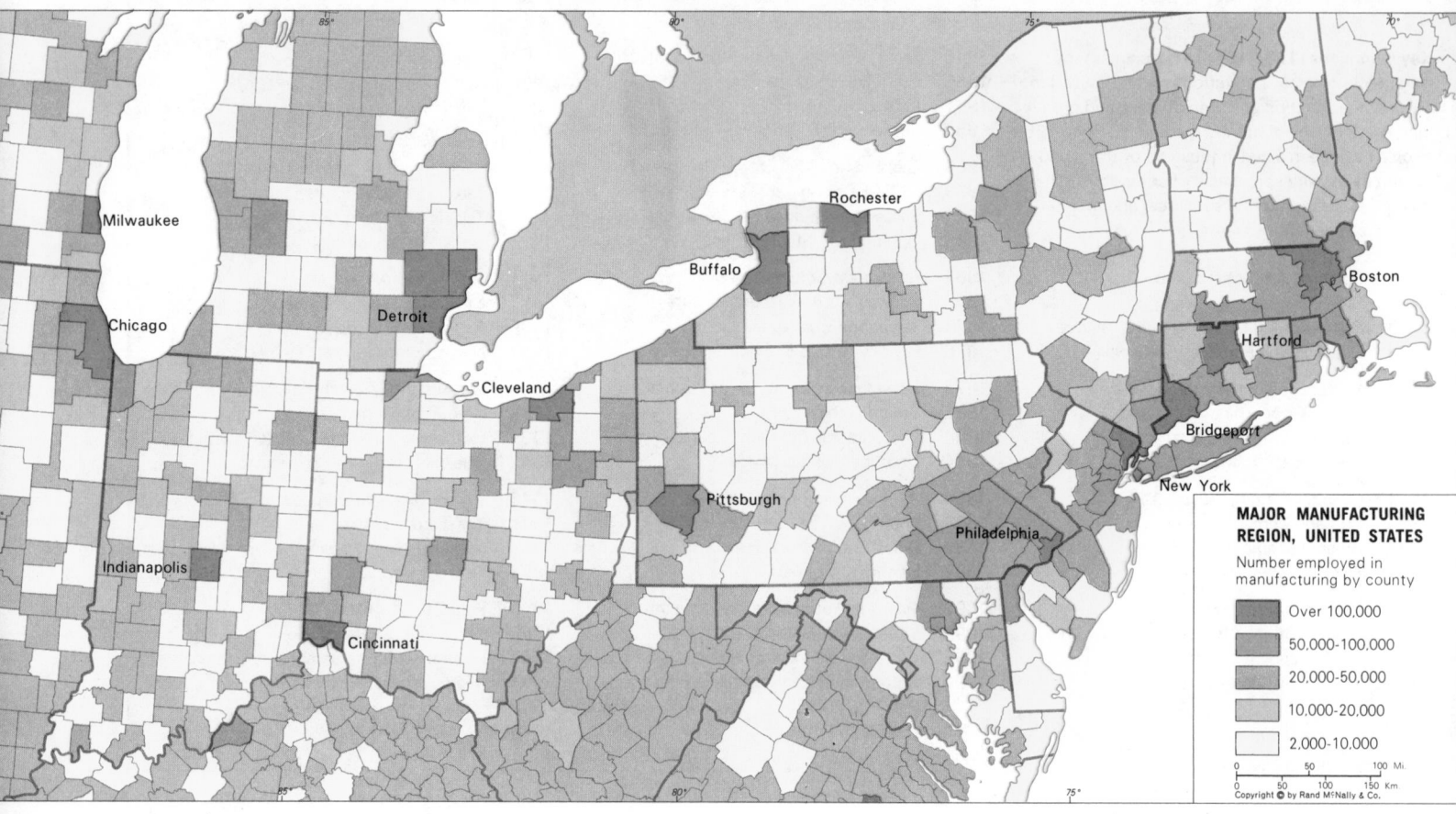

MAJOR MANUFACTURING REGION, UNITED STATES

Number employed in manufacturing by county

Over 100,000
50,000-100,000
20,000-50,000
10,000-20,000
2,000-10,000

Copyright © by Rand McNally & Co.

major population centers. Southwest Asia has no major manufacturing, while China is struggling to modernize its industries. But from an industrial point of view, Africa remains the least developed continent. The only exceptions are the mining industries in the Johannesburg region keyed to some of the world's richest deposits of gold, uranium, and diamonds.

Current Trends. In the past two decades, other patterns in industrial development have emerged. Light industries, such as electronics, food processing, even automotive assembly, have been moving to suburban areas outside major cities in the United States and parts of Western Europe. Suburbs offer low-cost labor and lower tax rates. However, this trend is highly dependent on the private automobile, since most workers cannot get to their jobs any other way. As a result, this type of population and industry shift is not feasible in many parts of the world.

Light industries are also moving their assembly and labor-intensive processes overseas to plants in Taiwan, the Philippines, Mexico, and Korea. In time, other industries may also transfer their operations to these countries to take advantage of lower tax rates and reduced labor costs. According to business observers, we are already entering the age of the "international product," whose various components are manufactured and assembled in factories all over the world.

Energy—Crisis and Opportunity

Energy resources are essential to industrial development in both advanced and less developed nations. The availability and cost of energy set limits on economic growth as much as the length of the growing season and available moisture restrict agriculture. Without fuel for transportation, most of the world would be paralyzed. Factories would close and cities eventually die. The very life of the world as we know it is highly dependent on adequate, cost-effective sources of energy.

Effects of the Crisis. Ironically, most of the world's major industrial countries, such as West Germany and Japan, are deficient in petroleum, while countries that export abundant quantities of oil, such as Libya and Nigeria, have little industrial development. Escalating energy costs have put pressure on many nations, creating problems of inflation and rising national debts. But industrialized countries can still afford to pay for imported fuel with goods that petroleum-exporting states want—automobiles, electrical goods, technical expertise, and so on.

Nations that suffer the most are both oil deficient and economically poor. They cannot pay the higher prices exacted by such oil cartels as OPEC (Organization of Petroleum Exporting Countries). While the industrialized nations must worry about reducing their use of auto-

mobiles, poorer nations must worry about growing enough food to feed their people.

In the past few decades, energy has expanded from the industrial arena into the political arena as well. Third-world countries are forming alliances to offset the industrial power of the more developed nations. For example, OPEC has been able to gain recognition as an international business and political force. Founded in 1960, the 18-member organization

...Nations that suffer the most are both oil deficient and economically poor...

includes not only Arab states but Venezuela, Nigeria, Indonesia, and Ecuador. But the industrialized nations have a potentially powerful cartel of their own. These countries, particularly the United States, produce the major share of food in the world. Grain embargoes can be as effective in some cases as oil embargoes. As a result, a tug of war involving food and energy may develop in the next decade or two, with poorer nations caught between these powerful international cartels.

The Search for New Sources. The energy crisis represents an opportunity as well. Most industrial nations are pursuing alternative means of generating the energy they need. It is important

to remember that petroleum dependency is relatively recent in human history, a product of 20th-century settlement and industrial technology. Since for many years petroleum and coal were relatively inexpensive, alternative forms of energy production were not explored. Now, with rising oil and gas prices, solar power, nuclear energy, shale oil, and wind and water

---

...A tug of war involving food and energy may develop in the next decade or two...

---

power are being seriously examined. Nations have invested heavily in nuclear energy, but recent accidents have dramatized some of the risks involved in using this form of energy; and no one has yet found a foolproof method for disposing of nuclear by-products. Solar, wind, water, and geothermal power represent clean, renewable sources of energy that can be used effectively in many parts of the world. Also, simply altering the way homes and commercial buildings are constructed can save energy and make use of solar collectors or prevailing winds.

Currently, even more sophisticated methods are being tried. In Hawaii, a state that must import petroleum for 92 percent of its electricity needs, 14,000 solar panels are used in heating water. A giant windmill on the north

coast of Oahu is part of a complex that will feed power to the Hawaiian Electric Company. Off the island of Hawaii, a floating rig draws its own power from the interaction of warm and cold sea water, a process known as ocean thermal energy conversion.

Weighing Our Choices. Our search for alternative energy sources means we are confronted with difficult choices regarding the environment. In many parts of the world, oil dependency can be lessened by using more coal; often this means accepting higher levels of air pollution. We can develop the vast reserves of oil shale found in the Rocky Mountains of the United States, but huge quantities of earth must be mined to extract the oil. As a result, we may destroy the natural environment in the process. How we choose to acquire additional energy will have considerable impact on the political, economic, and natural environment of the world. Energy solutions must benefit not only industrial and resource-rich nations but poorer countries as well if we are to create a stable and balanced world economy.

...How we choose to acquire additional energy will have considerable impact on the political, economic, and natural environment of the world...

Concentration and Dispersion. The original basis for the heavy industries locating in the northeastern United States was the iron ore of Michigan and Minnesota and the coking coal of the Appalachian Mountains. However, many light industries are moving to suburban areas or the southeastern and southwestern regions of the United States. These areas offer lower energy and labor costs and greater tax benefits. More recently, the same attractions are inducing companies to move their labor-intensive operations to plants overseas.

Complex Distribution of Industry. Many of the major industrial regions of the world are located close to the major industrial resource areas. However, it is a mistake to assume that natural resources always attract industry. A full range of factors must be considered—technology, politics, markets, labor force, as well as resources—to understand why industry locates where it does.

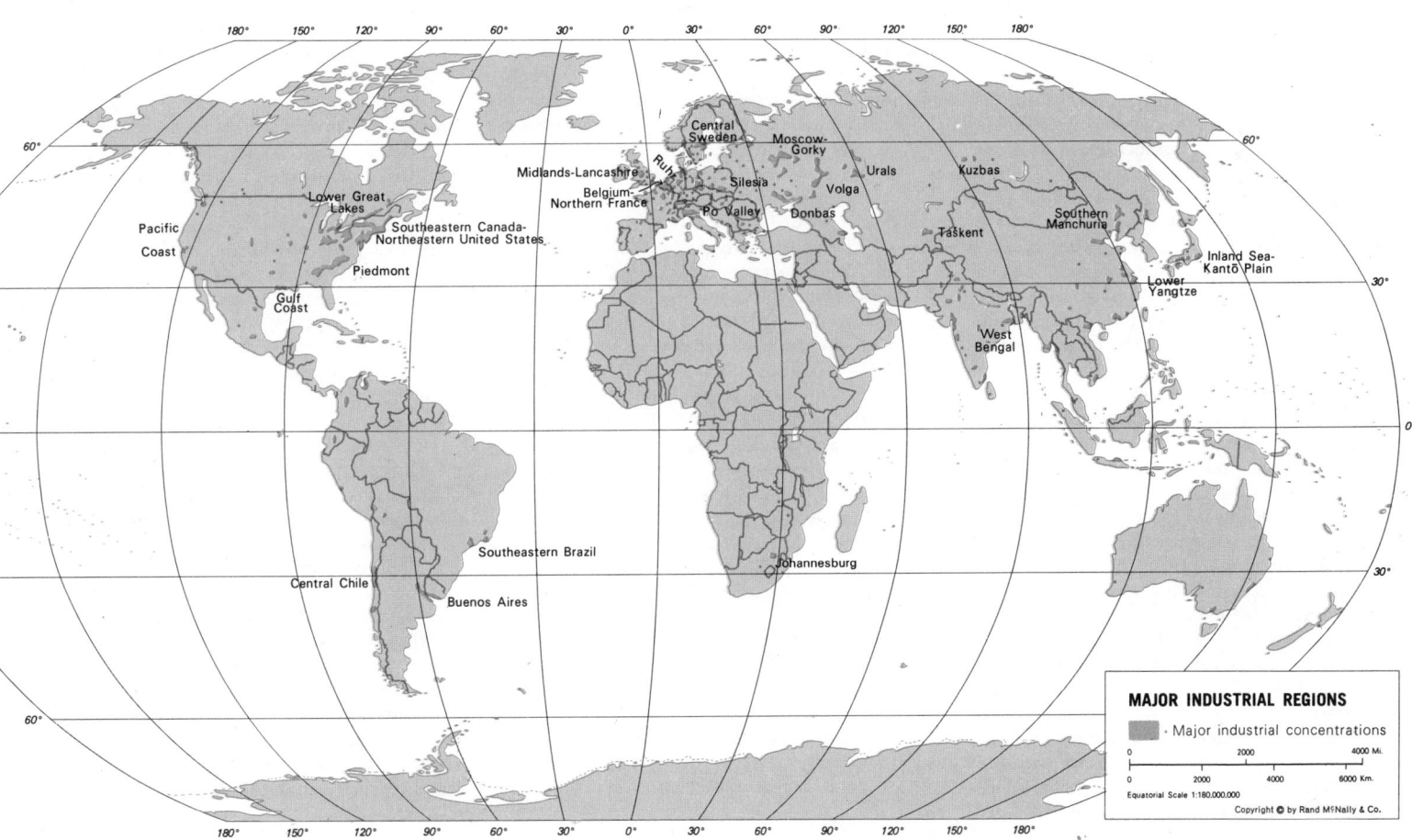

MAJOR INDUSTRIAL REGIONS

Major industrial concentrations

Equatorial Scale 1:180,000,000

Copyright © by Rand McNally & Co.

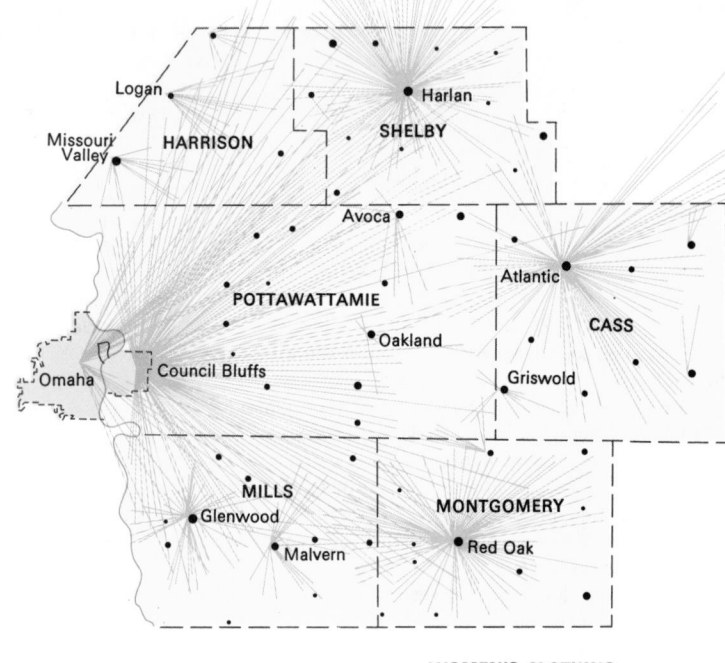

GROCERIES

WOMEN'S CLOTHING

Settlements as Trade Centers

So far in our attempt to understand human patterns and imprints, we have looked at some of the factors that influence the location and design of rural communities and cities. Now we need to consider another element: the role of towns as trade centers.

Each urban settlement acts as a central place offering goods and services to the people within its trade area. The number and type of goods or services available depends largely on the size of the town or urban settlement. Even the smallest towns will have a post office, grocery store, and perhaps a clothing shop, a doctor, a dentist, and church and school. However, the chances are remote that a large department store or hospital would be attracted to these small towns. There would not be enough business to make such facilities economical or profitable. Each of the goods or services offered by a town will attract people from a certain area or zone. When added together, these zones constitute the trade area, or "hinterland," of a center.

The Settlement Hierarchy. When you examine the trade patterns of villages, towns, and cities in a particular area, a type of "settlement hierarchy" emerges. This concept can be used to explain the size and spacing of these trade centers. In general, the principle of a "hierarchy" can be applied to most settled regions of the world. In well-populated areas, settlements tend to fall into distinctive categories. At the base of the system are rural villages of about 500 inhabitants; next come towns with 1,000 to 2,000 people, small cities with populations of 5,000 to 10,000, and finally larger cities with

perhaps 50,000. Each of these settlements is subordinate, both economically and culturally, to one or more metropolitan areas of 200,000 or more people. In turn, these areas are subordinate to national urban districts with up to several million inhabitants. That the larger centers with their wide range of goods and services have larger trade centers is not surprising. That they incorporate the functions of small centers is less obvious but true in most parts of the world. As a result, we can say that within a settlement hierarchy, cities, towns, and villages are both dependent on and independent of one another, since their functions and clientele tend to overlap somewhat. Naturally, the largest urban centers will draw customers from the widest area. These principles are illustrated in the accompanying maps of southwestern Iowa and northeastern Spain.

The study of trade areas and consumer patterns helps us understand how the settlement hierarchy evolves. Very often, improvements in transportation result in the concentration of goods and services within a few larger centers. A rural district with poor roads or few motor vehicles will have a number of small trading centers that serve a regular clientele. When the roads are improved and more people acquire trucks and automobiles, customers will bypass these smaller centers for the attractions of larger cities. Perhaps these cities offer a rich assortment of goods, more services, or lower

---

. . . The principle of a "(settlement) hierarchy" can be applied to most regions of the world . . .

---

prices. Also, the longer trip to a large center may be a matter of convenience; people can buy several goods or services in one place. These possibilities explain why smaller towns tend to decline as communications and transportation improve and why people within a city may pass up neighborhood shops in favor of a trip "downtown."

Market Centers. Not all cities in the world have central business districts like those in the United States. But most urban centers have at least one district that can be called commercial. Moreover, in regions where storage facilities are poor, cities provide markets where rural people can sell their produce to urban customers. Such markets are still found in some cities of Europe and are common in African, Asian, and Latin American towns.

Finally, it should be remembered that commerce in a particular trade area depends to some extent on the characteristics of production. In the mountains of southwestern Asia, the largest markets are found in regions where people raise or produce complementary goods. For example, one group may cultivate cereal crops, another fruits and vegetables, and still another may make pottery or special tools. The existence of such markets enables families engaged in subsistence farming to specialize in certain crops or products and trade their surplus. The situation in which families are totally self-sufficient, producing everything they need, is more mythical than real. Even in the most primitive areas, where the economy is small-scale and exchange based on barter, markets are a vital feature of people's livelihoods.

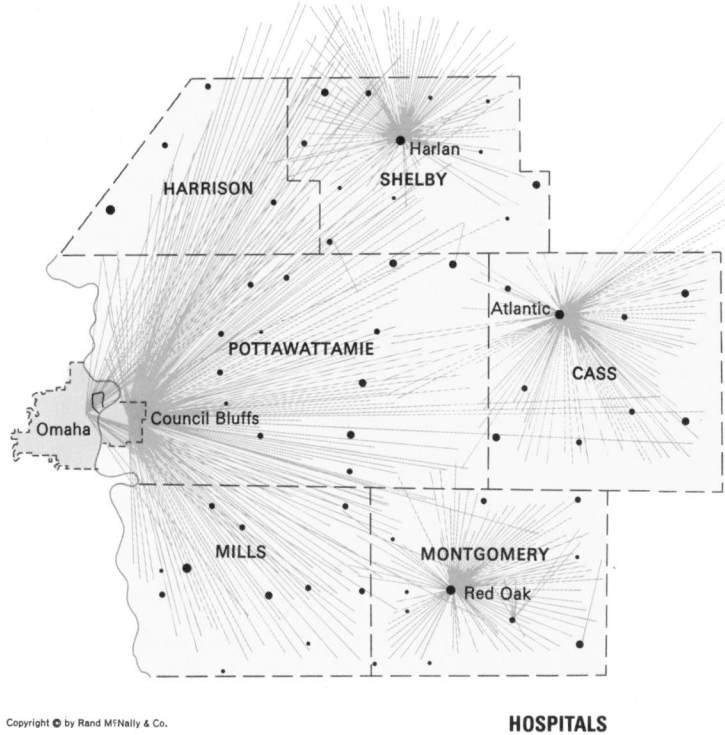

HARRISON

SHELBY

Harlan

POTTAWATTAMIE

Omaha

Council Bluffs

Atlantic

CASS

MILLS

MONTGOMERY

Red Oak

HOSPITALS

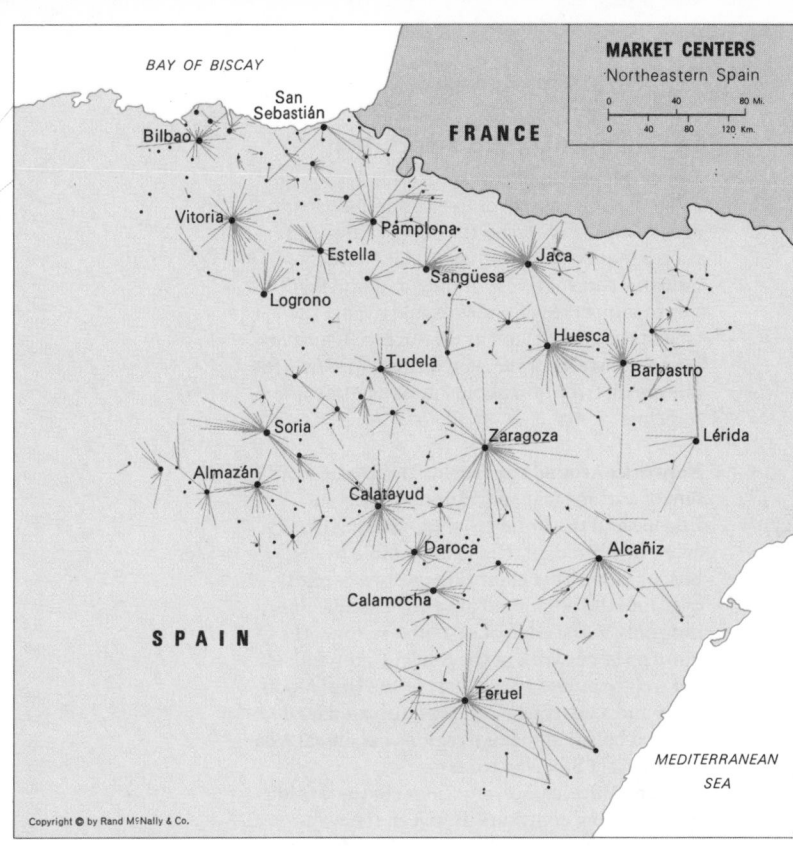

MARKET CENTERS
Northeastern Spain

0   40   80 Mi.

0   40   80   120 Km.

BAY OF BISCAY

FRANCE

San Sebastián

Bilbao

Vitoria

Pamplona

Estella

Jaca

Sangüesa

Logrono

Huesca

Tudela

Barbastro

Soria

Zaragoza

Lérida

Almazán

Calatayud

Daroca

Alcañiz

Calamocha

SPAIN

Teruel

MEDITERRANEAN
SEA

Trade Centers. The maps graphically portray the importance of trade centers in establishing a pattern of settlement within an area. Red lines show the travel of people to central places to buy goods and services. In Spain (map at right), as in Iowa, large centers grow to provide a greater range of goods and services than smaller centers and to attract customers from the widest area. The size and spacing of these interdependent places show an ordered pattern as it progresses from the smallest village to the largest city. Development of transportation and methods of food production and storage are among the factors that help create the settlement pattern.

Open-Air Market. Abidjan's market in Ivory Coast, Africa, provides an effective means for rural peoples to offer their products to urban consumers. Local markets of this nature are often the only method for exchanging goods in Africa, Asia, and Latin America, or wherever storage and transportation facilities are inadequate. Such markets are also found in some European cities.

The Modern Market. The modern shopping center of Europe and North America serves much the same purpose as an open-air market—the sale of goods and services to customers. But there the resemblance ends. A complex transportation network supplies the center with a wide variety of goods. Many centers, like the district in Stockholm, Sweden, pictured here, draw customers from a wide area and often replace neighborhood shopping districts or downtown centers.

Development of Transportation

The development of transportation is closely related to the growth of urban and industrial areas. Cities depend on the supply lines and routes that converge on them. Likewise, no industry can survive without adequate facilities to import raw materials and export finished products. A look at the surface transportation networks of the world clearly reveals the uneven distribution of our human patterns and imprints.

Networks Around the World. The greatest system of surface transportation appears in Europe and the United States, where virtually every inhabited district is accessible by car, bus, or train. This elaborate pattern carries over into the populated areas of Canada, thinning only at the edge of settled territory. The more open network of the Soviet Union follows the well-populated area west of the Ural Mountains and a narrower zone of cultivated land wedged between the dry regions of central Asia and the vast Siberian forests.

South America presents some of the world's most striking contrasts. Between the well-developed and generally accessible plains of Argentina and the underdeveloped interior of Brazil is an enormous difference in population density and level of economic organization. Development of the Amazon basin and huge rain forest area has spurred construction of more roads and highways. Previously, communication depended entirely on inland water

---

. . . Improvements in transportation result in the concentration of goods and services within a few larger centers . . .

---

routes. The Pan American Highway, stretching from Mexico through Central America and down the Pacific Coast to Chile, is a major link among Latin American nations. Feeder roads off this highway connect smaller cities and

Building a Transportation System. The Trans-Amazon Highway stretches from Recifé, Brazil, to Pucallapa, Peru. A portion of the "highway" in Amazonas, a state in northwestern Brazil, near the center of South America, pictured here, represents a country's transportation system in the early stages of development.

WORLD TRANSPORTATION

—— Railroad
—— Motorable road
(Areas within 25 miles)
—— Inland waterway
• Major port
○ Major airport

0   1000   2000 Mi.
0   1000   2000   3000 Km.

Copyright © by Rand McNally & Co.

Transportation Systems Related to Progress. World transportation networks are most heavily concentrated in the urban and industrial areas of Europe and North America. The communication system provided by such a network contributes to the rapid dissemination of ideas, methods, and tools, and thus to the cultural evolution of these areas. In sharp contrast, the lack of transportation and communication systems in less developed countries is as much a barrier to progress as overpopulation or lack of resources.

Sophisticated Surface Transportation. Trails of blurred light from moving automobiles on an expressway near Peoria, Illinois, close to the heart of the North American continent, serve to dramatize the advanced development of the surface transportation of the United States.

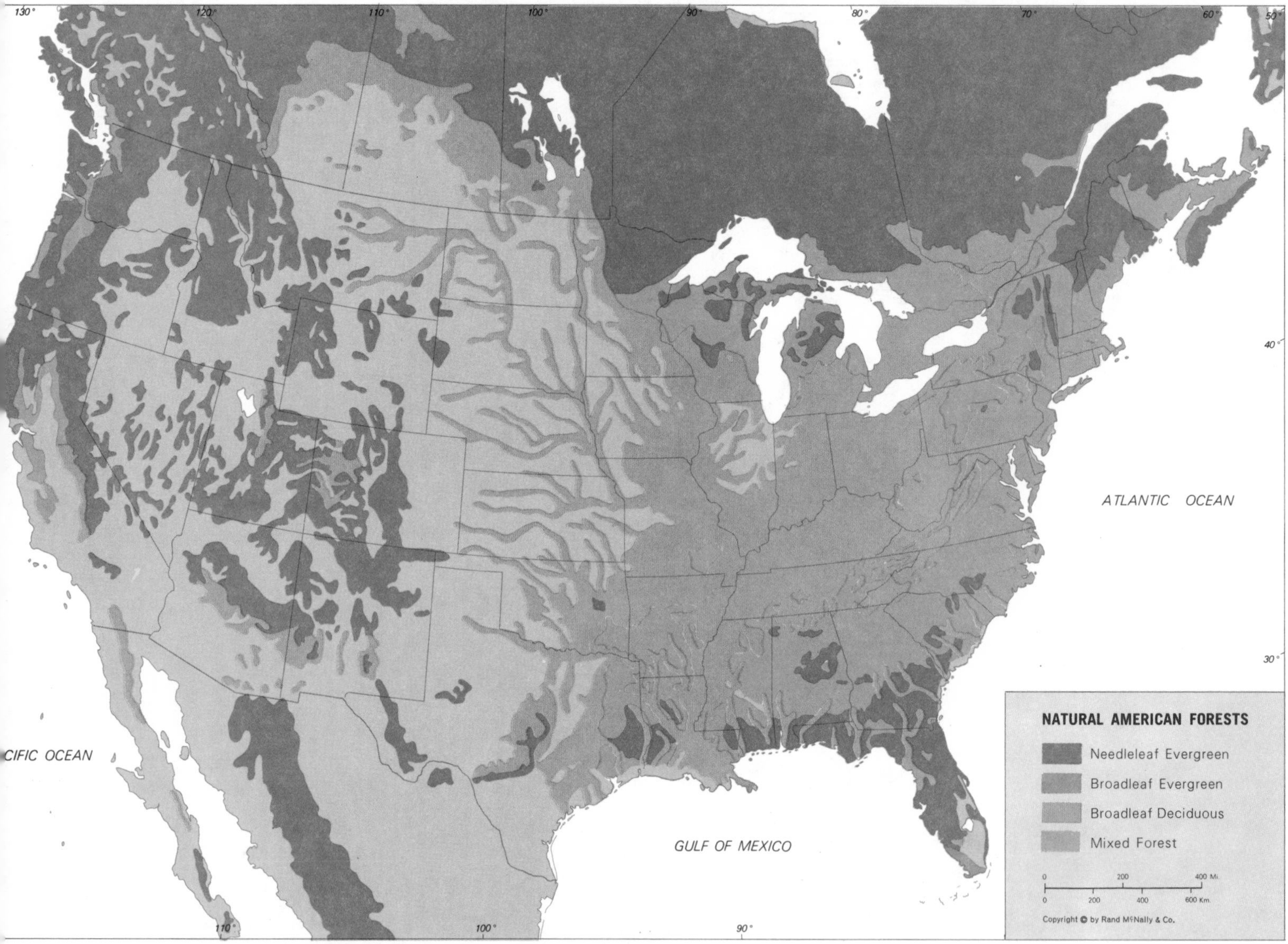

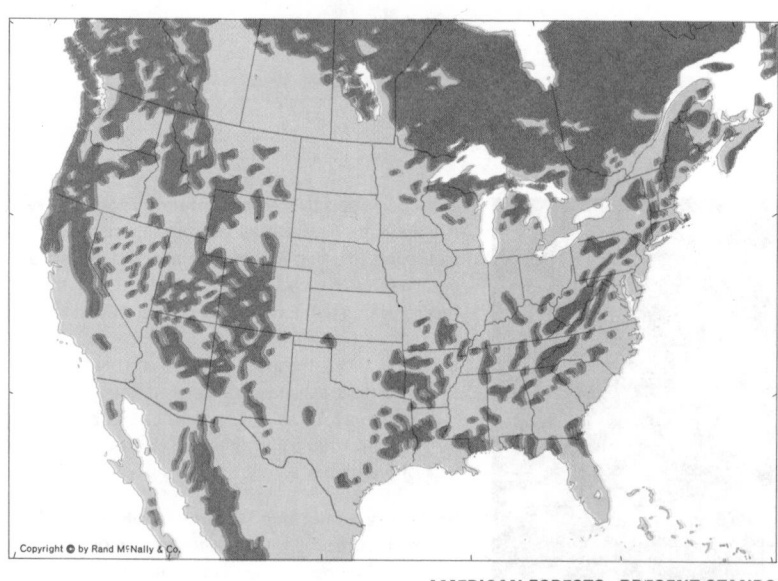

ATLANTIC OCEAN
CIFIC OCEAN
GULF OF MEXICO
NATURAL AMERICAN FORESTS
Needleleaf Evergreen
Broadleaf Evergreen
Broadleaf Deciduous
Mixed Forest
130°
120°
110°
100°
90°
80°
70°
60°
50°
40°
30°
0 200 400 Mi.
0 200 400 600 Km.
Copyright © by Rand McNally & Co.

Copyright © by Rand McNally & Co.

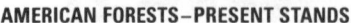

AMERICAN FORESTS–PRESENT STANDS

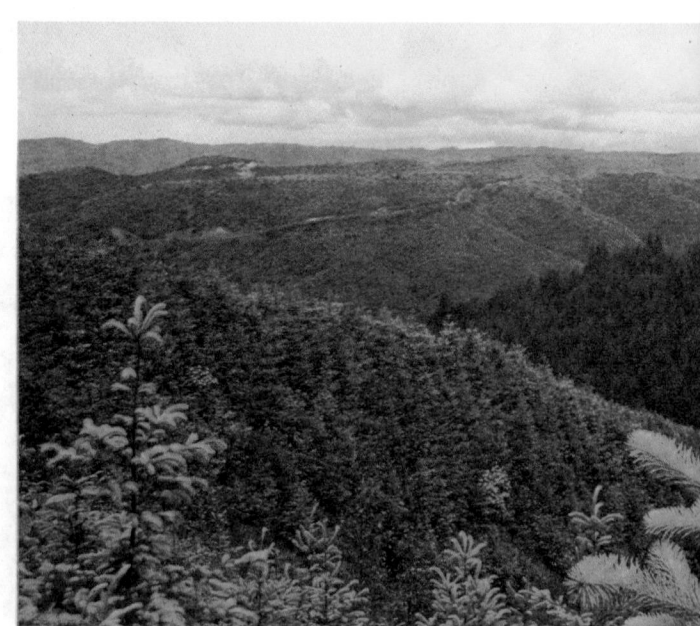

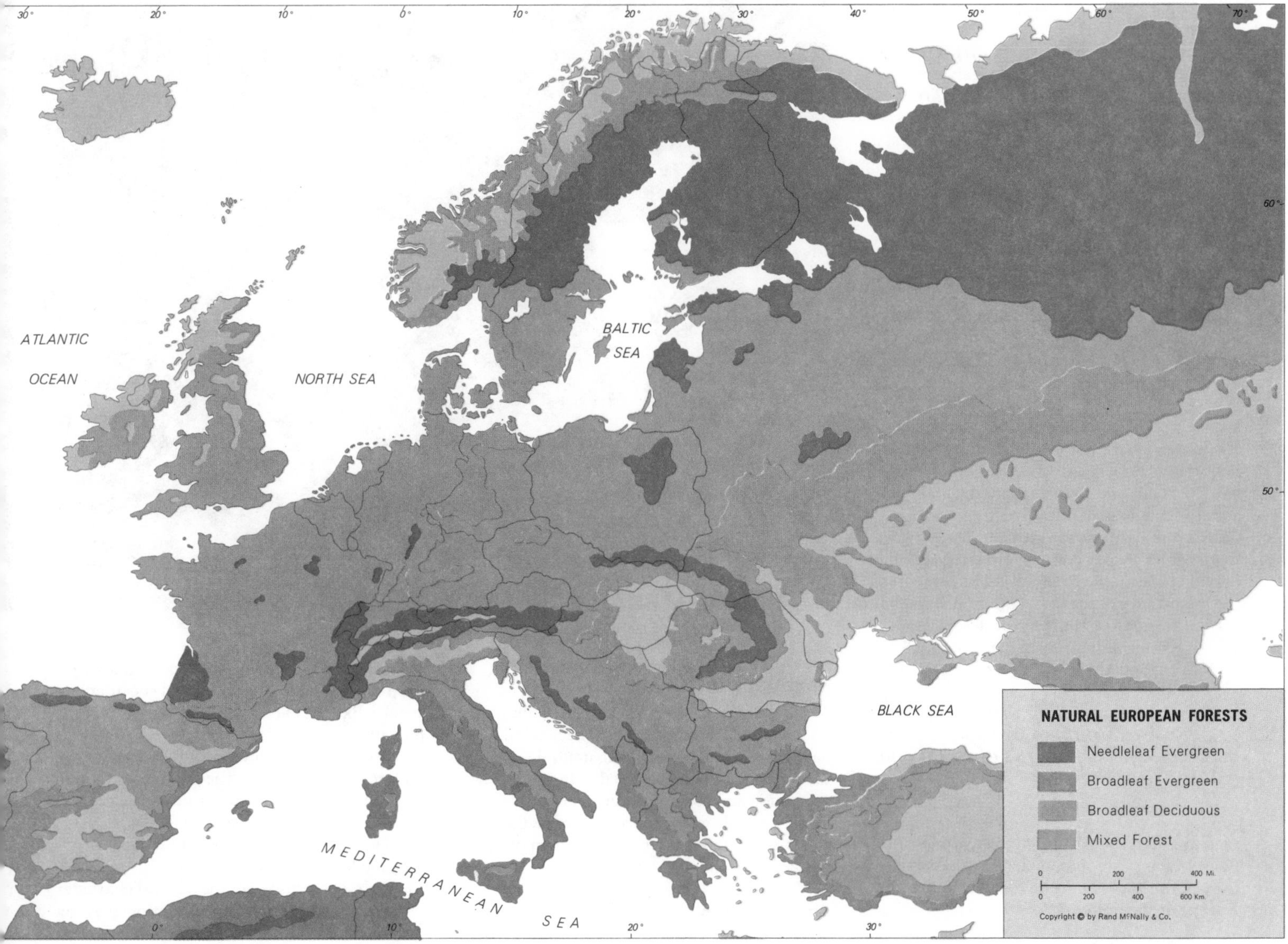

NATURAL EUROPEAN FORESTS

ATLANTIC

OCEAN

NORTH SEA

BALTIC
SEA

BLACK SEA

MEDITERRANEAN SEA

NATURAL EUROPEAN FORESTS

Needleleaf Evergreen

Broadleaf Evergreen

Broadleaf Deciduous

Mixed Forest

0   200   400 Mi.

0   200   400   600 Km.

Copyright © by Rand McNally & Co.

Deforestation. The larger maps on these pages show the probable extent of forest before humanity began clearing large areas for farming. Agriculture and industrial development have reduced the forest cover to the limited regions shown on the smaller maps. Deforestation of an equal magnitude has taken place in Asia, Africa, and other regions of the world where people have sacrificed forests for fuel as well as for farming and industry.

Reforestation. In this photograph, taken in western Washington, acres of new trees (foreground) are planted as mature trees are harvested. Reforestation of this type is now a standard procedure by which government and industry attempt to perpetuate renewable forest resources and stabilize the forest environment.

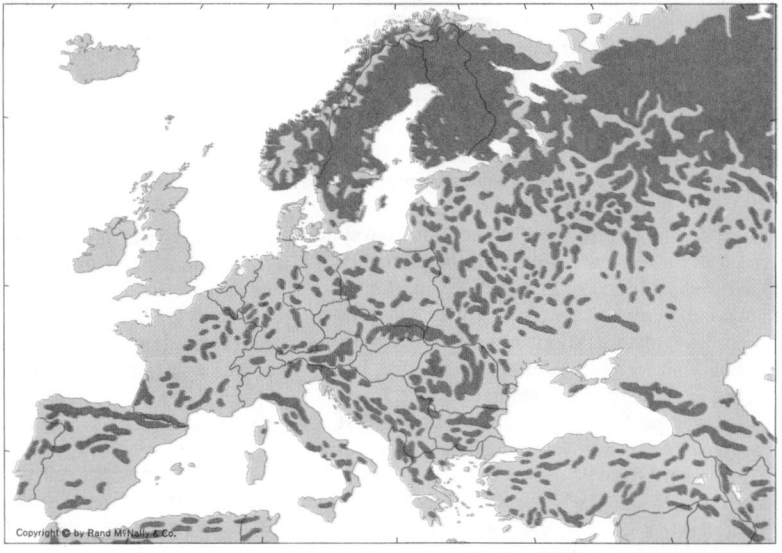

Copyright © by Rand McNally & Co.

EUROPEAN FORESTS—PRESENT STANDS

farm communities in remote areas to ports and market centers.

The transportation pattern of Africa is more complicated. The continent is largely under-developed, though the Union of South Africa and the northern parts of Morocco, Algeria, and Tunisia are exceptions. The greatest contrast in transportation patterns appears between the arid regions of the Sahara and the cultivated zone extending from Senegal across the continent to Ethiopia. Egypt is a special case. For countless centuries, the Nile River has served as a great natural highway, delaying the country's road and rail development. However, the government is beginning to construct settlements in outlying desert areas, and roadways will be vital in maintaining lines of communication with the Nile Delta.

Vast regions of the Asian continent are sparsely settled. In the mountainous and dry sections, transportation facilities are poor or nonexistent. The relatively well-developed network of roads and railways in India and Pakistan reflects British initiative in reproducing an essentially European pattern. The network in Australia clearly defines inhabited and uninhabited parts of the country and underscores the importance of the few roads and single railway cutting across the interior desert. However, if mining industries in the "outback" regions expand, there will be a corresponding

. . . The distribution of transportation facilities reflects patterns of social and cultural development . . .

increase in the number of highways and rail lines. In East Asia, Japan alone possesses a transportation system comparable to that of Europe or the United States.

Transportation, Economics, and Culture. Transportation facilities are perhaps not a refined indicator of economic development, but their patterns present a striking picture of the different concentrations of human activity around the globe. The fact that people find it easy to move from Hamburg to Rome or from New York to San Francisco but find it much harder to travel from Rio de Janeiro to the interior of Brazil or from Algiers to the Congo tells us a great deal about the state of economic development in these areas. Moreover, the distribution of transportation facilities reflects patterns of social and cultural development as well. The complex transportation network in France means that virtually every field, factory, and home in this country is connected into a nationwide system of communications. In contrast, people in areas not well served by roads and railways may not be exposed to new ideas and methods. In short, whether a nation is connected into a vital network of communication or relatively isolated has a significant impact on its rate of cultural evolution and economic development.

Modifying the Environment

As people have spread over the earth, they have not only settled and improved the land, they have destroyed it as well. Substantial regions of the planet have been stripped of their native vegetation and become desert and semidesert areas. Animals once numbering in the thousands or millions have become extinct or are now found mainly in zoos.

Clearing the Land. Perhaps the most conspicuous result of our efforts to modify the environment has been the removal or alteration of plant life. Except for the great forests of northern Canada and Siberia, all of the world's major vegetation zones show signs of clearing or burning, and the grazing of domestic animals. In the tropical rain forests, scattered groups may farm an area for a short time and then move on; to clear away forest, they burn off trees or kill them by stripping a complete circle of their bark. At the edge of these tropical rain forests is a zone of tall grass and scattered trees, usually referred to as "savanna." For the most part, savannas are created and maintained by fires set each year to clear the land for farming or pasture. In the drier parts of this zone, savanna gives way to grass and low shrubs (steppe). Beyond such vegetation lie desert zones consisting of plants that germinate

. . . The most conspicuous result of our efforts to modify the environment has been the removal or alteration of plant life . . .

quickly after infrequent rains, perennials with deep or widespreading roots, and succulent species like the cactus that can store up moisture.

One of the best known examples of how human activity has modified native vegetation can be found in the Mediterranean area of the Old World. In this region of ancient agricultural and pastoral livelihood, most of the original forest has been destroyed or reduced to scrub. That this is not the natural character of the land is suggested by vegetation growing on protected sites. Cemeteries in northwestern Africa are sacred ground, and trees found there are seldom disturbed. As a result, many cemeteries resemble small forests with their tall trees and deep, spreading shade. The removal of this shade from the surrounding land exposes the earth to the sun's heat and changes the climate at ground level. This change creates a favorable environment for the invasion of plants from nearby steppes or desert lands. Thus, the widely held belief that the Sahara is expanding is true. However, the cause is not a change in the atmosphere but centuries of clearing away forests to make room for human settlement.

The great, mid-latitude zones of both the Old World and New World were once covered with a mixed forest of evergreen and deciduous, broadleaf, and coniferous trees. Now this region is the most heavily populated in the world. Indeed, the process of clearing forests is so advanced in China that it is almost impossible to reconstruct that country's native vegetation patterns. Europe and the United States still have substantial forested regions, but most of these forests represent second or third growth

Soil Depletion. The severely eroded slope (far left) near Bab-Taza, Morocco, is the result of overgrazing and improper methods of cultivation. With protective vegetation gone, heavy rains carve a maze of gullies into the slope, making future cultivation increasingly difficult. Water erosion of this sort is one of several ways in which fertile soil has been depleted since the beginning of agriculture, approximately 10,000 years ago.

Water Pollution. The Cuyahoga River, pictured here as it enters Lake Erie, at Cleveland, Ohio, is an example of a river in a heavily populated area that carries industrial wastes, sewage, and detergents into the inland lakes and, finally, to the world's oceans. Recent legislation by federal, state, and local governments bordering the Great Lakes has curbed the discharge of such pollutants. This type of cooperative effort is essential if rivers, lakes, and their related marine environments are to be saved from extinction.

and may be of a different species than the original stands. This is especially true of parts of Western Europe and the "cut-over" districts around the Great Lakes in the United States.

In Europe, human settlements have replaced much of the continent's forests. In contrast, from the beginning of the Christian era until the 10th century, most of the area north of the Alps was so heavily forested that it presented a living barrier to agricultural settlement. The clearing of this vast forest represents one of the most impressive and difficult accomplishments of medieval society. In England, the process was carried out so vigorously that by the 17th century it was difficult to find enough timber for shipbuilding.

Soil Erosion. The clearing and destruction of the world's forests has had serious consequences for the soil. In some cases, it has meant a change in the structure of the chemical composition of the earth; in others, the loss of part or all of the soil through erosion. Some erosion is inevitable in any area where soil is exposed to running water or wind; nor is all erosion destructive. Earth washed from hilly or mountainous regions may enrich floodplains that sustain thousands, even millions, of people. Nevertheless, in many areas, accelerated soil erosion caused by human activity is one of the more obvious results of our modification of the earth and one of our most serious problems.

Erosion may take several forms. The most spectacular is gully erosion, whereby the earth is washed away to form deep channels that may evolve into intricate networks. This hazard is greatest where slopes are steep, protective vegetation has been cleared away, and poor cul-

tivation methods have been used or the area has been overgrazed. The land eventually becomes unfit for agriculture. If abandoned by farmers and herders, the slopes may be re-colonized by native vegetation. But nature, however forgiving, often requires centuries to repair what human cultivation may have destroyed in a single decade. Other forms of erosion include "sheet wash," when topsoil is removed without forming gullies. Landslides and mudslides carry away hundreds of square acres of productive land. Also, topsoil can be removed by wind, a process that in the 1930s created the famous Dust Bowl of the American Great Plains.

Each of these destructive processes has taken a heavy toll of productive land. To cope with the problem, farmers have built elaborate terraces, improved the soil with mud from river valleys, and used various types of fertilizer. As a result, areas of relatively low productivity have supported some of the largest populations in the world. Most areas of the earth, however, have suffered serious depletion of the soil. It is not an exaggeration to say that this vital resource has been continuously damaged since humanity first began practicing agriculture some 10,000 years ago. The implications of this fact are especially serious today, when we are faced with a population explosion and the prospect of widespread famine.

...Nature, however forgiving, often requires centuries to repair what human cultivation may have destroyed in a single decade...

Pollution: The High Cost of Progress

Our modifications of the environment are not restricted to vegetation, animal life, and the soil. We are now aware that the earth's air and water have also undergone radical changes at our hands. The term "pollution" covers a wide range of processes, from oil spills and automobile exhausts to nuclear and chemical wastes. The earth's atmosphere and hydrosphere are closed circulating systems, much like the circulatory system in a human being. At one time, the waste products of our civilization were probably insignificant enough to be dispersed by these systems without harming the air or water. But this is certainly not the case today. One of the consequences of urbanization and industrialization has been a rapid increase in air and water contamination.

Air Quality. Air pollution is especially serious in areas where temperature inversions occur. Occasionally, a layer of cooler air may form near the ground. Since this air is heavier and more stable than warm air, it forms a "lid," or temperature inversion, over an area. Pollutants cannot rise and disperse; they remain trapped in the colder air. Inversions like this are common in the Los Angeles area, which is also flanked on three sides by mountains that prevent the air from moving horizontally. When you consider that the city also has the world's greatest concentration of automobiles, numerous refineries and industries, and huge amounts of garbage and trash, it is not surprising that Los Angeles suffers from a severe smog problem. Similar problems plague other industrialized urban areas.

Although the most ominous feature of air pollution is its hazard to human health, it also damages buildings and crops. Air pollutants corrode, tarnish, and crack a wide variety of materials. The stone and statuary on the great medieval cathedrals of Europe have probably suffered more damage during the past century than in all of their previous history. Native vegetation and crops also suffer from the effects of pollution. Evergreen trees cannot grow in cities located within the industrial zone of the northeastern United States. Moreover, Los Angeles smog has damaged the vegetable and citrus crops of southern California. In many cities, wilted leaves on trees and shrubs and the corroded metal of buildings are mute testimony to the same process.

Scientists concerned with air quality have also taken a harder look at the effects of clearing away extensive tracts of vegetation. Plants provide much of the free oxygen in our atmosphere. As more forest areas are cut back or burned off, scientists worry that the loss of so much vegetation may lessen air quality. They are watching the commercial development of Brazilian rain forests with particular concern. The region of the Amazon basin is thought to provide a significant part of the oxygen for the Western hemisphere.

Water Pollution. The problem of water pollution is also most serious near cities and industrial establishments, though oceanographers have found contaminants in all the world's seas as well. Discharges of phosphates, pesticides, industrial wastes, and sewage into lakes and rivers damage fish and plant life and contaminate drinking water in most cities. Coastal areas are threatened by massive oil spills from offshore drilling or shipwrecks of supertankers carrying millions of gallons of petroleum. Most recently, chemical "dumping grounds" have been discovered where chemical wastes have been illegally or improperly buried near populated areas. These chemicals often seep into the earth and contaminate ground water or hidden springs and well water used for cooking and drinking. Also, containers of nuclear waste material disposed of in the sea are not always adequately sealed. Material leaking into the environment will remain radioactive for thousands of years before decaying into stable elements.

Restoring the Environment. Over the past two decades, environmentalists, consumer groups, and government agencies have focused their attention on the problem of pollution. Action by these groups has resulted in various environmental protection regulations, in some cases on both a national and international level. The results have been mixed, but promising. In Chicago, air quality has been dramatically improved over a 15-year period. Lake Erie, once considered devoid of life, has also made a striking comeback. Fish and plant life now flourish where once only sediment and decaying algae could be found.

. . . A clear distinction between a natural and an artificial environment is difficult to make, because the influence of humanity is evident almost everywhere . . .

Even more promising in the long run are experiments in the design of electrically powered vehicles, attempts to recycle liquid wastes, and the use of solid waste for building materials and landfill. Optimists point to technological breakthroughs in solar, wind, and geothermal power for private homes and small- to medium-sized businesses. Thanks to international agreements, the threat posed by fallout from thermonuclear explosions is less serious than it was previously. Many nations recognize the need for such agreements regarding the construction of nuclear power plants and the disposal of plutonium by-products.

Nevertheless, much remains to be done. If economic growth and development are carried on without adequate safeguards, the deterioration of our air, soil, and water is likely to continue. The quality of our environment in the future depends upon the priorities we choose and upon our ability to cooperate as a world community.

Artificial Environments

A clear distinction between a natural and an artificial environment is difficult to make, because the influence of humanity is evident almost everywhere. Nevertheless, we can start by pointing to the historic and even prehistoric efforts of people to create a more comfortable settlement.

Keeping Warm. Caves were probably the first artificial environments. They offered shelter and, with the discovery of fire, warmth to prehistoric peoples. Since the earliest times, people have lived in such forbidding regions as Alaska and southern Chile. The ice and snow huts built by Eskimos were well-insulated dwellings. While the Indians of southern Chile were less skilled in constructing shelters, they had the imagination and boldness to carry fires in their canoes. By the time of the Roman Empire, people had devised methods of heating large buildings and water used for public baths. The stone castles of medieval Europe may have been chilly and drafty, but there is reason to believe that the peasant huts clustered nearby were warm and relatively comfortable. Although people have often had to work and travel in harsh climates, they have long been able to create warm shelters.

Cooling Off. Defense against excessive heat is a more complicated affair. But even here it is easy to point out how human beings have dealt with the problem. In the Middle East, covered streets helped block the sun's rays. Wetted grass mats were placed over the doorways of

houses in India. In the American Southwest, Indians used thick adobe walls to keep out the oppressive summer heat. The use of fans and other devices to circulate the air or reduce humidity are refinements of an ancient quest.

Early methods of modern air conditioning began in the textile industry. Steam pots were used to increase humidity and help reduce breakage and static electricity. In the 1920s, new techniques of refrigeration began to appear. The first use of air conditioning for human comfort occurred in an American motion-picture theater in 1922.

Air conditioning is now a requirement of life in the hotter regions of the United States, especially the Southeast and the Southwest. Life during the torrid summer months may be a series of short trips from one air-conditioned place to another. Exposure to the "real world" may be as limited as in Alaska or Siberia during the bitterly cold winter months. Within the last few decades, air conditioning has been used in large shopping centers and sports arenas; often these facilities are enclosed under one roof or dome.

Evolution of Our Patterns and Imprints

The story of our gradual settlement of the planet can be divided into at least three distinctive phases, with a fourth phase slowly emerging.

Expansion Without Agriculture. The first phase began about 100,000 years ago, probably in Africa. Moving in small bands and supporting themselves by hunting and by gathering wild plants, various groups spread from tropical environments to all the earth's major climatic zones. Population remained low during this long migration, and vast areas were left unoccupied. Yet the remarkable adaptability of the human species enabled people to survive in dense rain forests, deserts, even on the edge of the Arctic Circle. Many experts feel that the isolation of these groups from one another, plus the high rate of infant deaths and the inbred genetic makeup of each people, helped create the physical characteristics still evident in our races. The precarious nature of hunting and gathering as a way of life did not permit any elaborate subdivision of labor or the development of more than subsistence skills. The family or clan remained the essential economic and social unit. If astronauts could have orbited the earth in 50,000 B.C., or even 15,000 B.C., they would not have seen any indications of modification of the environment.

Expansion and Concentration with Agriculture. The situation changed dramatically about 10,000 years ago, when humanity entered into the second phase—agricultural development. Plants and animals were domesticated, and people began to enjoy a relatively steady, abundant food supply. It is not known exactly where this crucial innovation took place. Most authorities favor the foothill region of the Near East, where they believe wheat and barley were the first cultivated crops and sheep and goats the first animals domesticated. Cultivation may also have begun several thousand years ago in the warm, humid environments of South and Southwest Asia. And in the New World, evidence suggests that corn (or maize) agriculture in Mexico is almost as ancient as wheat cultivation in the Near East.

The development of agriculture enabled human settlements to increase significantly. In some areas, population jumped a hundred-fold as people learned to plant, irrigate, and harvest crops. Abundant food production freed some people to develop skills such as pottery, crafts, tool manufacturing, and weaving. Societies began to separate into special castes of warriors, priests, and merchants. From the eight

---

. . . The story of our gradual settlement of the planet can be divided into at least three distinctive phases, with a fourth phase slowly emerging . . .

---

major centers of innovation, agriculture expanded to all areas of the earth where cultivation and raising livestock were possible. A major exchange of crops and animals occurred after the European conquest of the New World. European settlers and pioneers cultivated the last great agricultural frontiers in the 19th century. Similar pioneer settlements, though on a much smaller scale, are found in South America and regions of Canada and the Soviet Union.

This 10,000-year period of rapid progress also saw humanity alter and modify vast areas of the environment. Clearing forests for agriculture and overgrazing lands encouraged soil erosion and turned some regions into virtual desert. In our hypothetical orbiting of the earth, an astronaut in 5,000 B.C. would have spotted cultivated fields, clearings in forests, eroded slopes, and countless other signs of the beneficial and destructive aspects of human activity.

Concentration—Urbanization and the Industrial Age. The middle of the 19th century signaled the third phase in the great adventure of the human expansion and settlement over the earth. An era of rapid scientific innovation ushered in the industrial age. As industry and commerce developed, people moved from rural areas into crowded urban centers, abandoning agriculture for the more varied economic opportunities found in cities. The trend toward concentration marked a reversal of previous population movements, a fact often overlooked in accounts of humanity's use of the earth. As a result, many areas of the world are now less occupied than prior to the Industrial Revolution. Although the distinction between crowded and empty lands was always evident during the period of agricultural expansion, the difference became more pronounced after people could leave rural areas. Convergence on urban and industrial sites meant a concentrated and magnified impact on the environment—often with damaging results. Air and water pollution, thought to be a 20th century dilemma, plagued industrial areas of Europe and the United States in the latter half of the 19th century.

Suburbanization. The fourth stage, suburbanization, is not yet a global trend. However, it is such a striking feature in North America and many European cities that it may well foreshadow a worldwide pattern. City growth initially fostered a concentration of population and industry. But subsequent development led to a new phase of expansion. The process began with the first streetcar lines extending out from the heart of the city. Houses could be built along these lines, allowing people to live beyond walking distance from their places of work. Today, expressways and rail transport enable millions of American and European suburbanites to live miles from where they work, shop, or find recreation and entertainment. Where before people thought little of walking 2 or 3 miles to work, commuters today regard traveling 20 or 30 miles as equally routine.

Artificial Environments. The Yoyogi Sports Center in Tōkyō, Japan, was built for the 1964 Olympics. It is now used as a recreation center and stands as one of the first in an increasing number and variety of large, self-contained artificial environments.

Cities "Under Glass." If we have been able to air-condition entire shopping centers and sports complexes, why not larger areas? This prospect is made more intriguing by the development of structural domes, which are relatively inexpensive and can be built virtually to any scale. Thus, a dome comparable to the one housing the Civic Arena in Pittsburgh could be as high as the tallest skyscraper. In this case, it would be possible to air-condition an entire city.

This awesome prospect should not overshadow the obstacles still facing us in our efforts to build comfortable, healthy environments. Although air conditioning can filter out pollutant particles, gaseous contaminants pass through unimpeded. Nor are we likely to discover an effective substitute for the beneficial qualities of sunlight. Not even an artificial environment with total and infallible control of temperature and humidity would be without its problems and hazards. A world of aritificial environments may help us solve part of our problems in constructing comfortable habitats. But whether this is a desirable or even humane solution remains to be seen.

Suburban growth, unfortunately, has often meant inner city decay, a problem facing most major American and European cities. Also, the process has encouraged the development of shopping centers and industrial districts in widely scattered suburban areas. The congestion associated with "rush hour" is complicated by traffic moving from suburb to suburb.

It is too early to predict whether suburbanization will occur in other nations as well. Most people in African and Asian countries still live close to where they work or combine their shops and homes into one. Moreover, even between Europe and the United States, the trend toward suburban growth differs significantly, since in Europe more people must rely on public transportation. Regardless of the transportation network that supports it, suburban sprawl often encroaches on agricultural land. Strasbourg, France, is expanding into the vineyards of the Rhine Valley, and Tel Aviv, Israel, is slowly reducing the citrus orchards of the Mediterranean coast. The growth of the huge Los Angeles metropolitan area has been at the expense of one of the nation's richest agricultural counties. Also, escalating fuel costs may encourage a new era of population concentration as commuting becomes more and more expensive. On the other hand, if more inexpensive sources of energy are developed and transportation facilities expanded, the current trend of suburban sprawl may actually accelerate. In any case, the movement of people from urban districts to outlying areas is likely to be an important chapter in the story of human settlement on our planet.

Four Phases of Human Settlement

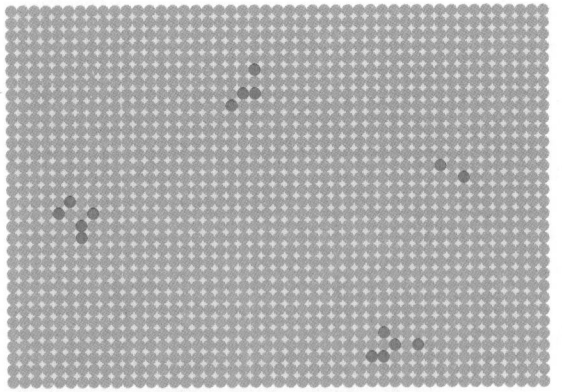

First Phase: Expansion without Agriculture. About 100,000 years ago, hunters and food gatherers spread from tropical environments to all the earth's major climatic regions, with insignificant modification of the environment.

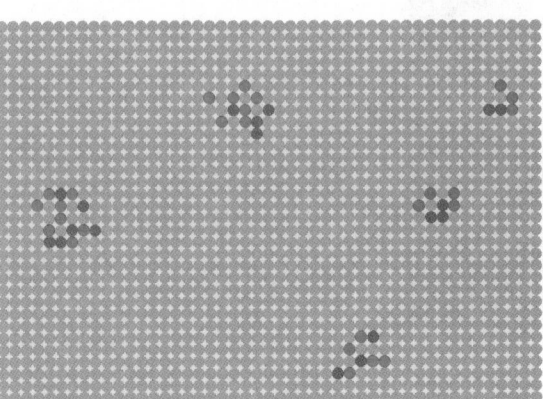

Second Phase: Expansion with Agriculture. Agricultural development evolved about 10,000 years ago and proceeded to expand to all areas where crop cultivation and livestock raising were possible, accompanied by deforestation and soil erosion.

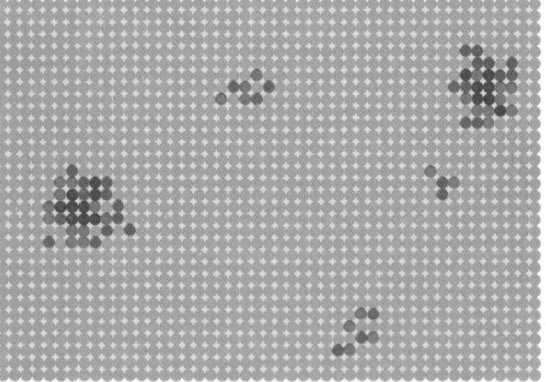

Third Phase: Concentration with Industrialization and Urbanization. Movement of the rural population to the urban centers began about 150 years ago and reversed the previous population movements. Convergence on urban and industrial sites accelerated pollution of air and water and the exhaustion of nonrenewable resources.

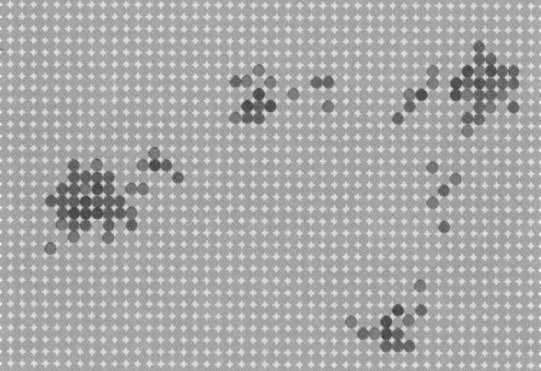

Fourth Phase: Suburbanization. A feature of urban industrial societies is the recent phase of expansion away from the cities, which has been facilitated by efficient transportation systems. Often, suburbs grow at the expense of agricultural land.

Epilogue

We began our look at the patterns and imprints of humanity with the observation that people have been virtually everywhere on the planet Earth. At times our presence has been beneficial, at times destructive. But it has always changed the appearance of the earth's surface. In the course of 100,000 years, humanity has developed from small hunting and gathering societies into nation states. Advanced methods of agriculture and industrialization have given us some measure of control over natural forces and have enabled us to increase our population dramatically. We have constructed elaborate artificial environments and intricate cultural landscapes. The imprint of our species is deep and widespread.

Our transformed human geography shows signs of failure as well. Environmental pollution and our consumption of nonrenewable resources are straining the earth's ability to support our expanding industrial economies. War and famine threaten the future of many nations, and the gap between rich and poor countries continues to widen at an alarming rate. Always, the specter of nuclear warfare hangs over each succeeding generation.

As we strive to create new patterns and imprints on the earth, we cannot tell if our evolving creation will result in a more attractive and productive world. We do know it will be different. We can hope that as we become more aware of our effect upon the environment, we will act more wisely in the future in order to live within the limits of our earth for the well-being of all humanity.

. . . We can hope that we will act more wisely in the future to live within the limits of our earth . . .

Environment Maps

The environment-map series shows the general nature of the environment, whether natural or modified by man. The appearance and/or general activity which characterize an area were the conditions for its being classified in one of the map categories. Inclusion in a category was determined largely by the percent of the area covered by urban development, crops (including pasture), trees, or grass. On these small-scale maps, no attempt was made to depict specific crops or the productivity of the area.

Ten major environments were depicted and the categories identified and described in the legend below. The colors and patterns for each category were chosen to illustrate the results of man's activity. Hill shading was used to show land configuration. Together, these design elements create a visual impression of the surface environment.

Naturally, when mapping any distribution it is necessary to limit the number of categories. Therefore, some gradations of meaning exist within the limits of the chosen categories. For example, the grassland, grazing-land category identifies the lush pampas of Argentina and the savanna of Africa as well as the steppes of the Soviet Union. Furthermore, in areas of cropland certain enclaves which might not be defined as cropland are included within the boundary. Tracts such as these, through the process of generalization were included within the boundary of the dominant environment surrounding them. Finally, it should be pointed out that boundaries on these maps, as on all maps, are never absolute but mark the center of transitional zones between categories.

Actual urban shapes were shown where metropolitan areas are of a large areal extent. A red dot indicates concentrated urbanized development where actual shapes would be indistinguishable at the map scale. Black dots were used to locate selected places important as locational reference points.

From these maps one may make comprehensive observations about the extent and distribution of the major world environments. For example, the urban areas of the world are limited in extent, although over 40 percent of the world's population lives in these areas. Together, the categories of cropland and cropland associated with woodland or grazing land apply to relatively small portions of the earth's surface. Conversely, vast areas of each continent show man's limited influence on the natural environment. The barren lands, wasteland, and tundra, the sparse grass and steppe land, and the tropical rain forests are notable in this respect.

Environment Map Legend

URBAN
Major areas of contiguous residential, commercial, and industrial development.

CROPLAND
Cultivated land predominates (includes pasture, irrigated land, and land in crop rotation).

CROPLAND AND WOODLAND
Cultivated land interrupted by small wooded areas.

CROPLAND AND GRAZING LAND
Cultivated land with grassland and rangeland.

GRASSLAND, GRAZING LAND
Extensive grassland and rangeland with little or no cropland.

OASIS
Important small areas of cultivation within grassland or wasteland.

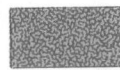
FOREST, WOODLAND
Extensive wooded areas with little or no cropland.

SWAMP, MARSHLAND
Extensive wetland areas (includes mangroves).

TUNDRA
Areas of lichen, shrubs, small trees, and wetland.

SHRUB, SPARSE GRASS; WASTELAND
Desert shrub and short grass, growing singly or in patches. Wasteland includes sand, salt flats, etc. (Extensive wastelands shown by pattern).

BARREN LAND
Icefields, glaciers, permanent snow, with exposed rock.

· Selected cities as points of reference.

Legend:
- Urban
- Cropland
- Cropland & Woodland
- Cropland & Grazing Land
- Grassland, Grazing Land
- Forest, Woodland
- Swamp, Marshland
- Tundra
- Shrub, Sparse Grass, Wasteland (pattern)
- Barren Land
- Oasis

Reykjavik

ATLANTIC

OCEAN

North Sea

Narvik

Murm

Trondheim

Bergen

Oslo

Göteborg

Stockholm

Tallinn

Helsinki

LENINGRAD

Gulf of Bothnia

Ume

Copenhagen

Rīga

Baltic Sea

Kaliningrad

Minsk

Glasgow

Belfast

MANCHESTER

Dublin

Amsterdam

Hamburg

Elbe

BERLIN

Oder

Warsaw

Popy

LONDON

Antwerp

Essen

Leipzig

Minsk

Brest

Frankfurt

Prague

Kraków

L'vov

CARPA

PARIS

Seine

Strasbourg

Loire

Rhine

Munich

VIENNA

BUDAPEST

Tisza

Bay of Biscay

La Coruña

Bordeaux

Zürich

Lyon

Garonne

Bilbao

PYRENEES

Douro

Ebro

MILAN

Venice

Save

Zagreb

Belgrade

Bucharest

Rhône

Genoa

Adriatic Sea

Danube

MADRID

Marseille

Sofia

Lisbon

BARCELONA

CORSICA

ROME

Tirane

Sevilla

SARDINIA

Naples

Tanger

ISLAS BALEARES

Tyrrhenian Sea

Athens

Oran

Algiers

Palermo

Aegean Sea

Casablanca

ATLAS MOUNTAINS

Tunis

SICILY

Mediterranean

Sea

MALTA

CRETE

Longitude West of Greenwich   0°   Longitude East of Greenwich

Scale 1: 16,000,000; one inch to 250 miles. Conic Projection

0   50   100   200   300   400   500 Miles

0   100   200   400   600   800 Kilometers

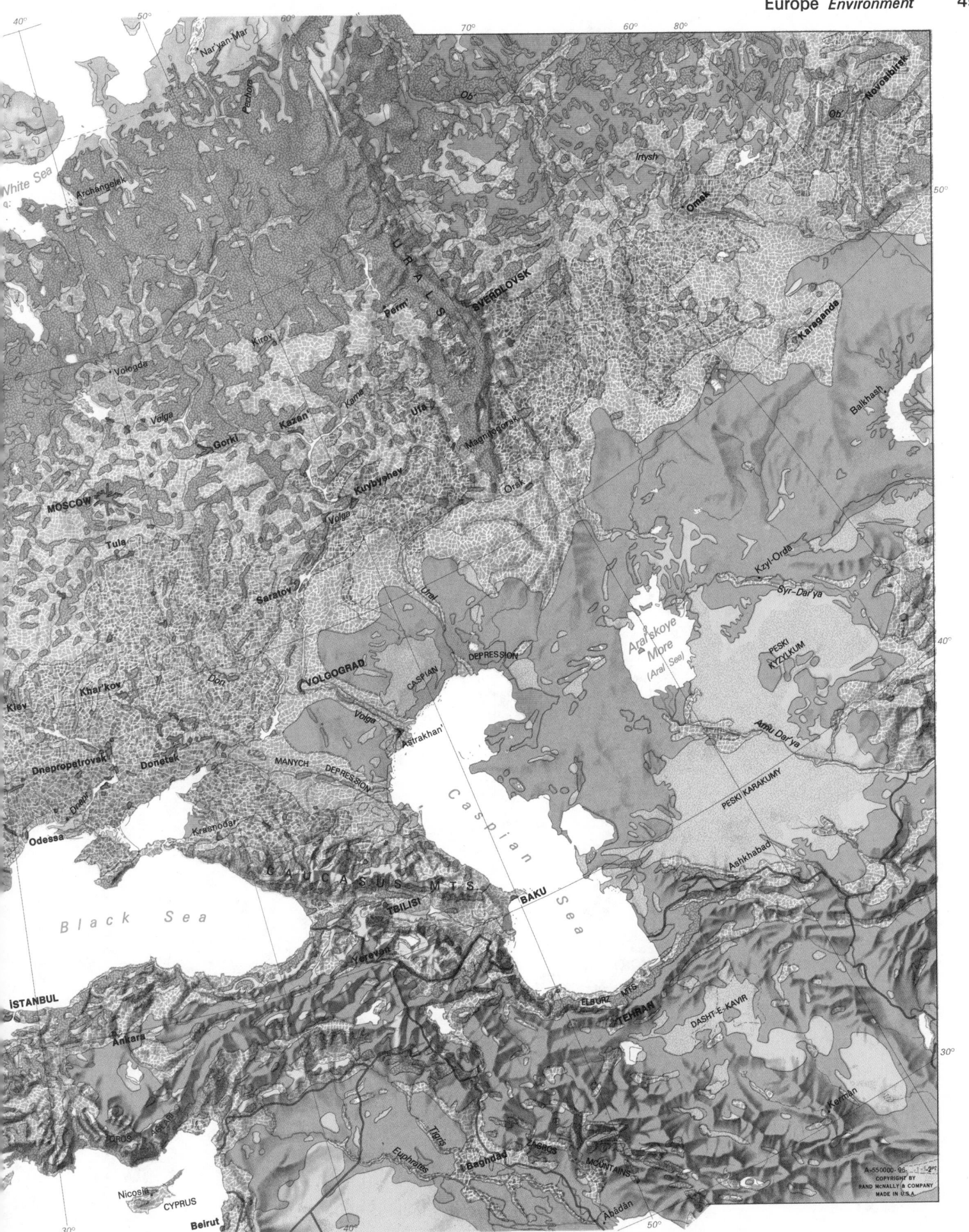

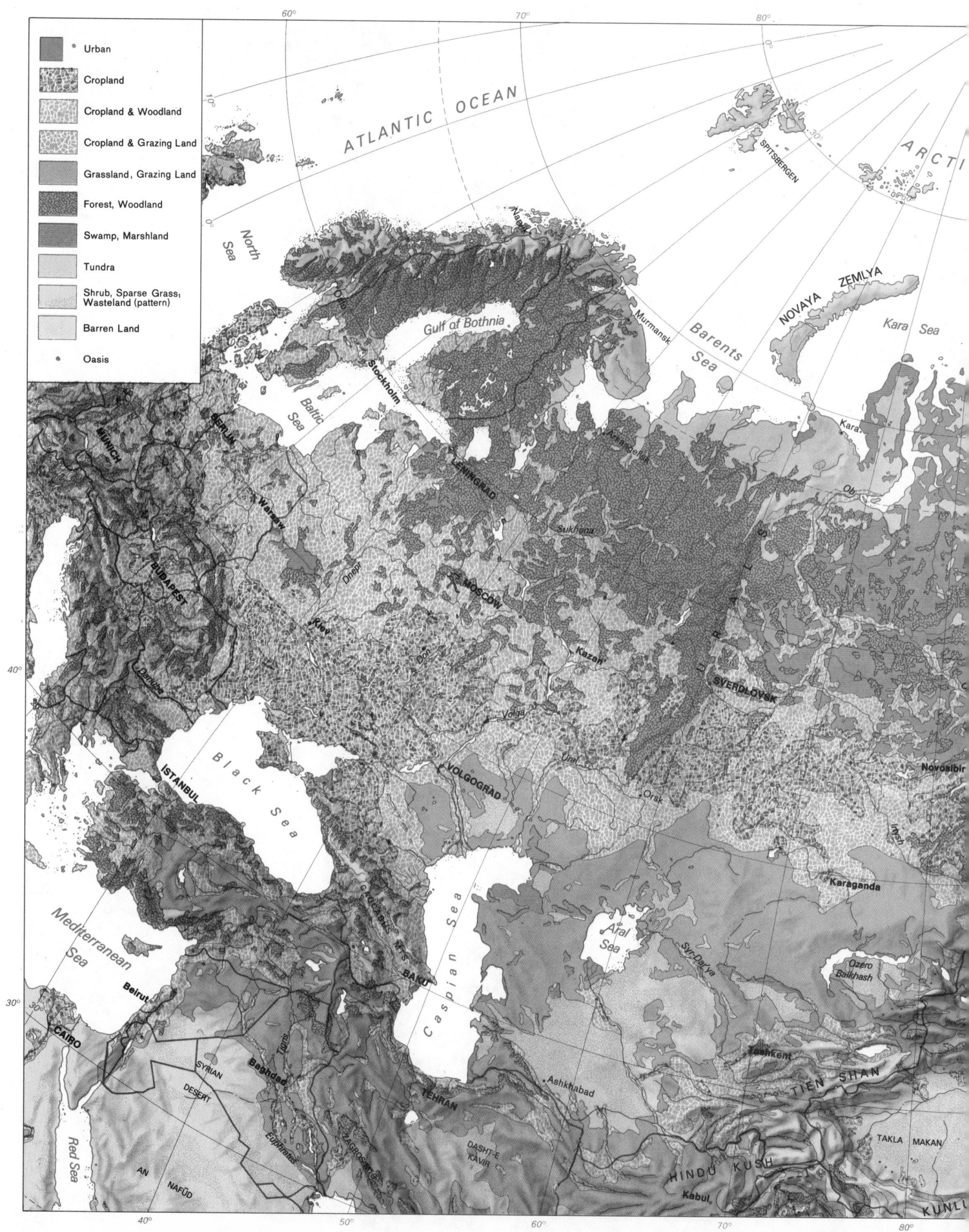

Urban
Cropland
Cropland & Woodland
Cropland & Grazing Land
Grassland, Grazing Land
Forest, Woodland
Swamp, Marshland
Tundra
Shrub, Sparse Grass, Wasteland (pattern)
Barren Land
Oasis

ATLANTIC OCEAN

ARCTIC

SPITSBERGEN

NOVAYA ZEMLYA

Barents Sea

Kara Sea

Murmansk

North Sea

Gulf of Bothnia

Stockholm

Baltic Sea

BERLIN

MUNICH

Warsaw

BUDAPEST

LENINGRAD

Sukhona

MOSCOW

Kiev

Dnepr

Don

Kazan

SVERDLOVSK

Novosibir

Danube

Volga

Ural

Orsk

ISTANBUL

Black Sea

VOLGOGRAD

Karaganda

Ob

Irtysh

Caucasus Mts

BAKU

Caspian Sea

Aral Sea

Ozero Balkhash

Mediterranean Sea

Belrut

CAIRO

SYRIAN

Baghdad

Tigris

Euphrates

DESERT

ZAGROS

TEHRAN

DASHT-E KAVIR

Ashkhabad

Tashkent

TIEN SHAN

TAKLA MAKAN

Red Sea

AN NAFUD

HINDU KUSH

Kabul

KUNLU

Scale 1:24,000,000; one inch to 380 miles. Lambert Azimuthal Equal-Area Projection

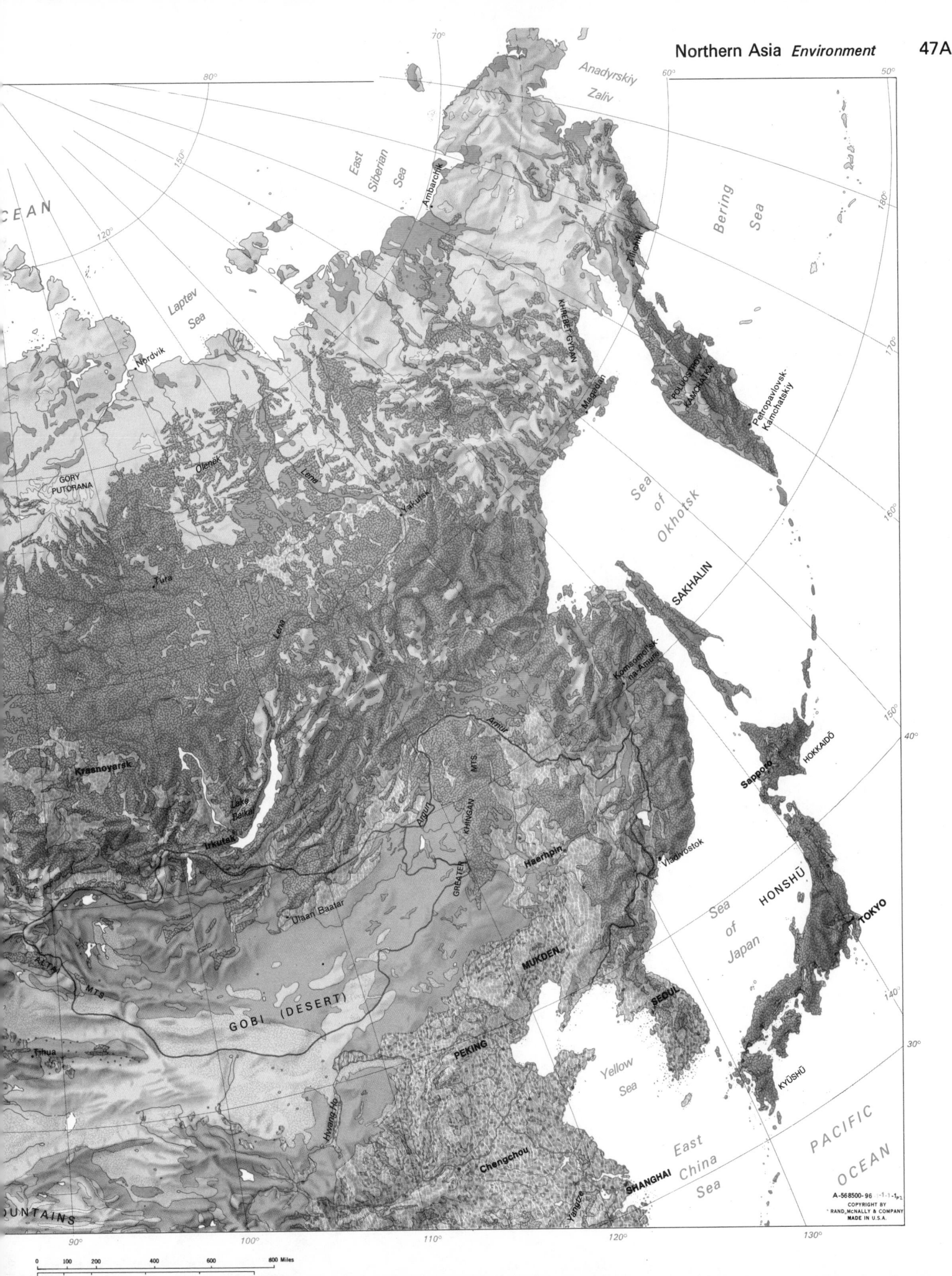

 CEAN

East Siberian Sea

Anadyrskiy Zaliv

Bering Sea

Laptev Sea

Nordvik

Ambarchik

KHREBET GYDAN

Magadan

Filippimy

Petropavlovsk-Kamchatskiy

POLUOSTROV KAMCHATKA

GORY PUTORANA

Olenek

Lena

Yakutsk

Sea of Okhotsk

Tura

SAKHALIN

Lena

Krasnoyarsk

Lake Baikal

Irkutsk

Komsomol'sk-na-Amure

Amur

MTS.

GREATER KHINGAN

Argun

Haerhpin

Vladivostok

HOKKAIDŌ

Sapporo

Sea of Japan

HONSHŪ

TOKYO

Ulaan Baatar

MUKDEN

SEOUL

ALTAI MTS.

GOBI (DESERT)

PEKING

Yellow Sea

KYŪSHŪ

Tihua

Hwang Ho

Chengchou

East China Sea

SHANGHAI

Yangtze

PACIFIC OCEAN

OUNTAINS

A-568500-96
COPYRIGHT BY
RAND McNALLY & COMPANY
MADE IN U.S.A.

0   100   200   400   600   800 Miles

0 150 300   600   900   1200 Kilometers

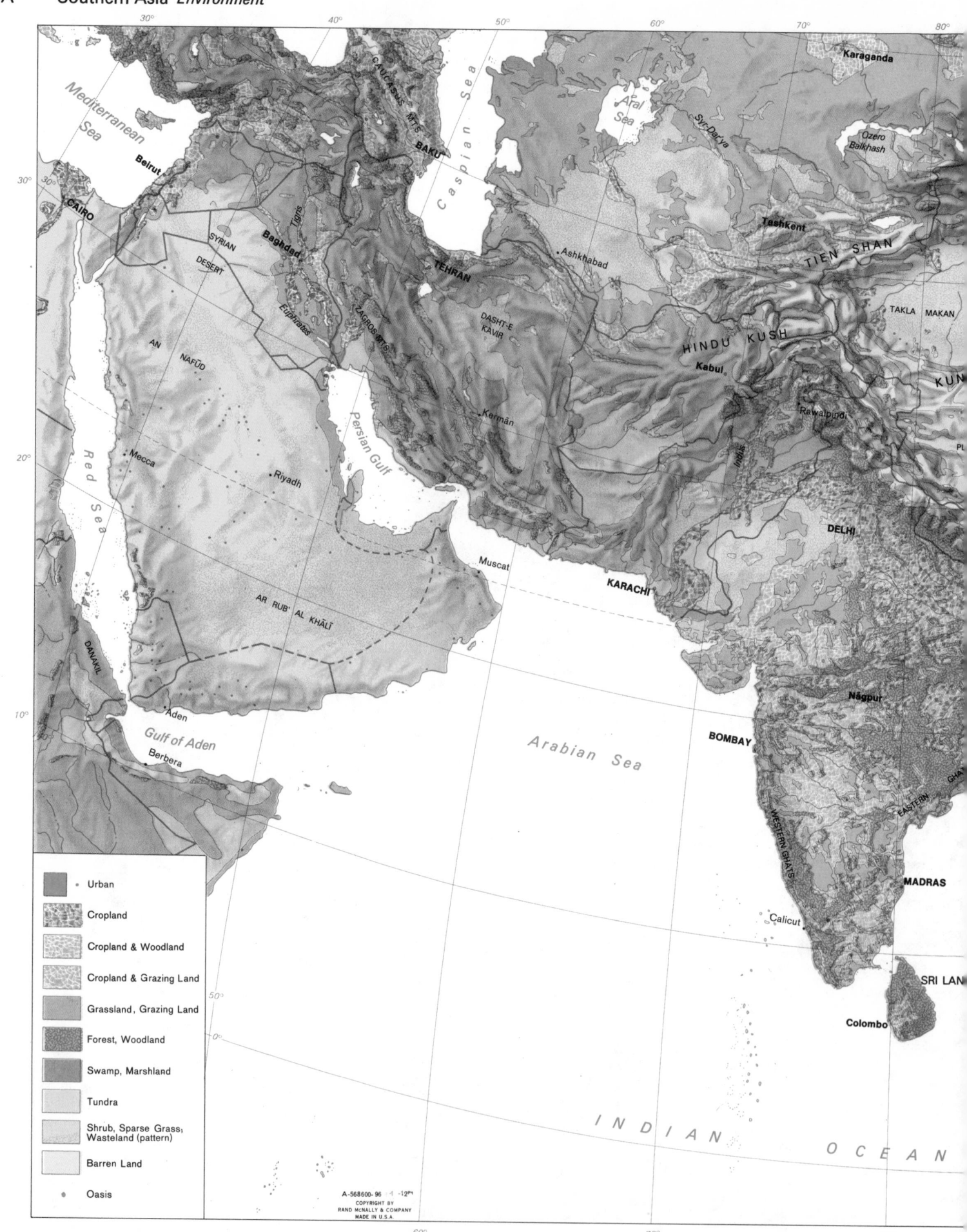

Urban

Cropland

Cropland & Woodland

Cropland & Grazing Land

Grassland, Grazing Land

Forest, Woodland

Swamp, Marshland

Tundra

Shrub, Sparse Grass, Wasteland (pattern)

Barren Land

• Oasis

A-568600-96   4   -12ᴾᴺ
COPYRIGHT BY
RAND McNALLY & COMPANY
MADE IN U.S.A.

Scale 1:24,000,000; one inch to 380 miles. Lambert Azimuthal Equal-Area Projection

ALTAI MTS

GREATER KHINGAN MTS

Haemhin

Vladivostok

GOBI (DESERT)

Ulaan Baatar

MUKDEN

Sea of Japan

HONSHŪ

TOKYO

Tihua

PEKING

SEOUL

KYŪSHŪ

Yellow Sea

PACIFIC OCEAN

Hwang Ho

Chengchou

East China Sea

SHANGHAI

OUNTAINS

WUHAN

TIBET

CHUNGKING

Mekong

Tropic of Cancer

T'aipei

TAIWAN

Philippine Sea

IMALAYAS

K'unming

CANTON

Ganges

Brahmaputra

CALCUTTA

Hohoi

HAINAN TAO

MANILA

Mandalay

Salween

Cebu

South China Sea

MINDANAO

Mekong

Bay of Bengal

Rangoon

HO CHI MINH CITY

BANGKOK

Celebes Sea

Andaman Sea

Gulf of Thailand

Kota Kinabalu

Manado

Kuching

BORNEO

Equator

Medan

SINGAPORE

CELEBES

SUMATRA

Ujung Pandang

Java Sea

JAKARTA

JAVA

0 100 200   400   600   800 Miles

0 150 300   600   900   1200 Kilometers

Red Sea

BERLIN

Athens

CRETE

ARABIAN DESERT

Alexandria

CAIRO

Nile

LONDON

PARIS

ROME

Banghazi

LIBYAN DESERT

Lake Nasser

NUBIAN DESERT

A

Nile

Tripoli

SICILY

MALTA

CORSICA

Tunis

R

ENNEDI

Al-Fash

SARDINIA

Algiers

MADRID

PYRENEES

ISLAS BALEAR

M e d i t e r r a n e a n   S e a

MOUNTAINS

GRAND ERG OCCIDENTAL

GRAND ERG ORIENTAL

A

TIBESTI

N

ATLAS

GRAND ERG OCCIDENTAL

AHAGGAR

H

A

D

Lake Chad

Ndjamena

Casablanca

Tamanrasset

A

U

Kano

S

ADRAR DES IFORAS

S

Yaoundé

CANARY ISLANDS

El Aaiun

EL DJOUF

S

Tombouctou

Niger

Lagos

ATLANTIC OCEAN

Niger

Gulf of Guinea

Tropic of Cancer

Bamako

Lake Volta

OCEAN

Dakar

Abidjan

Freetown

CAPE VERDE ISLANDS

ATLANTIC OCEAN

Scale 1:24,000,000; one inch to 380 miles. Lambert Azimuthal Equal-Area Projection

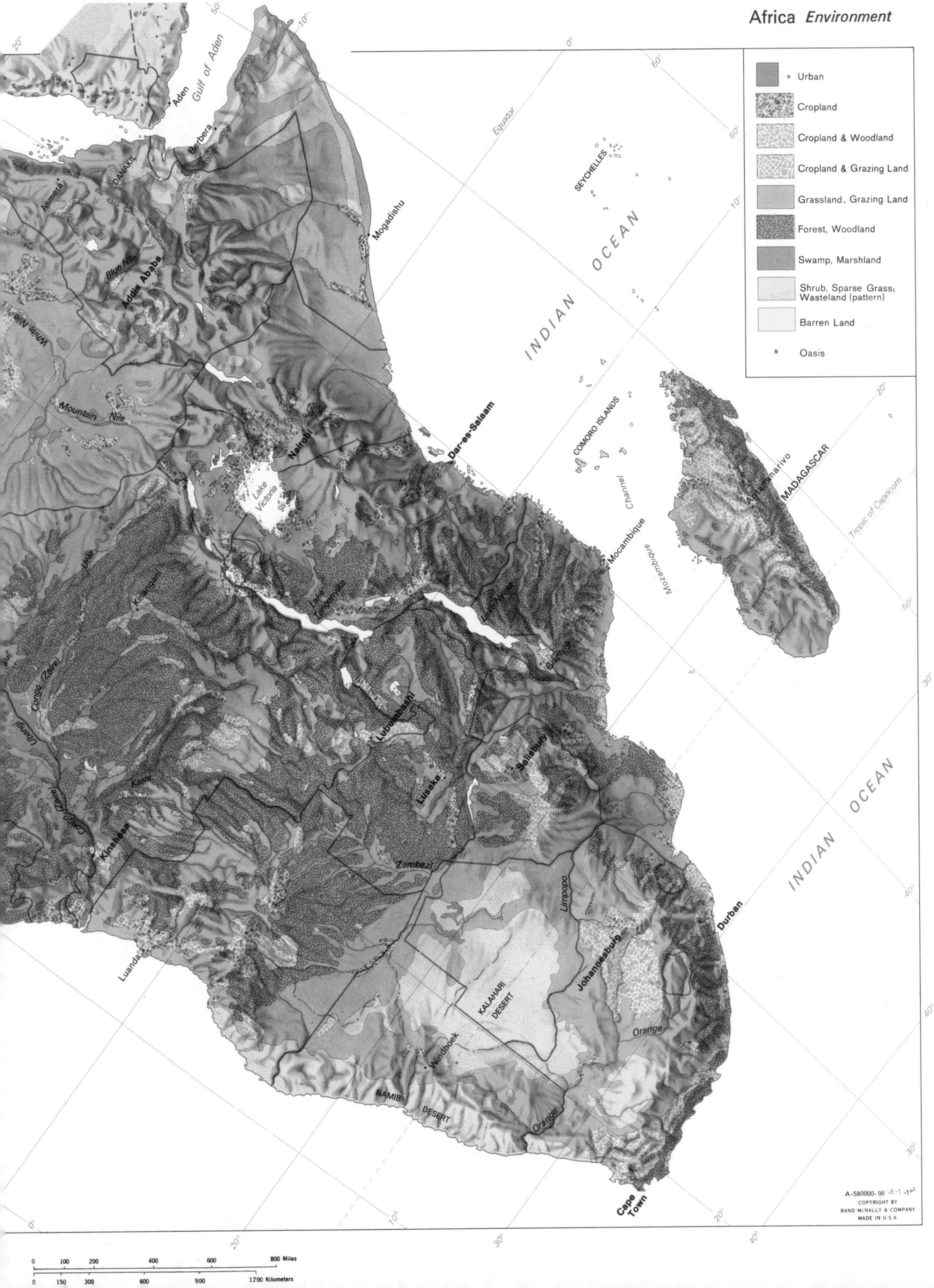

Legend

- Urban
- Cropland
- Cropland & Woodland
- Cropland & Grazing Land
- Grassland, Grazing Land
- Forest, Woodland
- Swamp, Marshland
- Shrub, Sparse Grass, Wasteland (pattern)
- Barren Land
- Oasis

INDIAN OCEAN

Gulf of Aden

Aden

Berbera

DANAKIL

Asmera

Blue Nile

Addis Ababa

White Nile

Mountain Nile

Mogadishu

SEYCHELLES

Equator

Nairobi

Lake Victoria

Dar-es-Salaam

COMORO ISLANDS

MADAGASCAR

Antananarivo

Tropic of Capricorn

Uele

Kisangani

Congo (Zaire)

Ubangi

Lake Tanganyika

Lake Nyasa

Mozambique Channel

Mozambique

Zaire (Congo)

Kasai

Lubumbashi

Blantyre

Kinshasa

Luanda

Lusaka

Salisbury

Zambezi

Limpopo

Durban

Johannesburg

KALAHARI DESERT

Orange

Windhoek

Orange

NAMIB DESERT

Cape Town

INDIAN OCEAN

| 0 | 100 | 200 | 400 | 600 | 800 Miles |

| 0 | 150 | 300 | 600 | 900 | 1200 Kilometers |

BORNEO

CELEBES

SERAM

Palembang

Banjarmasin

SUMATRA

Java Sea

Ujung Pandang

Arafura Sea

JAKARTA

Surabaya

JAVA

SUMBA

TIMOR

Timor Sea

Darwin

Gulf of

Carpentaria

PEN

KIMBERLEY
PLATEAU

Daly

Victoria

INDIAN OCEAN

Broome

Fitzroy

Mount Isa

GREAT SANDY DESERT

Alice Springs

GREA
ARTESIA
BASIN

GIBSON DESERT

SIMPSON

DESERT

Tropic of Capricorn

Carnarvon

GREAT VICTORIA DESERT

Lake
Eyre

Kalgoorlie

NULLARBOR PLAIN

Lake
Gairdner

FLINDERS RANGES

Broken
Hill

DARLING RA.

Murray

Perth

Adelaide

Great Australian Bight

INDIAN OCEAN

Legend

■	Urban
	Cropland
	Cropland & Woodland
	Cropland & Grazing Land
	Grassland, Grazing Land
	Forest, Woodland
	Swamp, Marshland
	Shrub, Sparse Grass, Wasteland (pattern)
	Barren Land

Scale 1:24,000,000; one inch to 380 miles. Lambert Azimuthal Equal-Area Projection

EW GUINEA

NEW BRITAIN

Moresby

SOLOMON ISLANDS

Equator

KIRIBATI

P A C I F I C   *O C E A N*

0°

Coral   Sea

Cairns

Townsville

VANUATU
(NEW HEBRIDES)

SAMOA ISLANDS

Pago Pago

10°

FIJI
ISLANDS

Suva

NEW
CALEDONIA

ÎLES
LOYAUTÉ

Rockhampton

Nouméa

TONGA ISLANDS

20°

Brisbane

DIVIDING RANGE

SYDNEY

Canberra

Tasman   Sea

30°

P A C I F I C

MELBOURNE

GREAT DIVIDING RANGE

Auckland

NORTH ISLAND

TASMANIA

O C E A N

Hobart

Wellington

SOUTHERN ALPS

Christchurch

SOUTH ISLAND

A-590200-96   1-1-2^P51
COPYRIGHT BY
RAND McNALLY & COMPANY
MADE IN U.S.A.

40°

STEWART
ISLAND

Dunedin

150°   160°   170°   180°   170°   160°

0   100   200   400   600   800 Miles
0   150   300   600   900   1200 Kilometers

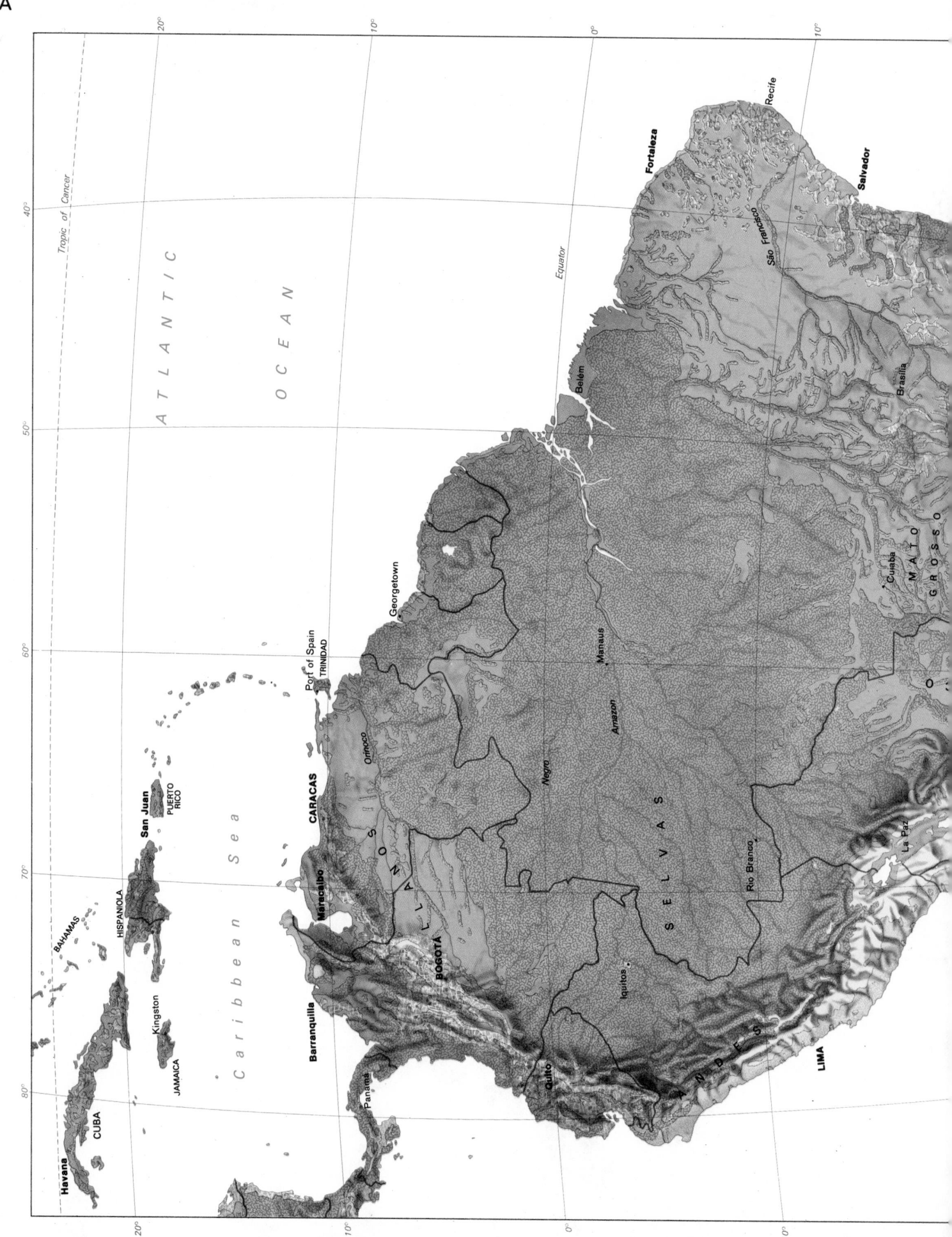

54A

Tropic of Cancer

40°

A T L A N T I C

O C E A N

50°

60°

Recife

Fortaleza

Salvador

Equator

São Francisco

Brasília

Belém

Georgetown

Port of Spain
TRINIDAD

San Juan

PUERTO
RICO

CARACAS

BAHAMAS

HISPANIOLA

Kingston

JAMAICA

Havana

CUBA

C a r i b b e a n   S e a

Barranquilla

Maracaibo

Orinoco

BOGOTÁ

Panamá

Quito

L L A N O S

Negro

Manaus

Amazon

S E L V A S

Iquitos

Rio Branco

Cuiabá

MATO GROSSO

La Paz

LIMA

A N D E S

70°

80°

20°

10°

0°

10°

20°

10°

0°

10°

Scale 1:24,000,000; one inch to 380 miles. Lambert Azimuthal Equal-Area Projection

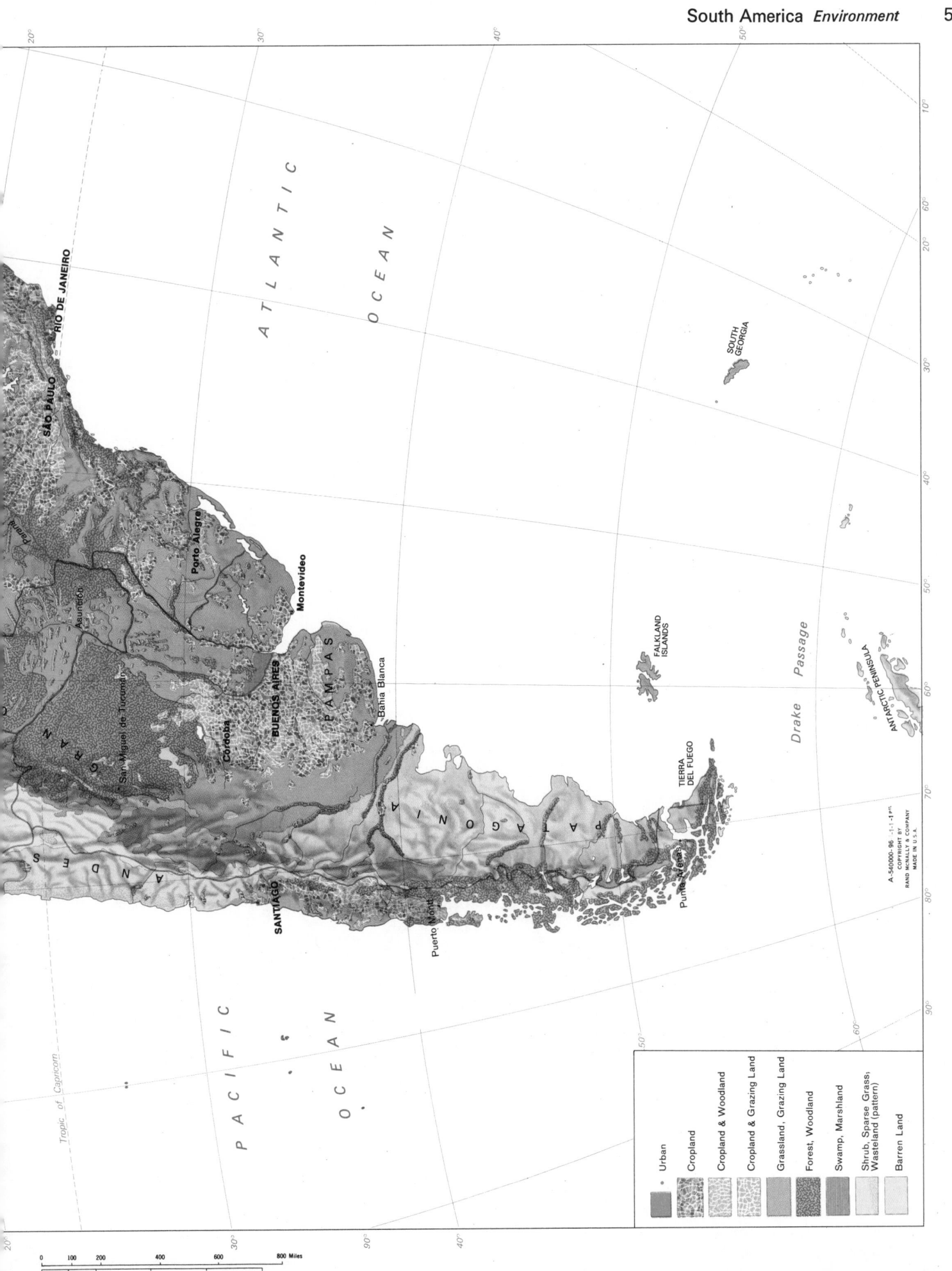

ATLANTIC

OCEAN

SOUTH
GEORGIA

RIO DE JANEIRO

SÃO PAULO

Porto Alegre

Montevideo

Asunción

Paraná

FALKLAND
ISLANDS

BUENOS AIRES

PAMPAS

Bahía Blanca

San Miguel de Tucumán

Córdoba

GRAN

Drake   Passage

ANTARCTIC PENINSULA

TIERRA
DEL FUEGO

SANTIAGO

P A T A G O N I A

A N D E S

Punta Arenas

Puerto Montt

PACIFIC

OCEAN

Tropic of Capricorn

A-540000-96 -1-1-1 PG
COPYRIGHT BY
RAND McNALLY & COMPANY
MADE IN U.S.A.

Urban

Cropland

Cropland & Woodland

Cropland & Grazing Land

Grassland, Grazing Land

Forest, Woodland

Swamp, Marshland

Shrub, Sparse Grass,
Wasteland (pattern)

Barren Land

0   100   200   400   600   800 Miles

0   150   300   600   900   1200 Kilometers

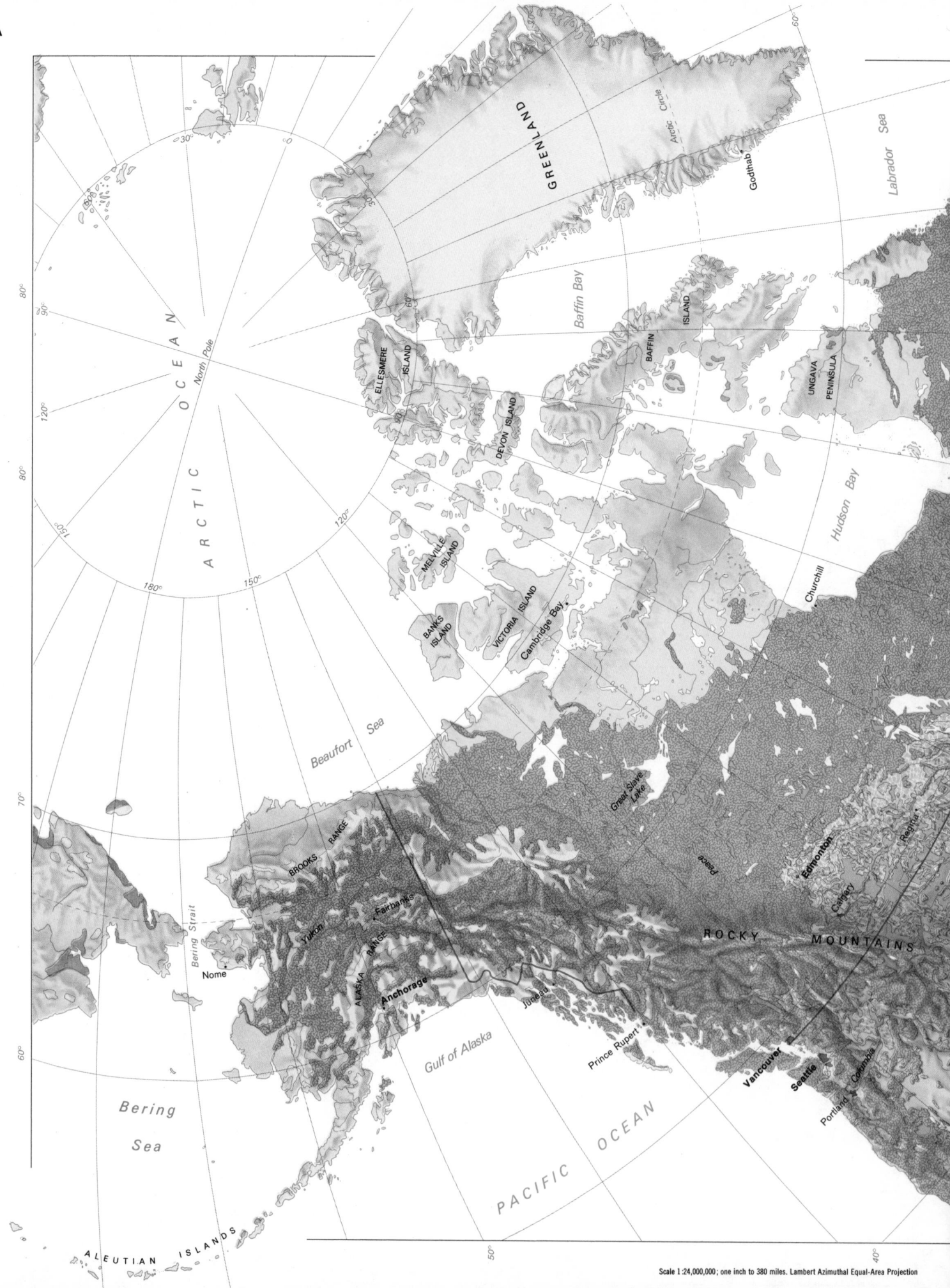

GREENLAND

Godthåb

Arctic Circle

Labrador Sea

Baffin Bay

BAFFIN ISLAND

ELLESMERE ISLAND

DEVON ISLAND

UNGAVA PENINSULA

Hudson Bay

Churchill

MELVILLE ISLAND

VICTORIA ISLAND

Cambridge Bay

BANKS ISLAND

OCEAN

ARCTIC

North Pole

Great Slave Lake

Peace

Edmonton

Regina

Calgary

ROCKY MOUNTAINS

Beaufort Sea

BROOKS RANGE

Yukon

Fairbanks

ALASKA RANGE

Anchorage

Nome

Bering Strait

Juneau

Prince Rupert

Vancouver

Seattle

Portland

Columbia

Gulf of Alaska

Bering

Sea

PACIFIC OCEAN

ALEUTIAN ISLANDS

Scale 1:24,000,000; one inch to 380 miles. Lambert Azimuthal Equal-Area Projection

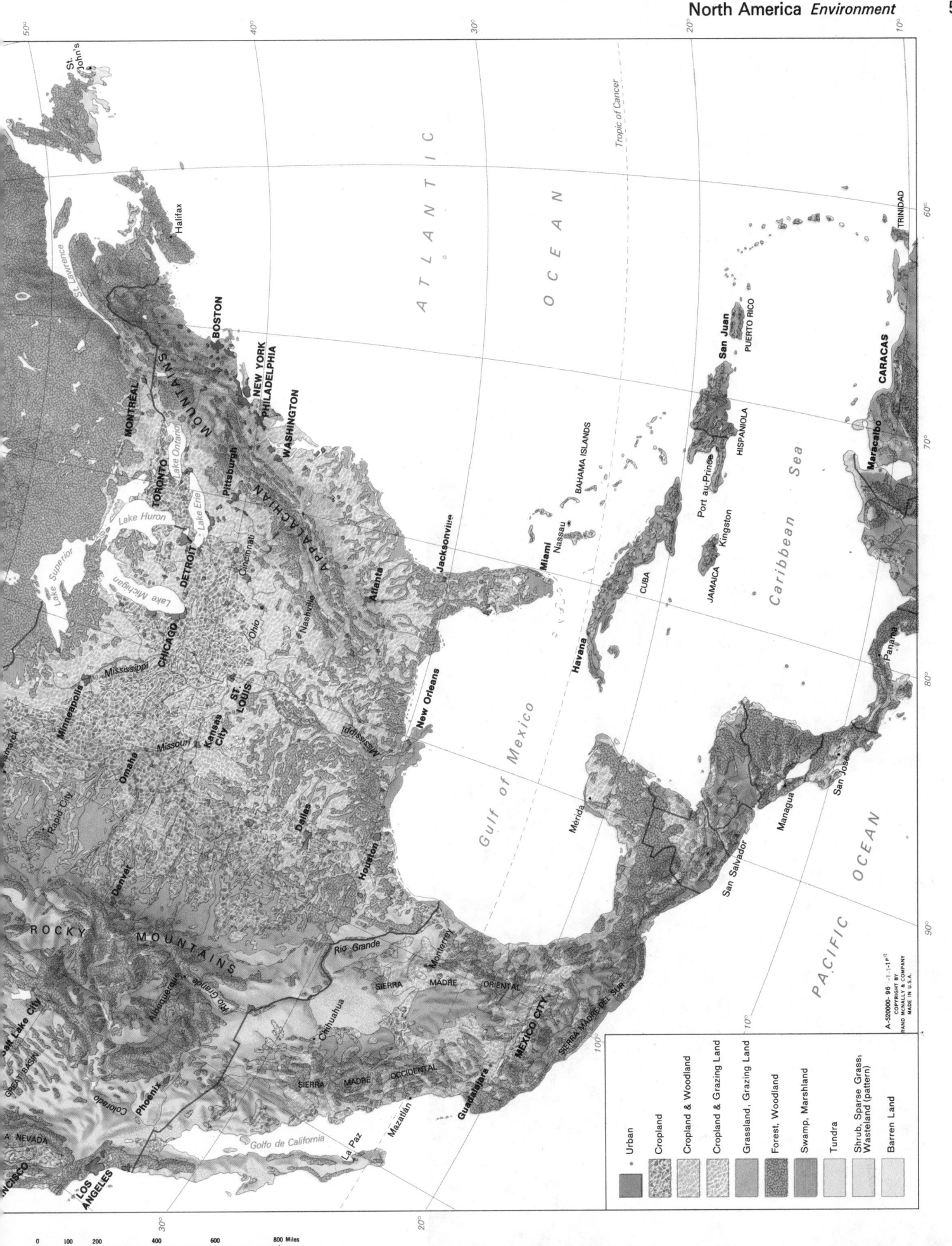

St. John's

Halifax

BOSTON
NEW YORK
PHILADELPHIA
WASHINGTON
MONTREAL
TORONTO
Pittsburgh
DETROIT
Cincinnati
CHICAGO
Nashville
Atlanta
Jacksonville

ATLANTIC
OCEAN

Tropic of Cancer

TRINIDAD

San Juan
PUERTO RICO

CARACAS

Maracaibo

HISPANIOLA

Port au-Prince
Kingston
JAMAICA

BAHAMA ISLANDS

Nassau

Miami

CUBA

Havana

Caribbean Sea

St. Lawrence

Lake Ontario
Lake Erie
Lake Huron
Lake Superior
Lake Michigan

APPALACHIAN MOUNTAINS

Ohio

ST. LOUIS
Kansas City
Minneapolis
Mississippi
Missouri
Omaha

New Orleans

Gulf of Mexico

Mérida

Panama

San José
Managua
San Salvador

PACIFIC OCEAN

Rapid City

Denver

ROCKY MOUNTAINS

Dallas

Houston

Rio Grande
Monterrey

SIERRA MADRE ORIENTAL

Chihuahua

MEXICO CITY

SIERRA MADRE OCCIDENTAL

SIERRA MADRE DEL SUR

Guadalajara

SIERRA NEVADA

Salt Lake City

GREAT BASIN

Albuquerque
Rio Grande
Colorado

Phoenix

Mazatlán
La Paz

Golfo de California

SAN FRANCISCO
LOS ANGELES

A-500000-96

COPYRIGHT BY
RAND McNALLY & COMPANY
MADE IN U.S.A.

■ Urban	
	Cropland
	Cropland & Woodland
	Cropland & Grazing Land
	Grassland, Grazing Land
	Forest, Woodland
	Swamp, Marshland
	Tundra
	Shrub, Sparse Grass; Wasteland (pattern)
	Barren Land

0   100   200   400   600   800 Miles
0   150   300   600   900   1200 Kilometers

United States Travel Maps

A United States travel map has been divided into ten regions—Hawaii, Northeastern U.S., Southeastern U.S., South Central U.S., Central U.S., North Central U.S., Southern Rocky Mountains, the Far West, Northwestern U.S., and Alaska, as a convenience to the traveler in planning a route between adjoining states.

The map shows all major highways and all major cities and towns. It shows the topography of the land, including mountains, lakes, and reservoirs. For the vacationer, the map also locates major National Park Service areas—national parks, monuments, seashores, and recreation areas.

Elevations are indicated in meters, Interstate highway distances in miles and kilometers, and other road distances in miles.

Explanation of Map Symbols

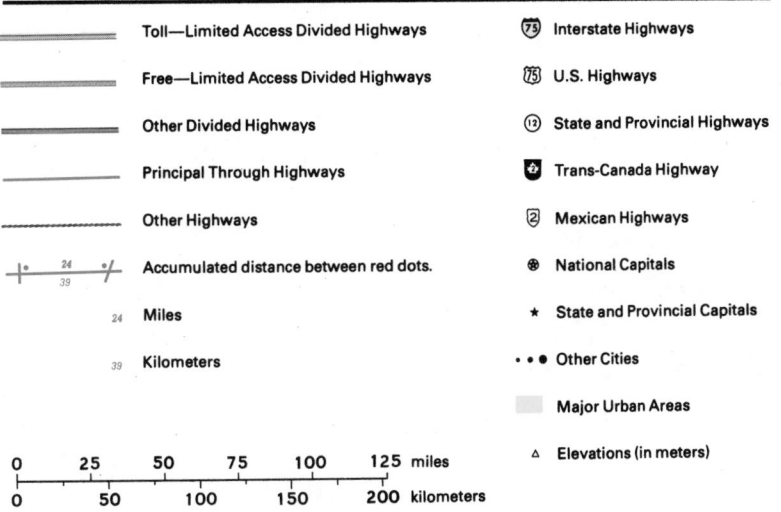

Toll—Limited Access Divided Highways	🛡75 Interstate Highways
Free—Limited Access Divided Highways	75 U.S. Highways
Other Divided Highways	12 State and Provincial Highways
Principal Through Highways	Trans-Canada Highway
Other Highways	2 Mexican Highways
⊢ 24 ⊣ Accumulated distance between red dots. 39	⊕ National Capitals
24 Miles	★ State and Provincial Capitals
39 Kilometers	• • ● Other Cities
	Major Urban Areas
0 25 50 75 100 125 miles	△ Elevations (in meters)
0 50 100 150 200 kilometers	

Scale 1:3,900,000 One inch equals approximately 62 miles.
One centimeter equals approximately 39 kilometers.

ALBERS CONICAL EQUAL AREA PROJECTION

Hawaii

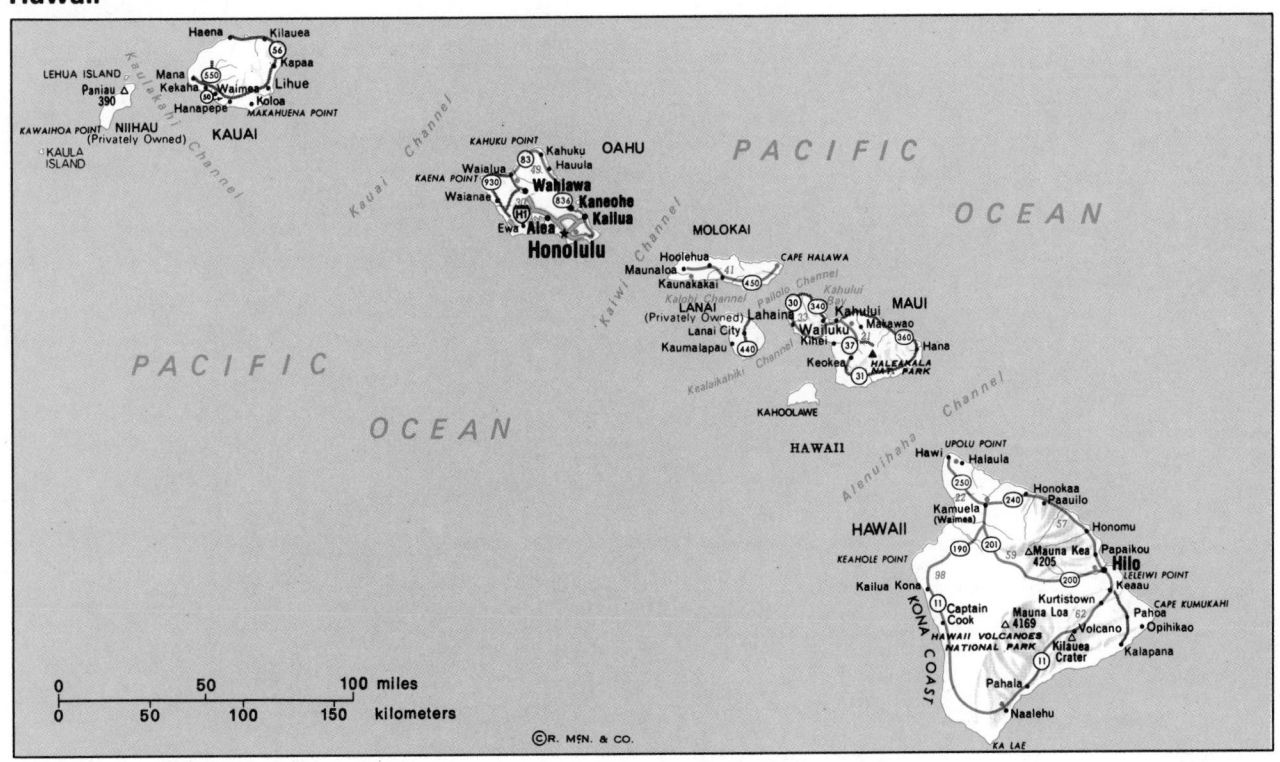

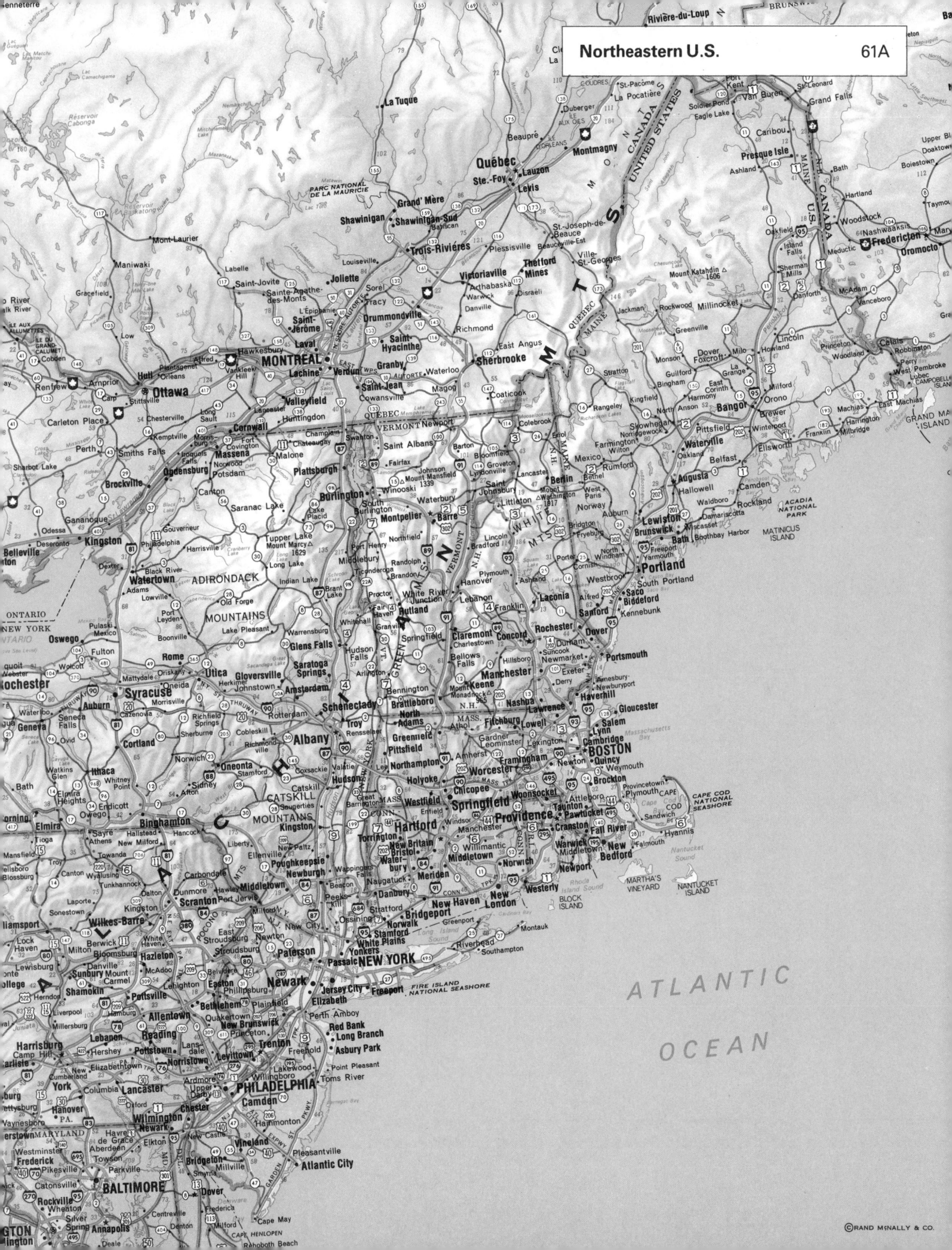

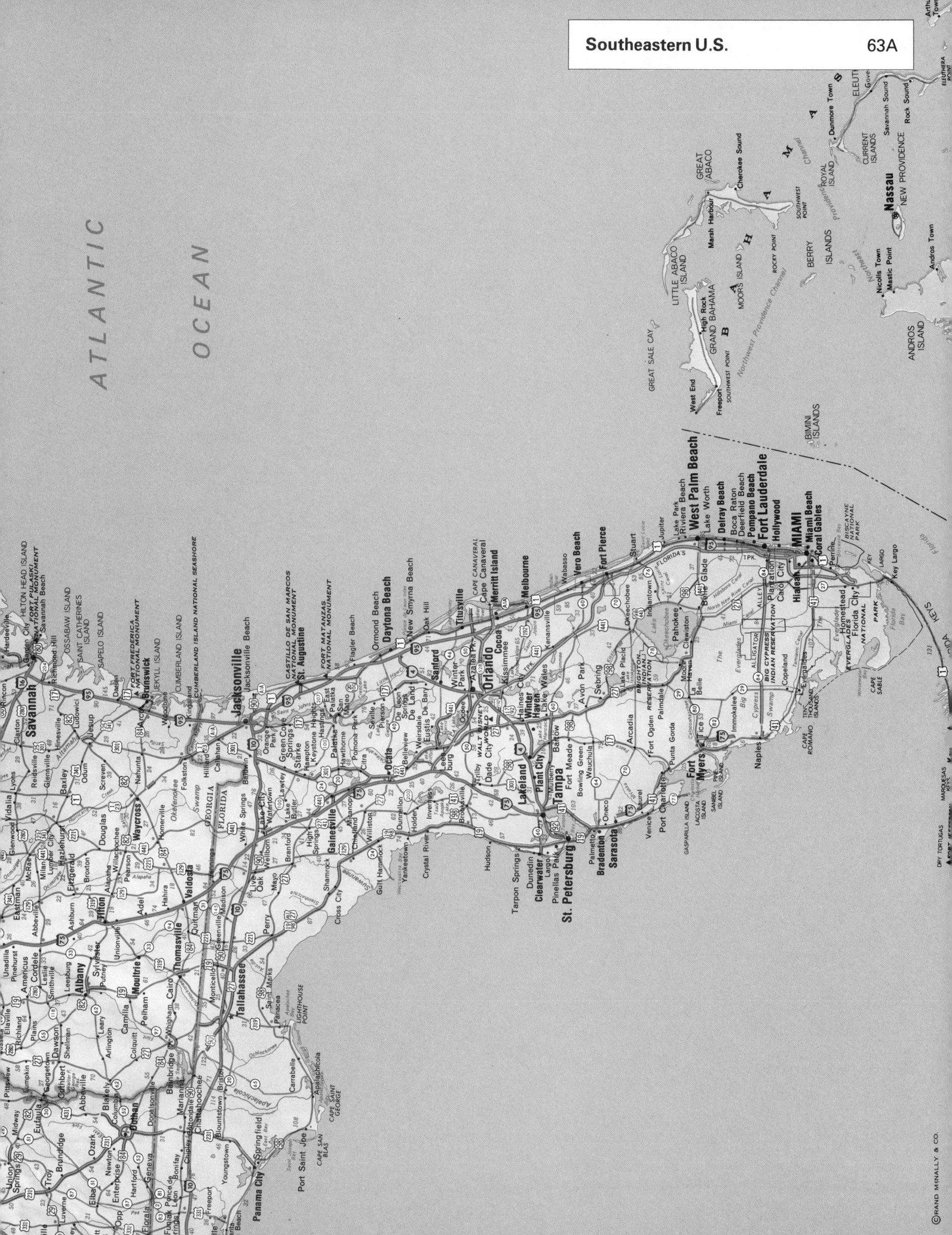

ATLANTIC

OCEAN

GREAT SALE CAY

LITTLE ABACO ISLAND
GREAT ABACO
Cherokee Sound
Marsh Harbour

MOORS ISLAND
ROCKY POINT
BERRY ISLANDS

High Rock
GRAND BAHAMA
West End
Freeport
SOUTHWEST POINT

Northwest Providence Channel

BIMINI ISLANDS

ELEUTHERA POINT
ELEUTHERA
Governor
Dunmore Town
CURRENT ISLANDS
Nassau NEW PROVIDENCE
Nicolls Town
Mastic Point
Andros Town
ANDROS ISLAND

West Palm Beach
Lake Park
Riviera Beach
Lake Worth
Delray Beach
Boca Raton
Deerfield Beach
Pompano Beach
Fort Lauderdale
Hollywood
MIAMI
Miami Beach
Coral Gables
Hialeah
Homestead
Florida City
BISCAYNE NATIONAL PARK
Key Largo
FLORIDA KEYS
CAPE SABLE
DRY TORTUGAS
MARQUESAS KEYS

Savannah
Jacksonville
St. Augustine
Daytona Beach
Ormond Beach
New Smyrna Beach
Titusville
CAPE CANAVERAL
Cape Canaveral
Cocoa
Merritt Island
Melbourne
Vero Beach
Fort Pierce
Stuart
Jupiter
Sanford
Orlando
Winter Park
Kissimmee
Lake Placid
Sebring
Avon Park
Okeechobee
Lake Okeechobee
Belle Glade
Pahokee
Clewiston
Brunswick
Waycross
Valdosta
Thomasville
Tallahassee
Ocala
Gainesville
Lakeland
Plant City
Tampa
St. Petersburg
Clearwater
Bradenton
Sarasota
Fort Myers
Naples
EVERGLADES NATIONAL PARK
BIG CYPRESS NATIONAL PRESERVE
ALLIGATOR ALLEY

GEORGIA
FLORIDA
Albany
Moultrie
Dothan
Panama City

GREAT ABACO

© Rand McNally & Co.

GULF OF MEXICO

© RAND McNALLY & CO.

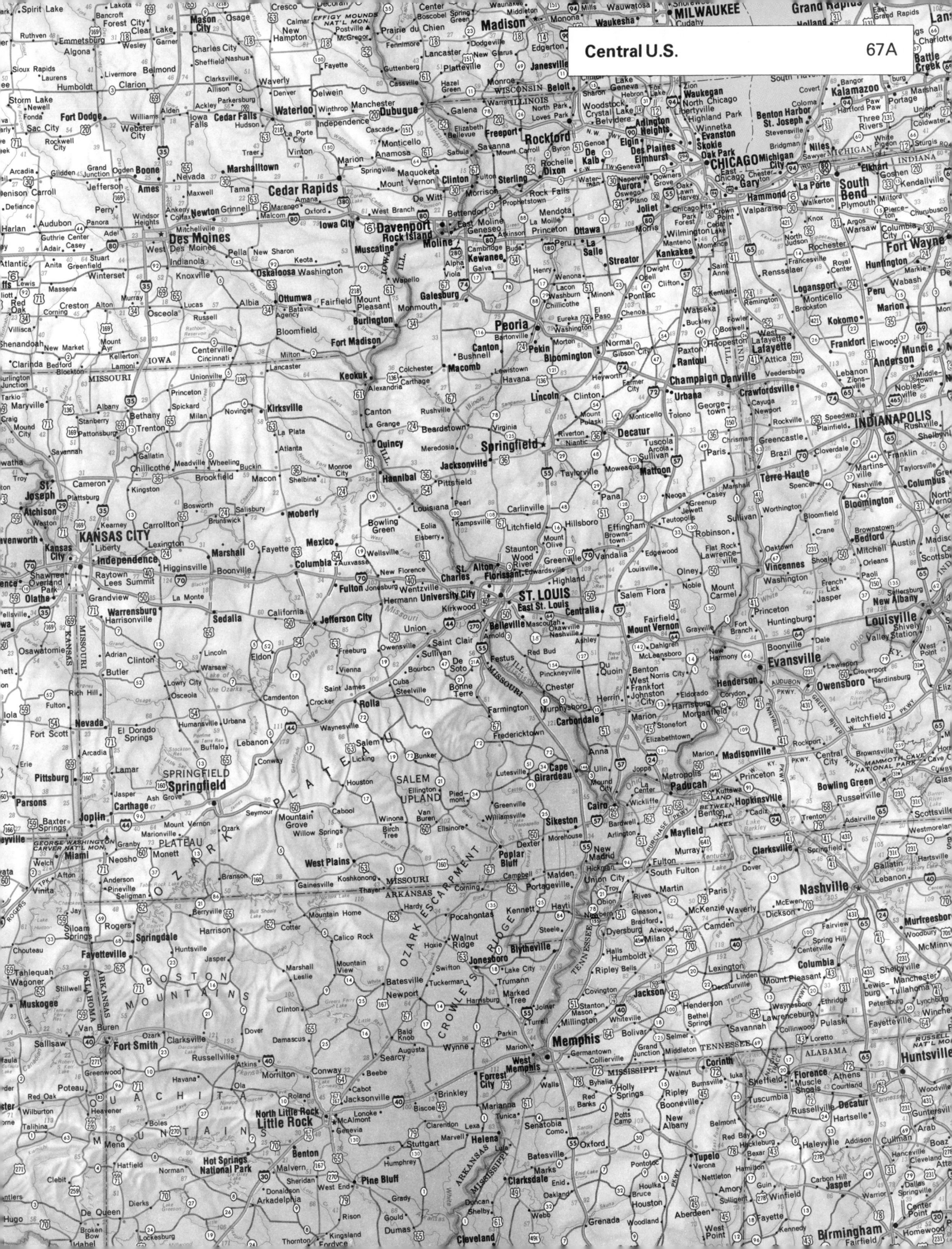

Conversion of
Meters to Feet

1 Meter = 3.28 Feet

Meters	Feet
6000	19685
4000	13124
3000	9843
2000	6562
1000	3281
500	1640
200	656
0	0

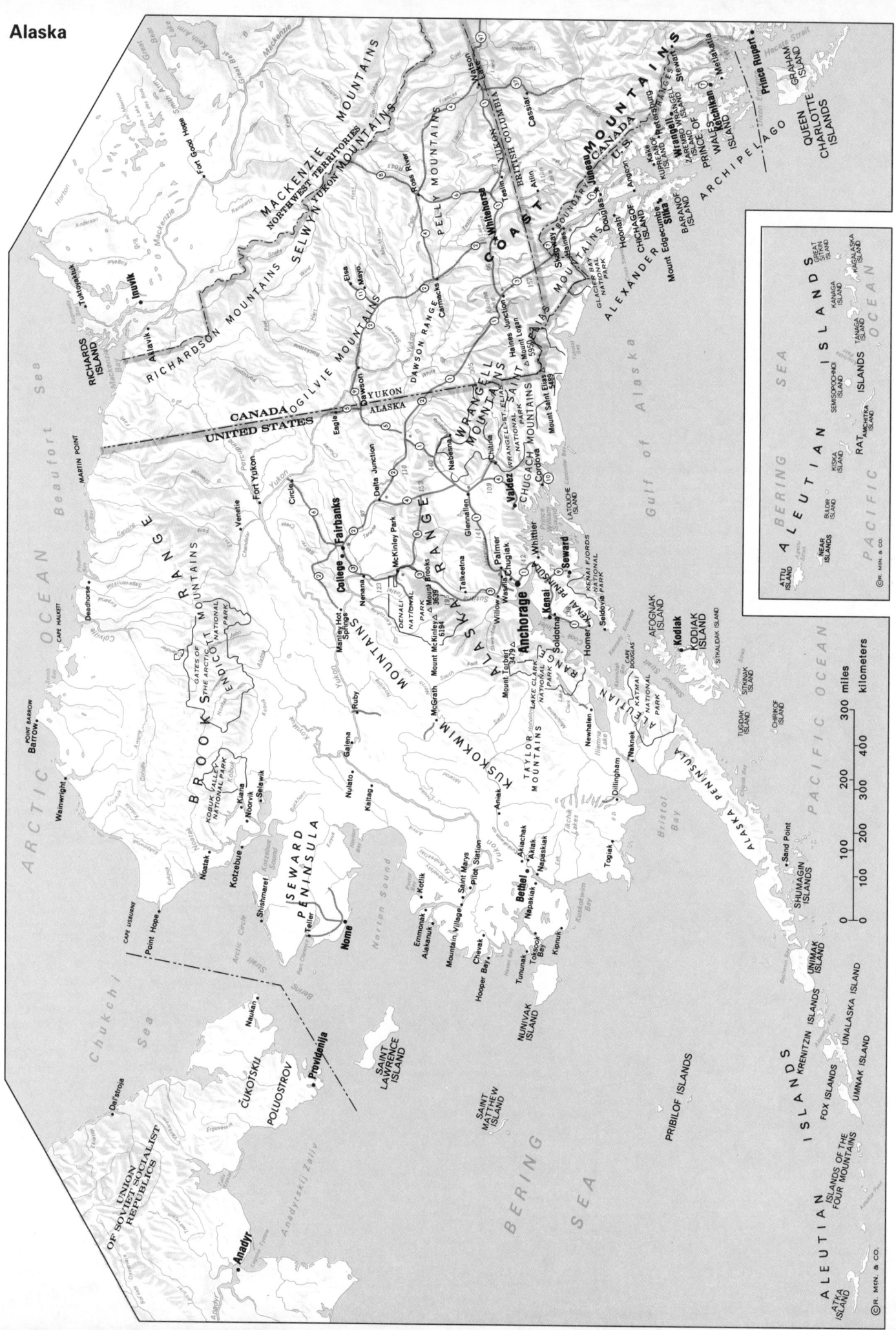

Alaska

Metropolitan Area Maps

Introduction

This section consists of 62 maps of the world's most populous metropolitan areas. In order to make comparison easier, all the metropolitan areas are shown at the same scale, 1:300,000.

Detailed urban maps are an important reference requirement for a world atlas. The names of many large settlements, towns, suburbs, and neighborhoods can be located on these large-scale maps. From a thematic standpoint the maps show generalized land-use patterns. Included were the total urban extent, major industrial areas, parks, public land, wooded areas, airports, shopping centers, streets, and railroads. A special effort was made to portray the various metropolitan areas in a manner as standard and comparable as possible.

Notable differences occur in the forms of cities. In most of North America these forms were conditioned by a rectangular pattern of streets; land-use zones (residential, commercial, industrial) are well defined. The basic structure of most European cities is noticeably different and more complex; street patterns are irregular and zones are less well defined. In Asia, Africa, and South America the form tends to be even more irregular and complex. Widespread dispersion of craft and trade activities has lessened zonation, there may be cities with no identifiable city centers, and sometimes there may be dual centers (old and modern). Higher population densities result in more limited, compact urban places in these areas of the world.

Explanation of Map Symbols

Inhabited Localities

The symbol represents the number of inhabitants within the locality

- · 0—10,000
- ○ 10,000—25,000
- ◉ 25,000—100,000
- ▣ 100,000—250,000
- ▣ 250,000—1,000,000
- ■ >1,000,000

The size of type indicates the relative economic and political importance of the locality

Écommoy
Trouville   St.-Denis
Lisieux   PARIS

■

Hollywood   Section of a City,
Westminster   Neighborhood
Northland ■
Center   Major Shopping Center

 Urban Area (area of continuous industrial, commercial, and residential development)

 Major Industrial Area

Wooded Area

Political Boundaries

International (First-order political unit)

━━ ━ ━━ Demarcated, Undemarcated, and Administrative

━━━━━ Demarcation Line

Internal

━━━━━ State, Province, etc. (Second-order political unit)

──────── County, Oblast, etc. (Third-order political unit)

─ ─ ─ ─ ─ Okrug, Kreis, etc. (Fourth-order political unit)

- - - - - - - City or Municipality (may appear in combination with another boundary symbol)

Capitals of Political Units

BUDAPEST Independent Nation

Recife State, Province, etc.

White Plains County, Oblast, etc.

Iserlohn Okrug, Kreis, etc.

Transportation

Road

PASSAIC EXPWY.   (I-80)   Primary

BERLINER RING   Secondary

Tertiary

Railway

CANADIAN NATIONAL   Primary

Secondary

Rapid Transit

Airport

LONDON (HEATHROW) AIRPORT

Rail or Air Terminal

■ SÜD BAHNHOF

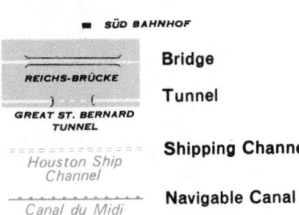
REICHS-BRÜCKE   Bridge

GREAT ST. BERNARD TUNNEL   Tunnel

Houston Ship Channel   Shipping Channel

Canal du Midi   Navigable Canal

TO MALMÖ   Ferry

Hydrographic Features

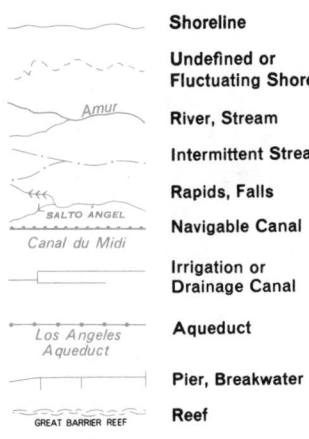
Shoreline

Undefined or Fluctuating Shoreline

Amur   River, Stream

Intermittent Stream

Rapids, Falls

SALTO ANGEL

Canal du Midi   Navigable Canal

Irrigation or Drainage Canal

Los Angeles Aqueduct   Aqueduct

Pier, Breakwater

GREAT BARRIER REEF   Reef

L. Victoria   Lake, Reservoir

Intermittent Lake

The Everglades   Swamp

Miscellaneous Cultural Features

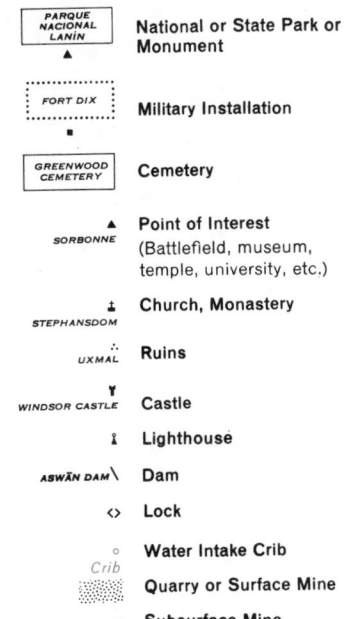
PARQUE NACIONAL LANÍN ▲   National or State Park or Monument

FORT DIX ■   Military Installation

GREENWOOD CEMETERY   Cemetery

▲ SORBONNE   Point of Interest (Battlefield, museum, temple, university, etc.)

STEPHANSDOM   Church, Monastery

UXMAL   Ruins

WINDSOR CASTLE   Castle

Lighthouse

ASWĀN DAM \   Dam

<>   Lock

○ Crib   Water Intake Crib

Quarry or Surface Mine

Subsurface Mine

Topographic Features

Mt. Kenya 5199 △   Elevation Above Sea Level

Elevations are given in meters

★   Rock

A N D E S KUNLUNSHANMAI   Mountain Range, Plateau, Valley, etc.

BAFFIN ISLAND   Island

POLUOSTROV KAMČATKA CABO DE HORNOS   Peninsula, Cape, Point, etc.

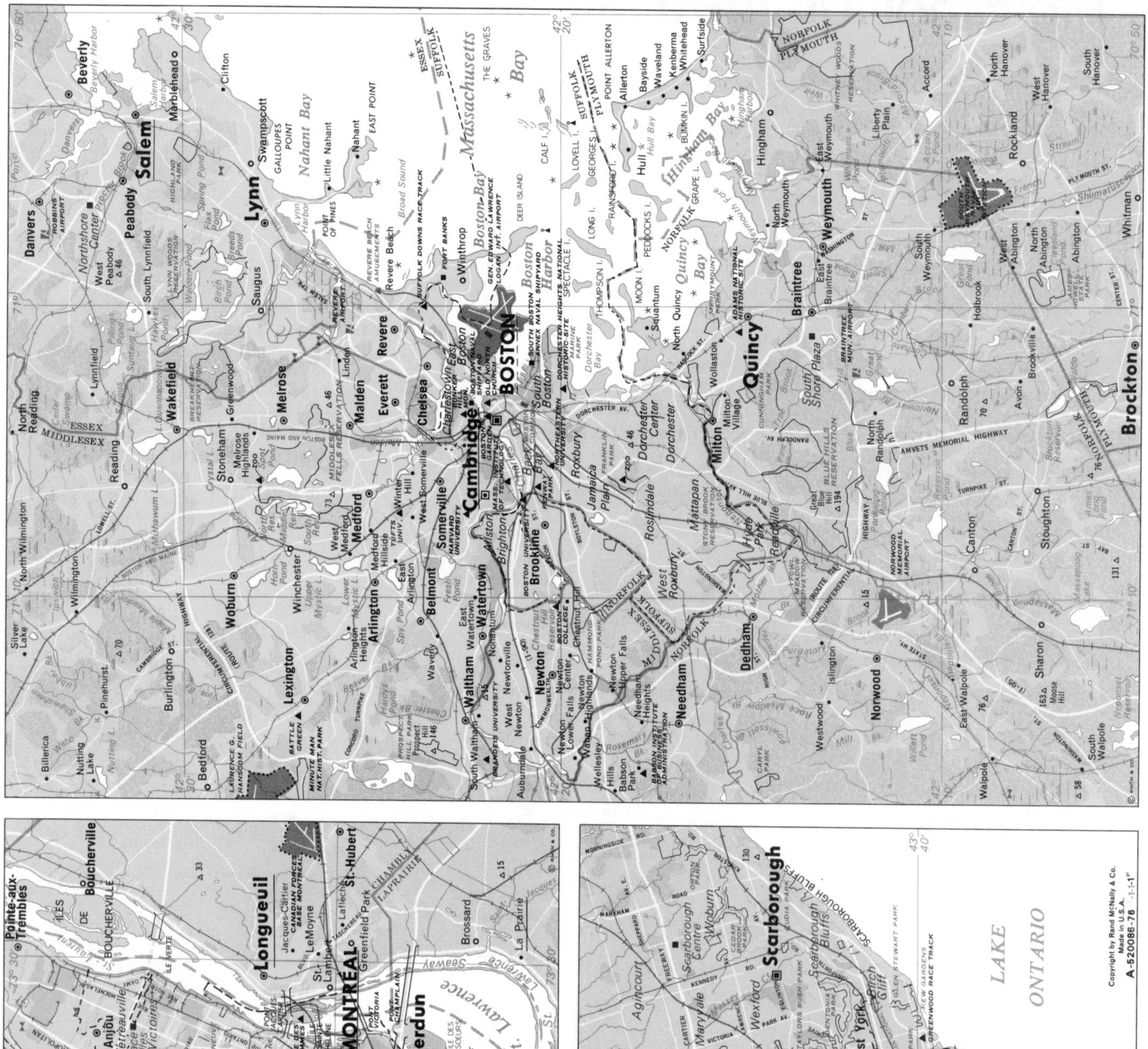

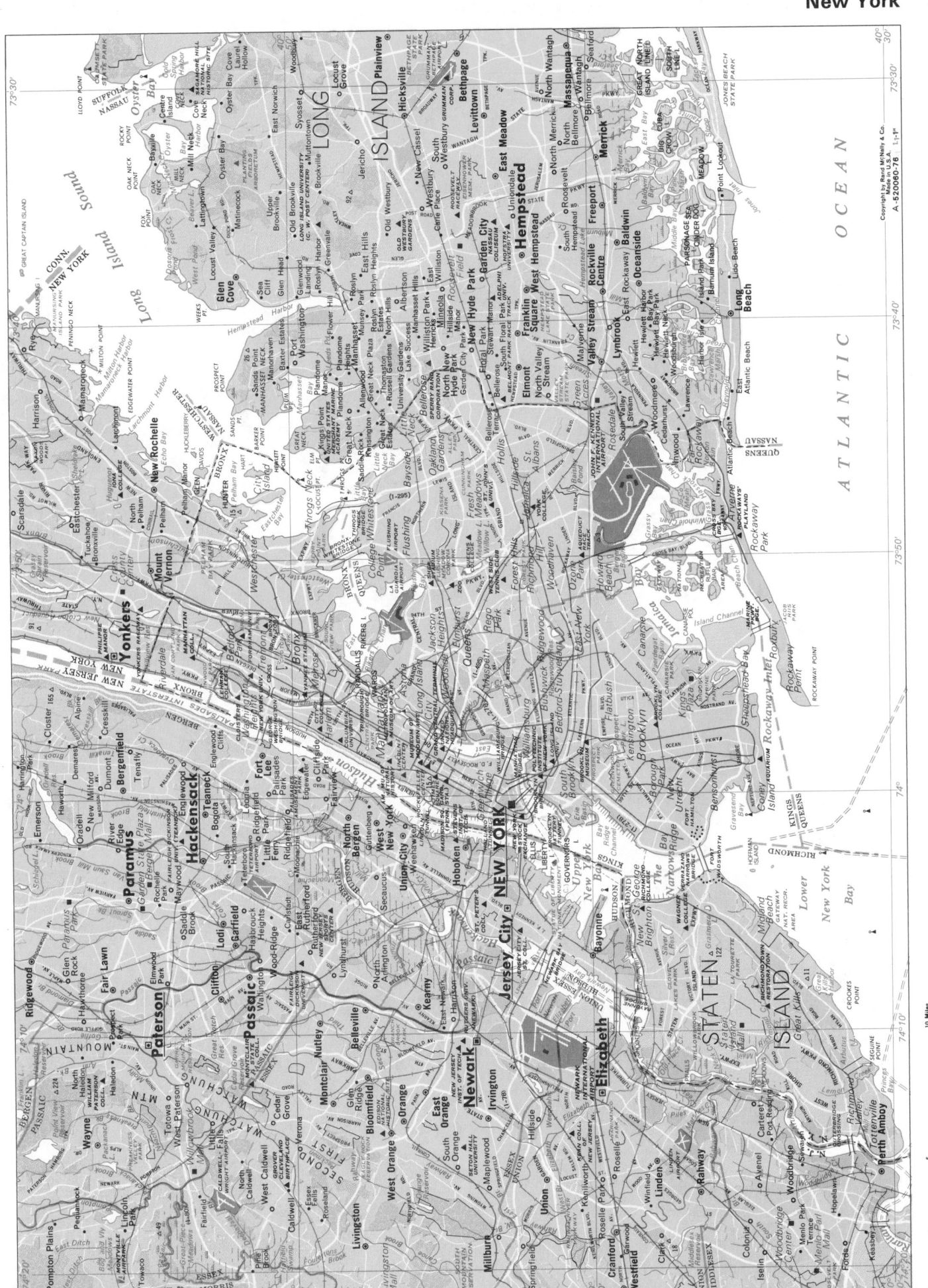

Copyright by Rand McNally & Co.
Made in U.S.A.
A-520060-76 1:1°

Scale 1:300,000; one inch to 4.7 miles.

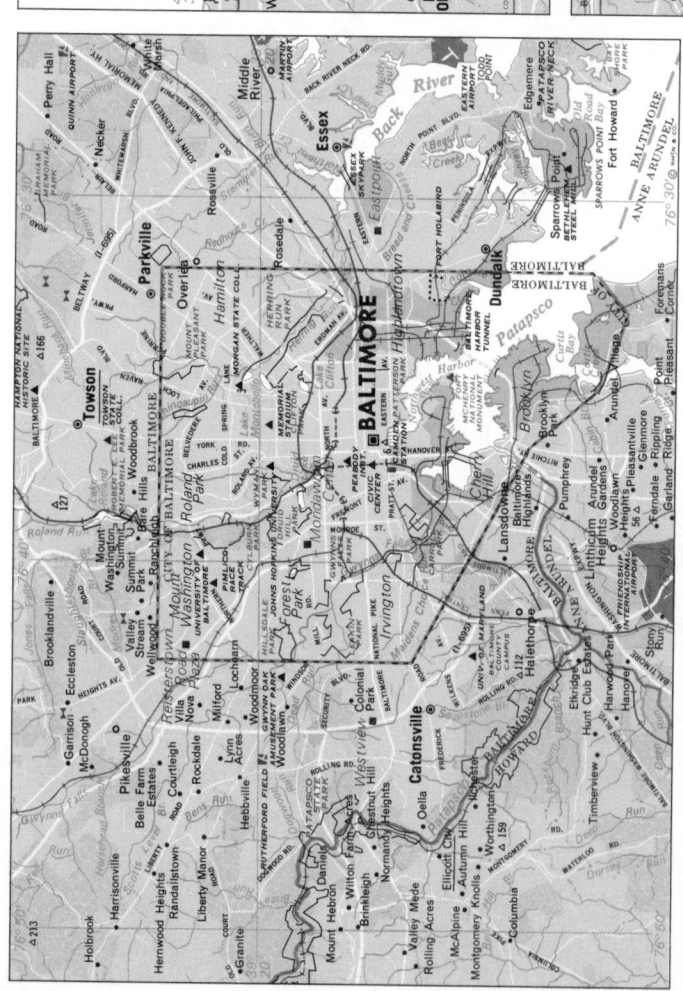

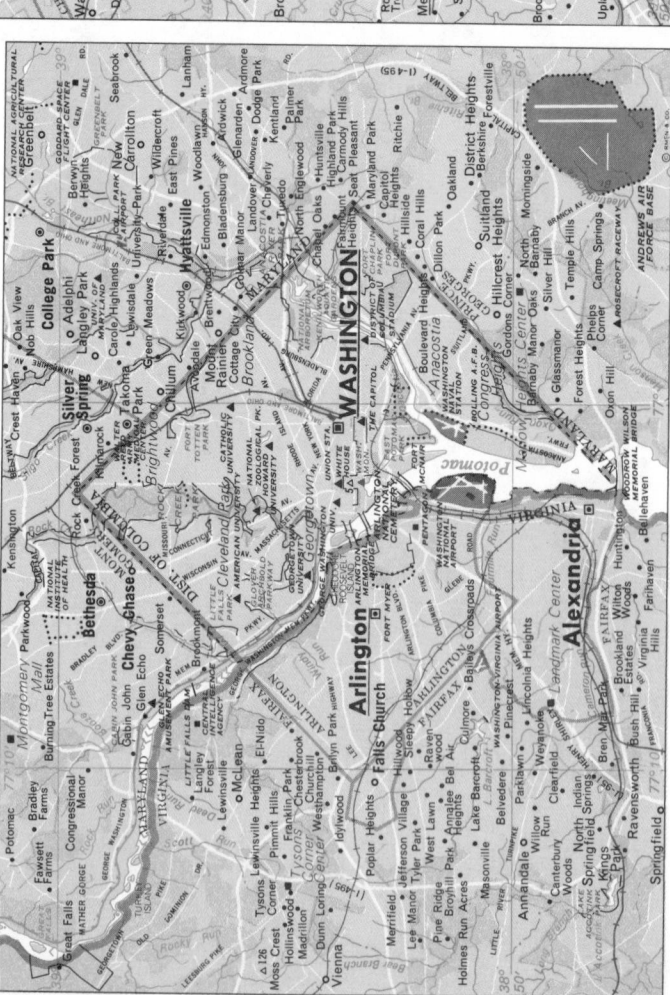

Scale 1:300,000; one inch to 4.7 miles.

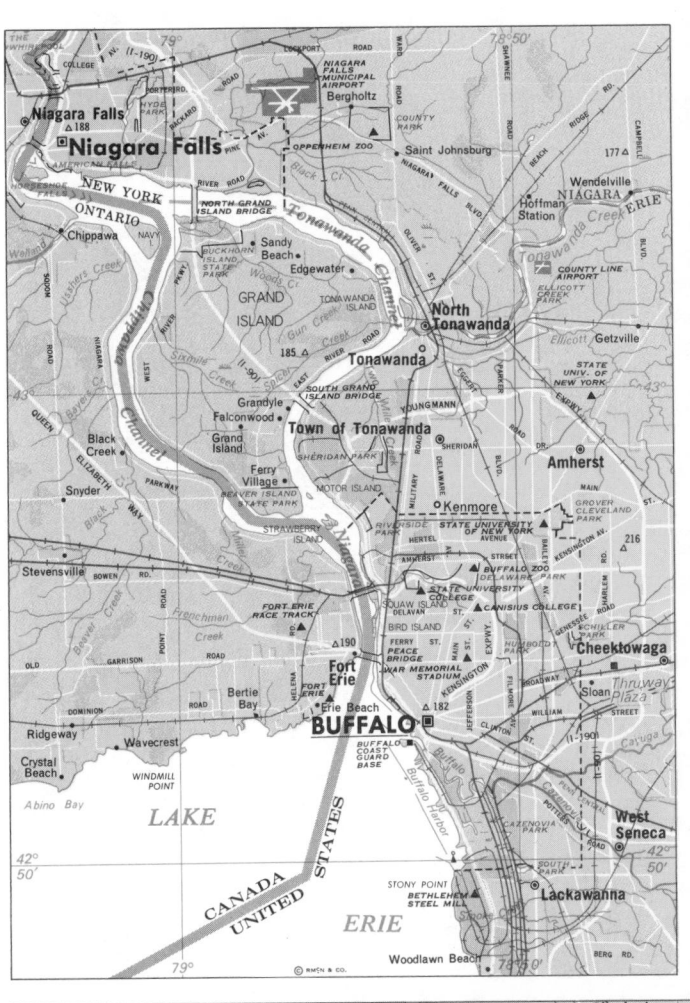

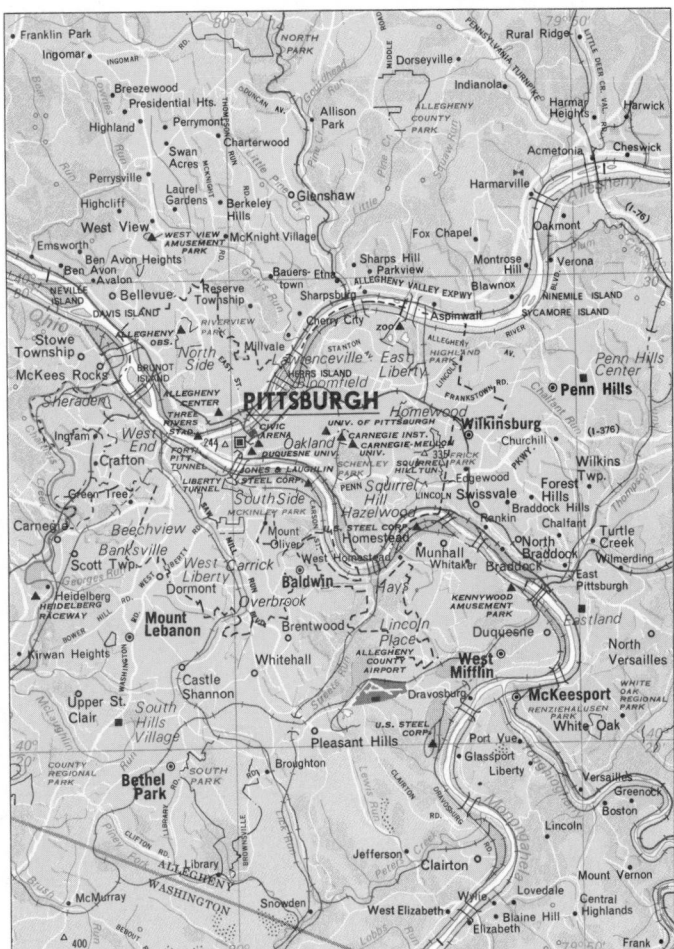

Buffalo (left map)

Niagara Falls
NEW YORK
ONTARIO
Chippawa
Navy Island
Sandy Beach
Edgewater
GRAND ISLAND
Grandyle
Falconwood
Grand Island
Ferry Village
Black Creek
Snyder
Stevensville
Bowen
Ridgeway
Wavecrest
Crystal Beach
Abino Bay
Bertie Bay
Dominion
Fort Erie
FORT ERIE
Erie Beach
BUFFALO
Woodlawn Beach
LAKE ERIE
CANADA
UNITED STATES
Windmill Point
Stony Point
Bethlehem Steel Mill
Lackawanna
West Seneca
Cheektowaga
Sloan
Kenmore
Amherst
Town of Tonawanda
Tonawanda
North Tonawanda
Getzville
Wendelville
Hoffman Station
NIAGARA
ERIE
Saint Johnsburg
Bergholtz
Niagara Falls Municipal Airport
College
North Grand Island Bridge
South Grand Island Bridge
Buckhorn Island State Park
Elliott Creek Park
County Line Airport
State Univ. of New York
Grover Cleveland Park
State University of New York
Canisius College
Buffalo Zoo
Delaware Park
War Memorial Stadium
Peace Bridge
Bird Island
Squaw Island
Fort Erie Race Track
Buffalo Coast Guard Base
Buffalo Harbor

Pittsburgh (right map)

Franklin Park
Ingomar
Ingomar
Breezewood
Presidential Hts.
Highland
Swan Acres
Perrysville
West View
Highcliff
Emsworth
Ben Avon Heights
Ben Avon
Avalon
Bellevue
NEVILLE ISLAND
DAVIS ISLAND
Stowe Township
McKees Rocks
Sheraden
Ingram
Crafton
Green Tree
Carnegie
Scott Twp.
Banksville
Beechview
West End
PITTSBURGH
Oakland
Dormont
Mount Lebanon
Kirwan Heights
Upper St. Clair
South Hills Village
Bethel Park
McMurray
North Park
Dorseyville
Indianola
Rural Ridge
Little Deer Cr.
Harwick
Harmar Heights
Acmetonia
Cheswick
Allison Park
Charterwood
Perrymont
Glenshaw
Berkeley Hills
McKnight Village
Fox Chapel
Harmarville
Montrose Hill
Verona
Oakmont
Sharps Hill
Parkview
Sharpsburg
Etna
Millvale
Cherry City
Aspinwall
Blawnox
NINEMILE ISLAND
SYCAMORE ISLAND
Penn Hills Center
Penn Hills
Homewood
Wilkinsburg
Churchill
Wilkins Twp.
Forest Hills
Swissvale
Edgewood
Rankin
Braddock Hills
Chalfant
Turtle Creek
Wilmerding
East Pittsburgh
North Braddock
Braddock
Munhall
Whitaker
Homestead
West Homestead
Hays
Baldwin
Overbrook
Brentwood
Whitehall
Castle Shannon
Pleasant Hills
Broughton
Lincoln Place
West Mifflin
Dravosburg
McKeesport
Port Vue
Liberty
Glassport
Versailles
North Versailles
Eastland
White Oak
Boston
Greenock
Lincoln
Jefferson
Clairton
Blaine Hill
Elizabeth
West Elizabeth
Mount Vernon
Central Highlands
Lovedale
Wylie
Snowden
WASHINGTON
Three Rivers
Civic Arena
Univ. of Pittsburgh
Carnegie Inst.
Carnegie-Mellon Univ.
Duquesne Univ.
Liberty Tunnel
Fort Pitt Tunnel
Allegheny County Airport
Kennywood Amusement Park
U.S. Steel Corp.
West View Amusement Park
Allegheny Valley Expwy.
County Regional Park
South Park
Allegheny County Park

Detroit (bottom map)

Wolverine Lake
Walled Lake
Wing Lake Shores
Birmingham
Bloomfield Village
Beverly Hills
Franklin
Bingham Farms
Berkley
Clawson
Madison Heights
Warren
Fraser
Macomb Mall
St. Clair Shores
Roseville
Center Line
East Detroit
Harper Woods
Grosse Pointe Woods
Grosse Pointe Shores
Grosse Pointe Farms
Grosse Pointe
Grosse Pointe Park
Lake St. Clair
Gaukler Point
Royal Oak
Huntington Woods
Lathrup Village
Pleasant Ridge
Ferndale
Hazel Park
Royal Oak Township
Oak Park
Southfield
Farmington Hills
Novi
Farmington
Clarenceville
Redford Township
Redford
Livonia
Northville
Plymouth
Westland
Garden City
Dearborn Heights
Inkster
Dearborn
Wayne
Melvindale
Lincoln Park
Allen Park
Romulus
Taylor
Sheldon
Highland Park
Hamtramck
DETROIT
Windsor
ONTARIO
MICHIGAN
UNITED STATES
CANADA
Belle Isle
Peche Isle
St. Clair Beach
Tecumseh
Riverside
Windsor Airport
Devonshire Plaza
Essex
La Salle
Fighting Island
River Rouge
Ecorse
Wyandotte
Lawrence Institute of Technology
Detroit Zoological Park
Michigan State Fair Grounds
Univ. of Detroit
Detroit City Airport
Chrysler Corp. Hamtramck Plant
Detroit Inst. of Arts Wayne State Univ.
Olympia Stadium
Tiger Stadium
Cobo Hall
Amtrak Sta.
Great Lakes Museum
Ford Museum Greenfield Village
Fairlane Town
Ford Motor Co. River Rouge Plant
Fort Wayne Military Museum
Great Lakes Steel Works
Windsor Raceway
Univ. of Windsor
Ambassador Bridge
Detroit-Windsor Tunnel
Detroit Metropolitan Wayne County Airport
National Airport
Mettetal Airport
Livonia Mall
Wonderland Center
Westland Center
Northland
Eastland
Universal Mall
Oakland Mall

Scale 1:300,000; one inch to 4.7 miles.
10 Miles
10 Kilometers
Copyright by Rand McNally & Co.
Made in U.S.A.
A-520089-76

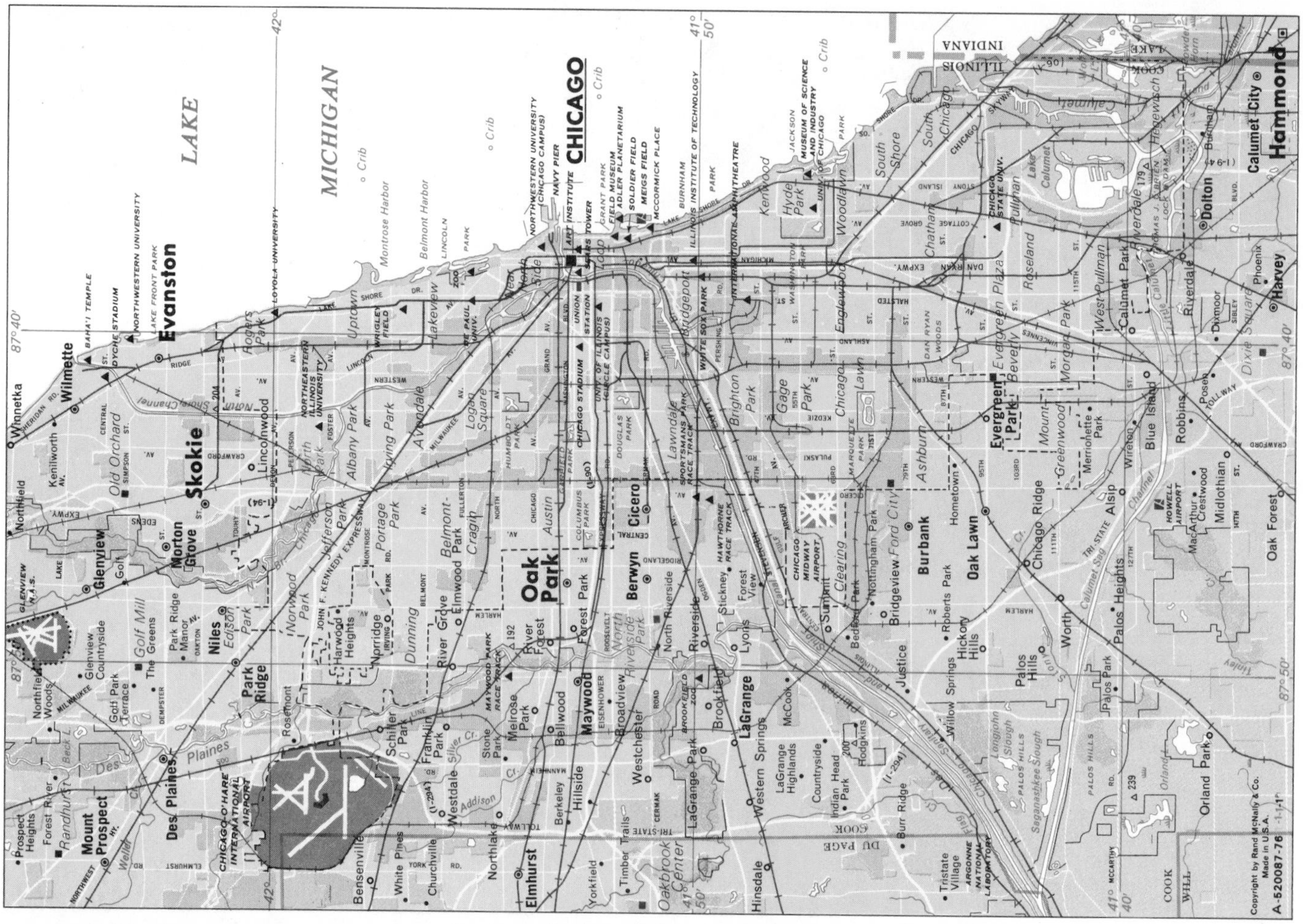

Chicago map

LAKE MICHIGAN

CHICAGO

Evanston · Wilmette · Winnetka · Skokie · Glenview · Morton Grove · Niles · Park Ridge · Des Plaines · Mount Prospect · Prospect Heights · Bensenville · Elmhurst · Oak Park · Berwyn · Cicero · Maywood · Melrose Park · Bellwood · Westchester · Broadview · Riverside · North Riverside · LaGrange · LaGrange Park · Brookfield · Hinsdale · Western Springs · LaGrange Highlands · Countryside · Indian Head Park · Burbank · Bridgeview · Summit · Clearing · Evergreen Park · Oak Lawn · Hickory Hills · Hometown · Justice · Willow Springs · Palos Hills · Palos Heights · Worth · Chicago Ridge · Greenwood · Merionette Park · Alsip · Blue Island · Calumet City · Dolton · Hammond · Harvey · Phoenix · Riverdale · West Pullman · Roseland · Beverly · Morgan Park · Robbins · Midlothian · Crestwood · Oak Forest · Orland Park · Posen · Dixmoor

INDIANA · ILLINOIS · COOK · DU PAGE

Chicago O'Hare International Airport · Chicago Midway Airport

Navy Pier · Soldier Field · Meigs Field · McCormick Place · Grant Park · Burnham Park · Jackson Park · Lincoln Park · Museum of Science and Industry · Northwestern University · Loyola University · Illinois Institute of Technology · University of Chicago · Sears Tower · Art Institute

Copyright by Rand McNally & Co. Made in U.S.A.
A-520087-76

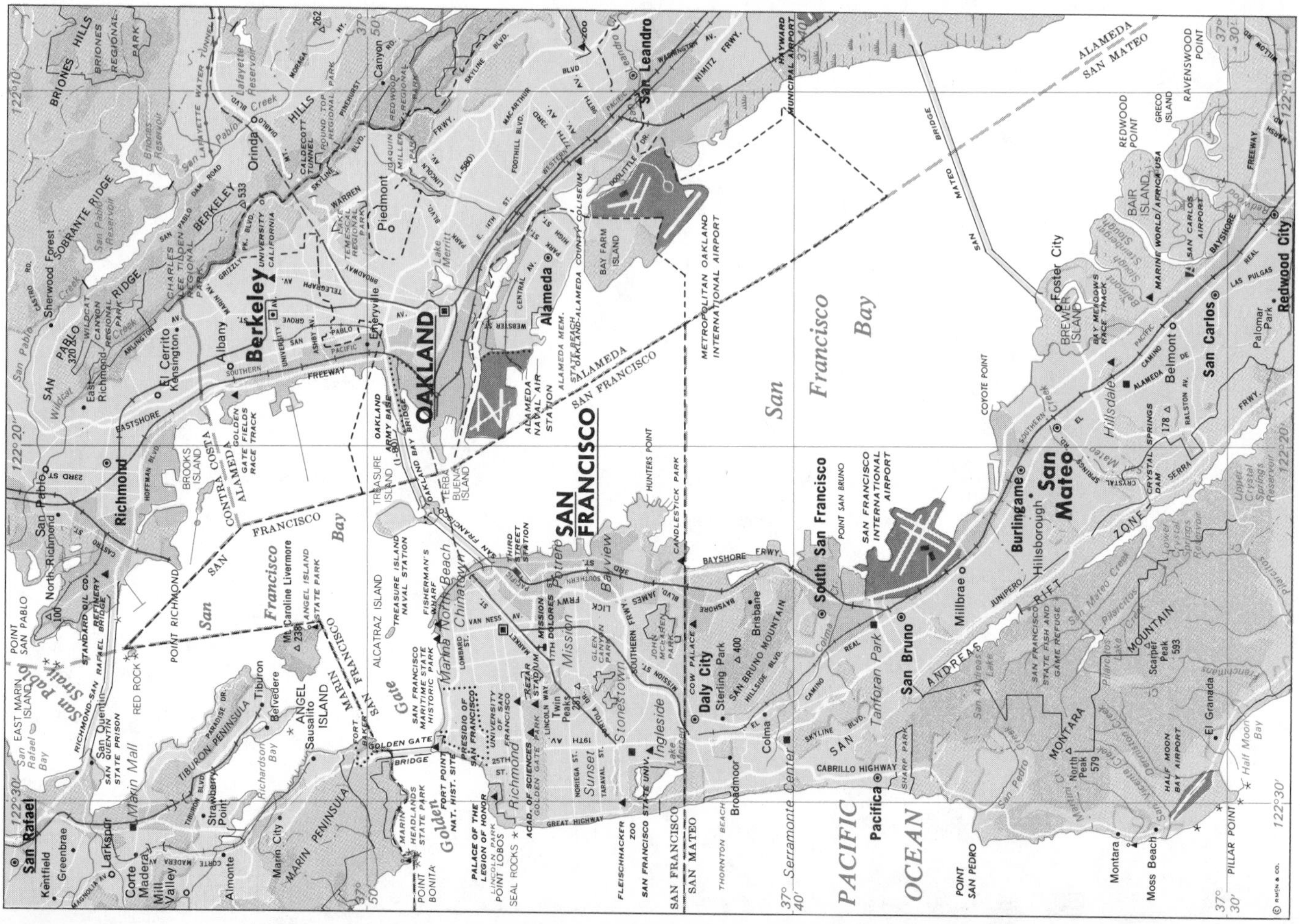

San Francisco map

PACIFIC OCEAN

SAN FRANCISCO BAY

SAN FRANCISCO · OAKLAND · Berkeley · Alameda · San Leandro · Richmond · North Richmond · Point Richmond · El Cerrito · Kensington · Albany · Emeryville · Piedmont · Orinda · Lafayette · San Rafael · Kentfield · Greenbrae · Larkspur · Corte Madera · Mill Valley · Sausalito · Belvedere · Tiburon · San Mateo · San Carlos · Redwood City · Belmont · Foster City · Burlingame · Hillsborough · Millbrae · San Bruno · South San Francisco · Brisbane · Daly City · Colma · Pacifica · Half Moon Bay · Moss Beach · El Granada · Montara

Golden Gate Bridge · San Francisco–Oakland Bay Bridge · San Mateo Bridge · Richmond–San Rafael Bridge

San Francisco International Airport · Metropolitan Oakland International Airport · Alameda Naval Air Station

Alcatraz Island · Angel Island · Treasure Island · Yerba Buena Island · Red Rock · Brooks Island · Bay Farm Island

University of California · San Francisco State University · Palace of the Legion of Honor · Acad. of Sciences · Golden Gate Park

ALAMEDA · CONTRA COSTA · MARIN · SAN FRANCISCO · SAN MATEO

Scale 1:300,000; one inch to 4.7 miles.
10 Miles
10 Kilometers

Scale 1:300,000; one inch to 4.7 miles.

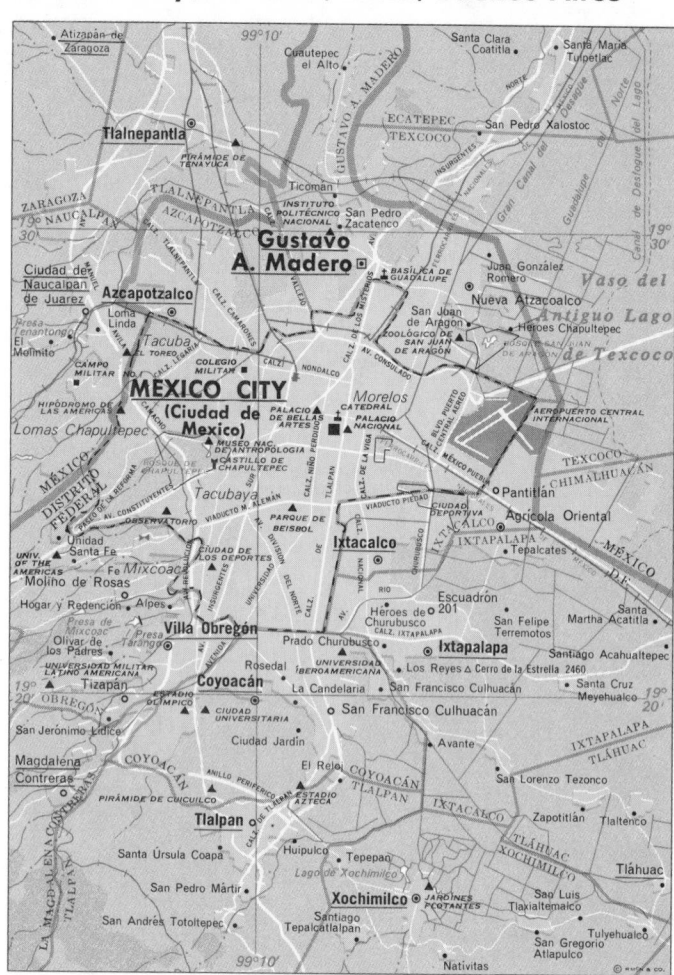

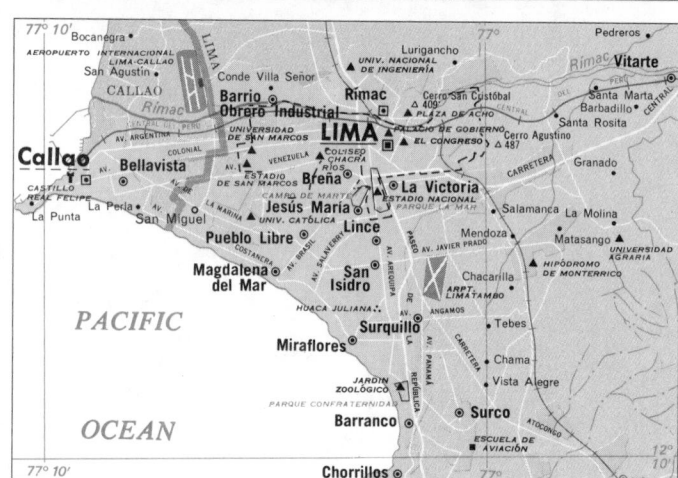

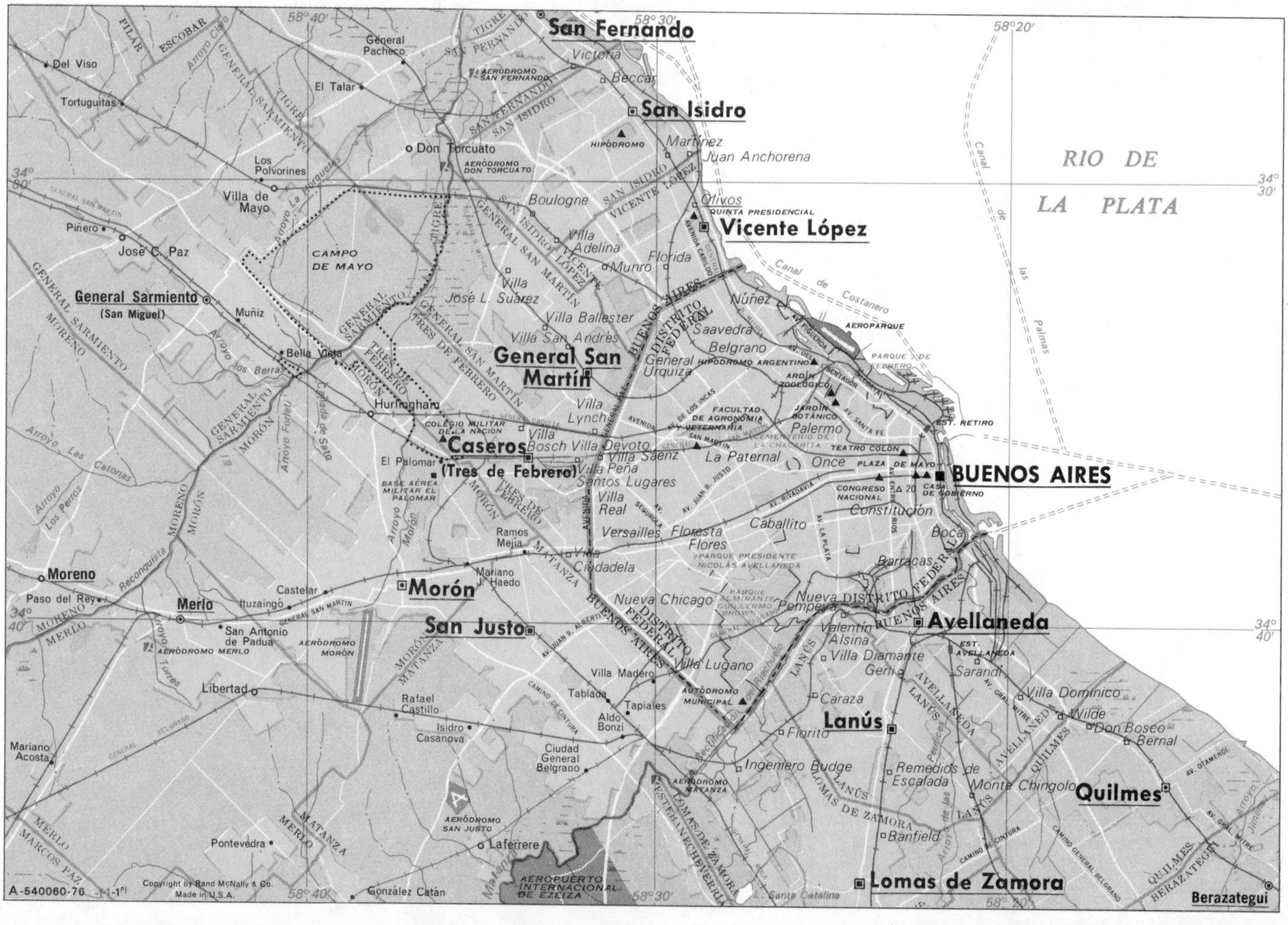

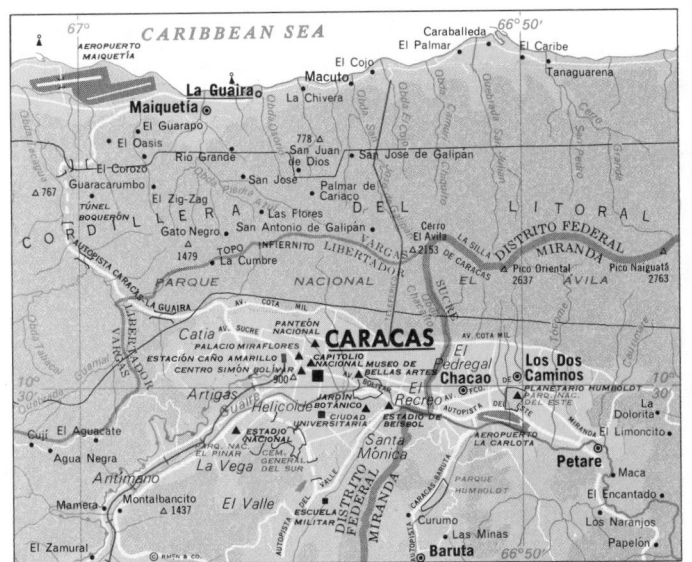

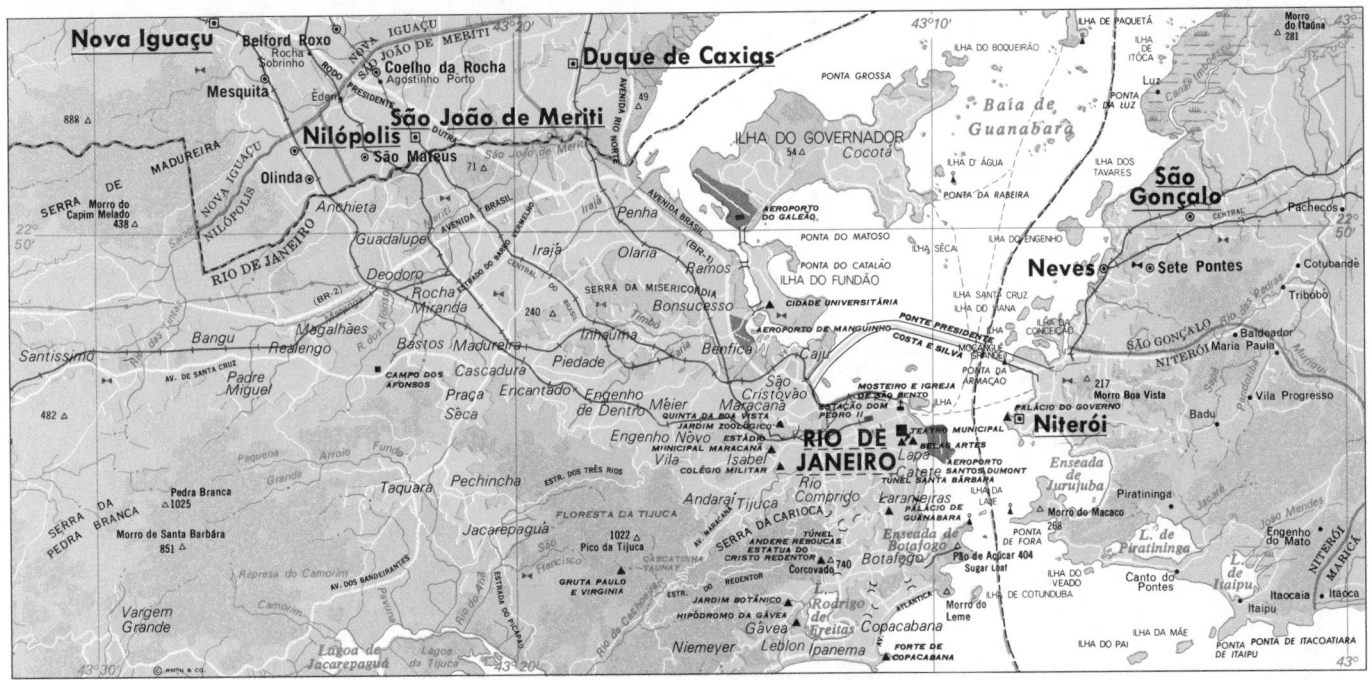

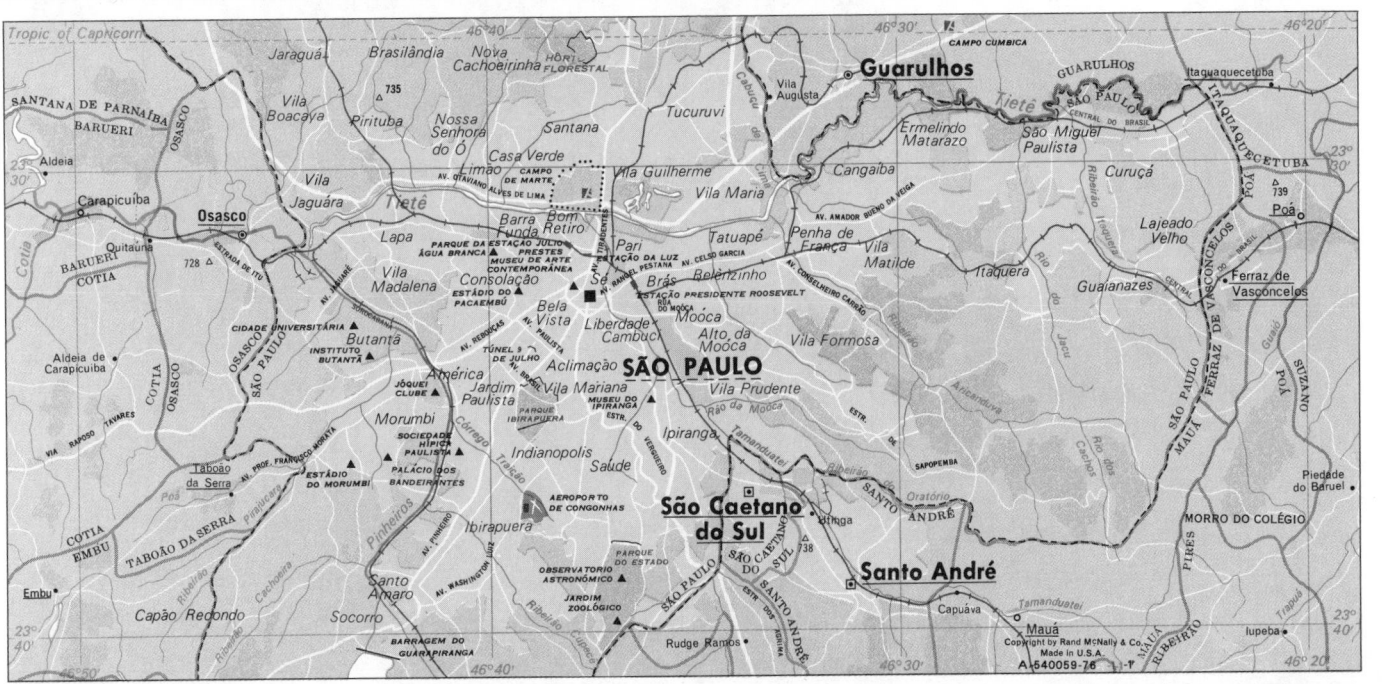

Scale 1:300,000; one inch to 4.7 miles.

Scale 1:300,000; one inch to 4.7 miles.

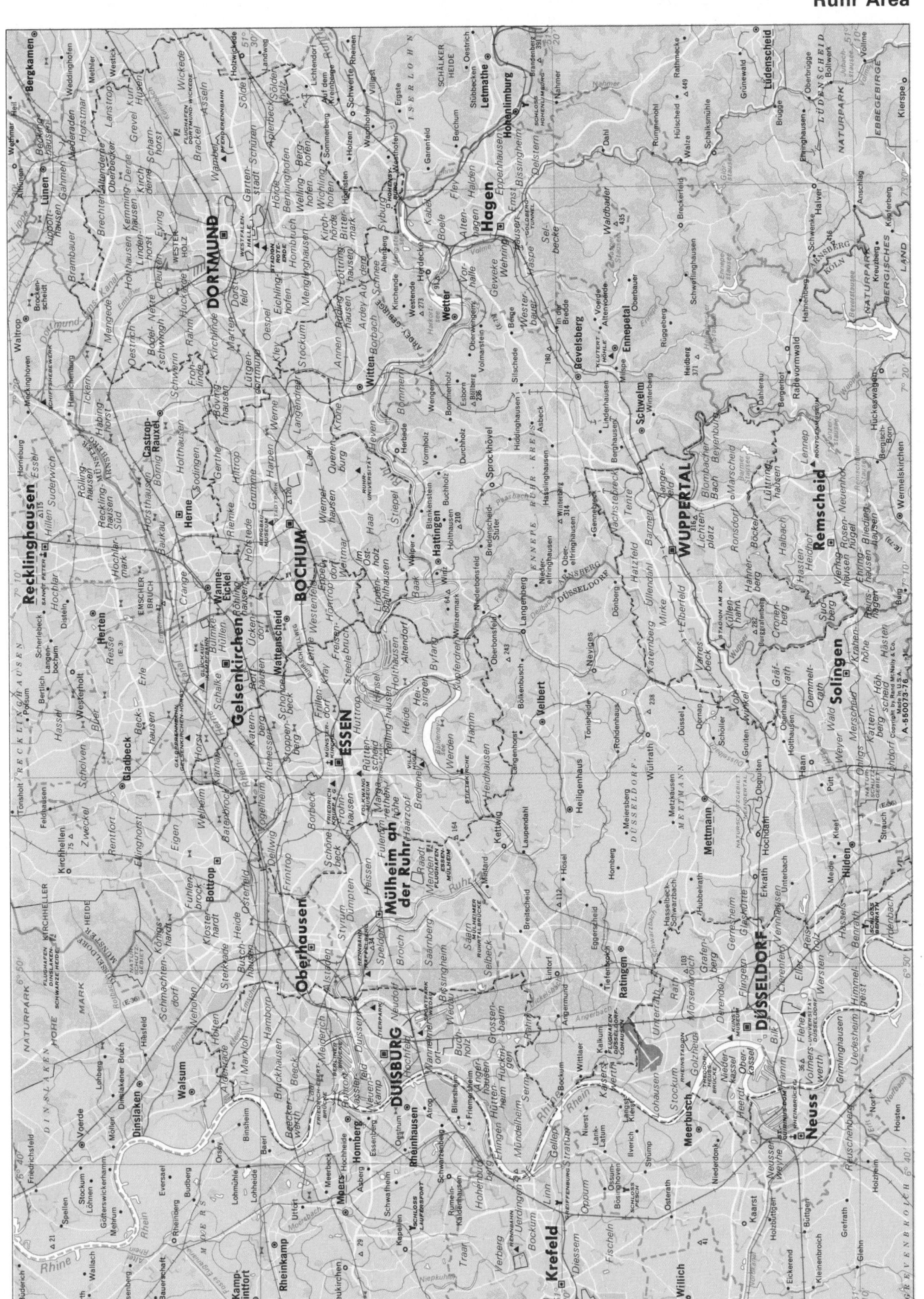

Copyright by Rand McNally & Co.
Made in U.S.A.
A-550073-76

Scale 1:300,000; one inch to 4.7 miles.

Scale 1:300,000; one inch to 4.7 miles.

10 Miles
10 Kilometers

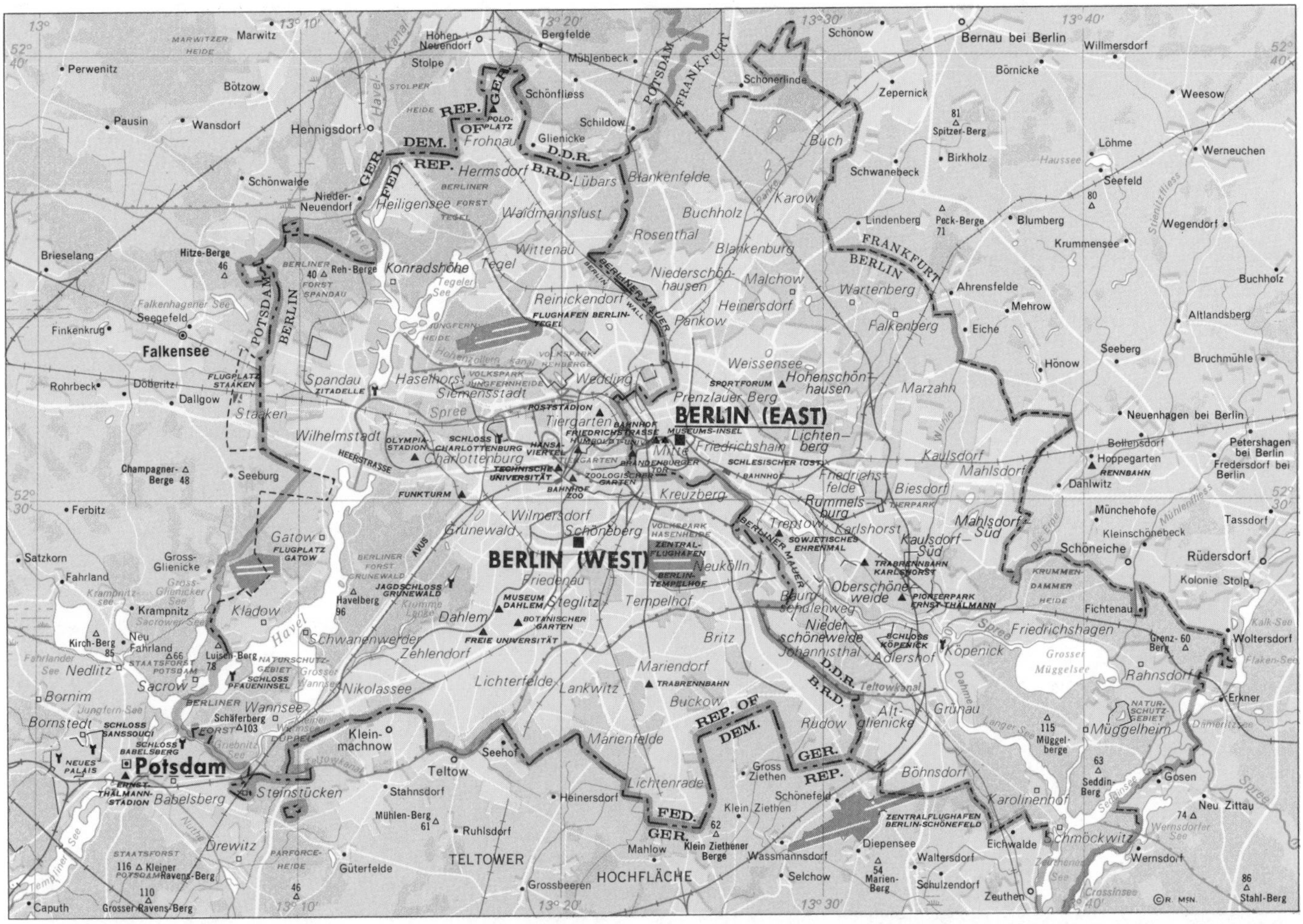

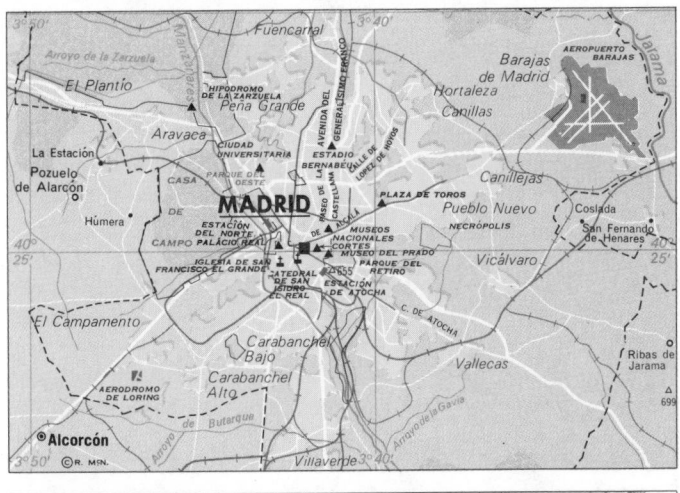

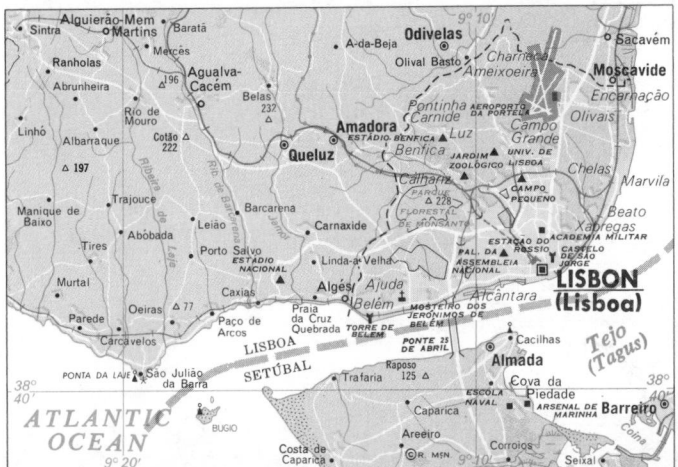
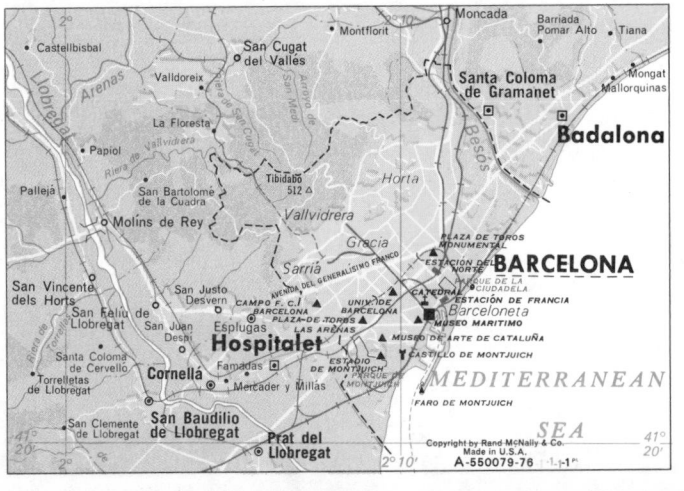

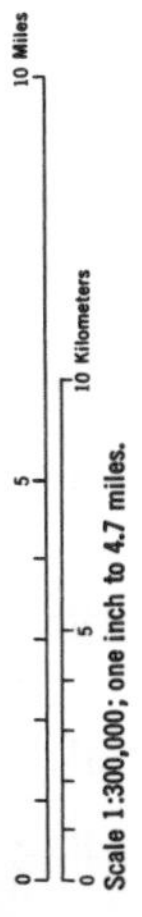

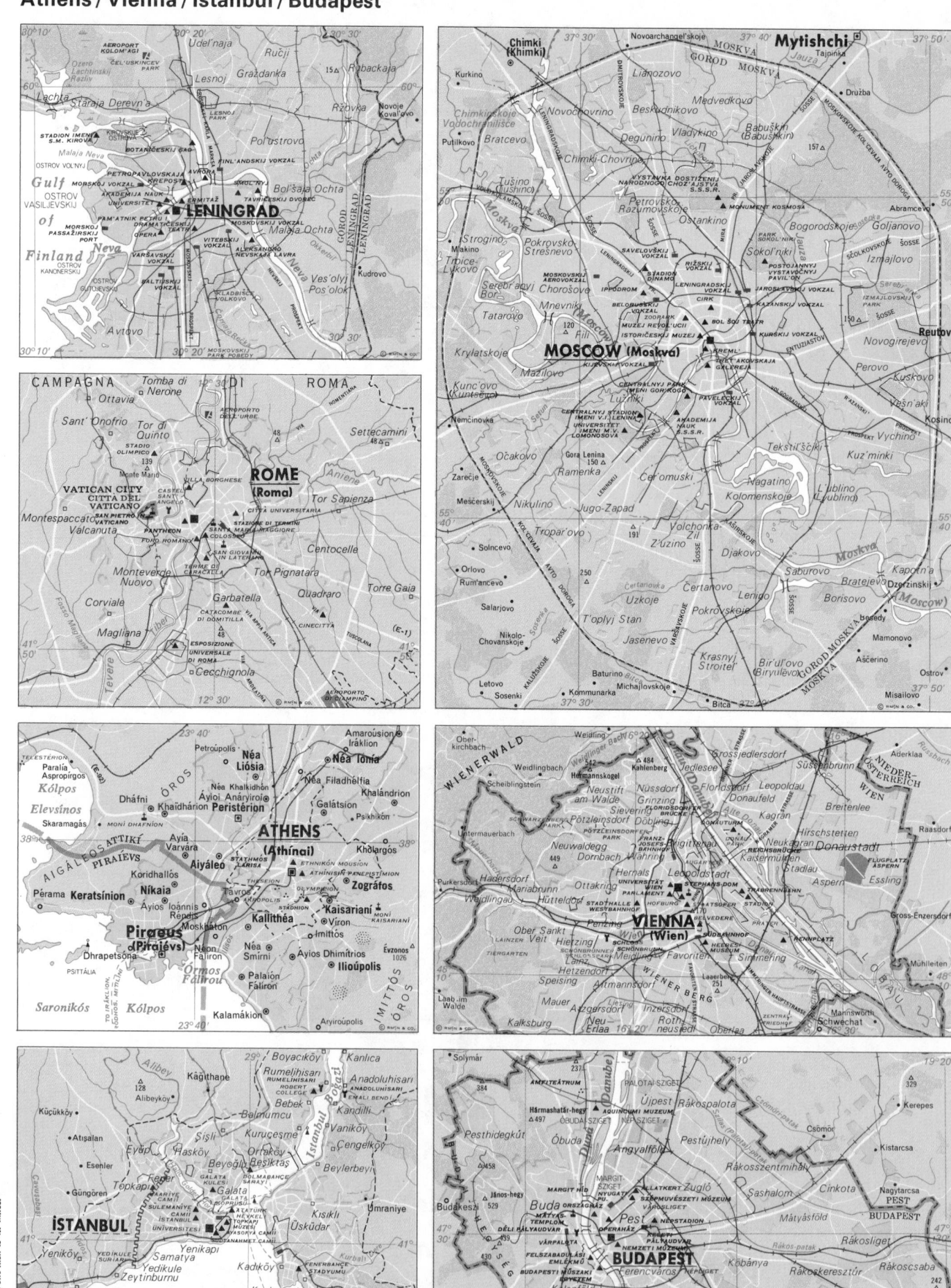

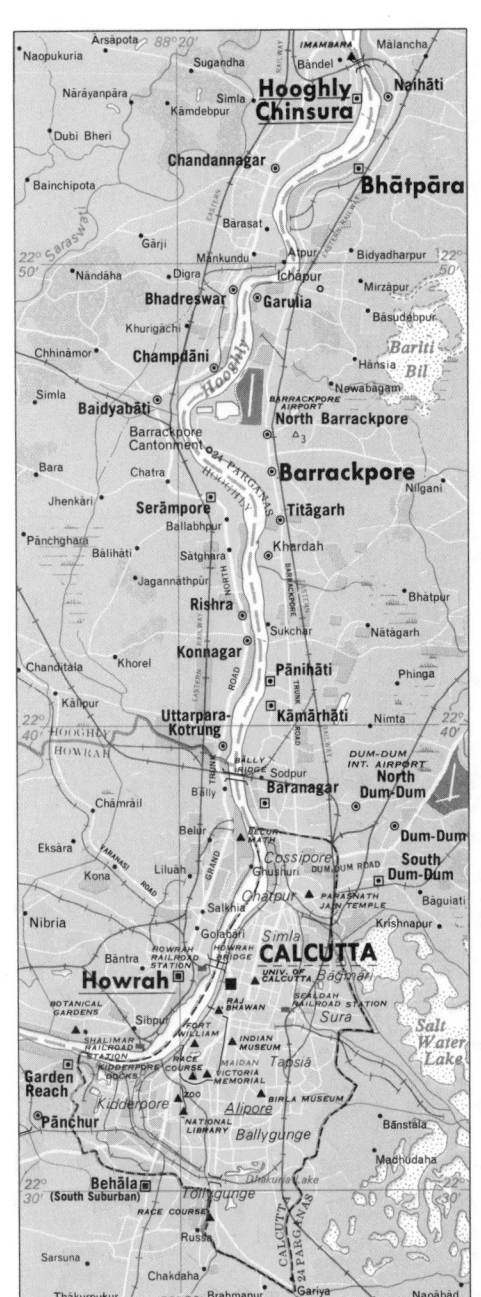

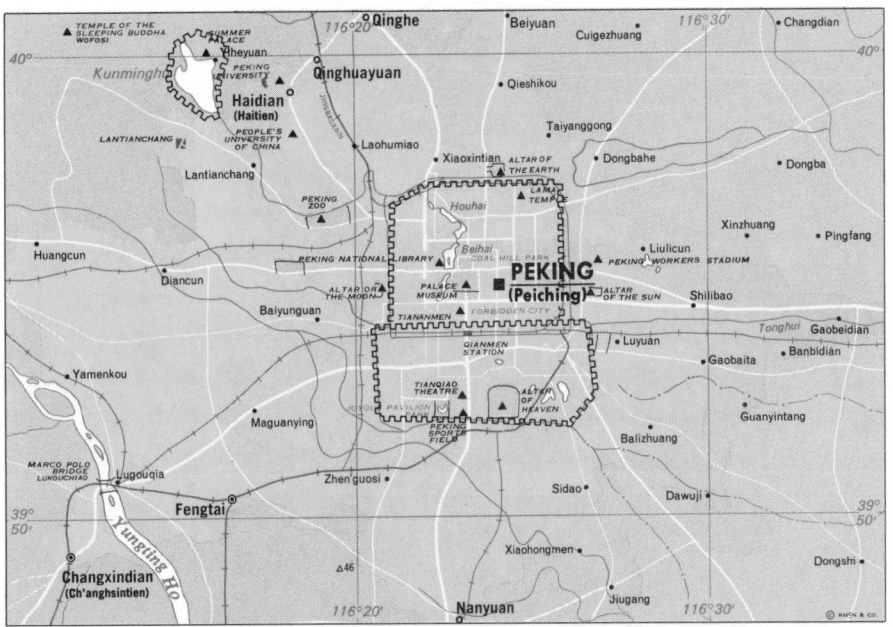

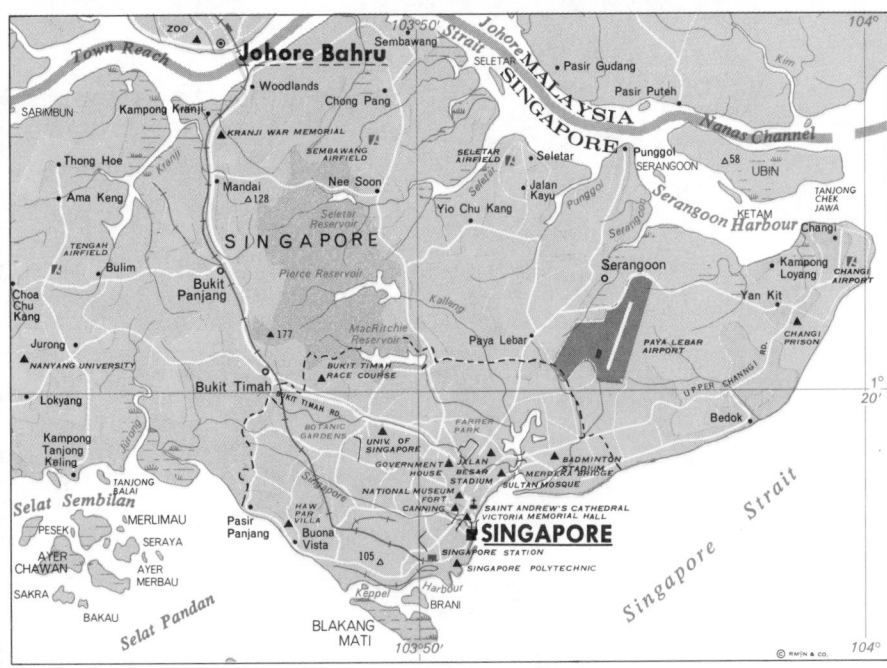

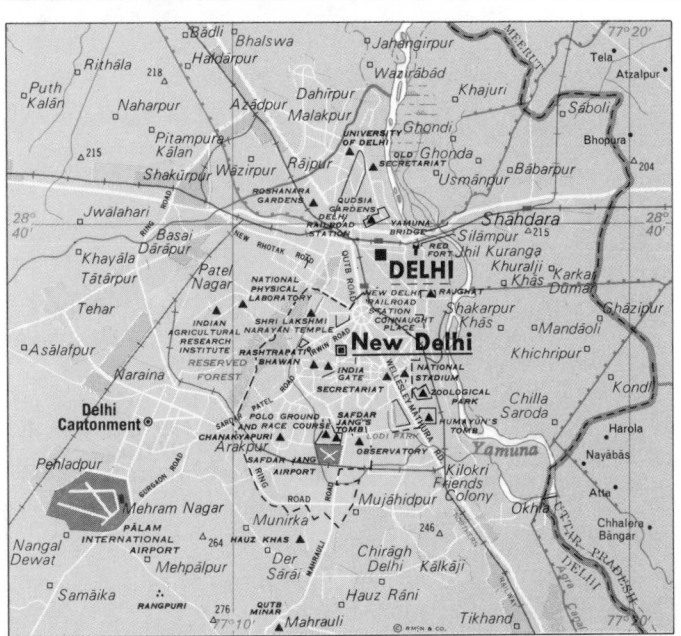

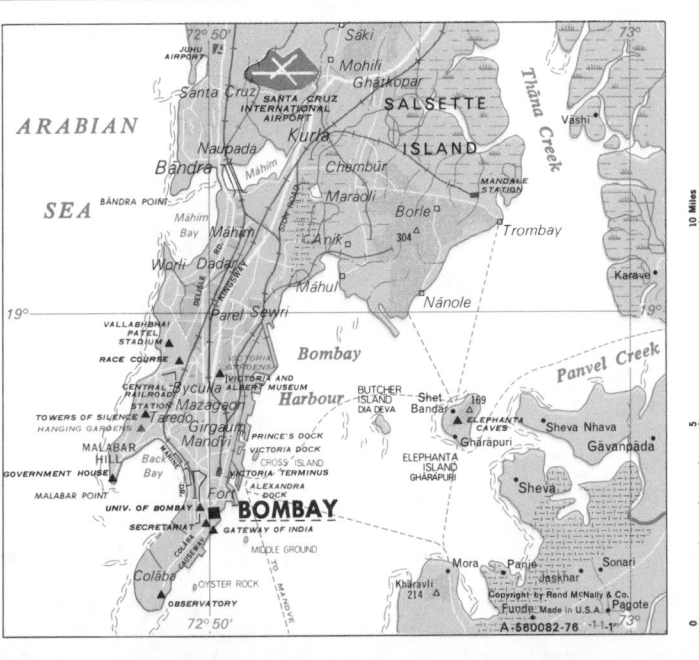

Scale 1:300,000; one inch to 4.7 miles.

10 Miles

10 Kilometers

Copyright by Rand McNally & Co.
Fuode Made in U.S.A.
A-580082-76

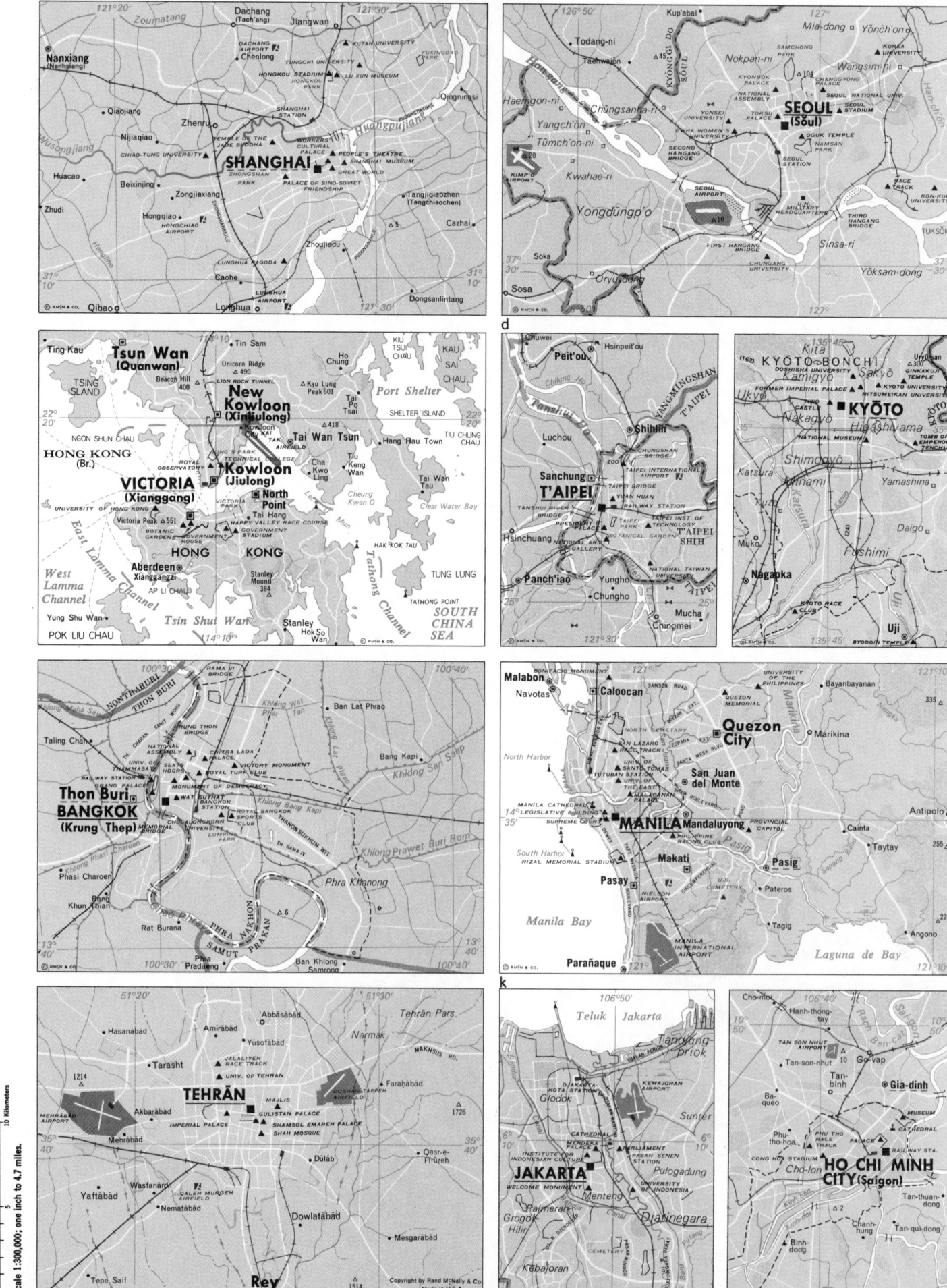

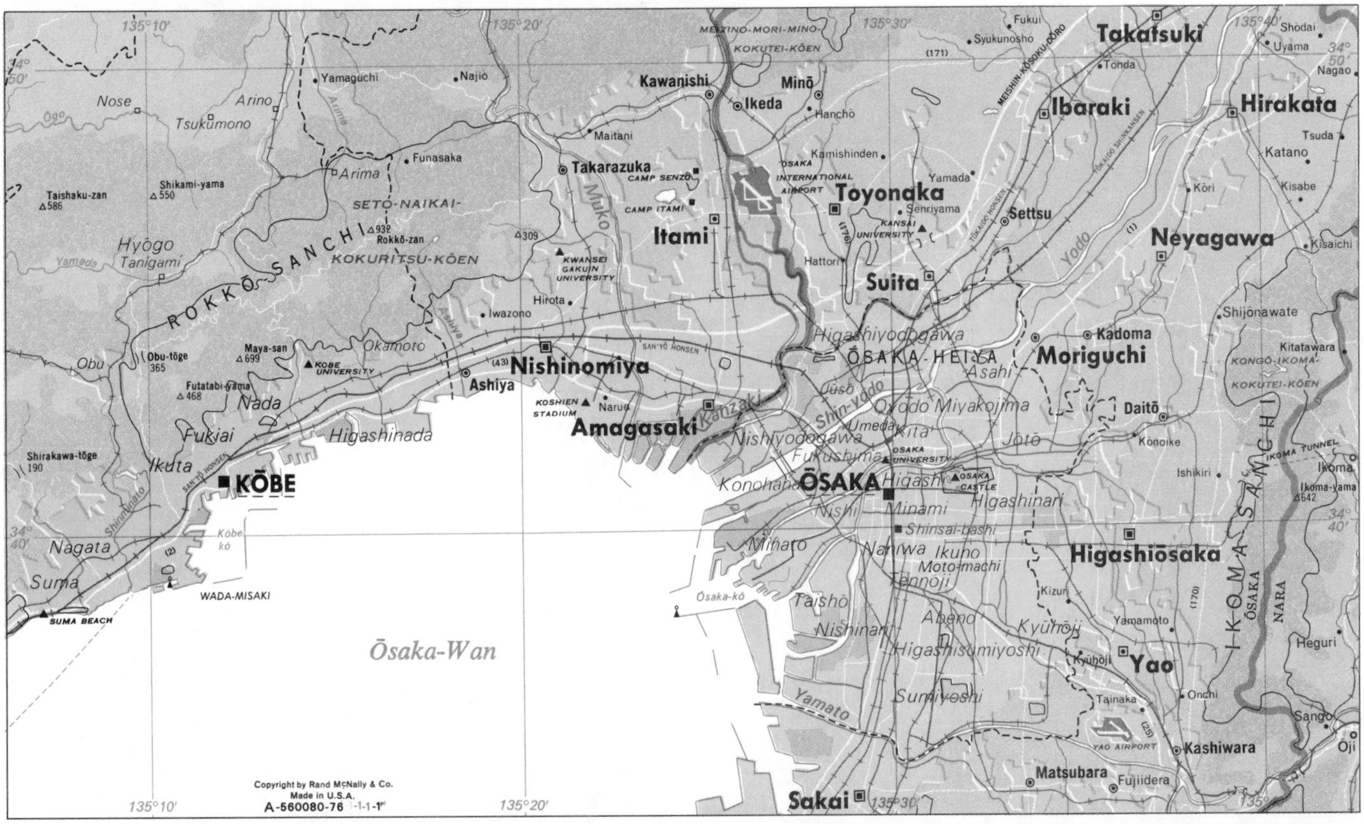

Tōkyō–Yokohama (top map)

139°30' 139°40' 139°50'

SAYAMA-KYŪRYŌ Tokorozawa Niiza Asaka Kawaguchi Matsudo
Kitano Kiyose Shimonikura Toda CHIBA
Yamaguchi-chosuiko CAMP ASAKA (U.S.) Yamato Kamiakatsuka Mabashi MATSUDO RACE TRACK
Mizuho Nakato Higashimurayama Katayama Kamiakatsuka (U.S.) Takenotsuka Kanamachi
YOKOTA AIR BASE (U.S.) Murayama Kurume Hōya Shimura Nishiarai Sugano
Jōgawara YAMATO AIR STATION (U.S.) Yamato Ogawa Shimoshakujii Higashiōizumi Kita Adachi Katsushika
Akishima Kodaira Suzuki-shinden Tanashi Nerima Egota Habashi CAMP ICHIGAYA Komagome Arakawa Ichikawa
TACHIKAWA AIR BASE (U.S.) Kokubunji KAMIIGUSA STADIUM Shimoigusa Ochiai TOKYO UNIV. OF EDUCATION Asakusa Edogawa Tōkagi
HITOTSUBASHI UNIVERSITY Koganei Musashino Kichijōji Asagaya OCHANOMIZU WOMEN'S UNIV. NATIONAL MUSEUM Sumida Mizue Hongyotoku
Tachikawa Hino Kunitachi Yaho Mitaka CHOFU ARPT. Suginami WASEDA UNIV. HONGO UNIV. OF TOKYO Taito Sumida Kameido
Hachiōji Toyoda Bubai FUCHU AIR STATION (U.S.) Kamishihara Takaido Shibuya Shinjuku HOSEI UNIV. MEIJI UNIV. Nihonbashi Kōtō Fukagawa Ukita
Manganji Fuchū Chōfu Shibasaki Kamikitazawa Akatsutsumi MEIJI SHRINE IMPERIAL PALACE NATIONAL DIET Chūō Ginza Kasai Urayasu
Tama Inagi Komae Soshigaya Setagaya Yoga KEIO UNIVERSITY TOKYO TOWER Minato TŌKYŌ
Shimoyugi Higashinakano Kaidori Sangenjaya Meguro Shinagawa
Kamiyugi Oyama Noborito Tamagawa Koyama Ōta
Seibeeshidan Kamioyamada Kanai Kamiasao Mizonokuchi Okusawa Denenchōfu Nakanobu Magome Ōmori
Kamimizo Sagamihara Kiso Kamoshida Eda Nakayama Hiyoshi Yaguchi Kamata TOKYO INTERNATIONAL AIRPORT
CAMP OCHINOBE (U.S.) Haramachida Nagatsuta Kizuki Tsunashima Yakō Rokugō KAWASAKI STADIUM Kawasaki
Ōnuma Machida Kanamori Kawawa Kōhoku Tsurumi Kawasaki-kō Tōkyō-wan
Shimomizo Kamitsuruma Nakayama Tsurumi Namamugi
CAMP ZAMA (U.S.) Shimotsuruma Seya Imajuku MITSUSAWA PARK X RACE TRACK Kanagawa Kanagawa
Sanda Zama Zama-iriya Yamato Fukami Kawashima Futatsubashi Putamatagawa YOKOHAMA
Kaneda Ebina ATSUGI N.A.S. (U.S.) HODOGAYA BASEBALL GROUND Hodogaya Yokohama-kō
Atsugi SAGAMIHARA-DAICHI Ayase Nishi YOKOHAMA PARK BASEBALL GROUND Nakajima

TAMA-KYŪRYŌ TAMAGAWA KANAGAWA Tōkyō-kō

35°40' 35°30'

Ōsaka–Kōbe (bottom map)

135°10' 135°20' 135°30' 135°40'

Nose Yamaguchi Najiō Kawanishi Minō Takatsuki Shōdai
Arino MEITŌ-MORI-MINŌ KOKUTEI-KŌEN Tonda Uyama Nagao
Tsukumono Ikeda Hancho Ibaraki Hirakata
Taishaku-zan Shikami-yama Funasaka Maitani Kamishinden Yamada Kōri Tsuda Katano Kisabe
Arima Takarazuka CAMP SENZO OSAKA INTERNATIONAL AIRPORT KANSAI UNIVERSITY Senriyama Kisaichi
SETO-NAIKAI- Rokkō-zan CAMP ITAMI Toyonaka Settsu Neyagawa
Hyōgo Tanigami KOKURITSU-KŌEN KWANSEI GAKUIN UNIVERSITY Itami Hattori Suita Shijonawate
ROKKŌ-SANCHI Iwazono Hirota Higashiyodogawa Asahi Kadoma KONGŌ-IKOMA KOKUTEI-KŌEN
Obu-tōge Maya-san KOBE UNIVERSITY ŌSAKA HEIYA Moriguchi Daitō
Futatabi-yama Okamoto Nishinomiya Jusō Jōtō Konoike Ishikiri IKOMA TUNNEL
Obu Nada Ashiya KOSHIEN STADIUM Narus Shin-Yodo Umeda OSAKA UNIVERSITY Ikoma-yama
Shirakawa-tōge Higashinada Amagasaki Nishiyodogawa Kita OSAKA CASTLE Higashiōsaka
Ikuta Fukiai Konohana ŌSAKA Higashi Higashinari
KŌBE Kōbe-kō Nishi Minami Higashinari IKOMA-SANCHI Ikoma-yama
Nagata Suma WADA-MISAKI Miharu Shinsai-bashi Naniwa Ikuno Moto-machi Tennōji Kizuri Yamamoto Heguri
SUMA BEACH Ōsaka-kō Taishō Nishinari Abeno Higashisumiyoshi Kyūhōji Yao NARA
Ōsaka-Wan Sumiyoshi YAO AIRPORT Tajihara Kashiwara Sango Ōji
Sakai Matsubara Fujiidera Oji

Neyagawa Moriguchi Higashiōsaka

34°50' 34°40'

Scale 1:300,000; one inch to 4.7 miles.
0 5 10 Miles
0 5 10 Kilometers

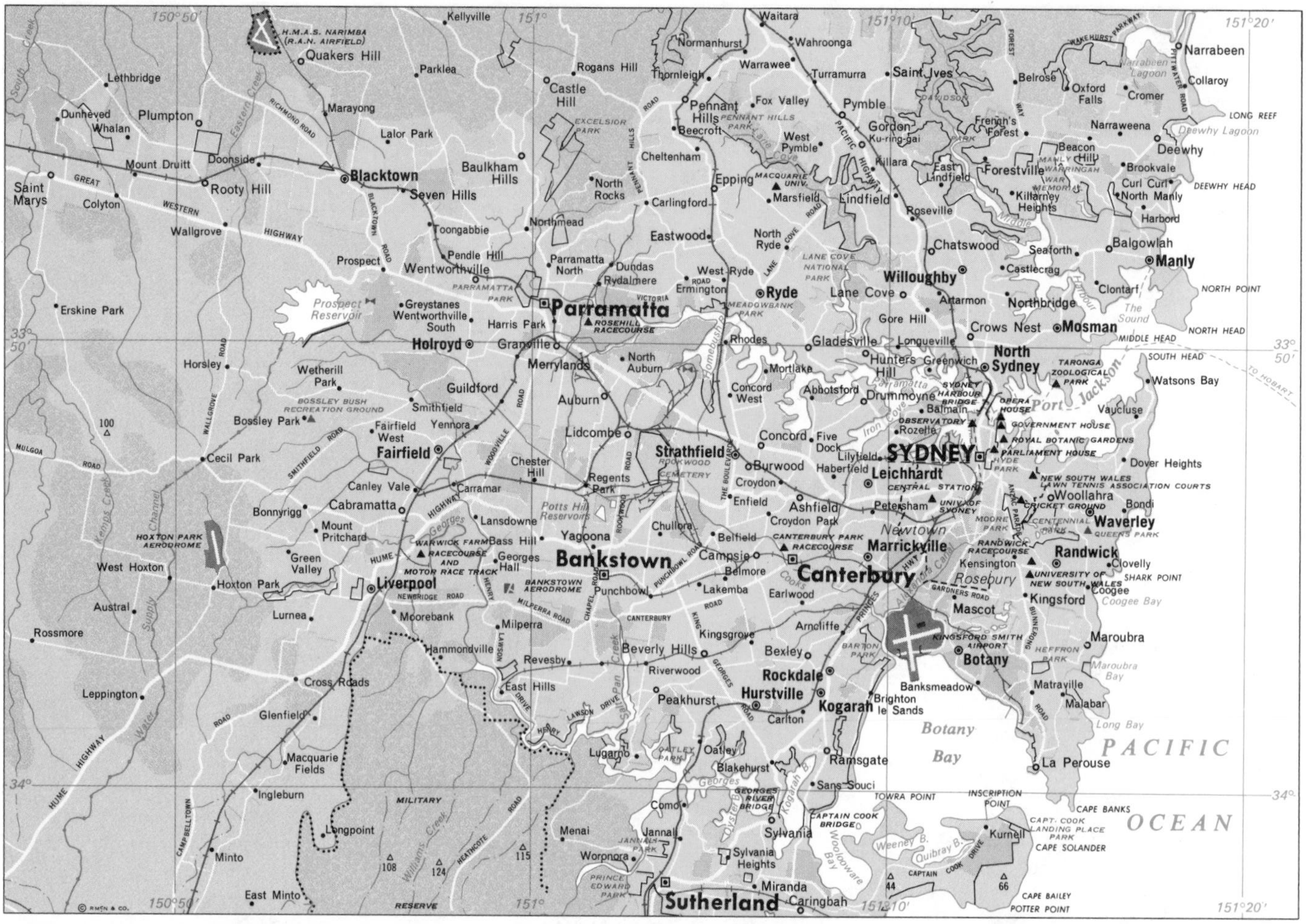

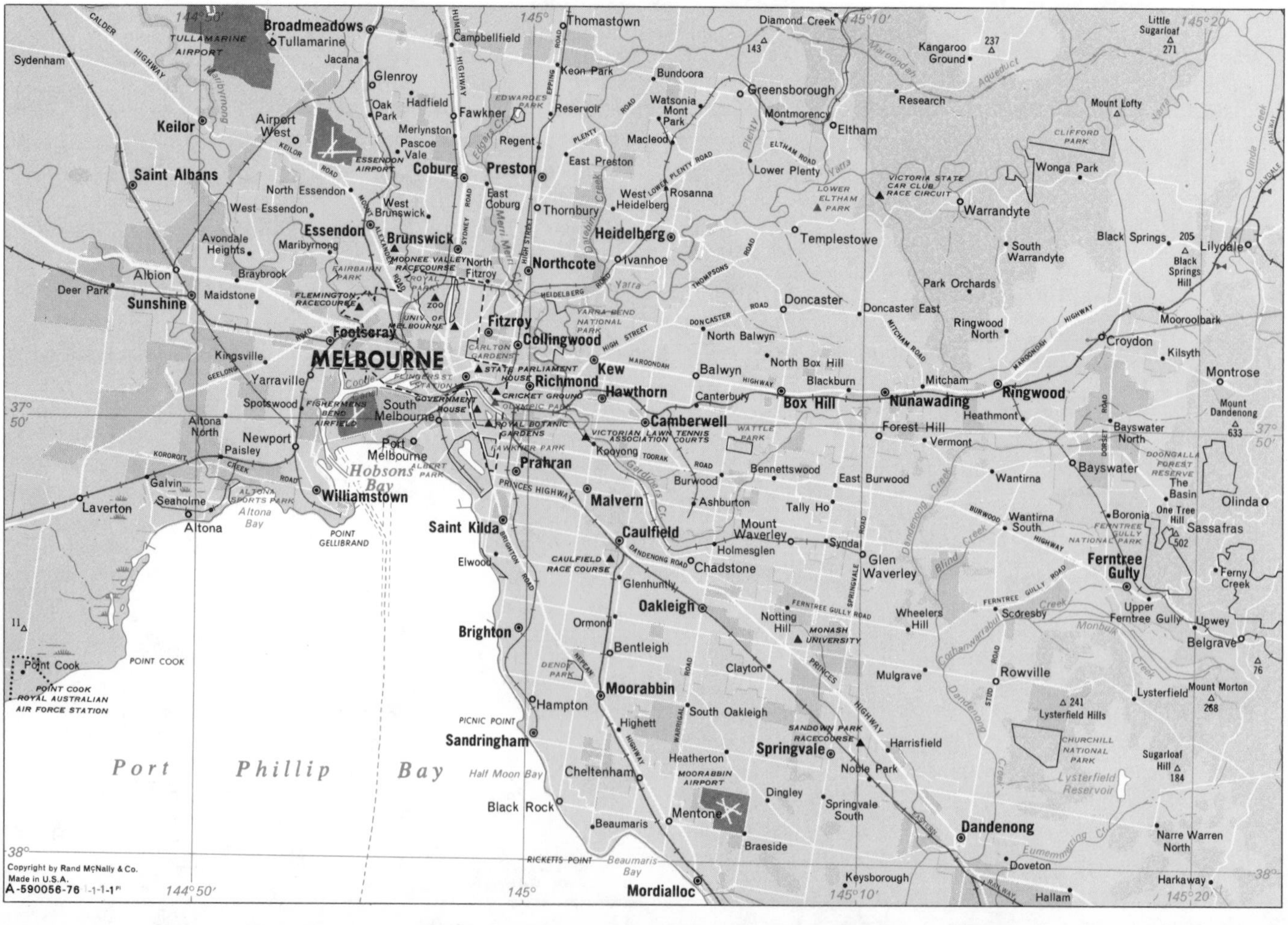

Sydney (top map)

Kellyville, Quakers Hill, Parklea, Rogans Hill, Normanhurst, Waitara, Wahroonga, Narrabeen, Collaroy, Oxford Falls, Cromer, Belrose, Saint Ives, Turramurra, Warrawee, Pennant Hills, Beecroft, Thornleigh, Fox Valley, Pymble, French's Forest, Narraweena, Deewhy, Killarney Heights, Beacon Hill, Brookvale, Curl Curl, North Manly, Harbord, Manly, Balgowlah, Seaforth, Clontart, Castlecrag, Northbridge, Willoughby, Crows Nest, Mosman, North Sydney, Chatswood, Roseville, Lindfield, Killara, Gordon, Ku-ring-gai, West Pymble, Marsfield, North Ryde, Epping, Cheltenham, Carlingford, Eastwood, Ermington, West Ryde, Ryde, Meadowbank, Rhodes, Gladesville, Hunters Hill, Greenwich, Lane Cove, Longueville, Drummoyne, Balmain, Rozelle, Observatory, Sydney, Leichhardt, Petersham, Newtown, Marrickville, Canterbury, Randwick, Waverley, Woollahra, Bondi, Vaucluse, Watsons Bay, Dover Heights, North Head, South Head, Middle Head, North Point, Long Reef, Deewhy Head, Deewhy Lagoon

Blacktown, Seven Hills, Baulkham Hills, Castle Hill, Marayong, Lalor Park, Toongabbie, Pendle Hill, Northmead, Parramatta North, Dundas, Rydalmere, Concord, Strathfield, Burwood, Croydon, Ashfield, Enfield, Belfield, Campsie, Belmore, Bankstown, Lakemba, Earlwood, Arncliffe, Kingsgrove, Bexley, Rockdale, Hurstville, Kogarah, Carlton, Brighton le Sands, Banksmeadow, Botany, Mascot, Kingsford, Maroubra, Matraville, Malabar, La Perouse

Mount Druitt, Doonside, Rooty Hill, Prospect, Wentworthville, Holroyd, Merrylands, North Auburn, Auburn, Lidcombe, Regents Park, Chullora, Punchbowl, Revesby, Beverly Hills, Riverwood, Peakhurst, Penshurst, Mortdale, Oatley, Como, Blakehurst, Sans Souci, Ramsgate, Sylvania, Miranda, Caringbah, Sutherland, Sylvania Heights, Woronora, Menai, Jannali, Kurnell

Saint Marys, Colyton, Erskine Park, Horsley, Wetherill Park, Bossley Park, Cecil Park, Cabramatta, Bonnyrigg, Mount Pritchard, Green Valley, West Hoxton, Austral, Rossmore, Leppington, Hoxton Park, Lurnea, Liverpool, Moorebank, Milperra, Hammondville, Cross Roads, Glenfield, Macquarie Fields, Ingleburn, Longpoint, Minto, East Minto

Fairfield, Fairfield West, Canley Vale, Carramar, Lansdowne, Yagoona, Georges Hall, Bass Hill, Chester Hill, Smithfield, Yennora, Guildford

PACIFIC OCEAN, Botany Bay, Coogee Bay, Maroubra Bay, Long Bay, Port Jackson, The Sound

Prospect Reservoir, Potts Hill Reservoir, Warwick Farm Racecourse, Rosehill Racecourse, Canterbury Park Racecourse, Randwick Racecourse, Rookwood Cemetery, Centennial Park, Hoxton Park Aerodrome, Bankstown Aerodrome, Kingsford Smith Airport, Captain Cook Bridge, Georges River Bridge, Sydney Harbour Bridge, Taronga Zoological Park, Lane Cove National Park, University of Sydney, University of New South Wales, Sydney Cricket Ground, New South Wales Lawn Tennis Association Courts, Royal Botanic Gardens, Government House, Parliament House, Hyde Park

Melbourne (bottom map)

Sydenham, Broadmeadows, Tullamarine, Tullamarine Airport, Campbellfield, Thomastown, Diamond Creek, Kangaroo Ground, Little Sugarloaf, Jacana, Glenroy, Keon Park, Bundoora, Greensborough, Research, Mount Lofty, Wonga Park, Keilor, Airport West, Oak Park, Hadfield, Fawkner, Reservoir, Watsonia, Mont Park, Montmorency, Eltham, Lower Plenty, Warrandyte, Saint Albans, North Essendon, Merlynston, Pascoe Vale, Regent, Preston, Macleod, West Heidelberg, Lower Eltham Park, Victoria State Car Club Race Circuit, Black Springs, Lilydale, West Essendon, Essendon, West Brunswick, Coburg, East Coburg, East Preston, Rosanna, Heidelberg, Templestowe, South Warrandyte, Park Orchards, Black Springs Hill, Avondale Heights, Maribyrnong, Brunswick, North Fitzroy, Thornbury, Northcote, Ivanhoe, Doncaster, Ringwood North, Croydon, Kilsyth, Montrose, Deer Park, Braybrook, Maidstone, Footscray, Fitzroy, Collingwood, Kew, Hawthorn, North Balwyn, Doncaster East, Mooroolbark, Albion, Sunshine, Melbourne, Richmond, Balwyn, North Box Hill, Blackburn, Mitcham, Nunawading, Ringwood, Bayswater North, Mount Dandenong, Kingsville, Spotswood, South Melbourne, Camberwell, Canterbury, Box Hill, Forest Hill, Vermont, Heathmont, Bayswater, The Basin, Yarraville, Newport, Paisley, Prahran, Burwood, Bennettswood, East Burwood, Wantirna, Boronia, Olinda, Altona North, Williamstown, Saint Kilda, Malvern, Ashburton, Mount Waverley, Tally Ho, Wantirna South, One Tree Hill, Sassafras, Galvin, Seaholme, Altona, Elwood, Caulfield, Glenhuntly, Chadstone, Holmesglen, Syndal, Glen Waverley, Scoresby, Upper Ferntree Gully, Ferntree Gully, Upwey, Laverton, Oakleigh, Notting Hill, Monash University, Wheelers Hill, Rowville, Belgrave, Ferny Creek, Brighton, Ormond, Bentleigh, Clayton, Mulgrave, Lysterfield, Mount Morton, Moorabbin, Highett, South Oakleigh, Sandown Park Racecourse, Harrisfield, Lysterfield Hills, Hampton, Sandringham, Heatherton, Springvale, Noble Park, Sugarloaf Hill, Black Rock, Cheltenham, Moorabbin Airport, Dingley, Springvale South, Dandenong, Narre Warren North, Beaumaris, Mentone, Braeside, Keysborough, Harkaway, Mordialloc, Doveton, Hallam

Port Phillip Bay, Hobsons Bay, Beaumaris Bay, Half Moon Bay, Point Cook, Point Gellibrand, Ricketts Point, Picnic Point, Rickett's Point

Flemington Racecourse, Moonee Valley Racecourse, Caulfield Race Course, Melbourne Cricket Ground, Royal Botanic Gardens, Government House, State Parliament House, Carlton Gardens, University of Melbourne, Melbourne Zoo, Victorian Lawn Tennis Association Courts, Yarra Bend National Park, Point Cook Royal Australian Air Force Station, Tullamarine Airport, Essendon Airport

Scale 1:300,000; one inch to 4.7 miles.
10 Miles, 10 Kilometers

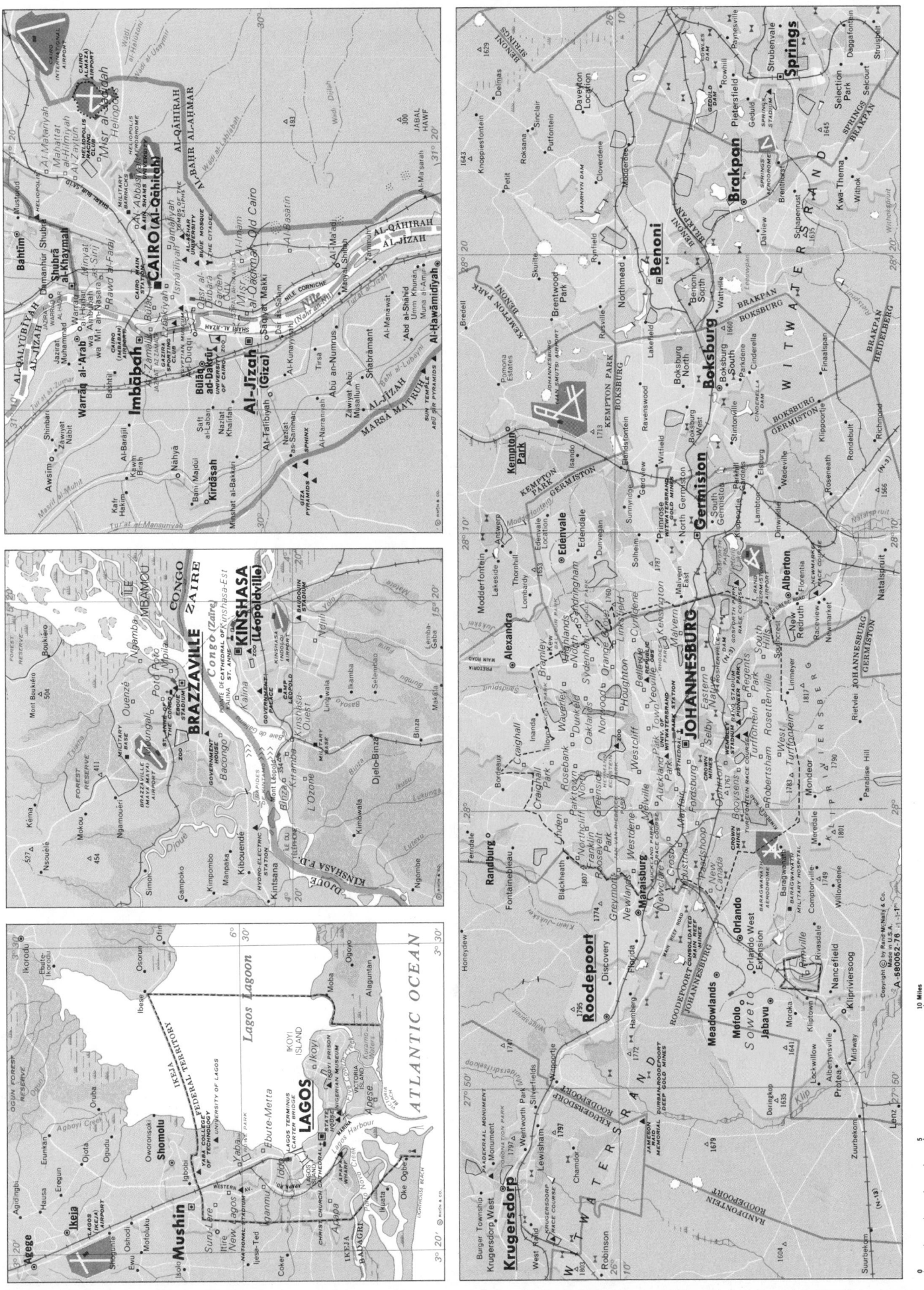

Scale 1:300,000; one inch to 4.7 miles.

Explanation of Map Symbols

CULTURAL FEATURES

Political Boundaries

━━━━━━ International

┈┈┈┈┈ Secondary (State, province, etc.)

┄┄┄┄┄ County

Populated Places

Cities, towns, and villages

• • • ● ● Symbol size represents population of the place

Chicago
Gary
Racine
Glenview
Edgewood

Type size represents relative importance of the place

Corporate area of large U.S. and Canadian cities and urban area of other foreign cities

Major Urban Area

Area of continuous commercial, industrial, and residential development in and around a major city

○ Community within a city

⊛ Capital of major political unit

☆ Capital of secondary political unit

◉ Capital of U.S. state or Canadian province

● County Seat

▲ Military Installation

⊙ Scientific Station

Miscellaneous

▭ National Park

▫ National Monument

▤ Provincial Park

▭ Indian Reservation

△ Point of Interest

∴ Ruins

■ ⌂ Buildings

⬭ Race Track

━━━━ Railroad

━┼─┼━ Tunnel

┈┈┈┈ Underground or Subway

⬥ Dam

⬢ Bridge

▱ Dike

LAND FEATURES

Passes =

Point of Elevation above sea level + 8,520 FT.

WATER FEATURES

Coastlines and Shorelines ⟶

Indefinite or Unsurveyed Coastlines and Shorelines ⟶

Lakes and Reservoirs ⟶

Canals ⟶

Rivers and Streams ⟶

Falls and Rapids ⟶

Intermittent or Unsurveyed Rivers and Streams ⟶

Directional Flow Arrow ⟶

Rocks, Shoals and Reefs ⟶

TYPE STYLES USED TO NAME FEATURES

A S I A	Continent
DENMARK CANADA	Country, State, or Province
BÉARN	Region, Province, or Historical Region
CROCKETT	County
PANTELLERIA (ITALY)	Country of which unit is a dependency in parentheses
SRI LANKA (CEYLON)	Former or alternate name
Rome (Roma)	Local or alternate city name
Naval Air Station	Military Installation
MESA VERDE SAN XAVIER	National Park or Monument, Provincial Park, Indian Res.,
UINTA DESERT	Major Terrain Features
MT. MORIAH	Individual Mountain
STROMBOLI NUNIVAK	Island or Coastal Feature
Ocean Lake River Canal	Hydrographic Features

Note: Size of type varies according to importance and available space. Letters for names of major features are spread across the extent of the feature.

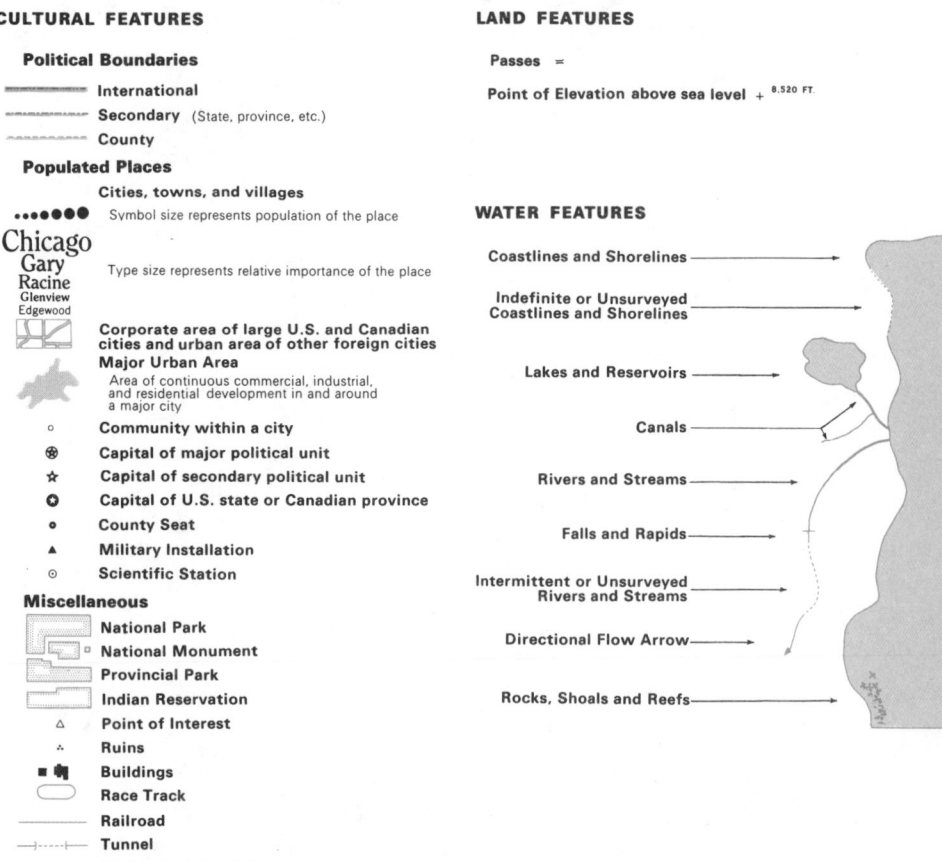

The Index Reference System

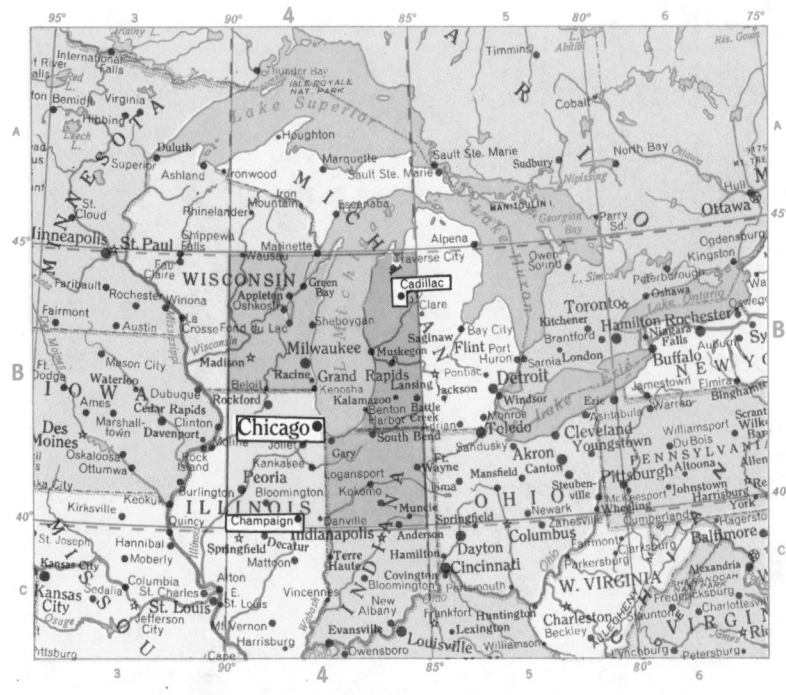

Place	Location	Index Key	Page
Cabinda, Ang.		B2	24
Cacequi, Braz.		D2	30
Cacouna, Que., Can.		B8	42
Caddo, Okla.		C5	79
Cadillac, Mich.		B4	58
Cadiz, Ky.		D2	62
Cadiz, Ohio		B4	78
Cádiz, Sp.		D2	8
Cadott, Wis.		D2	88
Cadyville, N.Y.		f11	75
Caen, Fr.		C3	5
Caernarvon, Wales		D4	4
Cagliari, It.		C4	9
Chambly, Que., Can.		D4	42
Chambly, co., Que., Can.		D4	42
Chambord, Que., Can.		A5	42
Champaign, Ill.		B4	58
Champaign, co., Ill.		C5	58
Champigny-sur-Marne, Fr.		g11	5
Champion, Ohio		A5	78
Champlain, N.Y.		f11	75
Charikar, Afg.		A4	20
Charleston, Ill.		D5	58
Chatham, Ont., Can.		E2	41
Cheyenne, Wyo.		E8	89
Cheyenne Wells, Colo.		C8	51
Chiang Mai, Thai.		B1	19
Chiang Rai, Thai.		B1	19
Chiapas, state, Mex.		D6	34
Chiari, It.		B2	9
Chiautla de Tapia, Mex.		n14	34
Chiba, Jap.		I10, n19	18
Chiba, pref., Jap.		*I10	18
Chicago, Ill.		B4	58
Chichester, Eng.		E6	4
Chichibu, Jap.		m18	18
Chickamauga, Ga.		B1	55
Chickasaw, Ala.		E1	46
Chickasaw, co., Iowa		A5	60
Chiclana, Sp.		D2	8
Chiclayo, Peru		C2	31
Chico, Calif.		C3	50

The indexing system used in this atlas is based upon the conventional pattern of parallels and meridians used to indicate latitude and longitude. The index samples beside the map indicate that the cities of *Chicago, Cadillac,* and *Champaign* are all located in *B4*. Each index key letter, *in this case "B,"* is placed between corresponding degree numbers of latitude in the vertical borders of the map. Each index key number, *in this case "4"* is placed between corresponding degree numbers of longitude in the horizontal borders of the map. Crossing of the parallels above and below the index letter with the meridians on each side of the index number forms a confining "box" in which the given place is certain to be located. It is important to note that location of the place may be anywhere in this confining "box."

Insets on many foreign maps are indexed independently of the main maps by separate index key letters and figures. All places indexed to these insets are identified by the lower case reference letter in the index key. A diamond-shaped symbol in the margin of the map is used to separate the insets from the main map and also to separate key letters and numbers where the spacing of the parallels and meridians is great.

Place-names are indexed to the location of the city symbol. Political divisions and physical features are indexed to the location of their names on the map.

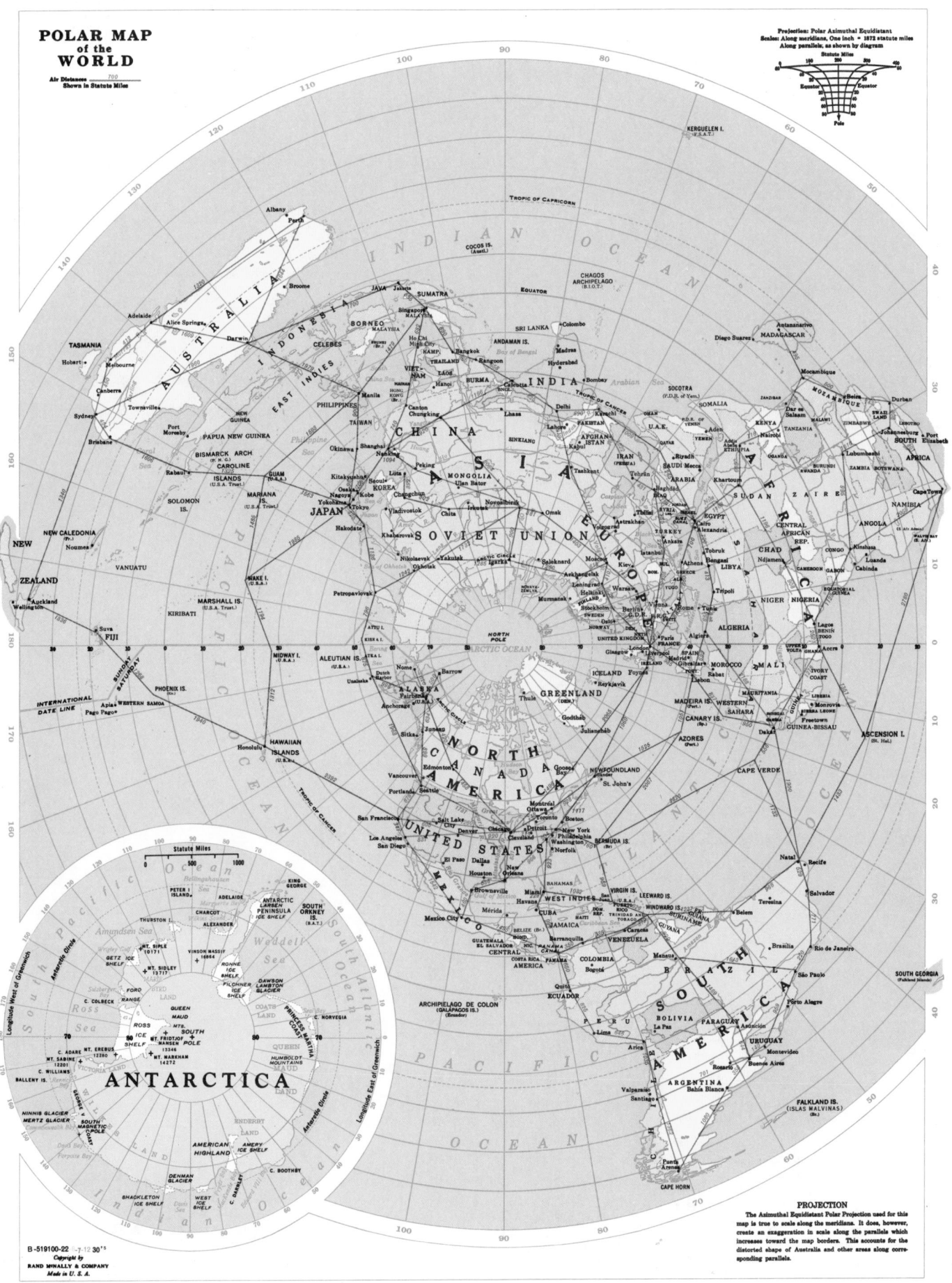

Polar Map
of the
WORLD

Air Distances ____700____
Shown in Statute Miles

Projection: Polar Azimuthal Equidistant
Scales: Along meridians, One inch = 1872 statute miles
Along parallels, as shown by diagram

Statute Miles

NORTH POLE

ANTARCTICA

Statute Miles
500   1000

PROJECTION

The Azimuthal Equidistant Polar Projection used for this map is true to scale along the meridians. It does, however, create an exaggeration in scale along the parallels which increases toward the map borders. This accounts for the distorted shape of Australia and other areas along corresponding parallels.

B-519100-22 5-7-12 30'5
Copyright by
RAND McNALLY & COMPANY
Made in U.S.A.

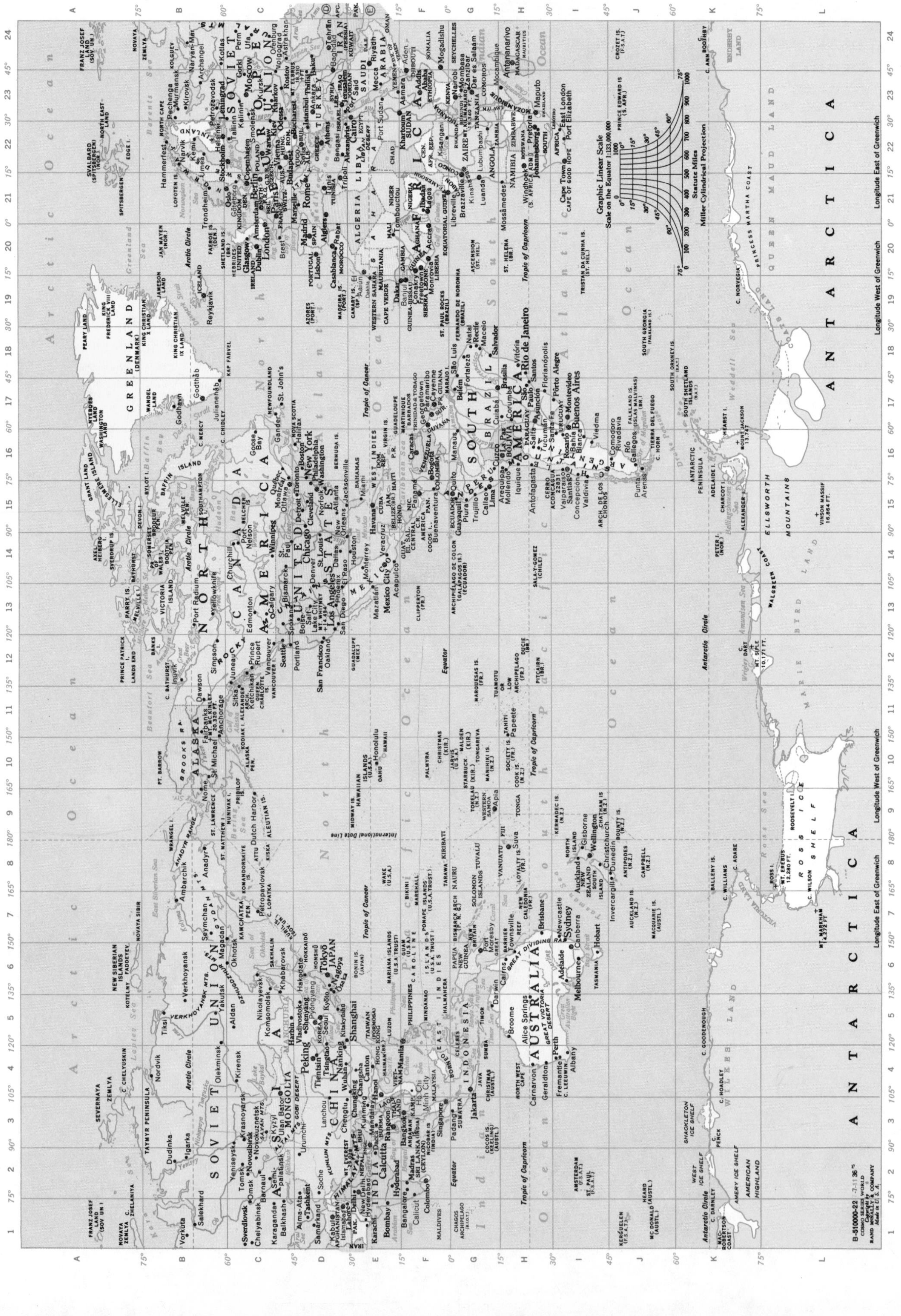
Graphic Linear Scale
Scale on the Equator 1:133,000,000
Statute Miles
Miller Cylindrical Projection
Longitude West of Greenwich
Longitude East of Greenwich
A N T A R C T I C A
Arctic Ocean
Atlantic Ocean
Pacific Ocean
Indian Ocean
Tropic of Cancer
Tropic of Capricorn
Equator
Arctic Circle
Antarctic Circle
NORTH AMERICA
SOUTH AMERICA
AFRICA
AUSTRALIA
SOVIET UNION
CHINA
UNITED STATES
CANADA
GREENLAND (DENMARK)
B-510000-22
RAND MCNALLY & COMPANY

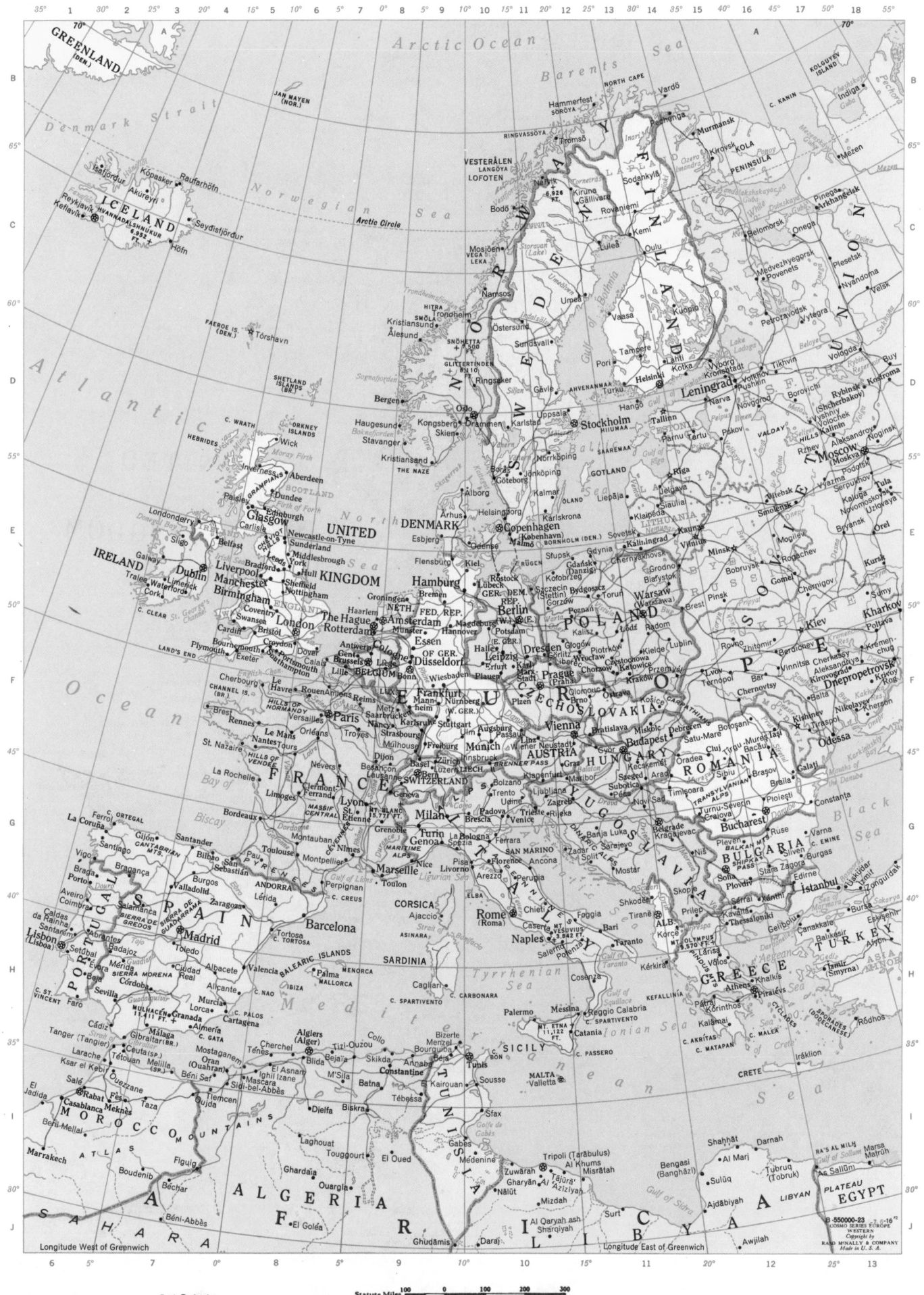

Statute Miles 100 0 100 200 300
Kilometers 100 0 100 200 300 400

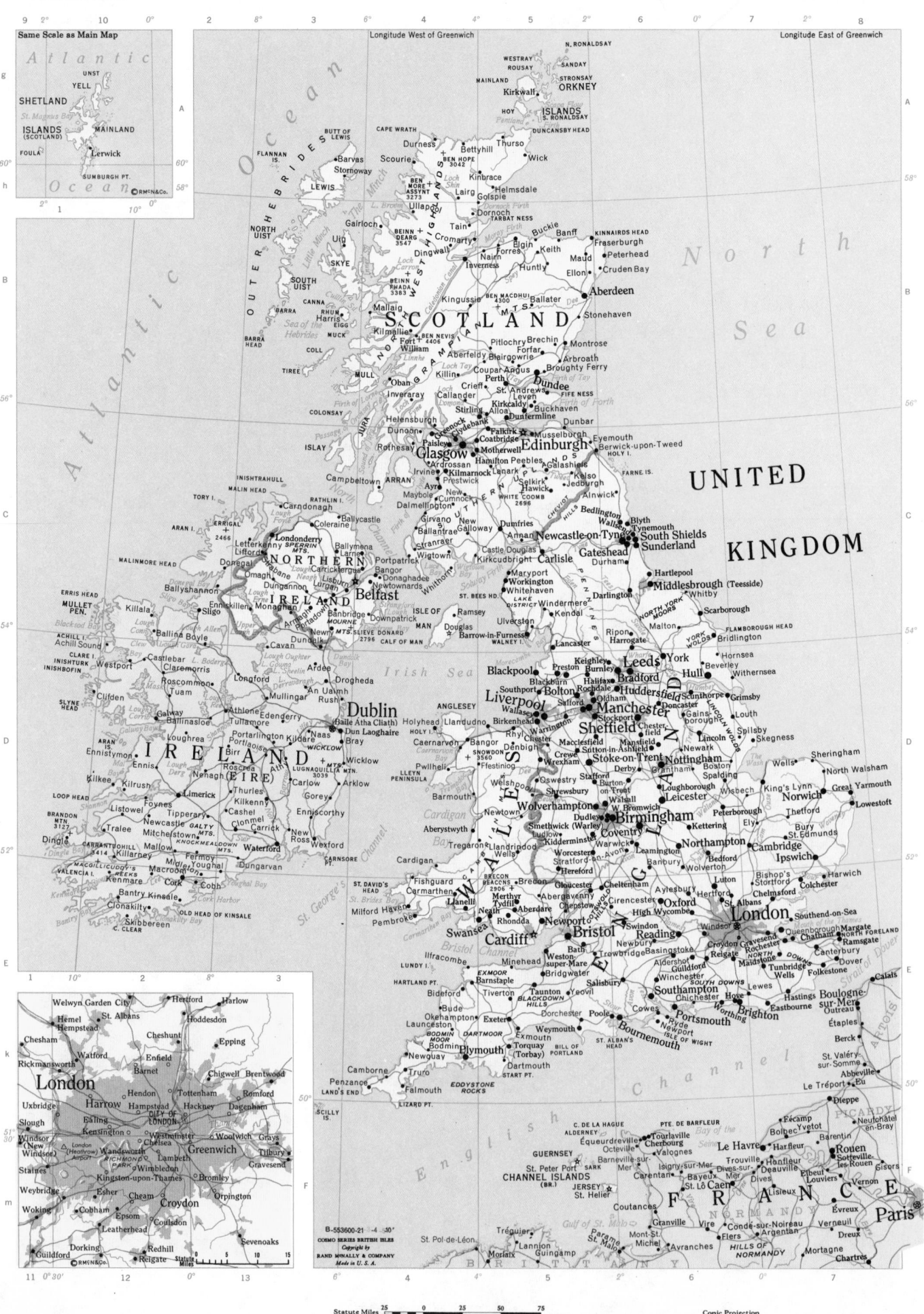

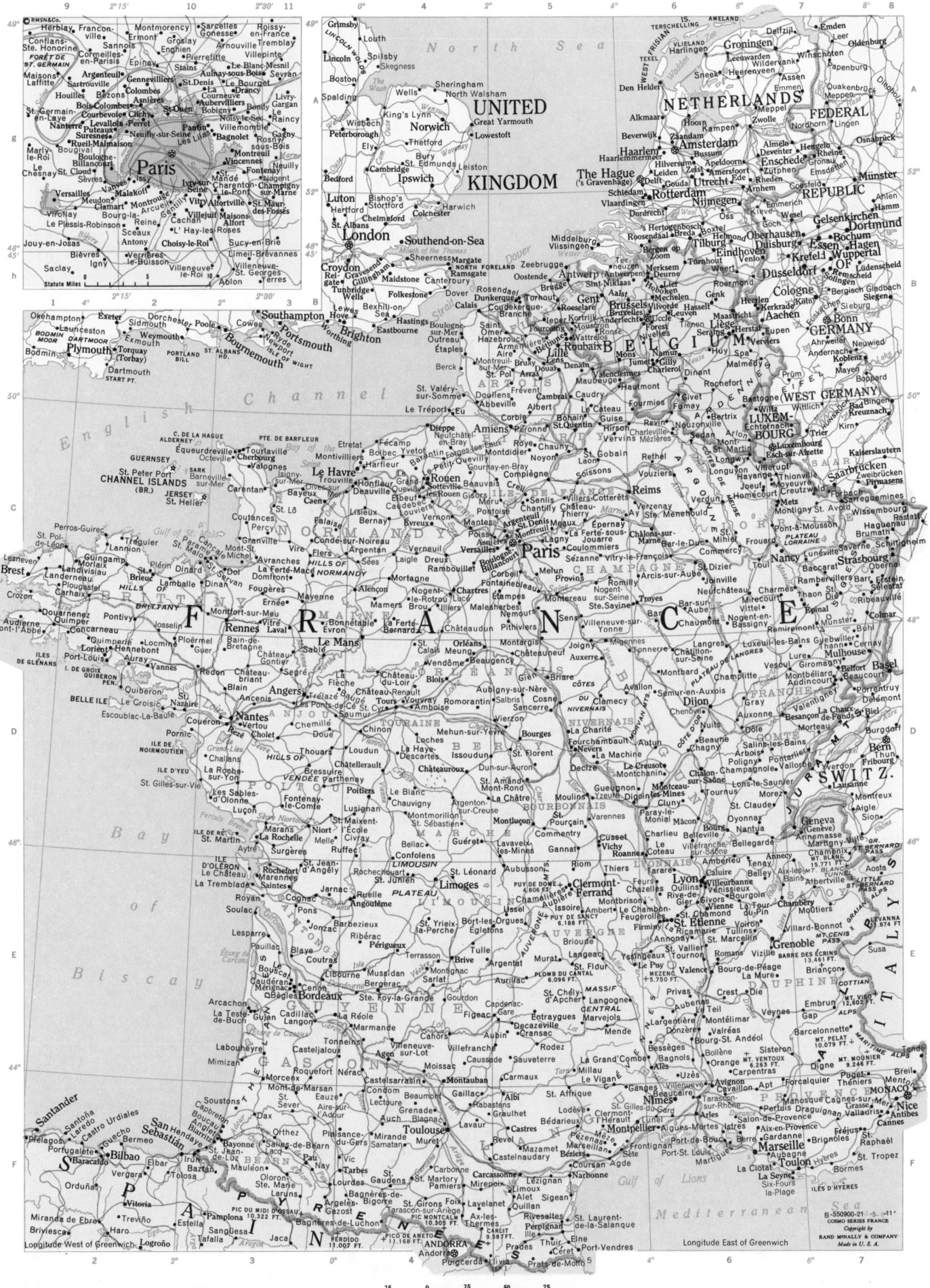

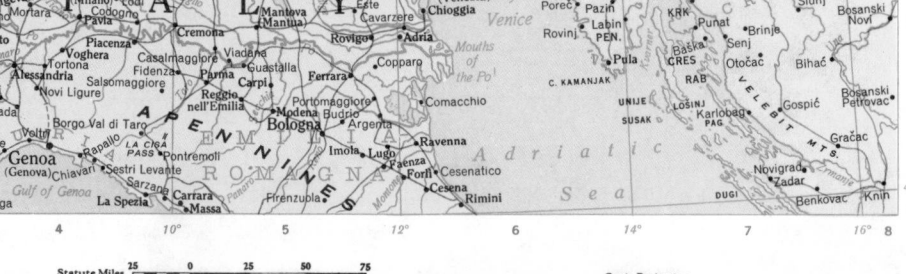

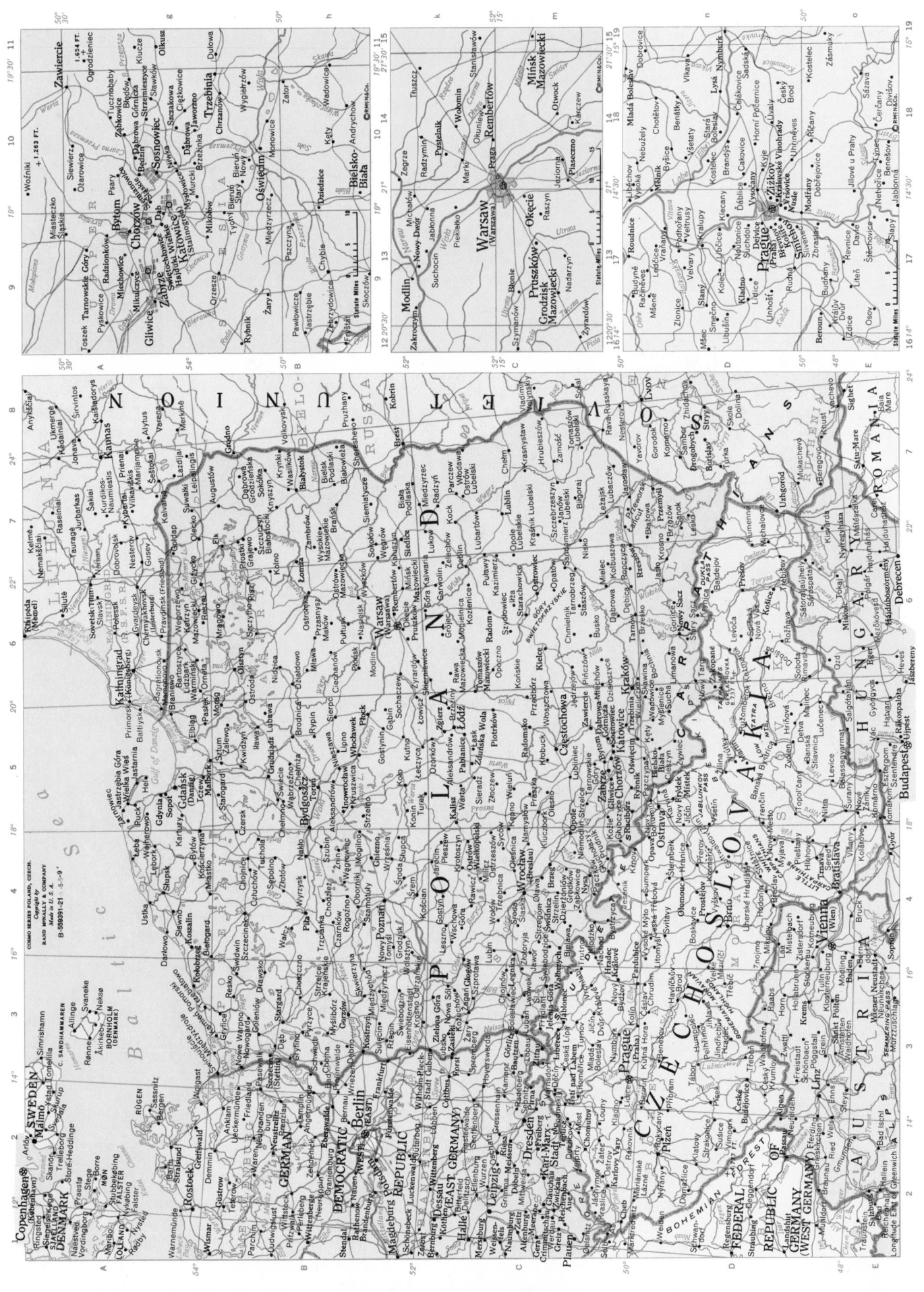

Conic Projection

Statute Miles

Kilometers

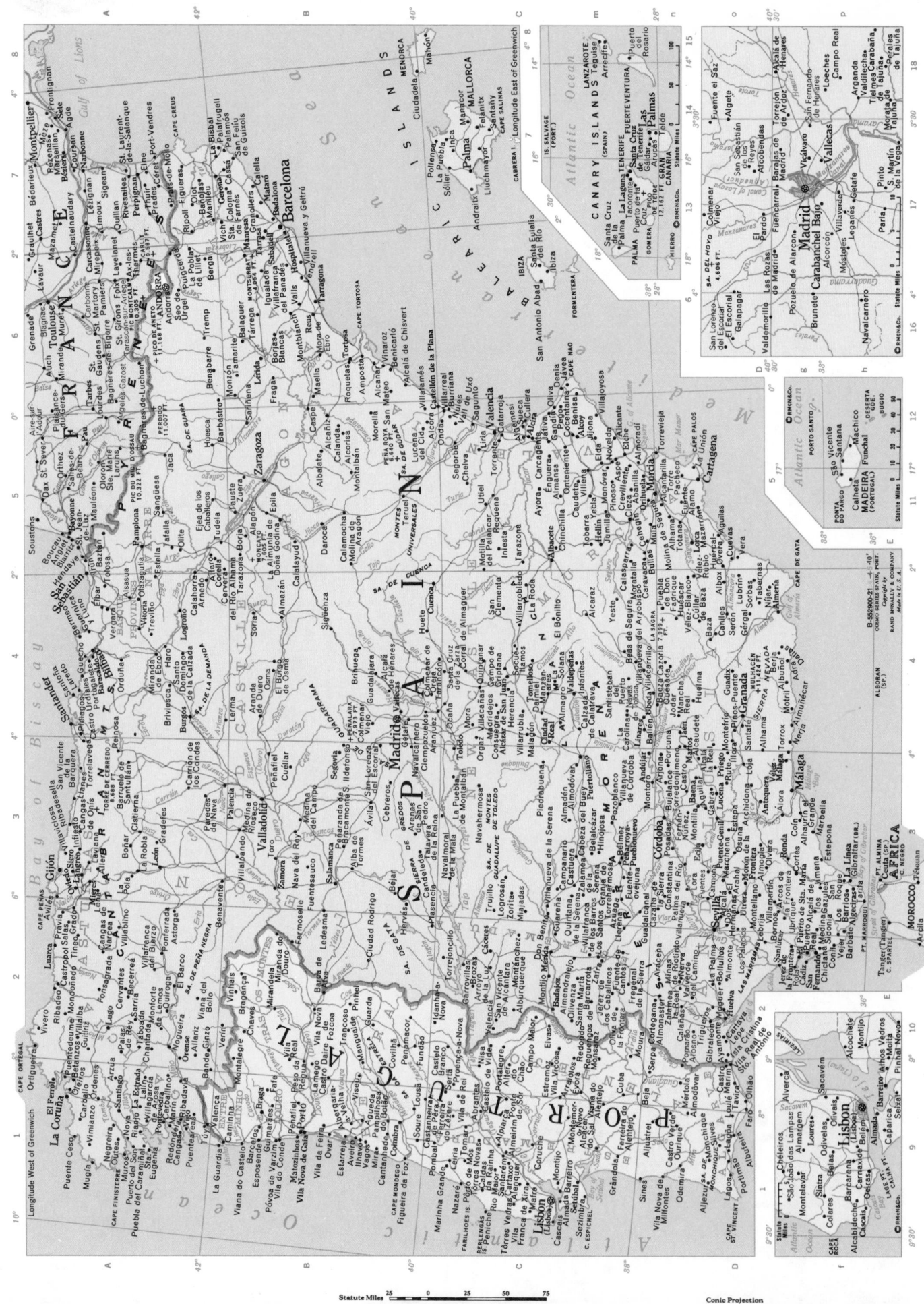

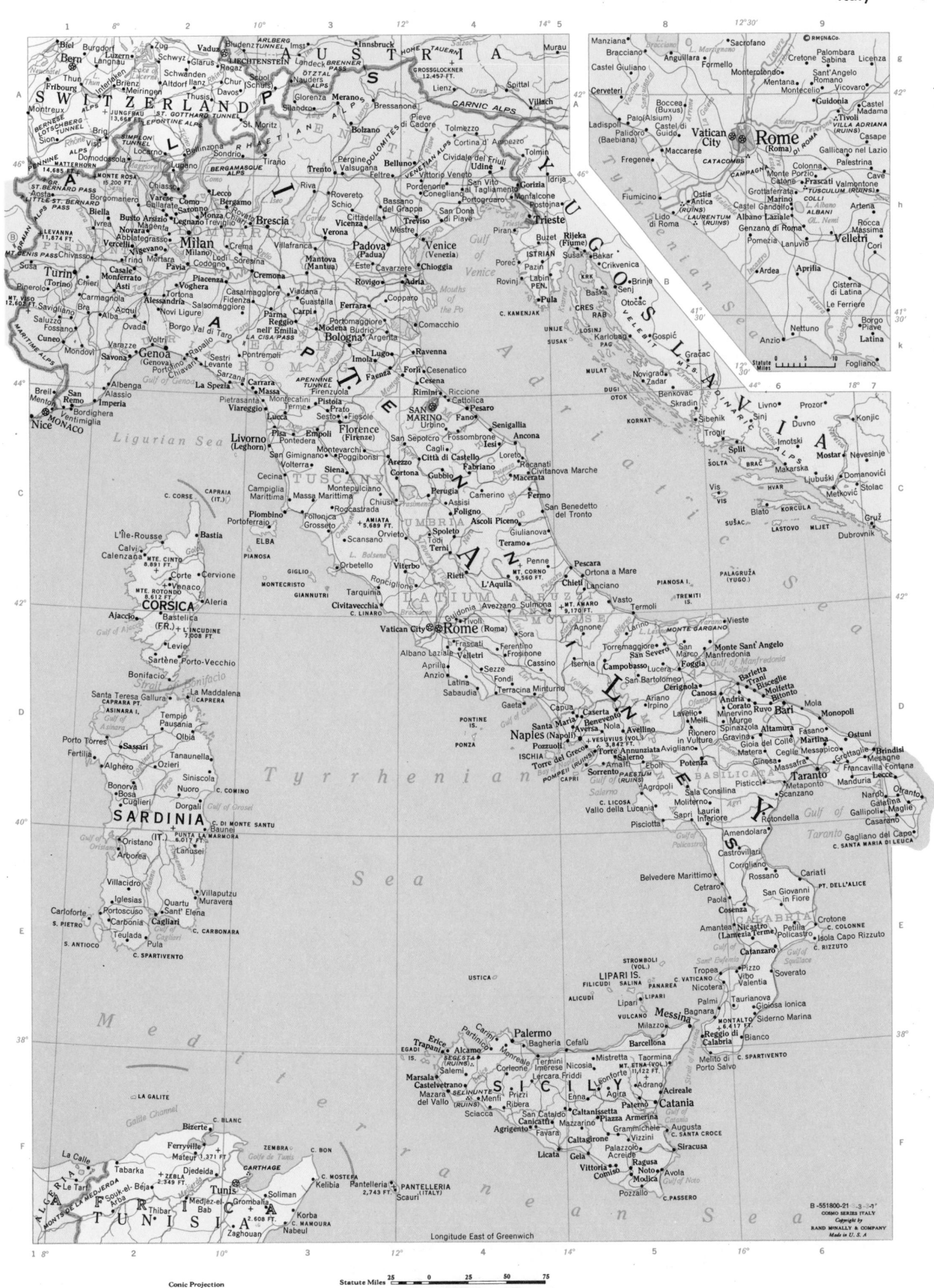

Conic Projection

Statute Miles
25   0   25   50   75

Kilometers
25 0 25 50   100

Longitude East of Greenwich

Statute Miles 25 0 25 50 75
Kilometers 25 0 25 50 100

Conic Projection

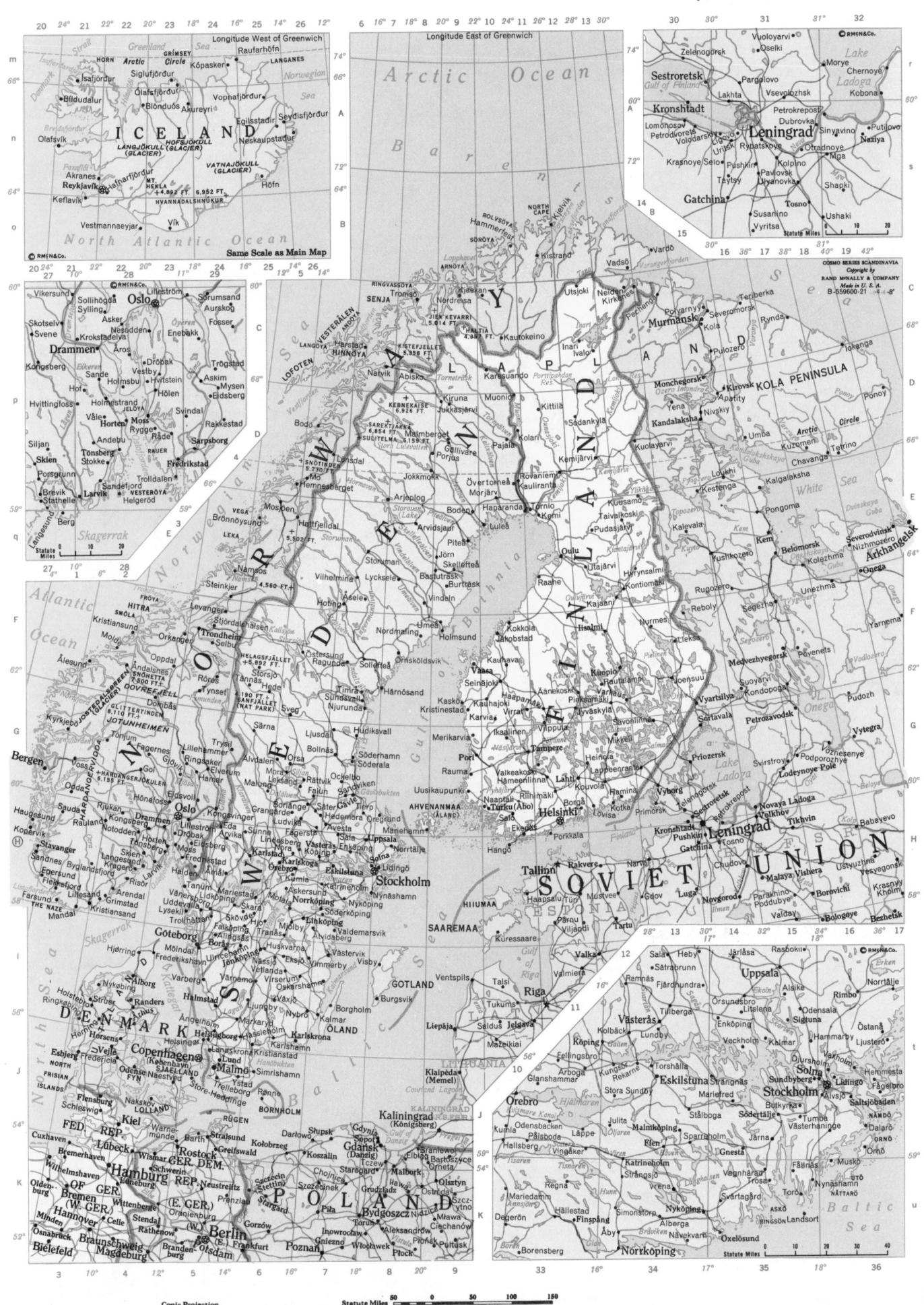

Conic Projection

Statute Miles

Kilometers

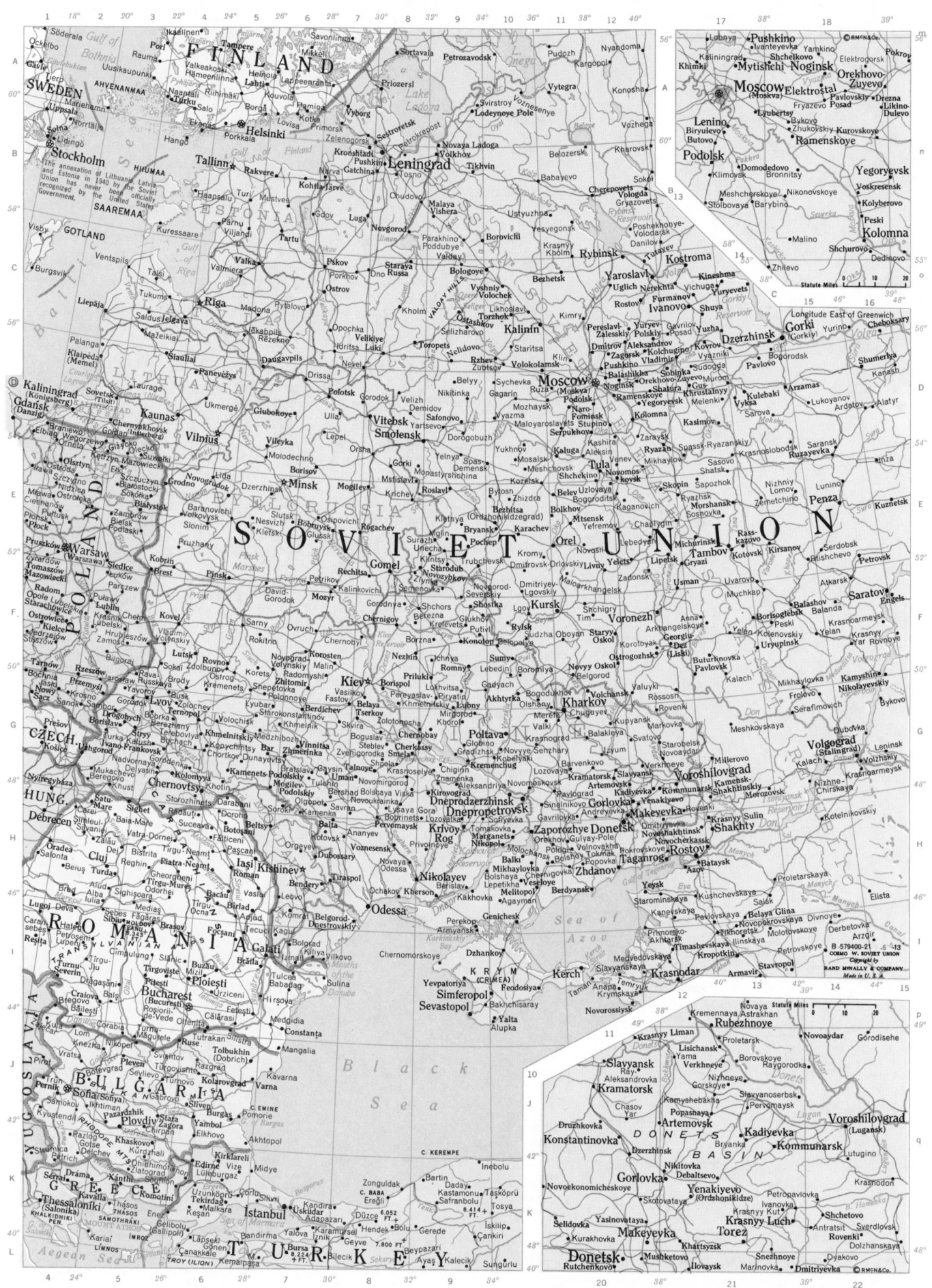

Lambert Azimuthal Equal Area Projection

Statute Miles
100 0 100 200 300 400 500

Kilometers
100 0 100 300 500 700

For Eastern Iraq, see map of Iran and Afghanistan.

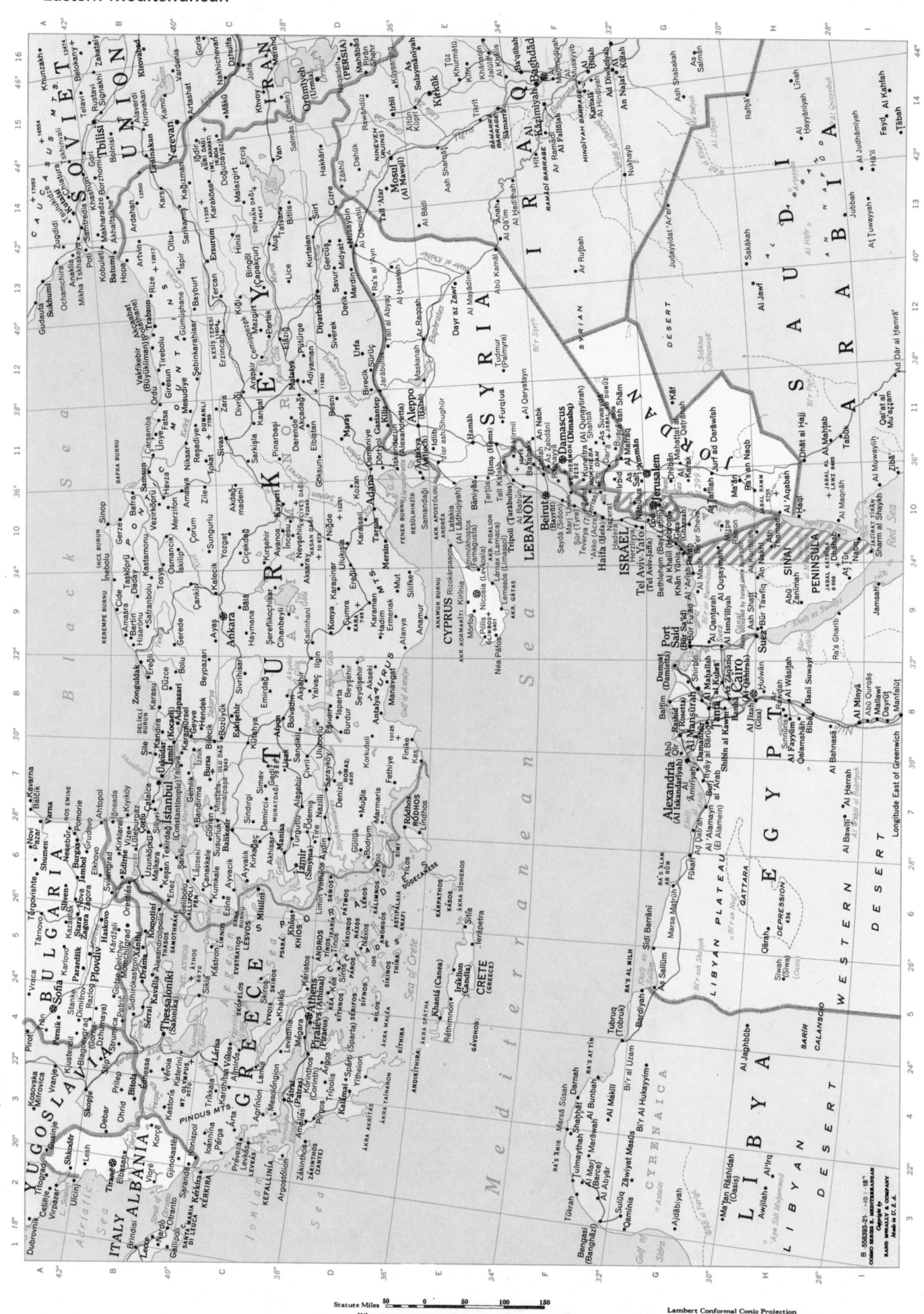

Statute Miles   50   0   50   100   150

Kilometers   50   0   50   100   200

Lambert Conformal Conic Projection

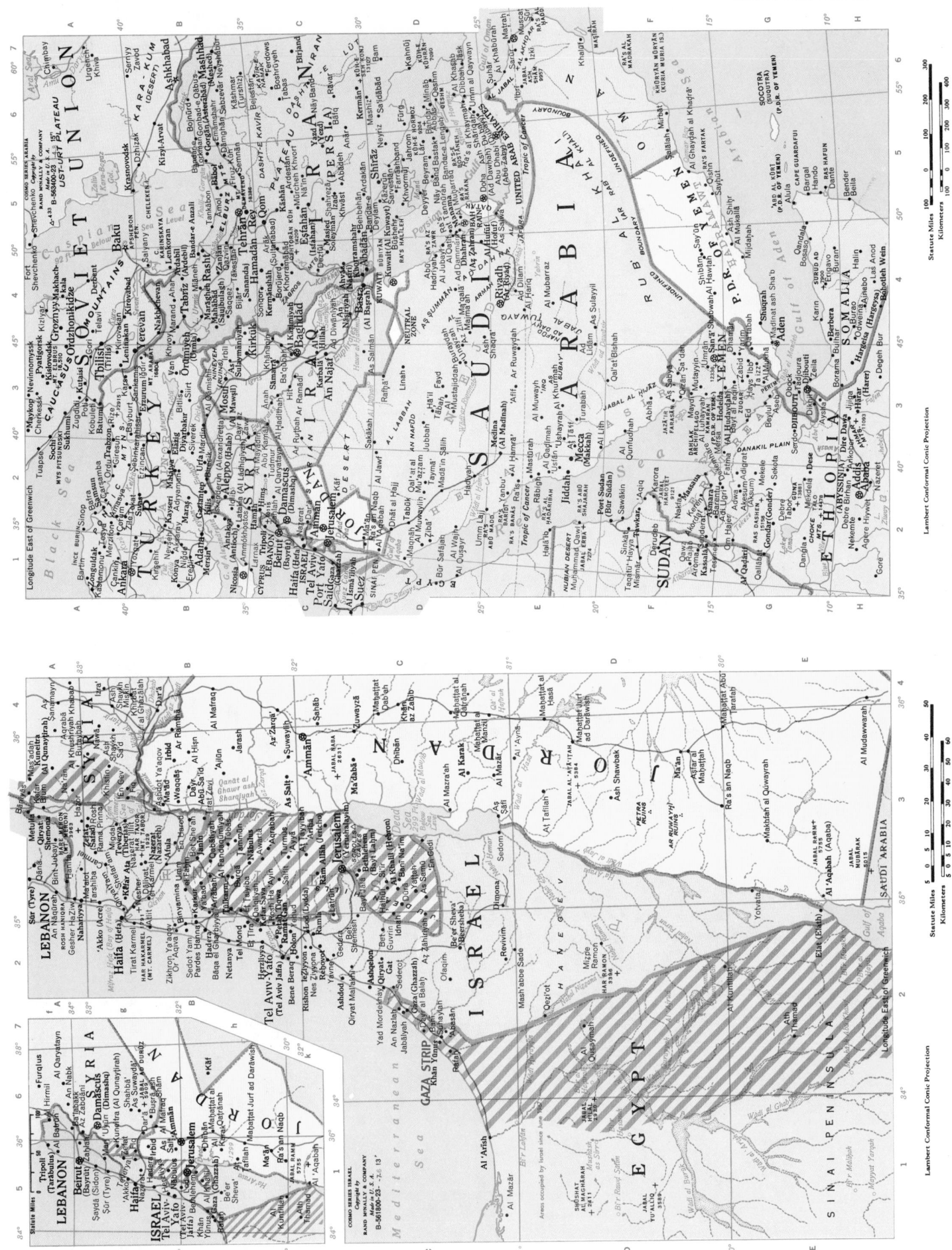

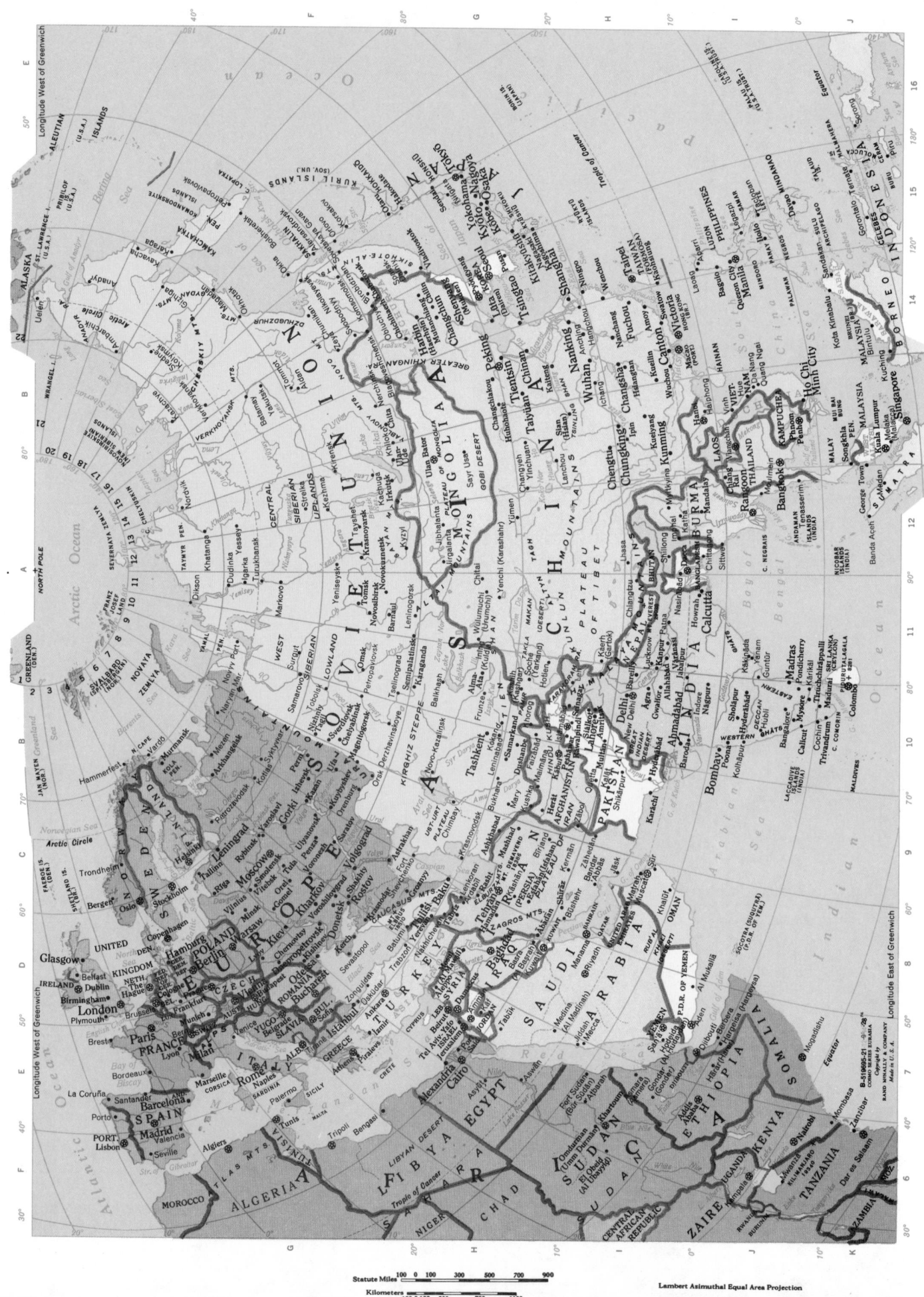

Statute Miles   100 0 100   300   500   700   900

Kilometers   100 0 100   300   700   1100

Lambert Azimuthal Equal Area Projection

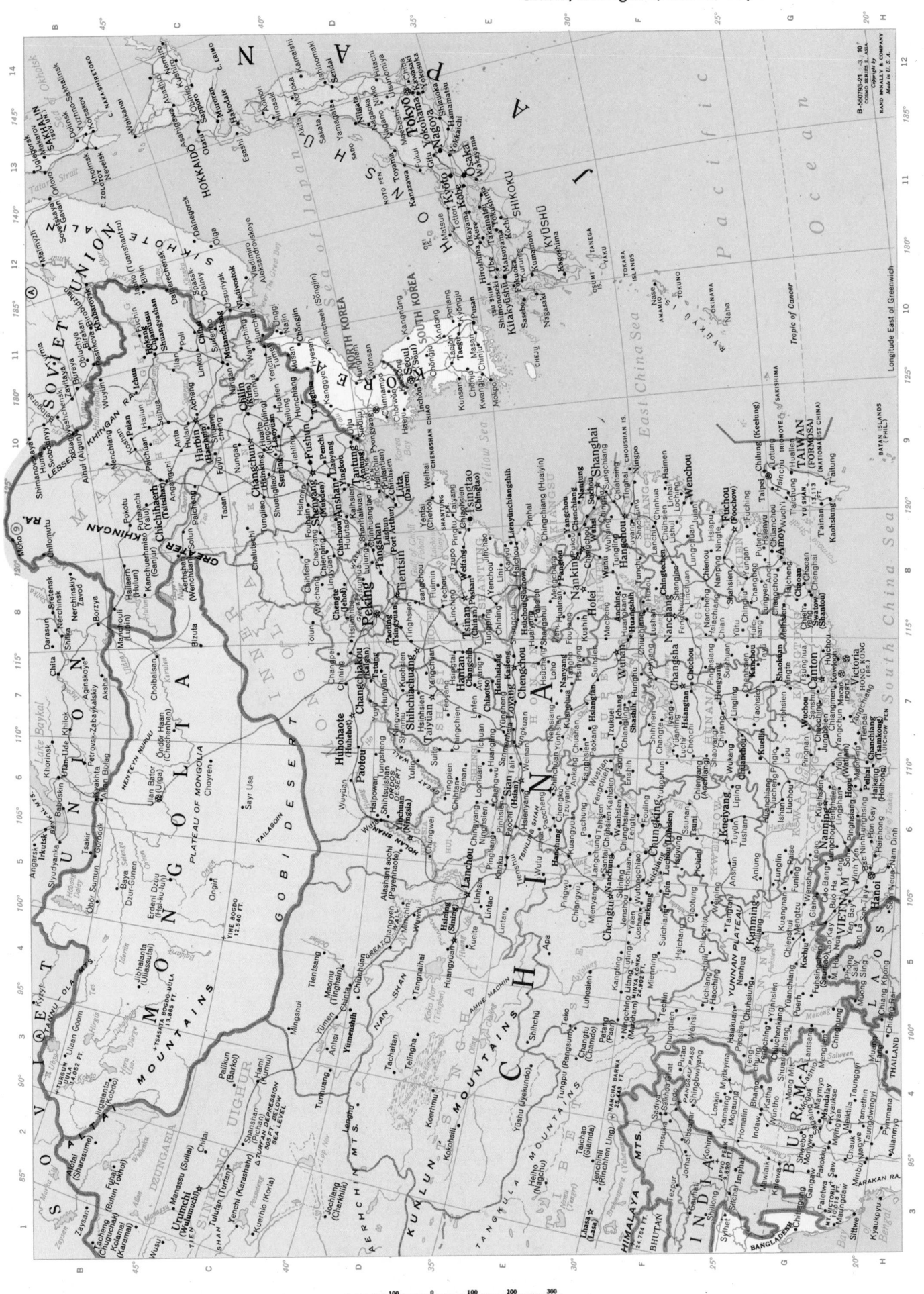

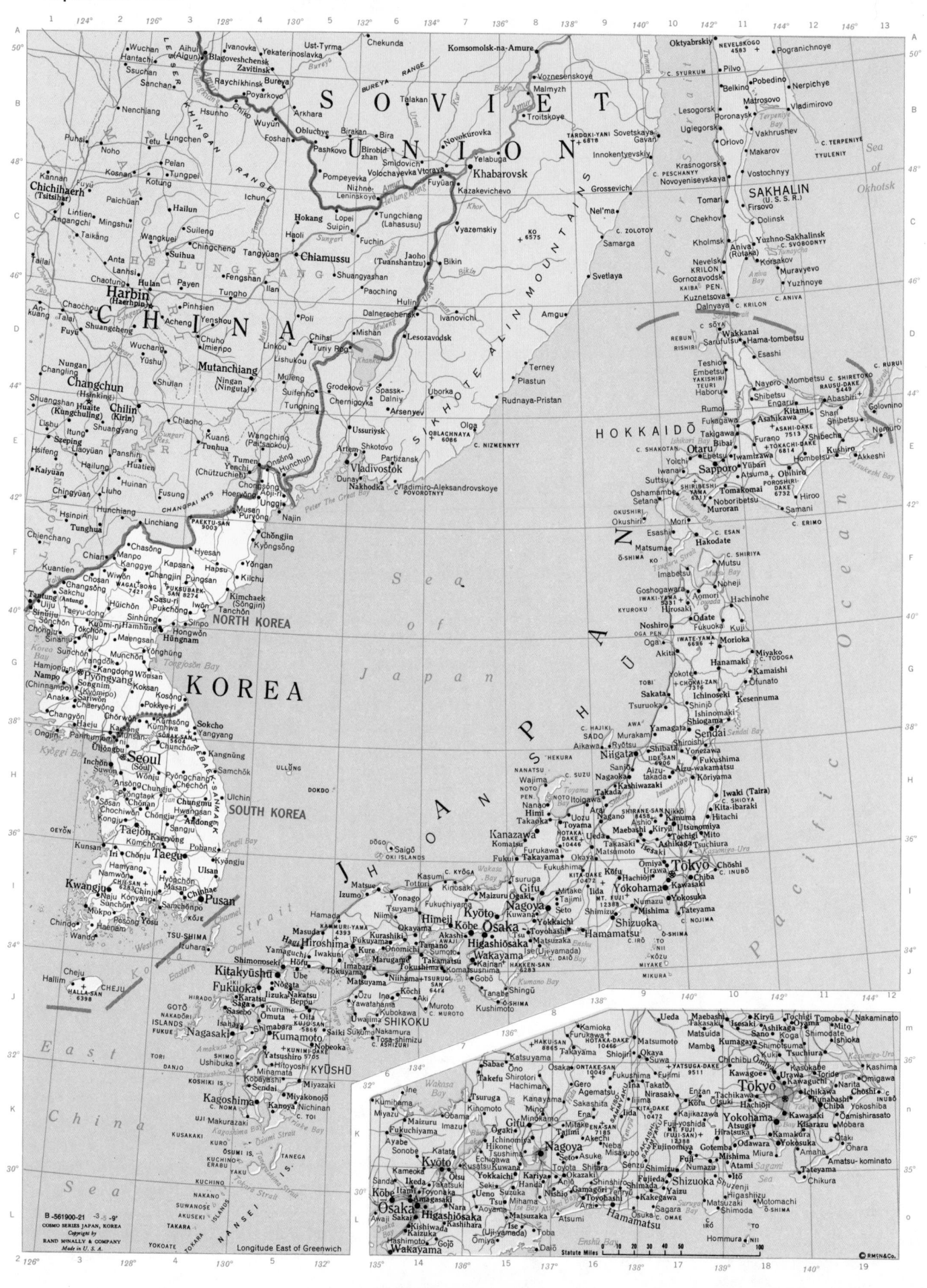

Longitude East of Greenwich

Statute Miles

Kilometers

Lambert Conformal Conic Projection

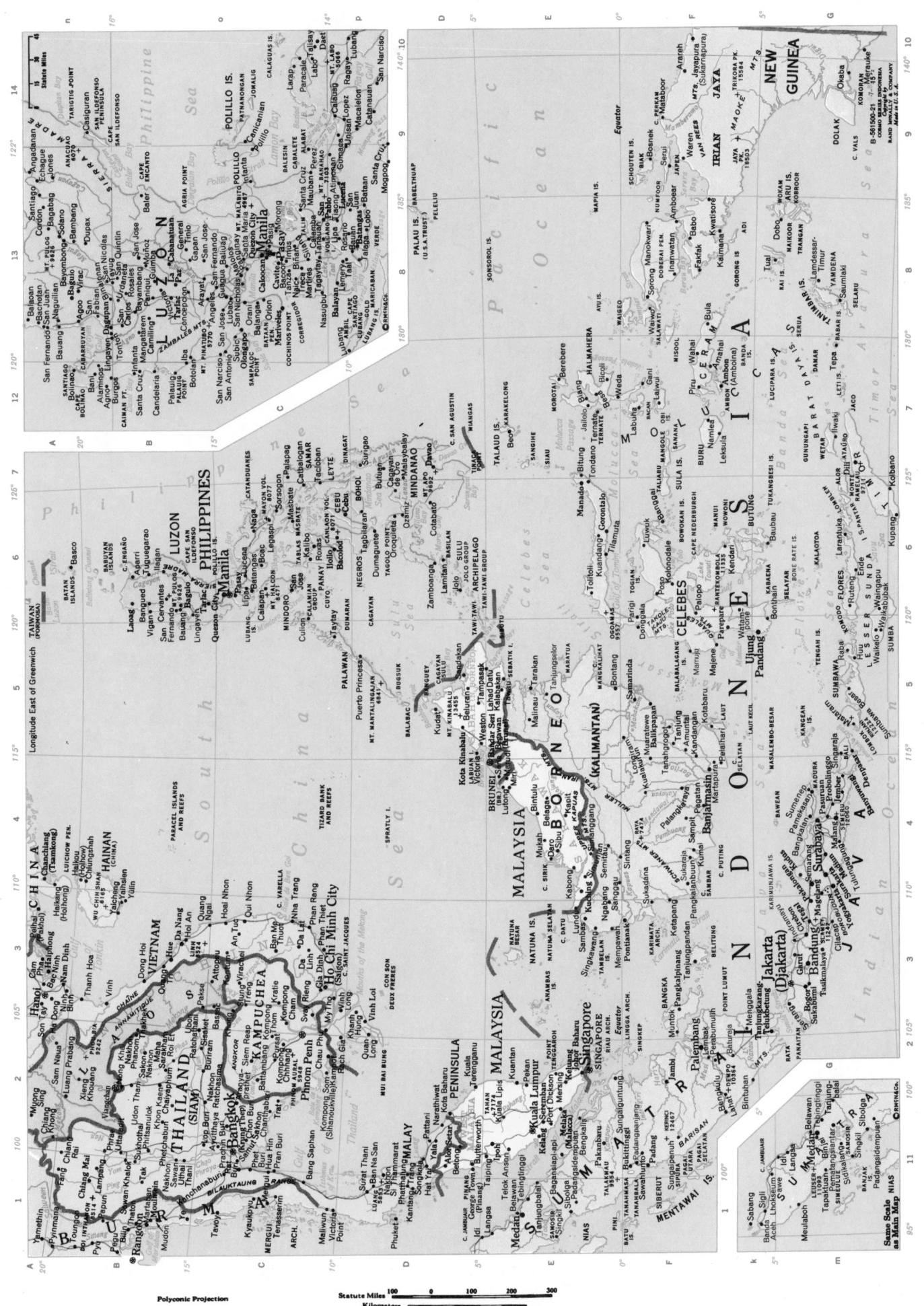

Polyconic Projection

Same Scale
as Main Map

Statute Miles 100 0 100 200 300
Kilometers 100 0 100 200 300 400

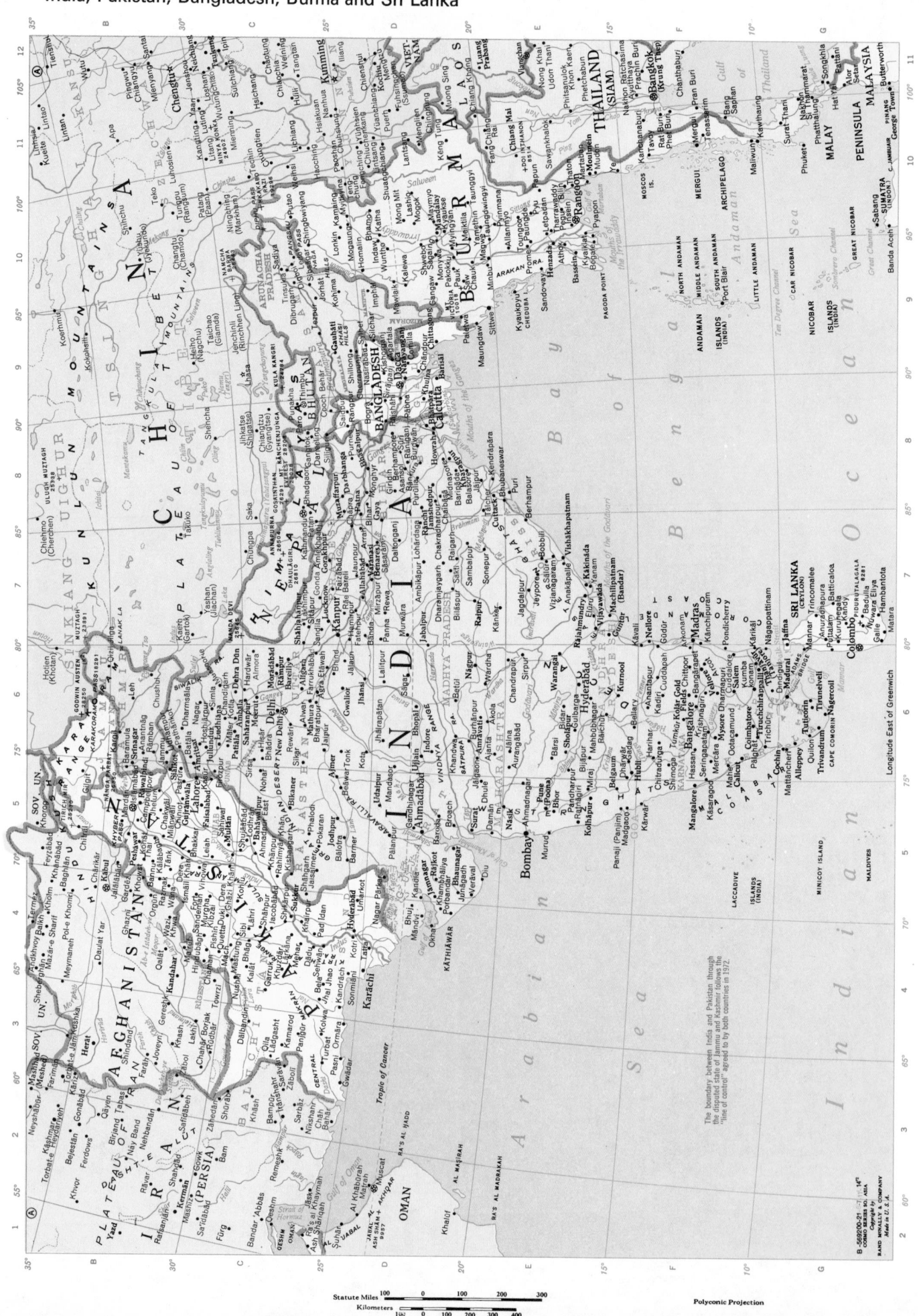

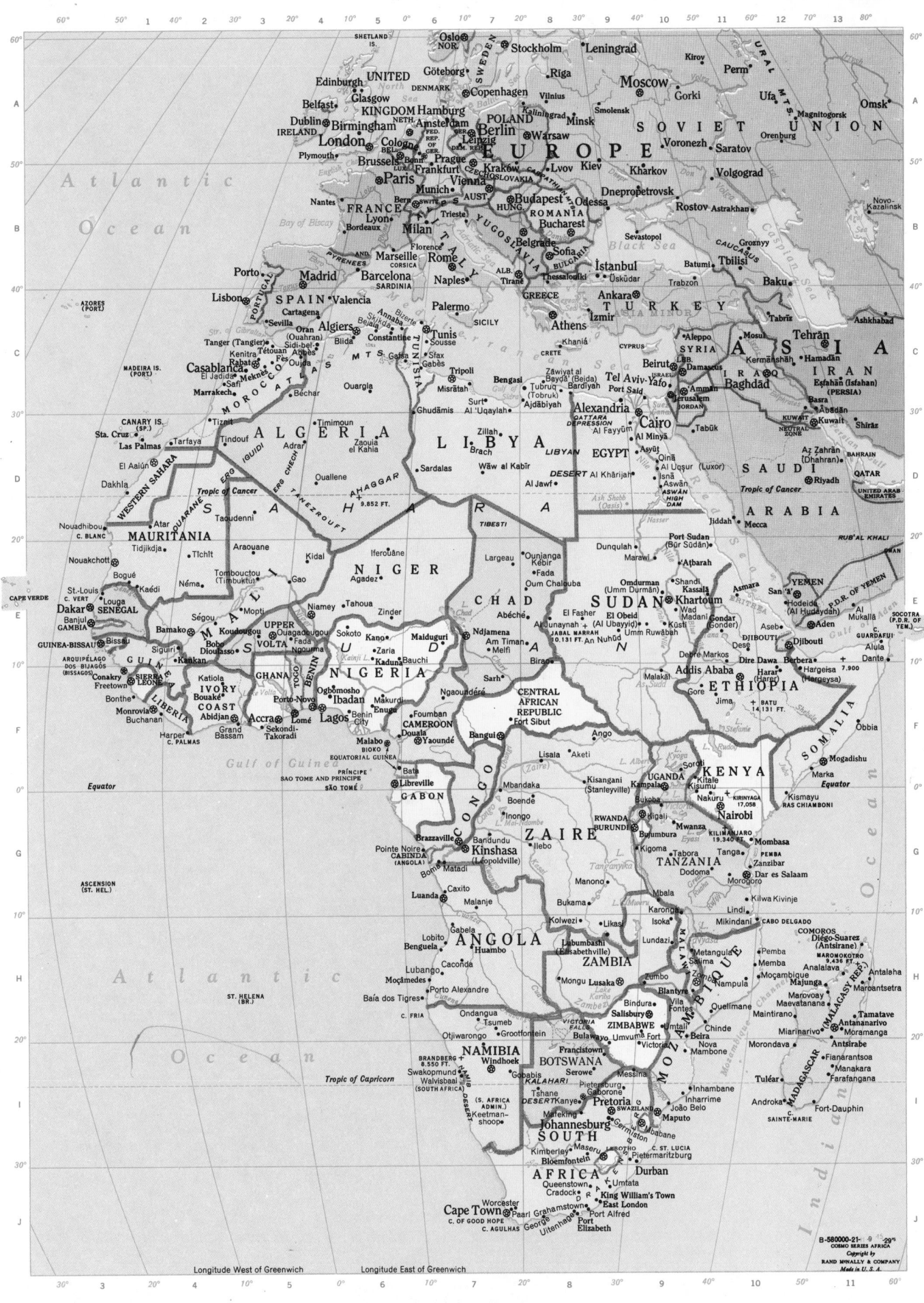

Sinusoidal Projection

Longitude West of Greenwich | Longitude East of Greenwich

Statute Miles   100 0 100   300   500   700   900

Kilometers   100 0 100 300 500 700 900 1100 1300

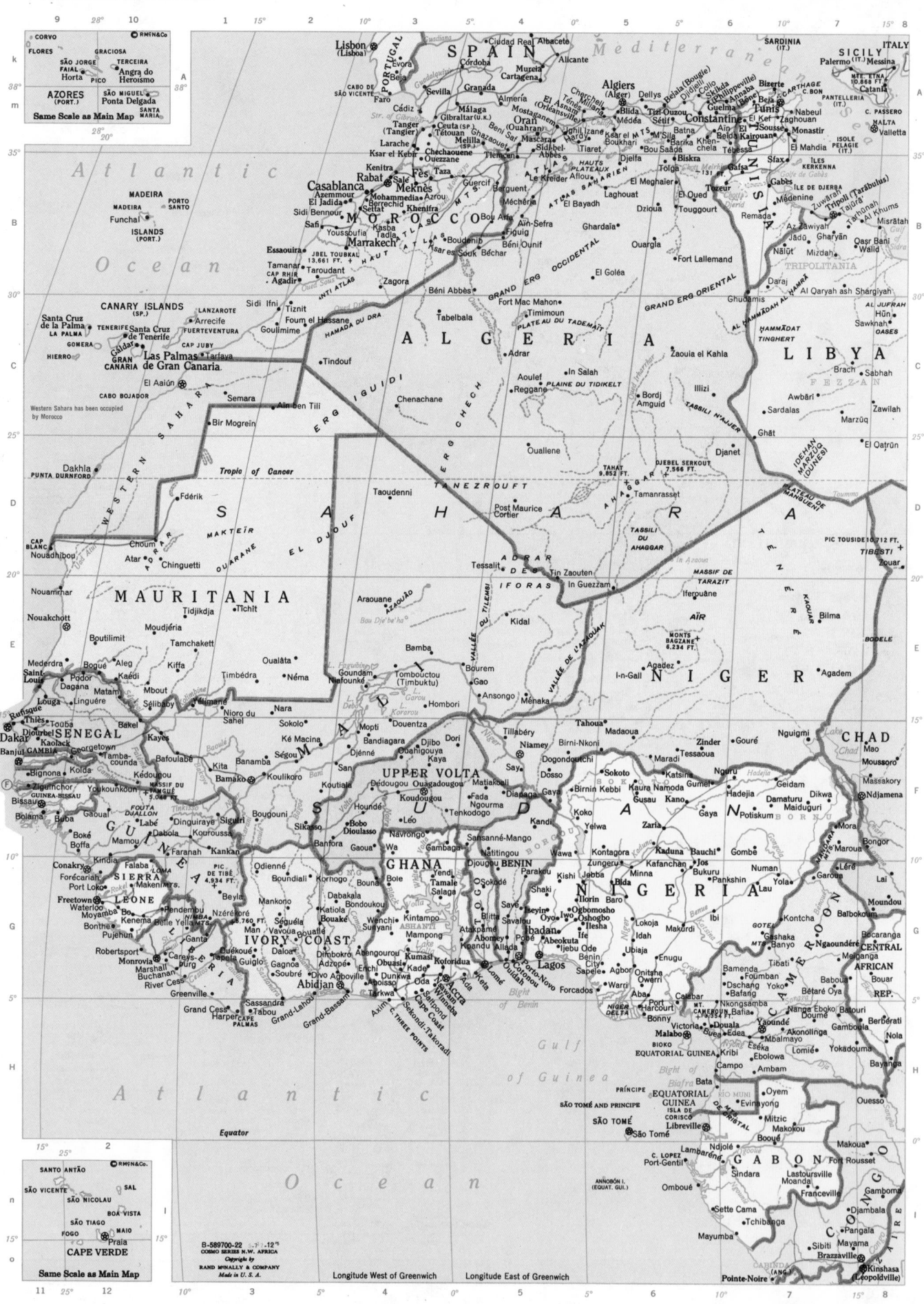

CORVO
FLORES
GRACIOSA
SÃO JORGE TERCEIRA
FAIAL   Angra do
HORTA   Heroismo
PICO
AZORES
(PORT.) SÃO MIGUEL
Ponta Delgada
SANTA
MARIA
Same Scale as Main Map

SANTO ANTÃO
SÃO VICENTE SAL
SÃO NICOLAU
BOA VISTA
SÃO TIAGO MAIO
FOGO
Praia
CAPE VERDE
Same Scale as Main Map

B-589700-22
COSMO SERIES N.W. AFRICA
Copyright by
RAND McNALLY & COMPANY
Made in U.S.A.

Longitude West of Greenwich
Longitude East of Greenwich

Statute Miles 100 0 100 200 300
Kilometers 100 0 100 200 300 400

Sinusoidal Projection

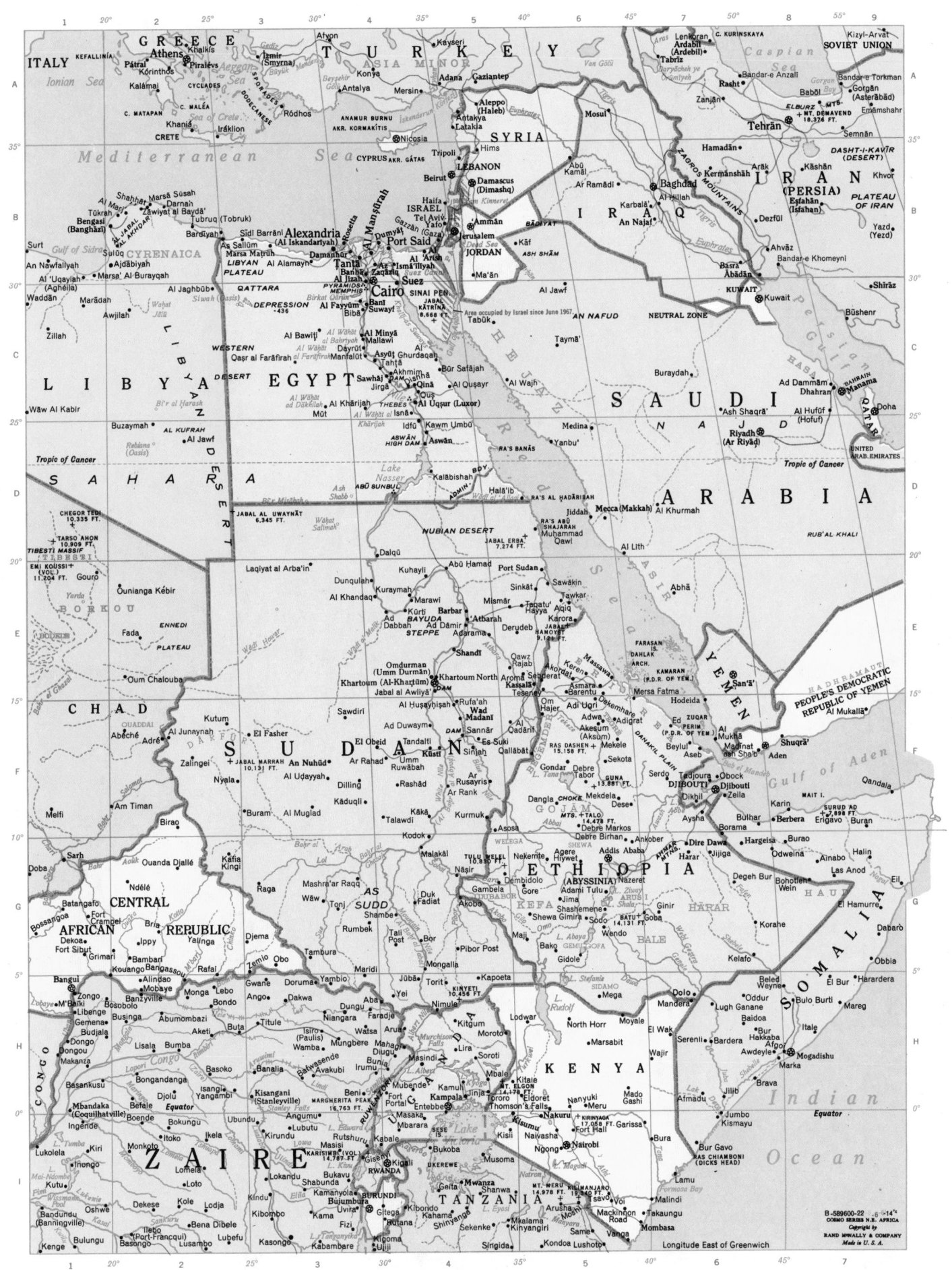

Sinusoidal Projection

Statute Miles   100   0   100   200   300
Kilometers   100   0   100   200   300   400

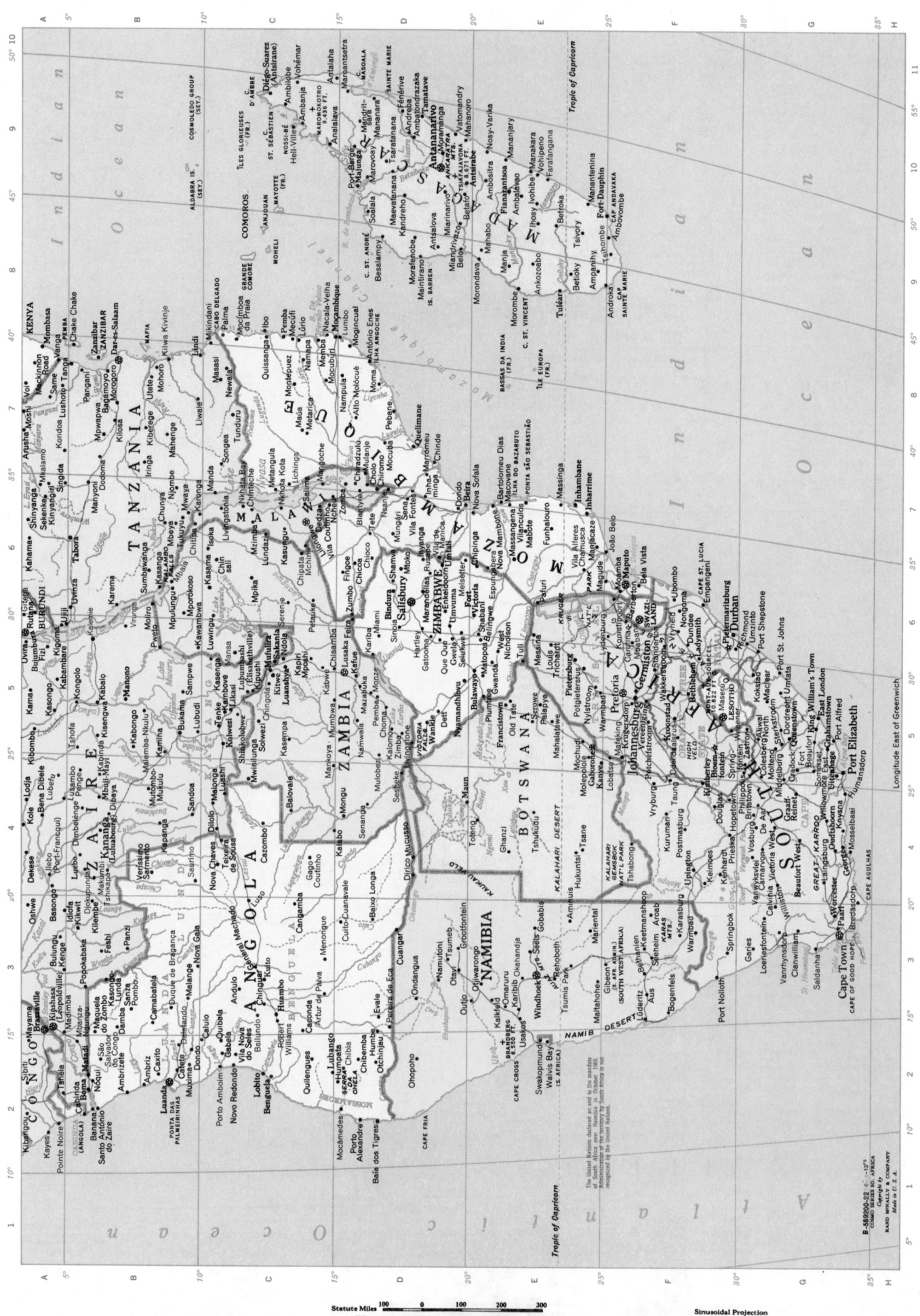

Statute Miles   Kilometers

Sinusoidal Projection

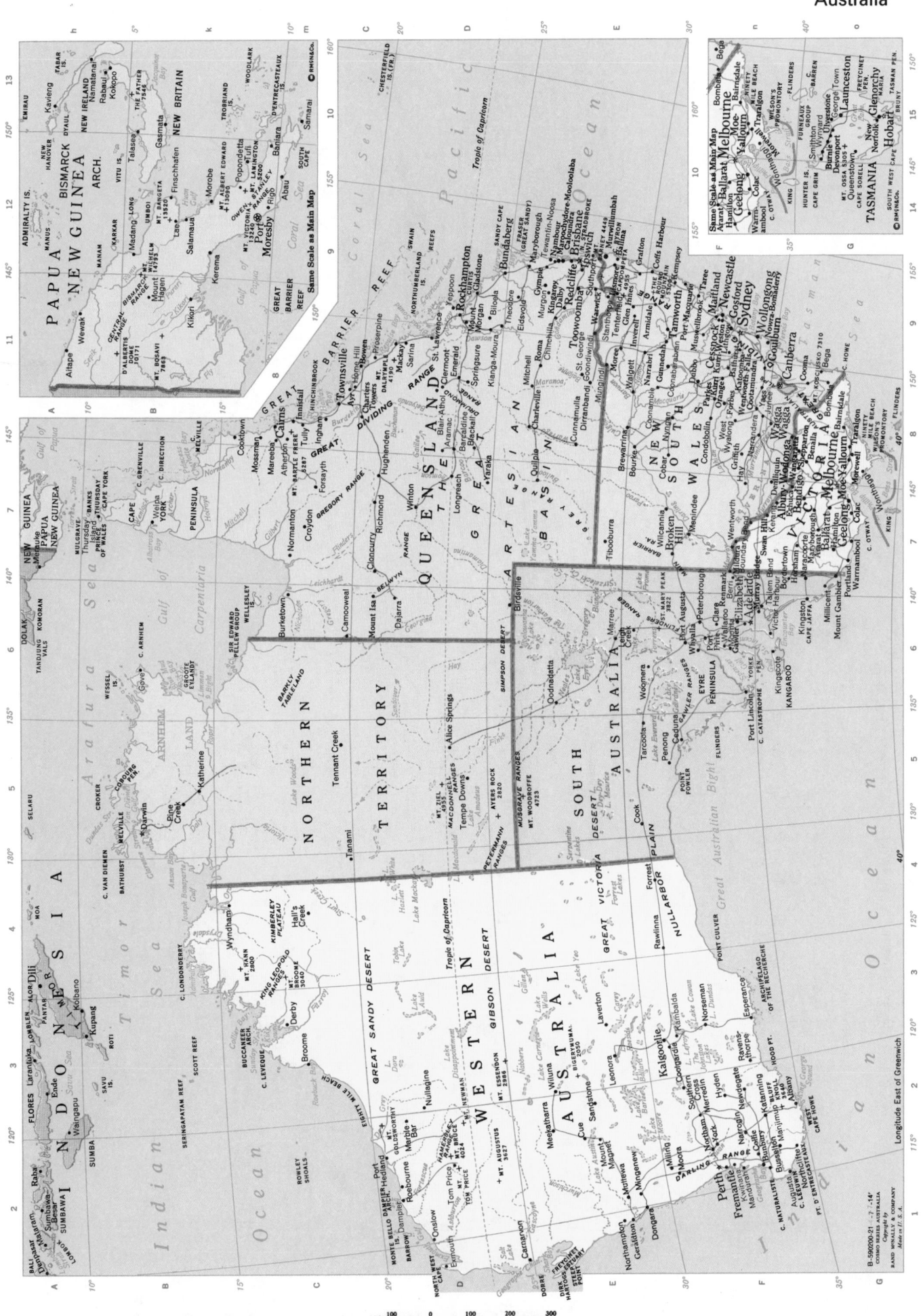

Statute Miles 50 0 50 100 150

Kilometers 50 0 50 100 150 200

Lambert Conformal Conic Projection

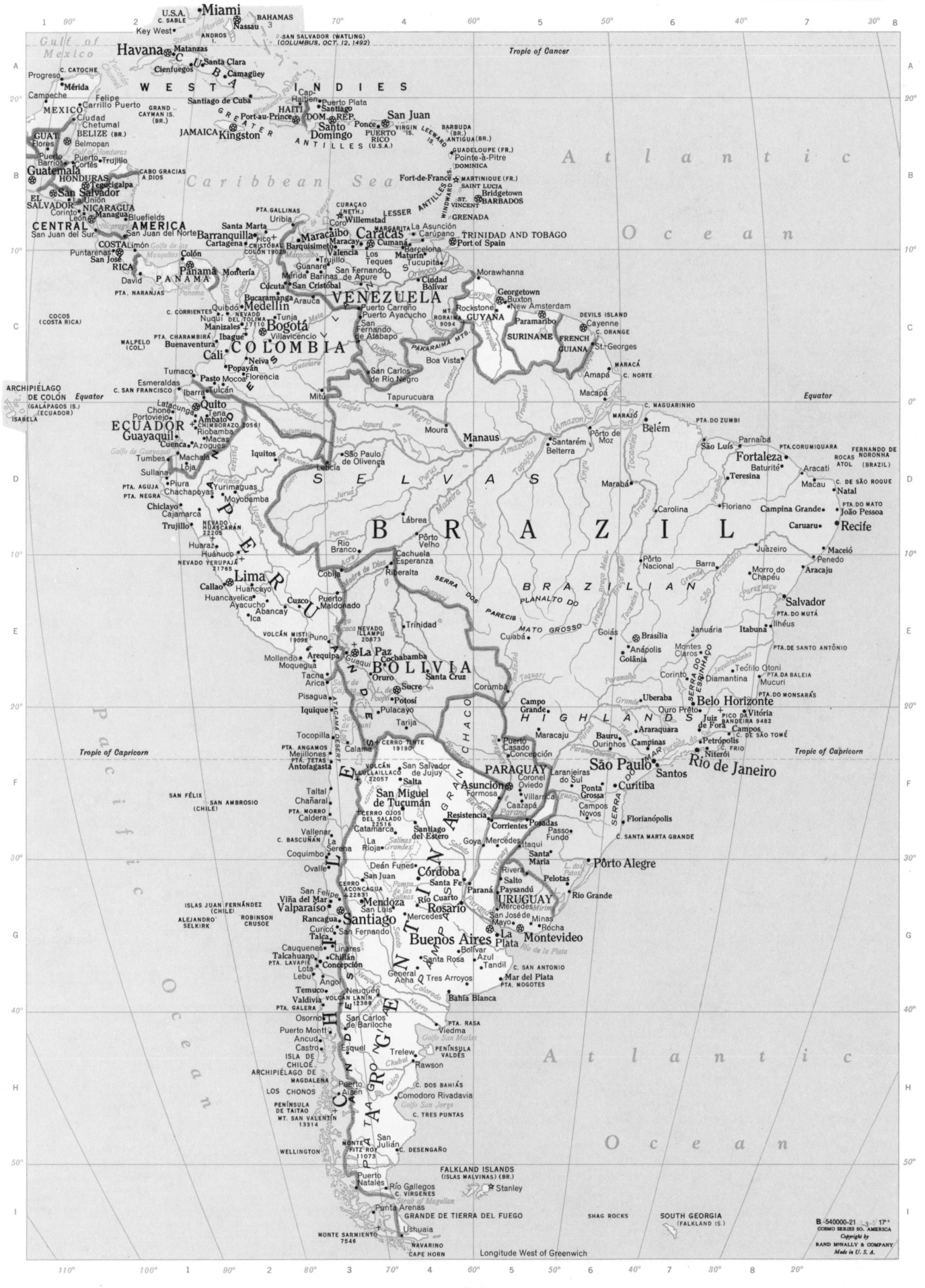

Gulf of Mexico

U.S.A. •Miami
C. SABLE
Key West BAHAMAS
ANDROS NASSAU

Tropic of Cancer

A
Havana •Matanzas
•Santa Clara
Cienfuegos C U B A •Camagüey
Progreso C. CATOCHE
Campeche Mérida
MEXICO Felipe
Carrillo Puerto
Ciudad Chetumal GRAND
CAYMAN IS.
(BR.)
Santiago de Cuba
SAN SALVADOR (WATLING)
(COLUMBUS, OCT. 12, 1492)
Puerto Plata
Haitien HAITI Santiago
DOM. REP.
Port-au-Prince
Santo Domingo
San Juan
Ponce PUERTO RICO (U.S.A.)
VIRGIN IS.
LEEWARD IS.

W E S T I N D I E S
GREATER ANTILLES
JAMAICA Kingston
LESSER ANTILLES

BARBUDA
(BR.)
ANTIGUA (BR.)
GUADELOUPE (FR.)
Pointe-à-Pitre
DOMINICA

Caribbean Sea

A t l a n t i c
O c e a n

BELIZE (BR.)
Flores Belmopan
GUAT. Puerto Barrios
Puerto Cortés
Guatemala
HONDURAS Tegucigalpa
San Salvador
EL SALVADOR La Unión
Corinto NICARAGUA Managua León
Bluefields
CENTRAL AMERICA
San Juan del Sur
Puntarenas COSTA RICA Limón
San José
David PTA. NARANJAS PANAMA Colón
COCOS (COSTA RICA)
Montería
Golfo del Panama

Fort-de-France
MARTINIQUE (FR.)
SAINT LUCIA
ST. VINCENT Bridgetown
BARBADOS
GRENADA

B

PTA. GALLINAS
Uribia
Santa Marta
Barranquilla
Cartagena
CRISTÓBAL
COLÓN 1902
Barquisimeto
Maracaibo
Coro CURAÇAO (NETH.)
Willemstad
Valencia
Caracas
MARGARITA
La Asunción
Carúpano
Cumaná Barcelona
TRINIDAD AND TOBAGO
Port of Spain

MALPELO (COL.)
C. CORRIENTES
Quibdó Medellín
Nuquí DEL TOLIMA
Manizales 17110
Bogotá
Buenaventura Cali COLOMBIA
Villavicencio
Ibagué Tunja
Los Teques
Maturín
Tucupita
Maracay Valencia
Trujillo
San Fernando de Apure
Guanare
Barinas
Mérida
San Cristóbal
Cúcuta
Bucaramanga
Arauca
VENEZUELA
Ciudad Bolívar
Puerto Ayacucho
San Fernando de Atabapo
Puerto Carreño
MT. RORAIMA 9094
PAKARAIMA MTS.
Morawhanna
Georgetown
Buxton
Rockstone
New Amsterdam
GUYANA
SURINAME
Paramaribo
FRENCH GUIANA
Cayenne
DEVILS ISLAND
C. ORANGE
St-Georges

C

PTA. CHARAMBIRÁ
Neiva
Popayán
Pasto Mocoa
Florencia
Tumaco
San Carlos de Río Negro
Boa Vista
MARACÁ
C. NORTE
Amapá
Macapá

ARCHIPIÉLAGO DE COLÓN Equator
(GALÁPAGOS IS.) (ECUADOR)
ISABELA

Esmeraldas
C. SAN FRANCISCO
Ibarra Tulcán
Quito
Latacunga Tena
Ambato CHIMBORAZO 20561
Riobamba Macas
ECUADOR
Guayaquil Cuenca
Azogues
Portoviejo
Chone
Mitú
Tapurucuara
Moura
Manaus
Santarém
Belterra
PORTO de Moz
MARAJÓ
C. MAGUARINHO
PTA. DO ZUMBI
Belém
Parnaíba
São Luís PTA. CORUMIQUARA
FERNANDO DE NORONHA
ROCAS ATOL (BRAZIL)
Equator

D

Tumbes
Machala
Loja
Sullana
Piura
PTA. AGUJA
PTA. NEGRA
Chiclayo
Cajamarca
Trujillo
NEVADO HUASCARÁN 22205
Huaraz
NEVADO YERUPAJÁ 21765
Iquitos
Leticia
São Paulo de Olivença
Yurimaguas
Moyobamba
Chachapoyas
SELVAS
B R A Z I L
Lábrea
Rio Branco
Pôrto Velho
Cachuela Esperanza
Riberalta
Carolina
Floriano
Marabá
Teresina
Baturité
Araçati
Macau
C. DE SÃO ROQUE
Natal
PTA. DO MATO
João Pessoa
Campina Grande
Caruaru Recife

HUÁNUCO
Cobija
SERRA DOS PARECIS
B R A Z I L I A N
PLANALTO DO
Juàzeiro
Barra
Morro do Chapéu
Pôrto Nacional
Penedo
Aracaju
Maceió
PTA. DO MUTÁ
Salvador

10°

Lima
Callao
Huancayo
Huancavelica
Ayacucho
Abancay
Ica
Cuzco
Puerto Maldonado
Trinidad
MATO GROSSO
Cuiabá
Goiás
Brasília
Anápolis
Goiânia
Januária
Montes Claros
Corinto
Uberaba
Diamantina
Teófilo Otoni
Mucuri
Itabuna
Ilhéus
PTA. DE SANTO ANTÔNIO

E

VOLCÁN MISTI 19098
Puno
NEVADO ILLIMANI 20873
La Paz
Cochabamba
Oruro
Santa Cruz
BOLIVIA
Sucre
Potosí
Corumbá
Campo Grande
Maracaju
Bauru
Araraquara
Campinas
Belo Horizonte
Ouro Prêto
PICO DA BANDEIRA 9482
Juiz de Fora
PTA. DA BALEIA
PTA. DO MONSARÁS
Campos
C. DE SÃO TOMÉ
Petrópolis
C. FRIO

20°
Mollendo
Moquegua
Arequipa
Tacna
Arica
Pisagua
Iquique
Tarija
Pulacayo
B R A Z I L I A N H I G H L A N D S
Puerto Casado
Concepción
Asunción
PARAGUAY
Laranjeiras do Sul
Coronel Oviedo
Ponta Grossa
Ourinhos
São Paulo
Curitiba
Santos
Rio de Janeiro
Niterói

Tropic of Capricorn

Tocopila
PTA. ANGAMOS
Mejillones
PTA. TETAS
Antofagasta
Taltal
CERRO TINTE 19190
Calama
San Salvador de Jujuy
VOLCÁN LLULLAILLACO 22057
Salta
San Miguel de Tucumán
CERRO OJOS DEL SALADO 22516
Catamarca
Santiago del Estero
Formosa
Resistencia
Corrientes
Goya
Mercedes
Posadas
Passo Fundo
Itaquí
Caazapá
Villarrica
Campos Novos
Florianópolis

Tropic of Capricorn

F

Chañaral
PTA. MORRO
Caldera
Vallenar
C. BASCUÑÁN
La Serena
Coquimbo
Ovalle
CERRO ACONCAGUA 22881
Deán Funes
San Juan
LA RIOJA
SALINAS GRANDES
Córdoba
Santa Fe
Paraná
Santa María
Santa Maria
Rivera
Salto
Paysandú
Mercedes
C. SANTA MARTA GRANDE
Pôrto Alegre
Rio Grande
URUGUAY
Pelotas

30°
SAN FÉLIX (CHILE)
SAN AMBROSIO (CHILE)
ISLAS JUAN FERNÁNDEZ (CHILE)
ALEJANDRO SELKIRK
ROBINSON CRUSOE
San Felipe
Viña del Mar
Valparaíso
Rancagua
Santiago
San Fernando
Curicó
Talca
Mendoza
San Luis
Río Cuarto
Rosario
Mercedes
San José de Mayo
Minas
Rocha
Montevideo
La Plata
Buenos Aires

G

Cauquenes
Talcahuano
PTA. LAVAPIE
Lota
Linares
Chillán
Concepción
Angol
Neuquén
Santa Rosa
Azul
Bolívar
Tandil
L. dos Patos
L. Mirim
C. SAN ANTONIO
PTA. MOGOTES
Mar del Plata

Temuco
VOLCÁN LANÍN 12389
PTA. GALERA
Valdivia
Osorno
Lebu
General Acha
Tres Arroyos
Bahía Blanca

40°

H

Puerto Montt
Ancud
ISLA DE CHILOÉ
Castro
ARCHIPIÉLAGO DE MAGDALENA
LOS CHONOS
San Carlos de Bariloche
Esquel
PTA. RASA
Viedma
Golfo San Matías
PENÍNSULA VALDÉS
Trelew
Rawson
A t l a n t i c
O c e a n

PENÍNSULA DE TAITAO
MT. SAN VALENTÍN 13314
Puerto Aisén
C. DOS BAHÍAS
Comodoro Rivadavia
Golfo San Jorge
C. TRES PUNTAS

50°
WELLINGTON
MONTE FITZ ROY 11073
San Julián
C. DESENGAÑO
Puerto Natales
Río Gallegos
C. VÍRGENES
Punta Arenas
FALKLAND ISLANDS (ISLAS MALVINAS) (BR.)
Stanley
SHAG ROCKS
SOUTH GEORGIA (FALKLAND IS.)

I

MONTE SARMIENTO 7546
GRANDE DE TIERRA DEL FUEGO
Ushuaia
NAVARINO
CAPE HORN
Longitude West of Greenwich

B-540000-21 -3- 17ª
COSMO SERIES SO. AMERICA
Copyright by
RAND McNALLY & COMPANY
Made in U.S.A.

Sinusoidal Projection

Statute Miles 100 0 100 300 500 700

Kilometers 100 0 100 300 500 700 900 1100

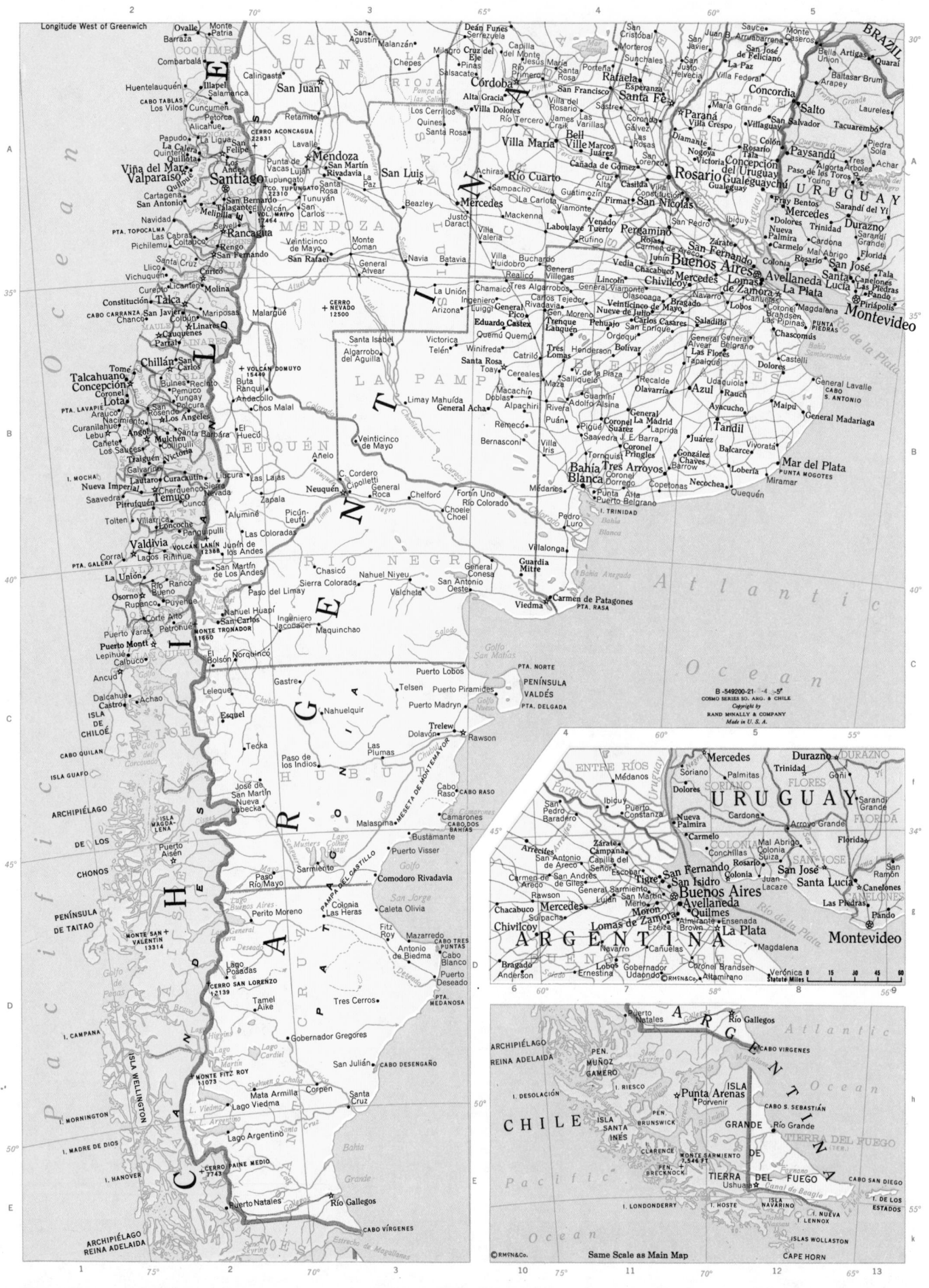

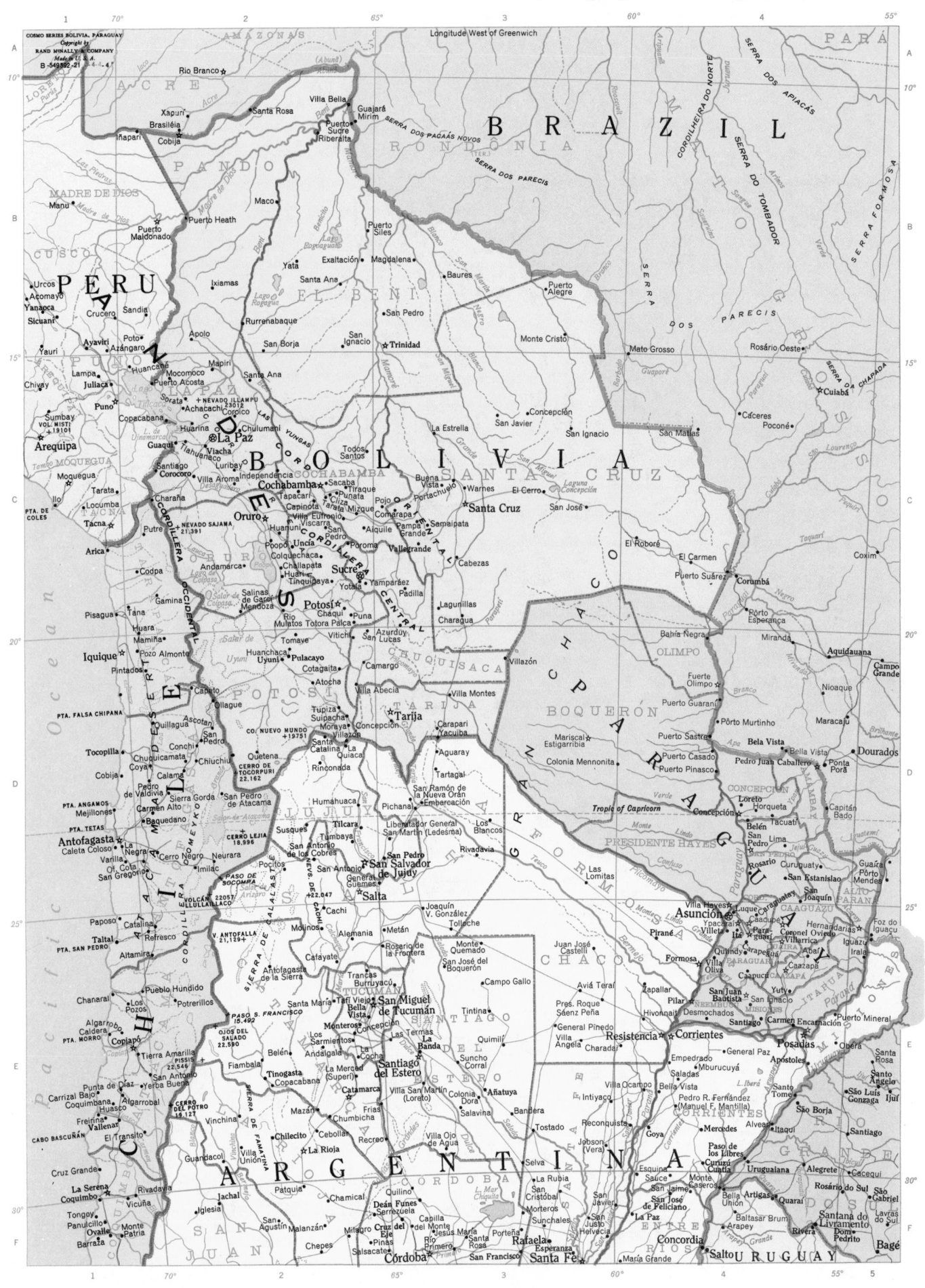

Oblique Conic Conformal Projection

Statute Miles
50   0   50   100   150

Kilometers
50 0 50 100 150 200

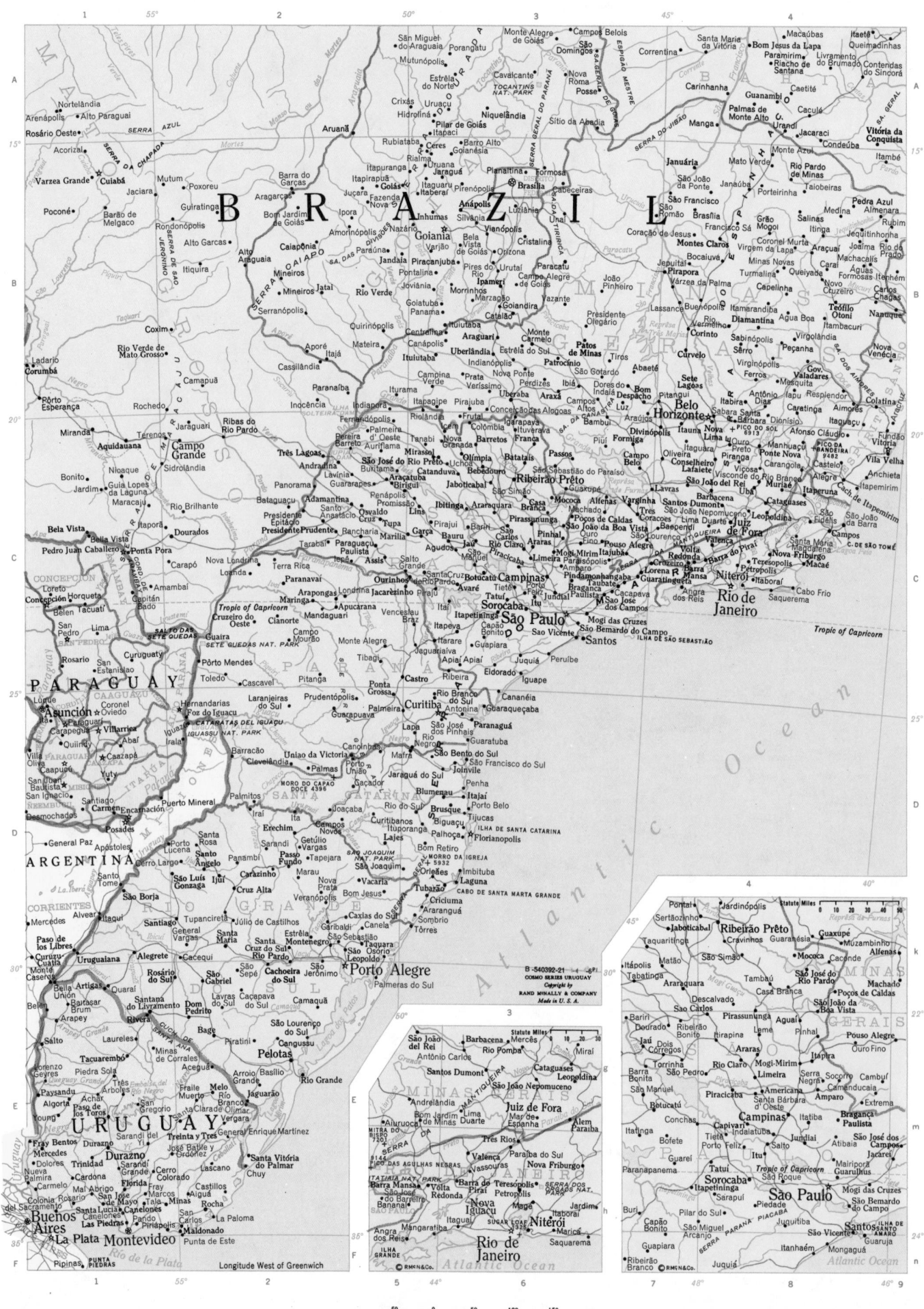

Oblique Conic Conformal Projection

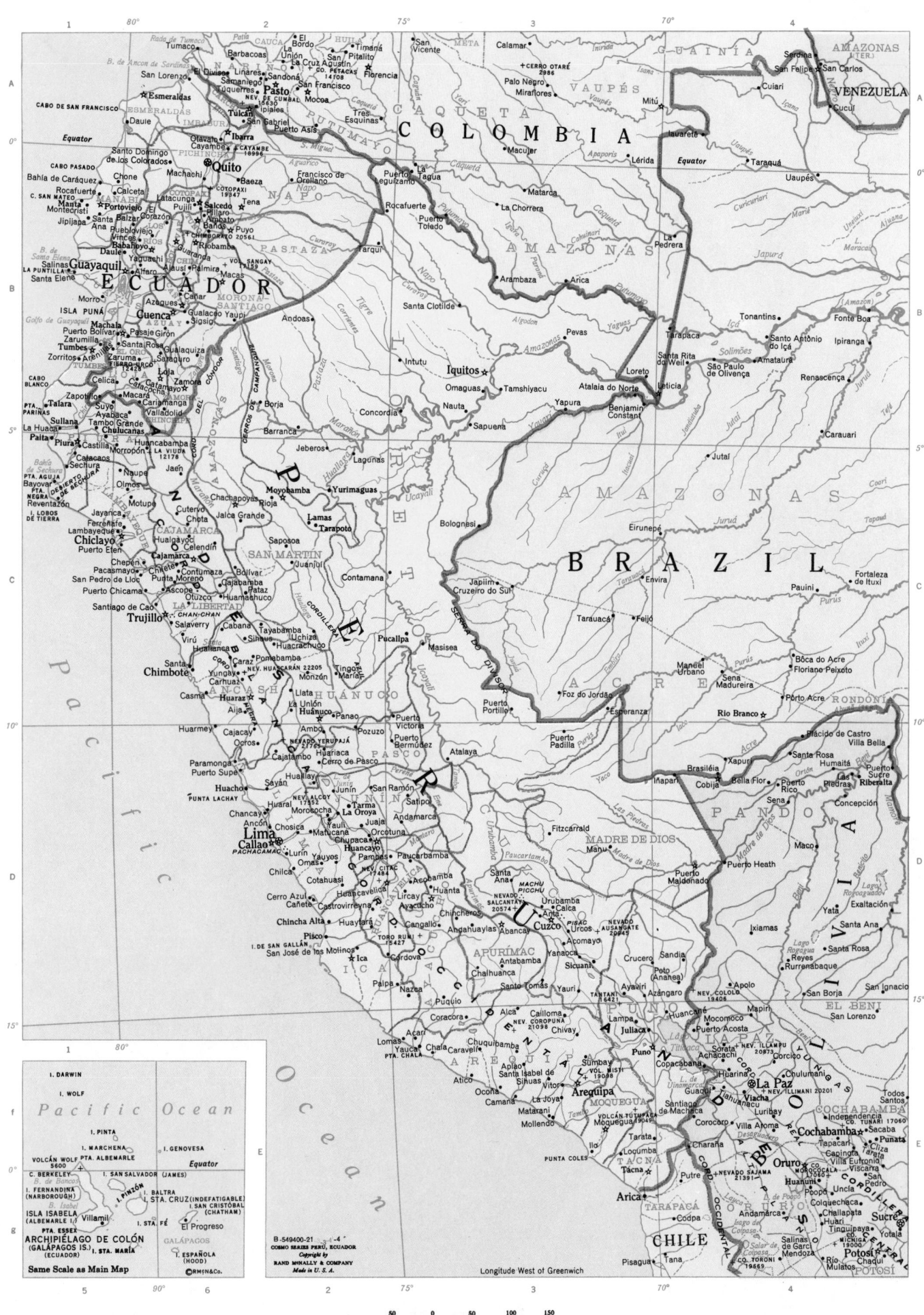

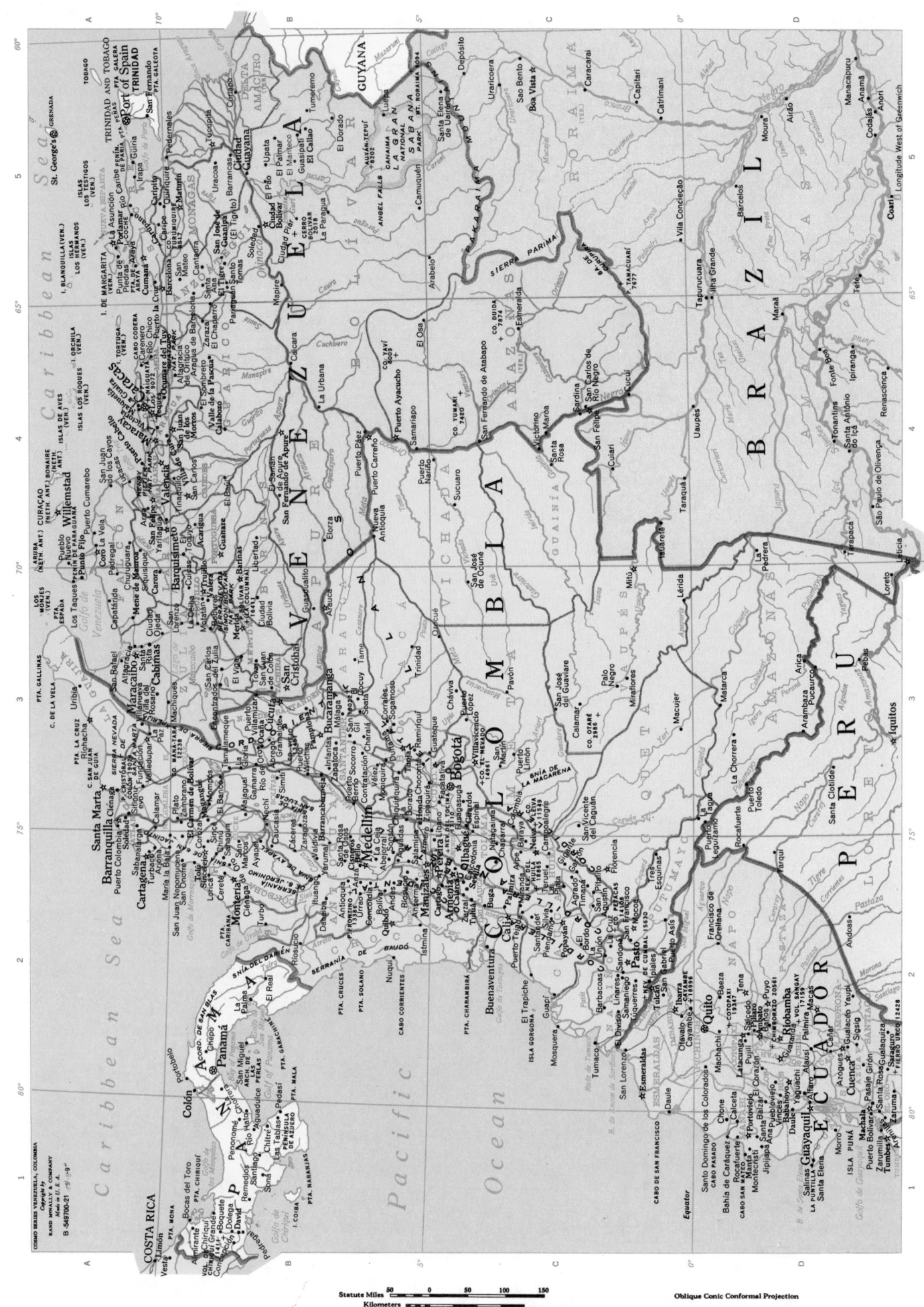

Statute Miles
50   0   50   100   150
Kilometers
50   0   50   100   150   200

Oblique Conic Conformal Projection

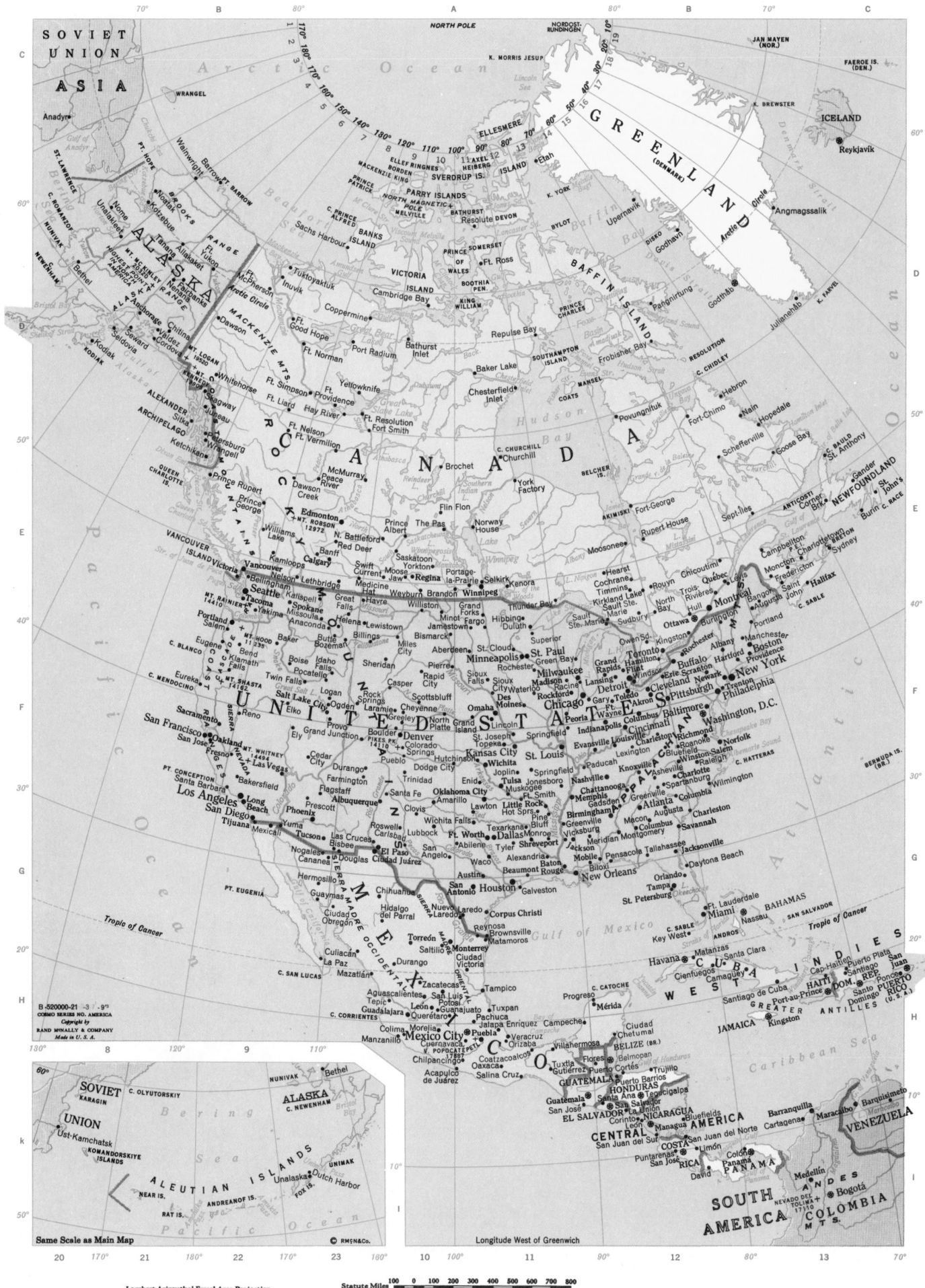

SOVIET UNION
ASIA

GREENLAND
(DENMARK)

ICELAND
Reykjavík

CANADA

ALASKA

UNITED STATES

MEXICO

CENTRAL AMERICA

WEST INDIES

CUBA

HAITI

JAMAICA

GUATEMALA
HONDURAS
EL SALVADOR
NICARAGUA
COSTA RICA
PANAMA

SOUTH AMERICA
COLOMBIA
VENEZUELA

SOVIET UNION
ALASKA
ALEUTIAN ISLANDS

Same Scale as Main Map

Longitude West of Greenwich

Lambert Azimuthal Equal Area Projection

Statute Miles
Kilometers

B-520000-21 -3 -9°
CORMO SERIES NO. AMERICA
Copyright by
RAND MCNALLY & COMPANY
Made in U.S.A.

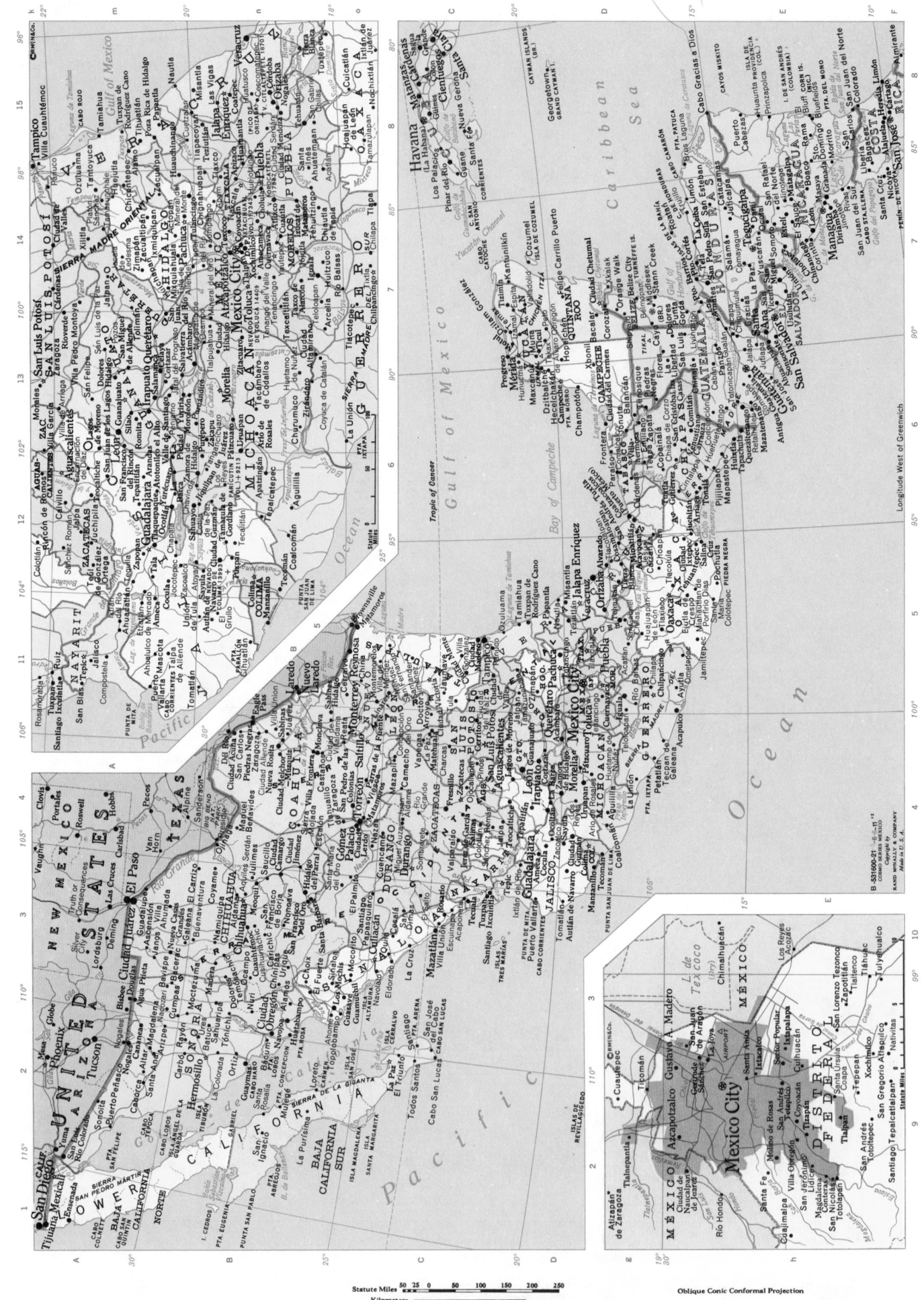

Statute Miles 50 25 0   50   100   150   200   250

Kilometers 50 0   100   200   300

Oblique Conic Conformal Projection

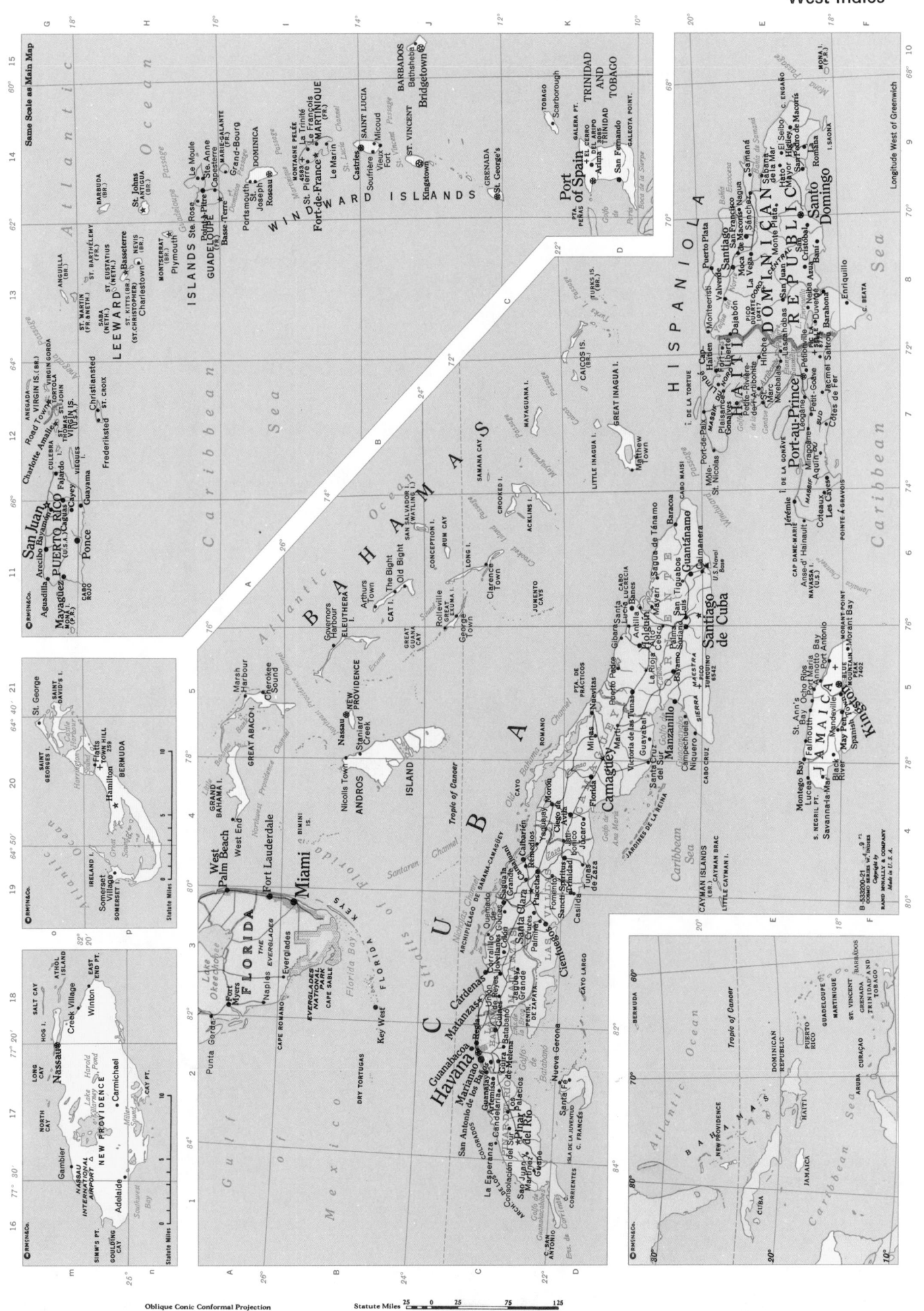

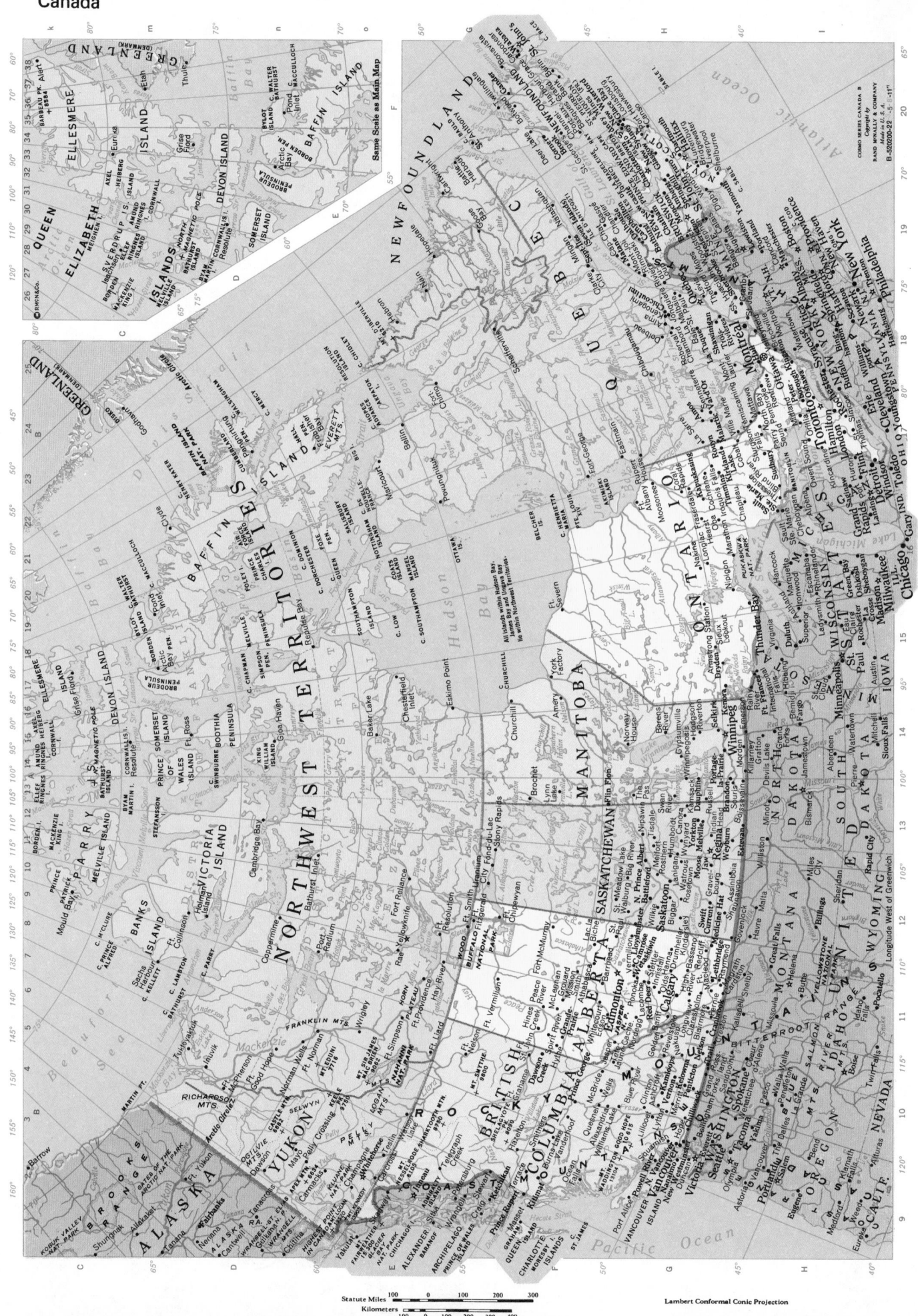

Statute Miles   100   0   100   200   300

Kilometers   100   0   100   200   300   400

Lambert Conformal Conic Projection

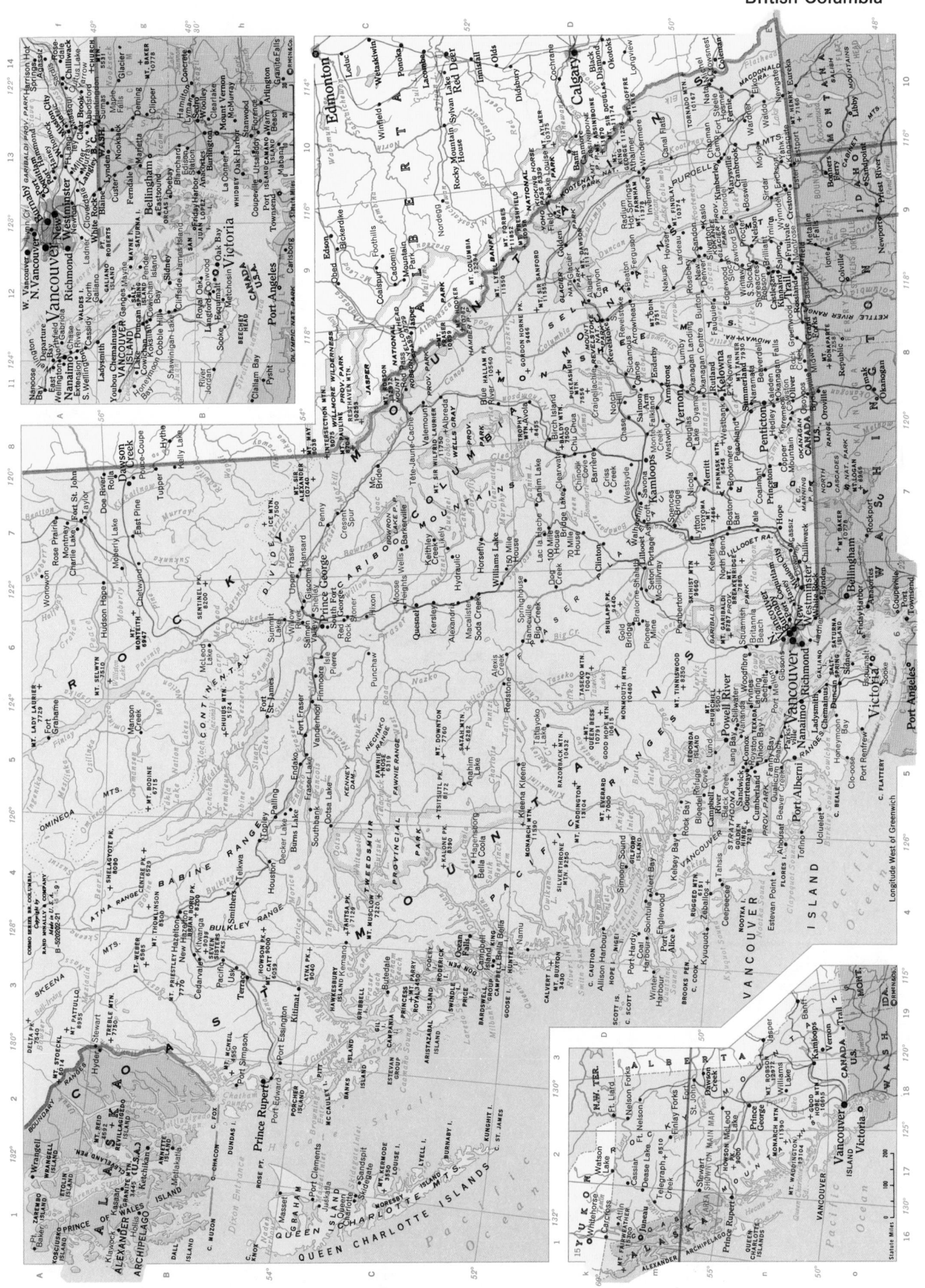

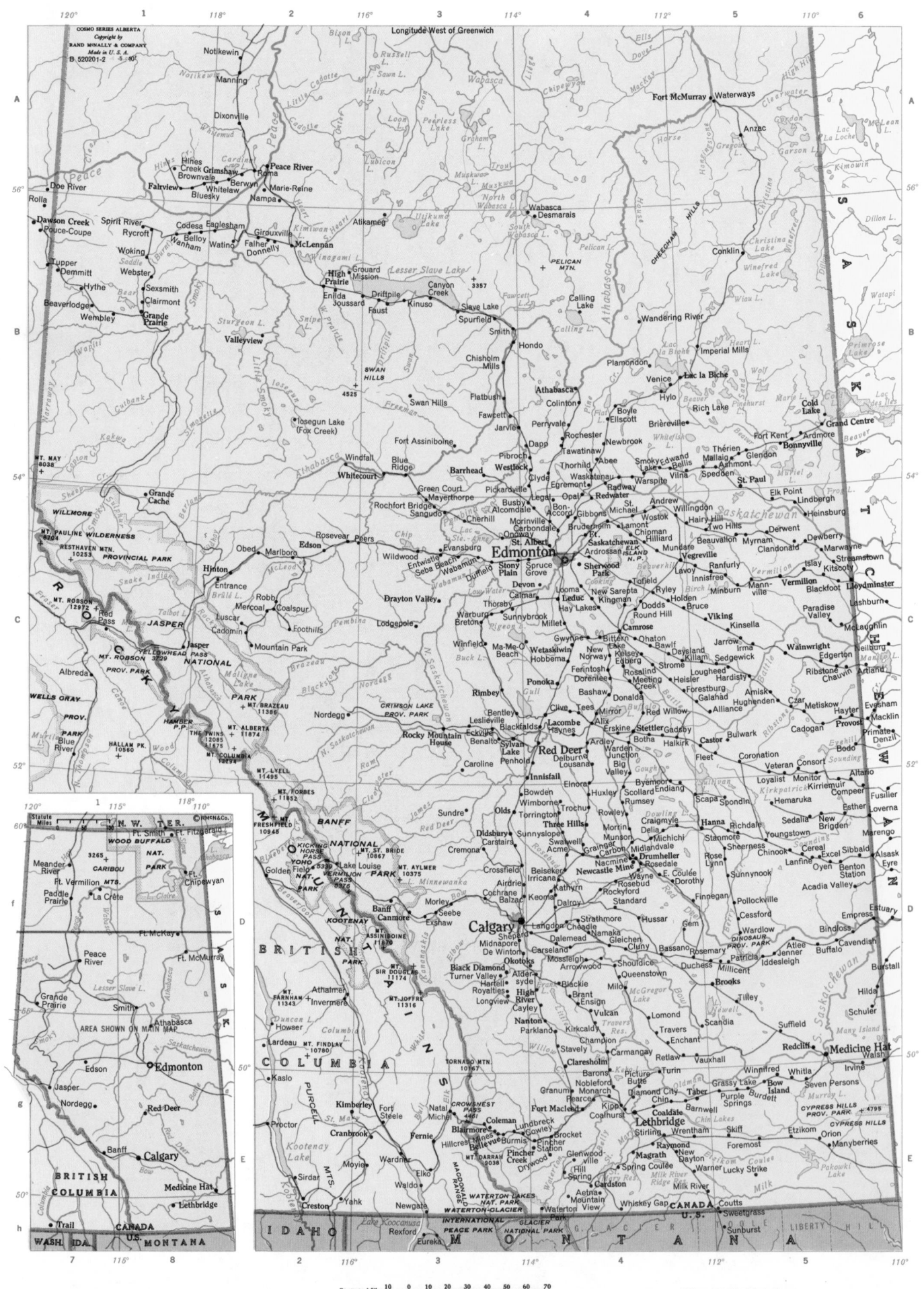

COSMO SERIES ALBERTA
Copyright by
RAND McNALLY & COMPANY
Made in U. S. A.
B 520201-2 4-40

Longitude West of Greenwich

Statute Miles 10 0 10 20 30 40 50 60 70
Kilometers 10 0 10 20 30 40 60 80 100

Oblique Cylindrical Projection

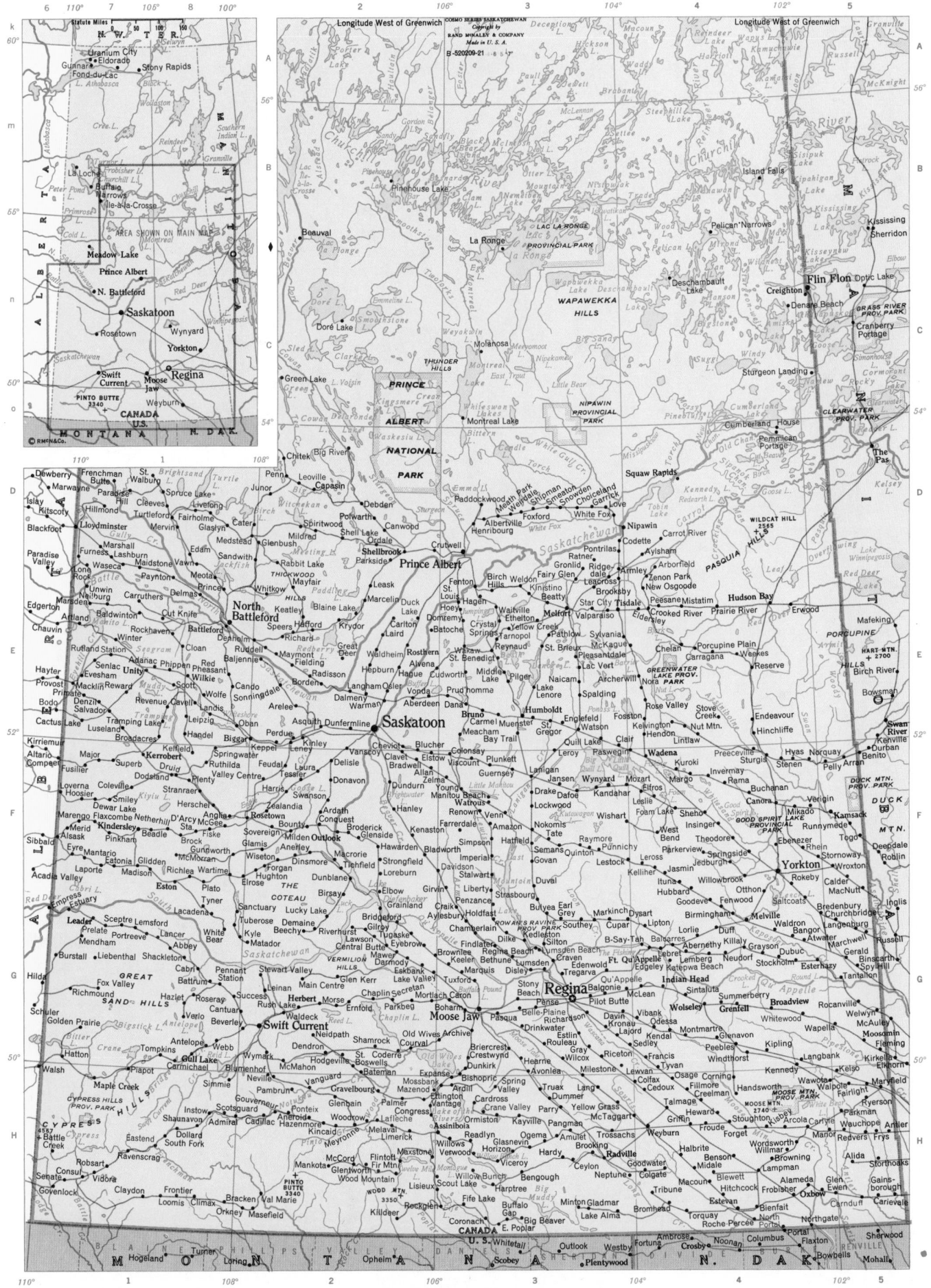

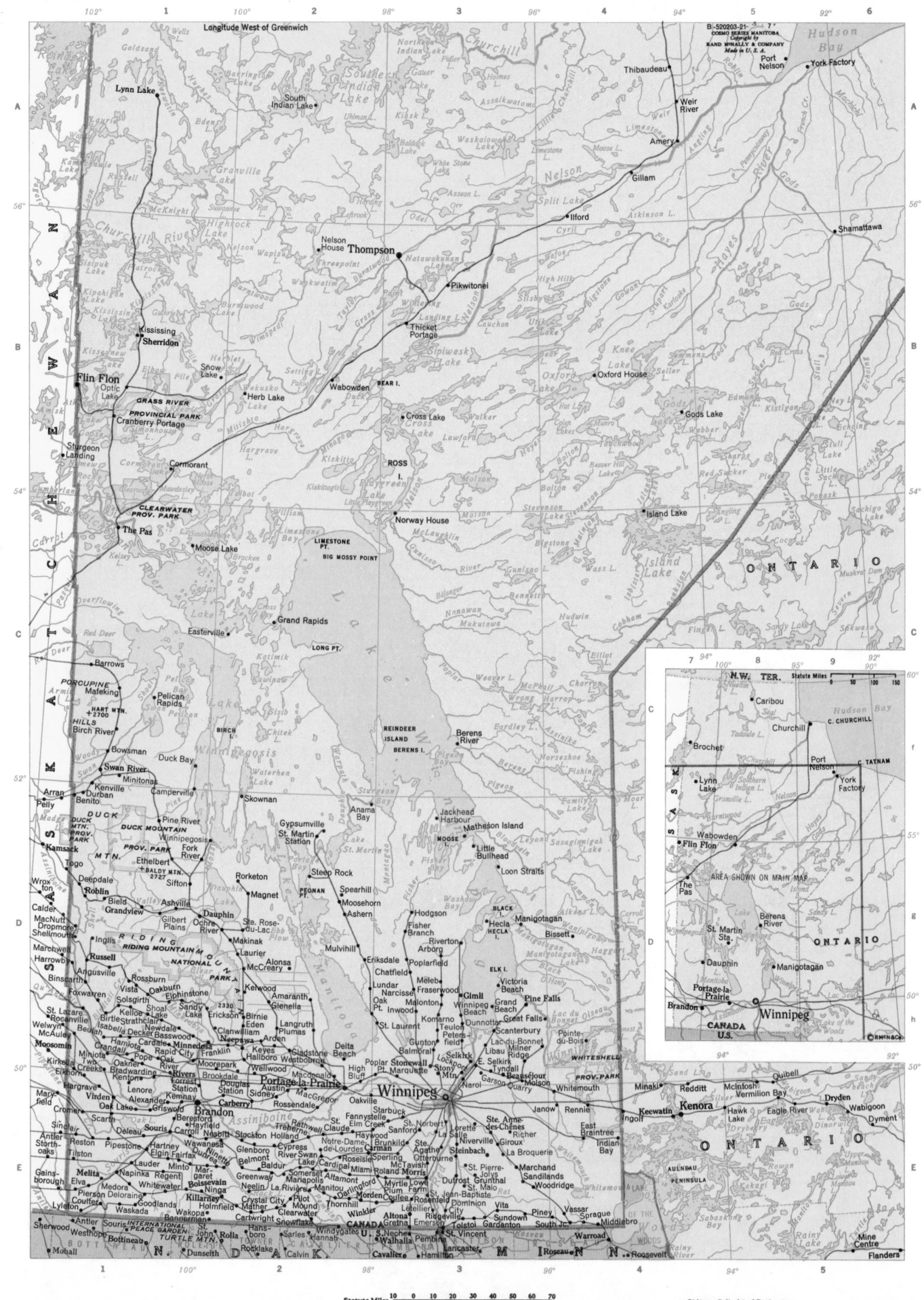

Longitude West of Greenwich

COSMO SERIES MANITOBA
Copyright by
RAND McNALLY & COMPANY
Made in U. S. A.
B-520203-21-

Statute Miles

Oblique Cylindrical Projection

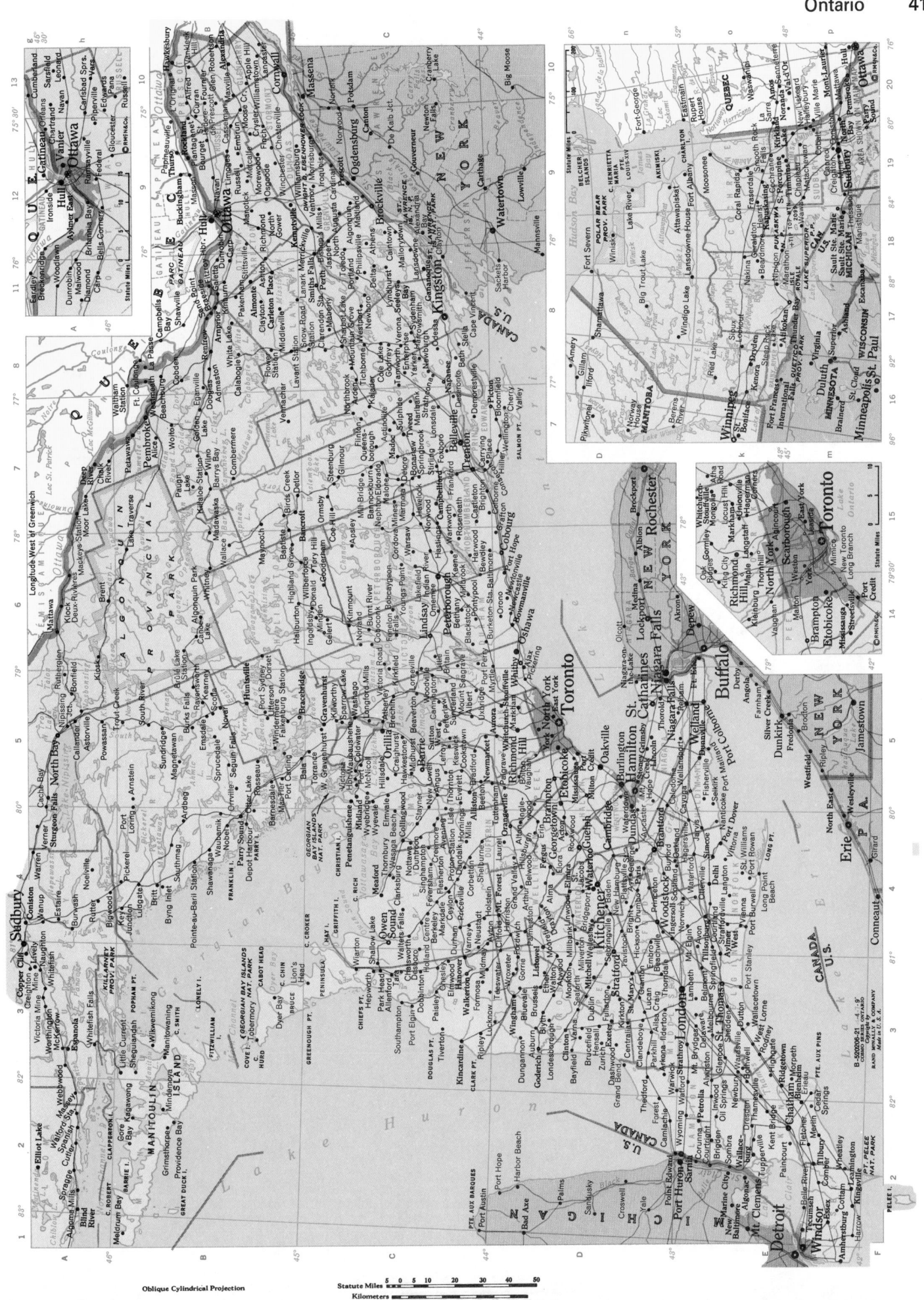

Oblique Cylindrical Projection

Statute Miles 5 0 5 10 20 30 40 50

Kilometers 5 0 5 15 25 35 45 55 65 75

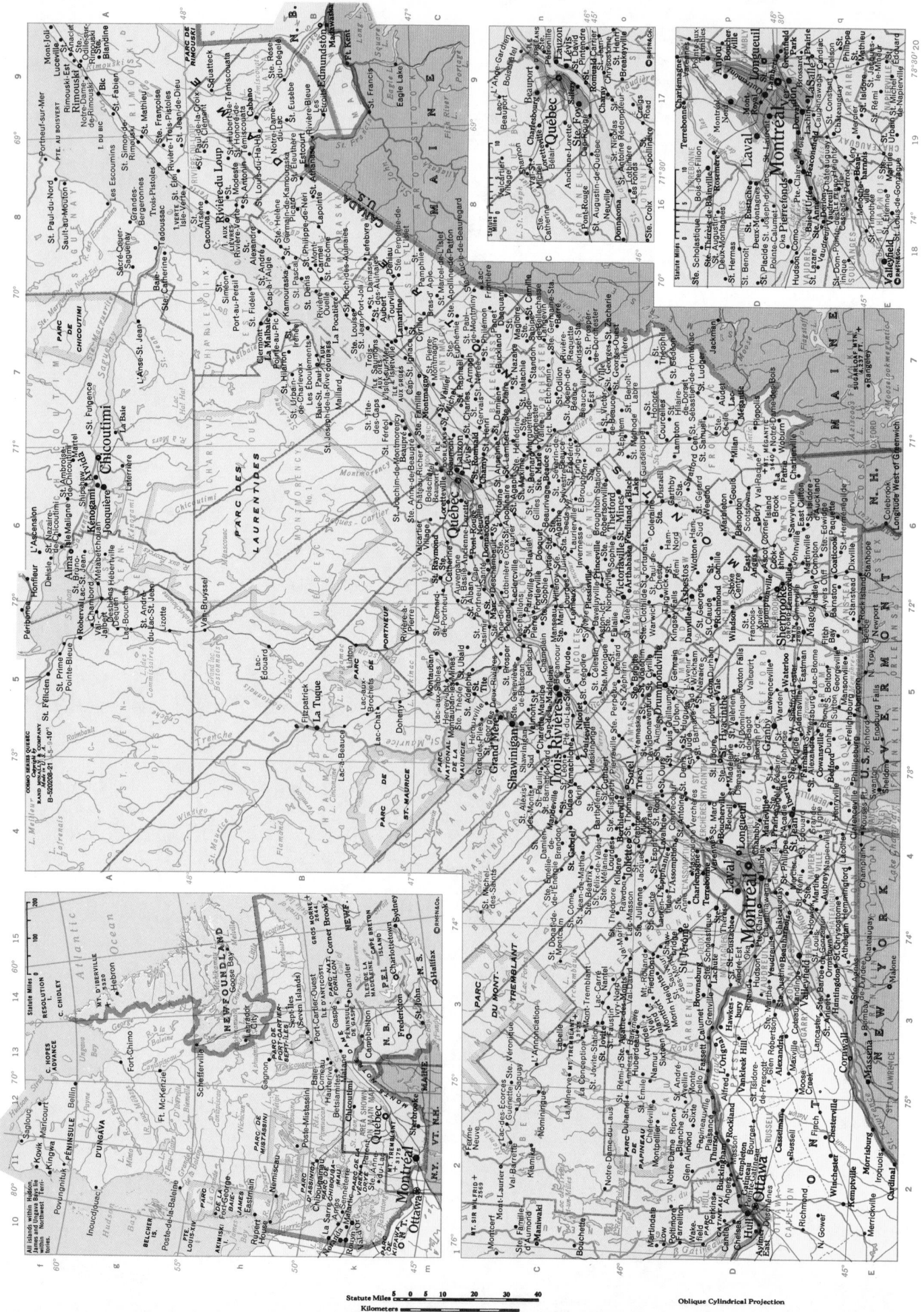

Statute Miles 5 0 5 10   20   30   40
Kilometers 5 0 5 15 25 35 45 55

Oblique Cylindrical Projection

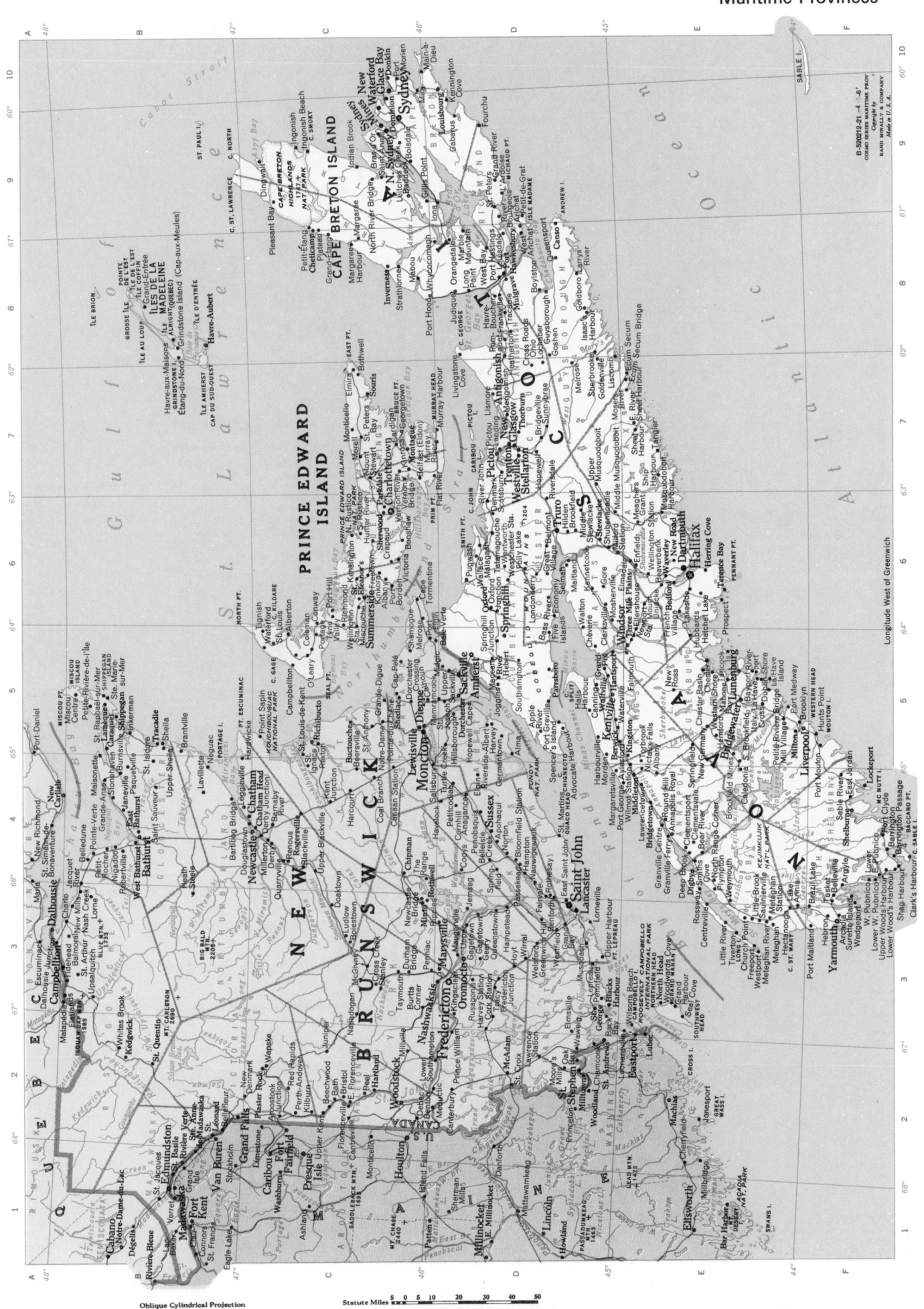

Oblique Cylindrical Projection

Statute Miles
Kilometers

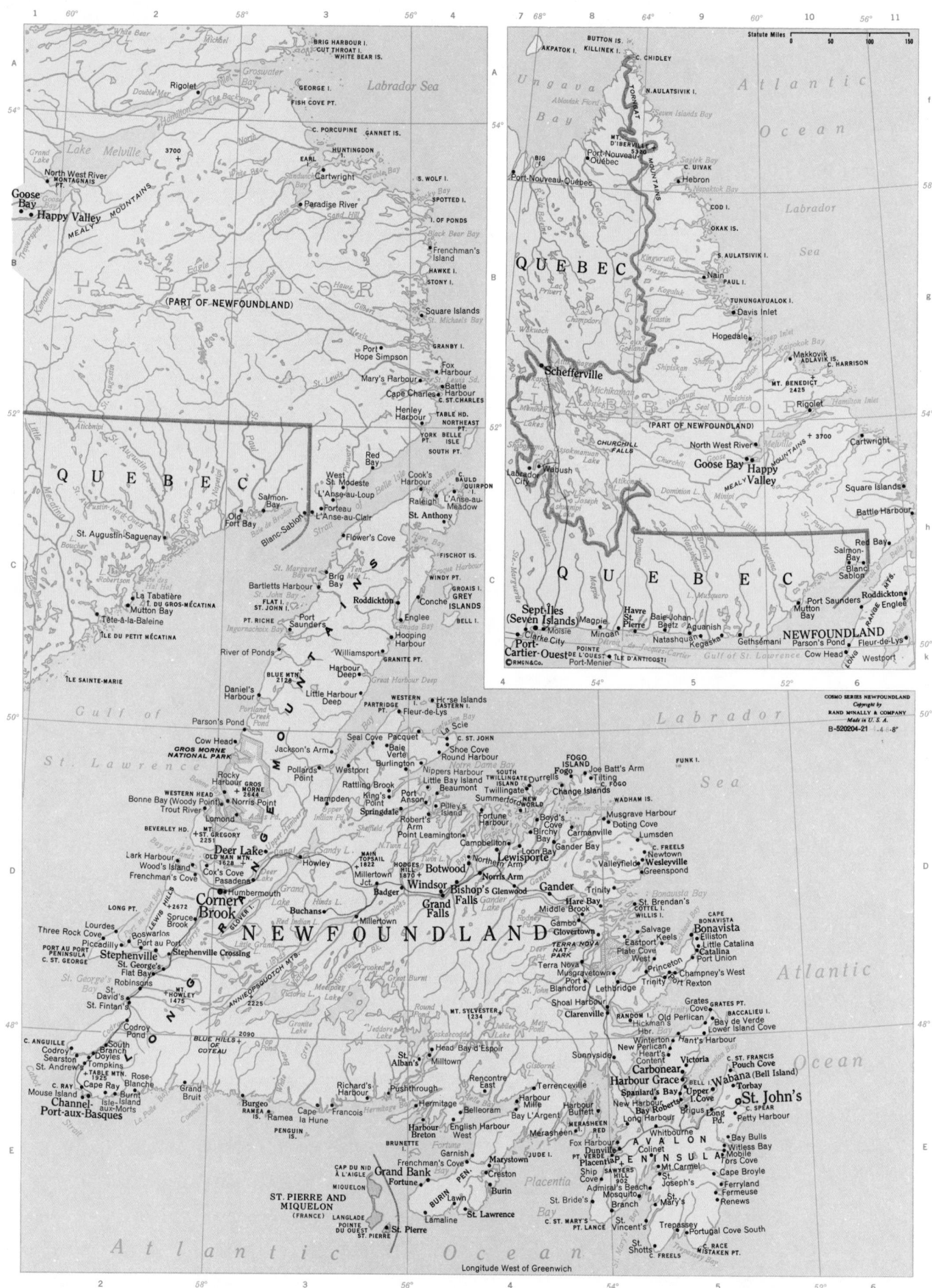

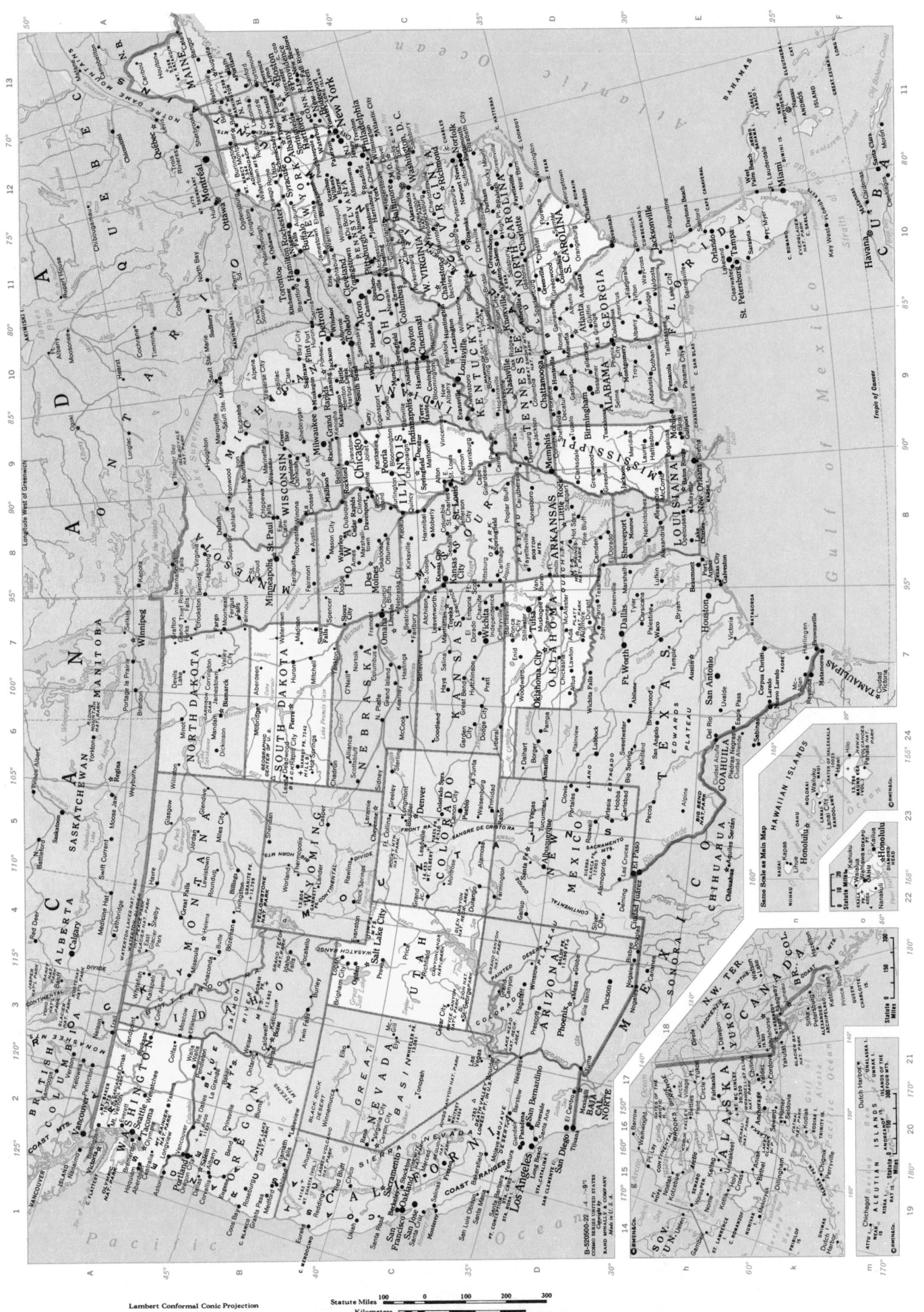

Lambert Conformal Conic Projection

Statute Miles
100   0   100   200   300

Kilometers
100 0 100 200 300 400

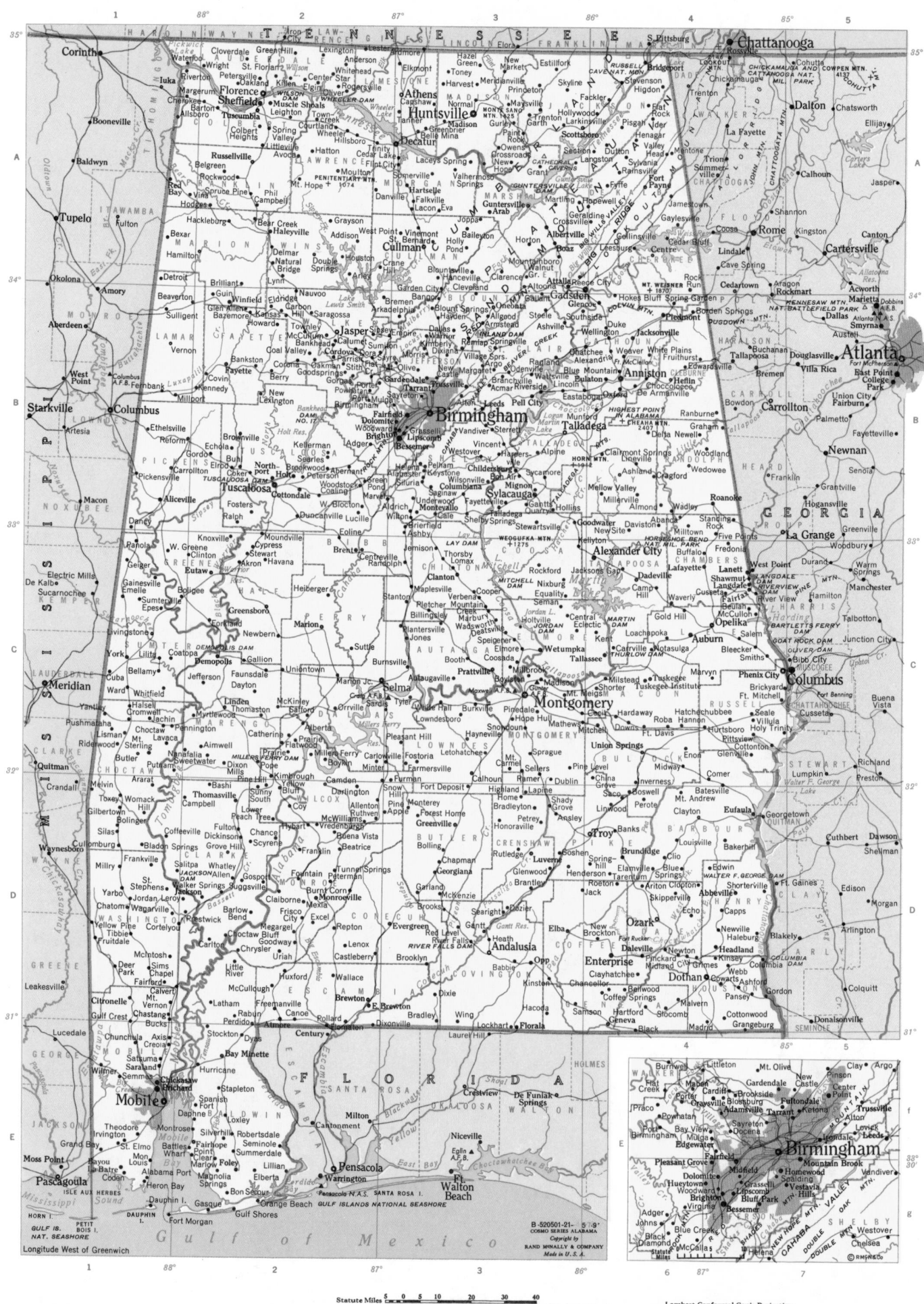

Statute Miles

Kilometers

Lambert Conformal Conic Projection

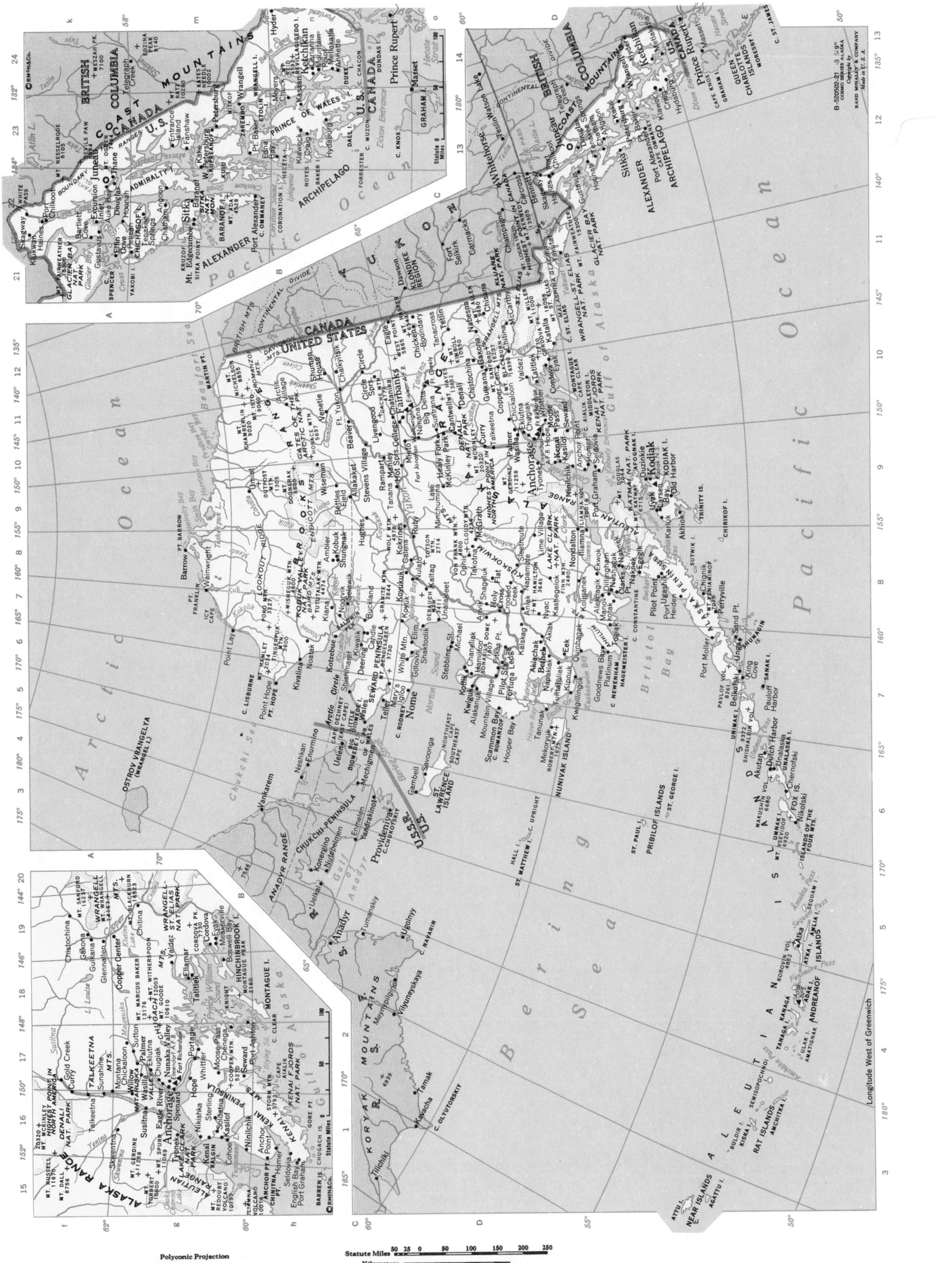

Polyconic Projection

Statute Miles

Kilometers

B-500502-21 -3 59°
COSMO SERIES ALASKA
RAND McNALLY & COMPANY
Made in U.S.A.

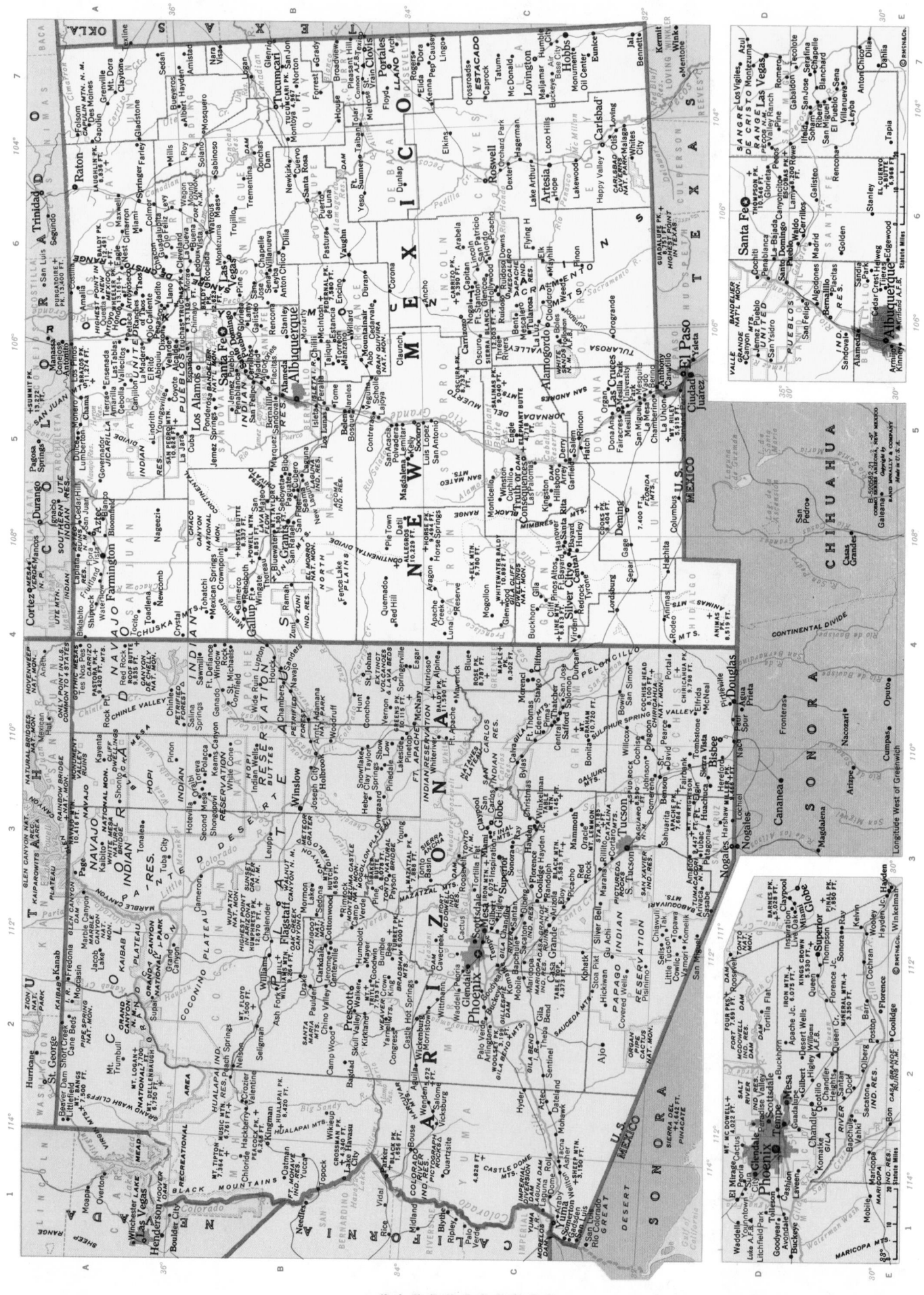

Statute Miles
10 0 0 10 20 30 40 50 60 70 80 90

Kilometers
10 0 10 20 40 60 80 100 120

Lambert Conformal Conic Projection

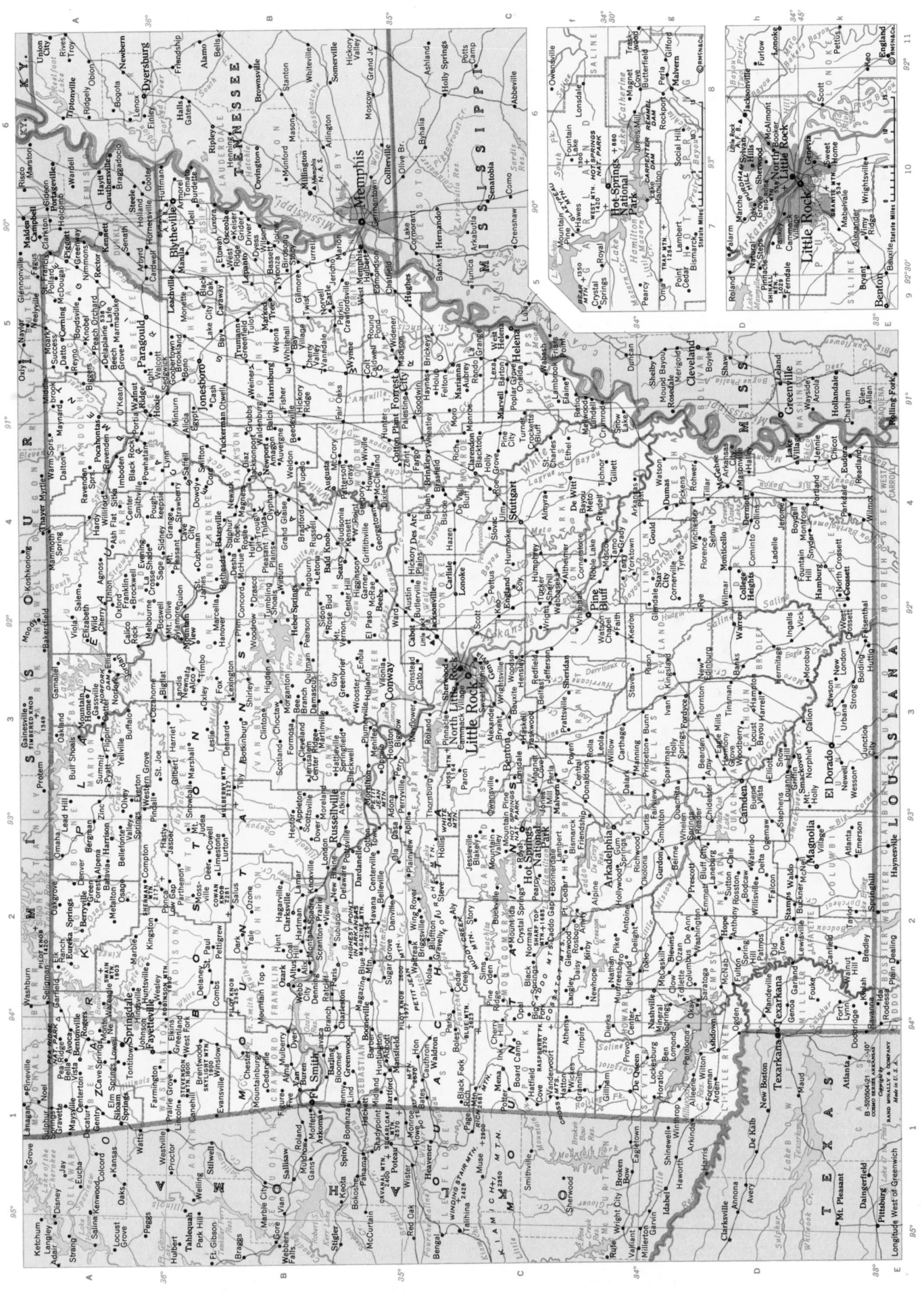

Lambert Conformal Conic Projection

Statute Miles

Kilometers

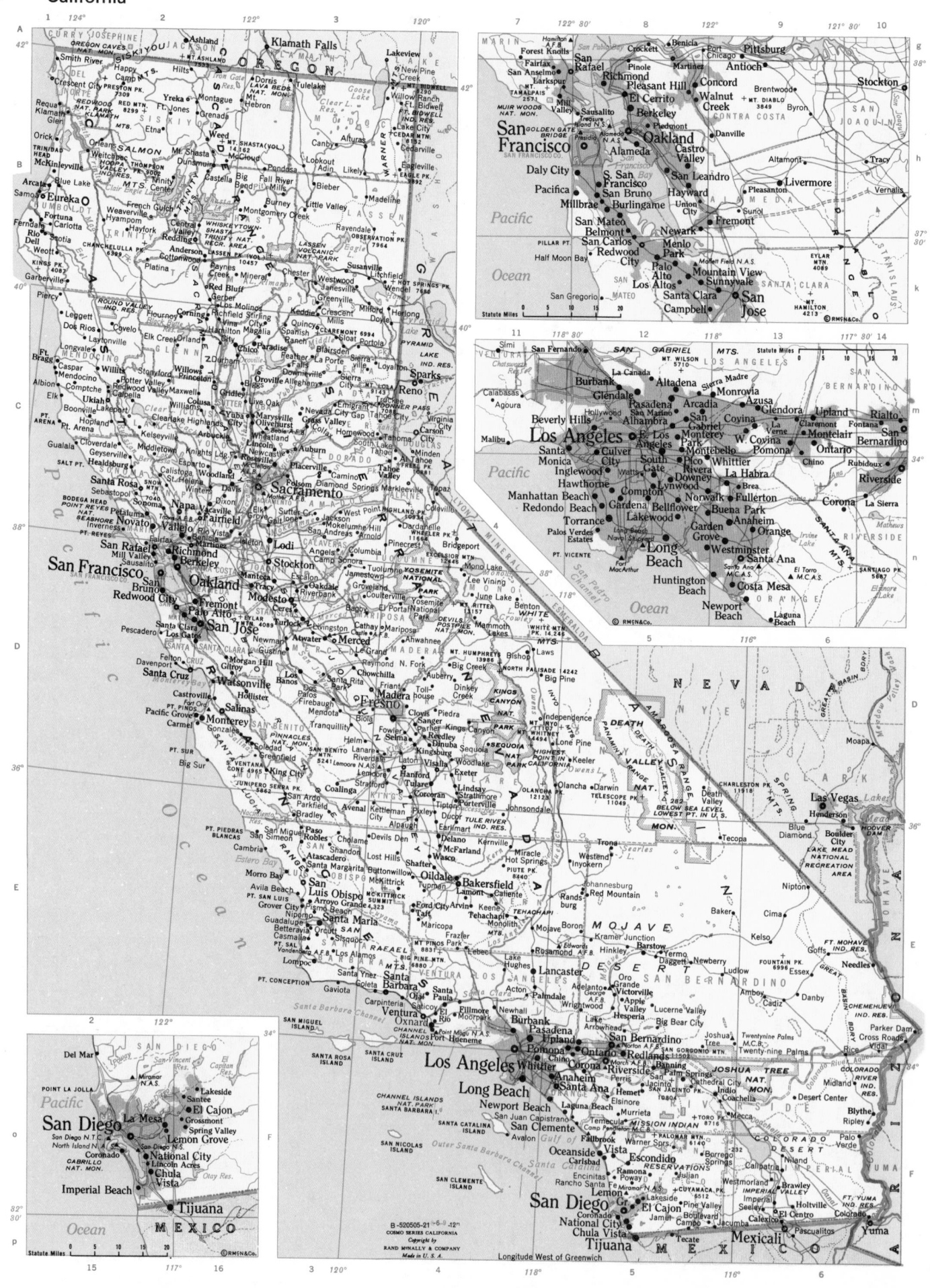

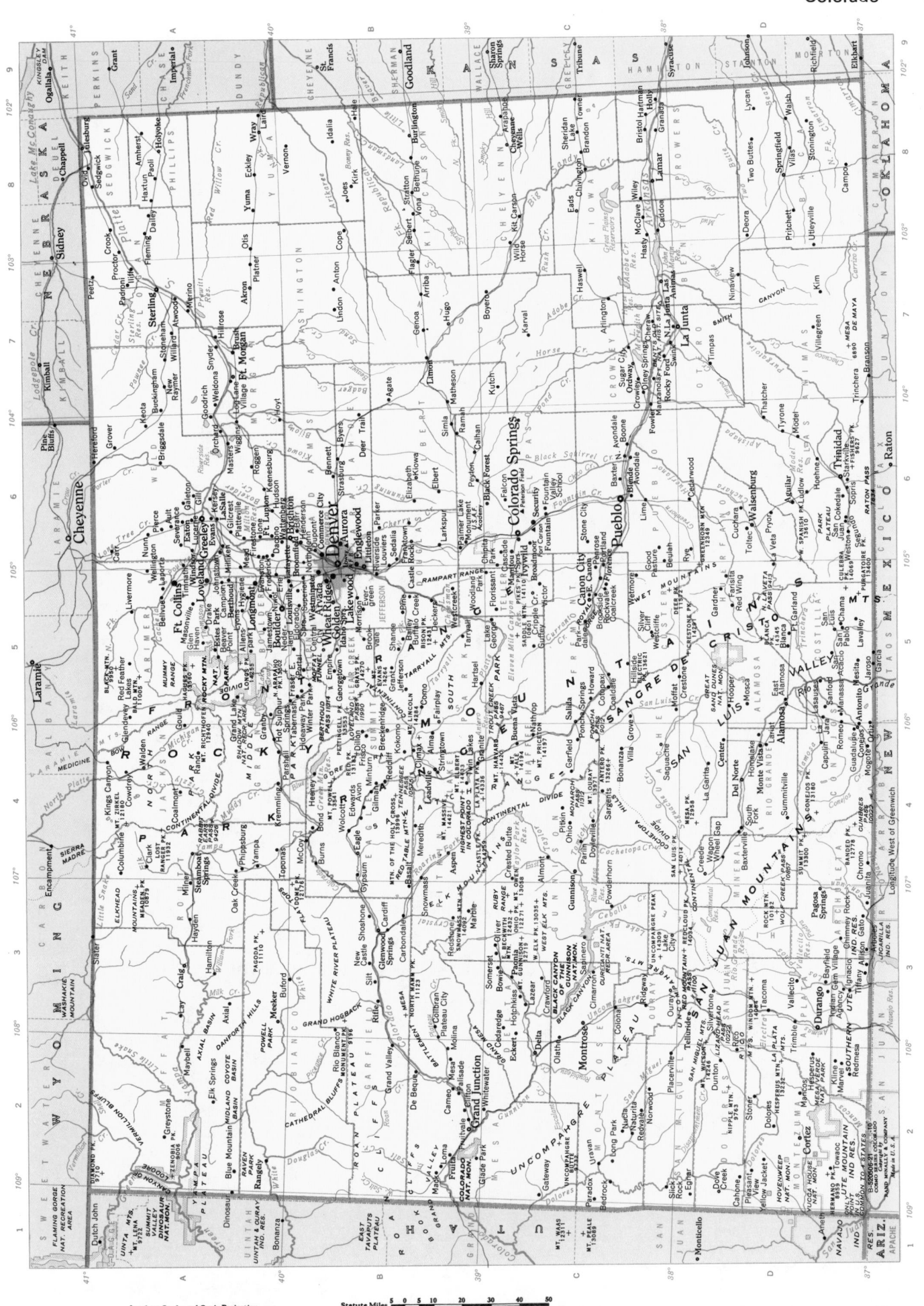

Lambert Conformal Conic Projection

Statute Miles 5 0 5 10 20 30 40 50

Kilometers 5 0 5 15 25 35 45 55 65 75

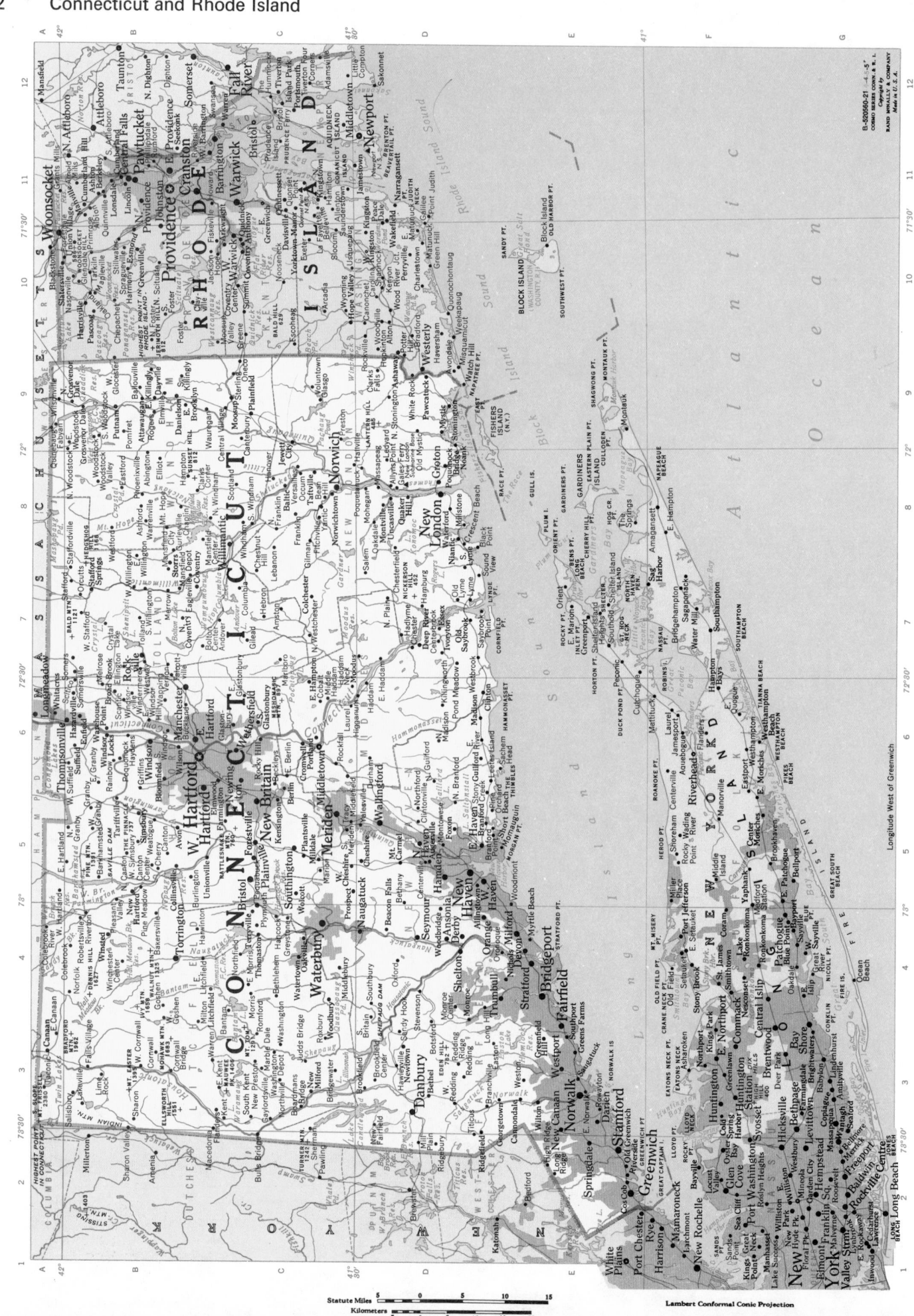

Statute Miles

Kilometers

Lambert Conformal Conic Projection

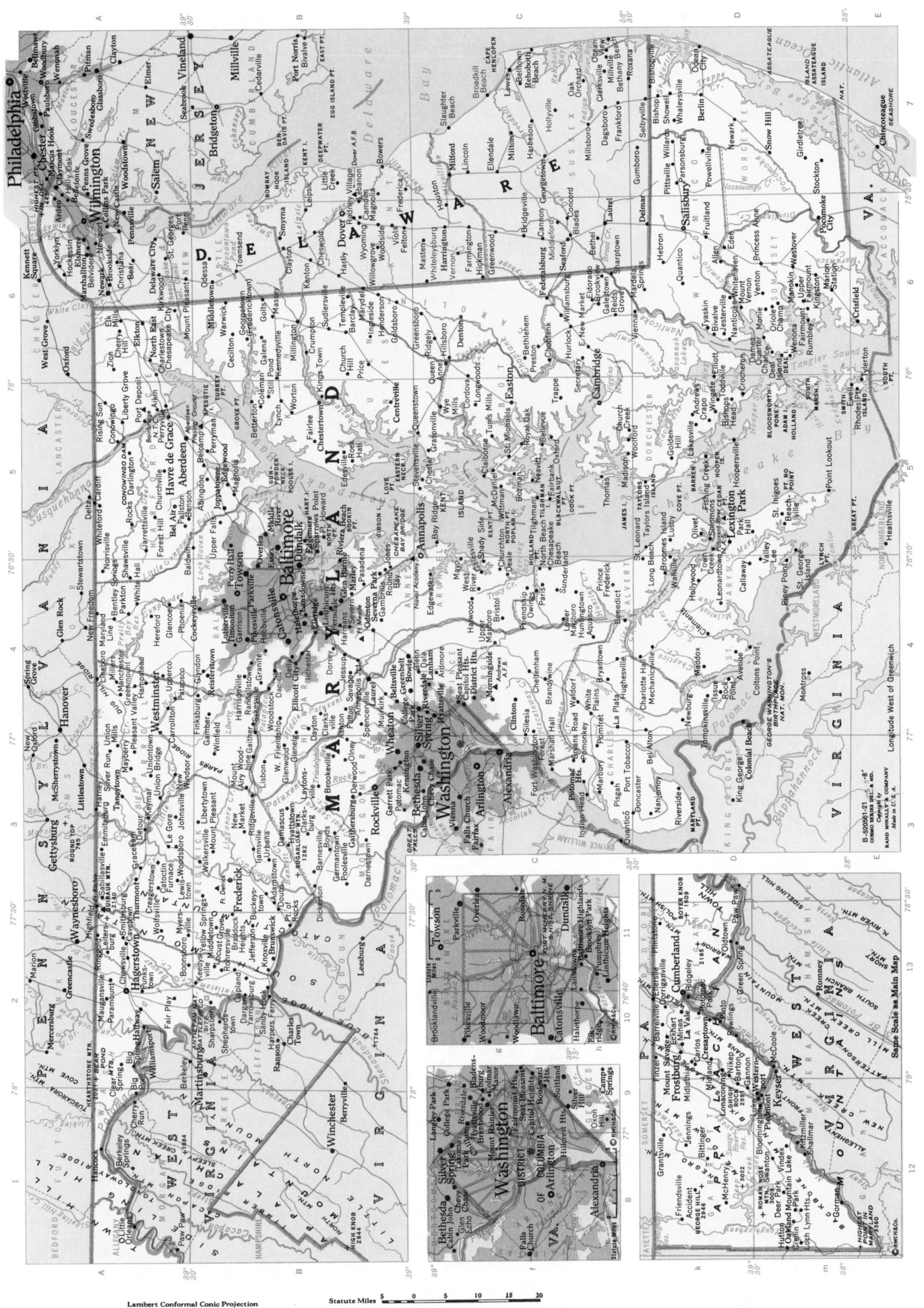

Lambert Conformal Conic Projection

Statute Miles 5 0 5 10 15 20

Kilometers 5 0 5 10 15 20 25 30

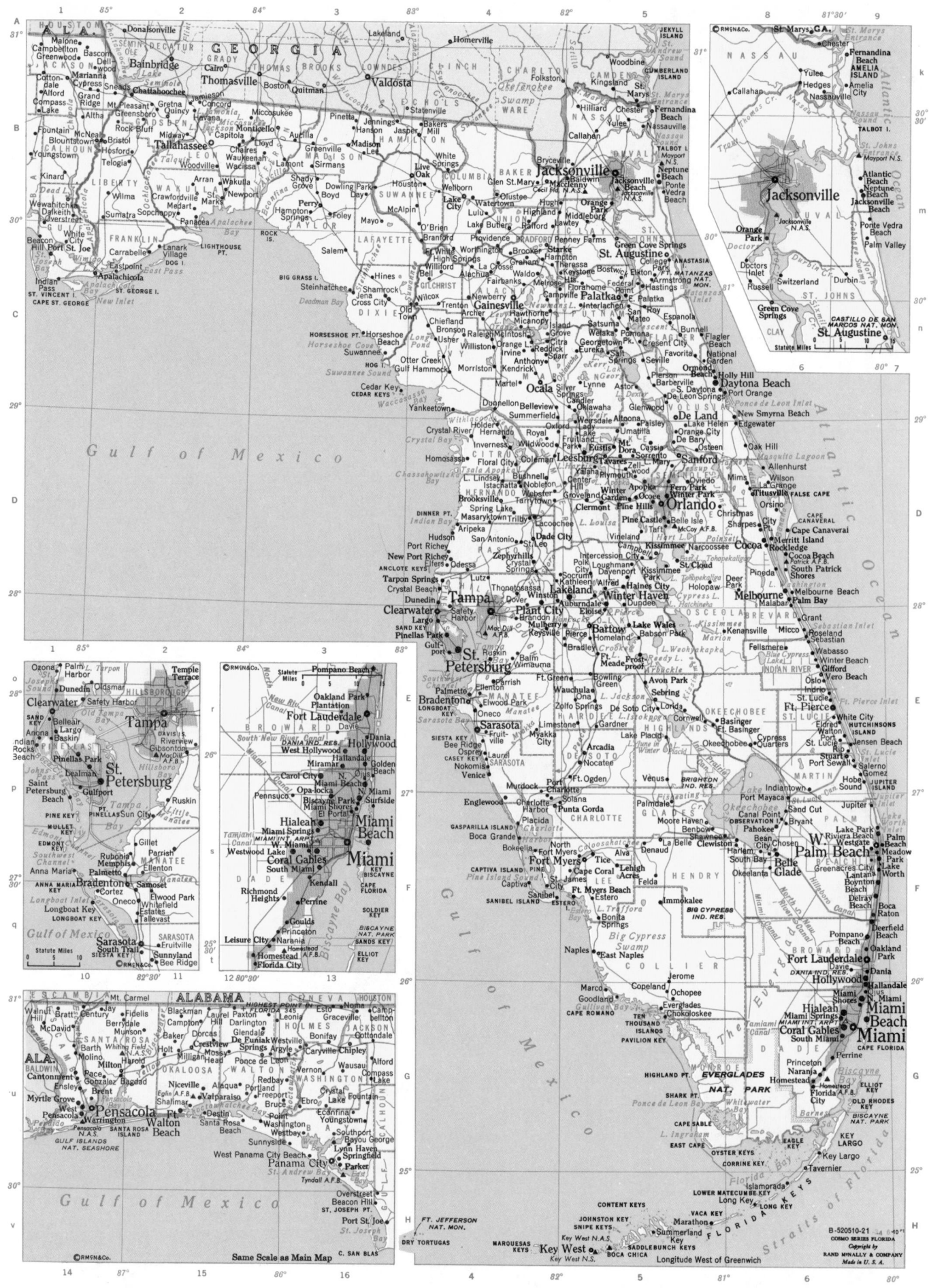

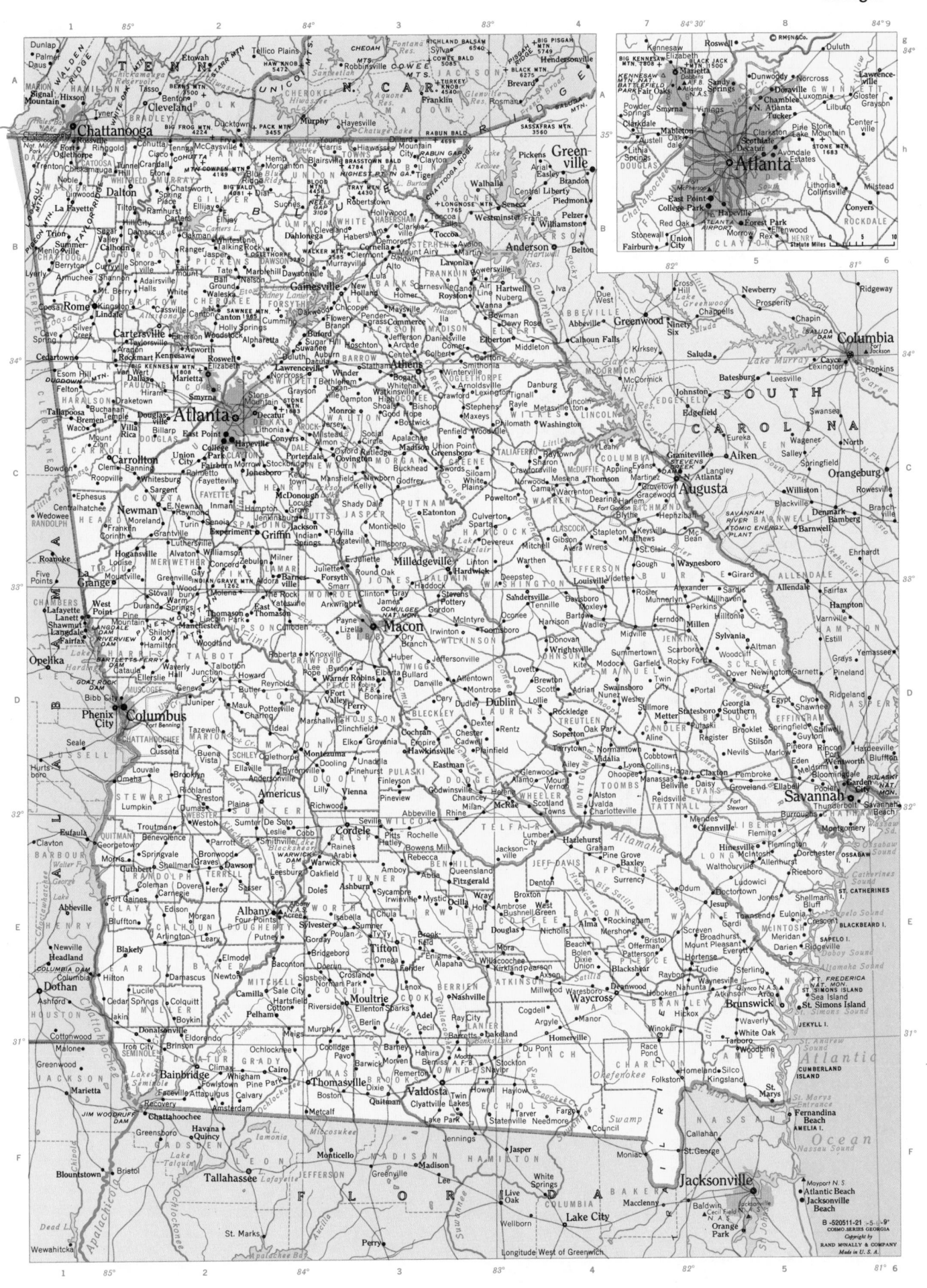

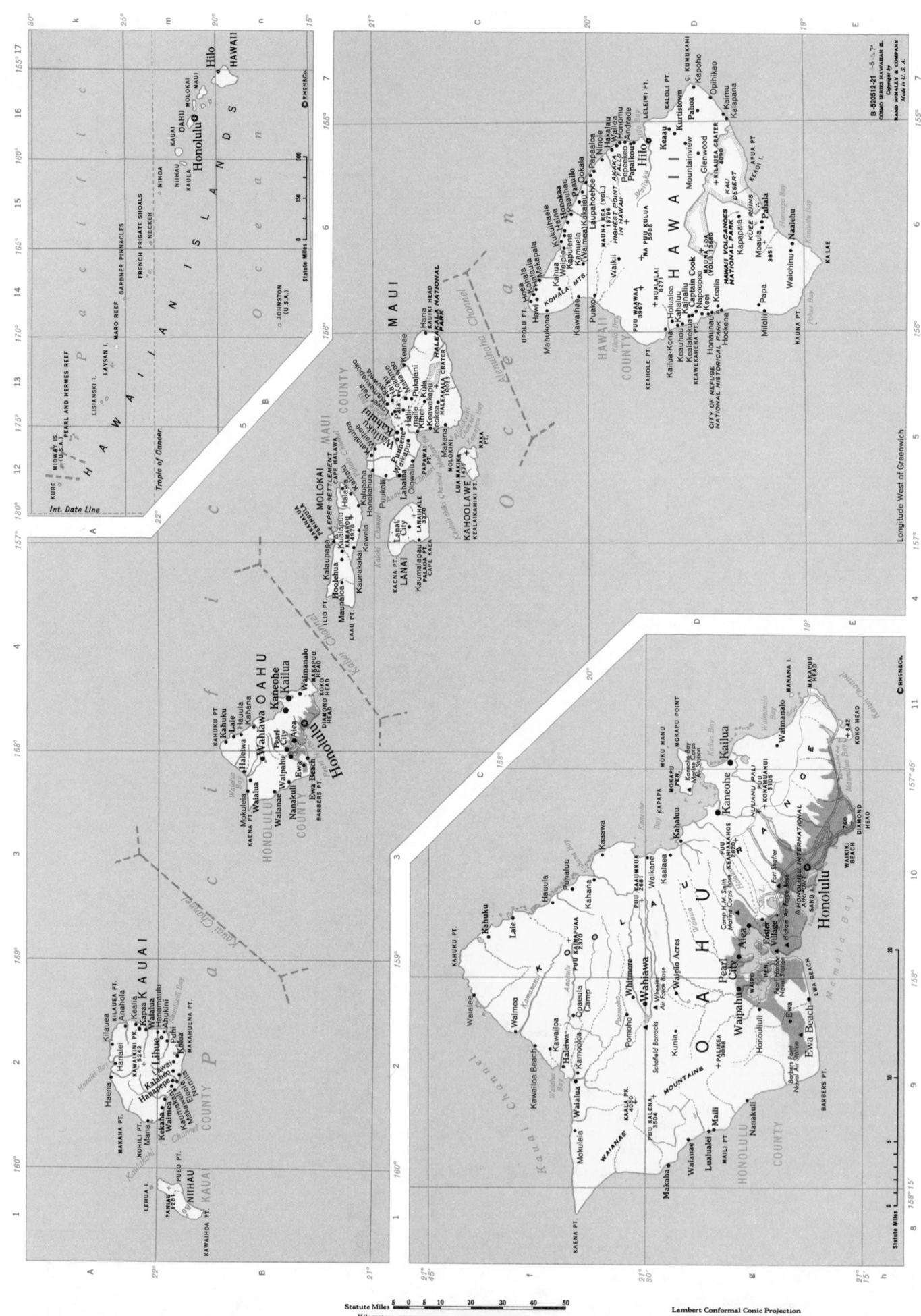

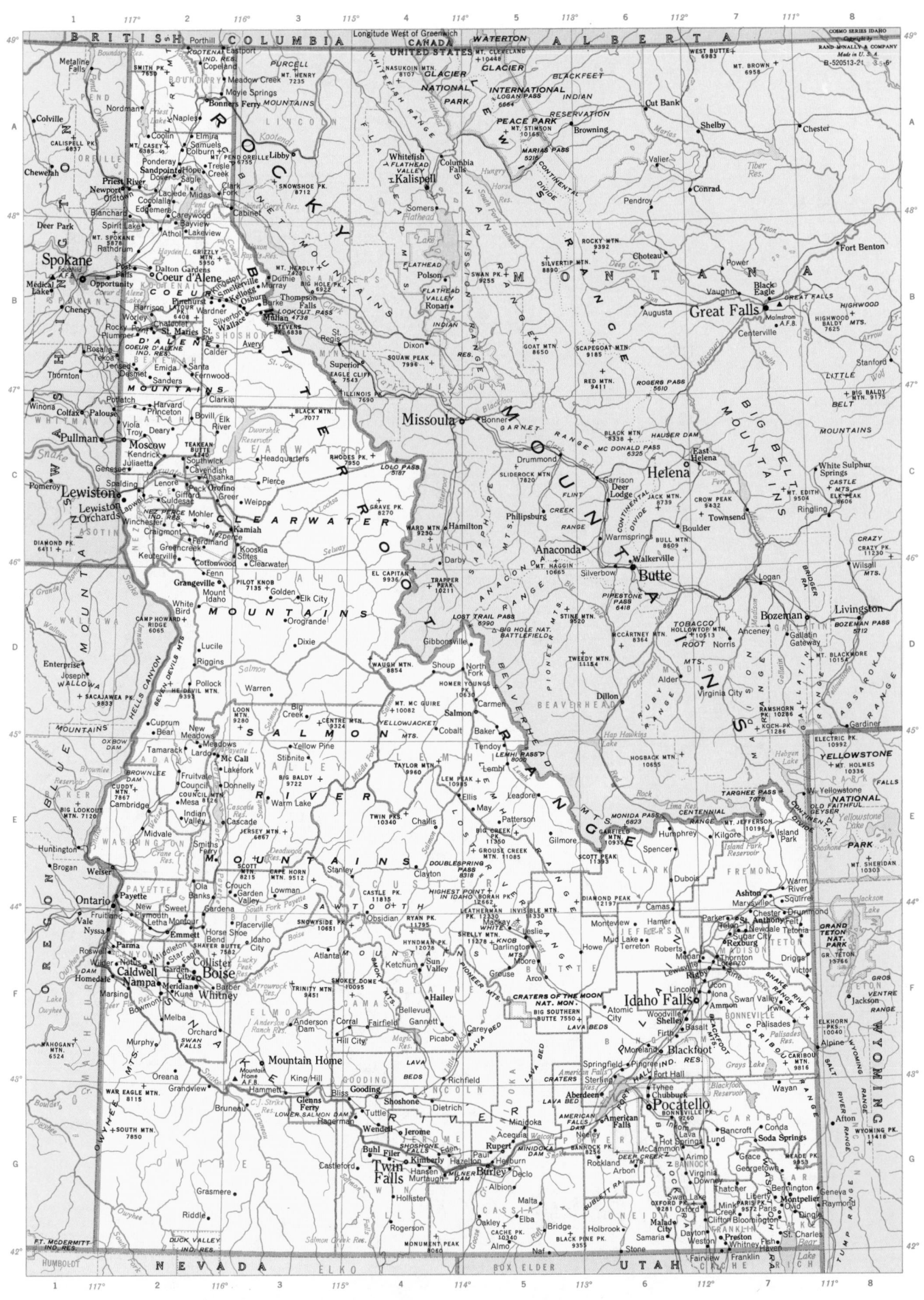

Lambert Conformal Conic Projection

Statute Miles
5 0 5 10   20   30   40   50   60

Kilometers
5 0 5 15 25 35 45 55 65 75

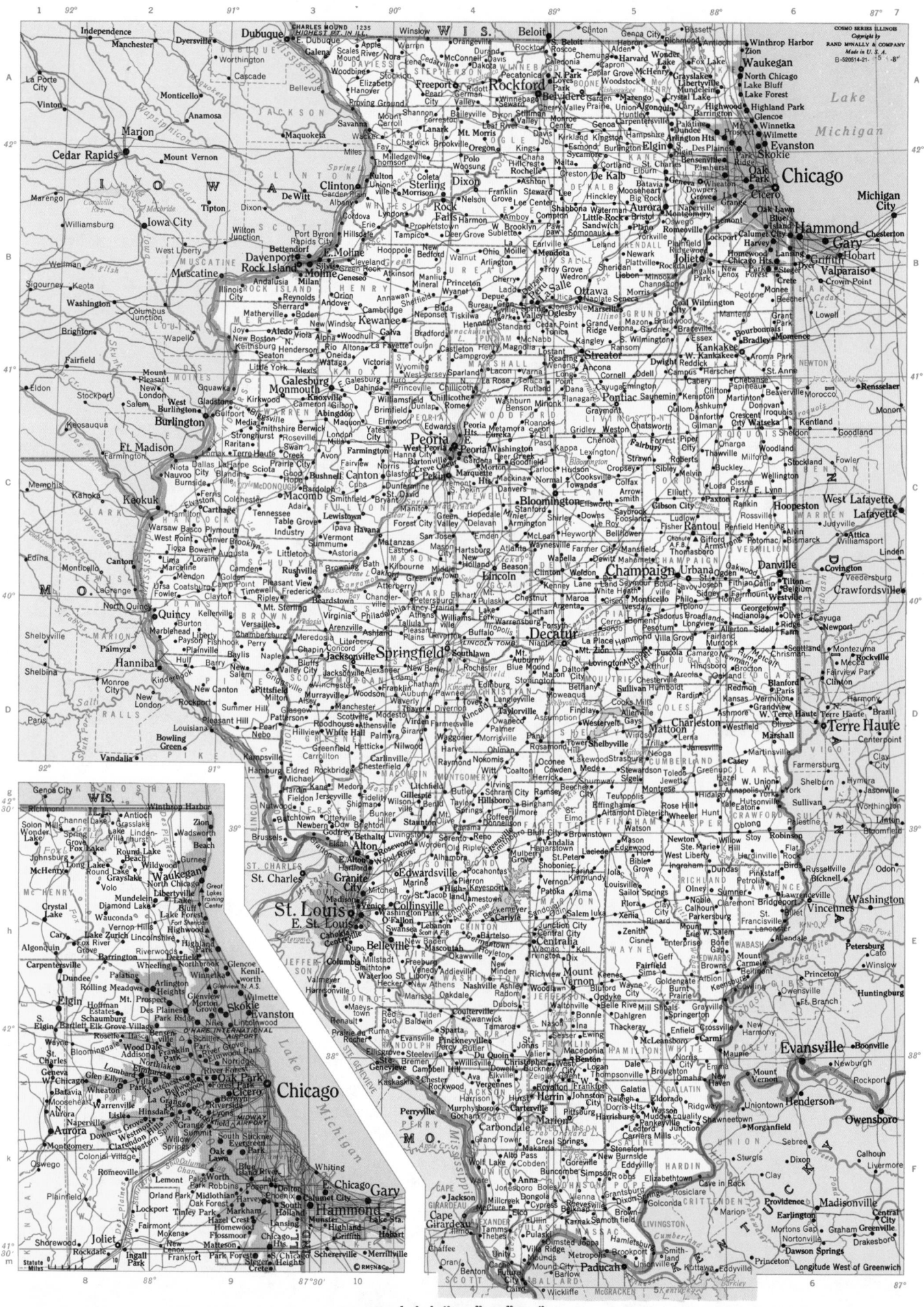

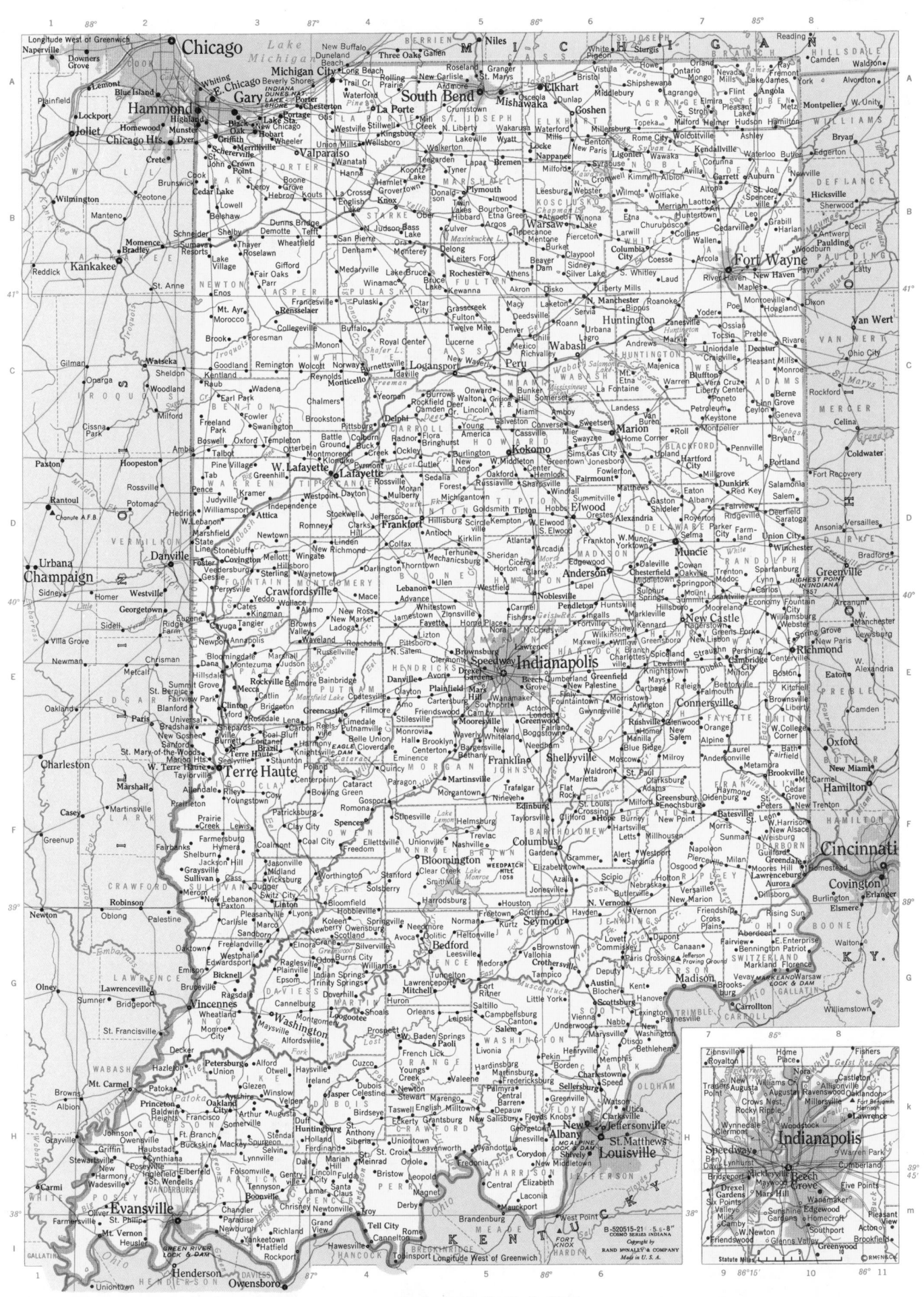

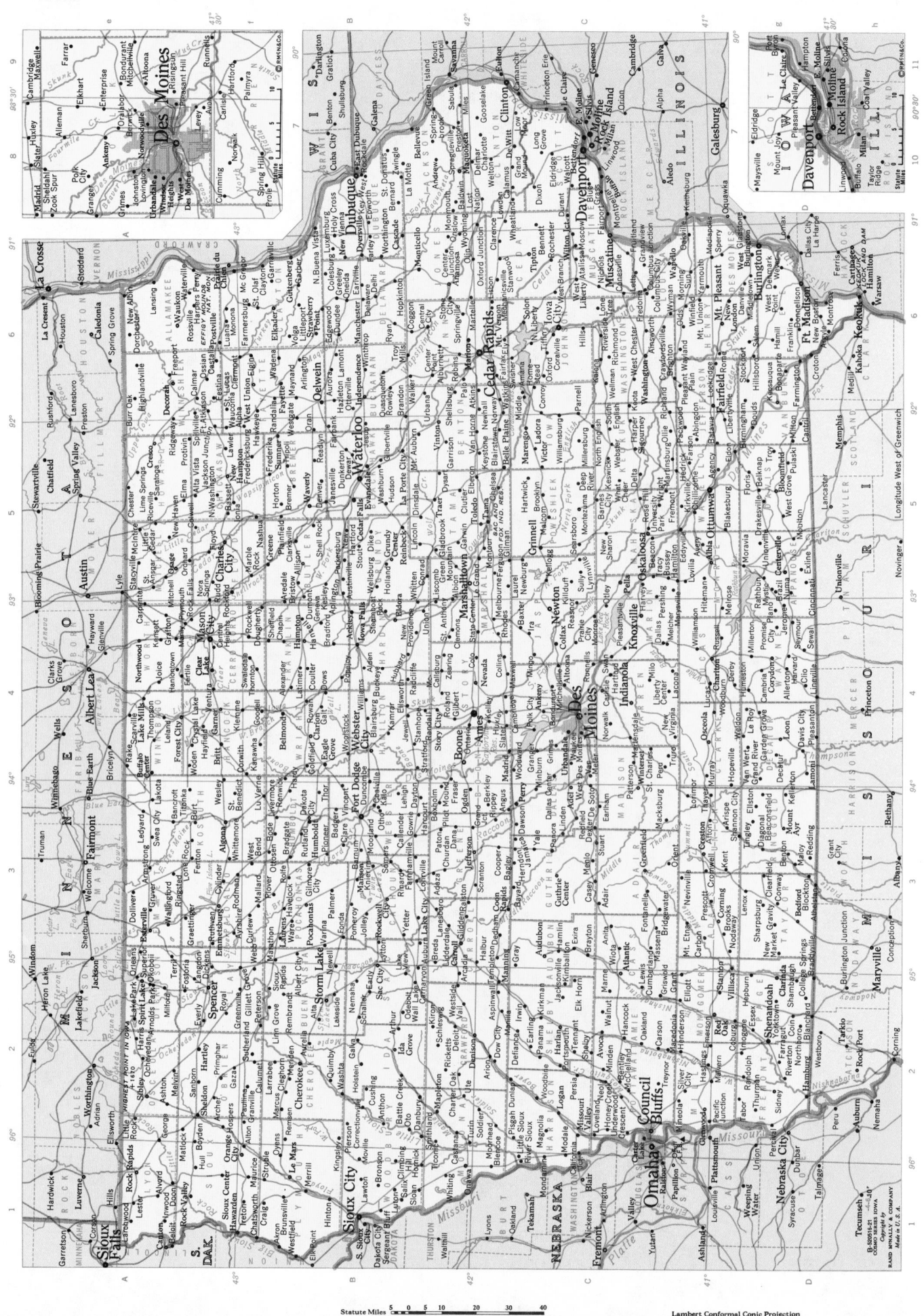

Statute Miles 5 0 5 10 20 30 40

Kilometers 5 0 5 15 25 35 45 55

Lambert Conformal Conic Projection

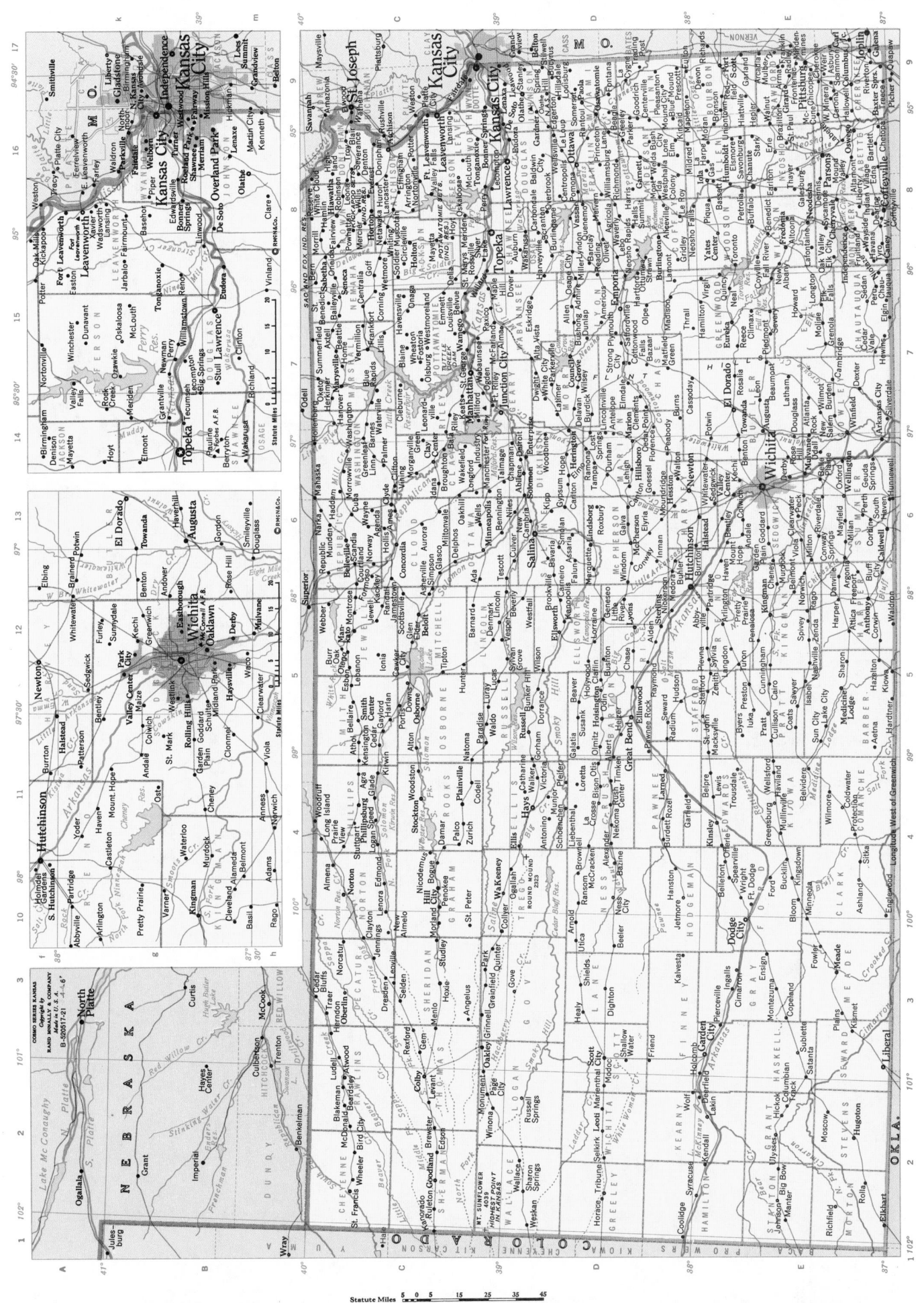

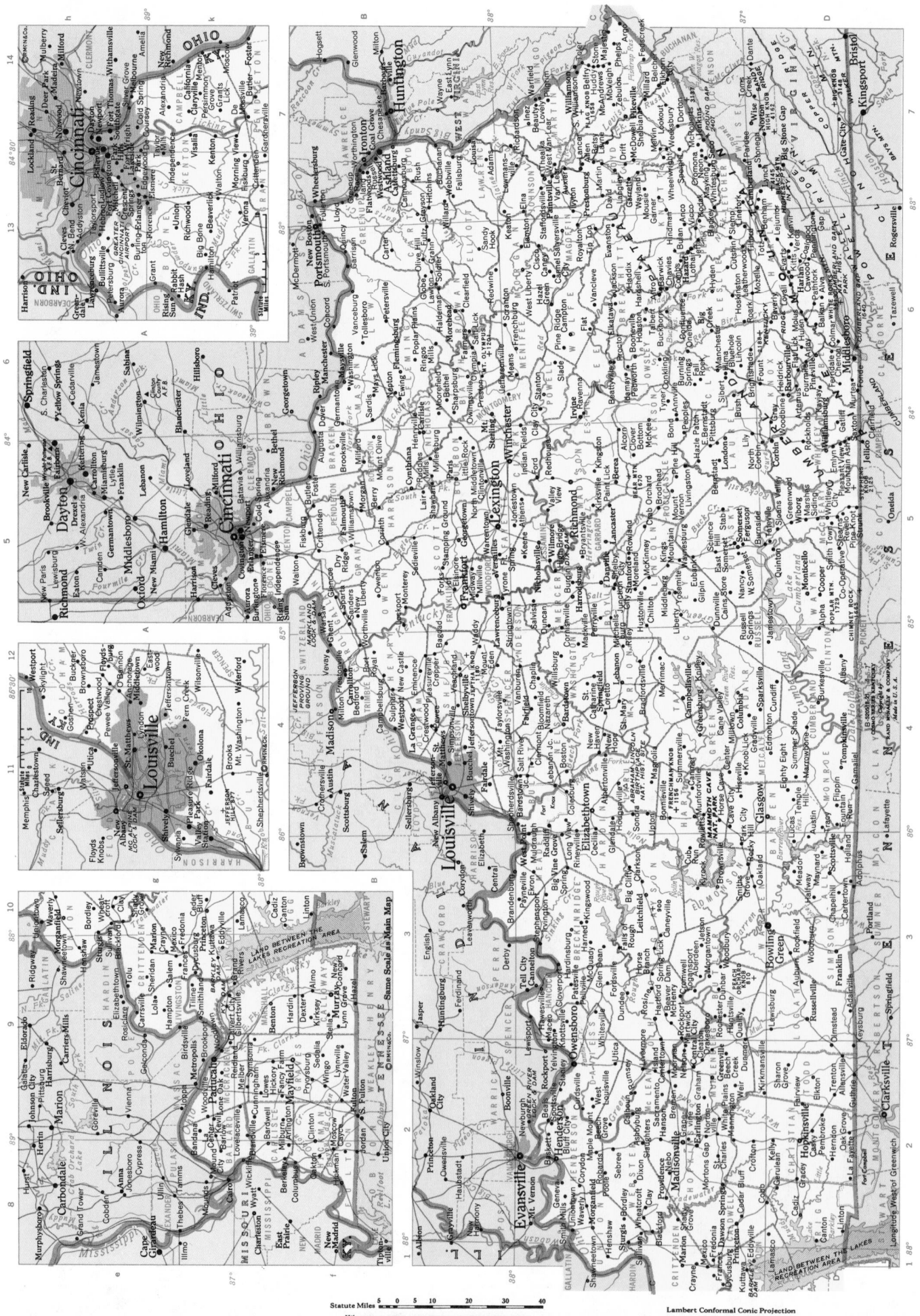

Statute Miles 5 0 5 10   20   30   40

Kilometers 5 0 5 10   20 30 40 50 60

Lambert Conformal Conic Projection

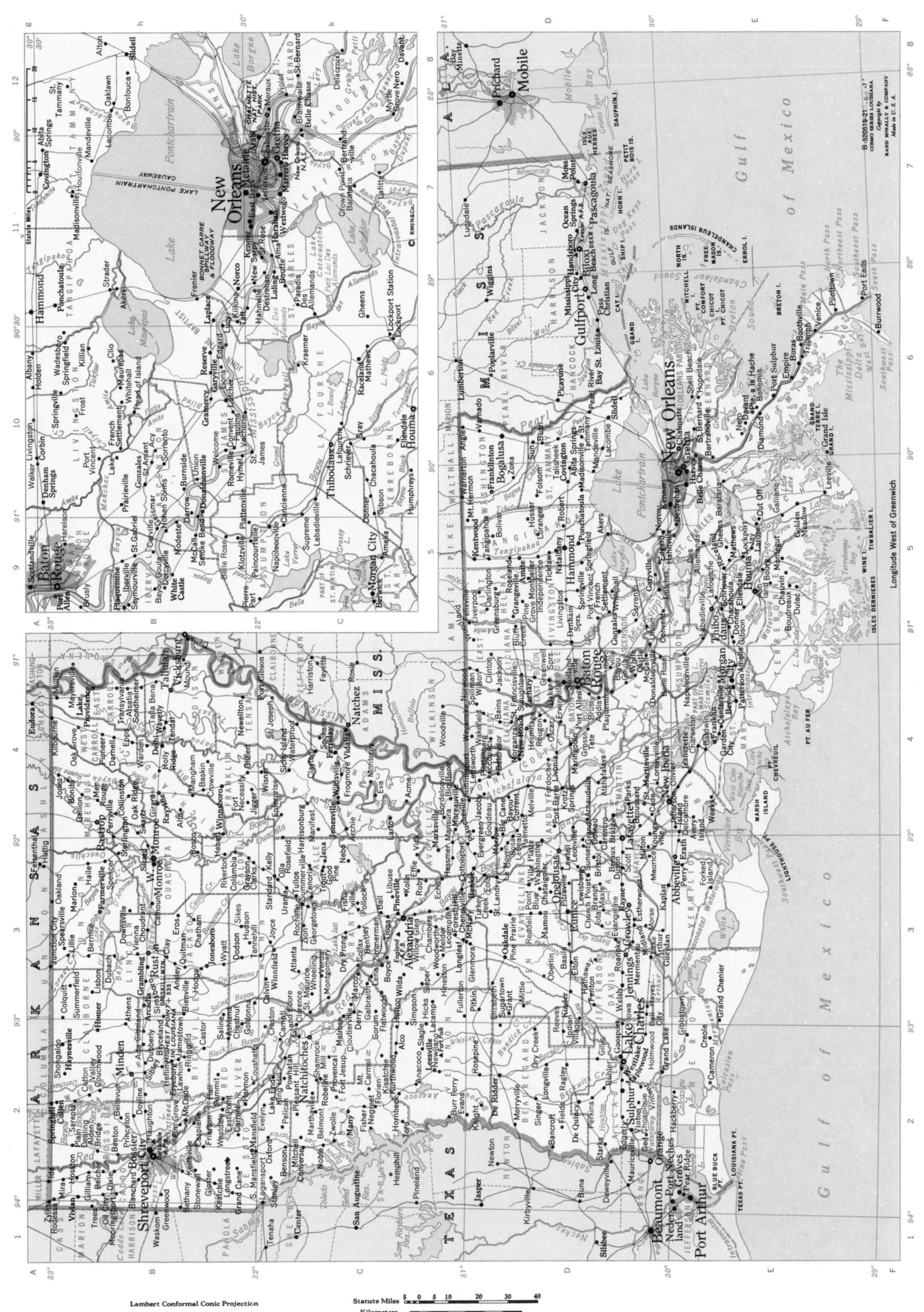

Lambert Conformal Conic Projection

Statute Miles 5 0 5 10 20 30 40

Kilometers 5 0 5 15 25 35 45 55

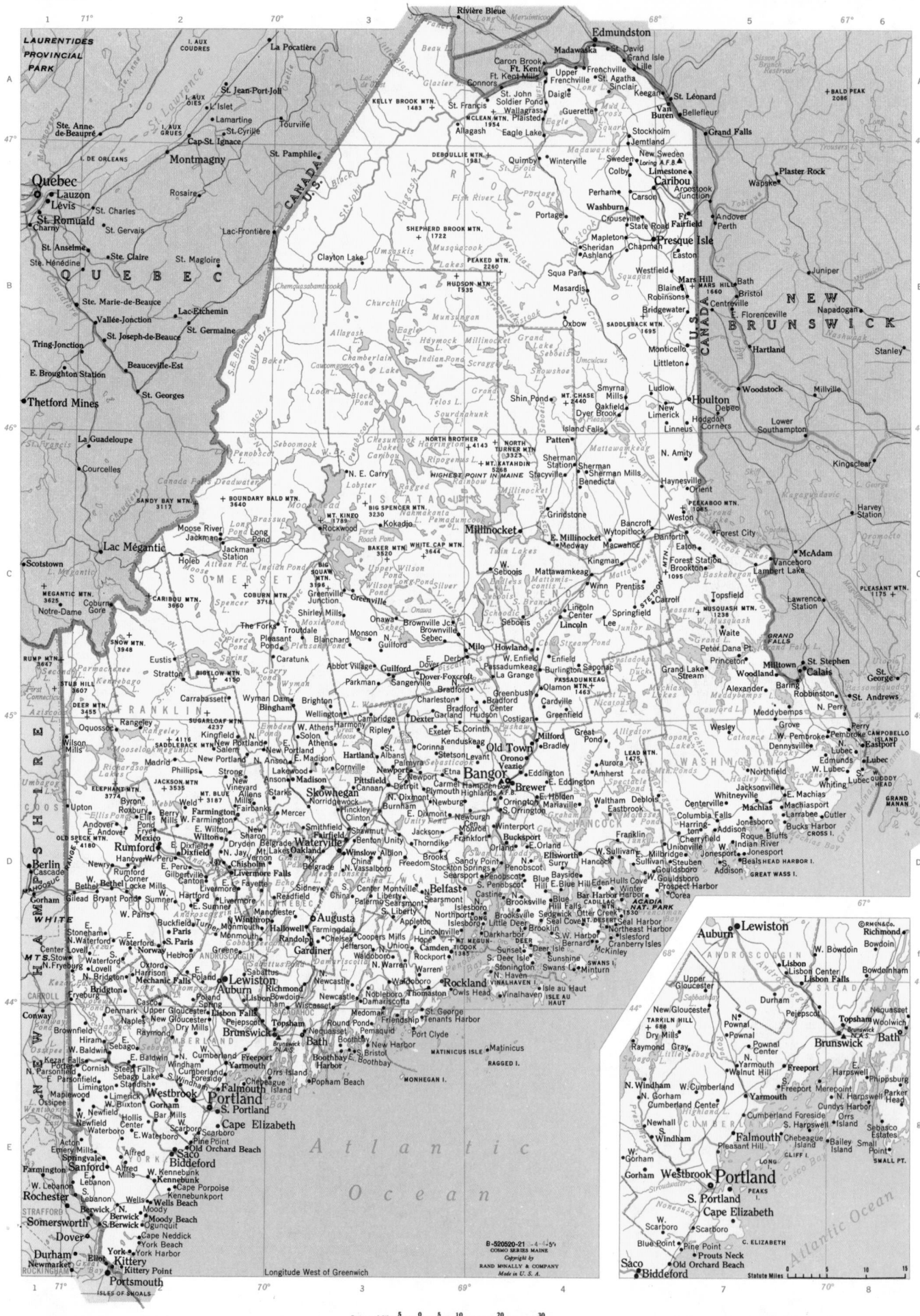

LAURENTIDES
PROVINCIAL
PARK

QUEBEC

NEW
BRUNSWICK

Québec

Atlantic
Ocean

Portland

Longitude West of Greenwich

Lambert Conformal Conic Projection

Statute Miles

Kilometers

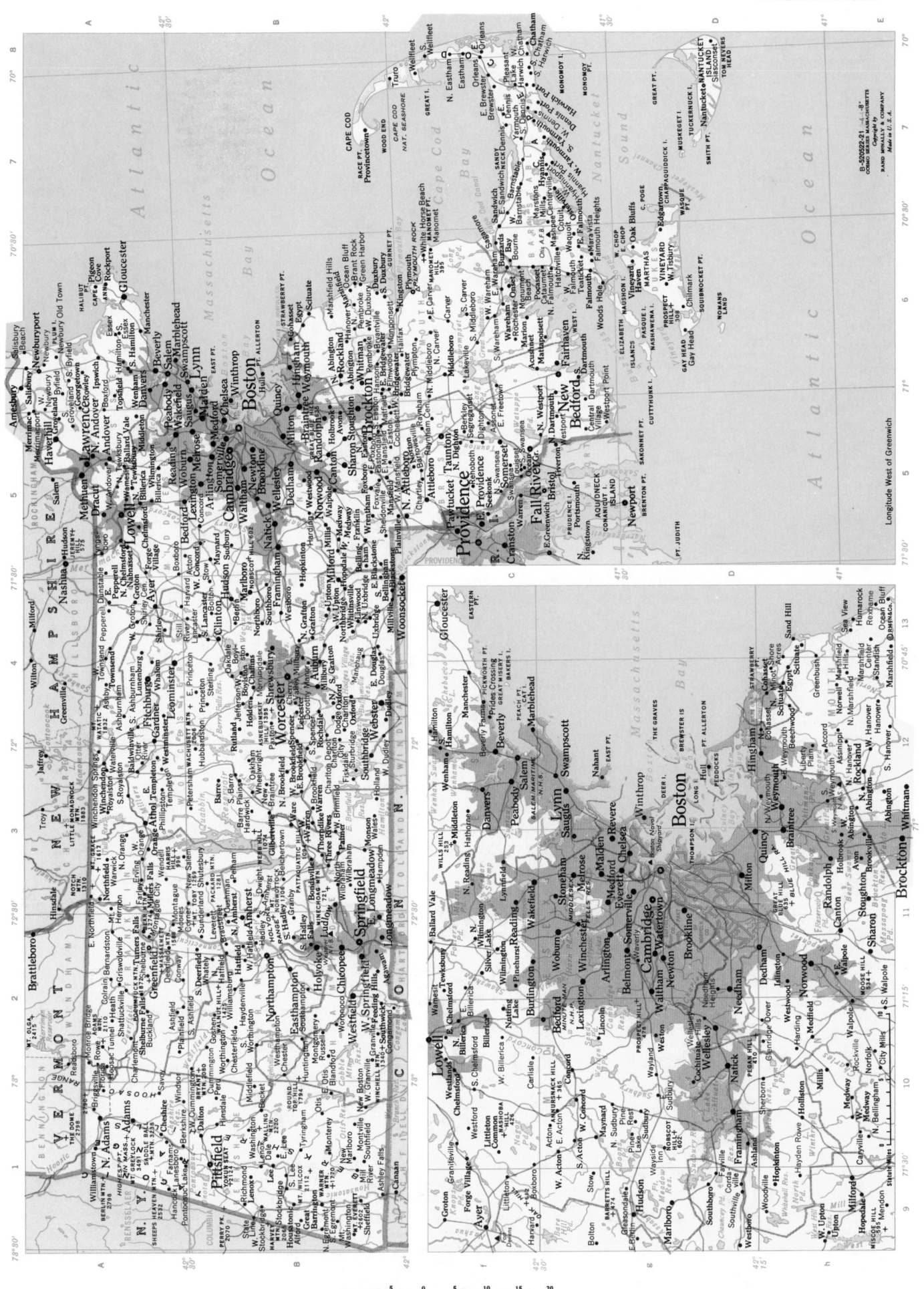

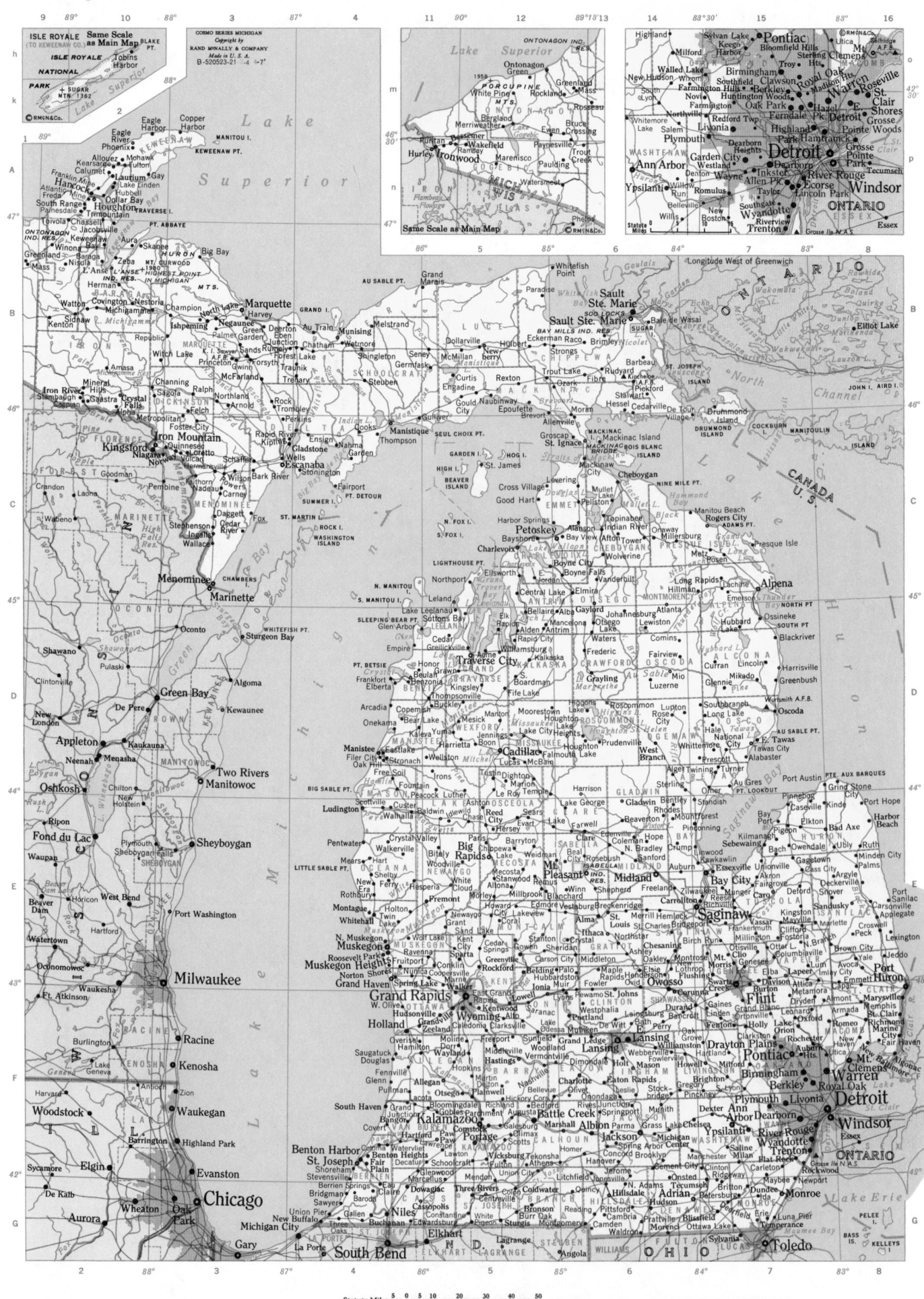

COSMO SERIES MICHIGAN
Copyright by
RAND MCNALLY & COMPANY
Made in U.S.A.
B-520523-21 -4 -7°

Lambert Conformal Conic Projection

Statute Miles 5 0 5 10 20 30 40 50
Kilometers 5 0 5 15 25 35 45 55 65 75

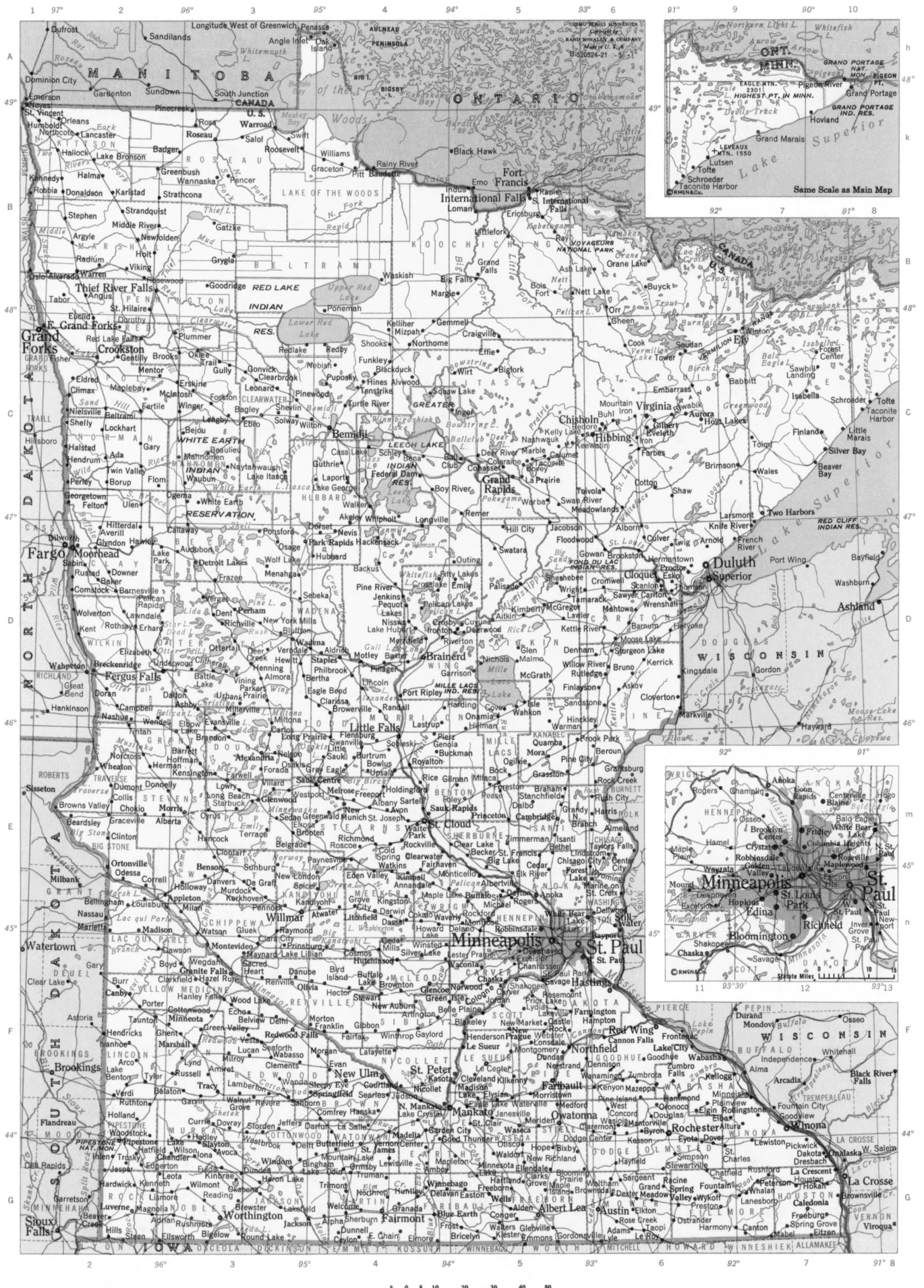

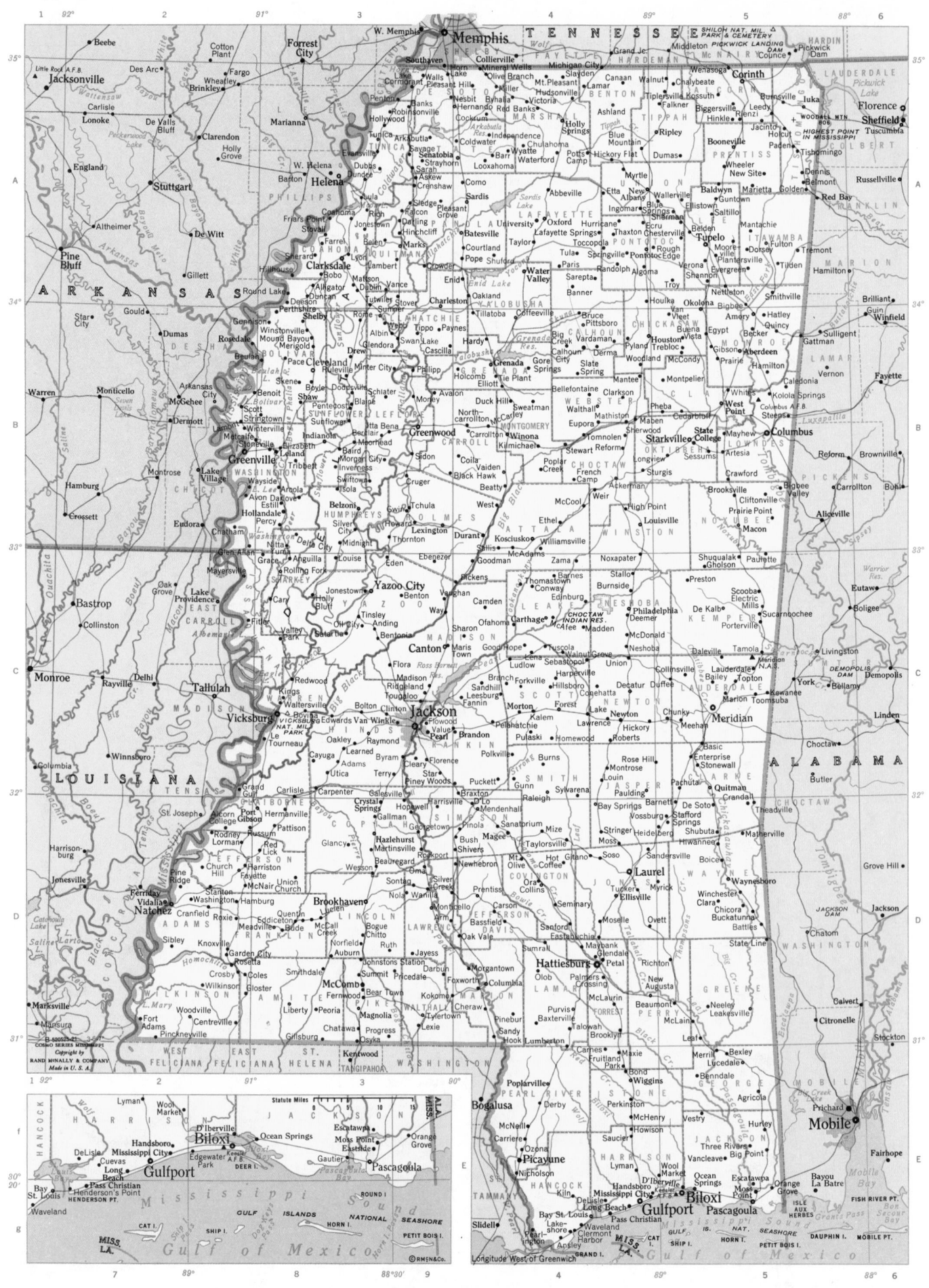

Lambert Conformal Conic Projection

Statute Miles

Kilometers

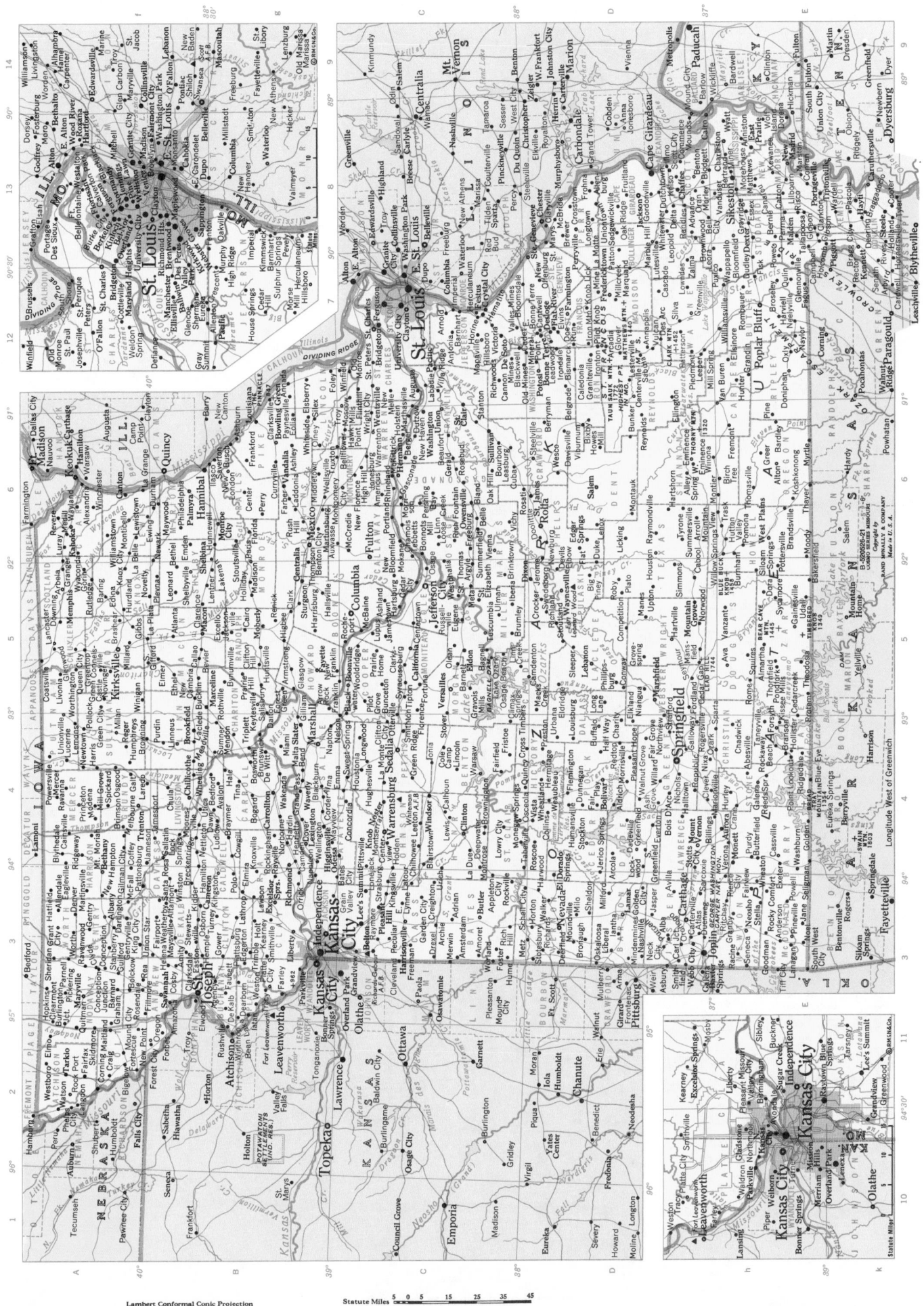

Statute Miles   10 0 10 20 30 40 50 60 70

Kilometers   10 0 10 30 50 70 90

Lambert Conformal Conic Projection

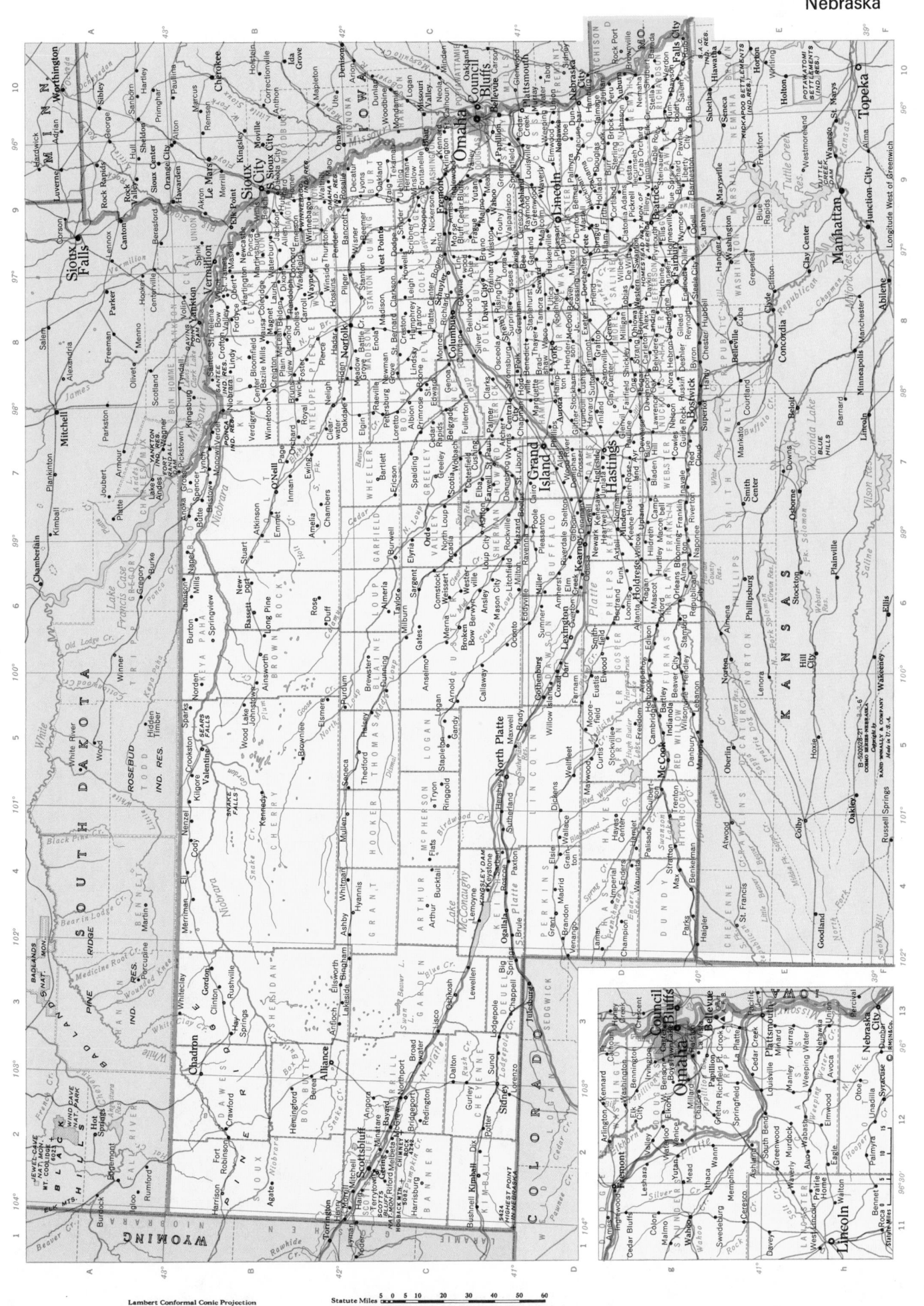

Statute Miles   5   0   5   10   20   30   40   50   60

Kilometers   5 0 5   15   35   55   75   95

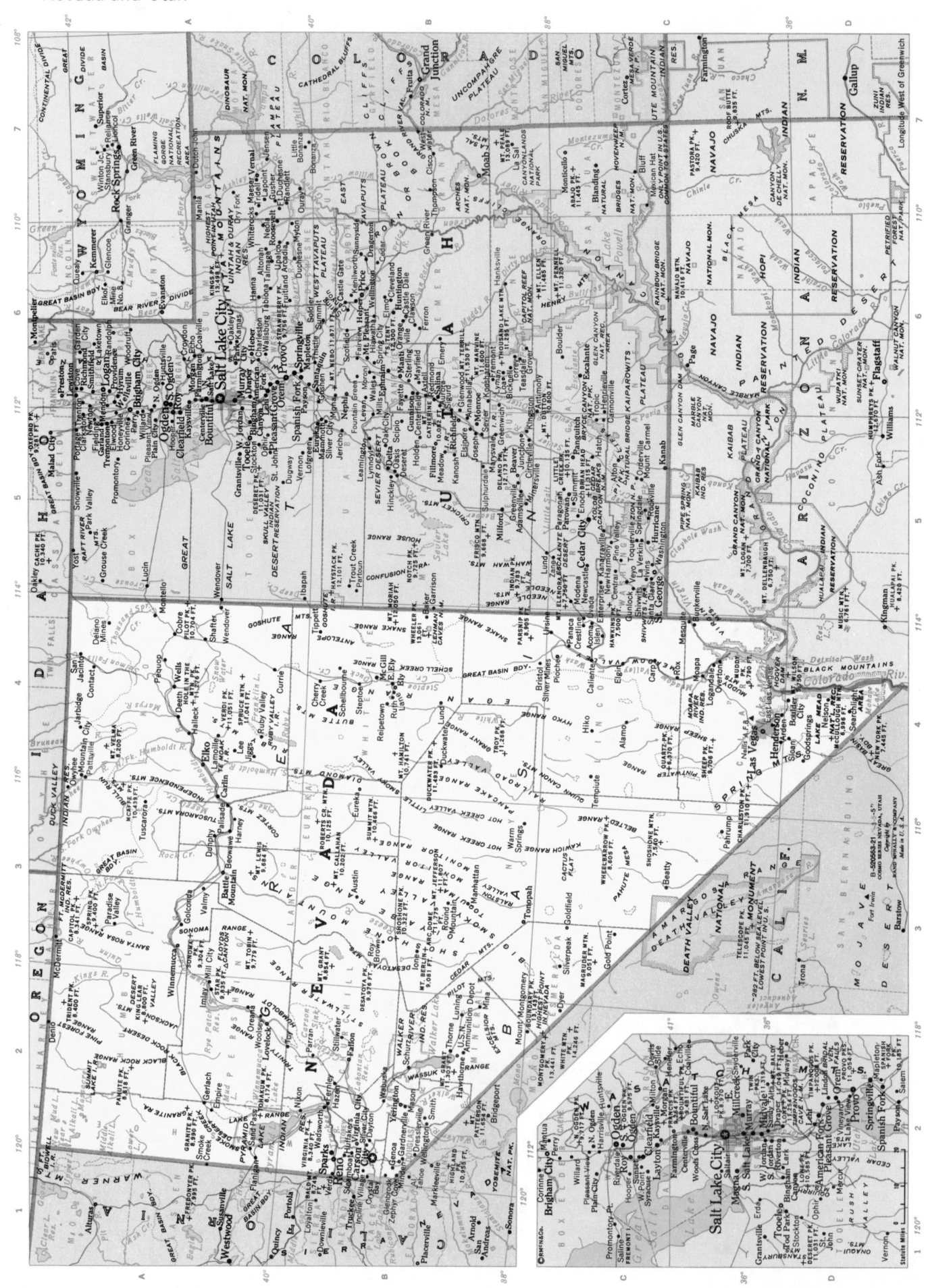

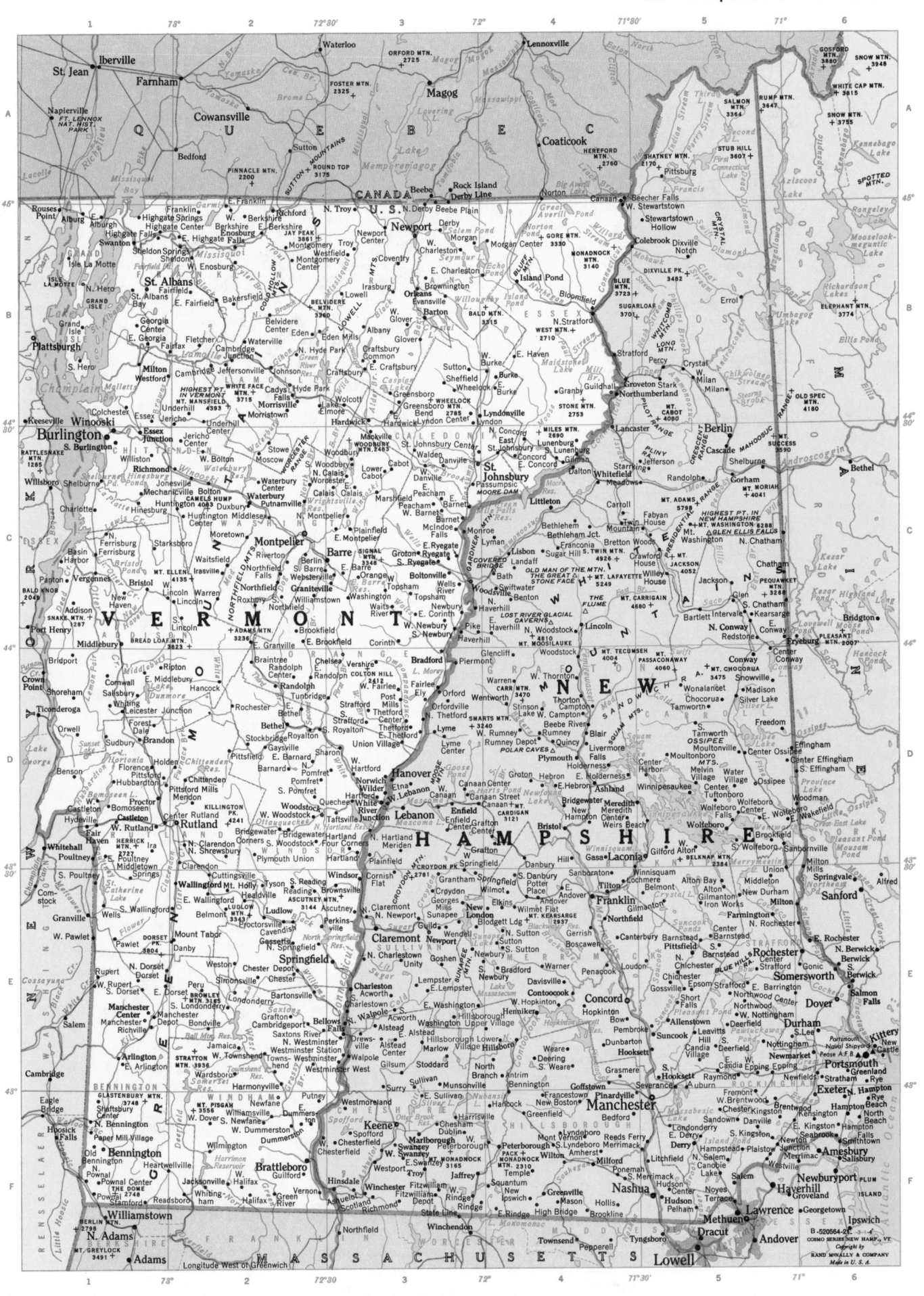

Lambert Conformal Conic Projection

Statute Miles
5   0   5   10   20

Kilometers
5   0   5   10   15   20   25

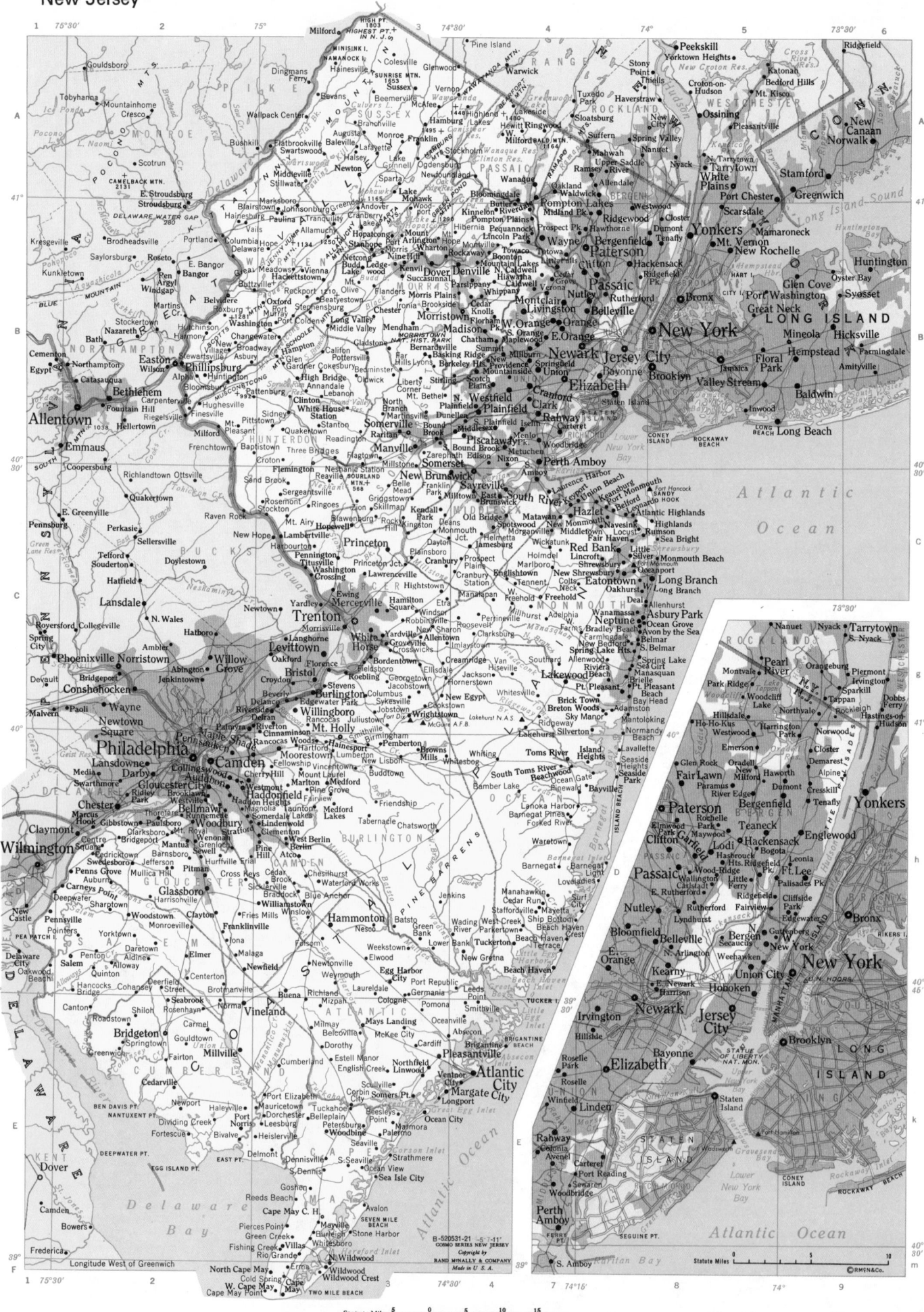

Longitude West of Greenwich

B-520531-21 —5/7-41
COSMO SERIES NEW JERSEY
Copyright by
RAND MCNALLY & COMPANY
Made in U.S.A.

Statute Miles
Kilometers

Lambert Conformal Conic Projection

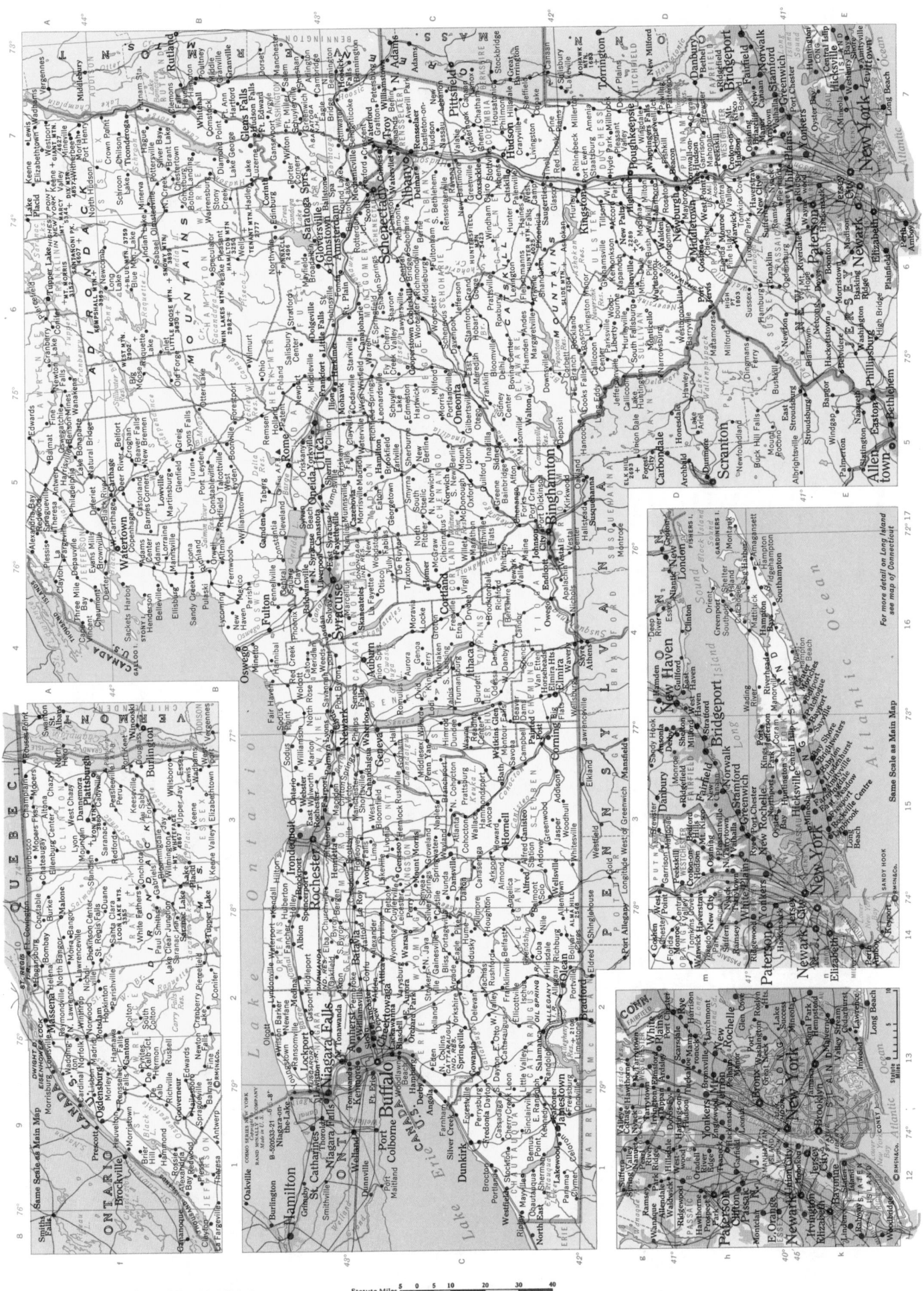

Lambert Conformal Conic Projection

Statute Miles

Kilometers

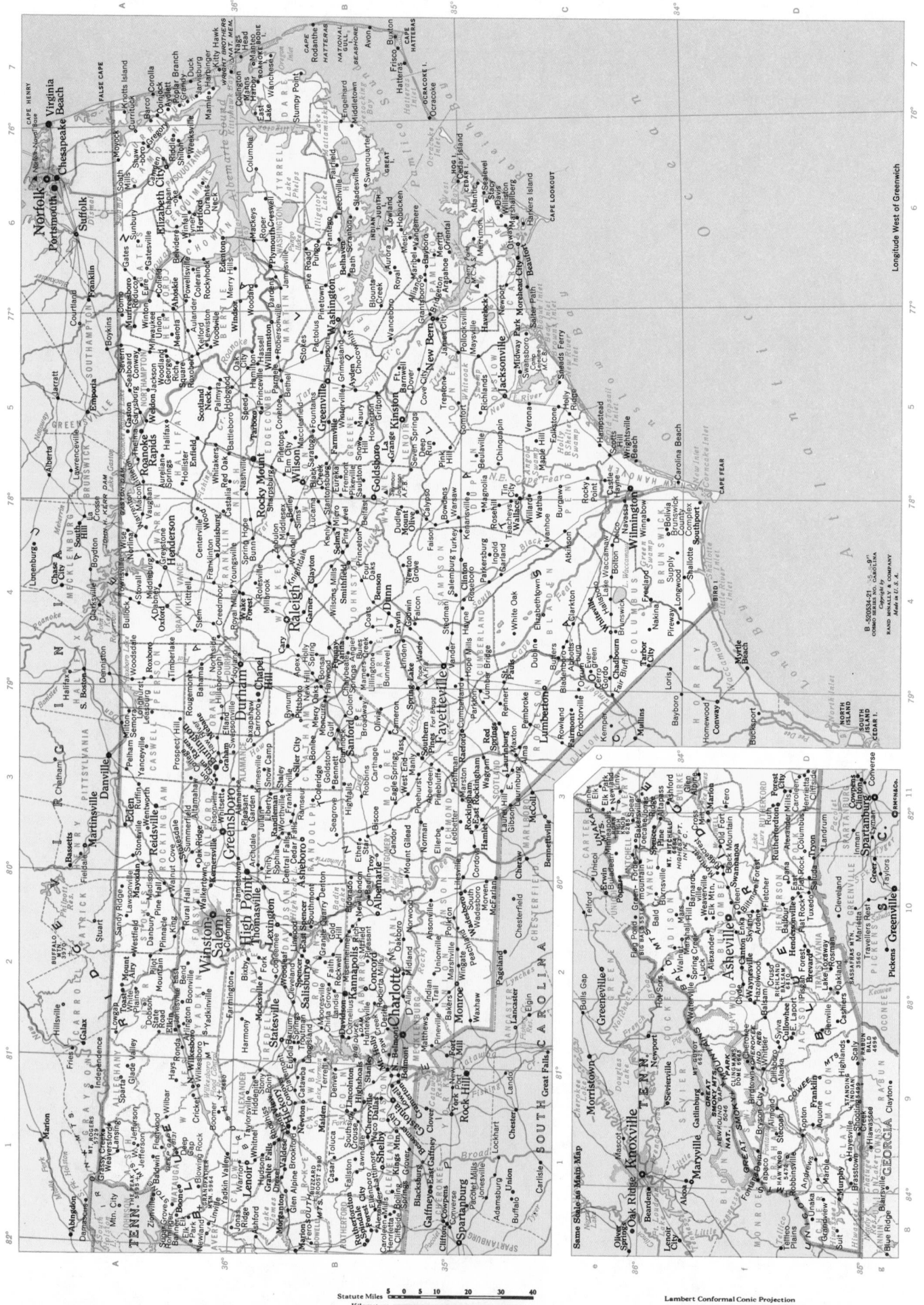

Statute Miles

Kilometers

Lambert Conformal Conic Projection

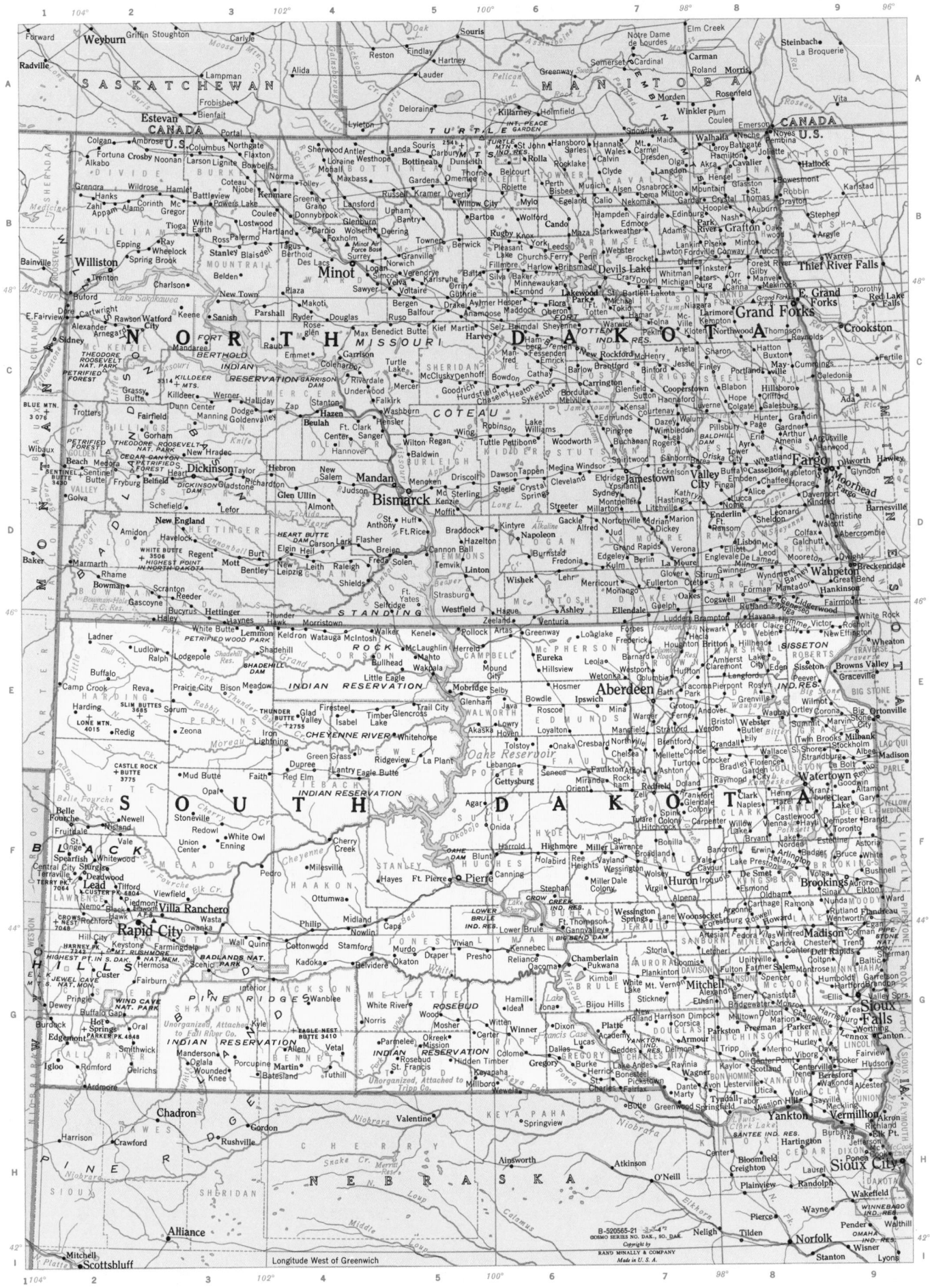

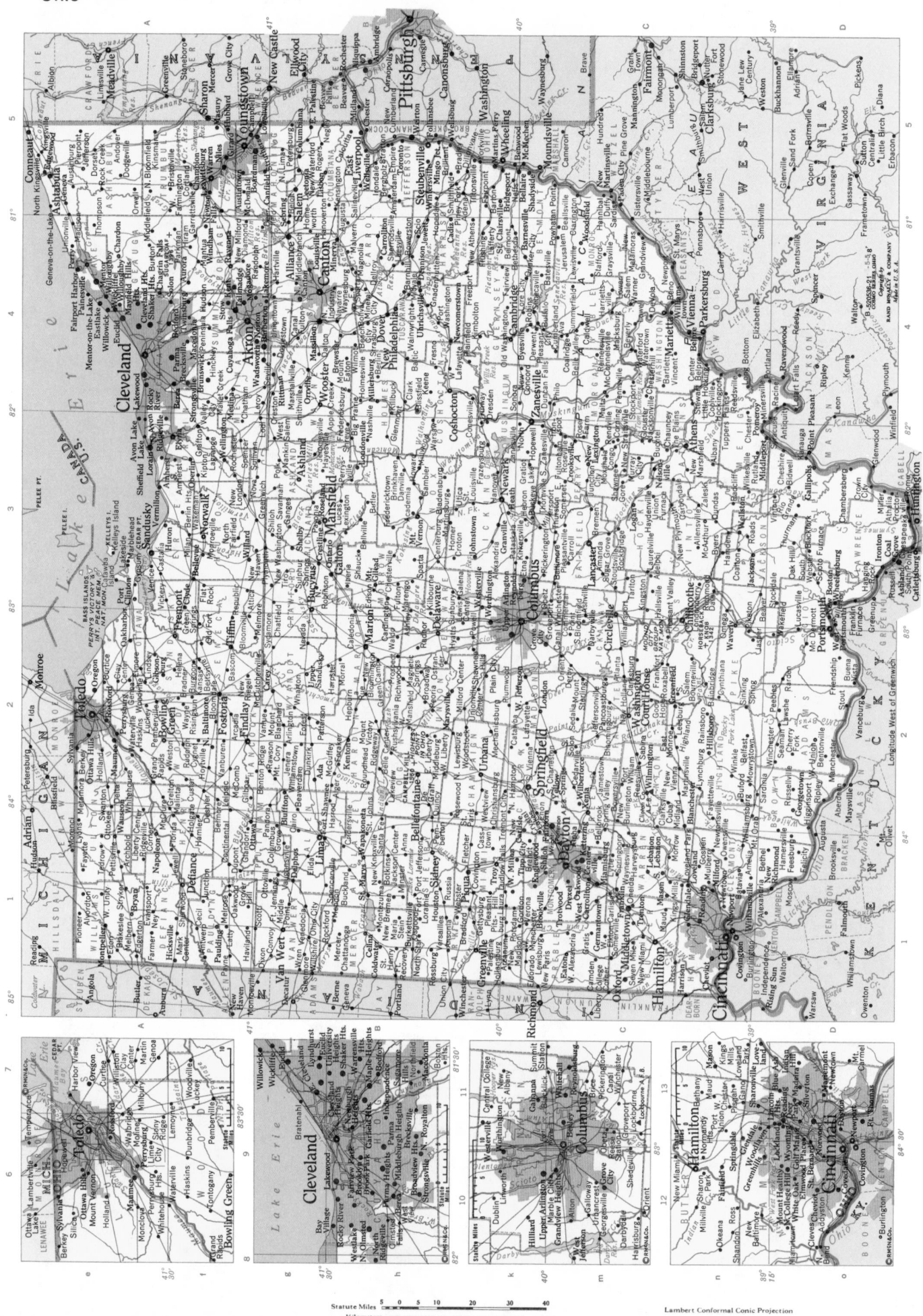

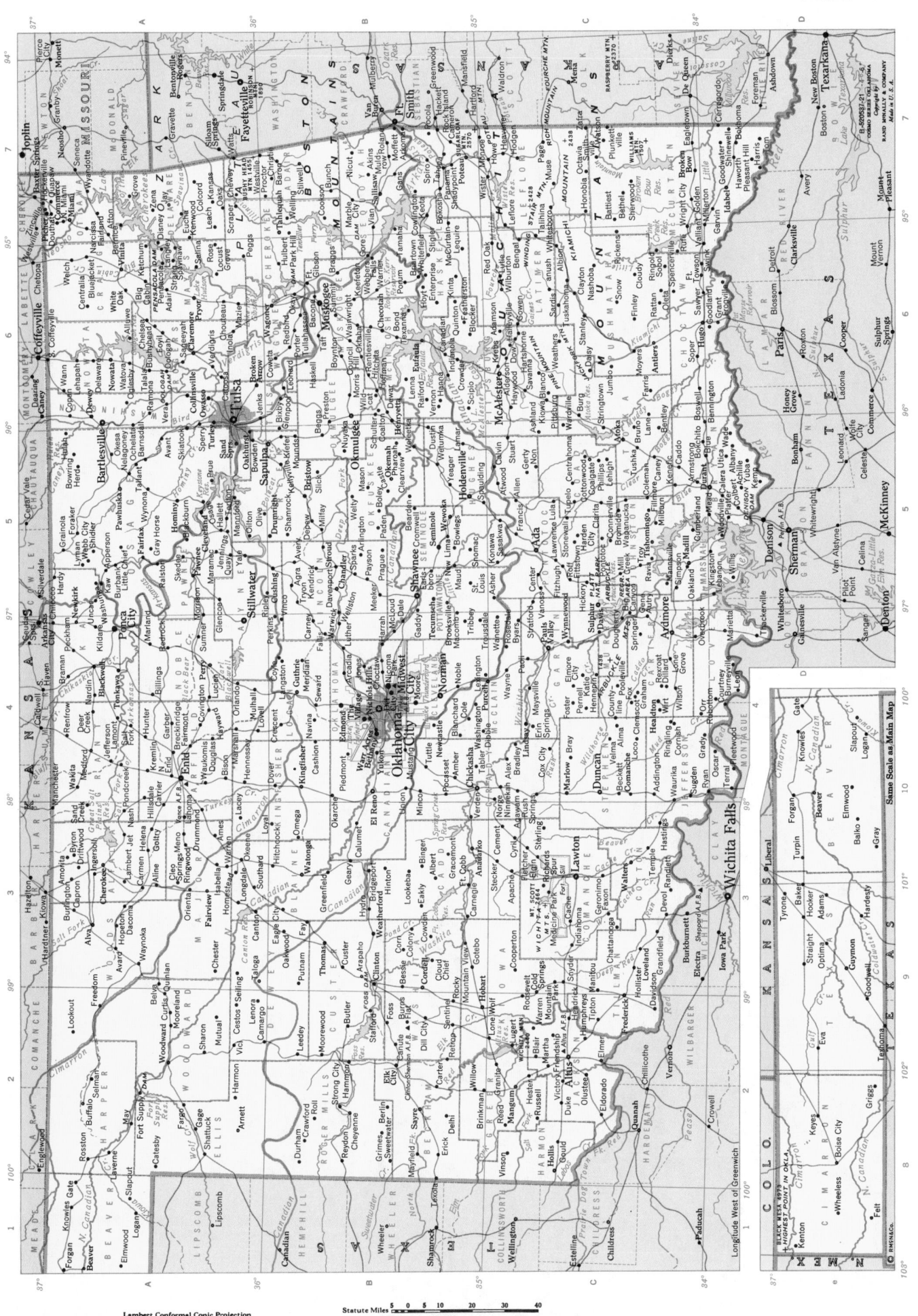

Lambert Conformal Conic Projection

Statute Miles 5 0 5 10 20 30 40
Kilometers 5 0 5 15 25 35 45 55

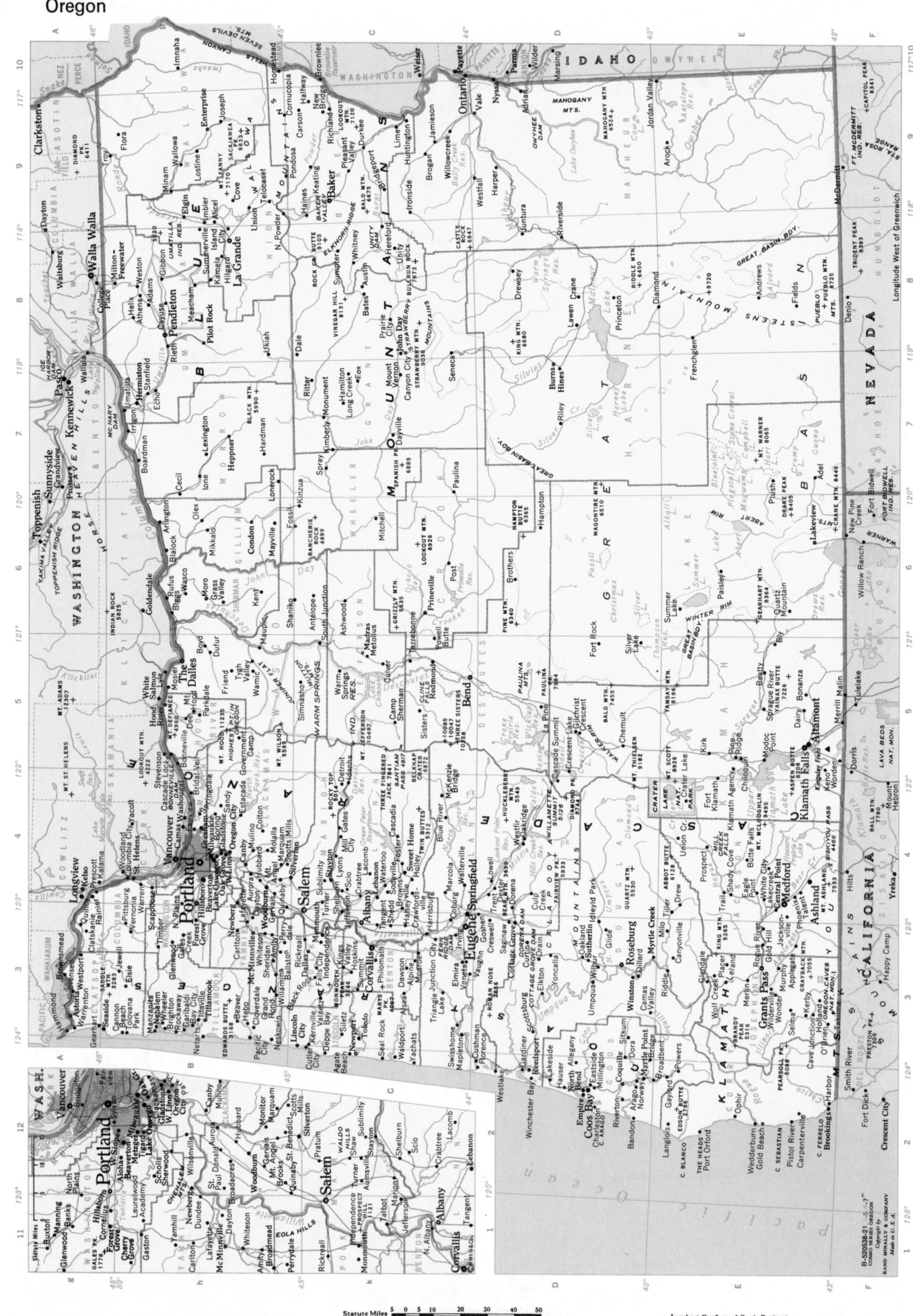

Statute Miles 5 0 5 10   20   30   40   50

Kilometers 5 0 5 15 25 35 45 55 65 75

Lambert Conformal Conic Projection

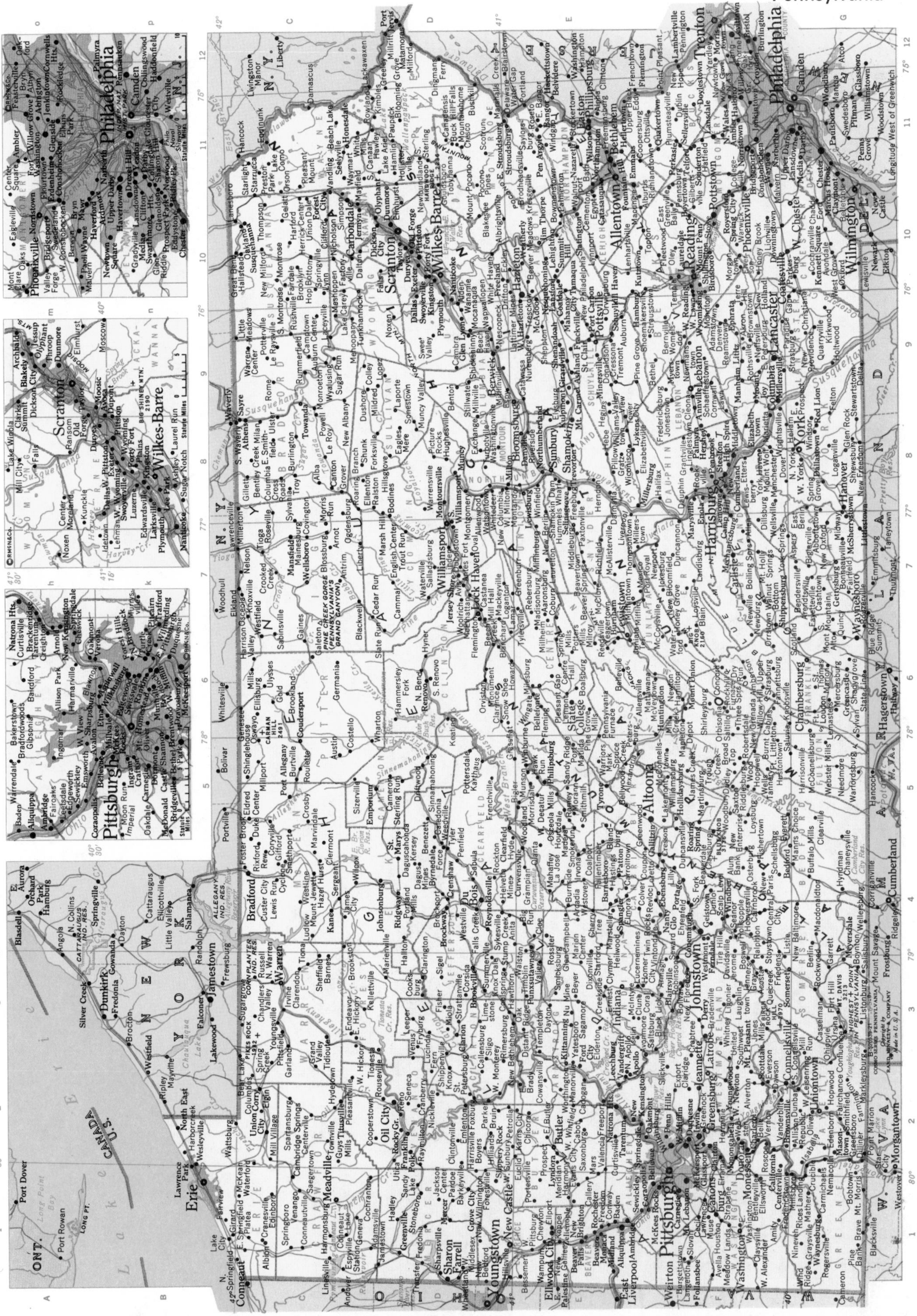

Pennsylvania

Philadelphia

Scranton

Wilkes-Barre

Pittsburgh

Lambert Conformal Conic Projection

Statute Miles

Kilometers

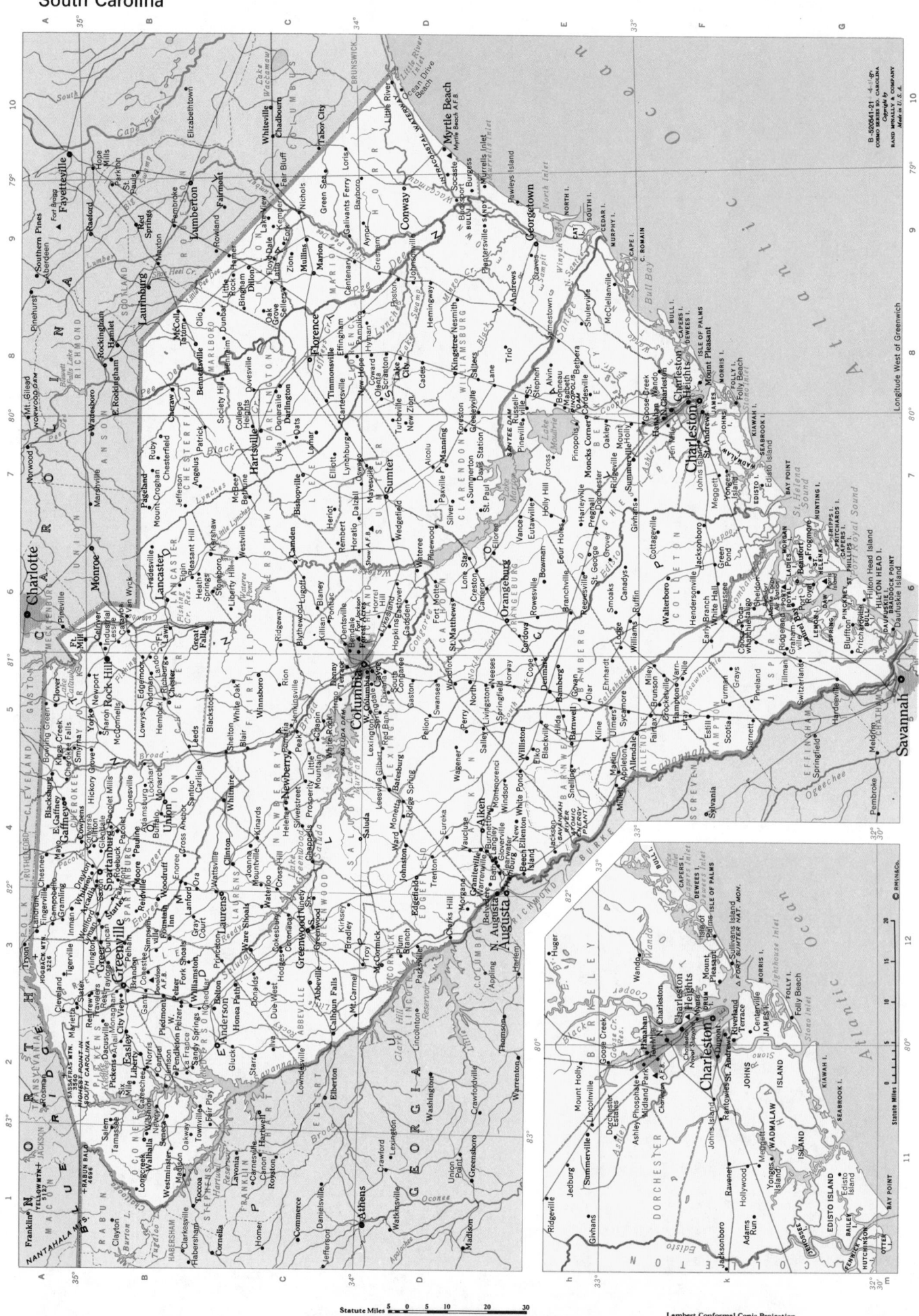

Statute Miles

0   5   10   20   30

Kilometers

5 0 5   15   25   35   45

Lambert Conformal Conic Projection

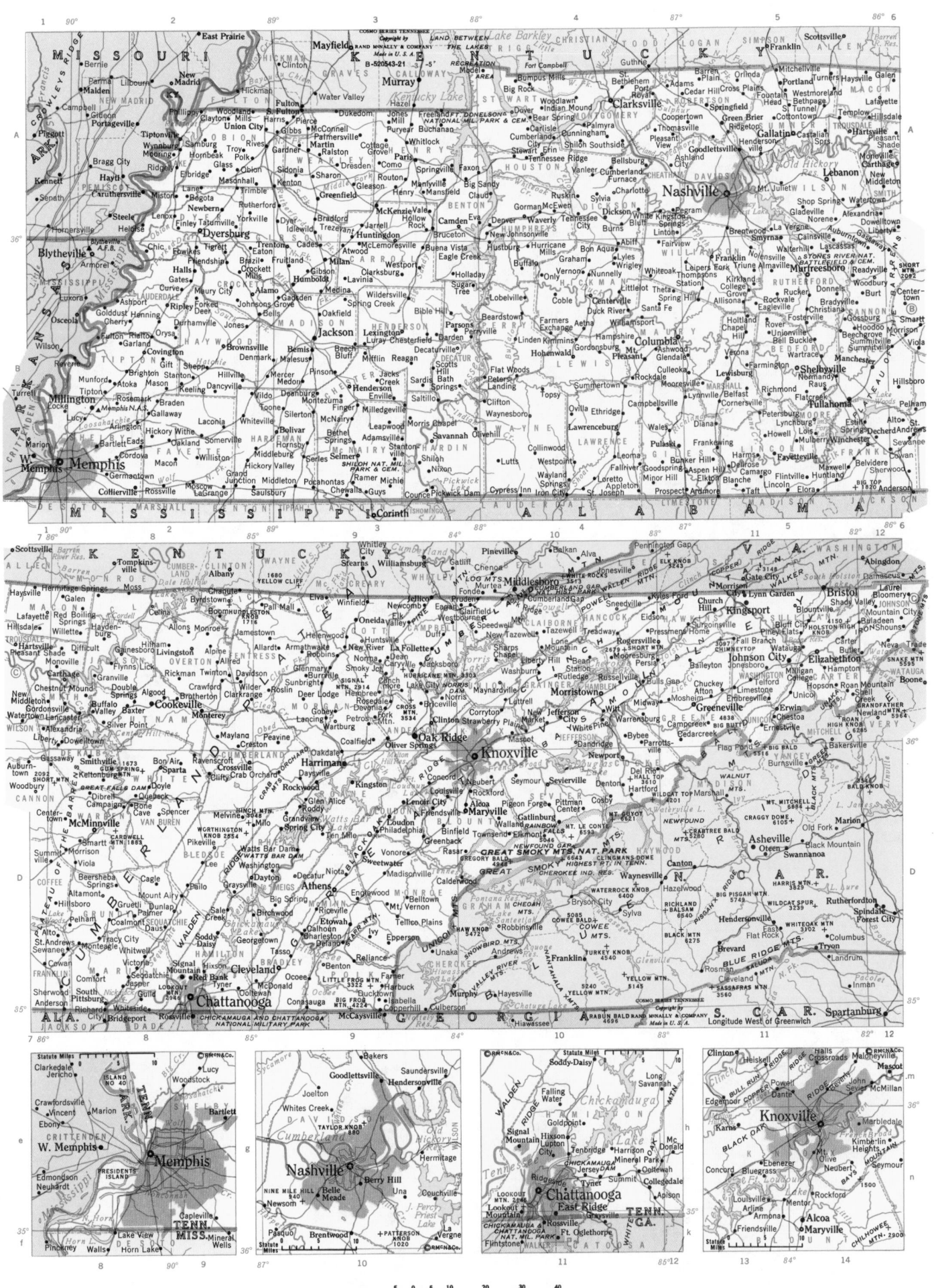

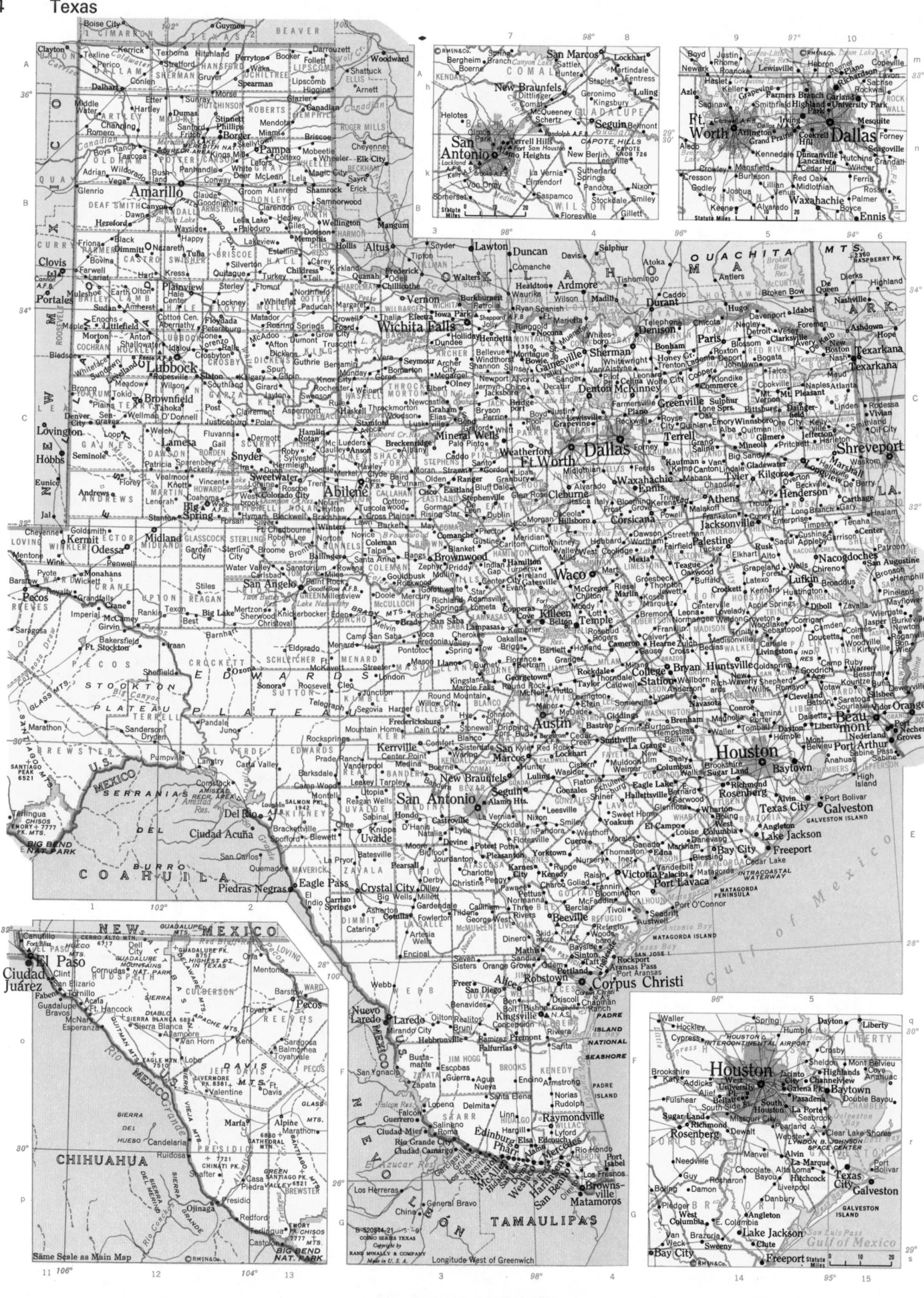

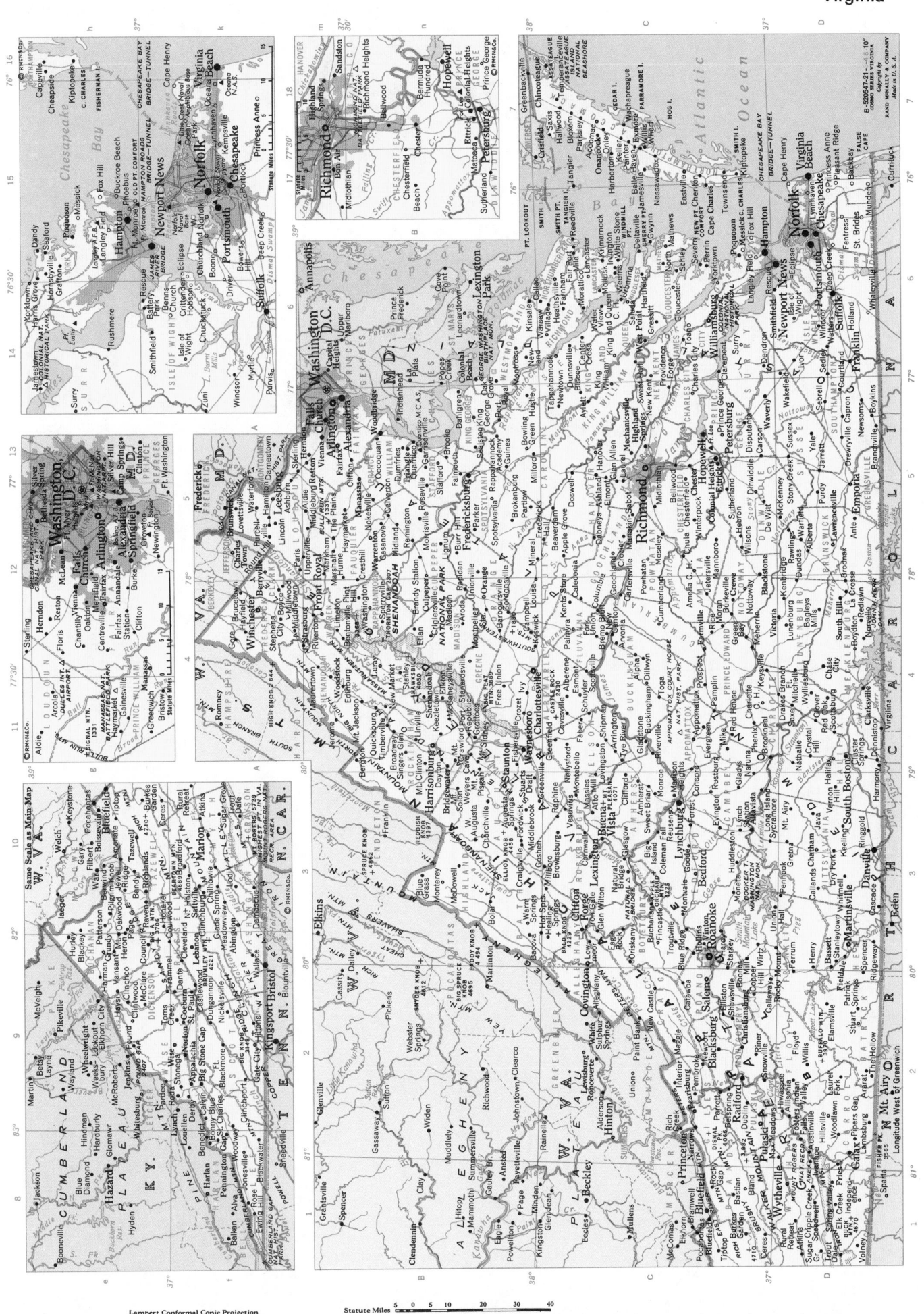

Statute Miles 5 0 5 10 20 30 40

Kilometers 5 0 5 15 25 35 45 55

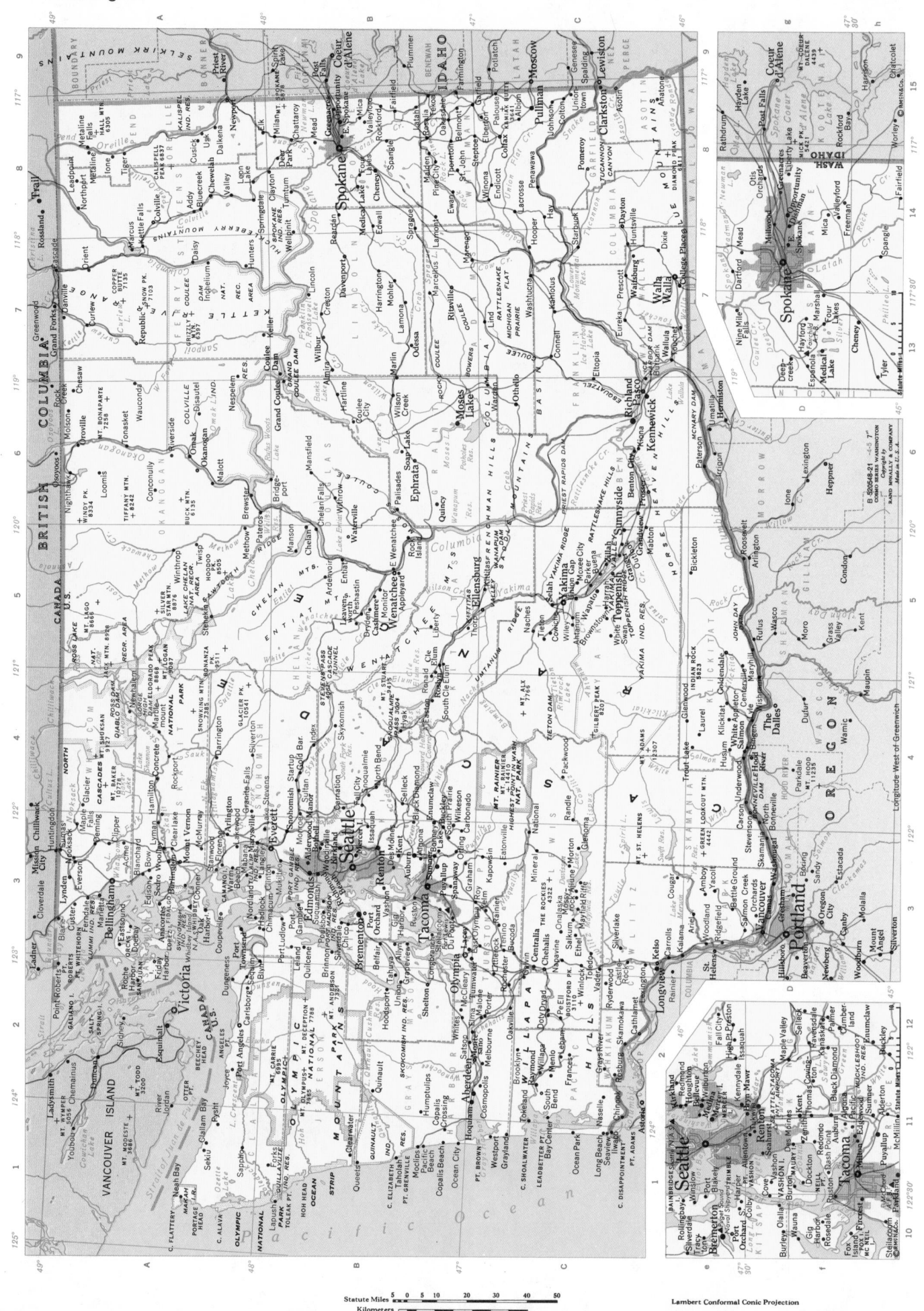

Statute Miles
Kilometers

Lambert Conformal Conic Projection

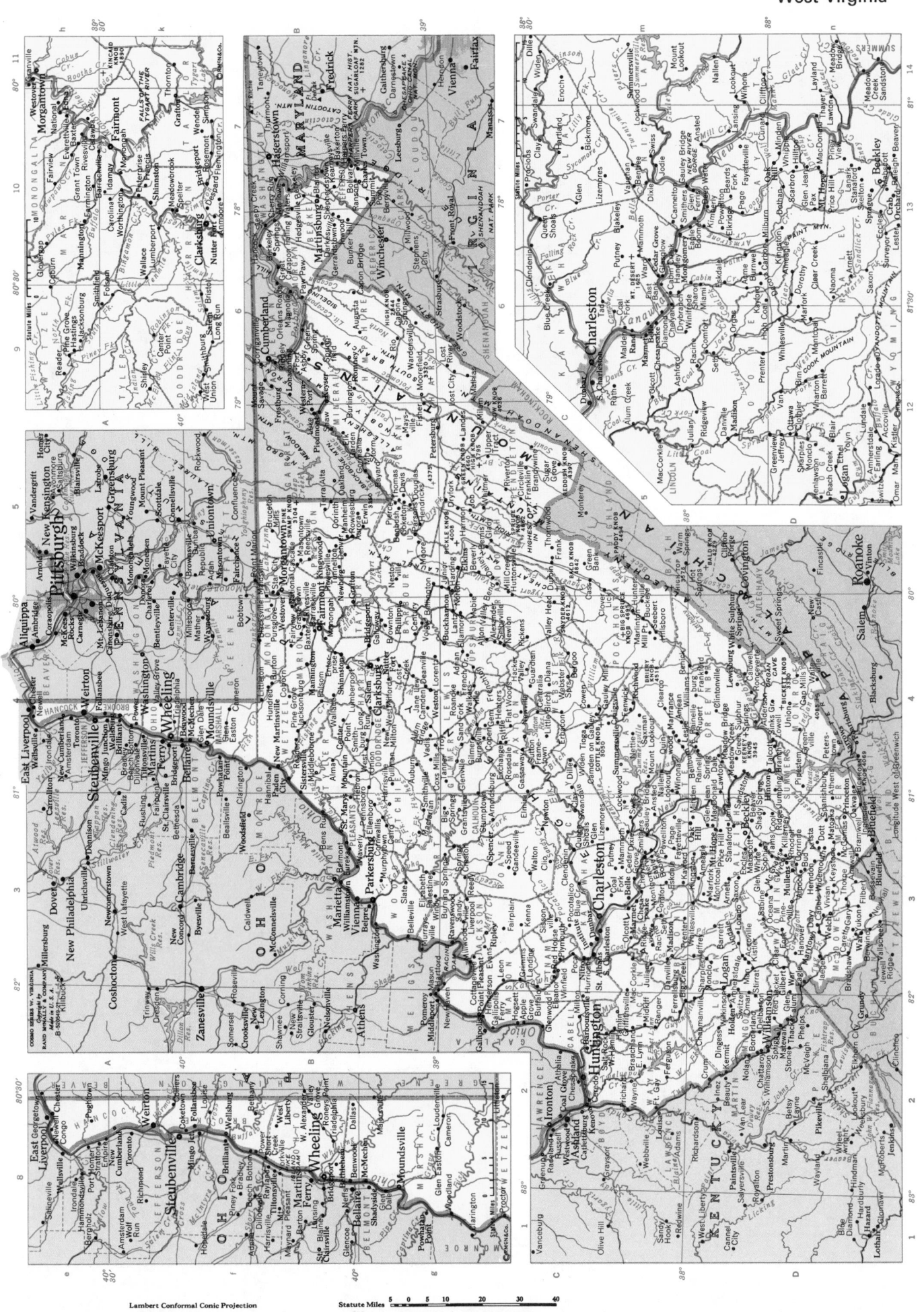

Lambert Conformal Conic Projection

Statute Miles

Kilometers

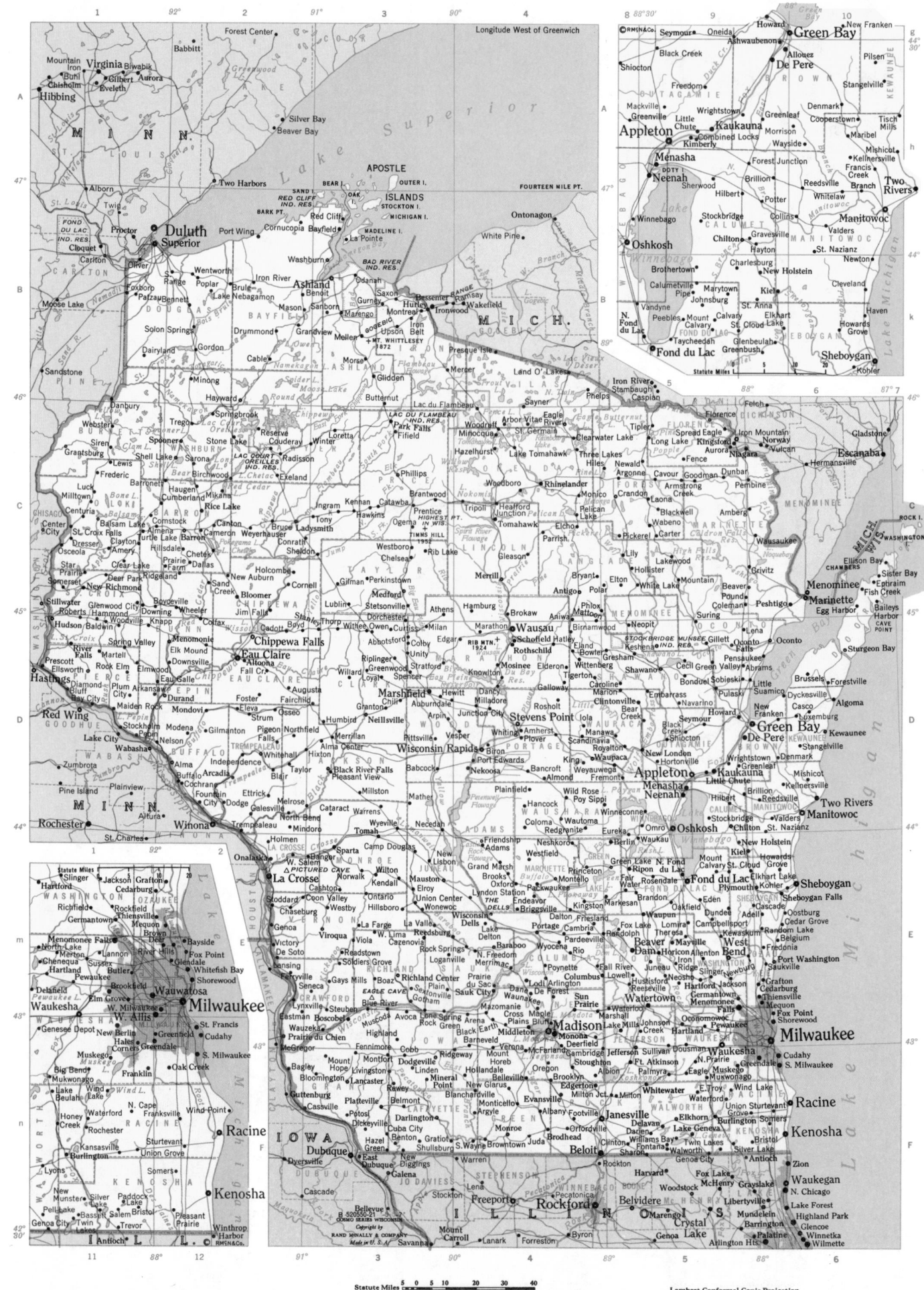

Longitude West of Greenwich

Lambert Conformal Conic Projection

Statute Miles
Kilometers

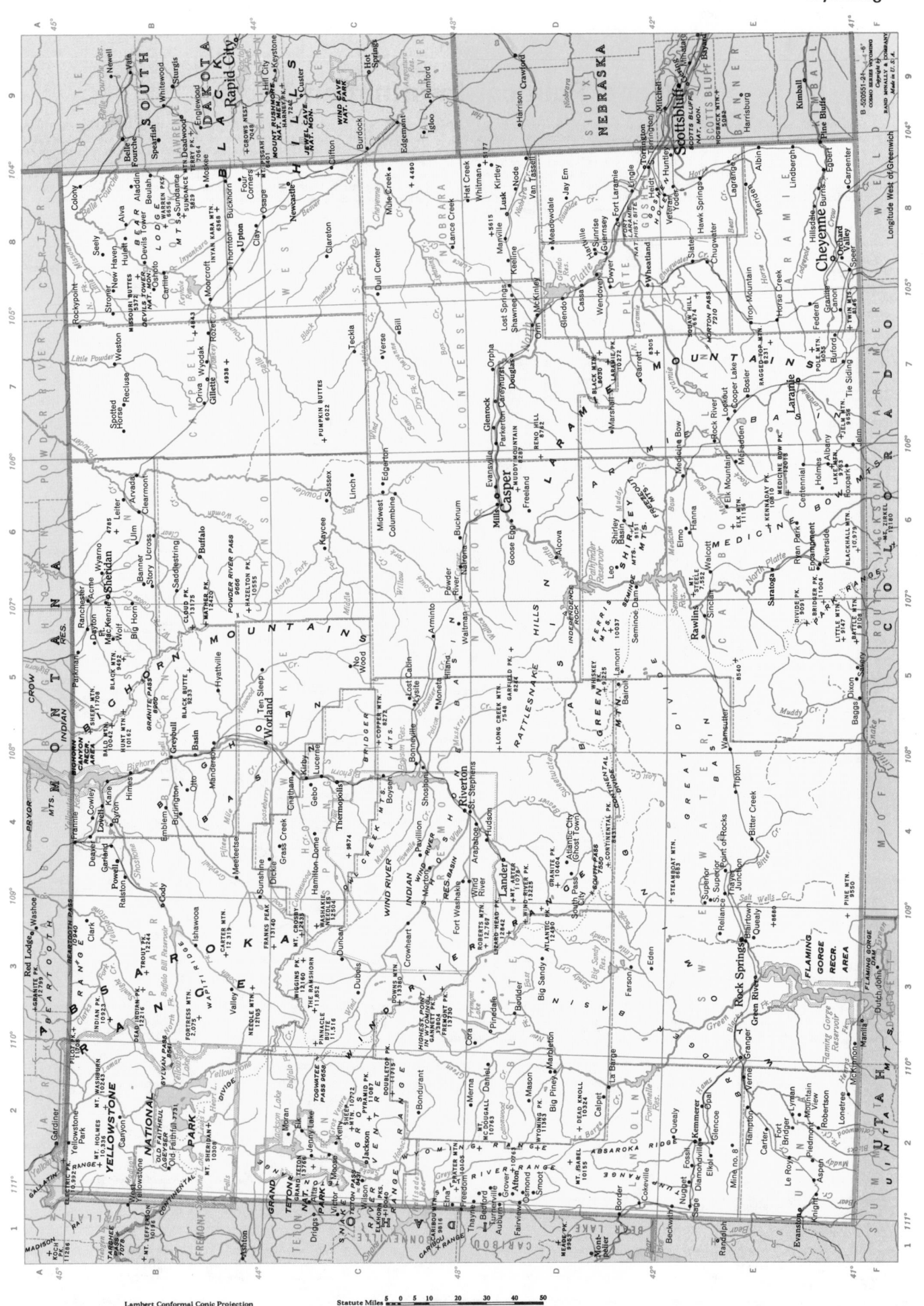

Lambert Conformal Conic Projection

Statute Miles 5 0 5 10 20 30 40 50

Kilometers 5 0 5 15 25 35 45 55 65 75

World Political Information Table

This table lists all countries and dependencies in the world, U.S. States, Canadian provinces, and other important regions and political subdivisions. Besides specifying the form of government for all political areas, the table classifies them into six groups according to their political status. Units labeled **A** are independent sovereign nations. (Several of these are designated as members of the British Commonwealth of Nations.) Units labeled **B** are independent as regards internal affairs, but for purposes of foreign affairs they are under the protection of another country. Units labeled **C** are colonies, overseas territories, dependencies, etc., of other countries. Together the **A**, **B**, and **C** areas comprise practically the entire inhabited area of the world. The areas labeled **D** are physically separate units, such as groups of islands, which are *not* separate countries, but form part of a nation or dependency. Units labeled **E** are States, provinces, Soviet Republics, or similar major administrative subdivisions of important countries. Units in the table with no letter designation are regions or other areas that do not constitute separate political units by themselves.

Region or Political Division	Area* in sq. miles	Estimated Population 1/1/1981	Pop. per sq. mi.	Form of Government and Ruling Power	Capital; Largest City (unless same)	Predominant Languages
Aden, see Yemen, P.D.R. of......	....	....	......			
Afars & Issas, see Djibouti......						
Afghanistan†	250,000	15,055,000	60	Republic.................................A	Kābul	Pushtu (Afghan), Persian
Africa	11,708,000	482,400,000	41		........; Cairo	
Alabama	51,609	3,920,000	76	State (U.S.).............................E	Montgomery; Birmingham	
Alaska	589,759	405,000	0.7	State U.S..............................E	Juneau; Anchorage	English, Indian, Eskimo
Albania†	11,100	2,725,000	245	People's Republic.......................A	Tiranë	Albanian
Alberta	255,285	1,920,000	7.5	Province (Canada)......................E	Edmonton	English
Algeria†	919,595	20,050,000	22	Republic................................A	Algiers (Alger)	Arabic, French, Berber
American Samoa	76	33,000	434	Unincorporated Territory (U.S.).........C	Pago Pago	Polynesian, English
Andaman & Nicobar Is.	3,202	195,000	61	Territory (India).......................D	Port Blair	Andaman, Nicobar Malay
Andorra	175	39,000	223	Principality............................	Andorra	Catalan
Angola†	481,353	7,155,000	15	Republic................................A	Luanda	Bantu languages, Portuguese
Anguilla	34	7,700	226	Associated State (U.K.)................B	The Valley; South Hill	English
Antarctica	5,100,000	....	......			
Antigua (incl. Barbuda)	170	75,000	441	Associated State (U.K.)................B	St. Johns	English
Arabian Peninsula	1,159,500	20,155,000	17		........; Kuwait	Arabic
Argentina†	1,068,301	27,235,000	25	Federal Republic.......................A	Buenos Aires	Spanish
Arizona	113,909	2,740,000	24	State (U.S.).............................E	Phoenix	
Arkansas	53,104	2,300,000	43	State (U.S.).............................E	Little Rock	
Armenia (S.S.R.)	11,506	3,075,000	267	Soviet Socialist Republic (Sov. Un.).....E	Yerevan	Armenian, Russian
Aruba	75	65,000	867	Division of Netherlands Antilles (Neth.)..........D	Oranjestad	Dutch, Spanish, English, Papiamento
Ascension	34	1,000	29	Dependency of St. Helena (U.K.).......D	Georgetown	English
Asia	17,297,000	2,631,600,000	152		........; Tōkyō	
Australia†	2,967,909	14,680,000	4.9	Parliamentary State (Federal) (Commonwealth of Nations)............................A	Canberra; Sydney	English
Australian Capital Territory	939	235,000	250	Territory (Australia)...................E	Canberra	English
Austria†	32,375	7,500,000	232	Federal Republic.......................A	Vienna (Wien)	German
Azerbaidzhan (S.S.R.)	33,436	6,145,000	184	Soviet Socialist Republic (Sov. Un.).....E	Baku	Turkic languages, Russian, Armenian
Azores	902	296,000	328	Part of Portugal (3 Districts)..........D	........; Ponta Delgada	Portuguese
Baden-Württemberg	13,804	9,250,000	670	State (Federal Republic of Germany).....E	Stuttgart	German
Bahamas†	5,382	250,000	46	Parliamentary State (Commonwealth of Nations)......A	Nassau	English
Bahrain†	256	285,000	1,113	Sheikdom...............................A	Manama	Arabic
Balearic Is.	1,936	700,000	362	Part of Spain (Baleares Province).......D	Palma	Catalan, Spanish
Baltic Republics	67,182	7,565,000	113	Soviet Union	........; Rīga	Lithuanian, Latvian, Estonian, Russian
Bangladesh†	55,598	89,595,000	1,611	Republic (Commonwealth of Nations)......A	Dacca	Bengali, English
Barbados†	166	275,000	1,657	Parliamentary State (Commonwealth of Nations)......A	Bridgetown	English
Basutoland, see Lesotho	....	....	......			
Bavaria (Bayern)	27,238	10,920,000	401	State (Federal Republic of Germany)......E	Munich (München)	German
Bechuanaland, see Botswana						
Belgium†	11,781	9,860,000	837	Monarchy...............................A	Brussels (Bruxelles)	Dutch, French, Flemish
Belize (British Honduras)	8,866	165,000	19	Colony (U.K.)..........................B	Belmopan; Belize City	English, Spanish, Indian languages
Benelux	28,672	24,400,000	851		........; Brussels	Dutch, French, Luxembourgeois
Benin†	43,484	3,610,000	83	Republic................................A	Porto-Novo; Cotonou	Native languages, French
Berlin, West	185	1,910,000	10,324	State (Federal Republic of Germany)......E	Berlin (West)	German
Bermuda	21	61,000	2,905	Colony (U.K.)..........................C	Hamilton	English
Bhutan†	18,147	1,340,000	74	Monarchy (Indian protection)...........B	Thimbu	Tibetan dialects
Bioko	785	92,000	117	Part of Equatorial Guinea..............D	Malabo (Santa Isabel)	Bantu languages, Spanish
Bolivia†	424,164	5,640,000	13	Republic................................A	Sucre and La Paz; La Paz	Spanish, Quechua, Aymará, Guaraní
Borneo, Indonesian (Kalimantan)	208,287	6,754,000	32	Part of Indonesia......................D	........; Banjarmasin	Bahasa Indonesia (Indonesian)
Botswana (Bechuanaland)†	231,805	870,000	3.8	Republic (Commonwealth of Nations)......A	Gaborone	Bechuana, other Bantu languages, English
Brazil†	3,286,487	123,795,000	38	Federal Republic.......................A	Brasília; São Paulo	Portuguese
Bremen	156	680,000	4,359	State (Federal Republic of Germany)......E	Bremen	German
British Antarctic Territory (excl. Antarctic mainland)	2,040	Winter pop. 85	0.04	Colony (U.K.)..........................C	Administered from Stanley, Falkland Islands	English
British Columbia	366,255	2,595,000	7.1	Province (Canada)......................E	Victoria; Vancouver	English
British Guiana, see Guyana	....	....	......			
British Indian Ocean Territory	23	....	......	Colony (U.K.)..........................C	Administered from London	
Brunei	2,226	230,000	103	Sultanate (U.K. protection).............B	Bandar Seri Begawan (Brunei)	Malay-Polynesian languages, English
Bulgaria†	42,823	9,110,000	213	People's Republic.......................A	Sofia (Sofiya)	Bulgarian
Burma†	261,228	33,585,000	129	Republic................................A	Rangoon	Burmese, English
Burundi (Urundi)†	10,747	4,560,000	424	Republic................................A	Bujumbura	Bantu and Hamitic languages, French
Byelorussia (Belorussia) (S.S.R.)†	80,155	9,725,000	121	Soviet Socialist Republic (Sov. Un.).....E	Minsk	Byelorussian, Polish, Russian
California	158,694	23,850,000	150	State (U.S.).............................E	Sacramento; Los Angeles	
Cambodia, see Kampuchea						
Cameroon†	183,569	8,525,000	46	Republic................................A	Yaoundé; Douala	Native languages, French
Canada†	3,831,033	24,005,000	6.3	Parliamentary State (Federal) (Commonwealth of Nations)............................A	Ottawa; Montréal	English, French
Canary Is.	2,808	1,605,000	572	Part of Spain (2 Provinces).............D	........; Las Palmas	Spanish
Cape Verde†	1,557	330,000	212	Republic................................A	Praia; Mindelo	Portuguese
Caroline Is.	446	89,000	200	Part of U.S. Pacific Is. Trust Ter. (4 Districts)........D	........; Koror	Malay-Polynesian languages, English
Cayman Is.	100	18,000	180	Colony (U.K.)..........................C	Georgetown	English
Celebes (Sulawesi)	73,057	11,206,000	153	Part of Indonesia......................D	........; Ujung Pandang	Bahasa Indonesia (Indonesian), Malay-Polynesian languages
Central African Republic†	240,535	2,020,000	8.4	Republic................................A	Bangui	Bantu languages, French
Central America	202,000	23,100,000	114		........; Guatemala	Spanish, Indian languages
Central Asia, Soviet	493,090	25,915,000	53	Soviet Union	........; Tashkent	Uzbek, Russian, Kirghiz, Turkoman, Tadzhik
Ceylon, see Sri Lanka						
Chad†	495,755	4,585,000	9.2	Republic................................A	Ndjamena (Fort Lamy)	Hamitic languages, Arabic, French
Channel Is. (Guernsey, Jersey, etc.)	75	132,000	1,760		........; St. Helier	English, French
Chile†	292,135	11,065,000	38	Republic................................A	Santiago	Spanish
China (excl. Taiwan)†	3,691,500	945,130,000	256	People's Republic.......................A	Peking (Peiping); Shanghai	Chinese, Mongolian, Turkic, Tungus
China (Nationalist), see Taiwan....						

† Member of the United Nations (1980).
* Areas include inland water.

Region or Political Division	Area* in sq. miles	Estimated Population 1/1/1981	Pop. per sq. mi.	Form of Government and Ruling Power	Capital; Largest City (unless same)	Predominant Languages
Christmas I. (Indian Ocean)	54	3,400	63	External Territory (Australia) C	; Flying Fish Cove	Chinese, Malay, English
Cocos (Keeling) Is.	5.4	300	56	External Territory (Australia) C		Malay, English
Colombia†	439,737	27,225,000	62	Republic A	Bogotá	Spanish
Colorado	104,248	2,910,000	28	State (U.S.) E	Denver	
Commonwealth of Nations	10,667,000	1,072,691,000	101		; London	
Comoros†	838	335,000	400	Republic A	Moroni	Swahili, French, Arabic
Congo†	132,047	1,550,000	12	Republic A	Brazzaville	Bantu languages, French
Congo, The, see Zaire						
Connecticut	5,009	3,130,000	625	State (U.S.) E	Hartford	
Cook Is.	91	16,000	176	Self-Governing Territory (New Zealand) B	Avarua	Malay-Polynesian languages, English
Corsica	3,352	200,000	60	Part of France (2 Departments) D	; Ajaccio	French, Italian
Costa Rica†	19,730	2,300,000	117	Republic A	San José	Spanish
Cuba†	44,218	9,700,000	219	Republic A	Havana (La Habana)	Spanish
Curaçao	171	165,000	965	Division of Netherlands Antilles (Neth.) D	Willemstad	Dutch, Spanish, English, Papiamento
Cyprus †	3,572	640,000	179	Republic (Commonwealth of Nations) A	Nicosia	Greek, Turkish, English
Czechoslovakia†	49,374	15,420,000	312	People's Republic A	Prague (Praha)	Czech, Slovak
Dahomey, see Benin						
Delaware	2,057	600,000	292	State (U.S.) E	Dover; Wilmington	
Denmark†	16,631	5,145,000	309	Monarchy A	Copenhagen (København)	Danish
Denmark and Possessions	857,175	5,239,000	6.1		Copenhagen (København)	Danish, Faeroese, Greenlandic
District of Columbia	67	640,000	9,552	District (U.S.) E	Washington	
Djibouti†	8,880	121,000	14	Republic A	Djibouti	Somali, French
Dominica†	290	83,000	286	Republic (Commonwealth of Nations) A	Roseau	English, French
Dominican Republic†	18,704	5,515,000	295	Republic A	Santo Domingo	Spanish
Ecuador†	109,483	8,625,000	79	Republic A	Quito; Guayaquil	Spanish, Quechua
Egypt (United Arab Republic)†	‡‡386,900	43,135,000	111	Republic A	Cairo (Al Qāhirah)	Arabic
Ellice Is., see Tuvalu						
El Salvador†	8,124	4,590,000	565	Republic A	San Salvador	Spanish
England (excl. Monmouthshire)	50,362	46,465,000	923	United Kingdom	; London	English
England & Wales	58,381	49,250,000	844	Administrative division of United Kingdom E	London	English, Welsh
Equatorial Guinea†	10,831	370,000	34	Republic A	Malabo	Bantu languages, Spanish
Estonia (S.S.R.)	17,413	1,525,000	88	Soviet Socialist Republic (Sov. Un.) E	Tallinn	Estonian, Russian
Ethiopia†	472,434	30,645,000	65	Provisional Military Government A	Addis Ababa	Amharic and other Semitic languages, English, various Hamitic languages
Eurasia	21,132,000	3,296,200,000	156		; Tōkyō	
Europe	3,835,000	664,600,000	173		; London	
Faeroe Is.	540	43,000	80	Self-Governing Territory (Denmark) B	Tórshavn	Danish, Faeroese
Falkland Is. (excl. Deps.)	4,700	2,000	0.4	Colony (U.K.) C	Stanley	English
Fernando Poo, see Bioko						
Fiji†	7,055	635,000	90	Parliamentary State (Commonwealth of Nations) A	Suva	English, Fijian, Hindustani
Finland†	130,129	4,785,000	37	Republic A	Helsinki	Finnish, Swedish
Florida	58,560	9,950,000	170	State (U.S.) E	Tallahassee; Miami	
France†	211,208	53,780,000	255	Republic A	Paris	French
France and Possessions	260,661	55,330,000	212		Paris	
Franklin	549,253	8,000	0.01	District of Northwest Territories, Canada E	; Frobisher Bay	English, Eskimo, Indian
French Guiana	35,135	63,000	1.8	Overseas Department (France) C	Cayenne	French
French Polynesia	1,544	150,000	97	Overseas Territory (France) C	Papeete	Malay-Polynesian languages, French
French Somaliland, see Djibouti						
French Southern & Antarctic Ter. (excl. Adélie Coast)	3,000	200	0.07	Overseas Territory (France) C		French
French West Indies	1,112	630,000	567		; Fort-de-France	French
Gabon†	103,347	555,000	5.4	Republic A	Libreville	Bantu languages, French
Galapagos Is. (Colón, Archipiélago de)	3,075	5,800	1.9	Province (Ecuador) D	Puerto Baquerizo Moreno	Spanish
Gambia†	4,361	610,000	140	Republic (Commonwealth of Nations) A	Banjul (Bathurst)	English, native languages
Georgia (S.S.R.)	26,911	5,105,000	190	Soviet Socialist Republic (Sov. Un.) E	Tbilisi	Georgic, Armenian, Russian
Georgia	58,876	5,505,000	94	State (U.S.) E	Atlanta	
Germany (Entire)	137,772	78,405,000	569		; Essen	German
German Democratic Republic (East Germany)†	41,768	16,715,000	400	People's Republic A	Berlin (East)	German
Germany, Federal Republic of (West Germany)†	96,004	61,690,000	643	Federal Republic A	Bonn; Essen	German
Ghana†	92,100	11,835,000	129	Republic (Commonwealth of Nations) A	Accra	English, native languages
Gibraltar	2.3	30,000	13,043	Colony (U.K.) C	Gibraltar	Spanish, English
Gilbert Is., see Kiribati						
Great Britain & Northern Ireland, see United Kingdom						
Greece†	50,944	9,565,000	188	Republic A	Athens (Athínai)	Greek
Greenland	840,004	51,000	0.06	Overseas Territory (Denmark) C	Godthåb	Greenlandic, Danish, Eskimo
Grenada†	133	114,000	857	Parliamentary State (Commonwealth of Nations) A	St. George's	English
Guadeloupe (incl. Dependencies)	687	320,000	466	Overseas Department (France) C	Basse-Terre; Pointe-à-Pitre	French
Guam	212	107,000	505	Unincorporated Territory (U.S.) C	Agana	English, Chamorro
Guatemala†	42,042	7,685,000	183	Republic A	Guatemala	Spanish, Indian languages
Guernsey (incl. Dependencies)	30	55,000	1,833	Bailiwick (U.K.) C	St. Peter Port	English, French
Guinea†	94,926	5,070,000	53	Republic A	Conakry	Native languages, French
Guinea-Bissau†	13,948	805,000	58	Republic A	Bissau	Native languages, Portuguese
Guyana†	83,000	921,000	11	Republic (Commonwealth of Nations) A	Georgetown	English
Haiti†	10,714	5,040,000	470	Republic A	Port-au-Prince	Creole, French
Hamburg	289	1,665,000	5,761	State (Federal Republic of Germany) E	Hamburg	German
Hawaii	6,450	970,000	150	State (U.S.) E	Honolulu	English, Japanese, Hawaiian
Hesse (Hessen)	8,152	5,615,000	689	State (Federal Republic of Germany) E	Wiesbaden; Frankfurt am Main	German
Hispaniola	29,418	10,555,000	359		; Port-au-Prince	French, Spanish
Holland, see Netherlands						
Honduras†	43,277	3,750,000	87	Republic A	Tegucigalpa	Spanish
Hong Kong	410	5,265,000	12,841	Colony (U.K.) C	Victoria	Chinese, English
Hungary†	35,920	10,945,000	305	People's Republic A	Budapest	Hungarian
Iceland†	39,769	229,000	5.8	Republic A	Reykjavík	Icelandic
Idaho	83,557	950,000	11	State (U.S.) E	Boise	
Illinois	57,926	11,505,000	199	State (U.S.) E	Springfield; Chicago	
India (incl. part of Kashmir)†	1,237,061	669,860,000	541	Republic (Commonwealth of Nations) A	New Delhi; Calcutta	Hindi and other Indo-Aryan languages, Dravidian languages, English
Indiana	36,519	5,530,000	151	State (U.S.) E	Indianapolis	
Indonesia (incl. West Irian)†	741,034	153,510,000	207	Republic A	Jakarta	Bahasa Indonesia (Indonesian), Chinese, English
Iowa	56,290	2,935,000	52	State (U.S.) E	Des Moines	
Iran (Persia)†	636,296	38,940,000	61	Republic A	Tehrān	Persian, Turkish dialects, Kurdish
Iraq†	167,925	13,230,000	79	Republic A	Baghdād	Arabic, Kurdish
Ireland†	27,136	3,455,000	127	Republic A	Dublin	English, Irish
Isle of Man	227	66,000	291	Possession (U.K.) C	Douglas	English
Israel†	‡‡7,848	3,920,000^	499	Republic A	Jerusalem; Tel Aviv-Yafo	Hebrew, Arabic
Italy†	116,318	57,230,000	492	Republic A	Rome (Roma); Milan (Milano)	Italian

† *Member of the United Nations (1980).*
‡‡ *Areas for Egypt, Israel, Jordan and Syria do not reflect de facto changes which took place since 1967.*
^ *Population excludes 1,100,000 people in territories administered by Israel.*
* *Areas include inland water.*

World Political Information Table *Continued*

Region or Political Division	Area* in sq. miles	Estimated Population 1/1/1981	Pop. per sq. mi.	Form of Government and Ruling Power	Capital; Largest City (unless same)	Predominant Languages
Ivory Coast†	123,847	8,390,000	68	Republic.................................A	Abidjan	French, native languages
Jamaica†	4,244	2,210,000	521	Parliamentary State (Commonwealth of Nations).....A	Kingston	English
Japan†	145,709	117,360,000	805	Monarchy................................A	Tōkyō	Japanese
Java (Jawa) (incl. Madura)	51,038	96,251,000	1,886	Part of Indonesia........................D	.........; Jakarta	Bahasa Indonesia (Indonesian), Chinese, English
Jersey	45	77,000	1,711	Bailiwick (U.K.).........................C	St. Helier	English, French
Jordan†	‡‡37,738	2,925,000	78	Monarchy................................A	'Ammān	Arabic
Kampuchea†	69,898	6,810,000	97	Republic................................A	Phnom Penh	Cambodian (Khmer), French
Kansas	82,264	2,380,000	29	State (U.S.)............................E	Topeka; Wichita	
Kashmir, Jammu &	86,024	9,700,000	113	In dispute (India & Pakistan)............	Srinagar	Kashmiri, Punjabi
Kazakh (S.S.R.)	1,049,155	14,960,000	14	Soviet Socialist Republic (Sov. Un.)......E	Alma-Ata	Turkic languages, Russian
Keewatin	228,160	5,000	0.02	District of Northwest Territories, Canada.....E	Baker Lake	English, Eskimo, Indian
Kentucky	40,395	3,690,000	91	State (U.S.)............................E	Frankfort; Louisville	
Kenya†	224,961	16,035,000	71	Republic (Commonwealth of Nations)........A	Nairobi	Swahili and other Bantu languages, English
Kerguelen Is.	2,700	90	0.03	Part of French Southern & Antarctic Ter. (Fr.)...D		French
Kirghiz (S.S.R.)	76,641	3,580,000	47	Soviet Socialist Republic (Sov. Un.)......E	Frunze	Turkic languages, Persian, Russian
Kiribati (Gilbert Is.)	291	59,000	203	Republic (Commonwealth of Nations)........A	Bairiki	Malay-Polynesian languages, English
Korea (Entire)	85,052‡	56,585,000	665		.........; Seoul (Sŏul)	Korean
Korea, North	46,540	18,115,000	389	People's Republic........................A	Pyŏngyang	Korean
Korea, South	38,025	38,470,000	1,012	Republic................................A	Seoul (Sŏul)	Korean
Kuwait†	6,880	1,380,000	201	Sheikdom................................A	Kuwait (Al-Kuwayt)	Arabic
Labrador	112,826	35,000	0.3	Part of Newfoundland Province, Canada.....D	.........; Labrador City	English, Eskimo
Laos†	91,429	3,760,000	41	People's Republic........................A	Viangchan	Lao, French
Latin America	7,938,600	367,960,000	46		.........; Mexico City	Spanish, Portuguese
Latvia (S.S.R.)	24,595	2,565,000	104	Soviet Socialist Republic (Sov. Un.)......E	Rīga	Latvian, Russian
Lebanon†	4,015	3,205,000	798	Republic................................A	Beirut (Bayrūt)	Arabic, French, English
Lesotho (Basutoland)†	11,720	1,360,000	116	Monarchy (Commonwealth of Nations)........A	Maseru	Sesotho, English
Liberia†	43,000	1,890,000	44	Republic................................A	Monrovia	Native languages, English
Libya†	679,362	3,030,000	4.5	Republic................................A	Tripoli	Arabic
Liechtenstein	61	26,000	426	Principality............................A	Vaduz	German
Lithuania (S.S.R.)	25,174	3,475,000	138	Soviet Socialist Republic (Sov. Un.)......E	Vilnius	Lithuanian, Polish, Russian
Louisiana	48,523	4,235,000	87	State (U.S.)............................E	Baton Rouge; New Orleans	
Lower Saxony (Niedersachsen)	18,308	7,280,000	398	State (Federal Republic of Germany).......E	Hannover	German
Luxembourg†	999	370,000	370	Grand Duchy.............................A	Luxembourg	Luxembourgeois, French, German
Macao	6.0	295,000	49,167	Overseas Province (Portugal).............C	Macao	Chinese, Portuguese
Macías Nguema Biyogo, see Bioko.						
Mackenzie	527,490	36,000	0.07	District of Northwest Territories, Canada.....E	.........; Yellowknife	English, Eskimo, Indian
Madagascar (Malagasy Republic)†	226,658	8,835,000	39	Republic................................A	Antananarivo	French, Malagasy
Madeira Is.	307	269,000	876	Part of Portugal (Funchal District).......D	Funchal	Portuguese
Maine	33,215	1,135,000	34	State (U.S.)............................E	Augusta; Portland	
Malawi (Nyasaland)†	45,747	6,045,000	132	Republic (Commonwealth of Nations)........A	Lilongwe; Blantyre	Bantu languages, English
Malaya	50,700	11,943,000	236	Part of Malaysia........................	Kuala Lumpur	Malay, Chinese, English
Malaysia†	128,430	14,185,000	110	Constitutional Monarchy (Comm. of Nations)........A	Kuala Lumpur	Malay, Chinese, English
Maldives†	115	155,000	1,348	Republic................................A	Male	Arabic, Divehi
Mali†	478,766	6,735,000	14	Republic................................A	Bamako	French, Bambara
Malta†	122	360,000	2,951	Republic (Commonwealth of Nations)........A	Valletta	English, Maltese
Manitoba	251,000	1,055,000	4.2	Province (Canada).......................E	Winnipeg	English
Mariana Is. (excl. Guam)	183	17,000	93	District of U.S. Pacific Is. Trust Ter.....D	Saipan (island); Chalon Kamoa	Malay-Polynesian languages, English
Maritime Provinces (excl. Newfoundland)	51,963	1,705,000	33	Canada	.........; Halifax	English
Marshall Is.	70	30,000	429	District of U.S. Pacific Is. Trust Ter.....D	Majuro (island); Ebeye	Malay-Polynesian languages, English
Martinique	425	310,000	729	Overseas Department (France)..............C	Fort-de-France	French
Maryland	10,577	4,250,000	402	State (U.S.)............................E	Annapolis; Baltimore	
Massachusetts	8,257	5,780,000	700	State (U.S.)............................E	Boston	
Mauritania†	397,955	1,655,000	4.2	Republic................................A	Nouakchott	Arabic, French
Mauritius (incl. Dependencies)†	790	960,000	1,215	Parliamentary State (Commonwealth of Nations).....A	Port Louis	French, Creole, English
Mayotte	144	50,000	347	Overseas Department (France)..............C	.........; Dzaoudzi	Malagasy, French
Mexico†	761,604	73,010,000	96	Federal Republic........................A	Mexico City	Spanish
Michigan	96,791	9,330,000	96	State (U.S.)............................E	Lansing; Detroit	
Middle America	1,055,600	124,860,000	118		.........; Mexico City	
Midway Is.	2.0	1,500	750	Unincorporated Territory (U.S.)...........C	Administered from Washington, D.C.	English
Minnesota	86,280	4,110,000	48	State (U.S.)............................E	St. Paul; Minneapolis	
Mississippi	47,716	2,540,000	53	State (U.S.)............................E	Jackson	
Missouri	69,686	4,955,000	71	State (U.S.)............................E	Jefferson City; St. Louis	
Moldavia (S.S.R.)	13,012	4,010,000	308	Soviet Socialist Republic (Sov. Un.)......E	Kishinev	Moldavian, Russian, Ukrainian
Monaco	0.6	25,000	41,667	Principality............................A	Monaco	French, Italian
Mongolia†	604,250	1,690,000	2.8	People's Republic........................A	Ulan Bator (Ulaanbaatar)	Mongolian
Montana	147,138	790,000	5.4	State (U.S.)............................E	Helena; Billings	
Montserrat	40	11,000	275	Colony (U.K.)...........................C	Plymouth	English
Morocco (excl. Western Sahara)†..	172,414	20,465,000	119	Monarchy................................A	Rabat; Casablanca	Arabic, Berber, French
Mozambique†	302,329	15,590,000	52	Republic................................A	Maputo	Bantu Languages, Portuguese
Namibia (excl. Walvis Bay)	318,261	1,035,000	3.3	Under South African Administration**......C	Windhoek	Bantu languages, Afrikaans, English, German
Nauru	8.2	7,700	939	Republic (Commonwealth of Nations)........A	Uaboe District; ...	Nauruan, English
Nebraska	77,227	1,580,000	20	State (U.S.)............................E	Lincoln; Omaha	
Nepal†	54,362	15,155,000	279	Monarchy................................A	Kathmandu	Nepali, Tibeto-Burman languages, English
Netherlands†	15,892	14,170,000	892	Monarchy................................A	Amsterdam and The Hague ('s-Gravenhage); Amsterdam	Dutch
Netherlands and Possessions	16,275	14,425,000	886		Amsterdam and The Hague; Amsterdam	
Netherlands Antilles	383	255,000	666	Self-Governing Territory (Netherlands).....C	Willemstad	Dutch, Spanish, English, Papiamento
Netherlands Guiana, see Suriname.						
Nevada	110,541	805,000	7.3	State (U.S.)............................E	Carson City; Las Vegas	
New Brunswick	28,354	720,000	25	Province (Canada).......................E	Fredericton; Saint John	English, French
New Caledonia (incl. Deps.)	7,358	139,000	19	Overseas Territory (France)...............C	Nouméa	Malay-Polynesian languages, French
New England	66,608	12,440,000	187	United States..........................	.........; Boston	English
Newfoundland	156,185	575,000	3.7	Province (Canada).......................E	St. John's	English
Newfoundland (excl. Labrador)	43,359	540,000	12		.........; St. John's	English
New Hampshire	9,304	925,000	99	State (U.S.)............................E	Concord; Manchester	
New Hebrides, see Vanuatu.						
New Jersey	7,836	7,420,000	947	State (U.S.)............................E	Trenton; Newark	
New Mexico	121,667	1,310,000	11	State (U.S.)............................E	Santa Fe; Albuquerque	English, Spanish
New South Wales	309,433	5,170,000	17	State (Australia).......................E	Sydney	English
New York	53,203	17,690,000	333	State (U.S.)............................E	Albany; New York	
New Zealand†	103,883	3,125,000	30	Parliamentary State (Commonwealth of Nations).....A	Wellington; Auckland	English, Maori
Nicaragua†	50,193	2,610,000	52	Republic................................A	Managua	Spanish
Niedersachsen, see Lower Saxony.						
Niger†	489,191	5,380,000	11	Republic................................A	Niamey	Hausa, Arabic, French

† *Member of the United Nations (1980).* ‡ *Includes 487 sq. miles of demilitarized zone, not included in North or South Korea figures.*
‡‡ *Areas for Egypt, Israel, Jordan, and Syria do not reflect de facto changes which took place since 1967.*
** *The United Nations declared an end to the mandate of South Africa over Namibia in October 1966. Administration of the territory by South Africa is not recognized by the United Nations.*
* *Areas include inland water.*

Region or Political Division	Area* in sq. miles	Estimated Population 1/1/1981	Pop. per sq. mi.	Form of Government and Ruling Power	Capital; Largest City (unless same)	Predominant Languages
Nigeria†	356,669	78,135,000	219	Republic (Commonwealth of Nations) ....A	Lagos	Hausa, Ibo, Yoruba, English
Niue	102	3,100	30	Self-Governing Territory (New Zealand) ....B	Alofi	Malay-Polynesian languages, English
Norfolk Island	14	2,300	164	External Territory (Australia) C	Kingston	English
North America	9,406,000	377,400,000	40	....	........; New York	....
North Borneo, see Sabah						
North Carolina	52,586	5,920,000	113	State (U.S.) ....E	Raleigh; Charlotte	....
North Dakota	70,665	660,000	9.3	State (U.S.) ....E	Bismarck; Fargo	....
Northern Ireland	5,452	1,545,000	283	Administrative division of United Kingdom ....E	Belfast	English
Northern Rhodesia, see Zambia						
Northern Territory	520,280	120,000	0.2	Territory (Australia) ....E	Darwin	English, Aboriginal languages
North Polar Regions	....	....	......	....		
North Rhine-Westphalia (Nordrhein-Westfalen)	13,154	17,090,000	1,299	State (Federal Republic of Germany) ....E	Dusseldorf; Essen	German
Northwest Territories	1,304,903	49,000	0.04	Territory (Canada) ....E	Yellowknife	English, Eskimo, Indian
Norway†	125,056	4,095,000	33	Monarchy ....A	Oslo	Norwegian (Riksmål and Landsmål)
Nova Scotia	21,425	865,000	40	Province (Canada) ....E	Halifax	English
Nyasaland, see Malawi						
Oceania (incl. Australia)	3,287,000	22,900,000	7.0		........; Sydney	....
Ohio	44,679	10,880,000	244	State (U.S.) ....E	Columbus; Cleveland	
Oklahoma	69,919	3,050,000	44	State (U.S.) ....E	Oklahoma City	
Oman†	82,030	900,000	11	Sultanate ....A	Muscat; Maṭraḥ	Arabic
Ontario	412,582	8,640,000	21	Province (Canada) ....E	Toronto	English
Oregon	96,981	2,650,000	27	State (U.S.) ....E	Salem; Portland	English
Orkney Is.	376	19,000	51	Part of Scotland, U.K. (Orkney Island Area).......D	Kirkwall	English
Pacific Islands Trust Territory	699	136,000	195	Administered by U.S. C	Saipan (island); Ebeye	Malay-Polynesian languages, English
Pakistan (incl. part of Kashmir)†	319,867	88,610,000	277	Republic ....A	Islāmābād; Karāchi	Urdu, English, Punjabi
Pakistan, East, see Bangladesh						
Panama†	29,762	2,000,000	67	Republic ....A	Panamá	Spanish
Papua New Guinea†	178,703	3,210,000	18	Republic (Commonwealth of Nations) ....A	Port Moresby	Papuan and Negrito languages, English
Paraguay†	157,048	3,100,000	20	Republic ....A	Asunción	Spanish, Guaraní
Pennsylvania	46,068	11,955,000	260	State (U.S.) ....E	Harrisburg; Philadelphia	
Persia, see Iran						
Peru†	496,224	17,995,000	36	Republic ....A	Lima	Spanish, Quechua
Philippines†	115,831	48,200,000	416	Republic ....A	Manila	Pilipino, English
Pitcairn (excl. Dependencies)	1.8	65	36	Colony (U.K.) C	Adamstown	English
Poland†	120,728	35,645,000	295	People's Republic ....A	Warsaw (Warszawa); Katowice	Polish
Portugal†	34,340	9,980,000	291	Republic ....A	Lisbon (Lisboa)	Portuguese
Portugal and Possessions	34,346	10,275,000	299		Lisbon (Lisboa)	
Portuguese Guinea, see Guinea-Bissau	....	....	......	....		
Prairie Provinces	757,985	3,945,000	5.2	Canada	........; Winnipeg	English
Prince Edward Island	2,184	120,000	55	Province (Canada) ....E	Charlottetown	English
Puerto Rico	3,435	3,223,000	938	Commonwealth (U.S.) C	San Juan	Spanish, English
Qatar†	4,247	225,000	53	Emirate ....A	Doha	Arabic
Quebec	594,860	6,480,000	11	Province (Canada) ....E	Québec; Montréal	French, English
Queensland	667,000	2,230,000	3.3	State (Australia) ....E	Brisbane	English
Reunion	969	500,000	516	Overseas Department (France) C	St. Denis	French
Rhineland-Palatinate (Rheinland-Pfalz)	7,660	3,640,000	475	State (Federal Republic of Germany) ....E	Mainz	German
Rhode Island	1,214	955,000	787	State (U.S.) ....E	Providence	English
Rhodesia, see Zimbabwe	....	....	......	....		....
Rio Muni, see Equatorial Guinea	....					
Rodrigues	42	29,000	690	Dependency of Mauritius (U.K.) ....D	........; Port Mathurin	English, French
Romania†	91,699	22,345,000	244	People's Republic ....E	Bucharest (Bucureşti)	Romanian, Hungarian
Russian Soviet Federated Socialist Republic	6,592,846	140,030,000	21	Soviet Federated Socialist Republic (Sov. Un.) ....E	Moscow (Moskva)	Russian, Finno-Ugric languages, various Turkic, Iranian, and Mongol languages
Russian S.F.S.R. in Europe	1,527,350	102,440,000	67	Soviet Union	........; Moscow	Russian, Finno-Ugric languages
Rwanda†	10,169	4,780,000	470	Republic ....A	Kigali	Bantu and Hamitic languages, French
Saar (Saarland)	993	1,050,000	1,057	State (Federal Republic of Germany) ....E	Saarbrücken	German
Sabah (North Borneo)	29,388	964,000	33	Administrative division of Malaysia ....E	Kota Kinabalu; Sandakan	Malay, Chinese, English
St. Helena (incl. Dependencies)	162	6,800	42	Colony (U.K.) C	Jamestown	English
St. Kitts-Nevis	104	53,000	510	Associated State (U.K.) ....B	Basseterre	English
Saint Lucia†	238	124,000	521	Parliamentary State (Commonwealth of Nations) ......A	Castries	English
St. Pierre & Miquelon	93	6,200	67	Overseas Department (France) C	St.-Pierre	French
St. Vincent†	150	126,000	840	Parliamentary State (Commonwealth of Nations) ......A	Kingstown	English
Samoa (Entire)	1,173	193,000	165		........; Apia	Samoan, English
San Marino	24	22,000	917	Republic ....A	San Marino	Italian
Sao Tome & Principe†	372	87,000	234	Republic ....A	São Tomé	Bantu languages, Portuguese
Sarawak	48,342	1,277,000	26	Administrative division of Malaysia ....E	Kuching	Malay, Chinese, English
Sardinia	9,301	1,600,000	172	Part of Italy (Sardegna Autonomous Region).........D	Cagliari	Italian
Saskatchewan	251,700	960,000	3.8	Province (Canada) ....E	Regina	English
Saudi Arabia†	830,000	8,465,000	10	Monarchy ....A	Riyadh	Arabic
Scandinavia (incl. Finland and Iceland)	510,000	22,612,000	44		........; Copenhagen (København)	Swedish, Danish, Norwegian, Finnish, Icelandic
Schleswig-Holstein	6,065	2,590,000	427	State (Federal Republic of Germany) ....E	Kiel	German
Scotland	30,416	5,150,000	169	Administrative division of United Kingdom ....E	Edinburgh; Glasgow	English, Gaelic
Senegal†	75,955	5,725,000	75	Republic ....A	Dakar	French, native languages
Seychelles†	171	67,000	392	Republic (Commonwealth of Nations) ....A	Victoria	French, Creole, English
Shetland Is.	551	23,000	42	Part of Scotland, U.K. (Shetland Island Area).......D	Lerwick	English
Siam, see Thailand						
Sicily	9,926	5,035,000	507	Part of Italy (Sicilia Autonomous Region).........D	Palermo	Italian
Sierra Leone†	27,925	4,125,000	148	Republic (Commonwealth of Nations) ....A	Freetown	English, native languages
Singapore†	224	2,465,000	11,004	Republic (Commonwealth of Nations) ....A	Singapore	Chinese, Malay, English, Tamil
Solomon Is.†	11,500	225,000	20	Parliamentary State (Commonwealth of Nations) ......A	Honiara	Malay-Polynesian languages, English
Somalia†	246,200	4,535,000	18	Republic ....A	Mogadishu (Muqdisho)	Somali, Arabic, English, Italian
South Africa (incl. Walvis Bay)†	471,447	29,645,000	63	Republic ....A	Pretoria and Cape Town; Johannesburg	English, Afrikaans, Bantu languages

† *Member of the United Nations (1980).*
* *Areas include inland water.*

World Political Information Table *Continued*

Region or Political Division	Area* in sq. miles	Estimated Population 1/1/1981	Pop. per sq. mi.	Form of Government and Ruling Power	Capital; Largest City (unless same)	Predominant Languages
South America	6,883,000	243,100,000	35		........; São Paulo	
South Australia	380,070	1,305,000	3.4	State (Australia)..........E	Adelaide	English
South Carolina	31,055	3,140,000	101	State (U.S.)..........E	Columbia; Charleston	
South Dakota	77,047	695,000	9.0	State (U.S.)..........E	Pierre; Sioux Falls	
Southern Rhodesia, see Zimbabwe.	....	....	....			
South Georgia	1,580	20	0.01	Dependency of Falkland Is. (U.K.)..........D		English, Norwegian
South West Africa, see Namibia...						
Soviet Union (Union of Soviet Socialist Republics)†	8,600,383	267,190,000	31	Federal Soviet Republic..........A	Moscow (Moskva)	Russian and other Slavic languages, various Finno-Ugric, Turkic, and Mongol languages, Caucasian languages, Persian
Soviet Union in Europe	1,920,789	174,400,000	91	Soviet Union	........; Moscow (Moskva)	Russian and other Slavic languages, various Finno-Ugric and Caucasian languages
Spain†	194,882	37,790,000	194	Monarchy..........A	Madrid	Spanish, Catalan, Galician, Basque
Spain and Possessions	194,894	37,921,000	195		Madrid	
Spanish North Africa	12	131,000	10,917	Five Possessions (no central government) (Spain)......C	........; Ceuta	Spanish, Arabic, Berber
Spanish Sahara, see Western Sahara.	....	....	....			
Sri Lanka (Ceylon)†	25,097	15,470,000	616	Republic (Commonwealth of Nations)..........A	Colombo	Sinhalese, Tamil, English
Sudan†	967,500	18,630,000	19	Republic..........A	Khartoum	Arabic, native languages, English
Sumatra (Sumatera)	182,860	28,092,000	154	Part of Indonesia..........D	........; Medan	Bahasa Indonesia, English, Chinese
Suriname†	63,037	425,000	6.7	Republic..........A	Paramaribo	Dutch, Creole, English
Svalbard and Jan Mayen	24,101	Winter pop. 3,000	0.1	Dependencies (Norway)..........C	........; Longyearbyen	Norwegian, Russian
Swaziland†	6,704	565,000	84	Monarchy (Commonwealth of Nations)..........A	Mbabane	Swazi and other Bantu languages, English
Sweden†	173,780	8,315,000	48	Monarchy..........A	Stockholm	Swedish
Switzerland	15,943	6,230,000	391	Federal Republic..........A	Bern (Berne); Zürich	German, French, Italian
Syria†	‡‡71,498	8,735,000	122	Republic..........A	Damascus (Dimashq)	Arabic
Tadzhik (S.S.R.)	55,251	3,875,000	70	Soviet Socialist Republic (Sov. Un.)..........E	Dushanbe	Tadzhik, Turkic languages, Russian
Taiwan (Formosa) (Nationalist China)	13,895	18,055,000	1,299	Republic..........A	Taipei	Chinese
Tanganyika, see Tanzania						
Tanzania (Tanganyika & Zanzibar)†	364,900	18,785,000	51	Republic (Commonwealth of Nations)..........A	Dar es Salaam	Swahili and other Bantu languages, English, Arabic
Tasmania	26,383	425,000	16	State (Australia)..........E	Hobart	English
Tennessee	42,244	4,625,000	109	State (U.S.)..........E	Nashville; Memphis	
Texas	267,339	14,335,000	54	State (U.S.)..........E	Austin; Dallas	
Thailand (Siam)†	198,114	47,845,000	242	Monarchy..........A	Bangkok (Krung Thep)	Thai
Tibet	471,700	1,700,000	3.6	Autonomous Region (China)..........E	Lasa (Lhasa)	Tibetan, Chinese
Togo†	21,925	2,565,000	117	Republic..........A	Lomé	Native languages, French
Tokelau (Union Is.)	3.9	1,600	410	Island Territory (New Zealand)..........C	........; Fakaofo	Malay-Polynesian languages, English
Tonga	270	97,000	359	Monarchy (Commonwealth of Nations)..........A	Nukualofa	Tongan, English
Transcaucasia	71,853	14,325,000	199	Soviet Union	........; Baku	
Trinidad & Tobago†	1,980	920,000	465	Republic (Commonwealth of Nations)..........A	Port of Spain	English
Tristan da Cunha	40	300	7.5	Dependency of St. Helena (U.K.)..........D	Edinburgh	English
Trucial States, see United Arab Emirates.	....	....	....			
Tunisia†	63,170	6,410,000	101	Republic..........A	Tunis	Arabic, French
Turkey†	300,948	45,955,000	153	Republic..........A	Ankara; İstanbul	Turkish
Turkey in Europe	9,175	3,965,000	432	Turkey	........; İstanbul	Turkish
Turkmen (S.S.R.)	188,456	2,805,000	15	Soviet Socialist Republic (Sov. Un.)..........E	Ashkhabad	Turkic languages, Russian
Turks & Caicos Is.	166	6,700	40	Colony (U.K.)..........C	Grand Turk	English
Tuvalu (Ellice Is.)	10	7,500	750	Parliamentary State (Commonwealth of Nations)......A	Funafuti	Malay-Polynesian languages, English
Uganda†	91,134	13,875,000	152	Republic (Commonwealth of Nations)..........A	Kampala	English, Swahili
Ukraine (S.S.R.)†	233,090	50,660,000	217	Soviet Socialist Republic (Sov. Un.)..........E	Kiev	Ukrainian, Russian
Union of Soviet Socialist Republics, see Soviet Union.						
United Arab Emirates†	32,278	1,055,000	33	Self-Governing Union..........A	Abu Dhabi; Dubai	Arabic
United Arab Republic, see Egypt.						
United Kingdom†	94,249	55,945,000	594	Monarchy (Commonwealth of Nations)..........A	London	English, Welsh, Gaelic
United Kingdom & Possessions	113,676	62,075,000	546		London	
United States†	3,678,896	228,340,000	62	Federal Republic..........A	Washington; New York	English
United States and Possessions	3,683,456	231,941,000	63		Washington; New York	English, Spanish
Upper Volta†	105,869	6,995,000	66	Republic..........A	Ouagadougou	French, native languages
Uruguay†	68,037	2,900,000	43	Republic..........A	Montevideo	Spanish
Utah	84,916	1,470,000	17	State (U.S.)..........E	Salt Lake City	
Uzbek (S.S.R.)	172,742	15,655,000	91	Soviet Socialist Republic (Sov. Un.)..........E	Tashkent	Turkic languages, Sart, Russian
Vanuatu (New Hebrides)	5,714	118,000	21	Parliamentary State (Commonwealth of Nations)..........A	Vila	Bislama, French, English
Vatican City (Holy See)	0.2	1,000	5,000	Ecclesiastical State..........A	Vatican City	Italian, Latin
Venezuela†	352,144	14,115,000	40	Federal Republic..........A	Caracas	Spanish
Vermont	9,609	515,000	54	State (U.S.)..........E	Montpelier; Burlington	
Victoria	87,884	3,920,000	45	State (Australia)..........E	Melbourne	English
Vietnam†	127,242	54,720,000	430	People's Republic..........A	Hanoi; Ho Chi Minh City (Saigon)	Vietnamese
Virginia	40,817	5,385,000	132	State (U.S.)..........E	Richmond; Norfolk	
Virgin Is., British	59	14,000	237	Colony (U.K.)..........C	Road Town	English
Virgin Is. (U.S.)	133	100,000	752	Unincorporated Territory (U.S.)..........C	Charlotte Amalie	English
Wake I.	3.0	200	67	Unincorporated Territory (U.S.)..........C	Administered from Washington, D.C.	English
Wales (incl. Monmouthshire)	8,019	2,785,000	347	United Kingdom	Cardiff	English, Welsh
Wallis & Futuna	98	12,000	122	Overseas Territory (France)..........C	Mata-Utu	Malay-Polynesian languages, French
Washington	68,192	4,160,000	61	State (U.S.)..........E	Olympia; Seattle	
Western Australia	975,920	1,275,000	1.3	State (Australia)..........E	Perth	English
Western Sahara	102,703	185,000	1.8	Occupied by Morocco..........C	El Aaiún	Arabic
Western Samoa†	1,097	160,000	146	Constitutional Monarchy (Comm. of Nations)..........A	Apia	Samoan, English
West Indies	92,000	28,750,000	313		........; Havana	
West Virginia	24,181	1,965,000	81	State (U.S.)..........E	Charleston; Huntington	
White Russia, see Byelorussia						
Wisconsin	66,216	4,740,000	72	State (U.S.)..........E	Madison; Milwaukee	
World	57,516,000	4,422,000,000	77		........; Tōkyō	
Wyoming	97,914	475,000	4.9	State (U.S.)..........E	Cheyenne; Casper	
Yemen†	75,290	5,995,000	80	Republic..........A	Ṣanʻāʼ	Arabic
Yemen, People's Democratic Republic of,†	128,560	1,850,000	14	People's Republic..........A	Aden	Arabic; English
Yugoslavia†	98,766	22,450,000	227	Socialist Federal Republic..........A	Belgrade (Beograd)	Serbo-Croatian, Slovenian, Macedonian
Yukon Territory	186,300	26,000	0.1	Territory (Canada)..........E	Whitehorse	English, Eskimo, Indian
Zaire (Congo, The)†	905,567	29,050,000	32	Republic..........A	Kinshasa	Bantu languages, French
Zambia (Northern Rhodesia)†	290,586	5,915,000	20	Republic (Commonwealth of Nations)..........A	Lusaka	Bantu languages, English
Zanzibar	950	535,000	563	Part of Tanzania..........D	........; Zanzibar	Arabic, English, Swahili
Zimbabwe (Rhodesia)	150,804	7,465,000	50	Republic (Commonwealth of Nations)..........A	Salisbury	Bantu languages, English

† *Member of the United Nations (1980).*
‡‡ *Areas for Egypt, Israel, Jordan and Syria do not reflect de facto changes which took place since 1967.*
* *Areas include inland water.*

World Facts and Comparisons

MOVEMENTS OF THE EARTH

The earth makes one complete revolution around the sun every 365 days, 5 hours, 48 minutes, and 46 seconds.

The earth makes one complete rotation on its axis in 23 hours and 56 minutes.

The earth revolves in its orbit around the sun at a speed of 66,700 miles per hour.

The earth rotates on its axis at an equatorial speed of more than 1,000 miles per hour.

MEASUREMENTS OF THE EARTH

Estimated age of the earth, at least 3 billion years.
Equatorial diameter of the earth, 7,926.68 miles.
Polar diameter of the earth, 7,899.99 miles.
Mean diameter of the earth, 7,918.78 miles.
Equatorial circumference of the earth, 24,902.45 miles.
Polar circumference of the earth, 24,818.60 miles.
Difference between equatorial and polar circumference of the earth, 83.85 miles.

Weight of the earth, 6,600,000,000,000,000,000,000 tons, or 6,600 billion billion tons.
Total area of the earth, 196,940,400 square miles.
Total land area of the earth (including inland water and Antarctica), 57,516,000 square miles.

THE EARTH'S INHABITANTS

Total population of the earth is estimated to be 4,422,000,000 (January 1, 1981).
Estimated population density of the earth, 77 per square mile.

THE EARTH'S SURFACE

Highest point on the earth's surface, Mount Everest, China (Tibet)–Nepal, 29,028 feet.
Lowest point on the earth's land surface, shores of the Dead Sea, Israel-Jordan, 1,299 feet below sea level.
Greatest ocean depth, the Marianas Trench, south of Guam, Pacific Ocean, 36,198 feet.

EXTREMES OF TEMPERATURE AND RAINFALL OF THE EARTH

Highest temperature ever recorded, 136.4°F. at Al 'Azīzīyah, Libya, Africa, on September 13, 1922.

Lowest temperature ever recorded, −126.9°F. at Vostok, Antarctica, on August 24, 1960.

Highest mean annual temperature, 88°F. at Lugh Ferrandi, Somalia.

Lowest mean annual temperature, −67°F. at Vostok, Antarctica.

At Cilaos, Réunion Island, in the Indian Ocean, 74 inches of rainfall was reported in a 24-hour period, March 15-16, 1952. This is believed to be the world's record for a 24-hour rainfall.

An authenticated rainfall of 366 inches in 1 month— July, 1861—was reported at Cherrapunji, India. More than 131 inches fell in a period of 7 consecutive days in June, 1931. Average annual rainfall at Cherrapunji is 450 inches.

The Continents

CONTINENT	Area (sq. mi.)	Population Estimated Jan. 1, 1981	Population per sq. mi.	Mean Elevation (feet)	Highest Elevation (Feet)	Lowest Elevation (Feet)	Highest Recorded Temperature	Lowest Recorded Temperature
North America	9,406,000	377,400,000	40	2,000	Mt. McKinley, United States (Alaska), 20,320	Death Valley, California, 282 below sea level	Death Valley, California, 134°F.	Snag, Yukon, Canada, −81°F.
South America	6,883,000	243,100,000	35	1,800	Mt. Aconcagua, Argentina, 22,831	Salinas Chicas, Argentina, 138 below sea level	Rivadavia, Argentina, 120°F.	Sarmiento, Argentina, −27.4°F.
Europe	3,835,000	664,600,000	173	980	Mt. Elbrus, Soviet Union, 18,510	Caspian Sea, Soviet Union—Iran, 92 below sea level	Sevilla (Seville), Spain, 122°F.	Ust-Shchugor, Soviet Union, −67°F.
Asia	17,297,000	2,631,600,000	152	3,000	Mt. Everest, China (Tibet)-Nepal, 29,028	Dead Sea, Israel-Jordan, 1,299 below sea level	Tirat Zvi, Israel, 129.2°F.	Oymyakon, Soviet Union, −89.9°F.
Africa	11,708,000	482,400,000	41	1,900	Mt. Kilimanjaro, Tanzania, 19,340	Lac Assal, Djibouti, 509 below sea level	Al 'Azīzīyah, Libya, 136.4°F.	Ifrane, Morocco, −11.2°F.
Oceania, incl. Australia	3,287,000	22,900,000	7	.....	Mt. Wilhelm, Papua New Guinea, 14,793	Lake Eyre, South Australia, 52 below sea level	Cloncurry, Queensland, Australia, 127.5°F.	Charlotte Pass, New South Wales, Australia, −8°F.
Australia	2,967,909	14,680,000	5	1,000	Mt. Kosciusko, New South Wales, 7,310	Lake Eyre, South Australia, 52 below sea level	Cloncurry, Queensland, 127.5°F.	Charlotte Pass, New South Wales, Australia, −8°F.
Antarctica	5,100,000	Uninhabited	...	6,000	Vinson Massif, 16,864	Unknown	Esperanza (Antarctic Peninsula), 58.3°F.	Vostok, −126.9°F.
World	57,516,000	4,422,000,000	77	.....	Mt. Everest, China (Tibet)-Nepal, 29,028	Dead Sea, Israel-Jordan, 1,299 below sea level	Al 'Azīzīyah, Libya, 136.4°F.	Vostok, −126.9°F.

Approximate Population of the World 1650-1981*

AREA	1650	1750	1800	1850	1900	1914	1920	1939	1950	1981
North America	5,000,000	5,000,000	13,000,000	39,000,000	106,000,000	141,000,000	147,000,000	186,000,000	219,000,000	377,400,000
South America	8,000,000	7,000,000	12,000,000	20,000,000	38,000,000	55,000,000	61,000,000	90,000,000	111,000,000	243,100,000
Europe	100,000,000	140,000,000	190,000,000	265,000,000	400,000,000	470,000,000	453,000,000	526,000,000	530,000,000	664,600,000
Asia	335,000,000	476,000,000	593,000,000	754,000,000	932,000,000	1,006,000,000	1,000,000,000	1,247,000,000	1,418,000,000	2,631,600,000
Africa	100,000,000	95,000,000	90,000,000	95,000,000	118,000,000	130,000,000	140,000,000	170,000,000	199,000,000	482,400,000
Oceania, incl. Australia	} 2,000,000	2,000,000	2,000,000	2,000,000	6,000,000	8,000,000	9,000,000	11,000,000	13,000,000	22,900,000
Australia					4,000,000	5,000,000	6,000,000	7,000,000	8,000,000	14,680,000
World	550,000,000	725,000,000	900,000,000	1,175,000,000	1,600,000,000	1,810,000,000	1,810,000,000	2,230,000,000	2,490,000,000	4,422,000,000

* Figures prior to 1981 are rounded to the nearest million.   Figures in italics represent very rough estimates.

Largest Countries of the World in Population

	Population 1/1/81		Population 1/1/81		Population 1/1/81
1 China (excl. Taiwan)	945,130,000	10 Nigeria	78,135,000	17 Philippines	48,200,000
2 India (incl. part of Kashmir)	669,860,000	11 Mexico	73,010,000	18 Thailand	47,845,000
3 Soviet Union	267,190,000	12 Germany, Federal Republic of (incl. West Berlin)	61,690,000	19 Turkey	45,955,000
4 United States	228,340,000	13 Italy	57,230,000	20 Egypt (United Arab Republic)	43,135,000
5 Indonesia	153,510,000	14 United Kingdom (Great Britain)	55,945,000	21 Iran	38,940,000
6 Brazil	123,795,000	15 Vietnam	54,720,000	22 Korea, South	38,470,000
7 Japan	117,360,000	16 France	53,780,000	23 Spain	37,790,000
8 Bangladesh	89,595,000			24 Poland	35,645,000
9 Pakistan (incl. part of Kashmir)	88,610,000			25 Burma	33,585,000

Largest Countries of the World in Area

	Area (sq. mi.)		Area (sq. mi.)		Area (sq. mi.)
1 Soviet Union	8,600,383	9 Sudan	967,500	18 Mongolia	604,250
2 Canada	3,831,033	10 Algeria	919,595	19 Peru	496,224
3 China (excl. Taiwan)	3,691,500	11 Zaire (The Congo)	905,567	20 Chad	495,755
4 United States	3,678,896	12 Greenland (Den.)	840,004	21 Niger	489,191
5 Brazil	3,286,487	13 Saudi Arabia	830,000	22 Angola	481,353
6 Australia	2,967,909	14 Mexico	761,604	23 Mali	478,766
7 India (incl. part of Kashmir)	1,237,061	15 Indonesia	741,034	24 Ethiopia	472,434
8 Argentina	1,068,301	16 Libya	679,362	25 South Africa (incl. Walvis Bay)	471,447
		17 Iran	636,296		

Principal Mountains of the World

North America

	Height (Feet)
McKinley, △Alaska (△United States; △North America)	20,320
Logan, △Canada (△St. Elias Mts.)	19,520
Citlaltépetl (Orizaba), △Mexico	18,701
St. Elias, Alaska–Canada	18,008
Popocatépetl, Mexico	17,887
Foraker, Alaska	17,400
Ixtacihuatl, Mexico	17,343
Lucania, Yukon, Canada	17,147
Whitney, △California	14,494
Elbert, △Colorado (△Rocky Mts.)	14,433
Massive, Colorado	14,421
Harvard, Colorado	14,420
Rainier, △Washington (△Cascade Range)	14,410
Williamson, California	14,375
Blanca Pk., Colorado (△Sangre de Cristo Range)	14,345
Uncompahgre Pk., Colorado (△San Juan Mts.)	14,309
Grays Pk., Colorado (△Front Range)	14,270
Evans, Colorado	14,264
Longs Pk., Colorado	14,255
Wrangell, Alaska	14,163
Shasta, California	14,162
Pikes Peak, Colorado	14,110
Colima, Nevado de, Mexico	13,993
Tajumulco, △Guatemala (△Central America)	13,846
Gannett Pk., △Wyoming	13,804
Mauna Kea, △Hawaii (△Hawaii I.)	13,796
Grand Teton, Wyoming	13,766
Mauna Loa, Hawaii	13,680
Kings Pk., △Utah	13,528
Cloud Pk., Wyoming (△Big Horn Mts.)	13,175
Wheeler Pk., △New Mexico	13,161
Boundary Pk., △Nevada	13,143
Gunnbjörn, △Greenland	13,120
Waddington, Canada (△Coast Mts.)	13,104
Robson, Canada (△Canadian Rockies)	12,972
Granite Pk., △Montana	12,799
Borah Pk., △Idaho	12,662
Humphreys Pk., △Arizona	12,633
Chirripó Grande, △Costa Rica	12,533
Adams, Washington	12,307
San Gorgonio, California	11,502
Chiriquí, △Panama	11,411
Hood, △Oregon	11,239
Lassen Pk., California	10,457
Duarte, Pico, △Dominican Rep. (△West Indies)	10,417
Haleakala, Hawaii (△Maui)	10,023
Parícutin, Mexico	9,213
La Selle, Pic, △Haiti	8,773
Guadalupe Pk., △Texas	8,751
Olympus, Washington (△Olympic Mts.)	7,965
Monte Cristo, △El Salvador–Guatemala–Honduras	7,936
Blue Mountain Pk., △Jamaica	7,402
Harney Pk., △South Dakota (△Black Hills)	7,242
Mitchell, △North Carolina (△Appalachian Mts.)	6,684
Clingmans Dome, North Carolina–△Tennessee (△Great Smoky Mts.)	6,643
Turquino, Pico, △Cuba	6,542
Washington, △New Hampshire (△White Mts.)	6,288
Rogers, △Virginia	5,729
Marcy, △New York (△Adirondack Mts.)	5,344
Katahdin, △Maine	5,268
Kawaikini, Hawaii (△Kauai)	5,243
Spruce Knob, △West Virginia	4,862
Pelée, △Martinique	4,583
Mansfield, △Vermont (△Green Mts.)	4,393
Punta, Cerro de, △Puerto Rico	4,389
Black Mtn., △Kentucky	4,145
Kaala Pk., Hawaii (△Oahu)	4,050

South America

	Height (Feet)
Aconcagua, △Argentina (△Andes Mts.; △South America)	22,831
Ojos del Salado, Argentina–△Chile	22,590
Tupungato, Argentina–Chile	22,310
Pissis, Argentina	22,241
Mercedario, Argentina	22,211
Huascarán, △Peru	22,205
Llullaillaco, Argentina–Chile	22,057
Yerupaja, Peru	21,765
Incahuasi, Argentina–Chile	21,719
Sajama, Nevado, △Bolivia	21,391
Illimani, Bolivia	21,201
Chimborazo, △Ecuador	20,561
Cotopaxi, Ecuador	19,347
Misti, Peru	19,098
Cristóbal Colón, △Colombia	19,029
Huila, Colombia (△Cordillera Central)	18,865
Bolívar (La Columna), △Venezuela	16,411
Fitz Roy, Argentina	11,073
Neblina, Pico da, △Brazil	9,888

Europe

	Height (Feet)
Elbrus, Soviet Union (△Caucasus Mts.; △Europe)	18,510
Dykh-Tau, Soviet Union	17,070
Shkhara, Soviet Union	16,594
Kazbek, Soviet Union	16,512
Blanc, Mont, △France–△Italy (△Alps)	15,771
Rosa, Monte (Dufourspitze) △Switzerland	15,200
Weisshorn, Switzerland	14,803
Matterhorn, Italy–Switzerland	14,685
Finsteraarhorn, Switzerland	14,026
Jungfrau, Switzerland	13,668
Grossglockner, △Austria	12,457
Teide, Pico de, △Spain (△Canary Is.)	12,162
Mulhacén, △Spain (continental)	11,424
Aneto, Pico de, Spain (△Pyrenees)	11,168
Etna, Italy (△Sicily)	11,122
Perdido (Perdu), Spain	11,007
Clapier, France-Italy (△Maritime Alps)	9,993
Zugspitze, Austria–△Germany, Fed. Rep. of	9,721
Coma Pedrosa, Andorra	9,665
Musala, △Bulgaria	9,592
Corno, Italy (△Apennines)	9,560
Olympus, △Greece	9,550
Triglav, △Yugoslavia	9,393
Korab, △Albania–Yugoslavia	9,068
Ginto, France (△Corsica)	8,891
Gerlachovka, △Czechoslovakia (△Carpathian Mts.)	8,737
Moldoveanu, △Romania	8,343
Rysy, Czechoslovakia–△Poland	8,199
Glittertinden, △Norway (△Scandinavia)	8,110
Parnassós, Greece	8,061
Idhi (Ida), Greece (△Crete)	8,058
Pico, △Portugal (△Azores Is.)	7,713
Hvannadalshnúkur, △Iceland	6,952
Kebnekaise, △Sweden	6,926
Estrela, △Portugal (continental)	6,539
Narodnaya, Soviet Union (△Ural Mts.)	6,184
Marmora, Punta la, Italy (△Sardinia)	6,017
Hekla, Iceland	4,747
Nevis, Ben, △United Kingdom (△Scotland)	4,406
Haltia, △Finland–Norway	4,357
Vesuvius, Italy	3,842
Snowdon, △Wales	3,560
Carrantuohill, △Ireland	3,414
Kékes, △Hungary	3,330
Scafell Pikes, △England	3,210

Asia

	Height (Feet)
Everest, △China (△Tibet)–△Nepal (△Himalaya Mts.; △Asia; △World)	29,028
Godwin Austen (K2), China–△Pakistan (△Kashmir) (△Karakoram Range)	28,250
Kanchenjunga, Nepal–△India	28,208
Makalu, China (Tibet)–Nepal	27,824
Dhaulagiri, Nepal	26,810
Nanga Parbat, Pakistan (Kashmir)	26,650
Annapurna, Nepal	26,504
Gasherbrum, Pakistan (Kashmir)	26,470
Gosainthan, China (Tibet)	26,291
Nanda Devi, India	25,645
Rakaposhi, Pakistan (Kashmir)	25,550
Kamet, India	25,447
Namcha Barwa, China (Tibet)	25,443
Gurla Mandhata, China (Tibet)	25,354
Ulugh Muztagh, China (△Kunlun Mts.)	25,338
Tirich Mir, Pakistan (△Hindu Kush)	25,230
Minya Konka, China	24,902
Muztagh Ata, China	24,787
Kula Kangri, △Bhutan	24,784
Communism Pk., △Soviet Union (△Pamir-Alay Mts.)	24,590
Pobeda Pk., China–Soviet Union (△Tien Shan)	24,406
Lenin Pk., Soviet Union	23,406
Api, Nepal	23,399
Khan-Tengri, Soviet Union	22,949
Kailas, China (Tibet)	22,031
Hkakabo Razi, △Burma–China	19,296
Demavend, △Iran	18,386
Ararat, △Turkey	17,011
Jaya Pk., △Indonesia (△New Guinea)	16,503
Klyuchevskaja Sopka, Soviet Union (△Kamchatka)	15,584
Trikora Pk., Indonesia	15,584
Belukha, Soviet Union	14,783
Tabun Bogdo (Khuitun), China–△Mongolia–Soviet Union (△Altai Mts.)	14,291
Turgun Uula, Mongolia	14,052
Kinabalu, △Malaysia (△Borneo)	13,455
Hsinkao, △Taiwan (Formosa)	13,113
Erciyeş, Turkey	12,848
Kerinci, Indonesia (△Sumatra)	12,467
Fuji, △Japan (△Honshu)	12,388
Hadūr Shu'ayb, △Yemen (△Arabian Peninsula)	12,336
Rindjani, Indonesia (△Lombok)	12,224
Semeru, Indonesia (△Java)	12,060
Munku-Sardyk, Mongolia–Soviet Union (△Sayan Mts.)	11,453
Rantekombola, Indonesia (△Celebes)	11,335
Sa'uda, Qurnet es, △Lebanon	10,131
Shām, Jabal ash, △Oman	9,957
Apo, △Philippines (△Mindanao)	9,692
Pulog, Philippines (△Luzon)	9,626
Bia, Phou, △Laos	9,242
Hermon, Lebanon–△Syria	9,232
Paektu-san, China–△Korea	9,003
Anai Mudi, △India (peninsular)	8,841
Inthanon, Doi, △Thailand	8,514
Pidurutalagala, △Sri Lanka	8,281
Mayon, Philippines (Luzon)	8,077
Asahi, Japan (△Hokkaido)	7,513
Tahan, Gunong, Malaysia (△Malaya)	7,174
Olimbos, △Cyprus	6,401
Kuju-San, Japan (△Kyushu)	5,866
Meron, △Israel	3,963
Carmel, Israel	1,791

Africa

	Height (Feet)
Kilimanjaro (Kibo), △Tanzania (△Africa)	19,340
Kirinyaga (Kenya), △Kenya	17,058
Margherita Pk., △Zaire–△Uganda	16,763
Ras Dashen, △Ethiopia	15,158
Meru, Tanzania	14,978
Elgon, Kenya–Uganda	14,178
Toubkal, Jbel, △Morocco (△Atlas Mts.)	13,665
Cameroun, △Cameroon	13,353
Thabana Ntlenyana, △Lesotho	11,425
Koussi, Emi, △Chad (△Tibesti Mts.)	11,204
Injasuti, △South Africa	11,182
Neiges, Piton des, △Reunion	10,069
Santa Isabel, △Equatorial Guinea (△Bioko)	9,868
Tahat, △Algeria (△Ahaggar Mts.)	9,852
Maromokotro, △Madagascar	9,436
Pico, △Cape Verde	9,281
Kātrīnā, Jabal, △Egypt	8,668
São Tomé, Pico de, △Sao Tome	6,640

Oceania

	Height (Feet)
Wilhelm, △Papua New Guinea	14,793
Giluwe, Papua New Guinea	14,330
Bangeta, Papua New Guinea	13,520
Victoria, Papua New Guinea (△Owen Stanley Range)	13,240
Cook, △New Zealand (△South Island)	12,349
Ruapehu, New Zealand (△North Island)	9,175
Balbi, △Solomon Is. (△Bougainville)	9,000
Egmont, New Zealand	8,260
Sinewit, Papua New Guinea (△Bismarck Archipelago)	8,000
Orohena, △Fr. Polynesia (△Tahiti)	7,352
Kosciusko, △Australia (△New South Wales)	7,310
Silisili, Mauga, △Western Samoa	6,095
Panié, △New Caledonia	5,341
Ossa, Australia (△Tasmania)	5,305
Bartle Frere, Australia (△Queensland)	5,287
Humboldt, New Caledonia	5,282
Woodroffe, Australia (△South Australia)	4,723
Tomaniivi (Victoria), △Fiji (△Viti Levu)	4,341
Bruce, Australia (△Western Australia)	4,024

Antarctica

	Height (Feet)
Vinson Massif (△Antarctica)	16,864
Kirkpatrick	14,856
Markham	14,272
Jackson	13,747
Sidley	13,717
Wade	13,396

△Highest mountain in state, country, range, or region named.

Great Oceans and Seas of the World

OCEANS AND SEAS	Area (sq. mi.)	Average Depth (feet)	Greatest Depth (feet)
Pacific Ocean	63,855,000	14,050	36,201
Atlantic Ocean	31,744,000	12,690	27,651
Indian Ocean	28,371,000	13,000	24,442
Arctic Ocean	5,427,000	5,010	17,880
Mediterranean Sea	967,000	4,780	16,420
South China Sea	895,000	5,420	18,090
Bering Sea	876,000	4,710	16,800
Caribbean Sea	750,000	7,310	24,580
Gulf of Mexico	596,000	4,960	14,360
Okhotsk, Sea of	590,000	2,760	11,400
East China Sea	482,000	620	9,840
Yellow Sea	480,000	150	300
Hudson Bay	476,000	402	850
Japan, Sea of	389,000	4,490	12,280
North Sea	222,000	310	2,170
Black Sea	178,000	3,610	7,360
Red Sea	169,000	1,610	7,370
Baltic Sea	163,000	180	1,440

Principal Lakes of the World

LAKES	Area (sq. mi.)
Caspian, Soviet Union–Iran (salt)	152,084
Superior, United States–Canada	31,820
Victoria, Kenya–Uganda–Tanzania	26,828
Aral, Soviet Union (salt)	26,518
Huron, United States–Canada	23,010
Michigan, United States	22,400
Great Bear, Canada	12,275
Baykal, Soviet Union	12,159
Great Slave, Canada	10,980
Tanganyika, Zaire–Tanzania–Burundi–Zambia	10,965
Nyasa, Malawi–Tanzania–Mozambique	10,900
Erie, United States–Canada	9,940
Winnipeg, Canada	9,465
Ontario, United States–Canada	7,540
Ladoga, Soviet Union	7,092
Balkhash, Soviet Union	6,678
Chad, Chad–Nigeria–Cameroon	△6,300
Onega, Soviet Union	3,821
Eyre, Australia (salt)	△3,700
Titicaca, Peru–Bolivia	3,500
Athabasca, Canada	3,120
Nicaragua, Nicaragua	2,972
Rudolf, Kenya–Ethiopia (salt)	2,473
Reindeer, Canada	2,467
Issyk-Kul, Soviet Union	2,393
Urmia, Iran (salt)	△2,229
Torrens, Australia (salt)	△2,200
Albert, Uganda–Zaire	2,162
Vänern, Sweden	2,156
Winnipegosis, Canada	2,103
Bangweulu, Zambia	△1,900
Nipigon, Canada	1,870
Manitoba, Canada	1,817
Great Salt, United States (salt)	1,700
Koko Nor (Ching Hai), China	1,650
Dubawnt, Canada	1,600
Gairdner, Australia (salt)	△1,500
Lake of the Woods, United States–Canada	1,485
Van, Turkey (salt)	1,470

△ Due to seasonal fluctuations in water level, areas of these lakes vary considerably.

Principal Rivers of the World

RIVER	Length (miles)
Nile, Africa	4,132
Amazon (Amazonas), South America	3,900
Mississippi–Missouri–Red Rock, North America	3,860
Ob-Irtysh, Asia	3,461
Yangtze (Chang), Asia	3,430
Huang Ho (Yellow), Asia	2,903
Congo (Zaïre), Africa	2,900
Amur, Asia	2,802
Irtysh, Asia	2,747
Lena, Asia	2,653
Mackenzie, North America	2,635
Mekong, Asia	2,600
Niger, Africa	2,590
Yenisey, Asia	2,566
Missouri, North America	2,466
Paraná, South America	2,450
Mississippi, North America	2,348
Plata-Paraguay, South America	2,300
Volga, Europe	2,293
Madeira, South America	2,060
Indus, Asia	1,980
Purús, South America	1,900
St. Lawrence, North America	1,900
Rio Grande, North America	1,885
Brahmaputra (Yalutsangpu), Asia	1,800
Orinoco, South America	1,800
São Francisco, South America	1,800
Yukon, North America	1,800
Danube, Europe	1,770
Darling, Australia	1,750
Salween, Asia	1,730
Euphrates (Fırat), Asia	1,675
Syr Darya, Asia	1,653
Zambezi, Africa	1,650
Tocantins, South America	1,640
Araguaia, South America	1,630
Amu Darya, Asia	1,628
Kolyma, Asia	1,615
Murray, Australia	1,600
Ganges, Asia	1,550
Pilcomayo, South America	1,550
Angara, Asia	1,549
Ural, Asia	1,522
Vilyuy, Asia	1,513
Arkansas, North America	1,450
Colorado, North America (U.S.–Mexico)	1,450
Irrawaddy, Asia	1,425
Dnepr, Europe	1,420
Aldan, Asia	1,392
Negro, South America	1,305
Paraguay, South America	1,290
Kama, Europe	1,261
Juruá, South America	1,250
Xingú, South America	1,230
Don, Europe	1,224
Ucayali, South America	1,220
Columbia, North America	1,214
Saskatchewan, North America	1,205
Peace, North America	1,195
Orange, Africa	1,155
Tigris, Asia	1,150
Sungari, Asia	1,140
Pechora, Europe	1,118
Tobol, Asia	1,093
Snake, North America	1,038
Uruguay, South America	1,025
Red, North America	1,018
Churchill, North America	1,000
Marañón, South America	1,000
Ohio, North America	981
Magdalena, South America	950
Roosevelt (River of Doubt), South America	950
Godavari, Asia	930
Si, Asia	930
Oka, Europe	920
Canadian, North America	906
Dnestr, Europe	876
Brazos, North America	870
Salado, South America	870
Fraser, North America	850
Parnaíba, South America	850
Colorado, North America (Texas)	840
Rhine, Europe	820
Narbada, Asia	800
Athabasca, North America	765
Donets, Europe	735
Pecos, North America	735
Green, North America	730
Elbe, Europe	720
James, North America	710
Ottawa, North America	696
White, North America	690
Cumberland, North America	687
Gambia, Africa	680
Yellowstone, North America	671
Tennessee, North America	652
Gila, North America	630
Vistula (Wisła), Europe	630
Loire, Europe	625
Tagus (Tajo) (Tejo), Europe	625
North Platte, North America	618
Albany, North America	610
Tisza (Tisa), Europe	607
Back, North America	605
Ouachita, North America	605
Cimarron, North America	600
Sava, Europe	585
Nemunas (Niemen), Europe	582
Branco, South America	580
Oder, Europe	565

Principal Islands of the World

ISLAND	Area (sq. mi.)
Greenland, Arctic Region	840,000
New Guinea, Oceania	316,856
Borneo, Indonesia–Malaysia–Brunei	286,967
Madagascar, Indian Ocean	227,800
Baffin, Canadian Arctic	183,810
Sumatra, Indonesia	182,860
Honshū, Japan	88,930
Great Britain, North Atlantic Ocean	88,756
Ellesmere, Canadian Arctic	82,119
Victoria, Canadian Arctic	81,930
Celebes, Indonesia	72,986
South Island, New Zealand	58,093
Java, Indonesia	50,745
North Island, New Zealand	44,281
Cuba, West Indies	44,218
Newfoundland, North Atlantic Ocean	43,359
Luzon, Philippines	40,814
Iceland, North Atlantic Ocean	39,800
Mindanao, Philippines	36,906
Ireland, North Atlantic Ocean	32,596
Novaya Zemlya, Soviet Arctic	31,390
Hokkaidō, Japan	29,950
Hispaniola, West Indies	29,530
Sakhalin, Soviet Union	29,344
Tasmania, Australia	26,383
Sri Lanka (Ceylon), Indian Ocean	25,332
Banks, Canadian Arctic	23,230
Devon, Canadian Arctic	20,861
Tierra del Fuego, Argentina-Chile	18,600
Kyūshū, Japan	16,215
Melville, Canadian Arctic	16,141
Southampton, Hudson Bay, Canada	15,700
West Spitsbergen, Arctic Region	15,260
New Britain, Oceania	14,592
Taiwan (Formosa), China Sea	13,885
Hainan, South China Sea	13,127
Timor, Timor Sea	13,094
Prince of Wales, Canadian Arctic	12,830
Vancouver, Canada	12,408
Sicily, Mediterranean Sea	9,926
Somerset, Canadian Arctic	9,370
Sardinia, Mediterranean Sea	9,301
Shikoku, Japan	7,245
North East Land, Svalbard Group	6,350
Ceram, Indonesia	6,046
New Caledonia, Oceania	5,671
Flores, Indonesia	5,513
Samar, Philippines	5,124
Negros, Philippines	4,903
Palawan, Philippines	4,500
Panay, Philippines	4,448
Jamaica, West Indies	4,232
Hawaii, Oceania	4,030
Cape Breton, Canada	3,970
Bougainville, Oceania	3,880
Mindoro, Philippines	3,794
Cyprus, Mediterranean Sea	3,572
Kodiak, Gulf of Alaska	3,569
Puerto Rico, West Indies	3,435
Corsica, Mediterranean Sea	3,352
Crete, Mediterranean Sea	3,217
New Ireland, Oceania	3,205
Leyte, Philippines	3,090
Wrangel, Soviet Arctic	2,819
Guadalcanal, Oceania	2,500
Long Island, United States	1,620

Population of Foreign Cities and Towns, Countries and Important Political Divisions

This table includes every urban center of 50,000 or more population in the world (excluding the United States), as well as many other important or well-known cities and towns. The table also lists major political subdivisions (states, provinces, etc.) of the leading countries.

The population figures are all from recent censuses (designated C) or official estimates (designated E), except for a few cities for which only unofficial estimates are available (designated UE). The date of the census or estimate is specified for each country. Individual exceptions are dated in parentheses or with a dagger symbol (‡ or †).

For many cities, a second population figure is given accompanied by a star (*). The starred population refers to the city's entire metropolitan area, including suburbs. These metropolitan areas have been defined by Rand McNally & Company, following consistent rules to facilitate comparisons among the urban centers of various countries. Where a place is part of the metropolitan area of another city, that city's name is specified in parentheses preceded by (*). Some important places that are considered to be secondary central cities of their areas are designated by (**) preceding the name of the metropolitan area's main city. A population marked with a triangle (▲) refers to an entire municipality, commune, or other district, which includes rural areas in addition to the urban center itself. The names of capital cities appear in CAPITALS; the largest city in each country is designated by the symbol (•).

AFGHANISTAN / Afghānestān

1973 E	**18,294,000**
Andkhvoy (1975 E)	46,000
Baghlān	29,000
Chārikār	19,000
Ghaznī	24,000
Herāt (1975 E)	157,000
Jalālābād (1975 E)	58,000
•KĀBUL (1975 E)	749,000
Kandahār (Qandahār) (1975 E)	209,000
Khānābād	18,000
Kholm	22,000
Mazār-e-Sharīf (1975 E)	97,000
Meymaneh (1975 E)	29,000
Pol-e-Khomrī	25,000
Qondūz	46,000
Sheberghān	17,000

ALBANIA / Shqipëri

1976 E	**2,482,000**
Berat (1975 E)	30,000
Durrës	61,000
Elbasan	50,700
Fier (1975 E)	28,000
Gjirokastër (1975 E)	22,000
Kavajë (1973 E)	19,900
Korçë	50,900
Lushnje (1975 E)	21,000
Shkodër	62,500
Stalin (Kuçovë) (1971 E)	14,300
•TIRANË	192,300
Vlorë (Valona)	58,400

ALGERIA / Algérie

1974 E	**16,275,000**
Aïn Beïda	40,011
Aïn Benian (*Algers) (1966 C)	17,653
Aïn M'Lila (1966 C) (44,662▲)	12,632
Aïn Sefra (26,234▲)	13,100
Aïn Taya (*Algiers) (1966 C)	22,542
Aïn Témouchent	47,977
•ALGIERS (ALGER) (*1,800,000)	1,503,720
Annaba (Bône)	313,174
Arzew (1966 C)	13,080
Barika (1966 C) (40,957▲)	13,689
Batna (115,138▲)	91,500
Béchar (Colomb-Béchar)	71,081
Bejaïa (Bougie) (103,996▲)	80,000
Béni Saf (1966 C) (23,368▲)	18,507
Biskra	84,971
Blida	158,947
Bordj Bou Arreridj (85,545▲)	66,400
Bordj Ménaïel (87,736▲)	38,700
Boufarik (109,234▲)	77,700
Bouguerra (1966 C) (21,401▲)	13,373
Bouira (50,007▲)	26,800
Bou Saâda	36,433
Chelghoum el Aïd (1966 C) (27,985▲)	15,031
Cherchell (40,308▲)	17,100
Collo (40,860▲)	14,100
Constantine	350,183
Dellys (31,729▲)	13,700
Djelfa (1966 C) (30,304▲)	25,472
Djidjelli (61,545▲)	43,500
Douéra	55,993
El Affroun (67,566▲)	47,500
El Arba (1966 C) (22,857▲)	14,415
El Asnam (Orléansville) (114,327▲)	80,500
El Bayadh (33,743▲)	21,200
El Eulma (54,406▲)	41,500
El Goléa (1966 C) (16,679▲)	13,708
El Meghaier (1966 C) (23,506▲)	11,324
El Oued (1966 C) (43,547▲)	11,429
Fouka (1966 C)	10,208
Frenda (23,349▲)	16,400
Ghardaïa (85,230▲)	55,200
Ghazaouet (29,592▲)	16,600
Guelma (1966 C)	39,817
Guerrara (1966 C) (14,173▲)	12,546
Hadjout (32,334▲)	27,100
Hamma Bouziane (1966 C) (21,040▲)	11,472
Hammam Bou Hadjar (1966 C) (14,637▲)	11,219
Khemis Miliana (63,370▲)	41,400
Khenchela (49,922▲)	40,900
Koléa (48,133▲)	35,900
Ksar el Boukhari (36,986▲)	18,400
Laghouat (60,249▲)	41,900
Lakhdaria (53,780▲)	30,800
Maghnia (44,777▲)	31,000
Mascara (82,468▲)	70,600
Mecheria	23,681
Médéa (102,336▲)	70,700
Mers el Kébir (1966 C) (20,193▲)	5,624
Mila (1966 C) (33,007▲)	12,733
Miliana (46,217▲)	27,200
Mohammadia (49,730▲)	30,000
Mostaganem	101,780
M'Sila (1966 C) (36,930▲)	19,883
Oran (Ouahran)	485,139
Ouargla (69,509▲)	26,200
Oued Zenati (81,036▲)	31,900
Relizane	65,918
Rouiba (*Algiers) (87,540▲)	20,300
Saïda (59,344▲)	51,800
Sétif	157,065
Sidi bel Abbès	151,148
Sig (41,725▲)	33,900
Skikda (Philippeville)	127,968
Souk Ahras (60,551▲)	48,800
Sour el Ghozlane (67,205▲)	32,100
Tébessa	58,008
Tiaret	63,039
Tighennif (1966 C) (25,839▲)	11,834
Tizi-Ouzou (223,702▲)	108,000
Tlemcen	115,054
Touggourt (65,935▲)	34,800

AMERICAN SAMOA

1970 C	**27,159**
•PAGO PAGO	2,451

ANDORRA

1971 C	**20,550**
•ANDORRA	2,000

ANGOLA

1970 C	**5,673,046**
Benguela	40,996
Cabinda	21,124
Huambo (Nova Lisboa)	61,885
Lobito	59,528
•LUANDA	475,328
Lubango (Sá da Bandeira)	31,674
Malanje	31,599

ANGUILLA

1974 C	**6,519**
•South Hill	774
THE VALLEY	760

ANTIGUA

1970 C	**65,525**
•ST. JOHNS	21,814

ARGENTINA

1970 C	**23,364,431**
Almirante Brown (*Buenos Aires)	245,017
Avellaneda (*Buenos Aires)	337,538
Azul	36,023
Bahía Blanca (1979 E)	253,000
Balcarce	26,461
Berazategui (*Buenos Aires)	127,740
Berisso (*La Plata)	58,833
Bolívar	18,643
Bragado	23,366
•BUENOS AIRES (1979 E) (*10,300,000)	2,978,000
Campana (*Buenos Aires)	33,919
Cañada de Gómez	20,611
Caseros (Tres de Febrero) (*Buenos Aires)	313,460
Catamarca (*64,410)	57,228
Chivilcoy	37,190
Cipolletti	23,768
Comodoro Rivadavia	72,906
Concepción del Uruguay	38,967
Concordia	72,136
Córdoba (1979 E) (*1,026,000)	985,000
Corrientes (1979 E)	186,000
Cruz del Eje	23,401
Curuzú-Cuatiá	20,636
Cutral-Có	19,404
Ensenada (*La Plata)	39,154
Esquel	13,771
Esteban Echeverría (*Buenos Aires)	111,150
Florencio Varela (*Buenos Aires)	98,446
Formosa	61,071
General Pico	21,897
General Roca	29,320
General San Martín (*Buenos Aires)	360,573
General Sarmiento (*Buenos Aires)	315,457
Godoy Cruz (*Mendoza)	112,481
Goya	39,367
Gualeguay	20,401
Gualeguaychú	40,661
Guaymallén (*Mendoza)	112,081
Junín	59,020
La Banda (*Santiago del Estero)	33,032
Lanús (*Buenos Aires)	449,824
La Plata (1979 E) (*557,000)	435,000
La Rioja	46,090
Las Heras (*Mendoza)	67,789
Lomas de Zamora (*Buenos Aires)	410,806
Luján (*Buenos Aires)	38,393
Maipú	34,839
Mar del Plata (1979 E)	417,000
Mendoza (1979 E) (*677,000)	125,000
Mercedes (*San Luis Prov.*)	40,052
Mercedes (*Buenos Aires Prov.*) (*Buenos Aires)	39,760
Merlo (*Buenos Aires)	188,868
Moreno (*Buenos Aires)	114,041
Morón (*Buenos Aires)	485,983
Necochea	39,868
Neuquén	43,070
Olavarría	52,453
Paraná	127,635
Pergamino	56,078
Pilar (*Buenos Aires)	34,372
Posadas	97,514
Presidencia Roque Sáenz Peña	38,620
Punta Alta	36,805
Quilmes (*Buenos Aires)	355,265
Rafaela	43,695
Reconquista	25,333
Resistencia (1979 E)	183,000
Río Cuarto	88,852
Río Gallegos	27,833
Rosario (1979 UE) (*975,000)	810,000
Salta (1979 E)	254,000
San Carlos de Bariloche	26,799
San Fernando (*Buenos Aires)	119,565
San Francisco (*48,896)	45,023
San Isidro (*Buenos Aires)	250,008
San Juan (1979 E) (*310,000)	115,000
San Justo (*Buenos Aires)	659,193
San Lorenzo (*Rosario)	56,487
San Luis	50,771
San Martín	24,300
San Miguel de Tucumán (1979 E) (*442,000)	375,000
San Nicolás de los Arroyos	64,730
San Rafael	58,237
San Salvador de Jujuy	82,637
Santa Fe (1979 E)	282,000
Santa Rosa	33,649
Santiago del Estero (*140,000)	105,127
Tandil	65,876
Tartagal	23,696
Tigre (*Buenos Aires)	152,335
Trelew	24,214
Tres Arroyos	37,991
Ushuaia	5,373
Venado Tuerto	35,677
Vicente López (*Buenos Aires)	285,178
Villa Krause (*San Juan)	47,794
Villa María	56,087
Zárate	54,772

AUSTRALIA

1979 E	**14,423,500**
Adelaide (*933,300)	13,400
Albury (*54,900)	36,600
Alice Springs (1976 C)	14,149
Ashfield (*Sydney)	42,850
Auburn (*Sydney)	48,400
Ballarat (*73,200)	38,400
Bankstown (*Sydney)	159,500
Bendigo (*59,600)	33,300
Blacktown (*Sydney)	179,350
Blue Mountains (*Sydney)	51,150
Botany (*Sydney)	36,150
Box Hill (*Melbourne)	49,200
Brighton (*Melbourne)	35,000
Brisbane (*1,014,700)	702,000
Brisbane Water (*Sydney) (1976 C)	54,819
Broadmeadows (*Melbourne)	112,300
Broken Hill	28,600
Brunswick (*Melbourne)	44,800
Bundaberg (*41,900)	32,500
Burnside (*Adelaide)	37,800
Cairns (*53,000)	36,000
Camberwell (*Melbourne)	88,700
Campbelltown (*Adelaide)	42,300
Campbelltown (*Sydney)	78,000
CANBERRA (*241,500)	221,000
Canning (*Perth)	48,350
Canterbury (*Sydney)	131,900
Caulfield (*Melbourne)	74,700
Coburg (*Melbourne)	57,100
Croydon (*Melbourne)	36,400
Dandenong (*Melbourne)	54,700
Darwin (1976 C) (*46,655)	39,193
Doncaster and Templestowe (*Melbourne)	89,100
Drummoyne (*Sydney)	32,700
Dubbo	22,850
Enfield (*Adelaide)	70,200
Essendon (*Melbourne)	50,300
Fairfield (*Sydney)	120,850
Footscray (*Melbourne)	51,700
Frankston (*Melbourne)	80,300
Fremantle (*Perth)	23,500
Geelong (*141,100)	15,200
Glenorchy (*Hobart) (1980 C)	42,400
Gosnells (*Perth)	46,850
Heidelberg (*Melbourne)	67,000
Hobart (1980 E) (*170,200)	49,020
Holroyd (*Sydney)	82,600
Hurstville (*Sydney)	66,950
Ipswich (*Brisbane)	71,200
Kalgoorlie (*19,300)	9,400
Keilor (*Melbourne)	76,800
Knox (*Melbourne)	83,100
Kogarah (*Sydney)	47,850
Ku-ring-gai (*Sydney)	103,100
Lake Macquarie (*Newcastle)	140,450
Launceston (1980 E) (*86,100)	32,300
Leichhardt (*Sydney)	62,550
Lismore	31,900
Liverpool (*Sydney)	95,950
Mackay (*44,800)	21,800
Maitland (*Newcastle)	38,950
Malvern (*Melbourne)	45,900
Manly (*Sydney)	36,350
Marion (*Adelaide)	69,700
Marrickville (*Sydney)	90,150
Melbourne (*2,739,700)	65,800
Melville (*Perth)	56,900
Mitcham (*Adelaide)	59,500
Moe	16,300
Moorabbin (*Melbourne)	102,900
Mount Gambier (*20,750)	18,950
Mount Isa	26,800
Newcastle (*379,800)	139,400
Northcote (*Melbourne)	53,000
North Sydney (*Sydney)	47,900
Nunawading (*Melbourne)	95,900
Oakleigh (*Melbourne)	55,400
Orange	30,650
Parramatta (*Sydney)	134,300
Penrith (*Sydney)	94,000
Perth (*883,600)	88,850
Port Adelaide (*Adelaide)	36,400
Port Augusta (*15,650)	14,400
Port Lincoln (*11,050)	10,250
Port Pirie (*14,900)	12,150
Prahran (*Melbourne)	47,900
Preston (*Melbourne)	87,900
Queanbeyan (*Canberra)	20,100
Randwick (*Sydney)	123,750
Redcliffe (*Brisbane)	41,200
Ringwood (*Melbourne)	37,900
Rockdale (*Sydney)	86,650
Rockhampton (*54,600)	53,900
Ryde (*Sydney)	91,900
St. Kilda (*Melbourne)	52,400
Salisbury (*Adelaide)	83,800
Sandringham (*Melbourne)	32,600
Shellharbour (*Wollongong)	41,650
Shepparton (*34,100)	23,200
South Perth (*Perth)	31,400
Southport (Gold Coast) (*128,000)	102,500
South Sydney (*Sydney)	32,100
Springvale (*Melbourne)	79,000
Stirling (*Perth)	169,350
Sunshine (*Melbourne)	94,600
•Sydney (*3,193,300)	49,750
Tamworth	32,650
Tea Tree Gully (*Adelaide)	63,300
Toowoomba	72,500
Townsville (*96,100)	84,900
Unley (*Adelaide)	35,700
Wagga Wagga	38,150
Waverley (*Melbourne)	121,500
Waverley (*Sydney)	64,050
West Torrens (*Adelaide)	46,100
Whyalla (*31,150)	31,000
Willoughby (*Sydney)	52,250
Wollongong (*223,950)	172,350
Woodville (*Adelaide)	76,600
Woollahra (*Sydney)	54,500

AUSTRIA / Österreich

1971 C	**7,456,745**
Bruck an der Mur (*50,000)	16,359
Dornbirn	33,810
Graz (1976 E) (*275,000)	250,900
Innsbruck (1976 E) (*150,000)	120,400
Kapfenberg (**Bruck)	26,001
Klagenfurt (1973 L)	82,512
Leoben (*48,000)	35,153
Linz (1976 E) (*290,000)	208,000
Salzburg (1976 E) (*165,000)	139,000
Sankt Pölten (1973 L)	50,144
Steyr (*54,000)	40,578
Stockerau (*Vienna) (1976 L)	12,768
Ternitz (1978 L)	16,343
Traun (*Linz)	20,843
•VIENNA (WIEN) (1979 E) (*1,925,000)	1,572,300
Villach (1973 L)	50,993
Wels (*59,000)	47,279
Wiener Neustadt (*41,000)	34,774
Wolfsberg (1974 L)	29,002

BAHAMAS

1970 C	**168,812**
Freeport	15,286
•NASSAU (*101,503)	3,233

BAHRAIN / Al-Bahrayn

1971 C	**216,078**
Al-Muḥarraq (*Manama)	37,577
•MANAMA (*145,000)	89,112

BANGLADESH

1974 C	**76,398,120**
Barisāl	98,127
Bhairab Bazar	43,702
Bogra	47,154
Brāhmanbāria	62,407
Chāndpur	51,668
Chittagong (*1,200,000)	497,026
Chuadanga	36,381
Comilla	86,446
•DACCA (*2,750,000)	1,563,517
Dinājpur	61,866
Doublemooring (*Chittagong)	125,453
Farīdpur	46,232
Ghorāsāl	34,321
Gopālpur	39,066
Jamālpur	60,261
Jessore (*82,817)	76,168
Jhenida	34,020
Khulna	521,543
Kishorganj	35,605
Kurigram	30,129
Kushtia	36,199
Mādārīpur	32,488
Mymensingh (*182,153)	76,036
Naogaon	34,395
Nārāyanganj (**Dacca)	201,450
Narsingdi	39,140
Nawābganj	46,059
Noākhāli	32,490
Pābna	62,254
Pānchlāish (*Chittagong)	127,839
Pārbatipur	10,604
Rājshāhi (Rampur Boalia) (*132,909)	96,645
Rangpur	72,829
Saidpur	90,132
Sātkhira	40,507
Sherpur	35,578
Sirājganj	74,457
Sitākunda (*Chittagong)	99,929
Sylhet	59,546
Tangail	51,863
Tongi (*Dacca)	67,420

BARBADOS

1970 C	**238,141**
•BRIDGETOWN (*115,000)	8,789

BELGIUM / Belgique / België

1980 E	**9,855,110**
Provinces	
Antwerpen (Anvers)	1,573,647
Brabant	2,220,699
Hainaut (Henegouwen)	1,308,931
Liège (Luik)	1,005,947
Limburg (Limbourg)	710,715
Luxembourg (Luxemburg)	222,317
Namur (Namen)	404,481
Oost-Vlaanderen; Flandre Orientale (East Flanders)	1,330,134
West-Vlaanderen; Flandre Occidentale (West Flanders)	1,078,239
Cities	
Aalst (Alost) (*Brussels)	79,340
Anderlecht (*Brussels)	95,969
Antwerp (Antwerpen) (*1,105,000)	194,073
Arlon (23,218▲)	17,400
Ath (Aat) (24,171▲)	14,400
Auderghem (*Brussels)	31,174
Bastogne (11,357▲)	6,700
Berchem (*Antwerp)	46,368
Berchem-Sainte-Agathe (Sint-Agatha-Berchem) (*Brussels)	18,792
Beveren (*Antwerp) (40,510▲)	20,300
Binche	33,743
Borgerhout (*Antwerp)	44,369
Braine-l'Alleud (*Brussels)	29,116
Brasschaat (*Antwerp)	31,663
Brugge (Bruges) (*217,000)	118,243
•BRUSSELS (BRUXELLES) (BRUSSEL) (*2,400,000)	143,957
Charlerol (*495 000)	221,911
Châtelet (*Charleroi)	38,753

C Census. E Official estimate. UE Unofficial estimate.
L Population within municipal limits of year specified. • Largest city in country.

* Population or designation of metropolitan area, including suburbs (see headnote).
▲ Population of an entire municipality, commune, or district, including rural area.
‡† Year of information specified at start of country.

Dendermonde 40,856
Deurne (★Antwerp) 78,646
Edegem (★Antwerp) 23,422
Eeklo 19,541
Ekeren (★Antwerp) 30,347
Etterbeek (★Brussels) 46,650
Eupen 17,072
Evere (★Brussels) 29,772
Forest (Vorst) (★Brussels) 51,314
Ganshoren (★Brussels) 21,593
Geel (31,450▲) 17,300
Genk (★★Hasselt) 61,512
Gent (Ghent) (★470,000) 241,695
Geraardsbergen (Grammont) (30,447▲) 14,900
Halle (Hal) (★Brussels) 32,124
Hamme 22,938
Harelbeke (★Kortrijk) 25,213
Hasselt (★275,000) 64,439
Herentals 23,682
Herstal (★Liège) 39,190
Hoboken (★Antwerp) 34,640
Huy 18,038
Ieper (Ypres) (34,446▲) 21,000
Ixelles (★Brussels) 76,545
Izegem 26,237
Jette (★Brussels) 40,361
Knokke-Heist 28,757
Kortrijk (Courtrai) (★200,000) 76,424
La Louvière (★148,000) 76,892
Leuven (Louvain) (★167,000) 85,632
Liège (Luik) (★765,000) 220,183
Lier (★Antwerp) 31,319
Lokeren 33,126
Maasmechelen 33,262
Mechelen (Malines) (★120,000) 77,667
Menen 33,972
Merksem (★Antwerp) 41,202
Mol (29,474▲) 16,600
Molenbeek St.-Jean (Sint-Jans-Molenbeek) (★Brussels) 70,958
Mons (Bergen) (★250,000) 96,784
Mortsel (★Antwerp) 26,834
Mouscron (Moeskroen) (★Lille, France) 54,553
Namur (★143,000) 100,712
Nivelles (21,318▲) 16,300
Oostende (Ostende) (★120,000) 70,125
Oudenaarde (Audenarde) (27,308▲) 13,600
Roeselare (Roulers) 51,752
Ronse (Renaix) 24,463
Saint-Gilles (Sint-Gillis) (★Brussels) 47,932
Schaerbeek (Schaarbeek) (★Brussels) 109,005
Schoten (★Antwerp) 31,180
Seraing (★Liège) 65,371
Sint-Niklaas (St.-Nicolas) 68,080
Sint-Truiden (St.-Trond) (36,160▲) 17,000
Soignies (23,344▲) 11,600
Spa 9,766
Tienen (Tirlemont) 32,842
Tongeren (Tongres) (29,375▲) 18,400
Tournai (Doornik) (69,862▲) 46,700
Turnhout 37,652
Uccle (Ukkel) (★Brussels) 75,861
Verviers (★103,000) 56,209
Veurne (Furnes) (11,212▲) 7,500
Vilvoorde (★Brussels) 33,644
Waregem 32,088
Waterloo (★Brussels) 24,536
Watermael-Boitsfort (★Brussels) 24,965
Wilrijk (★Antwerp) 43,161
Woluwe-St.-Lambert (★Brussels) 46,823
Woluwe-St.-Pierre (★Brussels) 39,166
Zottegem (25,152▲) 13,000

BELIZE

1972 E 127,200

•Belize City 41,500
BELMOPAN (1971 E) 5,000
Corozal 5,000
Orange Walk 6,100
Punta Gorda 2,200
San Ignacio 4,600
Stann Creek 7,400

BENIN (DAHOMEY)

1975 E 3,112,000

•Cotonou 178,000
PORTO-NOVO 104,000

BERMUDA

1970 C 52,330

•HAMILTON (★13,757) 2,060
St. George 1,604

BHUTAN / Druk-Yul

1977 E 1,232,000

THIMBU 8,982

BOLIVIA

1976 C 4,647,816

Cobija 3,636
Cochabamba 205,002
•LA PAZ 654,713
Oruro 124,121
Potosí 77,334
Santa Cruz 256,946
SUCRE 62,207
Tarija 39,087
Trinidad 27,583

BOTSWANA

1971 C 574,094

Francistown 18,613
•GABORONE (GABERONES) 18,799
Kanye 10,664
Lobatse 11,936
Mahalapye 12,056
Mochudi 6,945
Molepolole 9,448
Serowe 15,723

BRAZIL / Brasil

1975 E 107,145,200

States

Acre 249,100
Alagoas 1,786,200
Amapá (Ter.) 142,100
Amazonas 1,089,700
Bahia 8,438,900
Ceará 5,111,600
Distrito Federal (Brasília) 763,000
Espírito Santo 1,725,100
Fernando de Noronha (Ter.) (1970 C) 1,239
Goiás 3,558,100
Maranhão 3,330,000
Mato Grosso (1978 L) 753,700
Mato Grosso do Sul (1978 L) 1,253,200
Minas Gerais 12,550,600
Pará 2,544,300
Paraíba 2,675,100
Paraná 8,449,200
Pernambuco ‡5,853,400
Piauí 1,988,200
Rio de Janeiro 10,400,200
Rio Grande do Norte 1,855,700
Rio Grande do Sul 7,457,600
Rondônia (Ter.) 141,300
Roraima (Ter.) 48,200
Santa Catarina 3,351,400
São Paulo 20,636,900
Sergipe 992,400

‡Includes 1975 estimated population for Fernando de Noronha

Cities (1970 C or †1975 E)

Alagoinhas 53,891
Alegrete 45,522
Alvorada 39,485
Americana 62,387
Anápolis 89,405
Andradina 43,465
Anil 37,719
Apucarana 41,800
Aracaju 179,512
Araçatuba 85,660
Araguari 48,702
Arapiraça 43,875
Arapongas 36,628
Araraquara 82,607
Araras 40,945
Araxá 31,498
Arcoverde 33,308
Assis 45,531
Bagé 57,036
Barbacena 57,766
Barra do Piraí 42,713
Barra Mansa (★★Volta Redonda) 75,006
Barretos 53,050
Bauru 120,178
Bayeux (★João Pessoa) 34,681
Belém (★660,000) 565,097
Belford Roxo (★Rio de Janeiro) 173,427
Belo Horizonte (★1,945,000) †1,557,464
Blumenau 85,942
Boa Vista *(Roraima Ter.)* 16,720
Boa Vista *(Santa Catarina State)* 33,503
Botucatu 42,252
Bragança Paulista 39,573
BRASÍLIA (1975 UE) (★750,000) 350,000
Brusque 32,427
Cabedelo (★João Pessoa) 12,811
Cachoeira do Sul 50,001
Cachoeiro de Itapemirim 58,968
Camarajibe (★Recife) 41,216
Campina Grande 163,206
Campinas 328,629
Campo Grande 130,792
Campos 153,310
Campos Elyseos (★Rio de Janeiro) 104,636
Canoas (★Porto Alegre) 148,798
Carapicuíba (★São Paulo) 54,907
Caruaru 101,006
Cascavel 33,809
Cataguases 32,515
Catanduva 48,446
Cavaleiro (★Recife) 58,811
Caxias 31,089
Caxias do Sul 107,487
Coelho da Rocha (★Rio de Janeiro) 100,781
Colatina 46,012
Conselheiro Lafaiete 44,894
Corumbá 48,607
Crato 36,836
Criciúma 50,430
Cruz Alta 43,568
Cruzeiro 42,366
Cubatão (★Santos) 37,255
Cuiabá 83,621
Curitiba (★680,000) 483,038
Curvelo 30,225
Diadema (★São Paulo) 68,552
Divinópolis 69,872
Duque de Caxias (★Rio de Janeiro) 256,582
Erechim 32,426
Feira de Santana 127,105
Florianópolis 115,665
Fortaleza (★1,175,000) †1,109,837
Franca 86,852
Garanhuns 49,579
Goiânia 362,152
Governador Valadares 125,174
Guaratinguetá 55,069
Guarujá (★Santos) 30,741
Guarulhos (★São Paulo) 221,639
Ijuí 31,879
Ilhéus 58,529
Imperatriz 34,709
Inhomirim (★Rio de Janeiro) 40,322
Ipatinga 35,808
Ipiíba (★Rio de Janeiro) 55,486
Itabira 40,143
Itabuna 89,928
Itajaí 54,135
Itajubá 42,485
Itapetinga 30,578
Itapetininga 42,331
Itaquari (★Vitória) 64,559
Itaúna 32,731
Itu 35,907
Ituiutaba 46,784
Jaboatão (★Recife) 52,537
Jacareí 48,684
Jaú 40,989
Jequié 62,341
João Monlevade 38,689
João Pessoa (★310,000) 197,398
Joinvile 77,760
Juàzeiro 36,273
Juàzeiro do Norte 79,796
Juiz de Fora 218,832
Jundiaí 145,785
Lajes 82,325
Lavras 35,489
Limeira 77,243
Limoeiro 30,726
Lins 38,080
Londrina 156,675
Lorena 39,653
Macapá 51,567
Maceió 242,860
Manaus 284,118
Marília 73,165
Maringá 51,620
Mauá (★São Paulo) 101,569
Mesquita (★Rio de Janeiro) 93,926
Mogi das Cruzes (★São Paulo) 90,330
Monjolo (★Rio de Janeiro) 46,793
Montes Claros 81,572
Mossoró 77,251
Muriaé 34,118
Muribeca dos Guararapes (★Recife) 74,963
Nanuque 34,714
Natal 250,787
Neves (★Rio de Janeiro) 112,912
Nilópolis (★Rio de Janeiro) 86,720
Niterói (★Rio de Janeiro) †376,033
Nova Friburgo 65,732
Nova Iguaçu (★Rio de Janeiro) 331,457
Nôvo Hamburgo (★Porto Alegre) 81,248
Olinda (★Recife) 187,553
Olinda (★Rio de Janeiro) 41,378
Osasco (★São Paulo) 283,303
Ourinhos 40,733
Paranaguá 51,510
Parnaíba 57,031
Parque Industrial (★Belo Horizonte) 80,572
Passo Fundo 69,135
Passos 39,184
Patos 39,850
Patos de Minas 42,215
Paulo Afonso 38,494
Pelotas 150,278
Petrolina 37,801
Petrópolis (★Rio de Janeiro) 116,080
Pinheirinho (★Curitiba) 50,302
Piracicaba 125,490
Poços de Caldas 51,844
Ponta Grossa 92,344
Porto Alegre (★1,760,000) †1,043,964
Porto Velho 41,146
Presidente Prudente 91,188
Queimados (★Rio de Janeiro) 62,560
Recife (★2,100,000) †1,249,821
Ribeirão Prêto 190,897
Rio Branco 34,531
Rio Claro 69,240
Rio de Janeiro (★8,235,000) †4,857,716
Rio Grande 98,863
Salvador (★1,270,000) †1,237,373
Santa Maria 120,667
Santana do Livramento 48,448
Santarém 51,123
Santo André (★São Paulo) 415,025
Santo Ângelo 36,020
Santos (★610,000) 341,317
São Bernardo do Campo (★São Paulo) 187,368
São Caetano do Sul (★São Paulo) 150,171
São Carlos 74,835
São Gonçalo (★Rio de Janeiro) 161,392
São João del Rei 45,019
São João de Meriti (★Rio de Janeiro) 163,934
São José do Rio Prêto 108,319
São José dos Campos 130,118
São Leopoldo (★Porto Alegre) 62,861
São Luís 167,529
São Mateus (★Rio de Janeiro) 38,393
•São Paulo (★9,900,000) †7,198,608
São Vicente (★Santos) 116,075
Sapucaia do Sul (★Porto Alegre) 41,154
Sete Lagoas 61,063
Sete Pontes (★Rio de Janeiro) 53,766
Sobral 51,864
Sorocaba 165,990
Taboão da Serra (★São Paulo) 40,959
Taubaté 98,933
Teófilo Otoni 64,568
Teresina 181,071
Teresópolis 53,462
Três Lagoas 40,157
Tubarão 51,121
Uberaba 108,576
Uberlândia 110,463
Uruguaiana 60,667
Varginha 36,447
Vicente de Carvalho (★Santos) 59,767
Vila Velha (Espírito Santo) (★Vitória) 43,177
Vitória (★345,000) 121,978
Vitória da Conquista 82,477
Vitória de Santo Antão 41,130
Volta Redonda (★205,000) 120,645

BRITISH VIRGIN ISLANDS

See Virgin Islands, British

BRUNEI

1971 C 136,256

•BANDAR SERI BEGAWAN (BRUNEI) (★37,000) 17,410
Seria 20,824

BULGARIA / Bâlgarija

1979 E 8,846,417

Asenovgrad (1969 E) 38,500
Blagoevgrad (Gorna Dzhumaya) 57,457
Burgas 165,994
Dimitrovgrad (1969 E) 44,200
Gabrovo 78,092
Gorna Oryakhovitsa (1969 E) 28,300
Karlovo (Levskigrad) (1969 E) 22,900
Karnobat (Polyanovgrad) (1969 E) 20,500
Kazanlŭk 56,483
Khaskovo 82,630
Kŭrdzhali 52,487
Kyustendil 52,118
Lom (1969 E) 29,100
Lovech (1969 E) 40,000
Mikhaylovgrad (1969 E) 34,200
Nova Zagora (1969 E) 21,000
Panagyurishte (1969 E) 21,800
Pazardzhik 71,933
Pernik (Dimitrovo) 91,428
Petrich (1969 E) 21,900
Pleven 122,916
Plovdiv 342,000
Razgrad (1969 E) 35,600
Ruse 170,594
Samokov (1969 E) 23,800
Sevlievo (1969 E) 21,900
Shumen (Kolarovgrad) 92,157
Silistra 53,085
Sliven 96,090
Smolyan (1969 E) 20,300
•SOFIA (SOFIYA) (★1,133,733) 1,047,920
Stanke Dimitrov (1969 E) 37,800
Stara Zagora 133,201
Svishtov (1969 E) 22,900
Tolbukhin (Dobrich) 94,132
Tŭrgovishte (Eski Dzhumaya) (1969 E) 31,100
Varna 286,382
Veliko Tŭrnovo (Tŭrnovo) 62,565
Vidin 58,213
Vratsa 64,697
Yambol 81,477

BURMA / Myanma

1977 E 31,512,000

Bassein 138,000
Chauk (1953 C) 24,466
Henzada (1970 E) 85,000
Insein (★Rangoon) (1973 C) 143,625
Kanbe (★Rangoon) (1973 C) 253,600
Mandalay 458,000
Meiktila (1953 C) 25,180
Mergui (1953 C) 33,697
Monywa (1953 C) 26,172
Moulmein 188,000
Myaungmya (1953 C) 24,532
Myingyan (1970 E) 65,000
Myitkyina (1953 C) 12,833
Pakokku (1953 C) 30,943
Pegu 135,000
Prome (Pyè) (1970 E) 65,000
•RANGOON (★3,000,000) 2,276,000
Sagaing (1953 C) 15,439
Sittwe (Akyab) (1970 E) 82,000
Tavoy (1970 E) 53,000
Thaton (1953 C) 38,047
Thingangyun (★Rangoon) (1973 C) 141,210
Toungoo (1953 C) 31,589
Yenangyaung (1953 C) 24,416

BURUNDI

1976 E 3,864,000

•BUJUMBURA 157,000
Gitega (1970 E) 15,000
Muyinga (1970 E) 19,000

CAMBODIA

See Kampuchea

CAMEROON / Cameroun

1976 C 7,663,246

Bafoussam 62,239
Bamenda 48,111
•Douala 458,246
Foumban 33,944
Garoua 63,900
Kumba 44,175
Maroua 67,187
Ngaoundere 38,992
Nkongsamba 71,298
Victoria 27,016
YAOUNDÉ 313,706

CANADA

1976 C 22,992,604

CANADA/ALBERTA 1,838,037

Banff 3,410
Blairmore (★7,292) 2,321
Brooks 6,339
Calgary 469,917
Camrose 10,104
Cardston 3,043
Claresholm 3,276
Coaldale 3,654
Drayton Valley 4,303
Drumheller 6,154
Edmonton (★554,228) 461,361
Edson 4,038
Fort MacLeod 3,067
Fort McMurray 15,424
Fort Saskatchewan (★Edmonton) 8,304
Grand Cache 4,116
Grande Prairie 17,626
High River 3,598
Hinton 6,731
Jasper 3,404
Lacombe 3,888
Leduc 8,576
Lethbridge 46,752
Lloydminster *(Alta. and Sask.)* 10,311
Medicine Hat (★36,326) 32,811
Olds 3,658
Peace River 4,840
Pincher Creek 3,448
Ponoka 4,636
Redcliff (★Medicine Hat) 3,006
Red Deer 32,184
Rocky Mountain House 3,432
St. Albert (★Edmonton) 24,129
St. Paul 4,337
Sherwood Park (★Edmonton) 26,534
Slave Lake 3,561
Spruce Grove 6,907
Stettler 4,182
Taber 5,296
Vegreville 4,158
Wainwright 3,890
Westlock 3,721
Wetaskiwin 6,754
Whitecourt 3,878

CANADA/ BRITISH COLUMBIA 2,466,608

Burnaby (★Vancouver) 131,599
Campbell River 11,781
Castlegar 6,255
Chemainus 2,129
Chilliwack (★37,525) 8,634
Clear Brook 4,849
Comox (★Courtenay) 5,359
Courtenay (★19,012) 7,733
Cranbrook 13,510
Creston 3,552
Dawson Creek 10,528
Duncan (★20,410) 4,106
Esquimalt (★Victoria) 15,053
Fernie 4,608
Fort Nelson 2,916
Fort St. John 8,947
Kamloops 58,311
Kelowna 51,955
Kimberley 7,111
Kitimat 11,791
Ladysmith 4,004
Langley (★Vancouver) 10,123
MacKenzie 5,266
Merritt 5,680
Mission City 8,278
Nanaimo 40,336
Nelson 9,235
New Westminster (★Vancouver) 38,393
North Vancouver (★Vancouver) 31,934
Oak Bay (★Victoria) 17,658
Penticton 21,344
Port Alberni (★26,254) 19,585
Port Coquitlam (★Vancouver) 23,926
Port Moody (★Vancouver) 11,649
Powell River 13,694
Prince George 59,929
Prince Rupert 14,754
Quesnel 7,637
Richmond (★Vancouver) 80,034
Sidney (★Victoria) 6,732
Smithers 3,783
Summerland 6,724
Terrace (★15,000) 10,251
Trail (★15,649) 9,976
Vancouver (★1,166,348) 410,188
Vernon (★22,541) 17,546
Victoria (★218,250) 62,551
West Vancouver (★Vancouver) 37,144
White Rock (★Vancouver) 12,497
Williams Lake (★15,966) 6,199

CANADA/MANITOBA 1,021,506

Brandon 34,901
Churchill 1,699
Dauphin 9,109
Flin Flon *(Man. and Sask.)* (★10,306) 8,560
Morden 3,886
Neepawa 3,508
Portage-la-Prairie 12,555
Selkirk 9,862
Steinbach 5,979
Swan River 3,742
The Pas 6,602
Thompson 17,291
Winkler 3,749
Winnipeg (★578,217) 560,874

C Census. E Official estimate. UE Unofficial estimate.
L Population within municipal limits of year specified. • Largest city in country.

★ Population or designation of metropolitan area, including suburbs (see headnote).
▲ Population of an entire municipality, commune, or district, including rural area.
‡† Year of information specified at start of country.

CANADA/ NEW BRUNSWICK 677,250

Bathurst (★19,500)	16,301
Beresford (★Bathurst)	3,199
Campbellton (★11,144)	9,282
Caraquet (★5,678)	3,950
Chatham (★★Newcastle)	7,601
Dalhousie	5,640
Dieppe (★Moncton)	7,460
Edmundston (★15,851)	12,710
Fairvale (★Saint John)	3,258
Fredericton	45,248
Grand Falls	6,223
Minto	3,714
Moncton (★77,571)	55,934
Newcastle (★18,419)	6,423
Oromocto	10,276
Quispamsis (★Saint John)	4,968
Riverview (★Moncton)	14,177
Sackville	5,755
St. Basile (★Edmundston)	3,072
Saint John (★112,974)	85,956
St. Stephen	5,264
Shediac	4,216
Sussex	3,938
Woodstock	4,869

CANADA/ NEWFOUNDLAND 557,725

Bay Roberts (★5,640)	4,072
Bishop's Falls	4,504
Bonavista	4,299
Botwood	4,554
Carbonear (★11,326)	5,026
Channel-Port-aux-Basques	6,187
Conception Bay South (St. John's)	9,743
Corner Brook	25,198
Deer Lake	4,546
Gander	9,301
Grand Bank	3,802
Grand Falls (★15,078)	8,729
Happy Valley	8,075
Labrador City (★15,781)	12,012
Lewisporte	3,782
Marystown	5,915
Mount Pearl (★St. John's)	10,193
St. John's (★143,390)	86,576
Springdale	3,513
Stephenville	10,284
Wabana	4,824
Wabush (★Labrador City)	3,769
Windsor (★Grand Falls)	6,349

CANADA/ NORTHWEST TERRITORIES 42,609

Fort Smith	2,288
Frobisher Bay	2,320
Hay River	3,268
Inuvik	3,116
Pine Point	1,915
Yellowknife	8,256

CANADA/NOVA SCOTIA ... 828,571

Amherst	10,263
Antigonish	5,442
Bible Hill (★Truro)	4,266
Bridgewater	6,010
Dartmouth (★Halifax)	65,341
Glace Bay (★★Sydney)	21,836
Halifax (★267,991)	117,882
Kentville (★12,973)	5,056
Liverpool	3,336
Louisbourg	1,519
New Glasgow (★23,513)	10,672
New Waterford (★Sydney)	9,223
North Sydney (★★Sydney Mines)	8,319
Pictou	4,588
Port Hawkesbury	4,008
Sackville	14,590
Springhill	5,220
Stellarton (★New Glasgow)	5,366
Sydney (★88,614)	30,645
Sydney Mines (★35,455)	8,965
Truro (★27,551)	12,840
Westville (★New Glasgow)	4,251
Windsor	3,702
Yarmouth	7,801

CANADA/ONTARIO 8,264,465

Ajax (★Toronto)	20,774
Amherstburg	5,566
Amherstview	5,295
Ancaster (★Hamilton)	14,255
Arnprior (★10,662)	6,111
Atikokan	5,668
Aurora (★Toronto)	14,249
Aylmer West	5,125
Barrie (★49,228)	34,389
Belleville	35,311
Blackburn Hamlet (★Ottawa)	8,290
Bracebridge	8,428
Bradford	5,080
Brampton (★Toronto)	103,459
Brantford (★82,800)	66,950
Brockville (★26,883)	19,903
Burlington (★Hamilton)	104,314
Caledon (★Toronto)	22,434
Cambridge (Galt) (★★Kitchener)	72,383
Capreol	4,089
Carleton Place	5,256
Chatham	38,685
Cobourg (★20,256)	11,421
Cochrane	4,974
Collingwood	11,114
Collins Bay (★Kingston)	6,897
Cornwall	46,121
Deep River	5,565
Delhi	3,929
Dryden	6,799
Dundas (★Hamilton)	19,179
Dunnville	11,642
East York (★Toronto)	106,950
Elliot Lake	8,849
Elmira	7,034
Espanola	5,926
Essex (★Windsor)	5,577
Etobicoke (★Toronto)	297,109
Exeter	3,494
Fergus (★11,727)	6,001
Fort Erie	24,031
Fort Frances	9,325
Gananoque	5,103
Goderich	7,385
Gravenhurst	7,986
Grimsby (★Hamilton)	15,567
Guelph (★70,388)	67,538
Haileybury (★12,596)	4,939
Haldimand	16,375
Halton Hills	34,477
Hamilton (★529,371)	312,003
Hanover	5,691
Hawkesbury (★11,306)	9,789
Hearst	5,195
Huntsville	11,123
Ingersoll	8,198
Iroquois Falls	6,887
Kanata (★Ottawa)	6,304
Kapuskasing	12,676
Kenora (★12,519)	10,565
Kincardine	4,182
Kingston (★90,741)	56,032
Kingsville (★11,836)	4,692
Kirkland Lake	13,567
Kitchener (★272,158)	131,870
Lambeth (★London)	2,876
Leamington	11,169
Lincoln	14,460
Lindsay	13,062
Listowel	5,126
London (★270,383)	240,392
Manitouwadge Lake	3,507
Marathon	2,258
Markham (★Toronto)	56,206
Meaford	4,319
Midland (★26,239)	11,568
Milton	20,756
Mississauga (★Toronto)	250,017
Mount Forest	3,376
Nanticoke	19,489
Napanee	4,844
Newcastle	31,928
New Hamburg	3,628
New Liskeard (★Haileybury)	5,601
Newmarket (★Toronto)	24,795
Niagara Falls (★★St. Catharines)	69,423
Niagara-on-the-Lake (★St. Catharines)	12,485
Nickel Centre (★Sudbury)	13,157
North Bay (★53,961)	51,639
North York (★Toronto)	558,398
Oakville (★Toronto)	68,950
Onaping Falls	6,776
Orangeville	12,021
Orillia	24,412
Oshawa (★135,196)	107,023
OTTAWA (★693,288)	304,462
Owen Sound	19,525
Paris (★Brantford)	6,713
Parry Sound	5,501
Pelham (★St. Catharines)	10,071
Pembroke (★18,468)	14,927
Penetanguishene (★Midland)	5,460
Perth	5,675
Petawawa (★14,326)	5,815
Peterborough (★65,293)	59,683
Petrolia	4,393
Pickering (★Toronto)	27,879
Picton	4,629
Port Colborne (★St. Catharines)	20,536
Port Elgin (★9,481)	5,069
Port Hope	9,788
Prescott	4,975
Rayside-Balfour (★Sudbury)	16,035
Renfrew	8,617
Richmond Hill (★Toronto)	34,716
St. Catharines (★301,921)	123,351
St. Marys	4,843
St. Thomas	27,206
Sarnia (★81,342)	55,576
Sault Ste. Marie (★81,992)	81,048
Scarborough (★Toronto)	387,149
Simcoe	14,189
Smiths Falls (★13,327)	9,279
Stoney Creek (★Hamilton)	30,294
Stratford	25,657
Strathroy	7,769
Sturgeon Falls	6,400
Sudbury (★157,030)	97,604
Tecumseh (★Windsor)	5,326
Thorold (★St. Catharines)	14,944
Thunder Bay (★119,253)	111,476
Tilbury	4,248
Tillsonburg	9,404
Timmins	44,747
•Toronto (★2,803,101)	633,318
Trenton (★32,634)	15,465
Valley East (★Sudbury)	19,591
Vanier (Eastview) (★Ottawa)	19,812
Vaughan (Woodbridge) (★Toronto)	17,782
Walden (★Sudbury)	10,453
Walkerton	4,626
Wallaceburg	11,132
Waterloo (★Kitchener)	46,623
Wawa (Jamestown)	4,272
Welland (★★St. Catharines)	45,047
Whitchurch Stouffville (★Toronto)	12,884
Whitby (★Oshawa)	28,173
Windsor (★247,582)	196,526
Woodstock	26,779
York (★Toronto)	141,367

CANADA/PRINCE EDWARD ISLAND 118,229

Charlottetown (★24,837)	17,063
Kensington	1,150
Montague	1,827
Parkdale (★Charlottetown)	2,172
St. Eleanors (★Summerside)	2,495
Sherwood (★Charlottetown)	5,602
Souris	1,447
Summerside (★14,145)	8,592

CANADA/QUEBEC 6,234,445

Acton Vale	4,326
Alma	25,638
Amos	9,213
Amqui	3,949
Ancienne-Lorette (Notre-Dame-de-Lorette) (★Québec)	11,694
Anjou (★Montréal)	36,596
Arthabaska (★Victoriaville)	5,907
Asbestos (★14,395)	9,075
Aylmer East (★Ottawa)	25,714
Baie-Comeau (★26,635)	11,911
Baie-d'Urfé (★Montréal)	3,955
Baie-St. Paul	4,062
Beaconsfield (★Montréal)	20,417
Beauceville	4,276
Beauharnois (★Montréal)	7,665
Beauport (★Québec)	55,339
Beaupré (★7,490)	2,821
Bécancour	9,043
Beloeil (★Montréal)	15,913
Berthierville	4,249
Black Lake (★Thetford Mines)	4,051
Blainville (★Montréal)	12,517
Boisbriand (★Montréal)	10,132
Bois-des-Filion (★Montréal)	4,346
Boucherville (★Montréal)	25,530
Bromptonville	2,992
Brossard (★Montréal)	37,641
Brownsburg (★Lachute)	3,114
Buckingham	14,328
Cabano	3,193
Candiac (★Montréal)	7,166
Cap-aux-Meules (★6,847)	1,305
Cap-Chat	3,617
Cap-de-la-Madeleine (★Trois-Rivières)	32,126
Carignan (★Montréal)	3,585
Chambly (★Montréal)	11,815
Chandler	4,011
Chapais	3,147
Charlemagne (★Montréal)	4,025
Charlesbourg (★Québec)	63,147
Charny (★Québec)	6,461
Châteauguay (★Montréal)	36,329
Château-Richer (★Québec)	3,075
Chibougamau	10,536
Chicoutimi (★128,643)	57,737
Clermont	3,518
Coaticook	6,392
Côte-St.-Luc (★Montréal)	25,721
Cowansville	11,902
Deux-Montagnes (★Montréal)	8,957
Dolbeau (★13,924)	8,451
Dollard-des-Ormeaux (★Montréal)	36,837
Donnacona (★7,876)	5,800
Dorion-Vaudreuil (Dorion) (★Montréal)	5,843
Dorval (★Montréal)	19,131
Drummondville (★45,018)	29,286
Drummondville-Sud (★Drummondville)	9,420
East Angus	4,417
East Broughton Station (★2,562)	1,191
Farnham	6,476
Forestville (★4,358)	1,819
Gaspé	16,842
Gatineau (★Ottawa)	73,479
Granby (★41,462)	37,132
Grande-Rivière	4,390
Grand'Mere (★Shawinigan)	15,999
Greenfield Park (★Montréal)	18,430
Hampstead (★Montréal)	7,562
Hauterive (★Baie-Comeau)	14,724
Havre-St.-Pierre	3,208
Hébertville-Station (★3,621)	1,362
Hudson (★Montréal)	4,480
Hull (★Ottawa)	61,039
Iberville (★St.-Jean)	8,897
Île-Perrot (★Montréal)	5,272
Joliette (★30,116)	18,118
Jonquière (★★Chicoutimi)	60,691
Kirkland (★Montréal)	7,476
La Baie	20,116
Lac-Brome	4,117
Lachenaie (★Montréal)	7,118
Lachine (★Montréal)	41,503
Lachute (★15,042)	11,928
Lac-Mégantic	6,457
La Malbaie (★5,135)	4,069
La Pocatière	4,319
Laprairie (★Montréal)	9,173
La Salle (★Montréal)	76,713
La Sarre	4,978
L'Assomption (★Montréal)	4,832
La Tuque	12,067
Lauzon (★Québec)	12,663
Laval (Ville de Laval) (★Montréal)	246,243
LeMoyne (★Montréal)	7,202
Lévis (★Québec)	17,819
Longueuil (★Montréal)	122,429
Loretteville (★Québec)	14,767
Louiseville	3,993
Magog (★14,598)	13,290
Malartic	5,092
Maniwaki	5,969
Marieville (★Montréal)	4,853
Mascouche (★Montréal)	14,266
Matane	12,726
Mercier (Ste.-Philomène) (★Montréal)	4,957
Métabetchouan	3,016
Mirabel	13,486
Mistassini (★Dolbeau)	5,473
Mont-Joli	6,508
Mont-Laurier	8,565
Montmagny	12,326
Montréal (★2,802,485)	1,080,546
Montréal-Est (★Montréal)	4,372
Montréal-Nord (★Montréal)	97,250
Montréal-Ouest (★Montréal)	5,980
Mont-Royal (★Montréal)	20,514
Mont-St.-Hilaire (★Montréal)	7,688
Murdochville	3,704
Napierville	2,166
New Richmond	4,295
Nicolet	4,818
Noranda (★★Rouyn)	9,809
Notre-Dame-des-Prairies	5,714
Otterburn Park (★Montréal)	4,159
Outremont (★Montréal)	27,089
Percé	5,198
Pierrefonds (★Montréal)	35,402
Pierreville (★2,510)	1,311
Pincourt (★Montréal)	7,892
Plessisville	7,238
Pohénégamook	3,627
Pointe-aux-Trembles (★Montréal)	35,618
Pointe-Claire (★Montréal)	25,917
Pontiac	3,365
Pont-Rouge	3,342
Port-Cartier	8,139
Portneuf (★3,225)	1,320
Price	2,461
Princeville	3,852
Québec (★542,158)	177,082
Rawdon	2,808
Repentigny (★Montréal)	26,698
Richmond	4,021
Rimouski (★30,225)	27,897
Rivière-du-Loup	13,103
Roberval	8,543
Rock Island (★3,548)	1,230
Rosemère (★Montréal)	7,112
Rouyn (★27,487)	17,678
Roxboro (★Montréal)	7,106
Ste.-Adèle (★6,273)	4,186
Ste.-Agathe-des-Monts	5,435
St.-Ambroise-de-Chicoutimi	3,169
Ste.-Anne-de-Bellevue (★Montréal)	3,738
Ste.-Anne-des-Monts (★7,606)	5,945
St.-Antoine (★St.-Jérôme)	6,872
St.-Basile-le-Grand (★Montréal)	5,843
St.-Boniface-de-Shawinigan	2,680
St.-Bruno (★Montréal)	21,272
Ste.-Catherine (★Montréal)	5,036
St.-Césaire	2,701
St.-Constant (★Montréal)	7,659
St.-David-de-l'Auberivière (★Québec)	4,386
St.-Eustache (★Montréal)	21,248
St.-Félicien	4,985
St.-Ferdinand (Bernierville)	2,182
Ste.-Foy (★Québec)	71,237
Ste.-Geneviève (★Montréal)	2,869
St.-Georges-Ouest (★Ville-St.-Georges)	6,478
St.-Hubert (★Montréal)	49,706
St.-Hyacinthe (★40,202)	37,500
St.-Jacques	2,095
St.-Jean (★50,363)	34,363
St.-Jérôme (★36,489)	25,175
St.-Joseph-de-Beauce	3,213
St.-Joseph-de-Sorel (★Sorel)	2,811
St.-Jovite	3,595
Ste.-Julie (★Montréal)	8,666
St.-Lambert (★Montréal)	20,318
St.-Laurent (★Montréal)	64,404
St.-Léonard (★Montréal)	78,452
St.-Luc (★St.-Jean)	7,103
St.-Marc-des-Carrières	2,625
Ste.-Marie-de-Beauce	4,462
St.-Pamphile	3,450
St.-Paul-l'Ermite (★Montréal)	6,107
St.-Pierre (★Montréal)	6,039
St.-Raymond	3,742
St. Rémi	4,866
St.-Romuald-d'Etchemin (★Québec)	9,160
Ste.-Thérèse-de Blainville (★Montréal)	17,479
St.-Tite	3,128
Sayabec	1,818
Schefferville	3,429
Senneterre	4,289
Sept-Îles (Seven Islands)	30,617
Shawinigan (★55,414)	24,921
Shawinigan-Sud (★Shawinigan)	11,155
Sherbrooke (★104,505)	76,804
Sillery (★Québec)	13,580
Sorel (★37,029)	19,666
Témiscaming	2,165
Terrebonne (★Montréal)	11,204
Thetford Mines (★28,826)	20,784
Thurso	3,066
Tracy (★Sorel)	12,284
Trois-Pistoles	4,554
Trois-Rivières (★98,583)	52,518
Trois-Rivières-Ouest (★Trois-Rivières)	10,564
Val-Bélair (★Québec)	10,716
Val-d'Or (★21,378)	19,915
Valleyfield (Salaberry-de) (★35,920)	29,716
Vanier (Québec-Ouest) (★Québec)	10,683
Varennes (★Montréal)	6,469
Vaudreuil (★Montréal)	5,630
Verdun (★Montréal)	68,013
Victoriaville (★27,732)	21,825
Ville-St.-Georges (★15,083)	8,605
Warwick	2,865
Waterloo	4,746
Westmount (★Montréal)	22,153
Windsor	5,637

CANADA/ SASKATCHEWAN 921,323

Assiniboia	2,738
Battleford (★North Battleford)	2,569
Biggar	2,491
Canora	2,689
Esterhazy	2,894
Estevan	8,847
Hudson Bay	2,280
Humboldt	4,265
Kamsack	2,726
Kindersley	3,523
Lloydminster (*Sask. and Alta.*)	10,311
Maple Creek	2,330
Meadow Lake	3,662
Melfort	5,141
Melville	5,149
Moose Jaw (★34,829)	32,581
Nipawin	4,317
North Battleford (★16,124)	13,158
Prince Albert	28,631
Regina (★151,191)	149,593
Rosetown	2,551
Saskatoon	133,750
Shaunavon	2,183
Swift Current	14,264
Tisdale	3,026
Unity	2,244
Uranium City	1,765
Weyburn	8,892
Wynyard	2,045
Yorkton	14,119

CANADA/YUKON 21,836

Dawson	838
Elsa	456
Faro	1,544
Watson Lake	808
Whitehorse	13,311

CAPE VERDE / Cabo Verde

1970 C	**272,071**
•Mindelo	28,797
PRAIA	21,494

CAYMAN IS.

1970 C	**10,652**
•GEORGETOWN	3,975

CENTRAL AFRICAN REPUBLIC
République centrafricaine

1971 E	**1,637,000**
Bambari (1968 E)	35,300
•BANGUI	187,000
Bouar (1968 E)	24,600

CHAD / Tchad

1975 E	**4,030,000**
Abéché	32,000
Kélo	18,500
Koumra	18,800
Moundou	45,000
•NDJAMENA (FORT-LAMY)	224,000
Sarh (Fort-Archambault)	50,000

CHILE

1970 C	**8,880,889**
Angol	22,123
Antofagasta	138,821
Apoquindo (★Santiago)	90,722
Arica	87,726
Calama	45,863
Chillán	87,555
Concepción (★395,000)	175,853
Conchalí (★Santiago)	246,046
Copiapó	45,194
Coquimbo	50,405
Coronel	37,312
Curicó	41,262
Iquique	65,040
La Cisterna (★Santiago)	246,537
La Granja (★Santiago)	163,882
La Serena	61,897
Las Rejas (★Santiago)	44,681
Linares	37,913
Lo Prado Arriba (★Santiago)	112,548
Los Ángeles	49,175
Lota	48,166
Ñuñoa (★Santiago)	280,733
Osorno	68,815
Ovalle	31,756
Providencia (★Santiago)	85,678
Puente Alto (★Santiago)	61,077
Puerto Montt	62,726
Punta Arenas	61,813
Quillota	35,488
Quilpué (★Valparaíso)	40,163
Quinta Normal (★Santiago)	138,007
Rancagua	86,404
Renca (★Santiago)	68,440
San Antonio	46,744
San Bernardo (★Santiago)	100,225
San Fernando	27,997
San Miguel (★Santiago)	320,883
•SANTIAGO (★2,925,000)	517,473
Talca	94,449
Talcahuano (★★Concepción)	152,755
Temuco	110,335
Tocopilla	22,241
Tomé	29,597
Valdivia	82,362
Vallenar	26,800
Valparaíso (★530,000)	250,358
Victoria	16,509
Villa Alemana	29,605
Viña del Mar (★Valparaíso)	188,811

C Census. E Official estimate. UE Unofficial estimate.
L Population within municipal limits of specified year. • Largest city in country.

★ Population or designation of metropolitan area, including suburbs (see headnote).
▲ Population of an entire municipality, commune, or district, including rural area.
‡† Year of information specified at start of country.

CHINA / Zhongguo

1975 UE 930,500,000

Provinces

Anhwei 45,900,000
Chekiang 35,600,000
Fukien 21,000,000
Heilungkiang 29,300,000
Honan 67,200,000
Hopeh 55,100,000
Hunan 49,000,000
Hupeh 43,600,000
Inner Mongolia (Auton. Region) 8,000,000
Kansu 19,500,000
Kiangsi 26,400,000
Kiangsu 62,100,000
Kirin 20,900,000
Kwangsi Chuang (Auton. Region) 30,000,000
Kwangtung 51,200,000
Kweichow 24,800,000
Liaoning 43,000,000
Ningsia Hui (Auton. Region) 2,800,000
Peking (Auton. City) 8,000,000
Shanghai (Auton. City) 11,300,000
Shansi 23,000,000
Shantung 78,100,000
Shensi 27,700,000
Sinkiang Uighur (Auton. Region) 8,900,000
Szechwan 99,800,000
Tibet (Auton. Region) 1,600,000
Tientsin (Auton. City) 7,000,000
Tsinghai 3,600,000
Yünnan 26,100,000

Cities

Ach'eng 60,000
Amoy (Hsiamen) 300,000
Anching (Huaining) 135,000
Anshan 1,050,000
Anshun 50,000
Anta 60,000
Anyang 175,000
Canton (Kuangchou) 2,500,000
Chanchiang (Tsamkong) 200,000
Changchiakou (Kalgan) 300,000
Changchih 100,000
Changchou (Wuchin) 300,000
Changchou (Lungchi) 110,000
Changchun (Hsinking) 1,300,000
Changsha 840,000
Changshu 95,000
Changte 125,000
Chaoan 95,000
Chaoching 75,000
Chaotung (Tientsaokang) 65,000
Chaoyang (*Kwangtung Prov.*) 60,000
Chaoyang (*Liaoning Prov.*) 120,000
Chenchiang (Chinkiang) 225,000
Chengchou 1,100,000
Chenghai 50,000
Chengte (Jehol) 120,000
Chengtu 1,800,000
Chenhsien 60,000
Chiahsing 150,000
Chiamussu (Kiamusze) 300,000
Chian 110,000
Chiangmen (Sunwui) 120,000
Chiaohsien 45,000
Chiaotso 275,000
Chiawang 50,000
Chichihaerh (Tsitsihar) 850,000
Chiehyang (Kityang) 65,000
Chihfeng 75,000
Chihsi 325,000
Chilin (Kirin) 775,000
Chinan (Tsinan) 1,125,000
Chinchou 450,000
Chingchiang (Huaiyin) 100,000
Chingshih 65,000
Chingtechen (Fouliang) 300,000
Chinhsi 50,000
Chinhsien 75,000
Chinhua 55,000
Chinhuangtao 275,000
Chining (*Inner Mongolia A.R.*) 100,000
Chining (*Shantung Prov.*) 130,000
Chiuchiang (Kiukiang) 100,000
Choutsun 50,000
Chüanchou 130,000
Chuchou 250,000
Chühsien 50,000
Chungking (Chungching) 2,900,000
Chungshan (Shekki) 90,000
Erhlien 60,000
Foshan (Fatshan) 125,000
Fouhsin (Fusin) 350,000
Fouyang 90,000
Fuchou (Foochow) 725,000
Fuhsien 85,000
Fushun 1,150,000
Haerhpin (Harbin) 2,400,000
Haicheng 90,000
Haikou (Hoihow) 275,000
Hailaerh (Hulun) 85,000
Hami (Kumul) 50,000
Hanchung (Nancheng) 90,000
Hangchou 900,000
Hanku 100,000
Hantan 480,000
Hengyang 350,000
Hochuan 60,000
Hofei 450,000
Hokang (Haoli) 250,000
Hopi 100,000
Hopu 50,000
Hsian (Sian) 1,900,000
Hsiangfan 110,000
Hsiangtan (Siangtan) 325,000
Hsienyang 85,000
Hsikueitucht 50,000
Hsinghua 85,000
Hsingtai 115,000
Hsinhsiang (Sinsiang) 250,000
Hsinhui 50,000
Hsining (Sining) 300,000
Hsinwen 50,000
Hsinyang 100,000
Hsüanhua 140,000
Hsüchang 100,000
Hsüchou (Süchow) 800,000
Huaian 50,000
Huainan 400,000
Huaipei 75,000
Huaite (Kungchuling) 75,000
Huangshih 140,000
Huatien 55,000
Huhohaote (Huhehot) 450,000
Huichou (Huiyang) 80,000
Hulan 75,000
Hunchiang 50,000
Ichang 120,000
Ichun 90,000
Ining (Kuldja) 90,000
Ipin (Suifu) 250,000
Itu 50,000
Iyang 110,000
Kaifeng 350,000
Kaiyüan 50,000
Kanchou (Kanhsien) 140,000
Kashih (Kashgar) 100,000
Kochiu 100,000
Koerhchinyuichienchi (Ulanhot) 80,000
Kolamai (Karamai) 60,000
Kueilin 250,000
Kueiyang 800,000
Kunming (Yunnanfu) 1,225,000
Lanchou 950,000
Lasa (Lhasa) 80,000
Liaoyang 250,000
Liaoyüan (Shuangliao) 250,000
Lienyünchiangshih (Sinhai) 250,000
Linching 65,000
Linchuan 55,000
Linfen 50,000
Linshi 90,000
Linhsia 65,000
Liuan 55,000
Liuchou 300,000
Liyüchiang 50,000
Loho 60,000
Loshan 70,000
Loyang 750,000
Luchou (Luhsien) 175,000
Lüshun (Port Arthur) 40,000
Lüta (Dairen) (1,700,000▲) 1,100,000
Maanshan 60,000
Manchouli (Lupin) 65,000
Maoming 100,000
Meihsien 50,000
Mienyang 50,000
Minhang 60,000
Mukden (Shenyang) 3,300,000
Mutanchiang 350,000
Nancha 50,000
Nanchang 700,000
Nanchung 225,000
Nanking 1,800,000
Nanning (Yungning) 350,000
Nanping 50,000
Nantung 275,000
Nanyang 60,000
Neichiang 225,000
Nientzushan 50,000
Ningpo (Ninghsien) 300,000
Paicheng 125,000
Paiyin 50,000
Pangfou (Pangpu) 400,000
Paochi 250,000
Paoting (Tsingyuan) 350,000
Paotou 650,000
Paoying 50,000
Peian 80,000
Peihai (Pakhoi) 95,000
Peipiao 100,000
PEKING (PEIPING) (8,000,000▲) 5,400,000
Penchi 500,000
Pinghsiang 120,000
Pingliang 80,000
Pingtingshan 85,000
Pohsien 90,000
Poshan 100,000
Putehachi (Yalu) 55,000
Sanmenhsia 60,000
Sanming 55,000
Shangchiu 100,000
•Shanghai (11,300,000▲) 8,100,000
Shangjao 60,000
Shangshui (Chouchiakou) 90,000
Shaohsing 150,000
Shaokuan (Kükong) 100,000
Shaoyang 215,000
Shashih 120,000
Shihchiachuang 940,000
Shihkuaikou 50,000
Shuangyashan 150,000
Soche (Yarkand) 50,000
Ssuping (Szeping) 165,000
Suchou (Soochow) 750,000
Suhsien 50,000
Suihua 70,000
Suining 60,000
Sungchiang 60,000
Swatow (Shantou) 325,000
Tachangchen 50,000
Taian 50,000
Taichou (Tai) 175,000
Taiyüan (Yangkü) 1,350,000
Tangshan (1980 UE) 650,000
Tantung (Antung) 300,000
Taoan 75,000
Tatung 350,000
Techou 70,000
Teyang 50,000
Tiehling 75,000
Tienshui 85,000
Tientsin (Tienching) (7,000,000▲) 4,500,000
Tinghsien (Ting) 40,000
Titao 50,000
Tsangchou (Tsanghsien) 100,000
Tsaochuang 75,000
Tsingtao (Chingtao) 1,200,000
Tsuni 250,000
Tukou 120,000
Tunchi 65,000
Tungchuan 75,000
Tunghsien 80,000
Tunghua 175,000
Tungkuan 55,000
Tungliao 60,000
Tunglinghsien 65,000
Tungtai 50,000
Tunhua 60,000
Tuyün 75,000
Tzukung 325,000
Tzupo (Changtien) (900,000▲) 60,000
Wanhsien 120,000
Weifang 240,000
Wenchou 260,000
Wuchou (Tsangwu) 160,000
Wuhan 3,000,000
Wuhsi (Wusih) 700,000
Wuhsing 90,000
Wuhu 325,000
Wulumuchi (Urumchi) 400,000
Wutungchiao 45,000
Yaan 50,000
Yangchiang 60,000
Yangchou (Chiangtu) 175,000
Yangchüan 275,000
Yencheng 60,000
Yenchi 90,000
Yentai (Chefoo) 150,000
Yingchengtsu 50,000
Yinchuan (Ningsia) 125,000
Yingkou 175,000
Yingkou (Tashihchiao) 50,000
Yüehyang 60,000
Yümenshih 90,000
Yützu 90,000

COLOMBIA

1973 C 22,551,811

Armenia (1979 E) (★205,000) 164,000
Barrancabermeja (1979 E) 115,000
Barranquilla (1979 E) (★950,000) 859,000
Bello (★Medellín) 121,204
•BOGOTÁ (1979 E) (★4,150,000) 4,067,000
Bucaramanga (1979 E) (★470,000) 402,000
Buenaventura (1979 E) 144,000
Buga (84,057▲) 71,016
Caicedonia 23,567
Calarcá (★Armenia) (49,936▲) 29,349
Caldas 27,394
Cali (1979 E) (★1,340,000) 1,293,000
Cartagena (1979 E) 388,000
Cartago (77,890▲) 69,154
Ciénaga (89,723▲) 42,546
Cúcuta (1979 UE) 355,000
Dos Quebradas (★Pereira) 37,837
Duitama (48,459▲) 36,551
Envigado (★Medellín) 69,921
Espinal 32,475
Facatativá 27,892
Florencia 31,817
Floridablanca (★Bucaramanga) 38,446
Fusagasugá 25,456
Girardot (★78,000) 61,829
Ibagué (1979 E) 257,000
Ipiales 30,871
Itagüí (★Medellín) 96,972
La Dorada 30,962
Líbano (42,832▲) 19,132
Lorica (59,757▲) 18,251
Magangué (62,746▲) 34,396
Manizales (1979 UE) 252,000
Medellín (1979 E) (★2,025,000) 1,477,000
Montería (1979 E) 123,000
Neiva (1979 E) 145,000
Ocaña 38,352
Palmira (1979 E) 168,000
Pamplona 31,817
Pasto (1979 E) 171,000
Pereira (1979 UE)](★325,000) 260,000
Popayán (1977 E) 88,768
Pradera 15,732
Puerto Berrío 19,579
Quibdó (1977 E) 33,588
Ríohacha (1977 E) 35,000
Santa Marta (1979 UE) 155,000
Santa Rosa de Cabal (★Pereira) (42,717▲) 28,368
Sevilla 31,143
Sincelejo (1977 E) 86,569
Sogamoso (67,738▲) 48,891
Soledad (★Barranquilla) 64,469
Sonsón 15,990
Tuluá (1979 E) 113,000
Tumaco (87,448▲) 38,742
Tunja (1977 E) 64,551
Valledupar (1979 E) 164,000
Villavicencio (1979 E) 133,000

COMOROS / Comores

1974 E 292,000

•MORONI 12,000
Mutsamudu (1966 C) 7,652

CONGO (PEOPLE'S REPUBLIC OF THE CONGO)

1970 C 1,089,300

•BRAZZAVILLE 175,000
Jacob (1969 E) 18,000
Loubomo (1969 E) 15,000
Pointe-Noire 135,000

COOK IS.

1971 C 21,227

•AVARUA (1961 E) 4,000

COSTA RICA

1976 E 1,993,800

Alajuela 35,000
Cartago 23,100
Desamparados (★San José) 32,700
Guadalupe (★San José) 29,100
Heredia 24,200
Liberia (18,000▲) 11,600
Limón (43,800▲) 31,900
Puntarenas 29,000
•SAN JOSÉ (1978 E) (★519,400) 239,800
San Juan (★San José) 19,600
San Pedro (★San José) 25,100
San Vicente (★San José) 16,400

CUBA

1970 C 8,553,400

Amancio Rodríguez (37,900▲) 12,300
Artemisa 31,200
Banes (39,300▲) 27,100
Baracoa (35,600▲) 20,900
Bauta (★Havana) (25,400▲) 21,100
Bayamo (1976 E) (88,994▲) 68,900
Camagüey (1976 E) 230,891
Camajuaní (32,300▲) 15,900
Cárdenas 55,700
Chaparra (51,000▲) 8,400
Ciego de Avila (1976 E) (66,542▲) 57,700
Cienfuegos (1976 E) (92,210▲) 86,600
Colón (40,800▲) 26,000
Consolación del Sur (42,000▲) 15,100
Contramaestre (43,900▲) 22,900
Cruces (32,100▲) 19,100
Florida (37,500▲) 32,700
Fomento (33,600▲) 12,900
Guanabacoa (★Havana) 69,700
Guantánamo (1976 E) 155,217
Güines (45,300▲) 41,400
Guisa (44,100▲) 9,000
•HAVANA (LA HABANA) (1976 E) (★2,000,000) 1,961,674
Holguín (1976 E) (160,965▲) 129,800
Manzanillo (88,900▲) 77,900
Matanzas (1976 E) 99,003
Mayarí (34,000▲) 17,600
Mayarí Arriba (31,400▲) 2,300
Morón (31,100▲) 29,000
Niquero (36,500▲) 11,300
Nueva Gerona (1976 E) (28,342▲) 24,300
Nuevitas (21,500▲) 20,700
Palma Soriano (59,600▲) 41,200
Pinar del Río (1976 E) 89,978
Placetas (48,400▲) 32,300
Sagua la Grande (41,900▲) 35,800
San Antonio de los Baños (30,000▲) 25,300
Sancti-Spíritus (1976 E) (67,569▲) 58,600
San Germán (30,200▲) 12,400
San José de las Lajas (33,600▲) 24,900
San Juan y Martínez (45,700▲) 11,100
San Luis (35,000▲) 17,400
Santa Clara (1976 E) 152,361
Santiago de Cuba (1976 E) 326,066
Santiago de las Vegas (★Havana) 29,300
Trinidad (37,000▲) 31,500
Vertientes (32,600▲) 14,000
Victoria de las Tunas (1976 E) (65,767▲) 54,400

CYPRUS / Kípros / Kıbrıs

1974 E 639,000

Ammókhostos (Famagusta) 39,400
Kirínia 3,900
Lárnax (Larnaca) 19,800
Lemesós (Limassol) (★80,600) 55,000
•NICOSIA (LEVKOSÍA) (★117,100) 51,000
Páfos 9,100

CZECHOSLOVAKIA / Československo

1979 E 15,280,148

Banská Bystrica 66,279
Beroun (★26,000) 18,149
Bratislava 374,860
Břeclav 24,258
Brno 372,793
České Budějovice (Budweis) 89,399
Cheb 31,030
Chomutov 49,960
Děčín 48,424
Frýdek-Místek (★Ostrava) 54,112
Gottwaldov (Zlín) 82,926
Havířov (★Ostrava) 93,832
Havlíčkův Brod 24,859
Hlohovec (★26,000) 16,815
Hodonín 25,504
Hradec Králové 93,165
Humenné 26,885
Jablonec [nad Nisou] 39,692
Jihlava 50,995
Karlovy Vary (Karlsbad) 61,212
Karviná (★★Ostrava) 80,017
Kladno (★86,000) 66,370
Kolín 31,169
Komárno 30,886
Košice 200,943
Krnov 26,393
Kroměříž 26,166
Levice 25,610
Liberec (★96,000) 85,119
Liptovský Mikuláš 23,795
Litvínov 23,572
Lučenec 26,300
Martin 56,294
Michalovce 28,012
Mladá Boleslav 43,876
Most 61,411
Náchod 19,812
Nitra 72,140
Nové Zámky 32,694
Nový Jičín 31,101
Olomouc 102,501
Opava 59,481
Orlová (★Ostrava) 30,938
Ostrava (★745,000) 325,473
Pardubice 93,042
Piešťany 30,070
Písek 28,067
Plzeň (Pilsen) 169,466
Poprad 36,428
Považská Bystrica 24,747
•PRAGUE (PRAHA) (★1,275,000) 1,193,345
Přerov 47,933
Prešov 69,453
Příbram 36,441
Prievidza 38,948
Prostějov 48,516
Ružomberok 26,803
Sokolov 27,338
Spišská Nová Ves 31,537
Šumperk 29,872
Tábor 31,005
Teplice 53,822
Třebíč 27,708
Trenčín 47,832
Třinec 34,226
Trnava 61,617
Trutnov 27,402
Uherské Hradiště 35,909
Ústí nad Labem (★103,000) 80,309
Valašské Meziříčí 24,485
Vsetín 29,023
Žilina 67,204
Znojmo 35,711
Zvolen 35,754

DENMARK / Danmark

1980 E 5,122,065

Åbenrå (21,172▲) 18,200
Albertslund (★Copenhagen) 30,425
Ålborg 153,948
Århus 244,839
Ballerup-Måløv (★Copenhagen) 48,938
Brøndby (★Copenhagen) 38,034
•COPENHAGEN (KØBENHAVN) (★1,470,000) 498,850
Esbjerg 79,310
Fredericia 45,820
Frederiksberg (★Copenhagen) 88,287
Frederikshavn 35,038
Gentofte (★Copenhagen) 67,300
Gladsakse (★Copenhagen) 64,954
Glostrup (★Copenhagen) 19,573
Haderslev (29,973▲) 23,100
Helsingør (Elsinore) 56,566
Herlev (★Copenhagen) 28,530
Herning (56,033▲) 47,900
Hillerød 33,686
Hjørring (34,456▲) 24,900
Høje Tåstrup (★Copenhagen) 43,292
Holbæk (29,578▲) 23,300
Holstebro (36,777▲) 29,900
Horsens 54,533
Hvidovre (★Copenhagen) 50,608
Køge (34,511▲) 30,300
Kolding 55,769
Lyngby (Kongens Lyngby)-Tårbæk (★Copenhagen) 52,013
Middelfart 17,996
Næstved (45,237▲) 39,800
Odense 168,528
Randers 62,486
Rødovre (★Copenhagen) 38,020
Roskilde 48,746
Silkeborg (46,774▲) 40,300
Søllerød (★Copenhagen) 31,920
Sønderborg 27,790
Svendborg (37,996▲) 33,200
Tårnby (★Copenhagen) 42,075
Vejle 49,471
Viborg (38,757▲) 32,600

DJIBOUTI

1971 E 125,000

•DJIBOUTI 40,000

DOMINICA

1970 C 70,302

•ROSEAU 10,157

DOMINICAN REPUBLIC / República Dominicana

1976 E 4,835,207

Baní 31,763
Barahona 53,912
Bonao 32,132
La Romana 49,498
La Vega 41,658
Mao (Valverde) 32,723
Moca 32,621
Puerto Plata 44,113
San Cristóbal 36,504
San Francisco de Macorís 60,821
San Juan [de la Maguana] 43,417
San Pedro de Macorís 66,022
Santiago [de los Caballeros] 219,846
•SANTO DOMINGO 979,608

C Census. E Official estimate. UE Unofficial estimate.
L Population within municipal limits of year specified. • Largest city in country.

★ Population or designation of metropolitan area, including suburbs (see headnote).
▲ Population of an entire municipality, commune, or district, including rural area.
‡† Year of information specified at start of country.

ECUADOR

1974 C ... 6,521,710

Ambato (1976 E) ... 80,000
Azogues ... 10,939
Babahoyo ... 28,345
Chone ... 23,647
Cuenca (1978 E) ... 128,788
Esmeraldas ... 60,132
Guaranda ... 11,387
•Guayaquil (1978 E) ... 1,022,010
Ibarra ... 41,057
Jipijapa ... 19,719
Latacunga ... 22,106
Loja ... 47,268
Machala ... 68,379
Manta ... 63,514
Milagro ... 53,058
Pasaje ... 20,822
Portoviejo ... 59,404
Quevedo ... 43,123
QUITO (1978 E) ... 742,858
Riobamba ... 58,029
Santo Domingo ... 30,487
Tulcán ... 24,443

EGYPT / Miṣr

1966 C ... 30,083,419

Abnūb ... 31,195
Abū Kabīr ... 41,789
Abū Tīj ... 28,161
Akhmīm ... 44,829
Al-'Arīsh ... ††40,338
Al-Badārī ... 26,531
Alexandria (Al-Iskandarīyah) (1978 E) (★2,850,000) ... 2,409,000
Al-Fashn ... 27,746
Al-Fayyūm (1976 C) ... 167,081
Al-Ḥawāmidīyah (★Cairo) ... 36,227
Al-Ismā'īlīyah (Ismailia) (1976 C) (★185,000) ... 145,478
Al-Jīzah (Giza) (★Cairo) (1976 C) ... 1,246,713
Al Madīnah al Fikrīyah ... 21,504
Al-Maḥallah al Kubrā (1976 C) ... 292,853
Al-Manshāh ... 25,027
Al-Manṣūrah (El Mansura) (1976 C) (★290,000) ... 257,866
Al-Manzilah ... 33,298
Al-Maṭarīyah ... 41,105
Al-Minyā (1976 C) ... 146,423
Al Qanāṭir al Khayrīyah ... 22,477
Al-Quṣayr ... 5,525
Al-Qūṣīyah ... 25,991
Al-Uqṣur (Luxor) ... 77,578
Armant ... 38,308
Ashmūn ... 32,168
Ash Shuhadā' ... 21,947
As-Sallūm ... 2,483
As-Sinbillāwayn ... 40,686
Aswān (1976 C) ... 144,377
Asyūt (1976 C) ... 213,983
Aṭ Ṭalibīyah ... 20,438
Az-Zaqāzīq (1976 C) ... 202,637
Bahtīm (★Cairo) ... 32,510
Banhā ... 63,849
Banī Mazār ... 34,053
Banī Suwayf (1976 C) ... 118,148
Bibā ... 22,871
Bilbays ... 58,070
Bilqās Qism Awwal ... 41,067
Biyalā ... 33,008
Būsh ... 21,174
•CAIRO (AL QĀHIRAH) (1978 E) (★8,500,000) ... 5,278,000
Damanhūr (1976 C) ... 188,927
Dayrūt ... 27,646
Dishnā ... 21,857
Disūq ... 45,580
Dumyāt (Damietta) (1975 E) ... 113,200
Fāqūs ... 40,561
Fuwah ... 30,654
Giheina al Gharbiya ... 24,203
Ḥawsh 'Īsá ... 30,006
Idfū ... 27,326
Idkū ... 42,239
Isnā ... 27,383
Jirjā ... 44,150
Kafr ad-Dawwār (★Alexandria) (1976 C) ... 160,554
Kafr ash-Shaykh ... 51,544
Kafr az-Zayyāt ... 34,084
Kafr Salīm (★Alexandria) ... 40,381
Kawm Umbū ... 27,227
Maghāghah ... 33,211
Mallawī ... 59,938
Manfalūṭ ... 34,132
Minūf ... 48,256
Minyā al-Qamḥ ... 31,533
Mīt Ghamr (★82,000) ... 43,665
Nafīshah (★Al-Ismā'īlīyah) ... 29,483
Port Said (Bur Sa'īd) (1978 E) ... 271,000
Qalyūb ... 49,303
Qinā ... 68,536
Qūṣ ... 27,462
Rashīd (Rosetta) ... 36,711
Samālūṭ ... 37,861
Samannūd ... 29,749
Sāqiyat Makkī ... 22,967
Sawhāj (1976 C) ... 101,758
Shibīn al-Kawm (1976 C) ... 102,844
Shirbīn ... 25,089
Shubrā al-Khaymah (★Cairo) (1976 C) ... 393,700
Sīdī Sālim ... 21,096
Sinnūris ... 34,855
Suez (As Suways) (1978 E) ... 204,000
Ṭahṭā ... 38,915
Ṭalā ... 25,448
Ṭanṭā (1976 C) ... 284,636
Ṭimā ... 29,293
Warrāq al-'Arab (★Cairo) ... 31,263
Ziftá (★★Mīt Ghamr) ... 37,883

††31,733 per 1967 census taken by Israeli occupation authorities.

EL SALVADOR

1977 E ... 4,255,000

Ahuachapán (63,600▲) ... 18,100
Chalchuapa (51,200▲) ... 22,000
Delgado (★San Salvador) (77,100▲) ... 53,600
Mejicanos (★San Salvador) (85,000▲) ... 70,500
Nueva San Salvador (63,500▲) ... 44,000
San Miguel (144,900▲) ... 72,900
•SAN SALVADOR (★720,000) ... 397,100
Santa Ana (189,000▲) ... 112,800
San Vicente (56,900▲) ... 21,500
Sonsonate (61,000▲) ... 40,100
Soyapango (★San Salvador) (56,900▲) ... 32,700
Usulután (57,600▲) ... 25,100
Zacatecoluca (71,500▲) ... 20,200

EQUATORIAL GUINEA / Guinea Ecuatorial

1965 C ... 254,684

Bata (1960 C) (27,024▲) ... 4,000
•MALABO (SANTA ISABEL) (37,152▲) ... 17,500

ETHIOPIA / Yaltopya

1978 E ... 29,408,200

•ADDIS ABABA ... 1,125,340
Asmera ... 373,827
Bahir Dar ... 45,955
Dabra-Mārk'os ... 35,818
Debre Zeyt ... 43,654
Desē ... 65,571
Dirē Dawa ... 72,202
Gonder ... 67,790
Hārer ... 55,401
Jimā ... 56,278
Keren ... 33,368
Mak'alē ... 41,235
Mitsiwa ... 29,064
Nazreth (Adāmā) ... 61,468

FAEROE IS. / Føroyar

1977 E ... 41,575

•TÓRSHAVN ... 11,586

FALKLAND ISLANDS

1972 C ... 1,957

•STANLEY ... 1,081

FIJI

1976 C ... 588,068

Lautoka (★28,847) ... 22,672
•SUVA (★117,827) ... 63,628

FINLAND / Suomi

1978 E ... 4,758,088

Espoo (Esbo) (★Helsinki) ... 129,758
Hämeenlinna ... 41,303
•HELSINKI (HELSINGFORS) (★885,000) ... 484,879
Hyvinkää ... 37,104
Iisalmi ... 22,131
Imatra ... 36,593
Joensuu ... 43,940
Jyväskylä (★86,000) ... 62,937
Kajaani ... 33,662
Kotka ... 61,320
Kouvola (★53,000) ... 30,524
Kuopio ... 73,567
Kuusankoski (★★Kouvola) ... 22,649
Lahti (★109,000) ... 94,980
Lappeenranta ... 53,393
Mikkeli ... 27,919
Nokia (★Tampere) ... 23,612
Oulu (★112,000) ... 93,497
Pori ... 79,815
Rauma ... 30,429
Tampere (★241,000) ... 165,519
Turku (Åbo) (★221,000) ... 164,586
Vaasa (Vasa) ... 53,774
Vantaa (Vanda) (★Helsinki) ... 127,403
Varkaus ... 24,536

FRANCE

1980 E ... 53,589,000

Regions and Departments

ALSACE ... 1,560,000
Bas-Rhin ... 904,300
Haut-Rhin ... 655,700
AQUITAINE ... 2,576,700
Dordogne ... 365,800
Gironde ... 1,089,000
Landes ... 292,000
Lot-et-Garonne ... 287,800
Pyrénées-Atlantiques (Basses-Pyrénées) ... 542,100
AUVERGNE ... 1,319,500
Allier ... 365,400
Cantal ... 160,500
Haute-Loire ... 199,300
Puy-de-Dôme ... 594,300
BASSE-NORMANDIE ... 1,314,000
Calvados ... 579,100
Manche ... 444,600
Orne ... 290,300
BOURGOGNE ... 1,589,600
Côte-d'Or ... 474,100
Nièvre ... 239,500
Saône-et-Loire ... 569,000
Yonne ... 307,000
BRETAGNE ... 2,652,800
Côtes-du-Nord ... 531,700
Finistère ... 817,800
Ille-et-Vilaine ... 731,600
Morbihan ... 571,700
CENTRE ... 2,224,000
Cher ... 319,100
Eure-et-Loir ... 352,700
Indre ... 243,000
Indre-et-Loire ... 498,700
Loiret ... 521,900
Loir-et-Cher ... 288,600
CHAMPAGNE-ARDENNE ... 1,346,600
Ardennes ... 300,700
Aube ... 286,900
Haute-Marne ... 205,700
Marne ... 553,300
CORSE (CORSICA) ... 229,400
Corse-du-Sud ... 102,400
Haute-Corse ... 127,000
FRANCHE-COMTÉ ... 1,085,800
Belfort, Territoire de ... 132,000
Doubs ... 492,500
Haute-Saône ... 223,500
Jura ... 237,800
HAUTE-NORMANDIE ... 1,638,500
Eure ... 443,800
Seine-Maritime ... 1,194,700
ÎLE-DE-FRANCE ... 10,064,700
Essonne ... 1,087,600
Hauts-de-Seine ... 1,350,000
Paris ... 2,050,500
Seine-et-Marne ... 889,400
Seine-Saint-Denis ... 1,292,400
Val-de-Marne ... 1,226,000
Val-d'Oise ... 921,000
Yvelines ... 1,247,800
LANGUEDOC-ROUSSILLON ... 1,832,100
Aude ... 265,200
Gard ... 500,000
Hérault ... 685,500
Lozère ... 72,300
Pyrénées-Orientales ... 309,100
LIMOUSIN ... 733,500
Corrèze ... 238,600
Creuse ... 138,100
Haute-Vienne ... 356,800
LORRAINE ... 2,312,900
Meurthe-et-Moselle ... 716,500
Meuse ... 191,400
Moselle ... 1,007,200
Vosges ... 397,800
MIDI-PYRÉNÉES ... 2,272,100
Ariège ... 135,500
Aveyron ... 268,300
Gers ... 167,200
Haute-Garonne ... 816,600
Hautes-Pyrénées ... 222,200
Lot ... 148,300
Tarn ... 334,900
Tarn-et-Garonne ... 179,100
NORD-PAS-DE-CALAIS ... 3,920,300
Nord ... 2,521,300
Pas-de-Calais ... 1,399,000
PAYS DE LA LOIRE ... 2,860,800
Loire-Atlantique ... 977,700
Maine-et-Loire ... 652,700
Mayenne ... 264,700
Sarthe ... 499,500
Vendée ... 466,200
PICARDIE ... 1,714,600
Aisne ... 527,200
Oise ... 642,100
Somme ... 545,300
POITOU-CHARENTES ... 1,537,200
Charente ... 334,200
Charente-Maritime ... 499,800
Deux-Sèvres ... 338,000
Vienne ... 365,200
PROVENCE-ALPES-CÔTE D'AZUR ... 3,873,100
Alpes-de-Haute-Provence (Basses-Alpes) ... 115,800
Alpes-Maritimes ... 862,600
Bouches-du-Rhône ... 1,715,400
Hautes-Alpes ... 99,800
Var ... 667,300
Vaucluse ... 412,200
RHÔNE-ALPES ... 4,930,800
Ain ... 398,000
Ardèche ... 252,000
Drôme ... 366,700
Haute-Savoie ... 483,400
Isère ... 903,900
Loire ... 735,500
Rhône ... 1,478,900
Savoie ... 312,400

Cities (1975 C)

Aix-en-Provence ... 110,659
Aix-les-Bains ... 22,210
Ajaccio ... 50,726
Albi ... 46,162
Alençon ... 33,680
Alès (★67,513) ... 44,245
Alfortville (★Paris) ... 38,057
Amiens (★152,997) ... 131,476
Angers (★188,695) ... 137,587
Angoulême (★100,528) ... 47,221
Annecy (★103,543) ... 53,262
Antibes (★★Cannes) ... 55,960
Antony (★Paris) ... 57,540
Arcachon (★38,000) ... 13,892
Argenteuil (★Paris) ... 102,530
Arles (50,059▲) ... 37,340
Armentières (★58,000) ... 26,346
Arras (★79,783) ... 46,446
Asnières [-sur-Seine] (★Paris) ... 75,431
Athis-Mons (★Paris) ... 30,737
Aubervilliers (★Paris) ... 72,976
Aulnay-sous-Bois (★Paris) ... 78,137
Aurillac ... 30,863
Autun ... 21,556
Auxerre ... 38,342
Avignon (★162,562) ... 90,786
Avranches ... 10,136
Bagneux (★Paris) ... 40,674
Bagnolet (★Paris) ... 35,906
Barentin (★12,000) ... 10,773
Bar-le-Duc ... 19,288
Bastia (★56,984) ... 50,718
Bayeux ... 13,457
Bayonne (★121,474) ... 42,938
Beauvais ... 54,089
Belfort (★75,795) ... 54,615
Besançon (★126,349) ... 120,315
Béthune (★145,155) ... 26,982
Béziers (★88,619) ... 84,029
Biarritz (★★Bayonne) ... 27,595
Blois ... 49,778
Bobigny (★Paris) ... 43,125
Bois-Colombes (★Paris) ... 26,657
Bondy (★Paris) ... 48,333
Bordeaux (★612,456) ... 223,131
Boulogne-Billancourt (★Paris) ... 103,578
Boulogne-sur-Mer (★100,581) ... 48,440
Bourg-en-Bresse ... 42,181
Bourges (★86,041) ... 77,300
Brest (★190,812) ... 166,826
Briançon ... 9,489
Brive-la-Gaillarde ... 51,864
Bron (★Lyon) ... 44,563
Bruay-en-Artois (★116,340) ... 25,714
Caen (★181,390) ... 119,474
Cagnes [-sur-Mer] (★Nice) (29,538▲) ... 23,353
Cahors ... 20,311
Calais (★100,327) ... 78,820
Caluire-et-Cuire (★Lyon) ... 43,041
Cambrai (★51,357) ... 39,049
Cannes (★210,000) ... 70,527
Carcassonne ... 42,154
Carmaux (★23,000) ... 13,208
Castres ... 45,978
Châlons-sur-Marne (★63,407) ... 52,275
Chalon-sur-Saône (★72,407) ... 58,187
Chambéry (★88,081) ... 54,415
Chamonix-Mont-Blanc ... 6,285
Champigny-sur-Marne (★Paris) ... 80,291
Chantilly ... 10,552
Charleville-Mézières (★69,124) ... 60,176
Chartres (★72,246) ... 38,928
Châteauroux (★66,836) ... 53,429
Châtellerault (★66,836) ... 37,080
Châtenay-Malabry (★Paris) ... 30,497
Châtillon (★Paris) ... 26,574
Chatou (★Paris) ... 26,550
Chaumont ... 27,226
Chauny (★21,000) ... 14,405
Chelles (★Paris) ... 36,516
Cherbourg (★82,539) ... 32,536
Chinon ... 5,391
Choisy-le-Roi (★Paris) ... 38,705
Cholet ... 52,976
Clamart (★Paris) ... 52,952
Clermont-Ferrand (★253,244) ... 156,900
Clichy (★Paris) ... 47,764
Cognac ... 22,237
Colmar (★83,435) ... 64,771
Colombes (★Paris) ... 83,390
Compiègne (★57,210) ... 37,699
Concarneau (18,759▲) ... 15,096
Corbeil-Essonnes (★Paris) ... 38,859
Courbevoie (★Paris) ... 54,488
Coutances ... 8,349
Creil (★77,225) ... 32,509
Créteil (★Paris) ... 59,023
Dax (★27,000) ... 19,137
Deauville ... 5,664
Decazeville (★26,000) ... 10,231
Denain (★★Valenciennes) ... 26,204
Dieppe (★40,000) ... 25,822
Dijon (★208,432) ... 151,705
Dinard ... 9,234
Dives-sur-Mer (★11,500) ... 5,872
Dole ... 29,295
Douai (★210,508) ... 45,239
Douarnenez ... 19,096
Drancy (★Paris) ... 64,430
Dreux ... 33,101
Dunkerque (★186,314) ... 83,163
Elbeuf (★48,000) ... 19,116
Épernay ... 29,677
Épinal (★53,522) ... 39,525
Épinay-sur-Seine (★Paris) ... 46,578
Étaples (★22,000) ... 10,559
Eu (★21,000) ... 8,626
Évreux ... 47,412
Fécamp ... 21,910
Foix ... 9,599
Fontaine (★Grenoble) ... 25,036
Fontainebleau (★36,000) ... 16,778
Fontenay-sous-Bois (★Paris) ... 46,475
Forbach (★62,000) ... 25,244
Fougères ... 26,610
Fréjus (★50,000) ... 28,851
Gagny (★Paris) ... 36,772
Gap (28,233▲) ... 25,052
Garges-lès-Gonesse (★Paris) ... 37,927
Gennevilliers (★Paris) ... 50,290
Givors (★35,000) ... 21,968
Granville ... 13,330
Grasse (34,579▲) ... 24,442
Grenoble (★389,088) ... 166,037
Guebwiller (★25,566) ... 11,072
Guéret ... 14,855
Haguenau ... 25,147
Hayange (★75,000) ... 20,426
Hendaye ... 9,470
Hénin-Beaumont (Hénin-Liétard) (★★Lens) ... 26,359
Houilles (★Paris) ... 30,345
Hyères (★★Toulon) (36,123▲) ... 29,611
Issy-les-Moulineaux (★Paris) ... 47,561
Ivry-sur-Seine (★Paris) ... 62,856
Jœuf (★30,000) ... 10,649
La Baule-Escoublac (★St.-Nazaire) ... 15,006
La Ciotat (32,721▲) ... 29,319
La Courneuve (★Paris) ... 37,958
La Garenne-Colombes (★Paris) ... 24,038
La Grand' Combe (★17,500) ... 10,452
Lambersart (★Lille) ... 29,642
Laon ... 27,914
La Rochelle (★100,649) ... 75,367
La Roche-sur-Yon ... 44,713
La Seyne-sur-Mer (★Toulon) ... 51,155
Laval ... 51,544
Le Blanc-Mesnil (★Paris) ... 49,107
Le Creusot ... 33,366
Le Grand-Quevilly (★Rouen) ... 31,963
Le Havre (★264,422) ... 217,881
Le Mans (★192,057) ... 152,285
Lens (★328,741) ... 40,199
Le Perreux-sur-Marne (★Paris) ... 28,333
Le Puy-en-Velay (★41,000) ... 26,594
Les Sables-d'Olonne (★29,000) ... 17,463
Levallois-Perret (★Paris) ... 52,523
Le Vésinet (★Paris) ... 17,986
L'Hay-les-Roses (★Paris) ... 31,412
Libourne ... 21,651
Liévin (★Lens) ... 33,070
Lille (★1,015,000) ... 172,280
Limoges (★167,664) ... 143,689
Lisieux ... 25,521
Livry-Gargan (★Paris) ... 32,917
Loches ... 6,738
Lomme (★Lille) ... 29,255
Longwy (★83,000) ... 20,131
Lons-le-Saunier ... 20,942
Lorient (★105,797) ... 69,769
Lourdes ... 17,870
Lunéville ... 22,709
Lyon (★1,170,660) ... 456,716
Mâcon ... 39,344
Maisons-Alfort (★Paris) ... 54,146
Maisons-Laffitte (★Paris) ... 23,504
Malakoff (★Paris) ... 34,121
Mantes-la-Jolie ... 42,465
Marcq-en-Baroeul (★Lille) ... 36,126
Marignane (★Marseille) ... 26,477
Marseille (★1,070,912) ... 908,600
Martigues (38,373▲) ... 26,897
Massy (★Paris) ... 41,344
Maubeuge (★105,000) ... 35,399
Mazamet (★28,000) ... 14,440
Meaux ... 42,243
Melun (★77,272) ... 37,705
Mende ... 10,451
Menton (★34,000) ... 25,129
Mérignac (★Bordeaux) ... 51,306
Metz (★181,191) ... 111,869
Meudon (★Paris) ... 52,806
Millau ... 21,907
Montargis (★50,200) ... 18,380
Montauban (48,053▲) ... 35,940
Montbéliard (★132,343) ... 30,425
Montceau-les-Mines (★51,385) ... 28,177
Mont-de-Marsan ... 26,166
Montélimar ... 28,058
Montereau-faut-Yonne ... 21,568
Montigny-lès-Metz (★Metz) ... 24,519
Montluçon (★71,988) ... 56,468
Montmorency (★Paris) ... 20,860
Montpellier (★211,430) ... 191,354
Montreuil-sous-Bois (★Paris) ... 96,587
Montrouge (★Paris) ... 40,304
Morlaix (19,237▲) ... 17,256
Moulins (★42,000) ... 26,067
Moyeuvre-Grande (★77,000) ... 12,523
Mulhouse (★218,743) ... 117,013
Nancy (★280,569) ... 107,902
Nanterre (★Paris) ... 95,032
Nantes (★453,500) ... 256,693
Narbonne ... 39,342
Neuilly-sur-Seine (★Paris) ... 65,983
Nevers (★59,424) ... 45,480
Nice (★437,566) ... 344,481
Nîmes (★131,638) ... 127,933
Niort (★64,128) ... 62,267
Nogent-sur-Marne (★Paris) ... 25,634
Noisy-le-Grande (★Paris) ... 26,662
Noisy-le-Sec (★Paris) ... 37,734
Noyon ... 13,889
Orange (25,371▲) ... 20,779
Orléans (★209,234) ... 106,246
Orly (★Paris) ... 26,109
Oullins (★Lyon) ... 27,772
Oyonnax ... 23,007
Palaiseau (★Paris) ... 28,716
Pantin (★Paris) ... 42,739
Paray-le-Monial ... 11,545
•PARIS (1980 E) (★9,450,000) ... 2,050,500
Pau (★126,859) ... 83,498
Périgueux (★57,830) ... 35,120
Perpignan (★117,689) ... 106,426
Pessac (★Bordeaux) ... 51,360
Poissy (★Paris) ... 37,431
Poitiers (★98,554) ... 81,313
Pont-à-Mousson (★23,000) ... 14,830
Pontoise (★Paris) ... 27,240
Port-de-Bouc ... 21,424
Privas ... 10,808
Puteaux (★Paris) ... 35,514
Quimper ... 55,977
Reims (★197,021) ... 178,381
Rennes (★229,310) ... 198,305
Rezé (★Nantes) ... 35,730
Rive-de-Gier (★38,000) ... 17,706
Roanne (★83,561) ... 55,195
Rochefort ... 28,155
Rodez (★35,000) ... 25,550
Romainville (★Paris) ... 26,260
Romans-sur-Isère (★46,000) ... 33,030
Rosny-sous-Bois (★Paris) ... 35,784
Roubaix (★★Lille) ... 109,553
Rouen (★388,711) ... 114,927
Royan (★29,000) ... 18,062
Rueil-Malmaison (★Paris) ... 62,727
St.-Avold (★28,000) ... 17,955
St. Brieuc (★82,148) ... 52,559
St.-Chamond ... 40,250
St.-Cloud (★Paris) ... 28,139
St. Cyr-l'École (★Paris) ... 16,537
St.-Denis (★Paris) ... 96,132
St.-Dié ... 25,423
St.-Dizier ... 37,266
Saintes ... 26,891
St.-Étienne (★334,846) ... 220,070

C Census. E Official estimate. UE Unofficial estimate.
L Population within municipal limits of year specified. • Largest city in country.

★ Population or designation of metropolitan area, including suburbs (see headnote).
▲ Population of an entire municipality, commune, or district, including rural area.
‡† Year of information specified at start of country.

St.-Étienne-du-Rouvray (★Rouen) 37,242
St.-Germain-en-Laye (★Paris) 37,509
St.-Jean-de-Luz (★23,000) 11,854
St.-Lô 23,221
St.-Malo 45,030
St.-Martin-d'Hères (★Grenoble) 38,052
St.-Maur-des-Fossés (★Paris) 80,920
St.-Nazaire (★119,418) 69,251
St.-Omer (★27,000) 16,932
St.-Ouen (★Paris) 43,588
St.-Quentin (★75,056) 67,243
St.-Tropez 4,523
Salon-de-Provence 34,576
Sarcelles (★Paris) 55,007
Sarreguemines 25,729
Sartrouville (★Paris) 42,253
Saumur 32,515
Savigny-sur-Orge (★Paris) 34,607
Schiltigheim (★Strasbourg) 30,144
Sedan 23,995
Senlis 13,639
Sens 26,463
Sète 39,258
Sèvres (★Paris) 21,149
Soissons (★49,000) 30,009
Sotteville (★Rouen) 31,659
Stains (★Paris) 35,545
Strasbourg (★390,000) 253,384
Suresnes (★Paris) 37,537
Talence (★Bordeaux) 34,127
Tarbes (★78,645) 54,897
Thann (★28,187) 8,519
Thionville (★141,881) 43,020
Thonon-les-Bains 26,354
Toul (★23,000) 16,454
Toulon (★378,430) 181,801
Toulouse (★509,939) 373,796
Tourcoing (★★Lille) 102,239
Tours (★245,631) 140,686
Trouville-sur-Mer (★16,000) 6,618
Troyes (★126,611) 72,167
Tulle 20,100
Valence (★104,330) 68,460
Valenciennes (★350,599) 42,473
Vannes 40,359
Vanves (★Paris) 22,528
Vénissieux (★Lyon) 74,347
Verdun 23,621
Versailles (★Paris) 94,145
Vesoul 18,173
Vichy (★59,062) 32,117
Vienne 27,830
Vierzon 35,699
Villefranche (★Nice) 7,200
Villefranche-sur-Saône (★42,000) 30,341
Villejuif (★Paris) 55,606
Villemomble (★Paris) 28,727
Villeneuve-d'Ascq (★Lille) 36,769
Villeneuve-St.-Georges (★Paris) 31,664
Villeurbanne (★Lyon) 116,535
Vincennes (★Paris) 44,261
Viry-Châtillon (★Paris) 32,411
Vitry-le-François 19,372
Vitry-sur-Seine (★Paris) 87,316
Voiron (★31,000) 19,420
Wattrelos (★Lille) 45,440

FRENCH GUIANA / Guyane française

1974 C 55,125
•CAYENNE 30,461
St.-Laurent-du-Maroni 3,182

FRENCH POLYNESIA / Polynésie française

1977 C 137,382
•PAPEETE (★42,000) 23,453

GABON

1976 E 530,000
Lambaréné 24,000
•LIBREVILLE 251,000
Port-Gentil 85,000

GAMBIA

1978 E 569,000
•BANJUL (BATHURST) (★88,000) 45,600

GAZA STRIP

1967 C 356,261
•GAZA (GHAZZAH) 118,272
Jabālyah 43,604
Khān Yūnis 52,997
Rafaḩ 49,812

GERMAN DEMOCRATIC REPUBLIC (EAST GERMANY) / Deutsche Demokratische Republik

1978 E 16,751,375
Altenburg 54,281
Annaberg-Buchholz 25,584
Apolda 28,961
Arnstadt 29,820
Aschersleben 35,259
Aue 30,053
Bautzen 47,450
•BERLIN, EAST (OST-BERLIN) (★★Berlin) 1,128,983
Bernburg 43,221
Bitterfeld (★105,000) 24,644
Blankenburg 18,143
Borna 23,326
Brandenburg 94,505
Burg [bei Magdeburg] 28,805
Coswig (★Dresden) 26,250
Cottbus 107,623
Crimmitschau 27,208
Delitzsch 24,124
Dessau (★135,000) 101,322
Döbeln 27,549
Dresden (★640,000) 514,508
Eberswalde 50,994
Eilenburg 21,969
Eisenach 49,850
Eisenhüttenstadt 48,677
Eisleben 27,785
Erfurt 208,800
Falkensee (★Berlin) 24,442
Finsterwalde 23,335
Forst [Lausitz] 27,030
Frankfurt an der Oder 77,175
Freiberg 50,808
Freital (★Dresden) 46,626
Fürstenwalde [Spree] 33,570
Gera 121,251
Glauchau 29,690
Görlitz 81,963
Gotha 58,369
Greifswald 60,636
Greiz 36,606
Güstrow 36,794
Halberstadt 47,919
Halle (★485,000) 232,543
Halle-Neustadt (★Halle) 91,860
Heidenau (★Dresden) 20,644
Hennigsdorf bei Berlin (★Berlin) 26,899
Hettstedt 19,646
Hoyerswerda 70,133
Ilmenau 24,026
Jena 102,025
Karl-Marx-Stadt (Chemnitz) (★460,000) 313,850
Köthen [Anhalt] 34,651
Lauchhammer 25,710
Leipzig (★710,000) 563,980
Leuna (★Halle) (1977 E) 10,132
Limbach-Oberfrohna (★Karl-Marx-Stadt) 24,272
Lübbenau [Spreewald] 22,365
Luckenwalde 27,677
Ludwigsfelde 20,081
Magdeburg (★395,000) 283,109
Meissen 40,858
Merseburg (★★Halle) 51,684
Mühlhausen (Thomas-Müntzer-Stadt) 43,678
Naumburg [an der Saale] 34,675
Neubrandenburg 73,258
Neuruppin 25,258
Neustrelitz 27,342
Nordhausen 46,317
Oranienburg (★Berlin) 24,258
Parchim 22,998
Pirna 48,233
Plauen 79,190
Potsdam (★Berlin) 126,262
Prenzlau 22,283
Quedlinburg 29,179
Radebeul (★Dresden) 35,497
Rathenow 32,341
Reichenbach [Vogtland] 25,909
Riesa 51,411
Rostock 224,834
Rudolstadt 31,435
Saalfeld [Saale] 33,876
Salzwedel 22,732
Sangerhausen 33,494
Schneeberg 21,842
Schönebeck 44,485
Schwedt [Oder] 52,228
Schwerin 115,950
Senftenberg 31,447
Sömmerda 21,933
Sondershausen 23,148
Sonneberg 28,663
Spremberg 22,582
Stassfurt 26,404
Stendal 42,942
Stralsund 73,889
Strausberg (★Berlin) 22,930
Suhl 42,324
Torgau 21,627
Waren 23,322
Weimar 62,803
Weissenfels 40,958
Weisswasser 29,632
Werdau 21,028
Wernigerode 35,435
Wilhelm-Pieck-Stadt Guben 36,826
Wismar 57,055
Wittenberg [Lutherstadt] 53,211
Wittenberge 32,893
Wolfen (★★Bitterfeld) 34,284
Zeitz 44,135
Zittau 41,822
Zwickau (★170,000) 123,446

GERMANY, FEDERAL REPUBLIC OF (WEST GERMANY) / Bundesrepublik Deutschland

1979 E 61,439,342

States
BADEN-WÜRTTEMBERG 9,190,052
BAYERN (BAVARIA) 10,870,968
BERLIN (WEST) 1,902,250
BREMEN 695,115
HAMBURG 1,653,043
HESSEN (HESSE) 5,576,085
NIEDERSACHSEN (LOWER SAXONY) 7,234,000
NORDRHEIN-WESTFALEN (NORTH RHINE-WESTPHALIA) 17,017,075
RHEINLAND-PFALZ (RHINE-LAND-PALATINATE) 3,633,195
SAARLAND 1,068,555
SCHLESWIG-HOLSTEIN 2,599,004

Cities
Aachen (★540,000) 242,971
Aalen (★80,000) 62,854
Achern 20,442
Achim (★Bremen) 27,442
Ahaus 27,824
Ahlen 53,681
Ahrensburg (★Hamburg) 25,416
Albstadt 48,192
Alfeld (Leine) 23,447
Alsdorf (★Aachen) 46,328
Altena 24,729
Amberg 44,541
Andernach (★★Neuwied) 26,897
Ansbach 38,338
Arnsberg 78,282
Aschaffenburg (★145,000) 59,054
Augsburg (★390,000) 245,940
Aurich 34,344
Backnang 29,104
Baden-Baden 49,399
Bad Harzburg (★Goslar) 25,095
Bad Hersfeld 28,240
Bad Homburg (★Frankfurt) 50,909
Bad Honnef am Rhein (★Bonn) 20,877
Bad Kissingen 22,331
Bad Kreuznach 41,255
Bad Nauheim (★Frankfurt) 26,852
Bad Neuenahr-Ahrweiler 26,027
Bad Oeynhausen 44,126
Bad Oldesloe 20,009
Bad Reichenhall 17,919
Bad Salzuflen (★★Herford) 51,181
Bad Vilbel (★Frankfurt) 25,875
Baesweiler (★Aachen) 23,471
Balingen 29,638
Bamberg (★120,000) 71,993
Barsinghausen (★Hannover) 32,699
Bayreuth (★89,000) 70,210
Beckum 37,952
Bensheim 32,874
Berchtesgaden 8,276
Bergheim (Erft) (★Cologne) 53,205
Bergisch Gladbach (★Cologne) 101,007
Bergkamen (★Essen) 47,533
Berlin, West- (★3,775,000) 1,902,250
Biberach 28,122
Bielefeld (★525,000) 312,357
Bietigheim-Bissingen (★Stuttgart) 33,982
Bingen 23,837
Böblingen (★Stuttgart) 41,065
Bocholt 65,346
Bochum (★★Essen) 402,988
BONN (★555,000) 286,184
Borken 31,939
Bornheim (★Bonn) 33,819
Bottrop (★Essen) 114,510
Brake 17,511
Bramsche 23,762
Braunschweig (Brunswick) (★335,000) 261,669
Bremen (★800,000) 556,128
Bremerhaven (★190,000) 138,987
Bretten 22,615
Brilon 24,439
Bruchsal 37,232
Brühl (★Cologne) 43,012
Buchholz in der Nordheide (★Hamburg) 27,999
Bückeburg 20,626
Bünde 39,871
Burgdorf (★Hannover) 27,949
Butzbach 21,096
Buxtehude (★Hamburg) 31,162
Calw 22,881
Castrop-Rauxel (★Essen) 79,264
Celle 72,804
Cloppenburg 20,681
Coburg 45,906
Coesfeld 31,093
Cologne (Köln) (★1,815,000) 976,136
Crailsheim 24,636
Cuxhaven 58,891
Dachau (★Munich) 34,162
Darmstadt (★305,000) 138,661
Datteln (★Essen) 37,004
Deggendorf 30,455
Delmenhorst (★★Bremen) 72,140
Detmold 67,116
Dillingen (★Saarlouis) 20,722
Dinslaken (★Essen) 58,334
Dormagen (★Cologne) 55,826
Dorsten (★Essen) 68,862
Dortmund (★★Essen) 609,954
Duderstadt 22,886
Duisburg (★★Essen) 559,066
Dülmen 38,074
Düren (★110,000) 86,308
Düsseldorf (★1,225,000) 594,770
Einbeck 28,923
Elmshorn 41,628
Emden 51,607
Emmendingen 24,448
Emmerich 29,378
Emsdetten 30,900
Ennepetal (★Essen) 35,965
Erftstadt (★Cologne) 42,905
Erkelenz 35,579
Erkrath (★Düsseldorf) 42,637
Erlangen (★★Nürnberg) 100,760
Eschwege 24,097
Eschweiler (★★Aachen) 53,065
Espelkamp 23,124
•Essen (★5,125,000) 652,501
Esslingen (★Stuttgart) 91,733
Ettlingen (★Karlsruhe) 36,259
Euskirchen 44,593
Fellbach (★Stuttgart) 41,653
Filderstadt (★Stuttgart) 36,757
Flensburg (★103,000) 88,810
Forchheim 28,932
Frankenthal (★Mannheim) 43,511
Frankfurt am Main (★1,880,000) 628,203
Frechen (★Cologne) 43,161
Freiburg (★220,000) 174,121
Freising 34,252
Friedrichshafen 51,541
Fulda (★79,000) 57,114
Fürstenfeldbruck (★Munich) 31,354
Fürth (★★Nürnberg) 98,266
Gaggenau 28,611
Garbsen (★Hannover) 57,406
Garmisch-Partenkirchen 27,765
Geldern 25,730
Gelsenkirchen (★★Essen) 306,323
Georgsmarienhütte (★Osnabrück) 30,857
Gevelsberg (★Essen) 31,138
Giessen (★160,000) 76,485
Gifhorn 33,006
Gladbeck (★Essen) 80,434
Goch 28,634
Göppingen (★155,000) 53,034
Goslar (★84,000) 52,815
Göttingen 128,118
Greven 28,414
Grevenbroich (★Düsseldorf) 58,644
Gronau (★Enschede, Netherlands) 41,042
Gummersbach 48,344
Gütersloh (★★Bielefeld) 77,792
Hagen (★★Essen) 220,676
Haltern (★Essen) 30,783
Hamburg (★2,260,000) 1,653,043
Hameln (★72,000) 59,005
Hamm 171,595
Hanau [am Main] (★★Frankfurt) 86,144
Hannover (★1,005,000) 535,854
Hattingen (★Essen) 57,255
Heidelberg (★★Mannheim) 128,773
Heidenheim (★89,000) 48,470
Heilbronn (★230,000) 111,426
Heinsberg 36,343
Helmstedt 26,816
Hemer 32,891
Hennef (★Siegburg) 28,835
Heppenheim (★Mannheim) 23,908
Herford (★120,000) 62,977
Herne (★Essen) 183,065
Herten (★Essen) 69,400
Herzogenrath (★Aachen) 42,425
Hilden (★Düsseldorf) 52,708
Hildesheim (★139,000) 102,512
Hof 53,398
Hofheim am Taunus (★Frankfurt) 33,262
Homburg (★★Zweibrücken) 41,581
Höxter 32,457
Hückelhoven 34,919
Hürth (★Cologne) 50,654
Ibbenbüren 42,149
Idar-Oberstein 35,811
Ingolstadt (★135,000) 89,467
Iserlohn 94,478
Itzehoe 33,707
Jülich 30,495
Kaarst (★Düsseldorf) 37,595
Kaiserslautern (★138,000) 99,197
Kamen (★Essen) 43,278
Kamp-Lintfort (★Essen) 37,859
Karlsruhe (★485,000) 271,417
Kassel (★370,000) 196,224
Kaufbeuren 42,204
Kempen (★Essen) 30,101
Kempten 57,390
Kerpen (★Cologne) 53,932
Kiel (★335,000) 250,750
Kirchheim (★Stuttgart) 31,756
Kleve (Cleves) 44,036
Koblenz (★180,000) 113,795
Königswinter (★Bonn) 34,935
Konstanz 67,948
Krefeld (★★Essen) 222,750
Kreuztal (★Siegen) 30,295
Kulmbach 28,324
Laatzen (★Hannover) 33,919
Lage 32,044
Lahr 35,516
Lampertheim (★Mannheim) 31,307
Landau 36,502
Landshut 55,538
Langen (★Frankfurt) 29,198
Langenfeld (★Düsseldorf) 46,590
Langenhagen (★Hannover) 46,825
Leer 31,316
Lehrte (★Hannover) 38,271
Leichlingen (★Cologne) 24,616
Leinfelden-Echterdingen (★Stuttgart) 35,044
Lemgo 39,512
Leonberg (★Stuttgart) 37,848
Leverkusen (★Cologne) 161,453
Lingen 43,864
Lippstadt 61,692
Löhne 37,111
Lörrach (★Basel, Switzerland) 41,522
Lübeck (★265,000) 222,120
Lüdenscheid 74,561
Ludwigsburg (★Stuttgart) 81,049
Ludwigshafen (★★Mannheim) 160,479
Lüneburg 62,198
Lünen (★Essen) 85,685
Mainz (★★Wiesbaden) 186,200
Mannheim (★1,395,000) 303,247
Marburg an der Lahn 74,724
Marl (★Essen) 89,441
Meerbusch (★Düsseldorf) 49,794
Melle 40,757
Memmingen 37,885
Menden [Sauerland] 53,101
Meppen 28,062
Merzig 30,008
Meschede 31,352
Mettmann (★Düsseldorf) 36,724
Minden (★125,000) 77,989
Moers (★Essen) 100,110
Mönchengladbach (★410,000) 258,001
Monheim (★Düsseldorf) 39,932
Mülheim an der Ruhr (★Essen) 182,465
Münden 26,047
Munich (München) (★1,940,000) 1,299,693
Münster 267,478
Nettetal 37,366
Neuburg an der Donau 23,945
Neu Isenburg (★Frankfurt) 35,899
Neumarkt in der Oberpfalz 30,226
Neumünster 80,331
Neunkirchen (★135,000) 52,216
Neuss (★Düsseldorf) 149,333
Neustadt am Rübenberge (★Hannover) 37,941
Neustadt an der Weinstrasse 50,405
Neu-Ulm (★Ulm) 47,263
Neuwied (★150,000) 60,461
Niederkassel (★Cologne) 25,460
Nienburg 30,207
Nordenham (★★Bremerhaven) 30,320
Norderstedt (★Hamburg) 64,302
Nordhorn 48,580
Northeim 32,307
Nürnberg (★1,025,000) 484,184
Nürtingen (★Stuttgart) 35,046
Oberammergau 4,800
Oberhausen (★★Essen) 229,613
Oberursel (★Frankfurt) 39,477
Oelde 27,335
Oer-Erkenschwick (★Essen) 26,702
Offenbach (★Frankfurt) 111,310
Offenburg 50,471
Oldenburg 136,155
Osnabrück (★270,000) 158,150
Paderborn 109,218
Papenburg 27,420
Passau 50,323
Peine 47,559
Pforzheim (★220,000) 106,677
Pinneberg (★Hamburg) 36,823
Pirmasens 50,250
Pulheim (★Cologne) 43,501
Rastatt 36,942
Ratingen (★Düsseldorf) 89,039
Ravensburg (★74,000) 42,081
Recklinghausen (★Essen) 119,472
Regensburg (★200,000) 132,399
Remagen (★Bonn) 14,342
Remscheid (★★Wuppertal) 129,507
Rendsburg 32,860
Reutlingen (★155,000) 94,737
Rheda-Wiedenbrück (★Bielefeld) 37,723
Rheinbach (★Bonn) 21,609
Rheinberg (★Essen) 26,205
Rheine 71,525
Rodgau (★Frankfurt) 34,854
Rosenheim 51,485
Rottenburg am Neckar 31,468
Rottweil 23,732
Rüsselsheim (★★Wiesbaden) 62,606
Saarbrücken (★390,000) 194,452
Saarlouis (★115,000) 39,028
Salzgitter 113,427
Sankt Augustin (★Bonn) 47,288
Sankt Ingbert 41,896
Sankt Wendel 26,880
Schleswig 30,118
Schmallenberg 24,929
Schorndorf (★Stuttgart) 33,527
Schwabach (★Nürnberg) 34,693
Schwäbisch Gmünd 56,621
Schwäbisch Hall 31,548
Schweinfurt (★110,000) 53,035
Schwelm (★Wuppertal) 31,207
Schwerte (★Essen) 47,333
Seelze (★Hannover) 30,293
Seevetal (★Hamburg) 35,409
Selb 21,428
Siegburg (★160,000) 34,475
Siegen (★205,000) 112,740
Sindelfingen (★Stuttgart) 54,153
Singen 43,653
Soest 40,373
Solingen (★★Wuppertal) 166,654
Speyer 43,663
Springe 30,528
Stade 42,519
Steinfurt 32,090
Stolberg (★★Aachen) 57,552
Straubing 42,718
Stuttgart (★1,935,000) 581,989
Sundern (Sauerland) 25,400
Trier (★125,000) 95,736
Troisdorf (★★Siegburg) 57,733
Tübingen 72,167
Tuttlingen 31,555
Uelzen 36,536
Ulm (★210,000) 99,560
Unna (★Essen) 56,903
Velbert (★Essen) 93,302
Verden 24,275
Viernheim (★Mannheim) 29,645
Viersen (★★Mönchengladbach) 81,419
Villingen-Schwenningen 78,465
Voerde (★Essen) 31,442
Völklingen (★★Saarbrücken) 44,901
Waiblingen (★Stuttgart) 44,968
Warendorf 32,909
Warstein 28,413
Wedel (★Hamburg) 30,075
Weiden 44,319
Weinheim (★Mannheim) 41,498
Wermelskirchen (★Wuppertal) 34,730
Wesel 56,760
Wetzlar (★105,000) 52,138
Wiesbaden (★795,000) 273,267
Wilhelmshaven (★135,000) 99,426
Willich (★Essen) 38,916
Witten (★Essen) 106,185
Wolfenbüttel (★★Braunschweig) 50,218
Wolfsburg 126,942
Worms (★★Mannheim) 73,505
Wunstorf (★Hannover) 37,318
Wuppertal (★870,000) 394,605
Würselen (★Aachen) 34,802
Würzburg (★205,000) 127,370
Zweibrücken (★105,000) 35,074

C Census. E Official estimate. UE Unofficial estimate.
L Population within municipal limits of year specified. • Largest city in country.

★ Population or designation of metropolitan area, including suburbs (see headnote).
▲ Population of an entire municipality, commune, or district, including rural area.
‡‡ Year of information specified at start of country.

GHANA

1970 C 8,559,313

•ACCRA (*738,498) 633,880
Bawku 20,567
Bolgatanga 18,896
Cape Coast 71,594
Ho 24,199
Keta 14,446
Koforidua 46,235
Kumasi 345,117
Nkawkaw 23,219
Nsawam 25,518
Obuasi 31,005
Oda 20,957
Sekondi-Takoradi 160,868
Tamale 83,653
Tarkwa 14,702
Tema 60,767
Wa 21,374
Winneba 30,778
Yendi 22,072

GIBRALTAR

1979 E 29,760

•GIBRALTAR 29,760

GREECE / Ellás

1971 C 8,768,641

Agrinion (*41,794) 30,973
Aiyáleo (*Athens) 79,961
Aíyion (*23,756) 18,829
Akharnaí (Acharnae) 24,621
Alexandroúpolis 22,995
Amaliás 14,177
Amaroúsion (*Athens) 27,112
Ambelókipoi (*Thessaloníki) 24,892
Árgos 18,890
Árta 19,498
•ATHENS (ATHÍNAI) (*2,540,241) 867,023
Ayía Varvára (*Athens) 26,409
Áyioi Anáryiroi (*Athens) 26,094
Áyios Dhimítrios (*Athens) 40,968
Dháfni (*Athens) 26,608
Dráma 29,692
Édhessa 13,967
Elevsís (Eleusis) 18,535
Ermoúpolis (Síros) (*16,082) 13,502
Flórina (Phlorina) 11,164
Galátsion (*Athens) 27,240
Glifádha (*Athens) 23,449
Grevená 8,016
Ilioúpolis (*Athens) 49,215
Ioánnina (Yanina) 40,130
Iráklion (Candia) (*84,710) 77,506
Iráklion (*Athens) 24,302
Kaisarianí (*Athens) 26,833
Kalámai (*40,402) 39,133
Kalamákion (*Athens) 26,957
Kalamariá 36,978
Kallithéa (*Athens) 82,438
Kardhítsa 25,685
Kastoría 15,407
Kateríni (*30,512) 28,808
Kavála 46,234
Keratsínion (*Athens) 67,672
Kérkira (Corfu) 28,630
Khaïdhárion (*Athens) 34,673
Khalandrion (*Athens) 35,944
Khalkís (Chalcis) 36,300
Khaniá (Canea) (*53,026) 40,564
Khíos (Chios) (*30,021) 24,084
Kifisiá (*Athens) 20,082
Komotiní 28,896
Koridhallós (*Athens) 47,335
Kórinthos (Corinth) 20,773
Kozáni 23,240
Lamía 37,872
Lárisa 72,336
Levádhia (Lebadea) 15,445
Mégara 17,294
Néa Ionía (*Athens) 54,906
Néa Liósia (*Athens) 56,217
Néa Smírni (*Athens) 42,512
Níkaia (*Athens) 86,269
Palaión Fáliron (*Athens) 35,066
Pátrai (Patras) (*120,847) 111,607
Peristérion (*Athens) 118,413
Piraiévs (Piraeus) (**Athens) 187,362
Pírgos (Pyrgos) 20,599
Ródhos (Rhodes) 32,092
Salamís 18,256
Sérrai 39,897
Spárti (Sparta) (*13,432) 10,549
Thessaloníki (Salonika) (*557,360) 345,799
Thívai (Thebes) 15,971
Tríkkala 34,794
Trípolis (Tripolitza) 20,209
Véroia 29,528
Víron (*Athens) 44,021
Vólos (*88,096) 51,290
Xánthi 24,867
Zákinthos 9,339
Zografós (*Athens) 56,722

GREENLAND / Grønland

1977 E 49,719

Angmagssalik 1,023
Egedesminde 3,347
•GODTHÅB 8,545
Holsteinsborg 3,741
Julianehåb 2,670
Sukkertoppen 2,937
Thule 357

GRENADA

1976 E 109,609

•ST. GEORGE'S (*26,000) 10,000

GUADELOUPE

1974 C 324,530

BASSE-TERRE (*25,202) 15,457
Capesterre (18,143▲) 6,861
Les Abymes (*Pointe-à-Pitre) (53,605▲) 10,573
•Pointe-à-Pitre (*59,000) 23,889

GUAM

1980 C 105,816

•AGANA (*25,000) 881
Dededo 23,659

GUATEMALA

1973 C 5,211,929

Amatitlán 15,372
Antigua Guatemala 17,692
Chiquimula 16,181
Coatepeque 15,949
Escuintla 37,180
•GUATEMALA (*945,000) 717,322
Mazatenango 24,156
Puerto Barrios 19,696
Quezaltenango 45,977
Retalhuleu 20,222

GUERNSEY

1971 C 53,734

•ST. PETER PORT (*36,000) 16,303

GUINEA / Guinée

1967 E 3,702,000

•CONAKRY (1967 C) 197,267
Kankan 50,000
Kindia 45,000
Labé 26,000
Mamou 18,000
Nzérékoré 26,000
Siguiri 15,000

GUINEA-BISSAU

1970 C 487,448

•BISSAU 71,169

GUYANA

1976 E 783,000

•GEORGETOWN (*187,056) 72,049
New Amsterdam (1970 C) 17,782

HAITI / Haïti

1975 E 4,583,785

Cap-Haïtien 52,220
Gonaïves 33,837
Jérémie 19,227
Les Cayes 24,931
Pétionville (*Port-au-Prince) (1971 C) 35,257
•PORT-AU-PRINCE (1978 E) (*800,000) 745,700
Port-de-Paix 16,151
St.-Marc 19,354

HONDURAS

1977 E 2,998,700

Choluteca 29,300
Comayagua (1974 C) 15,941
El Progreso 32,800
La Ceiba 44,900
La Lima (1974 C) 14,631
Puerto Cortés 30,200
San Pedro Sula 172,900
•TEGUCIGALPA 316,800
Tela 22,700

HONG KONG

1976 C 4,402,990

Kowloon (**Victoria) 749,600
New Kowloon (*Victoria) 1,628,880
Tai Wan Tsun (Ngau Tau Kok) (*Victoria) (1961 C) 53,836
Tsun Wan (*Victoria) 455,270
•VICTORIA (HONG KONG) (*3,975,000) 1,026,870

HUNGARY / Magyarország

1980 C 10,710,000

Ajka 30,000
Baja 39,000
Békés (22,000▲) 17,900
Békéscsaba (66,000▲) 57,400
•BUDAPEST (*2,600,000) 2,060,000
Cegléd (40,000▲) 32,500
Csongrád (22,000▲) 19,100
Debrecen 195,000
Dunaújváros 60,000
Eger 60,000
Érd (*Budapest) 40,000
Esztergom 31,000
Gödöllő (*Budapest) 26,000
Gyöngyös 38,000
Győr 125,000
Gyula (34,000▲) 29,300
Hajdúböszörmény (32,000▲) 28,600
Hajdúszoboszló 24,000
Hatvan 24,000
Hódmezővásárhely (54,000▲) 45,100
Jászberény (31,000▲) 24,900
Kaposvár 73,000
Karcag 24,000
Kazincbarcika 37,000
Kecskemét (93,000▲) 74,200
Kiskunfélegyháza (36,000▲) 27,300
Kiskunhalas (31,000▲) 22,700
Komló 30,000
Makó 30,000
Miskolc 210,000
Mohács (21,000▲) 17,700
Mosonmagyaróvár 30,000
Nagykanizsa 48,000
Nagykőrös (27,000▲) 21,600
Nyíregyháza (107,000▲) 84,600
Orosháza (36,000▲) 31,500
Ózd 47,000
Pápa 32,000
Pécs 170,000
Salgótarján 49,000
Sopron 56,000
Szeged 175,000
Székesfehérvár 102,000
Szekszárd 34,000
Szentes (35,000▲) 30,600
Szolnok 77,000
Szombathely 82,000
Tata 24,000
Tatabánya 75,000
Törökszentmiklós (26,000▲) 22,500
Vác 34,000
Várpalota 28,000
Veszprém 55,000
Zalaegerszeg 55,000

ICELAND / Ísland

1979 E 226,724

Akureyri 13,137
Hafnarfjördur (*Reykjavík) 12,158
Keflavík 6,539
Kópavogur (*Reykjavík) 13,533
•REYKJAVÍK (*120,085) 83,536

INDIA / Bhārat

1976 E 609,264,000

(total excludes Sikkim, annexed in 1975)

States

Andaman and Nicobar Islands (Ter.) 128,000
Andhra Pradesh 47,944,000
Arunachal Pradesh (Ter.) 520,000
Assam 17,354,000
Bihār 61,790,000
Chandīgarh (Ter.) 285,000
Dādra and Nagar Haveli (Ter.) 83,000
Delhi (Ter.) 5,116,000
Goa, Damān and Diu (Ter.) 954,000
Gujarāt 30,269,000
Haryana 11,221,000
Himāchal Pradesh 3,657,000
Jammu and Kashmīr 5,120,000
Karnataka (Mysore) 32,448,000
Kerala 23,955,000
Lakshadweep (Ter.) 36,000
Madhya Pradesh 47,167,000
Mahārāshtra 56,341,000
Manipur (Ter.) 1,195,000
Meghalaya 1,125,000
Mizoram (pop. included with Assam)
Nāgāland 557,000
Orissa 24,391,000
Pondicherry (Ter.) 524,000
Punjab 14,954,000
Rājasthān 29,005,000
Sikkim (1971 E) 196,852
Tamil Nadu (Madras) 45,434,000
Tripura (Ter.) 1,731,000
Uttar Pradesh 96,172,000
West Bengal 49,788,000

Cities (1971 C)

Abohar 58,925
Achalpur (Ellichpur) (*66,451) 42,326
Adilābād 30,368
Ādoni 85,311
Agartala (*100,264) 59,625
Āgra (*634,622) 591,917
Āgra Cantonment (*Āgra) 37,074
Ahmadābād (*1,950,000) 1,585,544
Ahmadnagar (*148,405) 118,236
Aijal 31,740
Ajmer (*264,291) 262,851
Akola 168,438
Akot 41,534
Alandur (*Madras) 65,039
Alīgarh 252,314
Alīpur Duār (*54,454) 36,667
Allahābād (*513,036) 490,622
Alleppey 160,166
Almora (*20,881) 19,671
Alwar 100,378
Amalāpuram 30,518
Amalner 55,544
Ambāla (*186,126) 83,633
Ambāla Cantonment (*Ambāla) 102,493
Ambarnāth (*Bombay) 56,276
Ambāsamudram (*49,255) 27,709
Ambattur (*Madras) 45,586
Āmbūr 54,011
Amrāvati (Amraoti) (*221,277) 193,800
Amreli (*43,794) 39,520
Amritsar (*458,029) 407,628
Amroha 82,702
Anakapalle 57,273
Ānand 59,155
Anantapur 80,069
Arcot (*75,911) 30,230
Arkonam 43,347
Arni 38,664
Arrah 92,919
Aruppukkottai 62,223
Asansol (*925,000) 155,968
Ashoknagar-Kalyangarh (*Hābra) 41,916
Āttūr 41,569
Aurangābād (*165,253) 150,483
Avadi (*Madras) 77,413
Azamgarh 40,963
Badagara 53,938
Bāgalkot 51,746
Bahraich 73,931
Baidyabāti (*Calcutta) 54,130
Balasore 46,239
Ballarpur 34,268
Ballia 47,101
Balrāmpur 36,191
Bālurghāt 67,088
Bānda 50,575
Bangalore (*1,750,000) 1,540,741
Bangaon 50,538
Bānkura 79,129
Bansbāria (*Calcutta) 61,748
Bāpatla 41,947
Baranagar (*Calcutta) 136,842
Bārāsat (*Calcutta) 42,642
Baraut 31,264
Bareilly (*326,106) 296,248
Barmer 38,630
Barnāla 31,388
Baroda (Vadodara) (*467,487) 466,696
Barrackpore (*Calcutta) 96,889
Bārsi 62,374
Basīrhāt 63,816
Basti 49,635
Batāla (*76,488) 58,200
Beāwar 66,114
Begusarai (*44,084) 35,736
Behāla (South Suburban) (*Calcutta) 272,600
Belgaum (*213,872) 192,427
Bellampalle 30,290
Bellary 125,183
Berhampore (*West Bengal state*) (*78,909) 72,605
Berhampur (*Orissa state*) 117,662
Bettiah 51,018
Betūl 30,862
Bhadrakh 40,487
Bhadrāvati (*101,358) 40,203
Bhadreswar (*Calcutta) 45,586
Bhāgalpur 172,202
Bhandāra 39,423
Bharatpur (*69,902) 68,036
Bhatinda (*65,318) 53,684
Bhātpāra (*Calcutta) 204,750
Bhaunagar (*225,974) 225,358
Bhavāni (*56,696) 23,114
Bhilai (Bhilainagar) (*245,124) 157,173
Bhīlwāra 82,155
Bhīmavaram 63,762
Bhind (*45,794) 42,371
Bhiwandi (*Bombay) 79,576
Bhiwāni 73,086
Bhopāl (*384,859) 298,022
Bhubaneswar 105,491
Bhuj (*52,861) 52,177
Bhusāwal (*104,708) 96,800
Bīdar 50,670
Bihar 100,046
Bijāpur 103,931
Bijnor 43,290
Bīkaner (*208,894) 188,518
Bilāspur (*130,740) 98,410
Bīr (Bhir) 49,965
Bishnupur 38,135
Bodhan 37,589
Bodināyakkanūr 54,176
Bokāro Steel City (*107,159) 94,007
Bolāngīr 35,748
Bombay (*6,750,000) 5,970,575
Botād 32,179
Broach (Bharuch) (*92,251) 91,589
Budaun 72,204
Budge Budge (*Calcutta) 51,039
Bulandshahr 59,505
Bulsār (Valsad) (*54,966) 43,254
Būndi 34,279
Burdwān 143,318
Burhānpur (*105,335) 105,246
Buxar 31,691
•Calcutta (*9,100,000) 3,148,746
Calicut (Kozhikode) 333,979
Cambay 62,097
Cannanore (*59,912) 55,162
Chaibāsā 35,386
Chākdaha 46,345
Chakradharpur (*34,967) 22,709
Chālakudi 37,562
Chālisgaon 41,720
Champdāni (*Calcutta) 58,596
Chandannagar (Chandernagore) (*Calcutta) 75,238
Chandausi 53,393
Chandīgarh (*232,940) 218,743
Chandrapur 75,134
Changanācheri 48,545
Chāpra (*98,401) 83,101
Chhatarpur 32,271
Chhindwāra (*53,508) 53,492
Chidambaram (*57,658) 48,811
Chikmagalūr 41,639
Chilakalūrupet 41,543
Chingleput 38,419
Chīrālā 54,487
Chitradurga 50,254
Chittaranjan 40,736
Chittoor 63,035
Chopda 32,656
Churu (*53,185) 52,502
Cochin 439,066
Coimbatore (*750,000) 356,368
Cooch Behār (*62,664) 53,684
Coonoor (*70,813) 38,007
Cuddalore 101,335
Cuddapah 66,195
Cumbum 40,796
Cuttack (*205,759) 194,068
Dabhoi 37,892
Dabra (*21,430) 18,623
Dalhousie (*5,123) 4,296
Daltonganj 32,367
Damān 17,317
Damoh (*59,983) 59,489
Dānāpur (*Patna) 42,694
Darbhanga 132,059
Darjeeling 42,873
Datia 36,439
Dāvangere 121,110
Dehra Dūn (*203,464) 166,073
Dehri 46,037
Delhi (*4,500,000) 3,706,558
Delhi Cantonment (*Delhi) 57,339
Deoband 38,194
Deoghar (*45,060) 40,356
Deolāli (**Nāsik) 55,436
Deoria 38,161
Dewās (*51,866) 51,545
Dhānbād (*600,000) 79,838
Dhār 36,172
Dhārāpuram 34,500
Dharmapuri 40,086
Dholka 35,520
Dholpur 31,865
Dhorāji (*60,080) 59,773
Dhrāngadhra 40,791
Dhubri (*45,589) 36,503
Dhule 137,129
Dibrugarh 80,348
Digboi (*32,388) 16,538
Dindigul 128,429
Dohad (*51,406) 44,506
Dombivli (*Bombay) 51,108
Dum-Dum (*Calcutta) 31,363
Durg (**Bhilai) 67,892
Durgāpur 206,638
Dwarka 17,801
Elūru (Ellore) 127,023
English Bāzār (*68,026) 61,335
Erode (*169,613) 105,111
Etah 33,514
Etāwah 85,894
Faizābād (*109,806) 102,835
Farīdābād New Township (*Delhi) 85,762
Farrukhābād (*110,835) 102,768
Fatehābād 22,630
Fatehpur 54,665
Fatehpur Sīkri 13,561
Fāzilka 36,281
Fīrozābād 133,863
Fīrozpur (Ferozepore) (*97,709) 49,545
Gadag 95,426
Garden Reach (*Calcutta) 154,913
Garulia (*Calcutta) 44,271
Gauhāti (*200,377) 123,783
Gaya 179,884
Ghāziābād (*Delhi) 118,836
Ghāzīpur 45,635
Giridih 40,308
Godhra (*66,853) 66,403
Gonda 52,662
Gondal (*55,329) 54,928
Gondia 77,992
Gopichettipālaiyam 36,356
Gorakhpur 230,911
Govindpura (*Bhopāl) 53,922
Gūdalūr 32,843
Gudivāda 61,068
Gudiyāttam (*67,966) 63,007
Gūdūr 33,778
Gulbarga 145,588
Guna 40,006
Guntakal 66,320
Guntūr 269,991
Gurdāspur 32,064
Gurgaon 57,151
Gwalior (*406,140) 384,772
Hābra (*93,351) 51,435
Hājīpur 41,890
Haldwāni 52,205
Hālisahar (*Calcutta) 68,906
Hānsi 41,108
Hāpur 71,266
Hardoi 46,639
Hardwār (*79,277) 77,864
Harihar 33,888
Haripād 31,145
Hassan 51,325
Hāthras 74,349
Hazāribāgh 54,818
Hindupur 42,959
Hinganghāt 44,349
Hingoli 31,948
Hisār 89,437
Hooghly-Chinsura (*Calcutta) 105,241
Hoshiārpur 57,691
Hospet 65,196
Howrah (*Calcutta) 737,877
Hubli-Dhārwār 379,166
Hyderābād (*2,000,000) 1,607,396
Ichalkaranji 87,731
Imphāl 100,366
Indore (*560,936) 543,381
Itārsi (*46,866) 44,191
Jabalpur (*534,845) 426,224
Jabalpur Cantonment (*Jabalpur) 50,195
Jagādhri (*115,020) 35,094
Jagannāthnagar (*Rānchī) 55,663
Jagraon 32,999
Jagtiāl 30,900
Jaipur (*636,768) 615,258
Jālgaon 106,711
Jālna 91,099
Jalpaiguri 55,159
Jamālpur (**Monghyr) 61,731
Jammu (*164,207) 155,338
Jāmnagar (*227,640) 199,709
Jamshedpur (*456,146) 341,576
Jaora 37,235
Jaridih Bazar (*69,321) 33,084
Jaunpur 80,737
Jetpur (*41,943) 41,926

C Census. E Official estimate. UE Unofficial estimate.
L Population within municipal limits of year specified. • Largest city in country.

* Population or designation of metropolitan area, including suburbs (see headnote).
▲ Population of an entire municipality, commune, or district, including rural area.
‡† Year of information specified at start of country.

Jeypore 34,319
Jhānsi (*198,135) 173,292
Jharia (**Dhānbād) 45,236
Jīnd 38,161
Jodhpur 317,612
Jorhāt (*70,674) 30,247
Jullundur (*329,830) 296,106
Junāgadh (*95,900) 95,485
Kadaiyanallūr 50,295
Kadiri 33,810
Kairāna 32,353
Kaithal 45,199
Kākināda 164,200
Kālol (*Ahmadābād) 50,321
Kalyān (*Bombay) 99,547
Kamarhati (*Calcutta) 169,404
Kāmthi (*Nāgpur) 53,412
Kānchipuram (Conjeeveram) (*119,693) 110,657
Kānchrāpāra (*Calcutta) 78,768
Kānpur (*1,320,000) 1,154,388
Kānpur Cantonment (*Kānpur) . 69,452
Kapadvanj 30,748
Kapūrthala 35,482
Karād 42,329
Kāraikkudi (*88,371) 55,449
Kāranja 31,150
Karimganj 31,618
Karīmnagar 48,918
Karnāl 92,784
Karūr 65,706
Kāsaragod 34,984
Kāsganj 46,467
Kāshīpur 33,457
Katihār (*80,121) 67,014
Kayankulam (Kayamkulam) 54,102
Kerkend (*Dhānbād) 51,314
Khadki (Kirkee) (*Pune) 65,497
Khāmgaon 53,692
Khammam 56,919
Khandwa (*85,403) 84,517
Khanna 34,182
Kharagpur (*161,257) 61,783
Khargone 41,316
Khurja 50,245
Kilikollūr 41,871
Kishanganj 36,893
Kishangarh 37,405
Kohima 21,545
Kolār 43,418
Kolār Gold Fields (*118,861) 76,112
Kolhāpur (*267,513) 259,050
Konnagar (*Calcutta) 34,424
Kota 212,991
Kot Kapūra (*34,116) 33,907
Kottagūdem 75,542
Kottayam 59,714
Kovilpatti 48,509
Krishnanagar 85,923
Kulti (**Asansol) 29,665
Kumbakonam (*119,655) 113,130
Kundla 37,957
Kurichi (*Coimbatore) 40,537
Kurnool 136,710
Lakhīmpur 43,752
Lalitpur 34,462
Lātūr 70,156
Leh 5,519
Lucknow (*840,000) 749,239
Lucknow Cantonment (*Lucknow) 39,338
Ludhiāna (*401,176) 397,850
Machilīpatnam (Bandar) 112,612
Madras (*3,200,000) 2,469,449
Madakulam (*Madurai) 46,317
Madanapalle 36,458
Madgaon (Margao) (*48,593) 41,655
Madhubani 32,919
Madurai (*725,000) 549,114
Mahbūbnagar 51,756
Mahuva 39,497
Mainpurī 43,849
Mālegaon 191,847
Māler Kotla (*48,859) 48,536
Malkāpur 35,476
Manappārai 32,092
Mandasor (*56,988) 52,347
Mandya 72,132
Mangalagiri 32,850
Mangalore (*215,122) 165,174
Mannārgudi 42,783
Mānsa 31,351
Mathura (*140,150) 132,028
Maunath Bhanjan 64,058
Māyūram 60,195
Meerut (*367,754) 270,993
Meerut Cantonment (*Meerut) . . 85,415
Mehsāna (Mahesāna) (*51,713) . . 51,598
Melappālaiyam (*Tirunelveli) . . . 47,731
Mettupālaiyam 48,365
Mettūr 38,380
Mhow (*63,739) 59,037
Midnapore 71,326
Mira (**Sāngli) 77,606
Mirzāpur 105,939
Modinagar 43,470
Moga (*61,625) 55,270
Mokameh 38,164
Monghyr (*164,205) 102,474
Morādābād (*272,652) 258,590
Morena 44,901
Mormugão 44,065
Morvi 60,976
Motihāri (*40,352) 37,032
Muktsar 36,750
Murtazāpur 23,141
Murwāra (Katni) (*86,535) 54,864
Mussoorie 18,038
Muzaffarnagar 114,783
Muzaffarpur 126,379
Mysore 355,685
Nabadwip 94,204
Nābha 34,761
Nadiād 108,269
Nāgappattinam (*74,019) 68,026
Nāgaur 36,448
Nāgda 32,569
Nāgercoil 141,288
Nagīna 37,066
Nāgpur (*950,000) 866,076
Naihāti (*Calcutta) 82,080
Naini Tāl (*25,167) 23,986
Najībābād 42,586
Nalgonda 33,126
Nānded 126,538
Nandurbār 54,070
Nandyāl 63,193
Nangi (*Calcutta) 47,555
Narasapur 36,147
Narasaraopet 43,467
Nārnaul 31,875
Nāsik (*271,681) 176,091
Navsāri (*80,101) 72,979
Nawābganj 35,395
Neemuch (*49,748) 47,113
Nellikkuppam 37,638
Nellore 133,590
NEW DELHI (**Delhi) 301,801
Neyveli 58,285
Nipāni 35,116
Nizāmābād 115,640
North Barrackpore (*Calcutta) . . 76,335
North Dum-Dum (*Calcutta) 63,873
Nowgong 56,537
Ongole 53,330
Ootacamund 63,310
Orai 42,513
Outer Burnpur (*Asansol) 56,900
Pālakollu 36,196
Pālanpur 42,114
Pālayankottai (**Tirunelveli) . . . 70,070
Pālghāt 95,788
Pāli 49,834
Pallavaram (*Madras) 51,374
Palni (*51,664) 49,575
Palwal 36,207
Panaji (Panjim) (Nova Goa) (*59,258) 34,953
Pānchur (*Calcutta) 59,021
Pandharpur 53,638
Pandu (*Gauhati) 38,876
Pānihāti (*Calcutta) 148,046
Pānīpat 87,981
Panruti 34,065
Paramagudi 48,880
Parbhani 61,570
Parli 31,078
Pātan 64,519
Pattukkottai 37,682
Pathānkot (*78,192) 76,355
Patiāla (*151,041) 148,686
Patna (*625,000) 473,001
Periyakulam 41,561
Petlād 39,535
Phagwāra (*55,012) 50,863
Pīlībhīt 68,273
Pimpri-Chinchwad (*Pune) 83,542
Pithāpuram 31,391
Pollāchi (*93,838) 68,655
Pondicherry (*153,325) 90,637
Ponnāni 35,723
Porbandar (*106,727) 96,881
Port Blair 26,218
Proddatūr 70,822
Pudukkottai 66,384
Pulgaon 33,382
Puliyangudi 38,742
Pune (Poona) (*1,175,000) 856,105
Pune Cantonment (*Pune) 77,774
Puri 72,674
Purnea (*71,311) 56,484
Purūlia 57,708
Quilon 124,208
Rabkavi Banhatti 37,509
Rāe-Bareli 38,765
Rāichūr 79,831
Raiganj 43,191
Raigarh (*48,049) 46,745
Raipur (*205,986) 174,518
Rājahmundry (*188,805) 165,912
Rājapālaiyam 86,952
Rājkot 300,612
Rāj-Nāndgaon (*55,827) 41,183
Rājpur (*Calcutta) 34,393
Rāmanāthapuram 36,122
Rāmpur 161,417
Rānāghāt 47,815
Rānchī (*255,551) 175,934
Rānībennur 40,749
Rānīganj (**Asansol) 40,104
Ratangarh 31,506
Ratlām (*119,247) 106,666
Ratnāgiri 37,551
Raurkela (*172,502) 125,426
Rewa 69,182
Rewāri 43,885
Rishīkesh 17,646
Rishra (*Calcutta) 63,486
Rohtak 124,755
Roorkee (*62,456) 47,561
Sāgar (*154,785) 118,574
Sahāranpur 225,396
Sāhibganj 35,640
Salem (*416,440) 308,716
Sāmalkot 34,607
Sambalpur (*105,085) 64,675
Sambhal 86,323
Sāngli (*201,597) 115,138
Sāntipur 61,166
Sardārshahr 37,703
Sāsarām 48,282
Sātāra 66,433
Satna (*62,162) 57,531
Secunderābād Cantonment (*Hyderābād) 94,416
Sehore 35,657
Seoni 38,396
Serampore (*Calcutta) 102,023
Shāhābād 33,408
Shāhjahānpur (*144,065) 135,604
Shāmli 36,959
Shikohābād 31,442
Shillong (*122,752) 87,659
Shimoga 102,709
Shivpuri (*50,858) 42,120
Sholāpur 398,361
Sidhpur (*41,334) 40,521
Sīkar 70,987
Silchar 52,596
Silīguri (*136,343) 97,484
Simla 55,368
Sindri (**Dhānbād) 46,385
Singānallūr (*Coimbatore) 112,206
Sirsa 48,808
Sītāpur 66,715
Sivakāsi (*60,753) 44,883
Siwān 33,162
Sonīpat 62,393
South Dum-Dum (*Calcutta) . . 174,342
Sri Gangānagar (Gangānagar) . 90,042
Srīkākulam 45,179
Srīnagar (*423,253) 403,413
Srīrangam (*Tiruchchirāppalli) . 51,069
Srīvilliputtūr 53,855
Sūjāngarh 39,073
Sultānpur 32,330
Surat (*493,001) 471,656
Surendranagar (*97,251) 66,667
Sūri 30,110
Tādepallegūdem 43,610
Tādpatri 31,618
Tāmbaram (*Madras) 58,805
Tandā 41,611
Tanuku 34,197
Tellicherry 68,759
Tenāli 102,937
Tenkāsi 42,627
Tezpur 39,870
Thāna (*Bombay) 170,675
Thanjāvūr (Tanjore) 140,547
Theni-Allinagaram 34,854
Tindivanam 45,058
Tinsukia 54,911
Tiruchchirāppalli (Trichinopoly) (*475,000) 307,400
Tiruchendūr (*55,636) 18,126
Tiruchengodu 36,990
Tirunelveli (*266,688) 108,498
Tirupati (*71,984) 65,843
Tiruppattūr 40,357
Tiruppur (*151,127) 113,302
Tiruvannāmalai 61,370
Tiruvottiyūr (*Madras) 82,853
Titāgarh (*Calcutta) 88,218
Tonk 55,866
Trichūr 76,241
Trivandrum 409,627
Tumkūr 70,476
Tuticorin (*181,913) 155,310
Udaipur 161,278
Udamalpet 39,311
Udgīr 30,647
Ujjain (*208,561) 203,278
Ulhāsnagar (*Bombay) 168,462
Upleta 35,326
Uttarpara-Kotrung (*Calcutta) . . 67,568
Valparai 95,175
Vāniyambādi (*57,686) 51,810
Vārānasi (Benares) (*606,271) . . 583,856
Vellore (*178,554) 139,082
Verāval (*75,520) 58,771
Vidisha 43,212
Vijayawāda (*344,607) 317,258
Vikramasingapuram 40,274
Villupuram 60,242
Virāmgām 43,790
Virudunagar 61,902
Vishākhapatnam (*363,467) 352,504
Visnagar 34,863
Vizianagaram 86,608
Warangal 207,520
Wardha 69,037
Yādgīr 32,756
Yamunānagar (**Jagādhri) 72,594
Yavatmāl 64,836

INDONESIA

1979 E ..... †144,911,000

Island Groups

BORNEO, INDONESIAN (KALIMANTAN) 6,406,000
CELEBES 10,605,000
JAVA AND MADURA 90,780,000
LESSER SUNDA ISLANDS . . †8,153,000
MOLUCCAS 2,481,000
SUMATRA 26,486,000

†Total excludes Timor Timur, annexed in 1976

Cities (‡1971 C or 1961 C)

Amahai 18,256
Ambon (Amboina) (1976 E) 91,000
Amuntai 27,383
Balikpapan ..... ‡137,340
Banda Aceh (Kutaradja) ..... ‡53,668
Bandung (*1,250,000) ..... ‡1,201,730
Bangil 28,275
Bangkalan 22,514
Banjarmasin ..... ‡281,673
Bantul 30,572
Banyuwangi ..... ‡89,303
Baubau 21,060
Bekasi ..... ‡45,694
Bengkulu ..... ‡31,866
Binjai ..... ‡59,882
Blitar ..... ‡67,856
Blora ..... ‡53,504
Bogor ..... ‡195,882
Bojonegoro ..... ‡52,597
Bondowoso 35,760
Brebes ..... ‡44,456
Bukittinggi ..... ‡63,132
Ciamis 35,189
Cianjur (Tjiandjur) 62,546
Cilacap (Tjilatjap) ..... ‡82,043
Cimahi (Tjimahi) ..... ‡72,367
Cirebon (Tjirebon) ..... ‡178,529
Denpasar ..... ‡88,142
Dili (1970 C) (65,451▲) 6,730
Ende 26,843
Garut ..... ‡81,234
Gorontalo ..... ‡82,328
Gresik ..... ‡48,561
Indramayu 25,710
• JAKARTA (DJAKARTA) (1979 UE) (*6,500,000) 6,400,000
Jambi (Telanaipura) ..... ‡158,559
Jayapura (Sukarnapura) (1976 E) 61,054
Jember ..... ‡122,712
Jepara 18,921
Jombang ..... ‡45,450
Kediri ..... ‡178,865
Klaten 33,400
Kotabumi 37,496
Krawang ..... ‡61,361
Kualakapuas 18,573
Kudus ..... ‡87,767
Kuningan 21,542
Kupang ..... ‡52,698
Lahat ..... ‡41,030
Langsa ..... ‡55,016
Lawang 35,852
Lhokseumawe 28,386
Lumajang ..... ‡48,995
Madiun ..... ‡136,147
Magelang ..... ‡110,308
Magetan 26,818
Majalengka 14,361
Majene 24,259
Makale 32,578
Malang ..... ‡422,428
Manado ..... ‡169,684
Martapura ..... ‡69,729
Medan ..... ‡635,562
Mojokerto ..... ‡60,013
Nganjuk 23,499
Ngawi 29,220
Padang ..... ‡196,339
Padangpanjang ..... ‡30,711
Padangsidempuan ..... ‡49,090
Pakanbaru ..... ‡145,030
Palangkaraya ..... ‡27,132
Palembang ..... ‡582,961
Palopo 29,724
Palu 16,977
Pamekasan ..... ‡41,416
Pangkalpinang ..... ‡74,733
Parepare ..... ‡72,538
Pasuruan ..... ‡75,266
Pati ..... ‡46,037
Payakumbuh ..... ‡63,388
Pekalongan ..... ‡111,537
Pemalang ..... ‡77,672
Pematangsiantar ..... ‡129,232
Perabumulih 41,951
Pinrang 23,818
Ponorogo ..... ‡67,711
Pontianak ..... ‡217,555
Praya 26,729
Probolinggo ..... ‡82,008
Purbolinggo 22,698
Purwakarta ..... ‡49,703
Purwokerto ..... ‡94,023
Purworejo ..... ‡52,956
Raba 29,881
Rangkasbitung 30,822
Salatiga ..... ‡69,831
Samarinda ..... ‡137,521
Semarang ..... ‡646,590
Serang ..... ‡56,263
Sibolga ..... ‡42,223
Sidoarjo ..... ‡41,254
Singaraja ..... ‡42,289
Singkawang 35,169
Situbondo ..... ‡55,348
Solok ..... ‡24,771
Sragen 25,685
Subang ..... ‡42,437
Sukabumi ..... ‡96,242
Sungaipenuh 36,766
Surabaya (*1,400,000) ..... ‡1,332,249
Surakarta ..... ‡414,285
Tangerang ..... ‡50,893
Tanjungbalai ..... ‡33,604
Tanjungkarang-Telukbetung . . ‡198,986
Tanjungpandan 29,412
Tanjungpinang ..... ‡37,638
Tarutung 24,998
Tasikmalaya ..... ‡136,004
Tebingtinggi ..... ‡30,314
Tegal ..... ‡105,752
Ternate 24,287
Tidore 26,160
Tual 38,403
Tuban 38,575
Tulungagung ..... ‡68,899
Ujung Pandang (Makasar) ..... ‡434,766
Watampone ..... ‡54,720
Yogyakarta (Jogjakarta) ..... ‡342,267

IRAN / Īrān

1976 C 33,591,875

Ābādān 296,081
Ahvāz 329,006
Āmol 68,782
Arāk 114,507
Ardabīl 147,404
Bābol 67,790
Bandar 'Abbās 89,103
Bandar-e Anzalī (Bandar-e Pahlavī) 55,978
Behbehān (1966 C) 39,874
Behshahr (1966 C) 26,032
Bīrjand (1966 C) 25,854
Bojnūrd (1966 C) 31,248
Borūjerd 100,103
Dezfūl 110,287
Emāmshahr (Shahrūd) (1966 C) . 30,767
Eşfahān (Isfahan) 671,825
Golpāyegān (1966 C) 20,515
Gonbad-e Qābūs 59,868
Gorgān 88,348
Hamadān 155,846
Homāyunshahr (1966 C) 46,836
Jahrom (1966 C) 38,236
Karaj 138,774
Kāshān 84,545
Kāzerūn 51,309
Kermān 140,309
Kermānshāh 290,861
Khorramābād 104,928
Khorramshahr 146,709
Khvoy 70,040
Lāhījān (1966 C) 25,725
Lār (1966 C) 21,576
Mahābād (1966 C) 28,610
Malāyer (1966 C) 28,434
Marāgheh 60,820
Marand (1966 C) 23,818
Marv Dasht (1966 C) 25,498
Mashhad (Meshed) 670,180
Masjed Soleymān 77,161
Mīāneh (1966 C) 28,447
Najafābād 76,236
Neyshābūr 59,101
Orūmīyeh (Reẕā'īyeh) 163,991
Qā'emshahr (Shāhī) 63,289
Qazvīn 138,527
Qom 246,831
Qūchān (1966 C) 29,133
Rasht 187,203
Sabzevār 69,174
Sanandaj 95,834
Sārī 70,936
Semnān (1966 C) 31,058
Shīrāz 416,408
Tabrīz 598,576
• TEHRĀN (*4,700,000) 4,496,159
Torbat-e Ḩeydarīyeh (1966 C) . . . 30,106
Yazd 135,978
Zāhedān 92,628
Zanjān 99,967

IRAQ / Al-'Irāq

1970 E 9,465,800

Ad-Dīwānīyah 62,300
Al-'Amārah 80,100
Al-Başrah (Basra) 370,900
Al-Fallūjah (1965 C) 38,072
Al-Ḩillah (Hilla) 128,800
Al-Kūfah (1965 C) 30,862
Al-Mawşil (Mosul) 293,100
An-Najaf 179,200
An-Nāşirīyah 62,400
Ar-Ramādī (1965 C) 28,723
As-Samāwah (1965 C) 33,473
As-Sulaymānīyah 98,100
Az-Zubayr (1965 C) 41,408
• BAGHDĀD (*2,183,800) 1,300,000
Ba'qūbah (1965 C) 34,575
Irbīl 107,400
Karbalā' 107,500
Kirkūk 207,900
Kūt al-Imāra (Al-Kūt) (1965 C) 42,116
Sāmarrā (1965 C) 24,746
Tall 'Afar (1965 C) 36,837

IRELAND / Eire

1979 C 3,368,217

An Uaimh (Navan) (*7,000) 4,277
Arklow (Inbhear Mór) 8,446
Athlone (Áth Luain) (*12,500) 9,760
Ballina (Béal Átha an Fheadha) . . 6,941
Ballinasloe (Béal Átha na Sluagh) 6,461
Bray (Brí Chualann) (*Dublin) . . 21,672
Carlow (Ceatharlach) 11,404
Carrick-on-Suir (Carraig na Siúire) 5,510
Castlebar (Caisleán an Bharraigh) 6,482
Clonmel (Cluain Meala) 12,411
Cobh 6,670
Cork (Corcaigh) (*175,000) 138,267
Drogheda (Droichead Átha) 22,555
Droichead Nua (1971 C) 5,053
• DUBLIN (BAILE ÁTHA CLIATH) (*1,110,000) 544,586
Dundalk (Dún Dealgan) 25,281
Dungarvan (Dún Garbháin) 6,578
Dún Laoghaire (*Dublin) 54,244
Ennis (Inis) (*12,000) 6,277
Enniscorthy (Inis Coirthe) 5,253
Galway (Gaillimh) 36,824
Kilkenny (Cill Choinnigh) (*14,800) 10,075
Killarney (Cill Áirne) 7,724
Limerick (Luimneach) (*80,000) . 60,665
Mallow (Mala) 6,609
Monaghan (Muineachán) 6,173
Mullingar (Muileann Cearr) (1971 C) (*9,245) 6,790
Naas (Nás na Ríogh) (*Dublin) ... 7,740
Nenagh (Aonach Urmhumhan) . . 5,647
New Ross (Ros Mhic Treoin) 5,230
Portlaoise (1971 C) (*6,470) 3,902
Sligo (Sligeach) 16,836
Thurles (Durlas Éile) 7,436
Tipperary (Tiobrad Árann) 4,929
Tralee (Tráighlí) 15,011
Tuam (Tuaim) (1971 C) (*4,952) . . 3,808
Tullamore (Tulach Mhór) 7,720
Waterford (Port Láirge) (*42,000) 32,617
Wexford (Loch Garman) 11,848
Youghal (Eochaill) 5,739

ISLE OF MAN

1976 C 61,723

• DOUGLAS (*28,500) 20,262
Peel 3,338
Ramsey 5,458

C Census. E Official estimate. UE Unofficial estimate.
L Population within municipal limits of specified year. • Largest city in country.

* Population or designation of metropolitan area, including suburbs (see headnote).
▲ Population of an entire municipality, commune, or district, including rural area.
‡† Year of information specified at start of country.

ISRAEL / Yisra'el

1979 E	**†3,836,200**
'Afula	19,700
'Akko (Acre) (★Haifa)	37,900
Ashdod	62,300
Ashqelon	52,000
Bat Yam (★Tel Aviv-Yafo)	130,100
Be'er Sheva' (Beersheba)	107,000
Bene Beraq (★Tel Aviv-Yafo)	89,600
Dimona	27,800
Elat (Elath)	18,900
Giv'atayim (★Tel Aviv-Yafo)	49,300
Hadera	37,800
Haifa (Hefa) (★415,000)	229,300
Herzliyya (★Tel Aviv-Yafo)	56,400
Holon (★Tel Aviv-Yafo)	128,400
JERUSALEM (YERUSHALAYIM) (AL-QUDS) *(includes Old City area occupied in 1967)* (★420,000)	398,200
Kefar Ata (★Haifa)	31,400
Kefar Sava (★Tel Aviv-Yafo)	38,100
Lod (Lydda)	39,400
Nahariyya	28,200
Nazerat (Nazareth) (★63,000)	40,400
Nazerat 'Illit (★Nazerat)	21,400
Nes Ziyyona	13,700
Netanya	95,900
Or Yehuda (★Tel Aviv-Yafo)	19,400
Petah Tiqwa (★Tel Aviv-Yafo)	117,000
Qiryat Bialik (★Haifa)	27,500
Qiryat Gat	24,300
Qiryat Motzkin (★Haifa)	23,200
Qiryat Ono (★Tel Aviv-Yafo)	22,500
Qiryat Shemona	15,800
Qiryat Yam (★Haifa)	28,400
Ra'ananna (★Tel Aviv-Yafo)	29,700
Ramat Gan (★Tel Aviv-Yafo)	120,400
Ramat HaSharon (★Tel Aviv-Yafo)	30,100
Ramla	40,600
Rehovot	63,700
Rishon le Ziyyon (★Tel Aviv-Yafo)	87,800
•Tel Aviv-Yafo (Tel Aviv-Jaffa) (★1,350,000)	336,300
Teverya (Tiberias)	28,300
Tirat Karmel (★Haifa)	15,500
Umm el Fahm	18,600
Zefat	15,500

ITALY / Italia

1979 E	**56,999,047**
Regions and Provinces	
ABRUZZI	1,239,738
Chieti	372,791
L'Aquila	302,480
Pescara	291,592
Teramo	272,875
APULIA, see PUGLIA	
BASILICATA (LUCANIA)	618,703
Matera	204,273
Potenza	414,430
CALABRIA	2,078,264
Catanzaro	748,166
Cosenza	735,673
Reggio di Calabria	594,425
CAMPANIA	5,457,838
Avellino	440,712
Benevento	294,438
Caserta	753,207
Napoli (Naples)	2,945,181
Salerno	1,024,300
EMILIA-ROMAGNA	3,964,538
Bologna	937,136
Ferrara	385,503
Forlì	598,672
Modena	590,547
Parma	399,560
Piacenza	280,981
Ravenna	361,634
Reggio nell'Emilia	410,505
FRIULI-VENEZIA GIULIA	1,245,130
Gorizia	146,600
Pordenone	274,550
Trieste	291,581
Udine	532,399
LAZIO (LATIUM)	5,059,174
Frosinone	464,439
Latina	434,787
Rieti	143,983
Roma (Rome)	3,747,003
Viterbo	268,962
LIGURIA	1,844,779
Genova	1,065,846
Imperia	229,936
La Spezia	244,558
Savona	304,439
LOMBARDIA (LOMBARDY)	8,941,704
Bergamo	890,540
Brescia	1,015,350
Como	772,532
Cremona	333,403
Mantova	380,413
Milano	4,065,584
Pavia	519,369
Sondrio	175,188
Varese	789,325
MARCHE (MARCHES)	1,415,563
Ancona	434,091
Ascoli Piceno	354,667
Macerata	292,728
Pesaro e Urbino	334,077
MOLISE	334,091
Campobasso	238,564
Isernia	95,527
PIEMONTE (PIEDMONT)	4,531,141
Alessandria	472,865
Asti	217,982
Cuneo	548,236
Novara	509,830
Torino (Turin)	2,380,674
Vercelli	401,554
PUGLIA (APULIA)	3,917,029
Bari	1,471,563
Brindisi	400,092
Foggia	692,245
Lecce	778,830
Taranto	574,299
SARDEGNA (SARDINIA)	1,601,586
Cagliari	730,333
Nuoro	278,267
Oristano	157,151
Sassari	435,835
SICILIA (SICILY)	4,999,032
Agrigento	489,020
Caltanissetta	295,817
Catania	1,014,493
Enna	204,114
Messina	686,764
Palermo	1,206,291
Ragusa	276,312
Siracusa	397,818
Trapani	428,403
TOSCANA (TUSCANY)	3,600,233
Arezzo	313,801
Firenze	1,209,407
Grosseto	223,661
Livorno	346,395
Lucca	388,576
Massa-Carrara	205,535
Pisa	388,560
Pistoia	266,526
Siena	257,772
TRENTINO-ALTO ADIGE	876,249
Bolzano	432,073
Trento	444,176
UMBRIA	808,351
Perugia	579,311
Terni	229,040
VALLE D'AOSTA	114,591
VENETO (VENETIA)	4,351,313
Belluno	224,829
Padova	813,289
Rovigo	254,466
Treviso	716,250
Venezia (Venice)	844,391
Verona	774,347
Vicenza	723,741
Cities	
Abano Terme	16,115
Acerra (★Naples) (37,629▲)	33,100
Acireale (49,813▲)	30,600
Adrano	34,190
Afragola (★Naples)	58,927
Agrigento	51,725
Alassio	13,943
Alba	31,309
Albano Laziale (★Rome) (27,889▲)	22,000
Alberobello	9,983
Alcamo	43,593
Alessandria	101,684
Alghero (37,892▲)	31,700
Altamura	49,878
Amalfi	6,446
Ancona	108,371
Andria	83,734
Anzio	27,223
Aosta	39,072
Arezzo	92,245
Ascoli Piceno	56,200
Assisi (24,910▲)	19,400
Asti	79,407
Augusta	38,181
Avellino	59,324
Aversa (★Naples)	51,837
Avezzano (34,353▲)	29,800
Avola	30,565
Bagheria	41,373
Barcellona Pozzo di Gotto (37,737▲)	26,000
Bari (★460,000)	387,266
Barletta	81,414
Bassano del Grappa	37,801
Battipaglia (40,604▲)	32,200
Belluno	37,003
Benevento (62,524▲)	52,800
Bergamo (★340,000)	125,544
Biella	55,857
Bisceglie	46,962
Bitonto	48,052
Bollate (★Milan)	43,115
Bologna (★550,000)	471,554
Bolzano (Bozen)	106,199
Bordighera (12,014▲)	9,600
Brescia	212,265
Bresso (★Milan)	34,245
Brindisi	89,241
Busto Arsizio (★Milan)	81,139
Cagliari (★305,000)	241,472
Caltagirone	38,525
Caltanissetta (61,461▲)	54,700
Camaiore (31,110▲)	22,700
Camerino (8,085▲)	3,400
Campobasso	47,316
Canicattì	32,603
Canosa di Puglia	30,781
Cantù	36,664
Capannori (43,972▲)	36,900
Capua	18,435
Carbonia	33,162
Carpi (59,824▲)	51,800
Carrara (★★Massa)	70,227
Casale Monferrato	42,711
Cascina	35,073
Caserta	67,257
Casoria (★Naples)	67,242
Cassino (32,181▲)	27,200
Castel Gandolfo (★Rome) (5,953▲)	3,400
Castellammare di Stabia (★Naples)	74,452
Castelvetrano	31,382
Catania (★515,000)	398,426
Catanzaro	93,845
Cattolica	15,811
Cava de' Tirreni (★Salerno) (51,611▲)	45,500
Cefalù (13,624▲)	11,600
Cerignola (51,349▲)	45,300
Cesano Maderno (★Milan)	32,637
Cesena (90,269▲)	68,100
Cesenatico (20,222▲)	15,900
Chiavari	30,508
Chieri (31,012▲)	26,400
Chieti	57,140
Chioggia (53,611▲)	38,200
Chivasso	27,064
Ciampino (★Rome)	30,561
Cinisello Balsamo (★Milan)	80,387
Cittadella (17,182▲)	7,000
Città di Castello (37,497▲)	28,600
Civitanova Marche (36,002▲)	31,500
Civitavecchia	48,342
Collegno (★Turin)	46,326
Cologno Monzese (★Milan)	51,855
Como (★160,000)	96,665
Conegliano (36,000▲)	29,500
Corato	41,623
Corsico (★Milan)	43,769
Cortina d'Ampezzo	8,326
Cosenza (★130,000)	102,338
Crema	34,742
Cremona	82,056
Crotone	57,009
Cuneo	55,784
Desio (★Milan)	33,051
Domodossola	20,704
Eboli	29,044
Empoli	45,725
Enna	29,370
Ercolano (Resina) (★Naples)	57,114
Erice	26,282
Este	18,283
Faenza (55,538▲)	40,100
Fano (53,273▲)	44,000
Fasano (36,420▲)	23,300
Favara	33,046
Fermo (35,186▲)	27,000
Ferrara (152,752▲)	125,200
Fiesole (★Florence)	14,760
Florence (Firenze) (★660,000)	462,690
Foggia	157,727
Foligno (52,580▲)	46,300
Forlì (110,523▲)	92,500
Francavilla Fontana	34,565
Frascati (★Rome)	19,587
Frattamaggiore (★Naples)	38,134
Frosinone	45,725
Gaeta	24,437
Gallarate (★Milan)	47,741
Gela	75,201
Genoa (Genova) (★855,000)	782,476
Giugliano in Campania (★Naples)	42,347
Gorizia	42,580
Gravina in Puglia	36,628
Grosseto (69,699▲)	61,600
Grottaglie	28,477
Grugliasco (★Turin)	34,202
Gubbio (32,164▲)	9,900
Guidonia Montecelio (★Rome)	48,821
Iesi (Jesi) (41,974▲)	35,600
Iglesias	29,561
Imola (60,234▲)	48,000
Imperia	42,159
Isernia (19,121▲)	14,500
Ivrea	28,650
L'Aquila	66,644
La Spezia (★192,000)	117,761
Latina (94,910▲)	83,200
Lecce	90,121
Lecco	52,806
Legnago	27,044
Legnano (★Milan)	49,960
Lentini	34,350
Licata	42,250
Limbiate (★Milan)	32,815
Lissone (★Milan)	30,482
Livorno (Leghorn)	176,757
Lodi	43,927
Loreto (10,851▲)	6,000
Lucca	91,256
Lucera (33,307▲)	28,500
Lugo (34,518▲)	20,300
Macerata (44,492▲)	37,700
Maddaloni (33,228▲)	26,100
Magenta	23,627
Manduria	30,488
Manfredonia (53,052▲)	45,800
Mantova	64,008
Marino (★Rome)	30,464
Marsala (86,051▲)	50,400
Martina France (44,340▲)	32,600
Massa (★145,000)	66,060
Matera	50,424
Mazara del Vallo	43,825
Merano (Meran)	34,460
Messina	271,660
•Milan (Milano) (★3,800,000)	1,677,109
Milazzo (30,710▲)	20,500
Modena	180,428
Modica (47,742▲)	31,400
Molfetta	66,699
Moncalieri (★Turin)	65,066
Monfalcone	31,053
Monopoli (44,017▲)	29,800
Monreale	25,416
Montecatini Terme	21,843
Montepulciano (14,255▲)	9,500
Monte Sant'Angelo	17,421
Monza (★Milan)	123,834
Naples (Napoli) (★2,740,000)	1,223,228
Nardò (30,916▲)	24,200
Nettuno (29,321▲)	25,300
Nicastro (Lamezia Terme) (62,069▲)	29,800
Nichelino (★Turin)	45,092
Nocera Inferiore (51,533▲)	43,300
Nola (29,282▲)	22,400
Novara	101,947
Novi Ligure	31,783
Nuoro	36,503
Oristano	29,769
Orvieto (23,414▲)	17,500
Otranto	4,748
Paderno Dugnano (★Milan)	38,885
Padova (★280,000)	242,216
Pagani	32,713
Palermo	693,949
Parma	176,945
Partinico	28,162
Paternò	48,992
Pavia	87,005
Perugia	139,871
Pesaro	90,705
Pescara	137,059
Piacenza	108,888
Pinerolo	36,589
Piombino	39,659
Pisa	103,772
Pistoia (94,344▲)	84,300
Poggibonsi	26,743
Pompei (★Naples) (22,526▲)	13,300
Pontedera	28,254
Pordenone	52,106
Portici (★Naples)	83,372
Portoferraio	11,212
Portofino	773
Potenza	64,513
Pozzuoli (★Naples) (70,429▲)	61,400
Prato (★201,000)	158,229
Ragusa (66,545▲)	55,200
Rapallo	29,809
Ravello (2,387▲)	1,400
Ravenna (139,392▲)	102,300
Reggio di Calabria	181,293
Reggio nell'Emilia	130,005
Rho (★Milan)	49,657
Riccione	31,688
Rieti (43,277▲)	38,700
Rimini	127,714
Riva [del Garda]	13,240
Rivoli (★Turin)	50,992
ROME (ROMA) (★3,195,000)	2,911,671
Rosignano Marittimo	29,402
Rovereto	33,082
Rovigo	52,588
Salerno (★240,000)	161,997
Salsomaggiore Terme	17,982
San Benedetto del Tronto	46,256
San Donà di Piave (32,058▲)	22,500
San Gimignano (7,521▲)	2,800
San Giorgio a Cremano (★Naples)	65,245
San Remo (63,423▲)	52,400
San Severo	54,914
Santa Maria Capua Vetere	32,529
Saronno	36,683
Sassari	119,597
Sassuolo	39,471
Savona (★120,000)	78,216
Scandicci (★Florence)	54,102
Schio	36,388
Sciacca (36,148▲)	32,300
Senigallia (40,567▲)	34,500
Seregno (★Milan)	37,717
Sesto Fiorentino (★Florence)	44,862
Sesto San Giovanni (★Milan)	98,151
Settimo Torinese (★Turin)	44,895
Siena	63,961
Siracusa	116,755
Sorrento (★42,900)	16,868
Spoleto (37,593▲)	32,200
Taranto	247,681
Teramo (51,768▲)	41,000
Termini Imerese	26,815
Terni	113,241
Tivoli (★Rome)	46,201
Todi (17,244▲)	3,900
Torre Annunziata (★Naples)	57,659
Torre del Greco (★Naples)	101,905
Trani	43,243
Trapani (72,036▲)	62,400
Trento	99,052
Treviso	89,121
Trieste	260,291
Turin (Torino) (★1,670,000)	1,160,686
Udine (★128,000)	102,973
Urbino (16,211▲)	13,000
Varese	91,100
Venice (Venezia) (★445,000)	355,865
Verbania	33,384
Vercelli	54,063
Verona	269,763
Viareggio	59,600
Vicenza	117,571
Vigevano	67,034
Villa San Giovanni (12,106▲)	9,000
Viterbo (58,529▲)	50,000
Vittoria	50,739
Vittorio Veneto	30,897
Voghera	42,781

IVORY COAST / Côte d'Ivoire

1978 E	**7,613,000**
Abengourou (1975 C)	31,239
•ABIDJAN	1,100,000
Agboville (1975 C)	27,192
Bouaké	230,000
Daloa	70,000
Danane (1975 C)	19,872
Dimbokro (1975 C)	30,986
Divo (1975 C)	37,896
Gagnoa (1975 C)	42,362
Grand-Bassam (1975 C)	25,808
Korhogo (1975 C)	47,657
Man	55,000
Séguéla (1975 C)	12,587

JAMAICA

1978 E	**2,137,300**
•KINGSTON	665,050
Mandeville (1970 C)	14,421
May Pen (1970 C)	26,074
Montego Bay (1970 C)	43,754
Ocho Rios (1970 C)	6,900
Port Antonio (1970 C)	10,538
Savanna-la-Mar (1970 C)	11,759
Spanish Town (1970 C)	40,731

JAPAN

1979 E	**116,133,000**
Districts and Prefectures	
CHUBU	19,844,000
Aichi	6,176,000
Fukui	792,000
Gifu	1,945,000
Ishikawa	1,110,000
Nagano	2,071,000
Niigata	2,437,000
Shizuoka	3,420,000
Toyama	1,098,000
Yamanashi	795,000
CHUGOKU	7,557,000
Hiroshima	2,723,000
Okayama	1,865,000
Shimane	782,000
Tottori	599,000
Yamaguchi	1,588,000
HOKKAIDŌ	5,532,000
Hokkaidō	5,532,000
KANTŌ (KWANTŌ)	34,428,000
Chiba	4,617,000
Gumma	1,826,000
Ibaraki	2,503,000
Kanagawa	6,809,000
Saitama	5,309,000
Tochigi	1,768,000
Tōkyō	11,596,000
KINKI	21,158,000
Hyōgo	5,139,000
Kyōto	2,515,000
Mie	1,674,000
Nara	1,190,000
Ōsaka	8,487,000
Shiga	1,063,000
Wakayama	1,090,000
KYŪSHŪ	13,985,000
Fukuoka	4,527,000
Kagoshima	1,770,000
Kumamoto	1,776,000
Miyazaki	1,141,000
Nagasaki	1,592,000
Ōita	1,224,000
Okinawa	1,096,000
Saga	859,000
SHIKOKU	4,143,000
Ehime	1,499,000
Kagawa	995,000
Kōchi	828,000
Tokushima	821,000
TŌHOKU	9,486,000
Akita	1,251,000
Aomori	1,514,000
Fukushima	2,015,000
Iwate	1,411,000
Miyagi	2,054,000
Yamagata	1,241,000
Cities (1975 C or †1979 E)	
Abashiri (43,825▲)	34,900
Abiko (★Tōkyō)	76,218
Ageo (★Tōkyō)	†163,985
Aioi	42,008
Aizu-wakamatsu	†113,175
Akashi (★Ōsaka) (1980 C)	254,873
Akishima (★Tōkyō)	83,864
Akita (1980 C)	284,830
Akō	49,583
Amagasaki (★Ōsaka) (1980 C)	523,657
Amagi (42,725▲)	25,700
Anan (60,439▲)	37,200
Anjō	†121,178
Aomori (1980 C)	287,609
Arao (★Ōmuta) (58,296▲)	47,300
Arida	34,865
Asahikawa (1980 C)	352,620
Asaka (★Tōkyō)	81,755
Ashibetsu (36,520▲)	29,100
Ashikaga	†165,024
Ashiya (★Ōsaka)	76,211
Atami	51,437
Atsugi (★Tōkyō)	†136,652
Ayabe (43,490▲)	29,000
Ayase (★Tōkyō)	50,365
Beppu	†137,477
Bibai (38,416▲)	29,200
Bisai	54,247
Chiba (★Tōkyō) (1980 C)	746,428
Chichibu	61,798
Chigasaki (★Tōkyō)	†168,849
Chikugo	39,520
Chikushino (★Fukuoka)	47,741
Chiryū (★Nagoya)	47,209
Chita (★Nagoya)	56,560
Chitose	61,031
Chōfu (★Tōkyō)	†179,631
Chōshi	90,374
Daitō (★Ōsaka)	†115,678
Ebetsu	77,624
Ebina (★Tōkyō)	59,783
Fuchū *(Hiroshima pref.)*	50,217
Fūchū (★Hiroshima) *(Hiroshima pref.)*	47,538
Fuchū (★Tōkyō)	†190,048
Fuji (1980 C) (★325,000)	205,752
Fujieda (101,216▲)	†72,000
Fujiidera (★Ōsaka)	59,515
Fujimi (★Tōkyō)	70,391
Fujinomiya (★★Fuji) (106,524▲)	†82,800
Fujioka (49,169▲)	30,000
Fujisawa (★Tōkyō) (1980 C)	300,181
Fuji-yoshida	51,976
Fukaya (75,748▲)	53,100
Fukuchiyama (60,003▲)	43,000
Fukui (1980 C)	240,264
Fukuoka (1980 C) (★1,575,000)	1,088,617
Fukuroi (42,581▲)	25,700
Fukushima (1980 C)	262,847
Fukuyama (1980 C)	346,031
Funabashi (★Tōkyō) (1980 C)	479,437
Furukawa (54,356▲)	31,100
Fussa (★Tōkyō)	46,457
Futtsu	56,653

C Census. E Official estimate. UE Unofficial estimate.
L Population within municipal limits of year specified. • Largest city in country.

★ Population or designation of metropolitan area, including suburbs (see headnote).
▲ Population of an entire municipality, commune, or district, including rural area.
‡† Year of information specified at start of country.

Gamagōri........85,282
Gifu (1980 C)........410,368
Ginowan........53,835
Gose (★Ōsaka)........37,554
Gotemba (62,722▲)........49,300
Gushikawa........42,133
Gyōda........66,069
Habikino (★Ōsaka)........†102,217
Hachinohe (1980 C)........238,208
Hachiōji (★Tōkyō) (1980 C)........387,162
Hadano (★Tōkyō)........†118,528
Hagi (52,724▲)........42,100
Hakodate (1980 C)........320,152
Hamada........50,316
Hamakita (67,180▲)........49,600
Hamamatsu (1980 C)........490,827
Hanamaki (65,826▲)........38,200
Handa........85,824
Hannō (★Tōkyō)........55,926
Haranomachi (43,483▲)........26,800
Hashima (52,570▲)........40,500
Hatogaya (★Tōkyō)........56,693
Hekinan........60,680
Higashihiroshima
(★Hiroshima)........66,231
Higashikurume (★Tōkyō)........†106,566
Higashimatsuyama........57,684
Higashimurayama (★Tōkyō)........†119,684
Higashiōsaka (★Ōsaka)
(1980 C)........521,635
Higashiyamato (★Tōkyō)........58,464
Hikari (★Tokuyama)........48,794
Hikone........85,066
Himeji (1980 C)........446,255
Himi (61,789▲)........38,600
Hino (★Tōkyō)........†142,982
Hirakata (★Ōsaka) (1980 C)........353,360
Hiratsuka (★Tōkyō) (1980 C)........214,299
Hirosaki (173,550▲)........†112,300
Hiroshima (1980 C)
(★1,525,000)........899,394
Hisai........36,587
Hita (63,969▲)........47,300
Hitachi (1980 C)........204,612
Hōfu (109,762▲)........†86,100
Honjō........51,090
Hōya (★Tōkyō)........91,546
Hyūga (53,448▲)........40,600
Ibaraki (★Ōsaka) (1980 C)........234,059
Ichihara (★Tōkyō) (1980 C)........216,395
Ichikawa (★Tōkyō) (1980 C)........364,244
Ichinomiya (1980 C)........253,138
Ichinoseki (59,122▲)........36,000
Iida (77,112▲)........51,900
Iizuka (★103,000)........75,417
Ikeda (★Ōsaka)........†101,872
Ikoma (★Ōsaka)........48,848
Imabari........†123,928
Imaichi (46,760▲)........29,800
Imari (60,913▲)........36,600
Ina (54,468▲)........32,500
Inagi (★Tōkyō)........43,924
Inazawa (★Nagoya)........88,606
Innoshima........41,683
Inuyama (★Nagoya)........58,731
Iruma (★Tōkyō)........83,997
Isahaya (73,341▲)........49,400
Ise (Uji-yamada)........†105,624
Isehara (★Tōkyō)........61,616
Isesaki........†104,300
Ishinomaki........†119,758
Ishioka (43,679▲)........30,400
Itami (★Ōsaka)........†177,745
Itō........68,072
Itsukaichi (★Hiroshima)........64,885
Iwai........38,304
Iwaki (Taira) (1980 C)
(342,076▲)........271,800
Iwakuni........†112,200
Iwakura (★Nagoya)........41,935
Iwamizawa (72,305▲)........56,800
Iwata........67,665
Iwatsuki (★Tōkyō) (83,825▲)........60,900
Iyo-mishima........38,409
Izumi (★Ōsaka)........†122,464
Izumi *(Kagoshima pref.)*........37,483
Izumi (★Sendai)........70,087
Izumi-ōtsu (★Ōsaka)........66,250
Izumi-sano (★Ōsaka)........86,139
Izumo (71,568▲)........47,700
Joetsu........†126,474
Jōyō (★Ōsaka)........58,923
Kadoma (★Ōsaka)........†142,167
Kaga (61,599▲)........47,400
Kagoshima (1980 C)........505,077
Kainan........53,250
Kaizuka (★Ōsaka)........79,506
Kakamigahara........†112,802
Kakegawa (61,731▲)........38,600
Kakogawa (★Ōsaka) (1980 C)........212,232
Kamagaya (★Tōkyō)........63,288
Kamaishi........68,981
Kamakura (★Tōkyō)........†173,331
Kameoka (58,184▲)........36,400
Kamifukuoka (★Tōkyō)........58,332
Kanazawa (1980 C)........417,681
Kanonji (44,131▲)........31,700
Kanoya (67,951▲)........38,500
Kanuma (81,799▲)........55,800
Karatsu........75,224
Kariya (★Nagoya)........†103,643
Karuizawa........13,951
Kasai (50,161▲)........30,600
Kasaoka (63,413▲)........42,700
Kashihara (★Ōsaka)........†105,691
Kashiwa (★Tōkyō) (1980 C)........239,199
Kashiwara (★Ōsaka)........63,586
Kashiwazaki (80,351▲)........53,500
Kasuga (★Fukuoka)........55,160
Kasugai (★Nagoya) (1980 C)........244,114
Kasukabe (★Tōkyō)........†151,083
Katano (★Ōsaka)........52,732
Katsuta........79,996
Kawachi-nagano (★Ōsaka)........66,936
Kawagoe (★Tōkyō)........259,317
Kawaguchi (★Tōkyō) (1980 C)........379,357
Kawanishi (★Ōsaka)........†128,861

Kawanoe........35,961
Kawasaki (★Tōkyō) (1980 C)........1,040,698
Kazo (45,183▲)........27,900
Kesennuma........66,616
Kimitsu........76,016
Kiryū........†132,950
Kisarazu........†108,065
Kishiwada (★Ōsaka)........†179,038
Kitaibaraki (44,332▲)........33,500
Kitakami (48,759▲)........28,200
Kitakyūshū (1980 C)
(★1,515,000)........1,065,084
Kitami (91,519▲)........73,000
Kitamoto (★Tōkyō)........46,632
Kiyose (★Tōkyō)........60,574
Kobayashi........38,325
Kōbe (★★Ōsaka) (1980 C)........1,367,392
Kōchi (1980 C)........300,830
Kodaira (★Tōkyō)........†156,758
Kōfu........†197,803
Koga (★Tōkyō)........55,973
Koganei (★Tōkyō)........†103,487
Kokubunji (★Tōkyō)........88,159
Komae (★Tōkyō)........70,043
Komaki (★Nagoya)........†101,299
Komatsu........†103,606
Komatsushima (42,203▲)........32,300
Kōnan........90,426
Kōnosu (★Tōkyō)........51,632
Kōriyama (1980 C) (286,497▲)........195,700
Koshigaya (★Tōkyō) (1980 C)........223,243
Kudamatsu (★★Tokuyama)........55,825
Kuki (★Tōkyō)........45,797
Kumagaya........†134,347
Kumamoto (1980 C)........525,613
Kunitachi (★Tōkyō)........64,495
Kurashiki (1980 C)........403,785
Kurayoshi (50,785▲)........34,800
Kure (★★Hiroshima) (1980 C)........234,550
Kurume (1980 C)........216,974
Kusatsu (★Ōsaka)........64,873
Kushiro (1980 C)........214,694
Kuwana........83,440
Kyōto (★★Ōsaka) (1980 C)........1,472,993
Machida (★Tōkyō) (1980 C)........295,354
Maebashi (1980 C)........265,171
Maizuru (97,780▲)........82,600
Marugame........65,662
Masuda (50,734▲)........34,400
Matsubara (★Ōsaka)........†135,741
Matsudo (★Tōkyō) (1980 C)........400,870
Matsue........†134,190
Matsumoto........†190,780
Matsuyama (1980 C)........401,682
Matsuzaka (112,870▲)........†81,800
Mihara........83,679
Miki (★Ōsaka) (55,731▲)........41,200
Minamiashigara........36,928
Minō (★Ōsaka)........79,621
Mino-kamo........37,524
Misato (★Tōkyō)........79,355
Misawa (37,437▲)........28,600
Mishima (★★Numazu)........89,248
Mitaka (★Tōkyō)........†166,514
Mito (1980 C)........215,563
Mitsuke (40,954▲)........30,900
Miura........47,888
Miyako........61,912
Miyakonojō (127,528▲)........†82,200
Miyazaki (1980 C)........264,858
Mizusawa (52,266▲)........34,700
Mobara........64,942
Mōka (47,345▲)........20,700
Mombetsu (32,825▲)........28,000
Moriguchi (★Ōsaka)........†164,716
Morioka (1980 C)........229,123
Moriyama........41,439
Mukō (★Ōsaka)........45,886
Muroran (★220,000)........†162,731
Musashi-murayama (★Tōkyō)........50,842
Musashino (★Tōkyō)........†138,874
Mutsu........44,646
Nagahama........54,064
Nagano (1980 C) (324,360▲)........244,300
Nagaoka........†178,201
Nagaokakyo (★Ōsaka)........65,557
Nagareyama (★Tōkyō)........†103,864
Nagasaki (1980 C)........447,091
Nagoya (1980 C) (★3,700,000)........2,087,884
Naha (1980 C)........295,801
Nakama (★Kitakyūshū)........43,145
Nakatsu (59,111▲)........44,200
Nakatsugawa (51,183▲)........36,800
Nanao (49,493▲)........38,800
Nankoku (42,832▲)........25,500
Nara (★Ōsaka) (1980 C)........297,893
Narashino (★Tōkyō)........†120,257
Narita (50,915▲)........30,500
Naruto (61,959▲)........50,600
Natori (46,730▲)........29,700
Naze........46,335
Nemuro........45,817
Neyagawa (★Ōsaka) (1980 C)........255,864
Nichinan (52,171▲)........38,200
Niigata (1980 C)........457,783
Niihama........†133,178
Niitsu (58,970▲)........42,900
Niiza (★Tōkyō)........†119,991
Nikkō........26,279
Nishinomiya (★Ōsaka)
(1980 C)........410,329
Nishio (82,524▲)........62,600
Nishiwaki........38,108
Nobeoka........†136,572
Noboribetsu (★Muroran)........50,885
Noda (★Tōkyō)........78,193
Nōgata........58,551
Noshiro (59,215▲)........43,600
Numata (45,255▲)........32,000
Numazu (1980 C) (★435,000)........203,699
Obihiro........†150,337
Ōbu (★Nagoya)........56,211
Ōda........37,449
Ōdate (71,828▲)........50,200
Odawara........†177,047
Ōfunato (39,632▲)........32,700
Ōgaki........†141,877

Ōita (1980 C)........360,484
Ojiya (44,375▲)........26,900
Ōkawa........50,395
Okaya........61,776
Okayama (1980 C)........545,737
Okazaki (1980 C)........262,370
Okegawa (★Tōkyō)........48,034
Okinawa........91,347
Ōme (★Tōkyō)........86,152
Ōmi-hachiman (★Ōsaka)
(51,537▲)........34,100
Ōmiya (★Tōkyō) (1980 C)........354,082
Ōmura (60,919▲)........44,200
Ōmuta (★225,000)........†163,436
Ōno *(Fukui pref.)* (41,918▲)........25,800
Ōno *(Hyōgo pref.)*........40,576
Onojo (★Fukuoka)........52,169
Onoda (★Ube)........43,804
Onomichi........†102,190
Ōsaka (1980 C) (★15,200,000)........2,648,158
Ōta........†120,472
Ōtake........38,457
Otaru........†185,737
Ōtawara (42,332▲)........22,900
Ōtsu (★Ōsaka) (1980 C)........215,318
Ōtsuki........36,766
Oyama (125,565▲)........†81,000
Rumoi........36,882
Ryūgasaki (40,565▲)........25,000
Sabae (57,252▲)........45,700
Saga........†162,038
Sagamihara (★Tōkyō) (1980 C)........439,257
Saijō (52,615▲)........39,100
Saiki (52,863▲)........42,200
Sakado (★Tōkyō)........51,230
Sakai (★Ōsaka) (1980 C)........810,120
Sakaide........67,624
Sakaiminato........35,821
Sakata (101,454▲)........†73,900
Saku (56,143▲)........32,500
Sakura (★Tōkyō) (80,804▲)........61,500
Sakurai (54,314▲)........42,800
Sanda (★Ōsaka)........35,261
Sanjō........81,806
Sano........75,844
Sapporo (1980 C)
(★1,450,000)........1,401,758
Sasebo (1980 C)........251,188
Sawara (48,670▲)........26,000
Sayama (★Tōkyō)........†121,433
Seki........53,881
Sendai *(Kagoshima pref.)*
(61,788▲)........34,700
Sendai *(Miyagi pref.)*
(1980 C) (★925,000)........664,799
Sennan (★Ōsaka)........46,741
Seto........†119,473
Settsu (★Ōsaka)........76,704
Shibata (74,025▲)........48,700
Shibukawa........47,071
Shijōnawate (★Ōsaka)........52,368
Shimabara (45,179▲)........34,000
Shimada........68,820
Shimizu (★★Shizuoka)
(1980 C)........241,578
Shimminato (★Takaoka)........44,700
Shimodate (57,778▲)........36,500
Shimonoseki (★★Kitakyūshū)
(1980 C)........268,964
Shingū........39,023
Shinjō (42,227▲)........28,100
Shiogama (★Sendai)........59,235
Shiojiri (47,421▲)........29,200
Shirakawa (42,685▲)........32,300
Shizuoka (1980 C) (★735,000)........458,342
Sōja........47,027
Sōka (★Tōkyō)........†186,759
Suita (★Ōsaka) (1980 C)........332,413
Sukagawa (54,922▲)........33,700
Sumoto (44,137▲)........35,700
Suwa........49,594
Suzaka........49,513
Suzuka (152,431▲)........†106,900
Tachikawa (★Tōkyō)........†142,793
Tagajō (★Sendai)........44,862
Tajimi........68,901
Takaishi (★Ōsaka)........66,824
Takamatsu (1980 C)........316,662
Takaoka (★220,000)........†174,334
Takarazuka (★Ōsaka)........†179,394
Takasago (★Ōsaka)........77,080
Takasaki (1980 C)........221,432
Takatsuki (★Ōsaka) (1980 C)........340,722
Takawa........61,464
Takayama........60,504
Takefu (65,012▲)........48,700
Takehara........36,273
Takikawa........50,090
Tama (★Tōkyō)........65,466
Tamana (42,837▲)........28,100
Tamano........78,516
Tanabe (66,999▲)........51,800
Tanashi (★Tōkyō)........67,433
Tatebayashi........66,410
Tateyama (56,139▲)........40,700
Tatsuno........39,646
Tendō (48,082▲)........27,900
Tenri (62,909▲)........45,200
Toba........29,346
Tochigi........83,189
Toda (★Tōkyō)........77,137
Tokai (★Nagoya)........95,457
Tōkamachi (50,211▲)........33,400
Toki........63,324
Tokoname........54,865
Tokorozawa (★Tōkyō) (1980 C)........236,477
Tokushima (1980 C)........249,343
Tokuyama (★255,000)........†111,347
•TŌKYŌ (1980 C)
(★25,800,000)........8,349,209
Tomakomai........†146,088
Tomioka (46,821▲)........29,200
Tondabayashi (★Ōsaka)........91,393
Toride (★Tōkyō)........52,816
Tosu........50,733
Tottori........†128,789
Towada (54,365▲)........27,900

Toyama (1980 C)........305,054
Toyoake (★Nagoya)........45,837
Toyohashi (1980 C)........304,274
Toyokawa........†102,484
Toyonaka (★Ōsaka) (1980 C)........403,185
Toyooka (46,210▲)........33,000
Toyota (1980 C)........281,609
Tsu........†144,587
Tsubame........43,265
Tsuchiura........†110,912
Tsuruga........60,205
Tsuruoka (95,932▲)........74,600
Tsushima........58,241
Tsuyama (79,907▲)........56,500
Ube (★222,000)........†167,732
Ueda........†110,340
Ueno (59,716▲)........42,500
Uji (★Ōsaka)........†150,869
Uozu........48,419
Urawa (★Tōkyō) (1980 C)........358,180
Usa (50,677▲)........25,400
Usuki (39,163▲)........28,200
Utsunomiya (1980 C)........377,748
Uwajima........70,428
Wakayama (1980 C)........401,462
Wakkanai........55,464
Warabi (★Tōkyō)........76,311
Yachiyo (★Tōkyō)........†132,989
Yaizu........†103,544
Yamagata (1980 C)........236,984
Yamaguchi (111,725▲)........†80,800
Yamato (★Tōkyō)........†165,858
Yamato-kōriyama (★Ōsaka)........71,001
Yamato-takada (★Ōsaka)........58,637
Yame........38,843
Yao (★Ōsaka) (1980 C)........272,706
Yashio (★Tōkyō)........56,127
Yatsushiro (107,200▲)........†80,000
Yawata (★Ōsaka)........50,131
Yawatahama (45,259▲)........34,700
Yokkaichi (1980 C)........255,442
Yokohama (★★Tōkyō)
(1980 C)........2,773,322
Yokosuka (★Tōkyō) (1980 C)........421,112
Yonago........†125,291
Yonezawa (91,974▲)........71,400
Yono (★Tōkyō)........71,044
Yūbari........50,131
Yukuhashi (53,750▲)........39,300
Zama (★Tōkyō)........80,562
Zushi (★Tōkyō)........56,298

JERSEY

1976 C........74,470

•ST. HELIER (★45,000)........26,343

JORDAN / Al-Urdunn

1979 E........2,152,273

Al-'Aqabah ('Aqaba)........26,986
Al-Karak........11,805
Al-Khalīl (Hebron) (††1971 E)........43,000
Al-Mafraq (1973 E)........15,500
•AMMĀN........648,587
Arīḩā (Jericho) (††1967 C)........6,829
Ar-Ramthā (1973 E)........19,000
As-Salt........32,866
Az-Zarqā'........215,687
Bayt Laḩm (Bethlehem)
(††1971 E)........25,000
Irbid........112,864
Janīn (††1971 E)........20,000
Jerusalem (★Jerusalem, Israel)
(††1976 E)........90,000
Ma'ān........11,308
Nābulus (††1971 E)........64,000

††Located in area occupied by Israel in 1967. See note under Israel.

KAMPUCHEA / Kâmpŭchéa Prâchéathipâtéyy

1962 C........5,728,711

Battambang........38,780
Kompong Cham........28,532
•PHNUM PÉNH........393,995

KENYA

1979 C........15,322,000

Eldoret........50,000
Kisumu........150,000
Mombasa........342,000
•NAIROBI........835,000
Nakuru........93,000
Nyeri........36,000
Thika........41,000

KOREA, NORTH / Chosŏn Minjujuŭi In'min Konghwaguk

1967 E........12,700,000

Aoji (1944 C)........39,616
Ch'ŏngjin........265,000
Haeju........115,000
Hamhŭng (1944 C)........112,184
Hŭngnam (1944 C)........143,600
Kaesŏng........140,000
Kilchu (1944 C)........30,026
Kimch'aek (Sŏngjin)........265,000
Najin (1944 C)........34,338
Namp'o (Chinnamp'o)........130,000
Ongjin (1949 C)........32,965
Pukch'ŏng (1944 C)........30,709
•P'YONGYANG........840,000
Sariwŏn (1944 C)........42,957
Sinŭiju........165,000
Songnim (1944 C)........53,035
Tanch'ŏn (1944 C)........32,761
Wŏnsan........215,000

KOREA, SOUTH / Taehan-Min'guk

1978 E........37,019,000

Andong (101,494▲)........85,000
Anyang (★Seoul)........187,887
Bucheon (★Seoul)........163,341
Ch'angwŏn........70,707
Chech'ŏn (80,124▲)........55,400
Cheju (152,486▲)........83,100
Chinhae........108,730
Chinju........174,918
Ch'ŏnan (109,324▲)........76,800
Ch'ŏngju........223,016
Chŏngŭp (1975 C) (54,864▲)........37,600
Chŏnju........348,053
Ch'unch'ŏn........152,606
Ch'ungju (110,091▲)........76,500
Chungmu........71,511
Inch'ŏn (★★Seoul)........936,497
Iri (132,272▲)........109,800
Kangnŭng (102,153▲)........67,100
Kimch'ŏn (70,348▲)........53,200
Kumi........89,612
Kunsan........167,422
Kwangju........694,646
Kyŏngju (113,921▲)........68,100
Masan........391,874
Mokp'o........210,922
Namwŏn (55,043▲)........37,900
P'ohang (1975 C) (134,404▲)........110,000
Pusan........2,879,570
Pyŏngtaek........56,324
Samch'ŏnp'o (61,701▲)........37,100
Sangju (55,242▲)........29,500
Seongnam (★Seoul)........324,064
•SEOUL (SŎUL) (1979 E)
(★10,775,000)........8,114,000
Sŏkch'o........71,737
Songjŏng (47,070▲)........29,900
Sunch'ŏn (114,588▲)........76,900
Suwŏn (★Seoul)........266,135
Taegu........1,487,098
Taejŏn........508,574
Ŭijŏngbu (★Seoul)........117,849
Ulsan (364,456▲)........247,000
Wŏnju........131,047
Yŏngju (1975 C) (70,793▲)........50,800
Yŏsu........151,337

KUWAIT / Al-Kuwayt

1975 C........994,837

Abraq Khīţān (★Kuwait)........59,443
Al-Farwānīyah (★Kuwait)........44,875
Al-Jahrah (★Kuwait)........52,302
As-Sālimīyah (★Kuwait)........113,943
Ḩawallī (★Kuwait)........130,565
•KUWAIT (Al-Kuwayt)
(★780,000)........78,116

LAOS / Lao

1973 E........3,181,000

Louangphrabang........43,000
Pakxé........44,860
Savannakhet........50,691
Sayaboury........13,760
•VIANGCHAN (VIENTIANE)........174,229

LEBANON / Al-Lubnān

1970 E........2,126,355

Ba'labakk (Baalbek)........16,000
•BEIRUT (BAYRŪT)
(★1,010,000)........474,870
Şaydā (Sidon)........34,000
Şūr (Tyre)........12,500
Ţarābulus (Tripoli)........157,320
Zaḩlah........29,500

LESOTHO

1972 E........972,000

•MASERU........17,000

LIBERIA

1974 C........1,503,368

Buchanan........23,994
•MONROVIA........204,210

LIBYA / Lībiyā

1970 E........1,938,000

Ajdābiyah (1964 C)........15,400
Beida (1964 C)........12,800
Benghāzī (Bengasi)........170,000
Darnah (Derna) (1964 C)........21,400
Misrātah........44,000
•TRIPOLI (ŢARĀBULUS)........264,000
Ţubruq (Tobruk) (1964 C)........15,900

LIECHTENSTEIN

1977 E........24,715

•VADUZ........4,704

LUXEMBOURG

1976 E........358,000

Bettembourg........7,100
Clervaux (1970 C)........1,428
Diekirch........5,500
Differdange
(★Esch-sur-Alzette)........18,000
Dudelange........14,600
Echternach (1970 C)........3,792
Esch-sur-Alzette (★98,000)........27,600
Ettelbruck........6,100
•LUXEMBOURG (★110,000)........79,300
Pétange (★★Longwy, France)........12,100
Sanem (★Esch-sur-Alzette)........10,900
Wtilz (1970 C)........3,920

C Census. E Official estimate. UE Unofficial estimate.
L Population within municipal limits of year specified. • Largest city in country.

★ Population or designation of metropolitan area, including suburbs (see headnote).
▲ Population of an entire municipality, commune, or district, including rural area.
‡† Year of information specified at start of country.

MACAO

1970 C 248,636
•MACAO (*248,636) 241,413

MADAGASCAR / Madagasikara

1977 E 8,520,000
•ANTANANARIVO (TANANARIVE) 484,000
Antsirabe (85,000▴) 45,000
Diégo-Suarez (Antsirane) 43,000
Fianarantsoa 73,000
Majunga 71,000
Manakara (1972 E) (25,070▴) 23,225
Marovoay (1972 E) 20,780
Tamatave 83,000
Tuléar 49,000

MALAWI

1977 C 5,561,821
•Blantyre 229,000
LILONGWE 102,924
Mzuzu 16,000
Zomba 16,000

MALAYSIA

1970 C 10,319,324
Alor Setar (*85,748) 66,179
Ayer Itam (*Pinang) 25,640
Batu Pahat 53,291
Bentong 22,683
Bukit Mertajam 26,631
Butterworth (**Pinang) 61,187
Chukai 12,514
George Town (Pinang) (*450,000) 270,019
Ipoh (*257,309) 247,689
Johor Baharu (*Singapore) 136,229
Kajang 21,950
Kampar 26,591
Kangar 8,758
Kelang 113,607
Keluang 43,272
Kota Baharu (*69,756) 55,052
Kota Kinabalu (Jesselton) 40,939
•KUALA LUMPUR (*750,000) 451,728
Kuala Terengganu (*59,494) 53,353
Kuantan 43,358
Kuching 63,535
Kulim 18,505
Melaka (Malacca) (*99,782) 86,357
Miri 35,702
Muar (Bandar Maharani) 61,218
Petaling Jaya (*Kuala Lumpur) 93,447
Sandakan 42,413
Segamat 17,796
Seremban (*90,062) 79,915
Sibu 50,635
Sungai Petani 35,959
Sungai Siput 21,383
Taiping 54,645
Tawau 24,247
Telok Anson 44,524

MALDIVES

1978 C 143,046
•MALE 29,555

MALI

1972 E 5,257,000
•BAMAKO (1976 C) 404,022
Gao 17,000
Kati (1971 E) 13,800
Kayes 37,000
Kita (1971 E) 11,700
Koulikoro 15,000
Koutiala 16,000
Mopti 43,000
Nioro du Sahel (1971 E) 13,200
San 18,000
Ségou 40,000
Sikasso 29,000
Tombouctou (Timbuktu) (1971 E) 11,900

MALTA

1979 E 346,970
Birkirkara (*Valletta) 16,832
Cospicua (*Valletta) 9,440
Gzira (*Valletta) 10,046
Hamrun (*Valletta) 13,875
Msida (*Valletta) 12,448
Paola (*Valletta) 11,974
Qormi (*Valletta) 15,784
Rabat 11,823
Sliema (*Valletta) 20,095
•VALLETTA (*215,000) 14,042
Victoria (*Gozo I.*) 5,249
Zabbar (*Valletta) 10,366
Zejtun 10,252

MARTINIQUE

1974 C 324,832
•FORT-DE-FRANCE (*113,556) 98,807
Le Lamentin (23,145▴) 7,558
Saint-Pierre 5,358
Schœlcher (*Fort-de-France) (14,749▴) 13,792

MAURITANIA / Mauritanie

1971 E 1,190,000
Atar (1967 E) 8,500
Kaédi (1967 E) 10,000
Nouadhibou (1966 E) 11,000
•NOUAKCHOTT 35,000

MAURITIUS

1978 E 924,663
Beau Bassin (*Port Louis) 83,714
Curepipe (*Port Louis) 54,356
•PORT LOUIS (*405,000) 142,853
Quatre Bornes (*Port Louis) 53,835
Vacoas-Phoenix (*Port Louis) 51,793

MEXICO / México

1976 E 62,329,000

States

Aguascalientes 430,000
Baja California Norte 1,253,000
Baja California Sur 181,000
Campeche 337,000
Chiapas 1,933,000
Chihuahua 2,000,000
Coahuila 1,334,000
Colima 317,000
Distrito Federal (Federal District) 8,906,000
Durango 1,122,000
Guanajuato 2,811,000
Guerrero 2,013,000
Hidalgo 1,409,000
Jalisco 4,157,000
México 6,245,000
Michoacán 2,805,000
Morelos 866,000
Nayarit 699,000
Nuevo León 2,344,000
Oaxaca 2,337,000
Puebla 3,055,000
Querétaro 618,000
Quintana Roo 131,000
San Luis Potosí 1,527,000
Sinaloa 1,714,000
Sonora 1,414,000
Tabasco 1,054,000
Tamaulipas 1,901,000
Tlaxcala 498,000
Veracruz 4,917,000
Yucatán 904,000
Zacatecas 1,097,000

Cities (1970 C)

Acámbaro 32,257
Acaponeta 11,844
Acapulco [de Juárez] (1978 E) 421,100
Acayucan 21,173
Actopan 11,037
Agua Dulce 21,060
Agua Prieta 20,754
Aguascalientes (1978 E) 247,800
Alvarado 15,792
Ameca 21,018
Amecameca [de Juárez] 16,276
Apatzingán 44,849
Apizaco 21,189
Arandas 18 934
Arriaga 13,193
Atlixco 41,967
Atotonilco el Alto 16,271
Autlán de Navarro 20,398
Caborca 20,771
Campeche (1978 E) 103,600
Cananea 17,518
Cárdenas 15,643
Celaya (1978 E) 114,400
Cerro Azul 20,259
Chihuahua (1978 E) 369,500
Chilpancingo [de los Bravos] 36,193
Cholula [de Rivadabia] 15,399
Ciudad Acuña 30,276
Ciudad Camargo 24,030
Ciudad Chetumal 23,685
Ciudad del Carmen 34,656
Ciudad de Valles 47,587
Ciudad Guzmán 48,166
Ciudad Hidalgo 24,692
Ciudad Ixtepec 14,025
Ciudad Jiménez 18,095
Ciudad Juárez (**El Paso, Tex.) (1978 E) 597,100
Ciudad Lerdo (*Torreón) 19,803
Ciudad Madero (*Tampico) (1978 E) 135,100
Ciudad Mante 51,247
Ciudad Melchor Múzquiz 18,868
Ciudad Mendoza (*Orizaba) 18,696
Ciudad Obregón (1978 E) 173,000
Ciudad Serdán 9,581
Ciudad Victoria (1978 E) 121,400
Coatepec 21,542
Coatzacoalcos (1978 E) 120,100
Colima 58,450
Comalcalco 14,963
Comitán [de Domínguez] 21,249
Córdoba (1978 E) 116,100
Cortazar 25,794
Cosamaloapan 19,766
Cumauhtéoc 26,598
Cuautla 13,946
Cuernavaca (1978 E) 226,600
Culiacán (1978 E) 302,200
Delicias 52,446
Dolores Hidalgo 16,849
Durango (1978 E) 218,600
Ecatepec de Morelos (*Mexico City) 11,899
El Grullo 10,538
Empalme 24,927
Encarnación de Díaz 10,474
Ensenada 77,687
Escuinapa de Hidalgo 16,442
Fresnillo [de González Echeverría] 44,475
Garza García (*Monterrey) 20,934
Gómez Palacio (**Torreón) (1978 E) 100,200
Guadalajara (1978 E) (*2,350,000) 1,813,100
Guadalupe (*Monterrey) 51,899
Guamúchil 17,151
Guanajuato 36,809
Guasave 26,080
Guaymas 57,492
Hermosillo (1978 E) 299,700
Hidalgo del Parral 57,619
Huajuapan de León 13,822
Huamantla 15,565
Huatabampo 18,506
Huauchinango 16,826
Huixtla 15,737
Iguala 45,355
Irapuato (1978 E) 155,600
Izúcar de Matamoros 21,164
Jacona de Plancarte 22,724
Jalapa Enríquez (1978 E) 191,100
Jalostotitlán 11,719
Jerez de García Salinas 20,325
Juchitán [de Zaragoza] 30,218
La Barca 18,055
Lagos de Moreno 33,782
La Paz 46,011
La Piedad [Cavadas] 34,963
Las Choapas 20,166
Léon [de los Aldamas] (1978 E) 590,000
Linares 24,456
Loma Bonita 15,804
Los Mochis (1978 E) 111,800
Los Reyes 19,452
Magdalena 10,281
Manzanillo 20,777
Martínez de la Torre 17,203
Matamoros (**Brownsville, Tex.) (1978 E) 186,500
Matamoros de la Laguna 15,125
Matehuala 28,799
Matías Romero 13,200
Mazatlán (1978 E) 177,700
Meoqui 12,308
Mérida (1978 E) 263,200
Mesa de Tijuana (*San Diego, Calif.) 50,094
Mexicali (1978 E)(*355,000) 338,400
•MÉXICO CITY (CIUDAD DE MÉXICO) (1978 E) (*14,400,000) 8,988,200
Minatitlán (1978 E) 112,600
Mineral del Monte 8,887
Monclova (1978 E) 130,900
Montemorelos 18,642
Monterrey (1978 E) (*1,925,000) 1,054,000
Morelia (1978 E) 239,400
Moroleón 25,620
Motul de Felipe Carrillo Puerto 12,949
Navojoa 43,817
Netzahualcóyotl (*Mexico City) 580,438
Nogales (*Sonora*) 52,108
Nogales (*Veracruz*) (*Orizaba) 14,254
Nueva Rosita 34,706
Nuevo Casas Grandes 20,023
Nuevo Laredo (**Laredo, Tex.) (1978 E) 214,200
Oaxaca [de Juárez] (1978 E) 131,200
Ocotlán 35,367
Ojinaga 12,757
Orizaba (1978 E) (*265,000) 118,400
Pachuca [de Soto] (1978 E) 105,200
Pánuco 14,277
Papantla [de Olarte] 26,773
Parras de la Fuente 18,707
Pátzcuaro 17,299
Pénjamo 9,245
Piedras Negras 41,033
Poza Rica de Hidalgo (1978 E) 188,900
Progreso 17,518
Puebla [de Zaragoza] (1978 E) 678,000
Puerto Vallarta 24,155
Puruándiro 9,956
Querétaro (1978 E) 176,200
Reynosa (1978 E) 218,700
Río Bravo 39,018
Rioverde 16,804
Romita 11,947
Rosario 10,276
Sabinas 20,538
Sabinas Hidalgo 17,439
Sahuayo 28,727
Salamanca 61,039
Salina Cruz 22,004
Saltillo (1978 E) 245,700
Salvatierra 18,975
San Andrés Tuxtla 24,267
San Cristóbal de las Casas 25,700
San Francisco del Oro 12,116
San Francisco del Rincón 27,079
San Juan de los Lagos 19,570
San Juan del Río 15,422
San Juan Teotihuacán (*Mexico City) 2,238
San Luis de la Paz 12,654
San Luis Potosí (1978 E) 315,200
San Luis Río Colorado 49,990
San Martín Texmelucan 23,355
San Miguel de Allende 24,286
San Miguel el Alto 7,909
San Nicolás de los Garzas (*Monterrey) 28,803
San Pedro de las Colonias 26,882
Santa Ana Chiautempan 12,327
Santa Bárbara 16,978
Santa Cruz de Juventino Rosas 15,859
Santa Inés Zacatelco 14,117
Santa Rosalía 7,356
Santiago Ixcuintla 17,321
Sayula 14,339
Silao 31,825
Sombrerete 11,077
Tala 15,744
Tamazula de Gordiano 13,521
Tamazunchale 12,302
Tampico (1978 E) (*420,000) 240,000
Tangancícuaro [de Arista] 12,650
Tapachula 60,620
Taxco de Alarcón 27,089
Tecomán 31,625
Tecuala 12,461
Tehuacán 47,497
Tehuantepec 16,179
Teocaltiche 13,745
Tepatitlán [de Morelos] 29,292
Tepic (1978 E) 133,400
Tequila 11,839
Texcoco [de Mora] (*Mexico City) 18,044
Teziutlán 23,948
Ticul 14,341
Tierra Blanca 22,727
Tijuana (**San Diego, Calif.) (1978 E) 535,000
Tizimín 18,343
Tlalnepantla (*Mexico City) 45,575
Tlapacoyan 13,172
Tlaquepaque (*Guadalajara) 59,760
Tlaxcala [de Xicohténcatl] 9,972
Toluca [de Lerdo] (1978 E) 222,900
Tonalá 15,611
Torreón (1978 E) (*450,000) 268,700
Tulancingo 35,799
Tuxpan (*Jalisco*) 14,693
Tuxpan (*Nayarit*) 20,322
Tuxpan de Rodríguez Cano (*Veracruz*) 33,901
Tuxtepec 17,700
Tuxtla Gutiérrez (1978 E) 101,700
Umán 8,371
Unión de Tula 6,399
Uriangato 14,626
Uruapan [del Progreso] (1978 E) 138,300
Valladolid 14,663
Valle de Santiago 16,517
Valle Hermoso 19,278
Venustiano Carranza 23,624
Veracruz [Llave] (1978 E) (*365,000) 295,300
Vicente Guerrero (*Tlaxcala*) 18,280
Vicente Guerrero (*Veracruz*) (*Orizaba) 11,688
Villa Frontera 25,761
Villahermosa (1978 E) 165,500
Xicotepec de Juárez 12,656
Yautepec 13,952
Yurécuaro 13,611
Yuriria 10,085
Zaachila 7,270
Zacapu 31,989
Zacatecas 50,251
Zacatepec 16,839
Zacoalco de Torres 11,343
Zamora de Hidalgo 57,775
Zapopan (*Guadalajara) 18,512
Zapotiltic 11,733
Zihuatanejo 4,879
Zitácuaro 36,911
Zumpango 12,923

MONACO

1975 E 25,000
•MONACO (*50,000) 25,000

MONGOLIA / Mongol Ard Uls

1969 C 1,197,600
Cecerleg (Tsetserleg) 12,400
Choibalsan 20,500
Darchan 22,800
Jirgalanta (Chovd) 12,400
Süchbaatar 10,000
•ULAN BATOR (URGA) (1970 E) 287,000

MONTSERRAT

1970 C 11,458
•PLYMOUTH 1,267

MOROCCO / Al-Magreb

1971 C 15,379,259
Agadir 61,192
Beni-Mellal 53,826
Berkane 39,015
Berrechid 20,113
•Casablanca (Dar-el-Beida) (*1,575,000) 1,506,373
El-Jadida (Mazagan) 55,501
Essaouira (Mogador) 30,061
Fès (Fez) 325,327
Fkih Ben Salah 26,598
Jerada 30,633
Kenitra 139,206
Khemisset 21,811
Khenifra 25,526
Khouribga 73,667
Ksar-el-Kebir 48,262
Ksar-es-Souk 16,775
Larache 45,710
Marrakech 332,741
Meknès 248,369
Mohammedia (Fedala) 70,392
Nador 32,490
Ouarzazate 11,142
Oued-Zem 33,323
Ouezzane 33,267
Oujda 175,532
RABAT (*540,000) 367,620
Safi 129,113
Salé (**Rabat) 155,557
Sefrou 28,607
Settat 42,325
Sidi Ifni 13,650
Sidi Kacem 26,831
Sidi Slimane 20,398
Tanger (Tangier) 187,894
Taroudant 22,272
Taza 55,157
Tétouan 139,105
Villa Alhucemas (Al Hoceima) 18,686
Youssoufia 22,435

MOZAMBIQUE / Moçambique

1970 C 8,168,933
Beira 110,752
Inhambane 24,090
João Belo 63,494
•MAPUTO (LOURENÇO MARQUES) 341,922
Nampula 120,188
Quelimane 71,289
Tete 51,453
Villa Cabral 41,251

NAMIBIA

1970 C 722,867
Gobabis 4,428
Keetmanshoop 10,297
Lüderitz 6,642
Mariental 4,629
Otjiwarongo 8,018
Rehoboth 5,363
Swakopmund 5,681
Tsumeb 12,338
•WINDHOEK 61,260

NEPAL / Nepāl

1971 C 11,555,983
Bhaktapur 40,112
Birātnagar 45,100
•KATHMANDU (*215,000) 150,402
Lalitpur (*Katmandu) 59,049
Nepālganj 23,523

NETHERLANDS / Nederland

1980 E 14,091,014

(*Includes 1,546 persons with no fixed residence in any province*)

Provinces

Drenthe 418,479
Dronten 19,658
Friesland 583,989
Gelderland 1,694,416
Groningen 553,709
Lelystad 38,971
Limburg 1,069,038
North Brabant (Noord-Brabant) 2,051,195
North Holland (Noord-Holland) 2,307,646
Overijssel 1,018,208
Southern IJsselmeer Polders (Zuidelijke IJsselmeerpolders) (not part of any province) 6,872
South Holland (Zuid-Holland) 3,083,555
Utrecht 895,464
Zeeland 348,268

Cities

Aalsmeer 20,486
Alkmaar (*107,000) 71,245
Almelo 63,381
Alphen aan den Rijn 51,780
Amersfoort (*128,678) 88,097
Amstelveen (*Amsterdam) 69,488
•AMSTERDAM (*1,810,000) 716,919
Apeldoorn 138,164
Arnhem (*287,305) 127,846
Assen 45,036
Bergen op Zoom 43,715
Beverwijk (*Amsterdam) 35,980
Breda (*151,236) 117,259
Brunssum (*Heerlen) 26,281
Bussum (*Amsterdam) 35,316
Castricum (*Amsterdam) 22,783
De Bilt (*Utrecht) 32,397
Delft (*The Hague) 83,939
Delfzijl 25,433
Den Helder 61,761
Deventer 64,561
Doetinchem (36,995▴) 27,800
Dordrecht (*195,792) 107,453
Edam-Volendam (*Amsterdam) 23,091
Ede (82,829▴) 43,500
Eindhoven (*369,352) 194,451
Emmen (89,763▴) 35,500
Enschede (*285,000) 143,042
Geldrop (*Eindhoven) 26,474
Geleen (*181,250) 35,371
Goes 30,193
Gorinchem 28,957
Gouda 58,784
Groningen (*200,467) 161,322
Haarlem (*Amsterdam) 158,291
Haarlemmermeer (77,657▴) 10,600
Harderwijk 30,174
Harlingen 15,427
Heemstede (*Amsterdam) 26,729
Heerenveen (36,729▴) 20,400
Heerlen (*267,003) 71,102
Helmond 58,490
Hengelo (**Enschede) 75,216
Hilversum (*Amsterdam) 92,964
Hoensbroek (*Heerlen) 22,748
Hoogeveen (43,645▴) 33,000
Hoorn 39,300
IJmuiden (Velsen) (*Amsterdam) 61,202
Kampen 30,353
Katwijk aan Zee 38,163
Kerkrade (*Heerlen) 47,001
Leeuwarden 84,518
Leiden (*173,386) 103,046
Lelystad (38,971▴) 9,900
Maassluis (*Rotterdam) 32,937
Maastricht (*145,346) 109,285
Meppel 22,377
Middelburg 38,077
Nijmegen (*217,951) 147,614
Oldenzaal 28,134
Oss 43,462

C Census. E Official estimate. UE Unofficial estimate.
L Population within municipal limits of year specified. • Largest city in country.

* Population or designation of metropolitan area, including suburbs (see headnote).
▴ Population of an entire municipality, commune, or district, including rural area.
‡† Year of information specified at start of country.

Papendrecht (★Dordrecht) 24,995
Purmerend (★Amsterdam) 32,565
Renkum (★Arnhem) (34,168▲) 12,600
Rheden (★Arnhem) (48,637▲) 10,100
Ridderkerk (★Rotterdam) 45,908
Rijswijk (★The Hague) 52,605
Roermond 37,539
Roosendaal 54,838
Rotterdam (★1,085,000) 579,194
Schiedam (★Rotterdam) 74,895
's-Hertogenbosch (★183,583) 87,897
Sittard (★★Geleen) 33,702
Sliedrecht 22,504
Sneek 28,457
Soest (★Amersfoort) 40,581
Spijkenisse (★Rotterdam) 36,863
Tegelen (★Venlo) 18,079
Terneuzen (35,393▲) 22,200
THE HAGUE ('s-GRAVENHAGE) (★775,000) 456,886
Tiel 28,919
Tilburg (★216,873) 151,799
Utrecht (★481,875) 237,037
Valkenswaard (★Eindhoven) 27,441
Veendam 28,169
Veenendaal 39,210
Veldhoven (★Eindhoven) 33,382
Venlo (★86,000) 62,595
Vlaardingen (★Rotterdam) 79,531
Vlissingen (Flushing) (45,726▲) 26,200
Voorburg (★The Hague) 44,227
Vught (★'s-Hertogenbosch) 23,582
Waalwijk 28,514
Wageningen 30,447
Wassenaar (★The Hague) 26,989
Weert (38,311▲) 27,800
Winschoten 21,101
Woerden 23,715
Zaanstad (Zaandam) (★Amsterdam) 128,809
Zeist (★Utrecht) 61,532
Zoetermeer (★The Hague) 63,832
Zutphen 31,767
Zwijndrecht (★★Dordrecht) 39,641
Zwolle 82,190

NETHERLANDS ANTILLES / Nederlandse Antillen

1960 C 188,914

Kralendijk *(Bonaire)* (1953 E) 600
Oranjestad *(Aruba)* (1965 E) 14,700
•WILLEMSTAD *(Curaçao)* (★94,133) 43,547

NEW CALEDONIA / Nouvelle-Calédonie

1976 C 133,233

•NOUMEA (★70,600) 56,100

NEW HEBRIDES
see Vanuatu

NEW ZEALAND

1979 E 3,144,700

•Auckland (★775,000) 147,600
Birkenhead (★Auckland) 20,600
Blenheim 17,450
Christchurch (★309,000) 171,300
Dunedin (★113,000) 81,600
East Coast Bays (★Auckland) 24,500
Gisborne (★32,000) 30,000
Hamilton (★97,400) 90,900
Hastings (★★Napier) 35,500
Invercargill (★53,800) 49,900
Lower Hutt (★Wellington) 65,100
Manukau (★Auckland) 143,500
Masterton (★21,200) 19,650
Mount Albert (★Auckland) 28,300
Mount Eden (★Auckland) 19,500
Mount Roskill (★Auckland) 34,800
Mount Wellington (★Auckland) 20,500
Napier (★110,600) 47,900
Nelson (★42,800) 33,100
New Plymouth (★44,700) 38,300
Palmerston North (★64,900) 58,800
Papakura (★Auckland) 22,200
Papatoetoe (★Auckland) 23,100
Porirua (★Wellington) 42,500
Rotorua (★47,400) 37,700
Takapuna (★Auckland) 63,700
Tauranga (★49,000) 34,300
Timaru (★30,100) 29,500
Tokoroa 19,150
Upper Hutt (★Wellington) 31,300
Wainuiomata (★Wellington) (1978 E) 19,650
Waitemata (★Auckland) 81,900
Wanganui (★39,800) 37,500
WELLINGTON (★349,900) 137,600
Whangarei (★39,600) 35,900

NICARAGUA

1978 E 2,451,418

Bluefields 18,252
Chinandega 44,435
Granada 56,232
León 81,647
•MANAGUA 552,900
Masaya 47,276
Matagalpa 26,986
Rivas 16,222

NIGER

1977 E 5,098,000

Maradi 45,900
•NIAMEY 225,300
Tahoua 31,300
Zinder 58,400

NIGERIA

1963 C 55,670,052

Aba (1975 E) 177,000
Abeokuta (1975 E) 253,000
Ado-Ekiti (1975 E) 213,000
Afikpo 36,096
Agege 45,986
Akure 71,106
Awka 48,725
Bauchi 37,778
Benin City (1975 E) 136,000
Bida 55,007
Calabar (1975 E) 103,000
Deba 60,679
Ede (1975 E) 182,000
Effon-Alaiye 67,090
Ejigbo 46,410
Enugu (1975 E) 187,000
Epe 44,268
Gombe 47,265
Gusau 69,231
Ibadan (1975 E) 847,000
Ife (1975 E) 176,000
Igboho 46,776
Ihiala 40,198
Ijebu-Igbo 43,180
Ijebu-Ode 68,543
Ijero Ekiti 41,935
Ikare 61,696
Ikerre (1975 E) 145,000
Ikire 54,022
Ikirun 79,516
Ikorodu 81,024
Ikot Ekpene 38,107
Ila (1975 E) 155,000
Ilawe 80,833
Ilegboro 44,543
Ilesha (1975 E) 224,000
Ilobu 87,223
Ilorin (1975 E) 282,000
Inisa 52,482
Ise Ekiti 45,323
Iseyin (1971 E) 115,000
Iwo (1975 E) 214,000
Jos 90,402
Kaduna (1975 E) 202,000
Kano (1975 E) 399,000
Katsina (1971 E) 109,000
Kishi 42,374
Kumo 64,878
Lafia 53,667
•LAGOS (1975 E) (★1,450,000) 1,060,800
Maiduguri (1975 E) 189,000
Makurdi 53,967
Minna 59,988
Mushin (★Lagos) (1975 E) 197,000
Nguru 43,234
Offa 86,425
Ogbomosho (1975 E) 432,000
Oka 62,761
Ondo 74,343
Onitsha (1975 E) 220,000
Oshogbo (1975 E) 282,000
Owo 89,693
Oyo (1975 E) 152,000
Port Harcourt (1975 E) 242,000
Sapele 61,007
Shagamu 51,371
Shaki 76,290
Shomolu (★Lagos) 64,731
Sokoto 89,817
Ugep 44,945
Warri 55,254
Zaria (1975 E) 224,000

NORWAY / Norge

1979 E 4,073,000

Ålesund 34,744
Arendal (1980 E) (★20,000) 11,400
Bergen (1980 E) (★238,000) 209,000
Bodø 32,163
Drammen (1980 E) (★71,000) 49,700
Eigersund 11,694
Fredrikstad (1980 E) (★48,000) 28,000
Gjøvik 26,150
Grimstad 13,588
Halden 26,810
Hamar 16,053
Hammerfest 7,457
Harstad 21,579
Haugesund 27,081
Horten 13,476
Kongsberg 20,385
Kongsvinger 17,018
Kristiansand 60,722
Kristiansund 18,412
Larvik (1980 E) (★16,500) 8,300
Lillehammer 21,762
Mandal 11,847
Mo (1970 C) 21,033
Molde 20,886
Moss 25,407
Namsos 11,640
Narvik 19,202
Notodden 12,973
•OSLO (1980 E) (★725,000) 454,819
Porsgrunn (★★Skien) (1980 E) 31,365
Ringerike 26,839
Sandefjord 34,405
Sandnes (★Stavanger) (1980 E) 36,200
Sarpsborg (1980 E) (★37,500) 12,100
Skien (1980 E) (★78,815) 47,450
Stavanger (1980 E) (★128,000) 90,000
Steinkjer 20,526
Tønsberg (1980 E) (★35,000) 9,200
Tromsø 45,360
Trondheim 134,683
Vadsø 6,054

OMAN / 'Umān

1962 E 565,000

•Maṭraḥ 14,000
MUSCAT (MASQAṬ) 6,000

PACIFIC ISLANDS TRUST TERRITORY

1973 C 114,773

Island Groups

Caroline Islands 75,394
Mariana Islands (excl. Guam) 14,335
Marshall Islands 25,044

PAKISTAN / Pākistān

1972 C 64,979,732

(excl. population in section of Jammu and Kashmir occupied by Pakistan)

Abbottābād (★47,122) 27,963
Ahmadpur East 43,312
Bahāwalnagar 50,991
Bahāwalpur (★133,782) 115,660
Baldia (★Karāchi) 79,529
Bannu (★43,795) 33,000
Bhakkar 34,638
Burewala 57,741
Campbellpore (★29,172) 21,633
Chakwāl 29,143
Chārsadda 45,555
Chiniot 70,108
Dādu 30,184
Dera Ghāzi Khān 72,343
Dera Ismāīl Khān (★58,778) 57,296
Faisalabad (Lyallpur) 823,343
Gujrānwāla (★360,478) 323,880
Gujrāt 100,333
Gwādar 15,758
Hāfizābād 61,597
Hyderābād (★660,000) 600,796
ISLĀMĀBĀD (★★Rāwalpindi) 77,000
Jacobābād 57,596
Jhang Maghiāna 131,843
Jhelum (★70,157) 63,676
Kamālia 50,934
Kāmoke 50,257
•Karāchi (1975 E) (★4,500,000) 2,800,000
Karāchi Cantonment (★Karāchi) 133,176
Kasūr 102,531
Khānewāl 67,746
Khānpur 49,235
Kohāt (★65,202) 48,096
Lahore (★2,200,000) 2,022,577
Lahore Cantonment (★Lahore) 147,165
Landhi Korangi (★Karāchi) 551,236
Lārkāna 71,893
Leiah 33,549
Mardān (★115,194) 105,157
Miānwāli 48,304
Mīrpur-Khās 81,965
Multān (★538,949) 504,365
Nawābshāh 81,045
New Karāchi No. 1 (★Karāchi) 85,398
New Karāchi No. 2 (★Karāchi) 67,682
Nowshera (★55,916) 31,101
Okāra (★101,052) 84,334
Orangi (★Karāchi) 109,979
Peshāwar (★284,833) 219,562
Quetta (★158,026) 137,659
Rahīmyār Khān (★85,699) 74,262
Rāwalpindi (★725,000) 372,919
Rāwalpindi Cantonment (★Rāwalpindi) 241,890
Sāhiwāl (Montgomery) 106,648
Sargodha (★200,460) 166,391
Shekhūpura 80,560
Shikārpur 70,924
Shujāābād 24,422
Siālkot (★203,650) 183,685
Sibi 19,989
Sukkur 158,781
Turbat 27,671
Wah Cantonment 107,510

PANAMA / Panamá

1970 C †1,472,280

†Includes former Canal Zone

Balboa (★Panamá) 2,569
Balboa Heights (★Panamá) 232
Colón (1976 E) (★82,000) 73,600
David 35,677
Gamboa 2,102
La Chorrera 25,873
•PANAMÁ (1978 E) (★645,000) 439,800
Puerto Armuelles 12,015
San Miguelito (★Panamá) (1977 E) 135,100
Santiago 14,595

PAPUA NEW GUINEA

1977 E 2,905,000

Lae 45,100
Madang 20,100
•PORT MORESBY 106,600
Rabaul 13,400
Wewak 18,100

PARAGUAY

1972 C 2,357,955

•ASUNCIÓN (1978 E) (★655,000) 463,700
Caacupé 7,278
Concepción 19,392
Coronel Oviedo 13,786
Encarnación 23,343
Fernando de la Mora (★Asunción) 36,834
Lambaré (★Asunción) 31,656
Luque (★Asunción) 13,921
Paraguarí 5,036
Pedro Juan Caballero 21,033
Pilar 12,506
Villa Hayes 4,749
Villarrica 17,687

PERU / Perú

1972 C 13,572,052

Arequipa (★304,653) 98,605
Ayacucho (★43,304) 34,593
Barranco (★Lima) 46,449
Barrio Obrero Industrial (★Lima) 238,402
Breña (★Lima) 123,345
Cajamarca 37,608
Callao (★★Lima) 196,919
Cerro de Pasco (★47,178) 35,975
Chiclayo (★189,685) 148,932
Chimbote 159,045
Chorrillos (★Lima) 87,021
Cuzco (★120,881) 67,658
Huacho 36,697
Huancayo (★115,693) 64,777
Huánuco 41,123
Ica 73,883
Iquitos 111,327
Jesús María (★Lima) 82,988
Juliaca 38,475
La Victoria (★Lima) 265,157
•LIMA (★3,250,000) 340,339
Lince (★Lima) 82,749
Magdalena del Mar (★Lima) 54,855
Miraflores (★Lima) 93,926
Pisco 41,429
Piura (★126,702) 81,683
Pucallpa 57,525
Pueblo Libre (★Lima) 76,279
Puno 41,166
Rímac (★Lima) 165,340
San Isidro (★Lima) 61,682
Sullana 60,112
Surco (★Lima) 70,949
Surquillo (★Lima) 89,201
Tacna 55,752
Trujillo (★241,882) 127,535
Tumbes 32,972
Vitarte (★Lima) 54,417

PHILIPPINES / Pilipinas

1975 C 42,070,660

Angeles 151,164
Antipolo (40,944▲) 35,672
Bacolod 223,392
Bacoor (★Manila) 62,225
Baguio 97,449
Baliuag 61,624
Batangas (125,363▲) 18,592
Biñan (★Manila) 67,444
Bocaue 40,577
Butuan (132,682▲) 53,578
Cabanatuan (115,258▲) 32,003
Cadiz (127,653▲) 26,581
Cagayan de Oro (165,220▲) 37,272
Calamba (97,432▲) 33,321
Calapan (55,608▲) 13,982
Caloocan (★Manila) 397,201
Cavite (★160,000) 82,456
Cebu (★500,000) 413,025
Cotabato (67,097▲) 49,134
Dagupan 90,092
Davao (484,678▲) 214,849
General Santos (Dadiangas) (91,154▲) 37,527
Gingoog (66,577▲) 16,590
Iligan (70,075▲) 12,234
Iligan (118,778▲) 10,367
Iloilo 227,027
Iriga (75,885▲) 13,938
Isabela (Basilan) (27,261▲) 7,204
Jolo 37,623
Koronadal (62,764▲) 15,066
La Carlota (40,984▲) 20,251
Laoag (66,259▲) 31,336
Lapu-Lapu 79,484
Las Piñas (★Manila) 81,610
Legazpi (88,378▲) 37,724
Lingayen (59,034▲) 16,096
Lipa (106,094▲) 18,330
Lucena 92,336
Maasin (54,737▲) 12,348
Makati (★Manila) 334,448
Malabon (★Manila) 174,878
Malaybalay (65,198▲) 10,207
Malolos 83,491
Mandaluyong (★Manila) 182,267
Mandaue (★Cebu) 75,904
•MANILA (★5,500,000) 1,479,116
Marawi 63,332
Marikina (★Manila) 168,453
Mati (73,125▲) 18,188
Mecauayan (★Manila) 60,225
Muntinglupa (★Manila) 94,563
Naga 83,337
Navotas (★Manila) 97,098
Olongapo 147,109
Ormoc (89,466▲) 13,075
Ozamiz (71,559▲) 17,372
Pagadian (66,062▲) 28,645
Parañaque (★Manila) 158,974
Pasay (★Manila) 254,999
Pasig (★Manila) 209,915
Puerto Princesa (45,709▲) 18,480
Quezon City (★Manila) 956,864
Roxas (Capiz) (71,305▲) 18,869
Sagay (95,421▲) 32,417
San Carlos (*Negros Occidental Prov.*) (90,982▲) 23,950
San Carlos (*Pangasinan Prov.*) (90,882▲) 12,003
San Fernando (*La Union Prov.*) (61,166▲) 14,133
San Fernando (*Pampanga Prov.*) 98,382
San Juan del Monte (★Manila) 122,492
San Pablo (116,607▲) 42,489
San Pedro 43,439
Santa Cruz 52,672
Santa Rosa (★Manila) 47,639
Tacloban (80,707▲) 63,693
Tagbilaran 37,335
Tagig (★Manila) 73,702
Valenzuela (★Manila) 150,605
Zamboanga (265,023▲) 53,678

POLAND / Polska

1979 E 35,414,000

Będzin (★Katowice) 75,000
Biała Podlaska 38,100
Białystok 218,700
Bielawa (Langenbielau) (★★Dzierżoniów) 32,100
Bielsko-Biała 160,300
Bolesławiec (Bunzlau) 39,200
Brzeg (Brieg) 35,300
Bydgoszcz 343,800
Bytom (Beuthen) (★★Katowice) 231,600
Chełm 51,200
Chojnice 31,100
Chorzów (★★Katowice) 149,900
Częstochowa 232,400
Dąbrowa Górnicza (★Katowice) 137,300
Dzierżoniów (Reichenbach) (★85,000) 35,800
Elbląg (Elbing) 108,100
Ełk (Lyck) 37,300
Gdańsk (Danzig) (★820,000) 449,200
Gdynia (★★Gdańsk) 232,500
Gliwice (Gleiwitz) (★★Katowice) 195,300
Głogów (Glogau) 49,200
Gniezno 61,100
Gorzów Wielkopolski (Landsberg) 102,500
Grudziądz 88,700
Inowrocław 65,100
Jarosław 34,900
Jastrzębie Zdrój 97,800
Jaworzno (★Katowice) 88,200
Jelenia Góra (Hirschberg) 86,000
Kalisz 97,700
•Katowice (★2,590,000) 351,300
Kędzierzyn-Koźle (Heydebreck) 68,700
Kielce 181,000
Knurów (★Katowice) 40,200
Kołobrzeg (Kolberg) 37,500
Konin 65,300
Koszalin (Köslin) 90,000
Kraków (★780,000) 706,100
Krosno 38,000
Kutno 40,500
Legionowo (★Warsaw) 37,200
Legnica (Liegnitz) 88,400
Leszno 47,500
Łódź (★1,025,000) 830,800
Łomża 38,100
Lubin (Lüben) 63,000
Lublin (★345,000) 297,600
Mielec 41,300
Mysłowice (★Katowice) 78,100
Nowa Sól (Neusalz) 38,000
Nowy Sącz 62,600
Nysa (Neisse) 40,700
Olsztyn (Allenstein) 130,400
Opole (Oppeln) 114,000
Ostrowiec Świętokrzyski 62,300
Ostrów Wielkopolski 61,400
Oświęcim 44,200
Otwock (★Warsaw) 47,400
Pabianice (★Łódź) 69,800
Piekary Śląskie (★Katowice) 63,500
Piła (Schneidemühl) 57,200
Piotrków Trybunalski 70,900
Płock 99,800
Poznań (★610,000) 545,600
Pruszków (★Warsaw) 49,000
Przemyśl 60,100
Pszczyna 34,800
Puławy 44,800
Racibórz (Ratibor) 52,900
Radom 187,600
Radomsko 39,900
Ruda Śląska (★Katowice) 156,800
Rybnik 118,200
Rzeszów 116,900
Siedlce 52,500
Siemianowice Śląskie (★Katowice) 77,200
Skarżysko-Kamienna 43,100
Słupsk (Stolp) 84,200
Sopot (Zoppot) (★Gdańsk) 51,800
Sosnowiec (★★Katowice) 241,700
Stalowa Wola 52,200
Starachowice 48,400
Stargard Szczeciński 57,200
Starogard Gdański 43,300
Suwałki 38,500
Świdnica (Schweidnitz) 55,700
Świętochłowice (★Katowice) 57,700
Świnoujście (Swinemünde) 46,000
Szczecin (Stettin) (★425,000) 388,000
Szczecinek (Neustettin) 35,200
Tarnobrzeg 35,200
Tarnów 102,800
Tarnowskie Góry (★Katowice) 65,900
Tczew 52,300
Tomaszów Mazowiecki 62,800
Toruń 170,100
Tychy (★Katowice) 160,700
Wałbrzych (Waldenburg) (★195,000) 132,900
Wałcz (Deutsch Krone) 22,000
WARSAW (WARSZAWA) (★2,080,000) 1,576,600
Wejherowo 41,600
Włocławek 104,400
Wodzisław Śląski 104,500
Wołomin (★Warsaw) 30,600
Wrocław (Breslau) 609,100
Zabrze (Hindenburg) (★★Katowice) 195,000
Zamość 45,700
Żary (Sorau) 34,700
Zawiercie 61,600
Zduńska Wola 38,200
Zgierz (★Łódź) 52,100
Zgorzelec 32,800
Zielona Góra (Grünberg) 98,000
Żyrardów (★Warsaw) 36,700

C Census. E Official estimate. UE Unofficial estimate.
L Population within municipal limits of specified year. • Largest city in country.

★ Population or designation of metropolitan area, including suburbs (see headnote).
▲ Population of an entire municipality, commune, or district, including rural area.
‡† Year of information specified at start of country.

PORTUGAL

1970 C	8,568,703
Almada (★Lisbon)	38,714
Amadora (★Lisbon)	66,189
Angra do Heroísmo (*Azores Is.*)	14,328
Aveiro	20,651
Barreiro (★Lisbon)	53,200
Beja	15,909
Braga	49,693
Bragança	10,001
Coimbra	56,568
Covilhã	27,018
Évora	24,003
Faro	20,687
Funchal (*Madeira Is.*)	40,057
Guimarães	25,113
Horta (*Azores Is.*)	6,025
•LISBON (LISBOA) (1975 E) (★1,950,000)	829,900
Matosinhos (★Porto)	22,475
Montijo (★Lisbon)	25,949
Moscavide (★Lisbon)	21,647
Odivelas (★Lisbon)	25,978
Piedade (★Lisbon)	21,004
Ponta Delgada (*Azores Is.*)	21,262
Portimão	10,389
Porto (Oporto) (1975 E) (★1,150,000)	335,700
Póvoa de Varzim	17,555
Queluz (★Lisbon)	25,913
Santarem	18,069
Setúbal	50,730
Sintra (★Lisbon) (1960 C)	7,705
Vila do Conde	16,390
Vila Nova de Gaia (★Porto)	50,219
Viseu	16,636

PUERTO RICO

1980 C	3,187,570
Adjuntas (18,617▲)	5,184
Aguadilla (52,627▲)	20,879
Aibonito (22,230▲)	9,369
Arecibo (86,660▲)	48,586
Bayamón (★San Juan)	184,854
Cabo Rojo (33,909▲)	10,254
Caguas (★San Juan) (118,020▲)	87,218
Carolina (★San Juan)	147,100
Cataño (★San Juan)	26,318
Cayey (40,927▲)	23,315
Cidra (28,135▲)	6,065
Coamo (30,752▲)	12,834
Corozal (28,218▲)	5,891
Fajardo (32,011▲)	26,845
Guánica (18,784▲)	9,627
Guayama (40,137▲)	21,044
Guayanilla (21,012▲)	6,191
Guaynabo (★San Juan)	65,091
Humacao (45,916▲)	19,135
Isabela (37,451▲)	12,097
Juncos (25,433▲)	7,898
Manatí (36,480▲)	17,254
Mayagüez (★132,814)	82,703
Ponce (★252,420)	161,260
San Germán (32,941▲)	13,093
•SAN JUAN (★1,535,000)	422,701
San Lorenzo (32,333▲)	8,886
San Sebastian (35,877▲)	10,792
Trujillo Alto (★San Juan) (51,389▲)	41,097
Utuado (34,384▲)	11,049
Vega Alta (★San Juan) (28,225▲)	10,584
Vega Baja (★San Juan) (46,841▲)	18,020
Yabucoa (30,589▲)	6,782
Yauco (37,682▲)	14,598

QATAR / Qaṭar

1971 E	160,000
•DOHA (AD-DAWḤAH)	95,000

REUNION / Réunion

1974 C	476,675
Le Port (25,068▲)	21,621
•ST. DENIS (103,512▲)	80,802
St. Pierre (46,060▲)	22,022

RHODESIA see Zimbabwe

ROMANIA / România

1978 E	21,854,622
Aiud	25,929
Alba-Iulia	44,870
Alexandria	39,531
Arad	174,411
Bacău	135,841
Baia-Mare	107,945
Bîrlad	57,954
Bistrița	48,959
Blaj	21,465
Bocşa	21,317
Borşa	25,427
Botoşani	68,325
Brăila	200,435
Braşov	268,226
•BUCHAREST (BUCUREŞTI) (★2,050,000)	1,858,418
Buzău	102,868
Călăraşi	50,601
Caracal	31,433
Caransebeş	28,437
Carei	24,473
Cîmpia Turzii	23,750
Cîmpina	33,554
Cîmpulung	33,329
Cluj	273,199
Codlea	23,691
Constanța (★301,758)	267,612
Craiova	230,721
Cugir	27,892
Curtea de Argeş	26,081
Dej	33,350
Deva	65,009
Dorohoi	22,332
Drobeta-Turnu-Severin	80,200
Făgăraş	35,831
Feteşti	28,257
Focşani	60,038
Galați	252,592
Gheorghe Gheorghiu-Dej	43,282
Giurgiu	53,072
Hunedoara	81,963
Huşi	23,652
Iaşi	278,545
Lugoj	45,957
Lupeni	27,857
Mangalia	30,404
Medgidia	41,792
Mediaş	66,795
Miercurea Ciuc	33,884
Odorheiu Secuiesc	30,756
Oltenița	25,185
Oradea	179,780
Petroşani (★74,000)	41,720
Piatra-Neamț	83,168
Piteşti	133,081
Ploieşti (★270,000)	206,138
Rădăuți	22,750
Reghin	31,035
Reşița	90,664
Rîmnicu-Sărat	29,246
Rîmnicu-Vîlcea	72,915
Roman	53,797
Roşiori de Vede	29,462
Săcele	31,615
Satu-Mare	107,852
Sebeş	26,881
Sfîntu Gheorghe	45,739
Sibiu	157,519
Sighetul Marmației	39,095
Sighişoara	33,359
Slatina	50,683
Slobozia	33,701
Suceava	66,527
Tecuci	37,423
Timişoara	277,779
Tîrgovişte	67,024
Tîrgu-Jiu	67,694
Tîrgu-Mureş	136,679
Tîrnăveni	26,877
Tulcea	66,054
Turda	56,350
Turnu-Măgurele	33,404
Vaslui	42,718
Vulcan	29,216
Zalău	35,734
Zărneşti	24,317

RWANDA

1978 C	4,819,000
Butare	21,700
•KIGALI	117,700
Ruhengeri	16,000

ST. HELENA
(*excl. Dependencies*)

1976 C	5,147
•JAMESTOWN	1,516

ST. KITTS-NEVIS

1970 C	47,457
•BASSETERRE (*St. Kitts*)	13,055
Charlestown (*Nevis*)	1,880

SAINT LUCIA

1978 E	117,500
•CASTRIES	47,600

ST. PIERRE & MIQUELON / Saint-Pierre-et-Miquelon

1974 C	5,840
•ST.-PIERRE	5,232

ST. VINCENT

1970 C	89,129
•KINGSTOWN (★23,782)	17,258

SAN MARINO

1977 E	20,000
•SAN MARINO	4,628

SAO TOME & PRINCIPE / São Tomé e Príncipe

1970 C	73,631
•SÃO TOMÉ	17,380

SAUDI ARABIA / Al-'Arabīyah as-Sa'ūdīyah

1974 C	7,012,642
Abhā	30,150
Ad-Dammām	127,844
Al-Hufūf (Hofuf)	101,271
Al-Jawf (1961 UE)	20,000
Al-Khubar	48,817
Al-Madīnah (Medina)	198,186
Al-Mubarraz	54,325
Al-Qaṭīf (1961 UE)	30,000
At-Tā'if	204,857
Aẓ-Ẓahrān (Dhahran) (1974 UE)	25,000
Buraydah	69,940
Ḥā'il	40,502
Juddah (Jidda)	561,104
Khamīs Mushayṭ	49,581
Mecca (Makkah)	366,801
Najran	47,501
Qal'at Bīshah (1961 UE)	20,000
Qīzān	32,812
•RIYADH (AR-RIYĀḌ)	666,840
Tabūk	74,825
Yanbu' (1961 UE)	20,000

SENEGAL / Sénégal

1976 C	5,085,388
•DAKAR	798,792
Diourbel	51,000
Kaolack	106,899
Rufisque (★Dakar) (1973 E)	54,000
Saint-Louis	88,000
Thiès	117,333
Ziguinchor	73,000

SEYCHELLES

1971 C	52,437
•VICTORIA	13,622

SIERRA LEONE

1974 C	2,730,000
Bo	30,000
Bonthe (1963 C)	6,230
•FREETOWN (★335,000)	274,000
Kenema	15,000
Kissy (★Freetown) (1963 C)	13,143
Koidu (1963 C)	11,706
Lunsar (1963 C)	12,132
Makeni	12,000
Port Loko (1963 C)	5,809

SINGAPORE

1980 E	2,390,800
•SINGAPORE (★2,600,000)	2,390,800

SOLOMON ISLANDS

1976 C	196,823
•HONIARA	14,942

SOMALIA / Somaliya

1972 E	2,941,000
Afgoi (1964 C)	16,575
Berbera (1966 E)	14,000
Hargeisa (1966 E)	42,000
Kismayu (1968 C)	17,872
Marka (Merca) (1967 E)	17,700
•MOGADISHU (MOGADISCIO)	230,000

SOUTH AFRICA / Suid-Afrika

1970 C	21,794,328
Provinces	
Cape (Kaap)	6,827,756
Natal	4,315,847
Orange Free State (Oranje-Vrystaat)	1,749,671
Transvaal	8,901,054
Cities	
Alberton (★Johannesburg)	23,988
Alexandra (★Johannesburg)	57,040
Aliwal North	12,311
Beaufort West	17,862
Bellville (★Cape Town)	49,026
Benoni (★Johannesburg)	151,294
Bethal	17,337
Bethlehem	29,918
Bishop Levis (★Cape Town)	26,386
Bloemfontein (★182,329)	149,836
Boksburg (★Johannesburg)	106,126
Brakpan (★Johannesburg)	73,210
CAPE TOWN (KAAPSTAD) (★1,125,000)	697,514
Carletonville	93,096
Clermont (★Durban)	26,125
Cradock	20,822
De Aar	18,057
Dundee	17,162
Durban (★1,040,000)	736,852
East London (Oos-Londen) (★190,000)	119,727
Edendale (★Pietermaritzburg)	41,194
Edenvale (★Johannesburg)	25,126
Elsies River (★Cape Town)	64,539
Ermelo	19,036
Ga-Rankuwa	45,631
George	24,625
Germiston (★★Johannesburg)	221,972
Goodwood (★Cape Town)	31,592
Graaff-Reinet	22,392
Grahamstown	41,302
Grassy Park (★Cape Town)	32,709
Hammarsdale	21,657
Harrismith	16,082
•Johannesburg (★2,550,000)	654,232
Kempton Park (★Johannesburg)	37,205
Kimberley	105,258
Klerksdorp (★175,000)	63,558
Kroonstad	51,988
Krugersdorp (★Johannesburg)	92,725
Ladysmith	28,920
Mabopane	22,559
Madadeni	32,398
Mafeking	6,515
Mariannhill (★Durban)	22,484
Mdantsane (★East London)	67,501
Middelburg	26,942
Mosselbaai	17,574
Nelspruit	25,092
Newcastle	14,407
Nigel	41,179
Odendaalsrus (★29,026)	15,603
Orkney (★★Klerksdorp)	22,117
Oudtshoorn	26,907
Paarl	49,244
Parow (★Cape Town)	60,768
Parys	17,447
Pietermaritzburg (★160,855)	114,822
Pietersburg	27,174
Port Elizabeth (★475,869)	392,231
Potchefstroom	57,443
Potgietersrus	6,667
PRETORIA (★575,000)	545,450
Queenstown	39,304
Randburg (★Johannesburg)	46,011
Randfontein (★Johannesburg)	50,481
Roodepoort-Maraisburg (★Johannesburg)	115,366
Rustenburg	22,303
Sandton (★Johannesburg)	49,022
Sasolburg (★Vereeniging)	29,056
Soweto (★Johannesburg)	602,043
Springs (★Johannesburg)	142,812
Standerton	21,038
Stellenbosch	29,955
Stilfontein (★Klerksdorp)	70,661
Strand (★Cape Town)	24,503
Tembisa (★Johannesburg)	83,637
Uitenhage (★★Port Elizabeth)	70,517
Umlazi (★Durban)	123,495
Umtata	25,216
Upington	28,632
Vanderbijlpark (★★Vereeniging)	80,375
Vereeniging (★310,188)	172,549
Virginia	46,138
Welkom (★132,880)	67,472
Westonaria (★Johannesburg)	36,253
Witbank	37,456
Worcester	41,198
Zwelitsha	22,131

SOVIET UNION
See Union of Soviet Socialist Republics

SPAIN / España

1978 E	38,141,157
Regions and Provinces	
ANDALUSIA (ANDALUCÍA)	6,560,445
Almería	418,471
Cádiz	1,016,340
Córdoba	751,833
Granada	780,848
Huelva	427,991
Jaén	677,756
Málaga	1,013,346
Sevilla	1,473,860
ARAGON (ARAGÓN)	1,204,244
Huesca	218,364
Teruel	157,454
Zaragoza	828,426
ASTURIAS	1,172,301
Oviedo	1,172,301
BALEARIC IS. (BALEARES)	642,702
Baleares	642,702
BASQUE PROVINCES (VASCONGADAS)	2,192,755
Álava	256,883
Guipúzcoa	714,690
Vizcaya	1,221,182
CANARY IS. (CANARIAS)	1,410,665
Las Palmas	704,389
Santa Cruz de Tenerife	706,276
CATALONIA (CATALUÑA)	6,071,953
Barcelona	4,724,063
Gerona	467,749
Lérida	358,430
Tarragona	521,711
ESTREMADURA (EXTREMADURA)	1,110,457
Badajoz	666,389
Cáceres	444,068
GALICIA	2,895,467
La Coruña	1,126,202
Lugo	418,770
Orense	447,980
Pontevedra	902,515
LEON (LEÓN)	1,156,113
León	549,709
Salamanca	368,833
Zamora	237,571
MURCIA	1,300,878
Albacete	343,868
Murcia	957,010
NAVARRE (NAVARRA)	511,699
Navarra	511,699
NEW CASTILE (CASTILLA LA NUEVA)	6,010,575
Ciudad Real	498,205
Cuenca	226,496
Guadalajara	143,520
Madrid	4,659,478
Toledo	482,876
OLD CASTILE (CASTILLA LA VIEJA)	2,261,956
Ávila	194,913
Burgos	368,302
Logroño	252,110
Palencia	192,102
Santander	515,109
Segovia	153,771
Soria	104,595
Valladolid	481,054
VALENCIA	3,638,947
Alicante	1,142,323
Castellón	430,845
Valencia	2,065,779
Cities (1975 C or ‡1978 E)	
Aguilas (18,900▲)	16,900
Albacete	‡107,725
Alcalá [de Guadaira] (39,593▲)	33,500
Alcalá de Henares (★Madrid)	‡114,788
Alcalá la Real (20,184▲)	9,300
Alcantarilla	21,891
Alcázar de San Juan	26,930
Alcira	35,428
Alcobendas (★Madrid)	‡57,951
Alcorcón (★Madrid)	‡124,348
Alcoy	‡65,078
Algeciras	‡92,933
Algemesí	23,623
Algorta (66,306▲)	‡29,500
Alicante	‡235,868
Almadén	10,312
Almendralejo	22,074
Almería	‡136,720
Andújar (34,459▲)	28,400
Antequera (40,113▲)	27,500
Aranjuez	31,275
Arcos de la Frontera (24,867▲)	15,500
Arizgoiti (Basauri) (★Bilbao) (55,303▲)	‡46,800
Arrecife (*Canary Is.*)	25,201
Ávila	‡38,105
Avilés (★129,000)	‡90,458
Badajoz (112,573▲)	‡89,500
Badalona (★Barcelona)	‡216,041
Baracaldo (★Bilbao)	‡123,178
Barcelona (★3,975,000)	‡1,902,713
Baza (20,113▲)	14,400
Bilbao (★995,000)	‡452,921
Burgos	‡148,487
Burjasot (★Valencia)	30,739
Burriana	23,846
Cabra (20,140▲)	15,900
Cáceres	‡64,539
Cádiz (★230,000)	‡156,328
Camas (★Sevilla)	23,840
Carmona	21,548
Cartagena (165,557▲)	‡135,200
Castellón de la Plana	‡118,648
Chiclana [de la Frontera]	31,711
Cieza	28,228
Ciudad Real	‡48,871
Córdoba	‡276,255
Cornellá (★Barcelona)	‡95,933
Cuenca	‡39,064
Daimiel	16,986
Don Benito	26,117
Dos Hermanas	47,800
Écija (33,505▲)	25,400
Éibar	37,838
Elche (165,203▲)	‡136,400
Elda	‡53,558
El Ferrol del Caudillo (★126,000)	‡90,317
El Puerto de Santa María	‡52,350
Esplugas Llobregat (★Barcelona)	38,110
Figueras	28,102
Gandía (41,565▲)	32,600
Gavá (★Barcelona)	30,586
Gerona	‡85,522
Getafe (★Madrid)	‡128,523
Gijón	‡256,904
Granada	‡229,108
Granollers (★Barcelona)	36,366
Guadalajara	‡49,130
Guadix (19,234▲)	14,900
Guernica y Luno (17,271▲)	11,704
Hellín (22,327▲)	16,109
Hospitalet (★Barcelona)	‡294,280
Huelva	‡125,810
Huesca	‡38,986
Ibiza	20,552
Igualada	30,024
Irún	‡54,781
Jaén	‡91,198
Játiva	22,613
Jerez de la Frontera (183,534▲)	‡137,700
La Coruña	‡228,637
La Línea	‡57,940
Langreo (Sama de Langreo) (63,128▲)	‡10,600
La Orotava (*Canary Is.*) (30,190▲)	9,300
Las Palmas de Gran Canaria (*Canary Is.*)	‡357,158
Leganés (★Madrid)	‡151,353
Léon (★144,000)	‡122,827
Lérida (108,212▲)	‡86,100
Linares (56,356▲)	‡50,520
Logroño	‡104,928
Loja (22,001▲)	11,700
Lorca (65,806▲)	27,400
Lucena	29,373
Lugo (72,686▲)	‡60,900
•MADRID (★4,415,000)	‡3,367,438
Mahón	21,619
Málaga	‡467,637
Manacor	24,275
Manresa	‡68,213
Marbella (59,445▲)	‡35,200
Martos (21,375▲)	16,300
Mataró	‡98,589
Mérida	38,319
Mieres (62,826▲)	‡22,200
Miranda de Ebro	35,354
Mislata (★Valencia)	26,100
Morón de la Frontera (26,047▲)	22,700
Móstoles (★Madrid)	‡108,290
Motril (35,471▲)	28,100
Murcia (290,414▲)	‡190,600
Onteniente	26,297
Orense (89,485▲)	‡77,600
Orihuela (51,163▲)	‡20,000
Oviedo	‡181,556
Palencia	‡67,755
Palma [de Mallorca]	‡287,389
Pamplona	‡175,833

C Census. E Official estimate. UE Unofficial estimate.
L Population within municipal limits of year specified. • Largest city in country.

★ Population or designation of metropolitan area, including suburbs (see headnote).
▲ Population of an entire municipality, commune, or district, including rural area.
‡† Year of information specified at start of country.

Peñarroya-Pueblonuevo	13,579
Plasencia	28,574
Ponferrada	‡53,400
Pontevedra (64,722▲)	‡33,500
Portugalete (*Bilbao)	‡57,053
Prat de Llobregat (*Barcelona)	‡57,330
Priego [de Córdoba] (20,560▲)	12,300
Puente-Genil (25,277▲)	21,900
Puerto de la Cruz *(Canary Is.)* (50,173▲)	37,100
Puertollano	‡52,722
Rentería (*San Sebastián)	46,329
Reus	‡84,986
Ronda (30,099▲)	22,100
Rota	25,702
Rubí (*Barcelona)	35,855
Sabadell (*Barcelona)	‡188,344
Sagunto	‡57,840
Salamanca	‡144,446
San Adrián de Besós (*Barcelona)	37,286
San Baudilio de Llobregat (*Barcelona)	‡67,321
San Cristóbal de la Laguna (Canary Is.) (114,183▲)	‡24,900
San Fernando (**Cádiz)	‡69,123
Sanlúcar (43,867▲)	31,500
San Sebastián (*290,000)	‡176,023
Santa Coloma de Gramanet (*Barcelona)	‡143,568
Santa Cruz de Tenerife *(Canary Is.)*	‡186,949
Santander	‡176,363
Santiago de Compostela (83,841▲)	‡61,100
Santurce-Antiguo (*Bilboa)	‡55,159
Segovia	‡49,583
Sestao (*Bilbao)	41,399
Sevilla (Seville) (*740,000)	‡630,329
Soria	‡29,315
Sueca	22,522
Talavera de la Reina	‡60,964
Tarragona	‡109,969
Tarrasa (*Barcelona)	‡160,403
Telde *(Canary Is.)* (58,503▲)	‡17,300
Teruel	‡24,856
Toledo	‡56,414
Tomelloso	26,089
Torrejón de Ardoz (*Madrid)	‡63,500
Torrelavega (55,695▲)	‡25,900
Torrente (*Valencia)	46,686
Tortosa (47,246▲)	20,400
Ubeda	30,223
Valencia (*1,140,000)	‡750,994
Valladolid	‡315,486
Vall de Uxó	25,087
Vélez-Málaga (38,249▲)	18,700
Vich	27,615
Vigo	‡260,059
Villanueva y Geltrú	41,229
Vitoria	‡185,271
Zamora	‡55,822
Zaragoza (Saragossa)	‡563,375

SPANISH NORTH AFRICA / Plazas de Soberanía en el Norte de África

1978 E	**120,719**
•Ceuta	64,567
Melilla	56,152

SRI LANKA

1977 E	**13,940,000**
Anuradhapura	38,000
Badulla	38,000
Battaramulla (*Colombo) (1971 C)	43,057
Batticaloa	40,000
•COLOMBO (*1,540,000)	616,000
Dalugama (*Colombo) (1971 C)	41,200
Dehiwala-Mount Lavinia (*Colombo)	169,000
Galle	79,000
Jaffna	118,000
Kalutara	32,000
Kandy	103,000
Kegalla	14,000
Kotikawatta (*Colombo) (1971 C)	43,764
Kotte (*Colombo)	102,000
Kurunegala	28,000
Maharagama (*Colombo) (1971 C)	40,378
Matale	34,000
Matara	40,000
Moratuwa (*Colombo)	104,000
Negombo	63,000
Ratnapura	32,000
Trincomalee	46,000

SUDAN / As-Sūdān

1973 C	**12,427,795**
Al-Fāshir	51,932
Al-Junaynah	35,424
Al-Khurṭūm Baḥrī (Khartoum North (*Khartoum)	150,991
Al-Qaḍārif	66,465
Al-Ubayyiḍ (El Obeid)	90,060
'Aṭbarah	66,116
Būr-Sūdān (Port Sudan)	132,631
Jūbā	56,737
Kassalā	98,751
•KHARTOUM (AL-KHARṬŪM) (*790,000)	333,921
Kūstī	65,257
Malakál	34,898
Nyala	59,852
Umm Durmān (Omdurman) (**Khartoum)	299,401
Wad Madanī	106,776
Wāw	52,752

SURINAME

1971 C	**384,900**
•PARAMARIBO (*175,000)	102,300

SWAZILAND

1976 C	**494,534**
•Manzini (*26,000)	10,019
MBABANE	23,109

SWEDEN / Sverige

1979 E	**8,303,010**

Counties

Älvsborg	424,240
Blekinge	154,135
Gävleborg	293,959
Göteborg och Bohus	713,242
Gotland	55,261
Halland	229,211
Jämtland	134,653
Jönköping	302,475
Kalmar	241,448
Kopparberg	285,545
Kristianstad	278,917
Kronoberg	172,401
Malmöhus	743,133
Norrbotten	266,983
Örebro	274,223
Östergötland	392,390
Skaraborg	268,702
Södermanland	252,026
Stockholm	1,524,266
Uppsala	241,722
Värmland	284,615
Västerbotten	241,898
Västernorrland	267,895
Västmanland	259,670

Cities

Alingsås (29,109▲)	19,800
Angelholm (29,397▲)	16,700
Arvika (26,962▲)	13,600
Avesta (26,471▲)	18,600
Boden (28,770▲)	20,200
Bollnäs (27,683▲)	11,100
Borås	102,914
Borlänge	46,318
Enköping (32,286▲)	18,800
Eskilstuna	90,414
Eslöv (26,939▲)	14,000
Falkenberg (34,610▲)	14,800
Falun (50,079▲)	31,600
Gällivare (24,661▲)	8,500
Gävle	87,364
Göteborg (Gothenburg) (*665,000)	434,699
Halmstad (75,663▲)	50,400
Härnösand (27,616▲)	19,400
Hässleholm (48,751▲)	17,000
Helsingborg	101,370
Huddinge (*Stockholm)	66,038
Hudiksvall (37,336▲)	15,200
Järfälla (*Stockholm)	52,442
Jönköping	107,652
Kalmar (52,657▲)	32,200
Karlshamn (31,907▲)	17,400
Karlskoga	37,070
Karlskrona (60,270▲)	33,400
Karlstad	73,904
Katrineholm (32,308▲)	22,700
Kiruna	30,177
Koping (27,291▲)	19,700
Kristianstad (68,675▲)	31,300
Kristinehamn (27,166▲)	20,700
Kungsbacka (42,905▲)	13,400
Landskrona	37,027
Lidingö (*Stockholm)	37,390
Linköping	111,866
Ljungby (27,097▲)	13,400
Ludvika	31,976
Luleå	67,190
Lund	78,003
Malmö (*305,000)	235,111
Mariestad (24,377▲)	16,200
Mjölby (25,885▲)	12,700
Mölndal (*Göteborg)	47,692
Motala (41,945▲)	25,100
Nacka (*Stockholm)	56,825
Nässjö (31,891▲)	18,200
Norrköping	119,993
Norrtälje (40,400▲)	31,200
Nyköping (63,918▲)	31,000
Örebro	116,877
Örnsköldsvik (60,665▲)	29,600
Oskarshamn (28,021▲)	19,000
Östersund (55,440▲)	41,000
Piteå (38,146▲)	17,400
Ronneby (30,270▲)	12,000
Sandviken	43,139
Skellefteå (73,647▲)	29,800
Skövde (45,847▲)	30,200
Söderhamn (31,264▲)	14,200
Södertälje (*Stockholm)	79,396
Sollefteå (26,133▲)	8,900
Sollentuna (*Stockholm)	45,864
Solna (*Stockholm)	51,324
•STOCKHOLM (*1,384,310)	649,384
Sundyberg (*Stockholm)	25,676
Sundsvall (94,358▲)	52,500
Täby (*Stockholm)	46,142
Trelleborg (34,473▲)	22,300
Trollhättan	49,846
Uddevalla (46,139▲)	32,300
Umeå (79,930▲)	52,800
Uppsala	145,032
Vänersborg (34,613▲)	20,600
Varberg (43,829▲)	19,800
Värnamo (30,156▲)	15,700
Västerås	117,257
Västervik (41,303▲)	21,000
Växjö (63,763▲)	41,500
Vetlanda (28,714▲)	12,400
Visby (Gotland) (55,261▲)	20,200

SWITZERLAND / Schweiz / Suisse / Svizzera

1980 E	**6,314,200**
Aarau (*51,100)	15,900
Adliswil (*Zürich)	16,100
Allschwil (*Basel)	18,000
Altdorf	8,200
Appenzell	5,300
Arbon (*15,100)	11,500
Arosa (1970 C)	2,717
Baar (*Zug)	15,300
Baden (*67,300)	13,900
Basel (Bâle) (*575,000)	180,900
Bellinzona (*33,700)	17,200
BERN (BERNE) (*282,400)	141,300
Biel (Bienne) (*87,000)	56,800
Bolligen (*Bern)	32,500
Bülach	12,200
Burgdorf (*17,900)	14,900
Château d'Oex (1970 C)	3,203
Chiasso	8,900
Chur (Coire)	32,500
Davos	11,200
Delémont	11,600
Einsiedeln	9,700
Emmen (*Luzern)	22,800
Frauenfeld	18,600
Fribourg (Freiburg) (*51,800)	37,700
Genève (Geneva) (*425,000)	151,100
Glarus	5,800
Grenchen (*25,300)	16,800
Herisau	13,900
Illnau (*Zürich)	14,600
Interlaken (1970 C)	4,735
Köniz (*Bern)	34,400
Kreuzlingen	16,100
Kriens (*Luzern)	21,200
La Chaux-de-Fonds	38,100
Langenthal (*21,900)	13,400
Lausanne (*225,200)	128,800
Lauterbrunnen (1970 C)	3,431
Le Locle	12,600
Liestal (*Basel)	11,700
Locarno (*41,600)	15,100
Lugano (*69,100)	28,000
Luzern (Lucerne) (*156,400)	62,400
Martigny	11,100
Meiringen (1970 C)	3,759
Monthey	11,400
Montreux (**Vevey)	20,200
Morges (*19,100)	13,300
Neuchâtel (Neuenburg) (*59,000)	34,900
Nyon	12,500
Olten (*47,200)	19,200
Opfikon (*Zürich)	11,200
Riehen (*Basel)	20,600
Rorschach (*23,000)	9,800
Sankt Gallen (St.-Gall) (*112,000)	73,800
Schaffhausen (Schaffhouse) (*51,300)	31,900
Schwyz	12,100
Sierre	14,200
Sion (Sitten)	23,400
Solothurn (Soleure) (*34,500)	15,600
Thun (Thoune) (*65,400)	37,000
Uster	23,000
Vernier (*Genève)	28,000
Vevey (*60,400)	15,700
Wädenswil	18,300
Wettingen (*Baden)	18,200
Wil (*21,500)	15,100
Winterthur (*106,800)	86,100
Wohlen (*15,700)	11,600
Yverdon (Iferten)	20,800
Zug (Zoug) (*52,200)	21,900
•Zürich (*780,000)	374,200

SYRIA / As-Sūrīyah

1978 E	**8,401,100**
Aleppo (Ḥalab)	878,000
Al-Ḥasakah	29,900
Al-Lādhiqīyah (Latakia)	204,000
Al-Qāmishlī (1970 C)	47,714
Ar-Raqqah	48,500
As-Suwaydā'	30,400
•DAMASCUS (DIMASHQ) (1979 E) (*1,550,000)	1,156,000
Dayr az-Zawr	99,100
Dūmā (*Damascus) (1970 C)	30,980
Ḥamāh	180,000
Ḥimṣ (Homs)	306,000
Idlib	52,600
Mukhayyam al-Yarmūk (*Damascus) (1970 C)	64,273

TAIWAN / T'aiwan

1977 E	**16,813,127**
Changhua (166,612▲)	129,000
Chiai	252,972
Chilung (Keelung)	345,392
Chungho (*T'aipei)	175,778
Chungli (Chunli) (180,689▲)	151,000
Chutung	52,000
Fengshan (Kaohsiunghsien) (*Kaohsiung)	177,982
Fengyüan (T'aichunghsien) (121,491▲)	94,000
Hsichih	51,000
Hsinchu	233,459
Hsinchuang (*T'aipei)	124,609
Hsintien (*T'aipei)	145,809
Hsinying (T'ainanhsien)	45,000
Hualien	101,010
Ilan (78,983▲)	66,000
Kangshan	58,000
Kaohsiung (*1,480,000)	1,172,977
Lotung	49,000
Lukang (Luchiang)	32,000
Makung (Penghuhsien)	23,000
Miaoli	66,000
Nant'ou	60,000
Panch'iao (T'aipeihsien) (*T'aipei)	314,848
Peikang	31,000
P'ingtung	182,114
Sanch'ung (*T'aipei)	292,909
Shulin (*T'aipei)	54,000
T'aichung	585,205
T'ainan	572,590
•T'AIPEI (*3,825,000)	2,196,237
T'aitung (111,647▲)	78,000
T'aoyüan	163,404
Touliu (Yünlin)	31,000
Yungho (*T'aipei)	162,731

TANZANIA

1978 C	**17,557,000**
Arusha	48,000
•DAR-ES-SALAAM	870,000
Dodoma (1970 E)	28,000
Iringa (1967 C)	21,746
Morogoro (1970 E)	30,000
Moshi	52,000
Mwanza	171,000
Tabora (1970 E)	23,000
Tanga	144,000
Ujiji (1967 C)	21,369
Zanzibar (1975 E)	80,000

THAILAND / Prathet Thai

1972 E	**36,286,000**
Ayutthaya	46,664
•BANGKOK (KRUNG THEP) (*3,375,000)	3,133,834
Ban Pong	22,036
Chachoengsao	27,071
Chiang Mai	93,353
Chon Buri	46,368
Hat Yai	57,255
Hua Hin	24,041
Khon Kaen	35,055
Lampang	42,007
Lop Buri	33,302
Nakhon Phanom	21,019
Nakhon Pathom	37,807
Nakhon Ratchasima	77,397
Nakhon Sawan	51,378
Nakhon Si Thammarat	50,761
Narathiwat	24,069
Nong Khai	24,680
Nonthaburi (*Bangkok)	25,654
Pattani	26,243
Phayao	22,217
Phet Buri	32,928
Phitsanulok	70,649
Phuket	38,493
Rat Buri	34,966
Samut Prakan (*Bangkok)	44,916
Samut Sakhon	39,982
Sara Buri	23,300
Songkhla	50,687
Suphan Buri	20,128
Surat Thani (Ban Don)	35,560
Surin	27,995
Trang	35,859
Ubon Ratchathani	52,171
Udon Thani	70,110
Warin Chamrap	25,850
Yala	39,983

TOGO

1977 E	**2,348,000**
•LOMÉ	229,400
Palimé	25,500
Sokodé	33,500

TONGA

1976 C	**90,085**
•NUKUALOFA	18,312

TRINIDAD & TOBAGO

1977 E	**1,118,500**
Arima (1970 C)	11,792
Débé (*Port of Spain) (1970 UE)	13,200
Point Fortin (1970 C)	7,738
•PORT OF SPAIN (*395,000)	42,950
Princess Town (1970 C)	7,784
San Fernando (*73,000)	36,650
San Juan (*Port of Spain) (1970 C)	30,802
Scarborough *(Tobago)* (1970 C)	1,724
Tunapuna (*Port of Spain) (1970 C)	11,984

TUNISIA / Tunisie

1975 C	**5,588,209**
Ariana (*Tunis)	47,833
Béja	39,226
Bizerte (Binzert)	62,856
Gabès	40,585
Gafsa	42,225
Hammam Lif (*Tunis)	35,634
Kairouan	54,546
Kasserine	22,594
La Goulette (*Tunis)	41,912
Le Bardo (*Tunis)	49,367
Menzel Bourguiba	42,111
Moknine	26,035
Monastir	26,759
Msaken	33,559
Nabeul	30,476
Sfax (*260,000)	171,297
Sousse	69,530
•TUNIS (*915,000)	550,404

TURKEY / Türkiye

1980 C	**45,217,556**

(Cities designated (E) are in Turkey in Europe)

Adana	568,513
Adapazarı	131,400
Adıyaman	55,030
Afyonkarahisar	73,832
Akhisar	60,061
Aksaray	65,306
Akşehir	40,418
Alaşehir	25,605
Alibeyköy (*Istanbul) (1975 C)	33,387
Amasya	48,010
ANKARA (*2,290,000)	2,203,729
Antakya (Antioch)	91,551
Antalya	176,446
Aydin	71,576
Bafra	50,167
Balıkesir	124,122
Bandırma	53,187
Batman	86,034
Bayburt	22,540
Bayrampaşa (E) (*Istanbul) (1975 C)	157,367
Bergama	34,386
Bolu	38,400
Bolvadin	30,733
Bornova (*İzmir)	54,965
Buca (*Izmir) (1975 C)	70,715
Burdur	44,750
Bursa	466,178
Çamdibi (*İzmir) (1975 C)	42,376
Çanakkale	39,943
Çankiri	35,040
Çarşamba	28,524
Ceyhan	57,097
Çorlu (E)	45,675
Çorum	76,020
Denizli	134,673
Diyarbakır	233,289
Düzce	37,659
Edirne (E)	71,927
Elâziğ	142,787
Ereğli *(Konya prov.)*	61,100
Ereğli *(Zonguldak prov.)*	50,096
Erzincan	73,335
Erzurum	190,121
Esenler (E) (*İstanbul) (1975 C)	49,379
Eskişehir	309,335
Gaziantep	371,000
Gebza (*Izmit)	58,212
Gelibolu (Gallipoli) (E)	14,554
Giresun	46,068
Gölcük	45,006
İnegöl	45,314
İskenderun (Alexandretta)	120,985
Isparta	91,544
•İstanbul (E) (*4,765,000)	2,853,539
İzmir (Smyrna) (*1,190,000)	753,749
İzmit (Kocaeli)	191,340
Kadirli	38,125
Kâğithane (E) (*İstanbul) (1975 C)	164,448
Karabük	84,975
Karaköse (Ağri)	41,103
Karaman	51,868
Kars	58,651
Kartal (*İstanbul)	67,627
Kastamonu	35,636
Kayseri	273,362
Keşan (E)	28,428
Kilis	58,686
Kırıkhan	47,688
Kırıkkale	175,235
Kırklareli (E)	36,183
Kırşehir	50,063
Konya	325,850
Kozan	42,410
Küçukçekmece (*İstanbul) (1975 C)	58,709
Kütahya	101,087
Lüleburgaz (E)	35,643
Malatya	184,390
Manisa	93,970
Maraş	177,919
Mardin	37,750
Mersin	215,300
Merzifon	32,031
Muğla	27,162
Muş	40,297
Mustafakemalpaşa	30,099
Nazilli	64,015
Nevşehir	37,106
Niğde	39,972
Nizip	39,267
Ödemiş	40,652
Ordu	52,080
Osmaniye	84,338
Polatlı	43,514
Reyhanli	30,843
Rize	41,740
Salihli	51,638
Samsun	198,266
Siirt	42,692
Silvan	44,412
Sinop	18,381
Sivas	173,831
Siverek	30,000
Söke	37,362
Tarsus	120,270
Tatvan	40,324
Tekirdağ (E)	51,327
Tire	32,242
Tokat	60,369
Trabzon	107,412
Turgutlu	55,575
Turhal	47,364
Urfa	148,434
Uşak	70,822
Uzunköprü (E)	27,706
Van	93,823
Viranşehir	41,934
Yozgat	36,220
Zile	30,066
Zonguldak (*195,000)	108,661

C Census. E Official estimate. UE Unofficial estimate.
L Population within municipal limits of year specified. • Largest city in country.

* Population or designation of metropolitan area, including suburbs (see headnote).
▲ Population of an entire municipality, commune, or district, including rural area.
‡† Year of information specified at start of country.

TURKS & CAICOS IS.

1970 C 5,607
•GRAND TURK 2,287

UGANDA

1969 C 9,548,847
Arua 10,837
Bugembe 46,884
Entebbe 21,096
Fort Portal 7,949
Gulu 18,170
Jinja 52,509
Kabale 8,234
•KAMPALA 330,700
Lugazi 12,000
Masaka 12,987
Mbale 23,544
Soroti 12,398
Tororo 15,977

UNION OF SOVIET SOCIALIST REPUBLICS / Sojuz Sovetskich Socialističeskich Respublik

1980 E 264,486,000
UNION OF SOVIET SOCIALIST REPUBLICS IN EUROPE 172,022,000

Soviet Socialist Republics

Byelorussia (White Russia) 9,611,000
Estonia 1,474,000
Latvia 2,529,000
Lithuania 3,420,000
Moldavia 3,968,000
Russian Soviet Federated Socialist Republic (part) 101,067,000
Ukraine 49,953,000

Cities (1974 E, ‡1980 E)

Abdulino 25,000
Agryz 19,000
Akhtubinsk 44,000
Akhtyrka 43,000
Alatyr 46,000
Aleksandriya ‡84,000
Aleksandrov ‡61,000
Aleksin ‡68,000
Almetyevsk ‡111,000
Alytus ‡57,000
Anapa 30,000
Antratsit (**Krasnyy Luch) ‡62,000
Apatity ‡64,000
Apsheronsk 33,000
Arkhangelsk ‡387,000
Armavir ‡163,000
Artemovsk ‡88,000
Arzamas ‡95,000
Astrakhan ‡465,000
Atkarsk 30,000
Avdeyevka (*Donetsk) 33,000
Azov ‡76,000
Bakhchisaray 20,000
Balakhna (*Gorkiy) 37,000
Balakleya 31,000
Balakovo ‡156,000
Balashikha (*Moscow) ‡119,000
Balashov ‡94,000
Baranovichi ‡135,000
Bataysk (*Rostov-na-Donu) ‡91,000
Belaya Kalitva 35,000
Belaya Tserkov ‡157,000
Belebey 39,000
Belgorod ‡248,000
Belgorod-Dnestrovskiy 37,000
Belorechensk 38,000
Beloretsk ‡72,000
Beltsy ‡128,000
Bendery ‡104,000
Berdichev ‡81,000
Berdyansk ‡124,000
Berezniki ‡186,000
Bezhetsk 30,000
Bobruysk ‡197,000
Bogoroditsk 32,000
Bogorodsk (*Gorkiy) 37,000
Bologoye 34,000
Bor (*Gorkiy) ‡63,000
Borislav 36,000
Borisoglebsk ‡67,000
Borispol' 36,000
Borisov ‡115,000
Borovichi ‡60,000
Boyarka (*Kiev) 31,000
Brest ‡186,000
Brovary (*Kiev) ‡60,000
Bryanka (*Stakhanov) ‡63,000
Bryansk ‡401,000
Bugulma ‡81,000
Buguruslan ‡54,000
Buy 28,000
Buynaksk 42,000
Buzuluk ‡77,000
Chapayevsk ‡85,000
Chaykovskij ‡71,000
Cheboksary ‡323,000
Chekhov ‡53,000
Cherepovets ‡274,000
Cherkassy ‡234,000
Cherkessk ‡92,000
Chernigov ‡245,000
Chernovtsy ‡221,000
Chernyakhovsk (Insterburg) 34,000
Chervonograd ‡56,000
Chistopol ‡65,000
Chusovoy ‡57,000
Daugavpils ‡117,000
Debaltsevo 37,000
Derbent ‡71,000
Dimitrov (**Krasnoarmeysk) ‡59,000
Dimitrovgrad (Melekess) ‡108,000
Dmitrov ‡59,000
Dneprodzerzhinsk (**Dnepropetrovsk) ‡253,000
Dnepropetrovsk (*1,460,000) ‡1,083,000
Dobropolye 31,000
Dolgoprudnyy (*Moscow) ‡66,000
Domodedovo (*Moscow) 39,000
Donetsk *(Donetsk obl.)* (*2,075,000) ‡1,032,000
Donetsk *(Rostov obl.)* 42,000
Donskoy (*Novomoskovsk) 34,000
Drogobych ‡68,000
Druzhkovka (*Kramatorsk) ‡66,000
Dubna ‡56,000
Dzerzhinsk (*Gorkiy) ‡260,000
Dzerzhinsk (*Gorlovka) 46,000
Dzhankoy 46,000
Elektrostal ‡141,000
Elista ‡72,000
Engels (**Saratov) ‡165,000
Fastov ‡52,000
Feodosiya ‡78,000
Frolovo 38,000
Fryazino (*Moscow) 39,000
Furmanov 41,000
Galich 21,000
Gatchina (*Leningrad) ‡76,000
Gelendzhik 31,000
Georgiu-Dezh (Liski) ‡52,000
Georgiyevsk ‡55,000
Glazov ‡83,000
Glukhov 30,000
Gomel ‡393,000
Gorkiy (Gorki) (*1,900,000) ‡1,358,000
Gorlovka (*700,000) ‡337,000
Gorodets 35,000
Gremyachinsk 27,000
Grodno ‡202,000
Groznyy ‡377,000
Gryazi 42,000
Gubakha 32,000
Gubkin ‡65,000
Gudermes 34,000
Gukovo ‡69,000
Gusev 23,000
Gus-Khrustalnyy ‡72,000
Ilichevsk 43,000
Ingulets 35,000
Inta ‡51,000
Ishimbay ‡58,000
Ivano-Frankovsk ‡159,000
Ivanovo ‡466,000
Ivanteyevka (*Moscow) 41,000
Izberbash 20,000
Izhevsk ‡562,000
Izmail ‡84,000
Izyum ‡61,000
Jelgava ‡69,000
Jurmala (*Riga) ‡62,000
Kagul 31,000
Kakhovka 35,000
Kalinin ‡416,000
Kaliningrad (*Moscow) ‡135,000
Kaliningrad (Königsberg) ‡361,000
Kaluga ‡270,000
Kalush ‡61,000
Kamenets-Podolskiy ‡86,000
Kamenka 32,000
Kamensk-Shakhtinskiy ‡72,000
Kamyshin ‡112,000
Kanash 46,000
Kandalaksha 43,000
Kapsukas 33,000
Kashira 42,000
Kasimov 34,000
Kaspiysk 42,000
Kaunas ‡377,000
Kazan (*1,050,000) ‡1,002,000
Kerch ‡158,000
Kharkov (*1,750,000) ‡1,464,000
Khartsyzsk (*Donetsk) ‡59,000
Khasavyurt ‡67,000
Kherson ‡324,000
Khimki (*Moscow) ‡120,000
Khmelnitskiy ‡179,000
Kiev (Kiyev) (*2,430,000) ‡2,192,000
Kimovsk 44,000
Kimry ‡58,000
Kinel' 40,000
Kineshma ‡102,000
Kirishi 34,000
Kirov *(Kirov obl.)* ‡392,000
Kirov *(Kaluga obl.)* 30,000
Kirovo-Chepetsk ‡74,000
Kirovograd ‡242,000
Kirovsk *(Murmansk obl.)* 40,000
Kirovsk *(Voroshilovgrad obl.)* (*Stakhanov) 40,000
Kishinev ‡519,000
Kislovodsk ‡102,000
Kizel 42,000
Klaipėda (Memel) ‡178,000
Klimovsk (*Moscow) ‡55,000
Klin ‡92,000
Klintsy ‡69,000
Kobrin 28,000
Kohtla-Järve ‡73,000
Kolchugino 43,000
Kolomna ‡149,000
Kolomyya ‡53,000
Kolpino (*Leningrad) ‡118,000
Kommunarsk (*Stakhanov) ‡120,000
Konakovo 33,000
Kondopoga 32,000
Konotop ‡84,000
Konstantinovka ‡113,000
Korosten ‡66,000
Kostroma ‡255,000
Kotel'nich 31,000
Kotlas ‡63,000
Kotovsk *(Odessa obl.)* 39,000
Kotovsk *(Tambov obl.)* 36,000
Kovel 40,000
Kovrov ‡144,000
Kramatorsk (*445,000) ‡180,000
Krasnoarmeysk (*155,000) ‡61,000
Krasnodar ‡572,000
Krasnodon 46,000
Krasnogorsk (*Moscow) ‡80,000
Krasnokamsk ‡56,000
Krasnyy Luch (*230,000) ‡107,000
Krasnyy Sulin 43,000
Kremenchug ‡212,000
Krichev 28,000
Krivoy Rog ‡657,000
Kronshtadt (*Leningrad) (1970 C) 39,477
Kropotkin ‡71,000
Krymsk (Krymskaya) 43,000
Kstovo (*Gorkiy) ‡60,000
Kudymkar (1975 E) 27,000
Kulebaki 46,000
Kumertau ‡54,000
Kungur ‡80,000
Kupyansk 34,000
Kurganinsk 38,000
Kursk ‡383,000
Kuybyshev (*1,440,000) ‡1,226,000
Kuznetsk ‡94,000
Labinsk ‡55,000
Leningrad (*5,360,000) ‡4,119,000
Leninogorsk ‡68,000
Lida ‡67,000
Liepāja ‡108,000
Lipetsk ‡405,000
Lisichansk (*365,000) ‡120,000
Livny 42,000
Lobnya (*Moscow) ‡53,000
Lomonosov (*Leningrad) 43,000
Lozovaya ‡55,000
Lubny ‡55,000
Luga 35,000
Lutsk ‡146,000
Lvov ‡676,000
Lysva ‡75,000
Lytkarino (*Moscow) 42,000
Lyubertsy (*Moscow) ‡162,000
Lyubotin 33,000
Lyudinovo 36,000
Makeyevka (**Donetsk) ‡439,000
Makhachkala ‡261,000
Marganets ‡51,000
Marks 22,000
Maykop ‡130,000
Mednogorsk 36,000
Melitopol ‡163,000
Michurinsk ‡102,000
Mikhaylovka ‡59,000
Millerovo 37,000
Mineralnyye Vody ‡68,000
Minsk (*1,330,000) ‡1,295,000
Mogilev ‡300,000
Molodechno ‡74,000
Monchegorsk ‡53,000
Morshansk (1977 E) 50,000
•MOSCOW (MOSKVA) (*11,950,000) ‡7,915,000
Mozdok 33,000
Mozhga 41,000
Mozyr ‡75,000
Mtsensk 34,000
Mukachevo ‡74,000
Murmansk ‡388,000
Murom ‡116,000
Mytishchi (*Moscow) ‡143,000
Naberezhnyye Chelny ‡319,000
Nalchik ‡211,000
Naro-Fominsk ‡57,000
Narva ‡74,000
Neftekamsk ‡72,000
Nevinnomyssk ‡106,000
Nezhin ‡71,000
Nikolayev ‡449,000
Nikopol ‡149,000
Nizhnekamsk ‡139,000
Noginsk ‡120,000
Novaya Kakhovka ‡54,000
Novgorod ‡192,000
Novocheboksarsk ‡89,000
Novocherkassk ‡185,000
Novo-Ekonomicheskoye (**Krasnoarmeysk) (1970 C) 31,214
Novograd-Volynskiy 44,000
Novokuybyshevsk (*Kuybyshev) ‡110,000
Novomoskovsk *(Dnepropetrovsk obl.)* ‡70,000
Novomoskovsk *(Tula obl.)* (*370,000) ‡147,000
Novopolotsk ‡70,000
Novorossiysk ‡162,000
Novoshakhtinsk ‡105,000
Novo-Troitsk ‡97,000
Novovolynsk 44,000
Novozybkov 39,000
Obninsk ‡76,000
Odessa (*1,120,000) ‡1,057,000
Odintsovo (*Moscow) ‡104,000
Oktyabr'sk 33,000
Oktyabr'skiy ‡91,000
Onega 25,000
Ordzhonikidze *(Severo-Osetinsk obl.)* ‡283,000
Ordzhonikidze *(Dnepropetrovsk obl.)* 39,000
Orekhovo-Zuyevo (*200,000) ‡133,000
Orel ‡309,000
Orenburg ‡471,000
Orsha ‡113,000
Orsk ‡252,000
Otradnyy 46,000
Panevėžys ‡104,000
Pärnu ‡51,000
Pavlograd ‡111,000
Pavlovo ‡69,000
Pavlovskiy Posad ‡71,000
Pechora ‡57,000
Penza ‡490,000
Pereslavl-Zalesskiy 33,000
Pereval'sk (*Stakhanov) 32,000
Perm (*1,075,000) ‡1,008,000
Pervomaysk (*Stakhanov) *(Voroshilovgrad obl.)* 46,000
Pervomaysk *(Nikolayev obl.)* ‡73,000
Petrodvorets (*Leningrad) ‡74,000
Petrovsk 34,000
Petrozavodsk ‡238,000
Pinsk ‡93,000
Podolsk (*Moscow) ‡203,000
Polotsk ‡72,000
Poltava ‡282,000
Priluki ‡66,000
Prokhladnyy 44,000
Pskov ‡177,000
Pugachev 35,000
Pushkin (*Leningrad) ‡89,000
Pushkino ‡71,000
Pyatigorsk ‡112,000
Ramenskoye (*Moscow) ‡79,000
Rasskazovo 40,000
Rechitsa ‡62,000
Reutov (*Moscow) ‡62,000
Rēzekne 34,000
Rīga (*920,000) ‡843,000
Rodniki 30,000
Rogachëv 20,000
Romny ‡53,000
Roslavl ‡56,000
Rossosh' 38,000
Rostov 31,000
Rostov-na-Donu (*1,075,000) ‡946,000
Rovenki ‡62,000
Rovno ‡185,000
Rtishchevo 41,000
Rubezhnoye (**Lisichansk) ‡66,000
Ruzayevka 44,000
Ryazan ‡462,000
Rybinsk ‡241,000
Rybnitsa 39,000
Rzhev ‡69,000
Safonovo ‡53,000
Salavat ‡140,000
Salsk ‡58,000
Saransk ‡271,000
Sarapul ‡107,000
Saratov (*1,090,000) ‡864,000
Serdobsk 37,000
Serpukhov ‡141,000
Sevastopol ‡308,000
Severodonetsk (**Lisichansk) ‡115,000
Severodvinsk (Molotovsk) ‡203,000
Severomorsk ‡51,000
Shakhtersk (**Torez) ‡70,000
Shakhty ‡212,000
Shchekino ‡71,000
Shchelkovo (*Moscow) ‡101,000
Shebekino 36,000
Shepetovka 42,000
Shostka ‡82,000
Shumerlya 35,000
Shuya ‡72,000
Šiauliai ‡121,000
Sibay 40,000
Simferopol ‡307,000
Slantsy 42,000
Slavyansk (**Kramatorsk) ‡141,000
Slavyansk-na-Kubani ‡55,000
Slobodskoy 36,000
Slutsk 39,000
Smela ‡63,000
Smolensk ‡305,000
Snezhnoye (*Torez) ‡67,000
Sochi ‡291,000
Sokol 48,000
Soligorsk ‡68,000
Solikamsk ‡102,000
Solnechnogorsk (*Moscow) 37,000
Solntsevo (*Moscow) ‡62,000
Sovetsk 40,000
Stakhanov (Kadiyevka) (*590,000) ‡108,000
Staraya Russa 37,000
Staryy Oskol ‡123,000
Stavropol ‡265,000
Sterlitamak ‡224,000
Stryy ‡56,000
Stupino ‡71,000
Sumy ‡233,000
Suzdal (1959 C) 9,000
Sverdlovsk ‡75,000
Svetlogorsk ‡56,000
Svetlovodsk (Kremges) 41,000
Syktyvkar ‡175,000
Syzran ‡168,000
Taganrog ‡278,000
Tallinn ‡436,000
Tambov ‡270,000
Tartu ‡106,000
Ternopol ‡149,000
Teykovo 42,000
Tikhoretsk ‡64,000
Tikhvin ‡61,000
Timashevsk 31,000
Tiraspol 142,000
Tokmak 39,000
Tolyatti (Stavropol) ‡517,000
Torez (Chistyakovo) (*295,000) ‡87,000
Torzhok (1977 E) 50,000
Tuapse ‡61,000
Tula (*615,000) ‡518,000
Tuymazy 42,000
Ufa (*1,000,000) ‡986,000
Uglich 37,000
Ukhta ‡89,000
Ulyanovsk ‡473,000
Uman ‡80,000
Uryupinsk 39,000
Ust'-Labinsk 38,000
Uzhgorod ‡93,000
Uzlovaya (**Novomoskovsk) ‡65,000
Valuyki 30,000
Velikiye Luki ‡103,000
Velikiy Ustyug 38,000
Ventspils 44,000
Vichuga ‡52,000
Vidnoye 40,000
Vilnius ‡492,000
Vinnitsa ‡323,000
Vitebsk ‡303,000
Vladimir ‡301,000
Vogodonsk ‡109,000
Volgograd (Stalingrad) (*1,230,000) ‡939,000
Volkhov 48,000
Vologda ‡241,000
Volsk ‡65,000
Volzhsk ‡53,000
Volzhskiy (*Volgograd) ‡214,000
Vorkuta ‡101,000
Voronezh ‡796,000
Voroshilovgrad (Lugansk) ‡469,000
Voskresensk ‡77,000
Votkinsk ‡92,000
Voznesensk 39,000
Vyatskiye Polyany 35,000
Vyazma ‡52,000
Vyazniki 44,000
Vyborg ‡77,000
Vyksa ‡54,000
Vyshniy Volochek ‡71,000
Yalta ‡81,000
Yaroslavl ‡603,000
Yartsevo 39,000
Yasinovataya 39,000
Yefremov ‡53,000
Yegoryevsk ‡73,000
Yelabuga 35,000
Yelets ‡112,000
Yenakiyevo (**Gorlovka) ‡115,000
Yessentuki ‡79,000
Yevpatoriya ‡95,000
Yeysk ‡72,000
Yoshkar-Ola ‡207,000
Yuryev-Polskiy 23,000
Zagorsk ‡108,000
Zaporozhye ‡799,000
Zavolzh'ye 38,000
Zelenodolsk ‡85,000
Zelenograd (*Moscow) ‡132,000
Zelenokumsk 30,000
Zhdanov ‡507,000
Zheleznodorozhnyy (*Moscow) ‡78,000
Zheleznogorsk ‡67,000
Zheltyye Vody ‡53,000
Zhigulevsk (1977 E) 50,000
Zhitomir ‡250,000
Zhlobin 29,000
Zhmerinka 38,000
Zhukovskiy ‡92,000

UNION OF SOVIET SOCIALIST REPUBLICS IN ASIA 92,464,000

Soviet Socialist Republics

Armenia 3,074,000
Azerbaidzhan 6,112,000
Georgia 5,041,000
Kazakh S.S.R. 14,858,000
Kirghiz S.S.R. 3,588,000
Russian Soviet Federated Socialist Republic (part) 37,298,000
Tadzhik S.S.R. 3,901,000
Turkmen S.S.R. 2,827,000
Uzbek S.S.R. 15,765,000

Cities (1974 E, ‡1980 E)

Abakan ‡133,000
Abay 41,000
Abovyan (*Yerevan) 32,000
Achinsk ‡117,000
Akhaltsikhe 19,000
Aktyubinsk ‡197,000
Alapayevsk (1977 E) 52,000
Aldan 20,000
Aleysk 37,000
Ali-Bayramly 38,000
Alma-Ata (*970,000) ‡928,000
Almalyk ‡102,000
Andizhan ‡233,000
Angarsk ‡241,000
Angren ‡108,000
Anzhero-Sudzhensk ‡107,000
Aral'sk 39,000
Arkalyk (1975 E) 35,000
Arsenyev ‡61,000
Artem ‡69,000
Artemovskiy 38,000
Arys 28,000
Asbest ‡80,000
Asha 38,000
Ashkhabad ‡318,000
Asino 31,000
Atbasar 39,000
Ayaguz 40,000
Baku (*1,800,000) ‡1,030,000
Balkhash ‡78,000
Barabinsk 37,000
Barnaul (*600,000) ‡542,000
Batumi ‡124,000
Bayram-Ali 36,000
Bekabad (Begovat) ‡69,000
Belogorsk ‡64,000
Belovo ‡112,000
Berdsk (*Novosibirsk) ‡68,000
Berezovskiy (*Sverdlovsk) 39,000
Berezovskiy *(Kemerovo obl.)* 37,000
Birobidzhan ‡70,000
Biysk ‡213,000
Blagoveshchensk ‡175,000
Bratsk ‡219,000
Bukhara ‡188,000
Chardzhou ‡143,000
Chebarkul' 42,000
Chelkar 20,000
Chelyabinsk (*1,215,000) ‡1,042,000
Cheremkhovo ‡75,000
Chernogorsk ‡73,000
Chimkent ‡327,000
Chirchik (*Tashkent) ‡134,000
Chita ‡308,000
Chu 35,000
Chust 31,000
Dudinka (1975 E) 23,000
Dushanbe ‡501,000
Dzhalal-Abad ‡55,000
Dzhambul ‡270,000
Dzhetygara 39,000
Dzhezkazgan ‡92,000
Dzhizak ‡71,000
Echmiadzin (*Yerevan) 37,000
Ekibastuz ‡74,000

C Census. E Official estimate. UE Unofficial estimate.
L Population within municipal limits of year specified. • Largest city in country.

* Population or designation of metropolitan area, including suburbs (see headnote).
▲ Population of an entire municipality, commune, or district, including rural area.
‡† Year of information specified at start of country.

Fergana ‡177,000
Frunze ‡543,000
Gagra 22,000
Geokchay 30,000
Gori ‡57,000
Gorno-Altaysk (1975 E) 39,000
Gulistan (1975 E) 39,000
Guryev ‡134,000
Igarka 16,000
Irbit ‡52,000
Irkutsk ‡561,000
Ishim ‡62,000
Iskitim ‡60,000
Kachkanar 38,000
Kafan 31,000
Kagan 38,000
Kamen-na-Obi 40,000
Kamensk-Uralskiy ‡189,000
Kamyshlov 31,000
Kansk ‡100,000
Karaganda ‡577,000
Karpinsk 37,000
Karshi ‡113,000
Kartaly 44,000
Katta-Kurgan ‡54,000
Kemerovo ‡478,000
Kentau ‡52,000
Kerki (1967E) 18,000
Khabarovsk ‡538,000
Khanty-Mansiysk (1975 E) 26,000
Khiva 26,000
Khodzheyli 40,000
Kholmsk 43,000
Khorog (1975 E) 15,000
Kirovabad ‡237,000
Kirovakan ‡149,000
Kiselevsk (**Prokopyevsk) ‡122,000
Kokand ‡154,000
Kokchetav ‡106,000
Komsomolsk-na-Amure ‡269,000
Kopeysk (*Chelyabinsk) ‡146,000
Korkino ‡63,000
Korsakov 40,000
Krasnokamensk 54,000
Krasnotur'insk ‡61,000
Krasnoufimsk 40,000
Krasnouralsk 40,000
Krasnovodsk ‡53,000
Krasnoyarsk ‡807,000
Kuba 19,000
Kulyab ‡57,000
Kurgan ‡316,000
Kurgan-Tyube 39,000
Kushva 43,000
Kustanay ‡169,000
Kutaisi ‡197,000
Kuybyshev 44,000
Kyakhta 16,000
Kyshtym 39,000
Kyzyl ‡67,000
Kyzyl-Kiya 33,000
Kzyl-Orda ‡159,000
Leninabad ‡132,000
Leninakan ‡210,000
Leninogorsk ‡54,000
Leninsk 31,000
Leninsk-Kuznetskiy ‡133,000
Lenkoran 38,000
Lesozavodsk 38,000
Magadan ‡124,000
Magnitogorsk ‡410,000
Margelan ‡112,000
Mariinsk 40,000
Mary ‡76,000
Mezhdurechensk ‡93,000
Miass ‡152,000
Mingechaur ‡63,000
Minusinsk ‡61,000
Myski 38,000
Nakhichevan-na-Arakse (1975 E) 37,000
Nakhodka ‡136,000
Namangan ‡234,000
Naryn (1975 E) 26,000
Navoy ‡86,000
Nazarovo ‡55,000
Nazyvayevsk 15,000
Nebit-Dag ‡73,000
Nefteyugansk 51,000
Nev'yansk 31,000
Nikolayevsk-na-Amure 33,000
Nizhneudinsk 42,000
Nizhnevartovsk ‡122,000
Nizhniy Tagil ‡400,000
Norilsk ‡182,000
Novoaltaysk (*Barnaul) ‡50,000
Novokazalinsk (1970 C) 34,815
Novokuznetsk ‡545,000
Novosibirsk (*1,460,000) ‡1,328,000
Nukus ‡113,000
Omsk (*1,040,000) ‡1,028,000
Osh ‡173,000
Osinniki ‡60,000
Partizansk (Suchan) 49,000
Pavlodar ‡281,000
Pervouralsk ‡130,000
Petropavlovsk ‡209,000
Petropavlovsk-Kamchatskiy ‡219,000
Polevskoy ‡64,000
Poti (1977 E) 54,000
Prokopyevsk (*395,000) ‡266,000
Przhevalsk ‡52,000
Razdan 33,000
Revda ‡63,000
Rezh 34,000
Rubtsovsk ‡158,000
Rudnyy ‡111,000
Rustavi (*Tbilisi) ‡132,000
Rybachye 33,000
Samarkand ‡481,000
Saran ‡56,000
Satka 44,000
Semipalatinsk ‡286,000
Serov ‡101,000
Shadrinsk ‡82,000
Shakhtinsk ‡51,000
Shchuchinsk 46,000
Sheki (Nukha) 44,000
Shevchenko ‡116,000
Spassk-Dalniy ‡53,000
Sukhumi ‡116,000
Sumgait *Baku) ‡196,000
Surgut ‡121,000
Sverdlovsk (*1,450,000) ‡1,225,000
Svobodnyy ‡75,000
Taldy-Kurgan ‡91,000
Tashauz ‡87,000
Tashkent (*2,015,000) ‡1,816,000
Tavda 47,000
Tayshet 35,000
Tbilisi (*1,240,000) ‡1,080,000
Temirtau ‡215,000
Termez ‡58,000
Tobolsk ‡64,000
Tokmak ‡60,000
Tomsk ‡431,000
Troitsk ‡83,000
Tselinograd (Akmolinsk) ‡237,000
Tskhinvali (1975 E) 34,000
Tulun ‡52,000
Turkestan ‡69,000
Tyumen ‡369,000
Ulan-Ude ‡305,000
Uralsk ‡170,000
Ura-Tyube 36,000
Urgench ‡103,000
Usolye-Sibirskoye ‡104,000
Ussuriysk ‡148,000
Ust-Ilimsk ‡76,000
Ust-Kamenogorsk ‡280,000
Ust-Kut ‡51,000
Verkhniy Ufaley 38,000
Verkhnyaya Pyshma (*Sverdlovsk) 40,000
Verkhnyaya Salda ‡55,000
Vladivostok ‡558,000
Yakutsk ‡155,000
Yangi-Yul ‡64,000
Yerevan (*1,155,000) ‡1,036,000
Yermak 40,000
Yurga ‡80,000
Yuzhno-Sakhalinsk ‡143,000
Zima (1977 E) 51,000
Zlatoust ‡199,000
Zugdidi 41,000
Zyryanovsk ‡52,000

UNITED ARAB EMIRATES / Ittiḥād al-Imārāt al-'Arabīyah

1968 C 180,200

ABU DHABI (ABŪ ẒABY) (1973 E) 50,000
'Ajmān 3,725
Al Fujayrah 760
Ash Shāriqah 19,200
•Dubai (Dubayy) (1970 E) 60,000
Ra's al Khaymah 5,300
Umm al Qaywayn 2,900

UNITED KINGDOM

1979 E 55,880,000

Political Divisions

ENGLAND 46,396,100
WALES 2,774,700
SCOTLAND 5,167,000
NORTHERN IRELAND 1,542,200

ENGLAND

Metropolitan Counties

Greater London 6,877,100
Greater Manchester 2,648,300
South York 1,301,300
Tyne & Wear 1,155,900
West Midlands 2,696,000
West York 2,064,100

Non-metropolitan Counties

Avon 924,200
Bedford 498,800
Berks 682,000
Buckingham 535,800
Cambridge 579,300
Cheshire 926,500
Cleveland 568,600
Cornwall & Isles of Scilly 419,300
Cumbria 469,900
Derby 898,300
Devon 952,100
Dorset 591,100
Durham 603,200
East Sussex 654,600
Essex 1,446,700
Gloucester 497,100
Hampshire 1,459,500
Hereford & Worcester 617,900
Hertford 952,000
Humberside 849,600
Isle of Wight 115,300
Kent 1,456,100
Lancashire 1,369,700
Leicester 836,300
Lincoln 533,800
Merseyside 1,531,600
Norfolk 686,300
Northampton 523,300
Northumberland 289,800
North York 663,200
Nottingham 974,100
Oxford 542,100
Shropshire 369,500
Somerset 415,500
Stafford 999,900
Suffolk 597,600
Surrey 993,700
Warwick 468,900
West Sussex 643,800
Wilts 516,400

Cities *(1979 E or ‡1973 E)

Abingdon (*Oxford) ‡20,130
Accrington (Hyndburn) (**Blackburn) 79,400
Adur (*Brighton) 57,700
Aldershot (Rushmoor) (*London) 81,000
Aldridge-Brownhills (Walsall) ‡89,370
Andover ‡27,620
Ashford ‡36,380
Ashton-under-Lyne (Tameside) (**Manchester) 218,500
Aycliffe (1971 C) 20,190
Aylesbury ‡41,420
Banbury ‡31,060
Barnsley 221,800
Barnstaple ‡17,820
Barrow-in-Furness 71,100
Basildon (*London) 148,200
Basingstoke ‡60,910
Bath 83,900
Batley (*Leeds) ‡41,630
Battle (1971 C) 4,987
Bebington (Wirral) ‡62,500
Bedford ‡74,390
Bedworth (Nuneaton) ‡41,600
Beeston & Stapleford (*Nottingham) ‡65,360
Benfleet (Castle Point) (*London) 84,400
Berkhamsted (*London) ‡15,920
Berwick-upon-Tweed ‡11,610
Bexhill-on-Sea ‡34,680
Birkenhead (Wirral) (*Liverpool) 342,300
Birmingham (*2,660,000) 1,033,900
Bishop Auckland ‡32,940
Bishop's Stortford (*London) ‡21,720
Blackburn (*221,900) 142,500
Blackpool (*275,000) 145,400
Bletchley ‡33,450
Blyth (Blyth Valley) 75,700
Blyth Valley see Blyth
Bodmin ‡10,430
Bognor Regis ‡34,620
Bolton (**Manchester) 260,100
Bootle (*Liverpool) ‡71,160
Boston ‡26,700
Bournemouth (*315,000) 144,200
Bracknell (*London) (1971 C) 33,953
Bradford (**Leeds) 461,600
Bradford-on-Avon ‡8,310
Braintree ‡26,300
Brentwood (*London) ‡58,690
Bridgwater ‡26,700
Bridlington ‡26,920
Brighouse (*Halifax) ‡35,320
Brighton (*425,000) 152,700
Bristol (*635,000) 408,000
Broadstairs and St. Peters ‡21,670
Bromsgrove (*Birmingham) ‡41,430
Broxbourne see Cheshunt
Burgess Hill (*London) ‡20,030
Burnham-on-Sea ‡12,690
Burnley (*160,000) 92,300
Burton-upon-Trent ‡49,480
Bury (**Manchester) 178,600
Bury St. Edmunds ‡26,800
Buxton ‡20,050
Camborne-Redruth ‡43,970
Cambridge 101,600
Cannock (Cannock Chase) (*Birmingham) 83,600
Cannock Chase see Cannock
Canterbury ‡34,510
Carlisle ‡70,930
Carlton (Gedling) (*Nottingham) 102,800
Castleford (*Leeds) ‡37,650
Castle Point see Benfleet
Caterham & Warlingham (*London) ‡35,840
Chatham (Medway) (*London) 147,400
Cheadle and Gatley (Stockport) ‡62,460
Chelmsford (*London) ‡58,320
Cheltenham 85,000
Chertsey (Runnymede) (*London) 72,800
Chesham (*London) ‡20,830
Cheshunt (Broxbourne) (*London) 79,200
Chester ‡61,370
Chesterfield (*127,000) 96,300
Chester-le-Street (*Newcastle) ‡20,720
Chichester ‡20,940
Chigwell (*London) ‡54,220
Chippenham ‡18,550
Chorley (**Preston) ‡31,800
Christchurch (*Bournemouth) 38,600
Cirencester ‡14,500
Clacton-on-Sea ‡39,380
Cleethorpes (*Grimsby) ‡37,200
Clevedon ‡15,140
Coalville ‡28,740
Colchester ‡79,600
Consett (*Newcastle) ‡35,080
Corby 53,000
Coventry (*655,000) 339,300
Cowes ‡19,190
Crawley (*London) 71,800
Crewe ‡50,450
Crosby (*Liverpool) ‡56,750
Cuckfield (*London) ‡26,500
Darlington ‡85,120
Dartford (*London) ‡44,130
Dartmouth ‡6,720
Dawley ‡30,720
Deal ‡26,840
Derby (*270,000) 215,900
Dewsbury (**Leeds) ‡50,560
Doncaster (*160,000) ‡81,530
Dorchester ‡13,880
Dorking (*London) ‡22,410
Dover ‡34,160
Dronfield (*Sheffield) ‡20,000
Dudley (**Birmingham) 296,000
Dunstable (*Luton) ‡32,090
Durham ‡29,490
Eastbourne 73,100
East Grinstead (*London) ‡19,420
Eastleigh (*Southampton) ‡46,340
East Retford ‡18,260
Ellesmere Port (*Liverpool) ‡63,870
Elmbridge see Walton and Weybridge
Ely ‡10,630
Epsom and Ewell (*London) 70,500
Esher (Elmbridge) ‡63,970
Eton (*London) ‡4,950
Evesham ‡14,090
Exeter 95,600
Exmouth ‡26,840
Falmouth ‡17,530
Fareham (*Portsmouth) 85,000
Farnham (*London) ‡33,140
Faversham ‡15,010
Felixstowe ‡19,460
Fleet (*London) ‡22,930
Fleetwood (**Blackpool) ‡30,070
Folkestone ‡45,610
Formby (*Liverpool) ‡24,850
Frimley & Camberley (*London) ‡47,390
Frome ‡13,780
Gainsborough ‡17,440
Gateshead (*Newcastle) 212,200
Gedling see Carlton
Gillingham (*London) 92,800
Glastonbury ‡6,580
Glossop (*Manchester) ‡24,820
Gloucester (*115,000) 91,300
Goole ‡17,920
Gosport (*Portsmouth) 79,400
Grantham ‡27,830
Gravesend (Gravesham) (*London) 95,900
Gravesham see Gravesend
Great Yarmouth ‡49,410
Grimsby (*145,000) 91,900
Guildford (*London) ‡58,470
Halesowen (Dudley) ‡54,120
Halifax (*173,000) ‡88,580
Haltemprice (*Hull) ‡54,850
Halton see Widnes
Harlow (*London) 79,100
Harrogate ‡64,620
Hartlepool (**Middlesbrough) 95,100
Harwich ‡15,280
Hastings 74,200
Havant (*Portsmouth) 116,100
Haverhill ‡14,550
Heanor ‡24,590
Hemel Hempstead (*London) ‡71,150
Hemsworth ‡14,680
Henley-on-Thames ‡11,860
Hereford 46,800
Herne Bay ‡26,510
Hertford (*London) ‡20,760
Hertsmere (*London) 87,800
Hexham ‡9,820
High Wycombe ‡61,190
Hinckley (**Coventry) ‡49,310
Hitchin ‡29,190
Horsham (*London) ‡26,770
Hove (*Brighton) 87,800
Hucknall (*Nottingham) ‡27,110
Huddersfield (*209,000) ‡130,060
Huntingdon & Godmanchester ‡17,200
Huyton-with-Roby (Knowsley) (*Liverpool) 179,700
Hyndburn see Accrington
Hythe ‡12,210
Ilkeston (*Nottingham) ‡33,690
Ipswich 118,900
Keighley (Bradford) ‡56,040
Kendal ‡22,440
Kenilworth (*Coventry) ‡19,730
Keswick ‡4,790
Kettering ‡44,480
Kidderminster ‡49,960
King's Lynn ‡29,990
Kingston-upon-Hull (Hull) (*350,000) 274,500
Kingswood (*Bristol) 82,100
Kirkby (Knowsley) ‡59,100
Knowsley see Huyton-with-Roby
Lancaster (*100,000) ‡50,570
Leamington Spa (**Coventry) ‡44,950
Leatherhead (*London) ‡40,830
Leeds (*1,540,000) 724,300
Leek ‡19,460
Leicester (*480,000) 276,600
Leighton-Linslade ‡22,590
Letchworth ‡31,520
Lewes ‡14,170
Leyland (South Ribble) (*Preston) 96,100
Lichfield ‡23,690
Lincoln 71,900
Littlehampton ‡20,320
Liverpool (*1,535,000) 520,200
•LONDON (*11,050,000) 6,877,100
Longbenton (North Tyneside) ‡50,120
Long Eaton (*Nottingham) ‡33,560
Loughborough ‡49,010
Lowestoft ‡53,260
Ludlow (1971 C) 7,466
Luton (*215,000) 160,300
Lymington ‡36,760
Lytham St. Annes (*Blackpool) ‡42,120
Macclesfield ‡45,420
Maidenhead (*London) ‡48,210
Maidstone ‡72,110
Malvern ‡30,420
Manchester (*2,800,000) 479,100
Mansfield (*198,000) ‡58,450
Margate ‡50,290
Market Harborough ‡15,230
Marlborough ‡6,370
Matlock ‡20,300
Medway see Chatham
Melton Mowbray ‡20,680
Middlesbrough (*580,000) 153,000
Middleton (Rochdale) ‡53,340
Morecambe [& Heysham] (**Lancaster) ‡42,010
Morley (Leeds) ‡44,790
Nelson (**Burnley) ‡31,220
Newark-upon-Trent ‡24,760
Newbury ‡24,850
Newcastle-under-Lyme (**Stoke-on-Trent) ‡75,940
Newcastle-upon-Tyne (*1,295,000) 287,300
Newmarket ‡13,370
Newport ‡22,430
Newton Abbot ‡19,940
Northampton 154,900
North Tyneside see Tynemouth
Northwich ‡17,710
Norwich (*220,000) 119,300
Nottingham (*645,000) 278,600
Nuneaton (**Coventry) 110,300
Oadby and Wigston (*Leicester) 52,300
Oakengates ‡17,340
Oakham ‡7,280
Oldham (**Manchester) 223,500
Ormskirk (*Liverpool) ‡28,860
Oxford (*240,000) 122,400
Penrith ‡11,400
Penzance ‡19,360
Peterborough ‡72,270
Peterlee (1971 C) 21,836
Plymouth (*295,000) 255,500
Poole (**Bournemouth) 115,500
Portsmouth (*490,000) 191,000
Preston (*245,000) 126,200
Queenborough-in-Sheppey ‡31,550
Ramsgate ‡40,090
Rawtenstall ‡20,950
Rayleigh (*London) ‡26,740
Reading (*200,000) 138,400
Redditch (*Birmingham) 64,300
Reigate and Banstead (*London) 114,000
Rickmansworth (*London) ‡29,030
Ripon ‡12,580
Rochdale (**Manchester) 209,000
*Rochester (Medway) (*London)* ‡56,030
Rotherham (**Sheffield) 248,800
Rugby ‡60,380
Runnymede see Chertsey
Rushden ‡21,840
Rushmoor see Aldershot
Ryde ‡23,170
Rye ‡4,530
Saint Albans (*London) 124,300
St. Austell [with Fowey] ‡32,710
St. Helens 188,700
Sale (Trafford) ‡59,060
Salford (*Manchester) 252,600
Salisbury ‡35,460
Sandwell see Smethwick
Sandwich ‡4,420
Scarborough ‡43,300
Scunthorpe 67,200
Seaford ‡18,020
Seaham (*Newcastle) ‡22,470
Selby ‡11,590
Sevenoaks (*London) ‡18,160
Sheffield (*705,000) 544,200
Shrewsbury ‡56,120
Sittingbourne & Milton ‡32,830
Skelmersdale [& Holland] (*Manchester) ‡35,850
Slough (*London) 98,400
Smethwick (Sandwell) (*Birmingham) 306,900
Solihull (*Birmingham) 198,300
Southampton (*410,000) 207,800
Southend-on-Sea (*London) 154,700
Southport (**Liverpool) ‡86,030
South Ribble see Leyland
South Shields (South Tyneside) (**Newcastle) 162,600
South Tyneside see South Shields
Spenborough (*Leeds) ‡41,460
Spennymoor ‡19,050
Stafford ‡54,860
Staines (Spelthorne) (*London) 93,500
Stamford ‡14,980
Stanley (*Newcastle) ‡42,280
Stevenage 73,100
Stockport (*Manchester) 291,700
Stockton-on-Tees (**Middlesbrough) 171,800
Stoke-on-Trent (*445,000) 257,200
Stourbridge (Dudley) ‡56,530
Stratford-on-Avon ‡20,080
Stretford (Trafford) (*Manchester) 224,000
Stroud ‡19,600
Sudbury ‡8,860
Sunderland (**Newcastle) 300,800
Sutton Coldfield (Birmingham) ‡83,630
Sutton-in-Ashfield (**Mansfield) ‡40,330
Swadlincote ‡21,060
Swindon (Thamesdown) 143,800
Tameside see Ashton-under-Lyne
Tamworth 60,300
Taunton ‡37,570
Tewkesbury ‡9,210
Thamesdown see Swindon
Thetford ‡15,690
Thornton Cleveleys (*Blackpool) ‡27,090
Thurrock (*London) 127,100
Tiverton ‡16,190
Todmorden ‡14,540
Tonbridge (*London) ‡31,410
Torquay (Torbay) 108,700
Trafford see Stretford

(England continued)

C Census. E Official estimate. UE Unofficial estimate.
L Population within municipal limits of year specified. • Largest city in country.

★ Population or designation of metropolitan area, including suburbs (see headnote).
▲ Population of an entire municipality, commune, or district, including rural area.
‡† Year of information specified at start of country.

* Italicized place names are now a part of the city shown in parentheses following the place name. These changes are part of the April 1974 reorganization of local administrative areas.

(England continued)

Trowbridge ‡20,120
Truro ‡15,690
Tunbridge Wells ‡44,800
Tynemouth (North Tyneside) (*Newcastle) 193,000
Ulverston ‡12,370
Wakefield (**Leeds) ‡58,490
Wallasey (Wirral) *‡94,520*
Walsall (**Birmingham) 263,400
Walton and Weybridge (Elmbridge) (*London) 110,000
Wansbeck 61,000
Warrington 168,200
Warwick (**Coventry) ‡17,870
Watford (*London) 76,500
Wellingborough ‡39,570
Wells ‡8,960
Welwyn Garden City (*London) ‡39,900
West Bridgford (*Nottingham) ‡28,340
West Bromwich (Sandwell) *‡162,740*
Weston-super-Mare ‡51,960
Weymouth and Portland 57,700
Whitby ‡12,710
Whitehaven ‡26,260
Whitstable ‡26,980
Widnes (Halton) 120,700
Wigan (**Manchester) 311,200
Wilmslow (*Manchester) ‡31,250
Winchester ‡31,070
Windermere ‡7,860
Windsor (New Windsor) (*London) ‡29,660
Winsford ‡26,920
Wirral see Birkenhead
Woking (*London) 80,500
Wokingham ‡22,390
Wolverhampton (**Birmingham) 258,200
Worcester 75,000
Workington ‡28,260
Worksop ‡36,590
Worthing (**Brighton) 90,600
Yeovil ‡26,180
York (*140,000) 100,900

WALES

Counties

Clwyd 385,100
Dyfed 325,600
Gwent 435,900
Gwynedd 226,300
Mid Glamorgan 537,500
Powys 107,100
South Glamorgan 390,600
West Glamorgan 366,600

***Cities* (1973 E)**

Aberdare 38,030
Abertillery (*Newport) 20,550
Aberystwyth 10,900
Bangor 16,030
Barry (*Cardiff) 42,780
Brecon 6,460
Bridgend 14,690
Caernarfon 8,840
Caerphilly (*Cardiff) 42,190
•CARDIFF (1979 E) (*625,000) 282,000
Carmarthen 12,860
Colwyn Bay 25,370
Ebbw Vale 25,670
Flint 15,070
Islwyn (*Newport) (1979 E) 63,400
Llandudno 17,700
Llanelli 25,870
Merthyr Tydfil 53,680
Milford Haven 13,960
Monmouth 7,000
Neath (**Swansea) 27,280
Newport (1979 E) (*310,000) 132,800
Pembroke 14,570
Pontypool (Torfaen) (**Newport) (1979 E) 90,400
Pontypridd (*Cardiff) 34,180
Port Talbot (*132,000) 50,200
Prestatyn 15,480
Rhondda (**Cardiff) (1979 E) 81,800
Rhyl 22,150
Swansea (1979 E) (*270,000) 186,900
Torfaen see Pontypool
Wrexham 39,530

SCOTLAND

Regions (1979 E)

Borders 99,938
Central 271,177
Dumfries and Galloway 142,547
Fife 340,170
Grampian 469,168
Highland 190,507
Lothian 750,728
Orkney (Island Area) 18,134
Shetland (Island Area) 22,111
Strathclyde 2,431,101
Tayside 401,661
Western Isles (Island Area) 29,758

Cities (‡1979 E or 1974 E)

Aberdeen ‡209,189
*Airdrie (Monklands) (*Glasgow)* *38,833*
Alloa 13,498
Arbroath 23,207
Ardrossan (**Irvine) 11,166
Ayr (*97,000) 47,991
Bearsden and Milngavie (*Glasgow) ‡38,812
Clydebank (*Glasgow) ‡52,835
Cumbernauld (*Glasgow) ‡49,300
Dumbarton (*Glasgow) 25,440
Dumfries 29,431
Dundee ‡190,793
Dunfermline (*124,893) 53,418
East Kilbride (*Glasgow) ‡76,000
EDINBURGH (*635,000) ‡455,126
Elgin 17,589
Falkirk (*142,058) 36,589
Forfar 11,395
•Glasgow (*1,830,000) ‡794,316
Glenrothes (**Kirkcaldy) ‡36,500
Grangemouth (**Falkirk) 24,347
Hamilton (*Glasgow) ‡107,490
Hawick 16,378
Helensburgh (*Glasgow) 13,956
Inverclyde (Greenock) ‡102,598
Inverness 36,595
Irvine (*97,000) ‡57,900
Johnstone (*Glasgow) 23,603
Kilmarnock (*82,000) 50,318
Kirkcaldy (*148,028) 50,063
Kirkintilloch (*Glasgow) 26,845
Kirkwall 4,814
Lerwick 6,307
Livingston ‡35,900
Monklands (Coatbridge) ‡109,645
Montrose 10,112
Motherwell (*Glasgow) ‡150,857
Oban 6,410
*Paisley (Renfrew) (*Glasgow)* *94,025*
Perth 44,066
Peterhead 14,994
Port Glasgow (Inverclyde) *22,278*
Prestwick (*Ayr) 13,138
Renfrew (**Glasgow) ‡214,534
St. Andrews 13,137
Stirling (*58,000) 29,818
Stranraer 10,170
Thurso 9,107
Wick 7,842

NORTHERN IRELAND

***Cities* (1971 C)**

Armagh 13,606
•BELFAST (1978 E) (*710,000) 354,400
Castlereagh (*Belfast) (1978 E) 63,900
Enniskillen 9,679
Larne 18,482
Lisburn (*Belfast) 31,836
Londonderry (1973 E) (*87,000) 51,200
Lurgan (*59,000) 25,431
Newry 20,279
Newtownabbey (*Belfast) (1978 E) 75,000
North Down (Bangor) (*Belfast) (1978 E) 61,500
Omagh 14,594
Portadown (**Lurgan) 22,207

UPPER VOLTA / Haute-Volta

1977 E 6,390,000

Bobo Dioulasso 120,000
Koudougou 38,000
•OUAGADOUGOU 180,000
Ouahigouya 27,000

URUGUAY

1975 C 2,763,964

Artigas 29,256
Canelones (1963 C) 14,180
Colonia del Sacramento (1963 C) 12,839
Dolores (1963 C) 12,483
Durazno 25,811
Florida 25,030
Fray Bentos (1963 C) 20,755
La Paz (*Montevideo) (1963 C) 13,204
Las Piedras (*Montevideo) 53,983
Maldonado (1963 C) 15,361
Melo 38,260
Mercedes 34,667
Minas 35,433
•MONTEVIDEO (*1,350,000) 1,229 748
Paysandú 62,412
Rivera 49 013
Rocha (1963 C) 19,063
Salto 71,881
San Carlos (1963 C) 13,663
San José de Mayo 28,427
Santa Lucía (1963 C) 12,630
Tacuarembo 34,157
Treinta y Tres 25,757
Trinidad (1963 C) 15,460

VANUATU

1979 C 112,596

•VILA (*14,801) 10,158

VATICAN CITY / Città del Vaticano

1977 E 723

VENEZUELA

1971 C 10,721,522

Acarigua 56,743
Altagracia de Orituco 18,717
Anaco 29,003
Araure 22,466
Bachaquero 17,896
Barcelona 78,201
Barinas 56,329
Barquisimeto 330,815
Baruta (*Caracas) 121,066
Boconó 15,915
Cabimas 118,037
Cagua 29,601
Calabozo 38,360
Caraballeda (*Caracas) 20,725
•CARACAS (*2,475,000) 1,658,500
Caripito 19,053
Carora 36,115
Carúpano 50,935
Catia La Mar (*Caracas) 62,200
Chacao (*Caracas) 78,528
Chivacoa 19,210
Ciudad Bolívar 103,728
Ciudad Guayana (Santo Tomé de Guayana) 143,540
Ciudad Ojeda (Lagunillas) 83,083
Coro 68.701
Cumaná 119,751
El Tigre 49,801
El Tocuyo 19,351
El Vigía 20,970
Guacara 38,793
Guanare 34,148
Guarenas (*Caracas) 33,374
Guatire (*Caracas) 18,604
Güigüe 18,067
La Guaira (*Caracas) 20,344
La Victoria 40,731
Los Dos Caminos (*Caracas) 59,211
Los Teques (*Caracas) 63,106
Machiques 18,898
Maiquetía (*Caracas) 59,238
Maracaibo 651,574
Maracay 255,134
Mariara 24,284
Maturín 98,188
Mérida 74,214
Morón 19,451
Ocumare del Tuy 24,229
Palo Negro 19,173
Petare (*Caracas) 227,727
Porlamar 31,985
Pozuelos 44,011
Puerto Cabello 72,103
Puerto la Cruz 63,276
Punta Cardón 18,182
Punto Fijo 55,483
San Antonio del Táchira 20,342
San Carlos 21,029
San Carlos del Zulia 26,762
San Cristobal 151,717
San Felipe 42,905
San Fernando de Apure 38,960
San José de Guanipa 22,530
San Juan de Colón 16,615
San Juan de los Morros 38,265
San Mateo 17,389
Táriba 15,683
Trujillo 25,921
Tucupita 21,417
Turmero 43,832
Upata 22,793
Valencia 367,171
Valera 76,740
Valle de la Pascua 36,809
Villa de Cura 27,832
Villa del Rosario 17,491
Yaritagua 21,363
Zaraza 15,480

VIETNAM / Viet-nam Dan-chu Cong-hoa

1967 E 37,073,000

Bac-ninh (1960 C) 22,520
Ban-me-thuot 37,500
Bien-hoa 52,200
Cam-pha (1971 E) 90,000
Cam-ranh 46,600
Can-tho 61,100
Chau-phu (1971 E) 40,400
Da-lat (1971 E) 86,600
Da-nang (1971 E) 437,700
Gia-dinh (*Saigon) (1968 E) 151,100
Ha-dong (1960 C) 25,001
Hai-duong (1960 C) 24,752
Hai-phong (1971 E) (650,000▲) 400,000
HANOI (1971 E) 1,600,000
•Ho Chi Minh City (Than-pho Ho Chi Minh) (Saigon) (1971 E) (*2,750,000) 1,804,900
Hon-gai (1960 C) 35,412
Hue (1971 E) 199,900
Khanh-hung 40,300
Long-xuyen 45,800
My-tho 62,700
Nam-dinh (1960 C) 86,132
Nha-trang 59,600
Phan-rang 21,900
Phan-thiet 58,300
Phu-cuong (1971 E) 34,400
Phu-vinh (1971 E) 51,500
Pleiku 23,700
Quang-tri (1971 E) 16,900
Quan-long 33,500
Qui-nhon 50,000
Rach-gia 56,000
Sa-dec 34,800
Truc-giang 45,200
Vinh (1960 C) 43,954
Vinh-loi 41,700
Vinh-long (1971 E) 35,300
Vung-tau 54,200

VIRGIN ISLANDS, BRITISH

1970 C 10,484

•ROAD TOWN 2,183

VIRGIN ISLANDS OF THE U.S.

1970 C 62,468

•CHARLOTTE AMALIE 12,220
Christiansted 3,020

WALLIS AND FUTUNA
Wallis et Futuna

1976 C 9,192

MATA-UTU 558
•Ono 624

WESTERN SAHARA

1974 E 108,000

•EL AAIÚN (AIÚN) 20,000

WESTERN SAMOA

1976 C 151,983

•APIA 32,099

YEMEN / Al-Yaman

1979 E 5,785,000

Hodeida (Al Ḩudaydah) (1978 E) 106,080
Mocha (Al-Mukhā) (1975 C) 1,110
•ṢAN'Ā' 192,045
Ta'izz (1975 C) 81,000

YEMEN, PEOPLE'S DEMOCRATIC REPUBLIC OF / Al-Yaman ash-Sha'bīyah

1973 E 1,555,000

•ADEN (1977 E) 271,600
Al Mukallā (1970 E) 65,000
Madīnat ash Sha'b (Al-Ittiḩad) (1966 UE) 10,000

YUGOSLAVIA / Jugoslavija

1976 E 21,560,000

People's Republics

Bosnia-Hercegovina (Bosna i Hercegovina) 4,029,000
Croatia (Hrvatska) 4,530,000
Macedonia (Makedonija) 1,784,000
Montenegro (Crna Gora) 565,000
Serbia (Srbija) 8,860,000
Slovenia (Slovenija) 1,792,000

Cities (1971 C)

Banja Luka 89 866
Bečej 26,470
•BELGRADE (BEOGRAD) (*1,150,000) 770,140
Bihać 24,026
Bijeljina 24,722
Bitola 65,851
Bor 29,039
Brčko 25,422
Čačak 38,170
Celje 31,788
Cetinje 11,892
Djakovica 29,638
Dubrovnik 31,106
Karlovac 47,532
Kikinda 37,487
Kosovska Mitrovica 42,241
Kragujevac 71,180
Kraljevo 27,817
Kranj 27,209
Kruševac 29,469
Kumanovo 46,406
Leskovac 44,255
Ljubljana 173,662
Maribor 97,167
Mostar 47,606
Nikšić 28,547
Niš 127,178
Novi Pazar 29,072
Novi Sad 141,712
Ohrid 26,370
Osijek 93,912
Pančevo (*Belgrade) 54,269
Peč 42,113
Pirot 29,228
Požarevac 33,121
Prilep 48,242
Priština 69,524
Prizren 41,661
Pula 47,414
Rijeka 132,933
Šabac 42,307
Sarajevo 244,045
Šibenik 30,090
Sisak 38,421
Skopje 312,092
Slavonski Brod 38,762
Smederevo 40,289
Sombor 43,971
Split 151,875
Sremska Mitrovica 31,921
Štip 27,289
Subotica 88,787
Svetozarevo 27,542
Tetovo 35,792
Titograd 54,509
Titovo Užice 34,312
Titov Veles 36,026
Tuzla 53,825
Valjevo 26,367
Varaždin 34,270
Vinkovci 29,072
Vranje 25,685
Vršac 34,231
Vukovar 30,149
Zadar 43,187
Zagreb 566,084
Zaječar 27,677
Zenica 51,279
Zrenjanin 59 580

ZAIRE / Zaïre

1974 E 24,222,000

Bandundu (1970 C) 74,467
Boma (1970 E) 61,100
Bukavu 182 000
Gandajika (1970 E) 60,100
Goma (1970 E) 48,600
Isiro (1970 E) 49,300
Kabinda (1970 E) 60,500
Kalemie (Albertville) (1970 E) 62,300
Kamina (1970 E) 56,300
Kananga (Luluabourg) 601,000
Kikwit 150,000
•KINSHASA (LÉOPOLDVILLE) (1975 E) 2,202,000
Kisangani (Stanleyville) 311,000
Kolwezi (1970 E) 81,600
Likasi (Jadotville) (1970 C) 146,394
Lubumbashi (Élisabethville) 404,000
Matadi 144,000
Mbandaka (Coquilhatville) 134,000
Mbanza Ngungu (1970 E) 55,800
Mbuji-Mayi (Bakwanga) 337,000
Mwene-Ditu (1970 E) 71,100

ZAMBIA

1980 E 5,834,000

Chililabombwe (Bancroft) 77,000
Chingola 192,000
Kabwe (Broken Hill) 147,000
Kalulushi 60,000
Kitwe 341,000
Livingstone 80,000
Luanshya 164,000
•LUSAKA 641,000
Mufulira 187,000
Ndola 323,000

ZIMBABWE (RHODESIA)

1979 E 7,130,000

Bulawayo (*363,000) 85,700
Fort Victoria (*24,000) 11,300
Gatooma (*33,000) 4,700
Gwelo (*70,000) 22,500
Harari (*Salisbury) (1969 C) 58,007
Highfield (*Salisbury) (1969 C) 52,560
Que Que (*51,000) 17,700
•SALISBURY (*633,000) 118,500
Shabani (*20,000) 1,900
Sinoia (*27,000) 7,200
Umtali (*64,000) 20,800
Wankie (*33,000) 14,700

C Census. E Official estimate. UE Unofficial estimate.
L Population within municipal limits of year specified. • Largest city in country.
* Population or designation of metropolitan area, including suburbs (see headnote).
▲ Population of an entire municipality, commune, or district, including rural area.
‡† Year of information specified at start of country.
* Italicized place names are now a part of the city shown in parentheses following the place name. These changes are part of the April 1974 reorganization of local administrative areas.

Populations of United States Cities, Towns, Counties, and States

This table lists alphabetically by state populations for approximately 20,000 places in the United States. Most populations are from the 1980 census. Populations for unincorporated places, not available from the 1980 census, are Rand McNally estimates or 1970 census figures. These populations are identified by a circle ○.

Populations followed by a triangle (▲) represent township or New England "town" populations. These "town" populations usually include a central village of the same name as well as other nearby communities and surrounding rural areas.

If a place is within a metropolitan area, the name of the Ranally Metropolitan Area (RMA) is designated in an abbreviated form after the place name. Each RMA includes one or more central cities, as well as socially and economically integrated surrounding areas. A central city for each RMA is identified by the use of CAPITAL LETTERS.

ALABAMA

1980 Census 3,890,061

CITIES

Abbeville	3,155
Adamsville BIR	2,498
Addison	746
Akron	604
Alabaster BIR	7,079
Albertville	12,039
Aldrich	600○
Alexander City	13,807
Aliceville	3,207
Altoona	928
Andalusia	10,415
ANNISTON ANNI	29,523
Arab	5,967
Ardmore	1,096
Ariton	844
Ashford DOTH	2,165
Ashland	2,052
Ashville	1,489
Athens HNTS	14,558
Atmore	8,789
Attalla GAD	7,737
Auburn OP-AU	28,471
Autaugaville	843
Axis	600○
Babbie	553
Bay Minette	7,455
Bayou La Batre	2,005
Bayview BIR	830○
Beatrice	558
Bellamy	750○
Berry	916
Bessemer BIR	31,729
BIRMINGHAM BIR	284,413
Blountsville	1,509
Bluff Park BIR	12,000○
Boaz	7,151
Bon Secour	600○
Brantley	1,151
Brent	2,862
Brewton	6,680
Bridgeport	2,974
Brighton BIR	5,308
Brilliant	871
Brookside BIR	1,409
Brookwood	492
Brundidge	3,213
Butler	1,882
Cahaba Heights BIR	3,800○
Calera	2,035
Calvert	500○
Camden	2,406
Camp Hill	1,628
Carbon Hill	2,452
Carrollton	1,104
Carrville	820
Castleberry	847
Cedar Bluff	1,129
Center Point BIR	15,675○
Centre	2,351
Centreville	2,504
Chatom	1,122
Chelsea	600○
Cherokee	1,589
Chickasaw MOB	7,402
Childersburg	5,084
Citronelle	2,841
Clanton	5,832
Clayhatchee	560
Clayton	1,589
Cleveland	487
Clio	1,224
Coaling	500○
Coden	500○
Coffeeville	448
Colbert Heights FLO-	500○
Collinsville	1,383
Columbia	881
Columbiana	2,655
Coosada MTGY	980
Cordova	3,123
Cottondale TUSC	2,300○
Cottonwood	1,352
Courtland	456
Cowarts DOTH	418
Creola	673
Crossville	1,222
Cuba	486
Cullman	13,084
Dadeville	3,263
Daleville	4,250
Daphne MOB	3,406
Dayton	911
De Armanville ANNI	450○
DECATUR DEC	42,002
Demopolis	7,678
Dixiana BIR	600○
Docena BIR	1,140○
Dolomite BIR	2,400○
Dora BIR	2,327
DOTHAN DOTH	48,750
Double Springs	1,057
Dozier	494
East Brewton	2,964
Eclectic	1,124
Edgewater BIR	1,400○
Elba	4,355
Elberta	491
Elkmont	429
Enterprise	18,033
Eufaula	12,097
Eulaton ANNI	650○
Eutaw	2,444
Evergreen	4,171
Fairfax	2,772○
Fairfield BIR	13,040
Fairhope MOB	7,286
Falkville	1,310
Fayette	5,287
Flint City DEC	673
Flomaton	1,882
Florala	2,165
FLORENCE FLO-	37,029
Foley	4,003
Forkland	429
Fort Deposit	1,519
Fort Payne	11,485
Frisco City	1,424
Fulton	606
Fultondale BIR	6,217
Fyffe	1,305
GADSDEN GAD	47,565
Gallant	550○
Garden City	655
Gardendale BIR	7,928
Geneva	4,866
Georgiana	1,993
Geraldine	911
Glencoe GAD	4,648
Goodwater	1,895
Gordo	2,112
Grand Bay	650○
Grant	632
Graysville BIR	2,642
Greenhill	550○
Green Pond	500○
Greensboro	3,248
Greenville	7,807
Grove Hill	1,912
Guin	2,418
Gulf Shores	1,233
Guntersville	7,041
Gurley	735
Hackleburg	883
Haleyville	5,306
Hamilton	4,792
Hanceville	2,220
Harpersville	934
Hartford	2,647
Hartselle	8,858
Hayneville	592
Headland	3,327
Heflin ANNI	3,014
Helena BIR	2,130
Hokes Bluff GAD	3,216
Holly Pond	493
Hollywood	1,110
Holt TUSC	4,300○
Homewood BIR	21,271
Hoover BIR	15,064
Hueytown BIR	13,309
Huguley	1,000○
HUNTSVILLE HNTS	142,513
Hurtsboro	752
Irondale BIR	6,521
Irvington	450○
Jackson	6,073
Jacksons Gap	500○
Jacksonville ANNI	9,735
Jasper	11,894
Jemison	1,828
Kennedy	604
Kent	500○
Ketona BIR	600○
Killen FLO-	747
Kimberly BIR	1,043
Kinsey DOTH	1,239
Kinston	604
Lafayette	3,647
Lanett	6,897
Langdale	2,235○
Leeds BIR	8,638
Leighton FLO-	1,218
Lexington	884
Lillian	600○
Lincoln	2,081
Linden	2,773
Lineville	2,257
Lipscomb BIR	3,741
Littleville FLO-	1,262
Livingston	3,187
Lockhart	547
Louisville	791
Loxley	804
Luverne	2,639
Lynn	554
McCalla BIR	500○
McKenzie	605
Madison HNTS	4,057
Madison MTGY	500○
Malvern	558
Maplesville	754
Margaret	757
Marion	4,467
Mentone	476
Meridianville HNTS	800○
Midfield BIR	6,536
Midland City DOTH	1,903
Midway	593
Millbrook MTGY	3,101
Millport	1,287
Millry	956
MOBILE MOB	200,452
Monroeville	5,674
Montevallo	3,965
MONTGOMERY MTGY	178,157
Montrose MOB	500○
Morris BIR	623
Moulton	3,197
Moundville	1,310
Mountain Brook BIR	17,400
Mount Olive BIR	1,900○
Mount Vernon	1,038
Munford ANNI	600○
Muscle Shoals FLO-	8,911
New Brockton	1,392
New Castle BIR	1,000○
New Hope HNTS	1,546
New Market	550○
Newton	1,540
Newville	814
Normal HNTS	5,000○
Northport TUSC	14,291
Notasulga	876
Oakman	770
Odenville	724
Ohatchee	860
Oneonta	4,824
OPELIKA OP-AU	21,896
Opp	7,204
Owens Cross Roads HNTS	804
Oxford ANNI	8,939
Ozark	13,188
Parrish	1,583
Pelham BIR	6,759
Pell City	6,616
Perdido	900○
Peterman	500○
Peterson TUSC	550○
Petersville FLO-	600○
Phenix City COL	26,928
Phil Campbell	1,549
Piedmont	5,544
Pinckard	771
Pine Hill	510
Pinson BIR	1,600○
Pisgah	699
Plantersville	650○
Pleasant Grove BIR	7,102
Point Clear MOB	750○
Prattville MTGY	18,647
Prichard MOB	39,541
Ragland	1,860
Rainbow City GAD	6,299
Rainsville	3,907
Ranburne	417
Red Bay	3,232
Red Level	504
Reece City GAD	718
Reform	2,245
River Falls	669
Riverside	849
River View	1,109○
Roanoke	5,896
Robertsdale	2,306
Rockford	494
Rogersville	1,224
Russellville	8,195
Rutledge	496
St. Bernard	600○
St. Elmo	450○
Samson	2,402
Saraland MOB	9,833
Satsuma MOB	3,791
Sayreton BIR	550○
Scottsboro	14,758
Section	821
Selma	26,684
Semmes MOB	1,200○
Shawmut	2,181○
Sheffield FLO-	11,903
Shelby	600○
Silverhill	624
Sipsey BIR	678
Slocomb	2,153
Smiths COL	900○
Southside GAD	4,848
Spanish Fort MOB	2,364○
Springville	1,476
Spruce Pine	600○
Stapleton	900○
Steele	795
Stevenson	2,568
Sulligent	2,130
Sumiton BIR	2,815
Summerdale	546
Sycamore	900○
Sylacauga	12,708
Sylvania	1,156
Talladega	19,128
Tallassee	4,763
Tanner HNTS	550○
Tarrant BIR	8,148
Theodore MOB	1,200○
Thomaston	679
Thomasville	4,387
Thorsby	1,422
Tillmans Corner MOB	5,100○
Town Creek	1,201
Townley	500○
Trinity DEC	1,328
Troy	12,587
Trussville BIR	3,507
TUSCALOOSA TUSC	75,143
Tuscumbia FLO-	9,137
Tuskegee	12,716
Union Springs	4,431
Uniontown	2,112
Valhermoso Springs	550○
Valley Head	609
Vernon	2,609
Vestavia Hills BIR	15,733
Vincent	1,652
Vinemont	615
Vredenburgh	433
Wadley	532
Walnut Grove	510
Warrior BIR	3,260
Weaver ANNI	2,765
Webb DOTH	448
Wedowee	908
West Blocton	1,147
West End Anniston ANNI	5,515○
Wetumpka MTGY	4,341
Whatley	450○
Wilmer MOB	581
Wilsonville	914
Wilton	642
Winfield	3,781
York	3,392

COUNTIES

Autauga	32,259
Baldwin	78,440
Barbour	24,756
Bibb	15,723
Blount	36,459
Bullock	10,596
Butler	21,680
Calhoun	116,936
Chambers	39,191
Cherokee	18,760
Chilton	30,612
Choctaw	16,839
Clarke	27,702
Clay	13,703
Cleburne	12,595
Coffee	38,533
Colbert	54,519
Conecuh	15,884
Coosa	11,377
Covington	36,850
Crenshaw	14,110
Cullman	61,642
Dale	47,821
Dallas	53,981
De Kalb	53,658
Elmore	43,390
Escambia	38,392
Etowah	103,057
Fayette	18,809
Franklin	28,350
Geneva	24,253
Greene	11,021
Hale	15,604
Henry	15,302
Houston	74,632
Jackson	51,407
Jefferson	671,197
Lamar	16,453
Lauderdale	80,504
Lawrence	30,170
Lee	76,283
Limestone	46,005
Lowndes	13,253
Macon	26,829
Madison	196,966
Marengo	25,047
Marion	30,041
Marshall	65,622
Mobile	364,379
Monroe	22,651
Montgomery	197,038
Morgan	90,231
Perry	15,012
Pickens	21,481
Pike	28,050
Randolph	20,075
Russell	47,356
St. Clair	41,205
Shelby	66,298
Sumter	16,908
Talladega	73,826
Tallapoosa	38,676
Tuscaloosa	137,473
Walker	68,660
Washington	16,821
Wilcox	14,755
Winston	21,953

ALASKA

1980 Census 400,481

CITIES

Akiachak	438
Alakanuk	522
ANCHORAGE ANCH	173,017
Anderson	517
Angoon	465
Barrow	2,207
Bethel	3,576
Chevak	466
College FRBK	3,000○
Copper Center	900○
Cordova	1,879
Craig	527
Delta Junction	945
Emmonak	567
FAIRBANKS FRBK	22,645
Fort Yukon	619
Galena	765
Gambell	445
Glennallen	600○
Haines	993
Homer	2,209
Hoonah	680
Hooper Bay	627
Juneau	19,528
Kake	555
Kasilof	500○
Kenai	4,324
Ketchikan	7,198
King Cove	460
King Salmon	500○
Kodiak	4,756
Kotzebue	2,054
Kwethluk	454
Metlakatla	1,100○
Mountain Point	459○
Mountain Village	583
Nenana	470
Nome	2,301
Noorvik	492
Palmer	2,141
Petersburg	2,821
Point Hope	464
Quinhagak	412
St. Paul Island	551
Sand Point	625
Savoonga	491
Seldovia	479
Seward	1,843
Sitka	7,803
Skagway	768
Soldotna	2,320
Togiak	470
Tok	500○
Unalakleet	623
Unalaska	1,322
Valdez	3,079
Wasilla	1,559
Wrangell	2,184
Yakutat	449

ARIZONA

1980 Census 2,717,866

CITIES

Aguila	600○
Ajo	5,650○
Alpine	500○
Apache Junction PHOE	9,935
Arizona Sunsites	900○
Ash Fork	600○
Avondale PHOE	8,134
Bagdad	2,600○
Benson	4,190
Bisbee	7,154
Black Canyon City	600○
Bouse	450○
Bowie	600○
Buckeye	3,434
Bullhead City	2,000○
Bylas	1,125○
Cameron	500○
Camp Verde	1,500○
Casa Grande	14,971
Casas Adobes TUC	5,300○
Cashion PHOE	3,000○
Catalina Foothills TUC	1,500○
Cave Creek	1,200○
Central Heights	1,500○
Chandler PHOE	29,673
Chandler Heights PHOE	750○
Chinle	950○
Chino Valley	2,858
Cibecue	950○
Clarkdale	1,512
Claypool	2,800○
Clifton	4,245
Colorado City	450○
Congress	450○
Coolidge	6,851
Cornville	800○
Cottonwood	4,550
Crane YUMA	2,400○
Dennehotso	500○
Douglas	13,058
Dreamland Villa PHOE	2,000○
Duncan	603
Eagar	2,791
Ehrenberg	900○
El Mirage PHOE	4,307
Eloy	6,240
Flagstaff	34,641
Florence	3,391
Fort Defiance	950○
Fredonia	1,040
Gadsden	500○
Ganado	1,200○
Gila Bend	1,585
Gilbert PHOE	5,717
Glendale PHOE	96,988
Globe	6,708
Goodyear PHOE	2,747
Grand Canyon	1,300○
Greasewood	450○
Green Valley TUC	6,500○
Guadalupe PHOE	4,506
Hayden	1,205
Heber	600○
Holbrook	5,785
Hotevilla	700○
Houck	600○
Huachuca City	1,661
Indian Ridge Estates TUC	2,300○
Jerome	420
Joseph City	900○
Kayenta	1,500○
Keams Canyon	600○
Kearny	2,646
Kingman	9,257

○ Rand McNally estimate (not reported in census).
▲ Population of entire township or "town", including rural area.
● Independent city. Population not included in county total.

Lake Havasu City 15,737
Lakeside 1,500○
Laveen 600○
Litchfield Park PHOE 2,500○
Little Acres 600○
McNary 900○
Mammoth 1,906
Marana 1,674
Maricopa 900○
Mayer 950○
Mesa PHOE 152,453
Miami 2,716
Moenkopi 900○
Mohave Valley 750○
Morenci 950○
Mountainaire 700○
Naco 800○
NOGALES NOGLS 15,683
Oracle 1,700○
Oraibi 600○
Page 4,907
Paradise Valley PHOE 10,832
Parker 2,542
Patagonia 980
Payson 5,068
Peach Springs 600○
Peoria PHOE 12,251
PHOENIX PHOE 764,911
Picacho 550○
Pima 1,599
Pine 500○
Pinetop 1,500○
Plantsite 1,100○
Polacca 600○
Prescott 20,055
Quartzsite 600○
Riviera 2,500○
Sacaton 1,000○
Safford 7,010
Sahuarita 600○
St. David 950○
St. Johns 3,343
Salome 600○
San Carlos 2,542○
San Luis 1,946
San Manuel 4,600○
Scottsdale PHOE 88,364
Sedona 6,500○
Seligman 950○
Sells 1,300○
Shonto 600○
Show Low 4,298
Sierra Vista 25,968
Silver Bell 600○
Snowflake 3,510
Somerton 5,761
South Tucson TUC 6,554
Springerville 1,452
Stanfield 900○
Stargo 1,194○
Sun City PHOE 39,200○
Superior 4,600
Surprise PHOE 3,723
Tacna 500○
Taylor 1,915
Tempe PHOE 106,743
Thatcher 3,374
Tolleson PHOE 4,433
Tombstone 1,632
Tuba City 1,500○
TUCSON TUC 330,537
Twin Knolls PHOE 4,700○
Valencia 1,300○
Velda Rose Estates PHOE 1,450○
Wellton 911
Whiteriver 950○
Wickenburg 3,535
Willcox 3,243
Williams 2,266
Window Rock 1,500○
Winkelman 1,060
Winslow 7,921
Wittmann 700○
Yarnell 950○
Youngtown PHOE 2,254
YUMA YUMA 42,433

COUNTIES

Apache 52,083
Cochise 86,717
Coconino 74,947
Gila 37,080
Graham 22,862
Greenlee 11,406
Maricopa 1,508,030
Mohave 55,693
Navajo 67,709
Pima 531,263
Pinal 90,918
Santa Cruz 20,459
Yavapai 68,145
Yuma 90,554

ARKANSAS

1980 Census 2,285,513

CITIES

Alma FTSM 2,755
Altheimer 1,231
Altus 441
Amity 859
Arkadelphia 10,005
Arkansas City 668
Ashdown 4,218
Ash Flat 524
Atkins 3,002
Augusta 3,496
Bald Knob 2,756
Barling FTSM 3,761
Batesville 8,263
Bauxite 433
Bay 1,605
Bearden 1,191
Beebe 3,599
Bella Vista 950○
Belleville 571
Benton 17,437
Bentonville 8,756
Berryville 2,966
Biscoe 486
Black Rock 848
Blytheville 24,314
Bonanza 553
Bono 967
Booneville 3,718
Bradford 950
Bradley 790
Brinkley 4,909
Brookland 840
Bryant 2,682
Buckner 436
Bull Shoals 1,312
Cabot L.R. 4,806
Calico Rock 1,046
Calion 638
Camden 15,356
Cammack Village L.R. 920
Caraway 1,165
Carlisle 2,567
Carthage 568
Cave City 1,634
Cave Springs FAY- 429
Centerton 425
Charleston 1,748
Cherokee Village 1,200○
Cherry Valley 729
Clarendon 2,361
Clarksville 5,237
Clinton 1,284
Coal Hill 859
College City 432
Conway 20,375
Corning 3,650
Cotter 920
Cotton Plant 1,323
Crawfordsville 685
Crossett 6,706
Cushman 556
Danville 1,698
Dardanelle 3,621
Decatur 1,013
Delight 431
De Queen 4,594
Dermott 4,731
Des Arc 2,001
Desha 600○
De Valls Bluff 738
De Witt 3,928
Diaz 1,192
Dierks 1,249
Doddridge 500○
Donaldson 500○
Dover 948
Dumas 6,091
Dyer 608
Dyess 446
Earle 3,517
Elaine 991
El Dorado 26,685
Elkins 579
Elm Springs FAY- 781
Emerson 444
Emmet 475
England 3,081
Eudora 3,840
Eureka Springs 1,989
Farmington FAY- 1,283
FAYETTEVILLE FAY- 36,604
Flippin 1,072
Fordyce 5,175
Foreman 1,377
Forrest City 13,803
FORT SMITH FTSM 71,384
Garland 660
Gassville 859
Genevia L.R. 3,500○
Gentry 1,468
Gillett 927
Gilmore 503
Glenwood 1,402
Gosnell 2,745
Gould 1,671
Grady 488
Gravette 1,218
Greenbrier 1,423
Green Forest 1,609
Greenland FAY- 622
Greenwood 3,317
Grubbs 546
Gurdon 2,707
Hackett 505
Hamburg 3,394
Hampton 1,627
Hardy 643
Harrisburg 1,921
Harrison 9,567
Hartford 613
Hartman 517
Haskell 1,074
Hazen 1,636
Heber Springs 4,589
Hector 449
Helena 9,598
Hensley L.R. 450○
Hickory Ridge 478
Holly Grove 754
Hope 10,290
Horatio 989
HOT SPRINGS NATIONAL PARK HTSPR 35,166
Hoxie 2,961
Hughes 1,919
Humnoke 442
Humphrey 872
Huntington 662
Huntsville 1,394
Huttig 976
Imboden 661
Jacksonville L.R. 27,589
Jasper 519
Johnson FAY- 519
Joiner 725
Jonesboro 31,530
Jones Mill 850○
Judsonia 2,025
Junction City 813
Keiser 962
Kensett 1,751
Knobel 503
Lake City 1,842
Lake Hamilton HTSPR 900○
Lakeview 512
Lake Village 3,088
Lamar 708
Lavaca FTSM 1,092
Leachville 1,882
Leola 481
Lepanto 1,964
Leslie 501
Lewisville 1,476
Lexa 500○
Lincoln 1,422
LITTLE ROCK L.R. 158,461
Lockesburg 616
London 859
Lonoke 4,128
Lowell FAY- 1,078
Luxora 1,739
McAlmont L.R. 1,400○
McCrory 1,942
McGehee 5,671
McNeil 725
McRae 641
Madison 1,227
Magazine 799
Magnolia 11,909
Malvern 10,163
Mammoth Spring 1,158
Manila 2,553
Mansfield 1,000
Marianna 6,220
Marion MEM 2,996
Marked Tree 3,201
Marmaduke 1,168
Marshall 1,595
Marvell 1,724
Mayflower L.R. 1,381
Melbourne 1,619
Mena 5,154
Mineral Springs 936
Monette 1,165
Monticello 8,259
Montrose 641
Morrilton 7,355
Mountainburg 595
Mountain Home 7,447
Mountain Pine 1,068
Mountain View 2,147
Mount Ida 1,023
Mount Pleasant 438
Mulberry 1,444
Murfreesboro 1,883
Nashville 4,554
Newark 1,109
Newport 8,339
Norman 539
Norphlet 756
North Crossett 2,891○
North Little Rock L.R. 64,419
Norvell 440○
Ola 1,121
Oppelo 486
Osceola 8,881
Oxford 520
Ozark 3,597
Palestine 976
Pangburn 673
Paragould 15,214
Paris 3,991
Parkdale 471
Parkin 2,035
Patterson 567
Pea Ridge 1,488
Perryville 1,058
Piggott 3,762
PINE BLUFF PNBLF 56,576
Plainview 752
Plumerville 785
Pocahontas 5,995
Portia 480
Portland 701
Pottsville 564
Prairie Grove 1,708
Prescott 4,103
Quitman 556
Rector 2,336
Redfield 745
Reyno 521
Rison 1,325
Rogers 17,429
Russellville 14,000
Salem 1,424
Searcy 13,612
Sheridan 3,042
Sherwood L.R. 10,586
Siloam Springs 7,940
Smackover 2,453
Sparkman 622
Springdale FAY- 23,458
Stamps 2,859
Star City 2,066
Stephens 1,366
Strong 785
Stuttgart 10,941
Subiaco 744
Sulphur Springs 496
Summit 506
Sweet Home L.R. 950○
Swifton 859
Sylvan Hills L.R. 2,900○
Taylor 657
TEXARKANA TEXR- 21,459
Thornton 711
Tontitown FAY- 571
Traskwood 459
Trumann 6,044
Tucker 600○
Tuckerman 2,078
Turrell 1,041
Tyronza 777
Urbana 500○
Van Buren FTSM 12,020
Vilonia 736
Wabbaseka 428
Waldo 1,685
Waldron 2,642
Walnut Ridge 4,152
Ward 981
Warren 7,646
Watson 433
Watson Chapel PNBLF 900○
Weiner 750
West Crossett 800○
West Fork 1,526
West Helena 11,367
West Memphis MEM 28,138
Wheatley 523
White Hall PNBLF 2,214
Wickes 464
Wilmar 747
Wilmot 1,227
Wilson 1,115
Wilton 495
Woodson L.R. 500○
Wynne 7,805
Yellville 1,044

COUNTIES

Arkansas 24,175
Ashley 26,538
Baxter 27,409
Benton 78,115
Boone 26,067
Bradley 13,803
Calhoun 6,079
Carroll 16,203
Chicot 17,793
Clark 23,326
Clay 20,616
Cleburne 16,909
Cleveland 7,868
Columbia 26,644
Conway 19,505
Craighead 63,218
Crawford 36,892
Crittenden 49,097
Cross 20,434
Dallas 10,515
Desha 19,760
Drew 17,910
Faulkner 46,192
Franklin 14,705
Fulton 9,975
Garland 69,916
Grant 13,008
Greene 30,744
Hempstead 23,635
Hot Spring 26,819
Howard 13,459
Independence 30,147
Izard 10,768
Jackson 21,646
Jefferson 90,718
Johnson 17,423
Lafayette 10,213
Lawrence 18,447
Lee 15,539
Lincoln 13,369
Little River 13,952
Logan 20,144
Lonoke 34,518
Madison 11,373
Marion 11,334
Miller 37,766
Mississippi 59,517
Monroe 14,052
Montgomery 7,771
Nevada 11,097
Newton 7,756
Ouachita 30,541
Perry 7,266
Phillips 34,772
Pike 10,373
Poinsett 27,032
Polk 17,007
Pope 39,003
Prairie 10,140
Pulaski 340,613
Randolph 16,834
St. Francis 30,858
Saline 52,881
Scott 9,685
Searcy 8,847
Sebastian 94,930
Sevier 14,060
Sharp 14,607
Stone 9,022
Union 49,988
Van Buren 13,357
Washington 99,735
White 50,835
Woodruff 11,222
Yell 17,026

CALIFORNIA

1980 Census 23,668,562

CITIES

Acton 650○
Adelanto 2,164
Adin 500○
Ahwahnee 600○
Alameda SF-O- 63,852
Albany SF-O- 15,130
Alhambra L.A. 64,615
Alondra L.A. 12,193○
Alpaugh 800○
Altadena L.A. 39,400○
Alturas 3,025
Alum Rock SF-O- 18,355○
Anaheim L.A. 221,847
Anderson REDD 7,381
Angels Camp 2,302
ANTIOCH ANT-P 43,559
Apple Valley 7,500○
Aptos S.CRZ 8,704○
Arbuckle 1,037○
Arcade SAC 41,200○
Arcadia L.A. 45,994
Arcata EUR 12,338
Arden SAC 54,000○
Arnold 500○
Arroyo Grande 11,290
Artesia L.A. 14,301
Arvin 6,863
Ashland SF-O- 14,810○
Atascadero 15,930
Atherton SF-O- 7,797
Atwater MRCD- 17,530
Auburn SAC 7,540
Avalon 2,010
Avenal 4,137
Avocado Heights L.A. 9,810○
Azusa L.A. 29,380
Baker 500○
BAKERSFIELD BAK 105,611
Baldwin Park L.A. 50,554
Banning 14,020
Barstow 17,690
Beaumont 6,818
Bell L.A. 25,450
Bellflower L.A. 53,441
Bell Gardens L.A. 34,117
Belmont SF-O- 24,505
Benicia SF-O- 15,376
Berkeley SF-O- 103,328
Beverly Hills L.A. 32,367
Big Bear City 950○
Big Creek 450○
Biggs 1,413
Big Pine 950○
Biola 800○
Bishop 3,333
Bloomington SBDO- 12,300○
Blue Lake 1,201
Blythe 6,805
Bonnyview REDD 4,882○
Boonville 750○
Boron 2,500○
Borrego Springs 900○
Brawley 14,946
Brea L.A. 27,913
Brentwood ANT-P 4,434
Broderick SAC 9,900○
Buena Park L.A. 64,165
Burbank L.A. 84,625
Burlingame SF-O- 26,173
Burney 2,190○
Buttonwillow 1,193○
Byron 685○
Calavo Gardens SDGO 6,100○
CALEXICO CLEX 14,412
Calipatria 2,636
Calistoga 3,879
Calpella 700○
Calwa FRES 5,191○
Camarillo V-OX 37,732
Cambria 1,716○
Cambrian Park SF-O- 5,316○
Camino 900○
Campbell SF-O- 27,067
Canby 450○
Capitola S.CRZ 9,095
Cardiff By The Sea SDGO 6,800○
Carlsbad OC-V 35,490
Carmel MTRY 4,707
Carmichael SAC 43,800○
Carpinteria S.BAR 10,835
Carson L.A. 81,221
Caspar 500○
Castle Park SDGO 5,000○
Castro Valley SF-O- 42,000○
Castroville SLNS 3,235○
Cathedral City 3,640○
Cedarville 800○
Central Valley REDD 2,361○
Ceres MOD 13,281
Cerritos L.A. 52,756
Cherryland SF-O- 9,969○
Chester 1,531○
CHICO CHICO 26,601
Chino L.A. 40,165
Chowchilla 5,122
Chula Vista SDGO 83,927
Citrus Heights SAC 25,100○
City of Commerce L.A. 10,509
Claremont L.A. 30,950
Clearlake Highlands 2,836○
Cloverdale 3,989
Clovis FRES 33,021
Coachella 9,129
Coalinga 6,593
Colfax 981
Colton SBDO- 27,419
Columbia 600○
Colusa 4,075
Compton L.A. 81,286
Concord SF-O- 103,251
Corcoran 6,454
Corning 4,745
Corona L.A. 37,791
Coronado SDGO 16,859
Corte Madera SF-O- 8,074
Costa Mesa L.A. 82,291
Cottonwood REDD 1,288○
Covelo 950○
Covina L.A. 33,751
Crescent City 3,099
Crockett SF-O- 2,700○
Cucamonga L.A. 55,250
Cudahy L.A. 17,984
Culver City L.A. 38,139
Cupertino SF-O- 25,770
Cypress L.A. 40,391
Daggett 650○
Daly City SF-O- 78,519
Danville SF-O- 7,000○
Davis 36,640
Del Aire L.A. 5,500○
Delano 16,491
Del Mar SDGO 5,017
Desert Hot Springs 5,941
Diamond Bar L.A. 10,576○
Diamond Springs 900○
Dinuba 9,907
Dixon 7,541
Dorris 836

○ Rand McNally estimate (not reported in census).
▲ Population of entire township or "town", including rural area.
● Independent city. Population not included in county total.

Downey L.A. 82,602
Downieville 500 ○
Duarte L.A. 16,766
Dublin SF-O- 13,641 ○
Dunsmuir 2,253
Durham CHICO 950 ○
Earlimart 3,080 ○
East Los Angeles L.A. 100,800 ○
East Palo Alto SF-O- 18,099 ○
East Tustin L.A. 12,500 ○
El Cajon SDGO 73,892
El Centro 23,996
El Cerrito SF-O- 22,731
El Encanto Heights S.BAR 6,225 ○
Elk Grove SAC 3,721 ○
El Monte L.A. 79,494
El Portal 600 ○
El Rio V-OX 6,173 ○
El Segundo L.A. 13,752
El Sobrante SF-O- 11,500 ○
El Toro L.A. 8,654 ○
Encinitas SDGO 6,300 ○
Enterprise REDD 11,486 ○
Escalon 3,127
Escondido SDGO 62,480
Esparto 1,088 ○
Etna 754
EUREKA EUR 24,153
Exeter VISL 5,619
Fairfax SF-O- 7,391
FAIRFIELD FRFL- 58,099
Fair Oaks SAC 15,500 ○
Fallbrook OC-V 9,000 ○
Fall River Mills 600 ○
Farmersville VISL 5,544
Feather Falls 560 ○
Felton S.CRZ 2,062 ○
Ferndale 1,367
Fig Garden FRES 9,000 ○
Fillmore 9,602
Firebaugh 3,740
Florence L.A. 24,600 ○
Florin SAC 9,646 ○
Folsom SAC 11,003
Fontana SBDO- 37,109
Foothill Farms SAC 12,300 ○
Ford City 3,503 ○
Forest Knolls 500 ○
Fort Bragg 5,019
Fort Jones 544
Fortuna 7,591
Foster City SF-O- 23,287
Fountain Valley L.A. 55,080
Fowler FRES 2,496
Frazier Park 1,167 ○
Freedom 5,563 ○
Fremont SF-O- 131,945
FRESNO FRES 218,202
Fullerton L.A. 102,034
Galt 5,514
Garberville 900 ○
Gardena L.A. 45,165
Garden Grove L.A. 123,351
Georgetown 900 ○
Gerber 775 ○
Geyserville 750 ○
Gilroy 21,641
Glen Avon Heights SBDO- 5,759 ○
Glendale L.A. 139,060
Glendora L.A. 38,654
Goleta S.BAR 25,600 ○
Gonzales 2,891
Graham L.A. 9,400 ○
Grand Terrace SBDO- 8,498
Grass Valley 6,697
Greenfield 4,181
Greenville 1,073 ○
Gridley 3,982
Grossmont SDGO 2,000 ○
Grover City 8,827
Guadalupe 3,629
Gualala 600 ○
Gustine 3,142
Hacienda Heights L.A. 43,000 ○
Half Moon Bay SF-O- 7,282
Hamilton City 800 ○
Hanford 20,958
Happy Camp 800 ○
Hawaiian Gardens L.A. 10,548
Hawthorne L.A. 56,447
Hayfork 950 ○
Hayward SF-O- 94,167
Healdsburg 7,217
Hemet 23,211
Hercules SF-O- 5,963
Hermosa Beach L.A. 18,070
Hesperia 5,700 ○
Highland SBDO- 12,300 ○
Hillcrest Center BAK 32,500 ○
Hillsborough SF-O- 10,451
Hinkley 680 ○
Hollister 11,488
Holtville 4,399
Home Gardens L.A. 5,116 ○
Homewood 500 ○
Hopland 900 ○
Huntington Beach L.A. 170,505
Huntington Park L.A. 46,223
Imperial 3,451
Imperial Beach SDGO 22,689
Independence 950 ○
Indio 21,611
Inglewood L.A. 94,245
Inverness 600 ○
Inyokern 800 ○
Ione 2,207
Irvine L.A. 62,134
Isla Vista S.BAR 13,441 ○
Isleton 914
Jackson 2,331
Jacumba 600 ○
Jamestown 950 ○
Jamul 700 ○
Janesville 600 ○
Johnsondale 600 ○
Joshua Tree 1,300 ○
Julian 500 ○
June Lake 425 ○
Kelseyville 900 ○

Kensington SF-O- 5,823 ○
Kernville 950 ○
Kettleman City 500 ○
King City 5,495
Kingsburg 5,115
Klamath 500 ○
Klamath Glen 600 ○
Knights Landing 900 ○
La Crescenta L.A. 14,900 ○
La Canada Flintridge L.A. 20,153
Ladera Heights L.A. 6,535 ○
Lafayette SF-O- 20,879
Laguna Beach L.A. 17,860
Laguna Hills L.A. 12,000 ○
La Habra L.A. 45,232
Lake Elsinore L.A. 5,982
Lake Hughes 600 ○
Lakeport 3,675
Lakeside SDGO 15,300 ○
Lakewood L.A. 74,654
La Mesa SDGO 50,342
La Mirada L.A. 40,986
Lamont 7,007 ○
LANCASTER LANC 48,027
La Palma L.A. 15,663
La Puente L.A. 30,882
Larkspur SF-O- 11,064
Laton 1,071 ○
La Verne L.A. 23,508
Lawndale L.A. 23,460
Laytonville 900 ○
Lebec 600 ○
Leggett 500 ○
Le Grand 900 ○
Lemon Grove SDGO 20,780
Lemoore 8,832
Lennox L.A. 16,121 ○
Leucadia SDGO 6,500 ○
Liberty Acres L.A. 6,500 ○
Lincoln 4,132
Lincoln Acres SDGO 1,800 ○
Lincoln Village STOC 6,112 ○
Linda MRYS- 7,731 ○
Lindsay 6,924
Live Oak S.CRZ 5,400 ○
Live Oak 3,103
Livermore SF-O- 48,349
Livingston 5,326
Lodi STOC 35,221
Loma Linda SBDO- 10,694
Lomita L.A. 17,191
LOMPOC LOMP 26,267
Lone Pine 1,800 ○
Long Beach L.A. 361,334
Los Alamitos L.A. 11,529
Los Alamos 600 ○
Los Altos SF-O- 25,769
Los Altos Hills SF-O- 7,421
LOS ANGELES L.A. 2,966,763
Los Banos 10,341
Los Gatos SF-O- 26,593
Los Molinos 900 ○
Los Nietos L.A. 7,100 ○
Loyalton 1,030
Lucerne 1,300 ○
Lucerne Valley 1,000 ○
Lynwood L.A. 48,548
McCloud 1,643 ○
McFarland 5,151
McKinleyville EUR 2,000 ○
Madera 21,732
Malibu L.A. 7,000 ○
Mammoth Lakes 900 ○
Manhattan Beach L.A. 31,542
Manteca STOC 24,925
Maricopa 946
Marina MTRY 20,647
Marina Del Rey L.A. 5,100 ○
Mariposa 950 ○
Martinez SF-O- 22,582
MARYSVILLE MRYS- 9,898
Maxwell 700 ○
Maywood L.A. 21,810
Meiners Oaks V-OX 5,600 ○
Mendocino 950 ○
Mendota 5,038
Menlo Park SF-O- 25,673
MERCED MRCD- 36,499
Middletown 900 ○
Millbrae SF-O- 20,058
Mill Valley SF-O- 12,967
Milpitas SF-O- 37,820
Mira Loma SBDO- 8,482 ○
Mission Viejo 45,000 ○
MODESTO MOD 106,105
Mojave 2,573 ○
Mokelumne Hill 560 ○
Monrovia L.A. 30,531
Montague 1,285
Montclair L.A. 22,628
Montebello L.A. 52,929
Montecito S.BAR 7,500 ○
MONTEREY MTRY 27,558
Monterey Park L.A. 54,338
Moraga Town SF-O- 15,014
Morgan Hill SF-O- 17,060
Morro Bay 9,064
Mountain View SF-O- 58,655
Mount Shasta 2,837
Murphys 950 ○
Murrieta 600 ○
Muscoy SBDO- 7,200 ○
Napa SF-O- 50,879
National City SDGO 48,772
Needles 4,120
Nevada City 2,431
Newark SF-O- 32,126
Newberry Springs 650 ○
Newhall L.A. 9,651 ○
Newman 2,785
Newport Beach L.A. 63,475
Niland 950 ○
Nipomo S.MAR 3,642 ○
Norco L.A. 21,126
North Fair Oaks SF-O- 9,740 ○
North Fork 800 ○
North Highlands SAC 36,800 ○
North Oaks L.A. 5,800 ○
Norwalk L.A. 85,232

Novato SF-O- 43,916
Oakdale 8,474
Oakland SF-O- 339,288
OCEANSIDE OC-V 76,698
Oildale BAK 20,500 ○
Ojai V-OX 6,816
Olivehurst MRYS- 8,100 ○
Ontario L.A. 88,820
Opal Cliffs S.CRZ 5,425 ○
Orange L.A. 91,788
Orangevale SAC 16,493 ○
Orcutt S.MAR 1,700 ○
Orick 900 ○
Orinda SF-O- 18,700 ○
Orland 3,976
Orleans 600 ○
Oro Grande 700 ○
Oroville 8,683
Otay SDGO 5,100 ○
Oxnard V-OX 108,195
Pacifica SF-O- 36,866
Pacific Grove MTRY 15,755
Palmdale LANC 12,277
Palm Desert 11,801
Palm Springs 32,271
Palo Alto SF-O- 55,225
Palos Verdes Estates L.A. 14,376
Palo Verde 600 ○
Paradise 22,571
Paramount L.A. 36,407
Parkway SAC 12,200 ○
Parlier 2,680
Pasadena L.A. 119,374
Paso Robles 9,163
Perris 6,740
Pescadero 450 ○
Petaluma SF-O- 33,834
Pico Rivera L.A. 53,459
Piedmont SF-O- 10,498
Pinole SF-O- 14,253
Pismo Beach 5,364
Pittsburg ANT-P 33,034
Pixley 1,584 ○
Placentia L.A. 35,041
Placerville 6,739
Pleasant Hill SF-O- 25,124
Pleasanton SF-O- 35,160
Point Arena 425
Pomona L.A. 92,742
Porterville 19,707
Port Hueneme V-OX 17,803
Portola 1,885
Poway SDGO 15,000 ○
Princeton 500 ○
Quincy 2,500 ○
Ramona SDGO 4,200 ○
Rancho Cordova SAC 39,000 ○
Rancho Mirage 6,281
Rancho Palos Verdes L.A. 35,227
Rancho Rinconado SF-O- 5,149 ○
Rancho Santa Fe SDGO 2,500 ○
Randsburg 600 ○
Red Bluff 9,490
REDDING REDD 41,995
Redlands SBDO- 43,619
Redondo Beach L.A. 57,102
Redwood City SF-O- 54,965
Redwood Valley 500 ○
Reedley 11,071
Rialto SBDO- 35,615
Richmond SF-O- 74,676
Ridgecrest 15,929
Rio Dell 2,687
Rio Linda SAC 7,524 ○
Rio Vista 3,142
Ripley 500 ○
Riverbank MOD 5,695
Riverdale 1,722 ○
Riverside SBDO- 170,876
Rocklin SAC 7,344
Rodeo SF-O- 5,356 ○
Rohnert Park SF-O- 22,965
Rolling Hills Estates L.A. 9,412
Rosamond 2,281 ○
Roseland S.ROS 5,105 ○
Rosemead L.A. 42,604
Roseville SAC 24,347
Rossmoor L.A. 12,922 ○
Rowland Heights L.A. 23,200 ○
Rubidoux SBDO- 12,400 ○
SACRAMENTO SAC 275,741
St. Helena 4,898
SALINAS SLNS 80,479
Salyer 600 ○
Samoa EUR 600 ○
San Andreas 1,564 ○
San Anselmo SF-O- 11,927
SAN BERNARDINO SBDO- 118,057
San Bruno SF-O- 35,417
San Carlos SF-O- 24,710
San Clemente L.A. 27,325
SAN DIEGO SDGO 875,504
San Dimas L.A. 24,014
San Fernando L.A. 17,731
SAN FRANCISCO SF-O- 678,974
San Gabriel L.A. 30,072
Sanger FRES 12,558
San Jacinto 7,098
San Jose SF-O- 636,550
San Juan Capistrano L.A. 18,959
San Leandro SF-O- 63,952
San Lorenzo SF-O- 23,200 ○
San Luis Obispo 34,252
San Marcos SDGO 17,479
San Marino L.A. 13,307
San Mateo SF-O- 77,561
San Miguel 800 ○
San Pablo SF-O- 19,750
San Rafael SF-O- 44,700
Santa Ana L.A. 203,713
SANTA BARBARA S.BAR 74,542
Santa Clara SF-O- 87,746
SANTA CRUZ S.CRZ 41,483
Santa Fe Springs L.A. 14,559
Santa Margarita 730 ○
SANTA MARIA S.MAR 39,685
Santa Monica L.A. 88,314
Santa Paula V-OX 20,552
SANTA ROSA S.ROS 83,205

Santa Ynez 500 ○
Santee SDGO 37,400 ○
Saratoga SF-O- 29,261
Saugus L.A. 7,700 ○
Sausalito SF-O- 7,090
Scotia 950 ○
Scotts Valley S.CRZ 6,891
Seal Beach L.A. 25,975
Seaside MTRY 36,567
Sebastopol S.ROS 5,500
Seeley 950 ○
Selma 10,942
Shafter 7,010
Sierra Madre L.A. 10,837
Signal Hill L.A. 5,734
Simi Valley L.A. 77,500
Smith River 900 ○
Solana Beach SDGO 6,000 ○
Soledad 5,928
Sonoma SF-O- 6,054
Sonora 3,239
Soquel S.CRZ 5,795 ○
South Dos Palos 700 ○
South El Monte L.A. 16,623
South Gate L.A. 66,784
South Lake Tahoe 20,681
South Modesto MOD 7,889 ○
South Pasadena L.A. 22,681
South San Francisco SF-O- 49,393
South San Gabriel L.A. 5,051 ○
South San Jose Hills L.A. 12,386 ○
South Whittier L.A. 45,800 ○
Spring Valley SDGO 36,400 ○
Stanford SF-O- 8,691 ○
Stanton L.A. 21,144
STOCKTON STOC 149,779
Stratford 800 ○
Strathmore 1,221 ○
Suisun City FRFL- 11,087
Sun City 5,519 ○
Sunnymead SBDO- 6,708 ○
Sunnyvale SF-O- 106,618
Sunol 450 ○
Susanville 6,520
Sutter Creek 1,705
Taft 5,316
Tahoe City 1,394 ○
Tara Hills SF-O- 5,400 ○
Tarpey FRES 4,700 ○
Tehachapi 4,126
Temple City L.A. 28,972
Thousand Oaks L.A. 77,797
Tiburon SF-O- 6,685
Tipton 950 ○
Torrance L.A. 131,497
Tracy 18,428
Tranquillity 600 ○
Trona 1,500 ○
Truckee 1,392 ○
Tulare 22,475
Tulelake 783
Tuolumne 1,365 ○
Turlock 26,291
Tustin L.A. 32,073
Twentynine Palms 6,000 ○
Ukiah 12,035
Union City SF-O- 39,406
Upland L.A. 47,647
Vacaville FRFL- 43,367
Valinda L.A. 18,837 ○
Vallejo SF-O- 80,188
VENTURA V-OX 74,474
Victorville 14,220
View Park L.A. 6,000 ○
Villa Park L.A. 7,137
VISALIA VISL 49,729
Vista OC-V 35,834
Walnut L.A. 9,978
Walnut Creek SF-O- 53,643
Walnut Park L.A. 8,925 ○
Wasco 9,613
Watsonville 23,543
Weaverville 1,489 ○
Weed 2,879
Weott 450 ○
West Athens L.A. 8,400 ○
West Carson L.A. 15,918 ○
West Covina L.A. 80,094
West Hollywood L.A. 34,500 ○
Westminster L.A. 71,133
West Modesto MOD 6,135 ○
Westmont L.A. 24,000 ○
Westmorland 1,590
West Pittsburg ANT-P 5,969 ○
West Point 900 ○
West Puente Valley L.A. 20,300 ○
West Sacramento SAC 12,002 ○
West Whittier L.A. 13,700 ○
Westwood 1,862 ○
Wheatland 1,474
Whittier L.A. 68,872
Williams 1,655
Willits 4,008
Willow Brook L.A. 29,600 ○
Willows 4,777
Windsor Hills L.A. 6,300 ○
Winters 2,652
Wonderland 900 ○
Woodlake 5,375
Woodland 30,235
Woodside SF-O- 5,291
Wrightwood 950 ○
Yermo 1,304 ○
Yorba Linda L.A. 28,254
Yosemite National Park 900 ○
Yreka 5,916
Yuba City MRYS- 18,736
Yucaipa SBDO- 17,400 ○

COUNTIES

Alameda 1,105,379
Alpine 1,097
Amador 19,314
Butte 143,851
Calaveras 20,710
Colusa 12,791
Contra Costa 657,252
Del Norte 18,217
El Dorado 85,812
Fresno 515,013
Glenn 21,350
Humboldt 108,024
Imperial 92,110
Inyo 17,895
Kern 403,089
Kings 73,738
Lake 36,366
Lassen 21,661
Los Angeles 7,477,657
Madera 63,116
Marin 222,952
Mariposa 11,108
Mendocino 66,738
Merced 134,560
Modoc 8,610
Mono 8,577
Monterey 290,444
Napa 99,199
Nevada 51,645
Orange 1,931,570
Placer 117,247
Plumas 17,340
Riverside 663,923
Sacramento 783,381
San Benito 25,005
San Bernardino 893,157
San Diego 1,861,846
San Francisco 678,974
San Joaquin 347,342
San Luis Obispo 155,345
San Mateo 588,164
Santa Barbara 298,660
Santa Clara 1,295,071
Santa Cruz 188,141
Shasta 115,715
Sierra 3,073
Siskiyou 39,732
Solano 235,203
Sonoma 299,827
Stanislaus 265,902
Sutter 52,246
Tehama 38,888
Trinity 11,858
Tulare 245,751
Tuolumne 33,920
Ventura 529,899
Yolo 113,374
Yuba 49,733

COLORADO

1980 Census 2,888,834

CITIES

Adams City DEN 2,200 ○
Aguilar 624
Akron 1,716
Alamosa 6,830
Antonito 1,103
Applewood DEN 6,200 ○
Arvada DEN 84,576
Aspen 3,678
Ault 1,056
Aurora DEN 158,588
Avondale 800 ○
Basalt 529
Bayfield 724
Bennett 942
Berthoud 2,362
Beulah 500 ○
Black Forest CSPG 2,700 ○
Blende PUEB 1,500 ○
Boone 431
BOULDER BOUL 76,685
Bow Mar DEN 930
Breckenridge 818
Brighton DEN 12,773
Broadmoor CSPG 1,900 ○
Brookridge DEN 1,200 ○
Broomfield DEN 20,730
Brush 4,082
Buena Vista 2,075
Burlington 3,107
Byers 1,100 ○
Calhan 541
Canon City 13,037
Carbondale 2,084
Cascade CSPG 600 ○
Castle Rock 3,921
Cedaredge 1,184
Center 1,630
Cherry Hills Village DEN 5,127
Cheyenne Canon CSPG 1,100 ○
Cheyenne Wells 950
Clifton GDJC 900 ○
Colorado City 950 ○
COLORADO SPRINGS CSPG 215,150
Commerce City DEN 16,234
Cortez 7,095
Craig 8,133
Creede 610
Crested Butte 959
Cripple Creek 655
Dacono 2,321
Deer Trail 463
Del Norte 1,709
Delta 3,931
DENVER DEN 491,396
Dolores 802
Dove Creek 826
Dupont DEN 2,000 ○
Durango 11,426
Eads 878
Eagle 801
East Alamosa 1,040 ○
Eaton 1,932
Edgewater DEN 5,714
Eldorado Springs 500 ○
Elizabeth 789
El Jebel 900 ○
Empire 423
Englewood DEN 30,021
Erie 1,254
Estes Park 2,703
Evans GRLY 5,063

○ Rand McNally estimate (not reported in census).
▲ Population of entire township or "town", including rural area.
● Independent city. Population not included in county total.

Evergreen DEN 2,321 ○
Fairplay 421
Federal Heights DEN 7,846
Firestone 1,204
Flagler 550
Florence 2,987
FORT COLLINS FTCL 64,632
Fort Lupton DEN 4,251
Fort Morgan 8,768
Fountain CSPG 8,324
Fowler 1,227
Fraser 470
Frederick 855
Frisco 1,221
Fruita 2,810
Georgetown 830
Gilcrest 1,025
Glendale DEN 2,496
Glenwood Springs 4,637
Golden DEN 12,237
Granada 557
Granby 963
GRAND JUNCTION GDJC 28,144
GREELEY GRLY 53,006
Green Mountain Falls CSPG 607
Greenwood Village DEN 5,729
Gunnison 5,785
Gypsum 743
Haxtun 1,014
Hayden 1,720
Hideaway Park 450 ○
Holly 969
Holyoke 2,092
Hotchkiss 849
Hudson 698
Hugo 776
Idaho Springs 2,077
Ignacio 667
Indian Hills DEN 900 ○
Ivywild CSPG 4,000 ○
Johnstown 1,535
Julesburg 1,528
Keenesburg 541
Kersey 913
Kremmling 1,296
Lafayette DEN 8,985
La Jara 858
La Junta 8,338
Lakewood DEN 112,848
Lamar 7,713
Laporte FTCL 900 ○
La Salle GRLY 1,929
Las Animas 2,818
La Veta 611
Leadville 3,879
Limon 1,805
Lincoln Park 2,984 ○
Littleton DEN 28,631
Log Lane Village 709
Longmont 42,942
Louisville BOUL 5,593
Loveland 30,244
Lyons 1,137
Manassa 945
Mancos 870
Manitou Springs CSPG 4,475
Manzanola 459
Meeker 2,356
Milliken 1,506
Minturn 1,060
Monte Vista 3,902
Montrose 8,722
Monument CSPG 690
Morrison DEN 478
Mountain View DEN 584
Mountain View FTCL 1,693 ○
Naturita 819
Nederland 1,212
New Castle 563
Niwot BOUL 500 ○
Northglenn DEN 29,847
North La Junta 1,249 ○
Norwood 478
Nucla 1,027
Oak Creek 929
Olathe 1,262
Orchard City 1,914
Orchard Mesa GDJC 5,824 ○
Ordway 1,135
Otis 534
Ouray 684
Ovid 439
Pagosa Springs 1,331
Palisade 1,551
Palmer Lake CSPG 1,130
Paonia 1,425
Parker 700 ○
Peri-Mack DEN 7,576 ○
Pierce 878
Platteville 1,662
Pleasant View DEN 3,800 ○
PUEBLO PUEB 101,686
Rangely 2,113
Rifle 3,215
Rocky Ford 4,804
Saguache 656
Salida 4,870
Sanford 687
San Luis 842
Security CSPG 8,700 ○
Sheridan DEN 5,377
Sherrelwood DEN 8,600 ○
Silt 923
Silverton 794
Simla 494
Skyway CSPG 3,600 ○
Southglenn DEN 2,800 ○
Southwood DEN 2,600 ○
Springfield 1,657
Steamboat Springs 5,098
Sterling 11,385
Stratton 705
Stratton Meadows CSPG 6,223 ○
Swink 668
Telluride 1,047
Thornton DEN 40,343
Trinidad 9,663
United States Air Force Academy CSPG 8,000 ○
Uravan 800 ○
Vail 2,261
Walden 947
Walsenburg 3,945
Walsh 884
Wellington 1,215
Western Hills DEN 4,500 ○
Westminster DEN 50,211
Wheat Ridge DEN 30,293
Widefield CSPG 6,600 ○
Wiggins 531
Wiley 425
Windsor 4,277
Woodland Acres 800 ○
Woodland Park 2,634
Wray 2,131
Yampa 472
Yuma 2,824

COUNTIES

Adams 245,944
Alamosa 11,799
Arapahoe 293,621
Archuleta 3,664
Baca 5,419
Bent 5,945
Boulder 189,625
Chaffee 13,227
Cheyenne 2,153
Clear Creek 7,308
Conejos 7,794
Costilla 3,071
Crowley 2,988
Custer 1,528
Delta 21,225
Denver 491,396
Dolores 1,658
Douglas 25,153
Eagle 13,171
Elbert 6,850
El Paso 309,424
Fremont 28,676
Garfield 22,514
Gilpin 2,441
Grand 7,475
Gunnison 10,689
Hinsdale 408
Huerfano 6,440
Jackson 1,863
Jefferson 371,741
Kiowa 1,936
Kit Carson 7,599
Lake 8,830
La Plata 27,424
Larimer 149,184
Las Animas 14,897
Lincoln 4,663
Logan 19,800
Mesa 81,530
Mineral 804
Moffat 13,133
Montezuma 16,510
Montrose 24,352
Morgan 22,513
Otero 22,567
Ouray 1,925
Park 5,333
Phillips 4,542
Pitkin 10,338
Prowers 13,070
Pueblo 125,972
Rio Blanco 6,255
Rio Grande 10,511
Routt 13,404
Saguache 3,935
San Juan 833
San Miguel 3,192
Sedgwick 3,266
Summit 8,848
Teller 8,034
Washington 5,304
Weld 123,438
Yuma 9,682

CONNECTICUT

1980 Census 3,107,576

CITIES

Abington 500 ○
Addison 1,100 ○
Ansonia BRDG 19,039
Attawaugan 450 ○
Avon H-NB 11,201 ▲ 1,200 ○
Bakersville 450 ○
Ballouville 500 ○
Baltic N.LON- 1,500 ○
Bantam TORR 860
Beacon Falls WATB 3,995 ▲ 1,500 ○
Bel Aire Estates N.LON- 900 ○
Berlin H-NB 15,121 ▲ 2,000 ○
Bethany 4,330 ▲ 890 ○
Bethel DANB 16,004
Bethlehem WATB 2,573 ▲ 800 ○
Black Point Beach Club 500 ○
Bloomfield H-NB 18,608 ▲ 7,400 ○
Blue Hills H-NB 6,600 ○
Branford N.HAV- 23,363 ▲ 4,500 ○
Branford Hills 2,200 ○
Branford Point 700 ○
BRIDGEPORT BRDG 142,546
Bristol H-NB 57,370
Broad Brook H-NB 1,548 ○
Brookfield DANB 12,872 ▲ 1,000 ○
Brookfield Center DANB 900 ○
Brooklyn 5,691 ▲ 900 ○
Canaan 1,083 ○
Candlewood Isle DANB 750 ○
Candlewood Shores DANB 1,950 ○
Cannondale N.Y. 1,300 ○
Canton H-NB 7,635 ▲ 1,100 ○
Centerbrook 900 ○
Central Village 1,200 ○
Cheshire N.HAV- 21,788 ▲ 13,000 ○
Chester 3,068 ▲ 1,569 ○
Clinton N.HAV- 11,195
Colchester H-NB 7,761 ▲ 3,190
Collinsville H-NB 2,897 ○
Coventry H-NB 8,895 ▲ 3,735 ○
Cromwell H-NB 10,265
Crystal Lake 500 ○
DANBURY DANB 60,470
Danielson 4,553
Darien N.Y. 18,892
Dayville 1,100 ○
Deep River 3,994 ▲ 2,333 ○
Derby BRDG 12,346
Durham N.HAV- 5,143 ▲ 2,200 ○
Eagleville 450 ○
East Berlin H-NB 900 ○
East Brooklyn 1,377 ○
East Canaan 800 ○
Eastford 1,028 ▲ 500 ○
East Granby H-NB 4,102 ▲ 500 ○
East Haddam 5,621 ▲ 600 ○
East Hampton H-NB 8,572 ▲ 3,497 ○
East Hartford H-NB 52,563
East Hartland 700 ○
East Haven N.HAV- 25,028
East Lyme N.LON- 13,870 ▲ 700 ○
East River N.HAV- 1,800 ○
Ellington H-NB 9,711 ▲ 1,000 ○
Enfield H-NB 42,695 ▲ 12,900 ○
Essex 5,078 ▲ 2,473 ○
Fairfield BRDG 54,849
Fall Mountain Lake 730 ○
Falls Village 500 ○
Farmington H-NB 16,407 ▲ 2,000 ○
Field Crest Estates N.LON- 1,200 ○
Fitchville 600 ○
Gales Ferry N.LON- 900 ○
Georgetown N.Y. 1,600 ○
Giants Neck 1,150 ○
Glastonbury H-NB 24,327 ▲ 10,200 ○
Goshen 1,706 ▲ 450 ○
Granby H-NB 7,956 ▲ 1,000 ○
Green Manorville H-NB 3,250 ○
Greenwich N.Y. 59,578
Grosvenor Dale 700 ○
Groton N.LON- 41,062 ▲ 10,086
Groton Long Point N.LON- 800 ○
Guilford N.HAV- 17,375 ▲ 3,632 ○
Haddam H-NB 6,383 ▲ 600 ○
Hadlyme 450 ○
Hamden N.HAV- 51,071
HARTFORD H-NB 136,392
Harwinton TORR 4,889 ▲ 900 ○
Hazardville H-NB 4,900 ○
Hebron H-NB 5,453 ▲ 500 ○
Heritage Village WATB 5,200 ○
Higganum 950 ○
Hitchcock Lake WATB 1,600 ○
Honeypot Glen N.HAV- 900 ○
Huckleberry Hill 700 ○
Indian Neck 2,200 ○
Ivoryton 950 ○
Jewett City N.LON- 3,294
Kensington H-NB 7,500 ○
Kent 2,505 ▲ 500 ○
Lake Beseck H-NB 500 ○
Lakeside WATB 900 ○
Lakeville 1,200 ○
Leffingwell 450 ○
Litchfield TORR 7,605 ▲ 1,489
Lords Point 460 ○
Lyme 500 ○
Madison N.HAV- 14,031 ▲ 4,310 ○
Manchester H-NB 49,761
Mansfield Center H-NB 800 ○
Marion H-NB 800 ○
Marlborough H-NB 1,200 ○
Meriden N.HAV- 57,118
Middlebury WATB 5,995 ▲ 3,900 ○
Middlefield H-NB 3,796 ▲ 600 ○
Middle Haddam 500 ○
Middletown H-NB 39,040
Milford BRDG 49,101
Milldale H-NB 1,100 ○
Monroe BRDG 14,010 ▲ 760 ○
Monroe Center BRDG 6,950 ○
Montville N.LON- 16,455 ▲ 1,688 ○
Moodus H-NB 1,352 ○
Moosup 3,376 ○
Mystic N.LON- 5,650 ○
Naugatuck WATB 26,456
Nautilus Park N.LON- 6,300 ○
New Britain H-NB 73,840
New Canaan N.Y. 17,931
New Fairfield DANB 11,260 ▲ 2,150 ○
New Hartford H-NB 4,884 ▲ 1,076 ○
NEW HAVEN N.HAV- 126,109
Newington H-NB 28,841
NEW LONDON N.LON- 28,842
New Milford DANB 19,420 ▲ 5,000 ○
New Preston 800 ○
Newtown BRDG 19,107 ▲ 2,022
Niantic N.LON- 4,000 ○
Noank N.LON- 1,371 ○
Norfolk 2,156 ▲ 1,500 ○
North Branford N.HAV- 11,554 ▲ 5,200 ○
Northfield TORR 600 ○
Northford N.HAV- 2,800 ○
North Grosvenordale 2,156 ○
North Haven N.HAV- 22,080
North Windham 750 ○
Norwalk N.Y. 77,767
Norwich N.LON- 38,074
Oakville WATB 8,300 ○
Old Mystic 500 ○
Old Saybrook 9,287 ▲ 2,281 ○
Oneco 500 ○
Orange N.HAV- 13,237
Oxford BRDG 6,634 ▲ 900 ○
Pawcatuck N.LON- 5,255 ○
Pequabuck 1,400 ○
Pine Bridge WATB 870 ○
Pine Orchard N.HAV- 1,500 ○
Plainfield 12,774 ▲ 2,923 ○
Plainville H-NB 16,401
Plantsville H-NB 5,700 ○
Pleasure Beach N.LON- 1,394 ○
Plymouth WATB 10,732 ▲ 1,000 ○
Pomfret 2,775 ▲ 500 ○
Poquonock H-NB 900 ○
Poquonock Bridge N.LON- 2,500 ○
Portland H-NB 8,383
Prospect WATB 6,807
Putnam 8,580 ▲ 6,855
Quaker Hill N.LON- 2,480 ○
Quinebaug 800 ○
Redding N.Y. 7,272 ▲ 800 ○
Ridgefield N.Y. 20,120 ▲ 6,000 ○
Rockfall H-NB 500 ○
Rocky Hill H-NB 14,559
Rogers 500 ○
Salisbury 3,896 ▲ 900 ○
Sandy Hook BRDG 950 ○
Seymour BRDG 13,434
Sharon 2,623 ▲ 900 ○
Shelton BRDG 31,314
Sherwood Manor H-NB 6,400 ○
Short Beach N.HAV- 1,200 ○
Simsbury H-NB 21,161 ▲ 4,994 ○
Somers H-NB 8,473 ▲ 1,274 ○
Somersville H-NB 750 ○
Southbury WATB 14,156 ▲ 900 ○
South Glastonbury H-NB 1,600 ○
Southington H-NB 36,879 ▲ 17,400 ○
South Windham 825 ○
South Windsor H-NB 17,198 ▲ 10,200 ○
Southwood Acres H-NB 9,800 ○
South Woodstock 800 ○
Stafford 9,268 ▲ 500 ○
Stafford Springs H-NB 3,392
Staffordville 600 ○
Stamford N.Y. 102,453
Stevenson BRDG 450 ○
Stonington N.LON- 16,220 ▲ 1,228
Stony Creek N.HAV- 700 ○
Storrs H-NB 10,691 ○
Stratford BRDG 50,541
Suffield H-NB 9,294 ▲ 1,500 ○
Tariffville H-NB 1,337 ○
Terryville H-NB 4,100 ○
Thomaston WATB 6,276 ▲ 3,500 ○
Thompson 8,141 ▲ 500 ○
Tolland H-NB 9,694 ▲ 500 ○
TORRINGTON TORR 30,987
Trumbull BRDG 32,989
Uncasville N.LON- 1,350 ○
Unionville H-NB 4,900 ○
Vernon H-NB 27,974
Wallingford N.HAV- 37,274
Warehouse Point H-NB 1,850 ○
Washington 3,657 ▲ 600 ○
Washington Depot 600 ○
WATERBURY WATB 103,266
Waterford N.LON- 17,843 ▲ 4,400 ○
Watertown WATB 19,489 ▲ 6,000 ○
Wauregan 900 ○
Wequetequock 800 ○
Westbrook 5,216 ▲ 1,509 ○
Westogue H-NB 2,396 ○
West Goshen 600 ○
West Granby H-NB 600 ○
West Hartford H-NB 61,301
West Haven N.HAV- 53,184
West Mystic N.LON- 500 ○
Weston N.Y. 8,284 ▲ 1,200 ○
Westport N.Y. 25,290
West Simsbury H-NB 1,419 ○
West Stafford 450 ○
West Suffield H-NB 500 ○
Wethersfield H-NB 26,013
Whitacres H-NB 2,500 ○
Willimantic H-NB 14,652
Wilton N.Y. 15,351 ▲ 6,500 ○
Windham H-NB 21,062 ▲ 700 ○
Windsor H-NB 25,204 ▲ 16,100 ○
Windsor Locks H-NB 12,190
Winsted 8,954 ○
Wolcott WATB 13,008 ▲ 5,500 ○
Woodbridge N.HAV- 7,761
Woodbury WATB 6,942 ▲ 1,342 ○
Woodmont BRDG 1,797

COUNTIES

Fairfield 807,143
Hartford 807,766
Litchfield 156,769
Middlesex 129,017
New Haven 761,337
New London 238,409
Tolland 114,823
Windham 92,312

DELAWARE

1980 Census 595,225

CITIES

Arden PHIL- 516
Bear PHIL- 950 ○
Bellefonte PHIL- 1,279
Belvidere PHIL- 1,100 ○
Birchwood Park PHIL- 1,500 ○
Blades 664
Briar Park DOVR 570 ○
Bridgeville 1,238
Brookside PHIL- 6,400 ○
Camden DOVR 1,757
Canterbury DOVR 500 ○
Capitol Park DOVR 900 ○
Carrcroft PHIL- 800 ○
Castle Hills PHIL- 1,950 ○
Chalfonte PHIL- 2,200 ○
Chelsea Estates PHIL- 1,650 ○
Chestnut Hill Estates PHIL- 2,000 ○
Christiana PHIL- 500 ○
Clarksville 450 ○
Claymont PHIL- 17,600 ○
Clayton DOVR 1,216
Cleland Heights PHIL- 1,500 ○
Collins Park PHIL- 2,850 ○
Delaware City PHIL- 1,858
Delmar SLSB 948
Dewey Beach 1,500 ○
DOVER DOVR 23,512
Dunleith PHIL- 2,700 ○
Dupont Manor DOVR 1,256 ○
Du Ross Heights 600 ○
Edgemoor PHIL- 4,300 ○
Elsmere PHIL- 6,493
Fairfax PHIL- 2,850 ○
Felton DOVR 547
Frankford 686
Frederica DOVR 864
Garfield Park PHIL- 1,000 ○
Georgetown 1,710
Graylyn Crest PHIL- 5,000 ○
Greenwood 578
Gwinhurst PHIL- 1,400 ○
Harmony Hills PHIL- 1,350 ○
Harrington 2,405
Hockessin PHIL- 950 ○
Holloway Terrace PHIL- 1,000 ○
Jefferson Farms PHIL- 2,400 ○
Kent Acres 600 ○
Laurel 3,052
Leedom Estates PHIL- 1,350 ○
Lewes 2,197
Lincoln 500 ○
Manor Park Apartments PHIL- 825 ○
Marshallton PHIL- 3,950 ○
Meadowood PHIL- 2,260 ○
Middletown 2,946
Midway 500 ○
Milford 5,356
Millsboro 1,233
Milton 1,359
Minquadale PHIL- 1,700 ○
Newark PHIL- 25,247
New Castle PHIL- 4,907
Newkirk Estates PHIL- 600 ○
Newport PHIL- 1,167
Ocean View 495
Penn Acres PHIL- 1,950 ○
Penny Hill PHIL- 700 ○
Rambleton Acres PHIL- 1,500 ○
Rehoboth Beach 1,730
Rodney Village 900 ○
St. Georges PHIL- 500 ○
Seaford 5,256
Selbyville 1,251
Silview PHIL- 1,650 ○
Smyrna DOVR 4,750
Stratford PHIL- 2,100 ○
Swanwyck Estates PHIL- 1,700 ○
Talleyville PHIL- 4,550 ○
Todd Estates PHIL- 2,050 ○
Willow Run PHIL- 1,950 ○
Wilmington PHIL- 70,195
Wilmington Manor PHIL- 1,750 ○
Wilmington Manor Gardens PHIL- 1,600 ○
Windy Hills PHIL- 1,300 ○
Wyoming DOVR 960
Yorklyn PHIL- 600 ○

COUNTIES

Kent 98,219
New Castle 399,002
Sussex 98,004

DISTRICT OF COLUMBIA

1980 Census 637,651

CITIES

WASHINGTON WASH 637,651

FLORIDA

1980 Census 9,739,992

CITIES

Alachua 3,561
Alford 548
Altamonte Springs ORL 22,028
Altha 478
Altoona 500 ○
Anna Maria SAR-B 1,537
Anthony 900 ○
Apalachicola 2,565
Apopka ORL 6,019
Arcadia 6,002
Archer 1,230
Atlantic Beach JAX 7,847
Atlantis WPB 1,325
Auburndale WNHV 6,501
Avon Park 8,026
Azalea Park ORL 7,367 ○
Babson Park 900 ○
Bagdad 900 ○
Baker 500 ○
Baldwin JAX 1,526
Bartow 14,780
Baskins ST.PET- 500 ○
Bayshore Gardens SAR-B 9,255 ○
Bee Ridge SAR-B 900 ○
Bellair JAX 3,000 ○
Belle Glade 16,535
Belle Isle ORL 2,848
Belleview 1,913
Biscayne Gardens MIA- 8,200 ○
Biscayne Park MIA- 3,088
Blountstown 2,632
Boca Grande 600 ○
Boca Raton MIA- 49,505
Bokeelia 500 ○
Bonifay 2,534
Bonita Springs 1,932 ○
Bowling Green 2,310
Boynton Beach 35,624
Bradenton SAR-B 30,170
Bradley 1,276 ○
Brandon TAM 12,749 ○
Branford 622
Bratt 500 ○
Brent PENS 4,100 ○
Bristol 1,044
Broadview Park MIA- 6,049 ○

○ Rand McNally estimate (not reported in census).
▲ Population of entire township or "town", including rural area.
● Independent city. Population not included in county total.

Bronson 853
Brooker 429
Brooksville 5,582
Browardale MIA- 8,900○
Brownsville MIA- 27,900○
Buena Vista 3,407○
Bunche Park MIA- 5,773○
Bunnell 1,816
Bushnell 983
Callahan 869
Callaway PNCY 7,154
Campbell 600○
Canal Point 900○
Cantonment PENS 3,241○
Cape Canaveral COCO 5,733
Cape Coral 32,103
Carol City MIA- 33,100○
Carrabelle 1,304
Carver Ranch Estates MIA- 5,515○
Caryville 633
Casselberry ORL 15,247
Cedar Key 700
Center Hill 751
Century 495
Charlotte Harbor 900○
Chattahoochee 5,332
Chiefland 1,986
Chipley 3,330
Chosen 700○
Christmas 600○
Citra 600○
Clair-Mel City TAM 5,300○
Clearwater ST.PET- 85,450
Clermont 5,461
Clewiston 5,219
COCOA COCO 16,096
Cocoa Beach COCO 10,926
Cocoa West COCO 5,779○
Coconut Creek MIA- 6,288
Coleman 1,022
Conway ORL 10,800○
Cooper City MIA- 10,140
Copeland 800○
Coral Gables MIA- 43,241
Cortez SAR-B 900○
Cottondale 1,056
Crawfordville 750○
Crescent City SAR-B 1,722
Cresthaven MIA- 5,800○
Crestview 7,617
Cross City 2,154
Crystal Beach ST.PET- 700○
Crystal Lake LKLD 6,227○
Crystal River 2,778
Cutler Ridge MIA- 17,441○
Cypress Quarters 1,310○
Dade City 4,923
Dania MIA- 11,811
Davenport 1,509
Davie MIA- 20,877
DAYTONA BEACH D.BCH 54,176
De Bary 3,154○
Deerfield Beach MIA- 39,193
De Funiak Springs 5,563
De Land 15,354
De Leon Springs 1,134○
Delray Beach 34,325
Deltona 4,868○
Destin FTWL 3,600○
Doctors Inlet JAX 450○
Dover TAM 2,094○
Dundee 2,227
Dunedin ST.PET- 30,203
Dunnellon 1,427
East Naples 6,152○
East Palatka 1,446○
Eastpoint 1,188○
Edgewater 6,726
Ellenton SAR-B 1,421○
Eloise WNHV 1,504○
El Portal MIA- 1,819
Elwood Park 450○
Englewood 5,108○
Ensley PENS 2,200○
Estero 550○
Eustis 9,453
Fairview Shores ORL 5,200○
Fellsmere 1,161
Fernandina Beach 7,224
Flagler Beach 1,951
Floral City 950○
Florida City MIA- 6,174
Fort Lauderdale MIA- 153,256
Fort Meade 5,546
FORT MYERS FTMY 36,638
Fort Myers Beach 4,305○
FORT PIERCE FTPI 33,802
FORT WALTON BEACH FTWL 20,829
Fountain 500○
Freeport 669
Frostproof 2,995
Fruitland Park 2,259
Fruitville SAR-B 1,531○
GAINESVILLE GAIN 81,371
Gibsonton TAM 2,500○
Gifford 5,772○
Glen Saint Mary 462
Glenwood 500○
Golden Beach MIA- 612
Gonzalez PENS 800○
Goodland 800○
Goulds MIA- 6,690○
Graceville 2,918
Grand Ridge 591
Grant 500○
Greenacres City WPB 8,843
Green Cove Springs 4,154
Greensboro 562
Greenville 1,096
Greenwood 577
Gretna 1,448
Grove City 1,252○
Groveland 1,992
Gulf Breeze PENS 5,478
Gulf Gate Estates SAR-B 5,874○
Gulfport ST.PET- 11,180
Haines City 10,799
Hallandale MIA- 36,517
Hampton 466
Harlem 2,006○
Hastings 636
Havana 2,782
Hawthorne 1,303
Hernando 1,500○
Hialeah MIA- 145,254
High Springs 2,491
Hilliard 1,869
Hobe Sound 2,029○
Holden Heights ORL 6,206○
Holiday 20,000○
Holly Hill D.BCH 9,953
Hollywood MIA- 117,188
Holt 600○
Homeland 450○
Homestead MIA- 20,668
Homosassa 900○
Hosford 600○
Hudson 2,278○
Immokalee 3,764○
Indian Harbour Beach MELB 5,967
Indian Rocks Beach ST.PET- 3,717
Indiantown 2,500○
Intercession City 500○
Interlachen 848
Inverness 4,095
Inwood WNHV 7,716○
Islamorada 1,500○
JACKSONVILLE JAX 540,898
Jacksonville Beach JAX 15,462
Jasmine Estates 2,967○
Jasper 2,093
Jay 633
Jennings 749
Jensen Beach 900○
Jupiter WPB 9,868
Kathleen LKLD 800○
Kendall MIA- 41,100○
Key Largo 2,866○
Keystone Heights 1,056
Key West 24,292
Kissimmee 15,487
La Belle 2,287
Lacoochee 1,380○
Lady Lake 1,193
Lake Alfred WNHV 3,134
Lake Butler 1,830
Lake City 9,257
Lake Forest MIA- 5,216○
Lake Helen 2,047
LAKELAND LKLD 47,406
Lake Magdalene TAM 9,266○
Lake Mary 2,853
Lake Park WPB 6,909
Lake Placid 963
Lake Wales 8,466
Lake Worth WPB 27,048
Lanark Village 600○
Lantana WPB 8,048
Largo ST.PET- 58,977
Lauderdale Lakes MIA- 25,426
Lauderhill MIA- 37,271
Laurel 1,200○
Laurel Hill 610
Lawtey 692
Lealman ST.PET- 16,000○
Leesburg 13,191
Lehigh Acres 5,000○
Leisure City MIA- 5,600○
Lighthouse Point MIA- 11,488
Live Oak 6,732
Lockhart ORL 5,809○
Longboat Key SAR-B 4,843
Longwood ORL 10,029
Lorida 600○
Loughman 650○
Lutz TAM 720○
Lynn Haven PNCY 6,239
Macclenny 3,851
McDavid 500○
Madison 3,487
Maitland ORL 8,763
Malabar MELB 1,118
Malone 897
Marathon 4,397○
Marco 1,500○
Margate MIA- 36,044
Marianna 7,074
Masaryktown 600○
Mayo 891
MELBOURNE MELB 46,536
Melbourne Beach MELB 2,713
Melrose 800○
Melrose Park MIA- 6,111○
Memphis SAR-B 3,207○
Merritt Island COCO 31,200○
MIAMI MIA- 346,931
Miami Beach MIA- 96,298
Miami Shores MIA- 9,244
Miami Springs MIA- 12,350
Micanopy 737
Middleburg 900○
Milligan 900○
Milton 7,206
Mims TITUS 8,309○
Miramar MIA- 32,813
Molino 900○
Monticello 2,994
Moore Haven 1,250
Mount Dora 5,883
Mulberry 2,932
Myrtle Grove PENS 16,186○
Naples 17,581
Naranja MIA- 2,900○
Neptune Beach JAX 5,248
Newberry 1,826
New Port Richey 11,196
New Smyrna Beach 13,557
Niceville FTWL 8,543
Nocatee 900○
Nokomis 2,500○
Norland MIA- 25,400○
North Andrews Gardens MIA- 7,082○
North Fort Myers FTMY 8,798○
North Lauderdale MIA- 18,479
North Miami MIA- 42,566
North Miami Beach MIA- 36,481
North Naples 3,201○
North Palm Beach WPB 11,344
North Port 6,205
Oak Hill 938
Oakland 658
Oakland Park MIA- 21,939
Ocala 37,170
Ocean City FTWL 5,267○
Ocoee ORL 7,803
Okeechobee 4,225
Oklawaha 950○
Oldsmar TAM 2,608
Olympia Heights MIA- 14,000○
Oneco SAR-B 3,246○
Opa Locka MIA- 14,460
Orange City 2,795
Orange Lake 500○
Orange Park JAX 8,766
ORLANDO ORL 128,394
Ormond Beach D.BCH 21,378
Ormond By The Sea D.BCH 6,002○
Osprey SAR-B 1,115○
Osteen 550○
Oxford 490○
Pace 1,776○
Pahokee 6,346
Palatka 10,175
Palm Bay MELB 18,560
Palm Beach WPB 9,729
Palmetto SAR-B 8,637
Palm Harbor ST.PET- 4,500○
Palm Springs WPB 8,166
Panacea 700○
PANAMA CITY PNCY 33,346
Panama City Beach PNCY 2,148
Parker PNCY 4,298
Parrish 850○
Paxton 659
Pembroke Pines MIA- 35,776
Penney Farms 630
PENSACOLA PENS 57,619
Perrine MIA- 10,257○
Perry 8,254
Pierson 1,085
Pine Castle ORL 4,700○
Pine Crest TAM 8,458○
Pine Hills ORL 13,882○
Pinellas Park ST.PET- 32,811
Pinewood MIA- 7,800○
Plantation MIA- 48,501
Plant City 19,270
Plymouth 700○
Polk City 576
Pomona Park 791
Pompano Beach MIA- 52,618
Pompano Beach Highlands MIA- 5,014○
Ponce de Leon 454
Ponte Vedra Beach JAX 1,000○
Port Charlotte 13,500○
Port Orange D.BCH 18,756
Port St. Joe 4,027
Port St. Lucie FTPI 14,690
Port Richey 2,165
Port Salerno 1,161○
Princeton MIA- 1,300○
Punta Gorda 6,797
Quincy 8,591
Red Bay 500○
Reddick 657
Richmond Heights MIA- 6,663○
Rio 900○
Riverview TAM 2,225○
Riviera Beach WPB 26,596
Rockledge COCO 11,877
Rocky Creek TAM 5,700○
Roseland 500○
Rubonia SAR-B 500○
Ruskin 2,414○
Safety Harbor ST.PET- 6,461
St. Augustine 11,985
St. Cloud 7,840
St. James City 800○
St. Leo 899
St. Lucie FTPI 593
ST. PETERSBURG ST.PET- 236,893
St. Petersburg Beach ST.PET- 9,354
Salt Springs 900○
Samoset SAR-B 4,070○
San Antonio 529
Sanford 23,176
Sanibel 3,363
San Mateo 900○
Santa Rosa Beach 650○
SARASOTA SAR-B 48,868
Satellite Beach MELB 9,163
Satsuma 500○
Sebastian 2,831
Sebring 8,736
Seminole Park ST.PET- 5,300○
Seville 650○
Sharpes COCO 700○
Silver Springs 900○
Sneads 1,690
Solana 1,286○
Sopchoppy 444
Sorrento 500○
South Bay 3,886
South Daytona D.BCH 9,608
South Miami MIA- 10,884
South Miami Heights MIA- 14,000○
South Patrick Shores MELB 10,313○
Southport PNCY 1,560○
South Venice 3,000○
Sparr 550○
Springfield PNCY 7,220
Spring Hill 950○
Starke 5,306
Stuart 9,467
Summerland Key 500○
Sunnyland SAR-B 800○
Sunrise MIA- 39,681
Surfside MIA- 3,763
Sweetwater Creek TAM 13,700○
TALLAHASSEE TALL 81,548
Tamarac MIA- 29,142
TAMPA TAM 271,523
Tarpon Springs 13,251
Tavares 4,103
Tavernier 900○
Telogia 500○
Temple Terrace TAM 11,097
Thonotosassa TAM 800○
Tice FTMY 7,254○
TITUSVILLE TITUS 31,910
Treasure Island ST.PET- 6,316
Trenton 1,131
Trilby 600○
Uleta MIA- 5,200○
Umatilla 1,872
Valparaiso FTWL 6,142
Venice 12,153
Vernon 885
Vero Beach 16,176
Wabasso 600○
Waldo 993
Warrington PENS 15,848○
Wauchula 2,986
Webster 856
Weirsdale 900○
Welaka 492
West Bay 700○
Westchester MIA- 6,600○
Westgate WPB 1,900○
West Melbourne MELB 5,078
West Miami MIA- 6,076
WEST PALM BEACH WPB 62,530
West Pensacola PENS 22,100○
Westwood Lakes MIA- 12,811○
Wewahitchka 1,742
White City 700○
White City FTPI 1,000○
White Springs 781
Whitfield Estates SAR-B 1,362○
Wildwood 2,665
Williston 2,240
Wilton Manors MIA- 12,742
Wimauma 900○
Winston LKLD 4,505○
Winter Beach 700○
Winter Garden 6,789
WINTER HAVEN WNHV 21,119
Winter Park ORL 22,314
Winter Springs ORL 10,475
Woodville 800○
Yalaha 650○
Yankeetown 600
Zephyrhills 5,742
Zolfo Springs 1,495

COUNTIES

Alachua 151,348
Baker 15,289
Bay 97,740
Bradford 20,023
Brevard 272,959
Broward 1,014,043
Calhoun 9,294
Charlotte 59,115
Citrus 54,703
Clay 67,052
Collier 85,791
Columbia 35,399
Dade 1,625,979
De Soto 19,039
Dixie 7,751
Duval 570,981
Escambia 233,794
Flagler 10,913
Franklin 7,661
Gadsden 41,565
Gilchrist 5,767
Glades 5,992
Gulf 10,658
Hamilton 8,761
Hardee 19,379
Hendry 18,599
Hernando 44,469
Highlands 47,526
Hillsborough 646,960
Holmes 14,723
Indian River 59,896
Jackson 39,154
Jefferson 10,703
Lafayette 4,035
Lake 104,870
Lee 205,266
Leon 148,655
Levy 19,870
Liberty 4,260
Madison 14,894
Manatee 148,442
Marion 122,488
Martin 64,014
Monroe 63,098
Nassau 32,894
Okaloosa 109,920
Okeechobee 20,264
Orange 471,660
Osceola 49,287
Palm Beach 573,125
Pasco 194,123
Pinellas 728,409
Polk 321,652
Putnam 50,549
St. Johns 51,303
St. Lucie 87,182
Santa Rosa 55,988
Sarasota 202,251
Seminole 179,752
Sumter 24,272
Suwannee 22,287
Taylor 16,532
Union 10,166
Volusia 258,762
Wakulla 10,887
Walton 21,300
Washington 14,509

GEORGIA

1980 Census 5,464,265

CITIES

Abbeville 985
Acworth ATL 3,648
Adairsville 1,739
Adel 5,592
Adrian 756
Ailey 579
Alamo 993
Alapaha 771
ALBANY ALB 73,934
Allenhurst 606
Alma 3,819
Alpharetta ATL 3,128
Alto 618
Americus 16,120
Aragon 855
Arlington 1,572
Ashburn 4,766
ATHENS ATH 42,549
ATLANTA ATL 425,022
Attapulgus 623
Auburn ATL 692
AUGUSTA AUG 47,532
Austell ATL 3,939
Avondale Estates ATL 1,313
Baconton 763
Bainbridge 10,553
Baldwin 1,080
Ball Ground 640
Barnesville 4,887
Barwick 413
Baxley 3,586
Belvedere Park ATL 27,000○
Berlin 538
Bibb City COL 667
Blackshear 3,222
Blairsville 530
Blakely 5,880
Bloomingdale SAV 1,855
Blue Ridge 1,376
Bogart ATH 819
Boston 1,424
Bowdon 1,743
Bowman 890
Bremen 3,966
Bronwood 524
Brooklet 1,035
Broxton 1,117
BRUNSWICK BRUNS 17,605
Buchanan 1,019
Buena Vista 1,544
Buford ATL 6,697
Butler 1,959
Byromville 567
Byron MAC- 1,661
Cairo 8,777
Calhoun 5,335
Camilla 5,414
Canon 704
Canton 3,601
Carnesville 465
Carrollton 14,078
Cartersville 9,508
Cataula 500○
Cave Spring 883
Cedartown 8,619
Chamblee ATL 7,137
Chatsworth 2,493
Chickamauga CHTN 2,232
Chicopee 900○
Clarkdale ATL 550○
Clarkesville 1,348
Clarkston ATL 4,539
Claxton 2,694
Clayton 1,838
Cleveland 1,578
Cobbtown 494
Cochran 5,121
Colbert ATH 498
College Park ATL 24,632
Collins 639
Colquitt 2,065
COLUMBUS COL 169,441
Comer 930
Commerce 4,092
Conyers ATL 6,567
Coolidge 736
Cordele 10,914
Cornelia 3,203
Covington ATL 10,586
Crawfordville 594
Cumming ATL 2,094
Cusseta COL 1,218
Cuthbert 4,340
Dacula ATL 1,577
Dahlonega 2,844
Dallas ATL 2,440
Dalton 20,743
Danville 529
Darien 1,731
Davisboro 433
Dawson 5,699
Dearing 539
Decatur ATL 18,404
Demorest 1,130
Dexter 527
Dock Junction BRUNS 6,009○
Doerun 1,062
Donalsonville 3,320
Doraville ATL 7,414
Douglas 10,980
Douglasville ATL 7,641
Dublin 16,083
Dudley 425
Duluth ATL 2,956
Dunaire ATL 5,400○
Dunwoody ATL 4,400○
East Ellijay 469
Eastman 5,330
East Newnan 1,634○
East Point ATL 37,486
Eatonton 4,833
Eden SAV 450○
Edison 1,128
Elberton 5,686
Eldorado 1,000○
Elizabeth ATL 1,700○
Ellaville 1,684
Ellenwood ATL 500○
Ellijay 1,507
Emerson ATL 1,110
Enigma 574
Evans AUG 800○
Experiment 2,000○

○ Rand McNally estimate (not reported in census).
▲ Population of entire township or "town", including rural area.
● Independent city. Population not included in county total.

Fairburn ATL	3,466
Fairmount	842
Fair Oaks ATL	13,200○
Fargo	600○
Fayetteville ATL	2,715
Fitzgerald	10,187
Flovilla	458
Flowery Branch ATL	755
Folkston	2,243
Forest Park ATL	18,782
Forsyth	4,624
Fort Gaines	1,260
Fort Oglethorpe CHTN	5,443
Fort Valley	9,000
Franklin	711
Gainesville	15,280
Garden City SAV	6,895
Georgetown	935
Gibson	730
Glennville	4,144
Glenwood	824
Gordon	2,768
Gracewood AUG	500○
Grantville	1,110
Gray MAC-	2,145
Grayson ATL	464
Greensboro	2,985
Greenville	1,213
Gresham Park ATL	6,600○
Griffin	20,728
Grovetown AUG	3,491
Guyton	749
Haddock	700○
Hagan	880
Hahira	1,534
Hamilton	506
Hampton ATL	2,059
Hapeville ATL	6,166
Hardwick	6,000○
Harlem AUG	1,485
Harrison	456
Hartwell	4,855
Hawkinsville	4,372
Hazlehurst	4,249
Helena	1,390
Hephzibah	1,452
Hiawassee	491
Hiltonia	515
Hinesville	11,309
Hiram ATL	711
Hoboken	514
Hogansville	3,362
Holly Springs ATL	687
Homeland	683
Homer	734
Homerville	3,112
Hoschton	490
Ideal	619
Irwinton	841
Jackson	4,133
Jasper	1,556
Jefferson	1,820
Jeffersonville	1,473
Jesup	9,418
Jonesboro ATL	4,132
Kennesaw ATL	5,095
Kingsland	2,008
Kingston	733
La Fayette	6,517
La Grange	24,204
Lakeland	2,647
Lake Park VALD	448
Lakeview CHTN	8,000○
La Vista ATL	5,200○
Lavonia	2,024
Lawrenceville ATL	8,928
Leary	783
Leesburg	1,301
Lenox	965
Leslie	470
Lilburn ATL	3,765
Lincoln Park	1,852○
Lincolnton	1,406
Lindale ROME	2,768○
Linwood	417
Lithia Springs ATL	4,000○
Lithonia ATL	2,637
Lizella MAC-	600○
Locust Grove ATL	1,479
Loganville ATL	1,841
Louisville	2,823
Ludowici	1,286
Lula	857
Lumber City	1,426
Lumpkin	1,335
Luthersville	597
Lyerly	482
Lyons	4,203
Mableton ATL	12,900○
McCaysville	1,219
McDonough ATL	2,778
MACON MAC-	116,860
McRae	3,409
Madison	2,954
Manchester	4,796
Mansfield	435
Marietta ATL	30,805
Marshallville	1,540
Martinez AUG	7,300○
Maysville	619
Meigs	1,231
Menlo	611
Metter	3,531
Midville	670
Milan	1,115
Milledgeville	12,176
Millen	3,988
Milstead ATL	1,157○
Monroe	8,854
Montezuma	4,830
Monticello	2,382
Morrow ATL	3,791
Morven	471
Moultrie	15,708
Mountain City	701
Mount Airy	670
Mount Berry ROME	500○
Mount Vernon	1,737
Mount Zion	445
Nahunta	951
Nashville	4,831
Nelson	562
New Holland	800○
Newnan	11,449
Newton	711
Nicholls	1,114
Norcross ATL	3,317
Norman Park	757
North Atlanta ATL	19,700○
North Decatur ATL	10,700○
North Druid Hills ATL	7,200○
Oakdale ATL	800○
Oakwood	723
Ochlocknee	627
Ocilla	3,436
Oglethorpe	1,305
Omega	996
Oxford ATL	1,750
Palmetto ATL	2,086
Panthersville ATL	7,000○
Patterson	763
Pavo	830
Peach Orchard AUG	14,000○
Peachtree City	6,429
Pearson	1,827
Pelham	4,306
Pembroke	1,400
Pendley Hills ATL	5,800○
Perry MAC-	9,453
Pinehurst	431
Pine Lake ATL	901
Pine Mountain	984
Pineview	564
Plains	651
Pooler SAV	2,543
Portal	694
Porterdale ATL	1,451
Port Wentworth SAV	3,947
Poulan	818
Powder Springs ATL	3,381
Preston	429
Quitman	5,188
Raoul	1,400○
Ray City	658
Red Oak ATL	1,200○
Reidsville	2,296
Remerton VALD	443
Reynolds	1,298
Rhine	590
Richland	1,802
Richmond Hill	1,177
Rincon SAV	1,988
Ringgold CHTN	1,821
Riverdale ATL	7,121
Roberta	859
Rochelle	1,626
Rockmart	3,645
ROME ROME	29,654
Rossville CHTN	3,745
Roswell ATL	23,337
Royston	2,404
Rutledge	694
St. Marys	3,596
St. Simons Island BRUNS	5,346○
Sandersville	6,137
Sandy Springs ATL	16,000○
Sardis	1,180
Sargent	700○
SAVANNAH SAV	141,634
Tybee Island SAV	2,240
Scottdale ATL	9,200○
Screven	872
Senoia	900
Shannon ROME	1,563○
Shellman	1,254
Siloam	446
Smithville	867
Smyrna ATL	20,312
Snellville ATL	8,514
Social Circle	2,591
Soperton	2,981
South Decatur ATL	28,100○
Sparks	1,353
Sparta	1,745
Springfield	1,075
Statenville	650○
Statesboro	14,866
Statham	1,101
Stillmore	527
Stockbridge ATL	2,103
Stone Mountain ATL	4,867
Sugar Hill ATL	2,340
Summerville	4,878
Suwanee ATL	1,026
Swainsboro	7,602
Sycamore	474
Sylvania	3,352
Sylvester	5,860
Talbotton	1,140
Tallapoosa	2,647
Tate	900○
Temple	1,520
Tennille	1,709
Thomaston	9,682
Thomasville	18,463
Thomson	7,001
Thunderbolt SAV	2,165
Tifton	13,749
Tignall	733
Toccoa	9,104
Toomsboro	673
Trenton CHTN	1,636
Trion	1,732
Tucker ATL	12,500○
Tunnel Hill	867
Twin City	1,402
Ty Ty	618
Unadilla	1,566
Union City ATL	4,780
Union Point	1,750
Uvalda	646
VALDOSTA VALD	37,596
Vidalia	10,393
Vienna	2,886
Villa Rica ATL	3,420
Waco	471
Wadley	2,438
Waleska	450
Walthourville	905
Warm Springs	425
Warner Robins MAC-	39,893
Warrenton	2,172
Warwick	488
Washington	4,662
Watkinsville ATH	1,240
Waverly Hall	913
Waycross	19,371
Waynesboro	5,760
West Point	4,294
Whigham	507
White	501
Whitesburg	775
Willacoochee	1,166
Winder	6,705
Windsor Forest SAV	7,288○
Winterville ATH	621
Woodbine	910
Woodbury	1,738
Woodland	664
Woodstock ATL	2,699
Woodville	455
Wrens	2,415
Wrightsville	2,526
Young Harris	687
Zebulon	995

COUNTIES

Appling	15,565
Atkinson	6,141
Bacon	9,379
Baker	3,808
Baldwin	34,686
Banks	8,702
Barrow	21,293
Bartow	40,760
Ben Hill	16,000
Berrien	13,525
Bibb	151,085
Bleckley	10,767
Brantley	8,701
Brooks	15,255
Bryan	10,175
Bulloch	35,785
Burke	19,349
Butts	13,665
Calhoun	5,717
Camden	13,371
Candler	7,518
Carroll	56,346
Catoosa	36,991
Charlton	7,343
Chatham	202,226
Chattahoochee	21,732
Chattooga	21,856
Cherokee	51,699
Clarke	74,498
Clay	3,553
Clayton	150,357
Clinch	6,660
Cobb	297,694
Coffee	26,894
Colquitt	35,376
Columbia	40,118
Cook	13,490
Coweta	39,268
Crawford	7,684
Crisp	19,489
Dade	12,318
Dawson	4,774
Decatur	25,495
De Kalb	483,024
Dodge	16,955
Dooly	10,826
Dougherty	100,978
Douglas	54,573
Early	13,158
Echols	2,297
Effingham	18,327
Elbert	18,758
Emanuel	20,795
Evans	8,428
Fannin	14,748
Fayette	29,043
Floyd	79,800
Forsyth	27,958
Franklin	15,185
Fulton	589,904
Gilmer	11,110
Glascock	2,382
Glynn	54,981
Gordon	30,070
Grady	19,845
Greene	11,391
Gwinnett	166,903
Habersham	25,020
Hall	75,649
Hancock	9,466
Haralson	18,422
Harris	15,464
Hart	18,585
Heard	6,520
Henry	36,309
Houston	77,605
Irwin	8,988
Jackson	25,343
Jasper	7,553
Jeff Davis	11,473
Jefferson	18,403
Jenkins	8,841
Johnson	8,660
Jones	16,579
Lamar	12,215
Lanier	5,654
Laurens	36,990
Lee	11,684
Liberty	37,583
Lincoln	6,949
Long	4,524
Lowndes	67,972
Lumpkin	10,762
McDuffie	18,546
McIntosh	8,046
Macon	14,003
Madison	17,747
Marion	5,297
Meriwether	21,229
Miller	7,038
Mitchell	21,114
Monroe	14,610
Montgomery	7,011
Morgan	11,572
Murray	19,685
Newton	34,489
Oconee	12,427
Oglethorpe	8,929
Paulding	26,042
Peach	19,151
Pickens	11,652
Pierce	11,897
Pike	8,937
Polk	32,386
Pulaski	8,950
Putnam	10,295
Quitman	2,357
Rabun	10,466
Randolph	9,599
Richmond	181,629
Rockdale	36,747
Schley	3,433
Screven	14,043
Seminole	9,057
Spalding	47,899
Stephens	21,763
Stewart	5,896
Sumter	29,360
Talbot	6,536
Taliaferro	2,032
Tattnall	18,134
Taylor	7,902
Telfair	11,445
Terrell	12,017
Thomas	38,098
Tift	32,862
Toombs	22,592
Towns	5,638
Treutlen	6,087
Troup	50,003
Turner	9,510
Twiggs	9,354
Union	9,390
Upson	25,998
Walker	56,470
Walton	31,211
Ware	37,180
Warren	6,583
Washington	18,842
Wayne	20,750
Webster	2,341
Wheeler	5,155
White	10,120
Whitfield	65,780
Wilcox	7,682
Wilkes	10,951
Wilkinson	10,368
Worth	18,064

HAWAII

1980 Census 965,000

CITIES

Aiea HON	12,560○
Anahola	638○
Captain Cook	1,263○
Crestview HON	1,000○
Eleele	758○
Ewa HON	2,906○
Ewa Beach HON	7,765○
Foster Village HON	3,755○
Haiku	464○
Hakalau	742○
Halaula	600○
Halawa Heights HON	5,809○
Haleiwa	2,626○
Haliimaile	638○
Hana	459○
Hanamaulu	2,461○
Hanapepe	1,388○
Hauula HON	2,048○
Hawi	797○
Hilo	29,600○
Holualoa	800○
Honaunau	900○
Honokaa	1,555○
Honokahua	431○
HONOLULU HON	365,048
Honomu	737○
Kaaawa HON	848○
Kahaluu HON	1,657○
Kahuku HON	917○
Kahului	8,280○
Kailua HON	39,700○
Kalaheo	1,514○
Kamuela	756○
Kaneohe HON	35,600○
Kapaa	3,794○
Kaumakani	1,014○
Kaunakakai	1,070○
Keaau	951○
Kealakekua	740○
Kealia	600○
Kekaha	2,404○
Keokea	500○
Kihei	900○
Kilauea	671○
Koloa	1,368○
Kualapuu	441○
Kurtistown	700○
Lahaina	3,718○
Laie HON	3,009○
Lanai City	2,122○
Laupahoehoe	452○
Lawai	600○
Lihue	3,124○
Lower Paia	1,105○
Maili HON	4,397○
Makaha HON	4,644○
Makakilo HON	3,499○
Makawao	1,066○
Makaweli	500○
Maunaloa	872○
Maunawili HON	5,303○
Mililani Town HON	2,035○
Mountainview	419○
Naalehu	1,014○
Nanakuli HON	6,506○
Ookala	486○
Paauhau	450○
Paauilo	710○
Pacific Palisades HON	7,846○
Pahala	1,507○
Pahoa	924○
Paia	541○
Papaikou	1,888○
Pearl City HON	22,200○
Poipu	466○
Puhi	772○
Pukalani	1,629○
Puunene	1,132○
Sunset Beach	500○
Wahiawa HON	17,598○
Waialua	4,047○
Waianae HON	3,302○
Waikapu	598○
Wailua	1,379○
Wailuku	7,979○
Waimalu HON	2,982○
Waimanalo	2,081○
Waimanalo Beach HON	3,045○
Waimea	1,569○
Waipahu HON	29,200○
Waipio Acres HON	2,146○
Whitmore Village HON	2,015○

COUNTIES

Hawaii	92,053
Honolulu	762,874
Kauai	39,082
Maui	71,047

IDAHO

1980 Census 943,935

CITIES

Aberdeen	1,528
American Falls	3,626
Ammon IDFL	4,669
Arco	1,241
Ashton	1,219
Avery	430○
Bancroft	505
Basalt	414
Bellevue	1,016
Blackfoot	10,065
BOISE BOIS	102,451
Bonners Ferry	1,906
Buhl	3,629
Burley	8,761
Caldwell	17,699
Cambridge	428
Cascade	945
Challis	758
Chubbuck POC	7,052
Clark Fork	449
Coeur d'Alene	20,054
Collister BOIS	2,700○
Cottonwood	941
Council	917
Craigmont	617
Dalton Gardens	1,795
Deary	539
Downey	645
Driggs	727
Dubois	413
Eagle	2,620
Elk City	450○
Emmett	4,605
Filer	1,645
Firth	460
Fort Hall	600○
Franklin	423
Fruitland	2,456
Garden City BOIS	4,571
Genesee	791
Georgetown	544
Glenns Ferry	1,374
Gooding	2,949
Grace	1,216
Grangeville	3,666
Hagerman	602
Hailey	2,109
Hansen	1,078
Hayden	2,586
Hazelton	496
Heyburn	2,889
Homedale	2,078
Horseshoe Bend	700
IDAHO FALLS IDFL	39,590
Inkom	830
Iona IDFL	1,072
Jerome	6,891
Juliaetta	522
Kamiah	1,478
Kellogg	3,417
Ketchum	2,200
Kimberly	2,307
Kingston	500○
Kooskia	784
Kuna	1,767
Lapwai	1,043
Lava Hot Springs	467
Lewiston	27,986
Lewisville	502
McCall	2,188
McCammon	770
Mackay	541
Malad City	1,915
Marsing	786
Menan	605
Meridian BOIS	6,658
Middleton	1,901
Montpelier	3,107
Moscow	16,513
Mountain Home	7,540
Mullan	1,269
Nampa	25,112
New Meadows	576
New Plymouth	1,186

○ Rand McNally estimate (not reported in census); Hawaii populations are 1970 populations based on statistical boundaries established by the state.
▲ Population of entire township or "town", including rural area.
● Independent city. Population not included in county total.

Nezperce 517
Notus 437
Oakley 663
Orofino 3,711
Osburn 2,220
Paris 707
Parma 1,820
Paul 940
Payette 5,448
Pierce 1,060
Plummer 634
POCATELLO POC 46,340
Post Falls 5,736
Potlatch 819
Preston 3,759
Priest River 1,639
Rathdrum 1,369
Rexburg 11,559
Rigby 2,624
Riggins 527
Ririe 555
Roberts 466
Rupert 5,476
St. Anthony 3,212
St. Maries 2,794
Salmon 3,308
Sandpoint 4,460
Shelley 3,300
Shoshone 1,242
Silverton 800○
Smelterville 776
Soda Springs 4,051
Spirit Lake 834
Star 450○
Sugar City 1,022
Sun Valley 545
Teton 559
Troy 820
Twin Falls 26,209
Ucon 833
Wallace 1,736
Wardner 423
Weippe 828
Weiser 4,771
Wendell 1,974
Wilder 1,260

COUNTIES

Ada 173,036
Adams 3,347
Bannock 65,421
Bear Lake 6,931
Benewah 8,292
Bingham 36,489
Blaine 9,841
Boise 2,999
Bonner 24,163
Bonneville 65,980
Boundary 7,289
Butte 3,342
Camas 818
Canyon 83,756
Caribou 8,695
Cassia 19,427
Clark 798
Clearwater 10,390
Custer 3,385
Elmore 21,565
Franklin 8,895
Fremont 10,813
Gem 11,972
Gooding 11,874
Idaho 14,769
Jefferson 15,304
Jerome 14,840
Kootenai 59,770
Latah 28,749
Lemhi 7,460
Lewis 4,118
Lincoln 3,436
Madison 19,480
Minidoka 19,718
Nez Perce 33,220
Oneida 3,258
Owyhee 8,272
Payette 15,722
Power 6,844
Shoshone 19,226
Teton 2,897
Twin Falls 52,927
Valley 5,604
Washington 8,803

ILLINOIS

1980 Census 11,418,461

CITIES

Abingdon 4,210
Addison CHI 28,836
Albion 2,285
Aledo 3,881
Alexis 1,076
Algonquin CHI 5,834
Alsip CHI 17,134
Altamont 2,389
Alton ST.L 34,171
Amboy 2,377
Anna 5,408
Annawan 908
Antioch CHI 4,419
Arcola 2,714
Argenta DEC 994
Arlington Heights CHI 66,116
Aroma Park KANK 673
Arthur 2,122
Ashland 1,351
Ashton 1,140
Assumption 1,283
Astoria 1,370
Athens 1,371
Atkinson 1,138
Atlanta 1,807
Atwood 1,464
Auburn 3,616
Augusta 764
Aurora CHI 81,293
Ava 811
Avon 1,019
Barrington CHI 9,029
Barry 1,487
Bartlett CHI 13,254
Bartonville PEOR 6,110
Batavia CHI 12,574
Beardstown 6,338
Beckemeyer 1,119
Beecher 2,024
Belleville ST.L 42,150
Bellwood CHI 19,811
Belvidere RKFD 15,176
Bement 1,770
Benld 1,638
Bensenville CHI 16,124
Benton 7,778
Berkeley CHI 5,467
Berwyn CHI 46,849
Bethalto ST.L 8,630
Bethany 1,550
Blandinsville 886
Bloomingdale CHI 12,659
BLOOMINGTON BLMNG 44,189
Blue Island CHI 21,855
Blue Mound 1,338
Bolingbrook CHI 37,261
Boulder Hill CHI 6,500○
Bourbonnais 13,280
Bradford 924
Bradley KANK 11,008
Braidwood 3,429
Breese 3,516
Bridgeport 2,281
Bridgeview CHI 14,155
Brighton ST.L 2,364
Brimfield 890
Broadview CHI 8,618
Brookfield CHI 19,395
Brookport PAD 1,128
Brownstown 708
Buda 668
Buffalo Grove CHI 22,230
Bunker Hill 1,700
Burbank CHI 28,462
Bushnell 3,811
Byron 2,035
Cahokia ST.L 18,904
Cairo 5,931
Calumet City CHI 39,673
Calumet Park CHI 8,788
Cambridge 2,217
Camp Point 1,285
Canton 14,626
Carbondale 27,194
Carlinville 5,439
Carlyle 3,388
Carmi 6,264
Carol Stream CHI 15,472
Carpentersville CHI 23,272
Carriers Mills 2,268
Carrollton 2,816
Carterville 3,445
Carthage 2,978
Cary CHI 6,640
Casey 3,026
Catlin DANV 2,226
Central City 1,505
Centralia 15,126
Centreville ST.L 9,747
Cerro Gordo 1,553
CHAMPAIGN CH-U 58,133
Chandlerville 842
Charleston 19,355
Chatham SPRG 5,597
Chatsworth 1,187
Chebanse KANK 1,191
Chenoa 1,847
Cherry 541
Cherry Valley RKFD 946
Chester 8,027
CHICAGO CHI 3,005,072
Chicago Heights CHI 37,026
Chicago Ridge CHI 13,473
Chillicothe PEOR 6,176
Chrisman 1,413
Christopher 3,086
Cicero CHI 61,232
Cissna Park 825
Clarendon Hills CHI 6,857
Clay City 1,038
Clayton 889
Clifton 1,390
Clinton 8,014
Coal City 3,028
Cobden 571
Colchester 1,729
Colfax 920
Collinsville ST.L 19,613
Columbia ST.L 4,269
Coulterville 1,118
Country Club Hills CHI 14,676
Countryside CHI 6,538
Creal Springs 845
Crest Hill CHI 9,252
Crestwood CHI 10,712
Crete CHI 5,417
Creve Coeur PEOR 6,851
Crossville 944
Crystal Lake CHI 18,590
Crystal Lawns CHI 2,800○
Cuba 1,648
Dallas City 1,408
Danvers 921
DANVILLE DANV 38,985
Darien CHI 14,968
DECATUR DEC 94,081
Deerfield CHI 17,430
DE KALB DKLB 33,099
Delavan 1,973
Depue 1,873
De Soto 1,589
Des Plaines CHI 53,568
Divernon 1,081
Dixon 15,659
Dolton CHI 24,766
Dongola 611
Downers Grove CHI 39,274
Dundee CHI 3,502
Du Quoin 6,594
Durand 1,073
Dwight 4,146
Earlville 1,382
East Alton ST.L 7,123
East Chicago Heights CHI 5,347
East Dubuque DUB 2,194
East Galesburg GLSB 928
East Moline D-RI-M 20,907
East Peoria PEOR 22,385
East St. Louis ST.L 55,200
Edinburg 1,231
Edwardsville ST.L 12,460
Effingham 11,270
Elburn CHI 1,224
Eldorado 5,198
Elgin CHI 63,798
Elizabeth 772
Elizabethtown 478
Elk Grove Village CHI 28,907
Elkville 973
Elmhurst CHI 44,251
Elmwood 2,117
Elmwood Park CHI 24,016
El Paso 2,676
Enfield 890
Equality 831
Erie 1,725
Eureka PEOR 4,306
Evanston CHI 73,706
Evansville 863
Evergreen Park CHI 22,260
Fairbury 3,544
Fairfield 5,954
Fairmont CHI 2,600○
Fairview Heights ST.L 12,414
Farina 594
Farmer City 2,252
Farmington 3,118
Findlay 868
Fisher 1,572
Flanagan 978
Flat Rock 493
Flora 5,379
Flossmoor CHI 8,423
Forest Park CHI 15,177
Forrest 1,246
Forreston 1,384
Fox Lake CHI 6,831
Fox River Grove CHI 2,515
Frankfort CHI 4,357
Franklin Grove 965
Franklin Park CHI 17,507
Freeburg ST.L 2,989
Freeport 26,406
Fulton CLNT 3,936
Galatia 1,042
Galena 3,876
GALESBURG GLSB 35,305
Galva 3,185
Gardner 1,322
Geneseo 6,373
Geneva CHI 9,881
Genoa 3,276
Georgetown DANV 4,220
Gibson City 3,498
Gillespie 3,740
Gilman 1,913
Girard 2,246
Glasford PEOR 1,201
Glen Carbon ST.L 5,197
Glencoe CHI 9,200
Glendale Heights CHI 23,163
Glen Ellyn CHI 23,649
Glenview CHI 30,842
Glenwood CHI 10,538
Godfrey ST.L 2,600○
Golconda 960
Grafton 1,024
Grand Tower 748
Granite City ST.L 36,815
Grant Park 1,038
Granville 1,537
Grayslake CHI 5,260
Grayville 2,313
Greenfield 1,090
Greenup 1,655
Greenview 830
Greenville 5,271
Gridley 1,246
Griggsville 1,301
Gurnee CHI 7,179
Hamilton 3,509
Hampshire 1,735
Hanna City PEOR 1,361
Hanover 1,069
Hanover Park CHI 28,850
Hardin 1,107
Harrisburg 9,322
Harristown DEC 1,456
Hartford ST.L 1,887
Harvard 5,126
Harvey CHI 35,810
Harwood Heights CHI 8,228
Havana 3,682
Hazel Crest CHI 13,973
Hebron 786
Henry 2,740
Herrin 10,040
Heyworth 1,598
Hickory Hills CHI 13,778
Highland 7,122
Highland Park CHI 30,611
Highwood CHI 5,452
Hillsboro 4,408
Hillside CHI 8,279
Hinckley 1,447
Hinsdale CHI 16,726
Hoffman Estates CHI 38,258
Homer 1,279
Hometown CHI 5,324
Homewood CHI 19,724
Hoopeston 6,411
Hopedale 913
Huntley CHI 1,646
Hurst 938
Hutsonville 705
Illiopolis 1,118
Ipava 661
Itasca CHI 7,948
Jacksonville 20,284
Jerseyville 7,506
Johnston City 3,873
Joliet CHI 77,956
Jonesboro 1,842
Joppa 535
Justice CHI 10,552
KANKAKEE KANK 30,141
Kansas 791
Karnak 646
Keithsburg 936
Kenilworth CHI 2,708
Ken Rock RKFD 5,945○
Kewanee 14,508
Kincaid 1,591
Kinmundy 945
Kirkland 1,155
Kirkwood 1,008
Knoxville GLSB 3,432
Lacon 2,135
Ladd 1,337
La Grange CHI 15,681
La Grange Highlands CHI 7,100○
La Grange Park CHI 13,359
La Harpe 1,471
Lake Bluff CHI 4,434
Lake Forest CHI 15,245
Lake In The Hills CHI 5,651
Lake Zurich CHI 8,225
La Moille 734
Lanark 1,483
Lansing CHI 29,039
La Salle 10,347
Lawrenceville 5,652
Lebanon ST.L 3,245
Lemont CHI 5,640
Lena 2,295
Le Roy 2,870
Lewistown 2,758
Lexington 1,806
Libertyville CHI 16,520
Lincoln 16,327
Lincolnwood CHI 11,921
Lindenhurst CHI 6,220
Lisle CHI 13,625
Litchfield 7,204
Livingston 949
Lockport CHI 9,017
Lombard CHI 37,295
London Mills 587
Louisville 1,166
Loves Park RKFD 13,192
Lovington 1,313
Lyons CHI 9,925
McHenry CHI 10,908
Mackinaw 1,354
McLean 836
McLeansboro 2,960
Macomb 19,632
Macon DEC 1,300
Madison ST.L 5,915
Mahomet CH-U 1,986
Manito 1,869
Mansfield 921
Manteno 3,155
Marengo 4,361
Marine 957
Marion 14,031
Marissa 2,568
Markham CHI 15,172
Maroa 1,760
Marseilles 4,766
Marshall 3,655
Martinsville 1,298
Mascoutah ST.L 4,962
Mason City 2,719
Matteson CHI 10,223
Mattoon 19,787
Maywood CHI 27,998
Mazon 828
Melrose Park CHI 20,735
Mendon 979
Mendota 7,134
Meredosia 1,272
Metamora PEOR 2,482
Metropolis 7,171
Midlothian CHI 14,274
Milan D-RI-M 6,264
Milford 1,716
Milledgeville 1,209
Millstadt ST.L 2,736
Minier 1,261
Minonk 2,039
Mokena CHI 4,578
Moline D-RI-M 45,709
Momence 3,297
Monmouth 10,706
Montgomery CHI 3,363
Monticello 4,753
Mooseheart CHI 600○
Morris 8,833
Morrison 4,605
Morrisonville 1,208
Morton PEOR 14,178
Morton Grove CHI 23,747
Mound City 1,102
Mounds 1,669
Mount Carmel 8,908
Mount Carroll 1,936
Mount Morris 2,989
Mount Olive 2,357
Mount Prospect CHI 52,634
Mount Pulaski 1,783
Mount Sterling 2,186
Mount Vernon 16,995
Moweaqua 1,922
Mulberry Grove 707
Mundelein CHI 17,053
Murphysboro 9,866
Naperville CHI 42,330
Nashville 3,186
Nauvoo 1,133
Neoga 1,736
New Athens 1,937
New Baden 2,476
New Berlin 834
New Boston 731
New Haven 559
New Lenox CHI 5,792
Newman 1,079
Newton 3,186
New Windsor 863
Niles CHI 30,363
Noble 832
Nokomis 2,656
Normal BLMNG 35,672
Norridge CHI 16,483
Norris City 1,515
North Aurora CHI 5,205
Northbrook CHI 30,735
North Chicago CHI 38,774
Northfield CHI 5,807
Northlake CHI 12,166
North Park RKFD 15,679○
North Riverside CHI 6,764
Oak Brook CHI 6,641
Oak Forest CHI 26,096
Oakland 1,035
Oak Lawn CHI 60,590
Oak Park CHI 54,887
Oakwood DANV 1,627
Oblong 1,840
Odell 1,083
Odin 1,285
O'Fallon ST.L 10,217
Oglesby 3,979
Okawville 1,337
Olive Branch 550○
Olney 9,026
Onarga 1,269
Oneida 765
Oquawka 1,533
Oreana DEC 999
Oregon 3,559
Orient 480
Orion 2,013
Orland Park CHI 23,045
Oswego CHI 3,021
Ottawa 18,166
Palatine CHI 32,166
Palestine 1,718
Palmyra 864
Palos Heights CHI 11,096
Palos Hills CHI 16,654
Palos Park CHI 3,150
Pana 6,040
Paris 9,885
Park Forest CHI 26,222
Park Forest South CHI 6,245
Park Ridge CHI 38,704
Patoka 662
Pawnee 2,577
Pawpaw 839
Paxton 4,258
Pecatonica 1,732
Pekin PEOR 33,967
PEORIA PEOR 124,160
Peoria Heights PEOR 7,453
Peotone 2,832
Percy 1,053
Peru 10,886
Petersburg 2,419
Phoenix CHI 2,850
Pinckneyville 3,319
Piper City 905
Pittsfield 4,170
Plainfield CHI 4,485
Plano CHI 4,875
Pleasant Hill 1,112
Pleasant Plains 688
Plymouth 649
Pocahontas 866
Polo 2,643
Pontiac 11,227
Port Byron D-RI-M 1,289
Posen CHI 4,642
Prairie Du Rocher 701
Princeton 7,342
Princeville 1,712
Prophetstown 2,141
Prospect Heights CHI 11,808
QUINCY QUIN 42,352
Ramsey 1,058
Rankin 727
RANTOUL RNTL 20,161
Raymond 957
Red Bud 2,850
Richmond CHI 1,068
Richton Park CHI 9,403
Ridge Farm 1,096
Ridgway 1,245
Riverdale CHI 13,233
River Forest CHI 12,392
River Grove CHI 10,368
Riverside CHI 9,236
Roanoke 2,001
Robbins CHI 8,119
Robinson 7,285
Rochelle 8,982
Rockdale CHI 1,913
Rock Falls 10,624
Rockford RKFD 139,712
Rock Island D-RI-M 47,036
Rockton BLOIT 2,313
Rolling Meadows CHI 20,167
Romeoville CHI 15,519
Roodhouse 2,364
Roselle CHI 16,948
Roseville 1,254
Rosewood Heights ST.L 6,700○
Rosiclare 1,441
Rossville 1,363
Round Lake Beach CHI 12,921
Royalton 1,320
Rushville 3,348
St. Anne KANK 1,421
St. Charles CHI 17,492
St. David 786
St. Elmo 1,611
St. Francisville 1,040
St. Joseph CH-U 1,900
Salem 7,813
Sandoval 1,734
Sandwich CHI 3,675
San Jose 784
Sauk Village CHI 10,906

○ Rand McNally estimate (not reported in census).
▲ Population of entire township or "town", including rural area.
● Independent city. Population not included in county total.

Savanna 4,529
Saybrook 882
Schaumburg CHI 52,319
Schiller Park CHI 11,458
Schram City 708
Seneca 2,098
Sesser 2,238
Shabbona 851
Shannon 938
Shawneetown 1,841
Sheffield 1,130
Shelbyville 5,259
Sheldon 1,215
Silvis D-RI-M 7,130
Skokie CHI 60,278
Somonauk 1,344
South Beloit BLOIT 4,088
South Chicago Heights CHI 3,932
South Elgin CHI 6,218
South Holland CHI 24,977
South Jacksonville 3,382
South Pekin PEOR 1,243
South Streator 2,000 ○
South Wilmington 747
Sparta 4,957
SPRINGFIELD SPRG 99,637
Spring Valley 5,822
Staunton 4,744
Steeleville 2,240
Steger CHI 9,269
Sterling 16,273
Stewardson 745
Stickney CHI 5,893
Stockton 1,872
Stonington 1,184
Streamwood CHI 23,456
Streator 14,769
Stronghurst 865
Sullivan 4,526
Summit CHI 10,110
Sumner 1,238
Swansea ST.L 5,347
Sycamore DKLB 9,219
Tampico 966
Taylorville 11,386
Teutopolis 1,414
Tilden 1,025
Tilton DANV 2,405
Tinley Park CHI 26,171
Tiskilwa 990
Toledo 1,284
Tolono CH-U 2,434
Toluca 1,471
Tonica 695
Toulon 1,390
Tower Hill 715
Tremont PEOR 2,096
Trenton 2,504
Troy ST.L. 3,772
Tuscola 3,839
Urbana CH-U 35,978
Utica 1,067
Valmeyer 898
Vandalia 5,338
Venice ST.L 3,480
Vermont 885
Vernon Hills CHI 9,827
Vienna 1,420
Villa Grove 2,707
Villa Park CHI 23,185
Viola 1,144
Virden 3,899
Virginia 1,825
Walnut 1,513
Wamac 1,665
Warren 1,595
Warrenville CHI 7,519
Warsaw 1,842
Washburn 1,206
Washington PEOR 10,364
Washington Park ST.L 8,223
Waterloo ST.L 4,646
Waterman 943
Watseka 5,543
Wauconda CHI 5,688
Waukegan CHI 67,653
Waverly 1,537
Wayne City 1,132
Westchester CHI 17,730
West Chicago CHI 12,550
West City 886
Westdale CHI 10,300 ○
West End RKFD 7,554 ○
Western Springs CHI 12,876
West Frankfort 9,437
Westmont CHI 16,718
West Peoria PEOR 6,950 ○
West Salem 1,145
Westville DANV 3,573
Wheaton CHI 43,043
Wheeling CHI 23,266
White Hall 2,935
Williamsville 996
Willow Springs CHI 4,147
Wilmette CHI 28,229
Wilmington 4,424
Winchester 1,716
Windsor 1,228
Winnebago RKFD 1,644
Winnetka CHI 12,772
Winthrop Harbor CHI 5,438
Witt 1,205
Wood Dale CHI 11,251
Woodhull 901
Woodridge CHI 22,322
Wood River ST.L 12,449
Woodstock 11,725
Worden 953
Worth CHI 11,592
Wyanet 1,069
Wyoming 1,614
Yates City 860
Yorkville CHI 3,422
Zeigler 1,858
Zion CHI 17,861

COUNTIES

Adams 71,622
Alexander 12,264
Bond 16,224
Boone 28,630
Brown 5,411
Bureau 39,114
Calhoun 5,867
Carroll 18,779
Cass 15,084
Champaign 168,392
Christian 36,446
Clark 16,913
Clay 15,283
Clinton 32,617
Coles 52,992
Cook 5,253,190
Crawford 20,818
Cumberland 11,062
De Kalb 74,624
De Witt 18,108
Douglas 19,774
Du Page 658,177
Edgar 21,725
Edwards 7,961
Effingham 30,944
Fayette 22,167
Ford 15,265
Franklin 43,201
Fulton 43,687
Gallatin 7,590
Greene 16,661
Grundy 30,582
Hamilton 9,172
Hancock 23,877
Hardin 5,383
Henderson 9,114
Henry 57,968
Iroquois 32,976
Jackson 61,522
Jasper 11,318
Jefferson 36,354
Jersey 20,538
Jo Daviess 23,520
Johnson 9,624
Kane 278,405
Kankakee 102,926
Kendall 37,202
Knox 61,607
Lake 440,372
La Salle 109,139
Lawrence 17,807
Lee 36,328
Livingston 41,381
Logan 31,802
McDonough 37,236
McHenry 147,724
McLean 119,149
Macon 131,375
Macoupin 49,384
Madison 247,671
Marion 43,523
Marshall 14,479
Mason 19,492
Massac 14,990
Menard 11,700
Mercer 19,286
Monroe 20,117
Montgomery 31,686
Morgan 37,502
Moultrie 14,546
Ogle 46,338
Peoria 200,466
Perry 21,714
Piatt 16,581
Pike 18,896
Pope 4,404
Pulaski 8,840
Putnam 6,085
Randolph 35,566
Richland 17,587
Rock Island 165,968
St. Clair 265,469
Saline 27,360
Sangamon 176,089
Schuyler 8,365
Scott 6,142
Shelby 23,923
Stark 7,389
Stephenson 49,536
Tazewell 132,078
Union 16,851
Vermilion 95,222
Wabash 13,713
Warren 21,943
Washington 15,472
Wayne 18,059
White 17,864
Whiteside 65,970
Will 324,460
Williamson 56,538
Winnebago 250,884
Woodford 33,320

INDIANA

1980 Census 5,490,179

CITIES

Advance 559
Akron 1,045
Albany MUN 2,625
Albion 1,637
Alexandria AND 6,028
Amboy 450
Amo 444
ANDERSON AND 64,695
Andrews 1,243
Angola 5,486
Arcadia 1,801
Ardmore S.B.- 3,400 ○
Argos 1,547
Arlington 500 ○
Ashley 841
Atlanta 657
Attica 3,841
Auburn 8,122
Aurora 3,816
Austin 4,857
Avilla 1,272
Bainbridge 644
Bargersville IND 1,647
Bass Lake 1,500 ○
Batesville 4,152
Battle Ground LAF 812
Bedford 14,410
Beech Grove IND 13,196
Berne 3,300
Beverly Shores CHI 864
Bicknell 4,713
Birdseye 533
Black Oak CHI 10,000 ○
Blanford 700 ○
Bloomfield 2,705
BLOOMINGTON BLMNG 51,646
Bluffton 8,705
Boonville 6,300
Boswell 810
Bourbon 1,522
Brazil 7,852
Bremen 3,565
Bristol S.B.- 1,203
Brook 926
Brooklyn IND 889
Brookston 1,701
Brookville 2,874
Brownsburg IND 6,242
Brownstown 2,704
Butler 2,509
Cambridge City 2,407
Camden 618
Campbellsburg 695
Cannelton 2,373
Carlisle 717
Carmel IND 18,272
Carthage 886
Cayuga 1,258
Cedar Lake CHI 8,754
Centerville RICH 2,284
Chalmers 554
Chandler EV 3,043
Charlestown LOU 5,596
Chesterfield AND 2,701
Chesterton 900 ○
Chesterton CHI 8,531
Chrisney 537
Churubusco 1,638
Cicero 2,557
Clarks Hill 653
Clarksville LOU 15,164
Clay City 883
Claypool 464
Clayton IND 703
Clinton T.H. 5,267
Cloverdale 1,357
Coalmont 450 ○
Coatesville 474
Colfax 823
Collegeville 900 ○
Columbia City 5,091
COLUMBUS COL 30,292
Connersville 17,023
Converse 1,190
Corydon 2,724
Covington 2,883
Crawfordsville 13,325
Cromwell 458
Crothersville 1,747
Crown Point CHI 16,455
Culver 1,601
Cynthiana 874
Dale 1,693
Daleville AND 2,000 ○
Dana 803
Danville IND 4,220
Darlington 811
Dayton 781
Decatur 8,649
Delphi 3,042
Demotte CHI 2,559
Denver 589
Dillsboro 1,038
Dublin 979
Dubois 550 ○
Dugger 1,118
Dunkirk 3,180
Dunlap S.B.- 1,700 ○
Dyer CHI 9,555
Earl Park 469
East Chicago CHI 39,786
Eaton 1,804
Edgewood AND 2,215
Edinburg 4,856
Edwardsport 459
Elberfeld 640
Elizabethtown COL 603
Elkhart S.B.- 41,305
Ellettsville BLMNG 3,328
Elnora 756
Elwood AND 10,867
English 633
Etna Green 522
EVANSVILLE EV 130,496
Fairland 900 ○
Fairmount MRN 3,286
Fairview Park T.H. 1,545
Farmersburg 1,240
Farmland MUN 1,560
Ferdinand 2,192
Fillmore 550 ○
Fishers IND 2,008
Flora 2,303
Floyds Knobs LOU 500 ○
Fontanet T.H. 450 ○
Fort Branch 2,504
Fortville IND 2,787
FORT WAYNE FTWA 172,196
Fountain City RICH 839
Fowler 2,319
Francesville 944
Francisco 612
Frankfort 15,168
Franklin 11,563
Frankton AND 2,080
Freelandville 680 ○
Freetown 600 ○
Fremont 1,180
French Lick 2,265
Galveston 1,822
Garrett 4,874
Gary CHI 151,953
Gas City MRN 6,370
Gaston 1,150
Geneva 1,430
Georgetown LOU 1,494
Goodland 1,200
Goshen 19,665
Gosport 1,341
Grabill FTWA 658
Grandview 670
Greencastle 8,403
Greendale 3,795
Greenfield IND 11,439
Greensburg 9,254
Greens Fork 426
Greentown KOK 2,265
Greenville LOU 537
Greenwood IND 19,327
Griffith CHI 17,026
Hagerstown 1,950
Hamilton 587
Hamlet 738
Hammond CHI 93,714
Hanna 500 ○
Hanover 4,054
Harlan 1,000 ○
Harmony 613
Hartford City 7,622
Hatfield 600 ○
Haubstadt EV 1,389
Hebron CHI 2,696
Heltonville 500 ○
Henryville LOU 950 ○
Highland CHI 25,935
Hillsboro 561
Hoagland 650 ○
Hobart CHI 22,987
Holland 683
Holton 487
Home Corner MRN 500 ○
Homecroft IND 831
Home Place IND 2,000 ○
Hope COL 2,185
Howe 500 ○
Hudson 447
Hudson Lake 1,500 ○
Huntertown FTWA 1,265
Huntingburg 5,376
Huntington 16,202
Hymera 1,054
Idaville 625 ○
INDIANAPOLIS IND 700,807
Indian Heights KOK 5,000 ○
Ingalls AND 909
Ireland 450 ○
Jamestown 924
Jasonville 2,497
Jasper 9,097
Jeffersonville LOU 21,220
Jonesboro 2,279
Kendallville 7,299
Kennard 441
Kentland 1,936
Kewanna 711
Kingman 566
Kirklin 662
Knightstown 2,325
Knightsville 763
Knox 3,674
KOKOMO KOK 47,808
Koontz Lake 900 ○
Kouts 1,619
La Crosse 713
Ladoga 1,151
LAFAYETTE LAF 43,011
La Fontaine 946
Lagrange 2,164
Lagro 549
Lake Station CHI 14,294
Laketon 500 ○
Lake Village 650 ○
Lakeville S.B.- 629
Lanesville 570
Lapaz 651
Lapel AND 1,881
La Porte 21,796
Laurel 819
Lawrence IND 25,591
Lawrenceburg 4,403
Lebanon 11,456
Leesburg 629
Leo 800 ○
Lewisville 577
Liberty 1,844
Ligonier 3,134
Linden 700
Linton 6,315
Lizton 456
Logansport 17,899
Long Beach MICH 2,262
Loogootee 3,100
Lowell CHI 5,827
Lynn 1,250
Lynnville 566
Lyons 782
Madison 12,472
Marengo 892
MARION MRN 35,874
Markle 975
Markleville AND 427
Marshall 413
Martinsville 11,311
Matthews 745
Mecca 482
Medaryville 731
Medora 853
Memphis LOU 500 ○
Mentone 973
Merrillville CHI 27,677
Mexico 850 ○
MICHIGAN CITY MICH 36,850
Michigantown 453
Middlebury 1,665
Middletown AND 2,978
Milan 1,566
Milford 1,153
Millersburg 809
Milltown 1,006
Milroy 900 ○
Mishawaka S.B.- 40,224
Mitchell 4,641
Monon 1,540
Monroe 739
Monroe City 569
Monroeville 1,372
Monrovia 450 ○
Montezuma 1,352
Monticello 5,162
Montpelier 1,995
Mooreland 479
Moores Hill 566
Mooresville IND 5,349
Morgantown 897
Morocco 1,348
Morristown 989
Mount Vernon 7,656
Mulberry 1,225
MUNCIE MUN 77,216
Munster CHI 20,671
Nappanee 4,694
Nashville 705
New Albany LOU 37,103
Newburgh EV 2,906
New Carlisle 1,439
New Castle 20,056
New Goshen T.H. 500 ○
New Harmony 945
New Haven FTWA 6,714
New Market 608
New Palestine IND 749
New Paris 1,300 ○
Newport 704
New Washington 600 ○
New Whiteland IND 4,502
Noblesville IND 12,056
North Judson 1,653
North Liberty 1,211
North Manchester 5,998
North Salem 581
North Terre Haute T.H. 1,500 ○
North Vernon 5,768
North Webster 709
Oakland City 3,301
Oaktown 776
Odon 1,463
Oldenburg 770
Oolitic 1,495
Orestes AND 539
Orland 424
Orleans 2,161
Osceola S.B.- 1,987
Osgood 1,554
Ossian FTWA 1,945
Otterbein 1,118
Otwell 500 ○
Owensville 1,261
Oxford 1,327
Palmyra 692
Paoli 3,637
Paragon 538
Parker City MUN 1,414
Patoka 832
Pekin 1,125
Pendleton AND 2,130
Pennville 805
Perrysville 532
Pershing 438
Peru 13,764
Petersburg 2,987
Pierceton 1,086
Pittsboro IND 891
Plainfield IND 9,191
Plainville 556
Pleasant Lake 500 ○
Plymouth 7,693
Portage CHI 27,409
Porter CHI 2,988
Portland 7,074
Poseyville 1,247
Princes Lakes 937
Princeton 8,976
Ravenswood 424
Redkey 1,537
Remington 1,268
Rensselaer 4,944
Reynolds 632
Richland 550 ○
RICHMOND RICH 41,349
Ridgeville 933
Rising Sun 2,478
Riverhaven 700 ○
Roachdale 958
Roann 548
Roanoke 891
Rochester 5,050
Rockport 2,590
Rockville 2,785
Rocky Ripple 778
Rome City 1,319
Rosedale 744
Roseland S.B.- 832
Rossville 1,148
Royal Center 908
Royerton 650 ○
Rushville 6,113
Russiaville KOK 973
St. Bernice 900 ○
St. Joe 546
St. John CHI 3,974
St. Mary-of-the-Woods 650 ○
St. Marys S.B.- 1,700 ○
St. Meinrad 500 ○
St. Paul 976
Salem 5,290
Sandborn 576
Santa Claus 514
Schererville CHI 13,209
Scottsburg 5,068
Seelyville T.H. 1,374
Sellersburg LOU 3,211
Selma MUN 1,056
Seymour 15,050
Sharpsville KOK 617
Shelburn 1,259
Shelby 700 ○
Shelbyville 14,989

○ Rand McNally estimate (not reported in census).
▲ Population of entire township or "town", including rural area.
● Independent city. Population not included in county total.

Sheridan 2,200
Shipshewana 466
Shirley AND 919
Shoals 967
Silver Lake 576
SOUTH BEND S.B.- 109,727
South Haven CHI 6,500 ○
South Milford 500 ○
Southport IND 2,266
South Whitley 1,575
Speed LOU 650 ○
Speedway IND 12,641
Spencer 2,732
Spiceland 940
Spring Grove RICH 469
Star City 500 ○
Staunton T.H. 607
Stockwell 500 ○
Stroh 450 ○
Sullivan 4,774
Summitville 1,085
Sunman 924
Swayzee 1,127
Sweetser MRN 944
Syracuse 2,579
Taylorsville COL 1,200 ○
Tell City 8,704
TERRE HAUTE T.H. 61,125
Thorntown 1,468
Tipton 5,004
Topeka 876
Trafalgar 466
Trail Creek MICH 2,581
Tri Lakes 1,198 ○
Troy 550
Underwood LOU 500 ○
Union City 3,908
Union Mills 550 ○
Universal T.H. 428
Upland 3,335
Utica LOU 850 ○
Vallonia 500 ○
Valparaiso CHI 22,247
Van Buren 935
Veedersburg 2,261
Versailles 1,560
Vevay 1,343
Vincennes 20,857
Wabash 12,985
Wakarusa 1,281
Waldron 800 ○
Walkerton 2,051
Wallen FTWA 1,200 ○
Walton 1,202
Wanatah 879
Warren 1,254
Warren Park IND 1,803
Warsaw 10,647
Washington 11,325
Waterloo 1,951
Waveland 559
Waynetown 915
West Baden Springs 796
West College Corner 614
Westfield IND 2,783
West Lafayette LAF 21,247
West Lebanon 946
Westpoint 500 ○
Westport 1,450
West Terre Haute T.H. 2,806
Westville 2,887
Wheatfield 755
Wheatland 532
Wheeler 600 ○
Whitestown IND 497
Whiting CHI 5,630
Wilkinson 493
Williamsburg 425 ○
Williamsport 1,747
Winamac 2,370
Winchester 5,659
Windfall 911
Winona Lake 2,827
Winslow 1,017
Wolcott 923
Wolcottville 890
Wolflake 450 ○
Woodburn FTWA 1,002
Worthington 1,574
Yorktown MUN 3,945
Zanesville 550 ○
Zionsville IND 3,948

COUNTIES

Adams 29,619
Allen 294,335
Bartholomew 65,088
Benton 10,218
Blackford 15,570
Boone 36,446
Brown 12,377
Carroll 19,722
Cass 40,936
Clark 88,838
Clay 24,862
Clinton 31,545
Crawford 9,820
Daviess 27,836
Dearborn 34,291
Decatur 23,841
De Kalb 33,606
Delaware 128,587
Dubois 34,238
Elkhart 137,330
Fayette 28,272
Floyd 61,169
Fountain 19,033
Franklin 19,612
Fulton 19,335
Gibson 33,156
Grant 80,934
Greene 30,416
Hamilton 82,381
Hancock 43,939
Harrison 27,276
Hendricks 69,804
Henry 53,336
Howard 86,896
Huntington 35,596
Jackson 36,523
Jasper 26,138
Jay 23,239
Jefferson 30,419
Jennings 22,854
Johnson 77,240
Knox 41,838
Kosciusko 59,555
La Grange 25,550
Lake 522,965
La Porte 108,632
Lawrence 42,472
Madison 139,336
Marion 765,233
Marshall 39,155
Martin 11,001
Miami 39,820
Monroe 98,387
Montgomery 35,501
Morgan 51,999
Newton 14,844
Noble 35,443
Ohio 5,114
Orange 18,677
Owen 15,840
Parke 16,372
Perry 19,346
Pike 13,465
Porter 119,816
Posey 26,414
Pulaski 13,258
Putnam 29,163
Randolph 29,997
Ripley 24,398
Rush 19,604
St. Joseph 241,617
Scott 20,422
Shelby 39,887
Spencer 19,361
Starke 21,997
Steuben 24,694
Sullivan 21,107
Switzerland 7,153
Tippecanoe 121,702
Tipton 16,819
Union 6,860
Vanderburgh 167,515
Vermillion 18,229
Vigo 112,385
Wabash 36,640
Warren 8,976
Warrick 41,474
Washington 21,932
Wayne 76,058
Wells 25,401
White 23,867
Whitley 26,215

IOWA

1980 Census 2,913,387

CITIES

Ackley 1,900
Adair 883
Adel 2,846
Afton 985
Agency OTUM 657
Ainsworth 547
Akron 1,517
Albert City 818
Albia 4,184
Albion 739
Alburnett 411
Alden 953
Algona 6,289
Allerton 670
Allison 1,132
Alta 1,720
Alton 986
Altoona DES 5,764
Amana 600 ○
AMES AMES 45,775
Anamosa 4,958
Anita 1,153
Ankeny DES 15,429
Anthon 687
Aplington 1,027
Arcadia 454
Arlington 498
Armstrong 1,153
Arnolds Park 1,051
Ashton 441
Atlantic 7,789
Audubon 2,841
Aurelia 1,143
Avoca 1,650
Avon Lake DES 600 ○
Badger 653
Bancroft 1,082
Batavia 525
Battle Creek 919
Baxter 951
Bayard 637
Beacon 530
Bedford 1,692
Belle Plaine 2,903
Bellevue 2,450
Belmond 2,505
Bennett 458
Bettendorf D-RI-M 27,381
Blairstown 695
Bloomfield 2,849
Blue Grass D-RI-M 1,377
Bonaparte 489
Bondurant DES 1,283
Boone 12,602
Boyden 708
Breda 502
Brighton 804
Britt 2,185
Brooklyn 1,509
Buffalo D-RI-M 1,441
Buffalo Center 1,233
BURLINGTON BUR 29,529
Burt 689
Bussey 579
Calamus 452
Callender 446
Calmar 1,053
Camanche CLNT 4,725
Cambridge 732
Capitol Heights DES 815 ○
Carlisle DES 3,073
Carroll 9,705
Carson 716
Carter Lake OMA- 3,438
Cascade 1,912
Casey 473
Cedar Falls WATL 36,322
CEDAR RAPIDS CEDR 110,243
Center Point 1,591
Centerville 6,558
Central City 1,067
Chariton 4,987
Charles City 8,778
Charlotte 442
Charter Oak 615
Cherokee 7,004
Churdan 540
Cincinnati 598
Clarence 1,001
Clarinda 5,458
Clarion 3,060
Clarksville 1,424
Clearfield 433
Clear Lake MSCY 7,458
Clermont 602
CLINTON CLNT 32,828
Clive DES 5,906
Coggon 639
Colesburg 463
Colfax 2,211
Collins 451
Colo 808
Columbus Junction 1,429
Conrad 1,133
Coon Rapids 1,448
Coralville IACY 7,687
Corning 1,939
Correctionville 935
Corwith 480
Corydon 1,818
Council Bluffs OMA- 56,449
Crescent 547
Cresco 3,860
Creston 8,429
Dakota City 1,072
Dallas 451
Dallas Center 1,360
Danbury 492
Danville BUR 994
DAVENPORT D-RI-M 103,264
Dayton 941
Decorah 7,991
Delhi 511
Delmar 633
Delta 482
Denison 6,675
Denver WATL 1,647
DES MOINES DES 191,003
De Soto 1,035
De Witt 4,512
Dexter 678
Dike 987
Donnellson 972
Doon 537
Dow City 616
Dows 771
DUBUQUE DUB 62,321
Dumont 815
Duncombe 504
Dunkerton 718
Dunlap 1,374
Durant 1,583
Dyersville 3,825
Dysart 1,355
Eagle Grove 4,324
Earlham 1,140
Earling 520
Earlville 844
Early 670
Eddyville 1,116
Edgewood 900
Eldon 1,255
Eldora 3,063
Eldridge D-RI-M 3,279
Elgin 702
Elkader 1,688
Elk Horn 746
Elliott 493
Ellsworth 480
Elma 714
Ely CEDR 425
Emerson 502
Emmetsburg 4,621
Epworth 1,380
Essex 1,001
Estherville 7,518
Evansdale WATL 4,798
Exira 978
Fairbank 980
Fairfax CEDR 683
Fairfield 9,428
Farley 1,287
Farmington 869
Farnhamville 461
Farragut 603
Fayette 1,515
Fonda 863
Fontanelle 805
Forest City 4,270
FORT DODGE FTDO 29,423
Fort Madison 13,520
Fredericksburg 1,075
Fremont 730
Fruitland 461
Galva 420
Garnavillo 723
Garner 2,908
Garrison 411
Garwin 626
George 1,241
Gilbert AMES 805
Gilbertville WATL 740
Gilman 642
Gilmore City 626
Gladbrook 970
Glenwood 5,280
Glidden 1,076
Goldfield 789
Gowrie 1,089
Graettinger 923
Grand Junction 970
Grand Mound 674
Grandview 473
Granger 619
Greene 1,332
Greenfield 2,243
Greenfield Plaza DES 2,100 ○
Grimes DES 1,973
Grinnell 8,868
Griswold 1,176
Grundy Center 2,880
Guthrie Center 1,713
Guttenberg 2,428
Hamburg 1,597
Hampton 4,630
Harlan 5,357
Hartford 761
Hartley 1,700
Hawarden 2,722
Hawkeye 512
Hazleton 877
Hedrick 847
Hiawatha CEDR 4,825
Hills 547
Hinton 659
Holstein 1,477
Hopkinton 774
Hospers 655
Hubbard 852
Hudson WATL 2,267
Hull 1,714
Humboldt 4,794
Humeston 671
Huxley AMES 1,884
Ida Grove 2,285
Independence 6,392
Indianola DES 10,843
Inwood 755
IOWA CITY IACY 50,508
Iowa Falls 6,174
Ireton 588
Irwin 427
Janesville WATL 840
Jefferson 4,854
Jesup 2,343
Jewell 1,145
Johnston DES 2,617
Kalona 1,862
Kanawha 756
Kellogg 654
Keokuk 13,536
Keosauqua 1,003
Keota 1,034
Keystone 618
Kingsley 1,209
Klemme 620
Knoxville 8,143
Lake City 2,006
Lake Mills 2,281
Lake Park 1,123
Lakeside 589
Lake View 1,291
Lakewood DES 900 ○
Lamoni 2,705
Lamont 554
Lansing 1,181
La Porte City 2,324
Larchwood 701
Latimer 441
Laurens 1,606
Lawler 534
Lawton 447
Le Claire D-RI-M 2,899
Le Grand 921
Lehigh 654
Le Mars 8,276
Lenox 1,338
Leon 2,094
Letts 473
Lewis 497
Lime Springs 476
Lisbon CEDR 1,458
Little Rock 490
Livermore 490
Logan 1,540
Lohrville 521
Lone Tree 1,014
Long Grove 596
Lost Nation 524
Lovilia 637
Lovington DES 850 ○
Lowden 717
Lu Verne 418
McGregor 945
Madrid 2,281
Malcom 418
Malvern 1,244
Manchester 4,942
Manilla 1,020
Manly 1,496
Manning 1,609
Manson 1,924
Mapleton 1,495
Maquoketa 6,313
Marathon 442
Marble Rock 419
Marcus 1,206
Marengo 2,308
Marion CEDR 19,474
Marquette 528
Marshalltown 26,938
MASON CITY MSCY 30,144
Massena 518
Maxwell 783
Maynard 561
Mechanicsville 1,166
Mediapolis 1,685
Melbourne 732
Melcher 953
Merrill 737
Middletown BUR 487
Milford 2,076
Milo 778
Milton 567
Minden 419
Missouri Valley 3,107
Mitchellville DES 1,530
Mondamin 423
Monona 1,530
Monroe 1,875
Montezuma 1,485
Monticello 3,641
Montrose 1,038
Moravia 706
Morning Sun 959
Moulton 762
Mount Ayr 1,938
Mount Pleasant 7,322
Mount Vernon 3,325
Moville 1,273
Murray 703
Muscatine 23,467
Mystic 665
Nashua 1,846
Neola 839
Nevada AMES 5,912
New Albin 609
Newell 913
Newhall 899
New Hampton 3,940
New Hartford 764
New London 2,043
New Market 554
New Sharon 1,225
Newton 15,292
New Vienna 430
New Virginia 512
Nora Springs 1,572
North Cedar WATL 1,950 ○
North English 990
North Liberty IACY 2,046
Northwood 2,193
Norwalk DES 2,676
Norway 633
Norwoodville DES 1,400 ○
Oakland 1,552
Oakville 470
Ocheyedan 599
Odebolt 1,299
Oelwein 7,564
Ogden 1,953
Okoboji 559
Olin 735
Onawa 3,283
Orange City 4,588
Orient 416
Orleans 546
Osage 3,718
Osceola 3,750
Oskaloosa 10,629
Ossian 829
Otho FTDO 692
OTTUMWA OTUM 27,381
Oxford 676
Oxford Junction 600
Pacific Junction 511
Palo CEDR 529
Panora 1,211
Parkersburg 1,968
Paullina 1,224
Pella 8,349
Perry 7,053
Peterson 470
Plainfield 469
Pleasant Hill DES 3,493
Pleasant Valley D-RI-M 750 ○
Pleasantville 1,531
Plymouth 463
Pocahontas 2,352
Polk City DES 1,658
Pomeroy 895
Postville 1,475
Prairie City 1,278
Preston 1,120
Primghar 1,050
Princeton 965
Quasqueton 599
Quimby 424
Radcliffe 593
Readlyn 858
Redfield 959
Red Oak 6,810
Reinbeck 1,808
Remsen 1,592
Riceville 919
Richland 600
Ringsted 557
Riverdale D-RI-M 462
Riverside 826
Robins CEDR 726
Rockford 1,012
Rock Rapids 2,693
Rock Valley 2,706
Rockwell 1,039
Rockwell City 2,276
Roland 1,005
Rolfe 796
Royal 522
Rudd 460
Russell 593
Ruthven 769
Sabula 824
Sac City 3,000
St. Ansgar 1,100
St. Charles 507
Salem 463
Salix 429
Sanborn 1,398
Saydel DES 4,200 ○
Saylorville DES 780 ○
Schleswig 868
Scranton 748
Sergeant Bluff SXCY 2,416
Seymour 1,036
Sheffield 1,224
Shelby 665
Sheldon 5,003
Shell Rock 1,478
Shellsburg 771
Shenandoah 6,274

○ Rand McNally estimate (not reported in census).
▲ Population of entire township or "town", including rural area.
● Independent city. Population not included in county total.

Sibley	3,051
Sidney	1,308
Sigourney	2,330
Sioux Center	4,588
SIOUX CITY SXCY	82,003
Sioux Rapids	897
Slater AMES	1,312
Sloan	978
Solon IACY	969
Spencer	11,726
Spillville	415
Spirit Lake	3,976
Springville	1,165
Stacyville	538
Stanhope	492
Stanton	747
Stanwood	705
State Center	1,292
Storm Lake	8,814
Story City	2,762
Stratford	806
Strawberry Point	1,463
Stuart	1,650
Sully	828
Sumner	2,335
Sutherland	897
Swea City	813
Swisher CEDR	654
Tabor	1,088
Tama	2,968
Terril	420
Thompson	668
Thornton	442
Tiffin IACY	413
Tipton	3,055
Titonka	607
Toledo	2,445
Traer	1,703
Treynor	920
Tripoli	1,280
Underwood	448
Union	515
University Heights IACY	1,069
University Park	645
Urbana	574
Urbandale DES	17,869
Ute	479
Vail	490
Van Horne	682
Van Meter	747
Ventura MSCY	614
Victor	1,046
Villisca	1,434
Vinton	5,040
Walcott D-RI-M	1,425
Walker	733
Wall Lake	892
Walnut	897
Wapello	2,011
Washburn WATL	1,400 ○
Washington	6,584
WATERLOO WATL	75,985
Waukee DES	2,227
Waukon	3,983
Waverly	8,444
Wayland	720
Webster City	8,572
Wellman	1,125
Wellsburg	761
Wesley	598
West Bend	941
West Branch IACY	1,867
West Burlington BUR	3,371
West Des Moines DES	21,894
West Liberty	2,723
West Point	1,133
West Union	2,783
What Cheer	803
Wheatland	840
Whiting	734
Whittemore	647
Williamsburg	2,033
Wilton	2,502
Windsor Heights DES	5,632
Winfield	1,042
Winterset	4,021
Winthrop	767
Woodbine	1,463
Woodward	1,212
Worthington	432
Wyoming	702
Zearing	630

COUNTIES

Adair	9,509
Adams	5,731
Allamakee	15,108
Appanoose	15,511
Audubon	8,559
Benton	23,649
Black Hawk	137,961
Boone	26,184
Bremer	24,820
Buchanan	22,900
Buena Vista	20,774
Butler	17,668
Calhoun	13,542
Carroll	22,951
Cass	16,932
Cedar	18,635
Cerro Gordo	48,458
Cherokee	16,238
Chickasaw	15,437
Clarke	8,612
Clay	19,576
Clayton	21,098
Clinton	57,122
Crawford	18,935
Dallas	29,513
Davis	9,104
Decatur	9,794
Delaware	18,933
Des Moines	46,203
Dickinson	15,629
Dubuque	93,745
Emmet	13,336
Fayette	25,488
Floyd	19,597
Franklin	13,036
Fremont	9,401
Greene	12,119
Grundy	14,366
Guthrie	11,983
Hamilton	17,862
Hancock	13,833
Hardin	21,776
Harrison	16,348
Henry	18,890
Howard	11,114
Humboldt	12,246
Ida	8,908
Iowa	15,429
Jackson	22,503
Jasper	36,425
Jefferson	16,316
Johnson	81,717
Jones	20,401
Keokuk	12,921
Kossuth	21,891
Lee	43,106
Linn	169,775
Louisa	12,055
Lucas	10,313
Lyon	12,896
Madison	12,597
Mahaska	22,507
Marion	29,669
Marshall	41,652
Mills	13,406
Mitchell	12,329
Monona	11,692
Monroe	9,209
Montgomery	13,413
Muscatine	40,436
O'Brien	16,972
Osceola	8,371
Page	19,063
Palo Alto	12,721
Plymouth	24,743
Pocahontas	11,369
Polk	303,170
Pottawattamie	86,500
Poweshiek	19,306
Ringgold	6,112
Sac	14,118
Scott	160,022
Shelby	15,043
Sioux	30,813
Story	72,326
Tama	19,533
Taylor	8,353
Union	13,858
Van Buren	8,626
Wapello	40,241
Warren	34,878
Washington	20,141
Wayne	8,199
Webster	45,953
Winnebago	13,010
Winneshiek	21,876
Woodbury	100,884
Worth	9,075
Wright	16,319

KANSAS

1980 Census 2,363,208

CITIES

Abilene	6,572
Alma	925
Almena	517
Altamont	1,054
Alta Vista	430
Altoona	564
Americus	915
Andale	538
Andover WICH	2,801
Anthony	2,661
Arcadia	460
Argonia	587
Arkansas City	13,201
Arlington	631
Arma	1,676
Ashland	1,096
Assaria	414
Atchison	11,407
Attica	730
Atwood	1,665
Auburn	890
Augusta WICH	6,968
Axtell	470
Baldwin City	2,829
Basehor K.C.	1,483
Baxter Springs	4,773
Bellaire WICH	1,300 ○
Belle Plaine WICH	1,706
Belleville	2,805
Beloit	4,367
Bennington	579
Benton	609
Bird City	546
Blue Rapids	1,280
Bonner Springs K.C.	6,266
Bronson	414
Bucklin	786
Buhler	1,188
Burden	518
Burlingame	1,239
Burlington	2,901
Burrton	976
Caldwell	1,401
Callahan WICH	900 ○
Caney	2,284
Canton	926
Carbondale	1,518
Cawker City	640
Cedar Vale	848
Centralia	486
Chanute	10,506
Chapman	1,255
Chase	753
Cheney	1,404
Cherokee	775
Cherryvale	2,769
Chetopa	1,751
Cimarron	1,491
Claflin	764
Clay Center	4,948
Clearwater	1,684
Clifton	695
Clyde	909
Coffeyville	15,185
Colby	5,544
Coldwater	989
Colony	474
Columbus	3,426
Colwich WICH	935
Concordia	6,847
Conway Springs	1,313
Cottonwood Falls	954
Council Grove	2,381
Cunningham	540
Dearing	475
Deerfield	538
Delphos	570
Derby WICH	9,786
De Soto	2,061
Dighton	1,390
Dodge City	18,001
Douglass	1,450
Downs	1,324
Eastborough WICH	854
Easton	460
Edgerton	1,214
Edna	537
Edwardsville K.C.	3,364
Effingham	634
El Dorado	10,510
Elkhart	2,243
Ellinwood	2,508
Ellis	2,062
Ellsworth	2,465
Elwood ST.JO	1,275
Emporia	25,287
Enterprise	839
Erie	1,415
Eskridge	603
Eudora	2,934
Eureka	3,425
Fairway K.C.	4,619
Florence	729
Fort Scott	8,893
Fowler	592
Frankfort	1,038
Fredonia	3,047
Frontenac	2,586
Galena JOP	3,587
Galva	651
Garden City	18,256
Garden Plain	775
Gardner K.C.	2,392
Garnett	3,310
Gas	543
Geneseo	496
Girard	2,888
Glasco	710
Glen Elder	491
Goddard WICH	1,427
Goessel	421
Goodland	5,708
Grainfield	417
Great Bend	16,608
Greenleaf	462
Greensburg	1,885
Gypsum	423
Halstead	1,994
Hanover	802
Harper	1,823
Hartford	551
Haven	1,125
Haviland	770
Hays	16,301
Haysville WICH	8,006
Herington	2,930
Hesston	3,013
Hiawatha	3,702
Highland	954
Hill City	2,028
Hillsboro	2,717
Hoisington	3,678
Holcomb	816
Holton	3,132
Holyrood	567
Hope	468
Horton	2,130
Howard	965
Hoxie	1,462
Hoyt	536
Hugoton	3,165
Humboldt	2,230
HUTCHINSON HUCH	40,284
Independence	10,598
Inman	947
Iola	6,938
Jamestown	440
Jetmore	862
Jewell	589
Johnson	1,244
Junction City	19,305
Kanopolis	729
KANSAS CITY K.C.	161,087
Kensington	681
Kingman	3,563
Kinsley	2,074
Kiowa	1,409
La Crosse	1,618
La Cygne	1,025
La Harpe	687
Lakin	1,823
Lansing LEAV	5,307
Larned	4,811
LAWRENCE LAWR	52,738
LEAVENWORTH LEAV	33,656
Leawood K.C.	13,360
Lebanon	440
Lebo	966
Lecompton	576
Lenexa K.C.	18,639
Lenora	444
Leon	667
Leonardville	437
Leoti	1,869
Le Roy	701
Lewis	551
Liberal	14,911
Lincoln	1,599
Lindsborg	3,155
Linn	483
Little River	529
Logan	720
Louisburg	1,744
Lucas	524
Lyndon	1,132
Lyons	4,152
McCune	528
Macksville	546
McLouth	700
McPherson	11,753
Madison	1,099
Maize WICH	1,294
Manhattan	32,644
Mankato	1,205
Marion	1,951
Marquette	639
Marysville	3,670
Meade	1,777
Medicine Lodge	2,384
Melvern	481
Meriden	707
Merriam K.C.	10,794
Midland Park WICH	1,350 ○
Milford	465
Miltonvale	588
Minneapolis	2,075
Minneola	712
Mission K.C.	8,643
Mission Hills K.C.	3,904
Moline	553
Montezuma	730
Moran	643
Mound City	755
Moundridge	1,453
Mount Hope	791
Mulberry	647
Mulvane WICH	4,254
Natoma	515
Neodesha	3,414
Ness City	1,769
Newton	16,332
Nickerson	1,292
Norton	3,400
Nortonville	692
Norwich	476
Oaklawn WICH	4,200 ○
Oakley	2,343
Oberlin	2,387
Ogden	1,804
Olathe K.C.	37,258
Olpe	477
Onaga	752
Osage City	2,667
Osawatomie	4,459
Osborne	2,120
Oskaloosa	1,092
Oswego	2,218
Ottawa	11,016
Overbrook	930
Overland Park K.C.	81,784
Oxford	1,125
Ozawkie	472
Paola	4,557
Park City WICH	2,550 ○
Parsons	12,898
Peabody	1,474
Perry	907
Phillipsburg	3,229
Piper K.C.	730 ○
Pittsburg	18,770
Plains	1,044
Plainville	2,458
Pleasanton	1,303
Pomona	868
Potwin	563
Prairie Village K.C.	24,657
Pratt	6,885
Pretty Prairie	655
Protection	684
Quenemo	413
Quinter	951
Ransom	448
Richmond	510
Riley	779
Riverton JOP	550 ○
Roeland Park K.C.	7,962
Rolla	417
Rose Hill WICH	1,557
Rossville	1,045
Russell	5,427
Sabetha	2,286
St. Francis	1,610
St. John	1,346
St. Marys	1,598
St. Paul	746
SALINA SLN	41,843
Satanta	1,117
Scammon	501
Scandia	480
Scott City	4,154
Scranton	664
Sedan	1,579
Sedgwick	1,471
Seneca	2,389
Severy	447
Sharon Springs	982
Shawnee K.C.	29,653
Silver Lake TOP	1,350
Smith Center	2,240
Solomon	1,018
South Haven	439
South Hutchinson HUCH	2,226
Spearville	693
Spring Hill	2,005
Stafford	1,425
Sterling	2,312
Stockton	1,825
Strong City	675
Sublette	1,293
Sunset Park WICH	1,050 ○
Syracuse	1,654
Thayer	517
Tonganoxie	1,864
TOPEKA TOP	115,266
Toronto	466
Towanda	1,332
Tribune	955
Troy	1,240
Turon	481
Udall	891
Ulysses	4,653
Valley Center WICH	3,300
Valley Falls	1,189
Victoria	1,328
WaKeeney	2,388
Wakefield	803
Wamego	3,159
Washington	1,488
Waterville	694
Wathena ST.JO	1,418
Waverly	671
Weir	705
Wellington	8,212
Wellsville	1,363
Westmoreland	598
Westwood K.C.	1,783
White City	534
Whitewater	751
WICHITA WICH	279,272
Wilson	978
Winchester	570
Winfield	10,736
Yates Center	1,998

COUNTIES

Allen	15,654
Anderson	8,749
Atchison	18,397
Barber	6,548
Barton	31,343
Bourbon	15,969
Brown	11,955
Butler	44,782
Chase	3,309
Chautauqua	5,016
Cherokee	22,304
Cheyenne	3,678
Clark	2,599
Clay	9,802
Cloud	12,494
Coffey	9,370
Comanche	2,554
Cowley	36,824
Crawford	37,916
Decatur	4,509
Dickinson	20,175
Doniphan	9,268
Douglas	67,640
Edwards	4,271
Elk	3,918
Ellis	26,098
Ellsworth	6,640
Finney	23,825
Ford	24,315
Franklin	21,813
Geary	29,852
Gove	3,726
Graham	3,995
Grant	6,977
Gray	5,138
Greeley	1,845
Greenwood	8,764
Hamilton	2,514
Harper	7,778
Harvey	30,531
Haskell	3,814
Hodgeman	2,269
Jackson	11,644
Jefferson	15,207
Jewell	5,241
Johnson	270,269
Kearny	3,435
Kingman	8,960
Kiowa	4,046
Labette	25,682
Lane	2,472
Leavenworth	54,809
Lincoln	4,145
Linn	8,234
Logan	3,478
Lyon	35,108
McPherson	26,855
Marion	13,522
Marshall	12,720
Meade	4,788
Miami	21,618
Mitchell	8,117
Montgomery	42,281
Morris	6,419
Morton	3,454
Nemaha	11,211
Neosho	18,967
Ness	4,498
Norton	6,689
Osage	15,319
Osborne	5,959
Ottawa	5,971
Pawnee	8,065
Phillips	7,406
Pottawatomie	14,782
Pratt	10,275
Rawlins	4,105
Reno	64,983
Republic	7,569
Rice	11,900
Riley	63,505
Rooks	7,006
Rush	4,516
Russell	8,868
Saline	48,905
Scott	5,782
Sedgwick	366,531
Seward	17,071
Shawnee	154,916
Sheridan	3,544
Sherman	7,759
Smith	5,947
Stafford	5,539
Stanton	2,339
Stevens	4,736
Sumner	24,928
Thomas	8,451
Trego	4,165

○ Rand McNally estimate (not reported in census).
▲ Population of entire township or "town", including rural area.
● Independent city. Population not included in county total.

Wabaunsee . 6,867
Wallace . 2,045
Washington . 8,543
Wichita . 3,041
Wilson . 12,128
Woodson . 4,600
Wyandotte . 172,335

KENTUCKY
1980 Census 3,661,433

CITIES

Adairville . 1,105
Albany . 2,083
Alexandria CIN- . 4,735
Anchorage LOU . 1,726
Arjay . 650 ○
Arlington . 511
Artemus . 500 ○
Ashland HNTG- . 27,064
Auburn . 1,467
Augusta . 1,455
Auxier . 900 ○
Barbourville . 3,333
Bardstown . 6,155
Bardwell . 988
Barlow . 746
Beattyville . 1,068
Beauty . 450 ○
Beaver Dam . 3,185
Bedford . 835
Belfry . 900 ○
Bellevue CIN- . 7,678
Benham . 936
Benton . 3,700
Berea . 8,226
Betsy Layne . 900 ○
Bloomfield . 954
BOWLING GREEN BOWLG . 40,450
Brandenburg . 1,831
Brodhead . 686
Brooksville . 680
Brownsville . 674
Buechel LOU . 5,900 ○
Bulan . 440 ○
Burgin . 1,008
Burkesville . 2,051
Burlington . 550 ○
Burnside . 775
Butler . 663
Cadiz . 1,661
Calhoun . 1,080
Calvert City PAD . 2,388
Campbellsburg . 714
Campbellsville . 8,715
Campton . 486
Caneyville . 642
Cannonsburg . 600 ○
Carlisle . 1,757
Carrollton . 3,967
Catlettsburg HNTG- . 3,005
Cave City . 2,098
Cawood . 800 ○
Cecilia . 500 ○
Centertown . 462
Central City . 5,214
Clarkson . 666
Clay . 1,356
Clay City . 1,276
Clearfield . 900 ○
Clinton . 1,720
Cloverport . 1,585
Cold Spring CIN- . 2,117
Columbia . 3,710
Combs . 700 ○
Corbin . 8,075
Corydon . 874
Covington CIN- . 49,013
Crab Orchard . 843
Crescent Springs CIN- . 1,951
Crestwood LOU . 531
Crittenden . 597
Crofton . 823
Cromona . 700 ○
Cumberland . 3,712
Cynthiana . 5,881
Danville . 12,942
Dayton CIN- . 6,979
Dixon . 533
Dorton . 600 ○
Drakesboro . 798
Drift . 600 ○
Dry Ridge . 1,250
Earlington . 2,011
East Bernstadt . 700 ○
Eddyville . 1,949
Edgewood CIN- . 7,230
Edmonton . 1,401
Elizabethtown . 15,380
Elkhorn City . 1,446
Elkton . 1,815
Elsmere CIN- . 7,203
Eminence . 2,260
Erlanger CIN- . 14,433
Evarts . 1,234
Fairdale LOU . 4,100 ○
Falmouth . 2,482
Ferguson . 1,009
Fern Creek LOU . 6,000 ○
Flat Lick . 700 ○
Flatwoods HNTG- . 8,354
Flemingsburg . 2,835
Florence CIN- . 15,586
Fordsville . 561
Fort Mitchell CIN- . 7,297
Fort Thomas CIN- . 16,012
Fort Wright CIN- . 4,481
Fournile . 500 ○
Frankfort . 25,973
Franklin . 7,738
Fredonia . 535
Frenchburg . 550 ○
Fullerton PTSM . 500 ○
Fulton . 3,137
Gamaliel . 456

Garrison . 650 ○
Georgetown LEX . 10,972
Ghent . 439
Glasgow . 12,958
Grahn . 500 ○
Grand Rivers . 428
Grapevine . 900 ○
Gray . 750 ○
Grayson HNTG- . 3,423
Greensburg . 2,377
Greenup HNTG- . 1,386
Greenville . 4,631
Guthrie . 1,361
Hanson . 485
Hardin . 545
Hardinsburg . 2,211
Harlan . 3,024
Harrodsburg . 7,265
Hartford . 2,512
Hawesville . 1,036
Hazard . 5,429
Hazel . 465
Hebron CIN- . 500 ○
Heidrick . 600 ○
Henderson EV . 24,834
Hickman . 2,894
Highview LOU . 5,000 ○
Hillview LOU . 5,196
Hima . 700 ○
Hindman . 876
Hitchins . 700 ○
Hodgenville . 2,459
HOPKINSVILLE HPKNV . 27,318
Horse Cave . 2,045
Hyden . 488
Independence CIN- . 7,998
Inez . 500 ○
Irvine . 2,889
Irvington . 1,409
Island . 532
Jackson . 2,651
Jamestown . 1,441
Jeffersontown LOU . 15,795
Jeffersonville . 1,528
Jenkins . 3,271
Junction City . 2,045
Kenvir . 950 ○
Kitts . 500 ○
Kuttawa . 560
La Center . 1,044
La Grange . 2,971
Lakeside Park CIN- . 3,038
Lancaster . 3,365
Langley . 600 ○
Lawrenceburg . 5,167
Lebanon . 6,590
Lebanon Junction . 1,581
Leitchfield . 4,533
Lejunior . 600 ○
Lewisburg . 972
Lewisport . 1,832
LEXINGTON LEX . 204,165
Liberty . 2,206
Livermore . 1,672
London . 4,002
Lone Oak PAD . 443
Long View . 650 ○
Lookout . 550 ○
Loretto . 954
Lothair . 600 ○
Louisa . 1,832
LOUISVILLE LOU . 298,451
Lovely . 700 ○
Loyall . 1,210
Ludlow CIN- . 4,959
Lynch . 1,614
Lyndon LOU . 1,553
McHenry . 582
McKee . 759
McRoberts . 1,037 ○
McVeigh . 800 ○
Madisonville . 16,979
Magnolia . 450 ○
Manchester . 1,838
Maple Mount . 500 ○
Marion . 3,392
Marshes Siding . 500 ○
Martin . 827
Maryville LOU . 6,000 ○
Mayfield . 10,705
Maysville . 7,983
Melbourne CIN- . 628
Melvin . 700 ○
Middlesboro . 12,251
Middletown LOU . 414
Midway LEX . 1,445
Millersburg . 987
Milton . 718
Monticello . 5,677
Morehead . 7,789
Morganfield . 3,781
Morgantown . 2,000
Mortons Gap . 1,201
Mount Sterling . 5,820
Mount Vernon . 2,334
Mount Washington LOU . 3,997
Muldraugh . 1,752
Munfordville . 1,783
Murray . 14,248
Nazareth . 700 ○
New Castle . 832
New Haven . 926
Newport CIN- . 21,587
Nicholasville LEX . 10,400
North Corbin . 800 ○
North Middletown . 637
Nortonville . 1,336
Oak Grove . 2,088
Okolona LOU . 23,800 ○
Olive Hill . 2,539
Oneida . 600 ○
OWENSBORO OWNS . 54,450
Owenton . 1,341
Owingsville . 1,419
PADUCAH PAD . 29,315
Paintsville . 3,815
Paris . 7,935
Park City . 614
Park Hills CIN- . 3,500

Pembroke . 636
Perryville . 841
Petersburg CIN- . 430 ○
Pewee Valley LOU . 982
Phelps . 1,126
Pikeville . 4,756
Pine Knot . 900 ○
Pineville . 2,599
Pittsburg . 620 ○
Pleasure Ridge Park LOU . 24,300 ○
Pleasureville . 837
Prestonsburg . 4,011
Princeton . 7,073
Prospect LOU . 1,981
Providence . 4,434
Raceland HNTG- . 1,970
Radcliff . 14,519
Ravenna . 793
Revelo . 550 ○
Richmond . 21,705
Rineyville . 450 ○
Robards . 500 ○
Rockport . 511
Russell HNTG- . 3,824
Russell Springs . 1,831
Russellville . 7,520
Sacramento . 538
St. Matthews LOU . 13,354
Salem . 833
Salyersville . 1,352
Sandy Hook . 627
Science Hill . 655
Scottsville . 4,278
Sebree . 1,516
Shelbiana . 500 ○
Shelby City . 700 ○
Shelbyville . 5,308
Shepherdsville LOU . 4,454
Shively LOU . 16,819
Silver Grove CIN- . 1,260
Simpsonville . 642
Smithland . 512
Smith Mills . 420 ○
Smiths Grove . 767
Somerset . 10,649
Sonora . 416
Southgate CIN- . 2,833
South Portsmouth PTSM . 550 ○
South Williamson . 700 ○
Spottsville . 500 ○
Springfield . 3,179
Staffordsville . 700 ○
Stamping Ground . 562
Stanford . 2,764
Stanton . 2,691
Stearns . 950 ○
Sturgis . 2,293
Summersville . 450 ○
Symsonia . 550 ○
Tateville . 725 ○
Taylor Mill CIN- . 4,509
Taylorsville . 801
Thealka . 500 ○
Toler . 420 ○
Tollesboro . 808
Tompkinsville . 4,366
Trenton . 465
Union CIN- . 601
Uniontown . 1,169
Upton . 731
Valley Station LOU . 20,000 ○
Vanceburg . 1,939
Van Lear . 1,033 ○
Veachland . 700 ○
Verda . 950 ○
Versailles LEX . 6,427
Vicco . 456
Vine Grove . 3,583
Walton CIN- . 1,651
Warsaw . 1,328
Washington . 624
Waverly . 434
Wayland . 601
Weeksbury . 700 ○
West Liberty . 1,381
West Point . 1,339
West Van Lear . 900 ○
Westwood HNTG- . 5,500 ○
Wheelwright . 865
White Plains . 859
Whitesburg . 1,525
Whitesville . 788
Whitley City . 1,060 ○
Wickliffe . 1,044
Williamsburg . 5,560
Williamstown . 2,502
Wilmore LEX . 3,787
Winchester . 15,216
Wingo . 606
Woodbine . 500 ○
Woodlawn PAD . 750 ○
Worthington HNTG- . 1,948

COUNTIES

Adair . 15,233
Allen . 14,128
Anderson . 12,567
Ballard . 8,798
Barren . 34,009
Bath . 10,025
Bell . 34,330
Boone . 45,842
Bourbon . 19,405
Boyd . 55,513
Boyle . 25,066
Bracken . 7,738
Breathitt . 17,004
Breckinridge . 16,861
Bullitt . 43,346
Butler . 11,064
Caldwell . 13,473
Calloway . 30,031
Campbell . 83,317
Carlisle . 5,487
Carroll . 9,270
Carter . 25,060
Casey . 14,818
Christian . 66,878
Clark . 28,322

Clay . 22,752
Clinton . 9,321
Crittenden . 9,207
Cumberland . 7,289
Daviess . 85,949
Edmonson . 9,962
Elliott . 6,908
Estill . 14,495
Fayette . 204,165
Fleming . 12,323
Floyd . 48,764
Franklin . 41,830
Fulton . 8,971
Gallatin . 4,842
Garrard . 10,853
Grant . 13,308
Graves . 34,049
Grayson . 20,854
Green . 11,043
Greenup . 39,132
Hancock . 7,742
Hardin . 88,917
Harlan . 41,889
Harrison . 15,166
Hart . 15,402
Henderson . 40,849
Henry . 12,740
Hickman . 6,065
Hopkins . 46,174
Jackson . 11,996
Jefferson . 684,793
Jessamine . 26,653
Johnson . 24,432
Kenton . 137,058
Knott . 17,940
Knox . 30,239
Larue . 11,983
Laurel . 38,982
Lawrence . 14,121
Lee . 7,754
Leslie . 14,882
Letcher . 30,687
Lewis . 14,545
Lincoln . 19,053
Livingston . 9,219
Logan . 24,138
Lyon . 6,490
McCracken . 61,310
McCreary . 15,634
McLean . 10,090
Madison . 53,352
Magoffin . 13,515
Marion . 17,910
Marshall . 25,637
Martin . 13,925
Mason . 17,760
Meade . 22,854
Menifee . 5,117
Mercer . 19,011
Metcalfe . 9,484
Monroe . 12,353
Montgomery . 20,046
Morgan . 12,103
Muhlenberg . 32,238
Nelson . 27,584
Nicholas . 7,157
Ohio . 21,765
Oldham . 28,094
Owen . 8,924
Owsley . 5,709
Pendleton . 10,989
Perry . 33,763
Pike . 81,123
Powell . 11,101
Pulaski . 45,803
Robertson . 2,270
Rockcastle . 13,973
Rowan . 19,049
Russell . 13,708
Scott . 21,813
Shelby . 23,328
Simpson . 14,673
Spencer . 5,929
Taylor . 21,178
Todd . 11,874
Trigg . 9,384
Trimble . 6,253
Union . 17,821
Warren . 71,828
Washington . 10,764
Wayne . 17,022
Webster . 14,832
Whitley . 33,396
Wolfe . 6,698
Woodford . 17,778

LOUISIANA
1980 Census 4,203,972

CITIES

Abbeville . 12,391
Abita Springs N.O. . 1,072
Addis B.R. . 1,320
Albany . 857
ALEXANDRIA ALEX . 51,565
Ama . 875 ○
Amelia MRGCY . 3,000 ○
Amite . 4,301
Anandale ALEX . 2,000 ○
Arabi N.O. . 13,800 ○
Arcadia . 3,403
Arlington . 850 ○
Arnaudville . 1,679
Athens . 419
Avery Island . 575 ○
Avondale N.O. . 5,000 ○
Baker B.R. . 12,865
Baldwin . 2,644
Ball ALEX . 3,405
Barataria . 1,100 ○
Basile . 2,635
Bastrop . 15,527
BATON ROUGE B.R. . 219,486
Bawcomville MONR . 1,900 ○
Bayou Cane HOMA . 15,000 ○

Bayou Goula . 800 ○
Belcher . 436
Belle Chasse N.O. . 5,500 ○
Belle Rose . 700 ○
Benton . 1,864
Bernice . 1,956
Berwick . 4,466
Blanchard SHRE . 1,128
Bogalusa . 16,976
Bonfouca . 480 ○
Bonita . 503
Boothville . 600 ○
Bossier City SHRE . 49,969
Bourg HOMA . 1,200 ○
Boutte . 1,200 ○
Boyce . 1,198
Breaux Bridge LAF . 5,922
Bridge City N.O. . 2,500 ○
Broussard LAF . 2,923
Brownfields B.R. . 1,800 ○
Brownsville MONR . 2,400 ○
Brusly B.R. . 1,762
Bunkie . 5,364
Buras . 2,500 ○
Calhoun . 425 ○
Cameron . 1,500 ○
Campti . 1,069
Carencro LAF . 3,712
Carville . 950 ○
Centerville . 500 ○
Chalmette N.O. . 23,100 ○
Charenton . 950 ○
Chataignier . 431
Chatham . 714
Chauvin . 3,000 ○
Cheneyville . 865
Choudrant . 809
Church Point . 4,599
Claiborne MONR . 1,600 ○
Clarence . 612
Clarks . 931
Clayton . 1,204
Clinton . 1,919
Colfax . 1,680
Collinston . 439
Columbia . 687
Converse . 449
Cooper Road SHRE . 10,000 ○
Cottonport . 1,911
Cotton Valley . 1,445
Coushatta . 2,084
Covington N.O. . 7,892
Crowley . 16,036
Cullen . 1,869
Cut Off . 2,000 ○
Darrow . 425 ○
Delcambre . 2,216
Delhi . 3,290
Denham Springs B.R. . 8,412
De Quincy . 3,966
De Ridder . 11,057
Des Allemands . 2,400 ○
Destrehan N.O. . 1,760 ○
Dodson . 469
Donaldsonville . 7,901
Doyline . 801
Dry Prong . 526
Dubach . 1,161
Dubberly . 421
Duson . 1,253
Elizabeth . 454
Elton . 1,450
Empire . 630 ○
Epps . 672
Erath . 2,133
Erwinville . 475 ○
Estherwood . 691
Eunice . 12,479
Farmerville . 3,768
Fenton . 491
Ferriday . 4,472
Florien . 964
Fordoche . 676
Forest Glen . 600 ○
Forest Hill . 494
Forest Park MONR . 1,500 ○
Fountain Place B.R. . 9,200 ○
Franklin . 9,584
Franklinton . 4,119
French Settlement . 761
Galliano . 2,000 ○
Garyville . 2,600 ○
Gibsland . 1,354
Gilbert . 800
Glenmora . 1,479
Golden Meadow . 2,282
Goldonna . 526
Gonzales B.R. . 7,287
Good Pine . 600 ○
Grambling . 4,226
Gramercy . 3,211
Grand Caillou . 1,400 ○
Grand Coteau . 1,165
Grand Ecore . 450 ○
Grand Isle . 1,982
Gray . 4,000 ○
Grayson . 564
Greensburg . 662
Greenwood SHRE . 1,043
Gretna N.O. . 20,615
Grosse Tete . 749
Gueydan . 1,695
Hackberry . 800 ○
Hahnville N.O. . 3,000 ○
Hammond . 15,043
Hammond East . 1,350 ○
Harahan N.O. . 11,384
Harrisonburg . 610
Harvey N.O. . 13,350 ○
Haughton SHRE . 1,510
Hayes . 830 ○
Haynesville . 3,454
Henderson . 1,560
Hessmer . 743
Hodge . 708
Homer . 4,307
Hornbeck . 470
Hosston . 480 ○
HOUMA HOMA . 32,602

○ Rand McNally estimate (not reported in census).
▲ Population of entire township or "town," including rural area.
● Independent city. Population not included in county total.

Independence 1,684
Inniswold B.R. 1,800○
Iota 1,326
Iowa 2,437
Jackson 3,133
Jeanerette 6,511
Jefferson N.O. 16,500○
Jena 4,332
Jennings 12,401
Jonesboro 5,061
Jonesville 2,828
Joyce 900○
Junction City 727
Kaplan 5,016
Kennedy Heights N.O. 2,000○
Kenner N.O. 66,382
Kentwood 2,667
Killian 611
Killona 600○
Kinder 2,603
Kraemer 500○
Krotz Springs 1,374
Lacombe N.O. 2,160○
LAFAYETTE LAF 81,961
Lafayette Southwest LAF 5,500○
Lafitte 1,223○
Lafourche 600○
Lagonda MRGCY 6,200○
Lake Arthur 3,615
LAKE CHARLES LKCH 75,051
Lake Providence 6,361
La Place 10,000○
Larose 5,000○
Lawtell 900○
Lecompte 1,661
Leesville 9,054
Leonville 1,143
Libuse ALEX 700○
Live Oak Manor N.O. 1,500○
Livingston 1,260
Livonia 980
Lockport 2,424
Logansport 1,565
Loreauville 860
Lucy 450○
Luling N.O. 4,300○
Lutcher 4,730
Madisonville N.O. 799
Mamou 3,194
Mandeville N.O. 6,076
Mangham 867
Mansfield 6,485
Mansura 2,074
Many 3,988
Maringouin 1,291
Marion 989
Marksville 5,113
Marrero N.O. 47,300○
Martin 584
Mathews 900○
Maurice 478
Melville 1,764
Meraux N.O. 4,100○
Mermentau 771
Mer Rouge 802
Merryville 1,286
Metairie N.O. 172,200○
Mimosa Park N.O. 2,000○
Minden 15,074
MONROE MONR 57,597
Montegut 800○
Montgomery 843
Montz 500○
Mooringsport SHRE 911
Moreauville 853
MORGAN CITY MRGCY 16,114
Morganza 846
Morrow 460○
Morse 835
Moss Bluff LKCH 2,000○
Napoleonville 829
Natalbany 700○
Natchitoches 16,664
Newellton 1,726
NEW IBERIA NWIB 32,766
Newllano 2,213
NEW ORLEANS N.O. 557,482
New Roads 3,924
New Sarpy N.O. 1,643○
Norco N.O. 5,000○
North Merrydale B.R. 3,500○
Norwood 421
Oakdale 7,155
Oak Grove 2,214
Oberlin 1,764
Oil City 1,323
Olla 1,603
Opelousas 18,903
Paincourtville 450○
Paradis 800○
Parks 545
Patterson MRGCY 4,584
Paulina 980○
Pearl River N.O. 1,693
Pierre Part 900○
Pine Prairie 734
Pineville ALEX 12,034
Pitkin 750○
Plain Dealing 1,213
Plaquemine 7,521
Pointe a la Hache 600○
Ponchatoula 5,469
Port Allen B.R. 6,114
Port Barre 2,625
Port Sulphur 3,200○
Port Vincent 450
Provencal 695
Raceland 4,880○
Rayne 9,066
Rayville 4,610
Reddell 550○
Red Oaks B.R. 2,000○
Reserve 7,000○
Ringgold 1,655
River Ridge N.O. 15,713○
Roanoke 600○
Roseland 1,346
Rosepine 953
Ruston 20,585
St. Bernard 720○
St. Francisville 1,471
St. Joseph 1,687
St. Martinville 7,965
St. Rose N.O. 2,800○
Samtown ALEX 4,125○
Sarepta 831
Schriever 500○
Scotlandville B.R. 26,400○
Scott LAF 2,239
Seymourville 2,800○
SHREVEPORT SHRE 205,815
Sicily Island 691
Siegle MONR 1,400○
Simmesport 2,293
Simpson 534
Simsboro 553
Slaughter 729
Slidell N.O. 26,718
Sorrento 1,197
South Mansfield 419
Springfield 424
Springhill 6,516
Starks 780○
Sterlington MONR 1,400
Stonewall 1,175
Sulphur LKCH 19,709
Sunset 2,300
Swartz 450○
Tallulah 10,392
Tangipahoa 493
Thibodaux 15,810
Tickfaw 571
Tioga ALEX 1,200○
Triumph 1,600○
Trout 500○
Tullos 772
Union 600○
Urania 849
Vacherie 2,200○
Vidalia NCHZ 5,936
Vienna 519
Ville Platte 9,201
Vinton 3,631
Violet N.O. 1,600○
Vivian 4,146
Walker B.R. 2,957
Washington 1,266
Waterproof 1,339
Welcome 450○
Welsh 3,515
Westlake LKCH 5,246
West Monroe MONR 14,993
Westwego N.O. 12,663
White Castle 2,160
Willow Glen 500○
Wilson 656
Winnfield 7,311
Winnsboro 5,921
Wisner 1,424
Woodworth 412
Youngsville LAF 1,053
Zachary B.R. 7,297
Zwolle 2,602

PARISHES

Acadia 56,427
Allen 21,390
Ascension 50,068
Assumption 22,084
Avoyelles 41,393
Beauregard 29,692
Bienville 16,387
Bossier 80,721
Caddo 252,294
Calcasieu 167,048
Caldwell 10,761
Cameron 9,336
Catahoula 12,287
Claiborne 17,095
Concordia 22,981
De Soto 25,664
East Baton Rouge 366,164
East Carroll 11,772
East Feliciana 19,015
Evangeline 33,343
Franklin 24,141
Grant 16,703
Iberia 63,752
Iberville 32,159
Jackson 17,321
Jefferson 454,592
Jefferson Davis 32,168
Lafayette 150,017
Lafourche 82,483
La Salle 17,004
Lincoln 39,763
Livingston 58,655
Madison 14,733
Morehouse 34,803
Natchitoches 39,863
Orleans 557,482
Ouachita 139,241
Plaquemines 26,049
Pointe Coupee 24,045
Rapides 135,282
Red River 10,433
Richland 22,187
Sabine 25,280
St. Bernard 64,097
St. Charles 37,259
St. Helena 9,827
St. James 21,495
St. John The Baptist 31,924
St. Landry 84,128
St. Martin 40,214
St. Mary 64,395
St. Tammany 110,554
Tangipahoa 80,698
Tensas 8,525
Terrebonne 94,393
Union 21,167
Vermilion 48,458
Vernon 53,475
Washington 44,207
Webster 43,631
West Baton Rouge 19,086
West Carroll 12,922
West Feliciana 12,186
Winn 17,253

MAINE

1980 Census 1,124,660

CITIES

Alfred 1,890▲ 500○
Andover 470○
Anson 2,226▲ 900○
Ashland 1,865▲ 800○
Auburn LEW- 23,128
AUGUSTA AUG 21,819
Bailey Island BR-BA 650○
BANGOR BANG 31,643
Bar Harbor 4,124▲ 2,392○
Bar Mills 825○
Bath BR-BA 10,246
Beals 430○
Belfast 2,043▲ 6,243
Berwick DOV- 4,149▲ 1,765○
Bethel 2,340▲ 1,225○
Biddeford POR 19,638
Bingham 1,184▲ 1,184○
Blaine 922▲ 470○
Blue Hill 1,644▲ 700○
Boothbay 2,308▲ 450○
Boothbay Harbor 2,207▲ 1,800○
Bradley BANG 1,149▲ 625○
Brewer BANG 9,017
Bridgton 3,528▲ 1,779○
Brownville Junction 775○
BRUNSWICK BR-BA 17,366▲ 13,900○
Bucksport 4,345▲ 2,456○
Calais 4,262
Camden 4,584▲ 3,492○
Canton 500○
Cape Elizabeth POR 7,838○
Cape Neddick 425○
Cape Porpoise 500○
Caribou 9,916
Castine 1,304▲ 550○
Chisholm 1,530○
Clinton 2,696▲ 1,124○
Corinna 1,887▲ 950○
Cornish 600○
Cumberland Center 900○
Cumberland Foreside 1,000○
Damariscotta 1,493▲ 720○
Danforth 500○
Dexter 4,286▲ 2,732○
Dixfield 2,389▲ 1,535○
Dover-Foxcroft 4,323▲ 3,102○
Dryden 500○
Eagle Lake 600○
East Hampden BANG 950○
East Holden 570○
East Millinocket 2,372○
Eastport 1,982
East Wilton 500○
Eliot PTSM 4,948▲ 2,450○
Ellsworth 5,179
Fairfield WATRVL 6,113▲ 3,694○
Falmouth POR 6,853○
Farmingdale AUG 2,535▲ 1,832○
Farmington 6,730▲ 3,096○
Fort Fairfield 4,376▲ 2,322○
Fort Kent 4,826▲ 2,876○
Freeport 5,863▲ 1,822○
Frenchville 1,450▲ 615○
Friendship 585○
Fryeburg 2,715▲ 1,075○
Gardiner AUG 6,485
Gorham POR 10,101▲ 3,337○
Gouldsboro 1,574
Grand Isle 460○
Gray POR 4,344▲ 900○
Greenville 1,839▲ 1,320○
Greenville Junction 600○
Guilford 1,793▲ 1,216○
Hallowell AUG 2,502
Hampden BANG 5,250▲ 1,400○
Hampden Highlands BANG 730○
Harrison 1,667▲ 465○
Hartland 1,669▲ 1,000○
Houlton 6,766▲ 6,780○
Howland 1,602○
Island Falls 981▲ 650○
Jackman 1,003▲ 800○
Jay 5,080▲ 500○
Jonesport 1,512▲ 1,073○
Kennebunk 6,621▲ 2,764○
Kennebunkport 2,952▲ 1,097○
Kezar Falls 900○
Kingfield 1,083▲ 700○
Kittery PTSM 9,314▲ 7,363○
Kittery Point PTSM 1,172○
LEWISTON LEW- 40,481
Limestone 8,719▲ 1,572○
Lincoln 5,066▲ 3,482○
Lisbon LEW- 8,769▲ 1,075○
Lisbon Falls LEW- 3,257○
Littleton 1,009▲ 600○
Livermore Falls 3,572▲ 2,378○
Lubec 2,045▲ 990○
Machias 2,458▲ 1,368○
Madawaska 5,282▲ 4,452○
Madison 4,367▲ 2,920○
Manchester AUG 1,949▲ 600○
Mapleton 1,895▲ 500○
Mars Hill 1,892▲ 1,384○
Mattawamkeag 1,000▲ 750○
Mechanic Falls 2,616○
Medway 1,871▲ 525○
Mexico 3,698▲ 3,325○
Milbridge 1,306▲ 465○
Milford BANG 2,160▲ 1,519○
Millinocket 7,567○
Milo 2,624▲ 1,514○
Monmouth 2,888▲ 500○
Monson 500○
Monticello 950▲ 425○
Moody 515○
Newcastle 1,227▲ 470○
New Harbor 450○
Newport 2,755▲ 1,588○
Norridgewock 2,552▲ 1,067○
North Anson 600○
North Berwick 2,878▲ 1,449○
North Bridgton 500○
Northeast Harbor 550○
North Vassalboro WATRVL 850○
North Windham POR 1,000○
Norway 4,042▲ 2,430○
Oakfield 847▲ 500○
Oakland WATRVL 5,162▲ 2,261○
Ogunquit 1,492
Old Orchard Beach POR 6,291○
Old Town BANG 8,422
Orono BANG 10,578○
Orrs Island BR-BA 500○
Oxford 3,143▲ 625○
Patten 1,368▲ 1,068○
Phillips 1,092▲ 700○
Pine Point 700○
Pittsfield 4,125▲ 3,398○
Portage 450○
Port Clyde 500○
PORTLAND POR 61,572
Presque Isle 11,172
Princeton 994▲ 800○
Randolph AUG 1,834○
Rangeley 1,023▲ 700○
Raymond 2,251▲ 500○
Richmond 2,627▲ 1,449○
Rockland 7,919
Rockport 2,749▲ 1,000○
Rumford 8,240▲ 6,198○
Sabattus LEW- 3,081▲ 1,200○
Saco POR 12,921
St. Agatha 1,035▲ 425○
Sanford 18,020▲ 10,457○
Sangerville 1,219▲ 550○
Scarborough POR 11,347▲ 1,200○
Searsport 2,309▲ 1,110○
Sebago Lake 600○
Sherman Mills 450○
Sherman Station 425○
Skowhegan 8,098▲ 6,571○
South Berwick DOV- 4,046▲ 1,863○
South Bristol 600○
South Paris 2,315○
South Portland POR 22,712
Southwest Harbor 1,855▲ 900○
South Windham POR 1,453○
Springvale 2,914○
Stonington 1,273▲ 700○
Strong 1,506▲ 700○
Thomaston 2,900▲ 2,160○
Topsham BR-BA 6,431▲ 2,700○
Union 1,569▲ 500○
Unity 1,431▲ 445○
Van Buren 3,557▲ 3,429○
Veazie BANG 1,610○
Vinalhaven 1,211▲ 900○
Waldoboro 3,985▲ 1,070○
Washburn 2,028▲ 1,098○
Waterboro 2,943▲ 500○
WATERVILLE WATRVL 17,779
Wells 8,211▲ 850○
Westbrook POR 14,976
West Cumberland POR 800○
West Enfield 440○
West Paris 1,390▲ 500○
West Peru 435○
West Scarborough 700○
Wilton 4,382▲ 2,225○
Windham Center POR 500○
Winslow WATRVL 8,057▲ 5,389○
Winter Harbor 1,120▲ 900○
Winterport 2,675▲ 750○
Winthrop AUG 5,889▲ 2,571○
Wiscasset 2,832▲ 1,350○
Woodland 1,534○
Woolwich BR-BA 2,156▲ 500○
Yarmouth POR 6,585▲ 2,421○
York PTSM 8,465▲ 1,900○
York Beach PTSM 860○
York Harbor PTSM 1,000○

COUNTIES

Androscoggin 99,657
Aroostook 91,331
Cumberland 215,789
Franklin 27,098
Hancock 41,781
Kennebec 109,889
Knox 32,941
Lincoln 25,691
Oxford 48,968
Penobscot 137,015
Piscataquis 17,634
Sagadahoc 28,795
Somerset 45,028
Waldo 28,414
Washington 34,963
York 139,666

MARYLAND

1980 Census 4,216,446

CITIES

Aberdeen 11,533
Abingdon BAL 450○
ANNAPOLIS ANPLS 31,740
Annapolis Junction BAL 600○
Ardmore WASH 900○
Arundel Village BAL 6,500○
Ashton WASH 800○
Aspen Hill WASH 9,800○
Avenel WASH 5,600○
BALTIMORE● BAL 786,775
Baltimore Highlands BAL 6,900○
Barton CUMB 617
Bay Ridge ANPLS 800○
Bel Air BAL 7,814
Belcamp BAL 650○
Beltsville WASH 9,000○
Benedict 700○
Berlin 2,162
Bethesda WASH 78,300○
Birchwood City WASH 5,600○
Bladensburg WASH 7,691
Boonsboro 1,908
Boulevard Heights WASH 1,900○
Bowie WASH 33,695
Braddock Heights 950○
Bradshaw BAL 800○
Brandywine WASH 600○
Brentwood WASH 2,988
Brooklandville BAL 500○
Brooklyn Park BAL 3,000○
Broomes Island 450○
Brunswick 4,572
Bryans Road WASH 2,000○
Cabin John WASH 1,600○
Calverton WASH 6,800○
Cambridge 11,703
Camp Springs WASH 2,900○
Capitol Heights WASH 3,271
Cardiff BAL 450○
Catonsville BAL 47,700○
Cecilton 508
Centreville 2,018
Charlestown PHIL- 720
Chase BAL 700○
Cheltenham WASH 500○
Chesapeake Beach WASH 1,408
Chesapeake City 899
Chester 600○
Chestertown 3,300
Cheverly WASH 5,751
Chevy Chase WASH 24,000○
Chillum WASH 15,100○
Churchton WASH 800○
Clarksburg WASH 600○
Clear Spring 477
Clinton WASH 4,400○
Cockeysville BAL 4,900○
College Park WASH 23,614
Colmar Manor WASH 1,286
Coltons Point 500○
Columbia WASH 56,100○
Corriganville CUMB 950○
Cresaptown CUMB 1,900○
Crisfield 2,924
Crofton WASH 10,000○
CUMBERLAND CUMB 25,933
Damascus WASH 4,000○
Darlington BAL 500○
Dayton BAL 700○
Deale WASH 1,600○
Deal Island 500○
Deer Park 486
Delmar 1,232
Denton 1,927
Derwood WASH 550○
District Heights WASH 6,799
Dorsey BAL 950○
Dublin BAL 500○
Dundalk BAL 89,500○
Easton 7,536
Eckhart Mines CUMB 1,400○
Edgemere BAL 8,000○
Edgewater WASH 800○
Edgewood BAL 10,000○
Edmondson Heights BAL 5,000○
Elk Ridge BAL 2,100○
Elkton PHIL- 6,468
Ellerslie CUMB 1,150○
Ellicott City BAL 2,100○
Emmitsburg 1,552
Essex BAL 43,700○
Fairmount Heights WASH 1,616
Federalsburg 1,952
Ferndale BAL 3,900○
Fishing Creek 650○
Forest Hill BAL 550○
Forestville WASH 11,700○
Fort Howard BAL 950○
Fort Washington Forest WASH 1,300○
Frederick 27,557
Friendsville 511
Frostburg CUMB 7,715
Fruitland SLSB 2,694
Fulton WASH 600○
Funkstown HAG- 1,103
Gaithersburg WASH 26,424
Galesville WASH 600○
Gambrills ANPLS 650○
Garrett Park WASH 1,178
Garrison BAL 750○
Germantown WASH 500○
Glen Burnie BAL 42,400○
Glyndon BAL 1,100○
Grantsville 498
Grasonville 1,200○
Greenbelt WASH 16,000
Greensboro 1,253
HAGERSTOWN HAG- 34,132
Halethorpe BAL 25,300○
Halfway HAG- 7,500○
Hampstead BAL 1,293
Hancock 1,887
Harmans 600○
Havre de Grace 8,763
Hebron 714
Hereford BAL 600○
Hillcrest Heights 24,900○
Hillcrest Heights WASH 25,000○
Hughesville 800○
Hurlock 1,690
Hyattsville WASH 12,709
Indian Head WASH 1,381
Jarrettsville BAL 900○
Jessup BAL 1,000○
Joppa BAL 9,100○
Keedysville HAG- 476
Kensington WASH 1,822
Kettering WASH 6,000○
Kingstown 600○
Kingsville BAL 700○
Lake Shore BAL 1,500○
Langley Park WASH 11,564○
Lanham WASH 9,400○
Lansdowne BAL 10,100○
La Plata WASH 2,484
Laurel WASH 12,103
La Vale CUMB 4,000○
Lawsonia 900○

○ Rand McNally estimate (not reported in census).
▲ Population of entire township or "town", including rural area.
● Independent city. Population not included in county total.

Leonardtown 1,448
Lexington Park 11,000○
Libertytown 500○
Linthicum Heights BAL 11,200○
Loch Lynn Heights 503
Lonaconing CUMB 1,420
Londontowne WASH 2,750○
Long Bar Harbor 700○
Long Beach 900○
Lutherville-Timonium BAL 29,500○
Lynne Acres BAL 6,500○
McAlpine BAL 1,500○
Manchester BAL 1,830
Marbury 500○
Margate BAL 5,100○
Marion Station 500○
Marley BAL 5,100○
Maryland City WASH 7,102○
Maugansville HAG- 1,500○
Middle River BAL 25,500○
Middletown 1,748
Midland CUMB 601
Millington 546
Montgomery Village WASH 6,000○
Mountain Lake Park 1,597
Mount Airy BAL 2,450
Mount Rainier WASH 7,361
Mount Savage CUMB 1,400○
Myersville 432
Nanticoke 430○
New Carrollton WASH 12,632
New Windsor 799
North Beach WASH 1,504
North East PHIL- 1,469
Oakland 1,994
Ocean City 4,946
Odenton BAL 7,400○
Olney WASH 4,600○
Owings Mills BAL 7,500○
Oxford 754
Oxon Hill WASH 2,000○
Palmer Park WASH 8,400○
Paramount HAG- 900○
Parkville BAL 37,400○
Parsonsburg SLSB 500○
Pasadena BAL 1,700○
Perry Hall BAL 5,500○
Perryman BAL 1,200○
Perry Point 500○
Pikesville BAL 25,400○
Piney Point 900○
Pittsville 519
Pocomoke City 3,558
Poolesville 3,428
Port Deposit 664
Potomac WASH 2,000○
Potomac Heights WASH 2,400○
Preston 498
Prince Frederick 1,500○
Princess Anne 1,499
Pumphrey BAL 3,000○
Queenstown 491
Randallstown BAL 17,300○
Randolph Hills WASH 5,500○
Reisterstown BAL 13,200○
Ridgely 933
Rising Sun 1,160
Riverdale WASH 4,748
Riviera Beach BAL 4,000○
Rockdale BAL 3,500○
Rock Hall 1,511
Rockville WASH 43,811
Rosedale BAL 11,300○
St. Marys City 900○
St. Michaels 1,301
SALISBURY SLSB 16,429
Savage BAL 2,200○
Seabrook WASH 9,100○
Seat Pleasant WASH 5,217
Secretary 487
Shady Side WASH 2,000○
Sharpsburg HAG- 721
Sharptown 654
Silver Hill WASH 2,600○
Silver Spring WASH 84,300○
Smithsburg HAG- 833
Snow Hill 2,192
Solomons 500○
South Laurel WASH 6,700○
Spencerville WASH 900○
Stevensville 450○
Sudlersville 443
Suitland WASH 26,800○
Sykesville BAL 1,712
Takoma Park WASH 16,231
Taneytown 2,618
Thurmont 2,934
Tilghman 900○
Town Creek Manor 900○
Towson BAL 84,500○
Trappe 739
Union Bridge 927
Upper Marlboro WASH 828
Waldorf WASH 6,500○
Walkersville 2,212
Westernport 2,706
West Friendship BAL 500○
Westminster BAL 8,808
Westover 525○
Wheaton WASH 73,800○
White Plains WASH 900○
Willards 540
Williamsport HAG- 1,867
Woodlawn BAL 7,700○
Woodmoor BAL 7,400○
Woodsboro 506
Woodstock BAL 700○

COUNTIES

Allegany 80,548
Anne Arundel 370,775
Baltimore 655,615
Calvert 34,638
Caroline 23,143
Carroll 96,356
Cecil 60,430
Charles 72,751
Dorchester 30,623
Frederick 114,263
Garrett 26,498
Harford 145,930
Howard 118,572
Kent 16,695
Montgomery 579,053
Prince Georges 665,071
Queen Annes 25,508
St. Marys 59,895
Somerset 19,188
Talbot 25,604
Washington 113,086
Wicomico 64,540
Worcester 30,889

MASSACHUSETTS

1980 Census 5,737,037

CITIES

Abington BOS 13,517▲ 5,000○
Acton BOS 17,544▲ 2,500○
Acushnet N.BED 8,704▲ 6,400○
Adams PTSF 10,381○
Agawam SPRG- 26,271▲ 10,300○
Amesbury BOS 13,971○
AMHERST AMH 33,229▲ 26,300○
Andover BOS 26,370▲ 8,700○
Arlington BOS 48,219○
Ashburnham FTCH- 4,075▲ 1,150○
Ashby FTCH- 2,311▲ 600○
Ashfield 1,458▲ 600○
Ashland BOS 9,165○
Assinippi BOS 1,400○
Assonet F.R. 900○
Athol 10,634○
Attleboro PROV- 34,196
Auburn WORC 14,845○
Avon BOS 5,026○
Ayer 6,993○
Baldwinville 2,000○
Ballardvale BOS 1,300○
Barnstable 30,898▲ 1,200○
Barre 4,102▲ 1,300○
Barre Plains 550○
Becket 1,339▲ 500○
Bedford BOS 13,067○
Belchertown SPRG- 8,339▲ 2,800○
Bellingham BOS 14,300○
Belmont BOS 26,100○
Berkshire 500○
Berlin BOS 2,215▲ 550○
Bernardston 1,750▲ 700○
Beverly BOS 37,655
Billerica BOS 36,727▲ 6,400○
Blackstone PROV- 6,570▲ 5,100○
Blandford 1,038▲ 800○
Bolton BOS 2,530▲ 500○
Bondsville SPRG- 1,750○
BOSTON BOS 562,994
Bourne 13,874▲ 600○
Boxborough BOS 3,126▲ 500○
Boxford BOS 5,374▲ 3,000○
Boylston WORC 3,470▲ 750○
Braintree BOS 36,337○
Brant Rock 900○
Brewster 5,226▲ 900○
Bridgewater BOS 17,202▲ 4,300○
Brimfield 500○
Brockton BOS 95,172
Brookfield WORC 2,397▲ 1,500○
Brookline BOS 55,062○
Brooks Place BOS 500○
Brookville BOS 950○
Bryantville BOS 1,500○
Burlington BOS 23,486○
Buzzards Bay 3,000○
Byfield BOS 950○
Cambridge BOS 95,322
Canton BOS 18,182○
Carlisle BOS 3,306▲ 600○
Carver BOS 6,988▲ 650○
Cataumet 800○
Centerville 2,500○
Chaffin WORC 3,700○
Charlemont 1,149▲ 500○
Charlton City WORC 1,100○
Chartley PROV- 600○
Chatham 6,071▲ 1,800○
Chelmsford BOS 31,174▲ 9,400○
Chelsea BOS 25,431
Cherry Valley WORC 1,400○
Cheshire PTSF 3,124▲ 1,100○
Chester 1,123▲ 750○
Chesterfield 1,000▲ 550○
Chicopee SPRG- 55,112
Clinton 12,771○
Cochituate BOS 5,700○
Cohasset BOS 7,174▲ 5,300○
Concord BOS 16,293▲ 6,400○
Conway 1,213▲ 600○
Cordaville BOS 1,457○
Cotuit 1,300○
Dalton PTSF 6,797○
Danvers BOS 24,100○
Dedham BOS 25,298○
Deerfield 4,517▲ 550○
Dennis 12,360▲ 900○
Dennis Port 2,000○
Dighton TAUN 5,352▲ 900○
Dorothy Pond WORC 1,900○
Dover BOS 4,703▲ 1,881○
Dracut BOS 21,249○
Dudley 8,717▲ 3,700○
Dunstable BOS 1,671▲ 900○
Duxbury BOS 11,807▲ 2,477○
East Acton BOS 1,200○
East Billerica BOS 2,900○
East Brewster 700○
East Bridgewater BOS 9,945▲ 3,300○
East Brookfield WORC 1,955▲ 1,500○
East Chelmsford BOS 1,500○
East Dennis 800○
East Douglas 1,800○
East Falmouth 3,600○
East Foxboro BOS 500○
East Freetown 500○
Eastham 3,472▲ 1,100○
Easthampton SPRG- 15,580○
East Longmeadow SPRG- 12,905○
East Mansfield BOS 500○
East Millbury WORC 1,000○
Eastondale BOS 900○
East Orleans 1,200○
East Pepperell BOS 2,500○
East Sudbury BOS 1,500○
East Templeton 980○
East Walpole BOS 4,900○
East Wareham 1,000○
Edgartown 2,204▲ 1,100○
Egypt BOS 1,500○
Elmwood BOS 750○
Essex BOS 2,998▲ 1,626○
Everett BOS 37,195
Fairhaven N.BED 15,759○
FALL RIVER F.R. 92,574
Falmouth 23,640▲ 3,000○
Fayville BOS 1,000○
Feeding Hills SPRG- 8,500○
Fiskdale 2,000○
FITCHBURG FTCH- 39,580
Forge Village BOS 1,400○
Foxboro BOS 14,148▲ 4,600○
Foxvale BOS 500○
Framingham BOS 65,113○
Franklin BOS 18,217○
Gardner 17,900
Georgetown BOS 5,687▲ 2,600○
Gilbertville 1,500○
Gleasondale 500○
Gloucester BOS 27,768
Grafton WORC 11,238▲ 2,000○
Granby SPRG- 5,380▲ 1,700○
Graniteville BOS 1,000○
Great Barrington 7,405▲ 3,400○
Greenfield 18,436○
Green Harbor BOS 1,300○
Groton 6,154▲ 1,600○
Groveland BOS 4,300○
Hadley 4,125▲ 890○
Halifax BOS 5,513▲ 900○
Hamilton BOS 6,960▲ 1,000○
Hampden SPRG- 4,745▲ 700○
Hanover BOS 11,358▲ 2,500○
Hanover Center BOS 1,000○
Hanson BOS 8,617▲ 900○
Hardwick 2,272▲ 500○
Harvard 12,170▲ 900○
Harwich 8,971▲ 1,600○
Harwich Port 2,000○
Harwood BOS 900○
Hatfield 3,045▲ 800○
Haverhill BOS 46,865
Haydenville 900○
Hingham BOS 20,339▲ 12,800○
Hinsdale PTSF 1,707▲ 950○
Holbrook BOS 11,140▲ 10,300○
Holden WORC 13,336▲ 3,900○
Holliston BOS 12,662○
Holyoke SPRG- 44,678
Hopedale BOS 3,905○
Hopkinton BOS 7,114▲ 4,100○
Housatonic 1,400○
Hubbardston 1,797▲ 500○
Hudson BOS 16,408○
Hull BOS 9,714○
Huntington 1,804▲ 950○
Hyannis 9,000○
Hyannis Port 700○
Indian Mound Beach 800○
Ipswich BOS 11,158▲ 5,600○
Island Creek 450○
Islington BOS 5,100○
Jefferson WORC 800○
Kingston BOS 7,362▲ 4,200○
Lakeville BOS 5,931▲ 1,700○
Lancaster 6,334▲ 900○
Lanesboro PTSF 3,131▲ 950○
Lawrence BOS 63,175
Lee PTSF 6,247▲ 3,550○
Leicester WORC 9,446▲ 3,400○
Lenox PTSF 6,523▲ 2,500○
Lenox Dale PTSF 600○
Leominster FTCH- 34,508
Lexington BOS 29,479○
Lincoln BOS 7,098▲ 3,300○
Linwood 1,100○
Littleton BOS 6,970▲ 3,100○
Longmeadow SPRG- 16,301○
Lowell BOS 92,418
Ludlow SPRG- 18,150○
Lunenburg FTCH- 8,405▲ 1,800○
Lynn BOS 78,471
Lynnfield BOS 11,257○
Malden BOS 52,386
Manchaug 1,000○
Manchester BOS 5,424○
Manomet BOS 950○
Mansfield BOS 13,453▲ 5,900○
Marblehead BOS 20,126○
Marion N.BED 3,932▲ 1,350○
Marlborough BOS 30,617
Marshfield BOS 20,916▲ 3,300○
Marshfield Hills BOS 1,500○
Marstons Mills 600○
Mashpee 3,700▲ 500○
Matfield BOS 700○
Mattapoisett N.BED 5,597▲ 2,400○
Maynard BOS 9,590○
Medfield BOS 10,220▲ 6,800○
Medford BOS 58,076
Medway BOS 8,447▲ 4,300○
Melrose BOS 30,055
Mendon BOS 3,108▲ 900○
Merrimac BOS 4,451▲ 2,300○
Merrimacport 450○
Methuen BOS 36,701○
Middleboro BOS 16,404▲ 6,400○
Middleton BOS 4,135○
Milford BOS 23,390○
Millbury WORC 11,808▲ 5,700○
Millers Falls 1,200○
Millis BOS 6,908▲ 3,700○
Millville 1,693○
Milton BOS 25,860○
Minot BOS 800○
Monponsett 600○
Monson SPRG- 7,315▲ 2,200○
Montague 8,011▲ 900○
Monterey 818▲ 500○
Monument Beach 1,400○
Morningdale WORC 1,150○
Mount Hermon 600○
Nabnasset BOS 4,800○
Nahant BOS 3,947○
Nantucket 5,087▲ 2,600○
Natick BOS 29,461○
Needham BOS 27,901○
NEW BEDFORD N.BED 98,478
New Braintree 671▲ 600○
Newbury BOS 4,529▲ 900○
Newburyport BOS 15,900
Newton BOS 83,622
Norfolk BOS 6,363▲ 450○
North Abington BOS 4,700○
North Acton BOS 900○
North Adams 18,063
North Amherst 3,000○
NORTHAMPTON NHAMP 29,286
North Andover BOS 20,129○
North Attleboro PROV- 21,095○
North Billerica BOS 6,700○
Northborough WORC 10,568▲ 5,900○
Northbridge WORC 12,246▲ 3,321○
North Brookfield WORC 4,150▲ 2,800○
North Carver BOS 700○
North Chelmsford BOS 5,800○
North Cohasset BOS 900○
North Dartmouth N.BED 6,000○
North Dighton TAUN 1,500○
North Eastham 1,400○
North Easton BOS 6,100○
North Falmouth 1,800○
Northfield 2,386▲ 1,400○
North Grafton WORC 3,400○
North Hanover BOS 900○
North Hatfield 450○
North Marshfield BOS 450○
North Oxford WORC 1,550○
North Pembroke BOS 2,500○
North Reading BOS 11,455○
North Scituate BOS 4,000○
North Sudbury BOS 1,700○
North Swansea F.R. 950○
North Tewksbury BOS 1,400○
North Truro 700○
North Uxbridge 1,400○
North Wilmington BOS 4,200○
Norton PROV- 12,690▲ 2,400○
Norwell BOS 9,182▲ 800○
Norwood BOS 29,711○
Nutting Lake BOS 2,400○
Oak Bluffs 1,984○
Oakdale WORC 600○
Ocean Bluff BOS 1,750○
Ocean Grove F.R. 4,000○
Ocean Heights 500○
Oldham Village BOS 900○
Onset BOS 2,200○
Orange 6,844▲ 4,000○
Orleans 5,306▲ 1,200○
Osterville 1,400○
Otis 963▲ 500○
Otter River 600○
Oxford WORC 11,680▲ 6,350○
Palmer SPRG- 11,389▲ 3,900○
Paxton WORC 1,800○
Peabody BOS 45,976
Pelham 1,112▲ 500○
Pembroke BOS 13,487▲ 1,800○
Pepperell BOS 8,061▲ 950○
Petersham 1,024▲ 550○
Pigeon Cove BOS 1,700○
Pinehurst BOS 6,800○
Pine Lake BOS 800○
Pine Rest BOS 900○
PITTSFIELD PTSF 51,974
Plainville PROV- 5,857○
Plymouth BOS 35,913▲ 13,900○
Pocasset 2,000○
Point Independence BOS 700○
Princeton 2,425▲ 600○
Provincetown 3,536○
Quincy BOS 84,743
Randolph BOS 28,218○
Raynham TAUN 9,085▲ 2,400○
Raynham Center TAUN 2,526○
Reading BOS 22,678○
Revere BOS 42,423
Rexhame BOS 550○
River Pines BOS 3,700○
Rochdale WORC 1,400○
Rochester 3,205▲ 450○
Rock BOS 500○
Rockland BOS 15,695○
Rockport BOS 6,345▲ 4,600○
Rowley BOS 3,867▲ 1,400○
Russell SPRG- 1,570▲ 650○
Rutland WORC 4,334▲ 2,000○
Sagamore 1,000○
Sagamore Beach 800○
Salem BOS 38,220
Salisbury BOS 5,973▲ 2,439○
Sand Hill BOS 1,750○
Sandwich 8,727▲ 1,900○
Saugus BOS 24,746○
Scituate BOS 17,317▲ 3,738○
Seekonk PROV- 12,269○
Sharon BOS 13,601○
Sheffield 2,743▲ 1,100○
Shelburne Falls 2,500○
Sherborn BOS 4,049▲ 950○
Shirley 5,124▲ 1,750○
Shore Acres BOS 1,200○
Shrewsbury WORC 22,674○
Silver Lake BOS 3,400○
Somerset F.R. 18,813○
Somerville BOS 77,372
South Acton BOS 4,600○
South Amherst 900○
Southampton SPRG- 4,137▲ 500○
South Ashburnham FTCH- 1,190○
South Barre 900○
Southborough BOS 6,193▲ 1,600○
Southbridge 16,665○
South Carver BOS 600○
South Chatham 950○
South Chelmsford BOS 2,700○
South Dartmouth N.BED 7,000○
South Deerfield 2,000○
South Dennis 1,500○
South Duxbury BOS 2,700○
South Easton BOS 1,400○
South Egremont 600○
South Grafton WORC 3,000○
South Hadley SPRG- 16,399▲ 8,900○
South Hadley Falls SPRG- 5,100○
South Hamilton BOS 2,900○
South Hanover BOS 950○
South Harwich 800○
South Hingham BOS 5,200○
South Lancaster 3,000○
South Lee PTSF 500○
South Swansea F.R. 1,700○
South Walpole BOS 1,600○
South Wellfleet 600○
Southwick SPRG- 7,382▲ 1,400○
South Yarmouth 9,700○
Spencer WORC 10,774▲ 5,895○
SPRINGFIELD SPRG- 152,319
Sterling WORC 5,440▲ 1,200○
Stockbridge PTSF 2,328▲ 1,147○
Stoneham BOS 21,424○
Stoughton BOS 26,710○
Stow BOS 5,144▲ 1,100○
Sturbridge 5,976▲ 900○
Sudbury BOS 14,027▲ 2,200○
Sudbury Center BOS 2,900○
Sunderland 2,929▲ 600○
Sutton WORC 500○
Swampscott BOS 13,837○
Swansea F.R. 15,461▲ 750○
TAUNTON TAUN 45,001
Teaticket 2,000○
Templeton 6,070▲ 900○
Tewksbury BOS 24,635▲ 11,500○
Thorndike SPRG- 1,000○
Three Rivers SPRG- 3,600○
Topsfield BOS 5,709▲ 3,600○
Touisset F.R. 1,300○
Townsend FTCH- 7,201▲ 2,000○
Truro 1,486▲ 500○
Turners Falls 4,500○
Upton BOS 3,886▲ 1,500○
Uxbridge WORC 8,374
Vineyard Haven 2,972○
Wakefield BOS 24,895○
Wales 1,177▲ 500○
Walpole BOS 18,859▲ 7,100○
Waltham BOS 58,200
Wamesit BOS 2,700○
Ware 8,953▲ 6,900○
Wareham 18,457▲ 2,024○
Warren SPRG- 3,777▲ 1,800○
Watertown BOS 30,384○
Wayland BOS 12,170▲ 5,500○
Webster WORC 14,480○
Wellesley BOS 27,209○
Wellfleet 2,209▲ 950○
Wenham BOS 3,897○
West Abington BOS 2,000○
West Acton BOS 5,800○
West Andover BOS 3,700○
West Barnstable 500○
West Billerica BOS 2,000○
Westborough WORC 13,619○
West Boylston WORC 6,204▲ 3,500○
West Bridgewater BOS 6,359▲ 2,100○
West Brookfield 3,026▲ 1,700○
West Chatham 1,200○
West Chelmsford BOS 7,000○
West Concord BOS 4,200○
West Dennis 2,000○
West Falmouth 1,200○
Westfield SPRG- 36,465
Westford BOS 13,434▲ 1,000○
West Groton 950○
West Hanover BOS 1,600○
West Hyannisport 1,200○
Westlands BOS 5,500○
West Mansfield BOS 500○
West Medway BOS 2,269○
Westminster FTCH- 5,139▲ 950○
West Newbury BOS 2,861▲ 950○
Weston BOS 11,169○
West Pelham 13,763▲ 450○
Westport F.R. 1,850○
Westport Point 450○
West Springfield SPRG- 27,042○
West Stockbridge PTSF 1,280▲ 800○
West Townsend FTCH- 700○
West Upton BOS 1,000○
West Wareham 900○
West Warren SPRG- 1,200○
Westwood BOS 13,212▲ 6,500○
West Yarmouth BOS 6,600○
Weymouth BOS 55,601○
Whalom FTCH- 1,400○
Whately 1,341▲ 450○
White Horse Beach BOS 800○
White Island Shores 950○
Whitinsville 5,300○
Whitman BOS 13,534○
Wilbraham SPRG- 12,053▲ 3,800○
Williamsburg 2,237▲ 950○
Williamstown 8,741▲ 4,285○
Wilmington BOS 17,471▲ 4,200○
Winchendon 7,019▲ 3,997○
Winchendon Springs 420○
Winchester BOS 20,701○
Winthrop BOS 19,294○
Woburn BOS 36,626
Woods Hole 1,500○
WORCESTER WORC 161,799
Wrentham BOS 7,580▲ 1,400○
Yarmouth 18,449▲ 900○
Yarmouth Port 900○

COUNTIES

Barnstable 147,925
Berkshire 145,110
Bristol 474,641
Dukes 8,942

○ Rand McNally estimate (not reported in census).
▲ Population of entire township or "town", including rural area.
● Independent city. Population not included in county total.

Essex 633,632
Franklin 64,317
Hampden 443,018
Hampshire 138,813
Middlesex 1,367,034
Nantucket 5,087
Norfolk 606,587
Plymouth 405,437
Suffolk 650,142
Worcester 646,352

MICHIGAN

1980 Census 9,258,344

CITIES

Adrian 21,186
Akron 538
Alanson 508
Albion 11,059
Algonac DET 4,412
Allegan 4,576
Allen Park DET 34,196
Alma 9,652
Almont DET 1,857
Alpena 12,214
Amasa 600 ○
Ann Arbor DET 107,316
Armada DET 1,392
Ashley 570
Athens 960
Atlanta 650 ○
Auburn BC-M 1,921
Auburn Heights DET 4,000 ○
Au Gres 768
Augusta BTLCK 913
Bad Axe 3,184
Baldwin 674
Bancroft FLN 618
Bangor 2,001
Bangor Township BC-M 17,494 ○
Baraga 1,055
Baroda BNTH- 627
Barron Lake S.B.- 1,600 ○
Barryton 422
Bath LANS 600 ○
BATTLE CREEK BTLCK 35,724
BAY CITY BC-M 41,593
Bay Port 800 ○
Beaverton 1,025
Beecher FLN 21,000 ○
Belding 5,634
Bellaire 1,063
Belleville DET 3,366
Bellevue 1,289
BENTON HARBOR BNTH- 14,707
Benton Heights BNTH- 6,400 ○
Benzonia 466
Bergland 700 ○
Berkley DET 18,637
Berrien Springs S.B.- 2,042
Bertrand S.B.- 5,000 ○
Bessemer 2,553
Beulah 454
Beverly Hills DET 11,598
Big Rapids 14,361
Birch Run FLN 1,196
Birmingham DET 21,689
Blissfield 3,107
Bloomfield Hills DET 3,985
Bloomingdale 537
Boyne City 3,348
Breckenridge 1,495
Bridgeport SAG 3,500 ○
Bridgman BNTH- 2,235
Brighton DET 4,268
Brimley 500 ○
Britton 693
Bronson 2,271
Brooklyn JAC 1,110
Brown City 1,163
Buchanan S.B.- 5,142
Burr Oak 853
Burton FLN 29,976
Cadillac 10,199
Caledonia GDR 722
Calumet 1,013
Camden 420
Canton 5,000 ○
Capac 1,377
Carleton DET 2,786
Caro 4,317
Carrollton SAG 7,482 ○
Carson City 1,229
Carsonville 622
Caseville 851
Caspian 1,038
Cass City 2,258
Cassopolis 1,933
Cedar Springs GDR 2,615
Cement City JAC 539
Center Line DET 9,293
Central Lake 895
Centreville 1,202
Champion 500 ○
Charlevoix 3,296
Charlotte 8,251
Chassell 700 ○
Cheboygan 5,106
Chelsea DET 3,816
Chesaning FLN 2,656
Clare 3,300
Clarkston DET 968
Clawson DET 15,103
Climax BTLCK 619
Clinton 2,342
Clio FLN 2,669
Coldwater 9,461
Coleman 1,429
Coloma BNTH- 1,833
Colon 1,190
Columbiaville FLN 953
Comstock KZOO 5,310 ○
Concord 900
Constantine 1,680
Coopersville 2,889
Corunna 3,206
Covert 600 ○
Crystal 600 ○
Crystal Falls 1,965
Cutlerville GDR 6,400 ○
Davison FLN 6,087
Dearborn DET 90,660
Dearborn Heights DET 67,706
Decatur 1,915
Deckerville 887
Deerfield 957
De Tour Village 466
DETROIT DET 1,203,339
De Witt LANS 3,165
Dexter DET 1,524
Dimondale LANS 1,008
Dollar Bay 900 ○
Dorr GDR 500 ○
Douglas 948
Dowagiac 6,307
Drayton Plains DET 18,000 ○
Drummond Island 500 ○
Dryden 650
Dundee 2,575
Durand FLN 4,238
East Detroit DET 38,280
East Grand Rapids GDR 10,914
East Jordan 2,185
Eastlake 514
East Lansing LANS 48,309
East Tawas 2,584
Eastwood KZOO 9,800 ○
Eaton Rapids 4,510
Eau Claire S.B.- 573
Eben Junction 450 ○
Ecorse DET 14,447
Edmore 1,176
Edwardsburg S.B.- 1,135
Elberta 556
Elk Rapids 1,504
Elkton 953
Ellsworth 436
Elsie 1,022
Engadine 500 ○
Erie TOL 700 ○
Escanaba 14,355
Essexville BC-M 4,378
Evart 1,945
Ewen 500 ○
Fairgrove 691
Fair Haven DET 900 ○
Fair Plain BNTH- 8,176 ○
Fairview 500 ○
Farmington DET 11,022
Farmington Hills DET 58,056
Farwell 804
Fennville 934
Fenton FLN 8,098
Ferndale DET 26,227
Flat Rock DET 6,853
FLINT FLN 159,611
Flushing FLN 8,624
Fowler 1,021
Fowlerville 2,289
Frankenmuth SAG 3,753
Frankfort 1,603
Fraser DET 14,560
Frederic 500 ○
Freeland BC-M 1,500 ○
Freeport 479
Fremont 3,672
Fruitport MUS 1,143
Fulton 750 ○
Gagetown 428
Gaines FLN 440
Galesburg KZOO 1,822
Galien 692
Garden City DET 35,640
Gaylord 3,011
Genesee FLN 950 ○
Gladstone 4,533
Gladwin 2,479
Gobles 816
Grand Blanc FLN 6,848
Grand Haven MUS 11,763
Grand Ledge LANS 6,920
GRAND RAPIDS GDR 181,843
Grandville GDR 12,412
Grant 683
Grass Lake 900 ○
Grayling 1,792
Greenville 8,019
Greilickville 1,000 ○
Grosse Ile DET 9,320 ○
Grosse Pointe DET 5,901
Grosse Pointe Park DET 13,639
Grosse Pointe Woods DET 18,886
Gwinn 1,300 ○
Hamilton 800 ○
Hamtramck DET 21,300
Hancock 5,122
Hanover JAC 490
Harbor Beach 2,000
Harbor Springs 1,567
Harper Woods DET 16,361
Harrison 1,700
Harrisville 559
Hart 1,888
Hartford BNTH- 2,493
Hartland DET 450 ○
Harvey 900 ○
Haslett LANS 5,500 ○
Hastings 6,418
Hazel Park DET 20,914
Hemlock BC-M 900 ○
Hermansville 700 ○
Hesperia 876
Higgins Lake 500 ○
Highland DET 1,000 ○
Highland Park DET 27,909
Hillsdale 7,432
HOLLAND HLND 26,281
Holly FLN 4,874
Holt LANS 8,400 ○
Homer 1,791
Hopkins 536
Houghton 7,512
Houghton Lake 800 ○
Houghton Lake Heights 1,300 ○
Howard City 1,118
Howell DET 6,976
Hubbardston 421
Hubbell 1,251 ○
Hudson 2,545
Hudsonville GDR 4,844
Huntington Woods DET 6,937
Ida TOL 1,000 ○
Imlay City 2,495
Inkster DET 35,190
Ionia 5,920
Iron Mountain 8,341
Iron River 2,426
Ironwood 7,741
Ishpeming 7,538
Ithaca 2,950
JACKSON JAC 39,739
Jenison GDR 19,000 ○
Jonesville 2,172
KALAMAZOO KZOO 79,722
Kaleva 445
Kalkaska 1,654
Keego Harbor DET 3,083
Kent City 860
Kentwood GDR 30,438
Kinde 600
Kingsford 5,290
Kingsley 664
Kingston 417
Laingsburg 1,145
Lake City 843
Lake Linden 1,181
Lake Odessa 2,171
Lake Orion DET 2,907
Lakeview BTLCK 18,000 ○
Lakeview 1,139
Lambertville TOL 7,000 ○
L'Anse 2,500
LANSING LANS 130,414
Lapeer FLN 6,225
Laurium 2,678
Lawrence 903
Lawton 1,558
Leland 600 ○
Leonard DET 423
Leslie 2,110
Lewiston 600 ○
Lexington 765
Lincoln Park DET 45,105
Linden FLN 2,174
Litchfield 1,353
Livonia DET 104,814
Lowell GDR 3,707
Ludington 8,937
Luna Pier TOL 1,443
Luther 414
Luzerne 500 ○
Lyons 708
McBain 519
Mackinac Island 479
Mackinaw City 820
Madison Heights DET 35,375
Mancelona 1,432
Manchester 1,686
Manistee 7,566
Manistique 3,962
Manton 1,212
Maple Rapids 683
Marcellus 1,134
Marenisco 600 ○
Marine City 4,414
Marion 816
Marlette 1,761
Marne 500 ○
Marquette 23,288
Marshall 7,201
Martin 447
Marysville PTHU 7,345
Mason LANS 6,019
Maybee 490
Mayville 958
Mecosta 428
Melvindale DET 12,322
Memphis 1,171
Mendon 951
Menominee 10,099
Merrill BC-M 851
Metamora 552
Michigan Center JAC 5,000 ○
Middleton 500 ○
Middleville GDR 1,797
Midland BC-M 37,250
Milan DET 4,182
Milford DET 5,041
Millington FLN 1,237
Mio 500 ○
Mohawk 950 ○
Moline GDR 800 ○
MONROE MONR 23,531
Montague MUS 2,332
Montrose FLN 1,706
Morenci 2,110
Morley 507
Mount Clemens DET 18,806
Mount Morris FLN 3,246
Mount Pleasant 23,746
Muir 698
Mulliken 550
Munising 3,083
MUSKEGON MUS 40,823
Muskegon Heights MUS 14,611
Nashville 1,628
Negaunee 5,189
Newaygo 1,271
New Baltimore DET 5,439
Newberry 2,120
New Boston DET 1,500 ○
New Buffalo MICH 2,821
New Era 534
New Haven DET 1,871
New Hudson DET 800 ○
New Lothrop 646
Newport DET 900 ○
Niles S.B.- 13,115
North Adams 565
North Branch 896
North Lake 500 ○
North Muskegon MUS 4,024
Northport 611
Northville DET 5,698
Norton Shores MUS 22,025
Norway 2,919
Novi DET 22,525
Oak Hill 1,000 ○
Oakley FLN 412
Oak Park DET 31,537
Okemos LANS 10,000 ○
Olivet 1,604
Onaway 1,084
Onekama 582
Onsted 670
Ontonagon 2,182
Ortonville DET 1,190
Oscoda 2,170 ○
Otisville FLN 682
Otsego KZOO 3,802
Otter Lake FLN 456
Ovid 1,712
Owosso 16,455
Oxford DET 2,746
Painesdale 650 ○
Palmer 900 ○
Parchment KZOO 1,817
Parma JAC 873
Paw Paw 3,211
Peck 606
Pellston 565
Pentwater 1,165
Perry LANS 2,051
Petersburg 1,222
Petoskey 6,097
Pewamo 488
Pickford 500 ○
Pigeon 1,247
Pinckney DET 1,390
Pinconning BC-M 1,430
Plainfield Heights GDR 5,000 ○
Plainwell KZOO 3,751
Plymouth DET 9,986
Pontiac DET 76,715
Portage KZOO 38,157
Port Austin 839
PORT HURON PTHU 33,981
Portland 3,963
Port Sanilac 598
Powers 490
Pullman 500 ○
Quincy 1,569
Quinnesec 900 ○
Ramsay 1,068 ○
Rapid River 700 ○
Ravenna 951
Reading 1,203
Redford DET 58,441 ○
Reed City 2,221
Reese 1,645
Remus 450 ○
Republic 1,000 ○
Richland KZOO 486
Richmond DET 3,536
River Rouge DET 12,912
Riverview DET 14,569
Rives Junction JAC 450 ○
Rochester DET 7,203
Rock 475 ○
Rockford GDR 3,324
Rockwood DET 3,346
Rogers City 3,923
Romeo DET 3,509
Romulus DET 24,857
Roosevelt Park MUS 4,015
Roscommon 834
Rose City 661
Roseville DET 54,311
Rothbury 522
Royal Oak DET 70,893
Rudyard 900 ○
SAGINAW SAG 77,508
St. Charles SAG 2,276
St. Clair 4,780
St. Clair Shores DET 76,210
St. Ignace 2,632
St. Johns 7,376
St. Joseph BNTH- 9,622
St. Louis 4,107
Saline DET 6,483
Sanford BC-M 864
Saranac 1,421
Saugatuck 1,079
SAULT STE. MARIE SOO 14,448
Sawyer 500 ○
Schoolcraft KZOO 1,359
Scottville 1,241
Sebewaing 2,046
Shelby 1,624
Shepherd 1,534
Shoreham BNTH- 742
Southfield DET 75,568
Southgate DET 32,058
South Haven 5,943
South Lyon DET 5,214
South Range 861
Sparta GDR 3,373
Spring Arbor JAC 1,832 ○
Springfield BTLCK 5,917
Spring Lake MUS 2,731
Springport 675
Stambaugh 1,442
Standish 1,264
Stanton 1,315
Stephenson 967
Sterling 457
Sterling Heights DET 108,999
Stevensville BNTH- 1,268
Stockbridge 1,213
Sturgis 9,468
Sunfield 591
Suttons Bay 504
Swartz Creek FLN 5,013
Tawas City 1,967
Taylor DET 77,568
Tecumseh 7,320
Tekonsha 755
Temperance TOL 3,500 ○
Three Oaks 1,774
Three Rivers 7,015
Tower 500 ○
Traverse City 15,516
Trenton DET 22,762
Troy DET 67,102
Ubly 862
Union City 1,667
Union Lake DET 12,000 ○
Union Pier 1,200 ○
Unionville 578
Utica DET 5,282
Vanderbilt 525
Vandercook Lake JAC 5,000 ○
Vassar 2,727
Vermontville 832
Vicksburg KZOO 2,224
Vulcan 600 ○
Wakefield 2,591
Waldron 570
Walker 15,088
Walled Lake DET 4,748
Warren DET 161,134
Waterford DET 10,000 ○
Watersmeet 700 ○
Watervliet BNTH- 1,867
Waverly LANS 6,700 ○
Wayland 2,023
Wayne DET 21,159
Webberville 1,535
Weidman 450 ○
West Branch 1,785
Westland DET 84,603
Westphalia 896
West Willow DET 5,400 ○
Westwood KZOO 9,500 ○
White Cloud 1,101
Whitehall MUS 2,856
White Pigeon 1,478
White Pine 1,400 ○
Whitmore Lake DET 3,000 ○
Whittemore 438
Williamston LANS 2,981
Willow Run DET 6,400 ○
Winn 450 ○
Wixom DET 6,705
Wolf Lake MUS 2,500 ○
Woodhaven DET 10,902
Woodland 431
Wyandotte DET 34,006
Wyoming GDR 59,616
Yale 1,814
Ypsilanti DET 24,031
Zeeland HLND 4,764
Zilwaukee SAG 2,201

COUNTIES

Alcona 9,740
Alger 9,225
Allegan 81,555
Alpena 32,315
Antrim 16,194
Arenac 14,706
Baraga 8,484
Barry 45,781
Bay 119,881
Benzie 11,205
Berrien 171,276
Branch 40,188
Calhoun 141,557
Cass 49,499
Charlevoix 19,907
Cheboygan 20,649
Chippewa 29,029
Clare 23,822
Clinton 55,893
Crawford 9,465
Delta 38,947
Dickinson 25,341
Eaton 88,337
Emmet 22,992
Genesee 450,449
Gladwin 19,957
Gogebic 19,686
Grand Traverse 54,899
Gratiot 40,448
Hillsdale 42,071
Houghton 37,872
Huron 36,459
Ingham 272,437
Ionia 51,815
Iosco 28,349
Iron 13,635
Isabella 54,110
Jackson 151,495
Kalamazoo 212,378
Kalkaska 10,952
Kent 444,506
Keweenaw 1,963
Lake 7,711
Lapeer 70,038
Leelanau 14,007
Lenawee 89,948
Livingston 100,289
Luce 6,659
Mackinac 10,178
Macomb 694,600
Manistee 23,019
Marquette 74,101
Mason 26,365
Mecosta 36,961
Menominee 26,201
Midland 73,578
Missaukee 10,009
Monroe 134,659
Montcalm 47,555
Montmorency 7,492
Muskegon 157,589
Newaygo 34,917
Oakland 1,011,793
Oceana 22,002
Ogemaw 16,436
Ontonagon 9,861
Osceola 18,928
Oscoda 6,858
Otsego 14,993
Ottawa 157,174
Presque Isle 14,267
Roscommon 16,374
Saginaw 228,059
St. Clair 138,802
St. Joseph 56,038
Sanilac 40,789

○ Rand McNally estimate (not reported in census).
▲ Population of entire township or "town", including rural area.
● Independent city. Population not included in county total.

Schoolcraft 8,575
Shiawassee 71,140
Tuscola 56,961
Van Buren 66,814
Washtenaw 264,748
Wayne 2,337,240
Wexford 25,102

MINNESOTA
1980 Census 4,077,148

CITIES

Ada 1,971
Adams 797
Adrian 1,336
Aitkin 1,770
Akeley 486
Albany 1,569
Albert Lea 19,190
Albertville 564
Alden 687
Alexandria 7,608
Amboy 606
Andover MPLS- 9,387
Annandale 1,568
Anoka MPLS- 15,634
Appleton 1,842
Apple Valley MPLS- 21,818
Arden Hills MPLS- 8,012
Argyle 741
Arlington 1,779
Arnold DUL- 1,350 o
Ashby 486
Atwater 1,128
Aurora 2,670
Austin 23,020
Avon 804
Bagley 1,321
Balaton 752
Barnesville 2,207
Barnum 464
Battle Lake 708
Baudette 1,170
Baxter 2,625
Bayport MPLS- 2,932
Becker 601
Belgrade 805
Belle Plaine 2,754
Belview 438
Bemidji 10,949
Benson 3,656
Bertha 510
Big Falls 490
Bigfork 457
Big Lake MPLS- 2,210
Bird Island 1,372
Biwabik 1,428
Blackduck 653
Blaine MPLS- 28,558
Blooming Prairie 1,969
Bloomington MPLS- 81,831
Blue Earth 4,132
Bovey 813
Braham 1,015
Brainerd 11,489
Brandon 473
Breckenridge 3,909
Brewster 559
Bricelyn 487
Brooklyn Center MPLS- 31,230
Brooklyn Park MPLS- 43,332
Brooten 647
Browerville 693
Brownsdale 691
Browns Valley 887
Brownsville 418
Brownton 697
Buffalo MPLS- 4,560
Buffalo Lake 782
Buhl 1,284
Burnsville MPLS- 35,674
Butterfield 634
Byron ROCH 1,715
Caledonia 2,691
Calumet 469
Cambridge 3,170
Canby 2,143
Cannon Falls 2,653
Carlton 862
Carver MPLS- 642
Cass Lake 1,001
Center City MPLS- 458
Ceylon 543
Champlin MPLS- 9,006
Chanhassen MPLS- 6,359
Chaska MPLS- 8,346
Chatfield 2,055
Chisago City MPLS- 1,634
Chisholm 5,930
Chokio 559
Circle Pines MPLS- 3,321
Clara City 1,574
Claremont 591
Clarissa 663
Clarkfield 1,171
Clarks Grove 620
Clearbrook 579
Cleveland 699
Clinton 622
Cloquet 11,142
Cohasset 600 o
Cokato 2,056
Cold Spring 2,294
Coleraine 1,116
Cologne 545
Columbia Heights MPLS- 20,029
Comfrey 548
Cook 800
Coon Rapids MPLS- 35,826
Corcoran MPLS- 4,252
Cosmos 571
Cottage Grove MPLS- 18,994
Cottonwood 924
Crookston 8,628
Crosby 2,218

Crosslake 1,064
Crystal MPLS- 25,543
Danube 590
Dassel 1,066
Dawson 1,901
Dayton 4,070
Deer River 907
Deerwood 580
Delano MPLS- 2,480
Detroit Lakes 7,106
Dilworth FAR- 2,585
Dodge Center 1,816
DULUTH DUL- 92,811
Dundas 422
Eagan MPLS- 20,532
Eagle Bend 593
Eagle Lake MNKT 1,470
East Bethel MPLS- 6,626
East Grand Forks GDFK 8,537
Eden Prairie MPLS- 16,263
Eden Valley 763
Edgerton 1,123
Edina MPLS- 46,073
Elbow Lake 1,358
Elgin 667
Elk River MPLS- 6,785
Ellendale 555
Ellsworth 629
Elmore 882
Ely 4,820
Elysian 454
Emmons 465
Erskine 585
Esko 500 o
Evansville 571
Eveleth 5,042
Eyota 1,244
Fairfax 1,405
Fairmont 11,506
Falcon Heights MPLS- 5,291
Faribault 16,241
Farmington MPLS- 4,370
Fergus Falls 12,519
Fertile 869
Fisher 453
Floodwood 648
Foley 1,606
Forest Lake MPLS- 4,596
Fosston 1,599
Franklin 512
Frazee 1,284
Freeport 563
Fridley MPLS- 30,228
Fulda 1,308
Gaylord 1,933
Gibbon 787
Gilbert 2,721
Glencoe 4,396
Glenville 851
Glenwood 2,523
Glyndon 882
Golden Valley MPLS- 22,775
Goodhue 657
Good Thunder 560
Goodview 2,567
Graceville 780
Grand Marais 1,289
Grand Meadow 965
Grand Rapids 7,934
Granite Falls 3,451
Greenbush 817
Grove City 596
Hallock 1,405
Halstad 690
Ham Lake MPLS- 7,832
Hancock 877
Hanska 429
Harmony 1,133
Harris 678
Hastings MPLS- 12,827
Hawley 1,634
Hayfield 1,243
Hector 1,252
Henderson 739
Hendricks 737
Henning 832
Herman 600
Hermantown DUL- 6,759
Heron Lake 783
Hibbing 21,193
Hill City 533
Hills 598
Hinckley 963
Hoffman 631
Hokah 686
Holdingford 635
Hopkins MPLS- 15,336
Houston 1,057
Howard Lake 1,240
Hoyt Lakes 3,186
Hugo MPLS- 3,771
Hutchinson 9,244
International Falls 5,611
Inver Grove Heights MPLS- 17,171
Ironton 537
Isanti 858
Isle 573
Ivanhoe 761
Jackson 3,797
Janesville 1,897
Jasper 731
Jeffers 437
Jordan MPLS- 2,663
Kandiyohi 447
Karlstad 934
Kasota 739
Kasson 2,827
Keewatin 1,443
Kellogg 440
Kelly Lake 900 o
Kenyon 1,529
Kerkhoven 761
Kiester 670
Kimball Prairie 651
La Crescent LACRO 3,674
Lafayette 507
Lake Benton 869
Lake City 4,505
Lake Crystal 2,078

Lake Elmo MPLS- 5,296
Lakefield 1,845
Lake Park 716
Lakeville MPLS- 14,790
Lamberton 1,032
Lanesboro 923
La Prairie 536
Le Center 1,967
Le Roy 930
Lester Prairie 1,229
Le Sueur 3,763
Lewiston 1,226
Lindstrom MPLS- 1,972
Lino Lakes MPLS- 4,966
Litchfield 5,904
Little Canada MPLS- 7,102
Little Falls 7,250
Littlefork 918
Long Prairie 2,859
Lonsdale 1,160
Luverne 4,568
Lyle 576
Mabel 861
McGregor 447
McIntosh 681
Madelia 2,130
Madison 2,212
Madison Lake 592
Mahnomen 1,283
MANKATO MNKT 28,651
Mantorville 705
Maple Grove MPLS- 20,525
Maple Lake 1,132
Mapleton 1,516
Maplewood MPLS- 26,990
Marble 757
Marine On St. Croix 543
Marshall 11,161
Maynard 428
Mazeppa 680
Medford 775
Melrose 2,409
Menahga 980
Mendota Heights MPLS- 7,288
Milaca 2,104
Milan 417
MINNEAPOLIS MPLS- 370,951
Minneota 1,470
Minnesota Lake 744
Minnetonka MPLS- 38,683
Montevideo 5,845
Montgomery 2,349
Monticello 3,111
Moorhead FAR- 29,998
Moose Lake 1,408
Mora 2,890
Morgan 975
Morris 5,367
Morristown 639
Morton 549
Motley 444
Mound MPLS- 9,280
Mounds View MPLS- 12,593
Mountain Iron 4,134
Mountain Lake 2,277
Nashwauk 1,419
New Brighton MPLS- 23,269
New Hope MPLS- 23,087
New London 812
New Prague 2,952
New Richland 1,263
New Ulm 13,755
New York Mills 972
Nicollet 709
North Branch 1,597
Northfield 12,562
North Mankato MNKT 9,145
North St. Paul MPLS- 11,921
Norwood 1,219
Oakdale MPLS- 12,123
Ogilvie 423
Oklee 536
Olivia 2,802
Onamia 691
Orono MPLS- 6,845
Oronoco 574
Ortonville 2,550
Osakis 1,355
Osseo MPLS- 2,974
Owatonna 18,632
Parkers Prairie 917
Park Rapids 2,976
Paynesville 2,140
Pelican Rapids 1,867
Pequot Lakes 681
Perham 2,086
Pierz 1,018
Pike Lake DUL- 1,200 o
Pine City 2,489
Pine Island 1,986
Pine River 881
Pipestone 4,887
Plainview 2,416
Plymouth MPLS- 31,615
Preston 1,478
Princeton 3,146
Prinsburg 557
Prior Lake MPLS- 7,284
Proctor DUL- 3,180
Ramsey MPLS- 10,093
Randall 527
Raymond 723
Redlake 600 o
Red Lake Falls 1,732
Red Wing 13,736
Redwood Falls 5,210
Renville 1,493
Rice 499
Richfield MPLS- 37,851
Richmond 867
Robbinsdale MPLS- 14,422
ROCHESTER ROCH 57,855
Rockford MPLS- 2,408
Rockville 597
Rogers MPLS- 652
Rollingstone 528
Roseau 2,272
Rosemount MPLS- 5,083

Roseville MPLS- 35,820
Rothsay 476
Round Lake 480
Royalton 660
Rush City 1,198
Rushford 1,478
Russell 412
Sabin 446
Sacred Heart 666
St. Charles 2,184
St. Clair 655
ST. CLOUD ST.CLD 42,566
St. Francis 1,184
St. James 4,346
St. Joseph ST.CLD 2,994
St. Louis Park MPLS- 42,931
St. Michael MPLS- 1,519
St. Paul MPLS- 270,230
St. Peter 9,056
Sanborn 518
Sandstone 1,594
Sartell ST.CLD 3,427
Sauk Centre 3,709
Sauk Rapids ST.CLD 5,793
Scanlon 1,050
Sebeka 774
Shakopee MPLS- 9,941
Sherburn 1,275
Shoreview MPLS- 17,300
Shorewood MPLS- 4,646
Silver Bay 2,917
Silver Lake 698
Slayton 2,420
Sleepy Eye 3,581
Soudan 950 o
South International Falls 2,806
South St. Paul MPLS- 21,235
Spicer 909
Springfield 2,303
Spring Grove 1,275
Spring Valley 2,616
Staples 2,887
Starbuck 1,224
Stephen 898
Stewart 616
Stewartville ROCH 3,925
Stillwater MPLS- 12,290
Taylors Falls 623
Thief River Falls 9,105
Tower 640
Tracy 2,478
Trimont 805
Truman 1,392
Twin Valley 907
Two Harbors 4,039
Tyler 1,353
Ulen 514
Vadnais Heights MPLS- 5,111
Verndale 504
Virginia 11,056
Wabasha 2,372
Wabasso 745
Waconia MPLS- 2,638
Wadena 4,699
Waite Park ST.CLD 3,496
Walker 970
Walnut Grove 753
Wanamingo 717
Warren 2,105
Warroad 1,216
Waseca 8,219
Waterville 1,717
Watkins 757
Waverly 470
Welcome 855
Wells 2,777
Westbrook 978
West Concord 762
West St. Paul MPLS- 18,527
Wheaton 1,969
White Bear Lake MPLS- 22,538
Willmar 15,895
Windom 4,666
Winnebago 1,869
Winona 25,075
Winsted 1,522
Winthrop 1,376
Woodbury MPLS- 10,297
Wood Lake 420
Worthington 10,243
Wykoff 482
Wyoming MPLS- 1,559
Zimmerman 1,074
Zumbrota 2,129

COUNTIES

Aitkin 13,404
Anoka 195,998
Becker 29,336
Beltrami 30,982
Benton 25,187
Big Stone 7,716
Blue Earth 52,314
Brown 28,645
Carlton 29,936
Carver 37,046
Cass 21,050
Chippewa 14,941
Chisago 25,717
Clay 49,327
Clearwater 8,761
Cook 4,092
Cottonwood 14,854
Crow Wing 41,722
Dakota 194,111
Dodge 14,773
Douglas 27,839
Faribault 19,714
Fillmore 21,930
Freeborn 36,329
Goodhue 38,749
Grant 7,171
Hennepin 941,411
Houston 19,617
Hubbard 14,098
Isanti 23,600
Itasca 43,006
Jackson 13,690
Kanabec 12,161

Kandiyohi 36,763
Kittson 6,672
Koochiching 17,571
Lac qui Parle 10,592
Lake 13,043
Lake of the Woods 3,764
Le Sueur 23,434
Lincoln 8,207
Lyon 25,207
McLeod 29,657
Mahnomen 5,535
Marshall 13,027
Martin 24,687
Meeker 20,594
Mille Lacs 18,430
Morrison 29,311
Mower 40,390
Murray 11,507
Nicollet 26,929
Nobles 21,840
Norman 9,379
Olmsted 91,971
Otter Tail 51,937
Pennington 15,258
Pine 19,871
Pipestone 11,690
Polk 34,844
Pope 11,657
Ramsey 459,784
Red Lake 5,471
Redwood 19,341
Renville 20,401
Rice 46,087
Rock 10,703
Roseau 12,574
St. Louis 222,229
Scott 43,784
Sherburne 29,908
Sibley 15,448
Stearns 108,161
Steele 30,328
Stevens 11,322
Swift 12,920
Todd 24,991
Traverse 5,542
Wabasha 19,335
Wadena 14,192
Waseca 18,448
Washington 113,571
Watonwan 12,361
Wilkin 8,382
Winona 46,256
Wright 58,962
Yellow Medicine 13,653

MISSISSIPPI
1980 Census 2,520,638

CITIES

Abbeville 448
Aberdeen 7,184
Ackerman 1,567
Amory 7,307
Anguilla 950
Arcola 588
Artesia 526
Ashland 532
Baldwyn 3,427
Batesville 4,692
Bay Saint Louis 7,891
Bay Springs 1,884
Bear Town 1,085 o
Beaumont 1,112
Belmont 1,420
Belzoni 2,982
Benoit 499
Bentonia 518
Beulah 431
Biloxi GUL-B 49,311
Blue Mountain 867
Bogue Chitto 500 o
Bolton 664
Booneville 6,199
Brandon JAC 9,626
Brookhaven 10,800
Brooklyn 500 o
Brooksville 1,038
Bruce 2,208
Bude 1,092
Burnsville 889
Byhalia 757
Caledonia 497
Calhoun City 2,033
Candlestick JAC 5,000 o
Canton 11,116
Carriere 500 o
Carthage 3,453
Cary 470
Charleston 2,878
Clarksdale 21,137
Cleveland 14,524
Clinton JAC 14,660
Coffeeville 1,129
Coldwater 1,505
Collins 2,131
Columbia 7,733
COLUMBUS COL 27,383
Como 1,378
Corinth 13,839
Crawford 495
Crenshaw 1,019
Crowder 789
Cruger 540
Crystal Springs 4,902
Decatur 1,148
De Kalb 1,159
De Lisle 1,000 o
Derma 793
D'Iberville GUL-B 7,288 o
D'Lo 463
Drew 2,528
Duck Hill 706
Duncan 501
Durant 2,889
Ecru 687

○ Rand McNally estimate (not reported in census).
▲ Population of entire township or "town", including rural area.
● Independent city. Population not included in county total.

Edinburg 500 ○
Edwards 1,515
Elliott 900 ○
Ellisville LAUR 4,652
Enterprise 607
Escatawpa PSCG 1,579 ○
Ethel 486
Eupora 2,048
Fayette 2,033
Fernwood 600 ○
Flora 1,507
Florence JAC 1,111
Flowood JAC 943
Forest 5,229
Foxworth 950 ○
Friars Point 1,400
Fulton 3,238
Gautier PSCG 2,087 ○
Glendale 800 ○
Gloster 1,726
Goodman 1,285
GREENVILLE GRNV 40,613
Greenwood 20,115
Grenada 12,641
GULFPORT GUL-B 39,676
Gunnison 708
Hatley 497
HATTIESBURG HATT 40,829
Hazlehurst 4,437
Heidelberg 1,098
Hernando MEM 2,969
Hickory 670
Hickory Flat 458
Hollandale 4,336
Holly Springs 7,285
Horn Lake 4,326
Houlka 710
Houston 3,747
Indianola 8,221
Inverness 1,034
Isola 834
Itta Bena 2,904
Iuka 2,846
JACKSON JAC 202,895
Jonestown 1,231
Kilmichael 906
Kiln 600 ○
Kings VICK 950 ○
Kosciusko 7,415
Lake 524
Lakeshore 500 ○
Lambert 1,624
Lauderdale 600 ○
LAUREL LAUR 21,897
Leakesville 1,120
Leland 6,667
Lexington 2,628
Liberty 669
Long Beach GUL-B 7,967
Lorman 700 ○
Louisville 7,323
Lucedale 2,429
Lumberton 2,217
Lyon 531
Maben 855
McComb 12,331
McHenry 550 ○
McLain 688
McNeill 500 ○
Macon 2,396
Madison JAC 2,241
Magee 3,497
Magnolia 2,461
Mantachie 732
Marion MRID 771
Marks 2,260
Mathiston 632
Meadville 575
Mendenhall 2,533
MERIDIAN MRID 46,577
Merigold 574
Metcalfe GRNV 952
Monticello 1,834
Moorhead 2,358
Morgantown NCHZ 2,008 ○
Morton 3,303
Moselle 500 ○
Moss Point PSCG 18,998
Mound Bayou 2,917
Mount Olive 993
NATCHEZ NCHZ 22,015
Nettleton 1,911
New Albany 7,072
New Augusta 589
Newhebron 470
Newton 3,708
North Carrollton 859
North Gulfport GUL-B 6,996 ○
North Tunica 1,325 ○
Noxapater 516
Oakland 540
Ocean Springs GUL-B 14,504
Okolona 3,409
Olive Branch MEM 2,067
Orange Grove GUL-B 2,000 ○
Osyka 581
Oxford 9,882
Pace 519
Palmers Crossing HATT 2,000 ○
PASCAGOULA PSCG 29,318
Pass Christian GUL-B 5,014
Pearl JAC 20,778
Pearlington 500 ○
Pelahatchie 1,445
Petal HATT 8,476
Philadelphia 6,434
Picayune 10,361
Pickens 1,386
Piney Woods 500 ○
Plantersville 920
Pontotoc 4,723
Poplarville 2,562
Port Gibson 2,371
Potts Camp 525
Prentiss 1,465
Purvis 2,256
Quitman 2,632
Raleigh 998
Raymond JAC 1,967
Richton 1,205
Ridgeland JAC 5,461
Rienzi 423
Ripley 4,271
Rolling Fork 2,590
Rosedale 2,793
Roxie 591
Ruleville 3,332
Saltillo 1,271
Sanatorium 700 ○
Sandersville LAUR 800
Schlater 429
Scooba 511
Senatobia 5,013
Shannon 680
Shaw 2,461
Shelby 2,540
Sherman 499
Shubuta 626
Shuqualak 554
Sidon 450
Sledge 699
Smithville 866
Soso 434
Southaven MEM 8,931 ○
Starkville 15,169
State College 4,595 ○
State Line 484
Stonewall 1,345
Summit 1,753
Sumner 452
Sumrall 1,197
Sunflower 1,027
Taylorsville 1,387
Tchula 1,931
Terry JAC 655
Tie Plant 500 ○
Tougaloo JAC 1,300 ○
Tunica 1,361
Tupelo 23,905
Tutwiler 1,174
Tylertown 1,976
Union 1,931
Utica 865
Valden 924
Vancleave 900 ○
Vardaman 1,009
Verona 2,497
VICKSBURG VICK 25,434
Walnut 513
Walnut Grove 439
Waltersville 700 ○
Water Valley 4,147
Waveland 4,186
Waynesboro 5,349
Webb 782
Weir 553
Wesson 1,313
West Point 8,811
Wheeler 500 ○
Wiggins 3,205
Winona 6,177
Winstonville 486
Woodville 1,512
Woolmarket 600 ○
Yazoo City 12,426

COUNTIES

Adams 38,035
Alcorn 33,036
Amite 13,369
Attala 19,865
Benton 8,153
Bolivar 45,965
Calhoun 15,664
Carroll 9,776
Chickasaw 17,853
Choctaw 8,996
Claiborne 12,279
Clarke 16,945
Clay 21,082
Coahoma 36,918
Copiah 26,503
Covington 15,927
De Soto 53,930
Forrest 66,018
Franklin 8,208
George 15,297
Greene 9,827
Grenada 21,043
Hancock 24,537
Harrison 157,665
Hinds 250,998
Holmes 22,970
Humphreys 13,931
Issaquena 2,513
Itawamba 20,518
Jackson 118,015
Jasper 17,265
Jefferson 9,181
Jefferson Davis 13,846
Jones 61,912
Kemper 10,148
Lafayette 31,030
Lamar 23,821
Lauderdale 77,285
Lawrence 12,518
Leake 18,790
Lee 57,061
Leflore 41,525
Lincoln 30,174
Lowndes 57,304
Madison 41,613
Marion 25,708
Marshall 29,296
Monroe 36,404
Montgomery 13,366
Neshoba 23,789
Newton 19,944
Noxubee 13,212
Oktibbeha 36,018
Panola 28,164
Pearl River 33,795
Perry 9,864
Pike 36,173
Pontotoc 20,918
Prentiss 24,025
Quitman 12,636
Rankin 69,427
Scott 24,556
Sharkey 7,964
Simpson 23,441
Smith 15,077
Stone 9,716
Sunflower 34,844
Tallahatchie 17,157
Tate 20,119
Tippah 18,739
Tishomingo 18,434
Tunica 9,652
Union 21,741
Walthall 13,761
Warren 51,627
Washington 72,344
Wayne 19,135
Webster 10,300
Wilkinson 10,021
Winston 19,474
Yalobusha 13,139
Yazoo 27,349

MISSOURI

1980 Census 4,917,444

CITIES

Adrian 1,484
Advance 1,054
Affton ST.L 27,500 ○
Agency 419
Alba 474
Albany 2,152
Alexandria 417
Allenton ST.L 500 ○
Alma 445
Alton 721
Anderson 1,237
Antonia ST.L 500 ○
Appleton City 1,257
Arcadia 683
Archie 753
Arnold ST.L 19,141
Ash Grove 1,157
Ashland 1,021
Atlanta 441
Aurora 6,437
Auxvasse 858
Ava 2,761
Avondale K.C. 612
Ballwin ST.L 12,750
Barnhart ST.L 800 ○
Bell City 539
Belle 1,233
Bellefontaine Neighbors ST.L 12,082
Bel-Nor ST.L 2,047
Belton K.C. 12,708
Benton 674
Berkeley ST.L 16,146
Bernie 1,975
Bertrand 688
Bethany 3,095
Billings 911
Birch Tree 622
Bismarck 1,625
Black Jack ST.L 5,293
Bland 662
Bloomfield 1,795
Blue Springs K.C. 25,927
Bolivar 5,919
Bonne Terre 3,797
Boonville 6,959
Bourbon 1,259
Bowling Green 3,022
Braggadocio 450 ○
Branson 2,550
Braymer 986
Breckenridge 523
Breckenridge Hills ST.L 5,666
Brentwood ST.L 8,209
Bridgeton ST.L 18,445
Brookfield 5,555
Brunswick 1,272
Bucklin 713
Buckner K.C. 2,848
Buffalo 2,217
Bunceton 419
Bunker 673
Burke City ST.L 2,600 ○
Burlington Junction 657
Butler 4,107
Cabool 2,090
Cainsville 496
Calhoun 427
California 3,381
Calverton Park ST.L 1,717
Camdenton 2,303
Cameron 4,519
Campbell 2,134
Canton 2,435
CAPE GIRARDEAU CPGIR 34,361
Cardwell 831
Carl Junction JOP 3,937
Carrollton 4,700
Carterville JOP 1,973
Carthage 11,104
Caruthersville 7,958
Cassville 2,091
Castle Point ST.L 6,500 ○
Cedar City JFCY 665
Cedar Hill ST.L 950 ○
Center 596
Centralia 3,537
Chaffee 3,241
Chamois 546
Charleston 5,230
Chillicothe 9,089
Clarence 1,147
Clarksville 585
Clarkton 1,228
Clayton ST.L 14,219
Cleveland 485
Clever 551
Clinton 8,366
Cole Camp 1,022
COLUMBIA COL 62,061
Concordia 2,129
Conway 601
Cooter 479
Corder 483
Crane 1,185
Crestwood ST.L 12,815
Creve Coeur ST.L 12,694
Crocker 979
Crystal City ST.L 3,573
Cuba 2,120
Dearborn 547
Deepwater 475
Dellwood ST.L 6,200
Delta 524
Desloge 3,481
De Soto ST.L 5,993
Des Peres ST.L 8,254
Dexter 7,043
Dixon 1,402
Doe Run 900 ○
Doniphan 1,921
Doolittle 701
Downing 462
Drexel 908
Duenweg JOP 703
East Prairie 3,713
Edgerton 584
Edina 1,520
Eldon 4,342
El Dorado Springs 3,868
Ellington 1,215
Ellisville ST.L 6,233
Elsberry 1,272
Elvins 1,548
Eminence 614
Essex 545
Eureka ST.L 3,862
Excelsior Springs K.C. 10,424
Exeter 588
Fairfax 835
Fair Grove 863
Farber 503
Farmington 8,270
Fayette 2,983
Ferguson ST.L 24,740
Festus ST.L 7,574
Fisk 450
Flat River 4,443
Florissant ST.L 55,372
Fordland 569
Forsyth 1,010
Frankford 443
Fredericktown 4,036
Freeburg 554
Freeman 485
Fulton 11,046
Gainesville 707
Galena 423
Gallatin 2,063
Garden City 1,021
Gerald 921
Gideon 1,240
Gilman City 414
Gladstone K.C. 24,990
Glasgow 1,336
Glasgow Village ST.L 7,200 ○
Glencoe ST.L 500 ○
Glendale ST.L 6,035
Golden City 900
Goodman 1,030
Gower 1,276
Grain Valley K.C. 1,327
Granby 1,908
Grandview K.C. 24,502
Grant City 1,068
Gray Summit ST.L 500 ○
Green City 719
Greenfield 1,394
Green Ridge 488
Greenwood K.C. 1,315
Hale 529
Hallsville 457
Hamilton 1,582
Hannibal 18,811
Hardin 688
Harrisonville K.C. 6,372
Hartville 576
Hayti 3,964
Hayti Heights 1,023
Hazelwood ST.L 12,935
Henrietta 424
Herculaneum ST.L 2,293
Hermann 2,695
Higbee 817
Higginsville 4,595
High Ridge ST.L 900 ○
Hillsboro ST.L 1,508
Holcomb 632
Holden 2,195
Hollister 1,439
Hopkins 634
Horine ST.L 850 ○
Hornersville 704
Houston 2,157
Howardville 536
Humansville 907
Iberia 852
Illmo CPGIR 1,368
Imperial ST.L 950 ○
Independence K.C. 111,806
Ironton 1,743
Jackson CPGIR 7,827
Jamesport 651
Jasper 1,012
JEFFERSON CITY JFCY 33,619
Jennings ST.L 17,026
Jonesburg 614
JOPLIN JOP 38,893
Kahoka 2,101
KANSAS CITY K.C. 448,159
Kearney 1,433
Kelso CPGIR 455
Kennett 10,145
Keytesville 689
King City 1,063
Kinloch ST.L 4,455
Kirksville 17,167
Kirkwood ST.L 27,987
Knob Noster 2,040
La Belle 845
Laclede 445
Laddonia 726
Ladue ST.L 9,376
La Grange 1,217
Lake Ozark 427
Lamar 4,053
La Monte 1,054
Lanagan 440
Lancaster 855
La Plata 1,423
Lathrop 1,732
Lawson 1,688
Leadwood 1,371
Lebanon 9,507
Lees Summit K.C. 28,741
Leeton 604
Lemay ST.L 28,300 ○
Lewistown 502
Lexington 5,063
Liberal 701
Liberty K.C. 16,251
Licking 1,272
Lilbourn 1,463
Lincoln 819
Linn 1,211
Linneus 421
Lockwood 971
Lone Jack 420
Louisiana 4,261
Lowry City 676
Lutesville 865
Macon 5,680
Madison 656
Maitland 415
Malden 6,096
Manchester ST.L 6,191
Mansfield 1,423
Maplewood ST.L 10,960
Marble Hill 601
Marceline 2,938
Marionville 1,920
Marshall 12,781
Marshfield 3,871
Marston 742
Marthasville 543
Maryland Heights ST.L 13,800 ○
Maryville 9,558
Matthews 547
Maysville 1,187
Meadville 416
Mehlville ST.L 22,900 ○
Memphis 2,105
Mercer 442
Mexico 12,276
Milan 1,947
Miner 1,182
Moberly 13,418
Monett 6,148
Monroe City 2,557
Montgomery City 2,101
Montrose 498
Morehouse 1,220
Morley 745
Moscow Mills 484
Mound City 1,447
Mountain Grove 3,974
Mountain View 1,664
Mount Vernon 3,341
Murphy ST.L 1,300 ○
Naylor 602
Neelyville 474
Neosho 9,493
Nevada 9,044
New Bloomfield 519
Newburg 743
New Florence 731
New Franklin 1,228
New Haven 1,581
New London 1,161
New Madrid 3,204
Nixa SPRG 2,662
Noel 1,161
Norborne 931
Normandy ST.L 5,174
North Kansas City K.C. 4,507
Northmoor K.C. 506
Northwoods ST.L 5,831
Novinger 626
Oakville ST.L 1,100 ○
Odessa 3,088
O'Fallon ST.L 8,654
Olivette ST.L 8,039
Oran 1,266
Oregon 901
Oronogo JOP 525
Orrick 922
Osage Beach 1,992
Osceola 841
Otterville 472
Overland ST.L 19,620
Owensville 2,241
Ozark SPRG 2,980
Pacific ST.L 4,410
Palmyra 3,469
Paris 1,598
Parkville K.C. 1,997
Parma 1,081
Pattonsburg 502
Peculiar K.C. 1,571
Perry 836
Perryville 7,343
Pevely ST.L 2,732
Piedmont 2,359
Pierce City 1,391
Pilot Grove 745
Pilot Knob 722
Pine Lawn ST.L 6,662
Pineville 504
Platte City K.C. 2,114
Plattsburg 2,095
Pleasant Hill K.C. 3,301
Pleasant Valley K.C. 1,545
Point Lookout 900 ○
Polo 583
Poplar Bluff 17,139
Portage Des Sioux 488
Portageville 3,470
Potosi 2,528

○ Rand McNally estimate (not reported in census).
▲ Population of entire township or "town", including rural area.
● Independent city. Population not included in county total.

Princeton 1,264
Purdy 928
Puxico 833
Queen City 783
Qulin 545
Ravenwood 436
Raymore K.C. 3,154
Raytown K.C. 31,759
Reeds Spring 461
Republic SPRG 4,485
Rich Hill 1,471
Richland 1,922
Richmond 5,499
Richmond Heights ST.L 11,516
Ridgeway 516
Risco 446
Rock Hill ST.L 5,702
Rock Port 1,511
Rogersville SPRG 741
Rolla 13,303
Russellville 667
St. Ann ST.L 15,523
St. Charles ST.L 37,379
St. Clair 3,485
Ste. Genevieve 4,481
St. James 3,328
St. Johns ST.L 7,854
ST. JOSEPH ST.JO 76,691
ST. LOUIS● ST.L 453,085
St. Marys 565
St. Paul ST.L 607
St. Peters ST.L 15,700
Salem 4,454
Salisbury 1,975
Sappington ST.L 10,603○
Sarcoxie 1,381
Savannah ST.JO 4,184
Scott City CPGIR 3,262
Sedalia 20,927
Seligman 508
Senath 1,728
Seneca 1,853
Seymour 1,535
Shelbina 2,169
Shelbyville 645
Sheldon 491
Shrewsbury ST.L 5,077
Sikeston 17,431
Skidmore 437
Slater 2,492
Smithton 559
Smithville K.C. 1,873
South Shore 450○
South West City 516
Spanish Lake ST.L 15,647○
Sparta 743
SPRINGFIELD SPRG 133,116
Stanberry 1,387
Steele 2,419
Steelville 1,470
Stewartsville 832
Stockton 1,432
Stover 1,041
Strafford SPRG 1,121
Sturgeon 901
Sugar Creek K.C. 4,305
Sullivan 5,461
Summersville 551
Sweet Springs 1,694
Taos 759
Tarkio 2,375
Thayer 2,211
Tipton 2,155
Trenton 6,811
Troy 2,624
Union ST.L 5,506
Union Star 423
Unionville 2,178
University City ST.L 42,738
Urich 509
Valley Park ST.L 3,232
Van Buren 850
Vandalia 3,170
Verona 592
Versailles 2,406
Viburnum 836
Vienna 514
Walnut Grove 504
Warrensburg 13,807
Warrenton 3,219
Warsaw 1,494
Washington 9,251
Waverly 941
Wayland 498
Waynesville 2,879
Weaubleau 464
Webb City JOP 7,309
Webster Groves ST.L 23,097
Wedgewood ST.L 5,700○
Wellington 780
Wellsville 1,546
Wentzville ST.L 3,193
West Alton ST.L 500○
Weston 1,440
West Plains 7,741
Wheaton 548
Willard SPRG 1,799
Williamsville 418
Willow Springs 2,215
Windsor 3,058
Winfield 592
Winona 1,050
Wright City 1,179
Wyatt 441

COUNTIES

Adair 24,870
Andrew 13,980
Atchison 8,605
Audrain 26,458
Barry 24,408
Barton 11,292
Bates 15,873
Benton 12,183
Bollinger 10,301
Boone 100,376
Buchanan 87,888
Butler 37,693
Caldwell 8,660
Callaway 32,252
Camden 19,963
Cape Girardeau 58,837
Carroll 12,131
Carter 5,428
Cass 51,029
Cedar 11,894
Chariton 10,489
Christian 22,402
Clark 8,493
Clay 136,488
Clinton 15,916
Cole 56,663
Cooper 14,643
Crawford 18,300
Dade 7,383
Dallas 12,096
Daviess 8,905
De Kalb 8,222
Dent 14,517
Douglas 11,594
Dunklin 36,324
Franklin 71,233
Gasconade 13,181
Gentry 7,887
Greene 185,302
Grundy 11,959
Harrison 9,890
Henry 19,672
Hickory 6,367
Holt 6,882
Howard 10,008
Howell 28,807
Iron 11,084
Jackson 629,180
Jasper 86,958
Jefferson 146,814
Johnson 39,059
Knox 5,508
Laclede 24,323
Lâfayette 29,925
Lawrence 28,973
Lewis 10,901
Lincoln 22,193
Linn 15,495
Livingston 15,739
McDonald 14,917
Macon 16,313
Madison 10,725
Maries 7,551
Marion 28,638
Mercer 4,685
Miller 18,532
Mississippi 15,726
Moniteau 12,068
Monroe 9,716
Montgomery 11,537
Morgan 13,807
New Madrid 22,945
Newton 40,555
Nodaway 21,996
Oregon 10,238
Osage 12,014
Ozark 7,961
Pemiscot 24,987
Perry 16,784
Pettis 36,378
Phelps 33,633
Pike 17,568
Platte 46,341
Polk 18,822
Pulaski 42,011
Putnam 6,092
Ralls 8,911
Randolph 25,460
Ray 21,378
Reynolds 7,230
Ripley 12,458
St. Charles 143,455
St. Clair 8,622
St. Francois 42,600
St. Louis 974,815
Ste. Genevieve 15,180
Saline 24,919
Scotland 5,415
Scott 39,647
Shannon 7,885
Shelby 7,826
Stoddard 29,009
Stone 15,587
Sullivan 7,434
Taney 20,467
Texas 21,070
Vernon 19,806
Warren 14,900
Washington 17,983
Wayne 11,277
Webster 20,414
Worth 3,008
Wright 16,188

MONTANA

1980 Census 786,690

CITIES

Absarokee 750○
Anaconda 12,518
Augusta 450○
Baker 2,354
Belgrade 2,336
Belt 825
Bigfork 900○
Big Sandy 835
Big Timber 1,690
BILLINGS BIL 66,798
Billings Heights BIL 4,000○
Black Eagle GTFA 1,100○
Boulder 1,441
Bozeman 21,645
Bridger 724
Broadus 712
Browning 1,226
BUTTE BUT 37,205
Cascade 773
Chester 963
Chinook 1,660
Choteau 1,798
Circle 931
Columbia Falls 3,112
Columbus 1,439
Conrad 3,074
Crow Agency 750○
Culbertson 887
Cut Bank 3,688
Darby 581
Deer Lodge 4,023
Dillon 3,976
Drummond 414
East Glacier Park 500○
East Helena 1,647
Ekalaka 620
Ennis 660
Eureka 1,119
Fairfield 650
Fairview 1,366
Forsyth 2,553
Fort Belknap Agency 500○
Fort Benton 1,693
Fort Peck 600○
Fromberg 469
Gardiner 600○
Glasgow 4,455
Glendive 5,978
GREAT FALLS GTFA 56,725
Hamilton 2,661
Hardin 3,300
Harlem 1,023
Harlowton 1,181
Havre 10,891
Helena 23,938
Hot Springs 601
Hungry Horse 900○
Hysham 449
Joliet 580
Jordan 485
Kalispell 10,648
Lakeside 500○
Lame Deer 600○
Laurel 5,481
Lewistown 7,104
Libby 2,748
Lincoln 500○
Livingston 6,994
Lockwood BIL 1,600○
Lodge Grass 771
Lolo 500○
Malta 2,367
Manhattan 988
Martin City 500○
Miles City 9,602
MISSOULA MSLA 33,388
Nashua 495
North Havre 1,073○
Orchard Homes MSLA 3,500○
Philipsburg 1,138
Plains 1,116
Plentywood 2,476
Polson 2,798
Poplar 995
Red Lodge 1,896
Richey 417
Ronan 1,530
Roundup 2,119
Rudyard 600○
St. Ignatius 877
St. Regis 600○
Scobey 1,382
Seeley Lake 800○
Shelby 3,142
Sheridan 646
Sidney 5,726
Somers 800○
Stanford 595
Stevensville 1,207
Sunburst 476
Superior 1,054
Terry 929
Thompson Falls 1,478
Three Forks 1,247
Townsend 1,587
Troy 1,088
Twin Bridges 437
Valier 640
Victor 450○
Walkerville BUT 887
West Yellowstone 735
Whitefish 3,703
Whitehall 1,030
White Sulphur Springs 1,302
Wibaux 782
Wolf Point 3,074

COUNTIES

Beaverhead 8,186
Big Horn 11,096
Blaine 6,999
Broadwater 3,267
Carbon 8,099
Carter 1,799
Cascade 80,696
Chouteau 6,092
Custer 13,109
Daniels 2,835
Dawson 11,805
Deer Lodge 12,518
Fallon 3,763
Fergus 13,076
Flathead 51,966
Gallatin 42,865
Garfield 1,656
Glacier 10,628
Golden Valley 1,026
Granite 2,700
Hill 17,985
Jefferson 7,029
Judith Basin 2,646
Lake 19,056
Lewis and Clark 43,039
Liberty 2,329
Lincoln 17,752
McCone 2,702
Madison 5,448
Meagher 2,154
Mineral 3,675
Missoula 76,016
Musselshell 4,428
Park 12,660
Petroleum 655
Phillips 5,367
Pondera 6,731
Powder River 2,520
Powell 6,958
Prairie 1,836
Ravalli 22,493
Richland 12,243
Roosevelt 10,467
Rosebud 9,899
Sanders 8,675
Sheridan 5,414
Silver Bow 38,092
Stillwater 5,598
Sweet Grass 3,216
Teton 6,491
Toole 5,559
Treasure 981
Valley 10,250
Wheatland 2,359
Wibaux 1,476
Yellowstone 108,035
Yellowstone National Park 275

NEBRASKA

1980 Census 1,570,006

CITIES

Ainsworth 2,256
Air Park West LINC 3,100○
Albion 1,997
Alda GDIS 601
Alliance 9,869
Alma 1,369
Ansley 644
Arapahoe 1,107
Arcadia 412
Arlington 1,117
Arnold 813
Ashland 2,274
Atkinson 1,521
Auburn 3,482
Aurora 3,717
Axtell 602
Bancroft 552
Bassett 1,009
Battle Creek 948
Bayard 1,435
Beatrice 12,891
Beaver City 775
Beaver Crossing 458
Beemer 853
Bellevue OMA- 21,813
Benkelman 1,235
Bennet 523
Bennington OMA- 631
Bertrand 775
Big Springs 505
Blair 6,418
Bloomfield 1,393
Blue Hill 883
Blue Springs 521
Boys Town OMA- 622
Bridgeport 1,668
Broken Bow 3,979
Brule 438
Burwell 1,383
Butte 529
Cairo 737
Callaway 579
Cambridge 1,206
Campbell 441
Cedar Bluffs 632
Cedar Rapids 447
Central City 3,083
Ceresco 836
Chadron 5,933
Chappell 1,095
Chester 435
Clarks 445
Clarkson 817
Clay Center 962
Coleridge 673
Columbus 17,328
Cozad 4,453
Crawford 1,315
Creighton 1,341
Crete 4,872
Crofton 948
Crown Point OMA- 700○
Culbertson 767
Curtis 1,014
Dakota City SXCY 1,440
Davenport 445
David City 2,514
Debolt OMA- 800○
Decatur 723
Deshler 997
De Witt 642
Dodge 815
Doniphan 696
Dorchester 611
Eagle 832
Edgar 705
Elgin 807
Elkhorn OMA- 1,344
Elm Creek 862
Elmwood 598
Elwood 716
Emerson 874
Eustis 460
Ewing 520
Exeter 807
Fairfield 543
Fairmont 767
Falls City 5,374
Fort Calhoun 641
Franklin 1,167
Fremont 23,979
Friend 1,079
Fullerton 1,506
Geneva 2,400
Genoa 1,090
Gering 7,760
Gibbon 1,531
Gordon 2,167
Gothenburg 3,479
GRAND ISLAND GDIS 33,180
Grant 1,270
Greeley 597
Greenwood 587
Gretna OMA- 1,609
Hampton 419
Hartington 1,730
Harvard 1,217
Hastings 23,045
Hay Springs 794
Hebron 1,906
Hemingford 1,023
Henderson 1,072
Hershey 633
Hickman 687
Holdrege 5,624
Homer 564
Hooper 932
Howells 677
Humboldt 1,176
Humphrey 799
Imperial 1,941
Indianola 856
Irvington OMA- 500○
Juniata 703
Kearney 21,158
Kenesaw 854
Kimball 3,120
Laurel 508
La Vista OMA- 9,588
Leigh 509
Lexington 6,898
LINCOLN LINC 171,932
Lodgepole 413
Long Pine 521
Loomis 447
Louisville 1,022
Loup City 1,368
Lyman 551
Lyons 1,214
McCook 8,404
Macy 500○
Madison 1,950
Mead 506
Milford 2,108
Minatare 969
Minden 2,939
Mitchell 1,956
Morrill 1,097
Mullen 720
Murray 465
Nebraska City 7,127
Neligh 1,893
Nelson 733
Newman Grove 930
Niobrara 419
Norfolk 19,449
North Bend 1,368
North Oaks OMA- 600○
North Omaha OMA- 1,100○
North Platte 24,479
Oakland 1,393
Ogallala 5,638
OMAHA OMA- 311,681
O'Neill 4,049
Orchard 482
Ord 2,658
Orleans 527
Osceola 975
Oshkosh 1,057
Osmond 871
Overton 633
Oxford 1,109
Palmer 487
Palmyra 512
Papillion OMA- 6,399
Pawnee City 1,156
Paxton 568
Pender 1,318
Peru 998
Pierce 1,535
Plainview 1,483
Plattsmouth OMA- 6,295
Plymouth 506
Polk 440
Ponca 1,057
Ralston OMA- 5,143
Randolph 1,106
Ravenna 1,296
Red Cloud 1,300
Roanoke OMA- 900○
Rushville 1,217
St. Edward 891
St. Paul 2,094
Sargent 828
Schuyler 1,940
Scottsbluff 14,156
Scribner 1,011
Seward 5,713
Shelby 724
Shelton 1,046
Shickley 413
Sidney 6,010
Silver Creek 496
South Sioux City SXCY 9,339
Spalding 645
Spencer 596
Springfield 782
Stanton 1,603
Sterling 526
Still Meadow OMA- 950○
Stratton 499
Stromsburg 1,290
Stuart 641
Sunnyslope OMA- 770○
Superior 2,502
Sutherland 1,238
Sutton 1,416
Syracuse 1,638
Tecumseh 1,926
Tekamah 1,886
Terrytown 727
Tilden 1,012
Trenton 796

○ Rand McNally estimate (not reported in census).
▲ Population of entire township or "town", including rural area.
● Independent city. Population not included in county total.

Utica 689
Valentine 2,829
Valley 1,716
Valparaiso 484
Verdigre 617
Wahoo 3,555
Wakefield 1,125
Walthill 847
Waterloo 450
Wauneta 746
Wausa 647
Waverly LINC 1,726
Wayne 5,240
Weeping Water 1,109
West Point 3,609
Wilber 1,624
Winnebago 902
Winside 439
Wisner 1,335
Wood River 1,334
Wymore 1,841
York 7,723
Yutan 631

COUNTIES

Adams 30,656
Antelope 8,675
Arthur 513
Banner 918
Blaine 867
Boone 7,391
Box Butte 13,696
Boyd 3,331
Brown 4,377
Buffalo 34,797
Burt 8,813
Butler 9,330
Cass 20,297
Cedar 10,852
Chase 4,758
Cherry 6,758
Cheyenne 10,057
Clay 8,106
Colfax 9,890
Cuming 11,664
Custer 13,877
Dakota 16,573
Dawes 9,609
Dawson 22,162
Deuel 2,462
Dixon 7,137
Dodge 35,847
Douglas 397,884
Dundy 2,861
Fillmore 7,920
Franklin 4,377
Frontier 3,647
Furnas 6,486
Gage 24,456
Garden 2,802
Garfield 2,363
Gosper 2,140
Grant 877
Greeley 3,462
Hall 47,690
Hamilton 9,301
Harlan 4,292
Hayes 1,356
Hitchcock 4,079
Holt 13,552
Hooker 990
Howard 6,773
Jefferson 9,817
Johnson 5,285
Kearney 7,053
Keith 9,364
Keya Paha 1,301
Kimball 4,882
Knox 11,457
Lancaster 192,884
Lincoln 36,455
Logan 983
Loup 859
McPherson 593
Madison 31,382
Merrick 8,945
Morrill 6,085
Nance 4,740
Nemaha 8,367
Nuckolls 6,726
Otoe 15,183
Pawnee 3,937
Perkins 3,637
Phelps 9,769
Pierce 8,481
Platte 28,852
Polk 6,320
Red Willow 12,615
Richardson 11,315
Rock 2,383
Saline 13,131
Sarpy 86,015
Saunders 18,716
Scotts Bluff 38,344
Seward 15,789
Sheridan 7,544
Sherman 4,226
Sioux 1,845
Stanton 6,549
Thayer 7,582
Thomas 973
Thurston 7,186
Valley 5,633
Washington 15,508
Wayne 9,858
Webster 4,858
Wheeler 1,060
York 14,798

NEVADA
1980 Census 799,184

CITIES

Babbitt 1,800○
Battle Mountain 2,100○
Beatty 900○
Boulder City 9,590
Caliente 982
Carlin 1,232
Carson City● 32,022
Crystal Bay 900○
East Las Vegas LASV 15,000○
Elko 8,758
Ely 4,882
Eureka 500○
Fallon 4,262
Fernley 1,200○
Gabbs 811
Gardnerville 2,500○
Hawthorne 5,000○
Henderson LASV 24,363
Indian Springs 900○
Jackpot 500○
LAS VEGAS LASV 164,674
Lemmon Valley RENO 2,000○
Lovelock 1,680
McGill 1,900○
Mesquite 700○
Mina 425○
Minden 1,200○
New Washoe City 1,000○
North Las Vegas LASV 42,739
Overton 1,200○
Owyhee 700○
Pahrump 1,000○
Panaca 550○
Paradise LASV 43,500○
Pioche 700○
RENO RENO 100,756
Ruth 735○
Skyland 500○
Sparks RENO 40,780
Stateline 1,500○
Sunrise Manor LASV 15,000○
Sun Valley RENO 6,700○
Tonopah 1,650○
Topaz Ranch Estates 500○
Verdi RENO 800○
Virginia City 600○
Weed Heights 650○
Wells 1,218
Winchester LASV 20,000○
Winnemucca 4,140
Yerington 2,021
Zephyr Cove 2,000○

COUNTIES

Churchill 13,917
Clark 461,816
Douglas 19,421
Elko 17,269
Esmeralda 777
Eureka 1,198
Humboldt 9,434
Lander 4,082
Lincoln 3,732
Lyon 13,594
Mineral 6,217
Nye 9,048
Pershing 3,408
Storey 1,459
Washoe 193,623
White Pine 8,167

NEW HAMPSHIRE
1980 Census 920,610

CITIES

Alstead 1,461▲ 500○
Alton 2,440▲ 900○
Alton Bay 900○
Amherst NSHUA 8,243▲ 750○
Antrim 2,208▲ 950○
Ashland 1,807▲ 1,450○
Atkinson BOS 4,397▲ 900○
Bartlett 1,566▲ 700○
Bedford MNCH 9,481▲ 1,300○
Belmont 4,026▲ 900○
Bennington 890▲ 500○
Berlin 13,084
Bethlehem 1,784▲ 700○
Bow CONC 4,015▲ 500○
Bradford 1,115▲ 450○
Bristol 2,198▲ 1,080○
Campton 1,694▲ 600○
Canaan 2,456▲ 600○
Canobie Lake BOS 800○
Center Harbor 808▲ 500○
Center Ossipee 500○
Charlestown 4,417▲ 1,700○
Chester 2,006▲ 500○
Claremont 14,557
Colebrook 2,459▲ 1,070○
CONCORD CONC 30,400
Contoocook CONC 1,200○
Conway 7,158▲ 1,600○
Danville BOS 1,318▲ 500○
Derry BOS 18,875▲ 7,000○
DOVER DOV- 22,377
Dublin 1,303▲ 600○
Durham 10,652▲ 7,500○
East Derry 600○
East Hampstead BOS 900○
Enfield 3,175▲ 1,500○
Epping 3,460▲ 1,300○
Exeter 11,024▲ 6,600
Farmington 4,630▲ 2,884○
Fitzwilliam 1,795▲ 600○
Franconia 743▲ 600○
Franklin 7,901
Fremont 1,333▲ 450○
Gilmanton 1,941▲ 600○
Gilsum 652▲ 500○
Goffstown MNCH 11,315▲ 2,500○
Gorham 3,322▲ 2,020○
Greenfield 972▲ 500○
Greenland PTSM 2,129▲ 600○
Greenville NSHUA 1,988▲ 1,450○
Groveton 1,597○
Hampstead BOS 3,785▲ 500○
Hampton PTSM 10,493▲ 6,000○
Hampton Beach 900○
Hampton Falls PTSM 1,372▲ 500○
Hanover 9,119▲ 6,300○
Henniker 3,246▲ 1,400○
Hillsboro 3,437▲ 2,000○
Hinsdale 3,631▲ 1,300○
Hooksett MNCH 7,303▲ 1,303○
Hudson NSHUA 14,022▲ 7,500○
Jaffrey 4,349▲ 2,000○
Keene 21,449
Kingston BOS 4,111▲ 900○
Laconia 15,575
Lancaster 3,401▲ 2,350○
Lebanon 11,134
Lincoln 1,313▲ 950○
Lisbon 1,517▲ 1,300○
Little Boars Head 500○
Littleton 5,558▲ 4,500○
Londonderry MNCH 13,598▲ 950○
MANCHESTER MNCH 90,936
Marlborough 1,846▲ 1,231○
Meredith 4,646▲ 1,100○
Merrimack NSHUA 15,406▲ 1,200○
Milford NSHUA 8,685▲ 6,000○
Millville Lake BOS 600○
Milton 2,438▲ 1,000○
NASHUA NSHUA 67,865
New Castle PTSM 975○
Newfields PTSM 817▲ 700○
New Ipswich FTCH- 2,433▲ 500○
New London 2,935▲ 1,500○
Newmarket PTSM 4,290▲ 2,800○
Newport 6,229▲ 3,500○
Newton BOS 3,068▲ 450○
Newton Junction BOS 450○
North Branch 800○
North Conway 2,000○
Northfield 3,051▲ 1,500○
North Hampton PTSM 3,425▲ 1,000○
North Salem BOS 600○
North Stratford 650○
North Swanzey 950○
North Walpole 2,175▲ 950○
North Woodstock 600○
Pelham BOS 8,090▲ 500○
Peterborough 4,895▲ 2,000○
Pinardville MNCH 4,500○
Pittsfield CONC 2,889▲ 1,800○
Plaistow BOS 5,609▲ 1,800○
Plymouth 5,094▲ 3,200○
PORTSMOUTH PTSM 26,254
Raymond MNCH 5,453▲ 1,200○
Rochester DOV- 21,560
Rollinsford DOV- 2,319▲ 1,200○
Rye PTSM 4,508▲ 800○
Rye Beach PTSM 600○
Salem BOS 24,124▲ 11,500○
Sanbornville 800○
Seabrook BOS 5,917▲ 700○
Somersworth DOV- 10,350
South Hooksett MNCH 1,200○
Stratham PTSM 2,507▲ 500○
Sunapee 2,312▲ 900○
Suncook CONC 4,700○
Swanzey Center 700○
Tilton 3,387▲ 1,105○
Troy 2,131▲ 1,400○
Walpole 3,188▲ 700○
Warner 1,963▲ 700○
Warren 650▲ 450○
West Chesterfield 450○
Westport 450○
West Swanzey 900○
Westville BOS 700○
Whitefield 1,681▲ 1,150○
Wilton NSHUA 1,500○
Winchester 3,465▲ 950○
Winnisquam 600○
Wolfeboro 3,968▲ 2,000○
Wolfeboro Falls 500○
Woodsville 1,500○

COUNTIES

Belknap 42,884
Carroll 27,931
Cheshire 62,116
Coos 35,147
Grafton 65,806
Hillsborough 276,608
Merrimack 98,302
Rockingham 190,345
Strafford 85,408
Sullivan 36,063

NEW JERSEY
1980 Census 7,364,158

CITIES

Absecon ATCY 6,859
Adamston N.Y. 1,300○
Allendale N.Y. 5,901
Allenhurst N.Y. 912
Allentown PHIL- 1,962
Allenwood N.Y. 500○
Alloway 900○
Alpha AL-B-E 2,644
Alpine N.Y. 1,549
Andover N.Y. 892
Annandale N.Y. 700○
Arrowhead Village N.Y. 3,100○
Asbury Park N.Y. 17,015
Atco PHIL- 2,100○
ATLANTIC CITY ATCY 40,199
Atlantic Highlands N.Y. 4,950
Audubon PHIL- 9,533
Avalon 2,162
Avenel N.Y. 13,000○
Avon by the Sea N.Y. 2,337
Barnegat 950○
Barnegat Light 619
Barrington PHIL- 7,418
Basking Ridge N.Y. 4,800○
Bay Head N.Y. 1,340
Bayonne N.Y. 65,047
Bayville N.Y. 900○
Beach Haven 1,714
Beachwood N.Y. 7,687
Bedminster N.Y. 500○
Belford N.Y. 6,000○
Belle Mead 600○
Belleville N.Y. 35,367
Bellmawr PHIL- 13,721
Belmar N.Y. 6,771
Belvidere 2,475
Bergenfield N.Y. 25,568
Berkeley Heights N.Y. 13,078○
Berlin PHIL- 5,786
Bernardsville N.Y. 6,715
Beverly PHIL- 2,919
Blackwood PHIL- 6,600○
Blairstown 700○
Bloomfield N.Y. 47,792
Bloomingdale N.Y. 7,867
Bloomsbury 864
Blue Anchor PHIL- 500○
Bogota N.Y. 8,344
Boonton N.Y. 8,620
Bordentown PHIL- 4,441
Bossert Estates PHIL- 2,800○
Bound Brook N.Y. 9,710
Bradley Beach N.Y. 4,772
Branchville 870
Breton Woods N.Y. 1,300○
Brick Town N.Y. 3,200○
Bridgeport PHIL- 900○
BRIDGETON BRDGT 18,795
Bridgewater N.Y. 5,800○
Brielle N.Y. 4,068
Brigantine ATCY 8,318
Broadway 450○
Brooklawn PHIL- 2,133
Brookwood N.Y. 4,000○
Browns Mills 7,144○
Budd Lake N.Y. 3,168○
Buena 3,642
Burleigh 550○
Burlington PHIL- 10,246
Butler N.Y. 7,616
Caldwell N.Y. 7,624
Califon N.Y. 1,023
Camden PHIL- 84,910
Cape May 4,853
Cape May Court House 2,062○
Carlstadt N.Y. 6,166
Carmel 500○
Carneys Point PHIL- 2,500○
Carteret N.Y. 20,598
Cedar Brook PHIL- 500○
Cedar Grove N.Y. 15,582○
Cedar Knolls N.Y. 3,000○
Cedar Run 450○
Cedarville 990○
Centre City PHIL- 2,500○
Chatham N.Y. 8,537
Cherry Hill PHIL- 64,395○
Chesilhurst PHIL- 1,590
Chester N.Y. 1,433
Cinnaminson PHIL- 16,962○
Clark N.Y. 18,829○
Clarksboro PHIL- 800○
Clayton PHIL- 6,013
Clementon PHIL- 5,764
Cliffside Park N.Y. 21,464
Cliffwood Beach N.Y. 6,200○
Clifton N.Y. 74,388
Clinton N.Y. 1,910
Closter N.Y. 8,164
Cold Spring 850○
Collingswood PHIL- 15,838
Cologne ATCY 500○
Colonia N.Y. 23,200○
Colts Neck N.Y. 500○
Columbus PHIL- 700○
Cranberry Lake N.Y. 600○
Cranbury N.Y. 1,253○
Cranford N.Y. 27,391○
Cresskill N.Y. 7,609
Crestwood Village N.Y. 2,000○
Crosswicks PHIL- 550○
Dayton N.Y. 900○
Deal N.Y. 1,952
Deans 600○
Deepwater PHIL- 650○
Delanco PHIL- 4,157○
Delran PHIL- 10,065○
Demarest N.Y. 4,963
Denville N.Y. 14,045○
Dividing Creek 500○
Dorchester 500○
Dorothy 600○
Dover N.Y. 14,681
Dumont N.Y. 18,334
Dunellen N.Y. 6,593
East Brunswick N.Y. 33,100○
East Hanover N.Y. 7,734○
East Newark N.Y. 1,923
East Orange N.Y. 77,025
East Rutherford N.Y. 7,849
East Windsor N.Y. 15,000○
Eatontown N.Y. 12,703
Edgewater N.Y. 4,628
Edgewater Park PHIL- 7,412○
Edison N.Y. 67,120○
Egg Harbor City ATCY 4,618
Elizabeth N.Y. 106,201
Elmer PHIL- 1,569
Elmwood Park N.Y. 18,377
Elwood 800○
Emerson N.Y. 7,793
Englewood N.Y. 23,701
Englewood Cliffs N.Y. 5,698
Englishtown N.Y. 976
Erial PHIL- 900○
Erma 950○
Essex Fells N.Y. 2,363
Estell Manor 848
Ewing Township PHIL- 32,831○
Fairfield N.Y. 7,987○
Fair Haven N.Y. 5,679
Fair Lawn N.Y. 32,229
Fairton BRDGT 800○
Fairview N.Y. 10,519
Fanwood N.Y. 7,767
Far Hills N.Y. 677
Farmingdale N.Y. 1,348
Fellowship PHIL- 1,900○
Fieldsboro PHIL- 597
Flagtown N.Y. 800○
Flanders N.Y. 6,000○
Flemington N.Y. 4,132
Florence PHIL- 4,000○
Florham Park N.Y. 9,359
Folsom 1,892
Fords N.Y. 14,000○
Forked River 1,422○
Fort Lee N.Y. 32,449
Franklin N.Y. 4,486
Franklin Lakes N.Y. 8,769
Franklinville PHIL- 900○
Freehold N.Y. 10,020
Frenchtown 1,573
Garfield N.Y. 26,803
Garwood N.Y. 4,752
Gibbstown PHIL- 5,676○
Gladstone N.Y. 2,038
Glassboro PHIL- 14,574
Glendola N.Y. 2,300○
Glendora PHIL- 5,400○
Glen Gardner N.Y. 834
Glen Ridge N.Y. 7,855
Glen Rock N.Y. 11,497
Gloucester City PHIL- 13,121
Green Brook N.Y. 4,302○
Green Creek 500○
Groveville PHIL- 1,800○
Guttenberg N.Y. 7,340
Hackensack N.Y. 36,039
Hackettstown N.Y. 8,850
Haddonfield PHIL- 12,337
Haddon Heights PHIL- 8,361
Hainesport PHIL- 900○
Haledon N.Y. 6,607
Hamburg N.Y. 1,832
Hamilton Square PHIL- 10,000○
Hammonton 12,298
Hampton N.Y. 1,614
Hancocks Bridge 600○
Harrington Park N.Y. 4,532
Harrison N.Y. 12,242
Hasbrouck Heights N.Y. 12,166
Haworth N.Y. 3,509
Hawthorne N.Y. 18,200
Hazlet N.Y. 18,000○
Heislerville 600○
Helmetta N.Y. 955
High Bridge N.Y. 3,435
Highland Lakes N.Y. 800○
Highland Park N.Y. 13,396
Highlands N.Y. 5,187
Hightstown N.Y. 4,581
Hillsdale N.Y. 10,495
Hillside N.Y. 21,636○
Hoboken N.Y. 42,460
Ho-Ho-Kus N.Y. 4,129
Holmdel N.Y. 800○
Hopatcong N.Y. 15,531
Hope N.Y. 450○
Hopelawn N.Y. 2,300○
Hopewell PHIL- 2,001
Huntington AL-B-E 700○
Ironia N.Y. 900○
Irvington N.Y. 61,493
Iselin N.Y. 18,400○
Island Heights N.Y. 1,575
Jackson N.Y. 600○
Jamesburg N.Y. 4,114
Jersey City N.Y. 223,532
Keansburg N.Y. 10,613
Kearny N.Y. 35,735
Kendall Park N.Y. 7,412○
Kenilworth N.Y. 8,221
Kenvil N.Y. 1,700○
Keyport N.Y. 7,413
Kingston 900○
Kinnelon N.Y. 7,770
Lake Hiawatha N.Y. 11,389○
Lakehurst N.Y. 2,908
Lake Telemark N.Y. 1,086○
Lakewood N.Y. 25,223○
Lambertville PHIL- 4,044
Lanoka Harbor 700○
Laurence Harbor N.Y. 3,500○
Lavallette N.Y. 2,072
Lawnside PHIL- 3,042
Lawrenceville PHIL- 1,800○
Lebanon N.Y. 820
Ledgewood N.Y. 1,100○
Leesburg 700○
Leonardo N.Y. 3,600○
Leonia N.Y. 8,027
Liberty Corner N.Y. 800○
Lincoln Park N.Y. 8,806
Lincroft N.Y. 4,100○
Linden N.Y. 37,836
Lindenwold PHIL- 18,196
Linwood ATCY 6,144
Little Falls N.Y. 11,727○
Little Ferry N.Y. 9,399
Little Silver N.Y. 5,548
Livingston N.Y. 30,127○
Locust N.Y. 700○
Lodi N.Y. 23,956
Long Branch N.Y. 29,819
Longport ATCY 1,249
Long Valley N.Y. 1,645○
Lumberton PHIL- 700○
Lyndhurst N.Y. 22,729○
McAfee N.Y. 500○
McKee City 600○
Madison N.Y. 15,357
Magnolia PHIL- 4,881
Mahwah N.Y. 7,500○
Malaga VINL- 950○
Manasquan N.Y. 5,354
Mantua PHIL- 1,900○
Manville N.Y. 11,278
Maple Shade PHIL- 16,464○
Maplewood N.Y. 24,932○
Margate City ATCY 9,179
Marlboro N.Y. 850○
Marlton PHIL- 10,180○
Marmora 500○

○ Rand McNally estimate (not reported in census).
▲ Population of entire township or "town", including rural area.
● Independent city. Population not included in county total.

Matawan N.Y. 8,837
Mauricetown 500○
Mays Landing 1,272○
Maywood N.Y. 9,895
Medford PHIL- 1,448○
Medford Lakes PHIL- 4,958
Mendham N.Y. 4,899
Mercerville PHIL- 15,000○
Merchantville PHIL- 3,972
Metuchen N.Y. 13,762
Middlesex N.Y. 13,480
Middletown N.Y. 16,000○
Midland Park N.Y. 7,381
Milford 1,368
Millburn N.Y. 21,089○
Millstone N.Y. 530
Milltown N.Y. 7,136
Millville VINL- 24,815
Mine Hill N.Y. 3,557○
Mizpah 600○
Monmouth Beach N.Y. 3,318
Monmouth Junction N.Y. 950○
Montclair N.Y. 38,321
Montvale N.Y. 7,318
Montville N.Y. 2,700○
Moonachie N.Y. 2,706
Moorestown PHIL- 15,596○
Morganville N.Y. 900○
Morris Plains N.Y. 5,305
Morristown N.Y. 16,614
Mountain Lakes N.Y. 4,153
Mountainside N.Y. 7,118
Mount Arlington N.Y. 4,251
Mount Ephraim PHIL- 4,863
Mount Freedom N.Y. 1,621○
Mount Holly PHIL- 10,818○
Mullica Hill PHIL- 550○
National Park PHIL- 3,552
Navesink N.Y. 1,500○
Neptune N.Y. 24,800○
Neptune City N.Y. 5,276
Nesco 430○
Netcong N.Y. 3,557
Newark N.Y. 329,248
New Brunswick N.Y. 41,442
New Egypt 1,769○
Newfield VINL- 1,563
Newfoundland N.Y. 900○
New Gretna 550○
New Milford N.Y. 16,876
New Providence N.Y. 12,426
Newton N.Y. 7,748
Newtonville VINL- 500○
Norma VINL- 800○
North Arlington N.Y. 16,587
North Bergen N.Y. 47,019▲ 47,019○
North Brunswick N.Y. 16,691○
North Caldwell N.Y. 5,832
North Cape May 3,812○
Northfield ATCY 7,795
North Haledon N.Y. 8,177
North Plainfield N.Y. 19,108
Northvale N.Y. 5,046
North Wildwood 4,714
Norwood N.Y. 4,413
Nutley N.Y. 28,998
Oakhurst N.Y. 4,600○
Oakland N.Y. 13,443
Oaklyn PHIL- 4,223
Oak Valley PHIL- 7,000○
Ocean City ATCY 13,949
Ocean Gate N.Y. 1,385
Ocean Grove N.Y. 4,200○
Oceanport N.Y. 5,888
Oceanville ATCY 600○
Ogdensburg N.Y. 2,737
Old Bridge N.Y. 13,100○
Old Tappan N.Y. 4,168
Oldwick N.Y. 450○
Oradell N.Y. 8,658
Orange N.Y. 31,136
Oxford 1,411○
Palisades Park N.Y. 13,732
Palmyra PHIL- 7,085
Paramus N.Y. 26,474
Parkertown 500○
Park Ridge N.Y. 8,515
Parsippany N.Y. 7,488○
Passaic N.Y. 52,463
Paterson N.Y. 137,970
Paulsboro PHIL- 6,944
Pedricktown PHIL- 900○
Pemberton 1,198
Pennington PHIL- 2,109
Pennsauken PHIL- 36,394○
Penns Grove PHIL- 5,760
Pennsville PHIL- 11,014○
Pequannock N.Y. 5,900○
Perth Amboy N.Y. 38,951
Phillipsburg AL-B-E 16,647
Pine Hill PHIL- 8,684
Pinehurst ATCY 1,500○
Pinewald 900○
Piscataway N.Y. 36,418○
Pitman PHIL- 9,744
Plainfield N.Y. 45,555
Plainsboro N.Y. 800○
Pleasantville ATCY 13,435
Point Pleasant N.Y. 17,747
Point Pleasant Beach N.Y. 5,415
Pomona ATCY 900○
Pompton Lakes N.Y. 10,660
Pompton Plains N.Y. 8,000○
Port Elizabeth 500○
Port Monmouth N.Y. 3,600○
Port Morris N.Y. 600○
Port Norris 1,900○
Port Reading N.Y. 4,800○
Port Republic ATCY 837
Princeton 12,035
Princeton Junction N.Y. 2,000○
Princeton Township 13,651○
Prospect Park N.Y. 5,142
Quinton PHIL- 500○
Rahway N.Y. 26,723
Ramblewood PHIL- 3,600○
Ramsey N.Y. 12,899
Rancocas PHIL- 600○
Rancocas Woods PHIL- 1,400○
Raritan N.Y. 6,128
Red Bank N.Y. 12,031
Richland VINL- 800○
Ridgefield N.Y. 10,294
Ridgefield Park N.Y. 12,738
Ridgewood N.Y. 25,208
Ringoes PHIL- 650○
Ringwood N.Y. 12,625
Rio Grande 1,203○
Riverdale N.Y. 2,530
River Edge N.Y. 11,111
Riverside PHIL- 8,591○
Riverton PHIL- 3,068
River Vale N.Y. 8,883○
Riviera Beach N.Y. 2,000○
Robbinsville PHIL- 550○
Rochelle Park N.Y. 6,380○
Rockaway N.Y. 6,852
Rocky Hill 717
Roebling PHIL- 3,600○
Roosevelt 835
Roseland N.Y. 5,330
Roselle N.Y. 20,641
Roselle Park N.Y. 13,377
Rosenhayn VINL- 750○
Rumson N.Y. 7,623
Runnemede PHIL- 9,461
Rutherford N.Y. 19,068
Saddle Brook N.Y. 15,975○
Saddle River N.Y. 2,763
Salem PHIL- 6,959
Sayreville N.Y. 29,969
Scotch Plains N.Y. 22,279○
Sea Bright N.Y. 1,812
Seabrook BRDGT 1,569○
Sea Girt N.Y. 2,650
Sea Isle City 2,644
Seaside Heights N.Y. 1,802
Seaside Park N.Y. 1,795
Secaucus N.Y. 13,719
Sewaren N.Y. 2,600○
Sewell PHIL- 1,900○
Shiloh BRDGT 604
Ship Bottom 1,427
Shore Acres N.Y. 1,300○
Sicklerville PHIL- 850○
Silverton N.Y. 2,000○
Slackwood PHIL- 8,100○
Somerdale PHIL- 5,900
Somerset N.Y. 20,300○
Somers Point ATCY 10,330
Somerville N.Y. 11,973
South Amboy N.Y. 8,322
South Belmar N.Y. 1,566
South Bound Brook N.Y. 4,331
South Hackensack N.Y. 2,412○
South Orange N.Y. 16,971○
South Plainfield N.Y. 20,521
South River N.Y. 14,361
South Toms River N.Y. 3,954
Sparta N.Y. 6,262○
Spotswood N.Y. 7,840
Springfield N.Y. 15,740○
Spring Lake N.Y. 4,215
Spring Lake Heights N.Y. 5,424
Stanhope N.Y. 3,638
Stewartsville AL-B-E 900○
Stirling N.Y. 2,000○
Stockholm N.Y. 600○
Stockton PHIL- 643
Stone Harbor 1,187
Stratford PHIL- 8,005
Strathmore N.Y. 7,674○
Succasunna N.Y. 7,400○
Summit N.Y. 21,071
Surf City 1,571
Sussex 2,418
Sutton Park N.Y. 2,500○
Swedesboro PHIL- 2,031
Teaneck N.Y. 42,355○
Tenafly N.Y. 13,552
Thorofare PHIL- 1,400○
Three Bridges N.Y. 650○
Tinton Falls N.Y. 7,740
Titusville PHIL- 900○
Toms River N.Y. 7,303○
Totowa N.Y. 11,448
Towaco N.Y. 1,400○
Trenton PHIL- 92,124
Tuckahoe 650○
Tuckerton 2,472
Twin Rivers N.Y. 1,500○
Union N.Y. 53,077○
Union Beach N.Y. 6,354
Union City N.Y. 55,593
Upper Greenwood Lake N.Y. 1,505○
Upper Saddle River N.Y. 7,958
Ventnor City ATCY 11,704
Vernon N.Y. 900○
Verona N.Y. 14,166
Villas 3,155○
Vincentown PHIL- 800○
VINELAND VINL- 53,753
Waldwick N.Y. 10,802
Wallington N.Y. 10,741
Wanamassa N.Y. 4,000○
Wanaque N.Y. 10,025
Waretown 900○
Washington 6,429
Washington Crossing PHIL- 500○
Washington Township N.Y. 10,577○
Watchung N.Y. 5,290
Waterford Works PHIL- 600○
Wayne N.Y. 49,141○
Weehawken N.Y. 13,383○
Wenonah PHIL- 2,303
West Berlin PHIL- 3,300○
West Caldwell N.Y. 11,407
West Cape May 1,091
West Creek 500○
Westfield N.Y. 30,447
West Long Branch N.Y. 7,380
West Milford N.Y. 1,600○
Westmont PHIL- 5,700○
West New York N.Y. 39,194
West Orange N.Y. 39,510
West Paterson N.Y. 11,293
Westville PHIL- 4,786
Westwood N.Y. 10,714
Wharton N.Y. 5,485
Whippany N.Y. 6,800○
White Horse PHIL- 10,600○
White House Station N.Y. 1,019○
White Meadow Lake N.Y. 6,300○
Whitesboro 700○
Whiting 700○
Whitman Square PHIL- 2,600○
Wildwood 4,913
Wildwood Crest 4,149
Williamstown PHIL- 4,075○
Willingboro PHIL- 43,386○
Winfield N.Y. 2,184○
Winslow PHIL- 500○
Woodbine 2,809
Woodbridge N.Y. 14,200○
Woodbury PHIL- 10,353
Woodcliff Lake N.Y. 5,644
Woodlynne PHIL- 2,578
Woodport N.Y. 500○
Wood-Ridge N.Y. 7,929
Woodstown PHIL- 3,250
Wrightstown 3,031
Wyckoff N.Y. 16,039○
Yardville PHIL- 8,100○

COUNTIES

Atlantic 194,119
Bergen 845,385
Burlington 362,542
Camden 471,650
Cape May 82,266
Cumberland 132,866
Essex 850,451
Gloucester 199,917
Hudson 556,972
Hunterdon 87,361
Mercer 307,863
Middlesex 595,893
Monmouth 503,173
Morris 407,630
Ocean 346,038
Passaic 447,585
Salem 64,676
Somerset 203,129
Sussex 116,119
Union 504,094
Warren 84,429

NEW MEXICO

1980 Census 1,299,968

CITIES

Adobe Acres ALBU 2,600○
Agua Fria S.FE 850○
Alameda ALBU 6,000○
Alamogordo 24,024
ALBUQUERQUE ALBU 331,767
Alcalde 800○
Anthony ELP 1,728○
Arenas Valley 500○
Armijo ALBU 14,500○
Arroyo Seco 500○
Artesia 10,385
Aztec 5,512
Bayard 3,036
Belen 5,617
Bernalillo ALBU 2,763
Black Rock 2,454
Bloomfield 4,881
Capitan 762
Carlsbad 25,496
Carrizozo 1,222
Cedar Crest 900○
Central 1,968
Chama 1,090
Chamisal 600○
Chimayo 1,300○
Church Rock 500○
Cimarron 888
Clayton 2,968
Cloudcroft 521
CLOVIS CLOV 31,194
Columbus 414
Cordova 600○
Crownpoint 900○
Cuba 609
Deming 9,964
Dexter 882
Dulce 900○
Edgewood 600○
El Prado 700○
Espanola 6,803
Estancia 830
Eunice 2,970
Fairacres LSCR 600○
Farmington 30,729
Five Points ALBU 4,100○
Flora Vista 500○
Fort Sumner 1,421
Fort Wingate 900○
Fruitland 700○
Gallup 18,161
Grants 11,451
Hagerman 936
Hanover 500○
Happy Valley 630○
Hatch 1,028
High Rolls Mountain Park 650○
Hobbs 28,794
Hurley 1,616
Isleta ALBU 1,800○
Jal 2,675
Jemez Pueblo 1,197○
Kirtland 1,500○
Laguna 800○
La Luz 800○
La Mesa 900○
LAS CRUCES LSCR 45,086
Las Vegas 14,322
Logan 735
Lordsburg 3,195
Los Alamos 17,100○
Los Lunas ALBU 3,525
Los Padillas ALBU 1,800○
Los Ranchos de Albuquerque ALBU 2,702
Los Trujillos 500○
Loving 1,355
Lovington 9,727
Magdalena 1,022
Melrose 649
Mescalero 900○
Mesilla LSCR 2,029
Mexican Springs 500○
Milan 3,747
Mora 900○
Moriarty 1,276
Mountainair 1,170
Mountain View ALBU 1,900○
New Laguna 600○
Ojo Caliente 500○
Organ 500○
Pajarito ALBU 1,500○
Paradise Hills ALBU 5,000○
Pecos 885
Penasco 900○
Placitas 450○
Pojoaque Valley 900○
Portales 9,940
Questa 608
Ramah 600○
Ranches of Taos 1,200○
Raton 8,225
Reserve 439
Rio Rancho ALBU 5,000○
ROSWELL RSWL 39,676
Ruidoso 4,260
Ruidoso Downs 949
San Antonio 500○
San Juan Pueblo 600○
San Rafael 560○
Santa Clara Pueblo 450○
Santa Cruz 600○
SANTA FE S.FE 48,899
Santa Rosa 2,469
Santo Domingo Pueblo 1,662○
Shiprock 7,000○
Silver City 9,887
Socorro 7,576
Springer 1,696
Sunland Park ELP 1,402○
Taos 3,369
Taos Pueblo 1,030○
Tatum 896
Tesuque S.FE 800○
Texico 958
Thoreau 950○
Tierra Amarilla 800○
Tohatchi 800○
Truth or Consequences 5,219
Tucumcari 6,765
Tularosa 2,536
Tyrone 950○
University Park LSCR 3,700○
Vaughn 737
Wagon Mound 416
Waterflow 500○
Williamsburg 433
Zuni 3,958○

COUNTIES

Bernalillo 419,700
Catron 2,720
Chaves 51,103
Colfax 13,706
Curry 42,019
De Baca 2,454
Dona Ana 96,340
Eddy 47,855
Grant 26,204
Guadalupe 4,496
Harding 1,090
Hidalgo 6,049
Lea 55,634
Lincoln 10,997
Los Alamos 17,599
Luna 15,585
McKinley 54,950
Mora 4,205
Otero 44,665
Quay 10,577
Rio Arriba 29,282
Roosevelt 15,695
Sandoval 34,799
San Juan 80,833
San Miguel 22,751
Santa Fe 75,306
Sierra 8,454
Socorro 12,969
Taos 18,862
Torrance 7,491
Union 4,725
Valencia 60,853

NEW YORK

1980 Census 17,557,288

CITIES

Accord 500○
Adams 1,701
Adams Center 800○
Addison 2,028
Afton 982
Akron 2,971
ALBANY A-S-T 101,727
Albertson N.Y. 11,200○
Albion ROCH 4,897
Alden BUF- 2,488
Alexandria Bay 1,265
Alfred 4,967
Allegany 2,078
Almond 568
Altamont A-S-T 1,292
Amagansett 1,800○
Amenia 1,157○
Amherst BUF- 66,100○
Amityville N.Y. 9,076
Amsterdam A-S-T 21,872
Andover 1,120
Angelica 982
Angola BUF- 2,292
Antwerp 749
Apalachin BING 1,233○
Aquebogue 1,300○
Arcade 2,052
Ardsley N.Y. 4,183
Arkport 811
Arkville 600○
Arlington POK 11,203○
Armonk N.Y. 5,900○
Athens 1,738
Atlanta 750○
Attica 2,659
AUBURN AUB 32,548
Aurora 926
Au Sable Forks 2,100○
Averill Park A-S-T 1,500○
Avoca 1,144
Avon ROCH 3,006
Babylon N.Y. 12,388
Bainbridge 1,603
Baldwin N.Y. 35,100○
Baldwinsville SYR 6,446
Ballston Spa A-S-T 4,711
Balmville NWBG 3,214○
Barker 535
Barryville 600○
Batavia 16,703
Bath 6,042
Bayberry SYR 5,900○
Bayport N.Y. 8,900○
Bay Shore N.Y. 31,200○
Bayville N.Y. 7,034
Beacon POK 12,937
Bedford Hills N.Y. 3,200○
Belfast 900○
Bellmore N.Y. 18,431○
Bellport N.Y. 2,809
Belmont 1,024
Bemus Point JMST 444
Bergen ROCH 976
Bethpage N.Y. 29,900○
Big Flats ELM- 2,500○
BINGHAMTON BING 55,860
Black River WATN 1,384
Blasdell BUF- 3,288
Blauvelt N.Y. 5,426○
Bloomingdale 608
Bohemia N.Y. 9,800○
Bolivar 1,345
Bolton Landing 1,500○
Boonville 2,344
Brant Lake 700○
Brentwood N.Y. 48,800○
Brewster N.Y. 1,650
Briarcliff Manor N.Y. 7,115
Bridgehampton 950○
Brighton ROCH 35,776○
Broadalbin A-S-T 1,415
Brockport ROCH 9,776
Brocton 1,416
Bronxville N.Y. 6,267
Brookfield 600○
Brookville N.Y. 3,290
Brownville WATN 1,099
BUFFALO BUF- 357,870
Burnt Hills A-S-T 2,000○
Cairo 725○
Caledonia ROCH 2,188
Callicoon 500○
Cambridge 1,820
Camden 2,667
Canajoharie 2,412
Canandaigua 10,419
Canaseraga 700
Canastota 4,773
Candor 917
Canisteo 2,679
Canton 7,055
Cape Vincent 785
Carle Place N.Y. 6,300○
Carthage 3,643
Cassadaga 821
Castile 1,135
Castleton on Hudson A-S-T 1,627
Cato SYR 475
Catskill 4,718
Cattaraugus 1,200
Cayuga Heights ITH 3,170
Cazenovia SYR 2,599
Cedarhurst N.Y. 6,162
Celoron JMST 1,405
Centereach N.Y. 34,600○
Center Moriches N.Y. 4,000○
Central Bridge 500○
Central Islip N.Y. 26,000○
Central Square SYR 1,418
Central Valley N.Y. 1,200○
Chadwicks UT-R 1,500○
Champlain 1,410
Chappaqua N.Y. 5,100○
Chateaugay 869
Chatham A-S-T 2,001
Chaumont 620
Chautauqua 430○
Chazy 800○
Cheektowaga BUF- 100,400○
Chenango Bridge BING 2,600○
Chenango Forks BING 500○
Cherry Creek 677
Cherry Valley 684
Chester N.Y. 1,910
Chestertown 750○
Chili Center ROCH 5,300○
Chittenango SYR 4,290
Churchville ROCH 1,399
Cincinnatus 500○
Clayton 1,816
Cleveland SYR 855
Clifton Knolls A-S-T 4,000○
Clifton Springs 2,039
Clinton UT-R 2,107
Clyde 2,491
Clymer 500○
Cobleskill 5,272
Cohocton 902
Cohoes A-S-T 18,144
Cold Spring Harbor N.Y. 5,490○

○ Rand McNally estimate (not reported in census).
▲ Population of entire township or "town", including rural area.
● Independent city. Population not included in county total.

Colonie A-S-T	8,869
Colton	450 ○
Commack N.Y.	24,300 ○
Congers N.Y.	5,000 ○
Conklin BING	1,900 ○
Constantia SYR	900 ○
Cooperstown	2,342
Copake	700 ○
Copenhagen	656
Copiague N.Y.	21,000 ○
Coram N.Y.	5,400 ○
Corfu BUF-	689
Corinth	2,702
Corning ELM-	12,953
Cornwall on the Hudson NWBG	3,164
Cortland	20,138
Coxsackie	2,786
Croghan	703
Croton-on-Hudson N.Y.	6,889
Crown Point	900 ○
Cuba	1,739
Cutchogue	1,000 ○
Dalton	500 ○
Dannemora	3,770
Dansville	4,979
Deer Park N.Y.	33,400 ○
Delanson A-S-T	448
Delevan	1,113
Delhi	3,374
Delmar A-S-T	8,900 ○
Depew BUF-	19,819
Deposit	1,897
Derby BUF-	1,200 ○
De Ruyter	542
De Witt SYR	10,032 ○
Dexter WATN	1,053
Dix Hills N.Y.	10,500 ○
Dobbs Ferry N.Y.	10,053
Downsville	950 ○
Dryden ITH	1,761
Dundee	1,556
Dunkirk	15,310
Earlville	985
East Aurora BUF-	6,803
Eastchester N.Y.	22,600 ○
East Glenville A-S-T	11,800 ○
East Half Hollow Hills N.Y.	9,691 ○
East Hampton	1,886
East Hills N.Y.	7,160
East Islip N.Y.	13,700 ○
East Marion	900 ○
East Meadow N.Y.	47,300 ○
East Northport N.Y.	22,200 ○
East Patchogue N.Y.	8,300 ○
Eastport N.Y.	1,308 ○
East Randolph	655
East Rochester ROCH	7,596
East Rockaway N.Y.	10,917
East Vestal BING	5,300 ○
Eden BUF-	3,000 ○
Edmeston	600 ○
Edwards	561
Elba	750
Elizabethtown	659
Ellenville	4,405
Ellicottville	713
ELMIRA ELM-	35,327
Elmira Heights ELM-	4,279
Elmont N.Y.	30,000 ○
Elsmere A-S-T	5,500 ○
Elwood N.Y.	15,400 ○
Endicott BING	14,457
Endwell BING	15,999 ○
Etna ITH	500 ○
Evans Mills	651
Fair Haven	976
Fairmount SYR	8,700 ○
Fairport ROCH	5,970
Fairview POK	8,517 ○
Falconer JMST	2,778
Farmingdale N.Y.	7,946
Farmingville N.Y.	5,700 ○
Fillmore	563
Fishkill POK	1,555
Floral Park N.Y.	16,805
Florida MIDD	1,947
Flower Hill N.Y.	4,558
Fonda A-S-T	1,006
Forestville	804
Fort Ann GLFLS	509
Fort Covington	1,200 ○
Fort Edward GLFLS	3,561
Fort Plain	2,555
Frankfort UT-R	2,995
Franklin	440
Franklin Square N.Y.	32,800 ○
Franklinville	1,887
Fredonia	11,126
Freeport N.Y.	38,272
Freeville ITH	449
Frewsburg JMST	2,000 ○
Friendship	1,285 ○
Fulton SYR	13,312
Galeville SYR	5,600 ○
Gang Mills ELM-	1,258 ○
Garden City N.Y.	22,927
Garden City Park N.Y.	5,200 ○
Garrison N.Y.	650 ○
Gasport LOCK	950 ○
Gates ROCH	29,756 ○
Geneseo	6,746
Geneva	15,133
Ghent	600 ○
Gilbertsville	455
Glasco KNGST	1,169 ○
Glen Cove N.Y.	24,618
Glenham POK	2,720 ○
Glen Head N.Y.	6,800 ○
GLENS FALLS GLFLS	15,897
Gloversville	17,836
Gorham	800 ○
Goshen MIDD	4,874
Gouverneur	4,285
Gowanda	2,713
Grand Gorge	800 ○
Granville	2,696
Great Neck (P.O.) N.Y.	5,604
Great Neck N.Y.	9,168
Great Neck Estates N.Y.	2,936
Greece ROCH	63,700 ○
Greene	1,747
Green Island A-S-T	2,696
Greenlawn N.Y.	8,600 ○
Greenport	2,273
Greenville N.Y.	5,500 ○
Greenwich	1,955
Greenwood	450 ○
Greenwood Lake N.Y.	2,809
Groton	2,313
Hadley	500 ○
Haines Falls	700 ○
Half Hollow Hills N.Y.	12,800 ○
Hamburg BUF-	10,582
Hamilton	3,725
Hammondsport	1,065
Hampton Bays	3,550 ○
Hannibal SYR	680
Harrison N.Y.	23,046
Harrisville	937
Hartsdale N.Y.	12,226 ○
Hartwick	600 ○
Hastings-on-Hudson N.Y.	8,573
Hauppauge N.Y.	14,200 ○
Haverstraw N.Y.	8,800
Hawthorne N.Y.	4,900 ○
Hemlock ROCH	500 ○
Hempstead N.Y.	40,404
Henrietta ROCH	1,200 ○
Herkimer UT-R	8,383
Hermon	490
Heuvelton	777
Hewlett N.Y.	6,880 ○
Hicksville N.Y.	50,000 ○
Highland POK	2,184 ○
Highland Falls	4,187
Hillcrest N.Y.	5,357 ○
Hilton ROCH	4,151
Hobart	473
Holbrook N.Y.	12,800 ○
Holland BUF-	1,000 ○
Holland Patent UT-R	534
Holley ROCH	1,882
Homer	3,635
Honeoye Falls ROCH	2,410
Hoosick Falls	3,609
Hopewell Junction POK	2,055 ○
Hornell	10,234
Horseheads ELM-	7,348
Houghton	1,620 ○
Hudson	7,986
Hudson Falls GLFLS	7,419
Huntington N.Y.	12,601 ○
Huntington Bay N.Y.	3,943
Huntington Station N.Y.	30,300 ○
Hurley KNGST	4,081 ○
Hurleyville	500 ○
Hyde Park POK	2,805 ○
Ilion UT-R	9,190
Indian Lake	450 ○
Interlaken	685
Inwood N.Y.	8,200 ○
Irondequoit ROCH	57,648 ○
Irvington N.Y.	5,774
Island Park N.Y.	4,847
Islip N.Y.	12,100 ○
Islip Terrace N.Y.	5,200 ○
ITHACA ITH	28,732
JAMESTOWN JMST	35,775
Jasper	450 ○
Jay	500 ○
Jeffersonville	554
Jericho N.Y.	14,200 ○
Johnson City BING	17,126
Johnstown	9,360
Jordan SYR	1,371
Keene	450 ○
Keeseville	2,025
Kenmore BUF-	18,474
Kennedy	500 ○
Kerhonkson	1,243 ○
Kinderhook A-S-T	1,377
Kings Point N.Y.	5,234
KINGSTON KNGST	24,481
Lackawanna BUF-	22,701
Lacona	582
LaFargeville	500 ○
Lake Delta UT-R	2,400 ○
Lake Erie Beach BUF-	3,500 ○
Lake George	1,047
Lake Grove N.Y.	9,692
Lake Katrine KNGST	1,092 ○
Lake Luzerne	1,000 ○
Lake Placid	2,490
Lake Ronkonkoma N.Y.	9,600 ○
Lake View BUF-	4,600 ○
Lakeville ROCH	950 ○
Lakewood JMST	3,941
Lancaster BUF-	13,056
Larchmont N.Y.	6,308
Larchmont North N.Y.	11,500 ○
Latham A-S-T	8,000 ○
Lawrence N.Y.	6,175
Leicester	462
Leonardsville	500 ○
Le Roy	4,900
Levittown N.Y.	65,400 ○
Lewiston BUF-	3,326
Liberty	4,293
Lima ROCH	2,025
Limestone	466
Lindenhurst N.Y.	26,919
Little Falls	6,156
Little Valley	1,203
Livingston Manor	1,522 ○
Livonia ROCH	1,238
Lloyd Harbor N.Y.	3,405
Locke	500 ○
LOCKPORT LOCK	24,844
Locust Grove N.Y.	11,648 ○
Long Beach N.Y.	34,073
Long Lake	500 ○
Loudonville A-S-T	9,000 ○
Lowville	3,364
Lyndonville	916
Lyon Mountain	950 ○
Lyons	4,160
Lyons Falls	755
Macedon ROCH	1,400
McGraw	1,188
Machias	700 ○
Madrid	800 ○
Mahopac N.Y.	5,265 ○
Maine BING	700 ○
Malone	7,668
Malverne N.Y.	9,262
Mamaroneck N.Y.	17,616
Manchester ROCH	1,698
Manhasset N.Y.	8,530 ○
Manlius SYR	5,241
Mannsville	431
Manorhaven N.Y.	5,384
Marathon	1,046
Margaretville	755
Marion ROCH	950 ○
Marlboro NWBG	1,580 ○
Massapequa N.Y.	27,500 ○
Massapequa Park N.Y.	19,779
Massena	12,851
Mastic N.Y.	5,200 ○
Mastic Beach N.Y.	5,200 ○
Mattituck N.Y.	1,200 ○
Mattydale SYR	8,292 ○
Mayfield	944
Mayville	1,626
Mechanicville A-S-T	5,500
Medford N.Y.	5,000 ○
Medina	6,392
Melville N.Y.	8,550 ○
Menands A-S-T	4,012
Merrick N.Y.	26,400 ○
Mexico	1,621
Middleburg	1,358
Middle Granville	600 ○
Middleport LOCK	1,995
MIDDLETOWN MIDD	21,454
Middleville	647
Milford	514
Millbrook POK	1,343
Millerton	1,013
Mineola N.Y.	20,757
Minetto	900 ○
Mineville	1,000 ○
Mohawk UT-R	2,956
Monroe N.Y.	5,996
Monsey N.Y.	7,400 ○
Montauk	1,300 ○
Montgomery NWBG	2,316
Monticello	6,306
Montour Falls	1,791
Mooers	549
Moravia	1,582
Moriah	500 ○
Morris	681
Morrisonville	1,500 ○
Morristown	461
Morrisville	2,707
Mountain Dale	1,200 ○
Mount Kisco N.Y.	8,025
Mount Morris	3,039
Mount Upton	500 ○
Mount Vernon N.Y.	66,713
Munnsville	499
Nanuet N.Y.	8,300 ○
Napanoch	800 ○
Naples	1,225
Narrowsburg	700 ○
Nassau A-S-T	1,285
Nassau Shores N.Y.	5,500 ○
Natural Bridge	650 ○
Nedrow SYR	3,000 ○
Nesconset N.Y.	8,300 ○
Newark	10,017
Newark Valley BING	1,190
New Baltimore	700 ○
New Berlin	1,392
NEWBURGH NWBG	23,438
New Cassel N.Y.	8,817 ○
New City N.Y.	30,800 ○
Newcomb	800 ○
Newfane LOCK	2,700 ○
New Hyde Park N.Y.	9,801
New Lebanon	800 ○
New Paltz	4,941
Newport	746
New Rochelle N.Y.	70,794
Newton Falls	560 ○
New Windsor NWBG	8,803 ○
New Woodstock SYR	450 ○
NEW YORK N.Y.	7,071,030
Niagara Falls BUF-	71,384
Nichols BING	613
Niskayuna A-S-T	17,471 ○
Norfolk	1,379 ○
North Amityville N.Y.	11,936 ○
North Babylon N.Y.	23,000 ○
North Bellmore N.Y.	23,600 ○
North Collins BUF-	1,496
North Creek	950 ○
Northeast Henrietta ROCH	12,000 ○
North Great River N.Y.	12,400 ○
North Lindenhurst N.Y.	11,400 ○
North Massapequa N.Y.	23,100 ○
North Merrick N.Y.	13,650 ○
North New Hyde Park N.Y.	16,100 ○
North Norwich	500 ○
North Patchogue N.Y.	8,000 ○
Northport N.Y.	7,651
North Rose	700 ○
North Syracuse SYR	7,970
North Tarrytown N.Y.	7,994
North Tonawanda BUF-	35,760
North Valley Stream N.Y.	14,881 ○
Northville	1,304
North Wantagh N.Y.	15,117 ○
Norwich	8,082
Norwood	1,902
Nunda	1,169
Nyack N.Y.	6,428
Oakdale N.Y.	7,800 ○
Oakfield	1,791
Oceanside N.Y.	36,400 ○
Odessa	613
Ogdensburg	12,375
Olcott LOCK	1,650 ○
Old Bethpage N.Y.	7,160 ○
Old Forge	950 ○
Olean	18,207
Oneida	10,810
Oneonta	14,933
Ontario ROCH	750 ○
Orchard Park BUF-	3,671
Orient	800 ○
Oriskany UT-R	1,680
Oriskany Falls UT-R	802
Ossining N.Y.	20,196
Oswego	19,793
Otego	1,089
Ovid	666
Owego BING	4,364
Oxford	1,765
Oyster Bay N.Y.	7,200 ○
Painted Post ELM-	2,196
Palmyra ROCH	3,729
Panama	511
Parish SYR	535
Parksville	500 ○
Patchogue N.Y.	11,291
Patterson N.Y.	950 ○
Pavilion	550 ○
Pawling POK	1,996
Pearl River N.Y.	17,146 ○
Peconic	800 ○
Peekskill N.Y.	18,236
Pelham N.Y.	6,848
Pelham Manor N.Y.	6,130
Penfield ROCH	9,600 ○
Penn Yan	5,242
Perry	4,198
Peru	1,300 ○
Petersburg	500 ○
Phelps	2,004
Philadelphia	855
Philmont	1,539
Phoenicia	700 ○
Phoenix SYR	2,357
Pine Bush NWBG	1,200 ○
Pine Island MIDD	950 ○
Plainview N.Y.	32,300 ○
Plattsburgh	21,057
Pleasant Valley POK	1,372 ○
Pleasantville N.Y.	6,749
Poland	553
Port Byron AUB	1,400
Port Chester N.Y.	23,565
Port Dickinson BING	1,974
Port Ewen KNGST	2,600 ○
Port Henry	1,450
Port Jefferson N.Y.	6,731
Port Jefferson Station N.Y.	7,500 ○
Port Jervis	8,699
Portland	600 ○
Port Leyden	740
Portville	1,136
Port Washington N.Y.	15,923 ○
Potsdam	10,635
Pottersville	600 ○
POUGHKEEPSIE POK	29,757
Prattsburg	750 ○
Prattsville	500 ○
Pulaski	2,415
Randolph	1,398
Ransomville BUF-	1,500 ○
Ravena A-S-T	3,091
Raymondville	600 ○
Red Creek	645
Red Hook	1,692
Redwood	600 ○
Remsen UT-R	621
Rensselaer A-S-T	9,047
Rhinebeck POK	2,542
Richburg	494
Richfield Springs	1,561
Richmondville	792
Ridgemont ROCH	8,500 ○
Ripley	1,000 ○
Riverhead	7,400 ○
ROCHESTER ROCH	241,741
Rockville Centre N.Y.	25,405
Roessleville A-S-T	5,476 ○
Rome UT-R	43,826
Ronkonkoma N.Y.	20,200 ○
Roosevelt N.Y.	15,000 ○
Roslyn Heights N.Y.	7,270 ○
Rotterdam A-S-T	24,800 ○
Round Lake A-S-T	791
Rouses Point	2,266
Roxbury	700 ○
Rushford	500 ○
Rushville	548
Rye N.Y.	15,083
Sackets Harbor	1,017
Sag Harbor	2,581
St. James N.Y.	11,000 ○
St. Johnsville	2,019
St. Regis Falls	950 ○
Salamanca	6,890
Salem	959
Sandy Creek	765
San Remo N.Y.	8,700 ○
Saranac Lake	5,578
Saratoga Springs A-S-T	23,906
Saugerties KNGST	3,882
Savannah	636 ○
Savona ELM-	932
Sayville N.Y.	15,300 ○
Scarsdale N.Y.	17,650
Schaghticoke A-S-T	677
Schenectady A-S-T	67,972
Schenevus	625
Schoharie	1,016
Schroon Lake	1,000 ○
Schuylerville	1,256
Scotia A-S-T	7,280
Scottsville ROCH	1,789
Sea Cliff N.Y.	5,364
Seaford N.Y.	17,150 ○
Selden N.Y.	24,100 ○
Seneca Falls	7,466
Shandaken	500 ○
Shelter Island	1,000 ○
Sherburne	1,561
Sherman	775
Sherrill	2,830
Shirley N.Y.	8,200 ○
Shortsville ROCH	1,669
Sidney	4,861
Sidney Center	600 ○
Silver Creek BUF-	3,088
Silver Springs	801
Sinclairville	772
Skaneateles SYR	2,789
Sloan BUF-	4,529
Sloatsburg N.Y.	3,154
Smithtown N.Y.	23,000 ○
Sodus ROCH	1,790
Sodus Point	1,334
Solvay SYR	7,140
Sound Beach N.Y.	5,400 ○
Southampton	4,000
South Bethlehem A-S-T	500 ○
South Corning ELM-	1,195
South Dayton	661
South Fallsburg	1,590 ○
South Farmingdale N.Y.	20,500 ○
South Glens Falls GLFLS	3,714
South Huntington N.Y.	9,115 ○
South New Berlin	450 ○
South Nyack N.Y.	3,602
Southold	2,030 ○
South Otselic	450 ○
Southport ELM-	8,700 ○
South Stony Brook N.Y.	15,329 ○
South Valley Stream N.Y.	6,600 ○
South Westbury N.Y.	10,700 ○
Spencer	863
Spencerport ROCH	3,424
Spring Valley N.Y.	20,537
Springville	4,285
Springwater	500 ○
Staatsburg POK	950 ○
Stamford	1,240
Stillwater A-S-T	1,572
Stony Brook N.Y.	6,600 ○
Stony Creek	450 ○
Stony Point N.Y.	8,270 ○
Stottville	1,300 ○
Suffern N.Y.	10,794
Sylvan Beach UT-R	1,243
Syosset N.Y.	10,200 ○
SYRACUSE SYR	170,105
Tappan N.Y.	6,100 ○
Tarrytown N.Y.	10,648
Terryville N.Y.	5,900 ○
Theresa	827
Thornwood N.Y.	5,400 ○
Three Mile Bay	600 ○
Ticonderoga	2,938
Tillson KNGST	1,300 ○
Tivoli KNGST	711
Tomkins Cove N.Y.	700 ○
Tonawanda BUF-	18,693
Town of Tonawanda BUF-	78,100 ○
Troy A-S-T	56,638
Trumansburg ITH	1,722
Tuckahoe N.Y.	6,076
Tully SYR	1,049
Tupper Lake	4,478
Unadilla	1,367
Uniondale N.Y.	24,500 ○
Union Springs AUB	1,201
University Gardens N.Y.	5,400 ○
UTICA UT-R	75,632
Valatie A-S-T	1,492
Valhalla N.Y.	6,600 ○
Valley Cottage N.Y.	6,007 ○
Valley Stream N.Y.	35,769
Van Etten	559
Vestal BING	6,000 ○
Vestal Center BING	900 ○
Victor ROCH	2,370
Waddington	980
Wading River	2,500 ○
Walden NWBG	5,659
Wallkill NWBG	1,849 ○
Walton	3,329
Wampsville	569
Wantagh N.Y.	22,300 ○
Wappingers Falls POK	5,110
Warrensburg	2,743 ○
Warsaw	3,619
Warwick N.Y.	4,320
Waterford A-S-T	2,405
Waterloo	5,303
WATERTOWN WATN	27,861
Waterville UT-R	1,672
Watervliet A-S-T	11,354
Watkins Glen	2,440
Waverly	4,738
Wayland	1,846
Webster ROCH	5,499
Weedsport SYR	1,952
Wellsburg ELM-	647
Wellsville	5,769
West Amityville N.Y.	6,470 ○
West Babylon N.Y.	32,500 ○
West Bay Shore N.Y.	8,900 ○
Westbury N.Y.	13,871
West Carthage	1,824
West Chazy	700 ○
West Elmira ELM-	5,901 ○
Westfield	3,446
West Haverstraw N.Y.	9,181
West Hempstead N.Y.	26,500 ○
West Huntington N.Y.	6,170 ○
West Islip N.Y.	21,500 ○
Westmere A-S-T	5,500 ○
West Point	8,000 ○
Westport	613
West Sayville N.Y.	5,000 ○
West Seneca BUF-	51,210 ○
Westvale SYR	7,300 ○
West Webster ROCH	10,600 ○
West Winfield	979
Whitehall	3,241
White Plains N.Y.	46,999
Whitesboro UT-R	4,460
Whitesville	600 ○
Whitney Point BING	1,093
Willard	700 ○
Williamson ROCH	1,991 ○
Williamsville BUF-	6,017
Williston Park N.Y.	8,216
Willsboro	950 ○
Wilmington	500 ○
Wilson LOCK	1,259

○ Rand McNally estimate (not reported in census).
▲ Population of entire township or "town", including rural area.
● Independent city. Population not included in county total.

Winthrop	500 ○
Witherbee	1,000 ○
Wolcott	1,496
Woodbourne	1,155 ○
Woodmere N.Y.	19,700 ○
Woodstock KNGST	1,073 ○
Worcester	950 ○
Wyandanch N.Y.	17,900 ○
Wyoming	507
Yonkers N.Y.	195,351
Yorkshire	850 ○
Yorktown N.Y.	5,400 ○
Yorktown Heights N.Y.	5,900 ○
Yorkville UT-R	3,115
Youngstown BUF-	2,191

COUNTIES

Albany	285,909
Allegany	51,742
Bronx	1,169,115
Broome	213,648
Cattaraugus	85,697
Cayuga	79,894
Chautauqua	146,925
Chemung	97,656
Chenango	49,344
Clinton	80,750
Columbia	59,487
Cortland	48,820
Delaware	46,931
Dutchess	245,055
Erie	1,015,472
Essex	36,176
Franklin	44,929
Fulton	55,153
Genesee	59,400
Greene	40,861
Hamilton	5,034
Herkimer	66,714
Jefferson	88,151
Kings	2,230,936
Lewis	25,035
Livingston	57,006
Madison	65,150
Monroe	702,238
Montgomery	53,439
Nassau	1,321,582
New York	1,427,533
Niagara	227,101
Oneida	253,466
Onondaga	463,324
Ontario	88,909
Orange	259,603
Orleans	38,496
Oswego	113,901
Otsego	59,075
Putnam	77,193
Queens	1,891,325
Rensselaer	151,966
Richmond	352,121
Rockland	259,530
St. Lawrence	114,254
Saratoga	153,759
Schenectady	149,946
Schoharie	29,710
Schuyler	17,686
Seneca	33,733
Steuben	99,135
Suffolk	1,284,231
Sullivan	65,155
Tioga	49,812
Tompkins	87,085
Ulster	158,158
Warren	54,854
Washington	54,795
Wayne	85,230
Westchester	866,599
Wyoming	39,895
Yates	21,459

NORTH CAROLINA

1980 Census 5,874,429

CITIES

Aberdeen	1,945
Ahoskie	4,887
Albemarle	15,110
Alexander Mills	643
Alliance	616
Andrews	1,621
Angier RAL	1,709
Ansonville	794
Apex RAL	2,847
Arapahoe	467
Archdale GRNS-	5,305
Arden ASHE	500 ○
Arlington	872
Asheboro	15,252
ASHEVILLE ASHE	53,281
Aulander	1,214
Aurora	698
Badin	1,800 ○
Bailey	685
Balfour	500 ○
Banner Elk	1,087
Barker Heights	2,933 ○
Barnardsville	500 ○
Battleboro RKYMT	632
Bayboro	759
Beaufort	3,826
Belfast GLDS	950 ○
Belhaven	2,430
Belmont GAST	4,607
Benson	2,792
Bessemer City GAST	4,787
Bethel	1,825
Beulaville	1,060
Biltmore Forest ASHE	1,499
Biscoe	1,334
Black Creek	523
Black Mountain	4,083
Bladenboro	1,385
Blowing Rock	1,337
Boger City	2,300 ○
Boiling Springs	2,381
Bolton	563
Bonnie Doone FAY	4,600 ○
Boone	10,191
Boonville	1,028
Brevard	5,323
Bridgeton	461
Broadway	908
Brookford HICK	467
Bryson City	1,556
Buies Creek	2,300 ○
Bunn	505
Bunnlevel	500 ○
Burgaw	1,586
BURLINGTON BUR	37,266
Burnsville	1,452
Butner	3,700 ○
Buxton	700 ○
Calypso	689
Candor	868
Canton	4,631
Caroleen	1,000 ○
Carolina Beach WILM	2,000
Carrboro DUR-	7,517
Carthage	925
Cary RAL	21,612
Cashiers	533
Castle Hayne WILM	1,000 ○
Catawba	509
Chadbourn	1,975
Chapel Hill DUR-	32,421
CHARLOTTE CHRLT	314,447
Cherokee	600 ○
Cherryville	4,844
China Grove KANN-	2,081
Chocowinity	644
Claremont	880
Clarkton	664
Clayton RAL	4,091
Clemmons WNS	2,400 ○
Cleveland	595
Cliffside	600 ○
Clinton	7,552
Clyde	1,008
Coats	1,385
Cofield	465
Columbia	758
Columbus	727
Concord KANN-	16,942
Conover	4,245
Conway	678
Cooleemee	1,600 ○
Cordova	1,200 ○
Cornelius CHRLT	1,460
Cove City	500
Cramerton GAST	1,869
Creedmoor	1,641
Creswell	426
Cricket	950 ○
Cross Mill	1,200 ○
Crouse	900 ○
Cullowhee	2,000 ○
Cumberland FAY	900 ○
Dallas GAST	3,340
Dana	500 ○
Davidson CHRLT	3,241
Davis	500 ○
Delco	550 ○
Denton	949
Dobson	1,222
Dover	600
Drexel	1,392
Dublin	477
Dunn	8,962
DURHAM DUR-	100,831
East Bend	602
East Flat Rock	3,000 ○
East Laurinburg	536
East Rockingham	2,858 ○
East Spencer SLSB	2,150
Eden	15,672
Edenton	5,264
Efland	600 ○
Elizabeth City	13,784
Elizabethtown	3,551
Elkin	2,858
Elk Park	535
Ellenboro	560
Ellerbe	1,415
Elm City	1,561
Elon College BUR	2,873
Enfield	2,995
Engelhard	600 ○
Enka ASHE	1,650 ○
Erwin	2,828
Fair Bluff	1,095
Fair Grove GRNS-	1,500 ○
Fairmont	2,658
Faison	636
Faith SLSB	552
Fallston	614
Farmville	4,707
FAYETTEVILLE FAY	59,507
Flat Rock	1,200 ○
Fletcher	700 ○
Forest City	7,688
Fountain	424
Four Oaks	1,049
Franklin	2,640
Franklinton	1,394
Franklinville	607
Fremont GLDS	1,736
Fuquay-Varina RAL	3,110
Garland	885
Garner RAL	9,556
Garysburg	1,434
Gaston	883
GASTONIA GAST	47,333
Gibson	533
Gibsonville BUR	2,865
Glen Alpine	645
Glen Raven BUR	2,900 ○
Glenville	500 ○
GOLDSBORO GLDS	31,871
Graham BUR	8,415
Grandy	600 ○
Granite Falls HICK	2,580
Granite Quarry SLSB	1,294
Grantsboro	550 ○
GREENSBORO GRNS-	155,642
Greenville	35,740
Grifton	2,179
Grimesland	453
Grover	597
Hallsboro	500 ○
Hamilton	638
Hamlet	4,720
Hampstead	700 ○
Harkers Island	1,700 ○
Harmony	470
Hatteras	700 ○
Havelock	17,718
Haw River BUR	2,117
Hays	900 ○
Hazelwood	1,811
Henderson	13,522
Hendersonville	6,862
Henrietta	1,500 ○
Hertford	1,941
HICKORY HICK	20,757
Hiddenite	800 ○
Highlands	653
High Point GRNS-	64,107
High Shoals GAST	586
Hillsborough	3,019
Hobgood	483
Hobucken	450 ○
Holly Ridge	465
Holly Springs RAL	688
Hookerton	460
Hope Mills FAY	5,412
Hot Springs	678
Hudson	2,888
Indian Trail CHRLT	811
Jackson	720
JACKSONVILLE JAX	17,056
James City	600 ○
Jamestown GRNS-	2,148
Jamesville	604
Jefferson	1,086
Jonesville	1,752
KANNAPOLIS KANN-	36,000 ○
Kenansville	931
Kenly	1,433
Kernersville WNS	6,802
King WNS	1,500 ○
Kings Mountain GAST	9,080
Kinston	25,234
Kitty Hawk	600 ○
Knightdale RAL	985
Lafayette FAY	4,100 ○
La Grange	3,147
Lake Waccamaw	1,133
Landis KANN-	2,092
Laurel Hill	1,500 ○
Laurinburg	11,480
Lawndale	469
Lenoir	13,748
Lewiston	459
Lexington	15,711
Liberty	1,997
Lilesville	588
Lillington	1,948
Lincolnton	4,879
Littleton	820
Locust	1,590
Long View HICK	3,587
Louisburg	3,238
Lowell GAST	2,917
Lowland	600 ○
Lucama	1,070
Lumberton	18,340
MacClesfield	504
McGrady	500 ○
Madison	2,806
Magnolia	592
Maiden	2,574
Manteo	902
Maple Hill	550 ○
Marble	700 ○
Marion	3,684
Marshall	809
Marshallberg	600 ○
Mars Hill	2,126
Marshville	2,011
Matthews CHRLT	1,648
Maury	450 ○
Maxton	2,711
Mayodan	2,627
Maysville	877
Mebane BUR	2,782
Micro	438
Middlesex	837
Midland	600 ○
Mint Hill CHRLT	9,830
Misenheimer	1,250 ○
Mocksville	2,637
Moncure	600 ○
Monroe CHRLT	12,639
Montreat	741
Mooresville	8,575
Morehead City	4,359
Morganton	13,763
Morven	765
Mount Airy	6,862
Mount Gilead	1,423
Mount Holly CHRLT	4,530
Mount Olive HICK	4,876
Mount Pleasant KANN-	1,210
Moyock	700 ○
Mulberry	950 ○
Murfreesboro	3,007
Murphy	2,070
Nags Head	1,020
Nashville RKYMT	2,678
Navassa	439
New Bern	14,557
Newland	722
New London	454
Newport	1,883
Newton	7,624
Newton Grove	564
Norlina	901
North Belmont CHRLT	4,500 ○
North Wilkesboro	3,260
Norwood	1,818
Oakboro	587
Oak City	475
Oak Ridge GRNS-	950 ○
Ocracoke	600 ○
Old Fort	752
Olivia	500 ○
Oriental	536
Oteen ASHE	2,200 ○
Oxford	7,580
Parkton	564
Parkwood DUR-	3,000 ○
Parmele	484
Paw Creek CHRLT	1,700 ○
Peachland	506
Pembroke	2,698
Pikeville	662
Pilot Mountain	1,090
Pinebluff	935
Pine Hall	500 ○
Pinehurst	1,200 ○
Pine Level	953
Pinetops	1,465
Pineville CHRLT	1,525
Pink Hill	644
Pinnacle	600 ○
Pisgah Forest	950 ○
Pittsboro	1,332
Pleasant Garden GRNS-	1,000 ○
Plymouth	4,571
Polkton	762
Princeton	1,034
Princeville	1,508
Raeford	3,630
RALEIGH RAL	149,771
Ramseur	1,162
Randleman	2,156
Red Springs	3,607
Reidsville	12,492
Rhodhiss HICK	727
Richlands	825
Rich Square	1,057
Ridgecrest	500 ○
Roanoke Rapids	14,702
Robbins	1,256
Robbinsville	1,370
Robersonville	1,981
Rockingham	8,300
Rockwell SLSB	1,339
Rockwell Park CHRLT	2,600 ○
ROCKY MOUNT RKYMT	41,283
Rocky Point	600 ○
Ronda	457
Roper	795
Roseboro	1,227
Rose Hill	1,508
Rosman	512
Rougemont	500 ○
Rowland	1,841
Roxboro	7,532
Royal Pines ASHE	2,041 ○
Ruffin	600 ○
Rural Hall WNS	1,336
Rutherfordton	3,434
St. Pauls	1,639
Salemburg	742
Salisbury SLSB	22,677
Salter Path	600 ○
Saluda	607
Sanford	14,773
Saxapahaw	500 ○
Scotland Neck	2,834
Seaboard	687
Selma	4,762
Shallotte	680
Sharpsburg RKYMT	997
Shelby	15,310
Siler City	4,446
Skyland ASHE	2,200 ○
Smithfield	7,288
Sneads Ferry	600 ○
Snow Hill	1,374
Southern Pines	8,620
South Gastonia GAST	1,900 ○
South Mills	800 ○
Southmont	700 ○
Southport	2,824
Sparta	1,687
Spencer SLSB	2,938
Spindale	4,246
Spring Hope	1,254
Spring Lake FAY	6,273
Spruce Pine	2,282
Stanley CHRLT	2,341
Stanleyville WNS	3,000 ○
Stantonsburg	920
Star	816
State Road	800 ○
Statesville	18,622
Stedman	723
Stokesdale GRNS-	800 ○
Stoneville	1,054
Stony Point	1,200 ○
Stovall	417
Summerfield GRNS-	900 ○
Sunbury	500 ○
Swannanoa ASHE	2,500 ○
Swanquarter	450 ○
Swansboro	976
Swepsonville	900 ○
Sylva	1,699
Tabor City	2,710
Tarboro	8,634
Taylorsville	1,103
Thomasville GRNS-	14,144
Toast	2,800 ○
Troutman	1,360
Troy	2,702
Tryon	1,796
Turkey	417
Tuxedo	950 ○
Valdese	3,364
Vanceboro	833
Vander FAY	500 ○
Vass	828
Verona JAX	600 ○
Wade FAY	474
Wadesboro	4,119
Wagram	617
Wake Forest RAL	3,780
Walkertown WNS	2,100 ○
Wallace	2,903
Walnut	550 ○
Walnut Cove	1,147
Wanchese	950 ○
Warrenton	908
Warsaw	2,910
Washington	8,418
Waxhaw	1,208
Waynesville	6,765
Weaverville ASHE	1,495
Weeksville	450 ○
Weldon	1,844
Wendell	2,222
West Concord KANN-	3,400 ○
West End	900 ○
Westfield	600 ○
West Jefferson	822
West Marion	2,300 ○
Whitakers	924
Whiteville	5,565
Whitsett BUR	500 ○
Whittier	500 ○
Wilkesboro	2,335
Williamston	6,159
WILMINGTON WILM	44,000
Wilson	34,424
Wilsons Mills	580 ○
Windsor	2,126
Winfall	634
Wingate CHRLT	2,615
WINSTON-SALEM WNS	131,885
Winter Park WILM	5,000 ○
Winterville	2,052
Winton	825
Wise	500 ○
Woodland	861
Wrightsville Beach WILM	2,910
Yadkinville	2,216
Yanceyville	1,500 ○
Youngsville	486
Zebulon	2,055

COUNTIES

Alamance	99,136
Alexander	24,999
Alleghany	9,587
Anson	25,562
Ashe	22,325
Avery	14,409
Beaufort	40,266
Bertie	21,024
Bladen	30,448
Brunswick	35,767
Buncombe	160,934
Burke	72,504
Cabarrus	85,895
Caldwell	67,746
Camden	5,829
Carteret	41,092
Caswell	20,705
Catawba	105,208
Chatham	33,415
Cherokee	18,933
Chowan	12,558
Clay	6,619
Cleveland	83,435
Columbus	51,037
Craven	71,043
Cumberland	247,160
Currituck	11,089
Dare	13,377
Davidson	113,162
Davie	24,599
Duplin	40,952
Durham	152,785
Edgecombe	55,988
Forsyth	243,683
Franklin	30,055
Gaston	162,568
Gates	8,875
Graham	7,217
Granville	33,995
Greene	16,117
Guilford	317,154
Halifax	55,286
Harnett	59,570
Haywood	46,495
Henderson	58,580
Hertford	23,368
Hoke	20,383
Hyde	5,873
Iredell	82,538
Jackson	25,811
Johnston	70,599
Jones	9,705
Lee	36,718
Lenoir	59,819
Lincoln	42,372
McDowell	35,135
Macon	20,178
Madison	16,827
Martin	25,948
Mecklenburg	404,270
Mitchell	14,428
Montgomery	22,469
Moore	50,505
Nash	67,153
New Hanover	103,471
Northampton	22,584
Onslow	112,784
Orange	77,055
Pamlico	10,398
Pasquotank	28,462
Pender	22,215
Perquimans	9,486
Person	29,164
Pitt	83,651
Polk	12,984
Randolph	91,861
Richmond	45,481
Robeson	101,577
Rockingham	83,426
Rowan	99,186
Rutherford	53,787
Sampson	49,687
Scotland	32,273
Stanly	48,517
Stokes	33,086
Surry	59,449
Swain	10,283
Transylvania	23,417

○ Rand McNally estimate (not reported in census).
▲ Population of entire township or "town", including rural area.
● Independent city. Population not included in county total.

Tyrrell 3,975
Union 70,380
Vance 36,748
Wake 300,833
Warren 16,232
Washington 14,801
Watauga 31,678
Wayne 97,054
Wilkes 58,657
Wilson 63,132
Yadkin 28,439
Yancey 14,934

NORTH DAKOTA

1980 Census 652,695

CITIES

Arthur 445
Ashley 1,192
Beach 1,381
Belcourt 950 ○
Belfield 1,274
Berthold 485
Beulah 2,878
BISMARCK BIS- 44,485
Bottineau 2,829
Bowbells 587
Bowman 2,071
Burlington MNOT 762
Cando 1,496
Carrington 2,641
Carson 469
Casselton 1,661
Cavalier 1,505
Center 900
Cooperstown 1,308
Crosby 1,469
Devils Lake 7,442
Dickinson 15,924
Drake 479
Drayton 1,082
Dunseith 625
Edgeley 843
Edmore 416
Elgin 930
Ellendale 1,967
Emerado 596
Enderlin 1,151
Fairmount 480
FARGO FAR- 61,308
Fessenden 761
Finley 718
Forman 629
Fort Totten 750 ○
Fort Yates 771
Gackle 456
Garrison 1,830
Glenburn 454
Glen Ullin 1,125
Grafton 5,293
GRAND FORKS GDFK 43,765
Gwinner 725
Hankinson 1,158
Harvey 2,527
Hatton 787
Hazen 2,365
Hebron 1,078
Hettinger 1,739
Hillsboro 1,600
Horace 494
Jamestown 16,280
Kenmare 1,456
Killdeer 790
Kindred 568
Kulm 570
Lakota 963
La Moure 1,077
Langdon 2,335
Larimore 1,524
Leeds 678
Lidgerwood 971
Linton 1,561
Lisbon 2,283
McClusky 658
McVille 626
Maddock 677
Mandan BIS- 15,513
Mayville 2,255
Medina 521
Michigan 502
Milnor 716
Minnewaukan 461
MINOT MNOT 32,843
Minto 592
Mohall 1,049
Mott 1,315
Napoleon 1,103
Neche 471
New England 825
New Rockford 1,791
New Salem 1,081
New Town 1,335
Northwood 1,240
Oakes 2,112
Park River 1,844
Parshall 1,059
Pembina 673
Portland 627
Powers Lake 466
Ray 766
Richardton 699
Riverdale 500 ○
Rolette 667
Rolla 1,538
Rugby 3,335
St. Thomas 528
Sawyer 417
Scranton 415
Stanley 1,631
Stanton 623
Steele 796
Strasburg 623
Surrey MNOT 999
Thompson 785
Tioga 1,597
Towner 867
Turtle Lake 707
Underwood 1,329
Valley City 7,774
Velva 1,101
Wahpeton 9,064
Walhalla 1,429
Washburn 1,767
Watford City 2,119
West Fargo FAR- 10,099
Westhope 741
Williston 13,336
Wilton 950
Wishek 1,345
Wyndmere 550
Zap 511

COUNTIES

Adams 3,584
Barnes 13,960
Benson 7,944
Billings 1,138
Bottineau 9,338
Bowman 4,229
Burke 3,822
Burleigh 54,811
Cass 88,247
Cavalier 7,636
Dickey 7,207
Divide 3,494
Dunn 4,627
Eddy 3,554
Emmons 5,877
Foster 4,611
Golden Valley 2,391
Grand Forks 66,100
Grant 4,274
Griggs 3,714
Hettinger 4,275
Kidder 3,833
La Moure 6,473
Logan 3,493
McHenry 7,858
McIntosh 4,800
McKenzie 7,132
McLean 12,288
Mercer 9,378
Morton 25,177
Mountrail 7,679
Nelson 5,233
Oliver 2,495
Pembina 10,399
Pierce 6,166
Ramsey 13,048
Ransom 6,698
Renville 3,608
Richland 19,207
Rolette 12,177
Sargent 5,512
Sheridan 2,819
Sioux 3,620
Slope 1,157
Stark 23,697
Steele 3,106
Stutsman 24,154
Towner 4,052
Traill 9,624
Walsh 15,371
Ward 58,392
Wells 6,979
Williams 22,237

OHIO

1980 Census 10,797,419

CITIES

Aberdeen 1,566
Ada 5,669
Addyston CIN- 1,195
Adelphi 472
Adena 1,062
AKRON AKR 237,177
Albany 905
Alexandria 489
Alger 992
ALLIANCE ALLI 24,315
Amanda 720
Amelia CIN- 1,108
Amherst CLEV 10,638
Amsterdam 783
Andover 1,205
Anna 1,038
Ansonia 1,267
Antwerp 1,765
Apple Creek 741
Arcadia 580
Arcanum 2,002
Archbold 3,318
Arlington 1,187
Ashland 20,326
Ashley 1,057
ASHTABULA ASHT 23,449
Ashville COL 2,046
Athens 19,743
Attica 865
Aurora CLEV 8,177
Austintown YNGS- 24,900 ○
Avon CLEV 7,241
Avondale DAY- 5,240 ○
Avon Lake CLEV 13,222
Bainbridge 1,042
Baltic 563
Baltimore 2,689
Barberton AKR 29,751
Barnesville 4,633
Barton WHL 900 ○
Bascom 500 ○
Batavia CIN- 1,896
Bay Village CLEV 17,846
Beach City 1,083
Beachwood CLEV 9,983
Beallsville 601
Beavercreek 31,589
Beaverdam 492
Bedford CLEV 15,056
Bedford Heights CLEV 13,214
Bellaire WHL 8,241
Bellbrook DAY- 5,174
Belle Center 930
Bellefontaine 11,888
Bellevue 8,187
Bellville MANS 1,714
Belmont 714
Beloit ALLI 1,093
Belpre PRKB 7,193
Berea CLEV 19,567
Bergholz 914
Berlin Heights CLEV 756
Bethel CIN- 2,231
Bethesda 1,429
Bettsville 752
Beverly 1,471
Bexley COL 13,405
Blacklick Estates COL 6,400 ○
Blanchester 3,202
Bloomdale 744
Bloomingburg 869
Bloomville 1,019
Blue Ash CIN- 9,506
Bluffton 3,310
Boardman YNGS- 32,800 ○
Bolivar CAN- 989
Boston Heights CLEV 781
Botkins 1,372
Bowerston 487
Bowling Green 25,728
Bradford 2,166
Bradner 1,175
Bratenahl CLEV 1,485
Brecksville CLEV 10,132
Bremen 1,432
Brentwood CIN- 9,400 ○
Brewster 2,321
Bridgeport WHL 2,642
Bridgetown CIN- 13,352 ○
Brilliant STU- 1,751
Broadview Heights CLEV 10,920
Brooklyn CLEV 12,342
Brook Park CLEV 26,195
Brookville DAY- 4,322
Brunswick CLEV 27,689
Bryan 7,879
Buchtel 585
Buckeye Lake NWRK 2,961 ○
Bucyrus 13,433
Buffalo 700 ○
Burton CLEV 1,401
Butler MANS 955
Byesville 2,572
Cadiz 4,058
Cairo 596
Calcutta E.LIV- 4,500 ○
Caldwell 1,935
Caledonia MRN 759
Cambridge 13,573
Camden 1,971
Campbell YNGS- 11,619
Canal Fulton AKR 3,481
Canal Winchester COL 2,749
Canfield YNGS- 5,835
CANTON CAN- 94,730
Cardington 1,665
Carey 3,674
Carroll COL 641
Carrollton 3,065
Castalia SNDSK 973
Cedarville 2,799
Celina 9,137
Centerburg 1,275
Centerville DAY- 18,886
Chagrin Falls CLEV 4,335
Champion YNGS- 5,100 ○
Chardon CLEV 4,434
Chauncey 1,050
Chesapeake HNTG- 1,370
Cheviot CIN- 9,888
Chillicothe 23,420
Christiansburg 593
Churchill YNGS- 7,457 ○
CINCINNATI CIN- 385,457
Circleville 11,700
Clarington 558
Clarksburg 483
Clarksville 525
CLEVELAND CLEV 573,822
Cleveland Heights CLEV 56,438
Clyde 5,489
Coal Grove HNTG- 2,630
Coalton 639
Coldwater 4,220
Columbiana 4,987
COLUMBUS COL 564,871
Columbus Grove 2,313
Conesville 451
Conneaut 13,835
Continental 1,179
Convoy 1,140
Coolville 649
Corning 789
Cortland YNGS- 5,011
Coshocton 13,405
Covedale CIN- 6,639 ○
Covington 2,610
Crestline 5,406
Creston 1,828
Cridersville LIMA 1,843
Crooksville 2,766
Croton 455 ○
Crown City 513
Cumberland 461
Curtice TOL 600 ○
Cuyahoga Falls AKR 43,710
Cygnet 646
Dalton CAN- 1,357
Danville 1,132
DAYTON DAY- 203,588
Deer Park CIN- 6,745
Defiance 16,810
De Graff 1,358
Delaware 18,780
Delhi Hills CIN- 8,000 ○
Delphos 7,314
Delta 2,886
Dennison 3,398
Deshler 1,870
Dillonvale WHL 912
Dover 11,526
Doylestown AKR 2,493
Dresden 1,646
Drexel DAY- 2,280 ○
Duncan Falls ZAN 1,100 ○
Dunkirk 954
East Cleveland CLEV 36,957
East Fultonham 600 ○
Eastlake CLEV 22,104
EAST LIVERPOOL E.LIV- 16,687
East Palestine 5,306
East Sparta CAN- 868
Eaton DAY- 6,839
Edgerton 1,813
Edgewood ASHT 3,437 ○
Edison 504
Edon 947
Eldorado 509
Elida LIMA 1,349
Elmore 1,271
Elmwood Place CIN- 2,840
Elyria CLEV 57,504
Empire STU- 484
Englewood DAY- 11,329
Euclid CLEV 59,999
Fairborn DAY- 29,702
Fairfield CIN- 30,777
Fairlawn AKR 6,100
Fairpoint 500 ○
Fairport Harbor CLEV 3,357
Fairview Park CLEV 19,311
Fayette 1,222
Fayetteville 478
Felicity 929
FINDLAY FIND 35,594
Fletcher 498
Flushing 1,266
Forest 1,633
Forest Park CIN- 18,675
Fort Jennings 538
Fort Loramie 977
Fort McKinley DAY- 11,536 ○
Fort Recovery 1,370
Fort Shawnee LIMA 4,541
Fostoria 15,743
Frankfort 1,008
Franklin MIDD 10,711
Frazeysburg 1,025
Fredericksburg 511
Fredericktown 2,299
Freeport 525
Fremont 17,834
Friendship 500 ○
Gahanna COL 18,001
Galion 12,391
Gallipolis 5,576
Gambier 2,056
Garfield Heights CLEV 33,380
Garrettsville 1,769
Geneva 6,655
Genoa TOL 2,213
Georgetown 3,467
Germantown DAY- 5,015
Gettysburg 545
Gibsonburg 2,479
Girard YNGS- 12,517
Glandorf 746
Glendale CIN- 2,368
Glouster 2,211
Gnadenhutten 1,320
Golf Manor CIN- 4,317
Grafton CLEV 2,231
Grand Rapids 962
Grandview Heights COL 7,420
Granville NWRK 3,851
Gratis 809
Green Camp 475
Greenfield 5,034
Greenhills CIN- 4,927
Green Springs 1,568
Greenville 12,999
Greenwich 1,458
Groesbeck CIN- 7,400 ○
Grove City COL 16,793
Groveport COL 3,286
Grover Hill 486
Hamden 1,010
Hamersville CIN- 688
Hamilton CIN- 63,189
Hamler 625
Hannibal 525 ○
Hanover NWRK 926
Hanoverton 490
Harrison CIN- 5,855
Harrod LIMA 506
Hartville CAN- 1,772
Harveysburg 425
Haskins 568
Haydenville 500 ○
Hayesville 518
Heath NWRK 6,969
Hebron NWRK 2,035
Hicksville 3,742
Highland Heights CLEV 5,739
Hilliard COL 8,008
Hillsboro 6,356
Hiram 1,360
Holgate 1,315
Holland TOL 1,048
Holmesville 436
Homewood CIN- 2,300 ○
Homeworth ALLI 600 ○
Hopedale 857
Hubbard YNGS- 9,245
Huber Heights DAY- 18,943 ○
Huber South DAY- 5,000 ○
Hudson CLEV 4,615
Huron SNDSK 7,123
Independence CLEV 8,165
Irondale E.LIV- 535
Ironton HNTG- 14,290
Jackson 6,675
Jackson Center 1,310
Jacksonville 651
Jamestown 1,702
Jefferson 2,952
Jeffersonville 1,252
Jeromesville 582
Jewett 972
Johnstown 3,158
Junction City 754
Kent AKR 26,164
Kenton 8,605
Kenwood CIN- 23,258 ○
Kettering DAY- 61,186
Killbuck 937
Kings Mills CIN- 500 ○
Kingston 1,208
Kingsville ASHT 1,129 ○
Kinsman 700 ○
Kirtland CLEV 5,969
Lafferty 600 ○
Lagrange CLEV 1,258
Lakemore AKR 2,744
Lakeside 800 ○
Lakeview 1,089
Lakewood CLEV 61,963
LANCASTER LANC 34,953
La Rue 861
Laura DAY- 501
Laurelville 591
Leavittsburg YNGS- 2,150 ○
Lebanon DAY- 9,636
Leesburg 1,019
Leetonia 2,121
Leipsic 2,171
Lewisburg 1,450
Lexington MANS 3,823
Liberty Center 1,111
LIMA LIMA 47,381
Lincoln Heights CIN- 5,259
Lincoln Village COL 11,215 ○
Lindsey 571
Linworth COL 500 ○
Lisbon 3,159
Lockland CIN- 4,292
Lodi CLEV 2,942
Logan 6,557
London 6,958
Lorain CLEV 75,416
Lore City 443
Loudonville 2,945
Louisville CAN- 7,873
Loveland CIN- 9,106
Loveland Park CIN- 1,450 ○
Lowell 729
Lowellville YNGS- 1,558
Lucas MANS 753
Lucasville PTSM 1,500 ○
Luckey TOL 895
Lynchburg 1,205
Lyndhurst CLEV 18,092
Lyons 596
McArthur 1,912
McClure 694
McComb 1,608
McConnelsville 2,018
McDermott PTSM 550 ○
Macedonia CLEV 6,571
McGuffey 646
Madeira CIN- 9,341
Madison CLEV 2,291
Magnolia 986
Malta 956
Malvern 1,032
Manchester 2,313
MANSFIELD MANS 53,927
Mantua CLEV 1,041
Maple Heights CLEV 29,735
Marble Cliff COL 630
Marblehead 679
Mariemont CIN- 3,295
MARIETTA MRIET 16,467
MARION MRN 37,040
Marshallville AKR 788
Martins Ferry WHL 9,331
Martinsville 539
Marysville 7,414
Mason CIN- 8,692
Massillon CAN- 30,557
Masury SHAR 5,180 ○
Maud CIN- 700 ○
Maumee TOL 15,747
Mayfield Heights CLEV 21,550
Mechanicsburg 1,792
Medina CLEV 15,268
Mendon 749
Mentor CLEV 42,065
Mentor-on-the-Lake CLEV 7,919
Metamora 556
Miamisburg DAY- 15,304
Miamitown CIN- 700 ○
Middleburg Heights CLEV 16,218
Middlefield CLEV 1,997
Middle Point 709
Middleport 2,971
MIDDLETOWN MIDD 43,719
Midvale 654
Milan SNDSK 1,569
Milford CIN- 5,232
Milford Center 764
Millbury TOL 955
Millersburg 3,247
Millersport 844
Mineral City 884
Minerva 4,549
Mingo Junction STU- 4,834
Mogadore AKR 4,190
Monfort Heights CIN- 7,100 ○
Monroe MIDD 4,256
Monroeville 1,329
Montgomery CIN- 10,088
Montpelier 4,431
Moraine DAY- 5,325
Morral 454
Morrow CIN- 1,254
Mount Blanchard 492
Mount Carmel CIN- 750 ○
Mount Gilead 2,911
Mount Healthy CIN- 7,562
Mount Orab CIN- 1,573
Mount Sterling COL 1,623
Mount Vernon 14,380
Mount Victory 667
Mowrystown 475
Mulberry CIN- 650 ○

○ Rand McNally estimate (not reported in census).
▲ Population of entire township or "town", including rural area.
● Independent city. Population not included in county total.

Murray City . . . 579
Napoleon . . . 8,614
Navarre CAN- . . . 1,343
Neffs WHL . . . 1,400 ○
Negley . . . 550 ○
Nevada . . . 945
NEWARK NWRK . . . 41,200
New Athens . . . 440
New Boston PTSM . . . 3,188
New Bremen . . . 2,393
Newburgh Heights CLEV . . . 2,678
New Carlisle DAY- . . . 6,498
Newcomerstown . . . 3,986
New Concord . . . 1,860
New Holland . . . 783
New Knoxville . . . 760
New Lexington . . . 5,179
New London . . . 2,449
New Madison . . . 1,008
New Matamoras . . . 1,172
New Miami CIN- . . . 2,980
New Paris RICH . . . 1,709
New Philadelphia . . . 16,883
Newport . . . 700 ○
New Richmond CIN- . . . 2,769
New Straitsville . . . 937
Newton Falls YNGS- . . . 4,960
Newtown CIN- . . . 1,817
New Vienna . . . 1,133
New Washington . . . 1,213
New Waterford . . . 1,314
Niles YNGS- . . . 23,088
North Baltimore . . . 3,127
North Bend CIN- . . . 546
North Bloomfield . . . 500 ○
Northbrook CIN- . . . 7,600 ○
North Canton CAN- . . . 14,228
North College Hill CIN- . . . 10,990
North Fairfield . . . 525
Northfield CLEV . . . 3,913
North Industry CAN- . . . 3,200 ○
North Kingsville ASHT . . . 2,939
North Lewisburg . . . 1,072
North Lima YNGS- . . . 700 ○
North Olmsted CLEV . . . 36,486
Northridge DAY- . . . 4,850 ○
Northridge DAY- . . . 16,000 ○
North Ridgeville CLEV . . . 21,522
North Royalton CLEV . . . 17,671
Northwood TOL . . . 5,495
Norton AKR . . . 12,242
Norwalk . . . 14,358
Norwood CIN- . . . 26,342
Oak Harbor . . . 2,678
Oak Hill . . . 1,713
Oakwood CLEV . . . 9,372
Oakwood DAY- . . . 3,786
Oakwood . . . 886
Oberlin CLEV . . . 8,660
Obetz COL . . . 3,095
Ohio City . . . 881
Olmsted Falls CLEV . . . 5,868
Oneida MIDD . . . 1,500 ○
Ontario MANS . . . 4,123
Oregon TOL . . . 18,675
Orrville . . . 7,511
Orwell . . . 1,067
Ottawa . . . 3,874
Ottawa Hills TOL . . . 4,065
Ottoville . . . 833
Owensville CIN- . . . 858
Oxford . . . 17,655
Page Manor DAY- . . . 9,300 ○
Painesville CLEV . . . 16,391
Pandora . . . 977
Park Layne DAY- . . . 4,800 ○
Parkman CLEV . . . 500 ○
Parma CLEV . . . 92,548
Parma Heights CLEV . . . 23,112
Pataskala COL . . . 2,284
Paulding . . . 2,754
Payne . . . 1,399
Peebles . . . 1,790
Pemberville . . . 1,321
Peninsula CLEV . . . 604
Pepper Pike CLEV . . . 6,177
Perry CLEV . . . 961
Perry Heights CAN- . . . 5,300 ○
Perrysburg TOL . . . 10,215
Perrysville MANS . . . 836
Petersburg YNGS- . . . 800 ○
Pettisville . . . 450 ○
Philo ZAN . . . 799
Pickerington COL . . . 3,917
Piketon . . . 1,726
Piney Fork . . . 475 ○
Pioneer . . . 1,133
Piqua . . . 20,480
Pitsburg . . . 460
Plain City . . . 2,102
Pleasant City . . . 481
Pleasant Hill . . . 1,051
Pleasantville LANC . . . 780
Plymouth . . . 1,939
Pomeroy . . . 2,728
Portage Lakes AKR . . . 20,400 ○
Port Clinton . . . 7,223
Port Jefferson . . . 482
PORTSMOUTH PTSM . . . 25,943
Port Washington . . . 622
Powhatan Point . . . 2,181
Proctorville HNTG- . . . 975
Prospect . . . 1,159
Quaker City . . . 698
Quincy . . . 633
Racine . . . 908
Randolph AKR . . . 750 ○
Ravenna AKR . . . 11,987
Rawson . . . 477
Reading CIN- . . . 12,879
Redbird CLEV . . . 1,500 ○
Reedurban CAN- . . . 6,600 ○
Republic . . . 656
Reynoldsburg COL . . . 20,661
Richmond Dale . . . 500 ○
Richmond Heights CLEV . . . 10,095
Richwood . . . 2,181
Ridgeville Corners . . . 425 ○
Ripley . . . 2,174

Risingsun . . . 698
Rittman . . . 6,063
Rock Creek . . . 652
Rockford . . . 1,245
Rocky River CLEV . . . 21,084
Rootstown AKR . . . 600 ○
Roseland MANS . . . 3,700 ○
Roseville . . . 1,915
Rossford TOL . . . 5,978
Rushsylvania . . . 610
Russellville . . . 445
Rutland . . . 635
Sabina . . . 2,799
Sagamore Hills CLEV . . . 4,700 ○
St. Bernard CIN- . . . 5,396
St. Clairsville WHL . . . 5,452
St. Henry . . . 1,596
St. Marys . . . 8,414
St. Paris . . . 1,742
Salem . . . 12,869
Salineville . . . 1,629
SANDUSKY SNDSK . . . 31,360
Sardinia . . . 826
Sardis . . . 500 ○
Scio . . . 1,003
Seaman . . . 1,039
Sebring ALLI . . . 5,078
Senecaville . . . 458
Seven Hills CLEV . . . 13,650
Seven Mile CIN- . . . 841
Seville . . . 1,568
Shadyside WHL . . . 4,315
Shaker Heights CLEV . . . 32,487
Sharonville CIN- . . . 10,108
Shawnee . . . 924
Sheffield Lake CLEV . . . 10,484
Shelby . . . 9,645
Sherwood . . . 915
Shiloh DAY- . . . 4,700 ○
Shiloh . . . 857
Shreve . . . 1,608
Sidney . . . 17,657
Silverton CIN- . . . 6,172
Smithfield STU- . . . 1,308
Smithville . . . 1,467
Solon CLEV . . . 14,341
Somerset . . . 1,432
South Charleston . . . 1,682
South Euclid CLEV . . . 25,713
South Lebanon CIN- . . . 2,700
South Solon . . . 416
South Vienna . . . 464
South Webster . . . 886
South Zanesville ZAN . . . 1,739
Spencer . . . 764
Spencerville . . . 2,184
Springboro DAY- . . . 4,962
Springdale CIN- . . . 10,111
Springfield DAY- . . . 72,563
Spring Valley . . . 541
STEUBENVILLE STU- . . . 26,400
Stockport . . . 558
Stony Ridge TOL . . . 450 ○
Stoutsville . . . 537
Stow AKR . . . 25,303
Strasburg . . . 2,091
Streetsboro CLEV . . . 9,055
Strongsville CLEV . . . 28,577
Struthers YNGS- . . . 13,624
Stryker . . . 1,423
Summit Station COL . . . 500 ○
Sunbury COL . . . 1,911
Swanton TOL . . . 3,424
Sycamore . . . 1,059
Sylvania TOL . . . 15,527
Syracuse . . . 946
Tallmadge AKR . . . 15,269
The Plains . . . 1,568 ○
The Village of Indian Hill CIN- . . . 5,521
Thornville . . . 838
Thurston . . . 527
Tiffin . . . 19,549
Tiltonsville WHL . . . 1,750
Tipp City DAY- . . . 5,595
TOLEDO TOL . . . 354,635
Toronto STU- . . . 6,934
Trenton MIDD . . . 6,401
Trinway . . . 500 ○
Trotwood DAY- . . . 7,802
Troy . . . 19,086
Twinsburg CLEV . . . 7,632
Uhrichsville . . . 6,130
Union DAY- . . . 5,219
Union City . . . 1,716
Uniontown AKR . . . 1,450 ○
Unionville . . . 500 ○
University Heights CLEV . . . 15,401
Upper Arlington COL . . . 35,648
Upper Sandusky . . . 5,967
Urbana . . . 10,762
Urbancrest COL . . . 880
Utica . . . 2,238
Vandalia DAY- . . . 13,161
Van Wert . . . 11,035
Vermilion CLEV . . . 11,012
Verona DAY- . . . 571
Versailles . . . 2,384
Wadsworth AKR . . . 15,166
Wakeman CLEV . . . 906
Walbridge TOL . . . 2,900
Wapakoneta LIMA . . . 8,402
Warren YNGS- . . . 56,629
Warrensville Heights CLEV . . . 16,565
Warsaw . . . 765
Washington Court House . . . 12,682
Waterford . . . 480 ○
Waterville TOL . . . 3,884
Wauseon . . . 6,173
Waverly . . . 4,603
Wayne . . . 894
Waynesburg . . . 1,160
Waynesville DAY- . . . 1,796
Wellington . . . 4,146
Wellston . . . 6,016
Wellsville E.LIV- . . . 5,095
West Alexandria DAY- . . . 1,313
West Carrollton DAY- . . . 13,148
Westerville COL . . . 23,414
West Farmington . . . 563

Westfield Center CLEV . . . 791
West Jefferson COL . . . 4,448
West Lafayette . . . 2,225
Westlake CLEV . . . 19,483
West Liberty . . . 1,653
West Manchester . . . 448
West Mansfield . . . 716
West Milton DAY- . . . 4,119
Weston . . . 1,708
West Portsmouth PTSM . . . 3,396 ○
West Salem . . . 1,357
West Union . . . 2,791
West Unity . . . 1,639
Wheelersburg PTSM . . . 3,709 ○
Whitehall COL . . . 21,299
Whitehouse TOL . . . 2,137
White Oak CIN- . . . 4,900 ○
Wickliffe CLEV . . . 16,790
Wickliffe YNGS- . . . 8,800 ○
Wilberforce DAY- . . . 4,300 ○
Willard . . . 5,674
Williamsburg CIN- . . . 1,952
Williamsport . . . 792
Willoughby CLEV . . . 19,329
Willoughby Hills CLEV . . . 8,612
Willowick CLEV . . . 17,834
Wilmington . . . 10,431
Winchester . . . 1,080
Windham YNGS- . . . 3,721
Wintersville STU- . . . 4,724
Woodbourne DAY- . . . 5,720 ○
Woodlawn CIN- . . . 2,715
Woodsfield . . . 3,145
Woodville . . . 2,050
Wooster . . . 19,289
Worthington COL . . . 15,016
Wyoming CIN- . . . 8,282
Xenia DAY- . . . 24,653
Yellow Springs DAY- . . . 4,077
Yorkville WHL . . . 1,447
YOUNGSTOWN YNGS- . . . 115,436
ZANESVILLE ZAN . . . 28,655

COUNTIES

Adams . . . 24,328
Allen . . . 112,241
Ashland . . . 46,178
Ashtabula . . . 104,215
Athens . . . 56,399
Auglaize . . . 42,554
Belmont . . . 82,569
Brown . . . 31,920
Butler . . . 258,787
Carroll . . . 25,598
Champaign . . . 33,649
Clark . . . 150,236
Clermont . . . 128,483
Clinton . . . 34,603
Columbiana . . . 113,572
Coshocton . . . 36,024
Crawford . . . 50,075
Cuyahoga . . . 1,498,295
Darke . . . 55,096
Defiance . . . 39,987
Delaware . . . 53,840
Erie . . . 79,655
Fairfield . . . 93,678
Fayette . . . 27,467
Franklin . . . 869,109
Fulton . . . 37,751
Gallia . . . 30,098
Geauga . . . 74,474
Greene . . . 129,769
Guernsey . . . 42,024
Hamilton . . . 873,136
Hancock . . . 64,581
Hardin . . . 32,719
Harrison . . . 18,152
Henry . . . 28,383
Highland . . . 33,477
Hocking . . . 24,304
Holmes . . . 29,416
Huron . . . 54,608
Jackson . . . 30,592
Jefferson . . . 91,564
Knox . . . 46,309
Lake . . . 212,801
Lawrence . . . 63,849
Licking . . . 120,981
Logan . . . 39,155
Lorain . . . 274,909
Lucas . . . 471,741
Madison . . . 33,004
Mahoning . . . 289,487
Marion . . . 67,974
Medina . . . 113,150
Meigs . . . 23,641
Mercer . . . 38,334
Miami . . . 90,381
Monroe . . . 17,382
Montgomery . . . 571,697
Morgan . . . 14,241
Morrow . . . 26,480
Muskingum . . . 83,340
Noble . . . 11,310
Ottawa . . . 40,076
Paulding . . . 21,302
Perry . . . 31,032
Pickaway . . . 43,662
Pike . . . 22,802
Portage . . . 135,856
Preble . . . 38,223
Putnam . . . 32,991
Richland . . . 131,205
Ross . . . 65,004
Sandusky . . . 63,267
Scioto . . . 84,545
Seneca . . . 61,901
Shelby . . . 43,089
Stark . . . 378,823
Summit . . . 524,472
Trumbull . . . 241,863
Tuscarawas . . . 84,614
Union . . . 29,536
Van Wert . . . 30,458
Vinton . . . 11,584
Warren . . . 99,276
Washington . . . 64,266
Wayne . . . 97,408

Williams . . . 36,369
Wood . . . 107,372
Wyandot . . . 22,651

OKLAHOMA

1980 Census . . . 3,025,266

CITIES

Achille . . . 480
Ada . . . 15,902
Adair . . . 508
Afton . . . 1,174
Alex . . . 769
Allen . . . 998
Altus . . . 23,101
Alva . . . 6,416
Amber . . . 416
Anadarko . . . 6,378
Antlers . . . 2,989
Apache . . . 1,560
Arapaho . . . 851
Ardmore . . . 23,689
Arkoma FTSM . . . 2,175
Arnett . . . 714
Asher . . . 659
Atoka . . . 3,409
Avant . . . 461
Barnsdall . . . 1,501
Bartlesville . . . 34,568
Beaver . . . 1,939
Beggs . . . 1,428
Bethany O.C. . . . 22,130
Bethel Acres . . . 2,314
Billings . . . 632
Binger . . . 791
Bixby TUL . . . 6,969
Blackwell . . . 8,400
Blair . . . 1,092
Blanchard O.C. . . . 1,616
Boise City . . . 1,761
Bokchito . . . 628
Bokoshe . . . 556
Boley . . . 423
Boswell . . . 702
Bowlegs . . . 522
Boynton . . . 518
Bray . . . 591
Bristow . . . 4,702
Broken Arrow TUL . . . 35,761
Broken Bow . . . 3,965
Buffalo . . . 1,381
Burns Flat . . . 2,431
Byng . . . 833
Cache . . . 1,661
Caddo . . . 923
Calera . . . 1,390
Canton . . . 854
Canute . . . 676
Carmen . . . 516
Carnegie . . . 2,016
Carney . . . 622
Cashion . . . 547
Catoosa TUL . . . 1,772
Cement . . . 884
Chandler . . . 2,926
Checotah . . . 3,454
Chelsea . . . 1,754
Cherokee . . . 2,105
Cheyenne . . . 1,207
Chickasha . . . 15,828
Chilocco . . . 500 ○
Choctaw O.C. . . . 7,520
Chouteau . . . 1,559
Claremore TUL . . . 12,085
Clayton . . . 833
Cleo Springs . . . 514
Cleveland . . . 2,972
Clinton . . . 8,796
Coalgate . . . 2,001
Colbert . . . 1,122
Colcord . . . 530
Collinsville TUL . . . 3,556
Comanche . . . 1,937
Commerce . . . 2,556
Cookson . . . 500 ○
Copan . . . 960
Cordell . . . 3,301
Corn . . . 542
Countyline . . . 500 ○
Covington . . . 715
Coweta TUL . . . 4,554
Cowlington . . . 546
Crescent . . . 1,651
Crowder . . . 431
Cushing . . . 7,720
Custer . . . 530
Cyril . . . 1,220
Davenport . . . 974
Davidson . . . 501
Davis . . . 2,782
Delaware . . . 544
Del City O.C. . . . 28,424
Depew . . . 682
Dewar . . . 1,048
Dewey . . . 3,545
Dickson . . . 996
Dill City . . . 649
Disney . . . 464
Dover . . . 570
Drummond . . . 482
Drumright . . . 3,162
Duke . . . 484
Duncan . . . 22,517
Durant . . . 11,972
Dustin . . . 498
Eagletown . . . 500 ○
Eakly . . . 452
Edmond O.C. . . . 34,637
Eldorado . . . 688
Elgin . . . 1,003
Elk City . . . 9,579
Elmore City . . . 582
El Reno . . . 15,486
ENID ENID . . . 50,363
Erick . . . 1,375

Eufaula . . . 3,092
Fairfax . . . 1,949
Fairland . . . 1,073
Fairmont . . . 419
Fairview . . . 3,370
Fittstown . . . 500 ○
Fletcher . . . 1,074
Forgan . . . 611
Fort Cobb . . . 760
Fort Gibson MSKOG . . . 2,483
Fort Supply . . . 559
Fort Towson . . . 789
Frederick . . . 6,153
Gage . . . 667
Garber . . . 1,215
Geary . . . 1,700
Geronimo . . . 726
Glencoe . . . 490
Glenpool TUL . . . 2,706
Goldsby O.C. . . . 603
Goodwell . . . 1,186
Gore . . . 445
Gotebo . . . 457
Gracemont . . . 503
Grandfield . . . 1,445
Granite . . . 1,617
Grove . . . 3,378
Guthrie . . . 10,312
Guymon . . . 8,492
Haileyville . . . 832
Hammon . . . 866
Harrah O.C. . . . 2,897
Hartshorne . . . 2,380
Haskell . . . 1,953
Healdton . . . 3,769
Heavener . . . 2,776
Helena . . . 710
Hennessey . . . 2,287
Henryetta . . . 6,432
Hinton . . . 1,432
Hobart . . . 4,735
Holdenville . . . 5,469
Hollis . . . 2,958
Hominy . . . 3,130
Hooker . . . 1,788
Howe . . . 562
Hugo . . . 7,172
Hulbert . . . 633
Hydro . . . 938
Idabel . . . 7,622
Inola . . . 1,550
Jay . . . 2,100
Jenks TUL . . . 5,876
Jones O.C. . . . 2,270
Kansas . . . 491
Kellyville . . . 960
Keota . . . 661
Keyes . . . 557
Kiefer TUL . . . 912
Kingfisher . . . 4,245
Kingston . . . 1,171
Kiowa . . . 866
Konawa . . . 1,711
Krebs . . . 1,754
Lahoma . . . 537
Lake Station TUL . . . 800 ○
Lamont . . . 571
Langley . . . 582
Langston . . . 443
Laverne . . . 1,563
LAWTON LAWT . . . 80,054
Leedey . . . 499
Lexington . . . 1,731
Lindsay . . . 3,454
Locust Grove . . . 1,179
Lone Grove . . . 3,369
Lone Wolf . . . 613
Luther O.C. . . . 1,159
McAlester . . . 17,255
McCurtain . . . 549
McLoud O.C. . . . 4,061
Madill . . . 3,173
Mangum . . . 3,833
Mannford . . . 1,610
Mannsville . . . 568
Marietta . . . 2,494
Marlow . . . 5,017
Maud . . . 1,444
Maysville . . . 1,396
Medford . . . 1,419
Medicine Park . . . 437
Meeker . . . 1,032
Miami . . . 14,237
Midwest City O.C. . . . 49,559
Mill Creek . . . 431
Minco . . . 1,489
Moore O.C. . . . 35,063
Mooreland . . . 1,383
Morris . . . 1,288
Morrison . . . 671
Mounds TUL . . . 1,086
Mountain Park . . . 557
Mountain View . . . 1,189
Muldrow . . . 2,538
MUSKOGEE MSKOG . . . 40,011
Mustang O.C. . . . 7,496
Newcastle O.C. . . . 3,076
Newkirk . . . 2,413
Nichols Hills O.C. . . . 4,171
Nicoma Park O.C. . . . 2,588
Noble O.C. . . . 3,497
Norman O.C. . . . 68,020
North Enid ENID . . . 992
North Miami . . . 544
Nowata . . . 4,270
Oakhurst TUL . . . 2,000 ○
Oakland . . . 485
Oaks . . . 591
Ochelata . . . 480
Oilton . . . 1,244
Okarche . . . 1,064
Okay MSKOG . . . 554
Okeene . . . 1,601
Okemah . . . 3,381
OKLAHOMA CITY O.C. . . . 403,213
Okmulgee . . . 16,263
Olustee . . . 721
Oologah . . . 798
Owasso TUL . . . 6,149

○ Rand McNally estimate (not reported in census).
▲ Population of entire township or "town", including rural area.
● Independent city. Population not included in county total.

Paden	448
Panama	1,164
Paoli	573
Pauls Valley	5,664
Pawhuska	4,771
Pawnee	1,688
Perkins	1,762
Perry	5,796
Picher	2,180
Piedmont O.C.	2,016
Pocola	3,268
Ponca City	26,238
Pondcreek	949
Porter	642
Porum	668
Poteau	7,089
Prague	2,208
Prue	554
Pryor	8,483
Purcell	4,638
Quapaw	1,097
Quinton	1,228
Ralston	495
Ramona	567
Randlett	461
Ravia	487
Red Oak	676
Ringling	1,561
Ripley	451
Roff	729
Roland	1,472
Rush Springs	1,451
Ryan	1,083
Salina	1,115
Sallisaw	6,403
Sand Springs TUL	13,246
Sapulpa TUL	15,853
Savanna	828
Sayre	3,177
Seiling	1,103
Seminole	8,590
Sentinel	1,016
Shattuck	1,759
Shawnee	26,506
Shidler	708
Skiatook TUL	3,596
Snyder	1,848
Soper	465
South Coffeyville	873
Sparks	772
Spavinaw	623
Sperry TUL	1,276
Spiro	2,221
Springer	679
Sterling	702
Stigler	2,630
Stillwater	38,268
Stilwell	2,369
Stonewall	672
Stratford	1,459
Stringtown	1,047
Stroud	3,148
Sulphur	5,516
Taft MSKOG	489
Tahlequah	9,708
Talihina	1,387
Taloga	446
Tecumseh	5,123
Temple	1,339
Terral	604
Texhoma	785
Thackerville	431
The Village O.C.	11,049
Thomas	1,515
Tipton	1,475
Tishomingo	3,212
Tonkawa	3,524
Tryon	435
TULSA TUL	360,919
Tupelo	542
Turley TUL	6,300○
Turpin	425○
Tuttle	3,051
Tyrone	928
Union	558
Valliant	927
Velma	831
Verden	625
Vian	1,521
Vici	845
Vinita	6,740
Wagoner	6,191
Wakita	526
Walters	2,778
Wanette	473
Wapanucka	472
Warner	1,310
Warr Acres O.C.	9,940
Washington	477
Watonga	4,139
Waukomis	1,551
Waurika	2,258
Wayne	621
Waynoka	1,377
Weatherford	9,640
Webbers Falls	461
Welch	697
Weleetka	1,195
Wellston	802
Westville	1,049
Wetumka	1,725
Wewoka	5,480
Wilburton	2,996
Wilson	1,585
Wister	444
Woodward	13,610
Wright City	1,168
Wynnewood	2,615
Wynona	780
Yale	1,652
Yukon O.C.	17,112

COUNTIES

Adair	18,575
Alfalfa	7,077
Atoka	12,748
Beaver	6,806
Beckham	19,243
Blaine	13,443
Bryan	30,535
Caddo	30,905
Canadian	56,452
Carter	43,610
Cherokee	30,684
Choctaw	17,203
Cimarron	3,648
Cleveland	133,173
Coal	6,041
Comanche	112,456
Cotton	7,338
Craig	15,014
Creek	59,210
Custer	25,995
Delaware	23,946
Dewey	5,922
Ellis	5,596
Garfield	62,820
Garvin	27,856
Grady	39,490
Grant	6,518
Greer	6,877
Harmon	4,519
Harper	4,715
Haskell	11,010
Hughes	14,338
Jackson	30,356
Jefferson	8,183
Johnston	10,356
Kay	49,852
Kingfisher	14,187
Kiowa	12,711
Latimer	9,840
Le Flore	40,698
Lincoln	26,601
Logan	26,881
Love	7,469
McClain	20,291
McCurtain	36,151
McIntosh	15,495
Major	8,772
Marshall	10,550
Mayes	32,261
Murray	12,147
Muskogee	66,939
Noble	11,573
Nowata	11,486
Okfuskee	11,125
Oklahoma	568,933
Okmulgee	39,169
Osage	39,327
Ottawa	32,870
Pawnee	15,310
Payne	62,435
Pittsburg	40,524
Pontotoc	32,598
Pottawatomie	55,239
Pushmataha	11,773
Roger Mills	4,799
Rogers	46,436
Seminole	27,473
Sequoyah	30,749
Stephens	43,419
Texas	17,727
Tillman	12,398
Tulsa	470,593
Wagoner	41,801
Washington	48,113
Washita	13,798
Woods	10,923
Woodward	21,172

OREGON

1980 Census 2,632,663

CITIES

Agate Beach	700○
Albany	26,546
Aloha POR	7,200○
Altamont	15,746○
Amity	1,092
Applegate	800○
Arlington	521
Ashland	14,943
Astoria	9,998
Athena	965
Aumsville SAL	1,432
Aurora POR	523
Baker	9,471
Bandon	2,311
Banks POR	489
Barview	1,388○
Bay City	986
Beaverton POR	30,582
Belleview	750○
Bend	17,263
Bly	600○
Boardman	1,261
Brookings	3,384
Brownsville	1,261
Bunker Hill	1,549○
Burns	3,579
Butte Falls	428
Canby POR	7,659
Cannon Beach	1,187
Canyon City	639
Canyonville	1,288
Carlton	1,302
Cascade Locks	838
Cave Junction	1,023
Cedar Hills POR	5,200○
Central Point MEDF	6,357
Charleston	700○
Chenoweth	2,329○
Chiloquin	778
Clackamas POR	1,000○
Clatskanie	1,648
Coburg	699
Columbia City POR	678
Condon	783
Coos Bay	14,424
Coquille	4,481
Cornelius POR	4,055
CORVALLIS CORV	40,960
Cottage Grove	7,148
Cove	451
Crescent	450○
Creswell	1,770
Culver	514
Dallas	8,530
Dayton	1,409
Depoe Bay	723
Dillard	800○
Drain	1,148
Dufur	560
Dundee POR	1,223
Eagle Point MEDF	2,764
Eastside	1,601
Echo	624
Elgin	1,701
Elmira EUG	500○
Enterprise	2,003
Errol Heights POR	7,750○
Estacada	1,419
EUGENE EUG	105,624
Fairview POR	1,749
Falcon Heights	1,389○
Falls City	804
Florence	4,411
Forest Grove POR	11,499
Fossil	535
Four Corners SAL	5,823○
Garden Home POR	4,700○
Gardiner	500○
Garibaldi	999
Gaston	471
Gates	455
Gearhart	967
Gervais SAL	1,144
Gilbert POR	2,850○
Gilchrist	500○
Gladstone POR	9,500
Glendale	712
Glenwood EUG	1,400○
Glide	500○
Gold Beach	1,515
Gold Hill	904
Grants Pass	14,997
Grants Pass Southwest	3,431○
Green	1,612○
Gresham POR	33,005
Halsey	693
Hammond	516
Happy Valley POR	1,499
Harbor	500○
Harrisburg EUG	1,881
Hayesville SAL	5,518○
Heppner	1,498
Hermiston	9,408
Hillsboro POR	27,664
Hines	1,632
Hood River	4,329
Hubbard POR	1,640
Huntington	539
Independence SAL	4,024
Irrigon	700
Island City	477
Jacksonville MEDF	2,030
Jefferson	1,702
Jennings Lodge POR	3,600○
John Day	2,012
Jordan Valley	473
Joseph	999
Junction City EUG	3,320
Keizer SAL	11,405○
Kinzua	500○
Klamath Falls	16,661
Lafayette	1,215
La Grande	11,354
Lake Oswego POR	22,868
Lakeside	1,453
Lakeview	2,770
La Pine	900○
Lebanon	10,413
Lewisburg	700○
Lincoln City	5,469
Lowell EUG	661
Lyons	877
McMinnville	14,080
McNulty POR	1,017○
Madras	2,235
Malin	539
Manzanita	443
Mapleton	900○
Marcola	500○
Marlene Village POR	6,400○
Maupin	495
May Park	1,466○
Maywood Park POR	1,083
MEDFORD MEDF	39,603
Medford West MEDF	3,919○
Merrill	809
Metolius	451
Metzger POR	3,800○
Midway POR	17,600○
Mill City	1,565
Milton-Freewater	5,086
Milwaukie POR	17,931
Molalla	2,992
Monmouth SAL	5,594
Monroe	412
Mount Angel	2,876
Mount Vernon	569
Myrtle Creek	3,365
Myrtle Point	2,859
Netarts	900○
Newberg POR	10,394
Newport	7,519
North Albany	900○
North Bend	9,779
North Plains POR	715
North Powder	430
Nyssa	2,862
Oak Grove POR	5,500○
Oakland	886
Oakridge	3,729
Ontario	8,814
Oregon City POR	14,673
Parkrose POR	21,350○
Pendleton	14,521
Philomath CORV	2,673
Phoenix MEDF	2,309
Pilot Rock	1,630
PORTLAND POR	366,383
Port Orford	1,061
Powellhurst POR	8,200○
Powers	819
Prairie City	1,106
Prineville	5,276
Rainier LNGV	1,655
Raleigh Hills POR	6,800○
Redmond	6,452
Reedsport	4,984
Riddle	1,265
River Road EUG	12,000○
Rockaway	906
Rockwood POR	9,400○
Rogue River	1,308
Roseburg	16,644
Russellville POR	5,800○
St. Helens POR	7,064
SALEM SAL	89,233
Sandy POR	2,905
Santa Clara EUG	11,000○
Scappoose POR	3,213
Scio	579
Seaside	5,193
Shady Cove	1,097
Sheridan	2,249
Sherwood POR	2,386
Siletz	1,001
Silverton	5,168
Sisters	696
South Medford MEDF	3,497○
Springfield EUG	41,621
Stanfield	1,568
Stayton	4,396
Sublimity	1,077
Sutherlin	4,560
Svensen	800○
Sweet Home	6,921
Talent MEDF	2,577
Tangent	478
The Dalles	10,820
Tigard POR	14,286
Tillamook	3,981
Toledo	3,151
Tri City	1,039○
Troutdale POR	5,908
Tualatin POR	7,348
Turner SAL	1,116
Umatilla	3,199
Union	2,062
Vale	1,558
Valsetz	600○
Veneta EUG	2,449
Vernonia	1,785
Waldport	1,274
Wallowa	847
Warren POR	500○
Warrenton	2,493
Wasco	415
Welches	500○
Wemme	500○
West Haven POR	3,200○
West Linn POR	12,956
Weston	719
Westport	650○
West Slope POR	6,100○
White City MEDF	500○
Willamina	1,749
Wilsonville POR	2,920
Winchester Bay	500○
Winston	3,359
Wolf Creek	450○
Woodburn SAL	11,196
Yachats	482
Yamhill	690
Yoncalla	805

COUNTIES

Baker	16,134
Benton	68,211
Clackamas	241,919
Clatsop	32,489
Columbia	35,646
Coos	64,047
Crook	13,091
Curry	16,992
Deschutes	62,142
Douglas	93,748
Gilliam	2,057
Grant	8,210
Harney	8,314
Hood River	15,835
Jackson	132,456
Jefferson	11,599
Josephine	58,820
Klamath	59,117
Lake	7,532
Lane	275,226
Lincoln	35,264
Linn	89,495
Malheur	26,896
Marion	204,692
Morrow	7,519
Multnomah	562,640
Polk	45,203
Sherman	2,172
Tillamook	21,164
Umatilla	58,861
Union	23,921
Wallowa	7,273
Wasco	21,732
Washington	245,401
Wheeler	1,513
Yamhill	55,332

PENNSYLVANIA

1980 Census 11,866,728

CITIES

Abington PHIL-	7,900○
Adamstown	1,119
Akron	3,471
Albion	1,818
Alburtis AL-B-E	1,428
Alden SCR-	800○
Aliquippa PGH	17,094
ALLENTOWN AL-B-E	103,758
Allison	1,040○
Allison Park PGH	5,600○
ALTOONA ALT	57,078
Ambler PHIL-	6,628
Ambridge PGH	9,575
Annville LEB	4,493○
Apollo	2,212
Archbald SCR-	6,295
Ardmore PHIL-	13,600○
Arnold PGH	6,853
Ashland	4,235
Ashley SCR-	3,512
Aspinwall PGH	3,284
Aston PHIL-	6,900○
Athens	3,622
Auburn	999
Austin	740
Avalon PGH	6,240
Avella	1,109○
Avis	1,718
Avoca SCR-	3,536
Avondale PHIL-	891
Avonmore	1,234
Baden PGH	5,318
Bairdford PGH	950○
Bala-Cynwyd PHIL-	8,600○
Baldwin PGH	24,598
Bally	1,051
Bangor	5,006
Barnesboro	2,741
Bath AL-B-E	1,953
Beaver PGH	5,441
Beaverdale	1,579○
Beaver Falls PGH	12,525
Beaver Meadows HAZ	1,078
Bedford	3,326
Bellefonte	6,300
Belle Vernon PGH	1,489
Belleville	1,817○
Bellevue PGH	10,128
Bellwood ALT	2,114
Bentleyville	2,525
Benton	981
Berlin	1,999
Bernville	798
Berwick	12,189
Berwyn PHIL-	9,300○
Bessemer	1,293
Bethel Park PGH	34,755
Bethlehem AL-B-E	70,419
Biglerville	991
Big Run	822
Birdsboro	3,481
Black Lick	1,074○
Blairsville	4,166
Blakely SCR-	7,438
Blandburg	775○
Blawnox PGH	1,653
Bloomsburg	11,717
Blossburg	1,757
Blue Ridge Summit	800○
Bobtown	1,055○
Boiling Springs	1,521○
Bolivar	706
Boothwyn PHIL-	7,100○
Boswell	1,480
Boyertown	3,979
Brackenridge PGH	4,297
Braddock PGH	5,634
Bradenville	1,200○
Bradford	11,211
Brentwood PGH	11,907
Briarcliff PHIL-	9,300○
Bridgeville PGH	6,154
Bristol PHIL-	10,867
Brookhaven PHIL-	7,912
Brookville	4,568
Broomall PHIL-	23,642○
Brownsville	4,043
Bryn Mawr PHIL-	9,500○
Burgettstown	1,867
Burnham	2,457
BUTLER BUTL	17,026
Cadogan	459○
Cairnbrook	800○
California	5,703
Cambridge Springs	2,102
Camp Hill HRBG	8,422
Canadensis	800○
Canonsburg PGH	10,459
Canton	1,959
Carbondale	11,255
Carlisle	18,314
Carmichaels	630
Carnegie PGH	10,099
Carnot PGH	5,400○
Castanea	1,204○
Castle Shannon PGH	10,164
Catasauqua AL-B-E	7,944
Catawissa	1,568
Cecil	900○
Cementon AL-B-E	1,200○
Centerville	4,207
Central City	1,496
Centre Hall	1,233
Chambersburg	16,174
Charleroi PGH	5,717
Cheltenham PHIL-	7,700○
Chester PHIL-	45,794
Chester Township PHIL-	5,687○
Cheswick PGH	2,336
Chicora	1,192
Christiana	1,183
Clairton PGH	12,188
Clarendon	776
Claridge PGH	600○
Clarion	6,664
Clarks Summit SCR-	5,272
Claysburg	1,516○
Claysville WASH	1,029
Clearfield	7,580
Cleona LEB	2,003
Clifton Heights PHIL-	7,320
Clymer	1,761
Coaldale	2,762
Coalport	739
COATESVILLE COAT	10,698
Cochranton	1,240

○ Rand McNally estimate (not reported in census).
▲ Population of entire township or "town", including rural area.
● Independent city. Population not included in county total.

Collegeville PHIL- 3,406
Collingdale PHIL- 9,539
Colonial Park HRBG 10,000 ○
Columbia 10,466
Colver 1,175 ○
Conemaugh JNST 2,128
Confluence 968
Conneautville 971
Connellsville 10,319
Conshohocken PHIL- 8,475
Conway PGH 2,747
Coopersburg AL-B-E 2,595
Coplay AL-B-E 3,130
Coral 700 ○
Coraopolis PGH 7,308
Cornwall LEB 2,653
Cornwells Heights PHIL- 8,700 ○
Corry 7,149
Coudersport 2,791
Crabtree 1,021 ○
Crafton PGH 7,623
Creighton PGH 1,658 ○
Cresson 2,184
Cressona PTSVL 1,810
Croydon PHIL- 9,800 ○
Crucible 800 ○
Curtisville PGH 1,337 ○
Curwensville 3,116
Dagus Mines 425 ○
Dallas SCR- 2,679
Dallastown YORK 3,949
Dalton SCR- 1,383
Danville 5,239
Darby PHIL- 11,513
Dauphin HRBG 901
Dawson 661
Dayton 648
Delta 692
Denver 2,018
Derry 3,072
Devon PHIL- 6,700 ○
Dickson City SCR- 6,699
Dillsburg HRBG 1,733
Distant 575 ○
Dixonville 900 ○
Donaldson 465 ○
Donora PGH 7,524
Dormont PGH 11,275
Dover YORK 1,910
Downingtown COAT 7,650
Doylestown PHIL- 8,717
Drexel Hill PHIL- 29,600 ○
Drifton HAZ 600 ○
Du Bois 9,290
Duboistown WMSPT 1,218
Duke Center 900 ○
Dunbar 1,369
Duncannon HRBG 1,645
Duncansville ALT 1,355
Dunlo JNST 950 ○
Dunmore SCR- 16,781
Dupont SCR- 3,460
Duquesne PGH 10,094
Duryea SCR- 5,415
Dushore 692
East Bangor 955
East Berlin 1,054
East Brady 1,153
East Greenville 2,456
East Norriton PHIL- 12,711 ○
Easton AL-B-E 26,027
East Petersburg LANC 3,600
East Pittsburgh PGH 2,493
East Stroudsburg 8,039
East Washington WASH 2,241
Ebensburg 4,096
Economy PGH 9,538
Eddystone PGH 2,555
Edenborn 500 ○
Edgewood PGH 4,382
Edgeworth PGH 1,738
Edinboro 6,324
Edwardsville SCR- 5,729
Eldred 965
Elizabethtown HRBG 8,233
Elizabethville 1,531
Elkins Park PHIL- 14,000 ○
Elkland 1,974
Ellport 1,290
Ellsworth 1,228
Ellwood City 9,998
Elmhurst 953 ○
Elmora 950 ○
Elrama 800 ○
Elysburg 1,337 ○
Emmaus AL-B-E 11,001
Emporium 2,837
Emsworth PGH 3,074
Enola HRBG 3,600 ○
Ephrata 11,095
Erdenheim PHIL- 3,300 ○
ERIE ERIE 119,123
Espy 1,652 ○
Etna PGH 4,534
Evans City BUTL 2,299
Everett 1,828
Everson 1,032
Exeter SCR- 5,493
Export PGH 1,143
Factoryville SCR- 924
Fairchance UNTN 2,106
Fairless Hills PHIL- 12,500 ○
Fairoaks PGH 1,854 ○
Fairview ERIE 1,855
Falls Creek 1,208
Farrell SHAR 8,645
Fayetteville 2,449 ○
Feasterville PHIL- 6,900 ○
Ferndale JNST 2,204
Fleetwood 3,422
Flemington 1,416
Flourtown PHIL- 5,200 ○
Folcroft PHIL- 8,231
Folsom PHIL- 7,600 ○
Ford City 3,923
Forest City 1,924
Forest Hills PGH 8,198
Fort Washington PHIL- 4,500 ○
Forty Fort SCR- 5,590

Fountain Hill AL-B-E 4,805
Fox Chapel PGH 5,049
Frackville 5,308
Franklin 8,146
Franklin Park PGH 6,135
Fredericktown 1,067 ○
Freedom PGH 2,272
Freeland HAZ 4,285
Freemansburg AL-B-E 1,879
Freeport PGH 2,381
Galeton 1,462
Gallitzin ALT 2,315
Gap 1,022 ○
Garrett 563
Geistown JNST 3,304
Gettysburg 7,194
Girard ERIE 2,615
Girardville 2,268
Glassport PGH 6,242
Glen Lyon 3,408 ○
Glenolden PHIL- 7,633
Glen Rock 1,662
Glenshaw PGH 14,000 ○
Glenside PHIL- 17,400 ○
Grampian 464
Grassflat 750 ○
Great Bend BING 740
Greencastle 3,679
Greensburg PGH 17,558
Green Tree PGH 5,722
Greenville 7,730
Grove City 8,162
Halifax 909
Hallstead BING 1,280
Hamburg 4,011
HANOVER HANV 14,890
Harmony 1,334
HARRISBURG HRBG 53,264
Harrisville 1,033
Hastings 1,574
Hatboro PHIL- 7,579
Hatfield PHIL- 2,533
Haverford PHIL- 5,800 ○
Havertown PHIL- 36,000 ○
Hawk Run 750 ○
Hawley 1,181
Hawthorn 547
HAZLETON HAZ 27,318
Hegins 900 ○
Heilwood 700 ○
Hellam YORK 1,428
Hellertown AL-B-E 6,025
Herminie PGH 1,100 ○
Hermitage SHAR 16,365 ○
Herndon 483
Hershey HRBG 9,000 ○
High Spire HRBG 2,959
Hillsville 915 ○
Hollidaysburg ALT 5,892
Homer City 2,248
Homestead PGH 5,092
Honesdale 5,128
Honey Brook COAT 1,164
Hooversville JNST 863
Hopwood UNTN 2,190 ○
Horsham PHIL- 6,000 ○
Houston PGH 1,568
Houtzdale 1,222
Howard 838
Hughesville 2,174
Hummels Wharf 750 ○
Huntingdon 7,042
Huntingdon Valley PHIL- 10,400 ○
Hyndman 1,106
Imperial PGH 2,385 ○
Indiana 16,051
Ingram PGH 4,346
Irvona 644
Irwin PGH 4,995
Isabella 700 ○
James City 450 ○
Jamestown 854
Jeannette PGH 13,106
Jefferson PGH 8,643
Jenkintown PHIL- 4,942
Jenners 800 ○
Jermyn SCR- 2,411
Jerome JNST 1,158 ○
Jersey Shore WMSPT 4,631
Jessup SCR- 4,974
Jim Thorpe 5,263
Johnsonburg 3,938
JOHNSTOWN JNST 35,496
Jonestown LEB 814
Juniata Terrace 631
Kane 4,916
Kenmawr PGH 5,100 ○
Kennett Square PHIL- 4,715
Kersey 600 ○
King of Prussia PHIL- 18,200 ○
Kingston SCR- 15,681
Kittanning 5,432
Knox 1,364
Knoxville 650
Koppel PGH 1,146
Kulpmont 3,675
Kutztown 4,040
Lafayette Hill PHIL- 6,600 ○
Lake City ERIE 2,384
Lakemont ALT 1,800 ○
LANCASTER LANC 54,725
Lanesboro BING 465
Langeloth 950 ○
Langhorne PHIL- 1,697
Lansdale PHIL- 16,526
Lansdowne PHIL- 11,891
Lansford 4,466
Larksville SCR- 4,410
Latrobe 10,799
Lattimer Mines 650 ○
Laureldale READ 4,047
Laurel Run SCR- 725
Lawrence PGH 970 ○
LEBANON LEB 25,711
Leechburg 2,682
Leetsdale PGH 1,604
Lehighton AL-B-E 5,826
Levittown PHIL- 78,600 ○
Lewisburg 5,407

Lewis Run 677
Lewistown 9,830
Ligonier 1,917
Lilly 1,462
Linesville 1,198
Lititz LANC 7,590
Littlestown HANV 2,870
Liverpool 809
Lock Haven 9,617
Loretto 1,395
Lower Burrell PGH 13,200
Lucernemines 1,380 ○
Ludlow 800 ○
Luzerne SCR- 3,703
Lykens 2,181
Lyndora BUTL 1,900 ○
McAdoo HAZ 2,940
McCandless PGH 26,250
McClure 1,024
McConnellsburg 1,178
McKeesport PGH 31,012
McKees Rocks PGH 8,742
McSherrystown 2,764
Macungie AL-B-E 1,899
Madera 900 ○
Mahaffey 513
Mahanoy City 6,167
Manchester YORK 2,027
Manheim 5,015
Mansfield 3,322
Mapleton Depot 591
Marcus Hook PHIL- 2,638
Marienville 900 ○
Marietta 2,740
Mars PGH 1,803
Martinsburg 2,231
Marysville HRBG 2,452
Masontown 4,909
Matamoras 2,111
Mather 860 ○
Mayfield SCR- 1,812
Meadow Lands PGH 1,200 ○
Meadville 15,544
Mechanicsburg HRBG 9,487
Media PHIL- 6,119
Mercer 2,532
Mercersburg 1,617
Merion Station PHIL- 7,400 ○
Meyersdale 2,581
Middleburg 1,357
Middletown HRBG 10,122
Midland E.LIV- 4,310
Midway PGH 1,187
Mifflin 648
Mifflinburg 3,151
Mifflintown 783
Mifflinville 1,074 ○
Mildred 800 ○
Milesburg 1,309
Milford 1,143
Millcreek Township ERIE 44,303 ○
Millersburg 2,770
Millerstown 550
Millersville LANC 7,668
Mill Hall 1,744
Millheim 800
Millsboro 900 ○
Millvale PGH 4,754
Millville 975
Milroy 1,575 ○
Milton 6,730
Minersville PTSVL 5,635
Mocanaqua 990 ○
Mohnton READ 2,156
Monaca PGH 7,661
Monessen PGH 11,928
Monongahela PGH 5,950
Monroeville PGH 30,977
Mont Alto 1,197
Mont Clare PHIL- 1,274 ○
Montgomery 1,653
Montoursville WMSPT 5,403
Montrose 1,980
Moon Run PGH 700 ○
Moosic SCR- 6,068
Morrisdale 600 ○
Morris Run 425 ○
Morrisville PHIL- 9,845
Moscow SCR- 1,536
Mount Carmel 8,190
Mount Holly Springs 2,068
Mount Jewett 1,053
Mount Joy 5,680
Mount Lebanon PGH 34,414 ○
Mount Pleasant 5,354
Mount Pocono 1,237
Mount Union 3,101
Mount Wolf YORK 1,517
Muncy 2,700
Munhall PGH 14,532
Murrysville PGH 16,036
Muse PGH 1,358 ○
Myerstown LEB 3,131
Nanticoke SCR- 13,044
Nanty Glo 3,936
Narberth PHIL- 4,496
Natrona Heights PGH 13,252 ○
Nazareth AL-B-E 5,443
Neffsville LANC 1,300 ○
Nemacolin 1,273 ○
Nescopeck 1,768
Nesquehoning 3,346
New Bethlehem 1,441
New Bloomfield 1,109
New Brighton PGH 7,364
NEW CASTLE NWCS 33,621
New Cumberland HRBG 8,051
New Florence 855
New Freedom 2,205
New Holland 4,147
New Hope 1,473
New Kensington PGH 17,660
Newmanstown 1,532 ○
New Milford 1,040
New Oxford HANV 1,921
New Philadelphia 1,341
Newport 1,600
Newtown Square PHIL- 11,775 ○
Newville 1,370

New Wilmington 2,774
Nicholson 945
Norristown PHIL- 34,684
Northampton AL-B-E 8,240
North Apollo 1,487
North Bend 700 ○
North Braddock PGH 8,711
North East ERIE 4,568
Northumberland 3,636
North Versailles PGH 13,294 ○
North Wales PHIL- 3,391
North Warren 1,360 ○
North York YORK 1,755
Norwood PHIL- 6,647
Noxen 800 ○
Nuremberg 800 ○
Oakdale PGH 1,955
Oakland BING 734
Oakmont PGH 7,039
Ohioville E.LIV- 4,217
Oil City 13,881
Old Forge SCR- 9,304
Oliver UNTN 1,500 ○
Olyphant SCR- 5,204
Oreland PHIL- 9,000 ○
Orwigsburg PTSVL 2,700
Osceola Mills 1,466
Oxford 3,633
Palmerton AL-B-E 5,455
Palmyra HRBG 7,228
Paoli PHIL- 6,100 ○
Parker 808
Parkesburg COAT 2,578
Patton 2,441
Pen Argyl 3,388
Penbrook HRBG 3,006
Penn Hills PGH 57,632 ○
Pennsburg 2,339
Penn Valley PHIL- 6,100 ○
Perkasie PHIL- 5,241
Perrysville PGH 5,300 ○
PHILADELPHIA PHIL- 1,688,210
Philipsburg 3,464
Phoenixville PHIL- 14,165
Pilgrim Gardens PHIL- 8,400 ○
Pine Grove 2,244
Pitcairn PGH 4,175
PITTSBURGH PGH 423,938
Pittston SCR- 9,930
Plains SCR- 6,606 ○
Pleasant Gap 1,773 ○
Pleasant Hills PGH 9,676
Pleasantville 1,099
Plum PGH 25,390
Plymouth SCR- 7,605
Plymouth Meeting PHIL- 6,000 ○
Plymouth Valley PHIL- 8,200 ○
Point Marion 1,642
Polk 1,884
Portage 3,510
Port Allegany 2,593
Port Royal 835
Port Vue PGH 5,316
POTTSTOWN PTSTN 22,729
POTTSVILLE PTSVL 18,195
Prospect Park PHIL- 6,593
Punxsutawney 7,479
Quakertown 8,867
Quarryville 1,558
Rankin PGH 2,892
READING READ 78,686
Reamstown 1,050 ○
Red Lion YORK 5,824
Reedsville 950 ○
Renovo 1,812
Republic 1,500 ○
Revloc 800 ○
Reynoldsville 3,016
Ridgway 5,604
Ridley Park PHIL- 7,889
Rimersburg 1,096
Roaring Spring 2,962
Robertsdale 550 ○
Robinson 660 ○
Rochester PGH 4,759
Rockledge PHIL- 2,538
Rockwood 1,058
Roscoe PGH 1,123
Roseto 1,484
Roslyn PHIL- 13,400 ○
Rossiter 750 ○
Rothsville LANC 1,318 ○
Roulette 1,100 ○
Rouseville 734
Royersford PHIL- 4,243
Russell 800 ○
Saegertown 942
Sagamore 850 ○
St. Clair PTSVL 4,037
St. Marys 6,417
Salisbury 817
Saltsburg 964
Sandy Lake 779
Saxton 814
Sayre 6,951
Scalp Level 1,186
Schaefferstown 800 ○
Schuylkill Haven PTSVL 5,977
Scottdale 5,833
Scott Township PGH 20,413 ○
SCRANTON SCR- 88,117
Selinsgrove 5,227
Sellersville PHIL- 3,143
Sewickley PGH 4,778
Shamokin 10,357
Shamokin Dam 1,622
SHARON SHAR 19,057
Sharon Hill PHIL- 6,221
Sharpsburg PGH 4,351
Sharpsville SHAR 5,375
Sheffield 1,564 ○
Shenandoah 7,589
Sheppton 650 ○
Shickshinny 1,192
Shillington READ 5,601
Shinglehouse 1,310
Shippensburg 5,261
Shoemakersville 1,391
Shrewsbury 2,688

Simpson 2,200 ○
Slatington AL-B-E 4,277
Slickville PGH 1,066 ○
Sligo 798
Slippery Rock 3,047
Slovan 900 ○
Smethport 1,797
Smithfield 1,084
Somerset 6,474
Souderton PHIL- 6,657
Southampton PHIL- 9,500 ○
South Connellsville 2,296
South Fork JNST 1,401
South Renovo 663
South Waverly 1,176
South Williamsport WMSPT 6,581
Spangler 2,399
Spring City PHIL- 3,389
Springdale PGH 4,418
Springfield PHIL- 25,326 ○
Spring Garden Township YORK 11,127 ○
Spring Grove YORK 1,832
STATE COLLEGE STCOL 36,130
Steelton HRBG 6,484
Stewartstown 1,072
Stockertown AL-B-E 661
Stoneboro 1,177
Stowe PTSTN 4,038 ○
Stowe Township PGH 10,119 ○
Strabane PGH 1,900 ○
Strasburg LANC 1,999
Strattanville 555
Stroudsburg 5,148
Sugarcreek 5,954
Sugar Notch SCR- 1,191
Summerville 830
Summit Hill 3,418
Sunbury 12,292
Susquehanna BING 1,994
Swarthmore PHIL- 5,950
Swissvale PGH 11,345
Swoyerville SCR- 5,795
Sykesville 1,537
Tamaqua 8,843
Tarentum PGH 6,419
Taylor SCR- 7,246
Telford PHIL- 3,507
Temple READ 1,486
Templeton 700 ○
Terre Hill 1,217
Throop SCR- 4,166
Tidioute 844
Titusville 6,884
Tobyhanna 700 ○
Topton AL-B-E 1,818
Towanda 3,526
Tower City 1,667
Trafford PGH 3,662
Tremont 1,796
Tresckow HAZ 1,146 ○
Trevorton 2,196 ○
Trevose PHIL- 7,000 ○
Troy 1,381
Tunkhannock 2,144
Turtle Creek PGH 6,959
Twin Rocks 700 ○
Tyrone 6,346
Union City 3,623
UNIONTOWN UNTN 14,510
United PGH 950 ○
Upper Darby PHIL- 50,200 ○
Upper St. Clair PGH 19,023 ○
Valley Forge 950 ○
Valley View 1,585 ○
Vanderbilt 689
Vandergrift 6,823
Verona PGH 3,179
Villanova PHIL- 6,600 ○
Vintondale 697
Walnutport AL-B-E 2,007
Wampum PGH 851
Wanamie SCR- 600 ○
Warminster PHIL- 35,543 ○
Warren 12,146
Warrendale PGH 800 ○
WASHINGTON WASH 18,363
Waterford ERIE 1,568
Watsontown 2,366
Waymart 1,248
Wayne PHIL- 8,900 ○
Waynesboro 9,726
Waynesburg 4,482
Weatherly 2,891
Webster PGH 800 ○
Wellsboro 3,805
Wesleyville ERIE 3,998
Westbrook Park PHIL- 5,700 ○
West Chester PHIL- 17,435
West Decatur 600 ○
West Fairview HRBG 1,426
Westfield 1,268
West Grove PHIL- 1,820
West Hazleton HAZ 4,871
West Lawn READ 1,686
West Leisenring 700 ○
West Middlesex SHAR 1,064
West Mifflin PGH 26,279
West Milton 775 ○
Westmont JNST 6,113
West Newton PGH 3,387
West Norriton PHIL- 14,034 ○
West Pittsburg 950 ○
West Pittston SCR- 5,980
West Reading READ 4,507
West View PGH 7,648
West Wyoming SCR- 3,288
West York YORK 4,526
Whitehall PGH 15,206
Whitehall AL-B-E 7,908 ○
White Haven 1,217
White Oak PGH 9,480
Whitney 500 ○
Wiconisco 1,236 ○
Wilcox 900 ○
Wilkes-Barre SCR- 51,551
Wilkinsburg PGH 23,669
Williamsburg 1,400
WILLIAMSPORT WMSPT 33,401
Williamstown 1,664

○ Rand McNally estimate (not reported in census).
▲ Population of entire township or "town", including rural area.
● Independent city. Population not included in county total.

Willow Grove PHIL- 21,300
Wilmerding PGH 2,421
Wilson AL-B-E 7,564
Winburne 650○
Windber JNST 5,585
Windgap 2,651
Windsor YORK 1,205
Womelsdorf 1,827
Wood 500○
Woodland 600○
Woodlyn PHIL- 6,000○
Worthington 760
Wrightsville 2,365
Wyalusing 716
Wyncote PHIL- 5,300○
Wyndmoor PHIL- 5,800○
Wynnewood PHIL- 7,700○
Wyoming SCR- 3,655
Wyomissing READ. 6,551
Yardley PHIL- 2,533
Yatesboro 700○
Yeadon PHIL- 11,727
Yeagertown 1,363○
YORK YORK 44,619
York Haven HRBG 746
Youngsville 2,006
Youngwood PGH 3,749
Zelienople 3,502

COUNTIES

Adams 68,292
Allegheny 1,450,085
Armstrong 77,768
Beaver 204,441
Bedford 46,784
Berks 312,509
Blair 136,621
Bradford 62,919
Bucks 479,211
Butler 147,912
Cambria 183,263
Cameron 6,674
Carbon 53,285
Centre 112,760
Chester 316,660
Clarion 43,362
Clearfield 83,578
Clinton 38,971
Columbia 61,967
Crawford 88,869
Cumberland 178,037
Dauphin 232,317
Delaware 555,007
Elk 38,338
Erie 279,780
Fayette 160,395
Forest 5,072
Franklin 113,629
Fulton 12,842
Greene 40,355
Huntingdon 42,253
Indiana 92,281
Jefferson 48,303
Juniata 19,188
Lackawanna 227,908
Lancaster 362,346
Lawrence 107,150
Lebanon 109,829
Lehigh 273,582
Luzerne 343,079
Lycoming 118,416
McKean 50,635
Mercer 128,299
Mifflin 46,908
Monroe 69,409
Montgomery 643,621
Montour 16,675
Northampton 225,418
Northumberland 100,381
Perry 35,718
Philadelphia 1,688,210
Pike 18,271
Potter 17,726
Schuylkill 160,630
Snyder 33,584
Somerset 81,243
Sullivan 6,349
Susquehanna 37,876
Tioga 40,973
Union 32,870
Venango 64,444
Warren 47,449
Washington 217,074
Wayne 35,237
Westmoreland 392,294
Wyoming 26,433
York 312,963

RHODE ISLAND
1980 Census 947,154

CITIES

Albion PROV- 1,200○
Allenton PROV- 600○
Anthony PROV- 4,500○
Arnold Mills PROV- 600○
Ashaway N.LON- 1,559○
Ashton PROV- 875○
Barrington PROV- 16,174▲ 13,500○
Berkeley PROV- 930○
Block Island 620
Bradford N.LON- 1,333○
Bristol PROV- 20,128
Carolina 500○
Central Falls PROV- 16,995
Charlestown 4,800▲ 1,200○
Chepachet PROV- 900○
Coventry PROV- 27,065▲ 8,000○
Cranston PROV- 71,992
Cumberland Hill PROV- 5,300○
Davisville PROV- 550○
Diamond Hill PROV- 1,150○
East Greenwich PROV- 10,211
East Providence PROV- 50,980
Esmond PROV- 3,500○

Forestdale 450○
Glendale PROV- 600○
Greenville PROV- 5,300○
Harmony PROV- 800○
Harris PROV- 1,000○
Harrisville PROV- 1,053○
Hope 490○
Hope Valley 1,326○
Island Park NWPT 1,000○
Jamestown PROV- 4,040
Johnston PROV- 24,907
Kingston 5,601○
La Fayette PROV- 680○
Lonsdale PROV- 4,100○
Manville PROV- 3,100○
Mapleville PROV- 900○
Middletown NWPT 17,216
Mount View PROV- 560○
Narragansett PROV- 12,088▲ 2,686○
NEWPORT NWPT 29,259
North Kingstown PROV- 21,938▲ 3,100○
North Providence PROV- 29,188
Oakland PROV- 500○
Pascoag PROV- 3,132○
Pawtucket PROV- 71,204
Peace Dale 3,000○
Plum Beach 435○
Portsmouth NWPT 14,257▲ 4,300○
PROVIDENCE PROV- 156,804
Quidnessett PROV- 3,300○
Quidnick PROV- 2,300○
Saylesville PROV- 3,200○
Shannock 600○
Slatersville PROV- 2,000○
South Hopkinton 500○
Spragueville 430○
Tiverton F.R. 13,526▲ 7,600○
Union Village PROV- 2,400○
Valley Falls PROV- 9,400○
Wakefield 3,300○
Warren PROV- 10,640
Warwick PROV- 87,123
Watch Hill N.LON- 500○
West Barrington PROV- 3,700○
Westerly N.LON- 18,580▲ 13,900○
West Kingston 700○
West Warwick PROV- 27,026
Woonsocket PROV- 45,914
Wyoming 600○
Yorktown Manor PROV- 2,500○

COUNTIES

Bristol 46,942
Kent 154,163
Newport 81,383
Providence 571,349
Washington 93,317

SOUTH CAROLINA
1980 Census 3,119,208

CITIES

Abbeville 5,863
Aiken 14,978
Alcolu 700○
Allendale 4,400
ANDERSON AND 27,313
Andrews 3,129
Arcadia SPRT 1,885○
Arlington SPRT 700○
Aynor 643
Baldwin Mills 1,042○
Bamberg 3,672
Barnwell 5,572
Batesburg 4,023
Bath AUG 1,576○
Beaufort 8,634
Beech Island AUG 700○
Belton 5,312
Belvedere AUG 3,500○
Bennettsville 8,774
Berea GRNV 7,186○
Bethune 481
Bishopville 3,429
Blacksburg 1,873
Blackville 2,840
Bluffton 541
Bowling Green 700○
Bowman 1,137
Branchville 1,769
Brandon GRNV 2,000○
Brentwood CHAS 2,000○
Brooklyn 2,000○
Brunson 590
Bucksport 800○
Buffalo 1,461○
Calhoun Falls 2,491
Camden 7,462
Cameron 536
Campobello 472
Carlisle 503
Cayce COL 11,701
Central 1,914
CHARLESTON CHAS 69,510
Cheraw 5,654
Chesnee 1,069
Chester 6,820
Chesterfield 1,432
City View GRNV 1,662
Clearwater AUG 4,000○
Clemson 8,118
Clifton SPRT 900○
Clinton 8,596
Clio 1,031
Clover 3,451
COLUMBIA COL 99,296
Conestee GRNV 540○
Converse SPRT 900○
Conway 10,240
Coward 428
Cowpens SPRT 2,023
Cross Hill 604
Darlington 7,989
Denmark 4,434

Denny Terrace COL 1,700○
Dentsville COL 3,700○
Dillon 7,042
Donalds 1,417○
Drayton SPRT 1,400○
Due West 1,366
Duncan SPRT 1,259
Easley GRNV 14,264
East Gaffney 3,750○
Eastover 899
Edgefield 2,713
Elgin 500○
Elloree 909
Enoree 700○
Estill 2,308
Eutawville 615
Fairfax 2,154
FLORENCE FLO 30,062
Folly Beach CHAS 1,478
Forest Acres COL 6,033
Fort Lawn 471
Fort Mill 4,162
Fountain Inn GRNV 4,226
Gaffney 13,453
Gantt GRNV 1,200○
Gaston COL 960
Georgetown 10,144
Glendale SPRT 800○
Gloverville 1,682○
Gluck AND 650○
Goose Creek CHAS 17,811
Graniteville 2,464○
Gray Court 988
Great Falls 2,601
Greeleyville 593
GREENVILLE GRNV 58,242
Greenwood 21,613
Greer GRNV 10,525
Hampton 3,143
Hanahan CHAS 13,224
Hardeeville 1,250○
Harleyville 606
Hartsville 7,631
Heath Springs 979
Hemingway 853
Hemlock 1,524○
Hickory Grove 500○
Hilton Head Island 6,511○
Holly Hill 1,785
Hollywood CHAS 729
Honea Path 4,114
Hopkins COL 1,600○
Industrial RKHL 900○
Inman SPRT 1,554
Irmo COL 3,957
Isle of Palms CHAS 3,421
Iva 1,369
Jackson 1,771
James Island CHAS 21,600○
Jefferson 651
Jenkinsville 500○
Joanna 1,631○
Johnsonville 1,421
Johnston 2,624
Jonesville 1,188
Kershaw 1,993
Kingstree 4,147
Ladson CHAS 3,000○
La France AND 700○
Lake City 5,636
Lake View 939
Lamar 1,333
Lancaster 9,603
Lando 850○
Landrum 2,141
Lane 554
Langley AUG 1,400○
Latta 1,804
Laurel Bay 4,490○
Laurens 10,587
Leesville 2,296
Lexington COL 2,131
Liberty 3,167
Lincolnville CHAS 808
Loris 2,193
Lugoff 1,500○
Lyman SPRT 1,067
Lynchburg 534
McBee 774
McClellanville 436
McColl 2,677
McCormick 1,725
Manning 4,746
Marietta GRNV 1,000○
Marion 7,700
Mauldin GRNV 8,245
Mayesville SUMT 663
Midland Park CHAS 1,300○
Monarch 1,726○
Moncks Corner 3,699
Montmorenci 900○
Mount Pleasant CHAS 13,838
Mullins 6,068
Murrells Inlet 700○
Myers CHAS 950○
Myrtle Beach 18,758
Neeses 557
Newberry 9,866
New Ellenton 2,628
Newry 750○
Nichols 606
Ninety Six 2,249
Norris 903
North 1,304
North Augusta AUG 13,593
North Charleston CHAS 65,630
North Myrtle Beach 3,960
Norway 518
Olanta 699
Orangeburg 14,933
Pacolet 1,556
Pacolet Mills 686
Pageland 2,720
Pamplico 1,213
Parkersville 500○
Pawleys Island 700○
Pendleton AND 3,154
Pickens GRNV 3,199
Piedmont GRNV 2,242○

Pinewood 689
Port Royal 2,977
Prosperity 672
Ravenel CHAS 1,655
Reidville GRNV 460○
Ridgeland 1,143
Ridge Spring 969
Ridgeville 603
ROCK HILL RKHL 35,344
Roebuck SPRT 800○
St. Andrews CHAS 9,202○
St. Andrews COL 16,500○
St. George 2,134
St. Matthews 2,496
St. Stephen 1,316
Salley 584
Saluda 2,752
Saxon SPRT 1,100○
Scranton 861
Seneca 7,436
Shannontown SUMT 7,491○
Simpsonville GRNV 9,037
Six Mile 470
Slater GRNV 800○
Socastee 900○
Society Hill 848
South Congaree COL 2,113
SPARTANBURG SPRT 43,968
Springdale COL 2,985
Springfield 604
Startex SPRT 1,203○
Sullivans Island CHAS 1,867
Summerton 1,173
Summerville CHAS 6,368
SUMTER SUMT 24,890
Surfside Beach 2,522
Swansea 888
Taylors GRNV 6,831○
Timmonsville 2,112
Travelers Rest GRNV 3,017
Troy 705
Turbeville 549
Union 10,523
Valencia Heights COL 4,700○
Varnville 1,948
Vaucluse 500○
Wagener 903
Walhalla 3,977
Walterboro 6,036
Wando Woods CHAS 1,900○
Ware Shoals 2,370
Warrenville 1,059○
Wattsville 1,181
Waylyn CHAS 2,400○
Welcome GRNV 5,000○
Wellford SPRT 2,143
West Columbia COL 10,409
Westminster 3,114
West Pelzer 944
Whitmire 2,038
Whitney SPRT 1,100○
Williamston 4,310
Williston 3,173
Windy Hill FLO 1,671○
Winnsboro 2,919
Winnsboro Mills 2,312○
Woodfield COL 5,500○
Woodruff 5,171
Yemassee 1,048
York RKHL 6,412

COUNTIES

Abbeville 22,627
Aiken 105,625
Allendale 10,700
Anderson 133,235
Bamberg 18,118
Barnwell 19,868
Beaufort 65,364
Berkeley 94,727
Calhoun 12,206
Charleston 277,308
Cherokee 40,983
Chester 30,148
Chesterfield 38,161
Clarendon 27,464
Colleton 31,676
Darlington 62,717
Dillon 31,083
Dorchester 58,266
Edgefield 17,528
Fairfield 20,700
Florence 110,163
Georgetown 42,461
Greenville 287,913
Greenwood 57,847
Hampton 18,159
Horry 101,419
Jasper 14,504
Kershaw 39,015
Lancaster 53,361
Laurens 52,214
Lee 18,929
Lexington 140,353
McCormick 7,797
Marion 34,179
Marlboro 31,634
Newberry 31,111
Oconee 48,611
Orangeburg 82,276
Pickens 79,292
Richland 267,823
Saluda 16,150
Spartanburg 201,553
Sumter 88,243
Union 30,751
Williamsburg 38,226
York 106,720

SOUTH DAKOTA
1980 Census 690,178

CITIES

Aberdeen 25,956
Alcester 885

Alexandria 588
Arlington 991
Armour 819
Aurora 507
Avon 576
Baltic 679
Belle Fourche 4,692
Beresford 1,865
Big Stone City 672
Bison 457
Blunt 424
Bowdle 644
Box Elder RAP 3,186
Brandon SXFL 2,589
Bridgewater 653
Bristol 445
Britton 1,590
Brookings 14,951
Buffalo 453
Burke 859
Canistota 626
Canton 2,886
Castlewood 557
Centerville 892
Chamberlain 2,258
Clark 1,351
Clear Lake 1,310
Colman 501
Colton 757
Corsica 644
Crooks 594
Custer 1,830
Deadwood 2,035
De Smet 1,237
Dupree 562
Edgemont 1,468
Elk Point 1,661
Elkton 632
Estelline 719
Eureka 1,360
Faith 576
Faulkton 981
Flandreau 2,114
Fort Pierre 1,789
Freeman 1,462
Froehlich Addition SXFL 750○
Garretson 963
Gettysburg 1,623
Gregory 1,503
Groton 1,230
Harrisburg 558
Hartford 1,207
Hayward Addition SXFL 725○
Hecla 435
Herreid 595
Highmore 1,055
Hill City 535
Hot Springs 4,742
Hoven 615
Howard 1,169
Humboldt 487
Hurley 419
Huron 13,000
Ipswich 1,153
Irene 523
Jefferson 592
Kadoka 832
Kimball 752
Lake Andes 1,029
Lake Norden 417
Lake Preston 789
Lead 4,330
Lemmon 1,871
Lennox 1,827
Leola 645
McCook Lake SXCY 600○
McIntosh 418
McLaughlin 754
Madison 6,210
Marion 830
Martin 1,018
Menno 793
Milbank 4,120
Miller 1,931
Mission 748
Mitchell 13,916
Mobridge 4,174
Murdo 723
Newell 638
New Underwood 517
North Eagle Butte 1,351○
North Sioux City SXCY 1,992
Norton Acres SXFL 800○
Onida 851
Parker 999
Parkston 1,545
Philip 1,088
Pierre 11,973
Pine Ridge 2,768○
Plankinton 644
Platte 1,334
Presho 760
RAPID CITY RAP 46,492
Redfield 3,027
Rosebud 600○
Rosholt 446
St. Francis 766
Salem 1,486
Scotland 1,022
Selby 884
SIOUX FALLS SXFL 81,343
Sisseton 2,789
Spearfish 5,251
Springfield 1,377
Sturgis 5,184
Tabor 460
Tea 729
Timber Lake 660
Tripp 804
Tyndall 1,253
Valley Springs 801
Vermillion 9,582
Viborg 812
Volga 1,221
Wagner 1,453
Wall 542
Watertown 15,649
Waubay 675
Webster 2,417

○ Rand McNally estimate (not reported in census).
▲ Population of entire township or "town", including rural area.
● Independent city. Population not included in county total.

Webster Grove SXFL 540 ○
Wessington Springs 1,203
White 474
White Lake 414
White River 561
Whitewood 821
Wilmot 507
Winner 3,472
Wolsey 437
Woonsocket 799
Yankton 12,011

COUNTIES

Aurora 3,628
Beadle 19,195
Bennett 3,236
Bon Homme 8,059
Brookings 24,332
Brown 36,962
Brule 5,245
Buffalo 1,795
Butte 8,372
Campbell 2,243
Charles Mix 9,680
Clark 4,894
Clay 13,135
Codington 20,885
Corson 5,196
Custer 6,000
Davison 17,820
Day 8,133
Deuel 5,289
Dewey 5,366
Douglas 4,181
Edmunds 5,159
Fall River 8,439
Faulk 3,327
Grant 9,013
Gregory 6,015
Haakon 2,794
Hamlin 5,261
Hand 4,948
Hanson 3,415
Harding 1,700
Hughes 14,220
Hutchinson 9,350
Hyde 2,069
Jackson 3,437
Jerauld 2,929
Jones 1,463
Kingsbury 6,679
Lake 10,724
Lawrence 18,339
Lincoln 13,942
Lyman 3,864
McCook 6,444
McPherson 4,027
Marshall 5,404
Meade 20,717
Mellette 2,249
Miner 3,739
Minnehaha 109,435
Moody 6,692
Pennington 70,133
Perkins 4,700
Potter 3,674
Roberts 10,911
Sanborn 3,213
Shannon 11,323
Spink 9,201
Stanley 2,533
Sully 1,990
Todd 7,328
Tripp 7,268
Turner 9,255
Union 10,938
Walworth 7,011
Yankton 18,952
Ziebach 2,308

TENNESSEE

1980 Census 4,590,750

CITIES

Adams 600
Adamsville 1,453
Alamo 2,615
Alcoa KNOX- 6,870
Alexandria 689
Algood 2,406
Allardt 654
Altamont 679
Ardmore 835
Ashland City NASH 2,329
Athens 12,080
Atoka MEM 691
Atwood 1,143
Bartlett MEM 17,170
Baxter 1,411
Beersheba Springs 643
Bell Buckle 450
Bells 1,571
Bemis JAC 1,883 ○
Benton 1,115
Bethel Springs 873
Big Sandy 650
Blaine 1,147
Bloomingdale KNGSP 8,000 ○
Blountville KNGSP 900 ○
Bluff City BRIS- 1,121
Bolivar 6,597
Bradford 1,146
Brentwood NASH 9,431
Briceville KNOX- 800 ○
Brighton 976
BRISTOL BRIS- 23,986
Brownsville 9,307
Bruceton 1,579
Bulls Gap 821
Burns 777
Byrdstown 884
Calhoun 590
Camden 3,279
Campaign 500 ○
Carson Spring 600 ○
Carthage 2,672
Caryville 2,039
Cedar Bluff KNOX- 1,200 ○
Cedar Hill 420
Celina 1,580
Centerville 2,824
Chapel Hill 861
Charleston 756
Charlotte 788
CHATTANOOGA CHTN 169,565
Church Hill KNGSP 4,110
CLARKSVILLE CLRKV 54,777
Cleveland 26,415
Clifton 773
Clinton KNOX- 5,245
Coalmont 625
Collierville MEM 7,839
Collinwood 1,064
Colonial Heights KNGSP 3,300 ○
Columbia 25,767
Cookeville 20,350
Copperhill 418
Cornersville 722
Counce 600 ○
Covington 6,065
Cowan 1,790
Crab Orchard 1,065
Cross Plains 655
Crossville 6,394
Dandridge 1,383
Dayton 5,913
Decatur 1,069
Decaturville 1,004
Decherd 2,233
Dickson 7,040
Dover 1,197
Dresden 2,256
Ducktown 583
Dunlap 3,681
Dyer 2,419
Dyersburg 15,856
Eagleville 444
East Ridge CHTN 21,236
Elizabethton JNSC- 12,431
Elkton 540
Englewood 1,840
Erin 1,614
Erwin 4,739
Estill Springs 1,324
Ethridge 548
Etowah 3,758
Fairview NASH 3,648
Fall Branch KNGSP 850 ○
Fayetteville 7,559
Finley 800 ○
Franklin NASH 12,407
Friendship 763
Friendsville KNOX- 694
Gadsden 683
Gainesboro 1,119
Gallatin 17,191
Gallaway 804
Gates 729
Gatlinburg 3,210
Germantown MEM 20,459
Gibson 458
Gleason 1,335
Goodlettsville NASH 8,327
Gordonsville 893
Graysville 1,380
Greenback 546
Green Brier NASH 3,180
Greeneville 14,097
Greenfield 2,109
Grimsley 600 ○
Halls 2,444
Hampton JNSC- 1,000 ○
Harriman 8,303
Hartsville 2,674
Henderson 4,449
Hendersonville NASH 26,561
Henning 638
Hohenwald 3,922
Hollow Rock 955
Hornbeak 452
Humboldt 10,209
Huntingdon 3,962
Huntland 983
Huntsville 519
Iron City 482
Jacksboro 1,620
JACKSON JAC 49,131
Jamestown 2,364
Jasper 2,633
Jefferson City 5,612
Jellico 2,798
JOHNSON CITY JNSC- 39,753
Jonesboro JNSC- 2,829
Kenton 1,551
KINGSPORT KNGSP 32,027
Kingston KNOX- 4,441
Kingston Springs 1,017
KNOXVILLE KNOX- 183,139
Laager 550 ○
Lafayette 3,808
La Follette 8,176
Lake City KNOX- 2,335
Lake Tansi 600 ○
La Vergne NASH 5,495
Lawrenceburg 10,175
Lebanon 11,872
Lenoir City KNOX- 5,446
Lewisburg 8,760
Lexington 5,934
Linden 1,087
Livingston 3,372
Lobelville 993
Loretto 1,612
Loudon 3,940
Luttrell 962
Lynchburg 668
Lynn Garden KNGSP 7,000 ○
McEwen 1,352
McKenzie 5,405
McMinnville 10,683
Madisonville 2,884
Manchester 7,250
Martin 8,898
Maryville KNOX- 17,480
Mascot KNOX- 900 ○
Mason 471
Maury City 989
Maynardville 924
Medina 687
MEMPHIS MEM 646,356
Michie 530
Middleton 596
Milan 8,083
Milligan College JNSC- 1,200 ○
Millington MEM 20,236
Minor Hill 564
Monteagle 1,126
Monterey 2,610
Morgantown 600 ○
Morrison 587
Morrison City KNGSP 900 ○
Morristown 19,683
Moscow 499
Mosheim 1,539
Mountain City 2,125
Mount Juliet NASH 2,879
Mount Pleasant 3,375
Munford MEM 1,587
Murfreesboro 32,845
NASHVILLE NASH 455,651
Newbern 2,794
New Johnsonville 1,824
New Market 1,216
Newport 7,580
New Tazewell 1,677
Niota 765
Nolensville 500 ○
Norris KNOX- 1,374
Oakland 472
Oak Ridge KNOX- 27,662
Obion 1,282
Oliver Springs KNOX- 3,659
Oneida 3,029
Ooltewah CHTN 900 ○
Palmer 1,027
Paris 10,728
Parsons 2,422
Pegram NASH 1,081
Petersburg 681
Petros 850 ○
Philadelphia 507
Pigeon Forge 1,822
Pikeville 2,085
Pittman Center 488
Portland 4,030
Pulaski 7,184
Puryear 624
Ramer 429
Red Bank CHTN 13,297
Red Boiling Springs 1,173
Riceville 500 ○
Ridgely 1,932
Ripley 6,366
Roan Mountain 850 ○
Robbins 450 ○
Rockford KNOX- 567
Rockwood 5,767
Rogersville 4,368
Russellville 900 ○
Rutherford 1,378
Rutledge 1,058
St. Joseph 897
Sale Creek 900 ○
Saltillo 434
Samburg 465
Savannah 6,992
Scotts Hill 668
Selmer 3,979
Sevierville 4,566
Sewanee 1,900 ○
Sharon 1,134
Shelbyville 13,530
Sherwood 450 ○
Signal Mountain CHTN 5,818
Smithville 3,839
Smyrna NASH 8,839
Sneedville 1,110
Soddy-Daisy CHTN 8,388
Somerville 2,264
South Fulton 2,735
South Pittsburg 3,636
Sparta 4,864
Spencer 1,126
Spring City 1,951
Springfield 10,814
Spring Hill 989
Stanton 540
Summitville 600 ○
Sunbright 500 ○
Surgoinsville 1,536
Sweetwater 4,725
Tazewell 2,090
Tellico Plains 698
Tennessee Ridge 1,325
Tiptonville 2,438
Tracy City 1,356
Trenton 4,601
Trezevant 921
Trimble 722
Troy 1,093
Tullahoma 15,800
Unicoi 600 ○
Union City 10,436
Vonore 528
Wartburg 761
Wartrace 540
Watertown 1,300
Waverly 4,405
Waynesboro 2,109
Westmoreland 1,754
Westover 500 ○
White Bluff 2,055
White House 2,225
White Pine 1,900
Whiteville 1,270
Whitwell 1,783
Winchester 5,821
Woodbury 2,160

COUNTIES

Anderson 67,346
Bedford 27,916
Benton 14,901
Bledsoe 9,478
Blount 77,770
Bradley 67,547
Campbell 34,841
Cannon 10,234
Carroll 28,285
Carter 50,205
Cheatham 21,616
Chester 12,727
Claiborne 24,595
Clay 7,676
Cocke 28,792
Coffee 38,311
Crockett 14,941
Cumberland 28,676
Davidson 477,811
Decatur 10,857
De Kalb 13,589
Dickson 30,037
Dyer 34,663
Fayette 25,305
Fentress 14,826
Franklin 31,983
Gibson 49,467
Giles 24,625
Grainger 16,751
Greene 54,406
Grundy 13,787
Hamblen 49,300
Hamilton 287,740
Hancock 6,887
Hardeman 23,873
Hardin 22,280
Hawkins 43,751
Haywood 20,318
Henderson 21,390
Henry 28,656
Hickman 15,151
Houston 6,871
Humphreys 15,957
Jackson 9,398
Jefferson 31,284
Johnson 13,745
Knox 319,694
Lake 7,455
Lauderdale 24,555
Lawrence 34,110
Lewis 9,700
Lincoln 26,483
Loudon 28,553
McMinn 41,878
McNairy 22,525
Macon 15,700
Madison 74,546
Marion 24,416
Marshall 19,698
Maury 51,095
Meigs 7,431
Monroe 28,700
Montgomery 83,342
Moore 4,510
Morgan 16,604
Obion 32,781
Overton 17,575
Perry 6,111
Pickett 4,358
Polk 13,602
Putnam 47,601
Rhea 24,235
Roane 48,425
Robertson 37,021
Rutherford 84,058
Scott 19,259
Sequatchie 8,605
Sevier 41,418
Shelby 777,113
Smith 14,935
Stewart 8,665
Sullivan 143,968
Sumner 85,790
Tipton 32,747
Trousdale 6,137
Unicoi 16,362
Union 11,707
Van Buren 4,728
Warren 32,653
Washington 88,755
Wayne 13,946
Weakley 32,896
White 19,567
Williamson 58,108
Wilson 56,064

TEXAS

1980 Census 14,228,383

CITIES

Abernathy 2,904
ABILENE ABIL 98,315
Addison D-FW 5,553
Alamo MCAL 5,831
Alamo Heights SANT 6,252
Albany 2,450
Alice 20,961
Allen D-FW 8,314
Alpine 5,465
Alto 1,203
Alvarado 2,701
Alvin HOU 16,515
AMARILLO AMA 149,230
Anahuac 1,840
Andrews 11,061
Angleton FREP- 13,929
Anson 2,831
Anthony ELP 2,640
Aransas Pass CRPX 7,173
Archer City 1,862
Arlington D-FW 160,123
Arp 939
Asherton 1,574
Aspermont 1,357
Athens 10,197
Atlanta 6,272
AUSTIN AUS 345,496
Azle D-FW 5,822
Baird 1,696
Balch Springs D-FW 13,746
Ballinger 4,207
Bartlett 1,567
Bastrop 3,789
Bay City 17,837
Baytown HOU 56,923
BEAUMONT B-PA-O 118,102
Bedford D-FW 20,821
Beeville 14,574
Bellaire HOU 14,950
Bellmead WACO 7,569
Bellville 2,860
Belton TMPL 10,660
Benavides 1,978
Benbrook D-FW 13,579
Big Lake 3,404
Big Spring 24,804
Big Wells 939
Bishop 3,706
Bloomington 1,676 ○
Blossom 1,487
Boerne SANT 3,229
Boling 950 ○
Bonham 7,338
Borger 15,837
Bowie 5,610
Brackettville 1,676
Brady 5,969
Brazoria FREP- 3,025
Breckenridge 6,921
Bremond 1,025
Brenham 10,966
Bridge City B-PA-O 7,667
Bridgeport 3,737
Brookshire 2,175
Brownfield 10,387
BROWNSVILLE BRNS 84,997
Brownwood 19,203
BRYAN BRY 44,337
Burkburnett WIFL 10,668
Burleson D-FW 11,734
Burnet 3,410
Caldwell 2,953
Calvert 1,732
Cameron 5,721
Canadian 3,491
Canton 2,845
Canutillo ELP 1,588 ○
Canyon 10,724
Canyon Lake 6,000 ○
Carrizo Springs 6,886
Carrollton D-FW 40,591
Carthage 6,447
Castroville SANT 1,821
Cedar Hill D-FW 6,849
Celina 1,520
Center 5,827
Centerville 799
Channelview HOU 12,200 ○
Charlotte 1,443
Chico 890
Childress 5,817
Chillicothe 1,052
Cisco 4,517
Clarendon 2,220
Clarksville 4,917
Clear Lake City HOU 8,700 ○
Cleburne D-FW 19,218
Cleveland HOU 5,977
Clifton 3,063
Cloverleaf HOU 9,700 ○
Clute FREP- 9,577
Cockrell Hill D-FW 3,262
Coleman 5,960
College Station BRY 37,272
Colleyville D-FW 6,700
Colorado City 5,405
Columbus 3,923
Comanche 4,075
Comfort 900 ○
Commerce 8,136
Conroe HOU 18,034
Coolidge 810
Cooper 2,338
Copperas Cove KILL 19,469
CORPUS CHRISTI CRPX 231,999
Corrigan 1,770
Corsicana 21,712
Cotulla 3,912
Crandall 831
Crane 3,622
Crockett 7,405
Crosbyton 2,289
Cross Plains 1,240
Crowell 1,509
Crowley D-FW 5,852
Crystal City 8,334
Cuero 7,124
Daingerfield 3,030
Daisetta 1,177
Dalhart 6,854
DALLAS D-FW 904,078
Dawson 747
Dayton 4,908
Decatur 4,104
Deer Park HOU 22,648
De Kalb 2,217
De Leon 2,478
Del Rio 30,034
Denison SHRM- 23,884
Denton D-FW 48,063
Denver City 4,704
De Soto D-FW 15,538
Devine SANT 3,756
Diboll LUFK 5,227
Dickinson GLV- 7,505
Dilley 2,579
Dimmitt 5,019
Donna 9,952
Dublin 2,723
Dumas 12,194
Duncanville D-FW 27,781
Eagle Lake 3,921
Eagle Pass 21,407
Eastland 3,747
Edcouch 3,092
Eden 1,294
EDINBURG EDIN 24,075

○ Rand McNally estimate (not reported in census).
▲ Population of entire township or "town", including rural area.
● Independent city. Population not included in county total.

Edna 5,650
El Campo 10,462
Eldorado 2,061
Electra 3,755
Elgin 4,535
EL PASO ELP 425,259
Elsa 5,061
Encinal 704
Ennis 12,110
Euless D-FW 24,002
Everman D-FW 5,387
Fairfield 3,505
Falfurrias 6,103
Farmers Branch D-FW 24,863
Farmersville 2,360
Farwell 1,354
Ferris D-FW 2,228
Flatonia 1,070
Floresville 4,381
Floydada 4,193
Forest Hill D-FW 11,684
Forney D-FW 2,483
Fort Davis 850○
Fort Stockton 8,688
Fort Worth D-FW 385,141
Franklin 1,349
Frankston 1,255
Fredericksburg 6,412
FREEPORT FREP- 13,444
Freer 3,213
Friendswood HOU 10,719
Friona 3,809
Fritch 2,299
Gainesville 14,081
Galena Park HOU 9,879
GALVESTON GLV- 61,902
Garland D-FW 138,857
Gatesville 6,260
Georgetown 9,468
George West 2,627
Giddings 3,950
Gilmer 5,167
Gladewater LNGV 6,548
Glen Rose 2,075
Goldthwaite 1,783
Goliad 1,990
Gonzales 7,152
Gorman 1,258
Graham 9,055
Granbury 3,332
Grand Prairie D-FW 71,462
Grand Saline 2,709
Granger 1,236
Grapeland 1,634
Grapevine D-FW 11,801
Greenville 22,161
Groesbeck 3,373
Groves B-PA-O 17,090
Groveton 1,262
Grulla 1,442
Hale Center 2,297
Hallettsville 2,865
Hallsville LNGV 1,556
Haltom City D-FW 29,014
Hamilton 3,189
Hamlin 3,248
Harker Heights KILL 7,345
HARLINGEN HRL 43,543
Haskell 3,782
Hearne 5,418
Hebbronville 4,079○
Hemphill 1,353
Hempstead 3,456
Henderson 11,473
Henrietta 3,149
Hereford 15,853
Hewitt WACO 5,247
Hico 1,375
Highland Park D-FW 8,909
Highlands HOU 3,462○
Hillsboro 7,397
Hitchcock GLV- 6,655
Hondo 6,057
Honey Grove 1,973
HOUSTON HOU 1,594,086
Hubbard 1,676
Humble HOU 6,729
Huntington LUFK 1,672
Huntsville 23,936
Hurst D-FW 31,420
Idalou LUB 2,348
Ingleside CRPX 5,436
Iowa Park WIFL 6,184
Iraan 1,358
Irving D-FW 109,943
Italy 1,306
Itasca 1,600
Jacinto City HOU 8,953
Jacksboro 4,000
Jacksonville 12,264
Jasper 6,959
Jefferson 2,643
Johnson City 872
Jones Creek FREP- 2,634
Jourdanton 2,743
Junction 2,593
Karnes City 3,296
Katy 5,660
Kaufman 4,658
Keene D-FW 3,013
Keller D-FW 4,143
Kemp 1,035
Kenedy 4,356
Kennedale D-FW 2,594
Kerens 1,582
Kermit 8,015
Kerrville 15,276
Kilgore 10,968
KILLEEN KILL 46,296
Kingsville 28,808
Kirby SANT 6,385
Kirbyville 1,972
Klein HOU 8,000○
Knox City 1,546
Kountze 2,716
Kyle 2,093
Ladonia 761
La Feria HRL 3,495
La Grange 3,768

Lake Jackson FREP- 19,102
La Marque GLV- 15,372
Lamesa 11,790
Lampasas 6,165
Lancaster D-FW 14,807
La Porte HOU 14,062
LAREDO LAR 91,449
League City HOU 16,578
Leakey 468
Lefors 829
Leonard 1,421
Leon Valley SANT 8,951
Levelland 13,809
Lewisville D-FW 24,273
Liberty 7,945
Lindale 2,180
Linden 2,443
Littlefield 7,409
Little Mexico 600○
Live Oak SANT 8,183
Livingston 4,928
Llano 3,071
Lockhart 7,953
Lockney 2,334
Lometa 666
LONGVIEW LNGV 62,762
Loraine 929
Lott 865
LUBBOCK LUB 173,979
Lueders 420
LUFKIN LUFK 28,562
Luling 5,039
Lyford 1,618
Lytle SANT 1,920
Mabank 1,443
MCALLEN MCAL 67,042
McCamey 2,436
McGregor 4,513
McKinney D-FW 16,249
McLean 1,160
Madisonville 3,660
Malakoff 2,082
Mansfield D-FW 8,092
Marble Falls 3,252
Marfa 2,466
Marlin 7,099
Marshall 24,921
Mart 2,324
Mason 2,153
Matador 1,052
Mathis 5,667
Memphis 3,352
Menard 1,697
Mercedes 11,851
Meridian 1,330
Merkel 2,493
Mesquite D-FW 67,053
Mexia 7,094
MIDLAND MIDL 70,525
Midlothian D-FW 3,219
Miles 720
Mineola 4,346
Mineral Wells 14,468
Mission MCAL 22,589
Missouri City HOU 24,533
Monahans 8,397
Mont Belvieu HOU 1,730
Moody 1,385
Morton 2,674
Mount Pleasant 11,003
Mount Vernon 2,025
Muleshoe 4,842
Munday 1,738
Nacogdoches 27,149
Naples 1,908
Natalia SANT 1,264
Navasota 5,971
Nederland B-PA-O 16,855
Needville 1,417
New Boston 4,628
New Braunfels 22,402
Newcastle 688
Newton 1,620
Nixon 2,008
Nocona 2,992
North Richland Hills D-FW 30,592
Oakwood 606
Odem 2,363
ODESSA ODES 90,027
O'Donnell 1,200
Olmos Park SANT 2,069
Olney 4,060
Olton 2,235
Orange B-PA-O 23,628
Orange Grove 1,212
Overton 2,430
Ozona 2,864○
Paducah 2,216
Palacios 4,667
Palestine 15,948
Pampa 21,396
Panhandle 2,226
Paris 25,498
Pasadena HOU 112,560
Pearland HOU 13,248
Pearsall 7,383
Pecos 12,855
Perryton 7,991
Pharr MCAL 21,381
Phillips 2,515○
Pilot Point 2,211
Pineland 1,111
Pittsburg 4,245
Plainview 22,187
Plano D-FW 72,331
Pleasanton 6,346
Port Arthur B-PA-O 61,195
Port Isabel 3,769
Portland CRPX 12,023
Port Lavaca 10,911
Port Neches B-PA-O 13,944
Post 3,961
Poteet 3,086
Prairie View 3,993
Premont 2,984
Presidio 950○
Quanah 3,890
Queen City 1,748
Quitman 1,893

Ralls 2,422
Ranger 3,142
Raymondville 9,493
Refugio 3,898
Richardson D-FW 72,496
Richland Hills D-FW 7,977
Richmond HOU 9,692
Rio Grande City 5,676○
Rio Hondo 1,673
Rising Star 1,204
River Oaks D-FW 6,890
Robinson WACO 6,074
Robstown CRPX 12,100
Roby 814
Rockdale 5,611
Rockport 3,686
Rocksprings 1,317
Rockwall D-FW 5,939
Rogers 1,242
Roma 3,384
Roscoe 1,628
Rosebud 2,076
Rosenberg HOU 17,995
Rotan 2,284
Round Rock AUS 11,812
Rowlett D-FW 7,522
Royse City D-FW 1,566
Rule 1,015
Runge 1,244
Rusk 4,681
Sabinal 1,827
St. Jo 1,071
SAN ANGELO SANG 73,240
SAN ANTONIO SANT 785,410
San Augustine 2,930
San Benito HRL 17,988
Sanderson 1,229○
San Diego 5,225
Sanger 2,574
San Isidro 500○
San Juan MCAL 7,608
San Marcos 23,420
San Pedro CRPX 5,294○
San Saba 2,336
Santa Anna 1,535
Schertz SANT 7,262
Schulenburg 2,469
Seabrook HOU 4,670
Seagoville D-FW 7,304
Seagraves 2,596
Sealy 3,875
Seguin 17,854
Seminole 6,080
Seymour 3,657
Shallowater LUB 1,932
Shamrock 2,834
SHERMAN SHRM- 30,413
Shiner 2,213
Silsbee 7,684
Sinton 6,044
Slaton LUB 6,804
Smithville 3,470
Snyder 12,705
Somerville 1,814
Sonora 3,856
Sourlake 1,807
South Houston HOU 13,293
Southside Place HOU 1,366
Spearman 3,413
Spur 1,690
Stamford 4,542
Stanton 2,314
Stephenville 11,881
Sterling City 915
Stinnett 2,222
Stockdale 1,265
Stratford 1,917
Strawn 694
Sudan 1,091
Sugar Land HOU 8,826
Sulphur Springs 12,804
Sundown 1,511
Sunray 1,952
Sweeny 3,538
Sweetwater 12,242
Taft 3,686
Tahoka 3,262
Talco 751
Taylor 10,619
Teague 3,390
TEMPLE TMPL 42,483
Terrell D-FW 13,225
Terrell Hills SANT 4,644
TEXARKANA TEXR- 31,271
Texas City GLV- 41,403
The Colony 11,586
Thorndale 1,300
Thorntonville 717
Three Rivers 2,133
Throckmorton 1,174
Timpson 1,164
Trinidad 1,130
Trinity 2,452
Troup 1,911
Tuleta 450○
Tulia 5,033
Turkey 644
TYLER TYL 70,508
Universal City SANT 10,720
University Park D-FW 22,254
Uvalde 14,178
Valley Mills 1,236
Van 1,881
Van Alstyne 1,860
Van Horn 2,772
Vernon 12,695
VICTORIA VICT 50,695
Vidor B-PA-O 12,117
WACO WACO 101,261
Waelder 942
Wallis 1,138
Watauga D-FW 10,284
Waxahachie 14,624
Weatherford D-FW 12,049
Weimar 2,096
Wellington 3,043
Weslaco 19,331
West 2,485
West Columbia FREP- 4,109

West University Place HOU 12,010
Wharton 9,033
Wheeler 1,584
Whitesboro 3,197
White Settlement D-FW 13,508
Whitewright 1,760
Whitney 1,631
WICHITA FALLS WIFL 94,201
Willis 1,674
Windcrest SANT 5,332
Wink 1,182
Winnsboro 3,458
Winters 3,061
Wolfe City 1,594
Woodsboro 1,974
Woodville 2,821
Woodway WACO 7,091
Wortham 1,187
Yoakum 6,148
Yorktown 2,498
Zapata 2,102○

COUNTIES

Anderson 38,381
Andrews 13,323
Angelina 64,172
Aransas 14,260
Archer 7,266
Armstrong 1,994
Atascosa 25,055
Austin 17,726
Bailey 8,168
Bandera 7,084
Bastrop 24,726
Baylor 4,919
Bee 26,030
Bell 157,889
Bexar 988,800
Blanco 4,681
Borden 859
Bosque 13,401
Bowie 75,301
Brazoria 169,587
Brazos 93,588
Brewster 7,573
Briscoe 2,579
Brooks 8,428
Brown 33,057
Burleson 12,313
Burnet 17,803
Caldwell 23,637
Calhoun 19,574
Callahan 10,992
Cameron 209,680
Camp 9,275
Carson 6,672
Cass 29,430
Castro 10,556
Chambers 18,538
Cherokee 38,127
Childress 6,950
Clay 9,582
Cochran 4,825
Coke 3,196
Coleman 10,439
Collin 144,490
Collingsworth 4,648
Colorado 18,823
Comal 36,446
Comanche 12,617
Concho 2,915
Cooke 27,656
Coryell 56,767
Cottle 2,947
Crane 4,600
Crockett 4,608
Crosby 8,859
Culberson 3,315
Dallam 6,531
Dallas 1,556,549
Dawson 16,184
Deaf Smith 21,165
Delta 4,839
Denton 143,126
De Witt 18,903
Dickens 3,539
Dimmit 11,367
Donley 4,075
Duval 12,517
Eastland 19,480
Ector 115,374
Edwards 2,033
Ellis 59,743
El Paso 479,899
Erath 22,560
Falls 17,946
Fannin 24,285
Fayette 18,832
Fisher 5,891
Floyd 9,834
Foard 2,158
Fort Bend 130,846
Franklin 6,893
Freestone 14,830
Frio 13,785
Gaines 13,150
Galveston 195,940
Garza 5,336
Gillespie 13,532
Glasscock 1,304
Goliad 5,193
Gonzales 16,883
Gray 26,386
Grayson 89,796
Gregg 99,487
Grimes 13,580
Guadalupe 46,708
Hale 37,592
Hall 5,594
Hamilton 8,297
Hansford 6,209
Hardeman 6,368
Hardin 40,721
Harris 2,409,544
Harrison 52,265
Hartley 3,987
Haskell 7,725
Hays 40,594
Hemphill 5,304

Henderson 42,606
Hidalgo 283,229
Hill 25,024
Hockley 23,230
Hood 17,714
Hopkins 25,247
Houston 22,299
Howard 33,142
Hudspeth 2,728
Hunt 55,248
Hutchinson 26,304
Irion 1,386
Jack 7,408
Jackson 13,352
Jasper 30,781
Jeff Davis 1,647
Jefferson 250,938
Jim Hogg 5,168
Jim Wells 36,498
Johnson 67,649
Jones 17,268
Karnes 13,593
Kaufman 39,015
Kendall 10,635
Kenedy 543
Kent 1,145
Kerr 28,780
Kimble 4,063
King 425
Kinney 2,279
Kleberg 33,358
Knox 5,329
Lamar 42,156
Lamb 18,669
Lampasas 12,005
La Salle 5,514
Lavaca 19,004
Lee 10,952
Leon 9,594
Liberty 47,088
Limestone 20,224
Lipscomb 3,766
Live Oak 9,606
Llano 10,144
Loving 91
Lubbock 211,651
Lynn 8,605
McCulloch 8,735
McLennan 170,755
McMullen 789
Madison 10,649
Marion 10,360
Martin 4,684
Mason 3,683
Matagorda 37,828
Maverick 31,398
Medina 23,164
Menard 2,346
Midland 82,636
Milam 22,732
Mills 4,477
Mitchell 9,088
Montague 17,410
Montgomery 128,487
Moore 16,575
Morris 14,629
Motley 1,950
Nacogdoches 46,786
Navarro 35,323
Newton 13,254
Nolan 17,359
Nueces 268,215
Ochiltree 9,588
Oldham 2,283
Orange 83,838
Palo Pinto 24,062
Panola 20,724
Parker 44,609
Parmer 11,038
Pecos 14,618
Polk 24,407
Potter 98,637
Presidio 5,188
Rains 4,839
Randall 75,062
Reagan 4,135
Real 2,469
Red River 16,101
Reeves 15,801
Refugio 9,289
Roberts 1,187
Robertson 14,653
Rockwall 14,528
Runnels 11,872
Rusk 41,382
Sabine 8,702
San Augustine 8,785
San Jacinto 11,434
San Patricio 58,013
San Saba 5,693
Schleicher 2,820
Scurry 18,192
Shackelford 3,915
Shelby 23,084
Sherman 3,174
Smith 128,366
Somervell 4,154
Starr 27,266
Stephens 9,926
Sterling 1,206
Stonewall 2,406
Sutton 5,130
Swisher 9,723
Tarrant 860,880
Taylor 110,932
Terrell 1,595
Terry 14,581
Throckmorton 2,053
Titus 21,442
Tom Green 84,784
Travis 419,335
Trinity 9,450
Tyler 16,223
Upshur 28,595
Upton 4,619
Uvalde 22,441
Val Verde 35,910
Van Zandt 31,426
Victoria 68,807

○ Rand McNally estimate (not reported in census).
▲ Population of entire township or "town", including rural area.
● Independent city. Population not included in county total.

Walker 41,789
Waller 19,798
Ward 13,976
Washington 21,998
Webb 99,258
Wharton 40,242
Wheeler 7,137
Wichita 121,082
Wilbarger 15,931
Willacy 17,495
Williamson 76,521
Wilson 16,756
Winkler 9,944
Wise 26,575
Wood 24,697
Yoakum 8,299
Young 19,001
Zapata 6,628
Zavala 11,666

UTAH

1980 Census 1,461,037

CITIES

Alpine PRVO 2,649
American Fork PRVO 12,417
Annabella 463
Aurora 874
Ballard 558
Bear River City 540
Beaver 1,792
Belmont Heights 600○
Bennion 800○
Blanding 3,118
Bluffdale 1,300
Bountiful S.L.C. 32,877
Brigham City 15,596
Carbonville 500○
Castle Dale 1,910
Cedar City 10,972
Centerfield 653
Centerville S.L.C. 8,069
Circleville 445
Clarkston 562
Clearfield OGD 17,982
Cleveland 522
Clinton OGD 5,777
Coalville 1,031
Copperton 850○
Corinne 512
Cottonwood S.L.C. 30,600○
Cottonwood Heights S.L.C. 12,000○
Delta 1,930
Draper S.L.C. 5,530
Duchesne 1,677
East Carbon 1,942
East Layton OGD 3,531
Eastwood Hills S.L.C. 1,200○
Elsinore 612
Elwood 481
Enoch 678
Enterprise 905
Ephraim 2,810
Escalante 652
Eureka 670
Fairview 916
Farmington S.L.C. 4,691
Ferron 1,718
Fillmore 2,083
Fountain Green 578
Fruit Heights OGD 2,728
Garland 1,405
Genola 630
Glenwood 447
Goshen 582
Granger S.L.C. 30,700○
Granite 650○
Granite Park S.L.C. 9,500○
Grantsville 4,419
Green River 1,048
Gunnison 1,255
Harrisville OGD 1,371
Heber City 4,362
Helper 2,724
Henefer 547
Herriman 600○
Highland 2,435
Highlands 500○
Hildale 1,009
Hinckley 464
Holladay S.L.C. 28,700○
Honeyville 915
Hunter S.L.C. 12,000○
Huntington 2,316
Huntsville 577
Hurricane 2,361
Hyde Park LOGN 1,495
Hyrum LOGN 3,952
Ivins 600
Kamas 1,064
Kanab 2,148
Kanosh 435
Kaysville OGD 9,811
Kearns S.L.C. 17,000○
Lark 500○
La Verkin 1,174
Layton OGD 22,862
Lehi PRVO 6,848
Levan 453
Lewiston 1,438
Lindon PRVO 2,796
LOGAN LOGN 26,844
Maeser 1,850○
Magna S.L.C. 8,600○
Manti 2,080
Mantua 484
Mapleton PRVO 2,726
Mendon 663
Midvale S.L.C. 10,144
Midway 1,194
Milford 1,293
Millcreek S.L.C. 31,700○
Millville LOGN 848
Minersville 552
Moab 5,333
Mona 536
Monroe 1,476
Monticello 1,929
Morgan 1,896
Moroni 1,086
Mount Olympus S.L.C. 6,000○
Mount Pleasant 2,049
Murray S.L.C. 25,750
Myton 500
Nephi 3,285
Newton 623
Nibley 1,036
North Logan LOGN 2,258
North Ogden OGD 9,309
North Salt Lake S.L.C. 5,548
Oakley 470
OGDEN OGD 64,407
Orangeville 1,309
Orderville 423
Orem PRVO 52,399
Panguitch 1,343
Paradise 542
Park City 2,823
Park Terrace S.L.C. 850○
Parowan 1,836
Payson PRVO 8,246
Perry 1,084
Peruvian Park S.L.C. 600○
Plain City OGD 2,379
Pleasant Grove PRVO 10,669
Price 9,086
Providence LOGN 2,675
PROVO PRVO 73,907
Randolph 659
Redmond 619
Redwood S.L.C. 2,000○
Richfield 5,482
Richmond 1,705
Riverdale OGD 3,841
River Heights LOGN 1,211
Riverton S.L.C. 7,293
Roosevelt 3,842
Roy OGD 19,694
St. George 11,350
Salem PRVO 2,233
Salina 1,992
SALT LAKE CITY S.L.C. 163,033
Sandy S.L.C. 51,022
Santa Clara 1,091
Santaquin PRVO 2,175
Smithfield LOGN 4,993
South Jordan S.L.C. 7,492
South Ogden OGD 11,366
South Salt Lake S.L.C. 10,561
Spanish Fork PRVO 9,825
Spring City 671
Spring Glen 800○
Springville PRVO 12,101
Stockton 437
Sunnyside 611
Sunset OGD 5,733
Syracuse OGD 3,702
Taylorsville S.L.C. 9,200○
Tooele 14,335
Tremonton 3,464
Trenton 447
Uintah OGD 439
Union S.L.C. 3,100○
Val Verda S.L.C. 6,500○
Vernal 6,600
Washington 3,092
Washington Terrace OGD 8,212
Wellington 1,406
Wellsville 1,952
Wendover 1,099
West Bountiful S.L.C. 3,556
West Jordan S.L.C. 26,794
West Point OGD 2,170
White City S.L.C. 7,500○
Willard 1,241
Woods Cross S.L.C. 4,263

COUNTIES

Beaver 4,378
Box Elder 33,222
Cache 57,176
Carbon 22,179
Daggett 769
Davis 146,540
Duchesne 12,565
Emery 11,451
Garfield 3,673
Grand 8,241
Iron 17,349
Juab 5,530
Kane 4,024
Millard 8,970
Morgan 4,917
Piute 1,329
Rich 2,100
Salt Lake 619,066
San Juan 12,253
Sanpete 14,620
Sevier 14,727
Summit 10,198
Tooele 26,033
Uintah 20,506
Utah 218,106
Wasatch 8,523
Washington 26,065
Wayne 1,911
Weber 144,616

VERMONT

1980 Census 511,456

CITIES

Alburg 1,352▲ 496
Arlington 2,184▲ 800○
Barre MTPLR- 9,824
Barton 2,990▲ 1,062
Bellows Falls 3,456
Bennington 15,815▲ 8,600○
Bethel 1,715▲ 900○
Bomoseen (P.O.) RUTL 500○
Bradford 2,191▲ 831
Brandon 4,194▲ 1,720○
Brattleboro 11,886
Bristol 3,293▲ 1,793
BURLINGTON BUR 37,712
Castleton RUTL 3,637▲ 600○
Center Rutland RUTL 475○
Chelsea 1,091▲ 500○
Chester 2,791▲ 470○
Danville 1,705▲ 450○
Derby 4,222▲ 598
Derby Line 874
Dorset 1,648▲ 550○
East Arlington 600○
East Barre MTPLR- 900○
East Middlebury 550○
East Montpelier 2,205▲ 600○
East Poultney 450○
Enosburg Falls 1,207
Essex BUR 14,392▲ 800○
Essex Junction BUR 7,033
Fair Haven 2,819
Forest Dale 500○
Gilman 550○
Graniteville MTPLR- 600○
Groton 667▲ 438○
Hardwick 2,613▲ 1,476
Hartford 7,963▲ 600○
Hartland 2,396▲ 500○
Hyde Park 2,021▲ 475
Hydeville RUTL 500○
Island Pond 1,123○
Jeffersonville 491
Jericho BUR 3,575▲ 1,340
Johnson 2,581▲ 1,393
Ludlow 2,414▲ 1,352
Lyndon 4,924▲ 425○
Lyndonville 1,401
Manchester 3,261▲ 563
Manchester Center 1,060○
Middlebury 7,574▲ 4,000○
Milton BUR 6,829▲ 1,411
MONTPELIER MTPLR- 8,241
Morrisville 2,074
Newbury 1,699▲ 425
Newport 4,756
North Bennington 1,635
North Clarendon RUTL 500○
Northfield MTPLR- 5,435▲ 2,033
Northfield Falls MTPLR- 600○
North Springfield 750○
North Troy 717
Norwich 2,398▲ 1,000○
Orleans 983
Pittsford 2,590▲ 666
Plainfield MTPLR- 1,249▲ 599
Poultney 3,196▲ 1,554
Proctor RUTL 1,998
Putney 1,850▲ 1,100○
Quechee 500○
Randolph 4,689▲ 2,217
Richford 2,206▲ 1,471
Richmond BUR 3,159▲ 865
Riverton MTPLR- 500○
Rochester 1,054▲ 500○
RUTLAND RUTL 18,436
St. Albans 7,308
St. Johnsbury 7,938▲ 6,400○
St. Johnsbury Center 450○
Saxtons River 593
Shaftsbury 3,001▲ 700○
South Barre MTPLR- 900○
South Burlington BUR 10,679
South Royalton 700○
South Ryegate 450○
Springfield 10,190▲ 5,632○
Stamford 773▲ 500○
Stowe 2,991▲ 531
Swanton 5,141▲ 2,520
Vergennes 2,273
Wallingford 1,893▲ 800○
Warren 956▲ 500○
Waterbury 4,465▲ 1,892
Waterbury Center 500○
Websterville MTPLR- 600○
West Pawlet 500○
West Rutland RUTL 2,351
White River Junction 2,379○
Wilder 1,328○
Williamstown MTPLR- 2,284▲ 650○
Wilmington 1,808▲ 545○
Winooski BUR 6,318
Woodstock 3,214▲ 1,178

COUNTIES

Addison 29,406
Bennington 33,345
Caledonia 25,808
Chittenden 115,534
Essex 6,313
Franklin 34,788
Grand Isle 4,613
Lamoille 16,767
Orange 22,739
Orleans 23,440
Rutland 58,347
Washington 52,393
Windham 36,933
Windsor 51,030

VIRGINIA

1980 Census 5,346,279

CITIES

Abingdon 4,318
Accomac 522
Alexandria● WASH 103,217
Altavista 3,849
Amelia Court House 700○
Amherst LYNCH 1,135
Annalee Heights WASH 1,750○
Annandale WASH 35,300○
Appalachia 2,418
Appomattox 1,345
Arlington WASH 152,700○
Arvonia 700○
Ashland RICH 4,640
Atkins 500○
Austinville 800○
Baileys Crossroads WASH 4,600○
Bassett MRTNV 2,950○
Bedford● 5,991
Belle Haven 589
Belle View WASH 3,500○
Bellwood RICH 600○
Bensley RICH 3,300○
Berryville 1,752
Big Stone Gap 4,748
Blacksburg 30,638
Blackstone 3,624
Bland 450○
Bluefield 5,946
Blue Ridge ROAN 1,200○
Boissevain 900○
Bon Air RICH 13,000○
Bowling Green 665
Boydton 486
Boykins 791
Bridgewater 3,289
BRISTOL● BRIS- 19,042
Broadway 1,234
Brodnax 492
Brookfield WASH 2,500○
Brookneal 1,454
Broyhill Park WASH 3,600○
Buchanan 1,205
Bucknell Manor WASH 2,350○
Buena Vista● 6,717
Burke WASH 1,500○
Burkeville 606
Callao 450○
Cape Charles 1,512
Cave Spring ROAN 6,300○
Centreville WASH 950○
Chantilly WASH 950○
Chapel Square WASH 2,000○
Charlotte Court House 568
CHARLOTTESVILLE● CHRLTV 45,010
Chase City 2,749
Chatham 1,390
Cheriton 695
Chesapeake● NORF- 114,226
Chester RICH 7,000○
Chilhowie 1,269
Chincoteague 1,607
Christiansburg 10,345
Clarksville 1,468
Clifton Forge● 5,046
Clinchco 1,000○
Clintwood 1,369
Cloverdale ROAN 850○
Coeburn 2,625
Collinsville MRTNV 7,400○
Colonial Beach 2,474
Colonial Heights● PET- 16,509
Courtland 976
Covington● 9,063
Craigsville 845
Crewe 2,325
Crozet 1,433○
Culpeper 6,621
Dahlgren 575○
Dale City WASH 23,000○
Damascus 1,330
Dante 1,200○
DANVILLE● DANV 45,642
Dayton 1,017
Deltaville 600○
Dillwyn 637
Drakes Branch 617
Dublin 2,368
Dumfries WASH 3,214
Dunn Loring Woods WASH 2,800○
Edinburg 752
Elkton 1,520
Elliston 750○
Emporia● 4,840
Engleside WASH 21,400○
Ewing 500○
Exmore 1,300
Fairfax● WASH 19,390
Fairlawn 2,000○
Falls Church● WASH 9,515
Falmouth 970○
Farmville 6,067
Ferrum 500○
Ferry Farms 1,300○
Fieldale MRTNV 1,400○
Fishersville 700○
Floyd 411
Franklin● 7,308
Fredericksburg● 15,322
Fries 758
Front Royal 11,126
Gainesville 600○
Galax● 6,524
Gate City KNGSP 2,494
Glade Spring 1,722
Glasgow 1,259
Glen Allen RICH 1,100○
Glenwood DANV 1,000○
Glenwood Farms RICH 3,200○
Gloucester 900○
Gloucester Point NN-H 850○
Goochland 450○
Gordonsville 1,175
Grafton 900○
Greenbriar WASH 6,000○
Gretna 1,255
Grindall Creek RICH 1,900○
Grottoes 1,369
Groveton WASH 6,800○
Groveton Gardens WASH 2,800○
Grundy 1,699
Halifax 772
Hamilton 598
Hampton● NN-H 122,617
Harrisonburg● 19,671
Hayfield WASH 2,200○
Herndon WASH 11,449
Highland Springs RICH 7,500○
Hillsville 2,123
Hollins ROAN 11,000○
Honaker 1,475
Hopewell● PET- 23,397
Hurt 1,481
Hybla Valley WASH 4,350○
Independence 1,112
Iron Gate 620
Irvington 567
Ivanhoe 600○
Jarratt 614
Jefferson Manor WASH 2,550○
Jefferson Village WASH 2,800○
Jewell Ridge 600○
Jonesville 874
Kenbridge 1,352
Keysville 704
Kilmarnock 945
Kings Park WASH 4,450○
Kings Park West WASH 5,000○
La Crosse 734
Lake Barcroft WASH 2,250○
Lake Ridge 6,500○
Lakeside RICH 29,400○
Laurel RICH 1,500○
Lawrenceville 1,484
Lebanon 3,206
Leesburg WASH 8,357
Lexington● 7,292
Loch Lomond WASH 2,300○
Louisa 932
Lovettsville 613
Lovingston 550○
Lowmoor 700○
Luray 3,584
LYNCHBURG● LYNCH 66,743
McKenney 473
McLean WASH 22,000○
Madison Heights LYNCH 3,500○
Manassas● WASH 15,438
Manassas Park● WASH 6,524
Mantua Hills WASH 1,550○
Marion 7,029
Marlboro RICH 950○
Marshall 600○
MARTINSVILLE● MRTNV 18,149
Mathews 650○
Matoaca PET- 2,000○
Max Meadows 550○
Meadowview 600○
Mechanicsville RICH 9,000○
Merrifield WASH 2,100○
Middleburg 619
Middletown 841
Midlothian RICH 1,000○
Milford 500○
Montrose RICH 2,200○
Montross 456
Montvale 450○
Monument Heights RICH 3,100○
Mount Jackson 1,419
Mount Sidney 550○
Narrows 2,516
Nassawadox 630
New Market 1,118
NEWPORT NEWS● NN-H 144,903
Nickelsville 464
NORFOLK● NORF- 266,979
North Springfield WASH 8,631○
Norton● 4,757
Oakton WASH 900○
Occoquan WASH 512
Onancock 1,461
Onley 526
Orange 2,631
Parksley 979
Parrott 525○
Pearisburg 2,128
Pembroke 1,302
Pennington Gap 1,716
PETERSBURG● PET- 41,055
Pimmit Hills WASH 7,200○
Pocahontas 708
Poquoson● NN-H 8,726
Portsmouth● NORF- 104,577
Pound 1,086
Pulaski 10,106
Purcellville 1,567
Quail Oaks RICH 1,700○
Quantico WASH 621
Radford● 13,225
Raven 1,880○
Reedville 500○
Remington 425
Reston WASH 32,000○
Rich Creek 746
Richlands 5,796
RICHMOND● RICH 219,214
Ridgeway MRTNV 858
Riverdale 500○
ROANOKE● ROAN 100,427
Rocky Mount 4,198
Rose Hill WASH 5,700○
Rose Hill 800○
Rural Retreat 1,083
Rustburg LYNCH 600○
St. Paul 973
Salem● ROAN 23,958
Saltville 2,376
Sandston RICH 4,500○
Saxis 415
Seaford NN-H 1,700○
Shenandoah 1,861
Smithfield NORF- 3,649
South Boston● 7,093
South Hill 4,347
Springfield WASH 12,500○
Stafford WASH 650○
Stanley 1,204
Stanleytown MRTNV 650○
Staunton● 21,857
Stephens City 1,179
Sterling WASH 12,000○
Stonega 450○
Strasburg 2,311
Stratford Landing WASH 2,650○
Stuart 1,131
Stuarts Draft 950○
Suffolk● NORF- 47,621
Sugar Grove 500○
Sugarland Run 4,500○
Sugar Loaf ROAN 6,000○

○ Rand McNally estimate (not reported in census).
▲ Population of entire township or "town", including rural area.
● Independent city. Population not included in county total.

Sweet Briar LYNCH 900○
Tangier 771
Tappahannock 1,821
Tazewell 4,468
Temperanceville 425○
Timberlake LYNCH 2,700○
Timberville 1,510
Toano 750○
Trammel 500○
Triangle WASH 3,050○
Troutville ROAN 496
Urbanna 518
Vansant 600○
Varina RICH 2,000○
Victoria 2,004
Vienna WASH 15,469
Vinton ROAN 8,027
Virginia Beach● NORF- 262,199
Wakefield 1,355
Warm Springs 425○
Warrenton WASH 3,907
Warsaw 771
Waverly 2,284
Waynesboro● 15,329
Waynewood WASH 4,500○
Weber City KNGSP 1,543
Westham RICH 3,600○
West Point 2,726
West Springfield WASH 16,000○
Williamsburg● 9,870
Willston WASH 2,500○
Winchester● 20,217
Windsor 985
Wise 3,894
Woodbridge WASH 35,000○
Woodstock 2,627
Wytheville 7,135

COUNTIES

Accomack 31,268
Albemarle 50,689
Alleghany 14,333
Amelia 8,405
Amherst 29,122
Appomattox 11,971
Arlington 152,599
Augusta 53,732
Bath 5,860
Bedford 34,927
Bland 6,349
Botetourt 23,270
Brunswick 15,632
Buchanan 37,989
Buckingham 11,751
Campbell 45,424
Caroline 17,904
Carroll 27,270
Charles City 6,692
Charlotte 12,266
Chesterfield 141,372
Clarke 9,965
Craig 3,948
Culpeper 22,620
Cumberland 7,881
Dickenson 19,806
Dinwiddie 22,602
Essex 8,864
Fairfax 596,901
Fauquier 35,889
Floyd 11,563
Fluvanna 10,244
Franklin 35,740
Frederick 34,150
Giles 17,810
Gloucester 20,107
Goochland 11,761
Grayson 16,579
Greene 7,625
Greensville 10,903
Halifax 30,418
Hanover 50,398
Henrico 180,735
Henry 57,654
Highland 2,937
Isle of Wight 21,603
James City 22,763
King and Queen 5,968
King George 10,543
King William 9,327
Lancaster 10,129
Lee 25,956
Loudoun 57,427
Louisa 17,825
Lunenburg 12,124
Madison 10,232
Mathews 7,995
Mecklenburg 29,444
Middlesex 7,719
Montgomery 63,516
Nelson 12,204
New Kent 8,781
Northampton 14,625
Northumberland 9,828
Nottoway 14,666
Orange 17,827
Page 19,401
Patrick 17,585
Pittsylvania 66,147
Powhatan 13,062
Prince Edward 16,456
Prince George 25,733
Prince William 144,703
Pulaski 35,229
Rappahannock 6,093
Richmond 6,952
Roanoke 72,945
Rockbridge 17,911
Rockingham 57,038
Russell 31,761
Scott 25,068
Shenandoah 27,559
Smyth 33,366
Southampton 18,731
Spotsylvania 34,435
Stafford 40,470
Surry 6,046
Sussex 10,874
Tazewell 50,511
Warren 21,200
Washington 46,487
Westmoreland 14,041
Wise 43,863
Wythe 25,522
York 35,463

WASHINGTON

1980 Census 4,130,163

CITIES

Aberdeen 18,739
Albion 631
Algona SEAT- 1,467
Allyn 750○
Anacortes 9,013
Appleyard 1,500○
Arlington SEAT- 3,282
Asotin 943
Auburn SEAT- 26,417
Battle Ground POR 2,774
Bellevue SEAT- 73,903
BELLINGHAM BELNG 45,794
Benton City 1,980
Bingen 644
Black Diamond SEAT- 1,170
Blaine 2,363
Bonney Lake SEAT- 5,328
Bothell SEAT- 7,943
BREMERTON BREM 36,208
Brewster 1,337
Bridgeport 1,174
Bryn Mawr SEAT- 2,150○
Buckley SEAT- 3,143
Bucoda 519
Buena 630○
Burbank 650○
Burien SEAT- 14,250○
Burlington 3,894
Camas 5,681
Carbonado SEAT- 456
Carnation 913
Carson 600○
Cashmere 2,240
Castle Rock 2,162
Cathlamet 635
Centralia 10,809
Central Park 2,800○
Chehalis 6,100
Chelan 2,802
Cheney 7,630
Chewelah 1,888
Chico 700○
Chinook 430○
Clarkston 6,903
Clearlake 700○
Cle Elum 1,773
Clinton SEAT- 500○
Colfax 2,780
College Place 5,771
Colville 4,510
Concrete 592
Connell 1,981
Copalis Beach 450○
Cosmopolis 1,575
Coulee City 510
Coulee Dam 1,412
Country Homes SPOK 3,500○
Coupeville 1,006
Darrington 1,064
Davenport 1,559
Dayton 2,565
Deer Park 2,140
Deming 450○
Des Moines SEAT- 7,378
Dishman SPOK 9,079○
Du Pont SEAT- 559
Eastgate SEAT- 5,450○
East Olympia OLYM 500○
East Wenatchee 1,640
Eatonville 998
Edgewood SEAT- 1,600○
Edmonds SEAT- 27,526
Ellensburg 11,752
Elma 2,720
Entiat 445
Enumclaw SEAT- 5,427
Ephrata 5,359
Everett SEAT- 54,413
Everson 898
Fairfield 582
Fall City 1,500○
Federal Way SEAT- 17,850○
Ferndale BELNG 3,855
Fircrest SEAT- 5,477
Fords Prairie 2,250○
Forks 3,060
Friday Harbor 1,200
Fruitvale YAK 3,500○
Garfield 599
Gig Harbor SEAT- 2,429
Gold Bar 794
Goldendale 3,414
Grand Coulee 1,180
Grandview 5,615
Granger 1,812
Granite Falls SEAT- 911
Grayland 550○
Greenacres SPOK 3,300○
Hadlock 500○
Harrington 507
Hazel Dell POR 4,600○
Hoodsport 500○
Hoquiam 9,719
Ilwaco 604
Ione 594
Issaquah SEAT- 5,536
Kalama 1,216
Kelso LNGV 11,129
Kenmore SEAT- 8,000○
Kennewick P-K-R 34,397
Kennydale 1,000○
Kent SEAT- 23,152
Kettle Falls 1,087
Kirkland SEAT- 18,779
Kittitas 782
Klickitat 700○
Lacey OLYM 13,940
La Conner 633
Lake Stevens SEAT- 1,660
Lakewood Center SEAT- 51,400○
Langley SEAT- 650
La Push 450○
Leavenworth 1,522
Liberty Lake SPOK 800○
Lind 567
Long Beach 1,199
LONGVIEW LNGV 31,052
Lynden 4,022
Lynnwood SEAT- 21,937
Mabton 1,248
McCleary 1,419
Manson 500○
Marysville SEAT- 5,080
Mead SPOK 1,200○
Medical Lake 3,600
Medina SEAT- 3,220
Mercer Island SEAT- 21,522
Millwood SPOK 1,717
Milton SEAT- 3,162
Mineral 500○
Moclips 600○
Monroe SEAT- 2,869
Montesano 3,247
Morton 1,264
Moses Lake 10,629
Mossyrock 463
Mountlake Terrace SEAT- 16,534
Mount Vernon 13,009
Moxee City 687
Mukilteo SEAT- 1,426
Naches 644
Napavine 611
Naselle 500○
Neah Bay 600○
Newport 1,665
Newport Hills SEAT- 6,050○
Nooksack 429
Nordland 500○
North Bend 1,701
North City SEAT- 6,200○
Oakesdale 444
Oak Harbor 12,271
Oakville 537
Ocean City 500○
Ocean Park 825○
Odessa 1,009
Okanogan 2,302
OLYMPIA OLYM 27,447
Omak 4,007
Opportunity SPOK 16,604○
Orchards POR 3,050○
Oroville 1,483
Orting SEAT- 1,763
Othello 4,454
Otis Orchards SPOK 900○
Pacific SEAT- 2,261
Pacific Beach 900○
Packwood 1,100○
Palouse 1,005
Parkland SEAT- 22,500○
Parkwater SPOK 4,400○
PASCO P-K-R 17,944
Pateros 555
Pe Ell 617
Peshastin 700○
Point Roberts 700○
Pomeroy 1,716
Port Angeles 17,311
Port Orchard BREM 4,787
Port Townsend 6,067
Poulsbo BREM 3,453
Prosser 3,896
Pullman 23,579
Puyallup SEAT- 18,251
Quilcene 900○
Quincy 3,525
Rainier 891
Raymond 2,991
Reardan 498
Redmond SEAT- 23,318
Redondo 560○
Renton SEAT- 30,612
Republic 1,018
Richland P-K-R 33,578
Richmond Beach SEAT- 7,700○
Richmond Highlands SEAT- 21,000○
Ridgecrest SEAT- 5,100○
Ridgefield POR 1,062
Ritzville 1,800
Riverton Heights SEAT- 34,500○
Rockford 442
Rock Island 491
Rollingbay SEAT- 600○
Rosalia 572
Roslyn 938
Roy 417
Ruston SEAT- 612
St. John 529
Salmon Creek POR 1,500○
SEATTLE SEAT- 493,846
Seaview 600○
Sedro Woolley 6,110
Selah YAK 4,372
Sequim 3,013
Shelton 7,629
Silverdale BREM 1,500○
Skyway SEAT- 8,950○
Snohomish SEAT- 5,294
Snoqualmie SEAT- 1,370
Soap Lake 1,196
South Bend 1,686
South Broadway YAK 3,500○
South Cle Elum 449
Spanaway SEAT- 5,768○
SPOKANE SPOK 171,300
Sprague 473
Stanwood SEAT- 2,744
Steilacoom SEAT- 4,886
Stevenson 1,172
Sultan SEAT- 1,578
Sumas 712
Sumner SEAT- 4,936
Sunnyside 9,225
Suquamish BREM 1,400○
Tacoma SEAT- 158,501
Tekoa 854
Tenino 1,280
Thomas 900○
Tieton 528
Toledo 637
Tonasket 985
Toppenish 6,517
Town and Country SPOK 6,484○
Tracyton BREM 1,500○
Tukwila SEAT- 3,578
Tumwater OLYM 6,705
Twisp 911
Union Gap YAK 3,184
University Place SEAT- 13,230○
Vancouver POR 42,834
Waitsburg 1,035
Walla Walla 25,618
Wapato 3,307
Warden 1,479
Washougal 3,834
Waterville 908
Wenatchee 17,257
Westport 1,954
White Center SEAT- 18,600○
White Salmon 1,853
Wilbur 1,122
Winlock 1,052
Winslow SEAT- 2,196
Winthrop 413
Wishram 650○
Woodland 2,341
Yacolt 544
YAKIMA YAK 49,826
Yelm 1,294
Zillah 1,599

COUNTIES

Adams 13,267
Asotin 16,823
Benton 109,444
Chelan 45,061
Clallam 51,648
Clark 192,227
Columbia 4,057
Cowlitz 79,548
Douglas 22,144
Ferry 5,811
Franklin 35,025
Garfield 2,468
Grant 48,522
Grays Harbor 66,314
Island 44,048
Jefferson 15,965
King 1,269,749
Kitsap 146,609
Kittitas 24,877
Klickitat 15,822
Lewis 55,279
Lincoln 9,604
Mason 31,184
Okanogan 30,639
Pacific 17,237
Pend Oreille 8,580
Pierce 485,643
San Juan 7,838
Skagit 64,138
Skamania 7,919
Snohomish 337,016
Spokane 341,835
Stevens 28,979
Thurston 124,264
Wahkiakum 3,832
Walla Walla 47,435
Whatcom 106,701
Whitman 40,103
Yakima 172,508

WEST VIRGINIA

1980 Census 1,949,644

CITIES

Accoville 500○
Adrian 415○
Alderson 1,375
Alum Creek 500○
Amherstdale 800○
Anawalt 652
Ansted 1,952
Athens 1,147
Barboursville HNTG- 2,871
Barrackville FAIRM 1,815
Barrett 800○
Baxter FAIRM 500○
Bayard 540
Beaver BECK 1,400○
BECKLEY BECK 20,492
Beech Bottom STU- 507
Belington 2,038
Belle CHAS 1,621
Belmont 887
Benwood WHL 1,994
Berkeley Springs 789
Berwind 600○
Bethany STU- 1,336
Beverly 475
Blennerhassett PRKB 2,200○
Blue Creek 500○
Bluefield 16,060
Bluewell 1,000○
Bolivar 672
Boomer 1,100○
Bradley BECK 1,200○
Bradshaw 1,200○
Bramwell 989
Brenton 800○
Bridgeport CLRKB 6,604
Brookhaven MORG 1,200○
Brownton 600○
Buckhannon 6,820
Buffalo 1,034
Bunker Hill 500○
Bunker Hill CHAS 800○
Burnsville 531
Cabin Creek 900○
Cairo 428
Cameron 1,474
Cannelton 750○
Caretta 950○
Carolina 650○
Cedar Grove 1,479
Ceredo HNTG- 2,255
Chapmanville 1,164
CHARLESTON CHAS 63,968
Charles Town 2,857
Charlton Heights 600○
Charmco 800○
Chattaroy 1,200○
Chelyan CHAS 800○
Chesapeake CHAS 2,364
Chester E.LIV- 3,297
CLARKSBURG CLRKB 22,371
Clay 940
Clendenin 1,373
Clothier 600○
Coalwood 1,100○
Colliers STU- 600○
Corinne 500○
Cowen 723
Crab Orchard BECK 1,900○
Craigsville 900○
Cross Lanes CHAS 3,200○
Culloden CHAS 1,500○
Cunard 450○
Danville 727
Davis 979
Davy 882
Decota 600○
Deep Water 500○
Delbarton 981
Dellslow 700○
Despard CLRKB 1,200○
Diamond 500○
Dixie 450○
Drybranch CHAS 700○
Dunbar CHAS 9,285
Dupont City CHAS 900○
East Bank 1,155
East Pea Ridge HNTG- 1,900○
East View CLRKB 1,618○
Eccles BECK 1,100○
Eckman 700○
Eleanor CHAS 1,282
Elizabeth 856
Elkhorn 700○
Elkins 8,536
Elkview CHAS 1,486○
Enterprise 950○
Eskdale 500○
Fairlea 1,200○
FAIRMONT FAIRM 23,863
Fairview 759
Farmington 583
Fayetteville 2,366
Flemington 452
Follansbee STU- 3,994
Fort Ashby CUMB 1,200○
Fort Gay 886
Gary 2,233
Gassaway 1,225
Gauley Bridge 1,177
Gilbert 757
Glasgow 1,031
Glen Dale WHL 1,875
Glendale Heights WHL 700○
Glen Jean 500○
Glenville 2,155
Glen White 500○
Grafton 6,845
Grantsville 788
Grant Town 987
Granville MORG 992
Great Cacapon 500○
Guthrie CHAS 800○
Hamlin 1,219
Handley CHAS 633
Harrisville 1,673
Hartford 556
Harvey 500○
Henderson 604
Henlawson 950○
Hico 700○
Hinton 4,622
Holden 1,600○
Hooverson Heights STU- 1,500○
Hundred 485
HUNTINGTON HNTG- 63,684
Hurricane CHAS 3,751
Iaeger 833
Idamay 600○
Institute CHAS 1,500○
Jeffrey 900○
Jodie 450○
Julian 700○
Junior 591
Kearneysville 500○
Kenova HNTG- 4,454
Kermit 705
Keyser 6,569
Keystone 902
Kimball 871
Kimberly 800○
Kincaid 700○
Kingwood 2,877
Kistler 750○
Knollwood CHAS 700○
Lanark BECK 600○
Lansing 500○
Lester 626
Lewisburg 3,065
Lilly Grove 1,700○
Logan 3,029
Longacre 450○
Lost Creek 604
Lumberport 939
Mabscott BECK 1,668
McComas 800○
McMechen WHL 2,402
Madison 3,228
Malden CHAS 950○
Mammoth CHAS 750○
Man 1,333
Mannington 3,036
Marlinton 1,352

○ Rand McNally estimate (not reported in census).
▲ Population of entire township or "town", including rural area.
● Independent city. Population not included in county total.

Marlowe HAG- 700○
Marmet CHAS 2,196
Marrtown PRKB 900○
Martinsburg 13,063
Mason 1,432
Masontown 1,052
Matewan 822
Matoaka 613
Maxwell Acres WHL 1,000○
Maybeury 700○
Meadow Bridge 530
Meadowbrook CLRKB 500○
Miami 500○
Middlebourne 941
Mill Creek 801
Milton HNTG- 2,178
Minden 800○
Monongah FAIRM 1,132
Montgomery 3,104
Moorefield 2,257
MORGANTOWN MORG 27,605
Moundsville WHL 12,419
Mount Clare 900○
Mount Gay 1,650○
Mount Hope 1,849
Mullens 2,919
Naoma 600○
Nettie 600○
Newburg 418
New Cumberland STU- 1,752
Newell E.LIV- 1,900○
New Haven 1,723
New Manchester STU- 600○
New Martinsville 7,109
Nitro CHAS 8,074
Nutter Fort CLRKB 2,078
Oak Hill 7,120
Oceana 2,143
Odd 550○
Omar 950○
Paden City 3,671
PARKERSBURG PRKB 39,967
Parsons 1,937
Paw Paw 644
Peach Creek 600○
Pennsboro 1,652
Petersburg 2,084
Peterstown 648
Philippi 3,194
Piedmont 1,491
Pineville 1,140
Piney View BECK 800○
Poca CHAS 1,142
Pocatalico CHAS 900○
Point Pleasant 5,682
Powellton 1,200○
Pratt 821
Princeton 7,493
Prosperity BECK 1,000○
Pursglove MORG 600○
Quinwood 460
Racine 650○
Rainelle 1,983
Raleigh BECK 900○
Rand CHAS 2,500○
Ranson 2,471
Ravenswood 4,126
Reader 700○
Red Jacket 1,000○
Reedsville 564
Rhodell 472
Richwood 3,568
Ridgeley CUMB 994
Ridgeview 500○
Ripley 3,464
Rivesville FAIRM 1,327
Roderfield 1,100○
Romney 2,094
Ronceverte 2,312
Rowlesburg 966
Rupert 1,276
St. Albans CHAS 12,402
St. Marys 2,219
Salem 2,706
Seth 650○
Shady Spring 1,000○
Sharples 500○
Shepherdstown 1,791
Shinnston 3,059
Sissonville CHAS 500○
Sistersville 2,367
Smithers 1,482
Sophia BECK 1,216
South Charleston CHAS 15,968
Spelter 450○
Spencer 2,799
Sprague BECK 900○
Squire 900○
Stanaford BECK 1,000○
Star City MORG 1,464
Stollings 900○
Stonewood CLRKB 2,058
Summersville 2,972
Sutton 1,192
Switzer 1,000○
Tad CHAS 500○
Talcott 450○
Terra Alta 1,946
Thomas 747
Triadelphia WHL 1,461
Tunnelton 510
Tyler Heights CHAS 3,200○
Union 743
Valley Grove WHL 597
Vallscreek 900○
Van 500○
Verdunville 950○
Vienna PRKB 11,618
Wallace 900○
War 2,158
Wayne 1,495
Webster Springs 939
Weirton STU- 24,736
Welch 3,885
Wellsburg STU- 3,963
West Hamlin 643
West Liberty WHL 744
Weston 6,250
Westover MORG 4,884
West Union 1,090
WHEELING WHL 43,070
White Sulphur Springs 3,371
Whitesville 689
Whitman 950○
Wilkinson 700○
Williamson 5,219
Williamstown MRIET 3,095
Winifrede CHAS 800○
Yukon 500○

COUNTIES

Barbour 16,639
Berkeley 46,775
Boone 30,447
Braxton 13,894
Brooke 31,117
Cabell 106,835
Calhoun 8,250
Clay 11,265
Doddridge 7,433
Fayette 57,863
Gilmer 8,334
Grant 10,210
Greenbrier 37,665
Hampshire 14,867
Hancock 40,418
Hardy 10,030
Harrison 77,710
Jackson 25,794
Jefferson 30,302
Kanawha 231,414
Lewis 18,813
Lincoln 23,675
Logan 50,679
McDowell 49,899
Marion 65,789
Marshall 41,608
Mason 27,045
Mercer 73,942
Mineral 27,234
Mingo 37,336
Monongalia 75,024
Monroe 12,873
Morgan 10,711
Nicholas 28,126
Ohio 61,389
Pendleton 7,910
Pleasants 8,236
Pocahontas 9,919
Preston 30,460
Putnam 38,181
Raleigh 86,821
Randolph 28,734
Ritchie 11,442
Roane 15,952
Summers 15,875
Taylor 16,584
Tucker 8,675
Tyler 11,320
Upshur 23,427
Wayne 46,021
Webster 12,245
Wetzel 21,874
Wirt 4,922
Wood 93,648
Wyoming 35,993

WISCONSIN

1980 Census 4,705,335

CITIES

Abbotsford 1,901
Adams 1,744
Adell 545
Albany 1,051
Algoma 3,656
Allenton 550○
Allouez GRBY 13,753○
Alma 848
Alma Center 454
Almena 526
Almond 477
Altoona EAUC 4,393
Amery 2,404
Amherst 701
Antigo 8,653
APPLETON APP 59,032
Arcadia 2,109
Arena 451
Argyle 720
Arlington 440
Ashland 9,115
Ashwaubenon GRBY 14,486
Athens 988
Auburndale 641
Augusta 1,560
Avoca 505
Baldwin 1,620
Balsam Lake 749
Bangor 1,012
Baraboo 8,081
Barneveld 579
Barron 2,595
Bay City 543
Bayfield 778
Bayside MILW 4,724
Bear Creek 454
Beaver Dam 14,149
Belgium 892
Belleville 1,302
Belmont 826
BELOIT BLOIT 35,207
Beloit North BLOIT 5,912○
Benton 983
Berlin 5,478
Big Bend MILW 1,345
Birchwood 437
Birnamwood 688
Biron 698
Black Creek 1,097
Black Earth 1,145
Black River Falls 3,434
Blair 1,142
Blanchardville 803
Bloomer 3,342
Bloomington 743
Blue River 412
Bonduel 1,160
Boscobel 2,662
Boyceville 862
Boyd 660
Brandon 862
Brillion 2,907
Bristol 500○
Brodhead 3,153
Brookfield MILW 34,035
Brooklyn 627
Brown Deer MILW 12,921
Bruce 905
Buffalo 894
Burlington 8,385
Butler MILW 2,059
Butternut 438
Cadott 1,247
Cambria 680
Cambridge 844
Cameron 1,115
Campbellsport 1,740
Camp Douglas 589
Cascade 615
Casco 484
Cashton 827
Cassville 1,270
Cecil 445
Cedarburg MILW 9,005
Cedar Grove 1,420
Centuria 711
Chenequa MILW 532
Chetek 1,931
Chilton 2,965
Chippewa Falls EAUC 11,845
Clayton 425
Clear Lake 899
Cleveland 1,270
Clinton 1,751
Clintonville 4,567
Cochrane 512
Colby 1,496
Coleman 852
Colfax 1,149
Columbus 4,049
Combined Locks APP 2,573
Coon Valley 758
Cornell 1,583
Crandon 1,969
Crivitz 1,041
Cross Plains 2,156
Cuba City 2,129
Cudahy MILW 19,547
Cumberland 1,983
Dallas 477
Dane 518
Darien 1,152
Darlington 2,300
Deerfield 1,466
De Forest MAD 3,367
Delafield MILW 4,083
Delavan 5,684
Delavan Lake 2,124○
Denmark 1,475
De Pere GRBY 14,892
Dickeyville 1,156
Dodgeville 3,458
Dorchester 613
Dousman MILW 1,153
Dresser 670
Durand 2,047
Eagle 1,008
Eagle Lake 1,000○
Eagle River 1,326
East Troy MILW 2,385
EAU CLAIRE EAUC 51,509
Eau Claire Southeast EAUC 2,316○
Eden 534
Edgar 1,194
Edgerton 4,335
Elcho 450○
Eleva 593
Elkhart Lake 1,054
Elkhorn 4,605
Elk Mound 737
Ellsworth 2,143
Elm Grove MILW 6,735
Elmwood 885
Elroy 1,504
Embarrass 496
Ettrick 462
Evansville 2,835
Fairchild 577
Fall Creek 1,148
Fall River 850
Fennimore 2,212
Florence 575○
FOND DU LAC FDLC 35,863
Fontana 1,764
Footville 794
Forestville 455
Fort Atkinson 9,785
Fountain City 963
Fox Lake 1,373
Fox Point MILW 7,649
Francis Creek 538
Franklin MILW 16,871
Frederic 1,039
Fredonia MILW 1,437
Fremont 510
French Island LACRO 3,000○
Friendship 744
Galesville 1,239
Gays Mills 627
Genoa City CHI 1,202
Germantown MILW 10,729
Gillett 1,356
Gilman 436
Glenbeulah 423
Glendale MILW 13,882
Glenwood City 950
Glidden 550○
Goodman 600○
Grafton MILW 8,381
Grantsburg 1,153
GREEN BAY GRBY 87,899
Greendale MILW 16,928
Greenfield MILW 31,467
Green Lake 1,208
Greenwood 1,124
Gresham 534
Hales Corners MILW 7,110
Hallie EAUC 1,223○
Hammond 991
Hancock 419
Hartford 7,046
Hartland MILW 5,559
Hayward 1,698
Hazel Green 1,282
Hewitt 470
Highland 860
Hilbert 1,176
Hillsboro 1,263
Holmen LACRO 2,411
Horicon 3,584
Hortonville 2,016
Howard GRBY 8,240
Howards Grove SHEB 1,838
Hudson MPLS- 5,434
Hurley 2,015
Hustisford 874
Independence 1,180
Iola 957
Iron Belt 520○
Iron Ridge 766
Iron River 650○
Jackson MILW 1,817
JANESVILLE JNSV 51,071
Jefferson 5,647
Johnson Creek 1,136
Juda 450○
Junction City 523
Juneau 2,045
Kaukauna APP 11,310
Kendall 486
KENOSHA CHI 77,685
Keshena 500○
Kewaskum 2,381
Kewaunee 2,801
Kiel 3,083
Kimberly APP 5,881
King 750○
Knapp 419
Kohler SHEB 1,651
Lac du Flambeau 900○
LA CROSSE LACRO 48,347
Ladysmith 3,826
La Farge 746
Lake Butte des Morts OSH 1,111○
Lake Delton 1,158
Lake Geneva 5,607
Lake Mills 3,670
Lake Nebagamon 780
Lake Tomahawk 600○
Lake Wazeecha 1,285○
Lake Wissota EAUC 1,419○
Lancaster 4,076
Land O'Lakes 500○
Lannon MILW 987
Laona 700○
La Valle 412
Lena 585
Little Chute APP 7,907
Livingston 642
Lodi 1,959
Lomira 1,446
Lone Rock 577
Loyal 1,252
Luck 997
Luxemburg 1,040
Lyons 540○
McFarland MAD 3,783
MADISON MAD 170,616
Manawa 1,205
MANITOWOC MNTW- 32,547
Maple Bluff MAD 1,351
Marathon 1,552
Marinette 11,965
Marion 1,348
Markesan 1,446
Marshall 2,363
Marshfield 18,290
Mauston 3,284
Mayville 4,338
Mazomanie 1,248
Medford 4,010
Mellen 1,046
Melrose 507
Menasha APP 14,728
Menomonee Falls MILW 27,845
Menomonie 12,769
Mequon MILW 16,193
Mercer 1,250○
Merrill 9,578
Merrillan 587
Merton MILW 1,045
Middleton MAD 11,779
Milltown 732
Milton JNSV 4,092
MILWAUKEE MILW 636,212
Mineral Point 2,259
Minocqua 900○
Minong 557
Mishicot MNTW- 1,503
Mondovi 2,545
Monona MAD 8,809
Monroe 10,027
Montello 1,273
Montfort 616
Monticello 1,021
Montreal 887
Mosinee 3,015
Mount Calvary 585
Mount Horeb 3,251
Mukwonago MILW 4,014
Muscoda 1,331
Muskego MILW 15,277
Necedah 773
Neenah APP 23,272
Neillsville 2,780
Nekoosa 2,519
Neopit 1,122○
Neosho 575
New Auburn 466
New Berlin MILW 30,529
Newburg 783
New Glarus 1,763
New Holstein 3,412
New Lisbon 1,390
New London 6,210
New Richmond 4,306
Niagara 2,079
North Fond du Lac FDLC 3,844
North Freedom 616
North Hudson MPLS- 2,218
North Lake 600○
North Prairie MILW 938
Norwalk 517
Oak Creek MILW 16,932
Oakfield 990
Oconomowoc MILW 9,909
Oconto 4,505
Oconto Falls 2,500
Okauchee MILW 1,800○
Okauchee Lake MILW 1,400○
Omro OSH 2,763
Onalaska LACRO 9,249
Oostburg 1,647
Oregon MAD 3,876
Orfordville 1,143
Osceola 1,581
OSHKOSH OSH 49,678
Osseo 1,474
Owen 998
Oxford 432
Paddock Lake CHI 2,207
Palmyra 1,515
Pardeeville 1,594
Park Falls 3,192
Pell Lake CHI 1,400○
Pembine 475○
Pepin 890
Peshtigo 2,807
Pewaukee MILW 4,637
Phelps 700○
Phillips 1,522
Pittsville 810
Plain 676
Plainfield 813
Platteville 9,580
Pleasant Prairie 500○
Pleasant View 750○
Plover 5,310
Plum City 505
Plymouth 6,027
Poplar 569
Portage 7,896
Port Edwards 2,077
Port Washington MILW 8,612
Potosi 736
Poynette 1,447
Poy Sippi 500○
Prairie du Chien 5,859
Prairie du Sac 2,145
Prentice 605
Prescott MPLS- 2,654
Princeton 1,479
Pulaski 1,875
RACINE RAC 85,725
Randolph 1,691
Random Lake 1,287
Redgranite 976
Reedsburg 5,038
Reedsville 1,134
Reeseville 649
Rhinelander 7,873
Rib Lake 945
Rice Lake 7,691
Richland Center 4,923
Ridgeway 503
Rio 785
Ripon 7,111
River Falls 9,036
River Hills MILW 1,642
Roberts 833
Rochester 746
Rock Springs 426
Rosendale 725
Rosholt 520
Rothschild WAUS 3,338
St. Cloud 560
St. Croix Falls 1,497
St. Francis MILW 10,066
St. Nazianz 738
Salem 1,000○
Sauk City 2,703
Saukville MILW 3,494
Schofield WAUS 2,226
Seymour 2,530
Sharon 1,280
Shawano 7,013
SHEBOYGAN SHEB 48,085
Sheboygan Falls SHEB 5,253
Shell Lake 1,135
Shiocton 805
Shorewood MILW 14,327
Shorewood Hills MAD 1,837
Shullsburg 1,484
Silver Lake CHI 1,598
Siren 896
Sister Bay 564
Slinger MILW 1,612
Soldiers Grove 622
Solon Springs 590
Somerset 860
South Kenosha CHI 875○
South Milwaukee MILW 21,069
South Wayne 495
Sparta 6,934
Spencer 1,754
Spooner 2,365
Spring Green 1,265
Spring Valley 987
Stanley 2,095
Star Prairie 420
Stetsonville 487
Stevens Point 22,970
Stockbridge 567
Stoddard 762
Stoughton 7,589
Stratford 1,385
Strum 944
Sturgeon Bay 8,847
Sturtevant RAC 4,130
Sullivan 434

○ Rand McNally estimate (not reported in census).
▲ Population of entire township or "town", including rural area.
● Independent city. Population not included in county total.

Sun Prairie MAD 12,931
Superior DUL- 29,571
Suring 581
Sussex MILW 3,482
Taylor 411
Theresa 766
Thiensville MILW 3,341
Thorp 1,635
Three Lakes .... 600 ○
Tigerton 865
Tomah 7,204
Tomahawk 3,527
Trempealeau 956
Trevor .... 500 ○
Turtle Lake 762
Twin Lakes CHI 3,474
Two Rivers MNTW- 13,354
Union Grove CHI 3,517
Valders 973
Verona MAD 3,336
Vesper 554
Viola 696
Viroqua 3,716
Wabeno .... 700 ○
Walworth 1,607
Washburn 2,080
Waterford MILW 2,051
Waterloo 2,393
Watertown 18,113
Waukesha MILW 50,319
Waunakee MAD 3,866
Waupaca 4,472
Waupun 8,132
WAUSAU WAUS. 32,426
Wausaukee 648
Wautoma 1,629
Wauwatosa MILW 51,308
Wauzeka 580
Webster 610
West Allis MILW 63,982
West Bend 21,484
Westby 1,797
Westfield 1,033
West Milwaukee MILW 3,535
Weston WAUS .... 3,400 ○
West Salem 3,276
Weyauwega 1,549
Whitefish Bay MILW 14,930
Whitehall 1,530
Whitelaw 649
Whitewater 11,520
Whiting 2,050
Wild Rose 741
Williams Bay 1,763
Wilton 465
Wind Lake MILW .... 2,400 ○
Wind Point RAC 1,695
Winneconne OSH 1,935
Wisconsin Dells 2,521
Wisconsin Rapids 17,995
Withee 509
Wittenberg 997
Wonewoc 842
Woodruff .... 900 ○
Woodville 725

Wrightstown APP 1,169
Wyocena 548

COUNTIES

Adams 13,457
Ashland 16,783
Barron 38,730
Bayfield 13,822
Brown 175,280
Buffalo 14,309
Burnett 12,340
Calumet 30,867
Chippewa 51,702
Clark 32,910
Columbia 43,222
Crawford 16,556
Dane 323,545
Dodge 74,747
Door 25,029
Douglas 44,421
Dunn 34,314
Eau Claire 78,805
Florence 4,172
Fond du Lac 88,952
Forest 9,044
Grant 51,736
Green 30,012
Green Lake 18,370
Iowa 19,802
Iron 6,730
Jackson 16,831
Jefferson 66,152
Juneau 21,039
Kenosha 123,137
Kewaunee 19,539
La Crosse 91,056
Lafayette 17,412
Langlade 19,978
Lincoln 26,311
Manitowoc 82,918
Marathon 111,270
Marinette 39,314
Marquette 11,672
Menominee 3,373
Milwaukee 964,988
Monroe 35,074
Oconto 28,947
Oneida 31,216
Outagamie 128,726
Ozaukee 66,981
Pepin 7,477
Pierce 31,149
Polk 32,351
Portage 57,420
Price 15,788
Racine 173,132
Richland 17,476
Rock 139,420
Rusk 15,589
St. Croix 43,872
Sauk 43,469
Sawyer 12,843
Shawano 35,928
Sheboygan 100,935
Taylor 18,817

Trempealeau 26,158
Vernon 25,642
Vilas 16,535
Walworth 71,507
Washburn 13,174
Washington 84,848
Waukesha 280,326
Waupaca 42,831
Waushara 18,526
Winnebago 131,732
Wood 72,799

WYOMING

1980 Census 470,816

CITIES

Afton 1,481
Baggs 433
Basin 1,349
Big Piney 530
Buffalo 3,799
Byron 633
CASPER CASP. 51,016
CHEYENNE CHEY 47,283
Cody 6,790
Cokeville 515
Cowley 455
Dayton 701
Diamondville 1,000
Douglas 6,030
Dubois 1,067
Edgerton 510
Encampment 611
Evanston 6,421
Evansville CASP 2,652
Gillette 12,134
Glenrock 2,736
Green River 12,807
Greybull 2,277
Guernsey 1,512
Hanna 2,288
Hudson 514
Jackson 4,511
Kemmerer 3,273
Lander 9,126
Laramie 24,410
Lingle 475
Lovell 2,447
Lusk 1,650
Lyman 2,284
Marbleton 537
Medicine Bow 953
Meeteetse 512
Midwest 638

Mills CASP. 2,139
Moorcroft 1,014
Mountain View CASP .... 1,500 ○
Mountain View 628
Newcastle 3,596
Orchard Valley CHEY .... 800 ○
Paradise Valley CASP ...... 2,300 ○
Pine Bluffs 1,077
Pinedale 1,066
Powell 5,310
Ranchester 655
Rawlins 11,547
Reliance .... 500 ○
Riverton 9,588
Rock River 415
Rock Springs 19,458
Saratoga 2,410
Sheridan 15,146
Shirley Basin .... 450 ○
Shoshoni 879
Sinclair 586
South Laramie .... 1,500 ○
South Superior 586
Story .... 700 ○
Sundance 1,087
Thermopolis 3,852
Torrington 5,441
Upton 1,193
Wamsutter 681
West Laramie .... 2,000 ○
Wheatland 5,816
Worland 6,391

COUNTIES

Albany 29,062
Big Horn 11,896
Campbell 24,367
Carbon 21,896
Converse 14,069
Crook 5,308
Fremont 40,251
Goshen 12,040
Hot Springs 5,710
Johnson 6,700
Laramie 68,649
Lincoln 12,177
Natrona 71,856
Niobrara 2,924
Park 21,639
Platte 11,975
Sheridan 25,048
Sublette 4,548
Sweetwater 41,723
Teton 9,355
Uinta 13,021
Washakie 9,496
Weston 7,106

○ Rand McNally estimate (not reported in census).
▲ Population of entire township or "town", including rural area.
● Independent city. Population not included in county total.

Geographical Facts about the United States

ELEVATION

The highest elevation in the United States is Mount McKinley, Alaska, 20,320 feet.
The lowest elevation in the United States is in Death Valley, California, 282 feet below sea level.
The average elevation of the United States is 2,500 feet.

EXTREMITIES

Direction	Location	Latitude	Longitude
North	Point Barrow, Alaska	71°23′N.	156°29′W.
South	Ka Lae (point) Hawaii	18°56′N.	155°41′W.
East	West Quoddy Head, Maine	44°49′N.	66°57′W.
West	Cape Wrangell, Alaska	52°55′N.	172°27′E.

The two places in the United States separated by the greatest distance are Kure Island, Hawaii, and Mangrove Point, Florida. These points are 5,848 miles apart.

LENGTH OF BOUNDARIES

The total length of the Canadian boundary of the United States is 5,525 miles.
The total length of the Mexican boundary of the United States is 1,933 miles.

The total length of the Atlantic coastline of the United States is 2,069 miles.
The total length of the Pacific and Arctic coastline of the United States is 8,683 miles.
The total length of the Gulf of Mexico coastline of the United States is 1,631 miles.
The total length of all coastlines and land boundaries of the United States is 19,841 miles.
The total length of the tidal shoreline and land boundaries of the United States is 96,091 miles.

GEOGRAPHIC CENTERS

The geographic center of the United States (including Alaska and Hawaii) is in Butte County, South Dakota, at 44°58′N., 103°46′W.
The geographic center of North America is in North Dakota, a few miles west of Devils Lake, at 48°10′N., 100°10′W.

EXTREMES OF TEMPERATURE

The highest temperature ever recorded in the United States was 134°F., at Greenland Ranch, Death Valley, California, on July 10, 1913.

The lowest temperature ever recorded in the United States was −76°F., at Tanana, Alaska, in January, 1886.

PRECIPITATION

The average annual precipitation for the United States is approximately 29 inches.
Hawaii is the wettest state, with an average annual rainfall of 82.48 inches. Nevada, with an average annual rainfall of 8.81 inches, is the driest state.
The greatest local average annual rainfall in the United States is at Mt. Waialeale, Kauai, Hawaii, 460 inches.
Greatest 24-hour rainfall in the United States, 23.22 inches at New Smyrna, Florida, October 10–11, 1924.
Extreme minimum rainfall records in the United States include a total fall of only 3.93 inches at Bagdad, California, for a period of 5 years, 1909–13, and an annual average of 1.78 inches at Death Valley, California.
Heavy snowfall records include 76 inches at Silver Lake, Colorado, in 1 day; 42 inches at Angola, New York, in 2 days; 87 inches at Giant Forest, California, in 3 days; and 108 inches at Tahoe, California, in 4 days.
Greatest seasonal snowfall, 1,000.3 inches, more than 83 feet, at Paradise Ranger Station, Washington, during the winter of 1955–56.

Historical Facts about the United States

TERRITORIAL ACQUISITIONS

Accession	Date	Area (sq. mi.)	Cost in Dollars
Original territory of the Thirteen States	1790	888,685	
Purchase of Louisiana Territory, from France	1803	827,192	$11,250,000.00
By treaty with Spain: Florida	1819	58,560 }	$ 5,000,000.00
Other areas	1819	13,443 }	
Annexation of Texas	1845	390,144	
Oregon Territory, by treaty with Great Britain	1846	285,580	
Mexican Cession	1848	529,017	$15,000,000.00
Gadsden Purchase, from Mexico	1853	29,640	$10,000,000.00
Purchase of Alaska, from Russia	1867	586,412	7,200,000.00
Annexation of Hawaiian Islands	1898	6,450	
Puerto Rico, by treaty with Spain	1899	3,435	
Guam, by treaty with Spain	1899	212	
American Samoa, by treaty with Great Britain and Germany	1900	76	
Virgin Islands, by purchase from Denmark	1917	133	$25,000,000.00
Total		3,618,979	$73,450,000.00

Note: The Philippines, ceded by Spain in 1898 for $20,000,000.00, were a territorial possession of the United States from 1898 to 1946. On July 4, 1946 they became the independent republic of the Philippines.

Note. The Canal Zone, ceded by Panama in 1903 for $10,000,000.00, was a territory of the United States from 1903 to 1979. As a result of treaties signed in 1977, sovereignty over the Canal Zone reverted to Panama in 1979.

WESTWARD MOVEMENT OF CENTER OF POPULATION

Year	U.S. Population Total at Census	Approximate Location
1790	3,929,214	23 miles east of Baltimore, Md.
1800	5,308,483	18 miles west of Baltimore, Md.
1810	7,239,881	40 miles northwest of Washington, D.C.
1820	9,638,453	16 miles east of Moorefield, W. Va.
1830	12,866,020	19 miles southwest of Moorefield, W. Va.
1840	17,069,453	16 miles south of Clarksburg, W. Va.
1850	23,191,876	23 miles southeast of Parkersburg, W. Va.
1860	31,443,321	20 miles southeast of Chillicothe, Ohio
1870	39,818,449	48 miles northeast of Cincinnati, Ohio
1880	50,155,783	8 miles southwest of Cincinnati, Ohio
1890	62,947,714	20 miles east of Columbus, Ind.
1900	75,994,575	6 miles southeast of Columbus, Ind.
1910	91,972,266	Bloomington, Ind.
1920	105,710,620	8 miles southwest of Spencer, Ind.
1930	122,775,046	3 miles northeast of Linton, Ind.
1940	131,669,275	2 miles southeast of Carlisle, Ind.
1950	150,697,361	8 miles northwest of Olney, Ill.
1960	179,323,175	6 miles northwest of Centralia, Ill.
1970	204,816,296	5 miles southeast of Mascoutah, Ill.
1980	226,504,825	Near DeSoto, Mo.

State Areas and Populations

STATE	Land Area square miles	Water Area* square miles	Total Area square miles	Area Rank	1980 Resident Population	1980 Population per square mile	1970 Population	1960 Population	1950 Population	Population Rank 1980	1970	1960
Alabama	50,708	901	51,609	30	3,890,061	75	3,444,165	3,266,740	3,061,743	22	21	19
Alaska	569,602	20,157	589,759	1	400,481	0.7	302,173	226,167	128,643	50	50	50
Arizona	113,417	492	113,909	6	2,717,866	24	1,772,482	1,302,161	749,587	29	33	35
Arkansas	51,945	1,159	53,104	28	2,285,513	43	1,923,295	1,786,272	1,909,511	33	32	31
California	156,362	2,332	158,694	3	23,668,562	149	19,953,134	15,717,204	10,586,223	1	1	2
Colorado	103,767	481	104,248	8	2,888,834	28	2,207,259	1,753,947	1,325,089	28	30	33
Connecticut	4,862	147	5,009	48	3,107,576	620	3,032,217	2,535,234	2,007,280	25	24	25
Delaware	1,982	75	2,057	49	595,225	289	548,104	446,292	318,085	47	46	46
District of Columbia	61	6	67	..	637,651	9,517	756,510	763,956	802,178	7	9	10
Florida	54,090	4,470	58,560	24	9,739,992	166	6,789,443	4,951,560	2,771,305	7	9	10
Georgia	58,073	803	58,876	23	5,464,265	93	4,589,575	3,943,116	3,444,578	13	15	16
Hawaii	6,425	25	6,450	47	965,000	150	769,913	632,772	499,794	39	40	43
Idaho	82,677	880	83,557	14	943,935	11	713,008	667,191	588,637	41	42	42
Illinois	55,748	2,178	57,926	25	11,418,461	197	11,113,976	10,081,158	8,712,176	5	5	4
Indiana	36,097	422	36,519	38	5,490,179	150	5,193,669	4,662,498	3,934,224	12	11	11
Iowa	55,941	349	56,290	26	2,913,387	52	2,825,041	2,757,537	2,621,073	27	25	24
Kansas	81,787	477	82,264	15	2,363,208	29	2,249,071	2,178,611	1,905,299	32	28	28
Kentucky	39,650	745	40,395	37	3,661,433	91	3,219,311	3,038,156	2,944,806	23	23	22
Louisiana	44,930	3,593	48,523	31	4,203,972	87	3,643,180	3,257,022	2,683,516	19	20	20
Maine	30,920	2,295	33,215	39	1,124,660	34	993,663	969,265	913,774	38	38	36
Maryland	9,891	686	10,577	42	4,216,446	399	3,922,399	3,100,689	2,343,001	18	18	21
Massachusetts	7,826	431	8,257	45	5,737,037	695	5,689,170	5,148,578	4,690,514	11	10	9
Michigan	56,817	39,974	96,791	11	9,258,344	96	8,875,083	7,823,194	6,371,766	8	7	7
Minnesota	79,289	6,991	86,280	12	4,077,148	47	3,805,069	3,413,864	2,982,483	21	19	18
Mississippi	47,296	420	47,716	32	2,520,638	53	2,216,912	2,178,141	2,178,914	31	29	29
Missouri	68,995	691	69,686	20	4,917,444	71	4,677,399	4,319,813	3,954,653	15	13	13
Montana	145,587	1,551	147,138	4	786,690	5.3	694,409	674,767	591,024	44	43	41
Nebraska	76,483	744	77,227	16	1,570,006	20	1,483,791	1,411,330	1,325,510	35	35	34
Nevada	109,890	651	110,541	7	799,184	7.2	488,738	285,278	160,083	43	47	49
New Hampshire	9,027	277	9,304	44	920,610	99	737,681	606,921	533,242	42	41	45
New Jersey	7,521	315	7,836	46	7,364,158	940	7,168,164	6,066,782	4,835,329	9	8	8
New Mexico	121,413	254	121,667	5	1,299,968	11	1,016,000	951,023	681,187	37	37	37
New York	47,831	5,372	53,203	27	17,557,288	330	18,241,266	16,782,304	14,830,192	2	2	1
North Carolina	48,798	3,788	52,586	29	5,874,429	112	5,082,059	4,556,155	4,061,929	10	12	12
North Dakota	69,273	1,392	70,665	18	652,695	9.2	617,761	632,446	619,636	46	45	44
Ohio	40,975	3,704	44,679	34	10,797,419	242	10,652,017	9,706,397	7,946,627	6	6	5
Oklahoma	68,782	1,137	69,919	19	3,025,266	43	2,559,253	2,328,284	2,233,351	26	27	27
Oregon	96,184	797	96,981	10	2,632,663	27	2,091,385	1,768,687	1,521,341	30	31	32
Pennsylvania	44,966	1,102	46,068	33	11,866,728	258	11,793,909	11,319,366	10,498,012	4	3	3
Rhode Island	1,049	165	1,214	50	947,154	780	949,723	859,488	791,896	40	39	39
South Carolina	30,225	830	31,055	40	3,119,208	100	2,590,516	2,382,594	2,117,027	24	26	26
South Dakota	75,955	1,092	77,047	17	690,178	9.0	666,257	680,514	652,740	45	44	40
Tennessee	41,328	916	42,244	35	4,590,750	109	3,924,164	3,567,089	3,291,718	17	17	17
Texas	262,135	5,204	267,339	2	14,228,383	53	11,196,730	9,579,677	7,711,194	3	4	6
Utah	82,096	2,820	84,916	13	1,461,037	17	1,059,273	890,627	688,862	36	36	38
Vermont	9,267	342	9,609	43	511,456	53	444,732	389,881	377,747	48	48	47
Virginia	39,780	1,037	40,817	36	5,346,279	131	4,648,494	3,966,949	3,318,680	14	14	14
Washington	66,570	1,622	68,192	21	4,130,163	61	3,409,169	2,853,214	2,378,963	20	22	23
West Virginia	24,070	111	24,181	41	1,949,644	81	1,744,237	1,860,421	2,005,552	34	34	30
Wisconsin	54,464	11,752	66,216	22	4,705,335	71	4,417,933	3,951,777	3,434,575	16	16	15
Wyoming	97,203	711	97,914	9	470,816	4.8	332,416	330,066	290,529	49	49	48
United States	3,540,030	138,866	3,678,896	..	226,504,825	62	203,235,298	179,323,175	151,325,798	..	..	..

*Includes the United States area of the Great Lakes.

U.S. State General Information

STATE	CAPITAL	LARGEST CITY	ENTERED UNION AS STATE Date of Entry	Rank of Entry	Greatest N-S Measurement (miles)	Greatest E-W Measurement (miles)	HIGHEST POINT Location	Altitude (feet)	STATE FLOWER	STATE BIRD	STATE NICKNAME
Alabama	Montgomery	Birmingham	Dec. 14, 1819	22	330	200	Cheaha Mountain	2,407	Camellia	Yellowhammer	Yellowhammer
Alaska	Juneau	Anchorage	Jan. 3, 1959	49	1,332	2,250	Mt. McKinley	20,320	Forget-me-not	Willow Ptarmigan	Last Frontier
Arizona	Phoenix	Phoenix	Feb. 14, 1912	48	390	335	Humphreys Peak	12,633	Saguaro Cactus	Cactus Wren	Grand Canyon
Arkansas	Little Rock	Little Rock	June 15, 1836	25	240	275	Magazine Mtn.	2,753	Apple Blossom	Mockingbird	Land of Opportunity
California	Sacramento	Los Angeles	Sept. 9, 1850	31	800	375	Mt. Whitney	14,494	Golden Poppy	California Valley Quail	Golden
Colorado*	Denver	Denver	Aug. 1, 1876	38	270	380	Mt. Elbert	14,433	Rocky Mountain Columbine	Lark Bunting	Centennial
Connecticut*	Hartford	Hartford	Jan. 9, 1788	5	75	90	S. slope of Mt. Frissell	2,380	Mountain Laurel	Robin	Constitution
Delaware*	Dover	Wilmington	Dec. 7, 1787	1	95	35	Ebright Road, New Castle Co.	442	Peach Blossom	Blue Hen Chicken	First
District of Columbia	Washington	Washington	March 3, 1791		15	15	Tenleytown	410	American Beauty Rose	Wood Thrush	
Florida	Tallahassee	Jacksonville	March 3, 1845	27	460	400	N. boundary, Walton Co.	345	Orange Blossom	Mockingbird	Sunshine
Georgia*	Atlanta	Atlanta	Jan. 2, 1788	4	315	250	Brasstown Bald (mtn.)	4,784	Cherokee Rose	Brown Thrasher	Peach
Hawaii	Honolulu	Honolulu	Aug. 21, 1959	50	480	1,600	Mauna Kea	13,796	Red Hibiscus	Nene (Hawaiian Goose)	Aloha
Idaho	Boise	Boise	July 3, 1890	43	480	305	Borah Peak	12,662	Syringa	Mountain Bluebird	Gem
Illinois	Springfield	Chicago	Dec. 3, 1818	21	380	205	Charles Mound	1,235	Violet	Cardinal	Prairie
Indiana	Indianapolis	Indianapolis	Dec. 11, 1816	19	265	160	Near Spartanburg	1,257	Peony	Cardinal	Hoosier
Iowa	Des Moines	Des Moines	Dec. 28, 1846	29	205	310	N. W. corner Osceola Co.	1,670	Wild Rose	Eastern Goldfinch	Hawkeye
Kansas	Topeka	Wichita	Jan. 29, 1861	34	205	410	Mt. Sunflower	4,039	Sunflower	Western Meadowlark	Sunflower
Kentucky	Frankfort	Louisville	June 1, 1792	15	175	350	Black Mountain	4,145	Goldenrod	Kentucky Cardinal	Bluegrass
Louisiana	Baton Rouge	New Orleans	April 30, 1812	18	275	300	Driskill Mountain	535	Magnolia	Pelican	Pelican
Maine	Augusta	Portland	March 15, 1820	23	310	210	Mt. Katahdin	5,268	White Pine	Chickadee	Pine Tree
Maryland*	Annapolis	Baltimore	April 28, 1788	7	120	200	Backbone Mountain	3,360	Black-eyed Susan	Baltimore Oriole	Old Free
Massachusetts*	Boston	Boston	Feb. 6, 1788	6	110	190	Mt. Greylock	3,491	Mayflower	Chickadee	Old Bay
Michigan	Lansing	Detroit	Jan. 26, 1837	26	400	310	Mt. Curwood	1,980	Apple Blossom	Robin	Wolverine
Minnesota	St. Paul	Minneapolis	May 11, 1858	32	400	350	Eagle Mtn.	2,301	Showy Lady's-slipper	Loon	Gopher
Mississippi	Jackson	Jackson	Dec. 10, 1817	20	340	180	Woodall Mountain	806	Magnolia	Mockingbird	Magnolia
Missouri	Jefferson City	St. Louis	Aug. 10, 1821	24	280	300	Taum Sauk Mountain	1,772	Hawthorne	Bluebird	Show Me
Montana	Helena	Billings	Nov. 8, 1889	41	315	570	Granite Peak	12,799	Bitterroot	Western Meadowlark	Big Sky
Nebraska	Lincoln	Omaha	March 1, 1867	37	210	415	S.W. corner Kimball Co.	5,426	Goldenrod	Western Meadowlark	Cornhusker
Nevada	Carson City	Las Vegas	Oct. 31, 1864	36	485	315	Boundary Peak	13,143	Shrub Sagebrush	Mountain Bluebird	Silver
New Hampshire*	Concord	Manchester	June 21, 1788	9	185	90	Mt. Washington	6,288	Purple Lilac	Purple Finch	Granite
New Jersey*	Trenton	Newark	Dec. 18, 1787	3	166	70	High Point	1,803	Purple Violet	Eastern Goldfinch	Garden
New Mexico	Santa Fe	Albuquerque	Jan. 6, 1912	47	390	350	Wheeler Peak	13,161	Yucca	Roadrunner	Land of Enchantment
New York*	Albany	New York	July 26, 1788	11	310	330	Mt. Marcy	5,344	Rose	Bluebird	Empire
North Carolina*	Raleigh	Charlotte	Nov. 21, 1789	12	200	520	Mt. Mitchell	6,684	Dogwood	Cardinal	Tar Heel
North Dakota	Bismarck	Fargo	Nov. 2, 1889	39	210	360	White Butte	3,506	Wild Prairie Rose	Western Meadowlark	Flickertail
Ohio	Columbus	Cleveland	March 1, 1803	17	230	205	Campbell Hill	1,550	Scarlet Carnation	Cardinal	Buckeye
Oklahoma	Oklahoma City	Oklahoma City	Nov. 16, 1907	46	210	460	Black Mesa	4,973	Mistletoe	Scissor-tailed Flycatcher	Sooner
Oregon	Salem	Portland	Feb. 14, 1859	33	290	375	Mt. Hood	11,239	Oregon Grape	Western Meadowlark	Beaver
Pennsylvania*	Harrisburg	Philadelphia	Dec. 12, 1787	2	180	310	Mt. Davis	3,213	Mountain Laurel	Ruffed Grouse	Keystone
Rhode Island*	Providence	Providence	May 29, 1790	13	50	35	Jerimoth Hill	812	Violet	Rhode Island Red	Little Rhody
South Carolina*	Columbia	Columbia	May 23, 1788	8	215	285	Sassafras Mountain	3,560	Carolina Jessamine	Carolina Wren	Palmetto
South Dakota	Pierre	Sioux Falls	Nov. 2, 1889	40	240	360	Harney Peak	7,242	Pasque	Ringnecked Pheasant	Coyote
Tennessee	Nashville	Memphis	June 1, 1796	16	120	430	Clingmans Dome	6,643	Iris	Mockingbird	Volunteer
Texas	Austin	Houston	Dec. 29, 1845	28	710	760	Guadalupe Peak	8,751	Bluebonnet	Mockingbird	Lone Star
Utah	Salt Lake City	Salt Lake City	Jan. 4, 1896	45	345	275	Kings Peak	13,528	Sego Lily	Seagull	Beehive
Vermont	Montpelier	Burlington	March 4, 1791	14	155	90	Mt. Mansfield	4,393	Red Clover	Hermit Thrush	Green Mountain
Virginia*	Richmond	Norfolk	June 25, 1788	10	205	425	Mt. Rogers	5,729	Flowering Dogwood	Cardinal	Old Dominion
Washington	Olympia	Seattle	Nov. 11, 1889	42	230	340	Mt. Rainier	14,410	Rhododendron	Willow Goldfinch	Evergreen
West Virginia*	Charleston	Huntington	June 20, 1863	35	200	225	Spruce Knob	4,862	Rhododendron	Cardinal	Mountain
Wisconsin	Madison	Milwaukee	May 29, 1848	30	300	290	Timms Hill	1,952	Violet	Robin	Badger
Wyoming	Cheyenne	Cheyenne	July 10, 1890	44	275	365	Gannett Peak	13,804	Indian Paint Brush	Meadowlark	Equality
United States	Washington, D.C.	New York					Mt. McKinley, Alaska	20,320		Bald Eagle	

*One of the Thirteen Original States.

Abbreviations

admin	administered
Afg	Afghanistan
Afr	Africa
Ala	Alabama
Alb	Albania
Alg	Algeria
Alsk	Alaska
Alta	Alberta
Am	American
Am. Sam	American Samoa
And	Andorra
Ang	Angola
Ant	Antarctica
Arc	Arctic
arch	archipelago
Arg	Argentina
Ariz	Arizona
Ark	Arkansas
Atl. O	Atlantic Ocean
Aus	Austria
Austl	Australia, Australian
auton	autonomous
Az. Is	Azores Islands
Ba	Bahamas
Barb	Barbados
B. C.	British Columbia
Bel	Belgium, Belgian
Bhu	Bhutan
Bis. Arch	Bismarck Archipelago
Bngl	Bangladesh
Bol	Bolivia
Bots	Botswana
Br	British
Braz	Brazil
Bru	Brunei
Bul	Bulgaria
Bur	Burma
Calif	California
Cam	Cameroon
Can	Canada
Can. Is	Canary Islands
Cen. Afr. Rep	Central African Republic
Cen. Am	Central America
co	county
Col	Colombia
Colo	Colorado
Con	Congo
Conn	Connecticut
cont	continent
C. R.	Costa Rica
C. V.	Cape Verde
Cyp	Cyprus
Czech	Czechoslovakia
D.C.	District of Columbia
Del	Delaware
Den	Denmark
dep	dependency, dependencies
dept	department
dist	district
div	division
Dji	Djibouti
Dom. Rep	Dominican Republic
Ec	Ecuador
Eg	Egypt
Eng	England
Equat. Gui	Equatorial Guinea
Eth	Ethiopia
Eur	Europe
Falk. Is	Falkland Islands
Fed	Federation
Fin	Finland
Fla	Florida
Fr	France, French
Fr. Gu	French Guiana
Ga	Georgia
Gam	Gambia
Ger., Fed. Rep. of	Federal Republic of Germany
Ger. Dem. Rep	German Democratic Republic
Gib	Gibraltar
Grc	Greece
Grnld	Greenland
Guad	Guadeloupe
Guat	Guatemala
Guy	Guyana
Hai	Haiti
Haw	Hawaii
Hond	Honduras
Hung	Hungary
I.	Island
I.C.	Ivory Coast
Ice	Iceland
Ill	Illinois
incl	includes, including
Ind	Indiana
Indian res	Indian reservation
Indon	Indonesia
I. of Man	Isle of Man
Ire	Ireland
is	islands
isl	island
Isr	Israel
It	Italy
Jam	Jamaica
Jap	Japan
Kam	Kampuchea
Kans	Kansas
Ken	Kenya
Kor	Korea
Kuw	Kuwait
Ky	Kentucky
La	Louisiana
Leb	Lebanon
Le. Is	Leeward Islands
Leso	Lesotho
Lib	Liberia
Liech	Liechtenstein
Lux	Luxembourg
Mad	Madagascar
Mad. Is	Madeira Islands
Mala	Malaysia
Man	Manitoba
Mart	Martinique
Mass	Massachusetts
Maur	Mauritania
Md	Maryland
Medit	Mediterranean
Mex	Mexico
Mich	Michigan
Minn	Minnesota
Miss	Mississippi
Mo	Missouri
Mong	Mongolia
Mont	Montana
Mor	Morocco
Moz	Mozambique
mtn	mount, mountain
mts	mountains
mun	municipality
N.A.	North America
nat. mon	national monument
nat. park	national park
N.B.	New Brunswick
N.C.	North Carolina
N. Cal	New Caledonia
N. Dak	North Dakota
Nebr	Nebraska
Nep	Nepal
Neth	Netherlands
Nev	Nevada
Newf	Newfoundland
N.H.	New Hampshire
Nic	Nicaragua
Nig	Nigeria
N. Ire	Northern Ireland
N.J.	New Jersey
N. Mex	New Mexico
Nor	Norway, Norwegian
N.S.	Nova Scotia
N.W. Ter	Northwest Territories
N.Y	New York
N.Z.	New Zealand
occ	occupied area
Okla	Oklahoma
Om	Oman
Ont	Ontario
Oreg	Oregon
Pa	Pennsylvania
Pac. O	Pacific Ocean
Pak	Pakistan
Pan	Panama
Pap. N. Gui	Papua New Guinea
Par	Paraguay
par	parish
P.D.R. of Yem	Yemen, People's Democratic Republic of
P.E.I	Prince Edward Island
pen	peninsula
Phil	Philippines
Pol	Poland
pol. dist	political district
pop	population
Port	Portugal, Portuguese
poss	possession
P.R.	Puerto Rico
pref	prefecture
prot	protectorate
prov	province, provincial
pt	point
Que	Quebec
reg	region
rep	republic
res	reservation, reservoir
R.I.	Rhode Island
riv	river
Rom	Romania
S. A	South America
S. Afr	South Africa
Sal	El Salvador
Sask	Saskatchewan
Sau. Ar	Saudi Arabia
S.C.	South Carolina
Scot	Scotland
S. Dak	South Dakota
Sen	Senegal
S.L.	Sierra Leone
Sol. Is	Solomon Islands
Som	Somalia
Sov. Un	Soviet Union
Sp	Spain, Spanish
St., Ste	Saint, Sainte
Sud	Sudan
Sur	Suriname
Swaz	Swaziland
Swe	Sweden
Switz	Switzerland
Syr	Syria
Tan	Tanzania
Tenn	Tennessee
ter	territories, territory
Tex	Texas
Thai	Thailand
Trin	Trinidad & Tobago
trust	trusteeship
Tun	Tunisia
Tur	Turkey
U.A.E	United Arab Emirates
Ug	Uganda
U.K	United Kingdom
Ur	Uruguay
U.S.	United States
Va	Virginia
Ven	Venezuela
Viet	Vietnam
Vir. Is	Virgin Islands
vol	volcano
Vt	Vermont
Wash	Washington
W.I.	West Indies
Win. Is	Windward Islands
Wis	Wisconsin
W. Sah	Western Sahara
W. Sam	Western Samoa
W. Va	West Virginia
Wyo	Wyoming
Yugo	Yugoslavia
Zimb	Zimbabwe

Index

This universal index includes in a single alphabetical list all important names that appear on the reference maps. Each place name is followed by its location; the map index key; and the page number of the map.

State locations are given for all places in the United States. Province and country locations are given for all places in Canada. All other place name entries show only country locations.

The index reference key, always a letter and figure combination, and the map page number are the last items in each entry. Because some places are shown on both a main map and an inset map, more than one index key may be given for a single map page number. Reference also may be made to more than a single map. In each case, however, the index key *letter and figure* precede the map page number to which reference is made. A lower case key letter indicates reference to an inset map which has been keyed separately.

All major and minor political divisions are followed by both a descriptive term (co., dist., region, prov., dept., state, etc), indicating political status, and by the country in which they are located. U.S. counties are listed with state locations; all others are given with country references.

The more important physical names that are shown on the maps are listed in the index. Each entry is followed by a descriptive term (bay, hill, range, riv., mtn.,isl., etc), to indicate its nature.

Country locations are given for all names, except for features entirely within States of the United States or provinces of Canada, in which case these divisions are also given.

Some names are included in the index that were omitted from the maps because of scale size or lack of space. These entries are identified by an asterisk (*) and reference is given to the approximate location on the map.

A long name may appear on the map in a shortened form, with the full name given in the index. The part of the name not on the map then appears in italics, thus: St. Gabriel *-de-Brandon*.

The system of alphabetizing used in the index is standard. When more than one name with the same spelling is shown, place names are listed *first* and political divisions *second*.

A

B

C

Caacupé Par. ... E4 29
Caaguazú dept., Par. ... D4 29
Caapucú, Par. ... E4 29
Caazapá, Par. ... E4 29
Caazapá, dept., Par. ... E4 29
Cabaceiras, Braz. ... *D4 27
Cabana, Peru ... C2 31
Cabanatuan, Phil. ... o13 19
Cabano, Que., Can. ... B9 42
Cabarrus, co.,N.C. ... B2 76
Cabedelo, Braz. ... *D7 27
Cabell, co., W. Vir. ... C2 87
Cabeza, del Buey, Sp. ... C3 8
Cabimas, Ven. ... A3 32
Cabinda, Ang. ... B2 24
Cabinda, dist., Ang. ... B2 24
Cabin John, Md. ... C3, f8 53
Cabo, Braz. ... *D7 27
Cabo Frio, Braz. ... C4 30
Cabool, Mo. ... D5 69
Caboolture, Austl. ... *E9 25
Caborca, Mex. ... A2 34
Cabo Rojo, P.R. ... *G11 35
Cabo San Lucas, Mex. ... C3 34
Cabot, Ark. ... C3 49
Cacak, Yugo. ... D5 10
Caçapava, Braz. ... C3 30
Cacequi, Braz. ... D2 30
Cáceres, Sp. ... C2 8
Cáceres, prov., Sp. ... *C2 8
Cachan, Fr. ... G10 5
Cache, Okla. ... C3 79
Cache, co., Utah ... A6 72
Cache, peak, Idaho ... G5 57
Cache Bay, Ont., Can. ... A5 41
Cachi, Arg. ... E2 29
Cachoeira, Braz. ... *E7 27
Cachoeira do Sul, Braz. ... E2 30
Cachoeiro do Itapemirim, Braz. ... C4 30
Cacouna, Que., Can. ... B8 42
Caddo, Okla. ... C5 79
Caddo, co., Okla. ... B3 79
Caddo, par., La. ... B2 63
Cadillac, Mich. ... D5 66
Cadillac, mtn., Maine ... D4 64
Cadiz, Ky. ... D2 62
Cadiz, Ohio ... B4 78
Cádiz, Sp. ... D2 8
Cádiz, prov., Sp. ... *D2 8
Cadott, Wis. ... D2 88
Cadyville, N.Y. ... f11 75
Caen, Fr. ... C3 5
Caernarvon, Wales ... D4 4
Caernarvon, co., Wales ... *D4 4
Cagayan, de Oro, Phil. ... D6 19
Cagayan, prov., Phil. ... *B6 19
Cagli, It. ... C4 9
Cagliari, It. ... E2 9
Cagnes-sur-Mer, Fr. ... F7 5
Caguas, P.R. ... G12 35
Cahaba Heights, Ala. ... *B3 46
Cahokia, Ill. ... E3 58
Cahors, Fr. ... E4 5
Caibarién, Cuba ... C4 35
Caicedonia, Col. ... C2 32
Caicó, Braz. ... *D7 27
Cailloma, Peru ... E3 31
Cairnbrook, Pa. ... F4 81
Cairns, Austl. ... C8 25
Cairo, Ga. ... F2 55
Cairo, Ill. ... F4 58
Cairo, Eg. ... B4 23
Caithness, co., Scot. ... *A5 4
Cajabamba, Peru ... C2 31
Cajacay, Peru ... D2 31
Cajamarca, Peru ... C2 31
Cajamarca, dept., Peru ... C2 31
Cajatambo, Peru ... D2 31
Cajázeiras, Braz. ... *D7 27
Cakovec, Yugo. ... B3 10
Calabar, Nig. ... H6 22
Calabria, pol. dist., It. ... *E5 9
Calabria, reg., It. ... E6 9
Calafat, Rom. ... D6 10
Calahorra, Sp. ... A5 8
Calais, Fr. ... B4 5
Calais, Maine ... C5 64
Calamar, Col. ... A3 32
Calamba, Phil. ... C6 19
Calañas, Sp. ... D2 8
Calapan, Phil. ... C6 19
Cǎlǎrasi, Rom. ... C8 10
Calarcá, Col. ... C2 32
Calasparra, Sp. ... C5 8
Calauag, Phil. ... P14 19
Calaveras, co., Calif. ... C3 50

Calca, Peru ... D3 31
Calcasieu, par., La. ... D2 63
Calceta, Ec. ... B1 31
Calcutta, India ... D8 10
Calcutta, Ohio ... B5 78
Caldas, dept. Col. ... B2 32
Caldas da Rainha, Port. ... C1 8
Caldwell, Idaho ... F2 57
Caldwell, Kans. ... E6 61
Caldwell, N.J. ... B4 74
Caldwell, Ohio ... C4 78
Caldwell, Tex. ... D4 84
Caldwell, co., Ky. ... C2 62
Caldwell, co., Mo. ... B3 69
Caldwell, co., N.C. ... B1 76
Caldwell, co., Tex. ... E4 84
Caldwell, par., La. ... B3 63
Caledonia, Ont., Can. ... D5 41
Caledonia, Minn. ... G7 67
Caledonia, N.Y. ... C3 75
Caledonia, Ohio ... B3 78
Caledonia, co., Vt. ... C3 73
Calella, Sp. ... B7 8
Calera, Ala. ... B3 46
Calera, Chile ... A2 28
Calexico, Calif. ... F6 50
Calgary, Alta., Can. ... D3, g8 38
Calhoun, Ga. ... B2 55
Calhoun, co., Ala. ... B4 46
Calhoun, co., Ark. ... D3 49
Calhoun, co., Fla. ... B1 54
Calhoun, co., Ga. ... E2 55
Calhoun, co., Ill. ... D3 58
Calhoun, co., Iowa ... B4 60
Calhoun, co., Mich. ... F5 66
Calhoun, co., Miss. ... B4 68
Calhoun, co., S.C. ... D6 82
Calhoun, co., Tex. ... E4 84
Calhoun, co., W. Va. ... C3 87
Calhoun City, Miss. ... B4 68
Calhoun Falls, S.C. ... C2 82
Cali, Col. ... C2 32
Calico Rock, Ark. ... A3 49
Calicut, India ... F6 20
Caliente, Nev. ... C4 72
California, Mo. ... C5 69
California, Pa. ... F2 81
California, state, U.S. ... C2 50
California, co., Tex. ... C5 84
Calipatria, Calif. ... F6 50
Calispell, peak, Wash. ... A8 86
Calistoga, Calif. ... C2 50
Callahan, co., Tex. ... C3 84
Callander, Ont., Can. ... A5 41
Callander, Scot. ... B4 4
Callao, Peru ... D2 31
Callao, prov., Peru ... D2 31
Callaway, co., Mo. ... C6 69
Callicoon, N.Y. ... D5 75
Calloway, co., Ky. ... f9 62
Calmar, Alta., Can. ... C4 38
Calmar, Iowa ... A6 60
Caloundra, Austl. ... C9 26
Caltagirone, It. ... F5 9
Caltanissetta, It. ... F5 9
Caluire -et-Cuire, Fr. ... E6 5
Calumet, Que., Can. ... D3 42
Calumet, Mich. ... A2 66
Calumet, Pa. ... *F2 81
Calumet, co., Wis. ... D5 88
Calumet City, Ill. ... B6, k9 58
Calumet Park, Ill. ... *B6 58
Calvados, dept., Fr. ... *C3 5
Calvert, Tex. ... D4 84
Calvert, co., Md. ... C4 53
Calvert City, Ky. ... e9 62
Calverton Park, Mo., ... A8 69
Calvillo, Mex. ... m12 34
Calwa, Calif. ... *D4 50
Camacho, Mex. ... C4 34
Camagüey, Cuba ... D5 35
Camagüey, prov., Cuba ... D5 35
Camaná, Peru ... E2 31
Camanche, Iowa ... C7 60
Camargo, see Ciudad Camargo, Mex.
Camarillo, Calif. ... *E4 50
Camarines Norte, prov., Phil. ... *C6 19
Camarines Sur, prov., Phil. ... *C6 19
Camas, Wash. ... D3 86
Camas, co., Idaho ... F4 57
Cambay, India ... *D5 20
Cambodia, see Kampuchea, country, Asia
Camborne -Redruth, Eng. ... E4 4
Cambrai, Fr. ... B5 5
Cambria, Calif. ... E3 50

Cambria, co., Pa. ... E4 81
Cambrian Park, Calif. ... *D3 50
Cambridge, Eng. ... D7 4
Cambridge, Ill. ... B3 58
Cambridge, Md. ... C5 53
Cambridge, Mass ... B5, g11 65
Cambridge, Minn. ... E5 67
Cambridge, Nebr. ... D5 71
Cambridge, N.J. ... *C3 74
Cambridge, N.Y. ... B7 75
Cambridge, Ohio ... B4 78
Cambridge & Isle of Ely, co., Eng. ... *D7 4
Cambridge City, Ind. ... E7 59
Cambridge Springs, Pa. ... C1 81
Camden, Ala. ... D2 46
Camden, Ark. ... D3 49
Camden, Del. ... B6 53
Camden, Maine ... D3 64
Camden, N.J. ... D2 74
Camden, N.Y. ... B5 75
Camden, Ohio ... C1 78
Camden, S.C. ... C6 82
Camden, Tenn. ... A3 83
Camden, Tex. ... D5 84
Camden, co., Ga. ... F5 55
Camden, co., Mo. ... C5 69
Camden, co., N.J. ... D3 74
Camden, co., N.C. ... A6 76
Camdenton Mo. ... D5 69
Camerino, It. ... C4 9
Cameron, La. ... E2 63
Cameron, Mo. ... B3 69
Cameron, Tex. ... D4 84
Cameron, W. Va. ... B4, g8 87
Cameron, Wis. ... C2 88
Cameron, co., S.C. ... D5 81
Cameron, co., Tex. ... F4 84
Cameron, par., La. ... E2 63
Cameroon, country, Afr. ... G7 22
Cameroun, Mont, mtn., Cam. ... H6 22
Camiling, Phil. ... o13 19
Camilla, Ga. ... E2 55
Camillus, N.Y. ... *B4 75
Camino, Calif. ... C3 50
Cammack Village, Ark. ... C3, h10 49
Camocim, Braz. ... *D6 27
Camp, co., Tex. ... C5 84
Campagna di Roma, reg., It. ... h9 9
Campana, Arg. ... g7 28
Campanario, It. ... C3 8
Campania, pol. dist., It. ... *D5 9
Campania, reg., It. ... D5 9
Campbell, Calif. ... k8 50
Campbell, Mo. ... E7 69
Campbell, Ohio ... A5 78
Campbell, co., Ky. ... B5 62
Campbell, co., S. Dak. ... E5 77
Campbell, co., Tenn. ... C9 83
Campbell, co., Va. ... C3 85
Campbell, co., Wyo ... B7 89
Campbell, hill, Ohio ... B2 78
Campbellford, Ont., Can. ... C7 41
Campbellpore, Pak. ... B5 20
Campbell River, B.C. ... D5 37
Campbells Bay, Que., Can. ... B8 41
Campbellsport, Wis. ... E5 88
Campbellsville, Ky. ... C4 62
Campbellton, N.B., Can. ... A3 43
Campbelltown, Pa. ... *F9 81
Campbeltown, Scot. ... C4 4
Campeche, Mex. ... D6 34
Camp Hill, Ala. ... C4 46
Camp Hill, Pa. ... F8 81
Campiglia Marittima, It. ... C3 9
Campina Grande, Braz. ... D7 27
Campinas, Braz. ... C3, m8 30
Campoalegre, Col. ... C2 32
Campobasso, It. ... D5 9
Campo Belo, Braz. ... C3 30
Campo de Criptana, Sp. ... C4 8
Campo Grande, Braz. ... C2 30
Campo Maior, Braz. ... *D6 27
Campo Maior, Port. ... C2 8
Campos, Braz. ... C4 30
Camp Point, Ill. ... C2 58
Camp Springs, Md. ... f9 53
Campti, La. ... C2 63
Campton Heights, Calif. ... *B1 50
Camrose, Alta., Can. ... C4 38
Canaan, Conn. ... A3 52
Canada, country, N.A. ... D10 33
Cañada de Gómez, Arg. ... A4 28
Canadensis, Pa. ... D11 81
Canadian, Tex. ... B2 84
Canadian, co., Okla. ... B3 79

Canadian, riv., U.S. ... C6 45
Canajoharie, N.Y. ... C6 75
Çanakkale, Tur. ... B6 14
Canal Fulton, Ohio ... B4 78
Canal Point, Fla. ... F6 54
Canal Winchester, Ohio ... C3, m11 78
Canandaigua, N.Y. ... C3 75
Cananea, Mex. ... A2 34
Cañar, prov., Ec. ... B2 31
Canary Islands, reg., Sp. ... C1 22
Cañas, C.R. ... *E7 75
Canastota, N.Y. ... B5 34
Canavieiras, Braz. ... *E7 27
Canberra, Austl. ... G8 25
Canby, Minn. ... F2 67
Canby, Oreg. ... B4, h12 80
Candeleda, Sp. ... B3 8
Candia, see Iraklion, Grc.
Candiac, Que., Can. ... q19 42
Candler, co., Ga. ... D4 75
Cando, N. Dak. ... B6 77
Candor, N.Y. ... C4 75
Canea, see Khaniá, Grc.
Canelones, Ur. ... E1 30
Canelones, dept. Ur. ... *E1 30
Cañete, Peru ... D2 31
Caney, Kans. ... E8 61
Canfield, Ohio ... A5 78
Cangallo, Peru ... D3 31
Cangas, Sp. ... A1 8
Canicatti, It. ... F4 9
Caniles, Sp. ... D4 8
Canisteo, N.Y. ... C3 75
Çankiri (Changra), Tur. ... B9 14
Canmore, Alta, Can. ... D3 38
Cannelton, Ind. ... I4 59
Cannes, Fr. ... F7 5
Canning, N.S., Can. ... D5 43
Cannington, Ont., Can. ... C5 41
Cannon, co., Tenn. ... B5 83
Cannon Falls, Minn. ... F6 67
Canoas, Braz. ... *D2 30
Canoinhas, Braz. ... D2 30
Canon City, Colo ... C5 51
Canonsburg, Pa. ... F1 81
Canora, Sask., Can. ... F4 39
Canosa de Puglia, It. ... D6 9
Canso, N.S., Can. ... D8 43
Cantal, dept., Fr. ... *E5 5
Canterbury, Eng. ... E7 4
Can Tho, Viet. ... *C3 19
Cantilan, Phil. ... *D7 19
Canton, China ... G7 17
Canton, Ga. ... B2 55
Canton, Ill. ... C3 58
Canton, Mass. ... B5, h11 65
Canton, Miss. ... C3 68
Canton, Mo. ... A6 69
Canton, N.Y. ... F9 75
Canton, N.C. ... D3 76
Canton, Ohio ... B4 78
Canton, Okla. ... A3 79
Canton, Pa. ... C8 81
Canton, S. Dak. ... G9 77
Canton, Tex. ... C5 84
Cantonment, Fla. ... u14 54
Cantwell, Mo. ... D7 69
Canutillo, Tex. ... o11 84
Canyon, Tex. ... B2 84
Canyon, co., Idaho ... F2 57
Canyonville, Oreg. ... E3 80
Cao Bang, Viet. ... G6 17
Capac, Mich. ... F8 66
Cap Chat, Que., Can. ... G20 36
Cap-de-la-Madeleine, Que., Can. ... C5 42
Cape, prov., S. Afr. ... G4 24
Cape Breton, Can. ... G21 36
Cape Breton, co., N.S., Can. ... D9 43
Cape Canaveral, Fla. ... D6 54
Cape Charles, Va. ... C6 85
Cape Coast, Ghana ... G4 22
Cape Coral, Fla. ... F5 54
Cape Elizabeth, Maine ... E2, g7 64
Cape Girardeau, Mo. ... D8 69
Cape Girardeau, co., Mo. ... D8 69
Cape Horn, mtn., Idaho ... E3 57
Capels, W. Va. ... D3 87
Cape May, N.J. ... F3 74
Cape May, co., N.J. ... E3 74
Cape May Court House, N.J. ... E3 74
Cape Town (Kaapstad), S. Afr. ... G3 24
Cape Verde, country, Afr. ... o12 22
Cape Vincent, N.Y. ... A4 75
Cap-Haïtien, Hai. ... *E7 35
Capiata, Par. ... *E4 29

D

Dickens, co., Tex. ... C2 84
Dickenson, co., Va. ... e9 85
Dickey, co., N. Dak. ... D7 77
Dickinson, N. Dak. ... D3 77
Dickinson, Tex. ... *E5 84
Dickinson, co., Iowa ... A2 60
Dickinson, co., Kans. ... D6 61
Dickinson, co., Mich. ... B3 66
Dickson, Tenn. ... A4 83
Dickson, co., Tenn. ... A4 83
Dickson City, Pa. ... D10, m18 81
Didsbury, Alta., Can. ... D3 38
Diégo-Suarez (Antsirane), Mad. ... C9 24
Dien Bien Phu, Viet. ... *A2 19
Diepholz, Ger., Fed. Rep. of ... B4 6
Dieppe, N.B., Can. ... C5 43
Dieppe, Fr. ... C4 5
Dierks, Ark. ... C1 49
Digboi, India ... C10 20
Digby, N.S., Can. ... E4 43
Digby, co., N.S., Can. ... E4 43
Dighton, Kans. ... D3 61
Digne, Fr. ... E7 5
Digoin, Fr. ... D5 5
Dijon, Fr. ... D6 5
Dikson, Sov. Un. ... B11 16
Dili, Indon. ... G7 19
Dilley, Tex. ... E3 84
Dilligen an der Donau,
  Ger., Fed. Rep. of ... D5 6
Dillon, Mont. ... E4 70
Dillon, S.C. ... C9 82
Dillon, co., S.C. ... C9 82
Dillonvale, Ohio ... B5 78
Dillsburg, Pa. ... F7 81
Dilworth, Minn. ... D2 67
Dimitrovgrad, Bul. ... D7 10
Dimmit, co., Tex. ... E3 84
Dimmitt, Tex. ... E3 84
Dimona, Isr. ... C3 15
Dimondale, Mich. ... F6 66
Dinan, Fr. ... C3 5
Dinant, Bel. ... B6 5
Dinard, Fr. ... C2 5
Dindigul, India ... F6 20
Dingwall, Scot. ... B4 4
Dinh Lap, Viet. ... *G6 17
Dinuba, Calif. ... D4 50
Dinwiddie, co., Va. ... C5 85
Diourbel, Sen. ... F1 22
Dipolog, Phil ... *D6 19
Dire Dawa, Eth. ... G6 23
Diriamba, Nic. ... E7 34
Dirranbandi, Austl. ... E8 25
Dishman, Wash. ... g14 86
Dismal, peak, Va. ... C2 85
Disraéli, Que., Can. ... D6 42
District Heights, Md. ... *C4 53
District of Columbia, U.S. ... C3, f8 53
Distrito Federal, fed. dist., Mex. ... D5 34
Distrito Federal, fed. dist., Ven. ... A4 32
Disûq, Eg. ... *G8 14
Diu, India ... D5 20
Divernon, Ill. ... D4 58
Dives-sur-Mer, Fr. ... C3 5
Divide, co., N. Dak. ... *B2 77
Divide, peak, Wyo. ... E5 89
Divinópolis, Braz. ... C4 30
Divnoye, Sov. Un. ... I14 12
Dix, mtn., N.Y. ... A7 75
Dixfield, Maine ... D2 64
Dixiana, Ala. ... B3 46
Dixie, co., Fla. ... C3 54
Dixmoor, Ill. ... *B6 58
Dixon, Calif. ... C3 50
Dixon, Ill. ... B4 58
Dixon, Mo. ... D5 69
Dixon, co., Nebr. ... B9 71
Dixonville, Pa. ... E3 81
Diyarbakir, Tur. ... D13 14
Djajapura, see Jayapura, Indon.
Djakarta, see Jakarta, Indon.
Djakovica, Yugo. ... D5 10
Djakovo, Yugo. ... D4 10
Djelfa, Alg. ... B5 22
Djibouti, Dji. ... F6 23
Djibouti, country, Afr. ... F6 23
Djombang, Indon. ... *G4 19
Djurdjevac, Yugo. ... B3 10
Djursholm, Swe. ... t36 11
Dmitriyevka, Sov. Un. ... H12, r21 12
Dmitrov, Sov. Un. ... C11 12
Dmitrovsk-Orlovskiy, Sov. Un. ... E10 12
Dnepr, riv., Sov. Un. ... H9 12
Dneprodzerzhinsk, Sov. Un. ... G10 12
Dnepropetrovsk, Sov. Un. ... G10 12
Dnestr, riv., Sov. Un. ... H7 12
Dno, Sov. Un. ... C7 12
Dobbs Ferry, N.Y. ... g13 75
Döbeln, Ger. Dem. Rep. ... C6 6
Doboj, Yugo. ... C4 10
Dobrich, see Tolbukhin, Bul.

Dobrogea, reg., Rom. ... *C9 10
Dobruja, reg., Bul. ... C9 10
Dobruja, reg., Rom. ... D9 10
Docena, Ala. ... f7 46
Doddridge, co., W. Va. ... B4 87
Dodge, co., Ga. ... D3 55
Dodge, co., Minn. ... G6 67
Dodge, co., Nebr. ... C9 71
Dodge, co., Wis. ... E5 88
Dodge Center, Minn. ... F6 67
Dodge City, Kans. ... E3 61
Dodgeville, Wis. ... F3 88
Dodoma, Tan. ... B7 24
Doerun, Ga. ... E3 55
Doe Run, Mo. ... D7 69
Doha (Ad Dawḥah), Qatar ... D5 15
Doi Inthanon, mtn., Thai. ... E10 20
Dolbeau, Que., Can. ... G19 36
Dôle, Fr. ... D6 5
Dolgeville, N.Y. ... B6 75
Dolinsk (Ochiai), Sov. Un. ... C11 18
Dolina, Sov. Un. ... D8 7
Dolomite, Ala. ... B3, g7 46
Dolores, Arg. ... B5 28
Dolores, Ur. ... E1 30
Dolores, co., Colo. ... D2 51
Dolores Hidalgo, Mex. ... m13 34
Dolton, Ill. ... k9 58
Dolzhanskaya, Sov. Un. ... q22 12
Domažlice, Czech. ... D2 7
Dominguez, Calif. ... *F4 50
Dominica, country, N.A. ... I14 35
Dominican Republic,
  country, N.A. ... E8 35
Dominion, N.S., Can. ... C9 43
Domodossola, It. ... A2 9
Dom Pedrito, Braz. ... E2 30
Don, riv., Sov. Un. ... H13 12
Dona Ana, co., N. Mex. ... C5 48
Donaghadee, N. Ire. ... C4 4
Donaldsonville, La. ... D4, h10 63
Donalsonville, Ga. ... E2 55
Don Benito, Sp. ... C3 8
Doncaster, EnNg. ... D6 4
Donegal, co., Ire. ... *C2 4
Doneraile, S.C. ... C8 82
Donets, riv., Sov. Un. ... G13 12
Donetsk, Sov. Un. ... H11, r20 12
Donggala, Indon. ... F5 19
Dong Hoi, Viet. ... B3 19
Doniphan, Mo. ... E7 69
Doniphan, co., Kans. ... C8 61
Donkin, N.S., Can. ... C10 43
Donley, co., Tex. ... B2 84
Donna, Tex. ... F3 84
Donnacona, Que., Can. ... C6, o16 42
Donora, Pa. ... F2 81
Donzère, Fr. ... E6 5
Doolittle, Mo. ... D6 69
Dooly, co., Ga. ... D3 55
Door, co., Wis. ... D6 88
Dora, Ala. ... B2 46
Doraville, Ga. ... h8 55
Dorchester, N.B., Can. ... D5 43
Dorchester, Eng. ... E5 4
Dorchester, co., Que., Can. ... C7 42
Dorchester, co., Md. ... D5 53
Dorchester, co., S.C. ... E6 82
Dordogne, dept., Fr. ... *E4 5
Dordrecht, Neth. ... B6 5
Dores do Indaiá, Braz. ... B3 30
Dorgali, It. ... D2 9
Dorion-Vaudreuil, Que., Can. ... q18 42
Dorking, Eng. ... m12 4
Dormont, Pa. ... k13 81
Dornbirn, Aus. ... E4 6
Dornoch, Scot. ... B4 4
Dorohoi, Rom. ... B8 10
Dorris, Calif. ... B3 50
Dorset, co., Eng. ... *F5 4
Dortmund, Ger., Fed. Rep. of ... C3 6
Dorton, Ky. ... C7 62
Dörtyol, Tur. ... D11 14
Dorval, Que., Can. ... q19 42
Dos Hermanas, Sp. ... D3 8
Dos Palos, Calif. ... D3 50
Dothan, Ala. ... D4 46
Douai, Fr. ... B5 5
Douala, Cam. ... H6 22
Douarnenez, Fr. ... C1 5
Doubletop, peak, Wyo. ... C2 89
Doubs, dept., Fr. ... *D7 5
Dougherty, co., Ga. ... E2 55
Douglas, Alsk. ... D13, k22 47
Douglas, Ariz. ... D4 48
Douglas, Ga. ... E4 55
Douglas, I. of Man ... C4 4
Douglas, Wyo. ... D7 89
Douglas, co., Colo. ... B6 51
Douglas, co., Ga. ... C2 55
Douglas, co., Ill. ... D5 58
Douglas, co., Kans. ... D8 61

Douglas, co., Minn. ... E3 67
Douglas, co., Mo. ... E5 69
Douglas, co., Nebr. ... C9 71
Douglas, co., Nev. ... B2 72
Douglas, co., Oreg. ... D3 80
Douglas, co., S. Dak. ... G7 77
Douglas, co., Wash. ... B6 86
Douglas, co., Wis. ... B1 88
Douglass, Kans. ... E7 61
Douglasville, Ga. ... C2 55
Doullens, Fr. ... B5 5
Douro Litoral, prov., Port. ... *B1 8
Dove Creek, Colo. ... D2 51
Dover, Del. ... D4 53
Dover, Eng. ... E7 4
Dover, Fla. ... h10 65
Dover, Mass. ... h10 65
Dover, N.H. ... E6 73
Dover, N.J. ... B3 74
Dover, Ohio ... B4 78
Dover, Pa. ... F8 81
Dover, Tenn. ... A4 83
Dover-Foxcroft, Maine ... C3 64
Dover Plains, N.Y. ... D7 75
Dowagiac, Mich. ... G4 66
Down, co., N. Ire. ... *C4 4
Downers Grove, Ill. ... B5, k8 58
Downey, Calif. ... n12 50
Downington, Pa. ... F10 81
Downpatrick, N. Ire. ... C4 4
Downs, Kans. ... C5 61
Downs, mtn., Wyo. ... C3 89
Downton, mtn., B.C., Can. ... C5 37
Dows, Iowa ... B4 60
Doylestown, Ohio ... B4 78
Doylestown, Pa. ... F11 81
Doyline, La. ... B2 63
Dracut, Mass. ... A5 65
Draganovo, Bul. ... D7 10
Drăgăsani, Rom. ... C7 10
Dragerton, Utah ... *B6 72
Draguignan, Fr. ... F7 5
Drain, Oreg. ... D3 80
Drake, peak, Oreg. ... E6 80
Drakesboro, Ky. ... C2 62
Drama, Grc. ... B5 14
Drama, prov., Grc. ... *B5 14
Drammen, Nor. ... H4, p28 11
Drancy, Fr. ... g10 5
Draper, Utah ... A6, D2 72
Dravosburg, Pa. ... *E1 81
Drayton, N. Dak. ... A8 77
Drayton, S.C. ... B4 82
Drayton Plains, Mich. ... F7 66
Drayton Valley, Alta., Can. ... C3 38
Drenthe, prov., Neth. ... *A7 5
Dresden, Ont., Can. ... E2 41
Dresden, Ger. Dem. Rep. ... C6 6
Dresden, Ohio ... B3 78
Dresden, Tenn. ... A3 83
Dreux, Fr. ... C4 5
Drew, Miss. ... B3 68
Drew, co., Ark. ... D4 49
Drexel, N.C. ... B1 76
Drexel, Ohio ... C1 78
Drexel Hill, Pa. ... *G11 81
Drift, Ky. ... C7 62
Drifton, Pa. ... D10 81
Driggs, Idaho ... F7 57
Driskill, mtn., La. ... B3 63
Drissa, Sov. Un. ... D6 12
Drogheda, Ire. ... D3 4
Drogobych, Sov. Un. ... G4 12
Druid Hills, N.C. ... *f10 76
Drumheller, Alta., Can. ... D4 38
Drummond, co., Que., Can. ... D5 42
Drummond Range, mts., Austl. ... D8 25
Drummondville, Que., Can. ... D3 42
Drummondville Ouest, Que., Can. ... *D5 42
Drumright, Okla. ... B5 79
Druzhkovka, Sov. Un. ... q20 12
Dryden, Ont., Can. ... o16 41
Dryden, N.Y. ... C4 75
Duarte, Calif. ... *E5 50
Duarte, peak, Dom. Rep. ... E8 35
Dubach, La. ... B3 63
Dubai (Dubayy), U.A.E. ... D6 15
Dubawnt, lake, N.W. Ter., Can. ... D13 36
Dubbo, Austl. ... F8 25
Dublin, Ga. ... D4 55
Dublin, Ind. ... E7 59
Dublin (Baile Átha Cliath),
  Ire. ... D3 4
Dublin, Tex. ... C3 84
Dublin, Va. ... C2 85
Dublin, co., Ire. ... D3 4
Dubois, co., Ind. ... H4 59
Du Bois, Pa. ... D4 81
Duboistown, Pa. ... D7 81
Dubossary, Sov. Un. ... H7 12
Dubovka, Sov. Un. ... G15 12
Dubrovnik, Yugo. ... D4 10

Dubuque, Iowa ... B7 60
Dubuque, co., Iowa ... B7 60
Duchesne, co., Utah ... A6 72
Duchov, Czech. ... C2 7
Duck, mtn., Man., Can. ... D1 40
Ducktown, Tenn. ... D9 83
Dudinka, Sov. Un. ... C11 13
Dudley, Eng. ... D5 4
Dudley, Mass. ... B4 65
Due West, S.C. ... D3 82
Dufferin, co., Ont., Can. ... C4 41
Dugger, Ind. ... F3 59
Duisburg, Ger., Fed. Rep. of ... C3 6
Duitama, Col. ... B3 32
Dukes, co., Mass. ... B6 65
Dulawan, Phil. ... *D6 19
Duluth, Ga. ... B2, g8 55
Duluth, Minn. ... D6 67
Dumaguete, Phil. ... D6 19
Dumas, Ark. ... D4 49
Dumas, Tex. ... B2 84
Dumfries, Scot. ... B5 4
Dumfries, Va. ... B5 85
Dumfries, co., Scot. ... *C5 4
Dumont, N.J. ... B5, h9 74
Dumyât (Damietta), Eg. ... G8 14
Dunaföldvár, Hung. ... B4 10
Dunapataj, Hung. ... B4 10
Dunaujváros, Hung. ... B4 10
Dunayevsty, Sov. Un. ... G6 12
Dunbar, Pa. ... G2 81
Dunbar, Scot. ... B5 4
Dunbar, W. Va. ... C3, m12 87
Dunbarton, co., Scot. ... *B4 4
Duncan, Ariz. ... C4 48
Duncan, B.C., Can. ... E6, g12 37
Duncan, Okla. ... C4 79
Duncan, S.C. ... B3 82
Duncannon, Pa. ... F7 81
Duncansville, Pa. ... F5 81
Duncanville, Tex. ... n10 34
Dundalk, Ont., Can. ... C4 41
Dundalk, Ire. ... C3 4
Dundalk, Md. ... B4, g11 53
Dundas, Ont., Can. ... D5 41
Dundas, co., Ont., Can. ... B9 41
Dundee, Ill. ... A5, h6 58
Dundee, Fla. ... D5 54
Dundee, Mich. ... G7 66
Dundee, N.Y. ... C4 75
Dundee, Scot. ... B5 4
Dundee, S. Afr. ... F6 24
Dundy, co., Nebr. ... D4 71
Dunedin, Fla. ... D4, o10 54
Dunedin, N.Z. ... P13 26
Dunellen, N.J. ... B4 74
Dunfermline, Scot. ... B5 4
Dungannon, N. Ire. ... C3 4
Dungarvan, Ire. ... D3 4
Dungulah, Sud. ... E4 23
Dunkerque, Fr. ... B5 5
Dunkirk, Ind. ... D7 59
Dunkirk, N.Y. ... C1 75
Dunkirk, Ohio ... B2 78
Dunkirk, see Dunkerque, Fr.
Dunklin, co., Mo. ... E7 69
Dun Laoghaire, Ire. ... D3 4
Dunlap, Ind. ... A6 59
Dunlap, Iowa ... C2 60
Dunlap, Tenn. ... D8 83
Dunlo, Pa. ... F4 81
Dunmore, Pa. ... D10, m18 81
Dunn, N.C. ... B4 76
Dunn, co., N. Dak. ... C3 77
Dunn, co., Wis. ... D2 88
Dunnellon, Fla. ... C4 54
Dunn Loring, Va. ... *B5 85
Dunnville, Ont., Can. ... E5 41
Dunoon, Scot. ... C4 4
Dunseith, N. Dak. ... A5 77
Dunsmuir, Calif. ... B2 50
Dunville, Newf., Can. ... E5 44
Du Page, co., Ill. ... A5 58
Duparquet, Que., Can. ... *D3 42
Duplin, co., N.C. ... C5 76
Dupnitsa, see Stanke Dimitrov, Bul.
Dupo, Ill. ... E3 58
Dupont, Pa. ... n18 81
Duque de Caxias, Braz. ... *C4 30
Duquesne, Pa. ... F2, k14 81
Du Quoin, Ill. ... E4 58
Dûra, Jordan ... C3 15
Durand, Mich. ... F6 66
Durand, Wis. ... D2 88
Durango, Colo. ... D3 51
Durango, Mex. ... C4 34
Durango, state, Mex. ... C4 34
Durant, Iowa ... C7 60
Durant, Miss. ... B4 68
Durant, Okla. ... D5 79
Durazno, Ur. ... E1 30

E

Eisenhüttenstadt, Ger. Dem. Rep. B7 6
Eisenstadt, Aus. E8 6
Eisleben, Ger. Dem. Rep. C5 6
Ekalaka, Mont. E12 70
Eksjö, Swe. I6 11
El Aaiún, W. Sah. C2 22
El Arahal, Sp. D3 8
El Asnam (Orléansville), Alg. A5 22
Elâziğ, Tur. C12 14
Elba, Ala. D3 46
El Banco, Col. B3 32
El Barco, Sp. A2 8
Elbasan, Alb. B3 14
Elbasan, pref., Alb. *B3 14
Elbe, (Labe), riv., Eur. B5 6
Elbert, Colo. B4 51
Elbert, co., Colo. B6 51
Elbert, co., Ga. B4 55
Elberton, Ga. B4 55
Elbeuf, Fr. C4 5
Elbing, see Elblag, Pol.
Elbistan, Tur. C11 14
Elblag, Pol. A5 7
El Bonillo, Sp. C4 8
El Bordo, Col. C2 32
Elbow Lake, Minn. E3 67
Elbrus, mtn., Sov. Un. E7 13
Elburn, Ill. B5 58
El Cajon, Calif. F5, o16 50
El Campo, Tex. E4 84
El Camp South, Tex. *E4 84
El Capitan, mtn., Mont. D2 70
El Carmen de Bolivar, Col. B2 32
El Carrizo, Mex. B3 34
El Centro, Calif. F6 50
El Cerrito, Calif. h8 50
Elche, Sp. C5 8
El Cocuy, Col. B3 32
Elda, Sp. C5 8
Eldon, Iowa D5 60
Eldon, Mo. C5 69
Eldora, Iowa B4 60
El Dorado, Ark. D3 49
Eldorado, Ill. F5 58
El Dorado, Kans. E7, g13 61
Eldorado, Mex. C3 34
Eldorado, Tex. D2 84
El Dorado, co., Calif. C3 50
Eldorado, peak, Wash. A4 86
El Dorado Springs, Mo. D3 69
Eldoret, Ken. H5 23
Eldred, Pa. C5 81
Eldridge, Iowa C7, g10 60
Eleanor, W. Va. C3 87
Electra, Tex. C3 84
Electric, peak., Mont. D6 70
Eleele, Haw. B2 56
Elektrostal, Sov. Un. n18 12
Elephant, mtn., Maine D2 64
Elevsís (Eleusis), Grc. g11 14
El Fasher, Sud. F3 23
El Ferrol *del Caudillo*, Sp. A1 8
El Fuerte, Mex. B3 34
Elgin, Ill. A5, h8 58
Elgin, Iowa B6 60
Elgin, N. Dak. D4 77
Elgin, Oreg. B9 80
Elgin, Scot. B5 4
Elgin, Tex. D4 84
Elgin, co., Ont., Can. E3 41
Elgon, mtn., Ken., Ug. H4 23
El Grullo, Mex. n11 34
Elida, Ohio B1 78
Elim, Pa. *E4 81
Eliot, Maine E2 64
Elizabeth, Austl. F6 25
Elizabeth, Ga. C2, h7 55
Elizabeth, La. D3 63
Elizabeth, N.J. B4, k8 74
Elizabeth, Pa. *E1 81
Elizabeth City, N.C. A6 76
Elizabeth Lake Estates, Mich. *F7 66
Elizabethton, Tenn. C11 83
Elizabethtown, Ky. C4 62
Elizabethtown, N.C. C4 76
Elizabethtown, Pa. F8 81
Elizabethville, Pa. E8 81
El Jadida, Mor. B3 22
Elk, Pol. B7 7
Elk, co., Kans. E7 61
Elk, co., Pa. D4 81
Elk, mtn., Wyo. E6 89
Elk, peak, Mont. D6 70
Elkader, Iowa B6 60
El Kairouan, Tun. A6 22
Elk City, Okla. B2 79
El Kef, Tun. A6 22
Elk Grove, Calif. C3 50
Elk Grove Village, Ill. h9 58
Elkhart, Ind. A6 59
Elkhart, Kans. E2 61
Elkhart, co., Ind. A6 59
Elkhorn, W. Va. *D3 87
Elkhorn, Wis. F5 88
Elkhorn City, Ky. C7 62
Elkhovo, Bul. D8 10
Elkin, N.C. A2 76
Elkins, W. Va. C5 87
Elkins Park, Pa. o21 81
Elkland, Pa. C7 81
Elk Mountain, N.C. f10 76
Elko, Nev. A4 72
Elko, co., Nev. A4 72
Elk Point, S. Dak. H9 77
Elk Rapids, Mich. D5 66
Elkridge, Md. B4, h10 53
Elkridge, W. Va. m13 87
Elk River, Idaho C2 57
Elk River, Minn. E5 67
Elk Run Heights, Iowa *B5 60
Elkton, Ky. D2 62
Elkton, Md. A6 53
Elkton, Mich. E7 66
Elkton, Va. B4 85
Elkville, Ill. F4 58
Ellaville, Ga. D2 55
Ellendale, N. Dak. E7 77
Ellensburg, Wash. C5 86
Ellenton, Fla. E4, p10 54
Ellenville, N.Y. D6 75
Ellerbe, N.C. B3 76
Ellesmere, isl., N.W. Ter., Can. k34 36
Ellettsville, Ind. F4 59
Ellicott City, Md. B4 53
Ellicottville, N.Y. C2 75
Ellijay, Ga. B2 55
Ellington, Mo. D7 69
Ellinwood, Kans. D5 61
Elliott, co., Ky. B6 62
Ellis, Kans. D4 61
Ellis, co., Kans. D4 61
Ellis, co., Okla. A2 79
Ellis, co., Tex. C4 84
Ellisville, Miss. D4 68
Ellisville, Mo. f12 69
Ellon, Scot. B5 4
Ellport, Pa. E1 81
Ellsworth, Kans. D5 61
Ellsworth, Maine D4 64
Ellsworth, Pa. F1 81
Ellsworth, Wis. D1 88
Ellsworth, co., Kans. D5 61
Ellwangen, Ger., Fed. Rep. of D5 6
Ellwood City, Pa. E1 81
Elma, N.Y. *C2 75
Elma, Wash. C2 86
Ellwood City, Pa. E1 81
Elma, N.Y. *C2 75
Elma, Wash. C2 86
El Mahdia, Tun. A7 22
Elmali, Tur. *D7 14
Elmer, N.J. D2 74
Elm Grove, Wis. *m11 88
Elmhurst, Ill. B6, k9 58
Elmira, Ont., Can. D4 41
Elmira, N.Y. C4 75
El Mirage, Ariz. D1 48
Elmira Heights, N.Y. C4 75
Elmont, N.Y. *G2 52
El Monte, Calif. *E4 50
Elmora, Pa. E4 81
Elmore, Minn. G4 67
Elmore, Ohio A2 78
Elmore, co., Ala. C3 46
Elmore, co., Idaho F3 57
Elmore City, Okla. C4 79
Elmsford, N.Y. g13 75
Elmshorn, Ger., Fed. Rep. of B4 6
Elmwood, Ill. C4 58
Elmwood Park, Ill. k9 58
Elmwood Park, N.J. h8 74
Elmwood Place, Ohio o13 78
El Nevado, mtn., Col. C3 32
Elnora, Ind. G3 59
El Obeid, Sud. F4 23
Eloise, Fla. E5 54
Elon College, N.C. A3 76
Elora, Ont., Can. D4 41
El Oro, prov., Ec. B2 31
Eloy, Ariz. C3 48
El Paso, Ill. C4 58
El Paso, Tex. o11 84
El Paso, co., Colo. C6 51
El Paso, co., Tex. o11 84
El Portal, Fla. s13 54
El Porto Beach, Calif. *F4 50
El Puerto de Santa María, Sp. D2 8
Elrama, Pa. F2 81
El Reno, Okla. B4 79
El Rio, Calif. E4 50
Elroy, Wis. E3 88
Elsa, Tex. F3 84
El Salto, Mex. C3 34
El Salvador, country, N.A. E7 34
Elsberry, Mo. B6 69
El Segundo, Calif. *F4 50
El Seibo, Dom. Rep. E9 35
Elsie, Mich. E6 66
Elsinore, Calif. F5 50
Elsmere, Del. A6 53
Elsmere, Ky. B5, h13 62
El Sobrante, Calif. *D2 50
Elsterwerda, Ger. Dem. Rep. C6 6
El Tigre, Ven. B5 32
El Tocuyo, Ven. B4 32
Elton, La. D3 63
Elūru, India E7 20
Elvas, Port. C2 8
El Verano, Calif. *C2 50
Elverum, Nor. G4 11
El Viejo, mtn., Col. B3 32
Elvins, Mo. D7 69
Elwood, Ind. D6 59
Elwood, Kans. C9 61
Elwood, N.Y. n15 75
Elwyn, Pa. *G11 81
Ely, Eng. D7 4
Ely, Minn. C7 67
Ely, Nev. B4 72
Elyria, Ohio A3 78
Elysburg, Pa. E8 81
Emāmshahr, Iran B6 15
Emanuel, co., Ga. D4 55
Embetsu, Jap. E10 18
Embrun, Ont., Can. B9 41
Emden, Ger., Fed. Rep. of B3 6
Emerson, Man., Can. E3 40
Emerson, Nebr. B9 71
Emerson, N.J. H8 74
Emery, co., Utah B6 72
Emeryville, Calif. *D3 50
Emi Koussi, vol., Chad E1 23
Emilia, reg., It. B3 9
Emilia-Romagna, pol. dist., It. B3 9
Emiliano Zapata, Mex. D6 34
Eminence, Ky. B4 62
Emirdağ, Tur. C8 14
Emlenton, Pa. D2 81
Emmaus, Pa. E11 81
Emmen, Neth. A7 5
Emerald, Austl. D8 25
Emmerich, Ger., Fed. Rep. of C3 6
Emmet, co., Iowa A3 60
Emmet, co., Mich. C6 66
Emmetsburg, Iowa A3 60
Emmett, Idaho F2 57
Emmitsburg, Md. A3 53
Emmons, co., N. Dak. D5 77
Empire, Calif. *D3 50
Empire, La. E6 63
Empire, Nev. A2 72
Empoli, It. C3 9
Emporia, Kans. D7 61
Emporia, Va. D5 85
Emporium, Pa. D5 81
Emsdetten, Ger., Fed. Rep. of B3 6
Emsworth, Pa. h13 81
Ena, Jap. n16 18
Encarnación, Par. E4 29
Encarnación de Díaz, Mex. m12 34
Encinal, Tex. E3 84
Encinitas, Calif. F5 50
Ende, Indon. G6 19
Enderby, B.C., Can. D8 37
Enderlin, N. Dak. D8 77
Endicott, N.Y. C4 75
Endwell, N.Y. *C4 75
Enfield, Conn. B6 52
Enfield, Ill. E5 58
Enfield, N.H. D3 73
Enfield, N.C. A5 76
Engaru, Jap. D11 18
Engels, Sov. Un. F16 12
Enghien, Fr. g10 5
England, Ark. C4, k11 49
England, reg., U.K. D6 4
Englee, Newf., Can. C3, h10 44
Englewood, Colo. B6 51
Englewood, Fla. *B5 54
Englewood, Fla. F4 54
Englewood, Ind. *G5 59
Englewood, N.J. h9 74
englewood, Ohio C1 78
Englewood, Oreg. *D2 80
Englewood, Tenn. D9 83
Englewood Cliffs, N.J. B5 74
Englishtown, N.J. C4 74
Enguera, Sp. C5 8
Enhaut, Pa. *F8 81
Enid, Okla. A4 79
Enka, N.C. f10 76
Enköping, Swe. H7, t35 11
Enna, It. F5 9
Ennis, Ire. D2 4
Ennis, Tex. C4, n10 84
Enniscorthy, Ire. D3 4
Enniskillen, N.Ire. C3 4
Enns, Aus. D7 6
Enola, Pa. F8 81
Enon, Ohio C2 78
Enoree, S.C. B4 82
Enosberg Falls, Vt. B2 73
Enriquillo, Dom. Rep. F8 35
Enschede, Neth. A7 5
Ensenada, Arg. g8 28
Ensenada, Mex. A1 34
Ensenada, P.R. G11 35
Ensley, Fla. u14 54
Entebbe, Ug. H4 23
Enterprise, Ala. D4 46
Enterprise, Calif. *B2 50
Enterprise, Kans. D6 61
Enterprise, Oreg. B9 80
Entiat, mts., Wash. B5 86
Entre Minho e Douro, reg., Port. B1 8
Entre Ríos, prov., Arg. A5, f7 28
Enugu, Nig. G6 22
Enumclaw, Wash. B4, f12 86
Enzan, Jap. n17 18
Épernay, Fr. C5 5
Ephraim, Utah B6 72
Ephrata, Pa. F9 81
Ephrata, Wash. B6 86
Épila, Sp. B5 8
Épinal, Fr. C7 5
Épinay-*sur-Seine*, Fr. g10 5
Epirus, reg., Grc. *C3 14
Epping, Eng. k13 4
Epping, N.H. E5 73
Epsom (& Ewell) Eng. m12 4
Epworth, Iowa B7 60
Equatorial Guinea, country, Afr. H6 22
Erath, La. E3 63
Erath, co., Tex. C3 84
Ercis, Tur. C14 14
Erciyes Dagi, mtn., Tur. C10 14
Érd, Hung. B4 10
Erdek, Tur. *B6 14
Erdenheim, Pa. o21 81
Erding, Ger., Fed. Rep. of D5 6
Ereğli, Tur. B8 14
Ereğli, Tur. D10 14
Erfurt, Ger. Dem. Rep. C5 6
Erice, It. E4 9
Erick, Okla. B2 79
Erickson, B.C., Can. E9 37
Erie, Colo. A5 51
Erie, Ill. B3 58
Erie, Kans. E8 61
Erie, Pa. B1 81
Erie, co., N.Y. C2 75
Erie, co., Ohio A3 78
Erie, co., Pa. C1 81
Erie, lake, Can., U.S. B10 45
Erin, Tenn. A4 83
Eritrea, prov., Eth. E5 23
Erlangen, Ger., Fed. Rep. of D5 6
Erlanger, Ky. A5, h13 62
Ermenak, Tur. D9 14
Ermont, Fr. g10 5
Ernakulam, India *G6 20
Ernest, Pa. E3 81
Errigal, mtn., Ire. C2 4
Errol Heights, Oreg. *B4 80
Erstein, Fr. C7 5
Erwin, N.C. B4 76
Erwin, Tenn. C11 83
Erzincan, Tur. C12 14
Erzurum, Tur. C13 14
Esashi, Jap. D11 18
Esashi, Jap. F10 18
Esbjerg, Den. J3 11
Escada, Braz. *D7 27
Escalante, Utah C6 72
Escalón, Calif. D3 50
Escalón, Mex. B4 34
Escambia, co., Ala. D2 46
Escambia, co., Fla. u14 54
Escanaba, Mich. C3 66
Escatawpa, Miss. E5, f8 68
Esch-sur-Alzette, Lux. C7 5
Eschwege, Ger., Fed. Rep. of C5 6
Eschweiler, Ger., Fed. Rep. of C3 6
Escondido, Calif. F5 50
Escoublac-La-Baule, Fr. D2 5
Escuinapa *de Hidalgo*, Mex. C3 34
Escuintla, Guat. E6 34
Eşfahān (Isfahan) Iran C5 23
Esher, Eng. m12 4
Eskdale, W. Va. C3, m13 87
Eskilstuna, Swe. H7, t34 11
Eskisehir, Tur. C8 14
Esmeralda, co., Nev. C3 72
Esmeraldas, Ec. A2 31
Esmeraldas, prov., Ec. A2 31
Esmond, R.I. B10 52
Espanola, Ont., Can. A3 41

F

G

H

Place	Ref.	Pg.
Huelva, Sp.	D2	8
Huelva, prov., Sp.	*D2	8
Huércal-Overa, Sp.	D5	8
Huerfano, co., Colo.	C6	51
Huesca, Sp.	A5	8
Huesca, prov., Sp.	*A5	8
Huéscar, Sp.	D4	8
Hueytown, Ala.	g6	46
Hughes, Ark.	C5	49
Hughes, co., Okla.	B5	79
Hughes, co., S. Dak.	F6	77
Hughes Springs, Tex.	*C5	84
Hughestown, Pa.	*D9	81
Hughesville, Pa.	D8	81
Hughson, Calif.	*D3	50
Hugo, Colo.	B7	51
Hugo, Okla.	C6	79
Hugoton, Kans.	E2	61
Huhohaote (Huhehot), China	C7	17
Huichon, Kor.	F3	18
Huila, dept., Col.	C2	32
Huixtla, Mex.	D6	34
Hukou, China	F8	17
Hulan, China	B10	17
Hulen, Ky.	D6	62
Hull, Que., Can.	D2	42
Hull, Eng.	D6	4
Hull, Iowa	A1	60
Hull, Mass.	B6, g12	65
Hull, co., Que., Can.	D2	42
Hulmeville, Pa.	*F11	81
Humacao, P.R.	*G12	35
Humansville, Mo.	D4	69
Humble, Tex.	E5, q14	84
Humboldt, Sask., Can.	E3	39
Humboldt, Iowa	B3	60
Humboldt, Kans.	E8	61
Humboldt, Nebr.	D10	71
Humboldt, Tenn.	B3	83
Humboldt, co., Calif.	B2	50
Humboldt, co., Iowa	B3	60
Humboldt, co., Nev.	A2	72
Humenné, Czech.	D6	7
Humeston, Iowa	D4	60
Hummelstown, Pa.	*F8	81
Humphrey, Nebr.	C8	71
Humphreys, co., Miss.	B3	68
Humphreys, co., Tenn.	A4	83
Humphreys, peak, Ariz.	B2	48
Humpolec, Czech.	D3	7
Hunan, prov., China	F7	17
Hunchiang, China	C10	17
Hunchun, China	C11	17
Hunedoara, Rom.	C6	10
Hungary, country, Eur.	B4	10
Hungnam, Kor.	G3	18
Hunt, mtn., Wyo	B5	89
Hunt, co., Tex.	C4	84
Hunterdon, N.J.	B3	74
Huntersville, N.C.	B2	76
Huntingburg, Ind.	H4	59
Huntingdon, Que., Can.	D3	42
Huntingdon, Pa.	F6	81
Huntingdon, Tenn.	A3	83
Huntingdon, co., Que., Can.	D3	42
Huntingdon, co., Pa.	F5	81
Huntingdon & Peterborough, co., Eng.	*D7	4
Huntington, Ind.	C7	59
Huntington, Mass.	B2	65
Huntington, N.J.	B2	74
Huntington, N.Y.	E7, n15	75
Huntington, Oreg.	C9	80
Huntington, Tex.	D5	84
Huntington, Utah	B6	72
Huntington, W. Va.	C2	87
Huntington, co., Ind.	C6	59
Huntington Bay, N.Y.	*G3	52
Huntington Beach, Calif.	n13	50
Huntington Beach, N.Y.	*D3	75
Huntington Park, Calif.	F4	50
Huntington Station, N.Y.	F3	52
Huntington Woods, Mich.	p15	66
Huntingtown, Md.	C4	53
Huntley, Ill.	A5	58
Huntly, Scot.	B5	4
Huntsville, Ala.	A3	46
Huntsville, Ark.	A2	49
Huntsville, Ont., Can.	B5	41
Huntsville, Mo.	B5	69
Huntsville, Tex.	D5	84
Hupeh (Hupei), prov., China	E7	17
Hurley, N. Mex.	C4	48
Hurley, N.Y.	D6	75
Hurley, Wis.	B3	88
Hurleyville, N.Y.	D6	75
Hurlock, Md.	C3	53
Huron, Calif.	*D4	50
Huron, Ohio	A3	78
Huron, S. Dak.	F7	77
Huron, co., Ont., Can.	D3	41
Huron, co., Mich.	E7	66
Huron, co., Ohio	A3	78
Huron, lake, Can.	B10	45
Hurricane, Utah	C5	72
Hurricane, W. Va.	C2	87
Hurst, Ill.	F4	58
Hurst, Tex.	*C4	84
Hurtsboro, Ala.	C4	46
Huşi, Rom.	B9	10
Hustisford, Wis.	E5	88
Husum, Ger., Fed. Rep. of	A4	6
Hutchins, Tex.	n10	84
Hutchinson, Kans.	D6, f11	61
Hutchinson, Minn.	F4	67
Hutchinson, co., S. Dak.	G8	77
Hutchinson, co., Tex.	B2	84
Huttig, Ark.	D3	49
Huxley, Iowa	C4, e8	60
Huy, Bel.	B6	5
Hvannadalshnúkur, mtn., Ice.	o24	11
Hvittingfoss, Nor.	p28	11
Hyannis, Mass.	C7	65
Hyannis Port, Mass.	C7	65
Hyattsville, Md.	C4, f9	53
Hybla Valley, Va.	*B5	85
Hyde, Pa.	D5	81
Hyde, co., N.C.	B6	76
Hyde, co., S. Dak.	F6	77
Hyde Park, N.Y.	D7	75
Hyde Park, Pa.	*F9	81
Hyderābād, India	E6	20
Hyderābād, Pak.	C4	20
Hyde Villa, Pa.	*F9	81
Hydro, Okla.	B3	79
Hyères, Fr.	F7	5
Hymera, Ind.	F3	59
Hyndman, Pa.	G4	81
Hyogo, pref., Jap.	*I7	18
Hyopchon, Kor.	I4	18
Hyrum, Utah	A6	72
Hyrynsalmi, Fin.	E13	11
Hythe, Alta., Can.	B1	38
Hythe, Eng.	E7	4

I

Place	Ref.	Pg.
Iaeger, W. Va.	D3	87
Iasi, Rom.	B8	10
Iba, Phil.	*B5	19
Ibadan, Nig.	G5	22
Ibagué, Col.	C2	32
Ibaraki, Jap.	*o14	18
Ibaraki, pref., Jap.	*H10	18
Ibarra, Ec.	A2	31
Ibb, Yemen	G3	15
Iberia, Mo.	C5	69
Iberia, par., La.	E4	63
Iberville, Que., Can.	D4	42
Iberville, co., Que., Can.	D4	42
Iberville, par., La.	D4, h9	63
Iberville, mtn., Newf.	f9	44
Ibitinga, Braz.	C3	30
Ibiza, Sp.	C6	8
Ica, Peru	D2	31
Ica, dept., Peru	D2	31
Ice, mtn., B.C., Can.	B7	37
Iceland, country, Eur.	n23	11
Ichang, China	E7	17
Ichihara, Jap.	*n19	18
Ichikawa, Jap.	n18	18
Ichinomiya, Jap.	n15	18
Ichinoseki, Jap.	G10	18
Ichnya, Sov. Un.	F9	12
Ichun, China	C4	18
Ida, Mich.	G7	66
Ida, co., Iowa	B2	60
Idabel, Okla.	D7	79
Ida Grove, Iowa	B2	60
Idaho, co., Idaho	D3	57
Idaho, state, U.S.		57
Idaho Falls, Idaho	F6	67
Idaho Springs, Colo.	B5	51
Idahou, Tex.	C2	84
Idamay, W. VA.	k10	87
Idanha-a-Nova, Port.	C2	8
Idaville, Ind.	C4	59
Idrija, Yugo.	B2	10
Ieper (Ypres), Bel.	B5	5
Ierápetra, Grc.	E5	14
Iesi, It.	C4	9
Ife, Nig.	G5	22
Igarapava, Braz.	C3	30
Igarka, Sov. Un.	C11	13
Iğdir, Tur.	C15	14
Ighil Izane, Alg.	A5	22
Iglesias, It.	E2	9
Igloo, S. Dak.	G2	77
Igualada, Sp.	B6	8
Iguatu, Braz.	*D7	27
Ihsing, China	*E8	17
Iida, Jap.	I8, n16	18
Iide-san, mtn., Jap.	H9	18
Iijima, Jap.	n16	18
Iisalmi, Fin.	F12	11
Iizuka, Jap.	J5	18
Ijebu Ode, Nig.	G5	22
Ijuí, Braz.	D2	30
Ikeda, Jap.	D14	18
Ikerre, Nig.	*G6	22
Ikhtiman, Bul.	D6	10
Ila, Nig.	E5	22
Ilagan, Phil.	B6	19
Ilan, China	B10	17
Ilan, Taiwan	*G9	17
Ilawe, Nig.	*E6	22
Ile-a-la-Cross, Sask., Can.	m7	39
Ilebo (Port-Francqui), Zaire	I2	23
Ile-de-France, former prov., Fr.	C5	5
Ile-Perrot, Que., Can.	q19	42
Ilesha, Nig.	G5	22
Ilford, Eng.	k13	4
Ilfracombe, Eng.	E4	4
Ilgin, Tur.	C8	14
Ilhavo, Port.	B1	8
Ilhéus, Braz.	E7	27
Ilia (Elis), prov., Grc.	*D3	14
Iliang, China	D11	20
Ilinskaya, Sov. Un.	I13	12
Ilion, N.Y.	B5	75
Illampu, mtn., Bol.	C2	29
Illapel, Chile	A2	28
Ille-et-Vilaine, dept., Fr.	*C3	5
Illinois, state, U.S.		58
Illinois, peak, Idaho	B3	57
Illinois, peak, Mont.	C1	70
Illiopolis, Ill.	D4	58
Illmo, Mo.	D8	69
Illora, Sp.	D4	8
Ilmenau, Ger. Dem. Rep.	C5	6
Ilo, Peru	E3	31
Ilocos Norte, prov., Phil	*B6	19
Ilocos Sur, prov., Phil.	C6	19
Iloilo, Phil.	C6	19
Iloilo, prov., Phil.	*C6	19
Ilorin, Nig.	G5	22
Ilovaysk, Sov. Un.	r21	12
Imabari, Jap.	I6	18
Imabetsu, Jap.	F10	18
Imari, Jap.	*J4	18
Imazu, Jap.	n15	18
Imbâbah, Eg.	*G8	14
Imbabura, prov., Ec.	A2	31
Imlay City, Mich.	E7	66
Immenstadt, Ger., Fed. Rep. of	E5	6
Immokalee, Fla.	F5	54
Imola, It.	B3	9
Imperia, It.	C2	9
Imperial, Calif.	F6	50
Imperial, Sask., Can.	F3	39
Imperial, Mo.	C7, g13	69
Imperial, Nebr.	D4	71
Imperial, Pa.	k13	81
Imperial, co., Calif.	F6	50
Imperial Beach, Calif.	o15	50
Imperoyal, N.S.,Can.	E6	43
Imphâl, India	D9	20
Ina, Jap.	n16	18
Inca, Sp.	C7	8
Inchon, Kor.	H3	18
Indaw, Bur.	D10	20
Independence, Calif.	D4	50
Independence, Iowa	B6	60
Independence, Kans.	E8	61
Independence, La.	D5	63
Independence, Minn.	*F5	67
Independence, Mo.	B3, h11	69
Independence, Ohio	h9	78
Independence, Oreg.	C3, k11	80
Independence, Wis.	D2	88
Independence, co., Ark.	B4	49
Independence Hill, Ind.	*B3	59
India, country, Asia	D6	20
Indialantic, Fla.	*D6	54
Indian, ocean	G2	2
Indiana, Pa.	E3	81
Indiana, co., Pa.	E3	81
Indiana, state, U.S.		59
Indianapolis, Ind.	E5, k10	59
Indian Head, Sask., Can.	G4	39
Indian Head, Md.	C3	53
Indian Hill, Ohio	o13	78
Indian Lake, N.Y.	B6	75
Indian Mound Beach, Mass.	*C6	65
Indianola, Iowa	C4	60
Indianola, Miss.	B3	68
Indianola, Nebr.	D5	71
Indianola, Pa.	*E1	81
Indian, peak, Wyo.	B3	89
Indian River, co., Fla.	E6	54
Indian Rocks, Beach, Fla.	p10	54
Indiantown, Fla.	E6	54
Indio, Calif.	F5	50
Indochina, reg., Asia	B3	19
Indonesia, country, Asia	F6	19
Indore, India	D6	20
Indramayu, Indon.	G3	19
Indre, dept., Fr.	*D4	5
Indre-et-Loire, dept., Fr.	*D4	5
Indus, riv., Asia	C4	20
Industrial, S.C.	B6	82
Industry, Pa.	*E1	81
Ine, Jap.	n14	18
Infantes, Sp.	C4	8
Infiesto, Sp.	A3	8
Ingalls, Ind.	E6	59
Ingalls Park, Ill.	B5	58
Ingersoll, Ont., Can.	D4	41
Ingham, Austl.	C8	25
Ingham, co., Mich.	F6	66
Ingleside, Nebr.	D7	71
Ingleside, Tex.	F4	84
Inglewood, Calif.	n12	50
Inglewood, Nebr.	C9, g11	71
Ingolstadt, Ger., Fed. Rep. of	D5	6
Ingomar, Pa.	h13	81
Ingonish Beach, N.S., Can.	C9	43
Ingram, Pa.	k13	81
Inhambane, Moz.	E7	24
Inharrime, Moz.	E7	24
Inishbofin, isl., U.K.	D1	4
Inishtrahull, isl., U.K.	C3	4
Inishturk, isl., U.K.	D1	4
Inkerman, Pa.	*D9	81
Inkom, Idaho	G6	57
Inkster, Mich.	p15	66
Inman, Kans.	D6	61
Inman, S.C.	A3	82
Inman Mills, S.C.	*A3	82
Inner Mongolia, prov., China	C8	17
Innisfail, Alta., Can.	C4	38
Innisfail, Austl.	C8	25
Innsbruck, Aus.	E5	6
Ino, Jap.	J6	18
Inowroclaw, Pol.	B5	7
Insein, Bur.	E10	20
Institute, W. Va.	C3	87
Intercesion City, Fla.	D5	54
Intercity, Wash.	*B3	86
Interlaken, N.J.	*C4	74
International Falls, Minn.	B5	67
Intersection, mtn., B.C., Can.	C7	37
Invercargill, N.Z.	Q12	26
Inverell, Austl.	E9	25

Invermere, B.C., Can. ... D9 37
Inverness, Calif. ... C2 50
Inverness, N.S., Can. ... C8 43
Inverness, Fla. ... D4 54
Inverness, Ill. ... *B6 58
Inverness, Miss. ... B3 68
Inverness, Scot. ... B4 4
Inverness, co., N.S., Can. ... C8 43
Inverness, co., Scot. ... *B4 4
Invisible, mtn.,Idaho ... F5 57
Inwood, Iowa ... A1 60
Inwood, N.Y. ... k13 75
Inyan Kara, mtn., Wyo. ... B8 89
Inyo,co., Calif. ... D5 50
Inyokern, Calif. ... E5 50
Ioánnina, Grc. ... C3 14
Ioannina, prov.,Grc. ... *C3 14
Iola, Kans. ... E8 61
Iola, Wis. ... D4 88
Iona, Idaho ... F7 57
Ione, Calif. ... D3 50
Ionia, Mich. ... F5 66
Ionia, co., Mich. ... F5 66
Iosco, co., Mich. ... D7 66
Iota, La. ... D3 63
Iowa, La. ... D2 63
Iowa, co., Iowa ... C5 60
Iowa, co., Wis. ... E3 88
Iowa, state, U.S. ... 60
Iowa City, Iowa ... C6 60
Iowa Falls, Iowa ... B4 60
Iowa Park, Tex. ... C3 84
Ipameri, Braz. ... B3 30
Ipava, Ill. ... C3 58
Ipiales, Col. ... C2 32
Ipin, China ... F5 17
Ipoh, Mala. ... E2 19
Ipswich, Austl. ... E9 25
Ipswich, Eng. ... D7 4
Ipswich, Mass. ... A6 55
Ipswich, S. Dak. ... E6 77
Iquique, Chile ... D2 29
Iquitos, Peru ... B3 31
Iraan, Tex. ... D2 84
Iraklion (Candia), Grc. ... E5 14
Iraklion, prov., Grc. ... *E5 14
Iran, (Persia), country, Asia ... F8 16
Irapuato, Mex. ... C4, m13 34
Iraq, country, Asia ... C3 15
Irbid, Jordan ... B3, g5 15
Irbil, Iraq ... D15 14
Iredell, co., N.C. ... B2 76
Ireland (Eire), country, Eur. ... D3 4
Ireton, Iowa ... B1 60
Iri, Kor. ... I3 18
Iringa, Tan. ... B7 24
Irion, co.,Tex. ... D2 84
Irkutsk, Sov. Un. ... D13 13

Iron, co., Mich. ... B2 66
Iron, co., Mo. ... D7 69
Iron, co., Utah ... C5 72
Iron, co., Wis. ... B3 88
Iron, mts., Va. ... f10 85
Irondale, Ala. ... f7 46
Irondale, Ohio ... B5 78
Irondequoit, N.Y. ... B3 75
Ironia, N.J. ... B3 74
Iron Mountain, Mich. ... C2 66
Iron River, Mich. ... B2 66
Iron River, Wis. ... B2 88
Ironton, Minn. ... D5 67
Ironton, Mo. ... D7 69
Ironton, Ohio ... D3 78
Ironwood, Mich. ... nll 66
Iroquois, N.B., Can. ... *B1 43
Iroquois, Ont., Can. ... C9 41
Iroquois, co., Ill. ... C6 58
Iroquois Falls, Ont., Can. ... *o19 41
Irosin, Phil. ... *C6 19
Irrawaddy, riv., Bur. ... D10 20
Irtysh, riv., Sov. Un. ... D10 13
Irún, Sp. ... A5 8
Irvine, Ky. ... C6 62
Irvine, Scot. ... C4 4
Irving, Tex. ... n10 84
Irvington, Ky. ... C3 62
Irvington, N.J. ... k8 74
Irvington, N.Y. ... g13 75
Irvona, Pa. ... E4 81
Irwin, Pa. ... F2 81
Irwin, S.C. ... *B6 82
Irwin, co., Ga. ... E3 55
Irwindale, Calif. ... *E4 50
Isabell, mtn., Wyo. ... D2 89
Isabela, P.R. ... *G11 35
Isabela, prov.,Phil. ... *D6 19
Isabella, Pa. ... G2 81
Isabella, Tenn. ... D9 83
Isabella, co., Mich. ... E6 66
Isahaya, Jap. ... J5 18
Isanti, Minn. ... E5 67
Isanti,co., Minn. ... E5 67
Ise (Uji-yamada), Jap. ... I8, o15 18
Iselin, N.J. ... B4 74
Iselin, Pa. ... E3 81
Isère, dept., Fr. ... *E6 5
Iserlohn, Ger., Fed. Rep. of ... *C3 6
Isernia, It. ... D5 9
Isesaki, Jap. ... H9, m18 18
Iseyin, Nig. ... G5 22
Ishikawa, pref.,Jap. ... *H8 18
Ishim, Sov. Un. ... D9 13
Ishimbay, Sov. Un. ... *D8 13
Ishinomaki, Jap. ... G10 18
Ishioka, Jap. ... m19 18
Ishpeming, Mich. ... B3 66

Isigny-sur-Mer, Fr. ... C3 5
Isiro (Paulis), Zaire ... H3 23
Iskenderun (Alexandretta), Tur. ... D11 14
Iskilip, Tur. ... B10 14
Isla Cristina, Sp. ... D2 8
Islâmâbâd, Pak. ... B5 20
Islamorado,Fla. ... H6 54
Island, co., Wash. ... A3 86
Island Falls, Maine ... B4 64
Island Heights, N.J. ... D4 74
Island Lake, Ill. ... *E2 58
Island Park, N.Y. ... *E7 75
Island Pond, Vt. ... B4 73
Islav, isl, U.K. ... C3 4
Isle, Minn. ... D5 67
Isle, of Ely, co., Eng. ... *D7 4
Isle, of Man, Br. dep; Eur. ... *C4 4
Isle of Man, isl., U.K. ... C4 4
Isle of Palms, S.C. ... k12 82
Isle of Wight, co., Eng. ... *E6 4
Isle of Wight, co., Va. ... D6 85
Isle of Wight, isl, U.K. ... E6 4
Isle Royale, isl., Mich. ... h9 66
Isleton, Calif. ... C3 50
Isle-Verte, Que., Can. ... A8 42
Islington, Mass. ... h11 65
Islip, N.Y. ... n15 75
Islip Terrace, N.Y. ... *n15 75
Isola Capo Rizzuto, It. ... E6 9
Isparta, Tur. ... D8 14
Israel, country, Asia ... C2 15
Issaquah, Wash. ... e11 86
Issaquena, co., Miss. ... C2 68
Issoire, Fr. ... E5 5
Issoudun, Fr. ... D4 5
Issyk-kul, lake, Sov. Un. ... E10 13
Issy les-Moulineaux, Fr. ... g10 5
Istanbul (Constantinople),
  Tur. ... B7 14
Istmina, Col. ... B2 32
Itá, Par. ... E4 29
Itabaiana, Braz. ... *E7 27
Itabaiana, Braz. ... *D7 27
Itaberaba, Braz. ... *E6 27
Itabira, Braz. ... B4 30
Itabuna, Braz. ... E7 27
Itajaí, Braz. ... D3 30
Itajubá, Braz. ... C3 30
Italy, Tex. ... C4 84
Italy, country, Eur. ... 9
Itami, Jap. ... o14 18
Itaperuna, Braz. ... C4 30
Itapetininga, Braz. ... C3, m7 30
Itapeva, Braz. ... C3 30
Itápolis, Braz. ... k7 30
Itapúa, dept., Par. ... E4 29
Itaqui, Braz. ... D1 30

Itararé, Braz. ... C3 30
Itasca, Ill. ... k8 58
Itasca, Tex. ... C4 84
Itasca, co., Minn. ... C5 67
Itatiba, Braz. ... m8 30
Itaúna, Braz. ... C4 30
Itawamba, co., Miss. ... A5 68
Ithaca, Mich. ... E6 66
Ithaca, N.Y. ... C4 75
Itô, Jap. ... o18 18
Itoigawa, Jap. ... H8 18
Itta Bena, Miss. ... B3 68
Itu, Braz. ... C3, m8 30
Ituango, Col. ... B2 32
Ituiutaba, Braz. ... B3 30
Ituna, Sask., Can. ... F4 39
Itzehoe, Ger.,Fed. Rep. of ... B4 6
Iuka, Miss. ... A4 68
Iva, S.C. ... C2 82
Ivanhoe, Calif. ... *D4 50
Ivanhoe, Minn. ... F2 67
Ivanhoe, Va. ... D2 85
Ivano-Frankovsk, Sov. Un. ... G5 12
Ivanovka, Sov. Un. ... q21 12
Ivanovo, Sov. Un. ... C13 12
Ivanteyevka, Sov. Un. ... n17 12
Ivory Coast, country, Afr. ... G3 22
Ivoryton, Conn. ... D7 52
Ivrea, It. ... B1 9
Ivry-sur-Seine, Fr. ... g10 5
Ivywild, Colo. ... C6 51
Iwaki (Tairi), Jap. ... H10 18
Iwaki-yama, mtn., Jap. ... F10 18
Iwakuni, Jap. ... I6 18
Iwamizawa, Jap. ... E10 18
Iwanai, Jap. ... E10 18
Iwate, pref., Jap. ... *G10 18
Iwate-yama, mtn., Jap. ... G10 18
Iwo, Nig. ... G5 22
Ixmiquilpan, Mex. ... m14 34
Ixtacalco, Mex. ... h9 34
Ixtacihuatl, mtn., Mex. ... n14 34
Ixtapalapa, Mex. ... h9 34
Ixtlán de Juárez, Mex. ... o15 34
Ixtlán del Río, Mex. ... C4, m11 34
Izamal, Mex. ... C7 34
Izard, co., Ark. ... A4 49
Izhevsk, Sov. Un. ... D8 13
Izmail, Sov. Un. ... I7 12
Izmir (Smyrna), Tur. ... C6 14
Izmit (Kocaeli), Tur. ... B7 14
Izúcar de Matamoros, Mex. ... n14 34
Izuhara, Jap. ... I4 18
Izumo, Jap. ... I6 18
Izyum, Sov. Un. ... G11 12

J

Jabalpur (Jubbulpore), India ... D6 20
Jaboatão, Braz. ... *D7 27
Jaboticabal, Braz. ... C3, k7 30
Jaca, Sp. ... A5 8
Jacala de Ledesma, Mex. ... m14 34
Jacareí, Braz. ... m9 30
Jacarèzinho, Braz. ... C3 30
Jáchymov, Czech. ... C2 7
Jacinto City, Tex. ... r14 84
Jack, co., Tex. ... C3 84
Jack, mtn., Mont. ... D4 70
Jack, mtn., Va. ... B3 85
Jackfork, mtn., Okla. ... C6 79
Jacks, mtn., Pa. ... E6 81
Jacksboro, Tex. ... C3 84
Jackson, Ala. ... D2 46
Jackson, Calif. ... C3 50
Jackson, Ga. ... C3 55
Jackson, Ky. ... C6 62
Jackson, La. ... D4 63
Jackson, Mich. ... F6 66
Jackson, Minn. ... G3 67
Jackson, Miss. ... C3 68
Jackson, Mo. ... D8 69
Jackson, N.C. ... A5 76
Jackson, Ohio ... C3 78
Jackson, S.C. ... E4 82
Jackson, Tenn. ... B3 83
Jackson, Wyo. ... C2 89
Jackson, co., Ala. ... A3 46
Jackson, co., Ark. ... B4 49

Jackson, co., Colo. ... A4 51
Jackson, co., Fla. ... B1 54
Jackson, co., Ga. ... B3 55
Jackson, co., Ill. ... F4 58
Jackson, co., Ind. ... G5 59
Jackson, co., Iowa ... B7 60
Jackson, co., Kans. ... C8 61
Jackson, co., Ky. ... C5 62
Jackson, co., Mich. ... F6 66
Jackson, co., Minn. ... G3 67
Jackson, co., Miss. ... E5 68
Jackson, co., Mo. ... C3 69
Jackson, co., N.C. ... f9 76
Jackson, co., Ohio ... C3 78
Jackson, co., Okla. ... C2 79
Jackson, co., Oreg. ... E3 80
Jackson, co., S. Dak. ... G4 77
Jackson, co., Tenn. ... C8 83
Jackson, co., Tex. ... E4 84
Jackson, co., W. Va. ... C3 87
Jackson, co., Wis. ... D3 88
Jackson, par., La. ... B3 63
Jackson, mtn., Maine ... D2 64
Jackson Center, Ohio ... B1 78
Jacksonville, Ala. ... B4 46
Jacksonville, Ark. ... C3, h10 49
Jacksonville, Fla. ... B5, m8 54
Jacksonville, Ill. ... D3 58
Jacksonville, N.C. ... C5 76
Jacksonville, Oreg. ... E4 80
Jacksonville, Tex. ... D5 84

Jacksonville Beach, Fla. ... B5, m9 54
Jacmel, Hai. ... E7 35
Jacobâbâd, Pak. ... C4 20
Jacobina, Braz. ... *E6 27
Jacomino, Cuba. ... *C2 35
Jacques Cartier, mtn.,
  Que., Can. ... k13 42
Jaén, Sp. ... D4 8
Jaén, prov., Sp. ... *D4 8
Jaffna, Sri Lanka ... G7 20
Jaffrey, N.H. ... F3 73
Jaguarão, Braz. ... E2 30
Jagüey Grande, Cuba ... C3 35
Jaipur, India ... C6 20
Jaisalmer, India ... C5 20
Jajce, Yugo. ... C3 10
Jâjpur, India ... D8 20
Jakarta (Djakarta), Indon. ... G3 19
Jakobstad (Pietersaari), Fin. ... F10 11
Jal, N. Mex. ... C7 48
Jalalabad, Afg. ... B5 20
Jalapa, Guat. ... *F6 34
Jalapa Enríquez, Mex. ... D5, n15 34
Jalca Grande, Peru ... C2 31
Jâlgaon, India ... D6 20
Jalisco,state, Mex. ... C4, m12 34
Jâlna, India ... E6 20
Jalpa, Mex. ... C4, m12 34
Jalpan, Mex. ... C5, m14 34
Jamaica, country, N.A. ... E5 35
Jambi, Indon. ... F2 19

James, riv., S. Dak. ... F7 77
Jamesburg, N.J. ... C4 74
James City, N.C. ... B5 76
James City, co., Va. ... C6 85
Jamesport, Mo. ... B4 69
Jamestown, Calif. ... D3 50
Jamestown, Ind. ... E4 59
Jamestown, Ky. ... D4 62
Jamestown, N.Y. ... C1 75
Jamestown, N.C. ... B3 76
Jamestown, N. Dak. ... D7 77
Jamestown, Ohio ... C2 78
Jamestown, Pa. ... D1 81
Jamestown, R.I. ... D11 52
Jamestown, Tenn. ... C9 83
Jamesville, N.Y. ... *C4 75
Jamiltepec, Mex. ... D5 34
Jammu, India ... B5 20
Jammu and Kashmir, Disputed reg.,
  India, Pak. ... B6 20
Jâmnagar, India ... D5 20
Jamshedpur, India ... D8 20
Jämtland, co., Swe. ... *F6 11
Janesville, Iowa ... B5 60
Janesville, Minn. ... F5 67
Janesville, Wis. ... F4 88
Janin, Jordan ... B3 15
Janos, Mex. ... A3 34
Jánoshalma, Hung. ... B4 10
Janów, Lubelski, Pol. ... C7 7
Januária, Braz. ... B4 30

K

L

Name	Loc.	Pg.
Luwuk, Indon.	F6	19
Luxembourg, Lux.	C7	5
Luxembourg, country, Eur.	C7	5
Luxembourg, prov., Bel.	*C6	5
Luxembourg, Wis.	D6	88
Luxeuil-les-Bains, Fr.	D7	5
Luxor, see Al Uqsur, Eg.		
Luxora, Ark.	B6	49
Luzern, Switz.	E4	6
Luzern, canton, Switz.	*E4	6
Luzerne, Pa.	n17	81
Luzerne, co., Pa.	D9	81
Luzon, isl., Phil.	B6	19
Lvov, Sov. Un.	G5	12
Lyaskovets, Bul.	D7	10
Lycoming, co., Pa.	D7	81
Lydia Mills, S.C.	*C4	82
Lydick, Ind.	*A5	59
Lyell, mtn., B.C., Can.	D9	37
Lyford, Tex.	F4	84
Lykens, Pa.	E8	81
Lyle, Minn.	G6	67
Lyman, Nebr.	C1	71
Lyman, S.C.	B3	82
Lyman, co., S. Dak.	G6	77
Lyman, N.Y.	G2	52
Lynbrook, N.Y.	G2	52
Lynch, Ky.	D7	62
Lynchburg, Ohio	C2	78
Lynchburgh (Independent City), Va.	C3	85
Lynden, Wash.	A3	86
Lyndhurst, N.J.	h8	74
Lyndhurst, Ohio	g9	78
Lyndon, Kans.	D8	61
Lyndon, Ky.	g11	62
Lyndonville, N.Y.	B2	75
Lyndonville, Vt.	B3	73
Lyndora, Pa.	E2	81
Lynn, Ind.	D8	59
Lynn, Mass.	B6, g12	65
Lynn, co., Tex.	C2	84
Lynnfield, Mass.	f11	65
Lynn Garden, Tenn.	C11	83
Lynn Haven, Fla.	u16	54
Lynn Lake, Man.	A1, f7	40
Lynville, Ky.	f9	62
Lynnwood, Pa.	*D9	81
Lynnwood, Wash.	*B3	86
Lynwood, Calif.	n12	50
Lyon, Fr.	E6	4
Lyon, co., Iowa	A1	60
Lyon, co., Kans.	D7	61
Lyon, co., Ky.	C1	62
Lyon, co., Minn.	F3	67
Lyon, co., Nev.	B2	72
Lyon Mountain, N.Y.	f11	75
Lyonnais, former prov.,Fr.	E6	5
Lyons, Ga.	D4	55
Lyons, Ill.	k9	58
Lyons, Ind.	G3	59
Lyons, Kans.	D5	61
Lyons, Mich.	F6	66
Lyons, Nebr.	C9	71
Lyons, N.Y.	B4	75
Lyons Falls, N.Y.	B5	75
Lysá, Czech.	n18	7
Lysaya Gora, Sov. Un.	G8	12
Lysekil, Swe.	H4	11
Lyster Station, Que., Can.	C6	42
Lysva, Sov. Un.	D8	13
Lytle, Tex.	E3	84
Lyubar, Sov. Un.	G6	12
Lyubertsy, Sov. Un.	N17	12

M

Name	Loc.	Pg.
Ma'alot Tarshiha, Isr.	A3	15
Maastricht, Neth.	B6	5
Mabank, Tex.	C4	84
Mabel, Minn.	G7	67
Mableton, Ga.	h7	55
Mabscott, W. Va.	D3, n13	87
Mabton, Wash.	C5	86
McAdam, N.B., Can.	D2	43
McAdenville, N.C.	*B1	76
McAdoo, Pa.	E9	81
Macaé, Braz.	C4	30
McAlester, Okla.	C6	79
McAllen, Tex.	F3	84
Macamic, Que., Can.	*o20	41
Macao, Port. dep., Asia	G7	17
Macapá, Braz.	C5	27
McArthur, Ohio	C3	78
Macas, Ec.	D3	27
Macau, Braz.	D7	27
McBee, S.C.	C7	82
McBride, B.C., Can.	C7	37
McCall, Idaho	E2	57
McCamey, Tex.	D1	84
McCarthy, mtn., Mont.	E4	70
McCaysville, Ga.	B2	55
McChesneytown, Pa.	*F2	81
McClain, co., Okla.	C4	79
McCleary, Wash.	B2	86
MacClenny, Fla.	B4	54
Macclesfield, Eng.	D5	4
McCloud, Calif.	B2	50
McClure, Ohio	A2	78
McClure, Pa.	E7	81
McColl, S.C.	B8	82
McComas, W. Va.	D3	87
McComb, Miss.	D3	68
McComb, Ohio	A2	78
McCone, co., Mont.	C11	70
McConnellsburg, Pa.	G6	81
McConnelsville, Ohio	C4	78
McCook, Nebr.	D5	71
McCook, co., S. Dak.	G8	77
McCormick, S.C.	D3	82
McCormick, co., S.C.	D3	82
McCracken, co., Ky.	e9	62
McCreary, Man., Can.	D2	40
McCreary, co., Ky.	D5	62
McCrory, Ark.	B4	49
McCulloch, co., Tex.	D3	84
McCurtain, Okla.	B7	79
McCurtain, co., Okla.	C7	79
McDermott, Ohio	D2	78
McDonald, Ohio	A5	78
McDonald, Pa.	k13	81
MacDonald, W. Va.	D3, D7	87
McDonald, co., Mo.	E3	69
McDonough, Ga.	C2	55
McDonough, co., Ill.	C3	58
McDowell, co., N.C.	f10	76
McDowell, co., W. Va.	D3	87
McDuffie, co., Ga.	C4	55
Macedon, N.Y.	B3	75
Macedonia, reg., Eur.	*B4	14
Macedonia, rep., Yugo.	*D5	10
Maceió, Braz.	D7	27
Macerata, It.	C4	9
McEwen, Tenn.	A4	83
McFarland, Calif.	E4	50
McFarland, Wis.	E4	88
McGehee, Ark.	*D4	49
McGill, Nev.	B4	72
MacGillicuddy's Reeks, mts., Ire.	E2	4
McGrann, Pa.	*E2	81
McGraw, N.Y.	C4	75
MacGregor, Man., Cån.	E2	40
McGregor, Iowa	A6	60
McGregor, Tex.	D4	84
McGuffey, Ohio	B2	78
McGuire, mtn., Idaho	D4	57
Machado, Braz.	C3, k9	30
Machala, Ec.	B2	31
McHenry, Ill.	A5, h8	58
McHenry, co., Ill.	A5	58
McHenry, co., N. Dak.	B5	77
Machias, Maine	D5	64
Machida, Jap.	*n18	18
Machilipatnam (Bandar), India	E7	20
Măcin, Rom.	C9	10
McIntosh, Minn.	C3	67
McIntosh, co., Ga.	E5	55
McIntosh, co., N. Dak.	D6	77
McIntosh, co., Okla.	B6	79
Mack, Ohio	*D2	78
Mackay, Austl.	D8	25
Mackay, Idaho	F5	57
McKean, co., Pa.	C4	81
McKeesport, Pa.	F4, r14	81
McKees Rocks, Pa.	F1, k13	81
McKenney, Va.	D5	85
McKenzie, Tenn.	A3	83
McKenzie, co., N. Dak.	C2	77
Mackenzie, dist., N.W. Ter., Can.	D11	36
Mackenzie, mts., Can.	C7	33
Mackenzie, riv., N.W. Ter., Can.	C8	36
Mackinac, co., Mich.	B5	66
Mackinac Island, Mich.	C6	66
Mackinaw, Ill.	C4	58
Mackinaw City, Mich.	C6	66
McKinley, Minn.	C6	67
McKinley, co., N. Mex.	B4	48
McKinley, mtn., Alsk.	C9	47
McKinley Heights, Ohio	*A5	78
McKinleyville, Calif.	B1	50
McKinney, Tex.	C4	84
McKittrick Summit, mtn., Calif.	E4	50
Macklin, Sask., Can.	E1	39
McKnight, Pa.	*E1	81
McKnownville, N.Y.	*C7	75
McLaughlin, S. Dak.	E5	77
McLean, Tex.	B2	84
McLean, Va.	g12	85
McLean, co., Ill.	C5	58
McLean, co., Ky.	C2	62
McLean, co., N. Dak.	C4	77
McLean, mtn., Maine	A4	64
McLeansboro, Ill.	E5	58
McLennan, Alta., Can.	B2	38
McLennan, co., Tex.	D4	84
McLeod, co., Minn.	F4	67
McLeod Lake, B.C., Can.	B6, n18	37
McLoud, Okla.	B4	79
McLoughlin, mtn., Oreg.	E4	80
McLouth, Kans.	C8, k15	61
McMasterville, Que., Can.	*D4	42
McMechen, W. Va.	B4, g8	87
McMillan Manor, Calif.	*E4	50
McMinn, co., Tenn.	D9	83
McMinnville, Oreg.	B3, h11	80
McMinnville, Tenn.	D8	83
McMullen, co., Tex.	E3	84
McMurray, Alta., Can.	A5, f8	38
McNair, Tex.	E5	84
McNairy, co., Tenn.	B3	83
McNary, Ariz.	B4	48
McNeill, mtn., B.C., Can.	B2	37
Macomb, Ill.	C3	58
Macomb, co., Mich.	F8	66
Macon, Fr.	D6	5
Macon, Ga.	D3	55
Macon, Ill.	D5	58
Macon, Miss.	B5	68
Macon, Mo.	B5	69
Macon, co., Ala.	C4	46
Macon, co., Ga.	D2	55
Macon, co., Ill.	D5	58
Macon, co., Mo.	B5	69
Macon, co., N.C.	f9	76
Macon, co., Tenn.	C7	83
Macoupin, co., Ill.	D4	58
McPherson, Kans.	D6	61
McPherson, co., Kans.	D6	61
McPherson, co., Nebr.	C4	71
McPherson, co., S. Dak.	E6	77
McRae, Ga.	D4	55
McRoberts, Ky.	C7	62
McSherrystown, Pa.	G7	81
Macksville, Kans.	E5	61
MacTier, Ont., Can.	B5	41
Macungie, Pa.	E10	81
McVeigh, Ky.	C7	62
Ma'daba, Jordan	C3	15
Madagascar, country, Afr.	E9	24
Madawaska, Maine	A4	64
Madawaska, co., N.B., Can.	B1	43
Madeira, Ohio	o13	78
Madeira Beach, Fla.	*E4	54
Madeira Is., reg., Port.	B1	22
Madelia, Minn.	F4	67
Madera, Calif.	D3	50
Madera, Mex.	B3	34
Madera, Pa.	E5	81
Madera, co., Calif.	D4	50
Madgaon, India	E5	20
Madhya Pradesh, state, India	D6	20
Madīnat ash Sha'b, P.D.R. of Yem.	G4	15
Madison, Ala.	A3	46
Madison, Conn.	D6	52
Madison, Fla.	B3	54
Madison, Ga.	C3	55
Madison, Ill.	E3	58
Madison, Ind.	G7	59
Madison, Kans.	D7	61
Madison, Maine	D3	64
Madison, Minn.	E2	67
Madison, Mo.	B5	69
Madison, Nebr.	C8	71
Madison, N.J.	B4	74
Madison, N.C.	A3	76
Madison, Ohio	A4	78
Madison, S. Dak.	G9	77
Madison, W. Va.	C3, m12	87
Madison, Wis.	*E4	88
Madison, co., Ala.	A3	46
Madison, co., Ark.	B2	49
Madison, co., Fla.	B3	54
Madison, co., Ga.	B3	55
Madison, co., Idaho	F7	57
Madison, co., Ill.	E4	58
Madison, co., Ind.	D6	59
Madison, co., Iowa	C3	60
Madison, co., Ky.	C5	62
Madison, co., Miss.	C4	68
Madison, co., Mo.	D7	69
Madison, co., Mont.	E4	70
Madison, co., Nebr.	C8	71
Madison, co., N.Y.	C5	75
Madison, co., N.C.	f10	76
Madison, co., Ohio	C2	78
Madison, co., Tenn.	B3	83
Madison, co., Tex.	D5	84
Madison, co., Va.	B4	85
Madison, par., La.	B4	63
Madison Heights, Mich.	o15	66
Madison Heights, Va.	C3	85
Madisonville, Ky.	C2	62
Madisonville, La.	D5, h11	63
Madisonville, Tenn.	D9	83
Madisonville, Tex.	D5	84
Madium, Indon.	*G4	19
Madoc, Ont., Can.	C7	41
Madras, India	F7	20
Madras, Oreg.	C5	80
Madre de Dios, dept., Peru	D3	31
Madrid, Iowa	C4, e8	60
Madrid, N.Y.	f9	75
Madrid, Sp.	B4, p17	8
Madrid, prov., Sp.	*B4	8
Madridejos, Phil.	*C6	19
Madridejos, Sp.	C4	8
Madurai, India	G6	20
Maebashi, Jap.	H9, m18	18
Maeser, Utah	A7	72
Mafeking, S. Afr.	F5	24
Mafra, Braz.	D3	30
Magadan, Sov. Un.	D18	13
Magallanes, prov., Chile	E2, h11	28
Magangué, Col.	B3	32
Magdalena, Mex.	A2	34
Magdalena, N. Mex.	B5	48
Magdalena, dept., Col.	A3	32
Magdalena, riv., Col.	C3	27
Magdalena Contreras, Mex.	h9	34
Magdalen Islands, co., Que., Can.	B8	43
Magdeburg, Ger. Dem. Rep.	B5	6
Magé, Braz.	h6	30
Magee, Miss.	D4	68
Magelang, Indon.	G4	19
Magenta, It.	B2	9
Maglie, It.	D7	9
Magna, Utah	A5, C2	72
Magnitogorsk, Sov. Un.	D8	13
Magnolia, Ark.	D2	49
Magnolia, Miss.	D3	68
Magnolia, N.J.	D2	74
Magnolia, N.C.	C4	76
Magnolia, Ohio	B4	78
Magoffin, co., Ky.	C6	62
Magog, Que., Can.	D5	42
Magrath, Alta., Can.	E4	38
Magwe, Bur.	D9	20
Mahameru, mtn., Indon.	G4	19
Mahanoy City, Pa.	E9	81
Maharashtra, state, India	D5	20
Mahaska, co., Iowa	C5	60

N

O

P

Q

R

Robeson, co., N.C. C3 76
Robesonia, Pa. *F9 81
Robinson, Ill. D6 58
Robinson, Pa. F3 81
Robinson, Tex. *D4 84
Robinsonville, Miss. A3 68
Roblin, Man., Can. D1 40
Robson, mtn., Can. C1 38
Robstown, Tex. F4 84
Roby, Mo. D5 69
Roby, Tex. C2 84
Roccastrada, It. C3 9
Rocha, Ur. E2 30
Roch, dept., Ur. *E2 30
Rochdale, Eng. D5 4
Rochdale, Mass. B4 65
Rochefort, Fr. E3 5
Rochelle, Ga. E3 55
Rochelle, Ill. B4 58
Rochelle Park, N.J. h8 74
Rochester, Ind. B5 59
Rochester, Mich. F7 66
Rochester, Minn. F6 67
Rochester, N.H. E6 73
Rochester, N.Y. B3 75.
Rochester, Pa. E1 81
Rock, co., Minn. G2 67
Rock, co., Nebr. B6 71
Rock, co., Wis. F4 88
Rockaway, N.J. B3 74
Rockaway, Oreg. B3 80
Rockbridge, co., Va. C3 85
Rockcastle, co., Ky. C5 62
Rockcliffe Park, Ont., Can. *B9 41
Rock Creek Hills, Md. *B3 53
Rockdale, Ill. B5, m8 58
Rockdale, Md. *B4 53
Rockdale, Tex. D4 84
Rockdale, co., Ga. C2 55
Rock Falls, Ill. B4 58
Rockford, Ill. A4 58
Rockford, Iowa A5 60
Rockford, Mich. E5 66
Rockford, Ohio B1 78
Rockford, Tenn. D10, n14 83
Rock Hall, Md. B5 53
Rockhampton, Austl. D9 25
Rock Hill, Mo. *C7 69
Rock Hill, S.C. B5 82
Rockingham, N.C. C3 76
Rockingham, co., N.H. E5 73
Rockingham, co., N.C. A3 76
Rockingham, co., Va. B4 85
Rock Island, Que., Can. D5 42
Rock Island, Ill. B3 58
Rock Island, co., Ill. B3 58
Rockland, Ont., Can. B9 41
Rockland, Maine B3 64
Rockland, Mass. B6, h12 65
Rockland, co., N.Y. D6 75
Rockledge, Fla. D6 54
Rockledge, Pa. o21 81
Rocklin, Calif. *C3 50
Rockmart, Ga. B1 55
Rockport, Ind. I3 59
Rockport, Maine D3 64
Rockport, Mass. A6 65
Rock Port, Mo. A2 69
Rockport, Tex. F4 84
Rock Rapids, Iowa A1 60
Rocksprings, Tex. D2 84
Rock Springs, Wyo. E3 89
Rockton, Ill. A4 58
Rock Valley, Iowa A1 60
Rockville, Conn. B7 52
Rockville, Ind. E3 59
Rockville, Md. B3 53
Rockville Center, N.Y. n15 75
Rockwall, Tex. C4, n10 84
Rockwall, co., Tex. C4 84
Rockwell City, Iowa B3 60
Rockwood, Mich. F7 66
Rockwood, Pa. F3 81
Rockwood, Tenn. D9 83
Rocky Ford, Colo. C7 51
Rocky Grove, Pa. D2 81
Rocky Hill, Conn. C6 52
Rocky Mount, N.C. B5 76
Rocky Mount, Va. C3 85
Rocky Mountain House,
Alta., Can. C3 38
Rocky Point, N.Y. *n15 75
Rocky Point, Wash. *B3 86
Rocky Ripple, Ind. k10 59
Rocky River, Ohio A4, h9 78
Roddickton, Newf, Can. C3, h10 44
Rodeo, Calif. *D3 50
Roderfield,W. Va. D3 87
Rodessa, La. B1 63
Rodez, Fr. E5 5
Rodgers Forge, Md. *B4 53
Rodhópi (Rhodope), prov., Grc. *B5 14
Ródhos, Grc. D7 14
Rodney, Ont. Can. E3 41
Rodney Village, Del. B6 53
Roebling, N.J. C3 74
Roeland Park, Kans. B9 61
Roermond, Neth. B6 5
Roeselare, Bel. B5 5
Roessleville, N.Y. *C7 75
Rogachev, Sov. Un. E8 12
Rogaland, co., Nor. *H1 11
Rogatica, Yugo D4 10
Roger Mills, co., Okla. B2 79
Rogers, Ark. A1 49
Rogers, Tex. D4 84
Rogers, Va. f10 85
Rogers, co.,Okla. A6 79
Rogers City, Mich. C7 66
Rogers Heights, Md. *C4 53
Rogersville, Tenn. C10 83
Rogoźno, Pol. B4 7
Rohnerville, Calif. *B1 50
Rohtak, India *C6 20
Roi Et, Thai. B2 19
Rojas, Arg. A4 28
Rokitno, Sov. Un. F6 12
Rokycany, Czech. D2 7
Roland Terrace, Md. *B4 53
Rolette, co., N. Dak. B6 77
Rolfe, Iowa B3 60
Rolla, Mo. D6 69
Rolla, N. Dak. A6 77
Rolling Fork, Miss. C3 68
Rolling Hills, Kans. B5 61
Rolling Hills Estates, Calif. *F4 50
Rolling Meadows, Ill. h8 58
Rollingwood, Calif. *D2 50
Roma, Austl. E8 25
Roma, Tex. F3 84
Roma, see Rome, It.
Roman, Rom. B8 10
Romania, country, Eur. B7 10
Romans *-sur-Isère*, Fr. E6 5
Romblon, Phil. *C6 19
Romblon, prov., Phil. *C6 19
Rome, Ga. B1 55
Rome, Ill. C4 58
Rome (Roma), It. D4, h8 9
Rome, N.Y. B5 75
Rome, Ohio *A5 78
Romeo, Ill. *B5 58
Romeo, Mich. F7 66
Romilly *-sur-Seine*, Fr. C5 5
Romita, Mex. m11 34
Romney, W.Va. B6 87
Romny, Sov. Un. F9 12
Romorantin, Fr. D4 5
Romulus, Mich. p15 66
Ronan, Mont. C2 70
Roncerverte, W. Va. D4 87
Ronciglione, It. C4 9
Ronda, Sp. D3 8
Rondôia, ter., Braz. B3 29
Ronkonkoma, N.Y. F4 52
Rønne, Den. A3 7
Ronse, Bel. B5 5
Roodhouse, Ill. D3 58
Rooks, co., Kans. C4 61
Roosendaal, Neth. B6 5
Roosevelt, N.Y. G2 52
Roosevelt, Utah A6 72
Roosevelt, co., Mont. B11 70
Roosevelt, co., N. Mex. B7 48
Roosevelt, riv., Braz. B3 29
Roosevelt Park, Mich. E4 66
Roquetas, Sp. B6 8
Rorschach, Switz. E4 6
Rosa, mtn., It., Switz. B2 9
Roraima, ter., Braz. C5 32
Rosario, Arg. A4 28
Rosário, Braz. *D6 27
Rosario, Mex. C3 34
Rosario, Par. D4 29
Rosario, Ur. E1 30
Rosário do Sul, Braz. E2 30
Rosario Tala, Arg. A5 28
Rosburg, Wash. B5 89
Roscoe, N.Y. D6 75
Roscoe, Pa. F2 81
Roscoe, Tex. C2 84
Roscommon, co., Ire. *D2 4
Roscommon, co., Mich. D6 66
Roseau, Dominica I14 35
Roseau, Minn. B3 67
Roseau, co., Minn. B3 67
Roseboro, N.C. C4 76
Rosebud, Tex. D4 84
Rosebud, co., Mont. D10 70
Roseburg, Oreg. D3 80
Rosedale, Fla. *E4 54
Rosedale, Miss. B2 68
Rosedale Station, Alta, Can. D4 38
Rose Hill, Kans. E6 61
Rose Hill, N.C. C4 76
Roseland, Fla. E6 54
Roseland, Ind. A5 59
Roseland, La. D5 63
Roseland, N.J. *B4 74
Roseland, Ohio B3 78
Roselle, Ill. k8 58
Roselle, N.J. k7 74
Roselle Park, N.J. k7 74
Rosemead, Calif. *F4 50
Rosemère, Que., Can. p19 42
Rosemont, Ill. *E3 58
Rosemont, Pa. *F11 81
Rosemount, Minn. F5 67
Rosenberg, Tex. E5, r14 84
Rosendael, Fr. B5 5
Rosendale, N.Y. *C6 75
Rosenheim, Ger., Fed. Rep of E6 6
Roseto, Pa. E11 81
Rosetown, Sask., Can. F1, n7 39
Roseville, Calif. C3 50
Roseville, Ill. C3 58
Roseville, Mich. o16 66
Roseville, Minn. m12 67
Roseville, Ohio C3 78
Rosewood, Calif. *B1 50
Rosewood Heights, Ill. *E3 58
Rosiclare, Ill. F5 58
Rosiorii-de-Vede, Rom. C7 10
Roskilde, co., Den. *J5 11
Roslavl, Sov. Un. E9 12
Roslyn, N.Y. *E7 75
Roslyn, Pa. *F11 81
Roslyn, Wash. B4 86
Roslyn Estates, N.Y. *G2 52
Roslyn Harbor, N.Y. *E7 75
Roslyn Heights, N.Y. D2, h13 75
Rosny-sous-Bois, Fr. g10 5
Ross, Calif. *C2 50
Ross, co., Ohio C2 78
Ross and Cromarty, co., Scot. *B4 4
Rossano, It. E6 9
Rossford, Ohio A2, e6 78
Rossiter, Pa. E4 81
Rossland, B.C., Can. E9 37
Rossmoor, Calif. *F5 50
Rossmoyne, Ohio *C1 78
Rossosh, Sov. Un. F12 12
Rossville, Ga. B1 55
Rossville, Ill. C6 58
Rosthern, Sask., Can. E2 39
Rostock, Ger. Dem. Rep. A6 6
Rostov, Sov. Un. C12 12
Rostov *-na-Donu*, Sov. Un. H12 12
Roswell, Ga. B2 55
Roswell, N. Mex. C6 48
Rotan, Tex. C2 84
Rotenburg *an der Fulda*,
Ger., Fed. Rep of B4 6
Rothenburg ob der Tauber
Ger., Fed. Rep of D5 6
Rothesay, Scot. C4 4
Rothschild, Wis. D4 88
Rothsville, Pa. F9 81
Rotondella, It. D6 9
Rotorua, N.Z. M16 26
Rotterdam, Neth. B6 5
Rotterdam, N.Y. *C6 75
Rottweil, Ger., Fed. Rep of D4 6
Roubaix, Fr. B5 5
Roudnice *ned Labem*, Czech. n7 17
Rouen, Fr. C4 5
Roulette, Pa. C5 81
Round Lake, Ill. h8 58
Roundlake, Miss. A3 68
Round Lake Beach, Ill. h8 58
Round Lake Heights, Ill. *h8 58
Round Lake Park, Ill. *h8 58
Round Pond, Ark. B5 49
Round Rock, Tex. D4 84
Roundup, Mont. D8 70
Rouses Point, N.Y. f11 75
Rouseville, Pa. D2 81
Routt, co., Colo. A3 51
Rouville, co., Que., Can. D4 42
Rouzerville, Pa. G7 81
Rovaniemi, Fin. D11 11
Rovato, It. B2 9
Rovenki, Sov. Un. G12, q22 12
Rovereto, It. B3 9
Rovigo, It. B3 9
Rovinj, Yugo. C1 10
Rovno, Sov. Un. F6 12
Rovnoye, Sov. Un. F16 12
Rowan, co., Ky. B6 62
Rowan, co., N.C. B2 76
Rowan Mill, N.C. B2 76
Rowes Run, Pa. *F2 81
Rowland, N.C. C3 76
Rowland, Pa. D11 81
Rowlesburg, W. Va. B5 87
Rowlett, Tex. *C4 84
Rowley, Mass. A6 65
Roxana, Ill. f13 69
Roxas (Capiz), Phil. C6 19
Roxboro, N.C. A4 76
Roxburgh, co., Scot. *C5 4
Roxton Falls, Que., Can. D5 42
Roy, N. Mex. B6 48
Roy, Utah A5, C2 72
Royal, Fla. D4 54
Royal Center, Ind. C4 59
Royal Mills, N.C. A4 76
Royal Oak, Mich. F7, o15 66
Royal Oak Township, Mich. *F7 66
Royalton, Ill. F4 58
Royalton, Pa. *F8 81
Royan, Fr. E3 5
Royersford, Pa. F10 81
Royse City, Tex. C4 84
Royston, Ga. B3 55
Rožňava, Czech. D6 7
Rtishchevo, Sov. Un. E14 12
Ruapehu, mtn., N.Z. M15 26
Rubezhnoye, Sov. Un. p21 12
Rubidoux, Calif. n14 50
Ruda Slaska, Pol. *C5 7
Rudbar, Afg. B3 20
Rudolf, lake, Afr. F9 21
Rudolstadt, Ger. Dem. Rep. C5 6
Rueil-Malmaison, Fr. g9 5
Rufino, Arg. A4 28
Rufisque, Sen. F1 22
Rugby, Eng. D6 4
Rugby, N. Dak. B6 77
Ruidoso, N. Mex. C6 48
Rule, Tex. C3 84
Ruleville, Miss. B3 68
Ruma, Yugo C4 10
Rumford, Maine D2 64
Rumoi, Jap. E10 18
Rumson, N.J. C4 74
Runge, Tex. E4 84
Runnels, co., Tex. D3 84
Runnemede, N.J. D2 74
Rupert, Idaho G5 57
Rupert, W. Va. D4 87
Rural Hall, N.C. A2 76
Ruse (Ruschuk), Bul. *D7 10
Ruse (Ruschuk), co., Bul. *D8 10
Rush, co., Ind. E7 59
Rush City, Minn. E6 67
Rush, co., Kan. D4 61
Rushford, Minn. G7 67
Rush Springs, Okla. C4 79
Rushville, Ill. C3 58
Rushville, Ind. E7 59
Rushville, Nebr. B3 71
Rusk, Tex. D5 84
Rusk, co.,Tex. C5 84
Rusk, co., Wis. C2 88
Ruskin, Fla. E4, p11 54
Russas, Braz. *D7 27
Russell (Russell City), Calif. *D3 50
Russell, Man., Can. D1 40
Russell, Kans. D5 61
Russell, Ky. B7 62
Russell, co., Ala. C4 46
Russell, co., Ont. Can. B9 41
Russell, co., Kans. D5 61
Russell, co., Ky. C4 62
Russell, co., Va. f9 85
Russell Gardens, N.Y. *E7 75
Russells Point, Ohio *B2 78
Russell Springs, Ky. C4 62
Russellton, Pa. E2 81
Russellville, Ala. A2 46
Russellville, Ark. B2 49
Russellville, Ky. D3 62
Russian Soviet Federated Socialist
Republic, rep., Sov. Un. C8 12
Russiaville, Ind. D5 59
Rustavi, Sov. Un. B15 14
Ruston, La. B3 63
Rutchenkovo, Sov. Un. r20 12
Rute, Sp. D3 8
Ruteng, Indon. G6 19
Ruth, Miss. D3 68
Ruth, Nev. B4 72
Ruthenia, reg., Sov. Un. D7 7
Rutherford, N.J. B4, h8 74
Rutherford, Tenn. A3 83
Rutherford, co., N.C. B1 76
Rutherford, co., Tenn. B5 83
Rutherford Heights, Pa. *F8 81
Rutherfordton, N.C. B1, f11 76
Rutland, Mass. B4 65
Rutland, Vt. D2 73
Rutland, co., Eng. *D6 4
Rutland, co., Vt. D1 73
Rutledge, Pa. *G11 81
Ruvo *di Puglia*, It. D6 9
Ruxton, Md. *B4 53
Ruzayevka, Sov. Un. D15 12

S

T

Tabaco, Phil. *C6 19
Tabasco, state, Mex. D6 34
Taber, Alta., Can. E4 38
Taboada, Sp. A2 8
Tábor, Czech. D3 7
Tabor, Iowa D2 60
Tabor, N.J. *B4 74
Tabora, Tan. B6 24
Tabor City, N.C. C4 76
Tabrīz, Iran B4 15
Tabūk, Sau. Ar. D2 15
Tachikawa, Jap. n18 18
Táchira, state, Ven. B3 32
Tacloban, Phil. C6 19
Tacna, Peru E5 31
Tacna, dept., Peru E3 31
Tacoma, Wash. B3, f11 86
Tacuarembó, Ur. E1 30
Tacuarembó, dept., Ur. *E1 30
Tadoussac, Que., Can. A8 42
Tadzhik, rep., Sov. Un. F9 16
Taegu, Kor. I4 18
Taejon, Kor. H3 18
Tafalla, Sp. A5 8
Taff Viejo, Arg. E2 29
Tafí Viejo, Arg. E2 29
Taft, Calif. E4 50
Taft, Fla. D5 54
Taft, Tex. F4 84
Taft Heights, Calif. *E4 50
Taft Southwest, Tex. *F4 84
Taganrog, Sov. Un. H12 12
Tahat, mtn., Alg. D6 22
Tahlequah, Okla. B7 79
Tahoka, Tex. C2 84
Tahoua, Niger F6 22
Taian, China *D8 17
Taichou, China *E8 17
T'aichung, Taiwan G9 17
Taihsien, China E6 17
Taikang, China C2 18
Tailai, China C1 18
T'ainan, Taiwan G9 17
Taipei, Taiwan G9 17
Taiping, Mala. E2 19
T'aitung, Taiwan G9 17
Taiwan (Formosa), country
(Nationalist China), Asia G9 17
Taiyüan (Yangkü), China D7 17
Taizz, Yemen G3 15
Tajimi, Jap. I8, n16 18
Tajrīsh, Iran *B5 15
Tājūrā, Libya B7 22
Tak, Thai. *B1 19
Takada, Jap. H9 18
Takamatsu, Jap. I7 18
Takaoka, Jap. H8 18
Takasaki, Jap. H9, m17 18
Takatsuki, Jap. o14 18
Takawa, Jap. *J5 18
Takayama, Jap. H8, m16 18
Takefu, Jap. n15 18
Takeo, Camb. *C2 19
Takingeun, Indon. *m11 19
Takoma Park, Md. f8 53
Takut, Bur. *D10 20
Talā, Eg. *G8 14
Tala, Mex. m12 34
Tala, Ur. E1 30
Talagante, Chile A2 28
Talai, China D2 18
Talara, Peru B1 31
Talavera de la Reina, Sp. C3 8
Talbert, Ky. C6 62
Talbot, co., Ga. D2 55
Talbot, co., Md. C5 53
Talbotton, Ga. D2 55
Talca, Chile B2 28
Talca, prov., Chile B2 28
Talcahuano, Chile B2 28
Tālcher, India D8 20
Talco, Tex. C5 84
Taliaferro, co., Ga. C4 55
Talihina, Okla. C6 79
Talisayan, Phil. *D6 19
Talladega, Ala. B3 46
Talladega, co., Ala. B3 46
Tallahassee, Fla. B2 54
Tallahatchie, co., Miss. B3 68
Tallapoosa, Ga. C1 55
Tallapoosa, co., Ala. C4 46
Tallassee, Ala. C4 46
Talleyville, Del. *A6 53
Tallinn, Sov. Un. B5 12
Tallmadge, Ohio A4 78
Tallulah, La. B4 63
Talnoye, Sov. Un. G8 12
Talsi, Sov. Un. C4 12
Taltal, Chile E1 29
Tama, Iowa C5 60
Tama, co., Iowa B5 60
Tamale, Ghana G4 22
Taman, Sov. Un. I11 12
Tamano, Jap. I6 18
Tamanrasset, Alg. D6 22
Tamaqua, Pa. E10 81
Tamatave, Mad. D9 24
Tamaulipas, state, Mex. C5 34
Tamazula de Gordiano, Mex. n12 34
Tambov, Sov. Un. E13 12
Tamil Nadu, state, India F6 20
Tampa, Fla. E4, p11 54
Tampere, Fin. G10 11
Tampico, Mex. C5, k15 34
Tams, W.Va. D3 87
Tamworth, Austl. F9 25
Tanabe, Jap. J7 18
Tananarive, see Antananarive, Mad.
Tanchon, Kor. F4 18
Tandag, Phil. *D7 19
Tândărei, Rom. C8 10
Taney, co., Mo. E4 69
Taneytown, Md. A3 53
Tanga, Tan. B7 24
Tanganyika, lake, Afr. C6 24
Tanger (Tangier), Mor. A3 22
Tangermünde, Ger. Dem. Rep. B5 6
Tangier, Va. C7 85
Tangipahoa, par., La. D5 63
Tangshan, China *D8 17
Tangtan, China C11 20
Tangyüan, China C4 18
Tanjay, Phil. *D6 19
Tanjore, see Thanjāvūr, India
Tanjungkarang-Telukbetung, Indon. G3 19
Tanjungpandan, Indon. F3 19
Tānk, Pak. B5 20
Tanque Verde, Ariz. *C4 48
Tanshui, Taiwan *F9 17
Ţanţā, Eg. G8 14
Tantung (Antung), China C9 17
Tanzania, country, Afr. B6 24
Taoan, China B9 17
Taormina, It. F5 9
Taos, N.Mex. A6 48
Taos, co., N.Mex. A6 48
Tapachula, Mex. E6 34
Tappahannock, Va. C6 85
Tappan, N.Y. g13 75
Taquara, Braz. D2 30
Taquaritinga, Braz. k7 30
Tara, Mo. *C7 69
Tara, Sov. Un. D10 13
Tarābulus, see Tripoli, Leb.
Tarakan, Laos *B2 19
Tarancon, Sp. B4 8
Taranto, It. D6 9
Tarapacá, prov., Chile D1 29
Tarapoto, Peru C2 31
Tarare, Fr. E6 5
Tarascon-sur-Ariège, Fr. F6 5
Tarazona, Sp. B5 8
Tarbes, Fr. F4 5
Tarboro, N.C. B5 76
Taree, Austl. E9 26
Tarentum, Pa. E2, h14 81
Tarfaya, Mor. C2 22
Tarifa, Sp. D3 8
Tarija, Bol. D3 29
Tarija, dept., Bol. D3 29
Tarkio, Mo. A2 69
Tarkwa, Ghana G4 22
Tarlac, Phil. B6, o13 19
Tarlac, prov., Phil. *B6 19
Tarma, Peru D2 31
Tarn, dept., Fr. *F5 5
Tarn-et-Garonne, dept., Fr. *E4 5
Tarnobrzeg, Pol. C6 7
Tarnów, Pol. C6 7
Tarnowskie Góry, Pol. g9 7
Taroudant, Mor. B3 22
Tarpon Springs, Fla. D4 54
Tarquinia, It. C3 9
Tarragona, Sp. B6 8
Tarragona, prov., Sp. *B6 8
Tarrant, Ala. B3, f7 46
Tarrant, co., Tex. C4 84
Tarrasa, Sp. B7 8
Tarrytown, N.Y. D7, m15 75
Tarsney, Mo. k11 69
Tarsus, Tur. D10 14
Tartu, Sov. Un. B6 12
Tashkent, Sov. Un. E9 13
Tashkurghan, Afg. A4 20
Tasikmalaya, Indon. *G3 19
Tasmania, state, Austl. o14 25
Tatabánya, Hun. B4 10
Tatamagouche, N.S., Can. D6 43
Tatarbunary, Sov. Un. C9 10
Tate, Ga. B2 55
Tate, co., Miss. A4 68
Tateville, Ky. D5 62
Tateyama, Jap. I9, n18 18
Tatta, Pak. D4 20
Tattnall, co., Ga. D4 55
Tatuí, Braz. C3, m8 30
Tatum, N.Mex. C7 48
Tatung, China C7 17
Taubaté, Braz. C3 30
Taung, S.Afr. F4 24
Taungdwingyi, Bur. D10 20
Taunggyi, Bur. D10 20
Taunton, Eng. E5 4
Taunton, Mass. C5 65
Taurage, Sov. Un. D4 12
Tauranga, N.Z. L16 26
Taurianova, It. E6 9
Tauste, Sp. B5 8
Tavares, Fla. D5 54
Tavas, Tur. *D7 14
Tavda, Sov. Un. D9 13
Tavira, Port. D2 8
Tavistock, Ont., Can. D4 41
Tavoy, Bur. F10 20
Tavsanli, Tur. *C7 14
Tawas City, Mich. D7 66
Taylor, Mich. p15 66
Taylor, Pa. D10, m18 81
Taylor, Tex. D4 84
Taylor, co., Fla. B3 54
Taylor, co., Ga. D2 55
Taylor, co., Iowa D3 60
Taylor, co., Ky. C4 62
Taylor, co., Tex. C3 84
Taylor, co., W.Va. B4 87
Taylor, co., Wis. C3 88
Taylor Mill, Ky. k14 62
Taylors, S.C. B3 82
Taylorsport, Ky. h13 62
Taylorsville, Ky. B4 62
Taylorsville, Miss. D4 68
Taylorsville, N.C. B1 76
Taylorville, Ill. D4 58
Tayshet, Sov. Un. D12 13
Taza, Mor. B4 22
Tazewell, Tenn. C10 83
Tazewell, Va. e10 85
Tazewell, co., Ill. C4 58
Tazewell, co., Va. e10 85
Tbilisi, Sov. Un. E7 13
Tchula, Miss. B3 68
Tczew, Pol. A5 7
Teague, Tex. D4 84
Teaneck, N.J. h8 74
Tecuala, Mex. C3 34
Tecuci, Rom. C8 10
Tecumseh, Ont., Can. E2 41
Tecumseh, Mich. F7 66
Tecumseh, Nebr. D9 71
Tecumseh, Okla. B5 79
Tegal, Indon. *G3 19
Tegucigalpa, Hond. E7 34
Teguise, Sp. m15 8
Tehachapi, Calif. E4 50
Tehama, co., Calif. B2 50
Tehrān, Iran B5 15
Tehuacan, Mex. D5, n15 34
Tehuantepec, Mex. D5 34
Teide, Pico de, peak, Sp.(Can. Is.) m13 8
Tejo (Tagus), riv., Eur. C1 8
Tekamah, Nebr. C9 71
Tekax de Alvaro Obregón, Mex. C7 34
Tekirdağ, Tur. B6 14
Teko, China B10 20
Tekoa, Wash. B8 86
Tela, Hond. *D7 34
Tel Aviv-Yafo (Tel Aviv Jaffa),
Isr. B2, g5 15
Telde, Sp. m14 8
Telemark, co., Nor. *H3 11
Telfair, co., Ga. E3 55
Telford, Pa. F11 81
Tell, Wis. I4 59
Tell City, Ind. I4 59
Teller, co., Colo. C5 51
Telluride, Colo. D3 51
Telok Anson, Mala. E2 19
Teloloapan, Mex. D5, n14 34
Temirtau, Sov. Un. *D10 13
Témiscouata, co., Que., Can. B9 42
Temora, Austl. *F8 25
Tempe, Ariz. C3, D2 48
Temperance, Mich. G7 66
Tempio Pausania, It. D2 9
Temple, Okla. C3 79
Temple, Pa. F10 81
Temple, Tex. D4 84
Temple City, Calif. *F5 50
Temple Hill, Ky. D4 62
Temple Terrace, Fla. o11 54
Templeton, Que., Can. D2 42
Templeton, Mass. A3 65
Templin, Ger. Dem. Rep. B6 6
Temryuk, Sov. Un. I11 12
Temuco, Chile B2 28
Tenafly, N.J. B5, h9 74
Tenaha, Tex. D5 84
Tenāli, India *E7 20
Tenancingo, *de Degollado*, Mex. D5, n14 34
Tenango del Valle, Mex. n14 34
Tenasserim, Bur. F10 20
Tengchung, China F4 17
Tengri Khan, mtn., China E11 13
Tenino, Wash. C3 86
Tennessee, state, U.S. 83
Tennessee, riv., U.S. D9 45
Tensas, par., La. B4 63
Teocaltiche, Mex. C4, m12 34
Teófilo Otoni, Braz. B4 30
Tepatitán *de Morelos*, Mex. C4, m12 34
Tepic, Mex. C4, m11 34
Teplice, Czech. C2 7
Teramo, It. C4 9
Teresina, Braz. D6 27
Teresópolis, Braz. C4, h6 30
Termez, Sov. Un. F9 13
Termini Imerese, It. F4 9
Termoli, It. C5 9
Ternate, Indon. E7 19
Terneuzen, Neth. B5 5
Terney, Sov. Un. D8 18
Terni, It. C4 9
Ternopol, Sov. Un. G5 12
Terra Alta, W. Va. B5 87
Terrace, B.C., Can. B3 37
Terrace Park, Ohio *C1 78
Terracina, It. D4 9
Terra Linda, Calif. *D2 50
Terrebonne, Que., Can. D4, p19 42
Terrebonne, co., Que., Can. D3 42
Terrebonne, par., La. E5 63
Terre Haute, Ind. F3 59
Terre Hill, Pa. F9 81
Terrell, Tex. C4 84
Terrell, co., Ga. E2 55
Terrell, co., Tex. D1 84
Terrell Hills, Tex. k7 84
Terry, Mont. D11 70
Terry, co., Tex. C1 84
Terrytown, La. *k11 63
Terrytown, Nebr. C2 71
Terryville, Conn. C4 52
Teruel, Sp. B5 8
Teruel, prov., Sp. *B5 8
Tesanj, Yugo. C3 10
Teterow, Ger. Dem. Rep. B6 6
Teton, co., Idaho F7 57
Teton, co., Mont. C4 70
Teton, co., Wyo. C2 89
Tétouan, Mor. A3 22
Tetovo, Yugo. D5 10
Tetu, China B3 18
Teutopolis, Ill. D5 58
Teverya (Tiberias), Isr. B3, g5 15
Tewantin-Noosa, Austl. C9 26
Tewksbury, Mass. A5, f11 65
Texarkana, Ark. D1 49
Texarkana, Tex. C5 84
Texas, Md. B4 53
Texas, co., Mo. D5 69
Texas, co., Okla. e9 79
Texas, state, U.S. 84
Texas City, Tex. E5, r15 84
Texhoma, Okla. e9 79
Teziutlán, Mex. D5, n15 34
Thailand (Siam), country, Asia B2 19
Thames, N.Z. L15 26
Thamesville, Ont., Can. E3 41
Thāna, India *E5 20
Thanh Hoa, Viet. B3 19
Thanjāvūr (Tanjore), India F6 20
Thann, Fr. D7 5
Thaon *-les-Vosges*, Fr. C7 5
Tharptown, Pa. *E8 81

Tharrawaddy, Bur. E10 20
Thatcher, Ariz. C4 48
Thatcher, Idaho G7 57
Thaton, Bur. E10 20
Thayer, Mo. E6 69
Thayer, co., Nebr. D8 71
Thayetmyo, Bur. *E10 20
The Dalles, Oreg. B5 80
The Entrance, Austl. F8 26
The Father, mtn., N. Gui. k13 25
The Hague ('s Gravenhage), Neth. A6 5
The Pas, Man., Can. C1, g7 40
The Plains, Ohio C3 78
Theresa, N.Y. A5, f9 75
Thermalito, Calif. *C3 50
Thermopolis, Wyo. C4 89
Thesprotía, prov., Grc. *C3 14
Thessalon, Ont., Can. p19 41
Thessaloníki (Salonika), Grc. B4 14
Thessaloníki (Salonika), prov., Grc. *B4 14
Thessaly, reg., Grc. C4 14
Thetford Mines, Que., Can. C6 42
The Village, Okla. *B4 79
Thibodaux, La. E5, k10 63
Thief River Falls, Minn. B2 67
Thiensville, Wis. E6, m12 88
Thiers, Fr. E5 5
Thiès, Sen. F1 22
Thimbu, Bhu C8 20
Thionville, Fr. C7 5
Thisted, co., Den. *I3 11
Thivai (Thebes), Grc. C4 14
Thomas, Okla. B3 79
Thomas, W. Va. B5 87
Thomas, co., Ga. F3 55
Thomas, co., Kans. C2 61
Thomas, co., Nebr. C5 71
Thomason, Ga. D2 55
Thomaston, Ala. C2 46
Thomaston, Conn. C4 52
Thomaston, Maine D3 64
Thomaston, N.Y. *E7 75
Thomasville, Ala. D2 46
Thomasville, Ga. F3 55
Thomasville, N.C. B2 76
Thompson, Conn. B9 52
Thompson Falls, Mont. C1 70
Thompsonville, Conn. A6 52
Thomson, Ga. C4 55
Thon Buri, Thai. *C2 19
Thorburn, N.S., Can. D7 43
Thornbury, Ont., Can. C4 41
Thorndale, Tex. D4 84
Thornton, Colo. *B6 51
Thornton, Idaho F7 57
Thornton, Ill. *B6 58
Thornton, Miss. B3 68
Thorntown, Ind. D4 59
Thornwood, N.Y. *D7 75
Thorofare, N.J. D2 74
Thorold, Ont., Can. D5 41
Thorp, Wis. D3 88
Thorpe, W. Va. D3 87
Thorsby, Ala. C3 46
Thorshavn, Faer. Is. C6 3
Thouars, Fr. D3 5
Thousand Oaks, Calif. *E4 50
Three Forks, Mont. E5 70
Three Hills, Alta., Can. D4 38
Three Oaks, Mich. G4 66
Three Rivers, Mass. B3 65
Three Rivers, Mich. G5 66
Three Rivers, Miss. E5 68
Three Rivers, Tex. E3 84
Throckmorton, Tex. C3 84
Throckmorton, co., Tex. C3 84
Throop, Pa. m18 81
Thule, Grnld. *B14 33
Thun, Switz. E3 6
Thunder Bay, Ont., Can. o17 41
Thunder Bay, dist., Ont., Can. o17 41
Thunderbolt, Ga. D5 55
Thurgau, canton, Switz. *E4 6
Thüringia, former state, Ger. Dem. Rep. *C5 6
Thuringia, reg., Ger. Dem. Rep. C5 6
Thurles, Ire. D3 4
Thurmont, Md. A3 53
Thurrock, Eng. *E7 4
Thursday Island, Austl. B7 25
Thurso, Que., Can. D2 42
Thurso, Scot. A5 4
Thurston, co., Nebr. B9 71
Thurston, co., Wash. C3 86
Tibet, prov., China B8 20
Tiburon, Calif. *C2 50
Tice, Fla. F5 54
Ticino, canton, Switz. *E4 6
Tickfaw, La. D5 63
Ticonderoga, N.Y. B7 75
Ticul, Mex. C7 34
Tidioute, Pa. C3 81
Tiehling, China C9 17
Tienen, Bel. B6 5
Tienshui, China E6 17
Tientsin (Tienching), China D8 17
Tie Plant, Miss. B4 68
Tierra Blanca, Mex. D5, n15 34
Tierra del Fuego, isl., Chile h12 28
Tietê, Braz. C3, m8 30
Tiff City, Mo. E3 69
Tiffin, Ohio A2 78
Tiflis, see Tbilisi, Sov. Un.
Tift, co., Ga. E3 55
Tifton, Ga. E3 55
Tiftona, Tenn. *D8 83
Tigard, Oreg. h12 80
Tigil, Sov. Un. D18 13
Tignish, P.E.I., Can. C6 43
Tigre, Arg. g7 28
Tigris, riv., Asia F7 13
Tijuana, Mex. A1 34
Tikhvin, Sov. Un. B9 12
Tiksi, Sov. Un. B15 13
Tilburg, Neth. B6 5
Tilbury, Ont., Can. E2 41
Tilden, Ill. E4 58
Tilden, Nebr. B8 71
Tilghman, Md. C5 53
Tiline, Ky. e9 62
Tillamook, Oreg. B3 80
Tillamook, co., Oreg. B3 80
Tillicum, Wash. *B2 86
Tillman, co., Okla. C2 79
Tillsonburg, Ont., Can. E4 41
Tilton, Ill. C6 58
Tilton, N.H. E4 73
Tiltonsville, Ohio B5 78
Timaru, N.Z. P13 26
Timbaúba, Braz. *D7 27
Timberlake, Va. *C3 85
Times Beach, Mo. *C7 69
Timiskaming, dist., Ont., Can. o19 41
Timişoara, Rom. C5 10
Timmins, Ont., Can. o19 41
Timmonsville, S.C. C8 82
Timoneng, Guam *F6 2
Timor, isl., Indon. G6 19
Timor Portuguese, see Portuguese Timor, dep., Asia
Timpson, Tex. D5 84
Tineo, Sp. A2 8
Tinley Park, Ill. k9 58
Tinsley, Miss. C3 68
Tioga, N. Dak. B2 77
Tioga, co., N.Y. C4 75
Tioga, co., Pa. C7 81
Tippah, co., Miss. A5 68
Tipp City, Ohio C1 78
Tippecanoe, co., Ind. D4 59
Tipperary, Ire. D2 4
Tipperary, co., Ire. *D3 4
Tipton, Calif. D4 50
Tipton, Ind. D5 59
Tipton, Iowa C6 60
Tipton, Mo. C5 69
Tipton, Okla. C2 79
Tipton, co., Ind. D5 59
Tipton, co., Tenn. B2 83
Tiptonville, Tenn. A2 83
Tiranë (Tirana), Alb. B2 14
Tiranë (Tirana), pref., Alb. *B2 14
Tirano, It. A3 9
Tiraspol, Sov. Un. H7 12
Tire, Tur. C6 14
Tîrgoviste, Rom. C7 10
Tîrgu-Jiu, Rom. C6 10
Tîrgul-Neamt, Rom. B8 10
Tîrgul-Ocna, Rom. B8 10
Tîrgu-Mureş, Rom. B7 10
Tîrgu-Sacuesc, Rom. B8 10
Tîrnaveni, Rom. B7 10
Tírnavos, Grc. *C4 14
Tirol, state, Aus. E5 6
Tirol, reg., Aus. E5 6
Tiruchchirâppalli, India F6 20
Tirunelveli, India G6 20
Tiruppur, India *F6 20
Tisdale, Sask., Can. E3 39
Tishomingo, Okla. C5 79
Tishomingo, co., Miss. A5 68
Tiskilwa, Ill. B4 58
Tisza, riv., Hung., Yugo. B5 10
Tiszafüred, Hung. B5 10
Tiszakécske, Hung. B5 10
Titicaca, lake, Bol., Peru C2 29
Titograd, Yugo. D4 10
Titovo Užice, Yugo. D4 10
Titov Veles, Yugo. E5 10
Titus, co., Tex. C5 84
Titusville, Fla. D6 54
Titusville, N.J. C3 74
Titusville, Pa. C2 81
Tiverton, Eng. E5 4
Tiverton, R.I. C12 52
Tivoli, It. D4, h9 9
Tivoli, Tex. E4 84
Tixtla, Mex. o14 34
Tizapán, Mex. h9 34
Tizimín, Mex. C7 34
Tizi-Ouzou, Alg. A5 22
Tiznit, Mor. C3 22
Tjiandjur, Indon. *G3 19
Tjimahi, Indon. *G3 19
Tlalpan, Mex. h9 34
Tlaxcala, state, Mex. D5 34
Tlaxiaco, Mex. D5 34
Tlemcen, Alg. B4 22
Toast, N.C. A2 76
Toba, Jap. o15 18
Tobarra, Sp. C5 8
Tobol, riv., Sov. Un. D9 13
Tobolsk, Sov. Un. D9 13
Tobyhanna, Pa. D11 81
Tocantins, riv., Braz. D6 27
Toccoa, Ga. B3 55
Toccoa Falls, Ga. B3 55
Tochigi, Jap. H9, m18 18
Tochigi, pref., Jap. *H9 18
Tocopilla, Chile D1 29
Todd, co., Ky. D2 62
Todd, co., Minn. D4 67
Todd, co., S. Dak. G5 77
Togo, country, Afr. G5 22
Tokat, Tur. B11 14
Tokenon, Kor. G2 18
Toki, Jap. *n16 18
Tokorozawa, Jap. n18 18
Tokushima, Jap. I7 18
Tokushima, pref., Jap. *I7 18
Tokuyama, Jap. I5 18
Tôkyô, Jap. I9, n18 18
Tokyo, pref., Jap. *I9 18
Tolbukhin (Dobrich), Bul. D8 10
Toledo, Ill. D5 58
Toledo, Iowa B5 60
Toledo, Ohio A2, e6 78
Toledo, Oreg. C3 80
Toledo, Sp. C3 8
Toledo, prov., sp. *C3 8
Toler, Ky. C7 62
Tolima, dept., Col. C2 32
Tolland, co., Conn. B7 52
Tolleson, Ariz. D1 48
Tolmin, Yugo. B1 10
Tolna, Hung. B4 10
Tolna, co., Hung. *B4 10
Tolono, Ill. D5 58
Tolosa, Sp. A4 8
Toluca, Ill. B4 58
Toluca *de Lerdo*, Mex. D5, n14 34
Tolyatti, Sov. Un. *D7 13
Tomah, Wis. E3 88
Tomahawk, Wis. C4 88
Tomakomai, Jap. E10 18
Tomakovka, Sov. Un. H10 12
Tomar, Port. C1 8
Tomari, Sov. Un. E17 13
Tomaszow Lubelski, Pol. C7 7
Tomaszow Mazowiecki, Pol. C6 7
Tomball, Tex. D5 84
Tombouctou (Timbuktu), Mali E4 22
Tombstone, Ariz. D4 48
Tomé, Chile B2 28
Tomelloso, Sp. C4 8
Tom Green, co., Tex. D2 84
Tomkins Cove, N.Y. D7, m14 75
Tommot, Sov. Un. D15 13
Tompkins, co., N.Y. C4 75
Tompkinsville, Ky. D4 62
Tom Price, Austl. D2 25
Tomsk, Sov. Un. D11 13
Toms River, N.J. D4 74
Tonalá, Mex. D6 34
Tonasket, Wash. A6 86
Tonawanda, N.Y. B2 75
Tondano, Indon. E6 19
Tønder, Den. A4 6
Tønder, co., Den. *J3 11
Tonga, Br. dep., Oceania H9 2
Tonganoxie, Kans. C8, k15 61
Tonk, India C6 20
Tonka Bay, Minn. *F5 67
Tonkawa, Okla. A4 79
Tonkin, reg., Viet. A3 19
Tonopah, Nev. B3 72
Tönsberg, Nor. H4, p28 11
Tooele, Utah A5, D2 72
Tooele, co., Utah A5 72
Toole, co., Mont. B5 70
Toombs, co., Ga. D4 55
Toowoomba, Austl. E9 25
Topanga, Calif. *F4 50
Topeka, Kans. C8, k13 61
Topol'čany, Czech. D5 7
Topolovgrad, Bul. D8 10
Toppenish, Wash. C5 86
Topsfield, Mass. A6 65
Topsham, Maine E3, g8 64
Topton, Pa. F10 81
Torbay, Newf., Can. E5 44
Torez, Sov. Un. q21 12
Torhout, Bel. B5 5
Toride, Jap. n19 18
Torino, see Turin, It.
Toro, Sp. B3 8
Törökszentmiklós, Hung. B5 10
Toronto, Ont., Can. D5, m15 41
Toronto, Ohio B5 78
Toropets, Sov. Un. C8 12
Torquay (Torbay), Eng. E5 4
Torrance, Calif. n12 50
Torrance, co., N. Mex. B5 48
Torre Annunziata, It. D5 9
Torre del Greco, It. D5 9
Torredonjimeno, Sp. D4 8
Torrelavega, Sp. A3 8
Torremaggiore, It. D5 9
Torrens, lake, Austl. F6 25
Torrente, Sp. C5 8
Torreón, Mex. B4 34
Torre Pacheco, Sp. D5 8
Torres Novas, Port. C1 8
Torrevieja, Sp. D5 8
Torrington, Conn. B4 52
Torrington, Wyo. D8 89
Torrox, Sp. D4 8
Tortilla Flat, Ariz. C3 48
Tortona, It. B2 9
Tortosa, Sp. B6 8
Toruń, Pol. B5 7
Torzhok, Sov. Un. C10 12
Toscana, pol. dist., It. *C3 9
Tosno, Sov. Un. C10 12
Tosya, Tur. B10 14
Totana, Sp. D5 8
Totkomlós, Hung. B5 10
Totonicapán, Guat. D6 34
Totowa, N.J. B4 74
Tottori, Jap. I7 18
Tottori, pref., Jap. *I7 18
Totz, Ky. D6 62
Toubkal, Jbel, mtn., Mor. B3 22
Tougaloo, Miss. C3 68
Touggourt, Alg. B6 22
Toul, Fr. C3 68
Toulon, Fr. F6 5
Toulon, Ill. B4 58
Toulouse, Fr. F4 5
Toungoo, Bur. E10 20
Touraine, former prov., Fr. D4 5
Tourcoing, Fr. B5 5
Tourlaville, Fr. C3 5
Tours, Fr. D4 5
Towaco, N.J. B4 74
Towanda, Kans. E7, k12 61
Towanda, Pa. C9 81
Tower City, Pa. E8 81
Town and Country, Mo. *C7 69
Towner, N. Dak. B5 77
Towner, co., N. Dak. B6 77
Townley, Ala. B2 46
Town of Pines, Ind. *A4 59
Town of Tonawanda, N.Y. *B2 75
Towns, co., Ga. B3 55
Townsend, Mass. A4 65
Townsend, Mont. D5 70
Townsville, Austl. C8 25
Towson, Md. B4, g11 53
Toyama, Jap. H8 18
Toyama, pref., Jap. *H8 18
Toyohashi, Jap. I8, o16 18
Toyokawa, Jap. *I8 18
Toyonaka, Jap. o14 18
Toyota, Jap. n16 18
Tozeur, Tun. B6 22
Trabzon, Tur. B12 14
Tracadie, N.B., Can. B5 43
Tracy, Calif. D3, h10 50
Tracy, Minn. F3 67
Tracy City, Tenn. D7 83
Traer, Iowa B5 60
Trafford, Pa. k14 81
Traiguén, Chile B2 28
Trail, B.C., Can. E9, o19 37
Trail Creek, Ind. A4 59
Trailer Estates, Fla. *E4 54
Traill, co., N. Dak. C8 77
Trainer, Pa. *G11 81
Tralee, Ire. D2 4
Tranås, Swe. H6 11
Trani, It. D6 9
Transilvania, prov., Rom. *B6 10
Transvaal, prov., S. Afr. E5 24
Transylvania, co., N.C. f10 76
Transylvania, reg., Rom. B6 10
Trapani, It. E4 9
Trappe, Pa. *F11 81

Place	Ref	Pg
Traralgon, Austl.	I6	26
Trás-os-Montes, reg., Port.	B2	8
Trás-os-Montes e Alto Douro, prov., Port.	*B2	8
Traunstein, Ger., Fed. Rep. of	E6	6
Travelers Rest, S.C.	B3	82
Traverse, co., Minn.	E2	67
Traverse City, Mich.	D5	66
Travis, co., Tex.	D4	84
Travnik, Yugo.	C3	10
Treasure, co., Mont.	D9	70
Treasure Island, Fla.	*E4	54
Trebíč, Czech.	D3	7
Trebinje, Yugo.	D4	10
Trebišov, Czech.	D6	7
Trego, co., Kans.	D4	61
Treinta y Tres, Ur.	E2	30
Treinta y Tres, dept., Ur.	*E2	30
Trélazé, Fr.	D3	5
Trelew, Arg.	C3	28
Trelleborg, Swe.	J5	11
Tremont, Ill.	C4	58
Tremont, Pa.	E9	81
Tremonton, Utah	A5	72
Trempealeau, co., Wis.	D2	88
Trenčín, Czech.	D5	7
Trenggauu, state, Mala.	*D2	19
Trenque Lauquén, Arg.	B4	28
Trentino-Alto-Adige, pol. dist., It.	*A3	9
Trento, It.	A3	9
Trenton, N.S., Can.	D7	43
Trenton, Ont., Can.	C7	41
Trenton, Fla.	C4	54
Trenton, Ga.	B1	55
Trenton, Ill.	E4	58
Trenton, Mich.	F7, p15	66
Trenton, Mo.	A4	69
Trenton, Nebr.	D4	71
Trenton, N.J.	C3	74
Trenton, Ohio	C1	78
Trenton, Tenn.	B3	83
Trentwood, Wash.	*B8	86
Tres Arroyos, Arg.	B4	28
Tresckow, Pa.	E10	81
Três Corações, Braz.	C3	30
Três Lagoas, Braz.	C2	30
Treutlen, co., Ga.	D4	55
Treviglio, It.	B2	9
Treviso, It.	B4	9
Trevorton, Pa.	E8	81
Trevose, Pa.	*F12	81
Trevose Heights, Pa.	*F12	81
Treynor, Iowa	C2	60
Trezevant, Tenn.	A3	83
Triangle, Va.	B5	85
Tribbett, Miss.	*B3	68
Tribune, Kans.	D2	61
Trichinopoly, see Tiruchchiràppalli, India		
Trichūr, India	F6	20
Trier, Ger., Fed. Rep. of	D3	6
Trieste, It.	B4	9
Trigg, co., Ky.	D2	62
Triglav, mtn., Yugo.	B1	10
Trigueros, Sp.	D2	8
Trikkala, Grc.	C3	14
Trikkala, prov., Grc.	*C3	14
Tri Lakes, Ind.	*B7	59
Trimble, co., Ky.	B4	62
Trimont, Minn.	G4	67
Trincomalee, Sri Lanka	G7	20
Tring-Jonction, Que., Can.	C6	42
Trinidad, Bol.	B3	29
Trinidad, Colo.	D6	51
Trinidad, Cuba	D4	35
Trinidad, Tex.	C4	84
Trinidad, Ur.	E1	30
Trinidad & Tobago, country, N.A.	A5	32
Trinité, Mart.	I14	35
Trinity, Tex.	D5	84
Trinity, co., Calif.	B2	50
Trinity, co., Tex.	D5	84
Trinity, mts., Calif.	B2	50
Trino, It.	B2	9
Trion, Ga.	B1	55
Tripoli, Iowa	B5	60
Tripolis, Grc.	D4	14
Tripoli (Tarābulus), Leb.	f5	15
Tripoli (Tarābulus), Libya	B7	22
Tripp, S. Dak.	G8	77
Tripp, co., S. Dak.	G6	77
Tripura, state, India	D9	20
Tristate Village, Ill.	*B5	58
Triumph, La.	E6	63
Trivandrum, India	G6	20
Trnava, Czech.	D4	7
Trois-Pistoles, Que., Can.	A8	42
Trois-Rivières, Que., Can.	C5	42
Troitsk, Sov. Un.	D9	13
Trollhättan, Swe.	H5	11
Troms, co., Nor.	C8	11
Tromsö, Nor.	*C8	11
Trona, Calif.	E5	50
Trondheim, Nor.	F4	11
Troodos, mtn., Cyp.	E9	14
Tropea, It.	E5	9
Trotwood, Ohio	C1	78
Troup, Tex.	C5	84
Troup, co., Ga.	C1	55
Trousdale, co., Tenn.	A5	83
Trouville, Fr.	C3	5
Trowbridge, Eng.	E5	4
Troy, Ala.	D4	46
Troy, Ill.	E4	58
Troy, Kans.	C8	61
Troy, Mich.	o15	66
Troy, Mo.	C7	69
Troy, N.Y.	C7	75
Troy, N.C.	B3	76
Troy, Ohio	B1	78
Troy, Pa.	C8	81
Troyes, Fr.	C6	5
Trubchevsk, Sov. Un.	E9	12
Trucial States, see United Arab Emirates, country, Asia		
Trucksville, Pa.	*D10	81
Trujillo, Peru	C2	31
Trujillo, Sp.	C3	8
Trujillo, Ven.	B3	32
Trujillo, state, Ven.	B3	32
Truman, Minn.	G4	67
Trumann, Ark.	B5	49
Trumansburg, N.Y.	C4	75
Trumbull, Conn.	E4	52
Trumbull, co., Ohio	A5	78
Truro, N.S., Can.	D6	43
Truro, Eng.	E4	4
Trussville, Ala.	B3, f7	46
Truth or Consequences, N. Mex.	C5	48
Trutnov, Czech.	C3	7
Tryon, N.C.	f10	76
Trysil, Nor.	G5	11
Tsangwu, see Wuchou, China		
Tselinograd, Sov. Un.	D10	13
Tsinan (Chinan), China	D8	17
Tsinghai (Chinghai), prov., China	D8	17
Tsingtao (Chingtao), China	D9	17
Tsingyuan, see Paoting, China		
Tskhinvali, Sov. Un.	A14	14
Tsu, Jap.	I8, o15	18
Tsuchiura, Jap.	H10, m19	18
Tsuni, China	F6	17
Tsun Wan, Hong Kong	*G7	17
Tsuruga, Jap.	I8, n15	18
Tsuruoka, Jap.	G9	18
Tsushima, Jap.	n15	18
Tsuyama, Jap.	I7	18
Tubarão, Braz.	D3	30
Tübingen, Ger., Fed. Rep. of	D4	6
Tubruq, (Tobruk), Libya	B2	23
Tuchola, Pol.	B4	7
Tuckahoe, N.Y.	h13	75
Tucker, Ga.	h8	55
Tucker, co., W. Va.	B5	87
Tuckerman, Ark.	B4	49
Tuckerton, N.J.	D4	74
Tucson, Ariz.	C3	48
Tucumán, Arg.	E2	29
Tucumán, prov., Arg.	E2	29
Tucumcari, N. Mex.	B7	48
Tudela, Sp.	A5	8
Tuguegarao, Phil.	B6	19
Tuktoyaktuk, N.W. Ter., Can.	C7	36
Tukwila, Wash.	f11	86
Tula, Sov. Un.	D11	12
Tulancingo, Mex.	C5, m14	34
Tulare, Calif.	D4	50
Tulare, co., Calif.	D4	50
Tularosa, N. Mex.	C5	48
Tulcán, Ec.	A2	31
Tulcea, Rom.	C9	10
Tuléar, Mad.	E8	24
Tulelake, Calif.	B3	50
Tulia, Tex.	B2	84
Tūlkarm, Jordan	B3	15
Tullahoma, Tenn.	B5	83
Tullamore, Ire.	D3	4
Tulle, Fr.	E4	5
Tullytown, Pa.	*F12	81
Tulsa, Okla.	A6	79
Tulsa, co., Okla.	B6	79
Tuluá, Col.	C2	32
Tulufan (Turfan), China	C2	17
Tulun, Sov. Un.	D13	13
Tulungagung, Indon.	G4	19
Tumaco, Col.	C2	32
Tumbarumba, Austl.	G7	26
Tumbes, Peru	B1	31
Tumen, China	C10	17
Tumkūr, India	F6	20
Tumuti, Austl.	*G8	26
Tumwater, Wash.	B3	86
Tunbridge Wells, Eng.	E7	4
Tunchi, China	*F8	17
Tunghsien, China	*D8	17
Tunghua, China	F2	18
Tungliao, China	C9	17
Tungurahua, prov., Ec.	B2	31
Tunhua, China	C10	17
Tunica, Miss.	A3	68
Tunica, co., Miss.	A3	68
Tunis, Tun.	A7	22
Tunisia, country, Afr.	A6	22
Tunja, Col.	B3	32
Tunkhannock, Pa.	C10	81
Tuntutuliak, Alsk.	C7	47
Tuolumne, Calif.	D3	50
Tuolumne, co., Calif.	C4	50
Tupelo, Miss.	A5	68
Tupper Lake, N.Y.	A6, f10	75
Tupungato, mtn., Arg.	A3	28
Tura, Sov. Un.	C13	13
Turbaco, Col.	A2	32
Turčiansky Svaty Martin, Czech.	D5	7
Turda, Rom.	B6	10
Turek, Pol.	B5	7
Turfan, see Tulufan, China		
Turgay, Sov. Un.	E9	13
Turgovishte, Bul.	D8	10
Turgutlu, Tur.	C6	14
Turin (Torino), It.	B1	9
Turka, Sov. Un.	G4	12
Turkestan, Sov. Un.	E9	13
Türkeve, Hung.	B5	10
Turkey, Tex.	B2	84
Turkey, country, Asia, Eur.	C9	14
Turkmen, S.S.R., rep., Sov. Un.	*F8	16
Turks & Caicos Islands, Br. dep., N.A.	D8	35
Turku (Abo), Fin.	G10	11
Turku-Pori, prov., Fin.	*G10	11
Turley, Okla.	A6	79
Turlock, Calif.	D3	50
Turner, Kans.	B8	61
Turner, co., Ga.	E3	55
Turner, co., S. Dak.	G8	77
Turners Falls, Mass.	A2	65
Turner Valley, Alta., Can.	D3	38
Turnhout, Bel.	B6	5
Turnov, Czech.	C3	7
Turnovo, Bul.	D7	10
Turnu Măgurele, Rom.	D7	10
Turnu Severin, Rom.	C6	10
Turquino, peak, Cuba	D5	35
Turtkul, Sov. Un.	E9	13
Turtle Creek, Pa.	k14	81
Tuscaloosa, Ala.	B2	46
Tuscaloosa, co., Ala.	B2	46
Tuscany, reg., It.	C3	9
Tuscarawas, co., Ohio	B4	78
Tuscola, Ill.	D5	58
Tuscola, co., Mich.	E7	66
Tusculum College, Tenn.	*C5	83
Tuscumbia, Ala.	A2	46
Tuskegee, Ala.	C4	46
Tuskegee Institute, Ala.	C4	46
Tustin, Calif.	*F5	50
Tuticorin, India	G6	20
Tutrakan, Bul.	C8	10
Tuttlingen, Ger., Fed. Rep. of	E4	6
Tutwiler, Miss.	A3	68
Tuvalu, country, Oceania	G8	2
Tuxedo, Md.	C4	53
Tuxedo Park, N.Y.	D6, m14	75
Tuxpan, Mex.	C3, m11	34
Tuxpan, Mex.	n12	34
Tuxpan de Rodriguez Cano, Mex.	C5, m15	34
Tuxtla Gutiérrez, Mex.	D6	34
Tuy, Sp.	A1	8
Tuyün, China	F6	17
Tuzla, Yugo.	C4	10
Tweed, Ont., Can.	C7	41
Twenty-Nine Palms, Calif.	E5	50
Twig, Minn.	D6	67
Twiggs, co., Ga.	D3	55
Twillingate, Newf., Can.	D4	44
Twin City, Ga.	D4	55
Twin Falls, Idaho	G4	57
Twin Falls, co., Idaho	*G4	57
Twin Lakes, Calif.	*D2	50
Twin Lakes, Ohio	*A4	78
Twin Lakes, Wis.	F5, n11	88
Twin Oaks, Pa.	*G11	81
Twin Orchards, N.Y.	*C5	75
Twin Rocks, Pa.	F4	81
Twinsburg, Ohio	A4	78
Two Harbors, Minn.	C7	67
Two Rivers, Wis.	D6, h10	88
Tyler, Minn.	F2	67
Tyler, Tex.	C5	84
Tyler, co., Tex.	D5	84
Tyler, co., W. Va.	B4	87
Tyler Park, Va.	*B5	85
Tylertown, Miss.	D3	68
Tyndall, S. Dak.	H8	77
Tynemouth, Eng.	C6	4
Tyre, see Sūr, Leb.		
Tyrrell, co., N.C.	B6	76
Tyrone, Pa.	E5	81
Tyrone, co., N. Ire.	*C3	4
Tyumen, Sov. Un.	D9	13
Tzukung, China	F5	17

U

Place	Ref	Pg
Ubá, Braz.	C4, g6	30
Ube, Jap.	J5	18
Ubeda, Sp.	C4	8
Uberaba, Braz.	B3	30
Uberlândia, Braz.	B3	30
Ubon Ratchathani, Thai.	B2	19
Uccle, Bel.	B6	5
Udaipur, India	D5	20
Uddevalla, Swe.	H4	11
Udine, It.	A4	9
Udon Thani, Thai.	B2	19
Ueda, Jap.	H9, m17	18
Uelen, Sov. Un.	C21	13
Uelkal, Sov. Un.	C21	13
Uelzen, Ger., Fed. Rep. of	B5	6
Ueno, Jap.	o15	18
Ufa, Sov. Un.	D8	13
Uganda, country, Afr.	H4	23
Uglegorsk (Esutoru), Sov. Un.	B11	18
Uglich, Sov. Un.	C12	12
Uherské Hradiště, Czech.	*D4	7
Uhrichsville, Ohio	B4	78
Uijongbu, Kor.	H3	18
Uinta, co., Wyo.	E2	89
Uintah, co., Utah	B7	72
Uitenhage, S. Afr.	G5	24
Uji, Jap.	*o14	18
Ujjain, India	D6	20
Ujung Pandang, Indon.	G5	19
Ukhta, Sov. Un.	C8	13
Ukiah, Calif.	C2	50
Ukraine (S.S.R.), rep., Sov. Un.	*E6	16
Ulan Bator (Urga), Mong.	B6	17
Ulan-Ude, Sov. Un.	D13	13
Ulhasnagar, India	*E5	20
Ulla, Sov. Un.	D7	12
Ulm, Ger., Fed. Rep. of	D4	6
Ulman, Mo.	C5	69
Ulsan, Kor.	I4	18
Ulster, co., N.Y.	D6	75

V

Vénissieux, Fr. ... E6 5
Venlo, Neth. ... B7 5
Ventimiglia, It. ... C1 9
Ventnor City, N.J. ... E4 74
Ventspils, Sov. Un. ... C3 12
Ventura, Calif. ... E4 50
Ventura, co., Calif. ... E4 50
Ventura North (Chrisman), Calif. ... *E4 50
Veracruz Llave, Mex. ... D5, n15 34
Veracruz, state, Mex. ... D5, n15 34
Veradale, Wash. ... *B8 86
Verâval, India ... D5 20
Vercelli, It. ... B2 9
Verchères, Que., Can. ... D4 42
Verchères, Que., Can. ... D9 42
Verden, Ger., Fed. Rep. of ... B4 6
Verdun, Que., Can. ... g19 42
Verdun -Sur-Meuse, Fr. ... C6 5
Verdunville, W.Va. ... D2 87
Vereeniging, S.Afr. ... F5 24
Verga, N.J. ... *D2 74
Vergennes, Vt. ... C1 73
Verkhneye, Sov. Un. ... G12, q21 12
Verkhoyansk, Sov. Un. ... C16 13
Vermilion, Alta., Can. ... C5 38
Vermilion, Ohio ... A3 78
Vermilion, co., Ill. ... C6 58
Vermilion, par.,La. ... E3 63
Vermilion Heights, Ill. ... *C6 58
Vermillion, S. Dak. ... H9 77
Vermillion, co., Ind. ... E3 59
Vermilion Heights, Ill. ... *C6 58
Vermont, state, U.S. ... 73
Vernal, Utah ... A7 72
Vernon, Ala. ... B1 46
Vernon, B.C., Can. ... D8, n19 37
Vernon, Fr. ... C4 5
Vernon, N.Y. ... *B5 75
Vernon, Tex. ... B3 84
Vernon, co., Mo. ... D3 69
Vernon, co., Wis. ... E3 88
Vernon, par., La. ... C2 63
Vernonia, Oreg. ... B3 80
Vernon Valley, N.Y. ... n15 75
Vernona, N.J. ... B4 74
Vernona, Pa. ... k14 81
Vernona, Wis. ... E4 88
Vero Beach, Fla. ... E6 54
Véroia, Grc. ... B4 14
Verona, It. ... B3 9
Verona Park, Mich. ... *F5 66
Verplanck, N.Y. ... *D7 75
Versailles, Fr. ... C4, g9 5
Versailles, Ind. ... F7 59
Versailles, Ky. ... B5 62
Versailles, Mo. ... C5 69
Versailles, Ohio ... B1 78
Versailles, Pa. ... *F2 81
Verviers, Bel. ... B6 5
Veseloye, Sov. Un. ... H10 12
Vesoul, Fr. ... D7 5
Vest-Agder, co., Nor. ... *H2 11
Vestal, N.Y. ... C4 75
Vestavia Hills, Ala. ... g7 46
Vestfold, co., Nor. ... *H4 11
Vestry, Miss. ... E5 68
Vesuvius, vol., It. ... D5 9
Veszprém, Hung. ... B3 10
Veszprem, co., Hung. ... *B3 10
Veszto, Hung. ... B5 10
Vevay, Ind. ... G7 59
Vevey, Switz. ... E3 6
Vezirköprü, Tur. ... B10 14

Viadana, It. ... B3 9
Vian, Okla. ... B7 79
Viangchan, Laos ... B2 19
Viareggio, It. ... C3 9
Viborg, co., Den. ... *I3 11
Vibo Valentia, It. ... E6 9
Vicco, Ky. ... C6 62
Vicente López, Arg. ... *g7 28
Vicenza, It. ... B3 9
Vichada, comisaría, Col. ... C3 32
Vichy, Fr. ... D5 5
Vicksburg, Mich. ... F5 66
Vicksburg,Miss. ... C3 68
Victor, N.Y. ... C3 75
Victor Harbour, Austl. ... G2 26
Victoria, Arg. ... A4 28
Victoria, B.C., Can. ... E6, f12 37
Victoria, Newf., Can. ... E5 44
Victoria, Chile ... B2 28
Victoria, Hong Kong ... G7 17
Victoria, Kans. ... D4 61
Victoria, Tex. ... E4 84
Victoria, Va. ... D4 85
Victoria, co., N.B., Can. ... B2 43
Victoria, co., N.S., Can. ... C9 43
Victoria, co., Ont., Can. ... C6 43
Victoria, co., Tex. ... E4 84
Victoria, state, Austl. ... G7 25
Victoria, isl., Can. ... B11 36
Victoria, lake, Afr. ... I4 23
Victoria, mtn., Pap. ... k12 25
Victoria de las Tunas, Cuba ... D5 35
Victoria Harbour, Ont., Can. ... C5 41
Victoriaville, Que., Can. ... C6 42
Victor Mills, S.C. ... *B3 82
Victorville, Calif. ... E5 50
Victory Gardens, N.J. ... *B3 74
Victory Heights, N.Y. ... *C4 75
Vidalia, Ga. ... D4 55
Vidalia, La. ... C4 63
Vidin, Bul. ... D6 10
Vidor, Tex. ... D6 84
Vienna (Wien), Aus. ... D8 6
Vienna, Ga. ... D3 55
Vienna, Ill. ... F5 58
Vienna, Va. ... B5, g12 85
Vienna, W. Va. ... B3 87
Vienne, Fr. ... E6 5
Vienne, dept., Fr. ... *D4 5
Vierzon, Fr. ... D5 5
Vieste, It. ... D6 9
Vietnam, country, Asia ... B3 19
View Park, Calif. ... *E4 50
Vigan, Phil. ... B6 19
Vigevano, It. ... B2 9
Vigo, Sp. ... A1 8
Vigo, co., Ind. ... F3 59
Vijayawâda, India ... E7 20
Vila Nova de Gaia, Port. ... B1 8
Vilas, co., Wis. ... B4 88
Vila Velha, Braz. ... C4 30
Vileyka, Sov. Un. ... D6 12
Viljandi, Sov. Un. ... B5 12
Vilkovo, Sov. Un. ... I7 12
Villacarrillo, Sp. ... C4 8
Villa Dolores, Arg. ... A3 28
Villafranca, It. ... B3 9
Villafranca de los Barros, Sp. ... C2 8
Villafranca del Panadés, Sp. ... B6 8
Villafranca di Verona, It. ... B3 9
Villagarcía, de Arosa, Sp. ... A1 8
Village-Richelieu, Que., Can. ... *D4 42

Villa Grove, Ill. ... D5 58
Villaguay, Arg. ... A5 28
Villa Heights, Md. ... *C4 53
Villahermosa, Mex. ... D6 34
Villa María, Arg. ... A4 28
Villanova, Pa. ... *G11 81
Villanueva de Córdoba, Sp. ... C3 8
Villanueva del Arzobispo, Sp. ... C4 8
Villanueva de La Serena, Sp. ... C3 8
Villanueva y Geltrú, Sp. ... B6 8
Villa Obregón, Mex. ... h9 34
Villa Park, Ill. ... k8 58
Villa Rica, Ga. ... C2 55
Villarreal, Sp. ... C5 8
Villarrica, Par. ... E4 29
Villarrobledo, Sp. ... C4 8
Villas, N.J. ... E3 74
Villavicencio, Col. ... C3 32
Villefranche-sur-Saône, Fr. ... E6 5
Villejuif, Fr. ... g10 5
Ville Marie, Que., Can. ... p20 41
Villemomble, Fr. ... g10 5
Villeneuve-le-Roi, Fr. ... h10 5
Villeneuve-St. Georges, Fr. ... h10 5
Villeneuve-sur-Lot, Fr. ... E4 5
Ville Platte, La. ... D3 63
Ville St. Georges, Que., Can. ... C7 42
Villeta, Par. ... E4 29
Villeurbanne, Fr. ... E6 5
Villigen-Schwenningen, Ger.,
  Fed. Rep. of ... *D4 6
Villisca, Iowa ... D3 60
Vilnius, Sov. Un. ... D5 12
Vilvoorde, Bel. ... B6 5
Vilyuy, riv., Sov. Un. ... C15 13
Vilyuysk, Sov. Un. ... C15 13
Vimianzo, Sp. ... A1 8
Viña del Mar, Chile ... A2 28
Vinalhaven, Maine ... D4 64
Vincennes, Fr. ... g10 5
Vincennes, Ind. ... G3 59
Vincent, Ala. ... B3 46
Vincent, Ohio ... *A3 78
Vindeln, Swe. ... E8 11
Vine Grove, Ky. ... C4 62
Vine Hill (Martinez East), Calif. ... *C2 50
Vineland, N.J. ... E2 74
Vineyard Haven (Tisbury), Mass. ... D6 65
Vinh Yen, Viet. ... G6 17
Vinita, Okla. ... A6 79
Vinita Park, Mo. ... *C7 69
Vinkovci, Yugo. ... C4 10
Vinnitsa, Sov. Un. ... G7 12
Vinson Massif, mtn., Ant. ... L15 2
Vinton, Iowa ... B5 60
Vinton, La. ... D2 63
Vinton, Va. ... C3 85
Vinton, co., Ohio ... C3 78
Vintondale, Pa. ... F4 81
Virden, Man., Can. ... E1 40
Virden, Ill. ... D4 58
Virginia, Ill. ... D3 58
Virginia, Minn. ... C6 67
Virginia, state, U.S. ... 85
Virginia Beach
  (Independent City), Va. ... D7, k16 85
Virginia City, Nev. ... B2 72
Virginia Gardens, Fla. ... *G6 54
Virgin Islands, Br. dep., N.A. ... G12 35
Virgin Islands of the U.S.,
  dep., N.S. ... G12 35
Viroflay, Fr. ... g9 5
Viroqua, Wis. ... E3 88

Virovitica, Yugo. ... C3 10
Visalia, Calif. ... D4 50
Visby, Swe. ... I8 11
Vishâkhapatnam, India ... E7 20
Vista, Calif. ... F5 50
Vista Park, Calif. ... *E4 50
Vitanovak, Yugo. ... D5 10
Vitebsk, Sov. Un. ... D8 12
Viterbo, It. ... C4 9
Vitim, Sov. Un. ... D14 13
Vitória, Braz. ... C4 30
Vitoria, Sp. ... A4 8
Vitória da Conquista, Braz. ... A4 30
Vitry -sur-Seine, Fr. ... g10 5
Vittoria, It. ... F5 9
Vittorio Veneto, It. ... B4 9
Vivian, La. ... B2 63
Vizcaya, prov., Sp. ... *A4 8
Vizianagaram, India ... E7 20
Vizzini, It. ... F5 9
Vlaardingen, Neth. ... B6 5
Vladimir, Sov. Un. ... C13 12
Vladimiro Aleksandrovskoye,
  Sov. Un. ... E6 18
Vladimir Volynskiy, Sov. Un. ... F5 12
Vladivostok, Sov. Un. ... E5 18
Vlasotince, Yugo. ... D6 10
Vlissingen, Neth. ... B5 5
Vlonë, pref., Alb. ... *B2 14
Vlorë, Alb. ... B2 14
Vodnany, Czech. ... *D3 7
Voeune Sai, Camb. ... F7 22
Voghera, It. ... B2 9
Voiron, Fr. ... E6 5
Volga, riv., Sov. Un. ... E7 13
Volgograd, Sov. Un. ... G14 12
Volkhov, Sov. Un. ... B9 12
Volkovysk, Sov. Un. ... E5 12
Vologda, Sov. Un. ... B12 12
Volokolamsk, Sov. Un. ... C10 12
Volos, Grc. ... C4 14
Volsk, Sov. Un. ... *D7 13
Volta Redonda, Braz. ... C4, h5 30
Volterra, It. ... C3 9
Volusia, co., Fla. ... C5 54
Volzhskiy, Sov. Un. ... G15 12
Voorheesville, N.Y. ... *C7 75
Vorarlberg, state, Aus. ... E4 6
Vordingborg, Den. ... A1 7
Vorkuta, Sov. Un. ... C9 13
Voronezh, Sov Un. ... F12 12
Voroshilovgrad (Lugansk),
  Sov. Un. ... G12, q22 12
Vosges, dept., Fr. ... *C7 5
Votkinsk, Sov. Un. ... *D8 13
Voznesensk, Sov. Un. ... H8 12
Vranje, Yugo. ... D5 10
Vratsa, Bul. ... D6 10
Vratsa, co., Bul. ... D6 10
Vršac, Yugo. ... C5 10
Vsetín, Czech. ... D5 7
Vukovar, Yugo. ... C4 10
Vulcan, Alta., Can. ... D4 38
Vulcan, Mo. ... D7 69
Vung Tau, Viet. ... *C3 19
Vyazma, Sov. Un. ... D10 12
Vyazniki, Sov. Un. ... C14 12
Vyborg, Sov. Un. ... A7 12
Vyksa, Sov. Un. ... D14 12
Vyshniy Volochek, Sov. Un. ... C10 12
Vysoké Tatry, Czech. ... D6 7
Vytegra, Sov. Un. ... A11 12

W

Wabana (Bell Island), Newf., Can. ... E5 44
Wabash, Ind. ... C6 59
Wabash, co., Ill. ... E6 58
Wabash, co., Ind. ... C6 59
Wabasha, Minn. ... F6 67
Wabasha, co., Minn. ... F6 67
Wabasso, Fla. ... E6 54
Wabaunsee, co., Kans. ... D7 61
Wacissa, Fla. ... B3 54
Waco, Tex. ... D4 84
Waconia, Minn. ... F5 67
Waddington, B.C., Can. ... F8 36
Waddington, N.Y. ... f9 75
Wadena, Sask., Can. ... F4 39
Wadena, Minn. ... D3 67
Wadena, co., Minn. ... D4 67

Wadesboro, N.C. ... C2 76
Wadley, Ga. ... D4 55
Wad Madanî, Sud. ... F4 23
Wadsworth, Ohio ... A4 78
Waelder, Tex. ... E4 84
Wagga Wagga, Austl. ... G8 25
Wagner, S.Dak. ... G7 77
Wagoner, Okla. ... B6 79
Wagoner, co., Okla. ... B6 79
Wagon Mound, N.Mex. ... B6 48
Wagrowiec, Pol. ... B4 7
Wah Cantonment, Pak. ... *B5 20
Wahiawa, Haw. ... B3, f9 56
Wahkiakum, co., Wash. ... C2 86
Wahneta, Fla. ... *E5 54
Wahoo, Nebr. ... C9, g11 71

Wahpeton, N.Dak. ... D9 77
Waialua, Haw. ... B3, f9 56
Waianae, Haw. ... B3, g9 56
Waikabubak, Indon. ... G5 19
Wailua, Haw. ... A2 56
Wailuku, Haw. ... C5 56
Waimanalo, Haw. ... B4, g11 56
Waimea, Haw. ... B2 56
Waimea, Haw. ... f9 56
Wainwright, Alta., Can. ... C5 38
Waipahu, Haw. ... B3, g9 56
Waipio Acres, Haw. ... g9 56
Waite Park, Minn. ... E4 67
Waitsburg, Wash. ... C7 86
Wajima, Jap. ... H8 18
Wakarusa, Ind. ... A5 59

Wakaw, Sask., Can. ... E3 39
Wakayama, Jap. ... I7, o14 18
Wakayama, pref., Jap. ... *I7 18
Wake, co., N.C. ... B4 76
WaKeeney, Kans. ... C4 61
Wakefield, Mass. ... B5, f11 65
Wakefield, Mich. ... n12 66
Wakefield, Nebr. ... B9 71
Wakefield, R.I. ... D11 52
Wakefield, Va. ... D6 85
Wake Forest, N.C. ... B4 76
Wakkanai, Jap. ... D10 18
Wakulla, co., Fla. ... B2 54
Walbridge, Ohio ... e6 78
Walbrzych, Pol. ... C4 7
Walden, N.Y. ... D6 75

Waldo, Ark. D2 49
Waldo, co., Maine D3 64
Waldorf, Md. C4 53
Waldron, Ark. C1 49
Waldwick, N.J. A4 74
Wales, reg., U.K. D5 4
Walhalla, N.Dak. A8 77
Walhalla, S.C. B1 82
Walker, La. g10 63
Walker, Mich. E5 66
Walker, Minn. C4 67
Walker, co., Ala. B2 46
Walker, co., Ga. B1 55
Walker, co., Tex. D5 84
Walkersville, Md. B3 53
Walkerton, Ont., Can. C3 41
Walkerton, Ind. B5 59
Walkertown, N.C. A2 76
Walkerville, Mont. D4 70
Wall, Pa. *F2 81
Wallace, Idaho B3 57
Wallace, N.C. C4 76
Wallace, co., Kans. D2 61
Wallaceburg, Ont., Can. E2 41
Wallasey, Eng. D5 4
Walla Walla, Wash. C7 86
Walla Walla, co., Wash. C7 86
Walled Lake, Mich. o15 66
Waller, Tex. D5 84
Waller, co., Tex. E4 84
Wallingford, Conn. D5 52
Wallingford, Vt. E2 73
Wallington, Eng. m12 4
Wallington, N.J. h8 74
Wallis, Tex. E4 84
Wallkill, N.Y. D6 75
Wallowa, Oreg. B9 80
Wallowa, co., Oreg. B9 80
Wallsend, Eng. C6 4
Walnut, Calif. *F4 50
Walnut, Ill. B4 58
Walnut Cove, N.C. A2 76
Walnut Creek, Calif. h8 50
Walnut Heights, Calif. *D2 50
Walnut Park, Calif. *F4 50
Walnutport, Pa. E10 81
Walnut Ridge, Ark. A5 49
Walpole, Mass. B5, h10 65
Walsall, Eng. D6 4
Walsenburg, Colo. D6 51
Walsh, co., N.Dak. B8 77
Walterboro, S.C. F6 82
Walters, Okla. C3 79
Walthall, co., Miss. D3 68
Waltham, Mass. B5, g11 65
Walthill, Nebr. B9 71
Walton, Ind. C5 59
Walton, Ky. B5, k13 62
Walton, N.Y. C5 75
Walton, co., Fla. u15 54
Walton, co., Ga. C3 55
Walton Hills, Ohio *A4 78
Walvisbaai, S.Afr. E2 24
Walworth, Wis. F5 88
Walworth, co., S.Dak. E5 77
Walworth, co., Wis. F5 88
Wamac, Ill. E4 58
Wamego, Kans. C7 61
Wampum, Pa. E1 81
Wanamassa, N.J. C4 74
Wanaque, N.J. A4 74
Wanganui, N.Z. M15 26
Wangaratta, Austl. H6 26
Wangching, China C10 17
Wanhsien, China E6 17
Wankie, Zimb. D5 24
Wantagh, N.Y. G2 52
Wapakoneta, Ohio B1 78
Wapato, Wash. C5 86
Wapello, Iowa C6 60
Wapello, co., Iowa C5 60
Wappingers Falls, N.Y. D7 75
War, W.Va. D3 87
Warangal, India E6 20
Ward, W. Va. m13 87
Ward, co., N. Dak. B4 77
Ward, co., Tex. D1 84
Warden, Wash. C6 86
Ward Ridge, Fla. *C1 54
Wardville, La. *C3 63
Ware, Mass. B3 65
Ware, co., Ga. E4 55
Wareham, Mass. C6 65
Warehouse Point, Conn. B6 52
Waren, Ger. Dem. Rep. B6 6
Ware Shoals, S.C. C3 82
Warfield, B.C., Can. E9 37
Warner Robins, Ga. D3 55
Warr Acres, Okla. B4 79
Warragul, Austl. *G8 25
Warren, Ark. D3 49
Warren, Ill. A4 58
Warren, Ind. C7 59
Warren, Mass. B3 65
Warren, Mich. F7, p16 66
Warren, Minn. B2 67
Warren, Ohio A5 78
Warren, Pa. C3 81
Warren, R.I. C11 52
Warren, co., Ga. C4 55
Warren, co., Ill. C3 58
Warren, co., Ind. D3 59
Warren, co., Iowa C4 60
Warren, co., Ky. C3 62
Warren, co., Miss. C3 68
Warren, co., Mo. C6 69
Warren, co., N.J. B3 74
Warren, co., N.Y. B7 75
Warren, co., N.C. A4 76
Warren, co., Ohio C1 78
Warren, co., Pa. C3 81
Warren, co., Tenn. D8 83
Warren, co., Va. B4 85
Warrensburg, Mo. C4 69
Warrensburg, N.Y. B7 75
Warrensville Heights, Ohio h9 78
Warrenton, Ga. C4 55
Warrenton, Mo. C6 69
Warrenton, N.C. A4 76
Warrenton, Oreg. A3 80
Warrenton, Va. B5 85
Warrenville, Ill. k8 58
Warrenville, S.C. D4 82
Warri, Nig. G6 22
Warrick, co., Ind. H3 59
Warrington, Eng. D5 4
Warrington, Fla. u14 54
Warrior, Ala. B3 46
Warrnambool, Austl. G7, n14 25
Warroad, Minn. B3 67
Warsaw, Ill. C2 58
Warsaw, Ind. B6 59
Warsaw, Mo. C4 69
Warsaw, N.Y. C2 75
Warsaw, N.C. B4 76
Warsaw (Warszawa), Pol. B6, m14 7
Warson Woods, Mo. *C7 69
Warwick, Que., Can. D6 42
Warwick, Eng. D6 4
Warwick, N.Y. D6, m14 75
Warwick, R.I. C10 52
Warwick, co., Eng. *D6 4
Wasatch, co., Utah A6 72
Wasco, Calif. E4 50
Wasco, co., Oreg. B5 80
Waseca, Minn. F5 67
Waseca, co., Minn. F5 67
Washakie, co., Wyo. C5 89
Washburn, Ill. C4 58
Washburn, Maine B4 64
Washburn, Wis. B3 88
Washburn, co., Wis. C2 88
Washington, D.C. C3, f8 53
Washington, Ga. C4 55
Washington, Ill. C4 58
Washington, Ind. G3 59
Washington, Iowa C6 60
Washington, Kans. C6 61
Washington, La. D3 63
Washington, Mo. C6 69
Washington, N.J. B3 74
Washington, N.C. B5 76
Washington, Pa. F1 81
Washington, co., Ala. D1 46
Washington, co., Ark. A1 49
Washington, co., Colo. B7 51
Washington, co., Fla. u16 54
Washington, co., Ga. C3 55
Washington, co., Idaho E2 57
Washington, co., Ill. E4 58
Washington, co., Ind. G5 59
Washington, co., Iowa C6 60
Washington, co., Kans. C6 61
Washington, co., Ky. C4 62
Washington, co., Maine D5 64
Washington, co., Md. A2 53
Washington, co., Minn. E6 67
Washington, co., Miss. B3 66
Washington, co., Mo. D7 69
Washington, co., Nebr. C9 71
Washington, co., N.Y. B7 75
Washington, co., N.C. B6 76
Washington, co., Ohio C4 78
Washington, co., Okla. A6 79
Washington, co., Oreg. B3 80
Washington, co., Pa. F1 81
Washington, co., R.I. D10 52
Washington, co., Tenn. C10 83
Washington, co., Tex. D4 84
Washington, co., Utah C5 72
Washington, co., Vt. C2 73
Washington, co., Va. f9 85
Washington, co., Wis. E5 88
Washington, par., La. D5 63
Washington, state, U.S. 86
Washington, mtn., N.H. C5 73
Washington Court House, Ohio C2 78
Washington Heights, N.Y. *D6 75
Washington North, Pa. *F1 81
Washington Park, Ill. E3 58
Washington Terrace, Utah *A5 72
Washingtonville, N.Y. *D6 75
Washington West, Pa. *F1 81
Washita, co., Okla. B2 79
Washoe, co., Nev. A2 72
Washougal, Wash. D3 86
Washtenaw, co., Mich. F7 66
Waskom, Tex. C5 84
Watauga, co., N.C. A1 76
Watchung, N.J. *B4 74
Waterbury, Conn. C4 52
Waterbury, Vt. C2 73
Waterford, Calif. *D3 50
Waterford, Ont., Can. E4 41
Waterford, Conn. D8 52
Waterford, Ire. D3 4
Waterford, N.Y. C7 75
Waterford, Pa. C1 81
Waterford, Wis. F5, n11 88
Waterford, co., Ire. *D3 4
Waterloo, Ont., Can. D4 41
Waterloo, Que., Can. D5 42
Waterloo, Ill. E3 58
Waterloo, Ind. B7 59
Waterloo, Iowa B5 60
Waterloo, N.Y. C4 75
Waterloo, Wis. E5 88
Waterloo, co., Ont., Can. D4 41
Waterman, Ill. B5 58
Waterproof, La. C4 63
Watertown, Conn. C4 52
Watertown, Fla. B4 54
Watertown, Mass. g11 65
Watertown, Minn. *F5 67
Watertown, N.Y. B5 75
Watertown, S. Dak. F8 77
Watertown, Tenn. A5 83
Watertown, Wis. E5 88
Water Valley, Miss. A4 68
Waterville, Que., Can. D6 42
Waterville, Que., Can. D6 42
Waterville, Maine D3 64
Waterville, Minn. F5 67
Waterville, N.Y. C5 75
Waterville, Ohio A2, f6 78
Waterville, Wash. B5 86
Watervliet, Mich. F4 66
Watervliet, N.Y. C7 75
Watford, Ont., Can. E3 41
Watford City, N. Dak. C2 77
Watkins Glen, N.Y. C4 75
Watonga, Okla. B3 79
Watonwan, co., Minn. F4 67
Watrous, Sask., Can. F3 39
Watseka, Ill. C6 58
Watsontown, Pa. D8 81
Watsonville, Calif. D3 50
Wattrelos, Fr. B5 5
Wattsville, S.C. B4 82
Wauchope, Austl. E9 26
Wauchula, Fla. E5 54
Wauconda, Ill. h8 58
Waukegan, Ill. A6, h9 58
Waukesha, Wis. E5 88
Waukesha, co., Wis. E5 88
Waukon, Iowa A6 60
Waunakee, Wis. E4 88
Waupaca, Wis. D4 88
Waupaca, co., Wis. D5 88
Waupun, Wis. E5 88
Waurika, Okla. C4 79
Wausau, Wis. D4 88
Wauseon, Ohio A1 78
Waushara, co., Wis. D4 88
Wautoma, Wis. D4 88
Wauwatosa, Wis. m11 88
Waverly, Ill. D4 58
Waverly, Iowa B5 60
Waverly, N.Y. C4 75
Waverly, Ohio C3 78
Waverly, Tenn. A4 83
Waverly, Va. C5 85
Waxahachie, Tex. C4, n10 84
Waycross, Ga. E4 55
Wayland, Ky. C7 62
Wayland, Mass. g10 65
Wayland, Mich. F5 66
Wayland, N.Y. C3 75
Waymart, Pa. C11 81
Wayne, Mich. p15 66
Wayne, Nebr. B8 71
Wayne, N.J. B4 74
Wayne, Pa. F11, o20 81
Wayne, W. Va. C2 87
Wayne, co., Ga. E4 55
Wayne, co., Ill. E5 58
Wayne, co., Ind. E7 59
Wayne, co., Iowa D4 60
Wayne, co., Ky. D5 62
Wayne, co., Mich. F7 66
Wayne, co., Miss. D5 68
Wayne, co., Mo. D7 69
Wayne, co., Nebr. B8 71
Wayne, co., N.Y. B3 75
Wayne, co., N.C. B4 76
Wayne, co., Ohio B4 78
Wayne, co., Pa. C11 81
Wayne, co., Tenn. B4 83
Wayne, co., Utah B6 72
Wayne, co., W. Va. C2 87
Waynesboro, Ga. C4 55
Waynesboro, Miss. D5 68
Waynesboro, Pa. G6 81
Waynesboro, Tenn. B4 83
Waynesboro (Independent City), Va. B4 85
Waynesburg, Ohio B4 78
Waynesburg, Pa. G1 81
Waynesville, Mo. D5 69
Waynesville, N.C. f10 76
Waynesville, Ohio C1 78
Waynoka, Okla. A3 79
Wayzata, Minn. *F5 67
Weakley, co., Tenn. A3 83
Weatherford, Okla. B3 79
Weatherford, Tex. C4 84
Weatherly, Pa. E10 81
Weaver, Ala. B4 46
Weaverville, Calif. B2 50
Weaverville, N.C. f10 76
Webb, co., Tex. F3 84
Webb City, Mo. D3 69
Weber, co., Utah A6 72
Weber City, Va. *f9 85
Webster, Mass. B4 65
Webster, N.Y. B3 75
Webster, S. Dak. E8 77
Webster, co., Ga. D2 55
Webster, co., Iowa B3 60
Webster, co., Ky. C2 62
Webster, co., Miss. B4 68
Webster, co., Mo. D5 69
Webster, co., Nebr. D7 71
Webster, co., W. Va. C4 87
Webster, par., La. B2 63
Webster City, Iowa B4 60
Webster Groves, Mo. f13 69
Webster Springs (Addison), W. Va. C4 87
Wedgeport, N.S., Can. F4 43
Wedowee, Ala. B4 46
Weed, Calif. B2 50
Weed Heights, Nev. *B2 72
Weedon, Que., Can. D6 42
Weedsport, N.Y. B4 75
Weehawken, N.J. h8 79
Weeks, La. E4 63
Weeping Water, Nebr. D9, h12 71
Weert, Neth. B6 5
Weiden, Ger., Fed. Rep. of D6 6
Weifang, China D8 17
Weihai, China D9 17
Weilheim, Ger., Fed. Rep. E5 6
Weimar, Ger. Dem. Rep. C5 6
Weimar, Tex. E4 84
Weinan, China E6 17
Weinheim, Ger., Fed. Rep. of D4 6
Weippe, Idaho C3 57
Weirton, W. Va. A4, f8 87
Weiser, Idaho E2 57
Weissenburg *in Bayern*, Ger., Fed. Rep. of D5 6
Weissenfels, Ger. Dem. Rep. *C5 6
Wejherowo, Pol. A5 7
Welborn, Kans. B8 61
Welch, W. Va. D3 87
Welcome, S.C. *B3 82
Weld, co., Colo. A6 51
Weldon, N.C. A5 76
Weleetka, Okla. B5 79
Welkom, S. Afr. *F5 24
Welland, Ont., Can. E5 41
Wellesley, Mass. B5, g10 65
Wellford, S.C. B3 82
Wellington, Austl. F7 26
Wellington, Ont., Can. D7 41
Wellington, Kans. E6 61
Wellington, N.Z. N15 26
Wellington, Ohio A3 78
Wellington, Tex. B2 84
Wellington, Utah B6 72
Wellington, co., Ont., Can. D4 41
Wellman, Iowa C6 60
Wells, B.C., Can. C7 37
Wells, Minn. G5 67
Wells, Nev. A4 72
Wells, co., Ind. C7 59
Wells, co., N.Dak. C6 77
Wellsboro, Pa. C7 81

Wildwood, Pa. *E2 81
Wildwood Crest, N.J. F3 74
Wilhelm, mtn., N.Gui. k12 25
Wilhelmina, mtn., Indon. F9 19
Wilhelm-Pieck-Stadt Guben, Ger. Dem. Rep. C7 6
Wilhelmshaven, Ger., Fed. Rep. of B4 6
Wilkes, co., Ga. C4 55
Wilkes, co., N.C. A1 76
Wilkes-Barre, Pa. D10, n17 81
Wilkesboro, N.C. A1 76
Wilkie, Sask., Can. E1 39
Wilkin, co., Minn. D2 67
Wilkinsburg, Pa. F2, k14 81
Wilkinson, co., Ga. D3 55
Wilkinson, co., Miss. D2 68
Will, co., Ill. B6 58
Willacoochee, Ga. E3 55
Willacy, co., Tex. F4 84
Willamina, Oreg. B3 80
Willard, Ohio A3 78
Willcox, Ariz. C4 48
Willemstad, Neth. Antilles A4 32
Williams, Ariz. B2 48
Williams, Calif. C2 50
Williams, co., N.Dak. B2 77
Williams, co., Ohio A1 78
Williams Bay, Wis. F5 88
Williamsburg, Iowa C5 60
Williamsburg, Ky. D5 62
Williamsburg, Ohio C1 78
Williamsburg, Pa. F5 81
Williamsburg (Independence City), Va. C6 85
Williamsburg, co., S.C. D8 82
Williams Lake, B.C., Can. C6, n18 37
Williamson, N.Y. B3 75
Williamson, W.Va. D2 87
Williamson, co., Ill. F4 58
Williamson, co., Tenn. A5 83
Williamson, co., Tex. D4 84
Williamsport, Ind. D3 59
Williamsport, Md. A2 53
Williamsport, Pa. D7 81
Williamston, Mich. F6 66
Williamston, N.C. B5 76
Williamston, S.C. B3 82
Williamstown, Ky. B5 62
Williamstown, Mass. A1 65
Williamstown, N.J. D3 74
Williamstown, Pa. E8 81
Williamstown, W. Va. B3 87
Williamsville, N.Y. C2 75
Willimantic, Conn. C8 52
Willingboro (Levittown), N.J. *C3 74
Willis Beach, Nebr. B9 71
Williston, Fla. C4 54
Williston, N.Dak. B2 77
Williston, S.C. E5 82
Williston Park, N.Y. G2 52
Willits, Calif. C2 50
Willmar, Minn. E3 67
Willoughby, Ohio A4 78
Willow Brook, Calif. *F4 50
Willow Grove, Pa. F11 021 81
Willowick, Ohio A4, g9 78
Willow Run, Mich. p14 66
Willows, Calif. C2 50
Willow Springs, Ill. k9 58
Willow Springs, Mo. E6 69
Wills Point, Tex. *C5 84
Wilmer, Tex. n10 84
Wilmerding, Pa. B6 81
Wilmette, Ill. A6, h9 58
Wilmington, Del. A6 53
Wilmington, Ill. B5 58
Wilmington, Mass. A5, f11 65
Wilmington, N.C. C5 76
Wilmington, Ohio C2 78
Wilmington Manor, Del. *A6 53
Wilmore, Ky. C5 62
Wilson, Ark. B5 49
Wilson, Conn. B6 52
Wilson, Kans. D5 61
Wilson, N.Y. B2 75
Wilson, N.C. B5 76
Wilson, Okla. C4 79
Wilson, Pa. E11 81
Wilson, co., Kans. E8 61
Wilson, co., N.C. B5 76
Wilson, co., Tenn. A5 83
Wilson, co., Tex. E3 84
Wilton, Conn. E3 52
Wilton, Maine D2 64
Wilton, N.H. F4 73
Wilton Junction (Wilton), Iowa C6 60
Wilton Manors, Fla. *F6 54
Wiltshire, co., Eng. *F6 4
Winamac, Ind. B4 59
Winchendon, Mass. A3 65
Winchester, Ont., Can. B9 41
Winchester, Eng. E6 4
Winchester, Ill. D3 58
Winchester, Ind. D8 59
Winchester, Ky. C5 62
Winchester, Mass. g11 65
Winchester, Mo. *C7 69
Winchester, Tenn. B5 83
Winchester (Independent City), Va. A4 85
Windber, Pa. F4 81
Winder, Ga. C3 55
Windfall, Ind. D6 59
Windgap, Pa. E11 81
Windham, Ohio A4 78
Windham, co., Conn. B8 52
Windham, co., Vt. F3 73
Windhoek, Namibia E3 24
Wind Lake, Wis. F5 88
Windom, Minn. G3 67
Windsor, Newf., Can. D4 44
Windsor, N.S., Can. E5 43
Windsor, Ont., Can. E1 41
Windsor, Que., Can. D5 42
Windsor, Colo. *A6 51
Windsor, Conn. B6 52
Windsor, Ill. D5 58
Windsor, Mo. C4 69
Windsor, N.C. B6 76
Windsor, Pa. G8 81
Windsor, Vt. E3 73
Windsor, co., Vt. D2 73
Windsor Heights, Iowa e8 60
Windsor Hills, Calif. *F4 50
Windsor Locks, Conn. B6 52
Windward Islands, see Dominica, Grenada, St Lucia and St. Vincent, Br. dep., N.A.
Windy Hill, S.C. *C8 82
Windy Hills, Ky. *H6 62
Winfield, Ala. B2 46
Winfield, Ill. *B5 58
Winfield, Kans. E7 61
Winfield, N.J. k7 74
Wingate, N.C. C2 76
Wingham, Ont., Can. D3 41
Wink, Tex. D1 84
Winkelman, Ariz. C3 48
Winkler, Man., Can. E3 40
Winkler, co., Tex. D1 84
Winn, par., La. C3 63
Winneab, Ghana G4 22
Winnebago, Ill. A4 58
Winnebago, Minn. G4 67
Winnebago, co., Ill. A4 58
Winnebago, co., Iowa A4 60
Winnebago, co., Wis. H9 88
Winneconne, Wis. D5 88
Winnemucca, Nev. A3 72
Winner, S.Dak. G6 77
Winneshiek, co., Iowa A6 60
Winnetka, Ill. A6, h9 58
Winnfield, La. C3 63
Winnie, Tex. *E5 84
Winnipeg, Man., Can. E3, h8 40
Winnipeg, lake, Man., Can. C2 40
Winnipegosis, Man., Can. D2 40
Winnipegosis, lake, Man. Can. C2 40
Winnsboro, La. B4 63
Winnsboro, S.C. C5 82
Winnsboro, Tex. C5 84
Winnsboro Mills, S.C. *C5 82
Winona, Minn. F7 67
Winona, Miss. B4 68
Winona, co., Minn. F7 67
Winona Lake, Ind. B6 59
Winooski, Vt. C1 73
Winschoten, Neth. A7 5
Winslow, Ariz. B3 48
Winslow, Ind. H3 59
Winslow, Maine D3 64
Windslow, Wash. e10 86
Winsted, Conn. B4 52
Winsted, Minn. F4 67
Winston, Fla. D4 54
Winston, Oreg. *D3 80
Winston, co., Ala. A2 46
Winston, co., Miss. B4 68
Winston-Salem, N.C. A2 76
Winter Garden, Fla. D5 54
Winter Haven, Fla. D5 54
Winter Park, Fla. D5 54
Winters, Calif. C2 50
Winters, Tex. D3 84
Winterset, Iowa C4 60
Wintersville, Ohio B5 78
Winterthur, Switz. E4 6
Winterton, Newf., Can. E5 44
Winterville, N.C. B5 76
Winthrop, Maine D3 64
Winthrop, Mass. B6, g12 65
Winthrop, Minn. F4 67
Winthrop Harbor, Ill. A6, h9 58
Wirt, co., W. Va. B3 87
Wisbech, Eng. D7 4
Wiscasset, Maine D3 64
Wisconsin, state, U.S. B8 45
Wisconsin Dells, Wis. E4 88
Wisconsin Rapids, Wis. D4 88
Wise, Va. f9 85
Wise, co., Tex. C4 84
Wise, co., Va. e9 85
Wishek, N.Dak. D6 77
Wisla, riv., Pol. B5 7
Wismar, Ger. Dem. Rep. B5 6
Wisner, La. C4 63
Wisner, Nebr. C9 71
Withamsville, Ohio C1 78
Witt, Ill. D4 58
Wittenberg, Ger. Dem. Rep. C6 6
Wittenberge, Ger. Dem. Rep. B5 6
Wixom, Mich. o14 66
Włocławek, Pol. B5 7
Woburn, Mass. B5, g11 65
Wolcott, Conn. C5 52
Wolcott, N.Y. B4 75
Wolfe, co., Que., Can. D6 42
Wolfe, co., Ky. C6 62
Wolfeboro, N.H. D5 73
Wolfe City, Tex. C4 84
Wolfenbüttel, Ger., Fed. Rep. of B5 6
Wolf Lake, Mich. E4 66
Wolf Point, Mont. B11 70
Wolfsburg, Ger., Fed. Rep. of B5 6
Wolfville, N.S., Can. D5 43
Wollongong, Austl. F9 25
Wolseley, Sask., Can. G4 39
Wolverhampton, Eng. D5 4
Wolverine Lake, Mich. *F7 66
Wolverton, Eng. D6 4
Womelsdrof, Pa. F9 81
Wonder Lake, Ill. A5, h8 58
Wŏnju, Kor. H3 18
Wonsan, Kor. G3 18
Wood, co., Ohio A2 78
Wood, co., Tex. C5 84
Wood, co., W.Va. B3 87
Wood, co., Wis. D3 88
Woodbine, Iowa C2 60
Woodbine, N.J. E3 74
Woodbourne, N.Y. D6 75
Woodbridge, Conn. D4 52
Woodbridge, N.J. B4, k7 74
Woodbridge, Va. B5 85
Woodburn, Oreg. B4, h12 80
Woodbury, Conn. C4 52
Woodbury, Ga. D2 55
Woodbury, N.J. D2 74
Woodbury, N.Y. *E7 75
Woodbury, Tenn. B5 83
Woodbury, co., Iowa B1 60
Woodbury Heights, N.J. *D2 74
Woodcliff Lake, N.J. g8 74
Woodcroft, Ind. *E5 59
Wood Dale, Ill. k9 58
Woodford, Eng. k13 4
Woodford, co., Ill. C4 58
Woodford, co., Ky. B5 62
Wood Green, Eng. k12 4
Woodlake, Calif. D4 50
Woodland, Calif. C3 50
Woodland, Maine C5 64
Woodland, Pa. E5 81
Woodland, Wash. D3 86
Woodland Beach, Mich. *G7 66
Woodlawn, Ky. A2 62
Woodlawn, Md. *B4 53
Woodlawn, Md. *C4 53
Woodlawn, Ohio n13 78
Woodlawn Beach, N.Y. C2 75
Woodlawn Orchards, Mich. *F6 66
Woodley Hills, Va. *B5 85
Woodlyn, Pa. *B10 81
Wood Lynne, N.J. *D2 74
Woodmere, N.Y. G2 52
Wood-Ridge, N.J. h8 74
Woodridge, N.Y. *D6 75
Wood River, Ill. E3 58
Woodroffe, mtn., Austl. E5 25
Woodruff, S.C. B3 82
Woodruff, co., Ark. B4 49
Woodruff Place, Ind. *E5 59
Woods, co., Okla. A3 79
Woodsboro, Tex. E4 84
Woods Cross, Utah C2 72
Woodsfield, Ohio C4 78
Woodside, Calif. *D2 50
Woodson, co., Kans. E8 61
Woodson Terrace, Mo. *C7 69
Woodstock, N.B., Can. C2 43
Woodstock, Ont., Can. D4 41
Woodstock, Ill. A5 58
Woodstock, Vt. D2 73
Woodstock, Va. B4 85
Woodstown, N.J. D2 74
Woodsville, N.H. C3 73
Woodville, Calif. *D4 50
Woodville, Miss. D2 68
Woodville, Ohio A2, f7 78
Woodville, Tex. D5 84
Woodward, Ala. B3, g7 46
Woodward, Iowa C4 60
Woodward, Okla. A2 79
Woodward, co., Okla. A2 79
Woodway, Tex. *D4 84
Woolwich, Eng. m13 4
Woonsocket, R.I. A10 52
Woonsocket, S.Dak. F7 77
Wooster, Ohio B4 78
Worcester, Eng. D5 4
Worcester, Mass. B4 65
Worcester, N.Y. C6 75
Worcester, S.Afr G3 24
Worchester, co., Eng. *D5 4
Worcester, co., Md. D7 53
Worcester, co., Mass. A3 65
Worden, Ill. E4 58
Workington, Eng. C5 4
Worland, Wyo. B5 89
World 2
Wormleysburg, Pa. *F8 81
Worms, Ger., Fed. Rep. of D4 6
Worth, Ill. k9 58
Worth, co., Ga. E3 55
Worth, co., Iowa A4 60
Worth, co., Mo. A3 69
Wortham, Tex. D4 84
Worthing, Eng. E6 4
Worthington, Ind. F4 59
Worthington, Ky. B7 62
Worthington, Minn. G3 67
Worthington, Ohio B2, k10 78
Wrangel, isl., Sov. Un. B21 13
Wrangell, Alsk. D13, m23 47
Wrangell, mtn., Alsk. f19 47
Wray, Colo. A8 51
Wrens, Ga. C4 55
Wrentham, Mass. B5 65
Wrexham, Wales D5 4
Wright, co., Iowa B4 60
Wright, co., Minn. E4 67
Wright, co., Mo. D5 69
Wright City, Okla. C6 79
Wrightstown, N.J. C3 74
Wrightsville, Ga. D4 55
Wrightsville, Pa. F8 81
Wroclaw (Breslau), Pol. C4 7
Wuchou, China G7 17
Wuhan, China E7 17
Wuhsi (Wusih), China E9 17
Wuhsing, China E9 17
Wuhu, China E8 17
Wulumuchi, see Urumchi, China
Wuppertal, Ger., Fed. Rep. of C3 6
Württemberg, reg. Ger., Fed. Rep. of D4 6
Würzburg, Ger., Fed. Rep. of D4 6
Wurzen, Ger. Dem. Rep. C6 6
Wusu, China C1 17
Wutungchiao, China C11 20
Wyandanch, N.Y. *n15 75
Wyandot, co., Ohio B2 78
Wyandotte, Mich. F7, p15 66
Wyandotte, co., Kans. C9 61
Wyckoff, N.J. *A4 74
Wymore, Nebr. D9 71
Wyncote, Pa. *F11 81
Wyndmoor, Pa. *F11 81
Wynne, Ark. B5 49
Wynnewood, Okla. C4 79
Wynnewood, Pa. *F11 81
Wynyard, Austl. o15 25
Wynyard, Sask., Can. F3, n8 39
Wyoming, Del. B6 53
Wyoming, Ill. B4 58
Wyoming, Mich. F5 66
Wyoming, Minn. E6 67
Wyoming, Ohio c13 78
Wyoming, Pa. n17 81
Wyoming, co., N.Y. C2 75
Wyoming, co., Pa. D9 81
Wyoming, co., W. Va. D3 87
Wyoming, state, U.S. 89
Wyomissing, Pa. F10 81
Wythe, co., Va. D1 85
Wytheville, Va. D1 85

X

Y

Z